TRAFFIC ENGINEERING

Second Edition

TRAFFIC ENGINEERING

Second Edition

Roger P. Roess

Professor of Transportation Engineering
Dean of Engineering
Polytechnic University

William R. McShane

Professor of Transportation Engineering
Dean, Long Island Campus
Polytechnic University

Elena S. Prassas

Assistant Professor of Transportation Engineering
Polytechnic University

Prentice Hall
Upper Saddle River, New Jersey 07458

Library of Congress Cataloging-in-Publication Data

Roess, Roger P.
    Traffic engineering / Roger P. Roess, William R. McShane, Elena S.
  Prassas.—2nd ed.
      p. cm.
    McShane's name appears first on the earlier edition.
    Includes bibliographical references and index.
    ISBN 0-13-461336-8
    1. Traffic engineering—United States.   I. McShane, William R.
  II. Prassas, Elena S. III. Title.
  HE355.M43   1998
  388.3'12'0973—dc21   97-32531
                                            CIP

Acquistions Editor: Bill Stenquist
Editor-In-Chief: Marcia Horton
Production Manager: Bayani Mendoza de Leon
Director of Production and Manufacturing: David W. Riccardi
Creative Director: Jayne Conte
Cover Designer: Bruce Kenselaar
Full Service Coordinator/Buyer: Donna Sullivan
Editorial Assistant: Meg Weist
Composition/Production Service: Bookmasters, Inc.

© 1998, 1990 by Prentice-Hall, Inc.
Upper Saddle River, NJ 07458

Printed in the United States of America
10 9 8 7 6 5

ISBN 0-13-461336-8

Prentice-Hall International (UK) Limited, *London*
Prentice-Hall of Australia Pty. Limited, *Sydney*
Prentice-Hall of Canada, Inc., *Toronto*
Prentice-Hall Hispanoamericana, S. A., *Mexico*
Prentice-Hall of India Private Limited, *New Delhi*
Prentice-Hall of Japan, Inc., *Tokyo*
Prentice-Hall Asia Pte. Ltd., *Singapore*
Editora Prentice-Hall do Brasil, Ltda., *Rio de Janeiro*

Contents

Preface

———————————

Traffic engineering covers a broad range of engineering applications with a common focus: the nation's system of highways and streets. Often defined as the nation's "lifeblood circulation system," this most important part of the national infrastructure supports the vast majority of inter- and intra-city movement of goods and people. Thus, this system plays a role in every important aspect of our society, including the economy, the environment, assurance of public safety, basic mobility for all societal purposes, and basic access to even the most remote regions of the country.

Traffic engineering involves a variety of engineering and management skills, including design, construction, operation, maintenance, and system optimization. Because the focus of the traffic engineer's work is a most visible part of the public infrastructure, it is a field that also involves politics at virtually every level of government. Thus, the traffic engineer is called on to exercise a broad range of skills, and must be sensitive to a wide range of issues, to be effective.

Both the ownership and use of automobiles skyrocketed in the post-WW II economy, and with it the demand for vastly improved highway systems on which private vehicles could be used. The use of over-the-road trucks for goods movement also exploded during this period, providing a second group seeking improved highway systems. These trends culminated in the initial authorization of the National System of Interstate and Defense Highways—and the creation of the Highway Trust Fund, and a set of road user taxes to pay for it—in the 1956 Federal-Aid Highway Act. For the next two decades, the national focus was on the construction of this system, which constituted the single largest public works project in the history of the world.

Much was learned, and many mistakes were made, in the process of building this system. Entire neighborhoods were displaced or carved up as freeways were built through urban areas. Rapid suburbanization accompanied the growth of the system, creating massive traffic demand that gradually choked many urban areas in virtually constant congestion. Congestion brought with it problems of air pollution created by vehicles. As we entered the 1970s, it was with new recognition that continuing construction of new highways would not solve all of our mobility and congestion problems, particularly in urban areas.

In the 1990s, a new phenomenon appeared. As the primary structures of the Interstate System began to reach the end of their physical service lives, and with decades of policies fostering deferred maintenance, the nation was faced with the unique problem of having to rebuild many parts of the system with yet another major constraint: Traffic had to be maintained during the period of reconstruction.

The Interstate Surface Transportation Efficiency Act (ISTEA) has brought about many changes in the traffic engineer's focus. New emphasis has been placed on non-freeway highway facilities; intermodalism and the use of public transportation as part of an integrated transportation system has become a primary objective; maximization of the use of existing transportation rights of way is favored over new construction. Many of these new foci relate directly to the traditional strengths of the traffic engineer in control, operation, and management of urban, suburban, and rural street systems.

This text seeks to provide a basic overview of specific knowledge areas that traffic engineers must bring to the task of addressing modern problems of mobility, access, and congestion. The following functional areas are addressed:

1. *Traffic Characteristics:* Characteristics of drivers, pedestrians, vehicles, roadways, and control systems must be well understood, as these are the media in which the traffic engineer functions. Their interaction creates the critical traffic stream characteristics that we seek to control and manipulate.
2. *Traffic Studies:* To understand traffic behavior, it must be observed, quantified, modeled, and analyzed. This involves a variety of skills, from practical field techniques and modern data collection equipment, to statistical analysis and handling of data.
3. *Geometric Design:* While this is not a text on geometric highway design, basic components of high-

way geometry and their impact on operations are presented and discussed.

4. *Traffic Control:* The basic tools of the trade—markings, signs, and signals—and their use are central to the profession of traffic engineering. These are the media by which we communicate with the driver as we encourage the safe and efficient use of highways and streets.
5. *Traffic Operations and Management:* The vast area of operational and management policy has a tremendous impact on the efficiency of operation on highways and streets. The determination and implementation of effective policies is one of the critical areas of traffic engineering, affecting everything from curb management to parking programs; from special use lanes to one-way street systems; from taxi and transit policies to high-occupancy vehicle lanes.
6. *Capacity and Level of Service Analysis:* The ability to determine how much traffic a given facility can handle at various levels of operational quality is a critical evaluation process. Models and techniques for conducting such analyses are also a critical part of the traffic engineer's function.

The need for traffic engineers continues to grow. Federal, state, and local agencies dealing with traffic issues and systems, and a plethora of consulting firms providing expert advice on traffic and transportation issues, are the most likely employers of professional traffic engineers.

This text covers a great deal of ground that, in general, cannot be covered in detail in a single semester course. It is appropriate for one-semester undergraduate survey courses in the subject (although only about half the material can be covered in this format) and for two- to three-course sequences at the undergraduate or graduate level. It has been developed to be a relatively complete treatment of a complex subject to provide for the maximum flexibility in its use.

An Instructor's Guide, containing solutions to many of the problems in this text, is available for use.

Acknowledgement

The authors are indebted to Dr. Carroll Messer, Professor of Civil Engineering at Texas A&M University; Dr. Ageliki (Lily) Elefteriadou, Assistant Professor of Civil Engineering at Penn State University; and Dr. Charles E. Dare, University of Missouri-Rolla for their thorough, insightful, and timely review of the original manuscript. Their comments and suggestions led to many important improvements in content and presentation. We thank them for their yeoman efforts on our behalf.

1

Introduction to Traffic Engineering and Its Scope

Traffic engineering is concerned with the safety of the public, the efficient use of transportation resources, and the mobility of people and goods. While it is all too easy to become engrossed in operational details, these three purposes are the true foundation of the profession.

Traffic engineers are called upon to protect the environment while providing mobility, to preserve a scarce public resource (capacity) while working with others to assure economic activity, and to assure safety and security through both commonplace good practices and high-tech communications. These and other challenges make the profession exciting and the practitioner's role dynamic.

As this second edition is being written, some of the emerging themes in recent years have been: (1) a new emphasis on *intermodal* approaches, so that transit is considered much more explicitly; (2) the growth of *intelligent transportation systems* (ranging from vehicle location systems to route guidance to transportation management centers), motivated by Federal law and made feasible by advances in communications and computer technology; (3) attention to *access manage-*

ment as a means of preserving the function of an arterial system and other systems, by designing good practices into land access and facility design or re-design; (4) significant attention to *congestion management,* due to the great awareness that the potential to expand right of way for new roads is very limited, and often infeasible; (5) an approach to congestion management which is based upon *assuring mobility,* turning a limiting approach into a very positive goal.

The emphasis on *environmental impact assessments* continues. Traffic and transportation are often the most critical element in environmental impact statements, and two other key areas—noise and mobile source air quality—depend directly upon traffic and transportation.

As exciting as some of these topics are, traffic engineering also includes a number of very basic and essential tasks. Among these are establishing and implementing ways to communicate effectively to the public through standard signing, marking, and signal displays; maintaining inventories and inspection programs that assure that the devices are in place; analyzing data for trends in growth and problems in safety performance; and making sure that the proper legal and administrative procedures are followed, so that good intentions (adding a sign or signal, or other action) have a sound basis for enforcement.

Elements of traffic engineering and of this text

Transportation engineering is defined by the Institute of Transportation Engineers (ITE) as the application of technology and scientific principles to the planning, functional design, operation, and management of facilities for any mode of transportation in order to provide for the safe, rapid, comfortable, convenient, economical, and environmentally compatible movement of people and goods [1].

Traffic engineering is defined by ITE as the phase of transportation engineering that deals with the planning, geometric design and traffic operations of roads, streets and highways, their networks, terminals, abutting lands, and relationships with other modes of transportation [1].

This text is organized on the basis of traffic studies and principles that span facility types, and then on the capacity, design, and operation of key facility categories (freeways and other uninterrupted flow facilities, intersections, and then systems—freeway and arterial). The text includes:

1. *Introduction,* including an overview of the profession, sources of additional information, a discussion of several emerging issues in traffic and transportation, and an overview of traffic stream components and characteristics (with some geometric design issues addressed). Introductory material is covered in Chapters 1–3.

2. *Traffic studies,* including an overview of the trends in traffic data collection and technology, plus detailed treatments of studies for volume, demand, capacity, travel time, speed, delay, accidents, and parking. The overview includes a discussion of performance measures in general. Chapters 4–8 cover this area.

3. *Uninterrupted flow facilities,* with a strong emphasis on capacity and level of service on freeways, multilane highways, and two lane rural roads. The freeway treatment includes basic freeway sections and turbulent areas (ramps, weaving). There is a full

chapter on calibrating relations. Chapters 9–13 cover this material.

4. *Intersections,* including chapters on traffic control devices and hardware, unsignalized and signalized intersections (basics, capacity, level of service, and operation), and detection and detector location. There is a full chapter on calibrating the basic relationships. This section is covered in Chapters 14–19.

5. *Systems,* both freeway and arterial as well as networks. The freeway treatment includes assessment of congested conditions, an overall assessment of the facility, and special problems that may exist due to construction zones and weather. The arterial treatment includes access management, signal progression, computer traffic controls systems, and extensions to networks. Both treatments include congestion issues, traffic management centers, and recent trends (automated toll collection, etc.). Chapters 20–25 comprise this portion of the text.

The transportation system

The transportation system exists to move people *and* goods, to enable economic activity, and to provide for public needs. Work, shopping, education, recreation, social activity and other essential functions of society depend upon the transportation system.

A. Some basic numbers

It is useful to appreciate just how many people may be moved in vehicles of different sorts and on different types of facilities. Consider the following selection of facilities: an urban freeway, a major arterial, a lane of buses, a light rail transit system (one track per direction), and a heavy rail transit system (one track per direction).

At capacity, current estimates are that an *urban freeway* can handle approximately 2400 passenger cars per hour per lane (pcphpl) under ideal conditions [2]. Using 1.5 passengers per car as a representative number, a freeway with three lanes in each direction can carry at most $(2400)(3)(1.5) = 10,800$ people per hour in 7200 cars.

High occupancy vehicle (HOV) lanes requiring two or more people in each vehicle have demonstrated that the equivalent number of people *per lane* can be carried in fewer vehicles at lower travel times [3]. Such facilities increase the average car occupancy. However, there is little evidence that HOV lanes can attract enough vehicles with two or more people to result in a higher number of people/hour than a normal freeway lane operating at capacity.

Under favorable conditions, an *arterial street* can typically process approximately 600 passenger cars per lane. This takes into account that a given direction has only a fraction of the total green time at signalized intersections. Thus, three lanes can move some $(600)(3)(1.5) = 2700$ people in 1800 cars in one direction.

Buses obviously move more people per vehicle than passenger cars: 50 people can be seated in one bus, and 80 people per bus is possible at "crush" capacity, including standees, of a typical urban bus. On an urban street, a reserved bus lane can move approximately 100 buses per hour (sometimes more), and the maximum observed on a limited access facility is about 800 buses per hour [4].

Assuming 80 persons per bus on the surface street and 50 persons per bus on the limited access road, this yields person capacities of 8000 people per hour in a reserved lane on a surface street and 40,000 people per hour on the limited access facility. While these are somewhat theoretical values, the maximum number actually observed was 56,000 people per hour in one reserved bus lane of the Lincoln Tunnel, connecting New York and New Jersey. However, this facility is atypical; many bus routes converge on the lane, which provides eventual access to the Port Authority Bus Terminal in Manhattan.

Estimates also exist for the capacity of fixed right-of-way transit vehicles. For instance, a *light rail transit* line may handle up to 19,000 passengers per hour on a single track [4]. This is, however, an estimate of what such a line can logically handle; such high values have not been observed in the United States for a number of reasons, including the absence of "feeder" lines to drive a high-demand section of track to these limits.

A *heavy rail transit* line can handle approximately 2000 passengers per train, and headways of two minutes between trains are typical. This yields 40,000 people per hour on a single track in one direction. The highest actual observed volume is 65,000 persons/hour on the New York City Independent Subway in Queens; this again is atypical, and represents crush loads on every train, and headways of about 90 seconds between trains.

B. Goods movement

In addition to person movement, *goods movement* must also be considered. Too often, the general public *and* the traffic engineer think of trucks as "things that get in the way and reduce capacity." As a practical matter, however, trucks provide most of the goods transport that underlies an area's economy [5].

Trucks are the primary distribution mechanism—they deliver raw materials to businesses, carry away products, deliver food to community stores, serve maintenance functions, and remove waste. They also deliver and distribute consumer items, business supplies, and other products. They aid in efficient intermodal transportation, collecting and distributing containers for shipping by rail, sea, and air.

The most startling growth in recent years has been in small package express delivery services. Some of this is due to the increased pace of international business, but the evolution of high-tech, high value-added products (computers, electronic subsystems, etc.) has made such express services the favored mode for very competitive manufacturers and assemblers. The emphasis in modern industry on low inventories and "just in time" manufacturing adds to this traffic. At the same time, other forces shift some demand from conventional shipping. FAX and e-mail, for example, are eroding document transmittal by express services.

What should we conclude? First, there is a general level of goods activity that is vital to the local economy, and it must be incorporated into the plans for the transportation system. Second, each specific project—a new building, restaurant, etc.—generates its own goods movements that are site-specific and that put local traffic demands on street space.

C. The system of facilities

Traffic facilities include the roadways for moving vehicles, as well as the parking areas and terminals for transferring passengers and goods and for storing the vehicles. The principal focus in this subsection is on the facilities for moving vehicles. The AASHTO design policy for streets and highways [6] discusses *hierarchies of movements,* relating streets and highways to

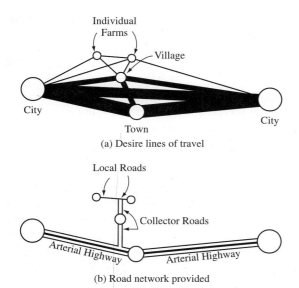

Figure 1-1 Channelization of trips in a rural area. [Used with permission of American Association of State Highway and Transportation Officials, from *A Policy on Geometric Design of Highways and Streets,* p. 6. Copyright © 1994 American Association of State Highway and Transportation Officials.]

the character of service they are to provide. Figure 1-1 shows roads matched to desire lines of travel in rural areas, where the thicker lines indicate stronger travel desire. Figure 1-2 shows a similar information for suburban areas, rendered somewhat differently.

The classic illustration relating the road to the service provided for mobility and for land access is shown in Figure 1-3. It illustrates the proportion of service provided by various categories of facilities in two critical categories: basic mobility (through movement), and land access (terminal functions).

AASHTO [6] identifies the *rural* hierarchy of facility types as:

- *rural principal arterial system,* stratified into two design types: (1) freeways and (2) other principal arterials;
- *rural minor arterial system,* which consists of numbered routes, with design characteristics that are expected to provide for relatively high travel speeds and minimum interference to through movement;
- *rural collector system,* which tends to serve intracounty travel at lower speeds than arterials. These are further refined into major and minor collector roads. "Major" collectors link significant local gen-

erators with larger towns or cities or with routes of higher classification, and "minor" collectors provide some collector function locally, or serve to link local generators with rural hinterlands;
- *local road system,* which provides local land access and constitutes some 65% to 75% of rural road mileage.

For *urbanized* areas, AASHTO defines the hierarchy of facilities as:

- *urban principal arterial system,* stratified as (1) interstate, (2) other freeways, and (3) other principal arterials, all with partial or full control of access. Even in the third subclass, land access should be incidental to the primary function of serving major circulation movements;
- *urban minor arterial street system,* which interconnects and augments the urban principal arterial system, with somewhat less travel mobility;
- *urban collector street system,* linking the arterial system to local streets and entering both residential and other areas, providing both land access and traffic circulation;

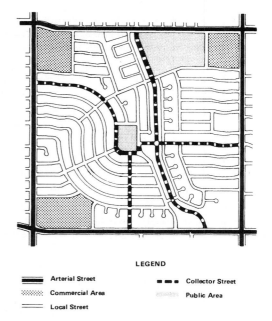

Figure 1-2 Schematic illustration of a suburban street network. [Used with permission of American Association of State Highway and Transportation Officials, from *A Policy on Geometric Design of Highways and Streets,* p. 8. Copyright © 1994 American Association of State Highway and Transportation Officials.]

PROPORTION OF SERVICE

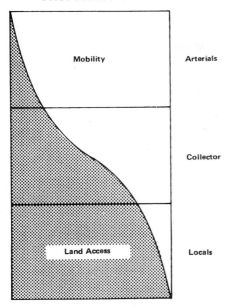

Figure 1-3 Road categories related to mobility and land access functions. [Used with permission of American Association of State Highway and Transportation Officials, from *A Policy on Geometric Design of Highways and Streets,* p. 9. Copyright © 1994 American Association of State Highway and Transportation Officials.]

- *urban local street system,* primarily delivering direct access to abutting lands and deliberately discouraging through traffic.

The use of the word "arterial" in these definitions is worthy of special note, because for many, the word has meant arterial *streets* with some or no limitation on local access, and "freeways" have been thought of as a separate category, with full access control.

The *Highway Capacity Manual* [2] focuses on facilities in terms of capacity and quality of service. It is organized in three facility categories: (1) freeways, (2) multilane and suburban highways, (3) urban streets. These also tend to conform to degrees of access control, ranging from full access control to limited or none.

The hierarchy of highway classification is important. Traffic mobility and land access service have conflicting requirements. The first demands high speed with few interruptions, while the second involves often time-consuming transfer of goods and/or people from vehicles to land or buildings. Land access

service also involves stopping and the storage of vehicles, operations which tend to inhibit through movement. Therefore, the design and control of a highway facility must be compatible with its intended functions, and must reinforce its specific safety and efficiency requirements.

D. Travel demand and transportation planning

Travel demand is generated by activity—people going places for work, shopping, recreation, and other purposes. Thus, much attention in transportation planning is focused on *spatial distribution* of residences and activity centers; *temporal distribution* of trips; *mode selection* for the trips. Indeed, one of the standard references [7] is a handbook listing trip generation rates for various activities.

In transportation planning work, there are a number of tools, e.g., References [8–10] for assigning traffic to a transportation network, knowing the capacities of the links, the spatial and temporal distribution of travel demand, and the rules for mode choice. There are also a number of texts and basic works on transportation planning and assignment, e.g., References [11–15], the details of which are beyond the scope of this text.

However, while this is not a transportation planning text, it is important to recognize that *demand* must be estimated, and that this is a difficult process. *Actual demand* can be much higher than observed volumes, simply because it includes those who would be passing during a given time period if there were no upstream or downstream capacity limitations. It can also include those who are presently using alternative routes, but would re-assign themselves if the route (or mode) became more attractive. These potential trips might be classified as *latent demand,* along with the trips of those people who are deferring trips to other periods—or foregoing them—because of present travel problems.

In traffic engineering, the focus is usually on making sure that the measure of the local demand is taken, not just the measure of a capacity-constrained volume. In some projects, re-routing is taken into account. Latent or unsatisfied demand is not usually added, unless there is a specific planning study or analysis undertaken to estimate it.

Three other points related to the transportation planning function and demand estimation are worthy of note:

1. *Proxies and Disaggregation.* The transportation planning literature often refers to "disaggregation" of trip making, with the intent of understanding the fundamental mechanism of why and how trips are made. For instance, if the population were disaggregated to a fine enough level (age, gender, employment category, etc.), then it might be possible to characterize the trip making of each group in detail, and then re-aggregate the trips from a sound base.

In fact, many studies continue to use the same "proxies" historically used in aggregated trip estimation, including auto ownership, household income, household size, trip purpose, and more recently, gender. The word "proxy" is used intentionally, because the individual traveler's decision making process *reflects* these parameters, but is not necessarily *explained* by them. The behavioral characterization is missing in good part because the extensive and detailed data bases needed to *explain* observed behavior do not yet exist.

2. *Land Use and Travel Demand.* It seems obvious that land use and the structure of the transportation network interact over time, and that each affects the other. Initially, some major development may justify adding or upgrading roads. Later, businesses and residences locate in new places because of the activity and the improved access to land provided by the upgraded roadway system. These businesses and residences then generate their own travel demand, which may cause additional transportation facility changes, which in turn feed the process again. At some point, an equilibrium is reached, wherein development and the transportation system are in balance. Predicting what balance will be reached, and how to reach it, however, are thorny questions to which only the most approximate answers can be given with the current state of the art.

Most traffic engineering work is done on the basis of "snapshots" in which development is known or estimated for some point in time (e.g., present year, future build year), with ancillary development taken into account only by using the most approximate of background growth factors.

3. *Selection of Origin or Destination.* This is somewhat like the "chicken and the egg" question,

and the answer may differ by job function/level, and may differ over the years. Do people pick the residence after the job is selected, or do they search out jobs within reasonable travel of the residence they have already chosen?

Why is this relevant? If trips are to be "distributed" from one end to all candidate "other ends," it is relevant to decide which end is "pinned" or fixed first—the residence or the job location. More precisely, the proportion of trips for which the work "end" is fixed vs. the proportion of trips for which the "home" end is fixed would be a most valuable piece of information. Such knowledge can be built into future disaggregation models and into land use/transportation interactive models.

E. Influencing the demand pattern

Figure 1-4 illustrates the interaction of much of what has been addressed above: travel demand exists because of the trip-making needs of the population; the transportation facilities exist; estimates of the mode choices are on based on historic patterns and/or the availability of supply. Transportation planners estimate the assignment and distribution of trips on the network, typically resulting in some overloaded links and perhaps unsatisfied demand.

The traffic engineer's job often starts with a given pattern of demand, which in at least some sections of the network exceeds capacity. Consider, for instance, the demand profile of Figure 1-5.

Before turning to what must be done if the demand cannot be influenced, it is appropriate to consider ways in which the demand *can* be influenced. Basically, these fall into three broad categories:

- Reduce the demand.
- Shift the temporal distribution of the demand.
- Repackage the demand.

Figure 1-4 shows these as a central step in the process. When this is resolved, one must then manage and operate the transportation system, and measure how well it performs.

Let us now consider each of the three measures:

1. *Reducing the Demand.* Travel demand is measured by some combination of total trips and length of trips (person miles traveled). It therefore follows that the travel demand can be reduced by such

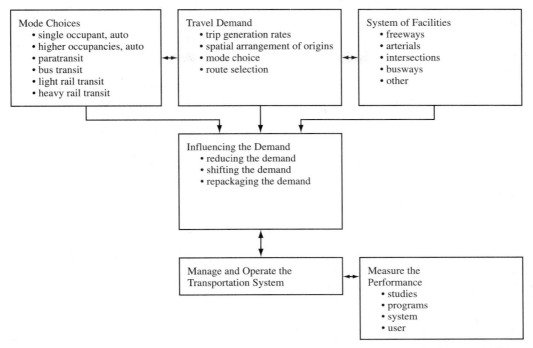

Figure 1-4   Key elements in addressing the transportation system. *Note:* The emphasis in this figure and the associated text is on person movement, not goods movement.

measures as shorter work weeks, shorter average trip lengths, and more work at home.

Shorter work weeks do not necessarily reduce peak demand periods. For instance, if workers were given the option of a four-day work week by taking either Mondays or Fridays off, the peak load on the other three weekdays would remain unaffected, and the basic problem would not be effectively addressed.

Nonetheless, combined with staggered hours and flexible days, some reductions in demand are cer-

tainly possible. The driving force, however, is likely to be economic and staffing in the business sector, rather than transportation-based master planning.

Shorter work trips are actually occurring as jobs shift to smaller cities and to decentralized locations, for the average trip lengths in these locations is shorter than the journey to work in older, larger cities. The concept of *more work at home,* encouraged by telecommunications and home computing, is still a vision rather than a reality for all but a small segment of workers. However, these same technological forces are aiding the decentralization of jobs into smaller clusters.

2. *Shifting the Demand.* Often the problem of congestion is not too much demand, but too much demand *at the same time.* Some of the means of shifting the temporal pattern of demand are *staggered work hours* and *variable work hours* (flex-time and other variations).

The benefits of such programs in reducing peak period load *and* making more efficient use of the capacity of roads and transit systems have been studied

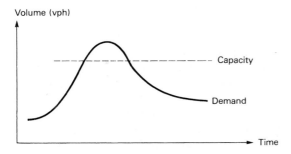

Figure 1-5   Demand pattern for a typical problem location.

and promoted [16,17]. The financial and energy advantages have also been addressed. At present, the use of such techniques is still limited, because the economic advantage to business has not been clearly established.

One very important force in encouraging varied work patterns has been the need of industry to attract workers, offering flexible hours to match the needs of workers and to provide a non-salary inducement to employment. It would not be surprising to see significant shifts to variable hours and variable schedules for these reasons, with consequent benefits to the transportation-demand profile. Note, however, that the driving force would not be concern for the transportation system but concern for attracting needed workers in competitive markets, or for matching schedules to home obligations, or some other business purpose.

3. *Repackaging the Demand.* Demand can be repackaged by a host of techniques related to *higher auto occupancies* and *shifts to transit and paratransit.* In many locations, this has been encouraged by allocating limited existing capacity to high-occupancy vehicle lanes, transit-ways, and other restricted-use lanes. Programs to encourage carpooling, vanpooling, park-and-ride, jitney service, express buses, and greater use of transit (transfers, fringe parking, etc.) have been employed throughout the United states and other countries. Activities to restrict parking opportunities in downtown areas or to introduce congestion-based pricing are also becoming more common.

The traffic engineer is clearly functioning in an environment in which labor availability and economic and business decisions lead to shifts in the demand profile and the demand level. The traffic engineer must be cognizant of these forces and can benefit from them, but it would be a mistake to expect that the demand pattern will be restructured solely for the benefit of the transportation system. Only in a time of extreme crisis (the fuel shortage of 1973–1974) has there been serious, politically viable consideration of shaping demand to match the transport capability.

Although future forces may once again raise the potential for transport allocation plans, the ability to shape demand in any major way is generally beyond the purview of the traffic engineer or even the transportation planner. However, allocating right of way to high occupancy vehicles and restricting access are means of shaping demand in which the traffic engineer is an active participant, perhaps even an initiator.

This text recognizes that these options exist, and that the traffic engineer works within this dynamic environment. However, it focuses on the techniques and procedures of traffic engineering, and not on these broader issues, except in this introduction. The traffic engineer, however, must always be aware of the environment in which he or she practices the profession, because the ways in which basic skills and techniques are applied is greatly influenced by this broader context.

ISTEA

The Intermodal Surface Transportation Efficiency Act (ISTEA) of 1991 [18] was landmark federal legislation, superseding the historic highway and transit legislation of previous eras [19,20] and putting a new emphasis on *intermodalism* and a strong focus on higher occupancies and transit use. The legislation is also notable for its urban orientation, the funding of a major intelligent transportation systems initiative, and the flexibility allowed to the states and localities in funds use.

The authorization is for a six-year period, so that the reauthorization legislation will be enacted about the time this text is published. The Institute of Transportation Engineers (ITE) has taken a position that this reauthorization (often called "ISTEA 2") should cover a minimum of another five years and should not involve another major overhaul of existing programs [21].

Most transportation professionals have spent their careers under the influence of the formative interstate highway program, begun in the 1950s. The National System of Interstate and Defense Highways (colloquially known as the "Interstate System") was formally authorized by the Federal-Aid Highway Act of 1956. This historic Act authorized construction of the 41,000 mile (later expanded to 42,500) interstate system, and created the Highway Trust Fund and a series of road user taxes to fund it and other highway programs. The ISTEA legislation recognizes that the interstate system is essentially finished, and incorporates the now 45,000 mile interstate system into a 155,000 mile *National Highway System.* The older designations of "primary, secondary, and urban system" components, key to previous funding legislation, have been dropped in this new national program.

The funding for the programs comes from the current Highway Trust Fund through 1999, including current balances and a federal gasoline excise tax of 2.5 cents per gallon, and from a requirement that the unobligated balances in the Trust Fund be spent down to approximately $2 billion by the end of 1997. Funding for highway programs increased by 63% in the ISTEA legislation, and for transit by 91%, with most of these increases taking place in the later years of the Act.

For the first time, states are *required* to have a statewide transportation planning process, and funding for the metropolitan area planning process has been increased. Under the press of the legislation, responsibility in many states is devolving onto the metropolitan planning organizations (MPOs), and these states are becoming more decentralized in their transportation programs.

The legislation also allows up to fifty percent of the funds designated for the National Highway System (NHS) to be shifted to Surface Transportation Program highway or transit projects, providing considerable flexibility. The Surface Transportation Program also has its own funding in the legislation, and includes any surface transportation capital project except local or rural minor collectors. Ten percent of the Surface Transportation Program funds are designated for safety, and another ten percent for transportation enhancement projects.

There are additional funds for congestion mitigation/air quality compliance, intelligent transportation, operational costs for traffic management, magnetically levitated trains, and the creation of transit planning and research programs. There are limits on projects which primarily benefit single-occupancy vehicles. At first there was a requirement that the states implement six management systems: for congestion, safety, public transportation, intermodal transportation, traffic monitoring, and bridges and pavements. Some of these have been implemented under federal rules promulgated since the passage of ISTEA, but there have also been some modifications because the Federal Highway Administration (FHWA), and the states have debated the implementation of the management systems, notably the congestion management system.

ITE noted in 1996 that many agencies were just then becoming comfortable with the new programs and policies [21], and recommended their continuation without radical change, but with a shift to a results-driven approach rather than a process-driven approach, saying that "Programs should not be judged on how they are carried out, but rather on what they accomplish and contribute. . . . "

In the same reference, ITE also notes that some $57 billion should be invested annually in capital programs for roads, bridges, and transit, but that the current funding level is less than $41 billion each year. ITE recommends funding ISTEA 2 entirely from user fees by returning to the Highway Trust Fund the allocation now used for deficit reduction, and by removing the Highway Trust Fund from the unified federal budget.

Environmental requirements

In addition to ISTEA, there are two other federal acts that greatly influence the practice of traffic engineering. These are the National Environmental Policy Act (NEPA) of 1969 as amended [22] and the Clean Air Act [23] as amended. There are also federal regulations [24] implementing policies and procedures for implementing NEPA and the regulation of the Council on Environmental Quality (CEQ). Further, there are various State Environmental Quality Acts (SEQR) or similarly named acts covering state practices, as well as similar laws or regulations on local levels.

The regulation identifies three classes of actions:

- *Class I actions* significantly affect the environment, and automatically require an environmental impact statement (EIS). Examples of such projects include construction of a new controlled access facility, a highway project of four or more lanes on a new location, new construction or extension of fixed rail transit facilities, or construction or extension of a separate roadway for buses or high occupancy vehicles (HOV) not within an existing highway facility.
- *Class II actions* do not involve significant environmental impacts, as suggested by past experience, and are given a categorical exclusion (CE). It is possible to review an action classified as Class II in unusual circumstances, including significant environmental

impacts and/or substantial controversy. Class II actions include landscaping, utility installations, activities to comply with a state's highway safety plan, installation of noise barriers, emergency repairs, accessibility improvements, and promulgation of rules, regulations, and directives (ministerial acts).

- *Class III actions* are all those which are not obviously Class I or II, and require an environmental assessment (EA), prepared by the applicant (for example, the state) to the appropriate federal agency, namely the Federal Highway Administration (FHWA) or the Federal Transit Administration (FTA). The environmental assessment is not as complete as an EIS, and may be used to determine whether an EIS is required. Public comment must be solicited, by hearing or by notice. If no significant impact is found, the appropriate federal administration may issue a finding of no significant impact (FONSI).

In the cases where an EIS is required, the lead agency (i.e., the applicant) must follow detailed procedures, which involve other agencies and the public. Procedures require a scoping stage in which the range of the EIS is determined; a draft environmental impact statement (DEIS); a review process, involving the public, for the DEIS; responses; a final environmental impact statement (FEIS); and appropriate reviews, comments, and approvals (or not). Both the DEIS and the FEIS must consider alternatives and mitigation of any negative impacts (or report inability to mitigate).

Impacts on the following must be considered:

- traffic and transportation
- noise
- air quality
- wetlands
- historic sites
- parklands, recreational facilities, wildlife and waterfowl refuges
- endangered species
- social, including impacts on neighborhoods and communities
- energy
- economic impact (positive and negative)

The process must include consideration of the construction and build-out stages. It is common to con-

sider the existing, the future no-build (without the project), the future build (with the project), and various alternatives. The range and coverage of the EIS is determined during the scoping process.

The Clean Air Act and its amendments are also very relevant, because the local area may be part of a non-attainment zone, in which case special attention is required.

There is no question that the process is lengthy and requires great care. Decades of abuse, including partitioning neighborhoods and failing to assess impacts, gave rise to the current legislation. Above all, it is critical that the process be followed in an orderly manner with good documentation, assuring that decision makers are fully informed when decisions are made.

Ethical aspects of impact work

The complex involvement with many interested parties and other professional disciplines in impact work presents special challenges to the transportation professional. Some of these are ethical issues.

The transportation professional will be functioning in an environment in which a number of participants do not understand the traffic and transportation issues or how they truly affect the project. This lack of understanding is not limited to the nontechnical people but includes other professionals, who sometimes have singularly narrow views and may overestimate their understanding of transportation. While it is truly a joy to work as part of an experienced complex team on such projects, there are occasions when the transportation professional encounters naive assumptions, design that is oblivious to transportation needs, and subtle (sometimes inadvertent) assumptions that an analysis can be simplified (oversimplified?) or an impact can be understated.

Experience has shown that the greatest risk to a project is an incomplete analysis. Major projects have been upset because an impact was overlooked or an analysis oversimplified. Sophisticated developers and experienced professionals know that the process calls for a fair statement of impacts and a *policy decision by the reviewers* on accepting the impacts, given an overall good. The process does *not* require zero impacts; it requires clear and complete identification, so that policymakers can make informed decisions.

Successful challenges to major projects have been based upon flawed analysis and overlooked or misstated impacts, not on disagreements with policymakers who made informed decisions. Indeed, such disagreement is not a valid basis for a legal challenge.

Ethical lapses are not only wrong in principle, they also have the potential of undermining the very objective they were intended to foster. The novice transportation professional is strongly advised not to misread the indifference or obliviousness of professionals in other disciplines or of clients (government or private) as subtle signals to "cut corners" or overlook things; it is quite possible that they simply do not understand the transportation issues, or that they view them as trivial.

In the long term, the transportation professional will be sought out for the quality of his or her work, and not for being compliant, because the professional's reputation for sound, thorough work is a great asset to the client in high-visibility projects.

Responsibility and liability in traffic engineering

The traffic engineer is in a very special relationship with the public at large. Perhaps more than any other engineer, the traffic engineer deals with the daily safety of a large segment of the public. Although it can be argued that any engineer who designs a product has this responsibility, few engineers have so many people using their product so routinely and frequently, and depending on it so totally. Therefore, the traffic engineer has a special obligation to employ the available knowledge and state of the art within existing resources in order to enhance public safety.

The traffic engineer also has a responsibility to protect the community from liability by good practice. While this section can make the engineer aware of this need and of some history, it is not intended as a substitute for legal advice on current obligations and practice, which should be sought from the agency's or corporation's lawyer. Indeed, it should motivate the engineer to seek such knowledge.

The engineer must be aware of the legal authority by which actions may be taken and the proper form in which they must be implemented. For instance, each state has legislation that establishes basic traffic law and assigns certain authority to the commissioner of transportation and to others. That authority frequently includes the establishment of detailed procedures, designation of manuals, and so forth.

There have been cases in which a community has installed numerous traffic control devices without following proper, clearly established procedures [25]. The question of whether obedience to these devices is enforceable is interesting, but the ambiguity that can be introduced in the case of a severe accident is quite serious. Should the device have been there? Did its presence cause the accident?

The traffic engineer must remember that controls put on the road (signs, signals, markings) are *communication devices* that provide the driver with a message. It is important that the message be given in a clear, unambiguous, and uniform way. This is done in day-to-day practice by the color, size, location, and content of the devices used. Frequently, markings are required to reinforce the message of a sign or signal. Failure to communicate the desired message in standard, well-established ways creates major problems for the public and for the community.

What is expected in the use of such devices? It is commonly expected that government bodies (and those who act for them) exercise due care in their planning, design, maintenance, and operational conduct.

A historic standard has been that due care be exercised in the preparation of plans, and that determinations made in the process be reasonable and not arbitrary. It is generally recognized that professional value judgments must be made, and key phrases are "due care" and "not arbitrary." These phrases, and the extent of their meaning, are continually under legal test.

Liability is associated with improper maintenance and operations, as well as improper design. Unsafe practices unfortunately exist, and sometimes show poor engineering judgment. Consider:

- safety barriers located behind fixed obstructions, such as telephone poles
- failure to replace a speed restriction sign on an exit ramp following a construction activity
- signals malfunctioning for excessive periods

Very often, such problems can be traced to a breakdown of communication between agencies or offices.

A police report of a signal failure is not passed along, or is not acted on; a maintenance or installation crew does not understand that a breakaway installation is supposed to be breakaway, and acts on its own to "correct" the "problem" of too many knockdowns.

It is important that there be a positive program to insure proper planning, design, construction, maintenance, and operation. This includes:

- assuring effective and efficient communications among agencies and/or offices
- following proper procedures in the installation of devices
- assuring reasonable checks (in terms of both frequency and detail of the check) on the operation of devices and equipment in the field
- planning for the discovery and remedy of traffic-hazard locations, by a program of field inspections, engineering study, and accident-history review

The fundamental issue is to provide for the public safety through positive programs, good practice, knowledge, and proper procedure. The negative (albeit important) side of this is the avoidance of liability problems.

Standard references for the traffic engineer

In order to keep up to date and aware, the traffic engineer should review on a regular basis the information and literature from the

- Institute of Transportation Engineers (ITE)
- Transportation Research Board (TRB)
- American Society of Civil Engineers (ASCE)

These and other organizations publish periodicals which can be quite valuable. Some of the prime documents of interest are *ITE Journal, Transportation Research Record (TRR), Transportation Journal of the ASCE,* and *Transportation Engineering.*

In addition, there are other reports of great interest:

- regular reports from the National Cooperative Highway Research Program (NCHRP) and the National Cooperative Transit Research Program (NCTRP)

- "synthesis of practice" reports from the same sources
- research reports from FHWA and FTA

There are other periodicals (such as *Transportation Research*) and series (such as those from Britain's Road Research Laboratory and the Australian Road Research Laboratory). In addition, there are newsletters from USDOT, states, technology transfer programs at universities, and commercial sources which help keep a traffic engineer current. The *McTrans Newsletter* is an excellent source of traffic, highway, transit, and other transportation software.

Several of the standard periodicals are becoming available on CD ROM, and a number of organizations have web sites on the internet (see next section).

In addition, there are several standard references to which the practicing traffic engineer should have ready access:

- **The Uniform Vehicle Code and the Model Traffic Ordinance.** *The Uniform Vehicle Code* (UVC) and *Model Traffic Ordinance* are prepared by the National Committee on Uniform Traffic Laws and Ordinances to encourage national uniformity. They have been published periodically since 1926 and are now issued in a single volume [26]. The purpose of these documents is to prescribe the required traffic control devices, the rules of the road, and the framework for state laws. This intent may be accomplished within a given state by passage of a Vehicle and Traffic Law or a similarly named law.
- **The Manual on Uniform Traffic Control Devices.** Specifically authorized in the UVC is a *Manual on Uniform Traffic Control Devices (MUTCD).* For instance, a state's Vehicle and Traffic Law may authorize the commissioner of transportation to have such a manual created and to cause its use to be required within the state. There is a federally sponsored MUTCD, issued by FHWA, with a national committee on the subject [27]. Because the "police power" required to mandate such a manual is reserved to the states by the U.S. Constitution, the federal government is limited to encouraging (albeit strongly) its adoption through federal-aid requirements and by having a model. It is the states which must decide and act to implement such a manual. Some states adopt the federal version with-

out modification, and others introduce additional detail or refinements, while keeping in substantial compliance.

- **The Highway Capacity Manual.** The *Highway Capacity Manual* (*HCM*) is published by TRB, after being recommended by the TRB Committee on Highway Capacity and Quality of Service. Again, the individual states may choose to adopt this manual as a standard for capacity and level of service analysis within the state. There have been three editions of the *HCM*: 1950, 1965, and 1985 (with an update in 1994). The purpose of the *HCM* is to provide the best available information in the capacity of traffic facilities and the quality of flow a driver experiences on them, as a function of traffic demand, geometric parameters, and other factors. The traffic facilities covered in the *HCM* include limited-access highways, rural two-lane and multilane highways, intersections, and arterial streets. There are chapters on pedestrians, transit, and bicycle capacity. The current edition (as of this writing) is the 1994 update to the third edition [2]. An additional update is expected in 1997, and a full fourth edition is expected in the year 2000. It will be a CD ROM version, with implementing software.

- **The AASHTO Green Book.** The AASHTO "Green Book," properly named *A Policy on the Geometric Design of Highways and Streets* [6], is the product of the American Association of State Highway and Transportation Officials. The common name derives from the color of the binding. The Green Book addresses the principles and policies for the geometric design of traffic facilities. It is rather detailed and has a very formal approval and endorsement process involving the AASHTO members, the states. FHWA references AASHTO standards for use. There is a 1994 metric edition which supersedes [6].

- **The Traffic Engineering Handbook.** The *Traffic Engineering Handbook* [28] is an ITE publication. It provides an overview of the several modes of transportation and has detailed chapters on various aspects of traffic and highway engineering. Individual chapters are written by experts in the specific topic.

- **Trip Generation.** *Trip Generation* [7] is another publication of ITE. It contains trip generation rates for a number of different land uses, in different areas, and has become the leading reference for this sort of data. The bases for the estimates are primarily empiric, and the handbook is updated periodically.

Additional references will prove valuable for specific applications, including the *Manual of Transportation Engineering Studies* [29], the *Manual of Traffic Signal Design* [30], and the state design manuals. The annual *Publications Catalog* of ITE is a good source for additional timely references. Additional key references are cited in chapters throughout this text.

Sources on the internet

In the mid-1990s, there has been an explosion of web sites for all sorts of businesses, agencies, and organizations. Any listing in this text will of necessity be dated, but it will also provide an excellent starting point, because many of the sites link to others. For instance, many university transportation programs can be reached from the ITS/America web site. With this caveat in mind, some good starting points are:

- *Institute of Transportation Engineers (ITE)* http://www.ite.org
- *U.S. Department of Transportation* http://www.dot.gov
- *ITS America (membership needed for some access)* http://www.itsonline.com
- *Transportation Research Board* http://www.nas.edu/trb/trb.html
- *McTrans Center* http://www-mctrans.ce.ufl.edu
- *Information on NEPA from USDOE* http://tis-nt.eh.doe.gov/nepa/

There are additional sites listed in References [31] and [32].

A comment on English vs. standard international (metric) units

At the current time, the U.S. is in the midst of a federally-mandated program to adopt standard international (SI) units. Some highways are now being constructed to metric standards—i.e., a standard 12-ft. lane becomes a standard 3.6 meter lane (which is slightly narrower than 12 ft.). At this juncture, however, virtually all signage is in English units, and all of the standard traffic engineering references are in English units, with the exception of the AASHTO Green Book. For this reason, the second edition of this text still uses primarily English units. Over the next several years, more and more standard references will be converted to SI units, and the third edition of this text will do the same. Where AASHTO standards and criteria are referenced, SI units are used.

Summary

This chapter provides an overview of what traffic engineers are involved in, some sense of the transportation system and related issues, relevant legislation, environmental impact considerations, ethical and liability issues, and key references. The next chapter addresses key issues and trends which were drawing significant attention as this edition of the text was written.

References

1. *Institute of Transportation Engineers Directory,* Institute of Transportation Engineers, Washington, DC, June 1995, p. A-29.
2. "Basic Freeway Segments" (Chapter 3), *Highway Capacity Manual, Special Report 209,* 3rd Edition, Transportation Research Board, National Research Council, Washington, DC, (revised) 1994.
3. *High Occupancy Vehicle Facility Development, Operation and Enforcement: Training Course,* U.S. Department of Transportation, Federal Highway Administration, Washington, DC, May 1981.
4. "Transit Capacity" (Chapter 12), *Highway Capacity Manual, Special Report 209,* 3rd Edition, Transportation Research Board, National Research Council, Washington, DC, (revised) 1994.
5. Sampson, R. J., Farris, M. T., and Shrock, D. L., *Domestic Transportation Practice, Theory and Policy,* 5th Edition, Houghton Mifflin, Boston, MA, 1985.
6. *A Policy on Geometric Design of Highways and Streets,* American Association of State Highway and Transportation Officials, Washington, DC, 1990.
7. *Trip Generation, Fifth Edition,* Institute of Transportation Engineers, Washington, DC, 1991 and 5th Edition Update, February 1995.
8. TRANPLAN, Version 7.1, Transportation modeling software, The Urban Analysis Group, Danville, CA, 1992.
9. MINUTP, Transportation modeling software, COMSIS Corporation, Sunnyvale, CA, 1989.
10. EMME/2, Release 6.3, INRO Consultants, Inc., Montreal, Canada, 1993.
11. Edwards, J. (editor), *Transportation Planning Handbook,* Prentice-Hall, Englewood Cliffs, NJ, 1992.
12. Manheim, M. L., *Fundamentals of Transportation System Analysis, Vol 1., Basic Concepts,* The MIT Press, Cambridge, MA, 1979.
13. Meyer, M. D., and Miller, E. J., *Urban Transportation Planning: A Decision-Oriented Approach,* McGraw-Hill, New York, NY, 1982.
14. Stopher, P. R., and Meyburg, A. H., *Urban Transportation Modeling and Planning,* Lexington Books, D.C. Heath, Lexington, MA, 1975.
15. "Forecasting Inputs to Transportation Planning," *NCHRP Report 266,* Transportation Research Board, National Research Council, Washington, DC, 1983.
16. *Alternatives for Improving Urban Transportation: A Management Overview,* U.S. Department of Transportation, Washington, DC, October 1977.
17. Desimone, V. R., "Four-Day Work Week and Transportation," *Transportation Engineering Journal,* ASCE, Vol. 98, No. TE3, August 1972, pp. 705–714.
18. *A Summary: Intermodal Surface Transportation Efficiency Act of 1991,* Publication No. FHWA-PL-92-008. U.S. Department of Transportation, Washington, DC.
19. *Federal Aid Highway Act of 1973,* Public Law 93-87, 93rd Congress, Sec. 502, August 1973.
20. *Urban Mass Transportation Act of 1964, U.S. Code,* Vol. 49, Secs. 1601 *et seq.,* 1976.
21. "Recommendations for ISTEA 2," *ITE Journal,* May 1996.
22. *National Environmental Policy Act of 1969,* as amended (NEPA).
23. *A Summary: Transportation Programs and Provisions of the Clean Air Act Amendments of 1990,* Publication No. FHWA-PD-92-023, U.S. Department of Transportation, Washington, DC.

24. Code of Federal Regulations, 23 CFR, Revised April 1, 1993.
25. "A Stop Is Put to Sign Hassle," *Newsday,* Tuesday, October 31, 1978.
26. *Uniform Vehicle Code and Model Traffic Ordinances,* National Committee on Uniform Traffic Laws and Ordinances, 1992.
27. *Manual on Uniform Traffic Control Devices,* U.S. Department of Transportation, Federal Highway Administration, Washington, DC, 1988.
28. Pline, J. (editor), *Traffic Engineering Handbook,* 4th Edition, Institute of Transportation Engineers, Prentice-Hall, Englewood Cliffs, NJ, 1991.
29. Robertson, H. D. (editor), *Manual of Transportation Engineering Studies,* Institute of Transportation Engineers, Washington, DC, 1994.
30. Kell, J., and Fullerton, I. J., *Manual of Traffic Signal Design,* 2nd Edition, Institute of Transportation Engineers, Prentice-Hall, Englewood Cliffs, NJ, 1991.
31. Messick, J., "A Transportation Engineer's Guide to the Internet," *ITE Journal,* March 1996.
32. Guensler, R., and Bernstein, D., "Transportation Resources on the Internet," *ITE Journal,* April 1996.

Problems

Problem 1–1

Consider the following vehicle occupancies, before and after a change in the downtown parking policy.

	Percent of Vehicles	
Occupancy	Before	After
1	55%	40%
2	35%	40%
3	10%	20%

The miles per vehicle trip do not change, nor does the number of people traveling. What is the change in the VMT?

Problem 1–2

Assume that the vehicle occupancies on a particular facility are as follows:

Percent of Vehicles	Occupancy (Persons)	
55%	1	55
31%	2	62
10%	3	30
4%	4 or more (say 4.2 average)	16

What percent of the vehicles have only one occupant? What percent of the people ride in single-occupant vehicles? What percent of the people ride with someone else?

Problem 1–3

Determine the total VMT under the two plans indicated below. Find the percent reduction of PLAN 2 relative to PLAN 1, in terms of VMT and PMT.

	Total Persons Traveling	In Vehicles of Occupancy	Average Miles Per Vehicle Per Week
Plan 1			
City	10,000	1	100
	10,000	2	120
Suburbs	10,000	1	170
	10,000	2	200
Plan 2			
City	7,000	1	90
	13,000	2	110
Suburbs	5,000	1	150
	15,000	2	160

Problem 1–4

Set Problem 1–3 up on a spreadsheet, so that changes in the indicated values will yield immediate results of the effect of Plan 2 relative to Plan 1 in terms of VMT, PMT, vehicle occupancy, fuel savings (gallons per year), and revenue changes (dollars per year).

For fuel computations, use 16 mpg as the consumption rate in urban travel and 18 mpg for suburban travel.

For revenue estimates, use the tax in your area on unleaded regular gasoline.

Experiment with shifts in people from one-person cars to two-person cars, plotting VMT (percent reduction) as a function of the shift. Also plot revenue changes (percent) on the same axis.

Problem 1–5

Consider "Year 1" as the base condition, and plot the change in the purchasing power of fuel-tax revenues as a function of year, given the news as stated below. All percent changes are relative to the immediately preceding year.

Year	Activity
1	Base year
2	3% reduction in VMT 5% inflation 2% increase in fuel efficiency
3	3% reduction in VMT 8% inflation 3% increase in fuel efficiency
4	1% reduction in VMT 9% inflation 2% increase in fuel efficiency
5	0% reduction in VMT 7% inflation 2% increase in fuel efficiency
6	1% reduction in VMT 4% inflation 3% increase in fuel efficiency
7	1% reduction in VMT 4% inflation 4% increase in fuel efficiency

Estimate the change in dollar revenues over the seven years. Plot and tabulate the revenues as a function of the year number. Use "100" as the Year 1 base-level revenues. Note that the fuel tax is specified as a fixed number of cents per gallon.

Estimate the total earning power of these revenues, and plot it on the same scale.

Estimate the impact of each factor on the change.

Problem 1–6

This problem is intended for use in term projects and not as part of a weekly assignment. Its purpose is to introduce a certain realism into Problems 1–3 and 1–4 and implement it on a spreadsheet.

For a given Standard Metropolitan Statistical Area (SMSA), as defined by the Census, obtain information on the VMT, and trip lengths within and among units within the SMSA (CBD, urban, suburban, etc.), disaggregated by auto occupancy. Also obtain information on fuel efficiency by area, fuel taxes, and trends in fuel efficiency. Not all of this information is available from one source.

Set up the format of a spreadsheet to allow you to shift groups of people from one auto-occupancy category to another, and to make other changes you deem appropriate. Note that it is important not to *accidentally* increase or decrease the total number of people, and this may influence your spreadsheet layout.

The spreadsheet should compute VMT, PMT, average occupanices, fuel consumption, and other results you deem appropriate. It should include comparisons (percentage changes) of three or more alternative plans.

Implement and use the spreadsheet for a range of studies, focusing on the impact of VMT, PMT, fuel consumption, and revenues of reducing the percent of single occupancy from its present level to 10 percent of all passenger cars.

Problem 1–7

This problem is intended for use in term projects and not as part of a weekly assignment. Its purpose is to introduce a certain realism into Problem 1–5 and implement it on a spreadsheet.

Obtain data on the age distribution of vehicles and the fuel efficiency of vehicles sold by year, such that you can generate a weighted average fuel efficiency of the fleet on the road in any calendar year. Note that assumptions are needed on the fuel efficiencies of future years. Note also that assumptions are needed on the *current* fuel efficiency of cars sold in Year *X,* relative to the manfacturer's data on fuel efficiency in the year of sale (i.e., when the cars were new).

Obtain data by state on the VMT, the mix or age distribution of cars in the state, and the fuel consumption and fuel revenues. If possible, obtain all these statistics broken out by urban versus rural.

Obtain as much of this information as possible by year for the period from 1975 to (estimates for) five years ahead of the present year.

Obtain information on inflation by year over the same period, as measured by the index most appropriate to measuring the earning power of construction moneys.

Set up the format of a spreadsheet to use this information to conduct the analysis of Problem 1–5, and do so.

2

Emerging Issues and Trends in Traffic Engineering

This chapter is devoted to issues that are at the forefront of attention in the mid-1990s, and are likely to continue to be so over the coming years. The first of these is *intelligent transportation systems* (ITS), made possible by advances in computing and communications technology and strongly supported by the 1991 ISTEA legislation. The original emphasis was on intelligent vehicle highway systems (IVHS), but the greater emphasis on other modes, also motivated by the ISTEA legislation, caused a renaming in the profession and a broader emphasis.

The second major theme is *preserving the function of the facilities*. Arterial streets are often the primary means of intercity travel by car and truck, and the prime component of state highway systems. Subsequent development, however, tends to load local traffic onto these facilities, degrading their primary function. *Access management* is the primary tool for preserving arterial function, and is addressed as a third major theme in this chapter. However, there are other function-preservation needs: residential areas need truly *local* streets, with traffic directed as quickly as possible to collector roads; in other areas, speeds

and volumes on minor collectors and minor arterials interfere with neighborhood function, and "traffic calming" projects seek to limit and direct flows to more suitable paths.

Next, there is a set of three interrelated themes. The first of these is *true attention to intermodalism*. Under the federal legislative emphasis (and perhaps the maturing of the profession), transit is being considered more actively as the mode by which additional *person*-trip needs can be satisfied. Likewise, greater attention is being paid to intermodal transfer points in the transportation system (availability, design, interlocking schedules, etc.). The second theme in this set is *performance measures*. There are a standard set of measures for assessing highway performance and even the need for highway improvements. However, in assessing a transportation network (including transit), the very absence of adequate transit—routes and schedules—may need to be reflected explicitly in the performance measures. These two themes lead to the third, namely *mobility and congestion*. The need for states to develop a congestion management system (CMS) as part of the ISTEA requirements focused attention on how to assess, address, and remedy congestion. The more attention some states paid to this, the more they realized the underlying issue was providing mobility, not just relieving—or reporting—congestion. This positive emphasis on meeting mobility needs allowed programs to be conceived that were more positive and, as it happens, often more multimodal.

The seventh theme selected for this chapter is *trends in population and transportation location.* Simply put, over several decades there has been a growth of suburb-to-suburb travel and proportionately less suburb-to-central-city travel. This is sometimes obscured by general growth, but is a very significant trend. Suburban highway systems must take loads previously associated with only urban arterials. Trips are on average shorter, and are often at less congested speeds. Business and industry are more decentralized within regions, and clustered in different ways in the suburbs (including industrial parks).

The last theme of the chapter is *metrication.* The United States is now on a schedule to switch to the metric system. AASHTO has already issued a metric edition of the "Green Book" in 1994 [1], and the fourth edition of the HCM (planned for the Year 2000) will be metric. As signs are added or upgraded, metric notation will be used.

The sections that follow discuss each of these significant theme areas in greater detail.

Intelligent transportation systems

In the 1960s, an idea arose that was ahead of its time: the fascinating concept of an electronic route guidance system (ERGS). As drivers passed through a network of roadside minicomputers (today's microprocessor-based computers were not even conceived), they would transmit their identity and destination, and receive guidance on an in-vehicle display on the best route. The network of minicomputers would be able to assemble the various requests, and obtain estimates of origin-destination patterns and network loading, including link travel times.

Unfortunately, the technology did not exist to cost-effectively implement this concept, and it faded. Other ideas, such as automated highways and collision avoidance, also hit technological and cost barriers.

By the late 1980s, a new generation of computers existed, and had revolutionized computing. People now had on their desktop the computing power of the mainframe computers of the 1960s and 1970s. Further, *integrated circuit* (IC) microprocessors were being put in cars, ovens, and a host of electronic devices as special-purpose computers. At the same time, the cost and power of communications changed radically. Wireless communications, cellular telephones, and many other innovations became commonplace.

Even more amazing, a global positioning system (GPS)—a network of satellites—allowed people on the ground to find their position within a few meters, and read that position on a device small enough to be hand-held. Designed for the U.S. military, GPS is now available commercially so that truckers on the road know exactly where they are at all times, and—thanks to wireless communications—dispatchers can know the exact location of every vehicle in their fleet. The same systems are available to passenger car drivers, and are already introduced as a standard feature on some high-end cars (circa 1996).

GPS can be used for these purposes because of another, related innovation—the *geographic information system* (GIS). By mapping the GIS coordinates of the road system, the GPS location of a vehicle can be mapped into a specific location on the map, and even displayed visually as a dot on a digital display. Various software packages are now available that also show theaters, hotels, hospitals, and other locations in a city, so that a traveler can use a GIS-coded network and pop-up menus to find desired destinations. The software also lays out the route to get to the destination from the user's present location.

The same routing features are available to the traveler. A driver can have an in-vehicle display, and receive route guidance based on the traveler's preferences (shortest route, shortest time, etc.), using stored information on the transportation system configuration and historic travel times for the time period, or—if available—current travel times.

The elements of this technology explosion were combined in 1991 by a strong federal mandate in the ISTEA legislation. The organization then known as IVHS/America (now ITS/America) played an important role in emphasizing the potential value of intelligent transportation systems, and in developing the strategic direction [1] of the legislated program. The strategic plan identified a number of directions and programs, including *advanced traffic management systems* (ATMS), *advanced traveler information systems* (ATIS), and *commercial vehicle operations* (CVO).

By 1996, a strong emphasis had developed on transportation management centers (TMCs), transit and intermodal applications, vehicle routing, collision avoidance, automated toll collection, and other elements. There has been major work done on a communications systems architecture for ITS, and an active program on the automated highway system (AHS). The remainder of this section addresses some of these foci, and related topics.

A. A new paradigm

Historically, transportation systems and their control have been in the jurisdiction of public agencies. The most advanced traffic management systems—ramp metering, variable message signing on freeways and arterials, central computer control facilities, and such—have also been major public works, administered by public agencies.

While individual travelers have always sought to optimize their own trip (according to their own objectives), the information flow to drivers has always been limited by technological feasibility of certain mechanisms—radio stations using helicopters or video cameras, variable message displays on some facilities, low power local highway advisory radio (HAR) on others, and CB radio. Modern technology, however, is actually fostering a shift from public sector dominance to the private sector as the primary focus in the new world of intelligent transportation systems. Public agencies will continue to operate facilities and provide support, but the information flow can now be totally independent, comprehensive, and driven by the competitive nature of the private sector marketplace. Even some features once spoken of as "... the government should ..." are now value-added features on cars and trucks, by which manufacturers make their products more attractive. Collision avoidance systems on buses are a case in point. Route guidance displays are yet another.

Even information on highway travel times could now be provided by the private sector, if there were a market and if certain regulatory restrictions were changed. It is now estimated that some 15–20% of

travelers have cellular telephones, and this percentage is growing rapidly. With the consent of the driver (or with approved safeguards), this information could be used for estimates—all by time of day—of link travel times, origins and destinations, and routings. The sample sizes involved would be phenomenal, far exceeding anything transportation professionals have had access to previously, or anything that a "probe vehicle" approach[1] could provide.

It is possible to see a future world in which virtually every driver is a fully informed and independent decision-maker, receiving network status information continually from a commercial wireless service, using it automatically in an on-board routing computer, which would be programmed to the individual's personal preferences in route selection. This will be equally true for commercial and private vehicles. Public agencies may administer the system, set ramp metering rates and signal progressions, but the drivers will be responding to a set of completely independent inputs, and dynamically adjusting their routes in response to them.

The same high level of expectation will affect the transit system, and travelers will expect detailed schedule and status information, information kiosks (already installed in a number of systems), and a generally higher level of information flow. Given the pervasive nature of cellular phones and potentially of wireless personal data assistants (PDAs), the private sector will surely provide services which are not yet conceived.

Likewise, the competitive nature of the automotive industry will lead to even further advances in on-board "smart" systems which add value and uniqueness to a particular manufacturer. Collision avoidance systems and route advisory systems are two examples already cited. In assessing the potential, one must remember that most vehicles now have on-board a powerful computer with excess capacity, to serve fuel consumption systems, various sensors, and other systems.

---

[1]Probe vehicles are used in some ITS applications. Basically, a limited number of vehicles agree to have their location transmitted periodically, thereby allowing the system administrator to generate estimates of current link travel times. Another approach to this estimation problem is to have successive wayside stations query passing vehicles that have a visible automatic toll debit card visible, thereby allowing travel time differences to be computed.

It is, therefore, clear that a paradigm shift is underway, the extent of which is not yet (as of 1996) fully recognized in the professional community. Private for-profit companies can and will provide many intelligent transportation features, ranging from network status to route guidance to collision avoidance. Public agencies will still manage the fixed infrastructure, coordinate emergency/incident responses, and undertake major capital experiments such as the AHS. But they will be in a supportive role in the information flow and personal decision-making of the future. The old paradigm of public sector dominance in managed systems is changing rapidly and dramatically.

B. Routing

The concept of vehicle routing has already been addressed. Circa 1996, there were some seventeen distinct automated vehicle navigation/guidance systems either commercially available, in demonstration projects, or in test [2]. Both Avis and Hertz had been making automated vehicle navigation available in test markets in their rental fleets, with Avis considering it as a key element in their safety initiative program. These were route guidance systems, advising the driver on when to turn in order to reach a selected destination. In 1994, a commercial system was available as an option on the Oldsmobile 88, and an alternative system was added as an option in select markets in 1995. Ford offered a system as an option on its Lincoln in 1996. Honda is offering an in-dash system on the Acura as an option [3]. Others are addressing the aftermarket for guidance systems (that is, systems installed after the vehicle has been purchased, hence the word derived from "*after* the initial *market*ing").

Figure 2-1 shows one system that was available in 1996, the Pathmaster™ System. Figure 2-2 shows the system used in the Avis rental cars. These systems have the visual displays shown, in addition to a computer-synthesized voice giving messages on required turns.

In addition to the technology, market and human factors must be considered.

ITS International reports one estimate of negligible growth of route guidance devices through the 1990s, with very rapid growth after that. Specifically, the estimate was for three million units to be in use in the United States by 2001, and over 22 million by

Figure 2-1   The Pathmaster System. [Courtesy of Rockwell Transportation Electronics.]

2005 [4]. The key was thought to be price: in 1985, cellular phones were priced at $2,050 and had some 280,000 units sold each year; by 1990, with a price of about $1,000 annually, 1.76 million units were being sold each year. Cellular phones are now (circa 1996) $200 or less, and are used as give-aways in service lease programs by most telecommunications providers. The marketing report on which the route guidance estimates are based assumes a similar price/sales curve.

Figure 2-2   Another In-Vehicle Navigation System. [Courtesy of ITS World.]

In the same issue, *ITS International* also notes another market analysis that distinguishes between "autonomous" and "advisory" systems, and makes different market projections for each [5]. Autonomous systems are defined as fully independent and navigation-focused, with no roadside infrastructure needed. Advisory systems are more fully linked to publicly funded infrastructure, which provides real time traffic information.[2] The same analysis reports that there was an installed base of some 800,000 autonomous units in Japan, and that 1995 sales were estimated at 500,000 for that year alone.

Ross and Burnett's work on human factor aspects of in-vehicle routing systems was reported in reference [6]. They note that design guidelines should not hinder innovative design by laying down detailed rules (screen size, etc.). They also note that drivers are likely to become more demanding over the years, and that manufacturers will address issues such as "heads-up" displays (projected in front of the driver), the design of low-cost systems with limited interfaces and options, and adaptability to individual drivers.

C. Dynamic assessment

The work on route guidance, the future size of that market, and the options needed, plus other ITS applications implicitly point to a major deficiency in transportation models presently in common use: they are inadequate to the task of predicting traffic behavior, having been designed for a totally different, primarily static traffic environment.

Conventional transportation planning models use historic traffic data, representing a peak hour for the design year. Traffic is distributed among available origins and destinations, and then assigned to the network as flow rates along specific paths by an iterative process. The traffic load assigned is usually for the peak hour, with no temporal distribution within the hour (the traffic engineer will later determine a peaking, based upon historic information). Overloads at the cordon—traffic that cannot load into the network during the peak hour—are simply relegated to the next hour contiguous to the peak. This process results in a static loading, representative (one hopes, and

verifies by calibration) of the design hour. Analytic and computer models are designed for this purpose.

The new environment, however, provides drivers with detailed information on the network, and virtually guarantees dynamic re-assignment as drivers learn of incidents, unexpected traffic loads due to special events, and such. Indeed, the advisory re-routing is done in an on-board computer and provided directly to the driver via the display. At every time increment, drivers can be re-assigning themselves *from their present locations to their destinations,* not just from their origins. There is yet another aspect to this: drivers with good knowledge of the network can change the time at which they leave the origin, as well as the routing. Thus, latent demand can move into the peak hour from other time periods, and vice-versa.

Models, therefore, are needed that can address a constant re-assignment of current locations to destinations, and to specific routes between these locations. The same models must be able to account for shifts in demand both in time and space in response to the real-time information base being provided to drivers.

For several years, traffic engineers have done significant work on dynamic assignment models that can meet some or all of these needs. Engineers focused on the issue in an FHWA-sponsored workshop [7], and the literature contains a number of models, e.g., References [8–10], some of which have been used in test applications.

D. Systems architecture

One of the focal points of the FHWA and ITS/America efforts has been on establishing a national ITS communications systems architecture, which can be used as the logical basis of all ITS systems. The logic is compelling, and is the same as establishing standards[3] for telephone jacks, the 110 volt plug configuration, and the interfaces between a personal computer and other devices: future growth can happen in a common environment, and not be hampered by needless inconsistency. Table 2-1 shows the anticipated benefits of conforming to the national ITS architecture (and risks of not doing so).

[2]In a preceding subsection, the authors have suggested that the private sector can take on this task very well, absent some regulatory limits.

[3]To date, the emphasis has been on the structure of the architecture. Standards are a later stage of development, but the analogy is valid.

Table 2-1 Benefits of Using the National ITS Architecture

Benefits of Using the Architecture to Guide Deployment

National compatibility: as travelers and commerical vehicles move within the United States, the equipment on their vehicle continues to support them at all locations.

Multiple suppliers: more vendors will be supplying compatible equipment, leading to competition and less expensive equipment.

Future growth: by following an "open systems" approach, the architecture allows migration paths for future system growth and expansion (i.e., you upgrade subsystems, you don't start from scratch.)

Support for ranges of functionality: the architecture supports high-end and low-end features. Basic services can be provided free, while value-added services can be provided on a fee basis.

Synergy: the architecture considers the requirements for multiple functions and allocates systems to optimally support those functions.

Risk reduction: the architecture's common framework reduces risk for implementors, manufacturers, and consumers alike.

Why is Conformance and the Architecture Important?

Following the architecture provides you with an evolutionary path. You won't be stuck with obsolete systems that can't be upgraded.

The architecture provides a common language for deployment. You want to be in step with current and evolving practices.

Standards Development Organizations are using requirements from the architecture to develop ITS and ITI standards.

Equipment builders are also relying on the architecture's requirements and the standards that are being developed.

The architecture has already done a lot of work for you in defining data flows and potential system configuration. Take advantage of it!

Consequences of Not Conforming to the Architecture

Future system upgrades (new features or replacements) may be difficult, if not impossible.

You may be locked into one supplier due to proprietary interfaces.

[From *Building the ITI: Putting the National Architecture into Action,* prepared for FHWA by Mitretek Systems, 1996.]

Despite this, some people do feel that "the market can't wait for the government to get its ITS infrastructure operational" and that the "private sector has the ability to get this out more quickly" [11] and can integrate the cost into route guidance systems or as a service provider billing. Nonetheless, there is now a concept for a national ITS architecture after a multi-year effort to involve all interested parties. That idea is now being translated into the Intelligent Transportation Infrastructure (ITI) being implemented in several metropolitan areas. A key reference is [12], which has the details of the architecture in its documentation [13].

Reference [12] defines 29 ITS user services within the architecture framework (refer to Table 2-2). Figure 2-3 shows the nineteen subsystems for the full ITS and the basic communication channels between these subsystems. These channels are:

• wide area wireless communications
• wireline communications
• dedicated short range communications

Table 2-2 Twenty-nine User Services within the National ITS Architecture

Travel and Transportation Management
En route Driver Information
Route Guidance
Travel Services Information
Traffic Control
Incident Management
Emissions Testing and Mitigation

Travel Demand Management
Demand Management and Operations
Pre-trip Travel Information
Ride Matching and Reservation

Public Transportation Operation
Public Transportation Management
En route Transit Information
Personalized Public Transit
Public Travel Security

Electronic Payment
Electronic Payment Services

Commercial Vehicle Operations
Commercial Vehicle Electronic Clearance
Automated Roadside Safety Inspections
On-board Safety Monitoring
Commercial Vehicle Administrative Processes
Hazardous Material Incident Response
Freight Mobility

Emergency Management
Emergency Notification and Personal Security
Emergency Vehicle Management

Advanced Vehicle Control and Safety Systems
Longitudinal Collision Avoidance
Lateral Collision Avoidance
Intersection Collision Avoidance
Vision Enhancement for Crash Avoidance
Safety Readiness
Pre-crash Restraint Deployment
Automated Highway Systems

Note: Italicized services comprise the basic capabilities of the ITI. Other services build upon them. Highway-Rail Intersection is a newly added user service which will be incorporated into the architecture.

[From *Building the ITI: Putting the National Architecture into Action,* Prepared for FHWA by Mitretek Systems, 1996.]

A channel is also available for vehicle-to-vehicle communications. Reference [12] also shows how the 29 ITS user services relate to the nine integrated components of the ITI, which is the infrastructure portion of ITS for metropolitan areas. Figure 2-4 shows the inter-relations between the nine metropolitan components. Note that the "Traffic Signal Control" and "Freeway Management" elements are closely linked, and may be implemented together.

E. ATMS

Advanced Traffic Management Systems (ATMS) work can include street networks and/or freeway management projects, or the combined system. Computerized traffic control has been implemented for decades, but in the ITS environment of the 1990s the emphasis has been on linkage of ATMS to advanced traveler information systems (ATIS) and other ITS elements.

Two of the national testbeds for what is now called ATMS have been the Urban Traffic Control System (UTCS) in Washington, DC [14] and the INFORM freeway corridor management project on Long Island, NY [15], previously known as the IMIS (integrated motorist information system) project. The UTCS project focused on advanced control policies for urban street networks, and was responsible for the first generation of what became the TRAF/NETSIM traffic simulation model. The INFORM project involved two freeways, one arterial street, and their various connections. It made extensive use of loop detectors, video cameras, and variable message signs. Both projects had centralized control centers, now often referred to as transportation management centers (TMCs) or traffic operations centers (TOCs). Other major projects have been undertaken in Toronto [16], Chicago [17], Dallas [18], Houston [19], New York [20], and a number of other cities. These projects continue to evolve to meet current needs and to make use of modern technology.

Under ISTEA funding, the federal government has supported a number of operational tests and deployments related to ATMS, some with strong ATIS and other elements. As cited in [21], these include the

- SMART Corridor project along 12.3 miles of the Santa Monica Freeway corridor in Los Angeles, California
- TRANSCOM Congestion Management Program in the New York Metropolitan Area, involving three states (NY, NJ, CT) and emphasizing inter-agency cooperation in sharing information on incidents

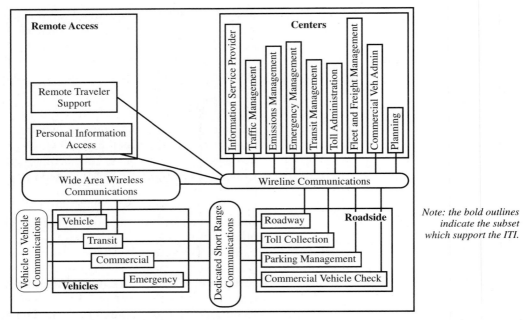

Figure 2-3 The nineteen subsystems of the full ITS. [From *Building the ITI: Putting the National Architecture into Action,* prepared for FHWA by Mitretek Systems, 1996.]

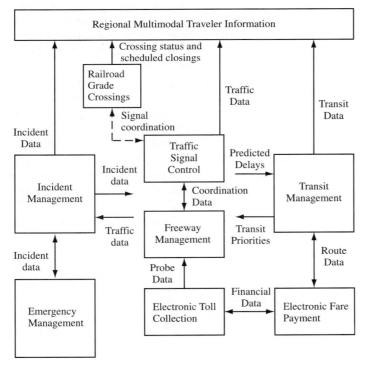

Figure 2-4 The intelligent transportation infrastructure (ITI) components and interconnections. [From *Building the ITI: Putting the National Architecture into Action,* prepared for FHWA by Mitretek Systems, 1996.]

and responses to them, as well as development of a regional strategy

• INFORM system on Long Island, already cited

FHWA is also involved in ATMS projects in Anaheim, California; Seattle, Washington; Montgomery County, Maryland; Irvine, California; Hartford, Connecticut; and other areas under ISTEA funding.

Figure 2-5 shows the transportation management center at Michigan DOT's MITS Center in Detroit. Notice the large screen display, the various video monitors, and the multi-position control desk. Figure 2-6 shows the INFORM network on Long Island. One of the most interesting challenges circa 1996 was the design of the ATMS control center in Atlanta, Georgia, built to accommodate the influx of traffic expected during the Summer Olympics of that year [22].

F. Tolls

One of the most dramatic "bottlenecks" on freeways is the toll plaza, with increased delays, extensive construction to widen the road and provide sufficient toll lanes, and significant queues. Accidents increase, as do emissions, due to stop-and-go traffic. In some areas, there is much controversy over which direction has the toll booths[4], just because of the air quality problem [23]. In addition, there are the problems of staffing levels and security (due to the cash being handled).

One very attractive solution has been electronic toll collection (ETC), also referred to as electronic toll and traffic management (ETTM). There are now some extensive systems, due in good part to the impetus under the federal ITS program and the ISTEA legislation. The basic concept is that the driver displays a debit card/device which is read by an infrared or other scanner as the vehicle passes through a toll station, and deducts the fee. Some systems require the driver to slow to 5 mph or less, and others allow higher speeds.

In the United States, electronic toll collection was pioneered in such states as Texas, Louisiana, and Oklahoma [24]. The largest installation is now in the

---

[4]Although many roads have toll booths in both directions, some just collect tolls in one direction. This is particularly suitable when no feasible non-toll path exists for the "other" direction.

Figure 2-5 The TMC in Detroit, Michigan. [Reprinted with permission of UK • International Press, from G. Revan and K. Johnson, "Big Image for Traffic Operations," *Traffic Technology International*, p. 52. Copyright © 1996 UK • International Press.]

New York area, where the toll facilities in several contiguous states represent more than half of the toll revenues collected annually in the United States. Figure 2-7 shows an EZ-PASS booth on the New York State Thruway, which is part of this extensive and growing system. The most fundamental design principle in the EZ-PASS system is commonality—several different authorities in three different states (New York, New Jersey, Pennsylvania) agreed on a functional design which allows a motorist to use the same pass on numerous facilities throughout the area. In October 1995, EZ-PASS was introduced on the Verrazano Bridge in New York, and is now (circa 1996) used in forty percent of the transactions on that facility. The MTA/Bridges and Tunnels Division expects several hundred thousand tags to be in use by the end of 1996, when all of its nine facilities will have EZ-PASS lanes. Add to these the New York State Thruway and other authorities, and the extensive network is growing rapidly. On the Tappan Zee Bridge, 75 percent of the morning toll transactions are electronic.

There have been problems with ETC implementation. Due to queues in other toll lanes, drivers have sometimes not been able to get to the more efficient ETC lanes easily. The EZ-PASS scanner does not see through some metal-oxide-tinted windows, creating additional problems. When cars follow trucks too closely through the scanner, some cars are erroneously charged the truck toll [25]. These technological problems have retarded the growth rate in use of the system.

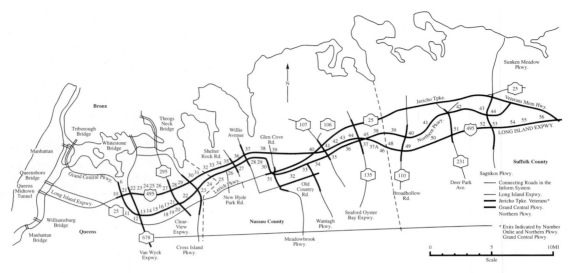

Figure 2-6   The INFORM Network on Long Island. [Courtesy of INFORM, New York State Department of Transportation.]

The pervasive use of vehicle tags also allows an opportunity to collect data in novel and extensive ways, particularly data regarding (1) portal-to-portal origins, destinations, and paths; (2) link travel times; and (3) incident detection, by deviations from the norm. TRANSCOM in the New York area is pursuing this potential.

One use of electronic vehicle tags not currently being discussed in great depth is to provide data for time-of-day variations in toll rates (variable pricing) and even congestion pricing, in which drivers are charged not just a differential toll but also for time spent in certain zones (by the addition of sensors at the cordon of the zones). While such economic theories have been advanced over the years, particularly by the late Professor Vickery of Columbia, the winner of the 1996 Nobel Prize in economics, the technology for their implementation has been lacking. ITS may revive interest in these concepts, which are often politically unpopular.

G. Collision avoidance

Historically, collision avoidance was viewed as one of the special advantages of an automated highway. Indeed, the first test of an automated highway system (AHS) was scheduled for August 1997 on a 7.6 mile segment of I-15 in San Diego, California [26]. At the same time, it is interesting that collision avoidance has taken on a life of its own, in the form of on-board sensors and systems which warn the driver when other vehicles get too close. NHTSA (National Highway and Transportation Safety Administration) is cur-

Figure 2-7   EZ-PASS lane on the New York State Thruway. [Courtesy of ITS: Intelligent Transport Systems, Rate 1 Publishing, Ltd.]

rently creating performance specifications for collision avoidance using advanced ITS technologies [27]. Products such as ultrasonic proximity detectors are advertised to address the problems of large vehicles changing lanes, and backing up, noting that some 18,000 traffic accidents each year involve large vehicles in such maneuvers [28].

H. Transit

The emphasis in much of the above has been on vehicular movement. Nonetheless, there is now a strong transit component to ITS efforts. Much of this takes the form of integrated information systems (kiosks, computer displays, internet postings, phone), common fare cards and smartcards, articulated schedules (bus-rail, other), electronic payment, and variable fares. ITS technology is being used to locate buses and improve schedule adherence, and research is underway on a new generation of traffic signal priority for transit, based upon more specific advance knowledge of arrival times.

Under ISTEA funding, USDOT has funded a number of ITS transit operational tests [21], including an assessment of how to apply a German flexible operation command and control system in Portland Oregon, an alternate bus routing project in New Jersey, and various electronic payment, smart bus, and smart card projects. (The smart card is an electronic fare card, most often intended to be used on various modes and/or systems.)

I. International activity

In anticipation of the audience for this text, as well as the significant effect of the 1991 ISTEA legislation, many of the examples and activities cited are based in the United States. However, in no way does this imply that the sole center of ITS activity is in the United States. In fact, Japan and Europe have had major ITS programs predating the U.S. effort and were discussion focal points for the first ITS/America meetings, so that valuable lessons could be learned [e.g., 29,30].

The attention to ITS is now truly international. The police in Seoul, Korea use a GPS-based system to locate and utilize police cars [31], and periodicals [e.g., *ITS International, ITS World*] report a major variable message sign (VMS) system on London-Midland routes, a full automatic vehicle identification (AVI) implementation on Swiss Rail, an ETC implementation

in Italy, growing efforts in Japan, smartcard implementations throughout Europe, a GPS-based taxi locator system in Singapore, a personal travel assistant (PTA) effort in Germany, a bus management system in Korea, and computer traffic control efforts in India.

Preserving the function of the facility

Another important theme is preserving the function and use for which traffic facilities were built. Even before preservation, the function must be built into the design, so that it is not easily modified later.

This section addresses three case studies: preserving local streets for neighborhood use, maintaining flow near a major traffic generator, and preserving arterial streets for through traffic. The last subject leads to access management, another emerging theme which is addressed in the next section.

A. Local streets and residential uses

One report aptly noted the attitude of drivers: "Many motorists simply regard any street in any location as, first and foremost, a place to drive. Further, they have certain expectations as to how a street system should operate, and if the street becomes congested beyond their tolerance, they will seek other paths."

Figure 2-8 highlights some of the problems experienced in a residential area due to external traffic, accentuated by the grid pattern of the streets. The essence of this problem, at the other extreme from the "state road" problem, is that local residents and traffic professionals intend the street for local access, but some motorists find other uses and alternative paths. How can one enhance the local-access character of the streets?

Conventional suburban practice includes initial design emphasizing curvilinear layouts, mazes, cul-de-sacs, and—eventually—extensive use of stop signs to control speed. Actually, practice has shown that mid-block speeds are frequently not changed [32], stop-sign compliance is lower than normal [33], and diversion depends upon the intensity of stop signs [32].

Reference [32] is an excellent compendium of conventional and innovative techniques used for defining and reinforcing the local-access character of a residential street system. Figure 2-9 illustrates some of the treatments applied to the case shown in

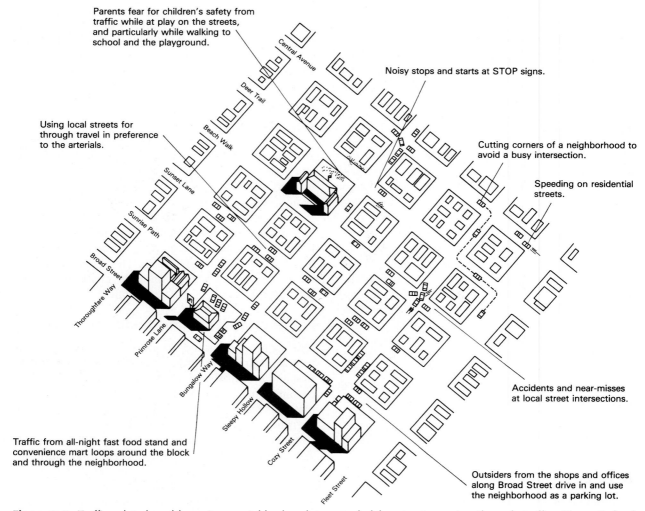

Parents fear for children's safety from traffic while at play on the streets, and particularly while walking to school and the playground.

Noisy stops and starts at STOP signs.

Using local streets for through travel in preference to the arterials.

Cutting corners of a neighborhood to avoid a busy intersection.

Speeding on residential streets.

Accidents and near-misses at local street intersections.

Traffic from all-night fast food stand and convenience mart loops around the block and through the neighborhood.

Outsiders from the shops and offices along Broad Street drive in and use the neighborhood as a parking lot.

Figure 2-8 Traffic-related problems in a neighborhood surrounded by streets serving through traffic. [From Federal Highway Administration, D. T. Smith, et al., *State of the Art: Residential Traffic Management,* 1980.]

Figure 2-8. Table 2-3 enumerates the treatments considered in [32] and lists the report's assessment of the probable effects on traffic.

The designation of the *function* of the roads, and a sense of what roads are intended to achieve is an important part of the process leading to a residential access system.

Reference [34] makes the point that in recent years the Neo-Traditional Neighborhood Development (NTND) movement has begun to redefine the criteria by which residential streets should be designed,

and cites several key references for residential street design [35,36,37] and summarizes the content of each. In addition, reference [38] presents a "toolbox" approach to residential traffic management.

B. Maintaining flow near a major generator

Major activity centers abutting arterials and other facilities present the potential for major problems, for they attract considerable numbers of trips and make

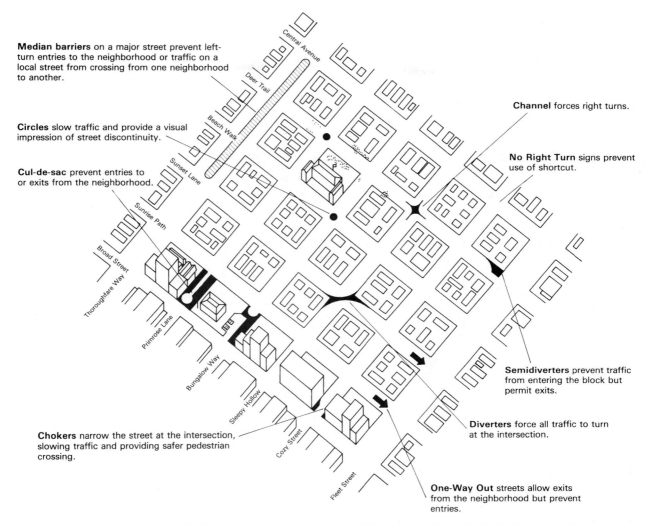

Median barriers on a major street prevent left-turn entries to the neighborhood or traffic on a local street from crossing from one neighborhood to another.

Circles slow traffic and provide a visual impression of street discontinuity.

Cul-de-sac prevent entries to or exits from the neighborhood.

Channel forces right turns.

No Right Turn signs prevent use of shortcut.

Semidiverters prevent traffic from entering the block but permit exits.

Diverters force all traffic to turn at the intersection.

One-Way Out streets allow exits from the neighborhood but prevent entries.

Chokers narrow the street at the intersection, slowing traffic and providing safer pedestrian crossing.

Figure 2-9 Some solutions applied to the neighborhood grid of Figure 2-8. [From Federal Highway Administration, D. T. Smith, et al., *State of the Art: Residential Traffic Management,* 1980.]

the use of capacity (number of lanes, etc.) and access of the arterial.

It is unrealistic simply to wish that such major generators did not exist, so that the arterial could maintain its original function and level of activity. The issue is then how to serve such generators while maintaining the arterial function.

Figure 2-9 shows one possible arrangement. Note that: (1) the through lanes are separated from storage areas which feed the complex with multiple-access lanes; and (2) the lane arrangements within the complex avoid the cross flows at the arterial interface which would normally dictate inefficient conflicts or multiphased signals.

C. The function of a state road

At the state level, state engineers and planners may take the view that the state system is intended for travel between major population clusters within the state, with other levels of government providing service within their jurisdictions (although with funding through federal–state programs in a number of cases). Within urban areas, state roads may be existing

Table 2-3 Methods Considered for Enhancing Local Access Character of Streets

Devices	Direct Traffic Effects						Emergency and Service Access
	Volume Reductions	Speed Reductions	Directional Control	Change In Composition	Noise	Safety	
Physical controls							
Speed bumps	Possible	Inconsistent	Unlikely	Unlikely	Increase	Adverse effects	Some problems
Undulations	Possible	Yes	Unlikely	Unlikely	No change	No problems documented	No problems documented
Rumble strips	Unlikely	Yes	Unlikely	Unlikely	Increase	Improved	No problems
Diagonal diverters	Yes	Likely	Possible	Possible	Decrease	Shifts accidents	Some constraints
Intersection cul-de-sac	Yes	Likely	Yes	Possible	Decrease	Shifts accidents	Some constraints
Midblock cul-de-sac	Yes	Likely	Yes	Possible	Decrease	Shifts accidents	Some constraints
Semidiverter	Yes	Likely	Yes	Possible	Decrease	Shifts accidents	Minor constraints
Forced-turn channelization	Yes	Likely	Yes	Possible	Decrease	Improved	Minor constraints
Median barrier	Yes	On curves	Possible	Possible	Decrease	Improved	Minor constraints
Traffic circle	Unclear	Minor	Unlikely	Possible	Little change	Questionable	Some constraints
Chokers and road narrowing	Rare	Minor	Unlikely	Unlikely	Little change	Improved ped. crossings	No problems
Passive controls							
Stop signs	Occasional	Some red.	Unlikely	Unlikely	Increase	Mixed results	No problems
Speed limit signs	Unlikely	Unlikely	Unlikely	Unlikely	No change	No change	No effect
Turn prohibition signs	Yes	Likely	Yes	Possible	Decrease	Improved	No effect
One-way streets	Yes	Inconsistent	Yes	Possible	Decrease	Possible imp.	No effect
Psycho-perception Controls							
Transverse markings	No change	Yes	No effect	No effect	Possible red.	Possible imp.	No effect
Crosswalks	No effect	Unlikely	No effect	No effect	No effect	Ineffective	No effect
Odd speed-limit signs	No effect	No effect	No effect	No effect	No effect	No effect	No effect
Novelty signs	No effect	Undocumented	No effect	No effect	Unlikely	No effect	No effect

[From Federal Highway Administration, D. T. Smith et al., *State of the Art: Residential Traffic Management*, FHWA Report RD-80-092, 1980.] Specific details of individual applications may result in performance substantially variant from characterizations in this matrix. See literature on individual devices for more complete performance data, assessments and qualifications.

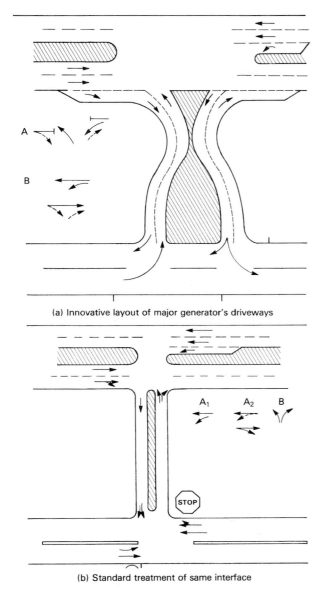

(a) Innovative layout of major generator's driveways

(b) Standard treatment of same interface

Figure 2-10 Driveways at a major generator along an arterial.

arterials with their own histories, or limited-access freeways. Outside of those areas, the state system may be arterials, with few limited-access facilities.

Note that zoning and land-use decisions are made at the *local* level, so that decisions on development (and the intensity of development) in the vicinity of state roads are not state-level decisions.

Enhanced access by virtue of a state arterial can actually lay the foundation for future development of the community. As years pass, such development has three dramatic impacts: (1) the traffic burden on the state road system increases; (2) the nature of local traffic and side frictions affects the original function of the arterial as serving through traffic; and (3) the development surrounds the existing right-of-way, making a simple upgrade infeasible due to the physical constraints and the cost of additional right-of-way acquisition.

In the extreme, this could lead to a growth pattern that would require (and has required, in cases) a major new facility, routed around the evolved developed community. Refer to Figure 2-11 for an illustration of this pattern.

How can this situation be anticipated and avoided? By initially reserving extra right-of-way width? By building with an inner roadway for through traffic, physically separated from the local traffic on outer lanes? The questions are rhetorical, but they are issues being faced today by many states. Part of the issue centers on whether traffic engineers have the tools to analyze and describe the problem.

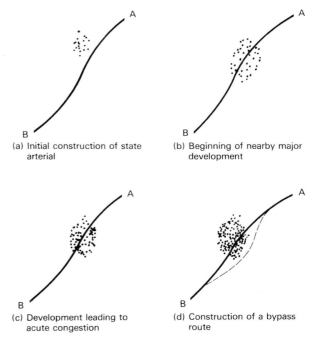

(a) Initial construction of state arterial

(b) Beginning of nearby major development

(c) Development leading to acute congestion

(d) Construction of a bypass route

Figure 2-11 Development of a community around a state road.

D. Insight from case studies

These cases in facility design and land-use interface are not intended to be comprehensive or to provide specific, generally applicable solutions. Rather, they are intended to acquaint the reader with the range of design situations and the considerations that enter into addressing them.

Access management

Because of the need to preserve facility function, there has been a major movement in the United States toward "access management," particularly to preserve arterial function. This has had two major elements:

- *Legal and Administrative.* To influence and redirect access, there must be a clear legislative mandate and a strong policy direction in the state. The leader in access management has been Colorado [39], followed by Florida [40] and more recently by New Jersey [41]. There have now been regular national access management conferences [42,43] in which professionals can share experiences in the legal, administrative, land use, and technical aspects of access management.
- *Technical.* There is some substantial literature on access management and its effects, including [44] and a major National Cooperative Research Program (NCHRP) project on the subject [45].

The remainder of this section addresses some conceptual issues related to access management. Figure 2-12 asserts that at the core of "access management" is a design philosophy for roads, intended to provide and preserve mobility. This implies the need for a consistent land use policy, for the two are intertwined. The design philosophy for roads is based upon some very basic traffic engineering principles, and yields considerable benefits when implemented.

A. Mobility as a goal

It is appropriate to clearly and unambiguously state that the preservation of mobility on primary systems should be the public policy, and that access management is part

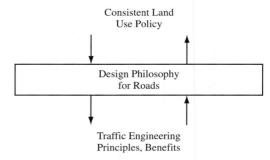

Figure 2-12 A design philosophy is at the core of access management.

of the design philosophy that implements that policy. This can be summarized as shown in Table 2-4.

In this context, we must understand that traffic engineering measures (VMT, turns, capacity, accidents) are not really driven by project-specific actions—a particular median construction, for instance—but rather by an overall readjustment in traffic assignments, driven by the public policy of preserving mobility.

Good access management is part of an overall design philosophy, a philosophy which most jurisdictions did not wish to accept for many decades. Who wanted to build a system that required intersections only every half mile, or quarter mile? Who wanted to limit access to parcels, or require interparcel access or backage roads or any such measure? Who had the authority to do so? The real answer is that "access management" in its current incarnation is a design philosophy for the road system which actually goes beyond the road system to a consistent land use policy. The need is clear, and adoption of such a philosophy is an essential element of a congestion management program.

No one should, however, underestimate the public volatility of access management policies. Such policies often retard development, and make development more costly, and thus less attractive to potential developers. In this arena, the need for better access control for traffic purposes is contrasted with the need for economic growth.

B. Transportation planning tools

A regional network is defined by the geography of the area, the land use pattern which has grown up, and

Table 2-4   Preservation of Mobility as a Public Policy Goal

Public Policy	Implementation	Effects
Preserve mobility on the designated system	By means of a design philosophy which includes access management	Short Term • VMT adjustment • Volume and turn changes • Preservation of capacity • Decreased accidents Longer Term • Land use adjustments • Rebalancing of short term effects

the transportation system which was provided. Over decades, these have evolved and interacted, always influenced by the underlying topography.

Planners can sketch out a "primary network" on this network in broad strokes, with the intent of providing mobility for the population. They can then lay out access management measures that can preserve this mobility. In this way, feasible paths and routes are defined.

Drivers then assign themselves to this network in ways that optimize their own trip making. The transportation assignment models can mimic the drivers' decision-making to some degree, with increasing realism if not perfection. Figure 2-13 illustrates the fact that each measure—such as a median construction—can be expected to affect paths taken to a particular destination.

The driver assignment results in a set of volumes, turn rates, and hence VMT. It also results in certain accident exposures throughout the region, and hence accident experiences. Further, it results in a certain pattern of vehicle emissions. Most importantly, if the original designation of the "primary network" were well done, that network can meet current and future mobility needs in an efficient and safe manner.

Complicating this picture is the reality that the land uses will shift, as businesses locate themselves to the opportunities presented by the defined system. In turn, the traffic pattern will shift. Most transportation models take the land use as a given, and are not suited to "play out" the dynamic of transportation/ land use interaction; our modeling talents are pressed in this area.

However, it is clear that there will be a new equilibrium, an equilibrium which is reached from a public policy statement that the primary system (by whatever name) has to be preserved for mobility.

C. The role of good traffic engineering

Some of the most dramatic effects of good access management were well known from traffic engineering theory and practice for decades, but were not considered feasible. If signals are properly spaced, the number of vehicles that can travel the entire facility without stopping can increase dramatically. Incidentally, this is not an increase in "capacity" as capacity is usually defined, but rather a very dramatic and important increase in the number of vehicles that do not get stopped. Likewise, facilities with raised medians are shown to have lower accident rates than facilities which do not have raised medians. It is good to see this confirmed, but it is also dictated by common sense.

What does complicate the analysis in the raised median example is the possibility that traffic is taking more circuitous routes to get to desired destinations, increasing VMT and/or having their accidents elsewhere, out of the analysis zone.

Of course, there is the other possibility, that the traffic stops going to certain destinations and goes to others. That is, that drivers simply go to another business of the same type which is now relatively easier to reach. This of course is one of the concerns of businesses on the arterial being improved.

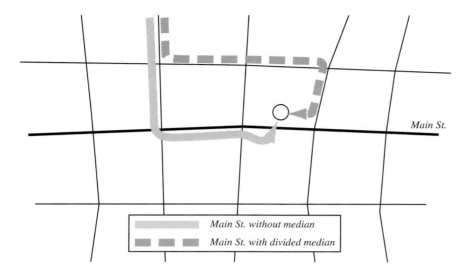

Figure 2-13 The defined network affects routing and influences land use.

Main St. without median
Main St. with divided median

Main St.

Rather than try to condense all of good traffic engineering practice into a few pages, let us simply observe that some of the most basic operational principles for use on the primary network are as follows:

- Provide excellent progression to major traffic flows.
- Provide proper intersection capacity.
- Avoid conflicting movements and separate flows.

These have tremendous benefits, and are responsible for much of the perceived increase in "capacity" reported in the literature.

D. Selecting proper performance measures

Although it may seem obvious, it is critical that performance measures selected to evaluate the quality of facility operation are capable of *detecting* the effects of actions which common sense says are important (if indeed they are), and of being *comprehensible* and *credible* to the general public as well as to transportation specialists.

It is essential that we recognize that some "measures" are best obtained by estimates and/or by use of computational tools. There are at least two very good reasons for this:

- Some effects happen over wider areas than we normally can afford to study; a case in point is VMT change due to re-routing of traffic following a median closure.

- Other effects are very real but buried within many other types of variability, such as daily fluctuations in traffic, driveway volumes, and such.

Nonetheless, it is essential that the need for such secondary estimates be highly credible to both professionals and the public.

As to the measures themselves: the access management literature makes use of average travel speeds, capacity, accident experience, and—to a lesser extent—VMT. This is quite consistent with existing practice in such a basic reference as the *Highway Capacity Manual.* It is best not to invent new measures, unless it is absolutely essential to accomplishing the task.

Table 2-5 summarizes a possible set of measures of performance for access management. For arterial traffic, it is strongly recommended that the focus be on the through vehicles, expressed as their average travel speed.

What is needed in some cases is more specific information on *how much* effect on speed or on capacity preservation results from a given measure, such as fewer driveways.

Why consider travel speed, and not travel rate or travel time? These are actually different ways of saying the same thing, and the distinction is only in the numeric form of the measure. In some presentations, it may be better to use one or the other of this set. However, they are merely different ways of saying the same thing. Nonetheless, in some presentations, one is more apt than the others.

Table 2-5 A Possible Set of Performance Measures for Access Management

Indicator	How to Observe in the Field	How to Estimate	Comments
Average travel speed or rate of the through vehicles	Travel time studies would be most common.	*Computation* Involves estimates of delay, and such procedures as those in the *HCM*. *Traffic Assignment Models* Rules vary, but sometime use *HCM* principles. *Simulation* In a model such as TRAF/NETSIM, based upon microscopic interaction of vehicles.	1) Refer to standard materials/sources for guidance on number of field observations needed; varies by purpose. 2) Use of average travel speed, travel rate, and/or travel time depends upon application.
Capacity	Observation of throughput when demand exceeds capacity.	Estimation of capacity is the primary subject of the *HCM*. Traffic assignment models use *HCM* or other inputs, or have the same rules imbedded. Throughput can be observed from TRAF/NETSIM, and interpreted with care.	1) Access management literature sometimes refers to "capacity" when "signal system bandwidth" is meant. 2) The issue is sometimes not capacity, but capacity preservation. If driveways prevent signal capacity being used, even when it exists, then it is a "capacity preservation" issue.
VMT or PMT	In principle, easy to measure VMT by observing volumes and PMT if occupancies are known. In practice, VMT effects may go beyond section being observed. Therefore, estimates may be more feasible.	Estimation by traffic assignment models may be the most appropriate technique, subject to some verification in the project area under consideration.	The emphasis on PMT has to be increased.
Accident experience	Requires measurement over an extended period (years) due to the nature of accidents and the need for sufficient observations.	Estimates linked to volumes, speeds, and site features (median, etc.) are possible. Look to the literature for a growing number of such relations.	The problem with empiric relations is that more things may be changing than are recorded (or summarized). Sight distances may have been improved, speed variance may have been reduced, and so forth.
Emissions	Limited opportunities with existing technology, due to point observations. Greater potential for area estimation based upon infrared (IR) sensors being considered in ITS efforts.	Estimates available in TRAF/NETSIM.	Even if only estimates are available, their use is a reminder that emissions is an important issue—and benefit—of access management.

Some display maps show different colors for various speeds, so that a person can get a sense of where the problems are. These maps actually show speed *and* distance, and also allow the person to visualize the effect of taking certain paths. While the psychology of how people process information from visual displays is a specialty (and of growing interest in computer science), clearly *rate* and *distance* are important.

The measures cited have the advantage that most of them can be observed relatively efficiently *and* are also available in traffic simulation models. While accident rates do require years of observation, there are relations for cases and situations which allow estimates to be made. For instance, there may be regression equations relating accident rates (by severity) to volume for given conditions (median, no median).

E. Summary

Access management is a critical and growing function associated with management of transportation systems, and the development of policies affecting them. There is clearly a great need for better understanding of the interrelated elements of land use, economic activity and growth, and traffic generation/distribution/assignment. This can be expected to be a major focus of transportation research over the next decade or more.

Attention to intermodal emphasis

This is a significant theme, and much has already been said about it in earlier materials in this chapter. The practicing traffic engineer must expect a much greater emphasis on person-movement, on accommodating (and giving preference to) transit, and on the design and operation of intermodal facilities. This will have implications for performance measures (see below) used in evaluating system performance.

Performance measures

Performance measures are parameters that describe, in various ways, the quality of service provided to the user of a facility. Think of this in terms of what the facility user experiences, and in terms of the kinds of experiences that affect user perceptions of service quality:

1. How good was *my* trip?
   • Travel time and delay can indicate this.
   • Speed is another way of expressing this.
2. How many of *us* did the system move?
   • Volume and people can indicate this.
3. How *well* did the system move us?
   • Travel time, delay, and speed seem to serve the purpose.
   • Some indication of crowding may be appropriate.
4. How *much* of the system resources were used up in the process?
   • Volume to capacity ratios may be appropriate.

Each of these thoughts is translated to standard parametric measures in later chapters. Their use is almost always to answer some of these fundamental questions.

The above questions, however, are oriented to a developed transportation system, where the trips *can* be made. What if the infrastructure is missing, so that the trips cannot even be conceived, or so that there is no historic record of the need?

Specifically, consider a well-developed vehicle-oriented corridor with no bus transit service (or one infrequent route). How does one construct a set of performance measures for *transit service availability*? That is, for assessing how well demand could be served, if it appeared? Is it relevant to be concerned about service availability if there is no demand? For the sake of discussion, consider the postulate that a corridor should have a choice of modes, and that it should be a real choice. Transit should then exist, have reasonable spatial coverage, plausible interarrival times, adherence to schedules, and other features. What are those features? What is expected by the traveling public? It need not be the flexibility of auto travel, or the same travel time, or . . . whatever . . . but it should be quantifiable. It may be necessary to assess transit *deficiency* as well as transit *service*. That is, if the routes are not there but should be, then the deficiency has to be quantified and reported. If there is demand, then how well it is served has to be reported as well.

This brief discussion highlights the difficulty in developing appropriate performance measures, and the need to consider measures for a wide range of potential conditions and situations.

Mobility and congestion

It has already been noted that both ISTEA and reality cause a major focus on congestion, but this is simply quantifying how bad things are. Indeed, the issue introduces an interesting problem: suppose a state was addressing a problem systematically for years, but then changes the definition of "congestion"—or does a better job of finding it, or faces natural growth—so that things suddenly look much worse. Has the multiyear allocation of public resources in the past years been a mistake?

There is another aspect to this problem: do we just fight tactical battles with tactical solutions to mitigate congestion, or do we make a strategic plan to address the mobility needs of the population? Asked this way, the answer seems clear, and establishes the value of focusing on mobility.

This issue will continue to evolve, as will the response of the profession to it. For present purposes, it is sufficient that the reader be aware of its importance.

Trends in population and transportation location

There is a strong pattern of job and population relocation, so that the historic trip to the central city is actually diminishing, at least on a percentage basis. Some of the new locations may represent true decentralization in the sense of dispersed job locations and dispersed, low density residences, both in the suburbs. However, even in the historic suburbs, there are concentrations in industrial parks, corridors, and other clusters. In larger metropolitan areas, these clusters would be cities in their own right in some areas of the

country. The future traffic engineer has to consider the implications of many smaller clusters interacting with each other, with shorter trips and less congestion (if adequate transportation capacity exists) than the historic trip to the central city.

Metrication

The federal government has mandated the use of the International System of units (SI units) in almost all its procurements, grants, and other business-related activities, based upon a 1988 amendment to the original legislation [47]. As a result, FHWA specified that all newly authorized federal contracts must use only metric units by September 30, 1996 [48]. In turn, AASHTO issued a revised, metric "Green Book" [49], also incorporating updates to *HCM* as available at the time the update was prepared. The fourth edition of the *HCM* is scheduled to be metric-only. This text uses some metric units (particularly related to AASHTO criteria) but will not be fully metric until the next edition.

Engineering students now use the metric system rather routinely in their undergraduate education, so that it is the practicing engineer who will be faced with the transition from the system most familiar to them. This will be complicated by a natural transition period in which certain references will have converted, but others will not have, primarily due to production cycles and/or anticipated revisions to the materials.

Without question, all key references and practices will be in the metric system very soon. Those with a need to refer to the literature, however, will encounter the older system with some regularity.

In addition to the technical use of the metric system amongst professionals, the use in signing and other areas will require a re-thinking by the public at large.

Summary

This chapter has provided an overview of some emerging issues and trends in traffic and transportation, so that the reader may approach the later chapters with a perspective of what is happening, before becoming immersed in different technical elements. The next chapter begins that process of immersion, focusing on traffic stream components and characteristics.

References

1. *Department of Transportation's IVHS Strategic Plan Report to Congress,* Publication No. FHWA-SA-93-009, U.S. Department of Transportation, Washington, DC, December 18, 1992.
2. Puentes, R., "In-Vehicle Navigation/Guidance Systems," *ITS America Fact Sheet (Draft),* June 28, 1996.
3. Cogan, R., "Wheels in Motion," *ITS World,* July/August 1996.
4. "Unit Prices Key to U.S. Market for In-Vehicle Guidance," *ITS International,* No. 5, June 1996.
5. "Autonomous v Advisory," *ITS International,* No. 5, June 1996.
6. "The Right Road to Take," *ITS International,* No. 5, June 1996.
7. *IVHS Dynamic Traffic Assignment and Simulation Workshop,* U.S. Department of Transportation, Federal Highway Administration, Washington, DC, March 1992.
8. Cascetta, E., et al., *A Dynamic Traffic Assignment Model for Real Time Applications, Proceedings of the First World Congress on Applications of Transport Telematics and Intelligent Vehicle-Highway Systems,* Vol. 3, Palais De Congres de Paris, Paris, France, 1994.
9. Janson, B., *Dynamic Traffic Assignment for Urban Road Networks,* Vol. 25B, Transportation Research Board, National Research Council, Washington, DC, April-June 1991, pp. 143–61.
10. Wie, B., et al., "The Augmented Lagrangian Method for Solving Dynamic Network Traffic Assignment Models in Discrete Time," *Transportation Science,* Vol. 28, August 1994.
11. Taylor, S. T., "Untangling Tie-ups in the ATIS Market," *ITS World,* July/August 1996.
12. *Building the ITI: Putting the National Architecture into Action,* prepared for Federal Highway Administration by Mitretek Systems, Washington, DC, April 1996.
13. *Architecture: Complete Set of the System Architecture Interim Program Review* (29 documents), ITS America, Washington, DC, 1996.
14. Stockfish, C. R., "The UTCS Experience," *Public Roads,* Vol. 48, No. 1, June 1984.
15. *Smart Highways: An Assessment of Their Potential to Improve Travel,* U.S. General Accounting Office, Report to the Chairman, Subcommittee on Transportation, Committee on Appropriations, U.S. Senate, GAO/PEMD-91-18, May 1991.
16. *Improved Operation of Urban Transportation Systems: Vol. 1,* Metropolitan Toronto Department of Roads and Traffic, November 1974.
17. Zavattero, D., Smoliak, A., and Sikaris, C., "Intelligent Transportation Systems Activities in Northeastern Illinois," Working Paper No. 95-10, Chicago Area Transportation Study, Chicago, IL, 1995.
18. "Looking to the Future," *Texas Transportation Researcher,* Vol. 32, No. 1, Texas Transportation Institute, The Texas A&M University, College Station, TX, spring 1996.
19. *Houston Transtar Brochure,* 6922 Old Katy Road, Houston, TX.
20. *ITS Executive Summaries,* The International Urban ITS Workshop, New York, NY, July 1996.
21. *Department of Transportation's Intelligent Transportation Systems (ITS) Projects,* U.S. Department of Transportation, Federal Highway Administration, Washington, DC, January 1995.
22. Pittman, R., "An Olympic-Sized Transportation Challenge," *Traffic Technology International,* June/July 1996.
23. Brooke, J., "One-way Verrazano Toll is Cutting Revenues," *New York Times,* Sunday, April 27, 1986, p. 43, Sec. 1.
24. Samuel, P., "ETC Storms Mid-Atlantic," *ITS International,* No. 5, June 1996.
25. McGarrett, J., "Controversies Hit Hong Kong," *ITS International,* No. 5, June 1996.
26. "AHS Project Installs Initial Sensors," *ITS America News,* Vol. 6, No. 8, August 1996.
27. Burgett, A. "Crash Avoidance Holds Key to Safer U.S. Highways," *Safety,* 1996.
28. "Sensory System to Reduce Accidents," *ITS International,* No. 5, June 1996.
29. *Surface Transportation and the Information Age,* Proceedings of the IVHS AMERICA, 1992 Annual Meeting, Newport Beach, CA, May 1992.
30. *Surface Transportation: Mobility, Technology, and Society,* Proceedings of the IVHS AMERICA, 1993 Annual Meeting, Washington, DC, April 1993.
31. *Report: Critical Design Review for Seoul Metropolitan Police Administration,* Grumman Data Systems, 1992.
32. Smith, D. T., et al., "State of the Art: Residential Traffic Management," *FHWA Report RD-80-092,* Federal Highway Administration, Washington, DC, December 1980.
33. De Leuw, Gather & Company, *Six Months' Experience: Berkeley Traffic Management Plan,* 1976.
34. Shaw, G. R., "Impact of Residential Street Standards on Neo-Traditional Neighborhood Concepts," *ITE Journal,* July 1994.
35. ITE Technical Council Committee 5A-25A, *Guidelines for Residential Subdivision Street Design, Proposed Revisions to a Recommended Practice,* Institute of Transportation Engineers, Washington, DC, 1990.

36. Homburger, W. S., et al., *Residential Street Design and Traffic Control,* Prentice-Hall, Englewood Cliffs, NJ, 1989.

37. American Society of Civil Engineers, National Association of Home Builders and Urban Land Institute, *Residential Streets,* 2nd Edition, ASCE, Washington, DC, 1990.

38. Savage, R. P. and MacDonald, R. D., "A Toolbox Approach to Residential Traffic Management," *ITE Journal,* June 1996.

39. "The State Highway Access Code," 2 CCR 601-1, amended by the Colorado Highway Commission, August 15, 1985.

40. "State Highway System Access Management Act of 1988," State of Florida, and "Rules of the Department of Transportation Chapter 14-97, State Highway System Access Management Classification System and Standards," Florida Department of Transportation, December 1990.

41. Eisendorfer, A. J., (NJDOT), "Access Permitting," The First National Conference on Access Management, Vail, CO, August 3, 1993.

42. The First National Conference on Access Management, Vail, CO, August 3, 1993.

43. The Second National Conference on Access Management, Vail, CO, August 11–14, 1996.

44. Levinson, Herbert, "Access Management on Suburban Roads," *Transportation Quarterly,* Vol. 48, Summer 1994, pp. 315–25.

45. "Impacts of Access Management Techniques," NCHRP Project 3-52, National Cooperative Highway Research Program.

46. Sackman, G. et al., "Vehicle Detector Placement for High-Speed, Isolated, Traffic-Actuated Intersection Control," *Manual of Theory and Practice,* Vol. 2, Federal Highway Administration, Washington, DC, May 1977.

47. The Metric Conversion Act of 1975, Public Law 94-168, 89 Stat. 1007, as amended by the Omnibus Trade and Competitiveness Act of 1988, Public Law 100-418, 102 Stat. 1107, 1451.

48. King, L., "The New AASHTO Metric Policy on Geometric Design of Highways and Streets," *ITE Journal,* August 1995.

49. *A Policy on Geometric Design of Highways and Streets,* American Association of State Highway and Transportation Officials, Washington, DC, 1994.

Problems

Problem 2–1

Explain the difference between a "highway" and an "arterial," as the terms are commonly used. Give a local example of each.

Problem 2–2

Consider an area that has four major employers, all located along the same arterial, one after the other. The demand for service, based upon the common starting time of 8:00 A.M., is as follows (expressed in *vehicles,* not vph):

Time	Firm A	Firm B	Firm C	Firm D
7:45–8:00 A.M.				
8:00–8:15 A.M.	5	10	10	5
8:15–8:30 A.M.	25	30	20	10
8:30–8:45 A.M.	300	150	350	125
8:45–9:00 A.M.	350	300	400	300
9:00–9:15 A.M.	15	6	15	6
9:15–9:30 A.M.	5	4	5	4
Totals	700	500	800	450

The average auto occupancy is 2.35 in all cases. Sixty percent of the demand comes from the west and 40% from the east (the arterial runs east-west).

(a) Estimate the total demand in the two directions, in vehicles and in people, by 15-minute period.

(b) If the four firms are each individually willing to start 15 or 30 minutes earlier (but not later, and not at any other interval, such as 23 minutes earlier), develop a plan that will best reduce the peak demand on the arterial. Summarize the resultant total demand as in (a).

(c) Discuss whether the plan you recommended might result in shifts in the pattern of people coming to work (that is, the temporal distribution for each firm) and/or in the auto occupancy.

Problem 2–3

Consider a state arterial in a suburban or outlying area, either selected by you or assigned by the instructor. Assess how much of the traffic is truly through traffic, in the sense of trips of several miles along the arterial, and how much the arterial is used for local traffic and local access. Extensive data is not required for this problem; field observation will suffice.

Be prepared for a class discussion of whether a problem exists, and whether a remedy is needed and feasible. Be prepared to take the view of a state planner and of a local traffic engineer.

Problem 2–4

For the jurisdiction in which this course is being given (or another, as assigned by the instructor), find out what the local review process is and summarize it for:

Land-development review

Zoning changes

Environmental impact assessments related to land development

For your own experience, find out which types of review meetings and hearings are open to the public, and plan to attend at least one of each type.

Problem 2–5

For the jurisdiction in which this course is being given (or another, as assigned by the instructor), identify four actual or potential TSM treatments, and enumerate them. Assess their potential for increasing efficiency or capacity and anticipated operating problems, if any.

Problem 2–6

Given:

There are 1.0 million autos in a given jurisdiction, each of which travels 200 miles per week at 17 miles per gallon.

The average gas station has a five-day inventory on hand, stored in underground tanks.

The typical auto has a gas tank that is 40% filled (capacity = 15 gallons).

(a) Compute the following:
   (1) The average daily deliveries to the gas stations to maintain the above equilibrium.
   (2) The "moving storage" expressed in total gallons in vehicle gas tanks *and* expressed in days of inventory onboard vehicles. (That is, how many days of supply is stored in vehicle gas tanks?)
(b) Given a *rumor* of an interruption in gas supply, assume the following takes place:
   (1) Drivers *immediately* increase their average percent filled to 70%.
   (2) Drivers reduce their usage to an average of 180 miles per week.

Can the gas stations meet the immediate demand created by the increase from 40% filled to 70% filled? How long will it be before the gas stations return to a five-day inventory, given 180 miles per week driving, constant gas supply, and tanks 70% filled?

3

Traffic Stream Components and Characteristics

Before studying the functional aspects of traffic engineering, it is reasonable to consider the various components of the traffic system, and how they interact to form traffic streams. Critical components of the traffic system are:

- drivers
- vehicles
- roads and highways
- the general environment
- control devices

It is also important to understand how various characteristics of traffic streams are quantified and manipulated in traffic engineering.

Every component of the traffic system influences the practice of traffic engineering. The *driver* has a variety of characteristics (reaction times, vision limits, walking times, etc.) that must be considered in designing safe and efficient systems; further, there is considerable *variability* in these characteristics, some of which may be correlated with identifiable factors (e.g., age) while some appear to be random. Likewise, the *vehicle* has characteristics that must be taken into

account, such as turning radii, acceleration patterns, deceleration patterns, tire conditions, and so forth. These characteristics differ by vehicle type, and also exhibit some randomness. Characteristics of the *roadway system* are also critical, including grades, curves, surface materials, and such.

The *environment* is frequently taken into account as a set of conditions that cause the driver, vehicle, or road characteristics to vary systematically. For instance, wet pavements result in different frictions and therefore different braking distances. Darkness influences vision.

Traffic control devices are mentioned for completeness, but later chapters (e.g., Chapter 14) are much more specific and detailed on the subject. The basic concept is that all control devices—markings, signs, and signals—communicate with the driver, and must do so in a uniform and comprehensible way. Moreover, they must be placed and sized so that a variety of drivers can make effective use of them under a variety of conditions.

Detailed knowledge—that is, real data—of driver and other characteristics continues to grow, but is sometimes limited for the task at hand. For instance, knowledge of variations in reaction time by age is useful, but presently age is taken into account by selecting higher percentiles from the distribution of times observed in a mixed population. The AASHTO Green Book, for instance, notes in part that "Because state-of-the-art knowledge about the elderly's impairments is incomplete, and given the lack of agreement on policy matters, it is not feasible to make specific recommendations on measures to aid the elderly. However, the following have been suggested as . . . having potential to aid the elderly driver. . . . Assess all standards to determine the feasibility of designing for the 95th or 99th percentile driver (i.e., the elderly) . . ." [1].

The challenge in system design is often in determining what characteristics to select for the design case: which vehicle types will exist on the particular facility? What mix of drivers? What special conditions must be considered? The authoritative reference on road design in the United States is the AASHTO Green Book [1], already cited in each chapter of this text. Further, each state has its own design manual, incorporating standards, procedures, and policies. Each of these represents an informed professional attempt to provide for safe, efficient, and economic facilities.

This chapter is merely an introduction to some of the basic elements considered in design and performance. It is certainly not intended to be used for design cases; for those, refer to [1] and to state practices.

One final introductory note: this chapter illustrates the transition underway in the mid-1990s. Several figures are shown with conventional units (feet, mph) whereas anything drawn from the latest AASHTO Green Book is shown in SI units. The next edition of this text will be in metric units completely, except for when historic data from studies pre-dating the conversion to metric are shown for educational reasons.

Road user characteristics

A. Addressing variability

In design, it is frequently necessary to use *a single* number to represent a characteristic, such as the re-

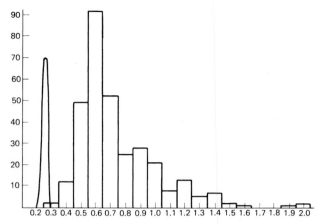

Figure 3-1   Brake reaction times from a study of 321 drivers. [Used with permission of Institute of Transportation Engineers, from S. Hulbert, "Human Factors in Transportation," *Transportation and Traffic Engineering Handbook,* p. 216. Copyright © 1982 Institute of Transportation Engineers.]

action time to an event. Figure 3-1 dramatically shows that there is a range of response times in the driver population to the simple task of responding to a brake light actuation. What single value should be used to characterize all drivers for design, and do we have enough data to estimate it properly?

This variability is reflected in many human characteristics. Figure 3-2 shows the distribution of walking times for pedestrians at crossing locations. Median walking speeds are about 5.0 fps, and 15th percentile values are in the range of 4.0 fps. Figure 3-3 shows the distribution of gap sizes in conflicting traffic selected by crossing pedestrians. It shows a median value of 84 ft and an 85th percentile of approximately 125 ft.

Most traffic engineering designs are based on a single characteristic value that can safely accommodate the vast majority of users. Timing a traffic signal for the *average* brake reaction time of drivers would be a risky proposition, given that a substantial number of users have a *longer* reaction time. For this reason, a high percentile value is used—most often the 85th percentile. Thus, a characteristic reaction time is selected such that 85% of all users have this reaction time or a faster reaction time. When necessary, even higher percentile values can be selected.

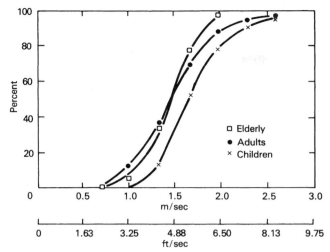

Figure 3-2 Typical pedestrian walking speeds at crossing locations. [Used with permission of John Wiley & Sons, Inc., from R. B. Sleight, "The Pedestrian," *Human Factors in Traffic Safety Research,* p. 237. Copyright © 1972 John Wiley & Sons, Inc.]

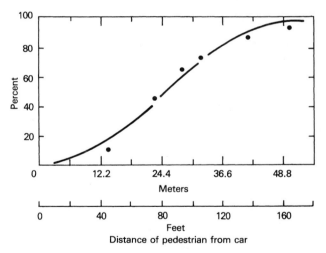

Figure 3-3 Pedestrian gap acceptance at crossing locations. [Used with permission of John Wiley & Sons, Inc., from R. B. Sleight, "The Pedestrian," *Human Factors in Traffic Safety Research,* p. 237. Copyright © 1972 John Wiley & Sons, Inc.]

Such a policy, however, requires that basic underlying characteristics be studied, quantified, and analyzed on a regular basis. Design and operational guides, such as the AASHTO Green Book, the Traffic Engineering Handbook, and others provide information on characteristic values for use in traffic engineering. They also provide references on the source studies used to arrive at the characteristic value or values. The traffic engineer, however, must always be cognizant of the underlying variability among road users. Ultimately, however, it is not possible to provide a system that exactly accommodates the individual characteristics of each user. The approach taken is to provide for a safe and efficient system that accommodates the vast majority of users, and to qualitatively consider those few users with characteristics outside the boundary of the design values used.

B. Critical characteristics for drivers

1. Perception-reaction time. One of the most basic numbers used to characterize drivers is the "*perception-reaction time*" or PRT. The perception time includes the detection, identification, and decision elements involved in responding to a stimulus. The reaction time is the time it takes to initiate the physical response.

Figure 3-4 shows the median and 85th percentile perception-reaction times from reference [1]—labeled reaction times—where three important concepts are introduced:

- Time varies with the complexity of the task: the more distinct elements of information (bits) to be resolved, the more complex the task, and the longer the time required for a response.
- Time also varies depending on whether the event (that is, the challenge or task) is expected or unexpected, with the unexpected events logically requiring more time; this is important, because early tests under controlled conditions often used scenarios (lights changing, etc.) which were expected by the subject.
- Median values are noticeably lower than the 85th percentile values, so that a condition designed for the "average" (in the sense of median, or 50th percentile) does not take into account many of the drivers in the traffic stream.

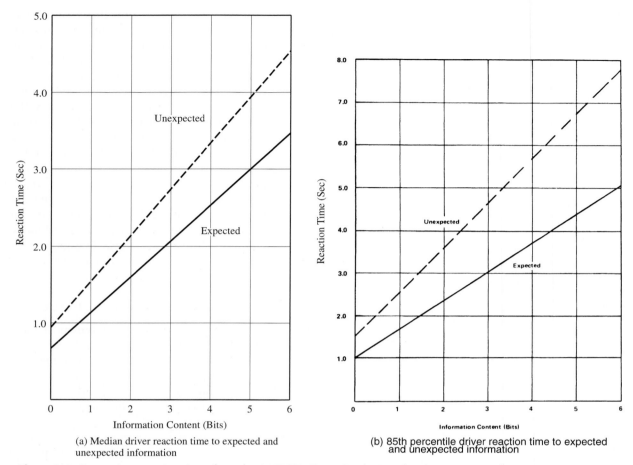

Figure 3-4 Perception-reaction times from the AASHTO Green Book. [Used with permission of American Association of State Highway and Transportation Officials, from *A Policy on Geometric Design of Highways and Streets,* p. 47 and 48. Copyright © 1994 American Association of State Highway and Transportation Officials.]

(a) Median driver reaction time to expected and unexpected information

(b) 85th percentile driver reaction time to expected and unexpected information

Even such a simple concept is complicated in many ways. Reference [2] notes that there is a fundamental difference between *design* and *actual* PRT, due primarily to the expectancy factor in the tests leading to design PRTs. It notes that actual PRTs are longer for this reason. At the same time, it cites a field-observed case in which the actual PRT in an accident reconstruction is estimated at 1.7 seconds, a rather fast value.

The literature also refers to the *perception-identification-emotion-volition* time, or PIEV. This is comparable in concept to the PRT. The *Manual on Uniform Traffic Control Devices* (MUTCD) [3] rec-

ommends PIEV times in the range of 3 to 10 seconds for the placement of some traffic control devices.

The AASHTO Green Book suggests a PRT of 2.5 seconds [1], but also contains guidance and observations on variations in driver population, conditions, and special circumstances. Note that based upon PRT = 2.5 seconds and a vehicle speed of 18 meters/sec, a vehicle would cover (2.5)(18) = 45 meters before any physical reaction is completed. This is referred to as the *reaction distance,* the distance traveled during the perception-reaction time. In English units, it is found as:

$$d_r = 1.468\, S\, t \qquad [3\text{-}1]$$

where: d_r = reaction distance, feet
S = speed, mph
t = perception-reaction time, secs
1.468 = conversion factor from mph to fps

In SI units, the equation becomes:

$$d_r = 0.278\,S\,t \qquad [3\text{-}2]$$

where: d_r = reaction distance, meters
S = speed, kph
t = perception-reaction time, secs
0.278 = conversion factor from kph to meters per sec

2. Visual acuity. *Visual acuity* is another driver characteristic of great importance. Drivers are now routinely tested for *static* acuity, namely the ability to read letters at certain distances, so that there is some assurance that signs can be seen and read. Other measures such as dynamic visual acuity, depth perception, glare recovery, and peripheral vision are not tested, but may be quite important in some driving tasks. (Given the standardization in signs by color, size, and shape, there may be compensation for some of these unmeasured factors).

Figure 3-5 illustrates the fields of vision: *clear (acute) vision* is in a cone some 3–5 degrees off the centerline, and allows characters and legends to be discerned; *fairly clear vision* extends to 10–12 degrees, and provides for shape and color but not legend; *peripheral vision* allows for motion detection. Reference [4] notes that peripheral vision is a critical factor in the driver's estimation of speed.

These vision fields play a major role in the placement of signs and other traffic displays. Drivers

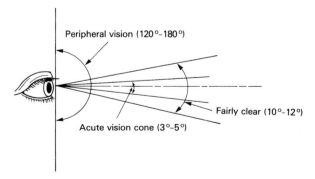

Figure 3-5 Fields of vision illustrated.

should not have to divert their eyes to "read" a sign or device to the extent that the roadway in front of them is no longer in their clear vision field. Thus, signs and devices are placed in locations where they would normally fall within the clear vision range of a driver focusing on the roadway ahead.

While drivers are normally tested periodically for *static visual acuity,* there are many other vision characteristics of importance to the driving task. *Dynamic visual acuity* is the ability to see objects in relative motion with the eye; *depth perception* is the ability to discern relative distances between objects; *glare recovery* relates to the ability to quickly respond to changing lighting conditions (such as the glare of oncoming headlights); *color vision* relates to the ability to discern colors. All of these characteristics are involved in the driving task, but none are monitored. It is also important to note that good static visual acuity does not guarantee good dynamic acuity, depth perception, glare recovery, or color vision.

C. Factors affecting human characteristics

There are a variety of factors that affect the human characteristics important to the driving task. Perception-reaction time increases with several factors, including age, fatigue, and the presence of alcohol or drugs. There are a number of practical aspects to this fact: longer PRTs may be appropriate for use in areas containing large numbers of senior citizens, for example.

Much has been written about drunk driving and its impact on society in general. The effect of alcohol and drugs on reaction time, however, does not wait until legal limits are surpassed. The first consumption of alcohol, for example, begins to degrade reaction capabilities. The driver may be totally unaware of this loss of reaction time, particularly if he or she is not beyond the legal limits, until it is needed in a critical situation, and is no longer available. The popular adage of "don't drink and drive" is wise advice indeed.

Other characteristics are also affected by other factors. For example, age affects almost every aspect of human activity, including various aspects of visual acuity. Glare recovery, for example, deteriorates greatly with age—which explains why many older drivers prefer not to drive at night.

Vehicle characteristics

A. Design vehicles: Basic dimensions

For what type of vehicle should a particular facility be designed? AASHTO has addressed this most critical question by defining a set of design vehicles, based upon the actual vehicle fleet. Table 3-1 shows the fifteen design vehicles defined by AASHTO [1] and their dimensions, including overhangs, wheelbases, and key distances from the hitch points of trucks and articulated buses (that is, buses with two sections, pinned together much as a tractor-trailer).

The basic dimensions of these vehicles allow minimum turning radii to be established. Minimum turning radii can be operationally achieved at speeds under 10 mph. At higher speeds, the minimum radius is controlled by the dynamics of the situation, not the turning capability of the vehicle. Minimum radii for slow-speed turns are shown in Table 3-2, and are a function only of the vehicle design characteristics. High-speed turns are covered in the section on "Horizontal Alignment."

For design work, a set of templates is available in reference [1]. Two of them are illustrated in Figure 3-6, for the design passenger car (P) and the design bus (BUS). These templates are available in CAD form also, so that standard CAD packages can make use of their features by overlay. Note that various turning radii are shown, for various angles of the final path (relative to the initial path).

The selection of design vehicles can have a profound effect on the later use of the facility, because these dimensions are literally "built into" the dimensions of the road. Future developments must also be taken into account. In the past, U-turns from left turn bays were frequently prohibited at many locations. However, with the growing popularity of access management techniques—especially raised medians—U-turns from left turn bays are not only allowed but thought of as an effective way for cars to reach destinations on the "other" side of the road, if they do not re-route themselves.[1]

[1]Of course, if the U-turning volume is too large, a prohibition may be used to force drivers to find another path.

In addition to the mechanics of the space taken by the vehicles in turning maneuvers, one must also consider the performance—acceleration and deceleration, particularly—and the implications for braking and safe stopping distances.

B. Acceleration performance of vehicles

Vehicles differ significantly in their weight-to-power ratios and thereby in their acceleration performance. Even though this applies most dramatically between passenger cars and trucks, it is also interesting to note the historic differences within the passenger car category.

Figure 3-7 shows trends in weight/power ratios of passenger cars during the transition period of the late 1970s and early 1980s, when federal mileage performance requirements in the wake of the 1973–74 fuel crisis caused major re-design (and downsizing) of passenger cars. Most fundamental was a downsizing of engines (number of cylinders, displacement). Weight/power ratios did not stabilize until engine efficiency was significantly improved, and the dual objectives of greater power and improved fuel efficiency could be simultaneously achieved.

Figure 3-8 shows the vehicle acceleration/deceleration curves presented in AASHTO [1] for passenger cars.

Reference [4] notes that AASHTO's change in the passenger car acceleration curves from 1984 to 1990 has substantial implications for the design and length of vertical curves. Refer to Figure 3-9, which compares the two sets of curves.[2]

The difference is dramatic. Whereas vehicles were thought to need 800 feet to reach 40 mph from zero in 1984, the estimate is 400 feet in 1990. For vehicles crossing a main road from an unsignalized cross street, the required sight distance is much less, and the main road's vertical curve can have a smaller radius (that is, be sharper).[3] Reference [4] discusses the full

[2]These curves are shown in standard (non-metric) units because neither the 1984 nor 1990 AASHTO book had made the conversion. The 1990 curves re-appear in the 1994 edition [1], with metric notation.

[3]There are other considerations, such as the braking distance on the main road, but the shortened requirement based upon the cross road is the issue under discussion.

Table 3-1 Fifteen AASHTO Design Vehicles and Their Dimensions

| Design Vehicle Type | Symbol | Dimensions (m) | | | | | | | | | | |
| | | Overall | | | Overhang | | | | | | | |
		Height	Width	Length	Front	Rear	WB$_1$	WB$_2$	S	T	WB$_3$	WB$_4$
Passenger car	P	1.3	2.1	5.8	0.9	1.5	3.4					
Single unit truck	SU	4.1	2.6	9.1	1.2	1.8	6.1					
Single unit bus	BUS	4.1	2.6	12.1	2.1	2.4	7.6					
Articulated bus	A-BUS	3.2	2.6	18.3	2.6	2.9	5.5		1.2[a]	6.1[a]		
Combination trucks												
Intermediate semitrailer	WB-12	4.1	2.6	15.2	1.2	1.8	4.0	8.2				
Large semitrailer	WB-15	4.1	2.6	16.7	0.9	0.6	6.1	9.1				
Double bottom semi-trailer–full trailer	WB-18	4.1	2.6	19.9	0.6	0.9	3.0	6.1	1.2[b]	1.6[b]	6.4	
Interstate semitrailer	WB-19*	4.1	2.6	21.0	1.2	0.9	6.1	12.8				
Interstate semitrailer	WB-20**	4.1	2.6	22.5	1.2	0.9	6.1	14.3				
Triple semitrailer	WB-29	4.1	2.6	31.0	0.8	1.0	4.1	6.3	1.0[d]	1.8[d]	6.6	6.6
Turnpike double semitrailer	WB-35	4.1	2.6	35.9	0.6	0.6	6.7	12.2	0.6[c]	1.8[c]	13.4	
Recreation vehicle												
Motor home	MH		2.4	9.1	1.2	1.8	6.1					
Car and camper trailer	P/T		2.4	14.9	0.9	3.0	3.4	6.1	1.5			
Car and boat trailer	P/B		2.4	12.8	0.9	2.4	3.4	4.6	1.5			
Motor home and Boat trailer	MH/B		2.4	16.1	1.2	2.4	6.1	4.6	1.8			

* = Design vehicle with 14.6 m trailer as adopted in 1982 STAA (Surface Transportation Assistance Act).

** = Design vehicle with 16.2 m trailer as grandfathered in 1982 STAA (Surface Transportation Assistance Act).

[a] = Combined dimension 7.3, split is estimated; [b] = Combined dimension 2.9, split is estimated; [c] = Combined dimension 2.4, split is estimated; [d] = Combined dimension 2.8, split is estimated.

WB$_1$, WB$_2$, WB$_3$, WB$_4$, are effective vehicle wheelbases; S is the distance from the rear effective axle to the hitch point; T is the distance from the hitch point to the lead effective axle of the following unit.

[Used with permission of American Association of State Highway and Transportation Officials, from *A Policy on Geometric Design of Highways and Streets*, p. 21. Copyright © 1994 American Association of State Highway and Transportation Officials.]

Table 3-2 Minimum Turning Radii of Design Vehicles

Design Vehicle Type	Passenger Car	Single Unit Truck	Single Unit Bus	Articulated Bus	Semitrailer Intermediate	Semitrailer Combination Large	Semitrailer Full Trailer Combination	Inter-State Semi-Trailer	Inter-State Semi-Trailer	Triple Semi-Trailer	Turnpike Double Semi-Trailer	Motor Home	Passenger Car with Travel Trailer	Passenger Car with Boat and Trailer	Motor Home and Boat Trailer
Symbol	P	SU	BUS	A-BUS	WB-12	WB-15	WB-18	WB-19*	WB-20**	WB-29	WB-35	MH	P/T	P/B	MH/B
Minimum design turning radius (m)	7.3	12.8	12.8	11.6	12.2	13.7	13.7	13.7	13.7	15.2	18.3	12.2	7.3	7.3	15.2
Minimum inside radius (m)	4.2	8.5	7.4	4.3	5.7	5.8	6.8	2.8	0	6.3	5.2	7.9	0.6	2.0	10.7

* Design vehicle with 14.6 m trailer as adopted in 1982 STAA (Surface Transportation Assistance Act).

** Design vehicle with 16.2 m trailer as grandfathered in 1982 STAA (Surface Transportation Assistance Act).

[Used with permission of American Association of State Highway and Transportation Officials, from *A Policy on Geometric Design of Highways and Streets*, p. 22. Copyright © 1994 American Association of State Highway and Transportation Officials.]

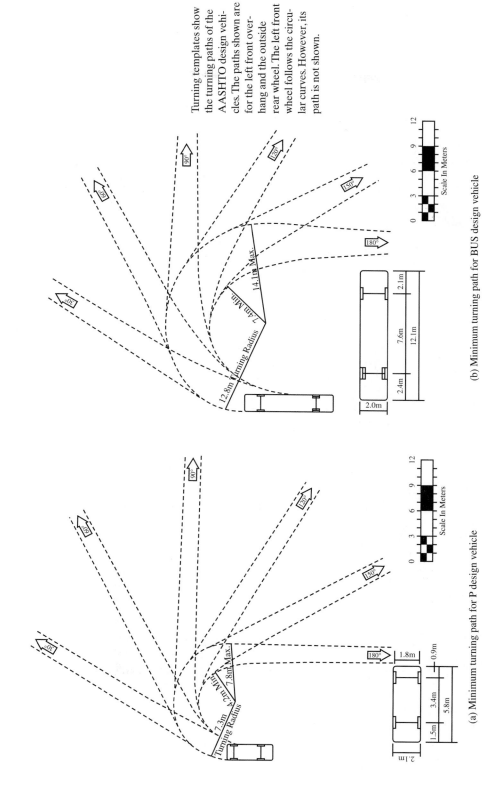

Turning templates show the turning paths of the AASHTO design vehicles. The paths shown are for the left front overhang and the outside rear wheel. The left front wheel follows the circular curves. However, its path is not shown.

(a) Minimum turning path for P design vehicle

(b) Minimum turning path for BUS design vehicle

Figure 3-6 Two illustrative templates for turning radii of design vehicles. [Used with permission of American Association of State Highway and Transportation Officials, from *A Policy on Geometric Design of Highways and Streets*, p. 24 and 25. Copyright © 1994 American Association of State Highway and Transportation Officials.]

49

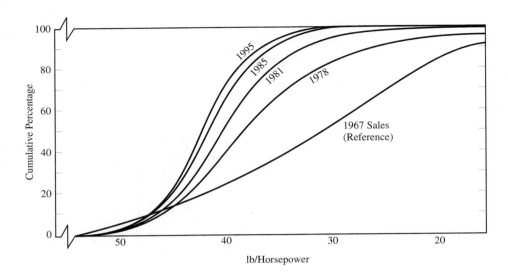

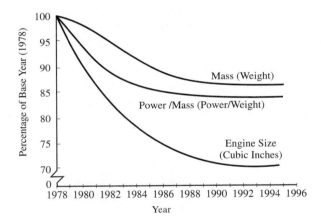

Figure 3-7 Power and weight trends for passenger cars. [Used with permission of Transportation Research Board, National Research Council, from *Highway Capacity Manual Special Report 209,* 3rd Edition, p. 2-24. Copyright © 1994 Transportation Research Board.]

range of implications of Figure 3-9 more fully. For present purposes, it is sufficient to note that recalibrations of basic relations can have profound impacts on a variety of traffic engineering practices.

C. Braking performance

Braking performance is related to a number of factors, including the type and condition of the tires, the condition and type of roadway surface, and the grade of the road. In general, the braking distance required to achieve a stop or deceleration (for locked wheels or maximum deceleration rates) is given by the following equation for English units:

$$d_b = \frac{S_i^2 - S_f^2}{30(F \pm G)} \qquad [3\text{-}3]$$

where: d_b = braking distance (ft)
   S_i = initial vehicle speed (mph)
   S_f = final vehicle speed (mph)
   F = coefficient of forward friction between tires and roadway
   G = grade, expressed as a decimal

In SI units, the equation becomes:

$$d_b = \frac{S_i^2 - S_f^2}{254(F \pm G)} \qquad [3\text{-}4]$$

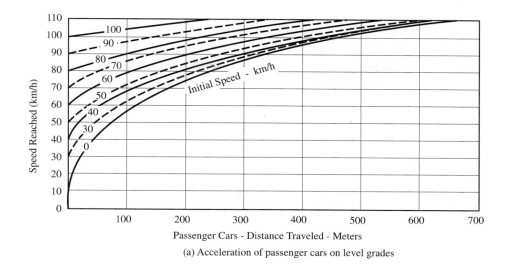

(a) Acceleration of passenger cars on level grades

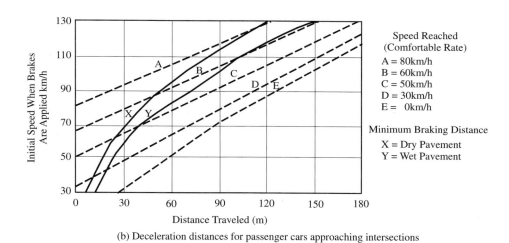

Speed Reached
(Comfortable Rate)
A = 80km/h
B = 60km/h
C = 50km/h
D = 30km/h
E = 0km/h

Minimum Braking Distance
X = Dry Pavement
Y = Wet Pavement

(b) Deceleration distances for passenger cars approaching intersections

Figure 3-8 Passenger car acceleration and deceleration curves. [Used with permission of American Association of State Highway and Transportation Officials, from *A Policy on Geometric Design of Highways and Streets,* p. 40. Copyright © 1994 American Association of State Highway and Transportation Officials.]

where: d_b = braking distance (meters)
         S_i = initial vehicle speed (km/h)
         S_f = final vehicle speed (km/h)
         F,G = as above

For the designation of grades, "+" is used for upgrades and the "−" is used for downgrades.

Figure 3-10 shows coefficients of friction for various pavement and tire conditions resulting from detailed field testing. Vehicle speed is an important factor. Extrapolations are clearly labeled.

The AASHTO Green Book [1] observes that friction factors should be based on wet pavements rather than dry, and on pavements nearing the end of

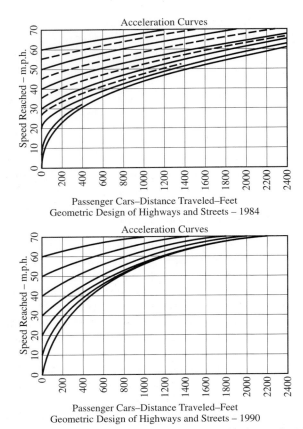

Passenger Cars–Distance Traveled–Feet
Geometric Design of Highways and Streets – 1984

Passenger Cars–Distance Traveled–Feet
Geometric Design of Highways and Streets – 1990

Figure 3-9 Comparison of acceleration profiles. [Used with permission of the Institute of Transportation Engineers, from R. P. Bhesania, "Changes in Intersection Sight Distance Standards and Their Implications," *ITE Journal.* Copyright © 1992 Institute of Transportation Engineers.]

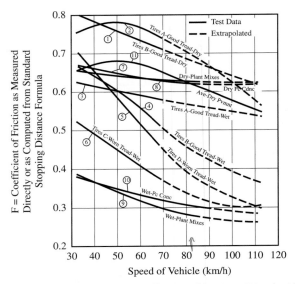

Figure 3-10 Variations in coefficient of friction. [Used with permission of American Association of State Highway and Transportation Officials, from *A Policy on Geometric Design of Highways and Streets*, p. 122. Copyright © 1994 American Association of State Highway and Transportation Officials.]

celeration cycle—from the point at which the brakes are engaged until the vehicle stops under maximum deceleration. To determine how far a vehicle will travel from the point at which a situation is first perceived to the time the deceleration is complete

their useful lives, noting that "(t)he values should encompass nearly all significant pavement surface types and the likely field conditions." Likewise, it notes that the factors should allow for worn tires rather than new, and encompass nearly all tread types and tire compositions.

Table 3-3 shows the coefficients of friction used in [1] for stopping sight distance computations, where it is noted that these values are conservative (i.e., rather low), compared to Figure 3-10 values and conditions.

D. Safe stopping sight distance

The braking distance defined in the previous section describes the distance covered by a vehicle in a de-

Table 3-3 Coefficients of Friction for Braking Distance Computations

Speed (km/h)	Coefficient of Friction, *F*
30	0.40
40	0.38
50	0.35
60	0.33
70	0.31
80	0.30
90	0.30
100	0.29
110	0.28
120	0.28

[Used with permission of American Association of State Highway and Transportation Officials, from *A Policy on Geometric Design of Highways and Streets,* p. 122. Copyright © 1994 American Association of State Highway and Transportation Officials.]

requires that the reaction distance, d_r, and the braking distance, d_b, be added. Together, this forms what is defined as the "safe stopping distance." In English units:

$$d = 1.468\, S_i t + \frac{S_i^2 - S_f^2}{30(F \pm G)} \qquad [3\text{-}5]$$

where d is in ft, and S_i and S_f are in mph.

In SI units:

$$d = 0.278\, S_i t + \frac{S_i^2 - S_f^2}{254(F \pm G)} \qquad [3\text{-}6]$$

where d is in meters, and S_i and S_f are in km/h.

The safe stopping distance is one of the most important measures in traffic engineering. Drivers must have adequate warning if they are to respond as intended to a device or situation. Thus, in design, a roadway must always provide the driver with a sight distance at least equal to the safe stopping distance. If this were not done, a situation could arise in which a driver rounds a curve to see a downed tree or other stationary obstacle in the roadway, but with insufficient distance to stop before colliding with it. Similarly, the "yellow" and "all red" intervals in a signal timing allow a driver who is too close to the intersection to stop (when the yellow appears) to safely proceed through the intersection. The following examples demonstrate just a few of the many applications of the safe stopping distance formula.

1. Safe stopping distance in highway design. As noted above, a cardinal rule of highway design is that the alignment must allow drivers to see a distance at least equal to the minimum *safe-stopping distance* for the highway. It is assumed that, in the worst case, a driver encounters an object stopped in his or her lane and evasive action is not possible. Thus, the driver must see the object in time to react and stop the vehicle.

Consider a highway with a design speed of 70 mph (112 km/h). Table 3-3 indicates that a coefficient of skidding friction of 0.28 should be used. This is indicative of a wet-pavement condition. AASHTO further recommends the use of 2.5 sec for reaction time. The safe-stopping distance is then computed from Equation [3-5], in English Units:

$$d_s = 1.468(70)(2.5) + \frac{70^2}{30(0.28)}$$

$$= 256.9 + 583.3 = 840.2 \text{ ft}$$

Thus, the highway must be designed such that drivers in either direction have a minimum of 840 ft of clear sight distance at all times. Failure to provide this would allow a driver to see a hazard initially at a point too close to allow a safe stop.

In earlier years it was assumed that drivers on wet pavements travel slower than on dry pavements. Safe-stopping-distance computations were based on an assumed wet-pavement vehicle speed that was lower than the design speed. For a 70-mph design speed, 58 mph would have been assumed, lowering the safe-stopping distance by over 200 ft. More recent studies have shown that vehicles travel just as quickly on wet pavements as on dry, and AASHTO criteria now reflect this.

2. Timing of change (yellow) and clearance (all red) intervals of traffic signals. A critical aspect of signal timing is the change or clearance intervals provided between conflicting phases. A green signal cannot be changed instantaneously from one street to another, as vehicles too close to the intersection when the light changes will not be able to stop safely. If vehicles are instantly released from the conflicting street, accidents will occur frequently. To avoid this, a *clearance and change interval* is provided between signal phases in the form of a YELLOW signal and a brief period when all the signals are RED—referred to as an ALL RED signal.

The total length of these intervals is related to safe-stopping distance. Any vehicle farther away than one safe-stopping distance from the signal when the YELLOW is flashed is assumed to be able to stop safely. Any vehicle just at or closer to the signal than one safe-stopping distance when the YELLOW is initiated will not be able to stop safely. Such a vehicle must be permitted to pass safely through the intersection before the conflicting flow is released.

Consider the case of an intersection with approach speeds of 30 mph, a coefficient of friction of 0.45, and an assumed driver perception-reaction time of 0.5 seconds. The safe-stopping distance is again given by Equation [3-5], in English Units:

$$d = 1.468(30)(0.5) + \frac{30^2}{30(0.45)}$$

$$= 22.0 + 66.7 = 88.7 \text{ ft}$$

For a vehicle to safely clear the intersection from a point just at the safe-stopping distance, it will have to travel the stopping distance, plus the width of the street, plus one car length (to clear the rear of the vehicle). If the street is 40 ft wide and a car is taken to be 18 ft long, such a vehicle must safely traverse 88.7 + 40 + 18 = 146.7 ft before vehicles from an opposing approach are released.

If it is assumed that the vehicle travels at its approach speed of 30 mph,

$$\text{time} = \frac{146.7 \text{ ft}}{30 \text{ mph} \times 1.468 \text{ fps/mph}} = 3.33 \text{ sec}$$

The YELLOW and ALL RED signal should be a total of 3.33 sec long to accommodate the safe clearance of vehicles unable to stop when the light changes. Note that this computation assumes that vehicles unable to stop continue at their approach speed, and that vehicles able to safely stop do so. Chapter 17 presents a full discussion of the timing of the clearance or change interval, as well as other basic principles of signalization.

3. Sign placement. Sign placement involves many issues that have been discussed in this chapter, including the human eye's visual field. Consider the placement of a sign indicating: "TOLL PLAZA AHEAD—BE PREPARED TO STOP." How far in advance of the toll plaza should such a sign be placed, given that it can be seen from a distance of 300 ft, and that queued vehicles from the toll plaza rarely extend more than 150 ft from the gates? Approach speed is 60 mph, the coefficient of friction is 0.35, and reaction time is 2.5 sec.

Clearly, the sign must be seen in time to allow vehicles to stop safely before the *end* of the vehicle queue at the toll plaza. Again, the safe-stopping distance is the key to the solution and is found by Equation [3-5]:

$$d_s = 1.468(60)(2.5) + \frac{60^2}{30(0.35)}$$

$$= 220.2 + 342.9 = 563.1 \text{ ft}$$

The vehicle queue extends 150 ft from the toll gates. Thus, the driver must see the sign a minimum of 563.1 + 150 = 713.1 ft from the gates. The sign itself, however, may be read from 300 ft. Thus, the sign must be placed a minimum of 713.1 − 300 = 413.1 ft in advance of the toll gates.

4. Accident investigations using skid distances. Accident investigators often make use of measured skid marks to estimate vehicle speeds before an accident. Such measurements are used together with knowledge of friction coefficients, estimates of collision speed, and the braking-distance formula to approximate the initial speed of vehicles.

Consider the following example. A vehicle hits a bridge abutment at a speed estimated by investigators as 15 mph. Skid marks of 100 ft on the pavement ($f = 0.35$) followed by skid marks of 200 ft on the gravel shoulder approaching the abutment ($f = 0.50$) are observed. The grade is level. What was the initial speed of the vehicle?

This problem involves only the braking distance, as skid marks indicate only the distance traveled after the brakes were engaged. Thus, perception-reaction time and distance are *not* factors in these computations.

Two braking distances are known: 100 ft on the pavement and 200 ft on the shoulder. Each has an initial and a final speed. As the only known speed is the final collision speed of 15 mph, the second braking distance (on gravel) is considered first:

$$d_b = \frac{S_i^2 - S_f^2}{30(f + g)}$$

$$d_b(\text{gravel}) = 200 = \frac{S_i^2 - 15^2}{30(0.50)}$$

$$S_i^2 = 200(30)(0.50) + 15^2$$

$$= 3225$$

$$S_i = 56.8 \text{ mph}$$

This, however, is not only the speed at the *beginning* of the gravel skid, but the speed at the *end* of the pavement skid. Thus, for the pavement skid:

$$d_b = 100 = \frac{S_i^2 - 56.8^2}{30(0.35)}$$

$$S_i^2 = 100(30)(0.35) + 3225 = 4275$$

$$S_i^2 = 65.4 \text{ mph}$$

The speed of the vehicle just prior to skidding on the pavement was, therefore, 65.4 mph. This information, along with other aspects of the accident investigation, can be used to help determine whether excessive speed was a contributory cause of the accident.

As can be seen from these sample calculations, braking and reaction distance computations are an important consideration in many traffic engineering applications. Stopping distance is a product of the characteristics of the driver, the vehicle, and the roadway. Because of this, the stopping distance of individual drivers and vehicles in various situations does vary considerably. Design values are chosen on the conservative side of observed behavior to provide for optimum safety of the road-user population.

Table 3-4 shows a range of stopping sight distances for various grades and speeds, making use of the formula (SI units) from AASHTO.

Reference [1] also notes that even though trucks require more stopping distance, Table 3-4 will generally suffice because the trucks have higher vantage points to see obstructions than do the passenger cars upon which Table 3-4 is based. Some caution is recommended in cases in which horizontal sight restrictions occur on downgrades, particularly at the end of a long downgrade, when trucks tend to have increased speeds.

E. Decision sight distance

AASHTO notes in [1] that in some cases, it is not the stopping distance that should control the design but rather the *decision sight distance*, observing that it

". . . is the distance required for a driver to detect an unexpected or otherwise difficult-to-perceive information source or hazard in a roadway environment that may be visually cluttered, recognize the hazard or its potential threat, select an appropriate speed and path, and initiate and complete the required safety maneuver safely and efficiently," citing [5]. Note that the decision sight distance is not based upon *stopping*, but rather upon maneuvering in an environment in which clutter yields higher perception-reaction time values. The AASHTO Green Book further observes that "Drivers need decision sight distances whenever there is a likelihood for error in either information reception, decision-making, or control actions."

Table 3-5 contains some decision sight distances, and the code for the five avoidance maneuvers cited in the table.

Geometric characteristics of roadways

The preceding sections have focused on the driver and on the vehicle, with attention to the road itself only when essential (e.g., in reference to the grade, or the friction during braking). As part of an overview, it is also useful to note some key issues as related to the

Table 3-4   Stopping Sight Distances, Wet Conditions

Design Speed (km/h)	Stopping Sight Distance (m) for Downgrades			Assumed Speed for Condition (km/h)	Stopping Sight Distance (m) for Upgrades		
	3%	6%	9%		3%	6%	9%
30	30.4	31.2	32.2	30	29.0	28.5	28.0
40	45.7	47.5	49.5	40	43.2	42.1	41.2
50	65.5	68.6	72.6	47	55.5	53.8	52.4
60	88.9	94.2	100.8	55	71.3	68.7	66.6
70	117.5	125.8	136.3	63	89.7	85.9	82.8
80	148.8	160.5	175.5	70	107.1	102.2	98.1
90	180.6	195.4	214.4	77	124.2	118.8	113.4
100	220.8	240.6	256.9	85	147.9	140.3	133.9
110	267.0	292.9	327.1	91	168.4	159.1	151.3
120	310.1	341.0	381.7	98	190.0	179.2	170.2

(See also Table 3-3 in this text for "f" values.) [Used with permission of American Association of State Highway and Transportation Officials, from *A Policy on Geometric Design of Highways and Streets*, p. 127. Copyright © 1994 American Association of State Highway and Transportation Officials.]

Table 3-5   Decision Sight Distances

Design Speed (km/h)	Decision Sight Distance for Avoidance Maneuver (meters)				
	A	B	C	D	E
50	75	160	145	160	200
60	95	205	175	205	235
70	125	250	200	240	275
80	155	300	230	275	315
90	185	360	275	320	360
100	225	415	315	365	405
110	265	455	335	390	435
120	305	505	375	415	470

- Avoidance Maneuver A: Stop on rural road.
- Avoidance Maneuver B: Stop on urban road.
- Avoidance Maneuver C: Speed/path/direction change on rural road.
- Avoidance Maneuver D: Speed/path/direction change on suburban road.
- Avoidance Maneuver E: Speed/path/direction change on urban road.

[Used with permission of American Association of State Highway and Transportation Officials, from *A Policy on Geometric Design of Highways and Streets,* p. 125. Copyright © 1994 American Association of State Highway and Transportation Officials.]

road directly, although all serious design should be done using reference [1] or appropriate state manuals, and not with this text.

A. Horizontal alignment

Roads are not perfectly straight, and do have curves in the horizontal plane. These are referred to as changes in the *horizontal alignment.* One of the most basic considerations is that as the road changes direction, the simple laws of physics tend to keep the vehicle in forward motion, thereby inducing what engineers call a "centrifugal force" although physicists take exception to the term.

Figure 3-11 shows the forces on a vehicle as it negotiates a simple curve on a *superelevated* ("banked" in colloquial terms) section of road. Consider that for small angles, the approximations $\sin \phi \simeq \phi$ and $\cos \phi \simeq (1 - \phi)$ are valid; it can be shown from Figure 3-11b that:

$$mg \sin \phi + F = (S^2/R)\cos \phi \qquad [3\text{-}7]$$

where "F" is the frictional force. This can be rearranged so that:

$$f = (S^2/127R) - e \qquad [3\text{-}8]$$

results in SI units, where 127 comes from the gravitational constant g of 9.807 m/s^2 and e is superelevation, expressed as a decimal, and f is the side friction factor.

Equation [3-8] can be manipulated into a more useful form, in which the minimum design radius of curvature is found from the desired speed, S, and the prevailing superelevation, e, and friction factor, f. In SI units:

$$R = \frac{S^2}{127(f + e)} \qquad [3\text{-}9]$$

where: R = minimum radius of curvature, meters
  S = speed, km/h
  f = coefficient of side friction (side friction factor)
  e = superelevation, expressed as a decimal

In English units:

$$R = \frac{S^2}{15(f + e)} \qquad [3\text{-}10]$$

where: R = minimum radius of curvature, ft
  S = speed, mph
  e, f = as above

Reference [1] contains values of f which are assumed for curve design, as well as guidance on maxi-

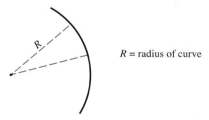

R = radius of curve

(a) Plan view (top view) of the change in horizontal alignment

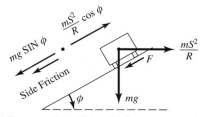

(b) Forces on the vehicle, with the curve superelevated

Figure 3-11 Effects of a change in horizontal alignment.

Figure 3-12 Illustration of spiral transition curves. [Used with permission of Yale University Press, from C. Tunnard and B. Pushkarev, *Manmade America,* p. 182. Copyright © 1963 Yale University Press.]

mum superelevation rates *e*. Representative values of *f* are:

$f = 0.16$ at 50 km/h, ranging to $f = 0.14$ at 80 km/h

$f = 0.14$ at 80 km/h, ranging to $f = 0.10$ at 110 km/h

Normal superelevation rates range between 0.02 and 0.12, with values above 0.10 rare in practice. Higher superelevation rates are used where higher speeds are expected. Values above this range are avoided, as every roadway will be used at low speeds during periods of congestion. Under slow speeds, high superelevations are uncomfortable to drivers. Refer to reference [1] for more details.

Horizontal highway curves are circular, and have a constant radius. Particularly at higher speeds, it is difficult for drivers to make an immediate transition from a straight path to one of constant radius *R*. To provide for this, *spiral transition curves* may be provided. A spiral transition curve is one that gradually and linearly changes its radius from infinity (straight) to the constant value of the circular curve over a specified distance. Figure 3-12 illustrates the visual effect of having a spiral transition, as compared to the situation without such a transition. Again, Reference [1] contains greater detail on the design and use of spiral transition curves.

B. Vertical alignment

Viewed from a distance, one can see the changes in *vertical alignment,* that is changes in the elevation of the roadway. The simplest case is a constant grade for a fixed distance (if one is allowed to ignore how the transition from level occurred). The braking distance formula has already assumed the existence of such a grade.

Figure 3-13 shows the forces acting on a vehicle in motion on a grade. It is interesting that the rolling resistance in particular can be very significant, depending on the road surface. Table 3-6 shows the grade that would be needed to have the same effect, if the rolling resistance did not exist and only the gravitational effect were responsible for the same result.

The more interesting changes in vertical alignment result from the need for transition curves between adjacent grades, as illustrated in Figure 3-14. Vertical curves are parabolic in shape, and therefore provide a natural transition with constantly changing radii. Sight distance considerations are critical in the design of such curves. *Crest* vertical curves (curves going from one grade to a *lower* grade) are limited by the driver's line of sight over the "hill." *Sag* vertical curves (curves going from one grade to a *higher* grade) are

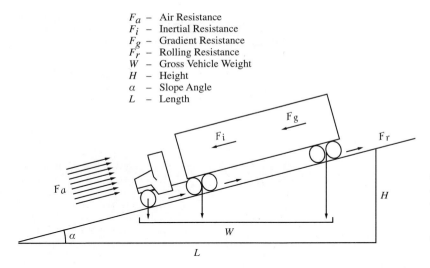

F_a – Air Resistance
F_i – Inertial Resistance
F_g – Gradient Resistance
F_r – Rolling Resistance
W – Gross Vehicle Weight
H – Height
α – Slope Angle
L – Length

Figure 3-13 Forces acting on a vehicle on a grade. [Used with permission of American Association of State Highway and Transportation Officials, from *A Policy on Geometric Design of Highways and Streets*, p. 269. Copyright © 1994 American Association of State Highway and Transportation Officials.]

Table 3-6   Equivalent Grades for Various Rolling Resistances

Surfacing Material	Rolling Resistance (kg/1000 kg GVM)	Equivalent Grade (%)[a]
Portland cement concrete	10	1.0
Asphalt concrete	12	1.2
Gravel, compacted	15	1.5
Earth, sandy, loose	37	3.7
Crushed aggregate, loose	50	5.0
Gravel, loose	100	10.0
Sand	150	15.0
Pea gravel	250	25.0

[a] Rolling resistance expressed as equivalent gradient.
[Used with permission of American Association of State Highway and Transportation Officials, from *A Policy on Geometric Design of Highways and Streets*, p. 270. Copyright © 1994 American Association of State Highway and Transportation Officials.]

limited by night visibility, for which headlight range is the determining factor. Again, the reader is referred to AASHTO [1] for more detail on the geometry and design of vertical curves.

C. Other geometric elements

Just as one has to design the vertical and horizontal curves, one has to consider their interaction. One critical consideration is *water drainage*. Virtually no section of road is perfectly level, or is not minimally superelevated. This is to allow water to drain to the side of the roadway, and longitudinally into catch basins and culverts.

The *cross section* of the road also requires detailed design consideration, including lane and roadway widths, shoulders, and median design. Accommodations for bus stops, HOV lanes and HOV entrances/ exits, median barriers, ramp design, and many other elements must be considered. Such level of detail, however, is the subject for texts on geometric design and for standard references.

D. Highway design

In addition to the various elements already addressed, some overall issues of facility design should be mentioned. The use of spiral curves to smooth the transitions in horizontal alignment and to improve the appearance of the road has been mentioned already.

The concepts of *basic number of lanes* and of *lane balance* on freeways as design principles are useful and functional. For the purpose of presenting the driver with a high level of expectancy, a basic number of lanes is established over a significant distance on a route, irrespective of variations in traffic demand and of lane balance requirements. However, for the integrity of the trip and the consistency of the design, some "additional" lanes may be needed for continuity in some sections.

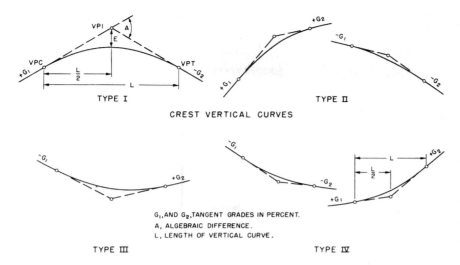

CREST VERTICAL CURVES

G₁, AND G₂, TANGENT GRADES IN PERCENT.
A, ALGEBRAIC DIFFERENCE.
L, LENGTH OF VERTICAL CURVE.

Figure 3-14 Types of vertical curves. [Used with permission of American Association of State Highway and Transportation Officials, from *A Policy on Geometric Design of Highways and Streets*, p. 281. Copyright © 1994 American Association of State Highway and Transportation Officials.]

Lane balance is a complementary concept, and is intended to minimize turbulence, confusion, and trapped drivers. At exits, the number of lanes should be such that one lane exists where the driver can make a choice, namely to use the exit or continue on the main line. This requires that the number of departing lanes (exit plus downstream main line) is one more than the number of approaching lanes. At entrances, the number of converging lanes should be a maximum of one more than the downstream main line. In this way, there can be one well-tapered merging lane.

Auxiliary lanes (lanes added for a limited distance, generally connecting consecutive on- and off-ramps) are often used to help provide for continuity and lane balance. The key point, however, is that lane continuity, lane balance, and the basic number of lanes are *functional concepts* that must be considered and planned prior to detailed design of any specific highway segment.

Another conceptual design worthy of special note is the *diamond interchange*. Figure 3-15a shows a traditional diamond interchange, often constructed as the most effective use of land and construction materials at a freeway-arterial street interchange when the demand is rather low. History shows, however, that demand grows over time, aided by the very existence of the freeway access. Land uses change, rural communities become suburban, and the development of land surrounding the interchange constrains future redesign options. At the same time, turning patterns

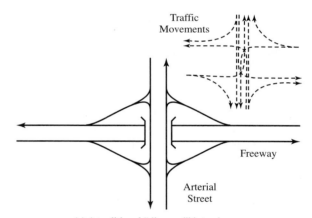

(a) A traditional "diamond" interchange

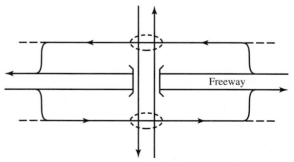

(b) Diamond interchange using parallel "service roads"

Figure 3-15 Diamond interchange designs illustrated.

within the "diamond" and the short distances between intersection of the diamond create major traffic problems that traffic engineers have generally addressed after the fact by some very creative (and complex) signal timing plans.

Figure 3-15b is only one of a set of alternative designs for a diamond interchange. Basically, the ramps form a pair of one-way streets that can serve the future community, and allow spacings that overcome the queue and phasing problems that occur in the traditional design.[4] Reference [6] addressed the cost-effectiveness of this design, assuming plausible traffic growth over twenty years, and found it to be a good alternative, saving future congestion costs at the expense of some additional right-of-way initially, in a present value analysis.

Traffic control devices

For completeness, one more basic element of the traffic system must be mentioned: traffic control devices. Much more will be said of markings, signs, and signals in later chapters, but an overview is appropriate.

Traffic control devices communicate with the driver, and should—indeed, must—follow certain specifications laid down in the individual state's *Manual on Uniform Traffic Control Devices (MUTCD),* many of which are simply adoptions of the federal *MUTCD* [3]. Even with the simplest controls—road *markings*—the driver can understand by the colors and patterns the message that is being transmitted. *Signs* are standardized in color, shape, symbols, location, size, and message format so that the driver has a high level of expectancy and comfort. *Signal* devices are standardized in the same way, including the sequence of indications. The three major categories of controls—markings, signs, signals—are also used in concert in some well-defined ways, so that left turn lanes are marked, signed, and signalized to provide a totally unambiguous environment.

The critical issue is *standardization* of the manner in which particular messages are transmitted to drivers. Similar messages must be consistently delivered in similar ways to avoid confusing the driver—effectly

increasing his/her reaction time. Both safety and efficiency require virtually immediate, conditioned responses by drivers to critical instructions, such as a "red" light or a STOP sign. Consistent color and shape codes can do much to accomplish this goal; federal and state *MUTCD*s guarantee uniformity on a statewide and national level. Even internationally, certain shapes and symbols have been standardized since the 1970s.

Traffic streams

Traffic streams are made up of individual drivers and vehicles, interacting in unique ways with each other and with elements of the roadway and general environment. Because the judgments and abilities of individual drivers come into play, vehicles in the traffic stream do not and cannot behave uniformly. Further, no two similar traffic streams will behave alike, even under equivalent circumstances, as driver behavior varies with local characteristics and driving habits.

Dealing with traffic, then, is quite different from dealing with purely physical phenomena. A given flow of water through channels and pipes of defined characteristics will behave in an entirely predictable fashion, according to the laws of hydraulics and fluid flow. A given flow of traffic through streets and highways of defined characteristics will vary by both location and time. This is the challenge of traffic engineering: to plan and design for a medium that is not predictable in exact terms—one that involves not only physical constraints, but the complex behavioral characteristics of humans.

There is, however, a reasonably consistent range of driver behavior, and therefore of traffic stream behavior. Drivers on a section of highway designed for a 60-mph maximum safe speed may select speeds in a fairly broad range (say 45 to 65 mph, for example), but few will travel at 80 mph or at 20 mph.

In describing traffic streams in quantitative terms, the purpose is both to understand the inherent variability in their characteristics and to define normal ranges in behavior. To do so, key parameters must be defined and measured. Traffic engineers will analyze, evaluate, and ultimately plan improvements in traffic facilities based upon such parameters and upon their knowledge of normal ranges of behavior. This section focuses on the definition and description

---

[4]In the extreme, the drivers would not recognize the basic diamond pattern as they drive it, because development can take place between the one-way pair.

of the parameters most often used for this purpose and the kinds of characteristics normally observed in traffic streams. These parameters are, in effect, the traffic engineer's measure of reality, and they constitute the language by which traffic streams are described and understood.

Traffic facilities are broadly separated into two principal categories:

- uninterrupted flow facilities
- interrupted flow facilities

These facility types relate to the interaction of traffic-stream elements that control the general character of flow along the facility.

Uninterrupted-flow facilities are those on which no external factors cause periodic interruption to the traffic stream. Such flow exists primarily on freeways and other limited-access facilities, where there are no traffic signals, STOP or YIELD signs, or surface intersections to interrupt flow. It may also exist on long sections of rural surface highway between signalized intersections, where characteristics approach those of a limited-access facility.

On uninterrupted flow facilities, the traffic stream is a product of individual vehicles interacting with each other and with the geometric and general environment of the roadway. The pattern of flow along the facility is controlled only by the characteristics of the land uses generating vehicular trips on the facility. Even when such a facility is experiencing extreme congestion, breakdowns are the result of internal interactions in the traffic stream, not external causes. Thus, even when a driver is in a traffic jam on a freeway, the facility is still classified as "uninterrupted flow."

Interrupted-flow facilities are those having external devices that periodically interrupt traffic flow. The principal device creating interrupted flow is the traffic signal, which periodically halts flow. Other devices, such as STOP and YIELD signs, also interrupt traffic, as do some uncontrolled intersections and driveways with significant usage.

On an interrupted flow facility, traffic engineers must deal with the constant stopping and restarting of a traffic stream. Flow depends not only on the interactions among vehicles and the roadway environment, but also on signal timing. Traffic signals, for example, allow designated movements to occur only part of the time. Because of the periodic interruption of flow on such a facility, flow occurs in "platoons." A platoon is a group of vehicles moving along a facility together, with significant gaps between one such group and the next. On signalized facilities, these platoons are formed by the pattern of green phases at successive intersections. In essence, an interrupted-flow facility is not available for continuous use, and *time* enters as a significant parameter affecting flow.

As platoons depart a traffic signal, they tend to disperse. When signals are far enough apart, the extent of dispersion becomes sufficient for essentially uninterrupted flow to exist on some part of the roadway between them. There is no exact criterion for the signal spacing at which this occurs. Many variables affect platoon dispersion, including quality of signal progression and the number and pattern of vehicles that enter the traffic stream from unsignalized intersections and driveways between the signals. As a general guide, signals two miles apart are thought to be sufficiently spaced for uninterrupted flow to exist at some point between them.

Traffic-stream parameters

Traffic-stream parameters fall into two broad categories: *macroscopic parameters* characterize the traffic stream as a whole; *microscopic parameters* characterize the behavior of individual vehicles in the traffic stream with respect to each other.

A traffic stream may be described macroscopically by three parameters:

1. Volume or rate of flow
2. Speed
3. Density

A. Volume and flow

Traffic *volume* is defined as the number of vehicles that pass a point on a highway, or a given lane or direction of a highway, during a specified time interval. The unit for volume is simply "vehicles," although it is often expressed as vehicles per unit time.

1. Daily volumes and their use. A common time interval for volumes is a day. Daily volumes are frequently used as the basis for highway planning and general observations of trends. Traffic volume projections are often based on measured daily volumes. Four daily volume parameters are widely used:

- *Average annual daily traffic* (AADT) is the average 24-hour traffic volume at a given location over a full 365-day year—that is, the total number of vehicles passing the site in a year divided by 365.
- *Average annual weekday traffic* (AAWT) is the average 24-hour traffic volume occurring on weekdays over a full year. This volume is of considerable interest where weekend traffic is light, so that averaging higher weekday volumes over 365 days would mask the impact of weekday traffic. AAWT is computed by dividing the total weekday volume for the year by 260.
- *Average daily traffic* (ADT) is an average 24-hour volume at a given location for some period of time less than a year. While an AADT is for a full year, an ADT can be measured for six months, a season, a month, a week, or as little as two days. An ADT is a valid number only for the period of time over which it was measured.
- *Average weekday traffic* (AWT) is an average 24-hour traffic volume occurring on weekdays for some period less than one year, such as for a month or a

season. The relationship between AAWT and AWT is analogous to that between AADT and ADT.

The unit by which all of these volumes are described is *vehicles per day* (vpd). Daily volumes generally are not differentiated by direction or lane, but are totals for an entire facility at the specified location.

Table 3-7 illustrates the relationship between the various daily volume parameters. It shows volume data for a sample location analyzed on a monthly basis. AWTs, shown in column 6, are computed for each month as the total weekday traffic for the month divided by the number of weekdays in the month. ADTs, shown in column 7, are computed for each month as the total traffic for the month divided by the number of days in the month. There are 12 values of AWT and ADT in Table 3-7, one for each month of the year. There is, however, only one value for AADT and one value for AAWT per year, based on yearly totals.

The sample data in Table 3-7 gives a capsule description of the character of the facility on which it was measured. Note that ADTs are significantly higher than AWTs in each month, and that the AADT is higher than the AAWT. This indicates that weekend traffic is heavy and that the facility probably

Table 3-7   Illustration of Daily Volume Parameters

1 Month	2 No. of Weekdays in Month (days)	3 Total No. of Days in Month (days)	4 Total Monthly Volume (veh)	5 Total Weekday Volume (veh)	6 AWT 5/2 (vpd)	7 ADT 4/3 (vpd)
Jan.	22	31	425,000	208,000	9,455	13,710
Feb.	20	28	410,000	220,000	11,000	14,643
Mar.	22	31	385,000	185,000	8,409	12,419
Apr.	22	30	400,000	200,000	9,091	13,333
May	21	31	450,000	215,000	10,238	14,516
Jun.	22	30	500,000	230,000	10,455	16,667
Jul.	23	31	580,000	260,000	11,304	18,710
Aug.	21	31	570,000	260,000	12,381	18,387
Sep.	22	30	490,000	205,000	9,318	16,333
Oct.	22	31	420,000	190,000	8,636	13,548
Nov.	21	30	415,000	200,000	9,523	13,833
Dec.	22	31	400,000	210,000	9,545	12,903
Year	260	365	5,445,000	2,583,000	—	—

AAWT = 2,583,000/260 = 9,935 vpd
AADT = 5,445,000/365 = 14,918 vpd

serves primarily recreational traffic. Note also that both AWTs and ADTs are highest during summer months, indicating that a warm-weather recreational area is most likely being served.

2. Hourly volumes and their use. While daily volumes are useful in highway planning, they cannot be used alone for design or operational analysis purposes. Volume varies considerably during the course of a 24-hour day, usually with periods of maximum volume occurring during the morning and evening commuter "rush" hours. The single hour of the day that has the highest hourly volume is referred to as the "peak hour." The traffic volume within this hour is of greatest interest to traffic engineers in design or operational analysis. The *peak hour volume* is generally a directional volume—that is, a volume in which the directions of flow are separated.

Peak hourly volumes are used as the basis for highway design and for many types of operational analysis. Highways must be designed to adequately serve the peak-hour traffic volume in the peak direction of flow. Since this traffic generally travels one way in the morning and the other at night, both directions are normally designed to accommodate the directional peak-hour volume. Most operational analyses, whether concerning imposition of control measures, safety, or capacity, must address conditions existing during periods of peak traffic volume. Peak hourly volumes are useful for this purpose, as are subhourly flows—discussed in the next section.

In design, peak hourly volumes are sometimes estimated from daily volume projections, using the following relationship:

$$DDHV = AADT \times K \times D \qquad [3\text{-}11]$$

where: $DDHV$ = directional design hour volume (vph)
$AADT$ = average annual daily traffic (vpd)
K = proportion of daily traffic occurring during the peak hour, expressed as a decimal
D = proportion of peak-hour traffic traveling in the peak direction, expressed as a decimal

For design purposes, K often represents the proportion of AADT occurring during the *thirtieth highest peak hour* of the year. The peak hours vary for each day and may be ranked in order of decreasing volume. The thirtieth highest peak-hour volume in such a listing is a criterion often used for rural design and analysis. Others, such as the fiftieth, are sometimes used in urban situations. This topic is discussed in greater detail later in this chapter.

The K and D factors usually are based on local or regional characteristics at existing locations. In general, the K factor decreases as the density of development surrounding the highway increases. In denser areas, there is more off-peak traffic, and capacity deficiencies tend to spread demand across a longer period than in more sparsely developed areas. The D factor is more variable; it depends on development density and on the specific relationship of the facility in question to major traffic generators in the area. Table 3-8 gives general ranges for these factors as an illustration.

For example, consider a rural highway on which it was projected that AADT in 20 years would reach 30,000 vpd. For the type of highway and region in question, it is known that peak-hour traffic currently is approximately 20% of the AADT, and that the peak direction generally carries 70% of the peak-hour traffic. An approximate DDHV could be estimated as

$$DDHV = AADT \times K \times D$$
$$= 30{,}000 \times 0.20 \times 0.70 = 4200 \text{ vph}$$

This value may now be used in design when the type and size of the facility to be provided are considered. The estimate assumes, however, that K and D do not change over time. If development is occurring, and volume is increasing as a result, the K and D factors may be expected to decline over time. If the area were expected to be suburban in character in 20 years, a more appropriate computation might be

$$DDHV = 30{,}000 \times 0.15 \times 0.60 = 2700 \text{ vph}$$

Table 3-8   General Ranges for K and D Factors

Facility Type	Normal Range of Factors	
	K Factor	**D Factor**
Rural	0.15–0.25	0.65–0.80
Suburban	0.12–0.15	0.55–0.65
Urban:		
Radial route	0.07–0.12	0.55–0.60
Circumferential route	0.07–0.12	0.50–0.55

based upon the values cited in Table 3-8. The resulting design hour volume would be a good deal less in this event, and the design process would be considerably altered.

This simple illustration points out the difficulty in projecting future traffic demands accurately. Not only does volume change over time, but the basic characteristics of volume variation may change as well. Accurate projections require the identification of causative relationships that remain stable over time. Such relationships are difficult to discern in the complexity of observed travel behavior.

3. Subhourly volumes and rates of flow. While hourly volume is the general basis for many forms of traffic design and analysis, the variation within a given hour is also of considerable interest. The quality of traffic flow is often related to short-term fluctuations in traffic demand. A facility may have capacity adequate to serve the peak-hour demand, but short-term peaks of flow within the peak hour may exceed capacity, thereby creating a breakdown.

Volumes observed for periods of less than one hour are generally expressed as equivalent hourly rates of flow. For example, 1000 vehicles observed in a 15-minute period would be expressed as

$$\frac{1000 \text{ veh}}{0.25 \text{ hr}} = 4000 \text{ vph}$$

The rate of flow, v, is 4000 vph for the 15-minute interval in which the 1000 vehicles were observed. Had traffic been observed for a full hour at the location in question, the hourly volume would *not* be 4000 vph. Table 3-9 illustrates the difference between an hourly volume and a rate of flow expressed as an hourly equivalent.

Table 3-9   Illustration of Hourly Volume and Rate of Flow

1 Time Interval	2 Volume for Time Interval (veh)	Col 2/0.25 Rate of Flow for Time Interval (vph)
5:00–5:15 P.M.	1000	4000
5:15–5:30 P.M.	1100	4400
5:30–5:45 P.M.	1200	4800
5:45–6:00 P.M.	900	3600
5:00–6:00 P.M.	4200 vph = hourly volume	

The volume observed over the full hour is the sum of the four 15-minute volumes comprising the hour. This value, 4200 vph, is an hourly volume. However, the rate of flow for each 15-minute period varies throughout the hour. The maximum value occurs between 5:30 and 5:45 P.M., when a volume of 1200 vehicles is observed. This is a rate of flow of 4800 vph, even though only 4200 vehicles are observed over the full hour. Vehicles arrive at a *rate* of 4800 vph for a 15-minute period.

These short-term fluctuations could be quite important in terms of operating conditions. If the facility on which the counts of Table 3-9 were observed had a capacity of 4200 vph, demand would exceed capacity for the 15-minute interval between 5:30 and 5:45 P.M., and a breakdown would occur. The recovery process from a breakdown is complex, often extending far beyond the period of the breakdown itself. Thus, for many types of traffic analysis, it is necessary to consider a maximum rate of flow within a peak hour.

What minimum time interval should be considered, then, for most traffic analyses? There is no standard answer. Various researchers have used flow rates for periods as short as one minute and as long as 30 minutes. For reasons of statistical stability, the 1997 *Highway Capacity Manual* suggests using 15 minutes for most operational and design analyses. The variation in flow rates for shorter periods is unstable, and relationships to other traffic-flow variables are difficult to establish. For time intervals of 15 minutes or longer, such relationships, which are critical to understanding traffic streams, can be established with a reasonable degree of statistical confidence. This text will work with 15-minute periods as the minimum for traffic analysis, although shorter periods will often be used in the research literature.

The relationship between hourly volume and the maximum rate of flow within the hour is defined by the *peak-hour factor (PHF),* as follows:

$$PHF = \frac{\text{hourly volume}}{\text{maximum rate of flow}} \qquad [3\text{-}12]$$

For 15-minute periods, the equation becomes

$$PHF = \frac{V}{4 \times V_{15}} \qquad [3\text{-}13]$$

where: V = hourly volume (vph)
V_{15} = maximum 15-minute volume within the hour (veh)

For the sample volumes given in Table 3-9, the peak-hour factor may be computed as

$$PHF = \frac{4200}{4 \times 1200} = 0.875$$

For 15-minute periods, the maximum value of the PHF is 1.00, which occurs when the volume in each 15-minute period is equal; the minimum value is 0.25, which occurs when the entire hourly volume occurs in one 15-minute interval. The normal range of values is between 0.70 and 0.98, with lower values signifying a greater degree of variation in flow during the peak hour.

The PHF is generally descriptive of trip-generation characteristics and may apply to an area or portion of a street and highway system. When known, the value may be used to convert a peak-hour volume to an estimated peak rate of flow within the hour:

$$v = \frac{V}{PHF} \qquad [3\text{-}14]$$

where: v = peak rate of flow within hour (vph)
V = peak hourly volume (vph)
PHF = peak-hour factor

This conversion will be used often in the methodologies and techniques covered throughout this text.

B. Speed and travel time

Speed is the second principal parameter describing the state of a given traffic stream. *Speed* is defined as a rate of motion, in distance per unit of time. It is the inverse of the time taken by a vehicle to traverse a given distance, or

$$S = \frac{d}{t} \qquad [3\text{-}15]$$

where: S = speed (mph or fps)
d = distance traversed (mi or ft)
t = time to traverse distance d (hr or sec)

In a moving traffic stream, each vehicle travels at a different speed.

Thus, the traffic stream does not have a single characteristic speed but rather a distribution of individual vehicle speeds. From a distribution of discrete vehicle speeds, a number of "average" or "typical" values may be used to characterize the traffic stream as a whole.

1. Time mean and space mean speed. Average or mean speeds can be computed in two different ways, yielding two different values with differing physical significance.

- *Time mean speed (TMS)* is defined as the average speed of all vehicles passing a point on a highway over some specified time period.
- *Space mean speed (SMS)* is defined as the average speed of all vehicles occupying a given section of a highway over some specified time period.

In essence, time mean speed is a point measure, while space mean speed is a measure relating to a length of highway or lane. Figure 3-16 illustrates the significance of these two averages.

In lane 1 of Figure 3-16, vehicles are spaced at exactly 88 ft and travel at exactly 44 fps (30 mph). In this lane, a vehicle would pass any stationary point every 88/44 or 2.0 sec. In lane 2 of the figure, vehicles are spaced at exactly 176 ft and travel at a speed of exactly 88 fps (60 mph). Thus, vehicles in this lane also pass any point at a rate of one every 176/88 or 2.0 sec. Thus, an observer stationed at any point within the section would observe as many vehicles passing a point in lane 1 as in lane 2—the lane volumes would be equal. In taking the average speed of these vehicles—the time mean speed—there would be equal numbers of vehicles traveling at 44 fps and 88 fps. The time mean speed of vehicles passing a point would therefore be

$$TMS = \frac{44 + 88}{2} = 66.0 \text{ fps}$$

To obtain a space mean speed, a given segment of the facility must be considered. Lane 1 in Figure 3-16 contains twice as many vehicles as lane 2. Given the

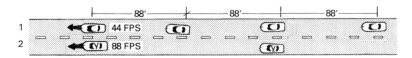

Figure 3-16 Comparison of time mean speed and space mean speed.

complete uniformity of the traffic stream shown, this will be true over any period of time considered. Thus, the space mean speed—the average speed of vehicles occupying the segment—includes twice as many vehicles traveling at 44 fps as at 88 fps, and the space mean speed is

$$SMS = \frac{2(44) + 88}{3} = 58.7 \text{ fps}$$

A space mean speed weights slower vehicles more heavily, as they occupy space in the segment for a longer period. Vehicles in lane 1 take twice as long to traverse the segment as vehicles in lane 2.

Both time mean speed and space mean speed may be computed from a series of measured travel times over a measured distance, according to the following formulas:

$$TMS = \frac{\sum \dfrac{d}{t_i}}{n} \qquad [3\text{-}16]$$

$$SMS = \frac{d}{\sum \dfrac{t_i}{n}} = \frac{nd}{\sum t_i} \qquad [3\text{-}17]$$

where: TMS = time mean speed (fps or mph)
SMS = space mean speed (fps or mph)
d = distance traversed (ft or mi)
n = number of travel times observed
t_i = travel time for the ith vehicle (sec or hr)

Mathematically, the space mean speed is a harmonic mean, while the time mean speed is a straightforward average of individual vehicle speeds. To compute space mean speed, the distance is divided by an average travel time. For time mean speed, each individual vehicle speed is computed as distance divided by time, and the results are averaged. Table 3-10 gives an illustration of these computations.

2. Average travel speed and average running speed. Average travel speed and average running speed are two forms of space mean speed that are frequently used as traffic engineering measures. Both are computed as distance divided by an average time to traverse a segment of highway. They differ in the components of time that are included in the speed computation.

Table 3-10 Computation of Time Mean Speed and Space Mean Speed

1 Vehicle No.	2 Distance (ft)	3 Travel Time (sec)	2/3 Speed (fps)
1	1000	18.0	1000/18 = 55.6
2	1000	20.0	1000/20 = 50.0
3	1000	22.0	1000/22 = 45.5
4	1000	19.0	1000/19 = 52.6
5	1000	20.0	1000/20 = 50.0
6	1000	20.0	1000/20 = 50.0
Totals	6000	119.0	303.7
Averages		119/6 = 19.8	303.7/6 = 50.6

TMS = 50.6 fps
SMS = 1000/19.8 or 6000/119 = 50.4 fps

Travel time is defined as the total time to traverse a given highway segment. *Running time* is defined as the total time during which the vehicle is in motion while traversing a given highway segment. The difference between the two is that running time does not include *stopped delays*, while travel time does. *Average travel speed* is based on an average travel time, while *average running speed* is based upon an average running time.

Consider the case of a one-mile segment of arterial. On the average, it takes a vehicle three minutes to traverse the section, one minute of which is stopped time experienced at signalized intersections. Then, the vehicle's average travel speed is

$$S_t = \frac{1 \text{ mi}}{3 \text{ min}} \times 60 \text{ min/hr} = 20 \text{ mph}$$

and its average running speed is

$$S_r = \frac{1 \text{ mi}}{2 \text{ min}} \times 60 \text{ min/hr} = 30 \text{ mph}$$

The difference in the two computations is a measure of the amount of stopped time in total travel time. Where there are no stopped delays in the segment, running time and travel time are equal, and the two speed measures will be equal.

3. Operating speed and percentile speeds. While average speeds are the measures most frequently used in characterizing a traffic stream, there are others as well. *Operating speed* is defined as the maximum safe speed at which a vehicle can be conducted in a given traffic stream, without exceeding the design speed of the highway segment. Operating speed is difficult to measure: it requires that a test car be driven through the traffic stream in a manner consistent with the definition. As "maximum safe speed" is a judgmental matter, consistent measurements among test-car drivers are not often achieved.

Percentile speeds are also used to describe the speed of traffic streams. A *percentile speed* is a speed below which the stated percent of vehicles in the traffic stream travel. Thus, an 85th-percentile speed means that 85% of the vehicles in the traffic stream travel at or below this speed. The *85th-percentile speed* is often used as a measure of the maximum reasonable speed for the traffic stream, while the *15th-percentile speed* may be used as a measure of the minimum reasonable speed for the traffic stream. The *50th-percentile* or *median speed* is also used to describe the midpoint of the speed distribution.

A more detailed discussion of percentile speeds is given in Chapter 7.

4. Uses of speeds and travel times. While speeds and travel times are inverse measures, their use as traffic engineering measures differs. Speeds are most often measured at a point, in a *spot speed study.* The intent of such studies is to determine the speeds that drivers select when unencumbered by traffic congestion. Thus, such studies are generally taken under conditions of free flow (light traffic). Segment *travel time studies* are generally taken specifically to evaluate the extent and causes of congestion or delay along a route. Speed and/or travel time are frequently used as measures of the quality of traffic service, as both are immediately discernible to the driver and affect his/her comfort and convenience.

The measurement and analysis of speeds and travel times is discussed in greater detail in Chapter 7.

C. Density

Density, a third measure of traffic stream conditions, is defined as the number of vehicles occupying a given length of highway or lane and is generally expressed as vehicles per mile (vpm) or vehicles per mile per lane (vpmpl).

Density is difficult to measure directly, as an elevated vantage point is required. It can be computed from speed and volume, however, as part of the relationship between these three key variables:

$$v = S \times D \qquad [3\text{-}18]$$

$$D = \frac{v}{S} \qquad [3\text{-}19]$$

where: v = rate of flow (vph)
S = space mean speed (mph)
D = density (vpm)

Thus, if the rate of flow for a given traffic stream were measured as 1000 vph, and the speed is 40 mph, the density would be computed as

$$D = \frac{1000 \text{ vph}}{40 \text{ mph}} = 25 \text{ vpm}$$

Density is perhaps the most important of the three traffic-stream parameters, because it is the measure most directly related to traffic demand. Demand does not occur as a rate of flow per se, although that is the way traffic engineers most often quantify it. Traffic is generated from various land uses, generating a number of vehicles that are placed on a limited segment of highway. Generated trips produce a traffic density, which in turn produces a rate of flow and a speed. Density is also an important measure of the quality of traffic flow, as it is a measure of proximity of vehicles, a factor which influences freedom to maneuver and psychological comfort of drivers.

D. Spacing and time headway

Flow, speed, and density are macroscopic measures, in that a traffic stream for a given time interval is described by a single value of each—which applies to the traffic stream as a whole. Spacing and headway are microscopic measures, because they apply to individual pairs of vehicles within the traffic stream.

Spacing is defined as the distance between successive vehicles in a traffic lane, measured from some common reference point on the vehicles, such as the front bumpers or front wheels. *Headway* is the time between successive vehicles as they pass a point along the lane, also measured between common reference points on the vehicles.

Average values of spacing and time headway are related to the macroscopic parameters as follows:

$$D = \frac{5280}{d_a}$$ [3-20]

$$v = \frac{3600}{h_a}$$ [3-21]

$$S = \frac{d_a}{h_a}$$ [3-22]

where: D = density (vpmpl)
S = average speed (fps)
v = rate of flow (vphpl)
d_a = average spacing (ft)
h_a = average headway (sec)

Microscopic measures are useful for many traffic analysis purposes. Because a spacing and/or a headway can be obtained for every pair of vehicles, the amount of data that can be collected in a short period is relatively large. Consider a traffic stream with a volume of 1000 vehicles over a 15-minute period. For this period, there would be *one* rate of flow, *one* density, and *one* average speed. There would, however, be 1000 headways and spacings, assuming that all vehicles were observed.

Use of microscopic measures also allows various vehicle types in the traffic stream to be isolated. Passenger-car flow rates and densities could be isolated in a mixed traffic stream by considering only pairs of passenger cars following each other. Trucks and other vehicle types could be similarly isolated, and their characteristics compared using headway and spacing measurements.

Characteristics of uninterrupted flow

Equation [3-18] states the relationship between the three principal variables describing an uninterrupted traffic stream: flow is equal to the product of speed and density. While this relationship holds for all stable traffic streams, the combinations of these variables that occur conform to additional two-dimensional relationships.

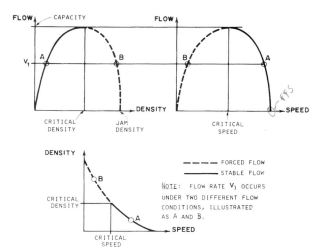

Figure 3-17   Relationships among flow, speed, and density. [Used with permission of Transportation Research Board, National Research Council, from *Highway Capacity Manual, Special Report 209,* 3rd Ed., p. 1-7. Copyright © 1994 Transportation Research Board.]

Figure 3-17 illustrates the general form of these relationships, which are valid not only for uninterrupted-flow traffic streams but also for interrupted flow between points of fixed interruption. The exact calibration of such relationships depends on prevailing conditions, which vary widely from location to location, and even over time at the same locations.

Note that a flow of "zero" occurs under two conditions. When there are no vehicles on the highway, density is zero, and no vehicles can be observed passing a point. Under this condition, speed is a theoretical value referred to as "free-flow speed" and is approximately the highest speed a single vehicle could safely achieve on the highway segment under study. Zero flow also occurs when density becomes so high that vehicular motion stops—a traffic jam. Under this condition, all vehicles are stopped, and no vehicles can be observed passing a point along the highway. The density at which this occurs is called *jam density.*

The peak of the speed-flow and density-flow curves is the maximum possible rate of flow, or *capacity.* The speed and density at which capacity occurs are called *critical speed* and *critical density.*

The peak of the speed-flow and density-flow curves, capacity, is a relatively unstable condition. As capacity is approached, there are fewer and fewer usable gaps in the traffic stream. At capacity, there are none, and any disruption or perturbation in the traffic stream sets off a chain reaction that cannot be effectively damped or dissipated. At this point, *forced* or *unstable flow* exists. The dashed portion of the curves in Figure 3-17, the region in which density exceeds critical density and speed is lower than critical speed, represents this forced-flow condition.

Note that any rate of flow less than capacity may occur under two different conditions: (1) high speed and low density, and (2) low speed and high density. These are represented by points *A* and *B*, respectively, in Figure 3-17. Obviously, point *A* is the more desirable operating condition, as point *B* is in the region of forced or unstable flow. The fact that a given flow may occur under two radically different operating conditions is important. It explains why volume or rate of flow cannot be used as a measure describing the operational quality of the traffic stream. Simply stating an observed volume does not uniquely describe the state of the traffic stream, as it can occur under two sets of circumstances. Speed and density, however, are good measures of the quality of operations, as both uniquely describe the state of the traffic stream. Further, both are directly discernible to the driver, while volume or flow is a point measure of no direct interest to the driver. Many historic and recent studies have examined the exact mathematical relationship that best describes these relationships. These are discussed in greater detail in subsequent chapters dealing with uninterrupted flow facilities. This introduction is intended to establish that such relation-ships exist, and are central to the description and understanding of traffic stream flow.

Characteristics of interrupted flow

On interrupted flow facilities, the most important aspects of flow occur at the points of interruption. For the most part, these are signalized intersections, although YIELD and STOP signs and other causes of fixed interruptions also qualify.

The details of flow at a signalized intersection are covered in Chapter 16. To summarize here, the dynamics of continually starting and stopping a traffic stream (with green and red signals) radically changes the flow regimen from that experienced under uninterrupted flow.

One important characteristic of uninterrupted flow facilities is the formation of platoons of moving vehicles. Platoons of vehicles can move along an arterial through "green windows" at each signalized intersection. The initiation of green at each successive intersection is timed relative to the previous intersection (offset) according to a desired speed. Because of this, flow along interrupted flow facilities is often unevenly distributed, with dense platoons of vehicles followed by periods of very light flow.

Within platoons, many of the same relationships governing uninterrupted flow are still valid. Such descriptions, however, fail to capture the essential nature of the interruptions that cause platoons to form, and which dominate the capacity and operational quality of the facility. Chapters 16 through 18 treat these subjects in great detail.

References

1. *A Policy on Geometric Design of Highways and Streets,* American Association of State Highway and Transportation Officials, Washington, DC, 1994.
2. Bates, J. T., "Perception-Reaction Time," *ITE Journal,* 1995.
3. *Manual on Uniform Traffic Control Devices,* U.S. Department of Transportation, Federal Highway Administration, Washington, DC, 1988, as amended.
4. Bhesania, R. P., "Changes in Intersection Sight Distance Standards and Their Implications," *ITE Journal,* August 1992.
5. Alexander, G. J., and Lunenfeld, H., *Positive Guidance in Traffic Control,* U.S. Department of Transportation, Federal Highway Administration, Washington, DC, 1975.
6. Oh, Y. T., "Cost-Effective Decisions and Life-Cycle Cost in Diamond Interchange Design," Ph.D. Dissertation, Polytechnic University, Brooklyn, NY, January 1989.

Problems

Problem 3–1

A driver takes 3.2 seconds to react to a complex situation while traveling at a speed of 90 km/hr. How far does the vehicle travel before the driver initiates a physical response to the situation (i.e., putting his/her foot on the brake)?

Problem 3–2

A driver traveling at 96 km/h rounds a curve on level grade to see a truck overturned across the roadway at a distance of 150 meters. If the coefficient of forward friction is 0.40, at what speed will the driver hit the truck? Plot the results for reaction times ranging from 0.50 to 5.00 seconds (in 0.50 second increments). Discuss the implications of the result.

Problem 3–3

A car hits a tree at an estimated speed of 35 mph on a 3% downgrade. If skid marks are observed of 100 ft on dry pavement (F = 0.45) followed by 250 ft on a grass-stabilized shoulder (F = 0.20), estimate the initial speed of the vehicle.

Problem 3–4

Drivers must slow from 110 km/h to 70 km/h to negotiate a severe curve on a rural highway. A warning sign for the curve is clearly visible for a distance of 30 meters. How far in advance of the curve must the sign be posted in order to insure that vehicles can safely decelerate? Assume a level grade, F = 0.30, and a perception-reaction time of 2 seconds.

Problem 3–5

What is the minimum radius that may be designed to provide for safe operation of vehicles at 110 km/h if f = 0.10 and e = 0.06?

Problem 3–6

The counts shown in the table were observed on a freeway. Compute (a) the hourly volume, (b) the peak rate of flow for a five-minute period, (c) the peak rate of flow for a 15-minute period, and (d) the peak hour factor based upon 15-minute periods.

Time	Count
5:00–5:05 P.M.	201
5:05–5:10	208
5:10–5:15	217
5:15–5:20	232
5:20–5:25	219
5:25–5:30	220
5:30–5:35	205
5:35–5:40	201
5:40–5:45	195
5:45–5:50	210
5:50–5:55	190
5:55–6:00	195

Problem 3–7

A volume of 900 vph is observed at an intersection approach. Plot the peak rate of flow within the hour as the PHF varies from 1.00 to 0.75.

Problem 3–8

The travel times shown were measured for vehicles as they traversed a 2.0-mile segment of highway. Compute the time mean speed and the space mean speed. Why is space mean speed always lower than time mean speed?

Vehicle	Travel Time (min)
1	2.6
2	2.4
3	2.4
4	2.8
5	2.2
6	2.1

Express both TMS and SMS in mph.

Problem 3–9

A traffic stream displays average vehicle headways of 2.2 sec at 50 mph. Compute the density and rate of flow for this traffic stream.

Problem 3–10

At a given location, space mean speed is found to be 40 mph and volume 1600 pcphpl. What is the density?

Problem 3–11

The AADT for a given highway location is 25,000 vpd. If the route is classified as an urban radial road, approximately what peak-hour volume would be expected?

Problem 3–12

Sketch the general form of the speed-density, speed-flow, and density-flow curves for an uninterrupted traffic stream. Show the following values on the curves: (a) capacity, (b) regions of stable and unstable flow, (c) critical speed and critical density, (d) jam density, and (e) free-flow speed.

4

Traffic Studies: Introduction and Overview

T raffic studies are conducted for a number of reasons, which can generally be classified as:

- *managing the physical system,* including inventories of control devices (signs, signals, markings), lighting fixtures, repair and maintenances activities, decisions and authorizations, permits, street maps, condition assessments;
- *investigating trends over time,* including volume, speeds, accidents, and needs assessments, so that actions can be anticipated, identified, and taken;
- *understanding the needs and choices of the public and industry* for mobility, including mode choices, routings, parking, trip-making by time of day, goods delivery, space utilization, and motivations for ride sharing;
- *calibrating basic relations or parameters,* such as the perception-reaction time, friction coefficients, discharge headways, lane utilization, and the many terms used in the equations presented in this text; this can include providing the factual basis for such measures as access management;

- *assessing the effectiveness of improvements,* such as accident reduction programs, specific geometric changes, HOV lanes, and other undertakings;
- *assessing potential impacts,* including traffic and environmental impact assessments, site developments, and access requests;
- *evaluating performance* of systems or subsystems, specifically focused on how well mobility is being delivered.

Many traffic engineers specialize in some of these areas, but it is safe to say that most have responsibilities which are dominated by three elements: evaluating performance, assessing potential impacts, and managing the physical system.

There has literally been a revolution in the technology of data collection and analysis, to the extent that many manual methods are simply not cost-effective in the modern traffic engineering office. The reader must understand the opportunities—and the challenges—provided by this technology. One of the challenges is to focus on how much data is enough, and on what can be reasonably established with a given amount of data. Therefore, Chapters 4–8 devote a considerable amount of attention to the *statistical* aspects of data interpretation.

Modern technology

Advances in computing and communications during the 1980s and 1990s have added substantial data collection, reduction, and analysis capabilities to traffic engineering studies. Spin-off sensor technologies from other fields—defense and the space program—have added to this capability. Lastly, the routine availability of such tools as low-cost, high-quality computer spreadsheet and data base programs have revolutionized the products that can be created.

Intersection controllers and even basic traffic counters are now routinely special-application computers, with their own CPU on board as well as considerable memory. Each device therefore can store—and transfer—data in machine readable form. Engineers now expect the data to be available in machine readable form, and to be efficiently transfered, and that spreadsheets and data base programs will analyze and present the data. Manufacturers who do not face this reality do not survive.

What elements must the traffic engineer consider? The specific technology will change, but the following elements seem to dominate:

- *Area Sensing:* Video and infrared sensors are in common use in traffic management centers (TMCs) and in specific applications. Both technologies are "passive" in that they do not radiate energy at the population, which radar does. Both can be installed at vantage points and "see" a territory that would take many in-ground loop detectors to cover. Infrared may have advantages over video in bad weather, because it depends upon the heat emissions of the traffic, not the visual image.
- *Imaging:* The key to the effective use of video and other sensors is capturing the image—and analyzing it—using software algorithms to identify the traffic, so that counts, speeds, and occupancies can be taken without human intervention. There is of course value in seeing the image in a traffic management center, but even in that environment, other sensors tend to identify the existence of a

problem, so that the operators can then look at the correct camera.

- *Sensors in the Software:* These are currently in use, and can be expected to become more sophisticated. Some systems depend upon motion past identified points [1], while other concepts use software algorithms to detect even stationary (queued) vehicles [2]. To the user, however, the appearance is the same: software allows the user to select several points in the display at which virtual loops are placed, and data collected as if the physical loop were in place. Refer to Figure 4-1 for an illustration. Comparable systems are also being developed in Korea, with some 32 "detectors" per intersection anticipated.
- *Wireless Communications:* The cellular phone is currently the most visible wireless communications device. Less visible but very important are lower powered versions of the same technology, so that sensors in traffic lanes can communicate with roadside receivers, and they in turn with the home base, potentially with no communications wires. This yields fast, flexible, and low cost installation.
- *Continued Miniaturization:* Electronics now allows some traffic sensors which are essentially the size of credit cards, as illustrated in Figure 4-2. In addition to the portability that comes with size (this unit is affixed directly to the pavement, with no cuts), the miniaturization also implies low power requirements, so that there are *no* communications or power links to the actual sensor.
- *Other Data Sources:* The obvious emphasis is on placing devices to get essential data, such as traffic counts. However, the entire emphasis on Intelligent Transportation Systems, including toll collection, smart cards, facility management (video, count and speed sensors, etc.) opens the door to vast amounts of data that can be used for traffic studies. Data bases created by trucking companies and by transit operators provide other sources. Cellular telephones, and even marketing studies by highly sophisticated credit card companies are sources of information.
- *Low Cost Computing:* It is given that computers become more powerful, smaller, and less expensive each year. The processors at the heart of desktop computers are also routinely installed in vehicles, sensors, and instruments.

Figure 4-1   Location of virtual detectors by software. [Courtesy of Image Sensing Systems.]

• *Value-Added Approaches Based on Commercial Products:* As much as we emphasize the *computer* revolution, the real driving force is the creation of new general-purpose software products such as data base programs and spreadsheets. In the very user-friendly environment created by Windows™ and such products, in which the user constructs systems by dragging icons, the traffic engineer—and related product developers—is freed from person-years of computer coding to do applications, using existing tools and products as the foundation.

The importance of this last item cannot be overstated. One manufacturer not only detects vehicles, but notes that different styles of vehicles have unique signatures, and that the signature varies by speed in predictable ways. Refer to Figure 4-3 for illustrations. Products can be developed that exploit this knowledge, if it matches the need of traffic engineers for information.

As one example of the potential of such products, the signatures in Figure 4-3 lead easily to: (1) counts and speeds, classified by vehicle type; and (2) headways between vehicles, classified by vehicle pairings (car-car, car-truck, truck-car, etc.). The former is a standard traffic engineering application. The latter is typically a research application, and a very expensive one using older technology and field observers.

Data fusion

One of the greatest challenges in the future will be the problem of "data fusion"—putting together data from different sources, and synthesizing it into a full and *accurate* picture of the system. The problem may be less acute for data analyzed at a later time, but it still exists. Did two different sources define and measure speed in the same way? Did they use time mean speed or space mean speed?[1] Was there a calibration? Were they measuring demand or some capacity-constrained volume?

In real time systems, such as TMCs, there are also questions of the *quality* of the data, and the *quantitative vs. qualitative nature* of the data. Information pours in from road sensors, video images, traveler telephone reports, cooperating agency observations, toll plaza congestion, and other sources. How does one manage this, and which data is more meaningful than other data, and for what purposes and decisions?

This is not an issue to be resolved here, but rather an issue which will arise continually in coming years, and require the attention of many in the profession.

[1]The difference is addressed in Chapter 7.

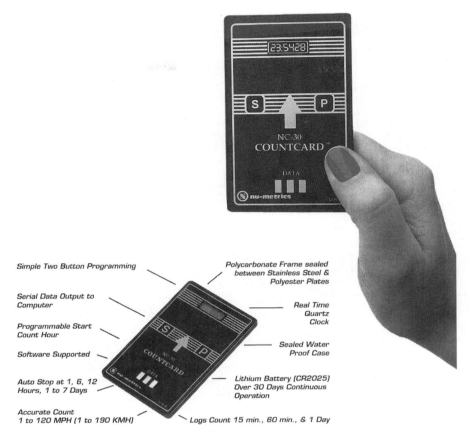

Figure 4-2   Miniaturization of traffic detectors. (See also Reference [3].) [Courtesy of Nu-Metrics, Inc.]

Performance assessment

In Chapter 1, four questions were posed as an introduction to performance assessment:

1. How good was *my* trip?
2. How many of *us* did the system move?
3. How *well* did the system move us?
4. How *much* of the system resources were used up in the process?

and the additional question was raised of whether these questions are sufficient when the infrastructure does not exist, as often is the case with public transportation.

Table 4-1 shows some candidate measures by which these questions can be addressed. *This table is neither complete nor definitive.* Indeed, in using this text, an excellent group exercise would be debating this table, filling it in as appropriate. Some of the questions raised in drafting Table 4-1 were:

- *Do we need a separate column for each facility type, and for each mode (particularly pedestrian and bicycle)?* Without question, there is merit to this, but the table size needs to be manageable for the purposes of this chapter. Nonetheless, a column on an HOV lane or a freeway versus a street would have been nice.[2]

- *Isn't the "Highway Facility, More Detailed" really an intersection?* Yes, that was the case used in constructing the illustration, but the spirit of the first three

---

[2]Of course, our solution is to add this work to the problems at the end of the chapter.

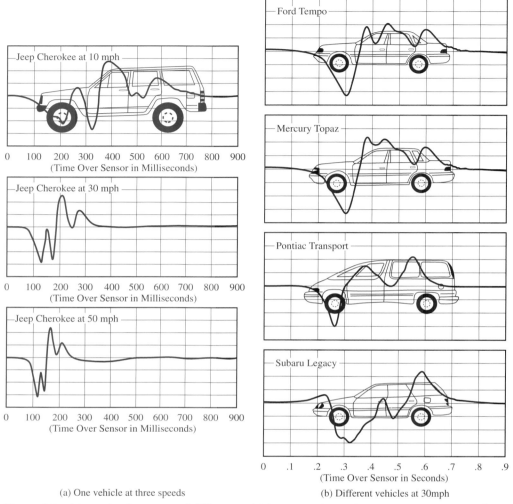

(a) One vehicle at three speeds

(b) Different vehicles at 30mph

Figure 4-3 Magnetic signatures of different vehicles. (See also Reference [4].) [Courtesy of Nu-Metrics, Inc.]

columns was: entire system, major subsystem (e.g., an arterial), and smaller element (e.g., an intersection).

• *Are there some performance measures shown which are really used for control mechanisms, and not for performance evaluations?* Yes. . . . and no. For instance, detector occupancy on a freeway is used as a good indicator of density, and is monitored for high values so that control measures (ramp metering, etc.) and advisories (variable message signs, etc.) can be instituted. This measure is not in general use as a performance indicator, but is used among professionals concentrating on freeway management

for just that purpose. It is uncertain whether it will migrate to general usage in coming years.

In the process of creating this table, there is a dramatic reminder of the totally different uses to which the word *occupancy* is put, even within the profession. Most of the time, the usage is clear, but there is great opportunity for confusion. For instance:

• *Occupancy* is used on freeways to mean the percentage (or fraction) of time a detector is covered by vehicles, and as such is directly related to density on the roadway.

Table 4-1 Candidate Performance Measures for Basic Questions

	Highway System	Highway Facility	Highway Facility, More Detailed	Transit
How good was *my* trip?	—	1) Travel time 2) Speed 3) Delay	1) Queues	1) Travel time 2) Schedule adherence
How many of *us* did the system serve?	1) VMT 2) PMT	1) Volume 2) People	1) Volume 2) People	1) Volume 2) People
How *well* did the system move us?	1) Total Travel Time 2) Map showing travel times or speeds, coded to ranges 3) Map showing congestion hotspots	1) Travel time and/or speed 2) Demand vs. Volume + demand/capacity ratios 3) Congestion + duration + spatial extent + average delay	Occupancy of detectors, as indicator of density	1) Interarrival times 2) Bus occupancies 3) Travel times 4) Schedule adherence
How *much* of the system resources were used up in the process?	Vehicle occupancies	1) Vehicle occupancies 2) v/c ratios and changes therein	1) Vehicle occupancies 2) v/c ratios and changes therein	Bus occupancies
Are there deficiencies in the infrastructure	Missing links	High v/c ratios	High v/c ratios	1) Missing routes 2) Missing links 3) Unrealistically high headways 4) High bus occupancies

Notes: VMT = Vehicle Miles Traveled; PMT = Person Miles Traveled; citations of "bus" could also be "rail."

- *Occupancy* is used with regard to vehicles to mean how many people are in the vehicle, so that *vehicle occupancy* (average or distribution) might be the better term, but most people simply are not that precise. The same is true of *bus occupancy*.
- *Occupancy* is sometimes used to indicate the percent (or fraction) coverage of a left turn bay or an intersection approach at some particular point in time. Some software uses this measure as an indicator of queueing and congestion.
- *Occupancy* is used in some traffic simulation models in another variation: *link occupancy* refers to the *number* of vehicles in the link. It can also be expressed as a fraction of the maximum number the link can hold.

Each of these usages is valid, and it is unfortunate—but true—that professionals in different specialties will use the term without full awareness of the other uses.

Classical studies

A number of traffic studies are used in the everyday practice of traffic engineering:

1. *Volume Studies.* Traffic counts are the most basic of all parametric studies, because volume (or rate of flow) is the unit used to quantify traffic demand or the amount of traffic. Counts are regularly sampled on all streets and highways, and for special purposes as needed. Chapter 6 discusses in detail the conduct and analysis of volume studies.
2. *Speed Studies.* Speed studies generally focus on the speed of vehicles passing a point under uncongested conditions. Such studies provide information on driver desires and their perception of "reasonable" operating speed. Speed data are critical inputs to many design, control, and safety aspects of traffic engineering. Chapter 7 presents a detailed discussion of speed studies and their application.
3. *Travel Time Studies.* While speeds are generally measured at a specific location or point along a highway, travel time to traverse a section of highway of significant length is also an important parameter. Travel time along a route section is used as a primary measure of traffic congestion and of the effectiveness of measures intended to facilitate through movement, such as progressive signal systems. Chapter 7 also presents a detailed discussion of travel-time studies.

4. *Delay Studies.* While point speeds and section travel times are useful measures, they cannot adequately describe the existence and extent of stopped delays. Because of this, traffic engineers are frequently interested in measuring the occurrence, locations, and amounts of stopped delay along a route or at a given location. Delay studies are frequently an adjunct to speed or travel time studies, with data being collected at the same time. Chapter 7 discusses delay studies and measurement techniques.
5. *Density Studies.* Density is rarely directly observed, as an elevated vantage point would be required. For any given traffic stream, however, measured speeds and volumes are sufficient to compute the corresponding density. Thus, many traffic studies yield density information via computation from other parameters.
6. *Headway and Spacing Studies.* Headways and spacings between individual pairs of vehicles in the traffic stream are frequently measured for a variety of purposes. Intersection departure headways are a basic measure of intersection capacity and performance, while spacing measurements can be used to compute densities. Like speed, headway and spacing are unique to each vehicle in the traffic stream, and averages are used to describe the stream as a whole. Individual headways and spacings are of great interest in studies of the interaction among different vehicle types in the traffic stream. The impact of trucks, for example, on trailing and preceding vehicles can be discerned through careful study of these parameters.

Special studies

Special-purpose data includes a wide range of information that does not neatly fit into any of the other categories. Often, such data cannot be collected by direct observation, and secondary sources or interviews must be used.

Studies frequently focus on problem areas that require special information in addition to inventory, population, and parametric data. The list that follows, although not exhaustive, illustrates many types of traffic studies that fall into this category.

1. *Accident Studies.* Traffic safety is the primary function of the traffic engineer. Therefore, the obser-

vation of traffic-accident occurrence is an ongoing process, which must yield (a) an identification of locations of unusually high or unacceptable number of accidents (b) sufficient information to describe each accident, (c) sufficient information to relate each accident to physical, environmental, and personal conditions involved in it. The traffic engineer must have global statistics available to relate overall accident occurrence to causative factors involving design and control, and specific information to fully analyze and correct problems at each location. Fortunately, accidents occur infrequently enough that they cannot be studied by direct observation. The traffic engineer must rely on state and local traffic accident records generated from motorist- and police-supplied accident reports, as well as insurance company records. Chapter 8 presents a detailed discussion of accident studies and their interpretation.

2. *Parking Studies.* Parking studies involve inventories of parking supply and a variety of counting techniques used to estimate demand. The gathering of additional information, such as trip purposes, tolerable walking distances, parking durations, and so on, requires interviews or other supplemental data-collection techniques.

3. *Goods Movement and Transit Studies.* Central business district (CBD) areas are centers of both goods movement and transit activity. A variety of study techniques are used to obtain information on transit-usage and goods-movement patterns. Both transit-vehicle and truck activities in CBD areas represent congesting elements, which are nevertheless vital to the businesses in the area. In order to make CBD traffic systems more efficient, the traffic engineer needs information on the demands for these elements, their operational characteristics, and their needs for special facilities. Such studies are often part of planning studies, and are not treated in detail in this text.

4. *Pedestrian Studies.* Pedestrians from a basic part of the traffic stream, interfacing with vehicles at intersections and other critical locations. All the parameters that describe vehicular flow characteristics can also be used to describe the movement of pedestrians. Pedestrians are, however, harder to observe. Interviews and other methods are used to obtain trip purpose, origin and destination,

and other information not obtainable by direct observation.

5. *Calibration Studies.* Traffic engineering often is based on basic values and relationships that have been observed and documented frequently in the field. Occasionally it becomes necessary to recalibrate these relationships to reflect unusual local conditions, or simply to update information to reflect new mixes of vehicles and drivers in the traffic stream. The calibration of basic relationships places special requirements on the data to be collected and its analysis.

While a virtually limitless number of values and relationships can be calibrated, Chapters 12 and 20 focus on the calibration of capacity and level-of-service relationships used for freeway and intersection analysis. These are good examples of calibration studies.

Clearly, the types and uses of traffic data and information are many and varied. Since they form the basis for virtually all types of traffic analyses, their accuracy is of critical importance. The output of planning, design, and operational management can only be as good as the data and information on which it is based.

Managing the system: Inventories

One of the most basic functions of traffic engineering is keeping track of the physical inventory, ranging from maps for street classification and traffic control device locations to details of each device installation.

Figure 4-4 shows a representative map from a standard reference, the ITE *Manual of Transportation Engineering Studies* [5]. These maps are often prepared as CAD drawings in modern practice.

There are also powerful computer-based inventory systems (signs, signals, bridges, etc.) that allow the engineer or technician to maintain a full and complete data base on the field installations, including conditions, date visited, actions taken, and so forth. To make these systems so effective, they are linked to computerized basemaps and GIS software, to get field locations precisely. Further, they receive input from digital cameras (for actual pictures of the installation) and bar code readers (to assure that the

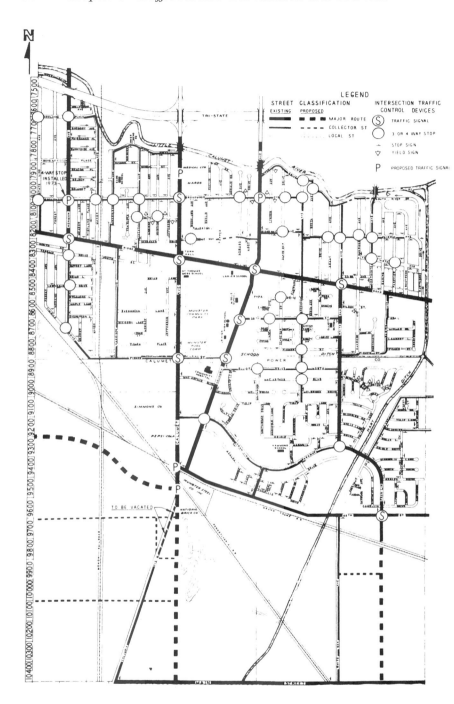

Figure 4-4   Representative map showing streets and controls. [Used with permission of Institute of Transportation Engineers, from P. C. Box and J. C. Oppenlander, *Manual of Traffic Engineering Studies,* 4th ed., p. 10. Copyright © 1976 Institute of Transportation Engineers.]

hardware was in place). Figure 4-5 shows one such sign inventory system. The same system makes custom field forms available, so that the data input can be assisted with a pen-based computer.

Figure 4-6 shows a comparable concept for the signal inventory element of an integrated but modular approach. It is now common that such products have the "look and feel" of the Windows™ operating system, and can produce both summary and detailed reports and analyses.

Figure 4-7 shows the product of a system developed to produce guide signs and other signs efficiently, working (for instance) in an AutoCAD™ environment.

This technology is a great aid in maintaining inventories, generating reports, and in general keeping on top of a daunting task. Standard interfaces allow plans to be updated to as-built drawings and imported into inventory systems.

Not every output is available in computer form, nor does every field application give rise to the need for it. Indeed, given the inefficiency of some pen-based systems (as of this writing, circa 1996), when much detailed information is required, the computer input mode may be inefficient. Figure 4-8 shows a *condition diagram* and associated checklist for which this may be the case. Of course, the final form can be scanned and put into an inventory/records system as a digital image.

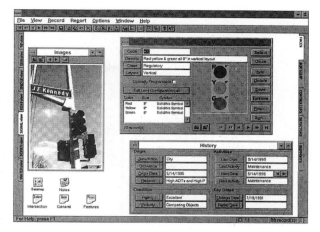

Figure 4-6 Illustration from a signal inventory system. [Courtesy of Cartè-Graph Systems, Inc.]

Condition diagrams are frequently used in accident investigations (see Chapter 8) and provide a complete inventory of the intersection in a visually effective mode. They are useful as a primary data display mode or as a supplement to computer files.

Inventory data, however, have a number of unique applications that are not so obvious. Sign and marking inventories, for example, can provide the basis for *maintenance planning.* Signs are subject to a number of hazards, including vandalism, theft, damage from accidents, fading of pigments, dirt, and so on. Markings are subject to traffic wear. For these reasons, sign and marking inventories should be checked each year. A field crew travels a specified route with a computer or hand-prepared sheet illustrating the types and locations of signs and markings. As observations are made, items still in good condition are checked, while those needing repair or replacement are noted.

Street lighting and traffic signals must also be periodically checked for burned-out bulbs or other operational defects. Signal failures are particularly dangerous and in the event of an accident can leave the traffic agency that has jurisdiction liable for damages.

Records of malfunctions and bulb burn-outs should also be kept to assist in planning regular bulb replacement and other maintenance procedures.

A critical aspect of the physical street and highway system is its structural condition and adequacy. Special inventories should be made annually, if possible, to check on a variety of *structural conditions*

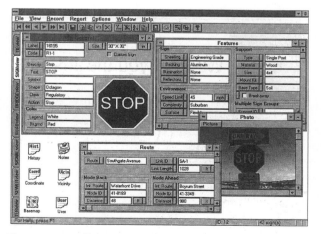

Figure 4-5 Illustration of a sign inventory system. [Courtesy of Carté-Graph Systems, Inc.]

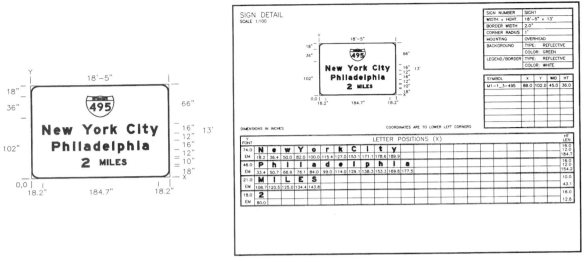

(a) Automatic Dimensioning   (b) Finished Sign Layout Drawing

Figure 4-7   The product of a system for creating signs. [Courtesy of Transoft Solutions, Inc.]

that can result in damage to the roadway and/or vehicles using it.

There are four key structural elements to a highway facility, each of which must be regularly checked:

1. Bridge structures
2. Drainage structures
3. Subsurface conditions
4. Pavement

Bridge structures have many components that deteriorate under constant loading, such as joints, cables, beams, and columns. Any or all could deteriorate owing to loading, excessive rusting, unanticipated changes in subsurface conditions, or defective materials. In recent years the number of bridge failures has increased, and the nation's bridge structures are generally considered to be in an average state of poor repair. Structural inspection is, however, a highly specialized skill, and expert consultants or staff members are generally used for this purpose.

Subsurface and/or drainage problems can cause roadway pavements to sag, heave, crack, or split. Subsurface conditions can cause embankments to collapse, or may weaken the sub-base to an extent that threatens the pavement. Often, subsurface problems are caused by drainage failures. A simple problem of a drain clogged by leaves or other material can result in excessive water seepage into the sub-base and eventual sub-base and pavement failure.

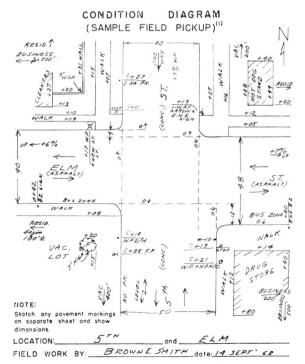

Figure 4-8   Condition diagram and checklist. [Used with permission of the Institute of Transportation Engineers, from P. C. Box and J. C. Oppenlander, *Manual of Traffic Engineering Studies*, 4th ed., p. 10. Copyright © 1976 Institute of Transportation Engineers.]

CHECKLIST FOR CONDITION FIELD DATA

1. Each street name and width of roadway
2. Each projected curb alignment:
   a. In line, or
   b. Offset
      (1) Position of offset (show on sketch)
      (2) Width of offset (measure)
   c. If streets are not at right angle, establish angle by measuring any even distance (20 feet, 30 feet, etc.) along two adjacent curbs from their point of intersection (legs of a triangle) and then distance between extreme points measured to (hypotenuse of triangle); show all three dimensions
3. Grades (if 5% or more)
4. Traffic regulations (one-way, turn prohibitions, etc.); measure and sketch on back any paint markings
5. In each quadrant, measure along each curb leg, beginning at projected intersection of curb lines

   Pickup: Corner radius
   Sidwalks (near and far edge)
   Signs (identify regulation)
   First major view obstruction and height
   Other items by type (poles, street lights, fire plugs, driveways, trees over 18″ in diameter, etc.)
   Usual distance measured from intersection is 75 to 100 feet

6. Check property frontage type one block each way
7. On sketch of area three blocks each way from intersection, indicate types of traffic control at each intersection (none, Yield or Stop, by directions controlled, signals, etc.); also indicate any significant *changes* in land use along each block (example: in residential area, note any school, church, industrial plant, business frontage, railroad crossing, etc.)

Figure 4-8   (continued)

Pavements are subject to many common problems, including surface scaling, chemical damage due to ice-salting in winter, simple wear, and—the most common of all—potholes. Roadway surfaces can be rated in general using several types of automated devices, which measure roughness and vibration when attached to the wheel of a test vehicle. Inspection by experts, however, if often needed to determine the cause and appropriate remedy for surfaces in poor condition.

Regular physical and structural evaluations are necessary if an efficient street-repair and repaving program is to be established. These programs involve high capital cost and much local disruption during construction and maintenance periods. Priorities must be clearly established and projects efficiently planned to make optimal use of available funds.

Observance studies

Another common traffic study involves the observance of driver responses to specific traffic regulations and controls. These studies are intended to record driver observance of these regulations and controls as a means of evaluating their effectiveness and the need for additional enforcement. They are conducted wherever ineffective or lax controls are suspected of being a problem—contributing to accidents, potential accidents, or congestion.

Field measurements are quite straightforward. Either drivers do or do not obey a specific regulation or control. Thus, for a speed-limit observance study, each driver is classified as traveling *above* the speed limit or *below* it.

For a STOP-sign observance study, four conditions are generally separately observed and recorded:

1. Voluntary full stop
2. Full stop caused by cross traffic
3. Rolling stop
4. No stop

For signal-observance studies, four conditions also are noted and recorded:

1. Vehicle crosses on green.
2. Vehicle crosses on yellow.
3. Vehicle crosses on red.
4. Vehicle "jumps" before green.

Recordings are made by simple check marks on field sheets of the types shown in Figure 4-9, and then summaries are prepared.

Results are generally quantified by the percentages of the traffic stream committing each action. Consider the following results of a signal-observance study:

Vehicles crossing on green	125
Vehicles crossing on yellow	38
Vehicles crossing on red	15
Vehicles "jumping" the green	27
	205

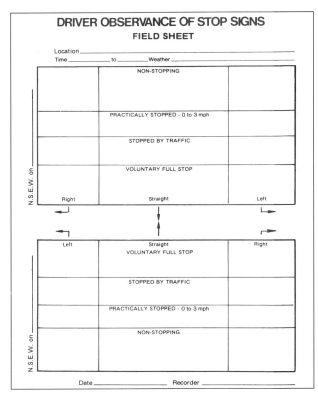

Figure 4-9 Observance study form for stop control. [Used with permission of the Institute of Transportation Engineers, from P. C. Box and J. C. Oppenlander, *Manual of Traffic Engineering Studies,* 4th ed., p. 184. Copyright © 1976 Institute of Transportation Engineers.]

Percentages for each action are:

Percent green = (125/205) × 100 = 60.98

Percent yellow = (38/205) × 100 = 18.54

Percent red = (15/205) × 100 =   7.32

Percent "jump" = (27/205) × 100 = 13.16

100.00

Once an observance rate is established for a given location, it is necessary to judge whether the rate is unusually low or approximates normal driver behavior. This requires knowledge of observance of various control devices over a wide range of representative sites. In general, regular observance studies should be made at random sites for such key controls as STOP or YIELD signs and traffic signals. This will provide a

basis for comparison for the results of any specific study where observance is thought to be a problem.

As a rule of thumb, observance rates of 15% or more lower than the generally existing norm for an area indicate a problem with the control itself: with its clarity, reasonableness, display, or enforcement. Increased enforcement is generally the last resort in improving observance of controls. Most drivers will obey reasonable controls that are clearly displayed and unambiguously applied. Well-designed control devices rarely require extraordinary enforcement to be observed.

Basic principles of probability and statistics

The last study leads us directly into the need for statistics, for the natural question is "How much data is required for a meaningful estimate of an observance rate (or any other parameter)?"

Rather than approach this question strictly with the assumption that "this is the appropriate formula (as you remember from your statistics course)," this section of the chapter reviews a number of basic principles, building the logical basis by which the reader can apply most of the statistical tests routinely used in traffic engineering. The review, however, will assume that the lecturer will supplement or expand the materials as needed by an individual class. Subsequent chapters present specific applications of statistics, and the basic material needed.

A. Randomness

Some events are very predictable, or should be predictable. If you add mass to a spring, or a force to a beam, you can expect it to deflect a predictable amount. If you depress the gas pedal a certain amount and you are on level terrain, you expect to be able to predict the speed of the vehicle.

Other events may be totally random. The emission of the next particle from a radioactive sample is said to be completely random, and is the subject for a basic experiment in introductory physics courses.

Other events may have very complex mechanisms, and *appear* to be random for all practical purposes. In some cases, the underlying mechanism cannot be perceived. In other cases, the underlying mechanism could be established with enough effort but we cannot (1) afford the time or the money necessary for the investigation, and/or (2) we cannot reasonably expect to measure the relevant variables later, in order to make use of our knowledge.

Consider the question of who turns north and who turns south after crossing a bridge. Most of the time, we simply say there is a probability p that a vehicle will turn north, and we treat the outcome as a random event. However, if we studied who was driving each car and where they worked, we might expect to make the estimate a very predictable event, for each and every car. In fact, if we kept a record of their license plates and their past decisions, we could also make very predictable estimates. The events—to a large extent—are not random.

The reader of course may object that "it isn't worth the trouble" or "we can't afford to waste that much time and money" or even that "the random assumption serves us well enough." That of course is the crux of engineering: model the system as simply (or as precisely) as possible (or necessary) *for all practical purposes*. Albert Einstein was quoted as saying "Make things as simple as possible, but no simpler."

In fact, a number of things are modeled as random *for all practical purposes*, given the investment we can afford and the process at hand. Most of the time, these judgments are just fine and are very reasonable but—like every engineering judgement—they can sometimes cause errors. For present purposes, past practice and experience in considering things to either *be random* or to *appear to be* random will be accepted.

B. The Bernoulli distribution

The Bernoulli Distribution has only two possible outcomes—yes—no, heads—tails, one—zero, with the first occurring with probability p (and therefore the other occurring with probability $(1 - p)$). This is modeled as

$$P(X = 1) = p$$
$$P(X = 0) = 1 - p$$

and the distribution is plotted as shown in Figure 4-10. This description of the probabilities is called the *probability mass function*.

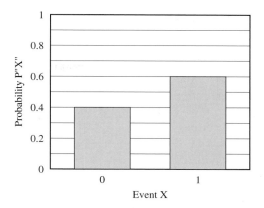

Figure 4-10 Bernoulli distribution for $p = 0.60$.

C. Measures of a distribution

For any distribution, there are several common descriptors, in addition to the mathematical and graphic presentation of the distribution relations. The most common of these is the *mean*, which has an expected value of:

$$\mu = \sum xP(x) \qquad [4\text{-}1]$$

summed over all x. This is also the (weighted) arithmetic average. It is equivalent to the center of gravity of the distribution.

The *variance* is a measure of dispersion of data around the mean:

$$\sigma^2 = \sum (x - \mu)^2 P(x) \qquad [4\text{-}2]$$

summed over all x. It is the second moment around the mean μ.

The *standard deviation* σ is the square root of the variance. It has the convenience of having the same dimensions as the mean, and certain other computational advantages which we will see when we discuss the normal distribution in Chapter 5.

Other measures include the *median,* which is the value exceeded fifty percent of the time, and the *mode,* which is the most frequently observed value. Various percentiles can also be used, such as the 50th, 85th, and 99th percentiles, where the Nth percentile has N percent of the values of x occurring below that level. It follows that the 50th percentile is the median. In some cases, the *range* (the difference between the highest and lowest values in the data) of the distribution is reported.

D. The binomial distribution

The binomial distribution can be thought of in two common ways:

1. Observe *N* outcomes of the Bernoulli Distribution, make a record of the number of events which have the outcome "1," and report that number as the outcome *X* or
2. The binomial distribution is characterized by the following properties:
   - There are *N* events, each with the same probability *p* of a positive outcome and $(1 - p)$ of a negative outcome.
   - The outcomes are independent of each other.
   - The quantity of interest is the total *number X* of positive outcomes, which may logically vary between 0 and *N*.
   - *N* is a finite number.

The two ways are equivalent, for most purposes.

Consider a situation in which people may choose "transit" or "auto," in which each person has the same probability *p* = 0.25 of choosing transit, and in which each person's decision is independent of all other persons. Defining "transit" as the positive choice for the purpose of this example, and choosing *N* = 8, note that:

- each person is characterized by the Bernoulli distribution, with *p* = 0.25;
- there are $2^8 = 64$ possible combinations of choices, and some of the combinations not only yield the same value of *X* but also have the same probability of occurring. For instance, the value of *X* = 2 occurs for

$$TTAAAAAA$$

and

$$TATAAAAA$$

and several other combinations, each with probability of $p^2 (1 - p)^6$, for a total of 28 such combinations based upon combinatorials.

Stated without proof is the result that the probability $P(X = x)$ is given by:

$$P(X = x) = \frac{N!}{(N - x)!x!} p^x (1 - p)^{N-x}, \quad [4\text{-}3]$$

with a mean of *Np* and a variance of *Npq*. The derivation may be found in any standard probability text, such as [6].

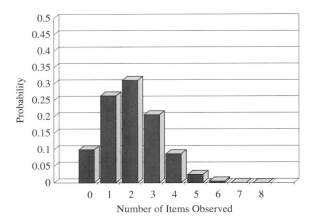

Figure 4-11   The binomial distribution for *p* = 0.25 and *N* = 8.

Figure 4-11 shows the plot of the binomial distribution for *p* = 0.25 and *N* = 8. Table 4-2 tabulates the probabilities of each outcome.

The mean may be computed as $\mu = 2.000$ and the standard deviation as $\sigma = 1.225$, using the formulas given above.

There is an important concept which the reader should master, in order to use statistics effectively throughout this text. Even though *on average* 2 out of 8 people will choose transit, there is absolutely no guarantee *what* the next eight randomly selected people will choose, even if they follow the rules (same *p*, independent decisions, etc.). In fact, the number

Table 4-2   Tabulated Probabilities for Binomial with *p* = 0.25 and *N* = 8

Outcome *X* People Choosing Transit	Probability of *X*
0	0.100
1	0.267
2	0.311
3	0.208
4	0.087
5	0.023
6	0.004
7	0.000
8	0.000

Table 4-3 Some Common Probability Distributions

Distribution Name	Shape	Mean μ	Variance σ^2	Number of Parameters	Typical Applications
Bernoulli	0 1	p	$p(1-p)$	1	single events of a binary (yes–no) nature
Binomial	0 1 2 ... N	Np	$Np(1-p)$	1	describing the probability of X out of N; building toward confidence bounds and estimating percentages
Poisson	0 1 2 3	$\alpha = (\lambda T)$	α	1	counting distribution of X events in a time period T. Uses the λ of the exponential.
Exponential		$1/\lambda$	$1/\lambda^2$	1	discharge and interarrival headways in traffic
Normal		μ	σ^2	2	speeds, volume, sometimes travel times
Erlang		$1/\lambda(c)$	$1/\lambda^2(c)$	2	more complicated headway distributions. c is an integer; $c > 0$

Note: The number of observations N in the binomial is not considered a parameter for these purposes, nor is the time period T in the Poisson.

could range anywhere from $X = 0$ to $X = 8$. Indeed, we can expect that the result $X = 1$ will occur 10.0% of the time, $X = 4$ will occur 8.7% of the time, and $X = 2$ will occur *only* 31.1% of the time.

This is the crux of the variability in survey results. If there were 200 people in the senior class, and each student surveyed eight people from the subject population, we would get different results. In general, our results—if plotted and tabulated—would conform to Figure 4-11 and Table 4-2 *but would not mimic them perfectly.* Likewise, if we average our results, the result would probably be close to 2.000, but would almost surely *not* be identical to it.

E. One- and two-parameter distributions

Two common distributions have been introduced to this point, the Bernoulli and the binomial. A number of other distributions are often used in traffic engineering, and in other applications.

Table 4-3 shows a number of the most common distributions, with the formulas for mean and variances. The equations for the distributions are not shown, but can be seen in Reference [6] or in later chapters as they are used. Common applications in traffic engineering are also noted.

In some cases, the specification of one parameter sets both the mean and the standard deviation. In others, two parameters can be specified independently (or estimated from data, given that the subject distribution is the correct one). *two parameter* distributions give the engineer more flexibility in matching the data, if they are justified by physical reasoning.[3]

---

[3]Three parameter—and higher—distributions also exist, but they are not commonly used in traffic engineering. A major conceptual problem is justifying the use of such distributions by physical reasoning. The reality is that some analysts prefer such distributions simply because they allow better *apparent* fits to the data, but that the amount of data

In practice, the proper distribution[4] is assumed and selected. Then the estimated mean and estimated variance (from data) are used to estimate the various parameters of the assumed distribution.

F. Histograms

Had there been 200 seniors in class, each collecting a sample X, we could plot the samples in the same format as Figure 4-11. This is called a *histogram* of the data. It is *not* what is theoretically expected, but rather what actually occurred. In general, even if the underlying distribution *were known* with its parameter(s), and we were able to plot the distribution and the histogram of the data on the same axis, they would not match exactly. For very large sample sizes, the histogram would approach the same shape. Of course, if the underlying distribution were *truly known,* we would not be collecting data, because that would be a waste of effort.

Applications

The introductory review of statistics in the preceding section is not sufficient to address some really interesting problems in statistics, such as: how many samples should we use? What confidence do we have in our estimate? How do we test whether this data could have come from that distribution? Subsequent chapters deal with specific aspects of statistics as they apply to various traffic engineering analyses.

---

available makes this a specious approach. The authors have great reservations about employing a three-parameter distribution just to have a good-looking fit.

[4]There is a statistical test concerning this assumption, to be discussed in a later chapter.

Summary

This chapter was designed to provide an overview of traffic studies, the related tools, and the use of modern technology. The tools include statistics, because the questions of how many samples are enough and

what confidence exists in the results pervade the use and presentation of traffic studies. These themes—studies, technology, and statistics—will be carried forward in Chapters 5–8.

References

1. Michalopoulos, P. G., "Vehicle Detection Video Through Image Processing: The Autoscope System," *IEEE Transactions on Vehicular Technology,* Vol. 40, February 1991.
2. Tzes, A., *Development of a Prototype Video-Based Sensor for Vehicle Detection from Stand Still Images,* submitted for publication, 1997.
3. *Nu-Metrics Product Guide,* Vol. 2, Nu-Metrics, Inc.
4. Sampey, H. R., "Vehicle Magnetic Imaging and Wireless Data Collection," *Nu-Metrics Technology Brief,* Nu-Metrics, Inc., Revised March 6, 1996.
5. Robertson, H. D. (editor), *Manual of Transportation Engineering Studies,* Institute of Transportation Engineers, Washington, DC, 1994.
6. Hayter, A. J., *Probability and Statistics for Engineers and Scientists,* PWS Publishing Co., Boston, MA, 1996.

Problems

Problem 4–1

Refer to Table 4-1 and the related questions in the text. Revise the table as needed, adding performance measures as appropriate, deleting others, and refining the set of basic questions. Discuss in class.

Problem 4–2

Refer to Table 4-1. Construct a column for an HOV reserved lane on a freeway. Is there a need to compare all measures to the other lanes in the same direction? Did you make this explicit?

Problem 4–3

Refer to Table 4-1. Construct columns for pedestrians, bicycles, downtown parking, and intermodal transfer points. Construct a column for goods movement. Is it necessary to distinguish between arterial use for goods purposes, delivery, and distribution center access?

Problem 4–4

There used to be a strong distinction between data collection, data reduction, and data analysis. Consider the task of collecting traffic counts in three lanes on one approach to an intersection, for three hours for 4p.m. to 7p.m. Estimate the labor for all phases (collection, reduction, analysis) assuming manual methods only. Compare this to an approach using the concepts and technology presented in this chapter, or—even better—the latest technology available at the time this assignment is given.

Problem 4–5

Run a compliance study at a STOP sign in a residential area, dividing the work amongst a group of 3–4 students, so that each group has about $N = 200$ observations. Estimate the fraction who are fully compliant, and compute the estimated 95% confidence bounds[5] on this fraction as $\pm 1.96\,s$, where s is the estimated standard deviation, the square root of $p(1 - p)/N$, where p is the estimated fraction who are fully compliant.

Problem 4–6

Plot the confidence bounds cited in Problem 4–5 for a range of p from 0.10 to 0.70 and for values of $N = 50, 100, 200,$ and 400. Comment.

Problem 4–7

Verify that the probabilities in Table 4-2 are correct, and compute the mean, variance, and standard deviation for this case.

Problem 4–8

Compute a table like Table 4-2, but for $p = 0.50$ and $N = 4$, and also plot the distribution. Then take 4 coins and flip them as a set. Count the number of heads and label this X. Repeat the experiment 100 times, and plot a histogram of the results, comparing it to the theoretic distribution and to other histograms from fellow students. Comment.

[5]This will be addressed in a later chapter, but the necessary formula is now given.

5

Statistics and Applications in Traffic Engineering

This chapter introduces commonly-used statistical analysis techniques in traffic engineering. Because traffic engineering and traffic engineering studies involve collection and analysis of large amounts of data, it is important to understand some of the statistical theory that underlies the handling and analysis of such information.

The science of statistics is required when it is not possible to directly observe or measure all of the values needed. If a room contained 100 people, the average weight of these people could be measured with 100% certainty and accuracy by weighing each one and computing the average. In traffic, this is often not possible. If the traffic engineer needs to know the average speed of all vehicles on a particular section of roadway, not all vehicles can be observed. Even if all speeds could be measured over a specified time period (a difficult accomplishment in many cases), speeds of vehicles arriving before or after the study period would be unknown. In effect, no matter how many speeds are measured, there are always more that are not. For all practical and statistical purposes, the number of vehicles using a particular section of roadway over time is infinite.

Because of this, traffic engineers often observe and measure the characteristics of a finite *sample* of vehicles in a *population* that is effectively infinite. When this is done, statistical analysis is commonly used to address the following questions:

- How many samples are required (i.e., how many individual measurements must be made)?
- What confidence should I have in this estimate (i.e., how good an estimate of a *population* characteristic is a *sample* measurement)?
- What statistical distribution best describes the observed data mathematically?
- Has a traffic engineering design resulted in a change in characteristics of the population? (For example, has a new speed limit resulted in reduced speeds?)

This chapter explores the statistical techniques used in answering these critical questions, and provides some common examples of their use in traffic engineering. Other chapters, particularly Chapter 7, explore additional applications, and give additional examples.

This chapter is not, however, intended to serve as a substitute for a course in statistics, nor for use as a text or reference on the subject. For some more basic references, see [1–4]. For some additional traffic references addressing statistical tests, see [5–6].

Statistics is fundamentally different from probability. In probability, models are based on physical reasoning, and the characteristics of distributions and relationships are derived and displayed. Numeric values—when used—are assumed to be known. In statistics, neither the numeric values nor the distributions[1] are known, and we must deal with the reality that *they will never be known* with complete certainty. The mathematics of statistics is used to *estimate* characteristics that cannot be established with absolute certainty, and to assess the degree of certainty of which does exist.

In traffic engineering, actions must be taken: geometric designs must be completed, speed limits set, signs and markings placed, signals placed and timed, etc. Average speeds, flow rates, and other characteristics are critical inputs to these actions. The inability to know this information with complete certainty, however, is not an excuse NOT to act. Statistical analysis enables the traffic engineer to make rational decisions based on estimated values, with full appreciation for the accuracy and reliability of those estimates.

Some basic principles

Before exploring some of the more complex statistical applications in traffic engineering, some basic principles of probability and statistics that are relevant to these analyses should be explored.

A. Addition of random variables

One of the most common occurrences in probability and statistics is the summation of random variables, often in the form $Y = a_1X_1 + a_2X_2$ or in the more general form:

$$Y = \sum a_i X_i \qquad [5\text{-}1]$$

where the summation is over i, usually from 1 to n.

It is easy to prove that the expected value (or mean) μ_Y of the random variable Y is given by:

$$\mu_Y = \sum a_i \mu_{Xi} \qquad [5\text{-}2]$$

[1]In some cases, we may have some physical reasoning from which to deduce the underlying distribution.

and that *if the random variables x_i are independent of each other,* the variance s_Y^2 of the random variable Y is given by:

$$\sigma_Y^2 = \sum a_i^2 \sigma_{Xi}^2 \qquad [5\text{-}3]$$

The fact that the coefficients a_i are multiplied has great practical significance for us in all our statistical work.

EXAMPLES:

ADDING TRAVEL TIMES: A trip is composed of three parts, each with its own mean and standard deviation as shown below. What is the mean, variance, and standard deviation of the total trip time?

Trip Components	Mean	Standard Deviation
1. Auto	7 min	2 min
2. Commuter Rail	45 min	6 min
3. Bus	15 min	3 min

The variance may be computed by squaring the standard deviation. The total trip time is the sum of the three components. Equations [5-2] and [5-3] may be applied to yield a mean of 67 minutes, a variance of $(2^2 + 6^2 + 3^2) = 49 \text{ min}^2$ and therefore a standard deviation of 7 minutes.

It is interesting that the standard deviation of the total trip is not much larger than the one component which has a standard deviation much larger than the other two. Inspection of the variance summation makes it clear why this is so.

PARKING SPACES: Based on observations of condos with 100 units, it is believed that the mean number of parking spaces desired is 70, with a standard deviation of 4.6. If we are to build a larger complex with 1000 units, what can be said about the parking?

In this situation, the information available is minimal. If X = the number of parking spaces for a condo with 100 units, then the mean (μ_x) of this distribution of values has been estimated to be 70 spaces, and the standard deviation (σ_x) has been estimated to be 4.6 spaces.

Since no other information is available, an assumption must be made that the number of parking spaces needed is proportional to the size of the condo development, i.e., that a condo with 1000 units will need 10 times as many parking spaces as one with

100 units. In equations [5-2] and [5-3], this becomes the value of *a*. Then, if *Y* = the number of parking spaces needed for a condo with 1000 units:

$$\mu_y = 10(70) = 700 \text{ spaces}$$

and:

$$\sigma_y^2 = (10^2)(4.6^2) = 2116$$

$$\sigma_y = 46 \text{ spaces}$$

Note that this estimates the *average* number of spaces needed by a condo of size 1000 units, but does not address the specific need for parking at any *specific* development of this size. The estimate is also based on the assumption that parking needs will be proportional to the size of the development, which may not be true. If available, a better approach would have been to collect information on parking at condo developments of varying size to develop a relationship between parking and size of development. The latter would involve regression analysis, a more complex type of statistical analysis.

B. The normal distribution

One of the most common statistical distributions is the *normal distribution,* known by its characteristic bell-shaped curve (see Figure 5-1).

In the introductory material on probability in Chapter 4, the binomial and Bernoulli distributions were shown. Each had distinct probabilities associated with each point, so that *P(X* = 1) had meaning. In continuous distributions, probability is indicated by the area under the *probability density function f(x)* between specified values, such as *P*(40 < *X* ≤ 50). The area may be found by integration between the two limits. Likewise, the mean *μ* and variance *σ²* can

be found from integration rather than summation as shown for discrete distributions in Chapter 4.

1. The standard normal. For the normal distribution, the integration cannot be done in closed form due to the complexity of the equation for *f(x)*, and tables for a "standard normal" distribution with zero mean (*μ* = 0) and unit standard deviation (*σ* = 1) are constructed. Refer to Table 5-1, which is one such table.

The standard normal is denoted *N*[0,1]. Any value of *x* on any normal distribution, denoted *N*[*μ*,*σ²*], can be converted to an equivalent value of *z* on the standard normal distribution. This can also be done in reverse when needed.

The translation of an arbitrary normal distribution of values of *x* to equivalent values of *z* on the standard normal distribution is accomplished as:

$$z = \frac{x - \mu}{\sigma} \qquad \text{[5-4]}$$

Figure 5-2 illustrates the translation for a distribution of spot speeds which has a mean of 55 mph and standard deviation of 7 mph to equivalent values of *z*. Consider the following problem: For the spot speed distribution of Figure 5-2a (*N*[55,49]), where the variance of 49 is the standard deviation of 7 squared, what is the probability that the next speed will be 65 mph or less? To answer this, translate and scale the *x*-axis as shown in Figure 5-2, so that the equivalent question for the standard normal distribution, *N*[0,1], is: Using Equation 5-4, determine the probability that the next value will be less than:

$$z = \frac{55 - 45}{7} = 1.43$$

According to Table 5-1, reading the vertical for the 1.4 and the horizontal for the 0.03, the probability of having a value less than 1.43 is 0.9236 or—as commonly if imprecisely expressed—92.36%.[2]

Another type of application frequently occurs: For the case just stated, what is the probability that the speed of the next vehicle is between 55 and 65 mph?

The probability that the speed is less than 65 mph has already been computed. We can now find the

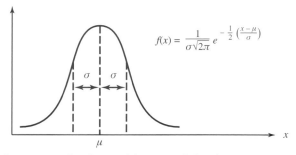

$$f(x) = \frac{1}{\sigma\sqrt{2\pi}} e^{-\frac{1}{2}\left(\frac{x-\mu}{\sigma}\right)}$$

Figure 5-1   The shape of the normal distribution.

[2]Probabilities are numbers between zero and one, inclusive, and not percentages. However, many people talk about them as percentages.

Table 5-1 Values of the Standard Normal Distribution

$$F(z) = \int_{-\infty}^{z} \frac{1}{\sqrt{2\pi}} e^{-z^2/2} \, dz$$

z	.00	.01	.02	.03	.04	.05	.06	.07	.08	.09
.0	.5000	.5040	.5080	.5120	.5160	.5199	.5239	.5279	.5319	.5359
.1	.5398	.5438	.5478	.5517	.5557	.5596	.5636	.5675	.5714	.5753
.2	.5793	.5832	.5871	.5910	.5948	.5987	.6026	.6064	.6103	.6141
.3	.6179	.6217	.6255	.6293	.6331	.6368	.6406	.6443	.6480	.6517
.4	.6554	.6591	.6628	.6661	.6700	.6736	.6772	.6808	.6844	.6879
.5	.6913	.6950	.6985	.7019	.7054	.7083	.7123	.7157	.7190	.7224
.6	.7257	.7291	.7324	.7357	.7389	.7422	.7454	.7486	.7517	.7549
.7	.7580	.7611	.7642	.7673	.7704	.7734	.7764	.7794	.7823	.7852
.8	.7881	.7910	.7939	.7967	.7995	.8023	.8051	.8078	.8106	.8133
.9	.8159	.8186	.8212	.8238	.8264	.8289	.8315	.8340	.8365	.8389
1.0	.8413	.8438	.8461	.8485	.8508	.8531	.8554	.8577	.8599	.8621
1.1	.8643	.8665	.8686	.8708	.8729	.8749	.8770	.8790	.8810	.8830
1.2	.8849	.8869	.8888	.8907	.8925	.8944	.8962	.8980	.8997	.9015
1.3	.9032	.9049	.9066	.9082	.9099	.9115	.9131	.9147	.9162	.9177
1.4	.9192	.9207	.9222	.9236	.9251	.9265	.9279	.9292	.9306	.9319
1.5	.9332	.9345	.9357	.9370	.9382	.9394	.9406	.9418	.9429	.9441
1.6	.9432	.9463	.9474	.9484	.9495	.9505	.9515	.9525	.9535	.9545
1.7	.9554	.9564	.9573	.9582	.9591	.9599	.9608	.9616	.9625	.9633
1.8	.9641	.9649	.9658	.9664	.9671	.9678	.9686	.9693	.9699	.9706
1.9	.9713	.9719	.9726	.9732	.9738	.9744	.9750	.9756	.9716	.9767
2.0	.9772	.9778	.9783	.9788	.9793	.9798	.9803	.9808	.9812	.9817
2.1	.9812	.9826	.9830	.9834	.9838	.9842	.9846	.9854	.9854	.9857
2.2	.9861	.9864	.9868	.9871	.9875	.9878	.9881	.9884	.9887	.9890
2.3	.9893	.9896	.9898	.9901	.9904	.9906	.9909	.9911	.9913	.9916
2.4	.9918	.9920	.9922	.9925	.9927	.9929	.9931	.9932	.9934	.9936
2.5	.9938	.9940	.9941	.9943	.9945	.9946	.9948	.9949	.9951	.9952
2.6	.9953	.9955	.9956	.9937	.9959	.9960	.9961	.9962	.9963	.9964
2.7	.9965	.9966	.9967	.9968	.9969	.9970	.9971	.9972	.9973	.9974
2.8	.9974	.9975	.9976	.9977	.9977	.9978	.9979	.9979	.9980	.9981
2.9	.9981	.9982	.9982	.9983	.9984	.9984	.9985	.9985	.9986	.9986
3.0	.9987	.9987	.9987	.9988	.9988	.9989	.9989	.9989	.9990	.9990
3.1	.9990	.9991	.9991	.9991	.9992	.9992	.9992	.9992	.9993	.9993
3.2	.9993	.9993	.9994	.9994	.9994	.9994	.9994	.9995	.9995	.9995
3.3	.9995	.9995	.9995	.9996	.9996	.9996	.9996	.9996	.9996	.9997
3.4	.9997	.9997	.9997	.9997	.9997	.9997	.9997	.9997	.9997	.9998

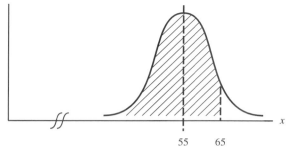

(a) The problem and normal distribution as specified

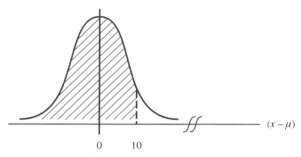

(b) The axis translated to a zero mean

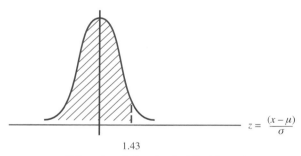

(c) The axis scaled so that the $N(0,1)$ is used

Figure 5-2   Translating a normal distribution to the $N[0,1]$.

probability that the speed is less than 55 mph, which on the z-axis is $(55–55)/7 = 0.00$ so that the probability is 0.50 or 50% exactly.[3] The probability of being between 55 and 65 mph is just the difference of the two probabilities: $(0.9236 − 0.5000) = 0.4236$ or 42.36%.

In a similar fashion, common sense and the application of the shaded area (and the fact of symmetry) can be used to find probabilities less than 0.5000. For

[3]Of course, given that the normal distribution is symmetric and the mean in this case is 55 mph, the probability of 0.50 could also have been found by inspection.

the case stated above, find the probability that the next vehicle's speed is less than 50 mph.

Translating to the z-axis, we wish to find the probability less than $(50–55)/7 = −0.72$. Negative values of z are not given in Table 5-1, but by symmetry it should be clear that the desired shaded area is the same size as the area *greater* than +0.72. Still, we can only find the shaded area less than +0.72 (it is 0.7642). Knowing that the area (or total probability) under the full curve is 1.00, the rest of the area—the desired quantity—is therefore $(1.000 − 0.7642)$ or 0.2358 or 23.48%.

From these illustrations, three important procedures have been presented: (a) the conversion of values from any arbitrary normal distribution to the standard normal distribution, (b) the use of the standard normal distribution to determine the probability of occurrences, and (c) the use of Table 5-1 to find probabilities less than both positive and negative values of z, and between specified values of z.

2. Quick facts about the normal. The above exercises allow one to compute relevant areas under the normal curve. Some numbers occur frequently in practice, and it is useful to have those in mind. For instance, what is the probability that the next observation will be within one standard deviation of the mean, given that the distribution is normal? That is, what is the probability that x is in the range $(\mu \pm 1.00 \ \sigma)$? By a similar process to those illustrated above, we can find that this probability is 68.3%.

The following ranges have frequent use in statistical analysis involving the normal distribution:

- 68.3% of the observations are within $\mu \pm 1.00 \ \sigma$
- 95.0% of the observations are within $\mu \pm 1.96 \ \sigma$
- 95.5% of the observations are within $\mu \pm 2.00 \ \sigma$
- 99.7% of the observations are within $\mu \pm 3.00 \ \sigma$
- 84.1% of the observations are less than $\mu + 1.00 \ \sigma$
- 97.7% of the observations are less than $\mu + 2.00 \ \sigma$
- 99.9% of the observations are less than $\mu + 3.00 \ \sigma$

The total probability under the normal curve is 1.00, and the normal curve is symmetric around the mean. It is also useful to note that the normal distribution is asymptotic to the x-axis, and extends to values of $\pm\infty$. These critical characteristics will prove to be useful throughout the text.

C. Central limit theorem

One of the most impressive—and useful—theorems in probability is that the sum of *n* similarly distributed random variables tends to the normal distribution, no matter what the initial, underlying distribution is. That is, the random variable $Y = \Sigma X_i$ where the X_i have the same distribution, tends to the normal distribution.

The words "tends to" can be read as "tends to look like" or "tends to be described by" the normal distribution. In mathematical terms, the actual distribution of the random variable Y approaches the normal distribution asymptotically. The only practical question is, how quickly?

Figure 5-3 shows a sketch in which the original distribution is a uniform distribution, with all values equally probable. It has sharp definition and no smoothness at the corners. Although not proven here, the sum of two random variables with the same uniform distribution is a triangular distribution, as indicated in the sketch. As more variables are added, the resulting distribution quickly develops smoothness and the characteristic shape of the normal distribution. By the time $n = 12$, the sum of uniform distributions tends to look quite like the normal curve.

Why is this happening? Consider a uniform distribution with the range (0,10). Extreme values are as probable as any other value. Adding only two such distributions, the range is (0,20), but in order to have an extremely high value (near 20), the first *and* second numbers must both be high. The same is true of very low numbers. However, for mid-range numbers, many combinations can yield a number in the vicinity of (say) ten. How fast is the tendency to approach the normal distribution, and has it been reached in a given case? As a practical matter, the resultant distribution can be inspected and the analyst can literally *see* if the case is plausible, based upon symmetry, smoothness, and tails. There are exceptional cases,[4] but frequently the numbers required for the distribution of such a summation process look normally distributed rather quickly.

1. Sum of travel times. Consider a trip made up of fifteen components, all with the same underlying distribution, each with a mean of 10 minutes and standard deviation 3.5 minutes. The underlying distribution is unknown. What can you say about the total travel time?

While there may be odd shapes which would contradict us, for reasonably smooth underlying distributions, $n = 15$ should be quite sufficient to say that the distribution of total travel times tends to look normal. Based upon basic relationships, it would have a mean of 150 minutes, a variance of 122.5 min[2] and a standard deviation of 11.1 minutes. These numbers, obtained from Equations [5-2] and [5-3], do not depend upon the appearance of normality.

However, if the total travel times do look normally distributed, it can also be said that 95% of the observations will fall within 150 ± 1.96 (11.1) minutes based upon the "quick facts" cited previously. That is, 95% of the observations will fall in the range 128 to 172 minutes.

2. Hourly volumes. Five minute counts are taken, and they tend to look rather smoothly distributed, but with some skewness (non-symmetry). Based upon many observations, the mean tends to be 45 vehicles in the 5-minute count, with a standard deviation of 7 vehicles. What can be said about the hourly volume?

---

[4]One of these exceptional cases can be the binomial distribution, with very small *p*, even when the *n* is very large. This is addressed in a later subsection.

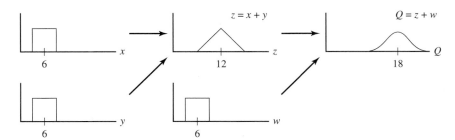

Figure 5-3 The sum of uniform distributions approaches the normal distribution.

The hourly volume is the addition of twelve such distributions, which should logically be basically the same if the traffic levels are stable. If so, the hourly volume will tend to look normal, have a mean of $(n\mu_x) = (12 \times 45) = 540$ vph and a variance of $(n\sigma_x^2)$ $(12 \times 7^2) = 588$ (vph)^2 due to the summation (see Equations [5-2] and [5-3]). The standard deviation is, therefore, 24.2 vph. Based upon normality, 95% of the observed hourly volumes would tend to be in the range 540 ± 48 vph ($\mu \pm 1.96\,\sigma$).

A special note: The summation has had an interesting effect. The σ/μ ratio for the 5-minute count distribution was $7/45 = 0.156$, but for the hourly volumes it was $48/540 = 0.089$. This is due to the summation, which tends to remove extremes by canceling "highs" with "lows" and thereby introduces stability. The mean of the sum grows in proportion to n but the standard deviation grows in proportion to the square root of n.

D. Sum of normal distributions

Although not proven here, it is true that the sum of any two normal distributions is itself normally distributed. By extension, if one normal is formed by n_1 summations of one underlying distribution and another normal is formed by n_2 summations of another underlying distribution, the sum of the total also tends to the normal. Thus, in the travel time example above, not all of the elements had to have exactly the

same distribution as long as subgroupings each tended to the normal.

E. The binomial distribution related to the Bernoulli distribution

Chapter 4 noted that the sum of n Bernoulli distributions *is* binomially distributed. This is not an approximation, but is exact in all cases, for all ranges of n. Note that the mean of the binomial is np and the variance is $np(1 - p)$, which could have been established by using Equations [5-2] and [5-3] on the addition of n Bernoulli distributions.

1. Asking people questions. Consider that the commuting population has two choices, $X = 0$ for auto and $X = 1$ for public transit. The probability p is generally unknown, and it is usually of great interest. Assuming the probability is the same for all people—to our ability to discern, at least—then each person is characterized by the Bernoulli distribution.

If we ask $n = 50$ people for their value of X, the resulting distribution of the random variable Y is binomial, and may tend to look like the normal (if the combination of p and N is suitable; more on this below). Figure 5-4 shows this exact distribution for $p = 0.25$. Without question, this distribution looks normal. Applying some "quick rules" from above, and noting that the expected value is 12.5 (50×0.25), the

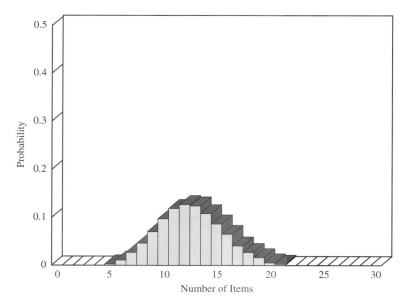

Figure 5-4   The binomial distribution for $p = 0.25$ and $n = 50$.

variance is 9.375 ($50 \times 0.25 \times 0.75$), and the standard deviation is 3.06, one can expect 95% of the results[5] to fall in the range 12.5 ± 6.0 or between 6.5 and 18.5.

Another random variable may be considered, namely $p_{est} = Y/n$, where Y is the binomially distributed number shown in Figure 5-4. Applying Equations [5-2] and [5-3], p_{est} has a mean of p, a variance of $p(1 - p)/n$, and a standard deviation which is the square root of that. Notice that the square root of n has appeared explicitly in the denominator of the standard deviation.

For the case at hand, p_{est} will have a mean of $12.5/50 = 0.25$ and 95% of its observations will fall in the range of 0.13 to 0.37. In a later section, p_{est} will be called the estimator of p and we will relate the range 0.13 to 0.37 to the confidence bounds on the estimate.

2. Increasing the number of people. If $n = 200$ had been selected, then the mean of Y would have been 50 when $p = 0.25$ (200×0.25) and the standard deviation would have been 6.1 (square root of $200 \times 0.25 \times 0.75 = 37.50$), so that 95% of the results would have fallen in the range of 38 to 62. For p_{est}, the mean would be 0.25 and the 95% range of results would be 0.19 to 0.31.

F. The binomial and the normal distributions

Without question, the Central Limit Theorem informs us that the sum of Bernoulli distributions—that

---

[5] *Each* result is *one* number, the sum of the fifty responses where each "transit" response adds one to the total.

is, the binomial—tends to the normal distribution. The only question is, how fast? A number of practitioners in different fields use a rule of thumb that says "for large n and small p," the normal approximation can be used without restriction. This is incorrect, and can lead to serious errors.

The most notable case in which the error occurs is when rare events are being described, such as auto accidents per million miles traveled, or aircraft accidents. Consider Figure 5-5, which is an *exact* rendering of the actual binomial distribution for $p = 0.7(10)^{-6}$ and two values of n, namely $n = 10^6$ and $n = 2(10)^6$ respectively. Certainly p is small and n is large in these cases.

Figure 5-5 is almost self-explanatory. For the (p,n) combinations chosen, the distribution does *not* have the characteristic symmetric shape of the normal distribution. In order for there to be some chance of this symmetry (and no significant probability near or below $X = 0$), a condition such as specified in Figure 5-6, namely $np/(1 - p) \geq 9$, is necessary.

Clearly, neither of the cases in Figure 5-5 satisfies such a condition. Note that the means in the two cases shown are $m = 0.7$ and 1.4, respectively, with standard deviations of 0.83 and 1.18. The normal distribution would have a significant part shown for $X < 0$, which is not physically meaningful in the applications at hand (e.g., accidents).

G. The Poisson distribution

The Poisson is known in traffic engineering as the "counting distribution." It has the clear physical

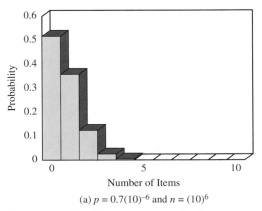

(a) $p = 0.7(10)^{-6}$ and $n = (10)^6$

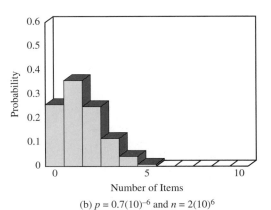

(b) $p = 0.7(10)^{-6}$ and $n = 2(10)^6$

Figure 5-5   The binomial can be far from the normal even with very low p and very high n.

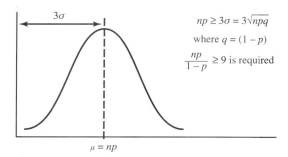

Figure 5-6 A necessary condition for the normal to approximate the binomial distribution.

meaning of a number of events X occurring in a specified counting interval of duration T, and is a one-parameter distribution with:

$$P(X = x) = \frac{m^x e^{-m}}{x!} \qquad [5\text{-}5]$$

with mean $\mu = m$ and variance $\sigma^2 = m$.

The fact that one parameter m specifies *both* the mean and the variance is a limitation, in that if we encounter field data where the variance and mean are clearly different, the Poisson does not apply.

The Poisson has at least two very interesting linkages to other distributions:

1. When interarrival times are exponentially distributed with mean $\mu = 1/\lambda$, the *number* of arrivals in an interval of duration T is Poisson distributed with mean $\mu = m = \lambda T$.
2. The binomial distribution tends to approach the Poisson distribution with parameter $m = np$.

Indeed, the Poisson would have been a suitable approximation to the "low p, high n" cases in the preceding subsection.

H. Correlation and dependence

To this point, much attention has been paid to basic relationships, and it was always assumed that the random variables involved (such as the X_i) were independent of each other. Of course, Y and the X_i are not independent of each other, but that has not been relevant to this point.

In Figure 5-7, two random variables are clearly related to each other. One of the most common measures of such relation is the linear correlation coefficient r, which can vary in the range of ± 1.0. The closer the magnitude of the coefficient to 1.0, the stronger the relationship. The sign ($\pm$) shows the direction of the trend: if Y increases when X does, the sign is positive. If Y increases as X decreases, the sign is negative.

Several multivariate analysis tools are used for investigating relationships between (and among) random variables. Those used most commonly in traffic engineering are regression, analysis of variance, and cluster analysis.

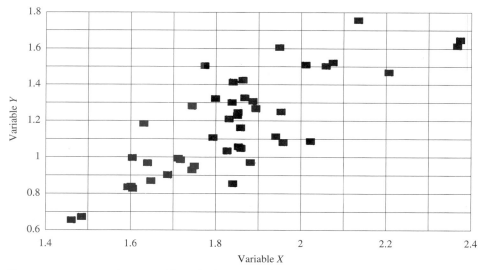

Figure 5-7 Two random variables which are correlated.

Common estimators

Three common point estimators are used extensively. All are unbiased estimators of desired quantities:

1) for the mean

$$\bar{x} = (1/n)\sum x_i \qquad [5\text{-}6]$$

2) for the variance

$$s^2 = \frac{\sum (x_i - \bar{x})^2}{n - 1} \qquad [5\text{-}7]$$

3) for percentanges[6]

$$\hat{p} = x/n \qquad [5\text{-}8]$$

They are referred to as "point" estimators simply because they estimate single numbers. They are "unbiased" because the expected value of the estimator—which is, after all, itself a random variable—are exactly the quantities they are estimating. That is,

$$E[x] = \mu \qquad E[s^2] = \sigma^2 \qquad E[p] = p$$

The standard deviation σ is usually estimated by s, the square root of the variance estimator. It is not an unbiased estimator, but is generally used as the most suitable.

The basic concept is that the random variables formed by Equations [5-6] to [5-8] can be used as effective measures of the unknown quantities μ, σ^2, and p. Indeed, in practice, they are essentially the best we can do.

Confidence bounds

This subject has already been introduced indirectly, in the "quick facts" about the normal distribution and some of the solved problems. It has been said that the probability of any random variable being within 1.96 standard deviations of the mean is 0.95 *if the normal distribution is a suitable descriptor of the situation.* Under those conditions:

$$P[(\mu - 1.96\sigma) < y \leq (\mu + 1.96\sigma)] = 0.95 \quad [5\text{-}9]$$

That result has been used (indirectly) to solve some problems earlier in this chapter.

[6]Actually, for fractions or probabilities.

Two questions are especially relevant: (1) for a given random variable Y, what are the μ and σ which we use? (2) What do we do if we do not know these quantities?

The answer to the first question is simple: use the μ and σ of the distribution of Y. Of course, these values must be known. The answer to the second question is straightforward: if we do not know a quantity, its estimator will be used (see the preceding section).

1. The mean. The random variable $\bar{x}$ defined in Equation [5-6] is equal to the sum of n random variables X_i, which is then multiplied by a constant $(1/n)$. Using Equation [5-2], it can be shown that $\mu_{\bar{x}} = \mu_{Xi}$. Using Equation [5-3], note that:

$$\sigma_{\bar{x}}^2 = (1/n)^2\{\sigma_{X1}^2 + \sigma_{X2}^2 + \sigma_{X3}^2 + \ldots + \sigma_{XN}^2\} = \sigma_X^2/n \qquad [5\text{-}10]$$

This demonstrates that a mean, $\bar{x}$, is itself a random variable from a distribution of similar means drawn from samples of size n. The true mean (μ) of such a distribution is the same as the true mean of the distribution of individual values from which the means are drawn. This is straightforward and logical. If 100 vehicle speeds are measured, their average can be directly computed. If, however, the 100 vehicles are separated into 10 groups of 10 speeds, the average of each group of 10 can be separately computed. The average of these averages, however, must be the same as the original average of the 100 speeds.

Of more use is Equation [5-10], which defines the variance of the distribution of means. The standard deviation is the square root of this, or:

$$\sigma_{\bar{x}} = \frac{\sigma_x}{\sqrt{n}} \qquad [5\text{-}11]$$

In fact, however, the true standard deviation of the original distribution is not known—only the estimate, s. Thus, σ_x is replaced by s_x in the equation. This value is often referred to as the *standard error of the mean*, and is given the symbol E. Thus:

$$E = \frac{s}{\sqrt{n}} \qquad [5\text{-}12]$$

Equation 5-9 can now be restated in terms of the distribution of sample means:

$$P[(\bar{x} - 1.96E) \leq \mu_{\bar{x}} \leq (\bar{x} + 1.96E)] = 0.95 \qquad [5\text{-}13]$$

In verbal terms, this means that *there is a 95% chance that true mean lies between* $\bar{x} \pm 1.96E$. In other words, the analyst is 95% confident that the true mean lies within the interval defined by $\bar{x} \pm 1.96E$. Further, while not proven here, any random variable consisting of sample means tends to be normally distributed for reasonably large n regardless of the original distribution of individual values.

A similar equation can be written for a probability of 0.997, which corresponds to 3 standard deviations around the mean:

$$P[(\bar{x} - 3E) \leq \mu_{\bar{x}} \leq (\bar{x} + 3E)] = 0.997 \quad [5\text{-}14]$$

These equations essentially allow the evaluation of *how good* the estimator of a mean is.

2. Application: Spot speeds. Speed data was taken at a fixed location on a road, using a radar meter. The observed data had an average of 63.2 mph and an estimated standard deviation of 8.4 mph; $n = 30$ observations were collected. What is the best single estimate of the true underlying mean μ_X of the spot speed distribution? What confidence do you have in that estimate?

The best single point estimate of μ_X is 63.2 mph, the computed average of the data. See Equation 5-6.

The 95% confidence bound involves the quantity $\pm 1.96\ E$, where $E = 8.4/30^{1/2} = 1.53$. The 95% confidence interval is $\pm 1.96\ (1.53) = 3.0$. See Equation [5-13]. Therefore the 95% confidence bounds are 63.2 ± 3.0 mph. Put another way, after collecting $n = 30$ samples we are 95% sure that the true mean speed is somewhere between 60.2 and 66.2 mph.

The 99.7% confidence interval is $\pm 3\ (1.53) = 4.6$. If 99.7% confidence is required, the true mean speed can only be placed in the interval 63.2 ± 4.6 mph, or 58.6 to 67.8 mph.

Neither of these estimates is very good, in that the intervals are quite large. It would not be possible to perform rational traffic engineering analyses without knowing the speed with greater precision. We *cannot, however,* provide a better estimate without additional data. **This is the most basic and immutable practical result of this entire exercise.** The limiting value in defining the intervals is the sample size n. The interval becomes smaller when the square root of n gets larger—i.e., *more data.*

3. The fraction $p_{est} = x/n$. Equations [5-13] and [5-14] hold for this case as well, with the standard deviation estimated from $E = \{p(1 - p)/n\}^{1/2}$. The only special requirement is that the binomial distribution of the sum (and thus of the fraction p_{est}) approach the normal distribution, as illustrated in Figure 5-6.

4. Application: Mode choice. Consider a survey in which 25% of 100 people interviewed had selected the transit mode. What is your best single estimate of the transit mode split? What are the 95% confidence bounds on this estimate?

The best single estimate of p is 0.25. See Equation [5-8]. The 95% confidence bounds are given by ± 1.96 $\{0.25\ (0.75)/100\}^{1/2}$ or ± 0.085. Therefore, it is 95% probable that the true mean is somewhere in the range from 0.165 and 0.335.

While this result may not excite us—and may even displease some people to whom we are presenting the information—the simple and immutable fact is that *these are the confidence bounds, given the sample size.*

Estimating sample sizes

The emphasis in the preceding section clearly motivates the next question, "So how many samples are needed?" Of course, the answer depends on desire, the confidence bounds and the standard deviation of the underlying distribution.

For cases in which the distribution of means can be considered to normal, the confidence range for 95% confidence is:

$$\pm 1.96 \frac{s}{\sqrt{n}}$$

If this value is called the tolerance, and given the symbol e, then the following equation can be solved for n, the desired sample size:

$$e = 1.96 \frac{s}{\sqrt{n}}$$

and:

$$n = 3.84 \frac{s^2}{e^2} \quad [5\text{-}15]$$

Similarly, for 99.7% confidence:

$$e = 3 \frac{s}{\sqrt{n}}$$

and:

$$n = 9 \frac{s^2}{e^2} \qquad [5\text{-}16]$$

Table 5-2 shows the required sample sizes for various desired 95% confidence bounds and standard deviations, for the case of spot speed estimates of the true mean speed. Inspection of the table leads to the obvious conclusion that great precision requires considerable sampling, and that the numbers become very large when we wish great precision in the face of large variation.

1. Application: Travel times. An arterial is to be studied, and it is desired to estimate the true mean travel time to a tolerance of ±5 seconds with 95% confidence. Based on prior knowledge and experience, it is estimated that the standard deviation of the travel times is about 15 seconds. How many samples are required?

Based on an application of Equation [5-15], $n = 3.84 (15^2)/(5^2) = 34.6$, which is rounded to 35 samples.

As the data is collected, the s computed is 22 seconds, not 15 seconds. What does this imply?

If the sample size is kept at $n = 35$, the confidence bounds will be ±1.96 $(22)/(35)^{1/2}$ or about ±7.3 seconds. If the confidence bounds must be kept at ±5 seconds, then the sample size must be increased so that $n \geq 3.84(22^2)/(5^2) = 74.4$ or 75. Additional data will have to be collected to meet the desired tolerance and confidence level.

2. Application: Vehicle occupancies. It is anticipated that a typical vehicle occupancy pattern of passenger cars is:

- 70% of the vehicles have one occupant
- 20% of the vehicles have two occupants
- 8% of the vehicles have three occupants
- 2% of the vehicles have more (say 4.2) occupants

Using this pattern, compute the number of observations needed to estimate the average vehicle occupancy to a tolerance of ±0.02 persons with 95% confidence. Assuming this pattern is correct, compute the mean and standard deviation of the vehicle occupancy. Assuming the pattern is correct, what percent of the riders are in vehicles with two or more occupants?

The first question cannot be answered without some knowledge of the underlying standard deviation of the vehicle occupancies. This sample problem is "different" in that information on σ or s is not provided, but rather information from which σ^2 can be computed.

Using the principles of Chapter 4 (Equations [4-1] and [4-2]), the mean and variance *for the assumed distribution* are computed as:

$$\mu = 0.70(1) + 0.20(2) + 0.08(3) + 0.02(4.2)$$
$$= 1.424 \text{ persons/vehicle}$$

$$\sigma^2 = 0.70(1 - 1.424)^2 + 0.20(2 - 1.424)^2$$
$$+ 0.08(3 - 1.424)^2 + 0.02(4.2 - 1.424)^2$$

or $s^2 = 0.545$ so that $s = 0.738$ persons/vehicle.

It is now possible to compute the required $n \geq 3.84 (0.738^2)/(0.02^2) \approx 5379$ samples are required. This is rather demanding, and does suggest knowing a

Table 5-2 Required Sample Sizes For Different Expectations (For 95% Confidence Levels)

Standard Deviation of Speeds	Desired Tolerance (mph)			
	±0.5 mph	±1.0 mph	±2.0 mph	±3.0 mph
5.0 mph	384	96	24	11
7.0 mph	753	188	47	21
9.0 mph	1245	311	78	35

Note: Table entries are required sample sizes.

number of about 1.424 (if the assumed distribution is plausible) to a tolerance of ±0.02.

The last part of the question set has nothing to do with sample sizes or confidence bounds. Note that 100 vehicles would carry on average 142.4 people, of whom 70 would be in single occupant vehicles, so that $(142.4 - 70) = 72.4$ people would be in vehicles carrying two or more people, or $(72.4/142.4)100\% = 50.8\%$ of the travelers.

The concept of hypothesis testing

Consider that there are two distinct choices, such as hypotheses H_0 and H_1. These are usually referred to as the *null hypothesis* and the *alternative hypothesis,* respectively. Of the two hypotheses, one is *true* and the other is *false.* Unfortunately, we do not know which is which. Therefore, we design a test, apply it, and make a judgment. The problem is that there is no guarantee that we are correct in our decision or judgment.

There are four possible outcomes in terms of whether or not the hypothesis is true. These are illustrated in Table 5-3. Clearly, for a given (but unknown) truth, there is one correct decision and one incorrect decision.

To illustrate the situation further, let us consider an example. An auto inspection program is going to be applied to 100,000 vehicles, of which 10,000 are "unsafe" and the rest are "safe." Any given vehicle is either safe or unsafe according to some definition. However, we do not *know* which is which.

We have a test procedure, but it is not perfect, due to the mechanics and test equipment used. In par-ticular, 15% of the unsafe vehicles are determined to be safe, and 5% of the safe vehicles are determined to be unsafe.

Let us define:

H_0: The vehicle being tested is "safe."

H_1: The vehicle being tested is "unsafe."

It therefore follows that a Type I error (rejecting a true null hypothesis) is labeling a safe vehicle as "unsafe." The probability of a Type I error is 0.05.

A Type II error (failure to reject a false null hypothesis) is labeling an unsafe vehicle as "safe." The probability of a Type II error is 0.15.

What are the consequences? In this particular case, a Type I error results in a failed inspection (and probably a repair bill) for a safe vehicle. A Type II error results in an unsafe vehicle being let out on the road.

Perhaps the most disturbing thing for the engineer to recognize is that *the decision is acted on without certainty of information.* The process outlined in this example results in $(90,000)(0.05) = 4500$ safe vehicles failing inspections and $(10,000)(0.15) = 1500$ unsafe vehicles passing inspections. Yet the decision maker does not *know* which is which.

The design of the test, and the tradeoff of Type I versus Type II error, is therefore a central part of any statistical investigation, whether the purpose is to decide on safe versus unsafe vehicles or on a mean travel time of 45 versus 60 minutes. In general, for a given test procedure (rules, number of samples, and so on), one can reduce Type I error only by living with a higher Type II error, and vice-versa. Of course, one can also modify the test procedure itself.

Table 5-3 Possible Outcomes in the Testing of a Hypothesis

The Unknown Truth: Two Possibilities	Test Procedure Results in a Determination That:	
	H_0 is TRUE	H_0 is FALSE
H_0 is TRUE	CORRECT	TYPE I ERROR: Reject a correct null hypothesis (False Negative)
H_0 is FALSE	TYPE II ERROR: Fail to reject a false null hypothesis (False Positive)	CORRECT

A. Hypothesis testing is action-oriented

Statistics are used so that people can make estimates, then judgments, and then act. In the preceding section, individual cars *were* judged and subjected to some action (repaired, put back on the road).

Hypothesis testing in particular is oriented towards making decisions, and moving ahead with actions. The basic concept recognizes that not all results will be "correct," but that the path for action is being prepared, nonetheless. The process is generally:

1. Formulate a hypothesis and—if appropriate—an alternative.
2. Design a test procedure by which a decision can be made.
3. Use statistics to refine or finalize the test procedure, recognizing the tradeoffs and making judgments about what levels of Type I and Type II errors are acceptable.
4. Apply the test to individual cases (or the one case at hand).
5. Based upon the results of the test, make decisions and/or take action.

Table 5-4 summarizes the key words for later use.

B. Before and after tests with two distinct choices

In a number of situations, there are two clear and distinct choices, and the hypotheses seem almost self-defining:

- auto inspection (acceptable, not acceptable)
- disease (have the disease, don't)
- speed reduction of 5 mph (it happened, it didn't)
- accident reduction of 10% (it happened, it didn't)
- mode shift by five percentage points (it happened, it didn't)

Table 5-4   Key Steps in an Action Plan

---

1. Formulate a Hypothesis
2. Design a Test Procedure
3. Refine/Finalize Test Procedure
4. Apply the Test
5. Make Decisions/Take Action

Of course there is the distinction between *the real truth* (reality, unknown to us) and *the decision* we make, as already discussed and related to Type I and Type II errors (sometimes referred to as "alpha" and "beta" errors). That is, we can decide that some healthy people have a disease and we can decide that some sick people do not have the disease.

There is also the distinction that people may not want to reduce the issue to a binary choice, or might not be able to do so. For instance, if an engineer expects a 10% decrease in the accident rate, should we test "H_0: no change" against "H_1: 10% decrease" against each other, and not allow the possibility of a 5% change? Such cases are addressed in the next section. For the present section, we will concentrate on binary choices.

1. Application: Travel time decrease. Consider a situation in which the existing travel time on a given route is known to average 60 minutes, and experience has shown the standard deviation to be about 8 minutes. An "improvement" is recommended which is expected to reduce the true mean travel time to 55 minutes. What test should be conducted? What decision rule should be included in the test? How much data should be collected in order to make the test? What are the probabilities of Type I and Type II error?

This is a rather standard problem, with what is now a fairly standard solution. The logical development of the solution follows.

The first question we might ask ourselves is whether we can consider the mean and standard deviation of the initial distribution to be truly *known* or whether they must be estimated. Actually, we will avoid this question, simply by focusing on whether the *after* situation has a true mean of 60 minutes or 55 minutes.

Note that we do *not* know the shape of the travel time distribution. If it were not for the Central Limit Theorem: a new random variable Y, formed by averaging[7] several travel time observations, will tend to the normal distribution, if enough observations are taken.

---

[7] That is, adding N observations X_i—in which case the Central Limit Theorem can be cited—and then dividing by n.

Figure 5-8 shows the shape of *Y* for two different hypotheses, which we now form:

H_0: The true mean of *Y* is 60 minutes.

H_1: The true mean of *Y* is 55 minutes.

Figure 5-8 also shows a logical decision rule: if the actual observation *Y* falls to the right of a certain point, *Y**, then accept H_0; if the observation falls to the left of that point, then accept H_1. Finally, Figure 5-8 shows shaded areas that are the probabilities of Type I and Type II errors.

Note that:

1. There really is only one observation *Y*, because the *n* travel time observations are all used to produce the one estimate *Y*.
2. If the point *Y** is fixed, then the only way the Type I and Type II errors can be changed is to increase *n*, so that the shapes of the two distributions become

narrower because the standard deviation of *Y* involves the square root of *n* in its denominator.

3. If the point Y* is moved, the probabilities of Type I and Type II errors vary, with one increasing while the other decreases.

To complete the definition of the test procedure, the point *Y** must be selected and the Type I and Type II errors determined.

It is common to require that the Type I error (also referred to as the "level of significance α") be set at 0.05, so that there is only a 5% chance of rejecting a true null hypothesis.

In the case of two alternative hypotheses, it is common to set both the Type I and Type II errors to 0.05, unless there is very good reason to imbalance them (both represent risks, and the two risks—repairing some cars needlessly versus having unsafe cars on the road, for instance—may not be equal).

Inspecting Figure 5-8, *Y** will be set at 57.5 mph in order to equalize the two probabilities. The only way these errors can be equal is if the value of *Y** is set at exactly half the distance between 55 mph and 60 mph. The symmetry of the assumed normal distribution requires that the decision point be equally distant from both 55 mph and 60 mph, assuming that the standard deviation of both distributions (before and after) remains 8 mph.

To insure that both errors are not only equal, but have an equal value of 0.05, *Y** must be 1.645 standard deviations away from 60 minutes, based upon the earlier "quick facts" concerning the normal distribution (which can be derived from Table 5-1). Therefore $n \geq (1.645^2)(8^2)/(2.5^2)$ or 28 observations, where 8 = the standard deviation, 2.5 = the tolerance (57.5 mph is 2.5 mph away from both 55 and 60 mph), and 1.645 corresponds to the *z* statistic on the standard normal distribution for a beta value of 0.05 (which corresponds to a probability of $z \leq 95\%$ on Table 5-1).

The test has now been established with a decision point of 57.5 mph. If the "after" study results in an average speed of under 57.5 mph, we will accept the hypothesis that the true average speed has been reduced to 55 mph. If the result of the "after" study is an average speed of more than 57.5 mph, the null hypothesis—that the true average speed has stayed at 60 mph—is accepted.

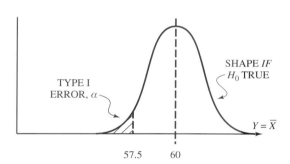

(a) Hypothesis H_0: True mean is 60 minutes

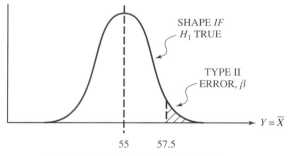

(b) Hypothesis H_1: True mean is 55 minutes

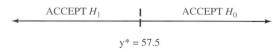

(c) Decision rule based upon *Y**

Figure 5-8   The shape of *Y* for each of the two hypotheses.

Was all of this analysis necessary to make the common-sense judgment to set the decision speed at 57.5 mph—half way between the existing average speed of 60 mph and the desired average speed of 55 mph? The answer is in two forms: the analysis provides the logical basis for making such a decision. This is useful. The analysis also provided the minimum sample size required for the "after" study to restrict both alpha and beta errors to 0.05. This is the most critical result of the analysis.

2. Application: Focus on the travel time difference. The preceding illustration assumed that we would focus on whether the underlying true mean of the "after" situation was either 60 minutes or 55 minutes. What are some of the practical objections that people could raise?

Certainly one objection is that we implicitly accepted at face value that the "before" condition truly had an underlying true mean of 60 minutes. Suppose, to overcome that, we focus on the *difference* between before and after observations.

The n_1 "before" observations can be averaged to yield a random variable Y_1 with a certain mean μ_1 and a variance of σ_1^2/n_1. Likewise, the n_2 "after" observations can be averaged to yield a random variable Y_2 with a (different?) certain mean μ_2 and a variance of σ_2^2/n_2. Another random variable can be formed as $Y = (Y_2 - Y_1)$ which has an underlying mean of $(\mu_2 - \mu_1)$ and variance $\sigma^2 = \sigma_2^2/n_1 + \sigma_1^2/n_2$. Figure 5-9 shows the distribution of Y, assuming two hypotheses.

What is the difference between this and the preceding illustration? The focus is directly on the difference, and does not implicitly assume that we know the initial mean. As a result, "before" samples are required. Also, there is more uncertainty, as reflected in the larger variance. There are a number of practical observations in using this result:

- it is common that the "before" and "after" variances are equal, in which case the total number of observations can be minimized if $n_1 = n_2$. If the variances are not known, the estimators s_i^2 are used in their place. The same is true in the preceding illustration;
- if the variances are not known, the estimators s_i^2 are used in their place, as in the previous illustration; and
- if the "before" data was already taken in the past and n_1 is therefore fixed, it may not be possible to reduce the total variance enough (by using just n_2)

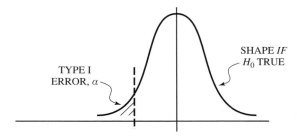

(a) Hypothesis H_0: True difference in means is "0"

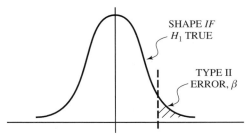

(b) Hypothesis H_1: True difference in means is –5 mph

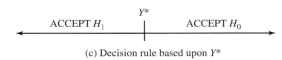

(c) Decision rule based upon Y^*

Figure 5-9   The shape of Y when focusing on the differences.

to achieve a desired level of significance α, say $\alpha = 0.05$.

By way of comparison to the preceding illustration, note that if both variances are 8^2 and $n_1 = n_2$ is specified, then $n_1 \geq 2*(1.645^2)(8^2)/(2.5^2)$ or 56 *and* $n_2 \geq 56$. The total required is 112 observations, and the fourfold increase is a direct result of focusing on the difference of -5 mph rather than the two rather absolute, binary choices (60 mph or 55 mph).

Before and after tests with generalized alternative hypothesis

It is also common to encounter situations in which the engineer states the situation as "there was a decrease" or "there was a change" versus "there was not," but does not state or claim the magnitude of the change. In these cases, it is standard practice to set up a null hypothesis of "there was no change" ($\mu = \mu_0$) and an alternative hypothesis of "there was a change" ($\mu \neq \mu_0$,). In such cases, a level of significance of 0.05 is generally used.

Figures 5-10 and 5-11 show the null hypotheses for two cases, both being "no change," but the first implicitly considering that *if* there were a change, it would be negative, and the second not having any sense (or suspicion) about the direction of the change, if it exists. Note that:

- The first is used when physical reasoning leads one to suspect that if there were a change, it would be a decrease.[8] In such cases, the Type I error probability is concentrated where the error is most likely to occur.
- The second is used when physical reasoning leads one to simply assert "there was a change" without any sense of its direction. In such cases, the Type I error probability is spread equally in the two tails.

The second case is often used in what might be called "reverse reasoning." We might *hope* that there was no change (or no difference), and really want to *not reject* the null hypothesis. That is, not rejecting the null hypothesis in this case is a measure of success. There are, however, other cases in which we wish to prove that there is a difference. The same logic can be used, but in such cases, rejecting the null hypothesis is "success." More will be said on this later in this chapter.

1. Application: Travel time differences. We have made some improvements (in our opinion and judgment) and suspect that there is a decrease in the true underlying mean travel time. Figure 5-10 applies.

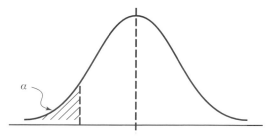

Figure 5-10   Null hypothesis: "There was no decrease."

---

[8]The same logic—and illustration—can be used for cases of suspected *increases,* just by a sign change.

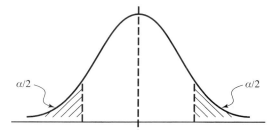

Figure 5-11   Null hypothesis of "there was no change."

Using the information from the previous illustrations, let us specify that we wish a level of significance $\alpha = 0.05$. The decision point depends upon the variances *and* the n_i. If the variances are as stated in the prior illustration and $n_1 = n_2 = 56$, then the decision point $Y^* = -2.5$ mph, as before.

Let us now go one step further. The data is collected, and $y = -3.11$ results. The decision is clear: reject the null hypothesis of "there is no decrease." But what risk did we take? Consider:

- Under the stated terms, had the null hypothesis been valid, we were taking a 5% chance of rejecting the truth. The odds favor (by 19–1, in case you are inclined to wager with us) not rejecting the truth in this case.
- At the same time, there is no stated risk of accepting a false hypothesis H_1, for the simple reason that no such hypothesis was stated.
- The null hypothesis was rejected because the value of Y was higher than the decision value of 2.5 mph. Since the actual value of -3.11 is considerably higher than the decision value, one could ask about the confidence level associated with the rejection. The point $Y = -3.11$ is 2.054 standard deviations away from the zero point, as can be seen from:

$$\sigma_Y = \sqrt{\frac{\sigma_1^2}{n_1} + \frac{\sigma_2^2}{n_2}} = \sqrt{\frac{8^2}{56} + \frac{8^2}{56}} = 1.51$$

and $z = 3.11/1.51 = 2.059$ standard deviations. Entering the N[0,1] table with $z = 2.059$ yields a probability of 0.9803. This means that if we had been willing to take *only* a 2% chance of rejecting a valid H_0, we *still* would have rejected the null hypothesis; we are 98% confident that our rejection of the null hypothesis is correct.

Since this reasoning is a little tricky, let us state it again: if the null hypothesis had been valid, you were initially willing to take a 5% chance of rejecting it. The data indicated a rejection. Had you been willing to take only a 2% chance, you still would have rejected it.

Table 5-5 shows two views of this situation: for $n_1 = n_2$ varying from 10 to 100. From the values in this table, note:

- If you wish to stay at a level of significance of 0.05, then the decision point Y^* varies from -5.89 to -1.86 for the values of n as shown. If you select $n_1 = n_2 = 10$, then the observed mean difference in the field has to be at least -5.89 for a rejection. There is an excellent chance that a true difference of -5 mph will not be detected most of the time in this scenario.
- If you wish to keep the decision point at $Y^* = -2.50$, then the level of significance varies from 0.24 to 0.01. If you select $n_1 = n_2 = 10$, there is a 24% chance that a valid hypothesis of "no decrease" will be rejected.

2. One-sided versus two-sided tests. The material just discussed appears in the statistics literature as "one-sided" tests, for the obvious reason that the probability is concentrated in one tail. If there is no rationale for this, a "two-sided" test should be executed, with the probability split between the tails. As a practical matter, this means that one does not use the probability tables with a significance level of 0.05, but rather with $0.05/2 = 0.025$.

3. Paired differences. In some applications—notably simulation, where the environment is controlled—data from the "before" and "after" situations can be paired and the differences taken immediately. In this way, the entire statistical analysis is done *directly* on the differences, and the overall variation can be much lower, because of the identity tags.

Another application of paired differences is pre-test and post-test in training activities. Consider the data of Table 5-6, first with no attempt at pairing the tests and then with the paired data.

Is it easy to see a significant difference in the paired data? Could it have been detected without the pairing? Using the approach of a one-sided tested on the null hypothesis "no increase," the following computations may be done:

$$s_1 = 7.74 \qquad s_2 = 7.26 \qquad n_1 = n_2 = 15$$

From this information, the standard deviation of the difference in means is found as:

$$s_Y = \sqrt{\frac{7.74^2}{15} + \frac{7.26^2}{15}} = 2.74$$

For a significance level of 0.05 (or 95% confidence) in a one-tailed test, the decision point is 1.65 standard

Table 5-5 Effects of Varying N_1 ($= N_2$) on Decision Point or Level of Significance

	a. Effect on Decision Point, Holding 0.05 Level of Significance		b. Effect on Level of Significance, Holding -2.50 Decision Point	
N	σ	Y^*	No. of Standard Deviations, σ	α
10	3.578	-5.89	0.699	0.24
20	2.530	-4.16	0.988	0.16
30	2.066	-3.40	1.210	0.11
40	1.789	-2.94	1.398	0.08
50	1.600	-2.63	1.563	0.06
60	1.461	-2.40	1.712	0.04
70	1.352	-2.22	1.849	0.03
80	1.265	-2.08	1.976	0.02
90	1.193	-1.96	2.096	0.02
100	1.131	-1.86	2.210	0.01

Table 5-6 Data Showing The Advantages of Pairing

Person	Pre-Test Score	Person	Post-Test Score	Person	Difference By Person
1	55	5	53	1	5
2	47	7	57	2	8
3	70	9	61	3	4
4	62	3	74	4	5
5	49	14	64	5	4
6	67	2	55	6	4
7	52	8	60	7	5
8	57	4	67	8	3
9	58	12	57	9	3
10	45	11	70	10	3
11	68	15	65	11	2
12	52	6	71	12	5
13	51	1	60	13	5
14	58	10	48	14	6
15	62	13	56	15	3
Estimated Mean =	56.9		61.2		4.3
Estimated STD =	7.74		7.26		1.50

STD = Standard Deviation.

deviations, or $1.65 \times 2.74 = 4.54$ mph. Given that the observed difference in average speeds is only $+4.3$ mph, the null hypothesis (no increase) is *not* rejected on the basis of this test.

However, inspection of the paired differences makes it clear—in this particular case—that *every* person had an increase. Application of the same basic approach using the paired differences shown in Table 5-6 yields:

$$s = 1.50 \qquad n = 15$$

The standard error of the mean for this case is:

$$E = \frac{1.50}{\sqrt{15}} = 0.388$$

For a level of significance 0.05, the decision point $Y^* = 1.65 \times 0.388 = 0.64$ mph. With an observed difference of 4.3 mph, the null hypothesis (no increase) is clearly rejected.

A hypothesis on the underlying distribution f(x)

One of the early problems stated was a desire to "determine" the underlying distribution, such as in a speed study. The most common test to accomplish this is the *goodness-of-fit test.*

In actual fact, the underlying distribution will not be *determined.* Rather, a hypothesis such as "H_0: The underlying distribution is normal" will be made, and we will secretly hope it is *not rejected,* for we wish to act as if the distribution were in fact normal.

The procedure is best illustrated (for the purposes of this text) by an illustration. Consider the spot speed data of Table 5-7 which was used in an earlier problem. The computed mean was 48 mph and the computed standard deviation 8.6 mph.

Consider the following hypothesis:

H_0: The underlying distribution is normal with $\mu = 48$ mph and $\sigma = 8.6$ mph.

Table 5-7 Data from a Speed Study

53	43	63	61	54
41	57	38	43	58
63	46	37	31	34
52	47	44	46	54
41	45	49	48	47
39	48	58	37	62
55	51	47	42	48
34	44	37	39	54
43	46	47	51	47
57	53	32	32	36
47	52	54	47	50
37	36	63	62	43
58	57	53	59	48

The steps in using the goodness-of-fit test on this hypothesis are as follows:

1. Define categories or ranges of the data, and assign the data to the categories.

   There should be at least five categories and at least five data entries in each category. The categories need not be the same width, although they often are. It is much more important that they represent the shape of the distribution.

   Define n_i = the number of samples in category i.
2. Compute the *expected* number of samples for each category, assuming that the hypothesized distribution is in fact true.

   Define e_i = expected number of samples in category i.
3. Compute the quantity

$$\chi^2 = \sum_{i=1}^{N} \frac{(n_i - e_i)^2}{e_i} \qquad [5\text{-}17]$$

where the summation is done over N categories.
4. As shown in any standard statistical text, the quantity χ^2 is chi-square distributed, and we expect low values if our hypothesis is correct. (If the observed samples exactly equal the expected, then the quantity is zero.) Therefore, refer to a table of the chi-square distribution (such as Table 5-8) and look up the number that we would not exceed more than 5% of the time (note: $\alpha = 0.05$ is being

used). To do this, we must also have the number of degrees of freedom, designated f. This is

$$f = N - 1 - g$$

where N is the number of categories and g is the number of things we estimated from the data in defining the hypothesized distribution. We defined μ and σ based upon information from the data, so that $g = 2$.
5. Make a decision and then proceed with other aspects of the analysis.

Note that categories are often defined in terms of histogram categories, as illustrated in Figure 5-12. For the case at hand, the hypothesized distribution is also shown, superimposed.

Table 5-9 shows the computations for the case at hand. Note that the probability of an outcome's falling into a given category can be found from the assumed normal distribution.

Had the hypothesis been a different distribution, then the reader would have had to consult a statistics reference for the table of that distribution, or compute the probabilities by directly using the formula for the distribution.

The decision is to *not reject* the hypothesis, comparing a computed chi-square value of 1.0209 with a tabular value of 9.488 ($\alpha = 0.05, f = 4$).

Note that if Engineer A had tested a hypothesis of the underlying distribution's being normal, and Engineer B had tested a hypothesis of the underlying distribution's being a "Student t" distribution, they *both* may have had their respective hypotheses not rejected. How could this happen? Remember that the test does not *prove* what the underlying distribution is in fact. At best, it does not oppose your desire to assume a certain distribution. Thus, both Engineers A and B can be happy. Of course, if the two distributions had radically different shapes, one would expect a rejection in at least one of the cases.

A final point on this type of hypothesis testing: the test is not directly on the hypothesized distribution, but rather on the expected versus observed number of samples. Table 5-9 shows this in very plain fashion: the computations involve the expected and observed number of samples; the actual distribution is important only to the extent that it influences the probability by category.

Table 5-8 Tabulation of the Chi-Square Distribution

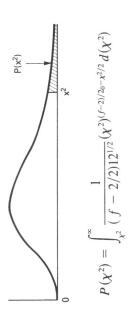

$$P(\chi^2) = \int_{\chi^2}^{\infty} \frac{1}{(f-2/2)12^{1/2}} (\chi^2)^{(f-2)/2_0 - \chi^2/2} \, d(\chi^2)$$

$P(\chi^2)$ i	.995	.990	.975	.950	.900	.750	.500	.250	.100	.050	.025	.010	.005
1	3927×10^{-2}	1571×10^{-7}	9821×10^{-7}	3932×10^{-8}	0.01579	0.1015	0.4549	1.323	2.706	3.841	5.024	6.635	7.879
2	0.01003	0.02010	0.05064	0.1026	0.2107	0.5754	1.386	2.773	4.605	5.991	7.378	9.210	10.60
3	.07172	.1148	.2158	.3518	.5844	1.213	2.366	4.108	6.251	7.815	9.348	11.34	12.34
4	.2070	.2971	.4844	.7107	1.064	1.923	3.357	5.585	7.779	9.488	11.14	13.28	14.86
5	.4117	.5543	.8312	1.145	1.610	2.675	4.351	6.626	9.236	11.07	12.83	15.09	16.75
6	.6757	.8721	1.237	1.635	2.204	3.455	5.348	7.841	10.64	12.59	14.45	16.81	18.55
7	.9893	1.259	1.690	2.167	2.833	4.255	6.346	9.037	12.02	14.07	16.01	18.48	20.28
8	1.344	1.646	2.180	2.733	3.199	5.071	7.344	10.22	13.36	15.51	17.53	20.09	21.98
9	1.735	2.088	2.700	3.325	4.168	5.899	8.343	11.39	14.68	16.92	19.02	21.67	23.59
10	2.150	2.558	3.247	3.940	4.865	6.737	9.342	12.55	15.99	18.31	20.48	23.21	25.19
11	2.603	3.053	3.816	4.575	5.578	7.584	10.34	13.70	17.28	19.68	21.92	24.72	26.76
12	3.074	3.571	4.404	5.226	6.304	8.458	11.34	14.85	18.55	21.03	23.34	26.22	28.30
13	3.565	4.107	5.009	5.892	7.042	9.299	12.34	15.98	19.81	22.36	24.74	27.69	29.82
14	4.075	4.660	5.629	6.571	7.790	10.17	13.34	17.12	21.06	23.68	26.12	29.14	31.32
15	4.601	5.229	6.262	7.261	8.547	11.04	14.34	18.25	22.31	25.00	27.49	30.58	32.80
16	5.142	5.812	6.908	7.962	9.312	11.91	15.34	19.37	23.54	26.30	28.85	32.00	34.27
17	5.697	5.408	7.564	8.672	10.09	12.79	16.34	20.49	24.77	27.59	30.19	33.41	35.72
18	6.265	7.015	8.231	9.390	10.86	13.68	17.34	21.60	25.99	28.87	31.53	34.81	37.16
19	6.844	7.644	8.907	10.12	11.65	14.56	18.34	22.72	27.20	30.14	32.85	36.19	38.58
20	7.434	8.260	9.591	10.85	12.44	15.45	19.34	23.83	28.41	31.41	34.17	37.57	40.00

21	8.034	8.897	10.28	11.59	13.24	16.34	20.34	24.93	29.62	32.67	35.48	38.93	41.40
22	8.643	9.542	10.98	12.34	14.04	17.24	21.34	26.04	30.81	33.92	36.78	40.29	42.80
23	9.260	10.20	11.69	13.09	14.85	18.14	22.34	27.14	32.01	35.17	38.08	41.64	44.18
24	9.886	10.86	12.40	13.85	15.66	19.04	23.24	28.24	33.20	36.42	39.36	42.98	45.58
25	10.52	11.52	13.12	14.61	16.47	19.94	24.34	29.34	34.38	37.65	40.65	44.31	46.93
26	11.16	12.20	13.84	15.38	17.29	20.84	25.34	30.43	35.56	38.89	41.92	45.64	48.29
27	11.81	12.88	14.57	16.15	18.11	21.75	26.34	31.53	36.74	40.11	43.19	46.96	49.64
28	12.46	13.56	15.31	16.93	18.94	22.66	27.34	32.62	37.92	41.34	44.46	48.28	50.99
29	13.12	14.26	16.05	17.71	19.77	23.57	28.34	33.71	39.09	42.58	45.72	49.59	52.34
30	13.79	14.95	16.79	18.49	20.60	24.48	29.34	34.80	40.26	43.77	46.98	50.89	53.67
40	20.71	22.16	24.43	26.51	29.05	33.66	39.34	45.62	51.80	55.76	59.34	63.69	66.77
50	27.99	29.71	32.36	34.76	37.69	42.94	49.33	56.33	63.17	67.50	71.42	76.15	79.49
60	35.53	37.48	40.48	43.19	46.46	52.29	59.33	66.98	74.40	79.08	83.30	88.38	91.95
70	43.28	45.44	48.76	51.74	55.33	61.70	69.33	77.58	85.53	90.53	95.02	100.42	104.22
80	51.17	53.54	57.15	60.39	64.28	71.14	79.33	88.13	96.58	101.88	106.63	112.33	116.32
90	59.20	61.75	65.65	69.13	73.29	80.62	89.33	98.65	107.56	113.14	118.14	124.12	128.30
100	67.33	70.00	74.22	77.93	82.36	90.13	99.33	109.14	118.50	124.34	129.56	135.81	140.17
	−2.576	−2.326	−1.960	−1.645	−1.28	−0.6745	0.0000	+0.6745	+1.282	+1.645	+1.960	+2.326	576

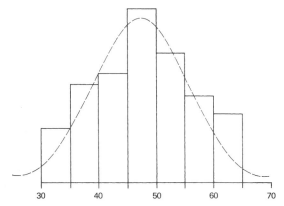

Figure 5-12 Histogram of the data and definition of categories.

Think of the process in the following way:

That is, the actual test is between two histograms. It is therefore important that the categories be defined in such a way that the "theoretic histogram" truly re-flects the essential features and detail of the hypothe-sized distribution. That is one reason why categories of different size are sometimes used: the categories should each match the fast-changing details of the un-derlying distribution.

Application: Discharge rates at a signalized intersection

Figure 5-13 shows the situation on an approach to a signalized intersection with a queue of vehicles stopped at a red indication. When the signal turns green, the first vehicle takes a certain amount of time to cross the stop line (that is, to discharge from the signal). The second vehicle takes less time on aver-age, and so forth. For the nth vehicle, the discharge time tends to stabilize—on average—as shown in Figure 5-13b.

It is common practice to observe discharge times for all vehicles, but to estimate the "saturation headway," h, based only upon the nth and higher vehicles. Although $n = 7$ is illustrated in Figure 5-13 by implication, it is often true that $n = 4$ or 5 is valid.

By observing a number of queues over several cy-cles, and by observing several lanes, it is possible to collect discharge headway data h_i for $1 \leq i \leq n$. Due

Table 5-9 Tabulation of Computations for Illustrative Problem

Category (1)	Actual Samples (2)	Cumulative Probability (3)	Probability of Category (4)	Expected Samples (5)	Chi-Square Term (6)
≤35 mph	5	0.078	0.078	5.07	0.00097
35.1–40	9	0.201	0.123	8.00	0.12500
40.1–45	10	0.400	0.199	12.94	0.66797
45.1–50	16	0.628	0.228	14.82	0.09395
51.1–55	12	0.818	0.190	12.35	0.00992
55.1–60	8	0.932	0.114	7.41	0.04698
≥60.1	5	1.000	0.068	4.42	0.07611
Sum =	65				1.0209

Column (3) is obtained from Table 5-1 by first transforming $X = 35, 40, \ldots$ by means of $Z = (X - 48)/8.6$. Table 5-1 is used because the hypothesized distribution is assumed to be normal.
Column (4) is obtained by taking differences of column (3) entries. For instance, $0.123 = 0.201 - 0.078$.
Column (5) is obtained by multiplying column (4) times $n = 65$ samples.
Column (6) is found by applying Equation 5-17, category by category.

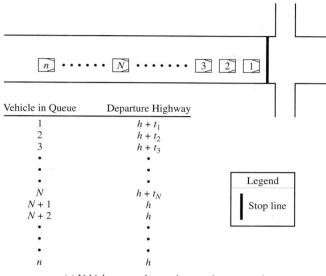

Vehicle in Queue	Departure Highway
1	$h + t_1$
2	$h + t_2$
3	$h + t_3$
$\bullet$	$\bullet$
$\bullet$	$\bullet$
$\bullet$	$\bullet$
N	$h + t_N$
$N + 1$	h
$N + 2$	h
$\bullet$	$\bullet$
$\bullet$	$\bullet$
$\bullet$	$\bullet$
n	h

Legend

| Stop line

(a) Vehicles queued on an intersection approach

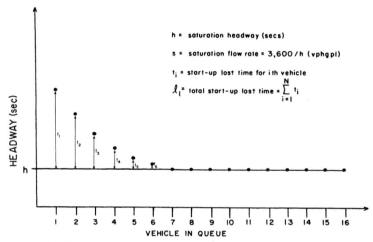

h = saturation headway (secs)

s = saturation flow rate = 3,600/h (vphgpl)

t_i = start-up lost time for i th vehicle

ℓ_1 = total start-up lost time = $\sum_{i=1}^{N} t_i$

(b) Discharge headways by position in the queue, averages only shown

Figure 5-13   Vehicle discharge headways at a signalized intersection. [Used with permission of Transportation Research Board, National Research Council, from *Highway Capacity Manual, Special Report 209,* 3rd Ed., pp. 2-3 and 2-4. Copyright © 1994 Transportation Research Board.]

to randomness in drivers and such, the discharge headway is a random variable.[9]

After the mean headway is established (that is, estimated), it may be subtracted from the earlier head-

[9]There are also systematic variations. For instance, different vehicle types (auto, van, truck) tend to have different mean discharge rates. The mean may also vary depending upon vehicle pairing (auto following auto, auto following truck, etc.). However, for the purposes of this section, these systematic variations will be dismissed, by assuming all vehicles are autos.

ways (first, second, etc., positions) so that the loss time shown in Figure 5-13b can be estimated.

For the present example, we will concentrate on the saturation headways for the nth and later vehicles.

A. Data base

It is typical that one or more field observers will collect a limited amount of data (say $n = 50$ or $n = 100$ individual headways), and do all estimations from that data. For educational reasons, we will assume that there are 45 distinct observers in a downtown area, each collecting 50 samples, independent of each other. An abbreviated form of the data is shown in Table 5-10.

If this were a class assignment, we would ask each student to collect such a set of 50 data points, analyze it, and bring the results to class for discussion.

In general, we would not have the luxury of collecting 45 different data sets and comparing them for pedagogical purposes. Nor would we be able to aggregate them without good arguments (and statistical tests, such as analysis of variance) that there is nothing obviously wrong with such aggregation. However, the authors created this data, and have the sole and unique advantage of *knowing* the true distribution, mean, and standard deviation. We can and will tell you that all 45 data sets came from the same distribution.

B. Basic statistics

For each of the 45 data sets, it is possible to compute the *estimates* of the true underlying mean and variance from Equations [5-6] and [5-7]. These results are shown in Table 5-11, with the standard deviation estimator s also shown.

For each of the 45 data sets, the 95% confidence bounds on the mean are also shown, using $n = 50$ observations. Consider the results for the sixth data set. The observer is stating in effect that he/she is 95% confident that the true mean is between 1.38 and 1.90 seconds.

Given that the authors happen to know the true mean, one of them questioned Observer #6: Are you willing to bet your grade that you are right when you say that the true mean lies between 1.38 and 1.90 seconds (Grade = A if you are correct, Grade = F if you are not)? What are the chances that Observer #6 will get an "A" under this rule?[10]

C. A rare insight: The distribution of the estimates of the mean

It is rare that we have so many data sets that we can actually see 45 different estimates of the same quan-

[10]The answer is 95% chance of an "A," 5% of an "F."

tity, namely the true mean μ_h. However, Table 5-11 shows exactly those results. Figure 5-14 presents a histogram of these values.

Based upon the fact that the random variable "estimator of true mean" is formed by adding 50 observations, each with the same distribution, it follows that this random variable tends to be normal, no matter what the distribution of h is. The reader may decide whether the histogram looks like it could have been generated from a normal distribution, and may test such a hypothesis (see the preceding section).

D. Pooling the data

Figure 5-15 shows two renderings of the $(45)(50) = 2250$ data points combined into one data set. Given that the authors know the data really came from the same source, there is no need to justify the pooling by an appropriate statistical test (an analysis of variance). Note that the two aggregations *of the same data* give two different impressions of the underlying distribution $f(x)$. In Part *a*, we might be tempted to propose a shifted exponential distribution. In Part *b*, we might be tempted to propose an Erlang distribution, just based upon shape.

We can and should consider the underlying physical mechanism in proposing a suitable distribution, and not just the observed shape. Given the two choices of Figure 5-15 and the fact that the variable under study is discharge headway (see Figure 5-13), the readers are encouraged to have a lively discussion.

Additional statistical tests

There are a number of very important statistical techniques not presented in this chapter. They include contingency tables, correlation analysis, analysis of variance (ANOVA), regression analysis, and cluster analysis. However, the material covered does allow a number of basic questions to be addressed.

Table 5-10 Abbreviation Table of Vehicle Headway Data: 45 Distinct Data Sets of 50 Headways Each

Survey	Data Point 1	2	3	4	—	49	50
1	1.32	1.60	0.71	2.84		0.82	0.93
2	1.86	1.94	1.06	0.72	—	1.12	2.73
3	1.10	2.41	0.80	0.87	—	1.39	1.78
4	2.20	5.72	2.00	2.19	—	1.35	1.28
5	1.15	2.45	1.38	4.86	—	1.99	0.80
6	1.45	1.22	1.06	1.03	—	1.03	1.18
7	0.92	1.41	1.75	1.05	—	2.73	1.34
8	0.92	0.74	1.85	1.83	—	4.17	1.18
9	1.36	1.56	0.77	1.19	—	3.03	0.94
10	0.97	1.77	0.70	0.96	—	2.48	1.15
11	0.91	1.93	0.72	0.92	—	1.03	4.00
12	0.89	1.45	1.56	1.32	—	0.95	0.83
13	1.85	1.77	3.47	1.29	—	1.74	1.13
14	3.62	1.88	0.96	1.08	—	4.74	0.74
15	2.52	1.14	0.73	1.46	—	1.02	0.84
16	3.04	0.93	0.94	0.83	—	1.21	1.76
17	0.75	0.80	1.01	2.82	—	4.77	1.59
18	3.81	5.12	2.60	0.83	—	0.89	0.71
19	2.58	1.92	1.52	5.15	—	1.67	0.89
20	2.39	1.12	2.13	5.09	—	3.25	3.80
21	0.80	1.14	1.68	1.83	—	1.33	0.92
22	2.74	1.32	8.46	1.74	—	3.40	6.69
23	0.98	0.82	1.70	2.46	—	0.99	1.50
24	1.63	1.00	1.29	1.62	—	1.50	1.54
25	1.27	2.98	1.98	3.99	—	1.65	2.75
26	1.35	3.84	1.06	2.97	—	0.75	0.72
27	1.13	1.26	1.89	0.93	—	1.51	2.90
28	0.91	1.78	2.88	1.66	—	0.86	4.81
29	2.81	1.64	1.62	1.06	—	1.09	1.13
30	2.67	2.70	1.11	1.13	—	1.98	1.18
31	1.74	1.38	1.17	2.50	—	3.37	0.91
32	2.84	1.14	3.13	0.74	—	6.67	0.98
33	1.70	1.43	1.44	1.09	—	2.26	2.13
34	1.14	1.71	0.74	1.72	—	0.79	1.44
35	2.71	1.47	1.65	1.31	—	0.94	1.96
36	8.16	1.52	1.68	1.05	—	1.65	1.23
37	5.83	3.76	4.35	4.44	—	1.13	1.18
38	1.53	5.00	2.11	1.68	—	3.19	0.93
39	0.72	4.22	1.39	0.85	—	1.28	2.41
40	1.24	1.66	1.03	2.25	—	1.50	2.74
41	2.26	1.58	2.47	1.50	—	1.90	2.53
42	0.99	0.74	2.25	1.30	—	3.26	1.48
43	1.43	1.68	1.27	1.06	—	2.39	0.96
44	3.28	0.85	1.50	0.99	—	2.45	1.00
45	2.07	0.79	4.00	1.18		1.83	3.24

Table 5-11   Some Results for Each of the 45 Data Sets

| Data Set | Estimators | | | 95% Conf Bounds |
	Mean	Variance	STD	
1	1.80	1.15	1.07	0.30
2	1.48	0.44	0.66	0.18
3	1.89	0.90	0.95	0.26
4	1.85	1.41	1.19	0.33
5	1.84	1.57	1.25	0.35
6	1.64	0.88	0.94	0.26
7	1.95	1.16	1.08	0.30
8	1.59	0.66	0.82	0.23
9	1.95	2.35	1.53	0.43
10	1.46	0.42	0.64	0.18
11	1.75	0.86	0.93	0.26
12	2.14	2.81	1.68	0.46
13	1.86	1.04	1.02	0.28
14	1.87	1.86	1.37	0.38
15	1.63	1.30	1.14	0.32
16	1.74	1.51	1.23	0.34
17	1.60	0.93	0.97	0.27
18	1.80	1.61	1.27	0.35
19	1.86	1.44	1.20	0.33
20	2.02	2.09	1.44	0.40
21	1.61	0.65	0.81	0.22
22	2.39	2.49	1.58	0.44
23	1.86	1.05	1.03	0.28
24	1.83	1.36	1.17	0.32
25	1.86	1.26	1.12	0.31
26	1.71	0.93	0.96	0.27
27	2.03	1.11	1.05	0.29
28	1.83	1.01	1.00	0.28
29	1.69	0.77	0.88	0.24
30	2.06	2.07	1.44	0.40
31	1.89	1.59	1.26	0.35
32	1.87	1.63	1.28	0.35
33	1.85	0.71	0.84	0.23
34	1.84	1.84	1.35	0.38
35	2.08	2.13	1.46	0.40
36	1.77	2.06	1.44	0.40
37	1.90	1.49	1.22	0.34
38	1.75	0.82	0.91	0.25
39	1.72	0.92	0.96	0.27
40	1.65	0.72	0.85	0.24
41	1.97	1.10	1.05	0.29
42	1.60	0.67	0.82	0.23
43	2.22	1.99	1.41	0.39
44	2.38	2.40	1.55	0.43
45	1.96	1.46	1.21	0.33

Note: These results are based on the data of Table 5-9, not all of which is shown therein.

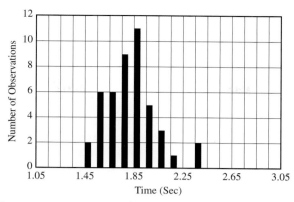

Figure 5-14 Histogram of "estimates of the true mean."

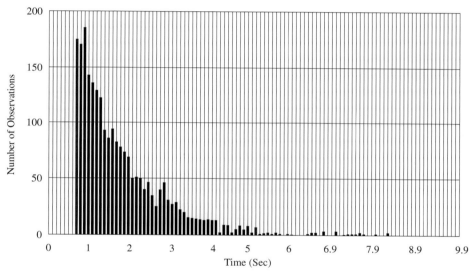

(a) Pooled headway data with 0.10 second interval

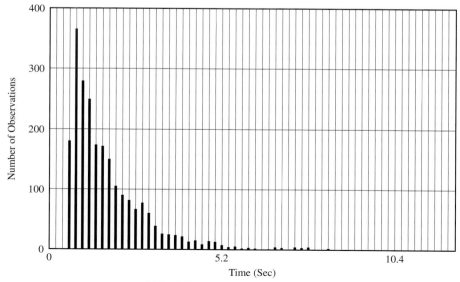

(b) Pooled headway data with 0.20 second interval

Figure 5-15 Pooled headway data in histograms.

Summary

Traffic studies cannot be done effectively without using some basic statistics. Sample sizes imply confidence bounds on the results, and vice-versa. The engineer frequently needs to explain that the confidence bounds are dictated by the sample size and the natural variability, and nothing can overcome this reality.

In using statistics, the engineer is often faced with the need to *act* despite the lack of certainty. Indeed, that is the reason why statistical analysis is employed. If two alternative hypotheses are presented, one is chosen, but there are generally non-zero probabilities of Type I and Type II errors—rejecting the truth or accepting the false.

If one hypothesis is presented (without a specific alternative), it is frequently to set up a "strawman" which we hope is rejected. For instance, a hypothesis of "zero change" when rejected leads us to some comfort that a change did occur.

One special application of hypothesis testing is asserting that a particular distribution was (could have been?) the source of the data observed. This is the chi-square goodness-of-fit test. When this hypothesis is not rejected (hopefully), the engineer then acts as if the proposed distribution were in fact the source of the data. Of course, it is possible that two different people can postulate two different distributions, both of which *could have* been the source of the data. In such a case, two results of "not rejected" could be obtained.

Note that we did not use the word "accepted" but rather carefully said "not rejected." They are not equivalent.

Likewise, it is wrong to say that hypothesis testing "proves" a result. It may allow an interpretation, but *proof* is an exercise in pure mathematics or probability theory, not statistical analysis.

A number of common applications were interspersed with various statistical techniques, so that the reader can gain a working knowledge of the techniques and be more prone to extend the applications.

References

1. Mendenhall, W., and Sincich, T., *Statistics for Engineering and the Sciences,* 3rd Edition, Dellen Publishing Company, 1992.
2. Mendenhall, W., Wackerly, D., and Scheaffer, R., *Mathematical Statistics with Applications,* 4th Edition, PWS-KENT Publishing Company, Boston, MA, 1990.
3. Crow, E. L., Davis, F. A., and Maxfield, M. W., *Statistics Manual,* Dover Publications, Mineola, NY, 1960.
4. Ostle, B., *Statistics and Research,* Revised 2nd Edition, Iowa State University Press, 1963.
5. *Manual of Transportation Engineering Studies,* Institute of Transportation Engineers, Prentice-Hall, Englewood Cliffs, NJ, 1994.
6. *Traffic Engineering Handbook,* Institute of Transportation Engineers, Prentice-Hall, Englewood Cliffs, NJ, 1992.

Problems

Problem 5–1

Experience suggests that spot speed data at a given location is normally distributed with a mean of 57 mph and a standard deviation of 7.6 mph. What is the speed below which 85% of the vehicles are traveling?

Problem 5–2

Consider a survey of n people asking whether they plan to use Route A or Route B, with an anticipated fraction p choosing Route A.

(a) Justify why the number X of people who say they will use Route A is binomially distributed.

(b) If $p = 0.30$, plot the 95% confidence bounds *and* the expected value of X as a function of n, for $n = 50$ to $n = 800$.

(c) Form the random variable $Y = X/n$ and plot its 95% confidence bounds and expected value over the same range of n. What is the random variable Y estimating?

(d) Explain how the answers to Parts b and c used the normal approximation to the binomial, if they did do so. Justify why this was a reasonable or plausible assumption.

Problem 5–3

For an $n = 100$ and various p values in the range from 0.10 to 0.90, plot the 95% confidence bounds and the expected value of Y as a function of p, where Y is defined as in Problem 2.

Note that the horizontal axis assumes that p is known and that one may enter the plot on the horizontal axis, draw a line upward, hit the curve(s), and estimate the 95% range of the *estimates* of p which will occur. If you knew the estimator p from data, can you enter the plot on the vertical axis, draw a line to the right, and find the range of true underlying p values which most likely caused this observed value? Relate this to the Equations [5-6] and [5-7] if possible.

Problem 5–4

Travel time data is collected on an arterial, and with 30 runs, an average travel time of 152 seconds is computed over the 2.00 mile length, with a computed standard deviation of 17.3 seconds.

Compute the 95% confidence bounds on your estimate of the mean. Was it necessary to make any assumption about the shape of the travel time distribution?

Problem 5–5

Vehicle occupancy data is taken in a high occupancy vehicle (HOV) lane on a freeway, with the following results:

Vehicle Occupancy	Number of Vehicles Observed
2 people	120
3	40
4	30
5	10

(a) Compute the estimated mean and standard deviation of the vehicle occupancy in the HOV. Compute the 95% confidence bounds on the estimate of the mean.
(b) When the HOV lane in question has an hourly volume of 900 vph, what is your estimate of how many people *on average* are being carried in the lane? Give a 95% confidence range.
(c) If we observe the lane tomorrow and observe a volume of 900 vph, what is the range of persons-moved we can expect in that hour? Use a range encompassing 95% of the likely outcomes. List any assumptions or justifications not made in Part b, but necessary in Part c, if any.

Problem 5–6

Based upon long-standing observation and consensus, the speeds on a curve are observed to average 57 mph with a 6 mph standard deviation. This is taken as a "given." Some active controls are put in place (signing, flashing lights, etc.), and the engineer is sure that the average will fall to at least 50 mph, with the standard deviation probably about the same.

(a) Formulate a null and alternative hypothesis based on taking "after" data only, and determine the required sample size n so that the Type I and II errors are each 0.05.
(b) Assume that data has been taken for the required N observations and that the average is 52.2 mph and the standard deviation is 6.0 mph. What is your decision? What error may have occurred, and what is its probability?
(c) If the data in Part b had been a mean of 52.2 mph and a standard deviation of 5.4 mph was observed, re-solve Part b.

Problem 5–7

For this problem, take the conditions of Problem 6, but this time there is no "long standing observation and consensus." Rather, there is some "before" data with an average of 57 mph, and standard deviation of 6.0 mph, and $n_1 = 67$ observations. You have been consulted only after the changes have been made, so that you cannot take more "before" data.

(a) Formulate a suitable hypothesis along the same lines as Problem 6, but recognize that n_1 is fixed. Assume that the Type I and II errors are to be equal, and plot or tabulate them as a function of n_2, the number of "after" samples.
(b) The agency can afford at most 150 "after" samples. What level of significance can you promise? Give a numeric answer and explain what it means, in terms a non-technical manager can understand. Attain $\alpha = 0.05$ if possible.

The data is taken and the average of the data is 52.2 mph, with 6.0 mph standard deviation. What is your conclusion? With what probability of error? Do you think that this will be good enough for the people who want the evaluation done? How can you improve the probability, if it is more than 0.05?

Problem 5–8

For the headway data addressed in the next-to-last section of the chapter, inspect the summary of the 45 distinct estimates of the mean in Table 5-11 (and the related statistics therein). For the histograms of means shown in Figure 5-14, what *should* the underlying distribution actually be?

(a) Based upon Table 5-11 information, what mean and standard deviation should this distribution have? Remember that it is the distribution of the means, *not* the distribution of headways.

(b) Use a goodness-of-fit test with a level of significance 0.05 to test the hypothesis that the underlying distribution for Figure 5-14 is the distribution specified in Part a of this problem.

Problem 5–9

Table P5-1 shows the histogram information shown in Figure 5-15a, for 0.10 increments. Each "bin" value shown is the beginning point of a range, so that there are 177 observations between 0.70 seconds and 0.80 seconds, with a mean of 0.75 (based on the midpoint).

Postulate an underlying distribution for the headways, based on the discussion in the text. Determine its parameters. (The Erlang has two. The shifted exponential also has two—the amount of the shift, and the mean of the part added to the shift).

Aggregating categories as needed for five or more samples per category, but at the same time identifying as much detail as possible, execute a goodness-of-fit test on the postulated distribution with $\alpha = 0.05$. Note that it will be necessary to compute the expected number of samples for each category, using the proposed distribution. Comment.

Table P5-1 Information for Problem 5–9

Bin	Frequency	Bin	Frequency	Bin	Frequency	Bin	Frequency
0	0						
0.1	0	2.6	25	5.1	4	7.6	1
0.2	0	2.7	40	5.2	6	7.7	2
0.3	0	2.8	43	5.3	1	7.8	1
0.4	0	2.9	32	5.4	2	7.9	0
0.5	0	3	28	5.5	3	8	0
0.6	0	3.1	29	5.6	2	8.1	1
0.7	177	3.2	20	5.7	3	8.2	0
0.8	172	3.3	19	5.8	2	8.3	0
0.9	186	3.4	13	5.9	0	8.4	3
1	141	3.5	12	6	2	8.5	0
1.1	133	3.6	12	6.1	1	8.6	0
1.2	125	3.7	12	6.2	0	8.7	0
1.3	119	3.8	11	6.3	0	8.8	0
1.4	89	3.9	12	6.4	0	8.9	0
1.5	82	4	11	6.5	1	9	0
1.6	90	4.1	11	6.6	3	9.1	0
1.7	79	4.2	3	6.7	3	9.2	0
1.8	75	4.3	8	6.8	0	9.3	0
1.9	71	4.4	8	6.9	4	9.4	0
2	52	4.5	6	7	0	9.5	0
2.1	53	4.6	3	7.1	0	9.6	0
2.2	50	4.7	5	7.2	4	9.7	0
2.3	41	4.8	8	7.3	0	9.8	0
2.4	44	4.9	5	7.4	1	9.9	0
2.5	36	5	8	7.5	1	10	0

6

Volume Studies and Characteristics

The most basic measurement in traffic engineering is counting—counting vehicles, passengers, people. These count measures are used to produce estimates of:

• volume and flow rate
• demand
• capacity

sometimes in conjunction with other measures or conditions. The three parameters are closely related and use the same units for description. They are not, however, the same, and the differences should be clearly understood. *Volume* is the number of vehicles (or persons) passing a point during a specified time period. Volume is generally expressed as a total number of vehicles for the period, or as an equivalent rate of *vehicles per hour*. *Demand* is the number of vehicles or people that desire to travel past a point during a specified period. Demand is frequently higher than actual volumes where congestion exists, as some trips are diverted to alternative routes, and some trips are simply not made because of constraints in the sys-

tem. *Capacity* is the maximum number of vehicles that can pass a point during a specified period. It is a characteristic of the roadway. Actual volume can never be observed at levels higher than the capacity of the facility, although there are situations in which this appears to occur because capacity has been computationally estimated and not directly observed.

This chapter introduces the basic concepts, and then considers volume variation over time (year, month, day, hour), followed by detailed sections on measuring volumes on a regional or state basis, for different purposes (origin-destinations, cordons, screenlines), and in small networks, arterials, and intersections.

One of the most commonly used gross indicators of traffic activity is the *annual average daily traffic* or AADT. It is the count for an entire year, around the clock, in both directions on the road being studied. It is a useful indicator of usage and need, but is subject to a number of caveats:

• Traffic varies systematically over the year, so that the AADT alone does not indicate volume levels in the busiest months of the year.

- Traffic variation patterns depend on the nature of the road (commuter, recreational, etc.) and on the overall traffic level.
- Even in the busiest period of the year, a daily variation must be taken into account, so that the peak period is properly identified.
- Within the peak period (actually, the peak hour) there is additional peaking, during short-term intervals; rates of flow for subhourly periods are introduced to identify and quantify peak flow periods as short as 5 or 15 minutes.

One of the liveliest points of debate is the appropriate hour within the year to use as the *design volume*.[1] Each day of the year has a peak hour. The volume in this peak hour is not the same each day. If they are ranked in descending order, the question becomes: which peak hour do we design for? The AASHTO Green Book in particular has historically cited the 30th highest hour as the design hour, but for urban applications where the "typical" rush hour is desired, some states and localities use the 100th highest hour.

Volume and demand

The *volume* on a road is by definition the number of vehicles passing the measurement point during a specified time interval. The most commonly-used interval is one hour, and volume for an hour is expressed as vehicles per hour (vph). In some cases, it is reported on a per-lane basis, and expressed as vehicles per hour per lane (vphpl). This can appear either as an average across all relevant lanes, or as individual lane numbers, depending on the context.

Per-lane measurements must be used carefully, because some studies report the average across all lanes and others report the number for the lane carrying the highest volume. Confusing the latter with the former is a fundamental mistake and can lead to serious error, because in general all lanes do *not* carry the same volume.

The *demand* is a measure of the number of vehicles (or passengers, or persons) waiting for service in the given time period, as distinct from the number that can be served. The *capacity* is the maximum number

that can *reasonably* be expected to be served in the given time period [4]. When the demand is less than the capacity, the volume equals the demand, and volume measurements *are* measurements of existing demand. Of course, it can be argued that demand should include re-routed trips, latent demand, and future growth. This has already been noted in Chapter 1, and must be considered on a case-by-case basis.

Figure 6-1 shows the two basic cases in which volume can be a misleading indicator of demand: (1) there is an upstream metering effect on the demand, due to signal timing or another capacity limitation, so that the demand does not reach the measurement point without being distorted; (2) a queue surrounds the measurement point, so that the observed volume reflects the downstream discharge, not the upstream demand. A great deal of care must be taken that neither case prevails when a *measured volume* is being used to *estimate demand*.

Figure 6-1 also highlights another point, related to performance evaluation: while volume is frequently a good indicator of performance, it is insufficient when demand exceeds capacity. This condition, known as level of service F on most facilities,[2] requires such measures as the existence, duration, and spatial extent of a queue. On freeways, such queues can stretch for miles. On surface systems, gridlock can extend over significant portions of the street network.

Figure 6-2 shows a simple case in which the demand and capacity are shown in Part a of the figure, where the demand is what *would have* occurred at the measurement point if the capacity allowed it. Because of the capacity limit, the measured volume is flattened by the capacity curve as shown in Part b, so that it spreads over more time *and* stays at a high level longer. This is because the backlog of vehicles cannot be processed, due to the demand limit. Part c shows an estimate of this queue (probably spread over three lanes), but it is actually an underestimate, because there are additional vehicles caught up in this queue just because they are on the upstream road encompassed by the backlogged vehicles.

---

[1]Actually, the design demand, but we will clarify this in an early section of this chapter.

[2]As will be explained in Chapter 18, intersection level of service F may occur (as of the 1997 definitions) in some conditions when demand is less than capacity, but the delay per vehicle is high.

UNDER SOME CIRCUMSTANCES, VOLUME DOES NOT MEASURE DEMAND

(a) Upstream metering

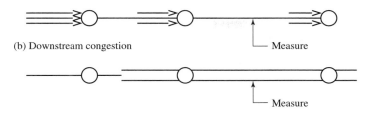

(b) Downstream congestion

└─ Measure

└─ Measure

UNDER SOME CIRCUMSTANCES, VOLUME DOES NOT SAY ENOUGH

Level of Service F

....Existence
....Duration
....Extent

Figure 6-1 Conditions under which volume does not reflect demand.

Figure 6-3 considers another case, where the real demand, the segment capacities, and the observed *output* volumes are shown in Parts a, b, and c respectively. The question is, why did these output volumes occur and why are they different than indicated by the demand?

Figure 6-3 can be used to illustrate another interesting point. Assume that the bottleneck in segment 3 is corrected, and capacity is increased to 4000 vph. In this case, the 3700 vph arriving at segment 3 proceed uninhibited. The 500 vph desiring to use the first off-ramp will do so, yielding a fourth-segment demand of 3200 vph. This segment has a capacity of only 3000 vph. A secondary bottleneck, not apparent initially from observed volumes, now appears. This is a "hidden bottleneck," because upstream constraints prevented sufficient volume from reaching this point to cause a breakdown. In designing corrective highway improvements, it is critical that all downstream points be properly evaluated to identify such hidden bottlenecks, and that all such points be improved as part of the project.

The case of a freeway bottleneck is relatively simple to analyze, because the number of entry and exit points is limited, and the number of available alternative routes available is generally small. On arterials, the situation is far more complex. Intersections are frequent, and midblock driveways allow for very diffused demand patterns. Every intersection represents a diversion opportunity, and the number of available alternative routes is generally very large. Thus, demand response to a bottleneck is more complex and almost impossible to discern. The number of

bottleneck points on a congested arterial also complicates matters. If several consecutive intersections are operating in a forced-flow mode, it is difficult to trace impacts. A downstream breakdown can influence the behavior of an upstream breakdown, and separation of the impacts is virtually impossible.

On arterial systems, it is often impossible to measure existing demand, except in cases were capacity does not constrain the demand. This chapter later presents a method for discerning intersection demand from observed volumes in a constrained case. This applies, however, only to an isolated breakdown, and does not account for the impact of diversion. Congestion in a surface network severely distorts demand patterns, and observed volumes are more a reflection of capacity constraints than of true demand.

The state of the practice is such that the term "volume" is used when "demand volume" or simply "demand" is meant. It would be nice if everyone were consistent, but that simply is not the case. Therefore, the reader must learn to function in a world in which the context *generally* makes the usage clear, but care should be exercised. For instance, the use of "volume" regarding intersections should be "demand volume," because the delay computation is based upon demand. The same should be true on the arterial, although in some contexts, the locations within the arterial are assessed on the volume that gets to them, not the demand that could get to them if an upstream limitation were removed.

The general caution to the reader is: be careful of when "demand" is meant and when "volume" is

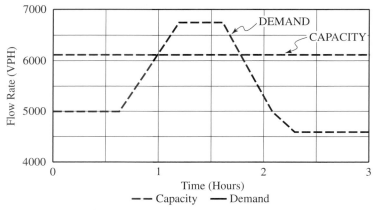

(a) Demand and capacity, as they would appear at the measurement point

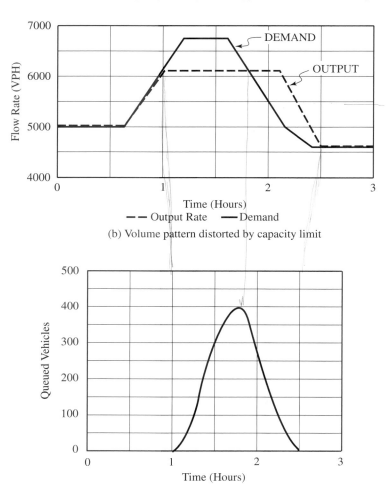

(b) Volume pattern distorted by capacity limit

(c) Queue that results if upstream extent is not taken into account

Figure 6-2 A simplified analysis of demand exceeding capacity.

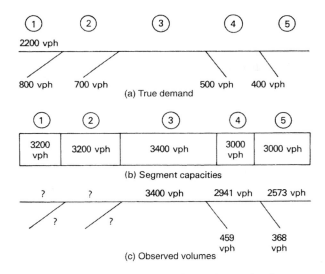

Figure 6-3   Effects of a bottleneck on observed volumes.

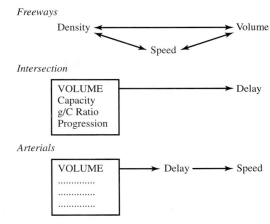

Figure 6-4   Volume is embedded in other measures

meant, because at the present time, many people depend upon the context to make it clear. There is a growing emphasis on using "demand volume" or "demand" when demand is meant, but this is not universally followed.

Volume and other stream flow parameters

Currently, some engineers are emphasizing that "volume isn't enough" (i.e., volume alone is insufficient to define the state of a traffic stream), which is absolutely true in many situations and certainly in most performance assessments. However, this does not mean that volume is a dated measure, nor does it need to be replaced by a different kind of measure.

In addition to its own merits, volume is embedded in many other measures. Figure 6-4 illustrates that on freeways, three key parameters interact—volume, speed, and density. In fact, it is common to describe a freeway's performance by speed *and* volume. Density alone might be sufficient—and technically, it is the measure by which freeway level of service is defined—but it is not as easy to measure as either speed or volume. Although "occupancy" (see Chapter 4) is a proxy for density, it has not caught on among a broad range of practitioners in the same way the

speed-volume combination has. Figure 6-5 shows some freeway speed-volume data, just for illustration.

Volume is also embedded in the assessment of intersection performance. Even though the defined level of service measure is stopped delay, demand volume is one of the key determinants of stopped delay. (Others are the capacity, the green-to-cycle-length or g/C ratio, and the progression quality, as shown in Figure 6-4 and addressed in detail in a later chapter.)

Likewise, volume is a prime determinant of arterial average travel speed, because of volume's impact on delay, which is a key component of arterial average travel speed, the defined level of service measure.

Temporal and spatial variation of volume

Chapter 3 introduced the types of volume statistics in common usage among traffic engineers: Daily volumes (vehicles per day) include the AADT and AAWT, as well as ADTs and AWTs. Peak hourly volumes are used for most design and operational analyses, with subhourly flow rates accounted for using the peak hour factor (PHF). For specific definitions and illustrations, review Chapter 3.

Volumes vary over time, often systematically. For instance, there generally is a significant variation in the ADT measured on a monthly basis over the year. Figure 6-6 shows the *monthly variation in ADT* at

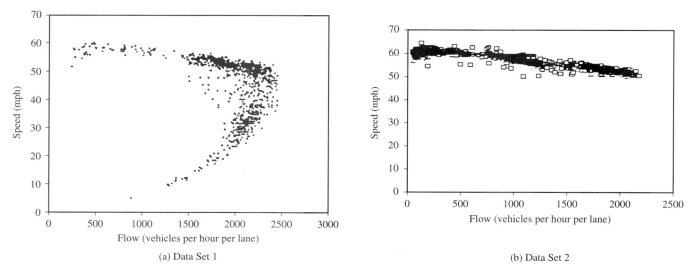

Figure 6-5   Some illustrative freeway speed-volume sets. [Used with permission of Transportation Research Board, National Research Council, from *Highway Capacity Manual, Special Report 209,* 3rd Ed., p. 2-29. Copyright © 1994 Transportation Research Board.]

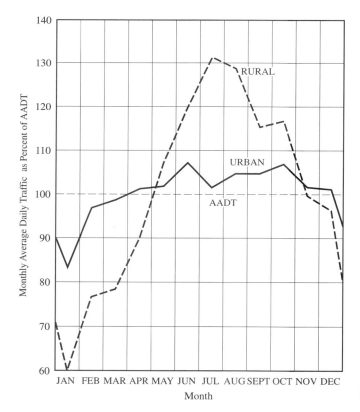

Figure 6-6   Monthly variation on some roads in Illinois. [Used with permission of Transportation Research Board, National Research Council, from *Highway Capacity Manual, Special Report 209,* 3rd Ed., p. 2-18. Copyright © 1994 Transportation Research Board.]

some illustrative measurement points, also showing the AADT (the average over the entire year) on the same graph. The rural and urban roads observed are markedly different, with the particular rural road observed having the peak months in the summer. The urban road, serving a different population, has much less variation over the year. It is quite feasible for a rural road to have a winter peak, if it is in an area dominated by winter sports.

Figure 6-7 shows the AWT by month, the Saturday-only traffic by month, and the Sunday/Holiday traffic by month for another area. Again, there are distinct differences between rural and urban roads, including different weekend uses.

The literature addresses two very important problems:

• finding ways in which roads can be grouped into categories, so that data need only be taken for a sample of roads from each category; the converse of this problem is deciding to which group an additional road belongs
• estimating AADT and/or K and D factors from shorter-term counting programs (week, month, etc.)

For instance, Reference [1] addresses the problem of estimating AADT from shorter term seasonal counts, and cites other work in which the task is to

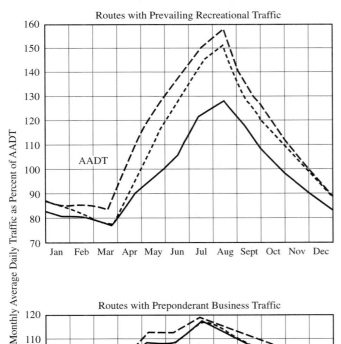

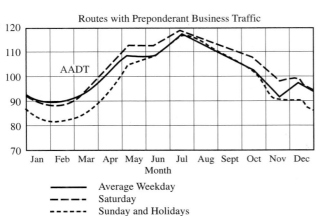

Figure 6-7 Monthly variation on some roads in Minnesota. [Used with permission of Transportation Research Board, National Research Council, from *Highway Capacity Manual, Special Report 209,* 3rd Ed., p. 2-17. Copyright © 1994 Transportation Research Board.]

establish patterns of short term counts that yield effective AADT estimates.

Given that the hourly counts are available from locations at which AADT data is taken (this would be routine), one may also rank-order the hourly data by volume level, express it as a fraction or percent of the AADT, and show (1) how many hours exceed a given level *or* (2) the percentage of the AADT in the nth highest hour.

Figure 6-8 shows data from Minnesota in the latter format: for a recreational access route (MN169), the highest hour in the entire year is about 30% of the AADT; for the same route, the 30th highest hour is about 22% of the AADT, and the 100th higher hour is about 18% of the AADT.

What volume should this or a similar road be designed to handle? The answer depends in part on the quality of flow that is the design target. If "very good

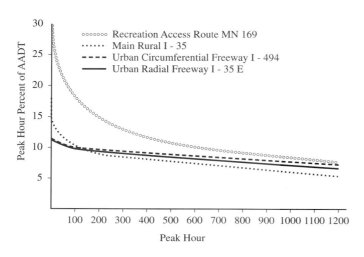

Figure 6-8 Ranked hourly volumes from Minnesota data. [Used with permission of Transportation Research Board, National Research Council, from *Highway Capacity Manual, Special Report 209,* 3rd Ed., p. 2-21. Copyright © 1994 Transportation Research Board.]

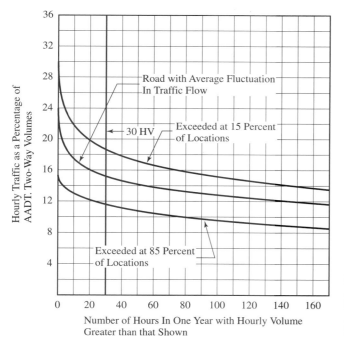

Figure 6-9 Relation between peak hour traffic and AADT. [Used with permission of Transportation Research Board, National Research Council, from *Highway Capacity Manual, Special Report 209,* 3rd Ed. Copyright © 1994 Transportation Research Board.]

flow, little delay, high average travel speed" is selected as the target and the design for the 30th highest hour, is this committing resources that are unavailable, and is it leaving too much capacity unused in other hours? On the other hand, are there too many hours with significantly higher volumes, so that situations much worse than the target performance level will often be experienced?

Figure 6-10 also shows the variation from *day to day* at the same time of day. To do this, data was collected over several months for weekdays at the four sites. (This was done at the Toronto traffic control center, and provided to the researchers). The shaded areas indicate the bounds within which 95% of the observations fell in a given five-minute period, by time of day.

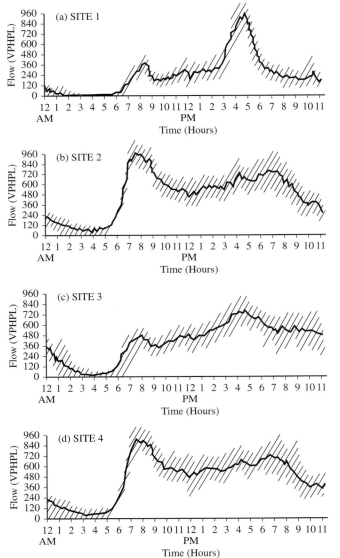

Note: (1) Sites 1 and 4 are one block apart on same street, in same direction (2) All sites are two moving lanes

Figure 6-10 Variation by time of day at four sites in Toronto, one direction only. [Used with permission of Transportation Research Board, National Research Council, from *Highway Capacity Manual, Special Report 209,* 3rd Ed., p. 2-20. Copyright © 1994 Transportation Research Board.]

Even though there is substantial variation in any five-minute period, Figure 6-10 may be considered in another way: At what time of day is a given traffic level first attained? This can be done by drawing a horizontal line at the level in question, to intersect the curves at various times. It happens that this time is very predictable at these sites, suggesting that the onset of the rush hour is very predictable and can be anticipated in planning and control.

Figure 6-11 shows a representative *variation within the peak period*, allowing both the peak hour and the peak 15 minutes within the peak hour to be identified. A previous section contained an example of such computations.

QUESTION: If the data allows the peak hour on any given day to be identified, and the use of AADT and K and D factors allows the design hour to be identified, are they different, and if so how? Should one be used for some purposes and the other for different purposes? This would be a useful class discussion.

Data collection techniques and technology

Traffic data is still taken by hand counts, checkoff forms, and mechanical hand counters in some applications. If the application is non-standard or infrequent, this may be particularly true. Also, some simple applications or field checks may not justify "going back to the shop" for more sophisticated equipment.

For the most part, however, the advantages of having the data in machine-readable form dictate that equipment with some electronic storage and a data interface be used. Figure 6-12 illustrates one such device, for counting all movements at an intersection (left, through, right, for each approach). The data is available through a data interface connection, and may be transferred "dumped" to a spreadsheet or other analysis program.

A. Short counts

In taking intersection and other counts with people in the field, even when automated recording equipment is used, it is common for an observer to take short

Location: Middle lane of Southbound Interstate 35W in Minneapolis, MN, 41 miles South of CBD, 3 lanes [one-way].
Time: Weekday morning, Metered, August 1983

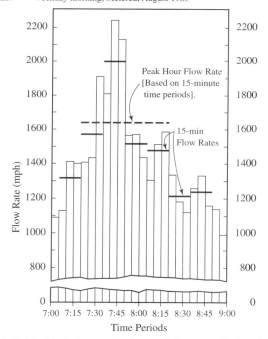

Figure 6-11 Variations with the peak hour, and identification of the peak hour from data. [Used with permission of Transportation Research Board, National Research Council, from *Highway Capacity Manual, Special Report 209,* 3rd Ed., p. 2-22. Copyright © 1994 Transportation Research Board.]

Figure 6-12 Illustrative intersection counter with data interface. [Courtesy of JAMAR Technologies, Inc.]

breaks during the counts and/or to alternate attention between approaches, movements, or lanes. This is done for practical reasons, including the cost associated with crew size and equipment.

The need to do short counts and/or alternation presents an interesting estimation problem. Table 6-1 shows some illustrative data, taken in one direction of an arterial street at midblock. Although the data shows only the counts, there may have been a classification count also, explaining why the one data person may have been very busy and in need of a four-minute on, one-minute off schedule.

The expansion from four to five minutes is straightforward, being simply a multiplication by (5/4) = 1.25. The counts are shown to tenths of vehicles to avoid later errors due to truncation at this point. Other aspects of the estimation are more difficult, and underlying mechanisms must be considered:

- Arterial (and freeway) traffic tends to distribute nonuniformly across the lanes, so that simply multi-

plying the count for one lane by two in order to estimate the total would not be correct; this would be equivalent to assuming a 50–50 split of traffic in the two lanes, which is not accurate.
- An assumption that the average of the observations also will be the average of the hour, including the missing counts. This is not accurate when the levels are in transition, which—as will be seen—is the case in this data.

The data shows that Lane 1 contains 41.2% of the traffic and Lane 2 contains 58.8% of the traffic. Simple straight-line interpolation between real observations in a given lane may be used to fill in almost all the blanks and maintain this split between the lanes, which itself is a direct product of the data.

However, this leaves the last point in Lane 1 and the first point in Lane 2 unspecified. Absent a better approach, extrapolation from the two nearest real observations is used. Refer to Figure 6-13. This does cause some divergence from the 41.2%/58.8% split

Table 6-1 Expanding Short Counts, Alternated between Lanes

	Time	Actual Count		Expanded by Time		Estimated Counts (veh)		Estimated Flow Rates (vphpl)	
		Lane 1	Lane 2	Lane 1	Lane 2	Lane 1	Lane 2	Lane 1	Lane 2
1	5:00pm	24	—	30.0	—	30.0	43.1	360	518
2	5:05	—	36	—	45.0	32.5	45.0	390	540
3	5:10	28	—	35.0	—	35.0	46.9	420	563
4	5:15	—	39	—	48.8	36.3	48.8	435	585
5	5:20	30	—	37.5	—	37.5	53.8	450	645
6	5:25	—	47	—	58.8	41.3	58.8	495	705
7	5:30	36	—	45.0	—	45.0	60.6	540	728
8	5:35	—	50	—	62.5	43.8	62.5	525	750
9	5:40	34	—	42.5	—	42.5	61.3	510	735
10	5:45	—	48	—	60.0	46.3	60.0	555	720
11	5:50	40	—	50.0	—	50.0	58.8	600	705
12	5:55	—	46	—	57.5	53.8	57.5	645	690
SUM =		192	266	240	332.5	494	657		
FRACTION OF TOTAL =		0.419	0.581	0.419	0.581				

Notes: (1) Counts taken for four minutes on, one minute off. (2) Classification count not shown. (3) Arrows indicate estimation in need of special attention, see text.

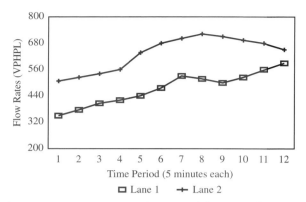

Figure 6-13 Presentation of estimated flow rates based on counts in Table 6-1.

between lanes, but this is reasonable, because the observations leading to it were technically from non-overlapping observation periods (5:00 to 5:54 and 5:05 to 5:59, to be precise).

B. Recording data in the field

It is critical to use field sheets to document data describing the site, conditions, date and time, and data recorder (by name). The field sheets must be thought of as official records, and the recorder—or engineer in charge—may be required to testify regarding what is on the sheets. It is standard for field data forms to require:

- location of count (e.g., intersection name)
- specific movements and/or classifications
- weather, roadway conditions, unusual conditions
- observer's name and title
- date and time of study
- counting periods, linked to clock time
- page *x* of *y* in data set

and to have sufficient space for clear data entry.

C. Historic methods

Manual data collection by direct observation in the field, with use of *standard paper forms,* was the most prevalent method for collecting volume data for many years. Reference [2] has many of the standard forms, both in its text and its appendices.

Mechanical hand counters have also been in wide use for decades: Buttons are depressed to advance in-

terlocking mechanical wheels. Different buttons are used for specific movements (left, through, right), for classification of vehicles (auto, truck, bus, other), or for other purposes. Figure 6-14 shows a set of such counters, used for an intersection count. Note that Figure 6-13 is the electronic version of this device. Single mechanical hand counters are also available, and are very convenient.

Roadside mechanical traffic counters, activated by a pressure tube (pneumatic) as wheels cross the tube, have been the mainstay of many traffic counting programs when extended counts (day, week, month) are needed but a more permanent installation is not economically justified.

Wire loops buried in the pavement have long served both traffic counting and traffic control purposes. A current running through the loop creates a magnetic field, and vehicles cause changes in the magnetic field and a detectable change in the current. Such loops are used for detecting vehicles on the minor street at semi-actuated signal locations, vehicles in turn bays and other locations for special signal phases, and vehicles on all approaches and/or movements at fully actuated signal locations.[3] Wire loops now come in various pre-formed shapes with some rigidity, to make the installation very efficient and cost-effective.

Wire loops, or *loop detectors* in common parlance, are not used in some locations because of frequent pavement construction, special disruptions (large metal structures nearby, disruptive magnetic fields), and/or frost heave of the pavement. Whether for these reasons or by historic preference, some jurisdictions use *radar, ultrasonic,* and *pressure plate* detectors to sense the presence or passage of vehicles.

Some historic (i.e., older) volume data was collected by *time-lapse photography,* usually as part of a research project in which other data was also of interest (discharge headways, interarrival times, speeds). However, this technology has been superseded by videotape in almost all cases.

Some of these detectors, particularly roadside counters activated using pneumatic tubes and pressure-

[3]Semi-actuated and actuated signals are covered in a later chapter. The basic concept is that green time is only given when the vehicles are detected and/or the green time's duration is adjusted.

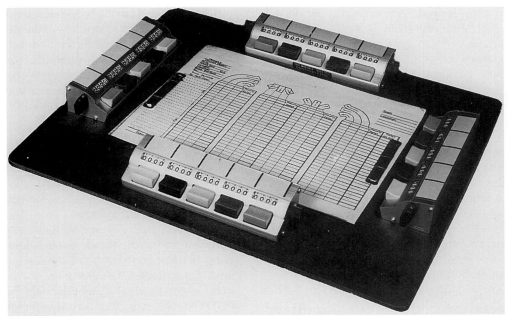

Figure 6-14 A set of mechanical hand counters for intersection counts. [Courtesy of The Denominator Company, Inc.]

plate detectors, do not count vehicles. Rather, axles are counted. This requires that sample classification counts be made to establish the average number of axles per vehicle at the study location, so that conversions from axle-counts to vehicle-counts can be made.

D. Modern methods

Chapter 4 has already addressed the evolving "modern" data collection technology in some detail, and its key features.

Some first-generation new technology has consisted of simple upgrading of existing, proven methods. The electronic counting board of Figure 6-13 has data interchange capability, but also the "look and feel" of an established tool (Figure 6-14). Roadside traffic counters may still appear as grey boxes chained to anything that doesn't move, but the mechanical innards are gone, replaced by electronics, memory, data interchange, and even wireless communication capability. Videotaping has superseded time-lapse photography.

The next generation of newer technology is already well-established. Video images are being "captured" and "imaged" so that volumes, classifications, and speeds can be identified by software algorithms. Virtual detectors are being "placed" on intersections and other locations by software linked to video, so that the function of many loop detectors is done. Some volume counting detectors are so small and low-powered that they are literally nailed down in the lane, and removed later. Some detectors transmit their data to a remote station by wireless communication, when queried.

Supplemental sources of volume data are also becoming available, as noted in Chapter 4. One such source is every traffic management center, many of which have had detailed data for decades; but the data is now being well integrated into regional or other data programs.

The sections that follow focus on the implementation of counting methodologies in specific applications common to the practice of traffic engineering.

Intersection volume studies

There is no single location more complex in a traffic system than the intersection. At a typical four-leg intersection there are twelve separate movements—left, through, and right from each leg. If a classification of each movement by cars, trucks, buses, and taxis were desired, *each* counting period would involve the observation of $4 \times 12 = 48$ separate pieces of data.

When intersections are counted manually, personnel must be positioned to properly see the movements they are counting. It is doubtful that an inexperienced counter could observe and classify more than one heavy or two light movements simultaneously. For heavily used multilane approaches, observers may have to concentrate on a single lane each. Short-break procedures are commonly used. Combining these with alternating periods, in which observers count different movements, can reduce the total manpower needed for such a study. Rarely, however, will an intersection be counted with fewer than four observers, and often more are needed. A "crew chief" is also required to time counting periods and call out break periods.

A. Special procedures for signalized intersections

At signalized intersections, the counting task is simplified because all movements do not occur simultaneously. Thus, a single observer may "double up" the number of movements or lanes counted, changing with the signal phase. One observer could count both a northbound and a westbound through movement, as these would move during different signal phases. The counts are separately recorded on different hand-counter registers, or on two different counters.

The count is complicated by the fact that *both* the counting period and the short-break periods must be even multiples of the cycle length. Thus, for a 60-second cycle, a four-out-of-five-minute pattern could be established. For a 90-second cycle this would not be possible, as neither five minutes nor four minutes are even multiples of 90 seconds.

Actuated signals present special problems, as both the cycle lengths and green splits vary on a cycle-by-cycle basis. Counting periods should be chosen to encompass a minimum of five cycles in each period, using the maximum cycle length as a guide. Counts arbitrarily proceed using this counting period. As the signal timing is assumed to be responding to actual demand, counts should approximately reflect it, despite variation in the signal timing.

The complexity of the field sheets used to record data is determined by the complexity of the study. In all cases, each observer is responsible for his or her own data, and the observer must be clearly identified on each sheet. If questions arise later, the observer can be contacted. As these field sheets become the basis for later traffic analyses, their accuracy and clarity is critical.

B. Arrival versus departure volumes

At most intersections, volumes are counted as they depart the intersection. This is done both for convenience and because turning movements cannot be fully resolved until vehicles depart the intersection. Where the capacity of an intersection approach is not sufficient to handle the demand volume, queues will form that cannot be cleared during a signal cycle. In such cases, departure counts do not reflect demand volumes, and arrival volumes should be observed.

Direct observation of arrival volumes is difficult, as the queue is dynamic. Arrival volumes can be estimated by counting departure volumes and the queue length at critical times during the count. Greatest accuracy is provided when the queue is counted during each signal phase. The queue, however, may be counted at the end of each counting period—that is, every 15 minutes for intersection approaches. In either case, the queue is counted at the *beginning of a red phase*. Table 6-2 illustrates how arrival counts can be estimated using such queue-length observations and departure counts.

The arrival count is computed for each counting period as the departure volume plus the net change in the size of the queue during the counting period. As Table 6-2 shows, the net change in the queue can be positive or negative. If a counting period ends with the same queue size it begins with, then the arrival volume is equal to the observed departure volume.

The conversion from departure to arrival volumes causes a different distribution of flow by counting period, even though the total two-hour flow in Table 6-2 is the same for arrivals and departures. The peak departure flow is 65 veh/15 min or 260 vph, while the peak arrival flow is 70 veh/15 min or 280 vph. Traffic analyses should be based on the latter figure.

The procedure is limited in that it can account only for the queuing at the intersection. Even observed arrival volumes do not account for diverted vehicles.

Table 6-2 Estimating Arrival Volumes from Departure Counts:
an Example

Time Period	Total Departure Count (veh)	Queue Length (veh)	Arrival Volume (veh)	
4:00–4:15 P.M.	50	0		50
4:15–4:30	55	0		55
4:30–4:45	62	5	62 + 5 =	67
4:45–5:00	65	10	65 + 10 − 5 =	70
5:15–5:30	60	12	60 + 12 − 10 =	62
5:30–5:45	60	5	60 + 5 − 12 =	53
5:45–6:00	62	0	62 − 5 =	57
	55	0		55
	469			469

Further, observation of the queue is practical only until it extends to the next intersection, after which the resolution of "arrival volumes" is a moot question.

C. Analysis and Presentation of Intersection Volumes

Of the many types of intersection volume data, most are presented in tabular form, since breakdowns by time interval, movement, and vehicle type are most easily shown in tables. More elaborate graphic presentations are most often prepared to depict peak-hour conditions or total volumes covering some other period of interest.

Figures 6-15 and 6-16 depict common forms for display of peak-hour or daily data. The first is a graphic intersection summary diagram that allows simple entry of data on a pre-designed graphic form. The second is an intersection flow diagram in which the thickness of flow lines is based on relative volumes.

Small-network volume studies

Such studies are intended to determine the amount and pattern of traffic flow over a limited network of street links and intersections during a specified interval. The size of such networks can range from a small community CBD with six to ten links to the hundreds of links involved in a large city CBD.

In addition to the CBD network, such studies are also taken in the vicinity of other major activity centers, such as airports and stadia. Such studies provide valuable information for traffic planning and control and may help in locating off-street parking facilities.

While the intent of such a study is to produce data to depict traffic-flow patterns in the entire network during a common time period, it will not generally be possible to count all links of the network at the same time, because of personnel and/or equipment limitations. For this reason, a *sampling* technique is used, wherein counts are made at various locations in the network at different times, while control locations are counted throughout the study to monitor hourly and daily variations in flow. The measured variations at control locations will be superimposed on sample counts taken throughout the network to adjust all data to represent a common period.

To implement such a procedure, two types of counts are conducted:

1. Control counts
2. Coverage counts

A. Control counts

Control counts are specifically established for the purpose of monitoring volume-variation patterns in the network under study. Because these data will be used to adjust the results of sample counts taken elsewhere in the network, it is critical that control-count locations be continuously counted for the entire duration of the study—that is, for the entire period that sample counts are taking place in the network.

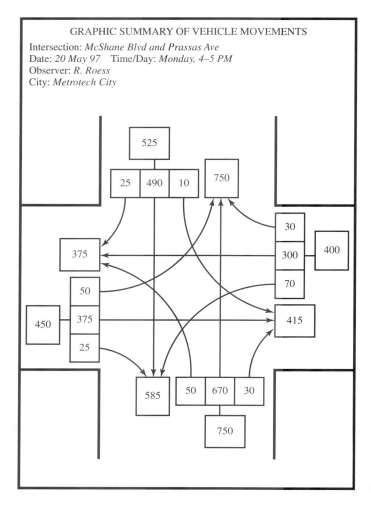

GRAPHIC SUMMARY OF VEHICLE MOVEMENTS

Intersection: *McShane Blvd and Prassas Ave*
Date: *20 May 97*   Time/Day: *Monday, 4–5 PM*
Observer: *R. Roess*
City: *Metrotech City*

Figure 6-15 A sample graphic intersection diagram.

The selection of control-count locations is very important. The locations must be representative in terms of hourly and daily volume-variation patterns. Remember that such variation patterns are generated by land-use patterns and by the character of traffic—particularly the percentages of through and local traffic in the traffic stream. Some general guidelines for choosing control-count locations are:

1. There should be one control-count location for every 10 to 20 locations to be sampled.
2. Different control-count locations should be established for each class of facility in the network—local streets, collectors, arterials, and so on—because these serve different mixes of through and local traffic and may exhibit different variation patterns.

3. Different control-count locations should be established for portions of the network with markedly different land-use characteristics.

These are only general guidelines. The engineer must exercise judgment and use his or her knowledge of the area under study to properly identify appropriate control-count locations.

B. Coverage counts

All locations at which sample counts will be taken are called *coverage counts.* All coverage counts, and control counts as well, are taken at midblock locations to avoid the difficulty of separately recording turning movements. Each link of the network is counted at

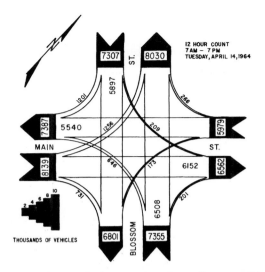

Figure 6-16 A sample intersection flow diagram. [Used with permission of Institute of Transportation Engineers, from *Transportation and Traffic Engineering Handbook,* 1st Ed., p. 410. Copyright © 1976 Institute of Transportation Engineers.]

least once during the study period. Intersection turning movements may be approximately inferred from successive link volumes, and, when necessary, supplementary intersection counts can be taken. The use of midblock locations allows for the use of portable automated counters, although the duration of some coverage counts may be too short to justify their use.

C. An illustration

Limited network studies can be best described by example. Figure 6-17 shows a small CBD network con-

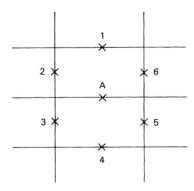

Figure 6-17 Network volume studies: An example.

sisting of six intersections and seven links. A count is needed for the eight-hour period 12:00 noon to 8:00 P.M. for the network. It will be assumed that one control-count location, noted as *A* in Figure 6-9, is sufficient to represent volume-variation patterns in the network, and that personnel and/or mechanical counters are available to count only two locations at a time.

1. A one-day study. It would be possible to complete the study in a single day by conducting a full eight-hour count at location *A*, the control count, while rotating a second field crew to count each coverage station for one hour within the eight-hour study period. Table 6-3a shows the data obtained for the study. Note that the data has already been expanded to cover full-hour periods, including the break periods during which the second crew records data and changes its location.

The control-count data is used to establish the hourly volume-variation pattern. The pattern is quantified by computing the proportion of total eight-hour volume occurring during each hour of the study for the control data. These proportions are computed in Table 6-3b.

It is now assumed that this pattern applies to all locations within the network. Thus, location 1, which was counted only between 12:00 noon and 1:00 P.M., is expected to have 0.117 of its eight-hour volume occur during this period. Thus, the full eight-hour volume may be computed as:

$$8\text{-hr vol} = \frac{1\text{-hr vol}}{0.117} = \frac{840}{0.117} = 7179 \text{ veh}$$

Table 6-3c illustrates this computation for the remainder of the coverage stations in the sample network.

Note that the analysis estimates the total volume both for the eight-hour period of interest and the peak hour. Both computations assume that the hourly volume distribution measured at the control-count location applies to all coverage counts within the network (or portion of the network) associated with the control location.

The results represent volumes that apply to the *day of the study.* Daily and seasonal variations have not been eliminated by this study technique. However, volumes for the entire network have been estimated for a common time period.

Table 6-3   Data and Computations for a One-Day Small
Network Volume Study

(a) Data from a one-day study

Control Station A		Coverage Station	Time of Count (P.M.)	Observed Count (vph)
Time (P.M.)	Count (vph)			
12–1	825	1	12–1	840
1–2	811	2	1–2	625
2–3	912	3	2–3	600
3–4	975	4	4–5	390
4–5	1056	5	5–6	1215
5–6	1153	6	6–7	1440
6–7	938			
7–8	397			

(b) Computation of hourly volume proportions from control-count data

Time	Count	Proportion of 8-Hour Total
12–1 P.M.	825 vph	825 / 7075 = 0.117
1–2	811	811 / 7075 = 0.115
2–3	912	912 / 7075 = 0.129
3–4	975	975 / 7075 = 0.138
4–5	1046	1046 / 7075 = 0.148
5–6	1153	1153 / 7075 = 0.163
6–7	938	938 / 7075 = 0.133
7–8	397	397 / 7075 = 0.056

Total = 7075 vph

(c) Expansion of hourly counts

Location	Time	Count	8-Hour Volume (est.)	Peak-Hour Volume (est.)
1	12–1	840	840 / 0.117 = 7179	× 0.163 = 1170
2	1–2	625	625 / 0.115 = 5435	× 0.163 = 886
3	2–3	600	600 / 0.129 = 4651	× 0.163 = 758
4	4–5	390	390 / 0.149 = 2617	× 0.163 = 431
5	5–6	1215	1215 / 0.163 = 7454	× 0.163 = 1215
6	6–7	1440	1440 / 0.133 = 10,827	× 0.163 = 1765

2. A multiday study. The previous example was based on the expansion of one-hour counts to represent an eight-hour study period. Since hourly volume-variation patterns from location to location are not as stable as daily or seasonal variations, greater accuracy might be achieved if each location in Figure 6-17 were counted for a full eight-hour day. This would mean that only one coverage-count location per day was counted, while the control-count location was counted on each of the six days necessary to complete coverage counts.

While this results in a full eight-hour count at each location, which does not have to be expanded, the counts cover *six* days, over which volume may vary considerably. The control-count data must be used to establish a daily variation pattern, so that all counts can be adjusted to reflect the average day of the study.

Daily volume variations are quantified in terms of factors defined as follows: The volume for a given day multiplied by the factor yields a volume for the average day of the study period. Stated mathematically:

$$V_a = V_i \times F_{vi}$$

where V_a = volume for the average day of the study (vpd)

V_i = volume for day i of the study (vpd)

F_{vi} = adjustment factor for day i

Thus, using data from the control-count location, at which the average volume will be known, volume adjustment factors for every day of the study can be computed as

$$F_{vi} = \frac{V_a}{V_i}$$

Table 6-4 shows sample study data and computations for a six-day study of the sample network. Again, it is assumed that the daily variation pattern

Table 6-4 Data and Computations for a Six-Day Small Network Volume Study

(a) Sample data for six-day study

Control Station A

Day	8-Hour Count (vph)	Coverage Station	Day Counted	8-Hour Count (vph)
Mon. 1	7000	1	Mon. 1	6500
Tue.	7700	2	Tue.	6200
Wed.	7700	3	Wed.	6000
Thu.	8400	4	Thu.	7100
Fri.	7000	5	Fri.	7800
Mon. 2	6300	6	Mon. 2	5400

(b) Computation of daily variation factors

Day	8-Hour Count (vph)	Factor
Mon. 1	7000	7350 / 7000 = 1.05
Tue.	7700	7350 / 7700 = 0.95
Wed.	7700	7350 / 7700 = 0.95
Thu.	8400	7350 / 8400 = 0.88
Fri.	7000	7350 / 7000 = 1.05
Mon.2	6300	7350 / 6300 = 1.17

Total = 44,100
Average = 7350

(c) Adjustment of coverage counts

Station	Day	8-Hour Count (vph)	Adjusted 8-Hour Count (vph)
1	Mon. 1	6500	× 1.05 = 6825
2	Tue.	6200	× 0.95 = 5890
3	Wed.	6000	× 0.95 = 5700
4	Thu.	7100	× 0.88 = 6248
5	Fri.	7800	× 1.05 = 8190
6	Mon. 2	5400	× 1.17 = 6318

measured at the control-count location applies to all coverage-count locations associated with it. The results represent volumes for the average of the six days of the study, but do not reflect seasonal variations or weekend traffic, since no counts were made on Saturday or Sunday.

3. Combining procedures. The two procedures illustrated above could be combined. For example, each coverage location could be counted for four hours, and two locations could be counted per day. The control location would be counted for the three days it would now take to count all control locations. Then, four-hour counts would be expanded to eight-hour counts, which would then be adjusted to represent the average day of the study. Table 6-5 illustrates such a study.

The examples shown in Tables 6-3 to 6-5 are illustrative. Obviously, such studies could be organized for any size network, for any period of time, using any appropriate number of control and coverage locations. The traffic engineer must use considerable judgment in designing the study to meet the information objectives at hand.

D. Estimating VMT

One output of most limited-network volume studies is an estimate of the total vehicle-miles traveled (VMT) on the network during the period of interest. The estimate is done roughly by assuming that a vehicle counted on a link travels the entire length of the link. This is a reasonable assumption, as some vehicles

Table 6-5 Data and Computations for a Three-Day Small Network Volume Study

(a) Control data and computation of hourly variation pattern

Time	Monday		Tuesday		Wednesday		Avg. % of 8 hr
	Count	% of 8 Hr	Count	% of 8 hr	Count	% of 8 hr	
12–4	3000	43	3200	43	2800	44	43
4–8	4000	57	4300	57	3600	56	57
Total	7000		7500		6400		

(b) Computation of daily variation factors

Day	8-Hour Count (vph)	Factor
Mon.	7000	6967/7000 = 0.99
Tue.	7500	6967/7500 = 0.93
Wed.	6400	6967/6400 = 1.09

Total = 20,900
Average = 6967

(c) Coverage data and adjustment of coverage counts

Station	Day	Time	Count (vph)	8-Hour Expanded Count (vph)	8-Hour Adjusted Count (vph)
1	Mon.	12–4	2213	2123/0.43 = 4937	× 0.99 = 4888
2	Mon.	4–8	3000	3000/0.57 = 5263	× 0.99 = 5210
3	Tue.	12–4	2672	2672/0.43 = 6214	× 0.93 = 5779
4	Tue.	4–8	2500	2500/0.57 = 4386	× 0.93 = 4079
5	Wed.	12–4	3500	3500/0.43 = 8140	× 1.09 = 8873
6	Wed.	4–8	3750	3750/0.57 = 6579	× 1.09 = 7171

Table 6-6   Estimating Vehicle Miles Traveled (VHT):
An example

Station	8-Hour Count	Link Length	Link VMT
A	6967 veh	× 0.25 mi	= 1741.75
1	4888	× 0.25	= 1222.00
2	5210	× 0.25	= 1302.50
3	5779	× 0.25	= 1444.75
4	4079	× 0.25	= 1019.75
5	8873	× 0.25	= 2218.25
6	7172	× 0.25	= 1792.75
		Total VMT =	10,741.75

traveling only a portion of a link will be counted while others will not, depending on whether they cross the counting location. Using the eight-hour volumes obtained in Table 6-5 as an example, and assuming that all links are 0.25 mile in length, Table 6-6 illustrates the estimation of VMT for the network during the eight-hour period of the study.

Table 6-6 results in the estimation of the total VMT for the seven-link network of Figure 6-17 for the average eight-hour study period over the three days of the study. This cannot be expanded to *annual* VMT without knowledge of the total daily and seasonal variations that exist at this location. Also, a 24-hour VMT estimate would have required that the study be conducted over 24-hour periods.

Statewide programs to estimate AADT and VMT

States generally have a special interest in observing trends in the AADT, shifts within the ADT pattern, and overall vehicle-miles traveled (VMT). More recently, there has been a growing attention to person-miles traveled (PMT) and to statistics for different modes. Similar programs at the local and/or regional level are desirable for non-state highway systems, although cost is often prohibitive.

Following some general guidelines (for instance, [3]) or local methodologies, the state road system is divided into functional classifications. Within each classification, a set of *permanent count stations* and *control count stations* are established, so that trends

can be observed, all roads in the group can be characterized, and expansions can be made where needed.

As the name implies, *permanent count stations* are fixed and always active, so that the annual pattern, the true AADT for that location, and other factors (such as K and D) are available. By comparing the data from different sites, the clustering rules for establishing the classifications can even be reviewed.

Control count stations are locations at which AADT is not measured, but shorter periodic observations allow the data to be factored by the group's pattern, so that AADT can be estimated. *Major control stations* may have a full one-week count (seven days) taken during each month of the year. *Minor control counts* may have one week (weekdays only) taken every other month.

A. Establishing daily and monthly variation factors

The objective of permanent and control counts in a statewide program is to establish volume variation patterns by day of the week (daily) and month of the year. It will later be assumed that all roads (in the same classification) grouped with the control location will have the same variation patterns. This will allow for the calibration of daily and monthly variation adjustment factors that can be applied to short-term coverage counts taken elsewhere within the group.

1. Daily factors. Consider the AADT from a permanent count station, or a group of them. Table 6-7

Table 6-7   Illustrative Computation of Daily
Variation Factors

Day	Average Yearly Volume for that Day	Daily Factor
Monday	1820 vpd	1430 / 1820 = 0.79
Tuesday	1588 vpd	1430 / 1588 = 0.90
Wednesday	1406 vpd	1430 / 1406 = 1.02
Thursday	1300 vpd	1430 / 1300 = 1.10
Friday	1289 vpd	1430 / 1289 = 1.11
Saturday	1275 vpd	1430 / 1275 = 1.12
Sunday	1332 vpd	1430 / 1332 = 1.07

Total = 10,010 veh in week

AADT est = 1430 vpd

shows a hypothetical year's data in which all fifty-two Mondays, Tuesdays, and so forth, are averaged so that an average pattern over the week is shown. The pattern is shown in Figure 6-18.

Note that the average of the daily averages *is* the same as the AADT, with some very minor difference because one of the days has 53 occurrences in a 365-day year, not just 52 (7*52 = 364, not 365). However, this is a rather small difference (see Problem 6-3).

Note also that the daily factors are computed in a format of WEEK/DAY, so that they can later be multiplied by the result for the DAY to estimate the WEEK.

For instance, suppose these factors were available and a Monday count of 1700 vpd were observed. What is the estimated traffic (ADT) for the week? Using the observed count and *assuming that the pattern shown in Figure 6-18 applies to this particular week,* one may estimate that the ADT = (0.79)(1700 vpd) = 1343 vpd in that week.

The key assumption is "assuming that the pattern shown in Figure 6-18 applies to this particular week." The weekly pattern may vary in a systematic way over the year, and this must be taken into account in such estimates.

2. Monthly factors from permanent count station data. Table 6-8 shows the monthly ADTs for a sec-

ond[4] hypothetical permanent count station, and a set of computations similar to the above by which monthly factors can be established.

If there were a road within the group represented by this second permanent count station, then its AADT could be estimated by applying the appropriate factor to the month's ADT observation for that road. If there were two different months observed at the other road, two distinct AADT estimates could be generated and averaged to yield one, better AADT estimate.

3. Monthly factors from major control count station. Consider a third count station, from still another grouping of roads, different from the preceding two examples. This one, however, is a major control count station, at which only one full week of days is taken per month.

In principle, the factors can be computed in a similar way, and the result (only) is shown in the solid line of Figure 6-19. The process is just like that of Table 6-9, but weekly sums are used rather than monthly, and the grand total of weeks is used rather than the AADT.

[4]A second *and different* permanent count station. Tables 6-7 and 6-8 come from different data sets, and cannot be cross-referenced or cross-checked.

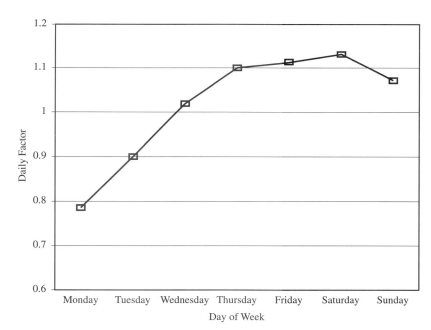

Figure 6-18 Display of daily factors from Table 6-7.

Table 6-8 Illustrative Computation of Monthly Adjustment Factors

Month	Total Traffic (veh)	ADT for Month (vpd)	Monthly Factors (AADT/ADT)
January	19,840	/31 = 640	797/640 = 1.25
February	16,660	/28 = 595	797/595 = 1.34
March	21,235	/31 = 685	797/685 = 1.16
April	24,300	/30 = 810	797/810 = 0.98
May	25,885	/31 = 835	797/835 = 0.95
June	26,280	/30 = 876	797/876 = 0.91
July	27,652	/31 = 892	797/892 = 0.89
August	30,008	/31 = 968	797/968 = 0.82
September	28,620	/30 = 954	797/954 = 0.84
October	26,350	/31 = 850	797/850 = 0.94
November	22,290	/30 = 743	797/743 = 1.07
December	21,731	/31 = 701	797/701 = 1.14

Total = 290,851

AADT = 290,851/365 = 797

Due to inspection/interpolation, these numbers add to 12.098 rather than 12.000. This can be corrected by a factor of (12.000/12.098) = 0.9918. The revised monthly factors of the last column take into account moving the estimates to the midpoint of the month *and* correcting by 0.9918.

Is this precision worth the trouble, given other randomness and uncertainty in the process? In this case, the shift and correction was viewed as a systematic error which could be avoided, and therefore worth the trouble.

B. Deciding upon inclusion in the group

An implicit assumption above has been that we know which stations—permanent or control—deserve to be grouped together. Analyzing this can be a very sophisticated problem in advanced statistics, including cluster analysis, but is generally beyond the scope of this text.

To alert the user to the nature of the problem, an example will be considered and an existing rule of thumb will be cited. The rule of thumb is: Contiguous control-count stations on similar highway types may be grouped if the factors at individual stations for a given day or month do not differ from the average by more than 0.10.

Consider as an example four consecutive stations on a given road, for which the daily factors have been computed and the average across the group has been computed, as shown in the top part of Table 6-10.

Plotting these results would reveal that Station 4 is noticeably different than the other stations. Establishing this one as a separate group (or part of one not discussed here, involving Stations 5, 6, etc.), the averages are recomputed and it is confirmed that Stations 1–3 are comparable to this new average.

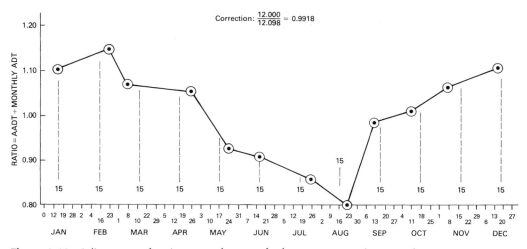

Figure 6-19 Adjustment of major control counts for known systematic corrections.

Table 6-9   Computations Related to Figure 6-19 and Resulting Monthly Factors

Month	Monthly Factor Based on Observed Weeks (M_i)	Monthly Midpoints (M)	Correction	Refined Monthly Factor Estimate (MF)
January	1.101	1.101	× 0.9918 =	1.094
February	1.144	1.139	× 0.9918 =	1.130
March	1.066	1.065	× 0.9918 =	1.056
April	1.051	1.056	× 0.9918 =	1.047
May	0.924	0.965	× 0.9918 =	0.957
June	0.906	0.906	× 0.9918 =	0.898
July	0.852	0.870	× 0.9918 =	0.863
August	0.801	0.818	× 0.9918 =	0.811
September	0.980	0.985	× 0.9918 =	0.977
October	1.010	1.019	× 0.9918 =	1.011
November	1.061	1.070	× 0.9918 =	1.061
December	1.104	1.104	× 0.9918 =	1.095
Totals	12.000	12.098		12.000

Correction = 12.000 / 12.098 = 0.9918

Table 6-10   An Illustration in Grouping Control Stations

	1	2	3	4	

Station Locations

Day	Station 1	Station 2	Station 3	Station 4	Average Factor
Monday	1.05	1.00	1.06	0.92	1.01
Tuesday	1.10	1.02	1.06	0.89	1.02
Wednesday	1.10	1.05	1.11	0.97	1.06
Thursday	1.06	1.06	1.03	1.00	1.04
Friday	1.01	1.03	1.00	0.91	0.98
Saturday	0.85	0.94	0.90	1.21	0.98
Sunday	0.83	0.90	0.84	1.10	0.92

Day	Station 1	Station 2	Station 3	Average Factor
Monday	1.05	1.00	1.06	1.04
Tuesday	1.10	1.02	1.06	1.06
Wednesday	1.10	1.05	1.11	1.09
Thursday	1.06	1.06	1.03	1.05
Friday	1.01	1.03	1.00	1.01
Saturday	0.85	0.94	0.90	0.90
Sunday	0.83	0.90	0.84	0.86

C. Coverage counts and their adjustment

Most states attempt to estimate the AADT for each two-mile segment of the state highway system each year. Low-volume roads—carrying less than 25–100 vpd—are generally not counted. Such roads usually make up 25% to 50% of the total mileage of state highways. For the remainder of the system, a 24–48 hour count is made each year, generally using portable counters.

These coverage counts, taken for one or two days, must be used to estimate the AADT at these locations. This is done by using the output of the control counting program undertaken by the state. For each contiguous grouping of control stations on each classification of highway, a set of daily and monthly variation factors is calibrated using the methods discussed previously. Table 6-11 illustrates such a table of factors.

Consider a coverage count taken at a location within the area covered by these adjustment factors. The count was 1000 vpd, and it was taken on a Tuesday in July. First, the adjustment factor for Tuesday would be used to estimate the ADT for the week of the study:

ADT (week of count) = 1000 × 1.121 = 1121 vpd

Table 6-11 Typical Daily and Monthly Variation Factors for a State Highway System Region

Daily Factors (DF)		Monthly Factors (MF)			
Day	Factor	Month	Factor	Month	Factor
Sunday	0.789	January	1.215	July	0.913
Monday	1.072	February	1.191	August	0.882
Tuesday	1.121	March	1.100	September	0.884
Wednesday	1.108	April	0.992	October	0.931
Thursday	1.098	May	0.949	November	1.026
Friday	1.015	June	0.918	December	1.114
Saturday	0.899				

Then, this ADT is adjusted for the month in which it occurred, using the adjustment factor for the month of July:

$$AADT = 1121 \times 0.913 = 1023 \text{ vpd}$$

This procedure can be generally expressed in the following form:

$$AADT = V_{24} \times DF \times MF \qquad [6\text{-}1]$$

D. VMT and PMT

Given estimates of AADT by road category or by road, the computation of an estimated VMT is straightforward, because one need only take the sum of volumes times distances, summed over the appropriate group or entire system.

Of course, the question of the precision or accuracy of this estimate is an interesting one. This is particularly true when one wants to study the "before and after" effects on VMT of a particular policy.

There are also other means of estimating VMT, including number of vehicles registered times reported mileages, with some corrections for out-of-state/ region mileages and for travelers to/through the state/region. Another common estimation procedure is to use fuel tax receipts by category of vehicle, and estimate VMT using average fuel consumption ratings for different types of vehicles.

PMT is another significant issue, because the historic way of estimating PMT was to simply multiply VMT by some estimated value of vehicle occupancy, weighted by the composition of the traffic (bus, auto, etc.). This, however, cannot be expected to suffice in a number of evaluations of current interest.

Origins and destinations

The volume pattern over the transportation system is not sufficient to do either a system, corridor, or even—in some cases—a facility analysis. When the network is changed (improved, disrupted due to construction or incidents, whatever), people re-route themselves. This can affect (self-assigned) road volumes, intersection turning rates, and such.

ITS technologies do hold the potential for great advances in origin-destination (O/D) data: paths by cellular phone, toll passes, and other means;[5] technology to read and process license plate data in studies; specific requests for routing information/ guidance. However, this technology is not yet endemic (in 1996, it was still in its infancy for these purposes). Some of the traditional means of acquiring O/D data include:

- lights-on studies
- license plate studies √
- post card studies
- roadside interview studies √
- other interviews

These are each reviewed briefly in this section.

A. Lights-on studies

Consider a situation in which two roads converge, and then diverge, allowing traffic from either entry roadway to use either departing roadway. This is a "weaving" section of highway, and the mix of weaving (i.e.,

[5]Subject to privacy safeguards and/or consent.

crossing) and non-weaving traffic greatly influences the performance of the facility.

One way of estimating the O/Ds in a weaving section is to conduct a lights-on study, in which the drivers on one of the approach roadways are asked—by special signing—to put their lights on. Signs on both departing roadways thank them, and indicate that their lights may be turned off.

Of course, not everyone on the selected approach roadway will comply. Further, some cars now have "lights on" as a matter of safety practice, so that both rates have to be taken into account. Nonetheless, the equations can be written, and estimates established.

The same logic can be applied to any section of roadway in which a limited number of movements are of interest.

Lights-on studies require preparation of signs, moderately large commitment of crew, and the involvement of the public. Some professionals are also concerned about such requests being the basis for needless litigation should an accident occur. Lower-cost, less staff-intensive methods are preferred.

B. License plate studies

License plates can be taken at any number of entrance and exit points on a facility such as a freeway, a downtown area, or a weaving section. If combined with volume counts, only a sampling of the license plates may be needed. Not all legs have to observed. For instance, the arriving and departing freeway traffic may not be sampled due to its speed and practical observation difficulties (finding a place to stand).

In principle, the task is straightforward. Volumes and matches are established, observation rates (percent plates actually) read by leg are taken into account, and estimates are generated. In practice, the match rates are sometimes very low, due to observer errors and the practical demands of reading six or more digits very quickly (three or four digits are sometimes used, but the match and error problems persist). Attempts to use tape recorders in the field (so more plates can be read) add another element to the reduction cost, as do observer-recorder pairs in the field. The technological solution needed is a low-cost license-plate reader, so that plates can be "imaged" and the logging automated, including linking the observation to the entry/exit leg and the time.

With improved technology, the effectiveness and economics of license plate studies will change dramatically, and wider areas (corridors, zones) or more complex areas (interchanges) can be studied efficiently.

Some facilities (for instance, the NYS Thruway) use toll cards keyed to entry and exit, and can provide O/D information such as a license plate study would do. Consideration of using the EZ-PASS cards in the same way has already been mentioned.

C. Post card studies

Post card studies can provide additional information on true O/D (rather than entry/exit points in the survey area), route selected, mode preference, and other items. As such, they have great value.

They do require a well designed and *pretested* form, staffing to hand out the form at all feasible (i.e., low speed) entry points, associated volume counts, and a budget for processing the forms. The authors have learned through a number of studies that it is *essential* to anticipate the analysis, and even to do a "dry run" of the final report. Are the questions asked sufficient to gain the insights you need in the final report? *This is the critical reality check on post card and all other surveys.*

Post card surveys—unlike field counts—are especially sensitive to the rule that "you only get one chance." If you make a mistake on Day One of a counting program, there are often later days to correct the deficiency. Post card surveys happen all at once, on a production schedule, with pre-printed cards. Further, they are uniquely tailored to the project, whereas volume counts usually follow a standard practice and use a standard format.

By their nature, post card surveys involve the public directly, both in the hand-out and in the response. The quality—and even quantity—of the latter can depend very much on the clarity and credibility of the form. Pretest! As a further practical matter, it is often necessary to coordinate such studies with the police, given the nature of interactions with motorists, and police assistance is of great value in slowing vehicles as they approach hand-out and collection areas.

D. Roadside interviews

Such interviews involve pulling drivers off the road, or approaching them at entrances or other points. For the peace of mind of the public (and the safety of all involved), this *always* involves the police. The advantages of the detail gained on trip-making must be weighed against the imposition on the public.

E. Other interviews

Each of the above studies focuses on a particular facility or the patterns in an entire area or corridor. It is also possible to focus on a particular destination, or a particular origin. Trips to certain work clusters, shopping malls, hospitals, and colleges can add much knowledge about the demand on the transportation system (and its patterns). The same is true of major residential clusters.

Cordon and screenline studies

A cordon is an imaginary boundary around a study area of interest. It is generally established to define a CBD or other major activity center, where the accumulation of vehicles within the area is of great importance in traffic planning. Cordon volume studies require counting all streets and highways that cross the cordon, classifying the counts by direction and by 15- to 60-minute time periods. Such counts will enable the estimation of vehicle accumulations within the area.

The cordon must be large enough to define the area of interest, yet small enough to define an area within which accumulation data will be useful for planning. The cordon is established to cross all streets and highways at *midblock* locations, to avoid the complexity of establishing whether turning vehicles are entering or leaving the area. The cordon should also be defined to minimize the number of crossing points. Natural barriers, such as rivers, railroads, or other points of limited crossing, can be used as part of the cordon, where available, to simplify the counting program.

Cordons usually define areas of similar land use. The accumulation information developed from a cordon study is used to estimate street capacity and parking needs. Thus, a very large cordon encompassing several different land-use activities will not be focused enough for these purposes.

The accumulation of vehicles within a cordon boundary is found by summarizing the total of all counts entering and leaving the area by time period. Table 6-12 illustrates the procedure. The cordon counts are generally begun at an hour when the street system is virtually empty. If this is not possible, then spot checks of off-street parking facilities and on-street sample counts are used to estimate the number of vehicles inside the cordon when the study begins.

Cordon studies are often coordinated with limited-network counts of the enclosed area. Using short counts and controls, the hourly volume on each link of the network can be estimated, as well as total VMT. These values can be used in conjunction with accumulation counts to determine the number of parked or standing vehicles within the cordon at any given time.

Note that an estimate of parking and standing vehicles may *not* reflect true parking demand if supply is inadequate and many moving vehicles are merely circulating looking for a place to park. Again, demand discouraged from entering the cordon area by congestion is also not evaluated using this study technique.

A screen-line study is a unique form of traffic count used to check and adjust the results of predicted origin-destination flows from a comprehensive home-interview planning study. Such surveys yield statistical predictions of vehicle-trips between various defined transportation zones within a study area.

Table 6-12 Accumulation Computations for a Cordon Study

Time	Vehicles Entering	Vehicles Leaving	Accumulation (veh)
4:00–5:00 A.M.	—	—	250
5:00–6:00	100	20	330
6:00–7:00	150	40	440
7:00–8:00	200	40	600
8:00–9:00	290	80	810
9:00–10:00	350	120	1040
10:00–11:00	340	200	1180
11:00–12:00 Noon	350	350	1180
12:00–1:00 P.M.	260	300	1140
1:00–2:00	200	380	960
2:00–3:00	180	420	720
3:00–4:00	100	350	470
4:00–5:00	120	320	270

A *screen line* is some form of natural or man-made barrier across which there are a limited number of crossing points. Rivers, railroads, limited-access facilities, and the like make excellent screen lines. Count stations are established at all points crossing the screen line, and hourly counts are made for the period of interest, which generally covers from 12 to 24 hours.

The total number of screen-line crossings (total, or by hour) is then compared to the total number of crossings predicted by the home-interview study. The comparison is used to "factor" or adjust all origin-destination flows predicted by the home-interview study.

Summary

Volume is the most basic of all traffic data. Virtually no traffic engineering function can be carried out without knowledge of present and/or future predicted traffic volumes. This chapter provides an overview of the subject, covering commonly-used study techniques, and providing insight into how volume data is organized, presented, and analyzed. In later chapters, such operational issues as intersection control (what kind is needed?), signal timing, performance analysis, and functional design all depend on volume data and information.

References

1. Sharma, S. C., and Leng, Y., "Seasonal Traffic Counts for a Precise Estimation of AADT," *ITE Journal,* September 1994.
2. *Manual of Transportation Engineering Studies,* Institute of Transportation Engineers, Prentice-Hall, Englewood Cliffs, NJ, 1994.
3. *Traffic Monitoring Guide,* U.S. Department of Transportation, Federal Highway Administration, Washington, DC, 1985.
4. *Highway Capacity Manual, Special Report 209,* Transportation Research Board, National Research Council, Washington, DC, (revised) 1997.

Problems

Problem 6–1

A volume of 900 vph is observed at an intersection approach. Plot the peak rate of flow within the hour as the PHF varies from 1.00 to 0.70.

Problem 6–2

If the peak hour volume on a freeway is 5000 vph and the PHF is 0.91, what is the maximum rate of flow within the hour, and what is the highest 15-minute count of vehicles?

Problem 6–3

The following data were collected during a study of two arterial lanes. Estimate the continuous 15-minute counts for the two-lane roadway as a whole, find the peak hour, and compute the PHF.

Time	Lane 1 (veh)	Lane 2 (veh)
3:30–3:40 P.M.	100	—
3:45–3:55	—	120
4:00–4:10	106	—
4:15–4:25	—	124
4:30–4:40	115	—
4:45–4:55	—	130
5:00–5:10	120	—
5:15–5:25	—	146
5:30–5:40	142	—
5:45–5:55	—	140
6:00–6:10	135	—
6:15–6:25	—	130
6:30–6:40	120	—
6:45–6:55	—	110
7:00–7:10	105	—

Problem 6–4

The following counts were observed on a freeway. Compute (a) the hourly volume, (b) the peak rate of flow for a five-minute period, (c) the peak rate of flow for a 15-minute period, and (d) the peak-hour factor based on 15-minute periods.

Time	Count
5:00–5:05 P.M.	201
5:05–5:10	208
5:10–5:15	217
5:15–5:20	232
5:20–5:25	219
5:25–5:30	220
5:30–5:35	205
5:35–5:40	201
5:40–5:45	195
5:45–5:50	210
5:50–5:55	190
5:55–6:00	195

Problem 6–5

What counting period would you select for a volume study at an intersection with a signal cycle of (a) 60 secs, (b) 90 secs, and (c) 120 secs.?

Problem 6–6

A small-network count was conducted for the network illustrated, using machine counts. Because only two machines were available, the count program was conducted over a period of several days, using Station A as a control count, and the following schedule of coverage counts:

Station	Count Scheduled
1	Mon., 6:00 A.M.–9:30 A.M.
2	Mon., 10:00A.M.–1:30 P.M.
3	Mon., 2:00 P.M.–5:30 P.M.
4	Tue., 6:00 A.M.–9:30 A.M.
5	Tue., 10:00 A.M.–1:30 P.M.
6	Tue., 2:00 P.M.–5:30 P.M.
7	Wed., 6:00 A.M.–9:30 A.M.
8	Wed., 10:00 A.M.–1:30 P.M.
9	Wed., 2:00 P.M.–5:30 P.M.
10	Thu., 6:00 A.M.–9:30 A.M.
11	Thu., 10:00 A.M.–1:30 P.M.
A	Mon.–Thu., 6:00 A.M.–6:00 P.M.

From the axle counts observed and shown below, estimate the 12-hour volume (6 A.M.–6 P.M.) at each station for the average day of the study.

Network and Data for Problem 6–6

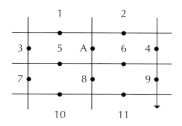

Axle Counts for Control Station A

Day	Time Period		
	6:00 A.M. to 10:00 A.M.	10:00 A.M. to 2:00 P.M.	2:00 P.M. to 6:00 P.M.
Mon.	4000	2800	4400
Tue.	3700	2600	4000
Wed.	3950	2680	4200
Thu.	4200	2950	4550

Axle Counts for Coverage Stations

Station	Count	Station	Count
1	2100	7	680
2	1200	8	1920
3	930	9	1230
4	872	10	2900
5	1100	11	2000
6	1000		

Sample Vehicle Classification Count

Vehicle Class	Number Observed
2-Axle	850
3-Axle	75
4-Axle	50
5-Axle	25

Problem 6–7

The following control counts were made at an urban count station to develop daily and monthly volume variation factors. Compute the factors from the following data:

24-Hr Counts

First Week in Month of	Mon.	Tue.	Wed.	Thu.	Fri.	Sat.	Sun.
January	2000	2200	2250	2000	1800	1500	950
April	1900	2080	2110	1890	1750	1400	890
July	1700	1850	1900	1710	1580	1150	800
October	2100	2270	2300	2050	1800	1550	1010

Standard Monthly Counts

Third Week in Month of	Average Daily Count
January	2250
February	2200
March	2000
April	2100
May	1950
June	1850
July	1800
August	1700
September	2000
October	2100
November	2150
December	2300

Problem 6–8

The following 24-hour counts were made at locations within the monthly and daily variation pattern defined by the control data of Table 6-11. Estimate the AADT of each of the following coverage counts:

Tuesday, March—15,000 vpd

Friday, August—21,000 vpd

Saturday, July—900 vpd

Problem 6–9

The following four control stations have been regrouped for the purposes of computing daily variation factors. Is the grouping appropriate, and if not, what grouping is? What are the combined daily variation factors for the appropriate group(s)? The stations are located sequentially along a state route.

	Mon.	Tue.	Wed.	Thu.	Fri.	Sat.	Sun.
Station 1	1.05	1.01	0.99	1.10	1.12	0.91	0.81
Station 2	1.10	1.05	0.97	1.10	1.08	0.89	0.88
Station 3	0.99	1.00	0.89	1.01	0.89	1.05	1.10
Station 4	1.04	1.02	1.01	1.09	1.12	0.89	0.83

Problem 6–10

For the interchange shown below, where would you station observers or road tubes to obtain volumes for flows A–B, B–A, B–C, C–B, A–C, and C–A?

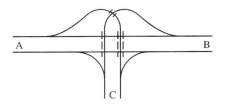

Problem 6–11

Estimate the annual VMT for a section of the state highway system represented by the variation factors of Table 6-11 if the following data are available for coverage stations in the section:

Station	Segment Length	Coverage–Count Date	24-Hr Count
1	2 miles	Tue., March	8,765 vpd
2	3	Mon., September	11,432
3	2.5	Fri., August	15,376
4	4	Sat., May	20,010
5	2	Wed., December	8,111
6	1.6	Wed., January	10,520

Problem 6–12

The following O&D results were obtained from license-plate observations. Expand and adjust the initial trip-table results to reflect the full distribution of vehicles.

Destination Station	Origin Station					Total Count at Destination Station
	1	2	3	4	5	
1	50	120	125	210	75	1200
2	105	80	143	305	100	2040
3	125	100	128	328	98	1500
4	82	70	100	125	101	985
5	201	215	180	208	210	2690
Total count at origin station	1820	1225	1750	2510	1110	8415

Table P6-1 Highest Peak Hour (see Figure 6-8)

Performance Target	1st	30th	100th
Good flows, high speed, low density, little delay (LOS B)			
Higher density, lower speeds, more delay, (LOS D)			
Highest densities, still lower speed, more delay, getting close to breakdown (LOS E)			

Problem 6–13

Refer to the section on Patterns and Variations and consider the four road types identified in Figure 6-8 and their related curves. Several combinations of design performance target and *n*th highest hour can be selected. Consider for instance Table P6-1. For *each* of the road types shown in Figure 6-8, fill in the blanks in the table above, providing one answer—overdesign, good design, inadequate design—and adding comments on your reasoning. Then, look for patterns in your tables, as well as differences which need to be explained.

After you have finished this task, consult the AASHTO Green Book and other sources, to better understand the interplay between target design performance and selection of the design hour volume.

Hint: To get you started, consider the recreational access route and the box in the upper left corner above. By selecting the 1st highest hour, you have specified $K = 0.30$ in the relation DDHV = $(K)(D)$(AADT). Assuming a $D = 0.70$ just for this discussion (see Table 6-2), this implies that DDHV = 0.21 (AADT). That is, we will build enough lanes to handle 21% of the entire AADT in one hour. Can we afford that? Can we do it? Is it reasonable to have so much unused capacity in the other hours, throughout the year? What is a reasonable target level and for which design volume, recognizing that there is some interplay?

Problem 6–14

Refer to the subsection on Short Counts within the section on *Data Collection Techniques and Technology* in this chapter. In developing the final estimates of counts and flow rates, one could have followed three rules:

(1) Keep the same apportionment between lanes, namely 41.2% and 58.8% in Lanes 1 and 2 respectively.
(2) Assure that the hourly totals in each lane are double the observed totals, given that 50% of the hour was observed.
(3) When data exists on either side of a missing point, simply interpolate between the two real points to estimate the missing point.

Following these rules, estimate the flow rates by time period and by lane, plot them on top of the Table 6-1 data that leads to Figure 6-13, and comment. More than that, suggest an alternative scheme that is logical, defensible, and better than the one specified above or the one used in the text of the chapter (if possible).

Problem 6–15

In the subsection Establishing Factors within *Estimating AADT and VMT,* refer to Table 6-6 and the associated text. The text points out that the average of the seven daily averages is *not quite* the AADT, because one of the days is represented 53 times in the year, but is very close in practice. Using the daily averages shown, compute *for each day of the week* (that is, assuming that ____ day is the one represented 53 times), the possible errors in the AADT which would arise from this procedural error. Comment.

Problem 6–16

Refer to Table 6-10 and the related discussion in the text. Plot the factors for each of the four stations *and* for the average, and then for the three stations and the revised average. Decide whether the analysis in the text is reasonable. Consider ways in which a set of fifty stations or locations could be studied for grouping.

7

Speed, Travel Time, and Delay Studies

Speed and travel time are the most commonly used indicators of performance for traffic facilities and networks. Travel time contours, speed trends, maps of link speeds (often color coded to suitable ranges), and various displays in transportation management centers emphasize the importance of these two parameters to the public and to the profession.

When facilities are congested, the amount of delay—and the extent of the congestion—are common supplemental indicators. The reader is cautioned, however, that both "delay" and "congestion" are generic terms. There are many kinds of "delay" that can be defined and measured, and the engineer must be careful to understand the specific measure being used in any specific reference. Similarly, "congestion" has many interpretations.

For some "point" facilities, such as intersections, average delay is the defined level of service indicator [1]. For arterial streets, the average travel speed of the *through* vehicles is the defined indicator [1], although the data is often taken by means of travel time runs. Even for freeways, where density is the defined level of service indicator, speed, delays, and related travel

times are also critical measures, particularly when describing congestion.

Travel time has the advantage that successive trip segments can be added directly, without concerns for weighted averages. Speeds, on the other hand, do not have to be linked so directly to trip length in the presentation, and are often used to describe performance at a particular point or short segment of a facility.

This chapter will cover basic field measurement techniques, and the applications of speed, travel time, and delay data in various types of analyses.

Presentations for areas and facilities

Table 7-1 is a simple statement of trends in the national speed profile through 1991, in terms of "spot" speeds (more will be said in the next section). It dramatically shows the difference between the posted speed limits on the measured facilities—all had 55 mph speed limits during the period depicted—and reality. On rural interstate highways, about 75% of all drivers

Table 7-1 A Tabulation of National Spot Speed Data

Fiscal Year	Average Speed (mph)	Median Speed (mph)	85th Percentile Speed (mph)	Percent > 55 mph
Urban Interstate Highways				
1985	57.2	57.4	64.0	64.1
1987	58.0	58.0	64.8	67.4
1989	58.9	59.0	66.1	71.3
1991	58.8	58.8	66.1	69.8
Rural Interstate Highways				
1985	59.5	59.4	66.1	75.4
1987	59.7	59.7	66.5	73.7
1989	60.1	60.3	67.2	76.8
1991	59.9	59.4	67.2	75.5
Rural Arterials				
1985	54.9	55.2	61.7	50.5
1987	55.9	56.1	62.8	54.3
1989	56.2	56.4	63.1	56.0
1991	56.4	56.3	63.1	56.5
Urban Principal Arterials				
1985	53.5	53.6	60.5	42.1
1987	54.0	54.1	60.7	44.7
1989	54.6	55.1	61.3	47.7
1991	54.0	53.9	60.8	42.2

Note: All highways have 55-mph speed limit.
[Used with permission of Transportation Research Board, National Research Council, from *Highway Capacity Manual, Special Report 209,* 3rd Ed., Copyright © 1994 Transportation Research Board.]

exceeded the speed limit. Such a display can spark much policy discussion about speed limits, compliance, safety, and other matters. In recent years, this trend has led to the abandonment of the 55-mph national speed limit amid concerns over the implications of the new policy on traffic accidents and fatalities. This concern is a critical reason to obtain good data on speeds, so that a comprehensive assessment of the new national policy can be made.

Figure 7-1 shows a travel time contour map in one metropolitan area, drawing attention to how long it takes to get to a certain point by a given mode. Such displays can highlight problems, and can define the situation without too many words. Shown as snapshots over time (particularly when superimposed), the growth of congestion can be illustrated very effectively.

Speed profiles on facilities can also effectively indicate the nature of the trip. Figure 7-2 shows the speed profile along an arterial, based on a test vehicle running the length of the facility. Significant delays are encountered at the intersections, perhaps indicating a problem with signal coordination. There appears to be significant queuing (and delay) approaching 3rd Street. In addition, there is a notable point of delay just after passing 2nd Street, at least in this one run.

The technology now exists to cost effectively obtain such machine-readable speed profiles. The primary cost of such collection is now very clearly the number of rental or other vehicles, plus the 1–2 people per vehicle on each travel time run. The logistics of arranging for N independent runs during the desired study period is also a practical problem. If $N = 30$,

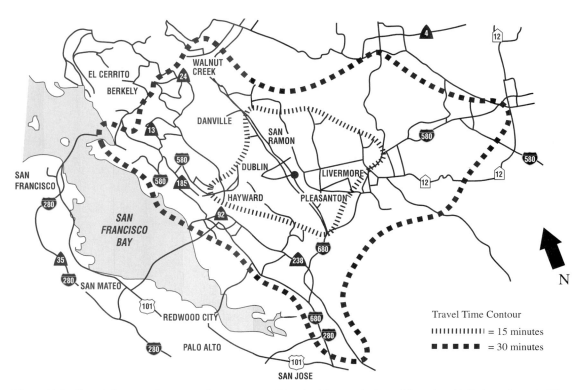

Figure 7-1   Travel time contour map for one area. [Used with permission of Prentice-Hall, Inc., from J. Pline (editor), *Traffic Engineering Handbook,* 4th Ed., Institute of Transportation Engineers, p. 69. Copyright © 1992 Prentice Hall, Inc.]

for instance, how many cars and people are needed, and how many rush hours should the collection be spread over?

The point of each of these displays is that speed and travel time communicate effectively, often dramatically. Anyone who has seen a real time display in a traffic management center can testify to its impact, especially as the speeds degrade over time, the color codes in links change, and the problem spreads.

The basic measurement

Taking speeds seems very straightforward: set up a radar meter or other device, and take speeds as the vehicles pass a fixed point. If necessary, correct the measurement for systematic error caused by the radar beam's angle to the actual vehicle path. If a radar meter is not used, two consecutive closely spaced loop detectors can serve the purpose by timing the differ-

ence between actuations. The same can be done with line-crossings on a video recording of a field site.

However, given that technology can make the actual data exercise so simple, it is perhaps even more important that we focus on *what* is *actually* being measured. There are speed indicators with subtle but systematic differences, and it is not always clear which measurement protocol is measuring which. The same is true of relating travel time and speed indicators.

A. Two speed indicators

Chapter 3 introduced the concepts of *time mean speed* and *space mean speed.* The concepts are reinforced here. Consider the illustration of Figure 7-3, in which 50% of the vehicles passing Point A have a speed of 60 mph and 50% have a speed of 40 mph. For simplicity in a later illustration, assume that each group has interarrival times of 2 seconds within the group.

Date/Time of Report: 7/31/90, 10:03 AM
Speed Profile for Run: 1 Pulse Date File; fryburg-pla
Run Title: Test Arterial with Multiple Delays

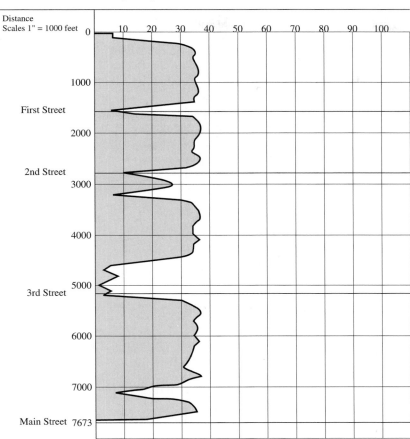

Figure 7-2 Sample travel time run on an arterial. [Used with permission of Prentice-Hall, Inc., from *Manual of Transportation Engineering Studies,* Institute of Transportation Engineers, p. 62. Copyright © 1994 Prentice Hall, Inc.]

For clarity, the two groups are shown in two distinct lanes in the illustrations. This is not a requirement.

What is the average speed? Clearly, it is 0.50(60) + 0.50(40) = 50.0 mph *at the measurement point.*

What is the average speed of vehicles over the next mile, assuming that the individual speeds do not change? Figure 7-4 shows an illustration of the pat-

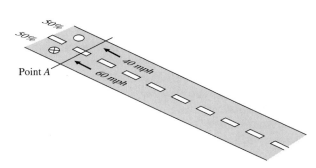

Figure 7-3 Collecting speed data at one illustrative location.

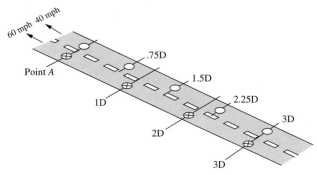

Figure 7-4 Relating the speed at one location to the speed of vehicles occupying a section of roadway.

tern with which each group occupies the *space* on the road. Due to their different travel times over the mile, there are more of the slower vehicles present than of the faster vehicles: The faster vehicles cover the mile and are gone sooner. Based on the pattern shown, the average is (3/7)(60) + (4/7)(40) = 48.57 mph.

The speed indicator measured at the point is often referred to as the *spot speed,* which is the *time mean speed* in more precise terms. The speed indicator defined by the average speed of all vehicles occupying a section of road is the *space mean speed.* The space mean speed is involved in characterizing freeway sections. It is important to note which speed is being observed, and which parameter is most appropriate for different applications.

Why bother? The difference between the two values is "only" 1.43 mph, which means that the spot speed is only about 2.9% higher than the space mean speed in this example. There are two reasons to bother: (1) when we are measuring speed differences, we do not want a 3% systematic error biasing the results; (2) as we change measurement techniques—using new technology or whatever—we do not want to accidentally switch from one speed indicator to the other without knowing it. We would like to compare "apples and apples," not "apples and oranges."

B. Another measurement technique

Let us continue the above illustration. Suppose we were on the top of a tall building and could see the entire mile of interest. Further, let us assume that we take two consecutive snapshots one second apart, note the distances Δ_t traveled by each vehicle in the picture, estimate speeds for each vehicle by $s_i = (\Delta_t/1.0 \text{ second})$ and average those speeds. What will we have computed?

Note that three-sevenths of the vehicles will be at 60 mph (see Figure 7-4) and four-sevenths will be at 40 mph. Therefore the computed speed is (3/7)(60) + (4/7)(40) = 48.57 mph, and the space mean speed has been obtained.

It is not necessary to actually take such snapshots. Video imaging systems can now estimate the speed of each vehicle in an area. The result is the space mean speed of vehicles occupying the area.

C. Yet another measurement technique

Suppose we once again were on top of the tall building, but this time visually "picked up" sample vehicles as they crossed the Point A boundary, followed them visually as they traversed the section, and then recorded their travel times. What would we have measured?

Note that 50% of the vehicles would have had 60 mph speeds[1] or 60 second travel times over the mile. The other 50% would have 40 mph speeds or 90 second travel times over the mile. Thus, the average travel time of speeds observed in this way is 75 seconds, which can be expressed as 48 mph. It is *neither* the space mean speed *nor* the spot speed.

What is it? It is exactly what was said—the average travel time of vehicles sampled in the way specified. That sampling does not have the same mix (4/3) as the vehicles in the section, and is therefore not precisely indicative of the vehicles *in* the section at a given time.

Can it relate to the spot speed? If we make the assumption that the speed does not change over the sample section, then the speed at entry is the same as the speed over the section and we can compute the spot speed from:

$$(1/n)\sum (D/TT_i)$$

where D is the section length and TT_i is the travel time of the *i*th observation. In practice, this means that 0.50(5280/60) + 0.50(5280/90) = 73.33 fps or 50 mph. This is the *time mean* or *spot speed.*

D. What is the point?

The point of proposing a set of travel time or speed measures that *look like* they are measuring the same thing is to raise the question, are they? The above illustrations show that the answer is, not always. Then the follow-on task is to determine the way in which they interrelate, so that we can match:

Field Technique ⟷ Desired Indicator(s)

The simple fact is that not every field technique will yield space mean speed directly, and we must understand what exactly is being measured.

This emphasis on matching the field technique to the desired indicator(s) is very important, particularly as new automated techniques emerge, yielding speed measures which are "obviously" space mean speed (or

---

[1]Under the assumption that they stay at the same speed throughout the section.

some other indicator) to the highly skilled developer who is not a traffic specialist.

The same applies to simulation models. Consider such measures as the average link travel time in the TRAF/NETSIM microscopic simulation model. Is it space mean speed, time mean speed, or neither? Does it matter? Is it closely related to one or the other?

E. Travel times by floating car

Consider one last measurement technique related to travel time and speed, particularly on arterial streets. It is very common to estimate travel time by instructing a driver to drive the street "normally," passing about the same number of cars that pass him or her, and so forth.[2] By driving in this way, the test car maintains its "average" position in the traffic stream, and is therefore assumed to be measuring speeds and travel times that are representative of average conditions.

This "floating car" approach then yields sample travel times. How do they relate to other indicators?

First, note from Figure 7-4 that if the vehicle is in fact "floating" in the stream so that the net cars passing the test driver are zero, then the vehicle is going at a rate that causes it to pass the slower vehicles—and causes the faster vehicles to pass it. The "net flux" of cars tends to be in the 4/3 ratio of this illustration, and the test car is measuring the travel time associated with the space mean speed.

Secondly, the literature has noted that such test cars tend to "fall in sync" with the signal progression, and are actually measuring the average travel time of the vehicles in the progressed, through traffic and not the weighted average of all vehicles (turners, those just entering, etc.) on the arterial. For the purpose of assessing arterial performance, this is desirable, because the defined measure is the average travel speed of through vehicles [1].

Spot speed studies

Spot speeds have been previously defined as the average speed of vehicles passing a point, or the time mean speed. Spot speed studies are intended to mea-

---

[2]The authors are not making a strong distinction between "floating" and "average" car instructions, because the driving task generally keeps the driver so busy that the best that is achieved is "representative."

sure this value, almost always under conditions of light flow. When measuring spot speeds, the traffic engineer is almost always interested in speeds that drivers freely select when not impeded by the density of traffic. For practical purposes, spot speed studies are generally conducted at times when traffic flow rates are less than 750–1000 vphpl for freeways.

A. Speed definitions

The speed measures of common interest in traffic studies are

- time mean speed
- space mean speed
- average travel speed
- average running speed
- 85th percentile speed

In addition, statistical terms such as the *pace* and the *modal* and *median* speeds are useful data points. Some definitions follow:

- *Average travel speed* on a facility is the speed including all delays and travel time, and is the same as the space mean speed over the section in question.
- *Average running speed* on a facility or link is the average speed of vehicles when only the time spent in motion is included; it does not include travel time lost when stopped at intersections or other obstructions.
- *85th percentile speed* is the speed not exceeded by 85% of the drivers, and is usually applied to the spot speed distribution.

The *pace* is the 10 mph interval containing the largest fraction of the speeds (again, spot speeds in most applications). The *mode* is the most frequent single value. The *median* is the speed that equally divides the distribution of spot speeds: There are as many vehicles traveling at higher speeds as at lower speeds.

B. Applications of spot speeds

In many situations, the speed of vehicles unimpeded by traffic is needed. Below is an illustrative list of the applications of such data in various traffic engineering analyses:

1. *Speed limit studies* to establish the effectiveness of new or existing speed limits and/or enforcement practices.

2. *Establishing trends* at the local, state, and national level to assess the effectiveness of national policy on speed limits and enforcement.
3. *Specific design applications,* including the establishment of appropriate sight distances; the relationship among speed, horizontal alignment, and superelevation; and speed performance related to grade and length of grade.
4. *Specific control applications,* including the timing of *yellow* and *all red* signal intervals, proper placement of signs, and establishing appropriate signal progressions.
5. *Investigation of high-accident locations* at which speed is suspected to be a causative factor.

The list is illustrative, and is not intended to be complete. Such studies, however, are of significant importance, and are among the most common conducted by traffic engineers.

C. Field techniques and practical considerations

The most common means of collecting speed data is through the use of radar meters (either hand-held or mounted on a vehicle). Since this methodology is the same as that used by police in speed enforcement, it is absolutely critical that the data collection operation be concealed from traffic. Once drivers know their speeds are being observed, they will slow down. From the point of view of a traffic engineering study, this is disastrous, as the measurements no longer reflect speeds freely selected by drivers, uninhibited by external factors other than the geometry and physical environment of the roadway.

Use of closely-spaced detectors, when these are available, is preferable. In some cases, it is desirable to measure travel times over a short "trap" distance—e.g., the distance between two pavement joints—manually with a stop-watch. The measurements will be less accurate (they involve random error and some systematic error caused by the angle of observation), but they are less likely to cause drivers to alter their behavior.

Even when radar meters are used, it is almost impossible to record the speed of every vehicle at a given location. Even for the period of the study, a *sample* of measurements is being taken. Care must be taken to avoid systematic errors in the data collection process. Common errors include (a) looking for the "fastest" vehicle—causing a bias to higher speeds in the data base; (b) disproportionate inclusion of trucks or other heavy vehicles in the sample—causing a bias to lower speeds; (c) inclusion of speeds of vehicles following a lead vehicle in platoon—causing a bias to lower speeds. The last is avoided by never including the speed of a vehicle traveling too closely behind another—200 ft for speeds less than 40 mph; 350 ft for speeds of 40 mph or higher. The first two are avoided by sampling on a systematic basis, such as every *n*th vehicle in each lane, depending on the collection capabilities.

In general, there is no attempt to record the exact speed of any given vehicle in the field, for two reasons: (1) None of the measurement techniques, except for the use of closely-spaced detectors, is accurate enough for an individual measurement; and (2) the mathematical descriptions of data distributions (see Chapter 5) cannot describe the occurrence of a single discrete value of speed. Rather, they describe the probability, or expected percentage of occurrences within a defined range of speeds. Practically speaking, this means that continuous probability functions cannot define the occurrence of a speed at exactly 36.55 mph. Such a function can, however, define the probability of an occurrence between 36 mph and 37 mph. For these reasons, field efforts concentrate on observing the number of vehicles traveling at speeds within various pre-defined ranges.

A sample field data sheet is included as Figure 7-5. The data shown is used in a continuing sample problem to illustrate typical analysis of spot speed data. The first two columns are used to pre-define the speed groups to be used. Ranges from as little as 1.0 mph to a maximum of 5 mph are acceptable. The smaller the range used in each group, the more accurate the resulting computations of average speed and other key statistics.

If measurements are to be made as time over a measured "trap," the limits of each speed group can be converted to an equivalent stop watch or timer reading in seconds. For example, if a 1,000 ft "trap" is set up, a speed of 30 mph translates to an elapsed time of:

$$t = \frac{1,000}{30 \times 1.468} = 22.7 \text{ sec}$$

The second set of columns allows pre-entry of elapsed times corresponding to each of the speed group limits. Once done, the stop watch or timer reading can be immediately placed in the correct group.

LOCATION	DATE	TIME
Route 10 @ MP 125.3	July 10, 1994	1:00 - 4:00 PM

WEATHER CONDITIONS	ROADWAY SURFACE CONDITIONS
Good - Clear, Dry	Asphaltic concrete - good.

SPEED GROUP		TIME GROUP		PASSENGER CARS	TRUCKS	OTHER	TOTALS			
Lower limit (mph)	Upper limit (mph)	Lower limit (secs)	Upper limit (secs)							
30	32									
32	34									
34	36			/l	)(	/	2	2	1	5
36	38			)(l	((	/	3	2	0	5
38	40			ЦHT	(	/	5	1	1	7
40	42			ЦHT ЦHT	l/l		10	3	0	13
42	44			ЦHT ЦHT ЦHT lll	)l/		18	3	0	21
44	46			ЦHT ЦHT ЦHT ЦHT ЦHT llll	/lll		29	4	0	33
46	48			ЦHT ЦHT ЦHT ЦHT ЦHT ЦHT ЦHT ЦHT ll	ll	//	42	2	2	46
48	50			ЦHT ЦHT ЦHT ЦHT ЦHT ЦHT ЦHT ЦHT ЦHT ЦHT ЦHT ЦHT	ll		60	2	0	62
50	52			ЦHT ЦHT ЦHT ЦHT ЦHT ЦHT ЦHT ll			37	0	0	37
52	54			ЦHT ЦHT ЦHT ЦHT lll			23	1	0	24
54	56			ЦHT ЦHT ll/		/	13	0	1	14
56	58			ЦHT ll	l	/	7	1	1	9
58	60			ЦHT			5	0	0	5
60	62			ll			2	0	0	2
62	64									
64	66									
66	68									
68	70									

METHOD OF MEASUREMENT

Signature *Ryan P. Roche*   7/10/94

_____ Radar
_____ Time over measured course length of _____ ft.
     _____ Stop watch/manual
     _____ Road tubes w/ timer
     _____ Electronic contact w/ timer

Figure 7-5   Data for an illustrative spot speed study.

The most common practice is to enter a "tick" in the appropriate row and column each time a vehicle speed is recorded. The last four columns of the worksheet can be used to enter totals as shown.

D. Presentation of data

1. Frequency distribution table. Spot speed data are presented in several standard formats. Table 7-2 shows a frequency distribution. This table shows the total number of vehicles observed in each speed group. For convenience of subsequent use, the table always includes one speed group at each extreme for which no vehicles were observed. The "middle speed, S" of the third column is taken as the midpoint value within the speed group. As individual speeds have not been recorded, it will be assumed that the *average speed of vehicles observed within any given speed group*

Table 7-2   Frequency Distribution Table for Illustrative Spot Speed Data

Speed Group		Middle Speed *S* (mph)	No. of Veh. in Group *n*	Veh. in Group (%)*	Cum. Veh. (%)*	*nS***	*nS²***
Lower Limit (mph)	Upper Limit (mph)						
32	34	33	0	0.0%	0.0%	0	0
34	36	35	5	1.8%	1.8%	175	6,125
36	38	37	5	1.8%	3.5%	185	6,845
38	40	39	7	2.5%	6.0%	273	10,647
40	42	41	13	4.6%	10.6%	533	21,853
42	44	43	21	7.4%	18.0%	903	38,829
44	46	45	33	11.7%	29.7%	1,485	66,825
46	48	47	46	16.3%	45.9%	2,162	101,614
48	50	49	62	21.9%	67.8%	3,038	148,862
50	52	51	37	13.1%	80.9%	1,887	96,237
52	54	53	24	8.5%	89.4%	1,272	67,416
54	56	55	14	4.9%	94.3%	770	42,350
56	58	57	9	3.2%	97.5%	513	29,241
58	60	59	5	1.8%	99.3%	295	17,405
60	62	61	2	0.7%	100.0%	122	7,442
62	64	63	0	0.0%	100.0%	0	0
			283	100.0%		13,613	661,691

*All percent computed to two decimal points and rounded to one; this may cause apparent "errors" in cumulative percents due to rounding.

**Computations rounded to the nearest whole number.

is the middle speed. This is why speed groups of more than 5 mph are not used. As the size of the speed group increases, the accuracy of this assumption decreases.

The fourth column shows the number of vehicles, or frequency, observed for each speed group. These are simply transcribed from the field data sheet of Table 7-2. The fifth column is the "percent of vehicles in group." For example, the 38–40 mph group has 7 out of a total of 283 observations, giving a percentage of $(7/283) \times 100 = 2.5\%$. The sixth column is the "cumulative percent vehicles," i.e., the percentage of vehicles traveling at or below the upper limit of the speed group. For the 42–44 mph speed group, this is the percentage of vehicles traveling at or below 44 mph, which included the vehicles in the 42–44 mph speed group and *all slower speed groups.* For this speed group, the value is 0.0% + 1.8% + 1.8% + 2.5% + 4.6% + 7.4% = 18.0%.

The last two columns are simple multiplications, as shown, used in subsequent computations.

2. Frequency and cumulative frequency distribution curves. Figure 7-6 shows two standard plots that are generally prepared from data in the Frequency Distribution Table. For convenience, they are usually plotted one above the other, using the same horizontal axis for speed.

The *Frequency Distribution Curve* plots points which represent the *middle speed* of each speed group vs. the % *frequency* in the speed group. Once again, the middle speed is taken to be the average of all speed observations in the group. The *Cumulative Frequency Distribution Curve* plots the *upper limit of the speed group* against the *cumulative % frequency* for the group. Because the cumulative % frequency is defined as the percentage of vehicles traveling at or below a given speed, the speed index must be the upper limit of speed for the group, NOT the middle speed.

In both cases, once the points are plotted, they are connected by a *smooth curve* that minimizes the total balance of points falling above the line and those

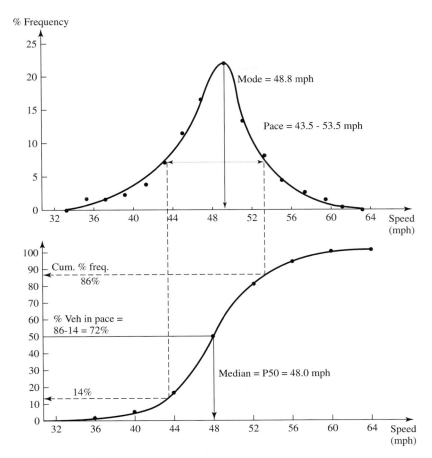

Figure 7-6 Frequency and cumulative frequency distribution curves for illustrative spot speed data.

falling below the line (on the vertical axis). A *smooth* curve requires that there be no breaks in the slope of the curve (i.e., no points or corners). The "best fit" is done by eye, generally lightly sketching in the curve freehand. When the "best fit" is approximated, a french curve may be used to darken the line.

E. Common statistics used to describe the distribution

A number of descriptive statistics can be computed from the data of the Frequency Distribution Table, or graphically scaled from the Frequency and Cumulative Frequency Distribution Curves. The statistics used generally describe two important characteristics of the distribution. Measures of *central tendency* define the approximate middle or center of the distribution; measures of *dispersion* define the extent to which data spreads around the center.

1. Measures of central tendency

a. The Average or Mean Speed. Like any other average or mean, the average speed of the distribution is computed by summing all of the individual observations and dividing by the number of observations. Unfortunately, data has been collected in groups, and the exact values of individual speeds are unknown. Thus, the assumption that the average speed within a given speed group represents the average speed of all observations within the group must now be used.

The sum of all speeds within group i may be estimated as:

$$n_i S_i \qquad [7\text{-}1]$$

where: n_i = frequency of observations in group i
S_i = middle speed of group i, mph

To get the total sum of all speeds in the study, this expression must be summed over all speed groups:

$$\Sigma n_i S_i \qquad [7\text{-}2]$$

This sum is then divided by N, the total number of individual speed observations made and recorded:

$$\bar{x} = \frac{\Sigma n_i S_i}{N} \qquad [7\text{-}3]$$

For the sample problem herein, this value is computed as:

$$\bar{x} = \frac{13,613}{283} = 48.10 \text{ mph}$$

where $\Sigma n_i S_i$ is the sum of the next-to-last column of the Frequency Distribution Table.

b. The Median Speed. The median speed is defined as the value of speed that divides the distribution into equal halves, i.e., there are as many drivers traveling at speeds higher than the median as are driving slower than it. Again, not having recorded discrete values of speed makes this determination more difficult. The median is best found graphically from the Cumulative Frequency Distribution Curve. As this curve plots the percentage of vehicles traveling at or below any given speed, the median is, by definition, the speed corresponding to 50% on this curve. This is commonly referred to as the "50th Percentile Speed" or P_{50}.

Refer to Figure 7-6: Enter the Cumulative Frequency Distribution Curve at 50% on the vertical axis. Draw a horizontal line to the curve, and drop a vertical line from the intersection of the first line with the curve. The resulting P_{50} is read from the horizontal axis at the crossing of the vertical line. For the sample problem, the median speed is:

$$P_{50} = 48.0 \text{ mph}$$

c. The Pace. The pace is a traffic engineering measure not commonly used for other statistical analyses. It is defined as *the 10 mph increment in speed in which the highest percentage of drivers were observed.* It is found using the Frequency Distribution Curve, recognizing that the area under this curve between any two boundaries represents the percent of vehicles traveling at speeds within those boundaries. This

area definition makes sense if the horizontal axis is thought of in terms of each speed group being *one* horizontal unit.

Refer to Figure 7-6: A 10 mph template is scaled from the horizontal axis. Keeping this template horizontal, place one end on the lower left side of the curve, and move slowly along the curve. When the right end of the template intersects the right side of the curve, the pace has been located. Obviously, the 10 mph range which intercepts the peak of the curve has the most area under it, and therefore the highest percentage of vehicles encompassed. For the sample problem, the pace is:

$$43.5 - 53.5 \text{ mph}$$

d. The Modal Speed. The modal speed is defined as the single value of speed that is most likely to occur. Since no discrete values of speed were recorded, this determination cannot be done directly.

Once again, refer to Figure 7-6: The modal speed can be scaled from the Frequency Distribution Curve by dropping a vertical line from the peak of the curve, reading the result from the horizontal axis. For the sample problem, the modal speed is:

$$48.8 \text{ mph}$$

If a curve is perfectly symmetric around the mean, then the average speed, the median speed, and the modal speed are all the same.

2. Measures of dispersion

a. The Standard Deviation. The most common measure of spread of data around a central value is the standard deviation. If discrete pieces of data are available, the equation for the standard deviation is:

$$s = \sqrt{\frac{\Sigma (x_i - \bar{x})^2}{N - 1}}$$

The difference between a given data point and the mean is a direct measure of dispersion. These differences are squared to avoid positive and negative differences canceling, and summed for all data points. They are then divided by $N - 1$. This is because one *degree of freedom* is lost because the mean of the distribution is known and used in the computation. A simple example of why one degree of freedom is lost can be constructed using the following three numbers: 3, 5, and 7. The average of these three numbers is 5. If the difference between the individual numbers and the mean (5) is computed, the results are $-2, 0,$ and $+2$. No matter what numbers are used, the sum of these differences must be "0." Thus, if the first two differences were stated, the third would be known. In the equation above, only the first $N - 1$ differences are statistically random. Once the first $N - 1$ differences are selected, the last is predetermined. The entire relationship is under a radical to reverse the effect of squaring the differences originally.

Because speed data is collected by groups, this equation is modified to:

$$s = \sqrt{\frac{\Sigma n_i(S_i - \bar{x})^2}{N - 1}} \qquad [7\text{-}4]$$

which may be manipulated into a more convenient form for use:

$$s = \sqrt{\frac{\Sigma n_i S_i^2 - N\bar{x}^2}{N - 1}} \qquad [7\text{-}5]$$

Conveniently, the first term of this equation is now the sum of the last column of the Frequency Distribution Table. Thus, the standard deviation of speed can be conveniently computed for the sample problem as:

$$s = \sqrt{\frac{661{,}691 - (283)(48.1)^2}{283 - 1}} = 4.94 \text{ mph}$$

The standard deviation of the distribution may also be roughly estimated using two values from the Cumulative Frequency Distribution Curve. Entering that curve (refer to Figure 7-6) on the horizontal axis at 85% and 15% yields values for the P_{85} and P_{15}. Using these values, the standard deviation can be roughly estimated as:

$$s_{est} = \frac{P_{85} - P_{15}}{2} = \frac{52.5 - 42.7}{2} = 4.9 \text{ mph} \quad [7\text{-}6]$$

This estimation is based on the assumption that speeds are normally distributed, and that the area under a Normal Distribution between the mean ± one standard deviation is approximately 70% (68.3% to be exact).

Most speed distributions will have standard deviations close to 5 mph, since this represents most driver behavior patterns reasonably well. Unlike average and other central speeds, which can vary widely from location to location, most speed distributions have similar standard deviations.

b. Percent Vehicles Within the Pace. If the pace itself is representative of the center of the distribution, the actual percentage of vehicles traveling within the pace is a measure of dispersion. The *smaller* the percentage of vehicles traveling within the 10 mph range of the pace, the *greater* degree of dispersion exists.

Refer to Figure 7-6 again: The pace limits, 43.0 and 53.0 mph, were determined from the Frequency Distribution Curve. These speeds are now used to enter the Cumulative Frequency Distribution Curve to determine the percentage of vehicles traveling at or below these speeds. Then:

% Under 53.0 mph	= 86.0%
% Under 43.0 mph	= 14.0%
% Between 43 and 53 mph	= 72.0%

Even though speeds between 34 and 62 mph were observed in this study, over 70% of the vehicles traveled in a 10 mph range of speed between 43.0 and 53.0 mph. This represents normal traffic behavior with a standard deviation of about 5.0 mph.

F. Applying the normal distribution to analysis of spot speed data

In most cases, speed distributions tend to be normal, that is, with a strong central tendency and decreasing probability of extreme values. Chapter 5 contains a detailed description of the normal distribution and its properties that should be reviewed in conjunction with this section.

If the speed distribution is assumed to be normal, several interesting analyses of the data may now take place. Recall that the notation x: $N[40, 25]$ signifies that the variable x is normally distributed with a mean of 40 and a variance of 25, which converts to a standard deviation of 5. Chapter 5 gives various examples of this notation and its interpretation. It also covers the conversion of values of any arbitrary normal distribution to equivalent values on the Standard Normal Distribution, z: $N[0, 1]$, which is shown in Table 5-1 (of Chapter 5).

1. Precision and confidence intervals. When a speed study is conducted, a single value of the mean speed is computed. For the sample study used herein, the value is 48.10 mph, based on a sample of 283 observations. This number is a sample mean of a finite number of observations that is being used to estimate the true mean of the underlying distribution of all vehicles traversing the site under uncongested conditions. The number of such vehicles is, for all practical purposes, infinite. In essence, the measured value of $\bar{x}$ is being used to estimate μ.

In Chapter 5, the standard error of the mean, E, was introduced as a means of estimating how good this estimate is:

$$E = \frac{s}{\sqrt{n}}$$

The standard error of the mean is the standard deviation of the distribution of sample means, where the total sample size is n. For the illustrative spot speed data:

$$E = \frac{4.94}{\sqrt{283}} = 0.294 \text{ mph}$$

From the characteristics of the Normal Distribution, it is known that 95% of all values lie between the mean ± 1.96 standard deviations; 99.7% of all values lie between the mean ± 3.00 standard deviations. Thus, for a single sample mean drawn from a distribution of sample means with fixed group size:

95% $\longrightarrow \bar{x} = \mu \pm 1.96 \, E$ or $\mu = \bar{x} \pm 1.96 \, E$

99.7% $\longrightarrow \bar{x} = \mu \pm 3.00 \, E$ or $\mu = \bar{x} \pm 3.00 \, E$

Thus, it can now be stated that the "true mean" of the distribution of vehicle speeds at the study location lies between the measured sample mean ± either 1.96 E or 3.00 E with a probability that such a statement is correct either 95% or 99.7% of the time respectively. The percentage is called the *confidence* level of the statement—i.e., we are this "confident" that our statement of the range within which the true mean lies is correct. The ± range to which we state the interval is called the *precision* to which the measurement of the true mean has been made.

For the sample study, in which an average speed of 48.10 mph was made, with a standard error of the mean (E) of 0.294 mph:

For 95% confidence:
    $\mu = 48.10 \pm 1.96(0.294) = 48.10 \pm 0.58$ mph

For 99.7% confidence:
    $\mu = 48.10 \pm 1.96(0.294) = 48.10 \pm 0.88$ mph

Notice that as the confidence increases, the precision range also increases. As we become more confident that the stated range of the true mean is correct, the size of the range becomes larger. Note that in the extreme, we can be 100% certain that the true mean of the distribution lies between $\pm\infty$. This, of course, would not be a meaningful or useful statement or measurement.

2. Estimating required sample size. Chapter 5 also illustrated how statements on accuracy can be inverted to determine an appropriate sample size for the study. Before the study is made, the analyst can specify the precision to which the average speed is to be measured, and the confidence level desired. The sample size may then be computed from these assumptions:

$$e = XE = X\frac{s}{\sqrt{n}}$$

where e = tolerance, ± mph and X = 1.96 for 95% confidence and 3.00 for 99.7% confidence. Solving this equation for n:

$$n = \frac{X^2 s^2}{e^2}$$

This equation, however, requires that the standard deviation be known before the study is made. To avoid this problem, a standard deviation from a previous study on the same facility may be used, or it may be assumed that a value of 5 mph is reasonable, as most field values will be close to this.

Consider the following problem: How many speeds must be measured to determine the average speed to within ±1.0 mph with 95% confidence? with 99.7% confidence? How do the answers change if the precision must be ±0.5 mph? Assuming a standard 5 mph standard deviation:

For 95% confidence, ±1.0 mph:

$$n = \frac{1.96^2(5^2)}{1.0^2} = 96 \text{ samples}$$

For 95% confidence, ±0.5 mph:

$$n = \frac{1.96^2(5^2)}{0.5^2} = 384 \text{ samples}$$

For 99.7% confidence, ±1.0 mph:

$$n = \frac{3^2(5^2)}{1.0^2} = 225 \text{ samples}$$

For 99.7% confidence, ±0.5 mph:

$$n = \frac{3^2(5^2)}{0.5^2} = 900 \text{ samples}$$

Note that in going from the relatively reasonable expectations of 1.0 mph precision with 95% confidence to the more severe 0.5 mph precision and 99.7% confidence, the required sample size increases from 96 to 900, a factor of almost 10! For most traffic engineering purposes, a 1.0 mph precision with 95% confidence is sufficient.

3. Before-and-after studies. Consider the following typical situation: An accident analysis at a critical location on a highway indicates that excessive speeds are a principal causative factor in the frequent accidents. As a result, new speed limit signs are installed, and a lower limit is applied. Enforcement procedures are intensified. Six months later, speed studies at the location show a 3 mph reduction in average speed. Were the new speed limit, signs, and enforcement procedures effective?

The following dilemma exists: Even if two different speed samples were taken at the location at the same time, the average speeds would be different. The question is whether or not the observed reduction in speeds reflects real changes in the underlying average speed of the population, or whether it was achieved through the chance selection of two different samples from the same population. If the former is true, the observed reduction in speeds is said to be "statistically significant"; if the latter is true, the observed reduction is said to be "statistically insignificant." This can be tested using a procedure called the Normal Approximation.

If two speed studies are conducted at the same location, and it is assumed that both samples *are selected from the same underlying population,* then the difference in sample means is normally distributed, with an average of "0" difference, and a standard deviation of:

$$s_Y = \sqrt{\frac{s_1^2}{n_2} + \frac{s_2^2}{n_2}}$$

where: s_Y = pooled standard deviation of the distribution of sample mean differences (when both samples are from the same distribution).

This distribution is called the Normal Approximation, as the distribution of the difference in sample means *approaches* normal. When n_1 and n_2 are both larger than 30, the approximation is acceptable. Since most traffic studies never deal with sample sizes smaller than this, the test is almost always valid. For those cases where smaller sample sizes exist, the *t-test* is applied, using the *Student's "t" Distribution,* which is described in most standard statistical references. The theory and applicability of the normal approximation were more completely described in Chapter 5.

In the testing for the statistical significance of an observed decrease in sample means, it is important to note that we are applying a *one-sided test* procedure. This means that the test is for a *decrease* in sample means, NOT a difference, which could be an increase or a decrease. Thus, if the "after" test shows an increase in sample average speeds, no test is needed—the traffic engineering measures intended to reduce speed obviously have failed.

When a decrease in average speeds is observed, subscript "1" refers to the "before" test and subscript "2" refers to the "after" test. The test is conducted by computing a z value for use in the Standard Normal Distribution. This is done by taking the observed difference in average speeds, subtracting the mean of the distribution (0), and dividing by the standard deviation of the difference in means (s_Y):

$$z_d = \frac{(\bar{x}_1 - \bar{x}_2) - 0}{s_Y}$$

Then, the probability of a value of z less than or equal to the observed value is obtained from the Standard Normal Distribution Table in the text (Table 5-1). If a value of 95% or greater is achieved, it can be said that 95% or more of all occurrences would be less than z_d, assuming both sample means were drawn from the same distribution. Conversely, a value as high or higher than z_d would be expected less than 5% of the time in such a situation. But z_d exists, computed from the observed difference in sample means. Thus, it is only 5% probable, or less, that the two sample means were from the same distribution and 95% probable, or more, that the two sample means came from different distributions.

The test is conducted using a Type I error (α) of 0.05. Before certifying that an observed reduction in sample speeds is "statistically significant," we wish to be 95% certain that our statement is correct; there should be no more than a 5% chance that we incorrectly reject the null hypothesis of "no change." Thus:

The observed difference in sample means is statistically significant if:

$$\text{Prob }(z \leq z_d) \geq 95\%$$

The observed difference in sample means is NOT statistically significant if:

$$\text{Prob }(z \leq z_d) < 95\%$$

Consider the following example: A speed study with $n = 50$ results in an average speed of 65.3 mph and a standard deviation of 5 mph. After making traffic improvements intended to reduce average speeds, a second study was made 6 months later. This study, with $n = 60$, resulted in an average speed of 64.5 mph and a standard deviation of 6 mph. Was the observed reduction in speeds statistically significant?

Step 1: Compute s_Y

$$s_Y = \sqrt{\frac{5^2}{50} + \frac{6^2}{60}} = 1.05 \text{ mph}$$

Step 2: Compute z_d

$$z_d = \frac{65.3 - 64.5}{1.05} = 0.76$$

Step 3: Find the Prob ($z \leq z_d$) from Text Table 5-1

$$\text{Prob }(z \leq 0.76) = 0.7764 = 77.64\%$$

Step 4: Compare Result to 95% Decision Criteria

As 77.64% is less than the minimum of 95% required to certify a statistically significant difference, the conclusion is that the observed reduction in average speeds *is not statistically significant.*

This result is important, in that it essentially implies that whatever traffic engineering measures were introduced to reduce speeds at this location were ineffective. The site must be reconsidered, and additional or different measures taken until a statistically significant reduction is achieved.

Even if the Normal Approximation results in a statistically significant reduction in observed average speeds, this result may be insufficient. Suppose a physical examination of the site in question determined that a safe average speed for vehicles traversing the site is 60 mph. Now the question is not whether or not the average speed of the population was re-

duced, but whether the observed "after" distribution has an average speed that can be considered statistically indistinguishable from 60 mph.

Note that the "after" study in the sample problem resulted in an average speed of 64.5 mph, with a standard deviation of 6 mph, based on 60 samples. If the "after" distribution is assumed to be normal, then:

$$\mu = \bar{x} \pm 1.96E$$

with 95% confidence. Thus, for the sample problem:

$$\mu = 64.5 \pm 1.96(6/\sqrt{60})$$

or:

$$\mu = 64.5 \pm 1.52 = 62.98 - 66.98 \text{ mph}$$

If the distribution is normal, then 95% of the time, the true mean speed of the population would be in this range. It is therefore less than 5% probable that the true mean of the population is the desired 60 mph. If the desired average speed lies outside the 95% confidence limits of the distribution, then it cannot be considered to have been achieved.

G. Testing for normalcy: The chi-square goodness-of-fit test

Many of the statistical analyses of the previous section rely on the assumption that the speed distributions in question are Normal. For completeness, it is therefore necessary to use the chi-square goodness-of-fit test (see Chapter 5) to verify this.

The statistic chi-squared is defined as:

$$\chi^2 = \sum_N \frac{(n_i - e_i)^2}{e_i}$$

where: e_i = theoretical frequency of observations in a particular speed group, assuming a normal distribution (in this case)

n_i = observed frequency of observations in a particular speed group, from field data

N = number of speed groups used

Table 7-3 illustrates the tabular implementation of this test for the illustrative spot speed data used throughout this section. Speed groups are already specified, and values of n_i can be taken directly from the Frequency Distribution Table of Table 7-2.

Table 7-3 Chi-Square Test on Illustrative Spot Speed Data

Average Speed (x) = 48.10 mph   Sample Size = 283

STD Speed (s) = 4.94 mph

Speed Group Upper Limit (mph)	Speed Group Lower Limit (mph)	Observed Frequency, n	Upper Limit IN < N[0.1] $x - \bar{x}$	Upper Limit IN < N[0.1] $z = \dfrac{x - \bar{x}}{s}$	Prob Of Occ $\leq z$ Table 5-1	Prob Of Occ In Group	Theoretical Frequency, e	n Comb Groups	e Comb Groups	Chi-Squared $\sum \dfrac{(n - e)^2}{e}$
∞	60	2	∞	∞	1.0000	0.0080	2.264 ⎫	7	6.452	0.0465
60	58	5	11.9	2.41	0.9920	0.0148	4.188 ⎭			
58	56	9	9.9	2.00	0.9772	0.0340	9.622	9	9.622	0.0402
56	54	14	7.9	1.60	0.9432	0.0602	17.037	14	17.0366	0.5412
54	52	24	5.9	1.19	0.8830	0.0978	27.677	24	27.6774	0.4886
52	50	37	3.9	0.79	0.7852	0.1372	38.828	37	38.8276	0.0860
50	48	62	1.9	0.38	0.6480	0.1560	44.148	62	44.148	7.2188
48	46	46	−0.1	−0.02	0.4920	0.1581	44.742	46	44.7423	0.0354
46	44	33	−2.1	−0.43	0.3339	0.1306	36.960	33	36.9598	0.4242
44	42	21	−4.1	−0.83	0.2033	0.0940	26.602	21	26.602	1.1797
42	40	13	−6.1	−1.23	0.1093	0.0588	16.640	13	16.6404	0.7964
40	38	7	−8.1	−1.64	0.0505	0.0298	8.433	7	8.4334	0.2436
38	36	5	−10.1	−2.04	0.0207	0.0136	3.849 ⎫	10	5.858	2.9285
36	34	5	−12.1	−2.45	0.0071	0.0071	2.009 ⎭			
						1.0000	283.000	283	283.000	14.0291

Chi-Square = 14.0291

Degs of Freedom = 12 − 3 = 9

For convenience, the speed groups are listed from highest to lowest. This is to coordinate with the Standard Normal Distribution table of this text (Table 5-1), which gives probabilities of z being less than or equal to a stated value. The upper limit of the highest speed group is adjusted to "infinity," as the theoretical Normal Distribution continues to both positive and negative infinity. The remaining columns of Table 7-3 focus on determining the theoretical frequencies, e_i, and computing the final value of X^2.

To find the theoretical frequency, i.e., the number of observations that would have occurred in each speed group if the distribution were perfectly Normal, we have to determine the probability of an occurrence within each of the speed group limits using the Standard Normal Distribution. Columns 4–8 of Table 7-3 do this, as follows:

1. Convert the upper limit of each speed group (in mph) to an equivalent value of z on the Standard Normal Distribution. This is done in two steps: (a) first the observed average value (48.10 mph) is subtracted from the upper limit of the speed group, resulting in the value shown in column 4; (b) the result of column 4 is divided by the observed standard deviation (4.94 mph). These two operations perform the standard transformation:

$$z = \frac{x - \bar{x}}{s}$$

2. Each value of z is now looked up in the Standard Normal Distribution table of the text. From this, the probability of z being less than the value shown is determined.

3. Consider the 58–56 mph speed group in Table 7-3: If the proportion of vehicles traveling at or below 58 mph is 0.9772 and the proportion of vehicles traveling at or below 56 mph is 0.9432, then the proportion of vehicles traveling between 58 and

56 mph is $0.9772 - 0.9432 = 0.0340$. Thus, the proportion of vehicles that theoretically should fall within any given group is found by successive subtractions of the proportions $\leq z$ in column 6 of Table 7-3.

4. Once the proportion of vehicles theoretically in each speed group is determined (col. 7, Table 7-3), the theoretical frequencies, e_i, are found by multiplying this value by the sample size of the study, 283 in this case. Fractional values of e_i are permitted.

5. The chi-square test is only valid when all values of e_i are greater than 5. In Table 7-3, the two highest and two lowest speed groups do not meet this criteria. To adjust, the two highest speed groups are combined, as are the two lowest. The resulting combined groups now each have values of e_i greater than 5. The values of n_i are also combined for these groups.

6. For each speed group, the value of $(n_i - e_i)^2/e_i$ may now be computed, and the values summed to find X^2. As shown in Table 7-3, for the sample speed study, the value is 14.0291.

7. To assess the meaning of this result, the number of *degrees of freedom* for the sample must be determined. It is found as the number of speed groups (after combinations have occurred) minus 3. One degree of freedom is lost for each piece of data from the distribution used in the computation of X^2. In this case, the mean, the standard deviation, and the sample size were used, causing the loss of 3 degrees of freedom. For the sample study of Table 7-3, degrees of freedom $= 12 - 3$ or 9.

The chi-square distribution is shown in Table 5-8 of the text. Probability values are shown on the horizontal axis of the table. The vertical axis shows degrees of freedom. The values of X^2 are in the body of the table. Because the computed value of X^2 is rarely an exact value shown in the table, interpolation is often required to find the correct probability. For the sample problem (d.f. $= 9$), 14.0291 falls between 11.39 (Prob $= 0.25$) and 14.68 (Prob $= 0.10$). Note also that the probability shown is that for a value being greater than or equal to X^2, the reverse of what is shown in the Standard Normal Distribution table. Interpolating:

$$\text{Prob } (\chi^2 \geq 14.0291) = 0.10 + (0.15)\frac{14.68 - 14.0291}{14.68 - 11.39}$$

$$= 0.130$$

Thus, it is 13% probable that a value of X^2 as high or higher than 14.0291 would occur if the sample distribution were Normal. We use the same criteria for acceptance of a statistically significant difference between the assumed and actual distribution as is used for testing for differences in sample means. In the Normal Approximation test, the probability of a value being *less than or equal to z* had to be 95% *or greater* to accept a statistically significant difference in sample means. This can be translated to a probability of a value *greater than z* being 5% *or less*. This, then, is the criteria applied to the chi-square test. To say that the assumed (Normal) distribution is statistically different from the sample data, the probability of X^2 being greater than or equal to the computed value must be *less than or equal to 5%*. Since this criteria is not met in our example (Prob $= 13\%$), the data and the assumed Normal Distribution are NOT statistically different, i.e., they may be considered to be the same. This determination validates previous analyses on the data that relied on the assumption of normality.

Barring a significant skew in the data caused by physical or regulatory constraints at the site, most speed distributions will be statistically Normal, validating the analyses previously discussed. If the distribution is NOT Normal, other statistical distributions can be fit, and other tests can be employed. These are not covered in this text, and the student is referred to standard statistical texts.

Travel time studies

While spot speed studies are generally used to determine driver-selected speeds unhindered by congestion, travel time studies are often used specifically to evaluate the extent and causes of congestion.

Travel time studies generally involve significant lengths of a facility, or group of facilities. Information on travel time between key points within the study section is sought, and is used to identify those sections or segments in need of improvement. Such studies are normally coordinated with *delay* observations, and *stopped delay* is the most easily observed measure.

Travel time information is used for many purposes:

- to identify problem locations on facilities by virtue of high travel times and delays
- to measure arterial level of service, based on average travel speeds and travel times

- to provide necessary input to traffic assignment models, which focus on link travel times as a key determinant of the route selected by the driver
- to provide travel time data for economic evaluations of transportation improvements, in which the economic value of travel time is a major factor
- to develop contour maps and other depictions of traffic congestion in an area or region

A. Field Techniques

Because travel time studies take place over an extended length of a facility, the most frequently-used methodology for collecting data is by running *test cars* through the section and making observations of intermediate travel times and stopped delays at key locations along the study route.

To assure some uniformity of data, drivers of test vehicles are instructed to use one of three driving strategies:

1. *Floating Car Technique:* In this procedure, the driver of the test car is instructed to pass as many vehicles as pass the test car. In this way, the average position of the vehicle in the traffic stream is maintained, and measurements tend to reflect average conditions within the traffic stream. Such a driving technique is productive when volumes are low, or when there is a single lane in each direction of travel. On a freeway, however, this could become very difficult, as passings occur frequently, and congestion may prevent a test-car driver from maintaining his/her position safely.
2. *Maximum Car Technique:* In this procedure, the driver is instructed to drive as fast as is safely practical in the traffic stream, without ever driving faster than the design speed of the facility. This is a less stressful procedure, but does not tend to estimate *average* conditions within the traffic stream. When using this technique, travel times reflect the faster range of the traffic stream, and often approximate 85th percentile average travel speeds.
3. *Average Car Technique:* In this procedure, the driver is asked to approximate the average conditions in the traffic stream, using his/her judgment only. This is a less stressful driving approach, but leaves a great deal to the judgment of individual drivers. Consistency of data may be somewhat compromised here, although the method will approximate average conditions in the traffic stream.

When using test-car study techniques, the vehicle may be equipped with a tape device that records speed vs. position throughout the route. The tape is analyzed later to obtain the desired information. If data is to be recorded manually, an observer with stop watches accompanies the driver and enters information into a field sheet of the type illustrated in Figure 7-7.

Issues related to sample size are handled similarly to spot speed studies. One of the reasons for specifying a driving strategy for test cars is to restrict the standard deviation of test-car results—leading to smaller required sample sizes. For most common applications, the required number of test-car runs ranges between 6–10 at the low end, to approximately 50 at the high end. The latter number is difficult to achieve without affecting traffic, and may require that runs be taken over an extended period of time, such as the evening rush hour over several days.

Other techniques may be used to estimate travel times. *License plates* can be used. Observers along a route record license plate numbers and the time each vehicle passed the checkpoint. License plates at various checkpoints must then be matched and travel times determined. This procedure leads to only travel time data, because the detail of individual stopped delays is lost. Sampling is quite difficult. If only 50% of the license plates are recorded at each checkpoint, then the probability of having a match at *only two checkpoints* is $(0.50 \times 0.50) = 0.25$. As there is no driving strategy to reduce the observed standard deviation, many more license plate matches are required than test-car runs to obtain similar precision and confidence in the results.

Where elevated observation points allow an entire study section to be observed, the progress of individual vehicles in the traffic stream may be directly observed. To insure adequate sample sizes, such studies usually involve videotaping the section so that many or even all vehicles can be traced in the laboratory.

B. Illustrative applications of travel time studies

This section presents two interesting cases for insight, using hypothetical but very plausible data bases for the first case. The second case is an interesting question of what to do when the "default" curves specified in some manuals and procedures need to be reconsidered.

Site _____ Run _____ Time Start _____ A.M./P.M.
Recorder _____ Comments _____
Note: Record of Checkpoints must be submitted.

- -

Checkpoint Number	Cumulative Section Length (ft, mi)	Cumulative Travel Time (min:sec)	Per Section		Special Notes	Section Travel Time (sec, min)
			Delay (sec, min)	Stops (#)		

The average travel speed for the sections may also be computed.

Figure 7-7   Typical field sheet for test-car runs.

1. Travel time data on an arterial. Given the cost and logistics of travel time studies (cars, drivers, multiple runs, maybe multiple days), there is a natural tendency to keep the number of observations N as small as possible. This case considers a hypothetical arterial in which the true mean running time is 196 seconds over a three-mile run, with a standard deviation of 15 seconds. The distribution of *this* variability is given as normal, just to keep the problem simple (one can also argue effectively that it is very plausible).

If the drivers were able to traverse the arterial at the running speed, the mean travel time would be 196 seconds and 95% of the observations would fall within $1.96(15) = 29.4$ seconds of that value. Consid-

ering the outer bounds of this range, the corresponding speeds would be:

223.4 seconds over 3 miles, or 47.9 mph

166.6 seconds over 3 miles, or 64.8 mph

The speed corresponding to the true average travel time of 196 seconds is 55 mph. Note that the average of the two outer limits is not 55 mph but rather 56.3 mph, but is not relevant. The speed should be computed from the average travel time as [3 mi/(196 secs/3600 secs/hr)] = 55 mph.[3]

[3]The discrepancy is due to the fact that whereas the travel times TT were specified as symmetric, the corresponding speed distribution L/TT is somewhat skewed.

However, this is not the end of this case. Consider that in addition to the natural variability of how the drivers chose to drive the arterial, there is a randomness due to stopping at signals. Specifically, it is postulated that:

Number of Signal Stops	Probability	Duration (red, plus decel/accel)
0	0.55	0 sec
1	0.30	40 sec
2	0.15	80 sec

Figure 7-8 shows some data that *could* result from the combination of the inherent driver randomness and the signal delay effects. There are $N = 20$ observations in the data displayed in Figure 7-8.

The estimated mean travel time is 224.1 seconds over three miles in this particular data, with an estimated standard deviation of 37.8 seconds over the three miles. The 95% confidence bounds on the mean are $\pm 1.96(37.8)/20^{0.5} = \pm 16.6$ seconds over the three miles. Expressing the travel time estimates in the form of space mean speeds:

Average Travel Speed (estimated)
= [3 mi/(224.1 secs/3600 secs/hr)] = 48.2 mph

95% confidence bounds
= [3 mi/(240.7 secs/3600 secs/hr)] = 44.9 mph
= [3 mi/(207.5 secs/3600 secs/hr)] = 52.0 mph

It is notable that $N = 20$ samples resulted in this rather broad range (given the stated assumptions on the underlying distribution).

Note that although the *data* of Figure 7-8 does not look normal, this is not a requirement in the above discussion. The distribution of the travel time distribution is in fact *not* normal, for it is the sum of a normally distributed travel time based on driver preference plus another distribution, described above for the signal delays. However, the **sum** of twenty observations from this distribution can—and probably does—look reasonably normally distributed.

2. Overriding default values. Figure 7-9 shows a default curve that might be used in a state handbook or other manual, drawn from [1] or other sources. In order to use another value, the case should be made that the proposed value is *significantly different* than the default curve's recommended value.

As a practical matter, the default values of running time (and thus running speed) contained in [1] are thought to be too low by some practitioners. They make the case that higher values are routinely expected. This implies that a one-sided error is expected, and thus a one-sided hypothesis test should be used.

For a certain volume V_1, let us say that the default curve of Figure 7-9 indicates an average travel speed of 40.0 mph. Based on three travel time runs over the two mile section, an applicant wishes to use the observed average travel speed of 43.0 mph. Is this acceptable? That is, is the 3.0 mph apparent difference actually *significantly* different?

Figure 7-10 shows the probable distribution of the random variable $Y = (\Sigma TT_i/N)$, the estimator of the

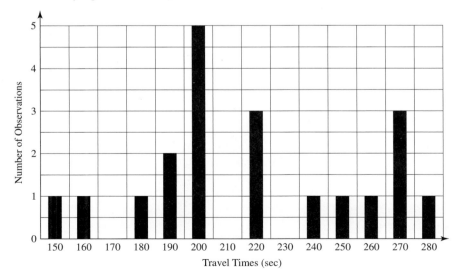

Figure 7-8 Histogram of hypothetical travel time data, $N = 20$ independent runs over three mile segment.

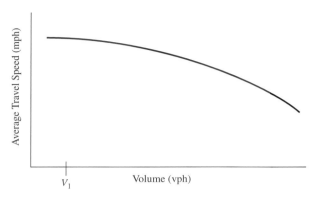

Figure 7-9   Default curve specified by agency (illustrative).

true average travel time, given the default and proposed average travel speeds. These are formulated as the null and alternative hypotheses, respectively, on an average travel time scale.

As can be seen from Figure 7-10, if the proposed difference is Δ, then Y^* must be set no more than $\Delta/2$, so that:

$$1.645\sigma_{TT}/n^{0.5} \leq \Delta/2$$

This assumes that the Type I and Type II error probabilities are equalized at 0.05. Assume that σ_{TT} has been measured to be 28 seconds over the two miles.

The specific values imply that $\Delta = 12.6$ seconds (Figure 7-10) so that $n \geq 54$ observations are required to balance the Type I and Type II errors at 0.05 and proceed. Given that the applicant has only $n = 3$ samples, the contention cannot even be considered.

For three values of proposed alternatives, with a default of 40 mph, one can compute:

Default (Null)	Proposed (Alternative)	Required N	Decision Pt Y*
40 mph	42 mph	≥115	41.0 mph
40 mph	43 mph	≥54	41.4 mph
40 mph	44 mph	≥32	41.9 mph
40 mph	45 mph	≥22	42.4 mph

That is, if a proposed change to 43 mph is suggested, at least 54 observations are required. However, ac-

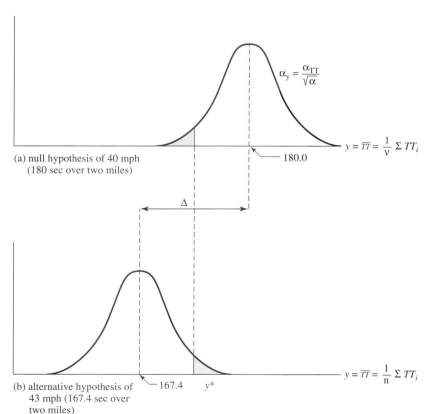

(a) null hypothesis of 40 mph (180 sec over two miles)

(b) alternative hypothesis of 43 mph (167.4 sec over two miles)

Figure 7-10   Default (null) and proposed (alternative) hypotheses.

cording to this formulation, an observed average travel speed of more than 41.4 mph will justify the switch to a new value of 43 mph. Note that the "decision point" values of speed are based on ½ the difference of the *travel times* implied by these speeds for the 2-mile test section.

It is strongly recommended that the student consider the implications of the above illustration *as formulated* and suggest a better or more appropriate formulation. Should the Type II error be equalized with the Type I error? Does the existence of a preferred or default value imply that it should not? Should we ever end up in a situation in which a larger substituted value is allowed than was ever seen? (For instance, suppose an average travel speed of 42.0 mph was seen with $N = 16$: Can we really agree to a revised value of 43 mph?)

3. Adequate sample sizes. Common practice is to use rather small numbers of travel time runs, simply because of the cost. The preceding examples show that rather large sample sizes are needed, unless data can support *much* smaller values of σ_{TT} than are being used in these cases.

Without such smaller values of σ_{TT}, it is difficult for applicants to propose and justify overriding default values *in individual cases,* due to the sample sizes required. However, a compendium of such cases—each individually with small sample sizes—can and should motivate an agency to review the default values/curves.

4. Defining the system. There are some practical aspects not directly related to the statistics applied above. For instance, the question sometimes arises as to the definition of the arterial in doing travel time runs—is the upstream delay at the first signal to be included or not? This question should be re-stated as, what is the system of interest? If it includes the first intersection, then the delay associated with that signal must be included, and the actual run must begin further upstream. It is convenient—but wrong—to eliminate the bottleneck intersection simply to make the defined "system" look good.

Intersection delay studies

Some types of delay are measured as part of a travel time study by noting the location and duration of stopped periods during the test run. Signalized intersections present a special problem, in that the sample sizes generally involved in test-car measurements are insufficient for a good estimate of delay at a *particular* signalized intersection.

Delay at a signalized intersection is of particular interest, because it is the *measure of effectiveness* used to quantify level of service. The 1985 *Highway Capacity Manual* and its 1994 update define intersection level of service on the basis of *average individual stopped-time delay* per vehicle. In its 1997 update, stopped delay will be replaced by control delay. A methodology for measuring delay in the field is of significant interest, needed for cases falling outside the boundaries of predictive algorithms and to collect data for calibration of predictive algorithms.

The measurement methodology relies on a technique in which stopped vehicles on an intersection approach are counted at intervals of 10 to 20 seconds. It is assumed that any vehicle counted as stopped during one of these intervals will be stopped (on average) for the length of the interval. Figure 7-11 shows a typical field sheet for recording these observations. The departing volume must also be separately observed and recorded.

In general, the technique follows these steps:

1. The maximum extent of the queue on the intersection approach during the study period must be observed in advance; observers must be able to count *all* stopped vehicles in the longest anticipated queue.
2. The count interval is set at 10, 15, or 20 seconds. Stopped vehicles within the queuing area are observed and recorded at each interval within the study period.
3. Discharge volumes are separately counted for the study period. A total count is usually sufficient, except for longer studies, where summaries every 15 minutes are useful.

Sample data for such a study is illustrated in Table 7-4, and is used to illustrate how the data is manipulated to produce a delay estimate.

The total of stopped-vehicle counts (sometimes referred to as *density counts,* although the usage is inconsistent with the traditional use of density in vehs/mi) for the sample study is:

$$33 + 34 + 31 + 24 = 122$$

It is assumed that each of these vehicles stopped for a period of time equal to the counting interval of

Minute into Collection	Seconds into the Minute							Vehicles Arriving (veh)	Vehicles Discharge (veh)

Column total = _____ _____ _____ _____ _____ _____

Arrival total = _____

Discharge total = _____

Figure 7-11 Typical field sheet for intersection delay study.

Table 7-4 Illustrative Intersection Delay Data

Minute	Seconds into Minute:			
	0 sec	15 sec	30 sec	45 sec
5:00 P.M.	2	4	1	3
5:01 P.M.	3	5	3	0
5:02 P.M.	6	3	2	1
5:03 P.M.	4	5	4	3
5:04 P.M.	2	2	6	4
5:05 P.M.	4	4	1	1
5:06 P.M.	5	2	5	5
5:07 P.M.	1	3	3	3
5:08 P.M.	4	5	2	2
5:09 P.M.	2	1	4	2
Totals	33	34	31	24

Total Exiting Vehicles: 100

15 seconds. Therefore, the aggregate delay for the 10-minute study period is:

$$122 \text{ vehs} \times 15 \text{ sec} = 1830 \text{ vehicle-seconds}$$

As the total count of exiting vehicles was 100 vehicles, the average stopped delay per vehicle is:

$$1830/100 = 18.3 \text{ sec/veh}$$

This procedure yields relatively good estimates of stopped delay, as long as the full extent of the queue has been observed, and exit counts are accurate. If flow is unstable, i.e., if a residual queue is growing through the study period, then the number of exiting vehicles will not be equal to the number of entering vehicles. In such cases, the growth of the queue should be noted, and the number of *entering* vehicles used as the divisor when average delay per vehicle is computed. Of course, in such cases, the queue will likely grow beyond limits that can be easily observed, and this technique would then not be employed.

Delay is one of the more complicated measures used in traffic engineering. In fact, there are many definitions of delay in addition to the stopped-time delay addressed by this study technique. Approach delay, travel time delay, time-in-queue delay, and other measures are also in use. Chapter 16 discusses the various types of delay and their definitions and applications in detail, and presents the analytic models used to predict them.

This procedure is easily modified to approximately measure approach delay by including *all* vehicles (whether moving or stopped) in the intersection area.

Summary

Speed, travel time, and delay are all critical measures used in characterizing traffic streams, and the quality of operations on traffic facilities. This chapter has provided an overview of how these parameters are measured in the field. Reference [3] provides additional general material of interest.

References

1. *Highway Capacity Manual, Special Report 209,* 3rd Edition, Transportation Research Board, National Research Council, Washington, DC, (revised) 1994.
2. *A Policy on Geometric Design of Highways and Streets,* American Association of State Highway and Transportation Officials, Washington, DC, 1994.
3. Robertson, H., Hummer, J., and Nelson, D. (editors), M*anual of Traffic Engineering Studies,* Institute of Transportation Engineers, Prentice-Hall, Englewood Cliffs, NJ, 1994.

Problems

Problem 7–1

Table P7-1 shows a number of measurement techniques, but has left blank the method(s) of estimating time mean speed and space mean speed. Complete the table, using formulas if appropriate. If it is not possible to estimate either of these quantities, state why and indicate what exactly is being measured. In every case, list any assumptions.

Problem 7–2

(a) Recognizing that the travel time over a two-mile segment *might* be normally distributed with a mean of 120 seconds and a standard deviation of σ seconds, how many travel time runs will be needed to estimate the average travel speed ±2 mph with 95% confidence? Repeat for ±3 mph and ±5 mph, in each case for $\sigma =$ 10, 15, and 20 seconds. As in the text, work with the travel time distribution directly if at all possible.
(b) Is the assumption that the travel times are normally distributed important in determining the sample sizes in "a"?

Problem 7–3

When manually observing travel times, *parallax error,* which occurs due to angles in the line of sight, must be corrected. Figure 7-12 illustrates parallax error from an observation point above the plane of the road (as on the roof of a building).

Note that the measured trap length is L, but that travel times will actually be recorded as the vehicles travel distance d, because of the systematic error introduced by the line of sight. Thus, a correction to measured travel times must be made, such that:

$$TT_{true} = TT_{obs} \times \frac{L}{d}$$

Observing that the tangent of θ is L/h, and—by similar triangles—is also $(L - d)/x$, it follows that the correction may also be stated as:

$$TT_{true} = TT_{obs} \times \frac{h}{h - x}$$

Table P7-1   Some Measurement Techniques and Their Relation to Commonly Desired Indicators

Measurement Technique	Time Mean Speed? How (Equation)?	Space Mean Speed? How (Equation)?	Notes and Assumptions
1. Radar measurements at a fixed point in the road, vehicles randomly selected.			
2. Speed trap on a freeway, using two loops one hundred feet apart. All vehicles measured.			
3. Area detector that senses the speed of all vehicles in a larger section of road, 0.25 miles or longer.			
4. Travel times of all vehicles entering a link, measured over the full length of the link.			
5. Arterial travel times taken by sampling the entering vehicles from a vantage point (or video imaging system), and observing their travel times on the section under study.			
6. Arterial travel times taken by test car, with the driver instructed to "float" with the traffic so that he/she maintains relative position (net cars passing/being passed approximates zero).			

For a range of x from 2 ft to 10 ft, and h from 20 ft to 40 ft, compute the correction factor. Present it as a table or graph, depending upon which you judge is more effective. Select values of the correction factor for a compact car and for a single-unit truck, using your best judgment.

Problem 7–4

Collect 45 speed samples by establishing a trap of appropriate length on an assigned section of road. Use a stopwatch or portable computer to collect the data, and estimate the mean and standard deviation of the spot speed and the confidence bounds on the mean. Present the data in a histogram and cumulative plot.

For this problem, work in groups of two. If the data are to be used in Problem 7-5 also , then work within an assigned time period, (e.g., 2–4 P.M.), along a certain section of

road. Do not work at the same place and time as another group.

Problem 7–5

Collect the Problem 7–4 data of all groups in the class (including your own). Specify and execute a test to the effect that "All the data came from the same distribution." Comment on why the result is reasonable. If the hypothesis was rejected, look for reasons.

Problem 7–6

A series of travel-time runs are to be done. Tabulate the number of runs required to estimate the overall average travel time with 95% confidence

$$\pm 2 \text{ min,} \qquad \pm 5 \text{ min,} \qquad \pm 10 \text{ min}$$

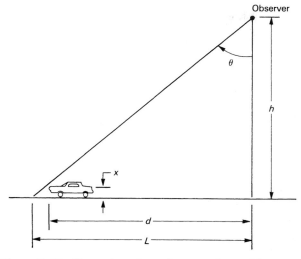

Figure 7-12   Illustration of parallax error for problem 7-3.

Travel Time	Vehicle Type
15.0 sec	Auto
14.4	Auto
14.4	Truck
16.3	Auto
15.5	Auto
13.9	Truck
15.0	Auto
14.6	Auto
16.3	Auto
11.8	Truck
15.5	Auto
15.9	Auto
12.6	Truck
13.7	Auto

for standard deviations of 5, 10, and 15 minutes. Note that a 3 × 3 table of values is desired.

Problem 7–7

For this problem, a section of arterial must be assigned or selected. The section should be at least three miles long and have five to seven signalized intersections. (If necessary, count only *major* intersections so as to achieve the five-to-seven number.) Execute five travel time runs in each direction using the "average car" method, completing the form in Figure 7-7. (If a one-way arterial is used, do the second direction on the street used for the return trip.)

(a) Tabulate and graphically present the results of travel time and delay runs. The equipment used may be stopwatches, computer, or other available hardware. Work in groups of two.
(b) Note that the number of runs suggested in this problem is not necessarily consistent with the results of Problem 7-6, but is set at five only to make it a reasonable assignment. How many groups will have to pool their results to achieve ±3 min on the 95% confidence bounds?

If it is not practical to organize the field studies called for in this problem, use the sample data from such a study provided in Table P7-2.

Problem 7–8

The following travel times were observed over a 1000-foot section from a vantage point on the tenth floor of a building:

The vehicles were selected by sampling whatever vehicle was entering the section, choosing one every 30 seconds.

Estimate the time mean speed and the space mean speed, by vehicle type, and overall. List any assumptions needed to provide any of the estimates. If possible, estimate the standard deviation of the speed(s).

Problem 7–9

The following stopped vehicles were observed as part of a delay study on the northbound approach of the Main Street–Church Street intersection:

Minute	Seconds Into Minute			
	0 sec	15 sec	30 sec	45 sec
7:20 A.M.	4	2	1	2
7:21	5	3	0	2
7:22	6	2	2	1
7:23	7	4	2	2
7:24	5	5	2	1
7:25	4	3	3	0
7:26	7	4	2	0
7:27	6	3	1	1
7:28	3	2	0	1
7:29	8	4	1	2

The discharge was 97 vehicles during the period, and the arrival was 101 vehicles. Estimate the total delay on the approach, and the delay per vehicle.

Problem 7–10

Consider the following spot speed data:

Speed Group (mph)	Number of Vehicles (f)
15–20	0
20–25	3
25–30	6
30–35	18
35–40	45
40–45	48
45–50	18
50–55	12
55–60	4
60–65	3
65–70	0

(a) Plot the frequency-distribution curve and cumulative frequency-distribution curve for these data.

(b) Find and identify on the curves: mean speed, standard deviation, modal speed, pace, and percent vehicles in the pace. (Show both computed values and values derived from the curves where applicable.)

(c) The true mean speed is between ____ mph and ____ mph with a confidence of 99.7%. What is the interval for a confidence of 95%?

Table P7-2   Travel time data for problem 7–7

Site ___Erin Blvd._____   Run ___Summary___   Time ___Start 5–7 P.M._____

Recorder ___XYZ_____   Comments _____

Note: Record of checkpoints must be submitted.

Checkpoint Number	Cumulative Section Length (mi)	Cumulative Travel Time (min:sec)	Per Section Delay (sec)	Stops (#)	Special Notes	Section Travel Time (sec, min)
1	—	—				
2	1.00	2:05	10	1		
3	2.25	4:50	30	1		
4	3.50	7:30	25	1		
5	4.00	9:10	42	2		
6	4.25	10:27	47	1		
7	5.00	11:54	—	—		

The average travel speed for the sections may also be computed.

(d) Based on this study, what is the sample size necessary to yield ±2.5 mph with 95% confidence?

(e) Another speed study was taken at this location after the imposition of a reduced speed limit. The study resulted in an average speed of 40.0 mph and a standard deviation of 6.91 mph for 100 speeds. Was the new speed limit successful in reducing speeds?

(f) Conduct a χ goodness-of-fit test to determine whether the data are normally distributed or not.

Problem 7–11

The following travel times were measured for vehicles as they traversed a 2.0 mile segment of highway. Compute the time mean speed and the space mean speed. Why is space mean speed always lower than time mean speed?

Vehicle	Travel Time (min)
1	2.6
2	2.4
3	2.4
4	2.8
5	2.2
6	2.1

Express TMS and SMS in mph.

Problem 7–12

Consider the following two spot speed samples conducted at a test location to determine whether or not prevailing speeds have been reduced to an average of 50 mph.

Before		After
55.3 mph	$\bar{x}$	52.8 mph
5.0 mph	s	5.6 mph
100	N	85

(a) Was the new speed limit effective in reducing average speeds at this location?

(b) Was the new speed limit effective in reducing average speeds to 50 mph at this location?

▶ **NOTE:** Problem 7–13 requires the use of a ball-bank indicator, and may require a permit or authorization from the agency responsible for the road used.

Problem 7–13

Working in teams of three at an assigned horizontal curve, do at least five runs in each direction, estimating the maximum comfortable speed in each direction. At the same time, let each person rate each run as "comfortable" or "uncomfortable." Report the results. Comment on (a) the variability of the data from run to run, (b) the difference in results (if any) in the two directions, and (c) the comparison of the subjective judgment of the occupants to the results obtained from the ball-bank test procedure. Compare the results to the posted advisory speed, if any.

▶ **NOTE:** Problems 7–14 through 7–18 require the use of a statistics text or reference and some background in statistics beyond that presented in this text.

Problem 7–14

An enforcement program is instituted along a rural four-lane road with a known speed problem. It is expected that the resulting reduction in average spot speed (time mean speed) will be at least 5 mph. Therefore, a null and alternative hypothesis are to be tested as follows:

H_o: There is no reduction in the average speed.

H_1: There is a 5 mph reduction in the average speed.

(a) Specify the test procedure such that the Type I and Type II errors are equal.

(b) Tabulate and plot the level of significance as a function of the number of samples, from $N = 10$ to $N = 300$. Assume the same number of samples before and after.

(c) Is the assumption of the same number of samples before and after the best one that could be made?

(d) If you can afford only the number of samples that will yield a level of significance of 0.50, is it worthwhile to run the test?

Problem 7–15

Specify a test procedure to investigate whether there is a change in the variance due to a new speed limit, such as the elimination of the national 55-mph limit. Is it necessary to assume that the mean has not changed?

Problem 7–16

Two different procedures are used to measure "delay" on the same intersection approach at the same time.

Both are expressed in terms of delay per vehicle. The objective is to see which procedure can be best used in the field. Assume that the following data are available from the field:

Delay (sec/veh)	
Procedure 1	Procedure 2
8.4	7.2
9.2	8.1
10.9	10.3
13.2	10.3
12.7	11.2
10.8	7.5
15.3	10.7
12.3	10.5
19.7	11.9
8.0	8.7
7.4	5.9
26.7	18.6
12.1	8.2
10.7	8.5
10.1	7.5
12.0	9.5
11.9	8.1
10.0	8.8
22.0	19.8
41.3	36.4

(a) A statistician, asked whether the data "are the same," conducts tests on the mean and the variance to determine "whether they are the same" at a level of significance of 0.05. Use the appropriate tests on the hypothesis that the difference in the means is zero and the variances are equal. Do the computations. Present the conclusions.

(b) Would it have been more appropriate to use the "paired-*t*" test in part (a) (rather than a simple *t* test)? Why or why not? What are the advantages of the paired-*t* test. If the paired *t*-test is used, what variance test is used (if any)?

(c) Reflect on the basic purpose of the field tests. Is it necessary that the results have the same mean and standard deviation in order for one field procedure to be substituted for the other? Plot a scatter diagram of the data. Compute the correlation coefficient. Suggest a means of estimating procedure 1 values while using procedure 2 in the field (or vice-versa).

Problem 7–17

Specify a procedure for estimating the confidence bounds on the 85th-percentile speed.

Problem 7–18

Consider the following two spot-speed samples conducted at a test location at which a new speed limit has been installed:

Before		After
62.3 mph	$\bar{x}$	60.5 mph
5.2 mph	s	6.1 mph
20	n	15

Is the reduction in mean speeds significant? Are the standard deviations statistically equivalent?

8

Accident Studies

In 1996, 43,300 people were killed on U.S. highways in a staggering 11,200,000 accidents. More people have been killed in the United States in traffic accidents than in all of the wars in which this nation has been involved, from the Revolutionary War to Vietnam. These facts vividly illustrate the over-riding importance of traffic safety as the primary professional objective of the traffic engineer. Table 8-1 provides additional sobering statistics for 1996 [1].

Obviously, a great deal of effort on every level of the profession is focused on the reduction of these numbers. U.S. highways have become increasingly safe for a variety of reasons. Highway design has incorporated many safety improvements, including better alignments, safer roadside and guardrail design, breakaway sign and lighting supports, impact attenuating devices, and similar features. Vehicle design has also improved, with padded dashboards, seat belts and harnesses, air bags, anti-lock brakes, side beams, and other features. While it is difficult to say that drivers have improved, it is clear that they have become more familiar with driving on freeways and in congested urban areas. All of these improvements have led to

steadily decreasing fatality and accident *rates* nationwide. Americans, however, continue to drive more each year, leaving total fatality and injury numbers frighteningly high. Americans have now exceeded *2 trillion vehicle miles of travel* each year. The trend of increasing vehicle use has continued for over 30 years, except for a brief perturbation in the 1970s during the years of the fuel crisis.

While federal efforts aimed at improving highway safety are significant, the efforts are hardly proportional to the attention paid to safety in other transportation modes. A single aircraft accident results immediately in thorough and costly investigations by several agencies, and a full review of policies and regulations when the cause is identified. The tragic explosion of the *Challenger* spacecraft resulted in an investigation of more than a year, and significant design modifications were made before another shuttle flight took place. Certainly, this type of attention is justified. On the other hand, in 1996, 119 people were killed in motor vehicle accidents every day—a rate of one every 12.1 minutes. Despite this, the scale of public attention and focus on highway safety remains

Table 8-1 Accident Statistics for 1996

Accident Type	Number of Deaths/ Disabling Injuries	Number of Accidents	Number of Vehicles Involved
Fatal	43,300	38,200	57,400
Disabling Injuries*	2,600,000	1,600,000	2,900,000
Property Damage Only (PDO)	N/A	9,600,000	15,900,000

*Injuries occurring in both fatal and disabling injury accidents. [From *Accident Facts,* National Safety Council, 1997.]

relatively low compared to that of other modes. The challenge for the traffic engineer is clear: The statistics of Table 8-1 represent a massive loss of life and a significant cost to society. They can never be accepted as the inevitable "cost of doing business" and must always be the focus of attention when traffic engineering issues are considered.

Approaches to highway safety

Improving highway safety requires consideration of the three elements influencing traffic operations: the driver, the vehicle, and the roadway. Unfortunately, the traffic engineer has effective control over only one of these elements—the roadway. Indirectly, by conducting studies and influencing state and federal legislation, the traffic engineer can influence driver licensing procedures, vehicle design, and vehicle registration programs.

There are several different ways in which improvements in traffic safety can be approached.

A. Reducing accident occurrence

Preventing accidents from occurring is the most effective means to improve highway safety. It is also the most difficult and complex task to accomplish. The causes of traffic accidents are many and complex, but studies show that 96% of all accidents involve some form of driver error. Thus, the most effective means to prevent accidents from occurring is the improvement of driver skills through training and testing programs,

and the removal of drivers with bad accident and/or violation records from the highways.

The traffic engineer can also provide designs that minimize the risk of driver error. Proper signing and marking reduce driver confusion and the risk of error. Highway designs that avoid sudden changes in geometry, provide good sight distance, and provide for smooth transitions between geometric elements can also reduce the chance of driver error. It is no "accident" that the lowest accident rates occur on freeways, where the standards for geometry, signing, and marking are the highest.

Many traffic controls, such as signals and STOP signs, eliminate or reduce conflicts in the traffic stream that could lead to accidents. The proper implementation of controls is the traffic engineer's most effective means of eliminating accidents.

Driver training and removal of "bad" drivers from the highways are complex issues involving licensing and enforcement procedures. These are usually treated as programmatic measures, which are discussed in greater detail later in this chapter.

B. Reducing the severity of accidents

While preventing the occurrence of accidents is difficult, many highway design and traffic engineering measures are aimed at reducing the severity of accidents when they occur.

A "forgiving highway" is one that is designed recognizing those locations at which accidents are most likely to occur. These locations are designed in such a way as to give drivers time and space to "recover" from errors and to minimize the severity of the accident when it occurs. Proper use of guardrail, median barriers, impact attenuators, and breakaway signpost and light standards, for example, can reduce the damage done when a vehicle leaves the travel lane. Gore areas on freeway off-ramps are kept free of objects, because indecisive drivers often encroach into the area and require the opportunity to recover from their error.

These and other measures reduce the severity of accidents and can affect injury and fatality rates, even where accidents still occur.

C. Improving crash survivability

Crash survivability primarily involves vehicle design. Vehicles should be designed to absorb most of the impact of an accident without transferring it to the occupants. Such design features as energy-absorbing bumper systems, padded dashboards, seat belts, air bags, and similar measures are all attempts to improve crash survivability. Except through legislative influence, the traffic engineer has little to do with this aspect of safety.

D. Programmatic safety efforts

A number of federal and state programs attempt to address traffic safety on a policy level. These legislative measures attack various aspects of safety that have been identified through study and research. The listing below is a sampling of some of the more notable programs influencing traffic safety:

• state vehicle inspection programs
• national speed limit (eliminated in 1996)
• national 21 year-old drinking age
• state DWI programs
• federal vehicle design standards

Traffic engineers need to be involved in the development of these programs and to provide guidance and input to policy-makers through professional and community organizations. As long as traffic accidents occur, all levels of government will attempt to deal with the problem programmatically. The programs must be well founded in research, and must concentrate on specific ways to improve safety.

E. Design aspects of safety

Highway design can significantly impact traffic safety. While it would take an entire text to adequately cover the highway design features influencing safety, several are particularly vital:

• horizontal and vertical alignment
• roadside design
• median barriers
• gore areas

Horizontal and vertical alignment are controlled by design speed—the maximum safe speed at which a vehicle can operate along a highway. A vehicle traveling at the design speed always has sufficient sight distance to stop if a stopped vehicle or other obstruction suddenly appears at the limit of the driver's sight line. The more sight distance provided, the safer the highway will be, particularly if drivers do not increase their speed to the safety limit. The reduction of accident rates observed after imposition of the 55-mph national speed limit in 1974 was also influenced by the fact that most newer U.S. freeways and rural highways are designed to 70-mph standards. Given sight distances adequate for 70-mph operation, slower operation provided for an even greater margin of error.

Roadside design is a critical safety feature, as this area is often encroached on by drivers in an accident. Clear shoulders, gentle side slopes, and absence of solid objects give the driver time to recover. Signposts and other roadside objects should be either protected by guardrails or of the "breakaway" type that minimizes impact damage.

Much research effort has focused on the design of barrier systems. Familiar barrier types, such as the W-beam, box-beam, and reinforced concrete barriers, all serve various functions, depending on the degree of flexibility or impenetrability required. The box-beam system is extremely flexible and is designed to deflect as much as 10 to 15 feet when impacted. It gently forces a vehicle to a stop or back into the traffic stream in the proper orientation. It requires, however, sufficient space to accommodate such deflections.

The W-beam design is also flexible, but does not deflect nearly as much as the box-beam, so it is employed where space prohibits any substantial encroachment. Where impenetrability is the issue, such as in many urban facility medians, reinforced concrete is used. It is not designed to deflect at all. Rather, it forces the vehicle into the general direction of traffic and stops it through friction. Concrete barriers are the most difficult to cross; they can be crossed only by breaking through the barrier or by "jumping" over it.

Gore areas have been noted previously. Their design is critical, as this area will frequently be crossed by vehicles. Thus, it is important that there be few objects to hit, and that all signing and other features located there be on breakaway supports. In extreme cases, where heavy abutments or other structures must be located in the gore area, impact attenuators are a must.

The important subject of highway safety can be covered only in overview in a general text such as this. The preceding sections have provided a brief introduction. The sections that follow focus on three aspects of traffic safety that directly concern traffic engineers: data collection and record systems, accident statistics and their interpretation, and site analysis.

Accident data collection and record systems

In order to further improve the safety of the highway system, the traffic engineer must have information and data on the location, frequency, severity, and types of accidents that are occurring. There can be no hope of determining *why* such accidents occur, and of developing corrective measures, unless details describing their occurrence are recorded.

The study of traffic accidents is fundamentally different from that employed to observe other traffic-stream parameters. Because accidents occur relatively infrequently, and at unpredictable times and locations, they cannot be objectively observed as they occur. Thus, all accident data come from secondary sources—motorist and police accident reports. A system for gathering, storing, and retrieving such information in a useful form must be carefully designed and monitored to provide the traffic engineer with the data needed to properly evaluate and correct traffic-safety deficiencies.

Such an information base must allow the following critical analyses to take place:

1. Identification of locations at which unusually high numbers of accidents occur

2. Detailed functional evaluation of high-accident locations to determine contributing causes of accidents at the location
3. Development of general statistical measures of various accident-related factors to give insight into general trends, common causal factors, driver profiles, and similar information
4. Development of procedures that allow the identification of hazards *before* large numbers of accidents occur

Accident data-collection and record systems accomplish the first of these important requirements.

A. Accident reporting

The ultimate basis for all accident data and information is the individual accident report. Every state requires any motorist involved in an accident that causes property damage above a stated limit to report that accident to the state motor vehicle bureau. In addition, more serious accidents, particularly those involving injury or death, will be investigated by a police officer, who will also file an accident report.

The police accident report is more useful, as often the officer has been trained in filling these out and is an impartial observer of the accident. Motorist forms are clearly *not* unbiased, and various participants in the accident may turn in markedly different versions of the facts.

Figure 8-1 illustrates a typical accident form to be filled out by a police officer. In the narrative portion, the officer is expected to provide details of the accident and to provide interpretations as to likely contributing causes of the accident.

Central to any accident form is a diagram schematically illustrating the accident. While these are often poorly done, they are a principal source of information for the traffic engineer in the study of individual accident locations.

It must be noted that many accidents go unreported. An early study of accidents in Illinois [2] estimated that as many as 71% of all auto involvements and 80% of all truck involvements go unreported. An "involvement" is one vehicle involved in an accident—a three-car accident is *one* accident and *three* involvements. This includes all those property-damage-only accidents falling below legal reporting limits, and many that should be reported but are not.

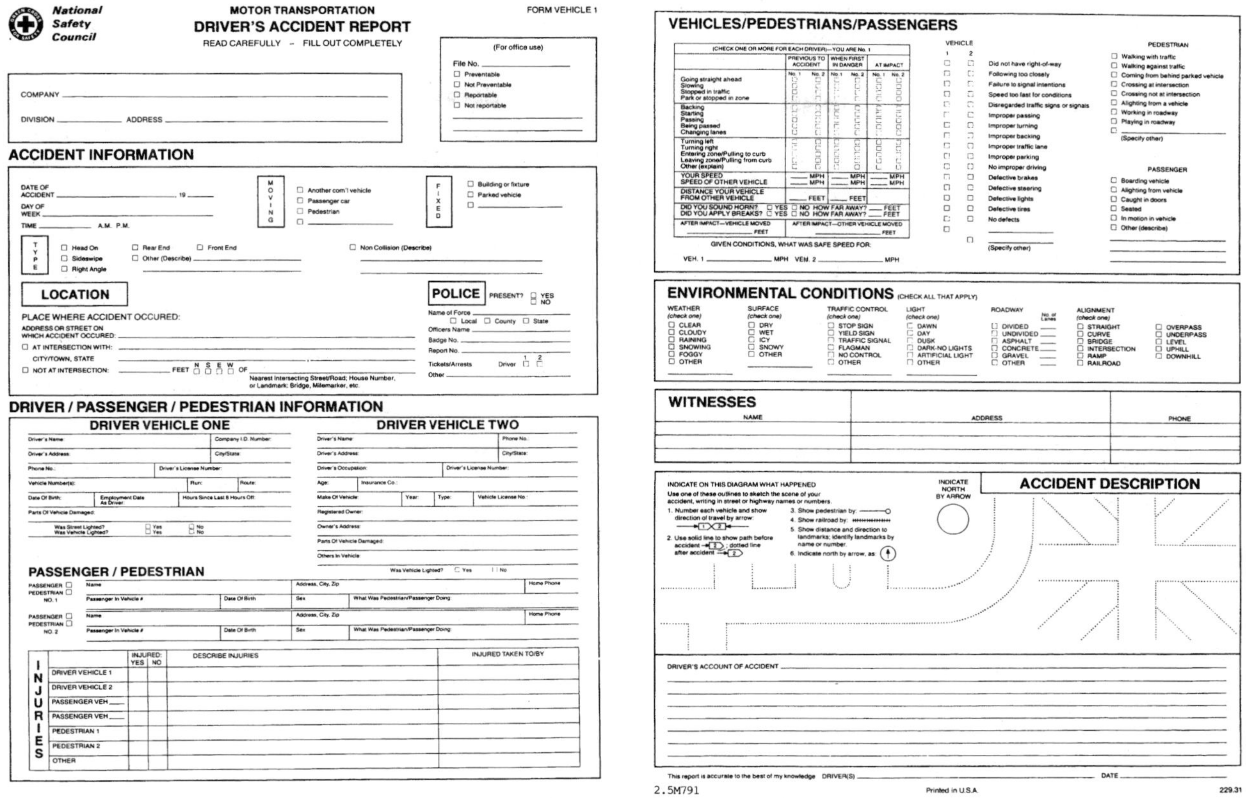
National Safety Council

MOTOR TRANSPORTATION
DRIVER'S ACCIDENT REPORT
READ CAREFULLY - FILL OUT COMPLETELY
FORM VEHICLE 1

(For office use)
File No.
Preventable
Not Preventable
Reportable
Not reportable

COMPANY
DIVISION ADDRESS

ACCIDENT INFORMATION

DATE OF ACCIDENT 19
DAY OF WEEK
TIME A.M. P.M.

MOVING: Another com'l vehicle; Passenger car; Pedestrian
FIXED: Building or fixture; Parked vehicle

TYPE: Head On; Sideswipe; Right Angle; Rear End; Other (Describe); Front End; Non Collision (Describe)

LOCATION

PLACE WHERE ACCIDENT OCCURED:
ADDRESS OR STREET ON WHICH ACCIDENT OCCURED:
AT INTERSECTION WITH:
CITY/TOWN, STATE
NOT AT INTERSECTION: FEET N S E W OF
Nearest Intersecting Street/Road; House Number, or Landmark: Bridge, Milemarker, etc.

POLICE PRESENT? YES NO
Name of Force
Local County State
Officers Name
Badge No.
Report No.
Tickets/Arrests Driver 1 2
Other

DRIVER / PASSENGER / PEDESTRIAN INFORMATION

DRIVER VEHICLE ONE
DRIVER VEHICLE TWO

PASSENGER / PEDESTRIAN

INJURIES
DRIVER VEHICLE 1
DRIVER VEHICLE 2
PASSENGER VEH
PASSENGER VEH
PEDESTRIAN 1
PEDESTRIAN 2
OTHER
INJURED: YES NO
DESCRIBE INJURIES
INJURED TAKEN TO/BY

VEHICLES/PEDESTRIANS/PASSENGERS

GIVEN CONDITIONS, WHAT WAS SAFE SPEED FOR:
VEH. 1 MPH VEH. 2 MPH

ENVIRONMENTAL CONDITIONS (CHECK ALL THAT APPLY)
WEATHER: CLEAR, CLOUDY, RAINING, SNOWING, FOGGY, OTHER
SURFACE: DRY, WET, ICY, SNOWY, OTHER
TRAFFIC CONTROL: STOP SIGN, YIELD SIGN, TRAFFIC SIGNAL, FLAGMAN, NO CONTROL, OTHER
LIGHT: DAWN, DAY, DUSK, DARK-NO LIGHTS, ARTIFICIAL LIGHT, OTHER
ROADWAY: DIVIDED, UNDIVIDED, ASPHALT, CONCRETE, GRAVEL, OTHER
ALIGNMENT: STRAIGHT, CURVE, BRIDGE, INTERSECTION, RAMP, RAILROAD, OVERPASS, UNDERPASS, LEVEL, UPHILL, DOWNHILL

WITNESSES
NAME ADDRESS PHONE

ACCIDENT DESCRIPTION
INDICATE NORTH BY ARROW

DRIVER'S ACCOUNT OF ACCIDENT

This report is accurate to the best of my knowledge DRIVER(S) DATE
2.5M791 Printed in U.S.A. 229.31

Figure 8-1 A typical police accident report form. [Courtesy of National Safety Council.]

Many property-damage accident cases are settled privately by drivers not wishing their insurance companies or the state licensing bureau to know of the accident.

While the traffic engineer's data base on accidents is limited, owing to the number of unreported cases, virtually all serious accidents—those involving substantial property damage, injury, or death—are reported. These are the cases in which the traffic engineer is chiefly interested. Many of these accidents involve correctable design, control, or operational features. The information on accidents must allow these to be identified, so that improvements may be prescribed.

B. Manual filing systems

All motorist accident-report forms are sent to the state motor vehicle bureau and entered into the state's central computer accident data system. Police accident forms, however, are generally sent and stored in three different locations:

1. A copy of each form goes to the state motor vehicle bureau for entry into the state's computer accident data system.
2. A copy of the form is sent to the central filing location for the municipality or district in which the accident occurred.
3. A copy of the form is retained by the officer in his or her precinct as a reference for possible court testimony.

The central municipal or district accident file is frequently the traffic engineer's most useful source of information for the detailed examination of high-accident locations, while state and/or municipal computer files are most useful for the generation and analysis of general statistical information.

Central files may be administered in a variety of ways. Often, a single filing system is centrally maintained for a city, county, or state region. In larger areas, separate files may be maintained for various subdivisions of the jurisdiction. Such systems may be maintained by a traffic department, a separate agency established for the purpose, or by a police department. In the latter case, a separate traffic division is often established within the police agency.

1. Location files. For any individual accident report to be useful, it must be easily retrievable for some time after the accident. Since the traffic engineer is interested in the correction of observed safety deficiencies at particular locations, any filing system must be organized by *location*—that is to say, the engineer should be able to retrieve reports of all accidents occurring at a specific location over a specified interval. This allows patterns in the types, times, and circumstances of accidents occurring at the location to be examined.

In urban systems, accident files are established for intersections and midblock sections. A determination is made as to whether N–S streets or E–W streets are to take precedence. This is required to avoid *two* files, one for the intersection of First Ave. and Main St., and another for Main St. and First Ave. A main file is established for each facility in the primary direction. Subfiles are then established for each intersection street and each midblock section. Midblock sections may be identified by the street addresses they encompass or by the intersections they lie between. Thus, the file for a facility might be established as follows:

Main Street
First Avenue
Second Avenue
Third Avenue
Foster Blvd.
Fourth Avenue
Lincoln Road
Fifth Avenue
100–199 Main St.
200–299 Main St.
300–399 Main St.
Etc.

Primary files would also be established for facilities in the secondary direction as well. These would *not*, however, contain subfiles for intersections. They would only contain subfiles for midblock locations.

In rural situations, distances between intersections and defined addresses may be too long to define midblock sections in the manner described above. Many of these rural situations are equipped with tenth-mile markers, denoting the mileage from the facilities terminus every tenth of a mile. In such cases, the number of the milepost is used as a location system. Where there are no mileposts, roadside landmarks, recognizable natural features, addresses, and crossroads are used to define midblock sections of highway.

2. Retention of records. Central accident files are generally kept current for one year, using one of two basic systems:

(a) Records are kept for one calendar year, at which time the entire file is "cleaned out" to start a new year.
(b) Records are kept for a 12-month rotating period. As each month begins, the records for the same month in the previous year are removed.

The latter system requires more manpower to maintain but assures that at least 11 months of accident records are readily available at all times.

After records are removed from the "active" file, they are retained in a "dead file" system—organized exactly in the same way as the "active" file—for a period of three to five years. To preserve space, such records may be microfilmed. After three to five years, most accident records will be discarded, or removed to a warehouse location.

3. Accident summary sheets. A common approach to retaining records for a longer period is to prepare summary sheets of each year's accident records. These may be kept indefinitely, while the individual accident forms are discarded after three to five years.

Figure 8-2 illustrates such a summary sheet, on which all of the year's accidents at one location can be reduced to a single coded sheet. The form retains the basic type of accident, the number and types of vehicles involved, their cardinal direction, weather and roadway conditions, and numbers of injuries and/or fatalities.

Number	Date	Time	Private Car	Private Car	Private Car	Private Car	Commercial	Omnibus	Bicycle	Pedestrian	Other	Accident Type	Weather	Road Conditions	Road Surface	Injured	Fatal
267	1·23·78	1645	N				N					E	C	W			
282	1·24·78	1300	S				S					E	C	Slush			
463	2·11·78	1805	S	S	S	S						B	C	W		1	
855	3·11·78	1205	N	N								B	C	D			
1462	5·6·78	1612	W	S								A	C	D		1	
1513	5·11·78	1315	N/W	S								A	C	D			
1528	5·12·78	1645	S	S	S							B	C	D			
1569	5·15·78	1525	S	W								A	C	D		2	
1675	5·24·78	1130	W	S								A	R	W		1	
1801	6·3·78	2039	W	S ←Bicycle								A	R	W		1	
1831	6·6·78	1510	N				N/E					A	C	D			
2216	7·8·78	1201	N	W								A	C	D			
2219	7·8·78	0720	S	W								A	C	D		2	
2248	7·10·78	1700	E	E								B	C	D			
2375	7·21·78	1610	S/E								MC/N	A	C	D		1	
2759	8·19·78	2015	N	E								A	C	D			
2787	8·22·78	0850	S	W								A	C	D			
2791	8·22·78	1715	S					School S				B	C	D			
3310	10·1·78	1920	S				W					A	R	W			
3432	10·11·78	1235	S	N/W								A	C	D			
3531	10·19·78	0950	W	W								E	C	D			
4217	12·7·78	0925	S				S					B	C	D			
4234	12·8·78	1030	S	E/S								A	R	W		2	
4281	12·10·78	1900	S	N/W								A	C	D			

TRAFFIC ACCIDENT RECORD

LOCATION MARCUS AVE. & NEW HYDE PARK RD.   T3L

VILLAGE N. NEW HYDE PARK   PRECINCT

Figure 8-2 Illustrative accident summary sheet. [Courtesy of Nassau County Traffic Safety Board, Mineola, NY.]

Table 8-2 lists the accident codes used in the accident summary sheet illustrated in Figure 8-2.

C. Computer record systems

All states, and many large municipalities and counties, maintain a computer accident record system. These supplement, but do not replace, manual filing systems. The computer has the advantage of being able to maintain a large number of accident records, keyed to locations, and to correlate these to other related traffic data. It is limited, however, to information that can be reduced to alphanumeric codes, and the detail of individual accident diagrams and descriptions is lost.

The computer is most useful in generating regular statistical reports at regular intervals, and in sorting data in ways that provide overall insight into accident trends and problems.

Most computer record systems maintain various data bases, including accident reports, a highway system network code, volume files from regular counting programs, and project improvement data. These can all be correlated to compute statistics and to perform

Table 8-2 Accident Type Codes for Accident Summary Sheet

A —right-angle collision
B —rear-end collision
C —head-on collision
D —m.v.'s sideswiped (opposite direction)
E —m.v.'s sideswiped (same direction)
F —m.v. leaving curb
G —m.v. collided with parked m.v.
H —m.v. collided with fixed object
I —m.v. executing U-turn
J —m.v. turned over
K —m.v. executing improper left turn
L —m.v. executing improper right turn
M—left turn, head-on collision
N —right turn, head-on collision
O —pedestrian struck by m.v.
P —unknown
Q —hole in roadway
R —m.v. backing against traffic
S —operator or occupant fell out of m.v.
T —person injured while hitching ride on m.v.
U —m.v. collided with separated part or object of another m.v.
V —m.v. and train in collision
W—m.v. struck by thrown or fallen object
X —parked m.v. (unattended) rolled into another m.v. or object
Y —towed m.v. or trailer broke free of towing vehicle
Z —m.v. and bicycle in collision

before–after comparisons and other analyses. Most computer systems are programmed to regularly provide statistical reports on the following:

- numbers of accidents by location
- accident rates by highway location and/or segment
- accident frequency versus driver, vehicle, and environmental characteristics
- accident summary statistics by type of location
- analysis of types of accidents versus types of location.
- correlation of improvement projects with accident experience

Computer systems can provide many types of useful outputs. Most states will accommodate requests for special reports. These take longer, as the system must be specially programmed to provide a particular form of output. The regular statistical reports of most states, however, provide a broad range of useful information for the engineer, who should always be aware of the capabilities of the specific state and local systems in his or her vicinity.

Accident statistics: Providing systematic insight

In 1994, there were 43,000 fatalities and 2,100,000 disabling injuries in the United States as a result of 11,200,000 accidents involving 20,000,000 vehicles. This resulted in a fatality rate of 1.83 deaths per 100 million vehicle-miles, and an involvement rate of 1.79 vehicles per accident.

These are examples of accident statistics based on factual data. They are intended to provide insight into the general state of highway safety and into systematic contributing causes of accidents. A thorough use of statistics and statistical analysis can yield valuable information for the engineer providing insights that help in the development of corrective measures. Care must be taken, however, because incomplete or partial statistics can be very misleading.

A. Types of statistics

Accident statistics are most often used to quantify and describe three principal informational elements:

- accident occurrence
- accident involvements
- accident severity

Accident *occurrence* is generally described in terms of the types and numbers of accidents that occur, often as a rate based on population or vehicle-miles of travel. *Involvement* statistics often concentrate on the categories of vehicles and drivers involved in accidents, with population-based rates a very popular method of expressing these statistics. *Severity* is generally expressed as the numbers of deaths and/or injuries occurring. Rates based on the number of accidents, population, or vehicle-miles of travel are also valuable in the presentation of severity rates.

Statistics in each of these three categories can be stratified and analyzed in an almost infinite number of ways, depending on the factors of interest to the analyst. Some common analyses include the examination of:

- trends over time
- stratification by highway type or geometric element
- stratification by driver characteristics
- stratification by contributing cause
- stratification by accident type
- stratification by environmental conditions

Such analyses allow the correlation of accident types with highway types and geometric elements, the identification of high-risk driver populations, quantification of the extent of the "driving while impaired" influence in accidents, and other important determinations. Many of these factors can be addressed through policy or programmatic means. Changes in guardrail design may result from correlation of accident occurrence and severity with certain types of installations. Changes in legal drinking age have frequently been a policy response to drunk-driving statistics. Legislation of vehicle design requirements has often resulted from studies linking fatalities and injuries to identifiable vehicle deficiencies. Over the years, legislation has required such safety features as directional signals, energy-absorbing bumper systems, seat belts and harnesses, padded dashes, dual master brake cylinders, and other improvements in vehicle design.

Accident statistics, and their proper analysis, reveal commonalities and trends concerning the underlying causes of accidents. These provide the information from which systematic improvements in policy, design, control, and enforcement can be developed and implemented.

B. Accident rates and their use

1. Bases for accident rates. Simple statistics citing total numbers of accidents, involvements, injuries, or deaths can be quite misleading, as they ignore the base from which these statistics arise. An increase in any of these totals of 10% from one year to the next may appear to depict a serious problem. However, if in the same year, vehicle-miles of travel increased by 25%, the rise in accident totals does not appear to be as serious. For this reason, many accident statistics are presented in the form of rates.

Accident rates generally fall into one of two broad categories: population-based rates and exposure-based rates. Some common bases for population-based rates include:

- area population
- number of registered vehicles
- number of licensed drivers
- highway mileage

These values are static and do not depend on vehicle usage or the total amount of travel. They are useful in quantifying overall risk to individuals on a comparative basis. Insofar as numbers of registered vehicles and licensed drivers reflect changes in usage, rates based on these bases can also partially reflect usage.

Exposure-based rates attempt to account for the amount of travel as a surrogate measure for the individual's exposure to potential accident situations. The two most common bases used for exposure-based rates are

1. Vehicle-miles of travel
2. Vehicle-hours of travel

The two can vary widely depending on the speed of travel, and comparisons based on mileage can yield different results from those based on hours of exposure. For point locations, such as intersections, vehicle-miles or vehicle-hours have very little meaning. Exposure rates in such cases are "event-based," using total volume passing through the point.

True "exposure" to risk, of course, involves a great deal more than just time or mileage. Exposure to vehicular and other conflicts that are susceptible to accident occurrence varies with many factors, including volume levels, roadside activity, intersection frequency, degree of access control, alignment, and many others. Data requirements make it difficult to quantify all of these factors in defining exposure. The traffic engineer should be cognizant of these and other factors when interpreting exposure-based accident rates.

In computing accident rates, numbers should be scaled to produce meaningful values. A fatality rate per vehicle-mile would yield values with many decimal points before the first significant digit and would be difficult to conceptualize. The listing that follows indicates commonly used rate bases:

Population-Based Accident Rates

- Deaths or accidents per 100,000 area population
- Deaths or accidents per 10,000 registered vehicles
- Deaths or accidents per 10,000 licensed drivers
- Deaths or accidents per 1000 miles of highway

Exposure-Based Accident Rates

- Deaths or accidents per 100,000,000 vehicle-miles
- Deaths or accidents per 10,000,000 vehicle-hours
- Death or accidents per 1,000,000 entering vehicles

While these constitute the most commonly used rates, care should be taken when reviewing statistics from various sources, as the bases may not always be uniform.

2. Basic accident rates. Three types of accident rates are characteristically computed for most jurisdictions annually: (a) general accident rates describing total accident occurrence, (b) fatality rates describing accident severity, and (c) involvement rates describing the types of vehicles and drivers involved in accidents. Consider the following data for City X for the year 1996:

Fatalities: 75

Fatal accidents: 60

Injury accidents: 300

PDO accidents: 2000

Total involvements: 4100

Vehicle-miles: 1,500,000,000

Registered vehicles: 100,000

Licensed drivers: 150,000

Area population: 300,000

The following fatality rates may be computed for City X during 1996, based on these statistics:

$$\text{Rate } 1 = 75 \times \frac{100,000}{300,000}$$

$$= 25 \text{ deaths per 100,000 population}$$

$$\text{Rate } 2 = 75 \times \frac{10,000}{100,000}$$

$$= 7.5 \text{ deaths per 10,000 registered vehicles}$$

$$\text{Rate } 3 = 75 \times \frac{10,000}{150,000}$$

$$= 5.0 \text{ deaths per 10,000 licensed drivers}$$

$$\text{Rate } 4 = 75 \times \frac{100,000,000}{1,500,000,000}$$

$$= 5.0 \text{ deaths per 100,000,000 veh-mi}$$

Similar rates could have been based on the total number of accidents or involvements. In general, the fatality or accident rate for a given year is computed as

$$\text{rate} = \text{total} \times \text{scale/base} \qquad [8\text{-}1]$$

where: rate = accident or fatality rate desired
  total = total number of accidents or fatalities during year
  scale = scale of the base, as in a rate per *scale* veh-mi
  base = total base statistic for year

Accident and fatality rates for a given county, city, or other subdivision should be compared against previous years, as well as against state and national norms for the analysis year. Such rates may also be subdivided by highway type, driver age and sex groupings, time of day, and other useful breakdowns for analysis.

3. Severity index. A widely used statistic for the description of relative accident severity is the *severity index (SI)*, defined as the number of fatalities per accident. For the data of the sample problem discussed previously, there were 75 fatalities in 2630 total accidents. The severity index for City X in 1996 is, therefore,

$$SI = \frac{75}{2630} = 0.0285 \text{ deaths/accident}$$

C. Examples of statistical displays and their use

Graphic and tabular displays of accident statistics can be most useful in transmitting information in a clear and understandable manner. If a picture is worth 1,000 words, then a skillfully-prepared graph of table is at least as useful in forcefully depicting facts. However, in preparing and reviewing statistical displays, the engineer must know what they *do not* say as well as what they *do* say. What follows is an example of a statistical display.

Figure 8-3 depicts time trends related to national accident experience, showing trends of vehicle-miles of travel, total deaths, the death rate per 100 million vehicle-miles, and the death rate per 100,000 population.

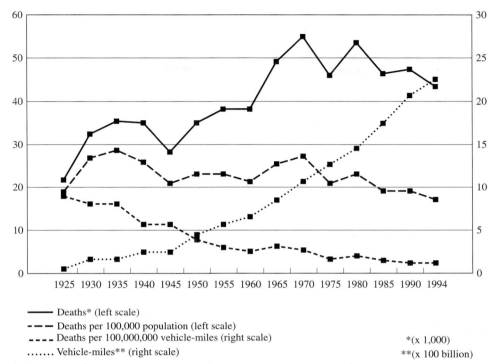

Figure 8-3 National trends in traffic fatalities. [From *Accident Facts,* National Safety Council, p. 105, 1995.]

Death rates have steadily declined since the 1930s, even though the number of total deaths has generally risen, at least through the early 1970s. This apparent anomaly is explained by the enormous growth in vehicle-miles traveled. The leveling off and moderate reduction in total deaths in the 1970s and 1980s reflects slower growth in vehicle use as a result of the fuel crises of the 1970s, as well as the imposition of the 55-mph national speed limit during the same period.

The continuing decrease in the number of deaths in the 1990s partially reflects the increased use of seat belts, spurred by tougher seat-belt laws and enforcement. Reference [1] indicates that 5000 lives were saved in 1993 by the use of seat belts.

One of the principal issues in highway safety at this writing is the elimination of the 55-mph national speed limit, and the return of many speed limits to 65 and 70 mph in rural and some suburban areas. Montana has no specific daytime speed limit at all, although state lawmakers were considering one at this writing. While there have been a number of studies in recent years trying to relate accident experience to speed limits, no clear consensus has emerged, and the careful study will continue as drivers adjust to the new higher speed limits.

D. Determining high-accident locations

A primary function of an accident record system is to regularly identify locations with an unusually high number of rate of accidents. As part of a manual filing system, most jurisdictions also maintain an *accident spot map.* Each time an accident report is filed, a color-coded pin or other symbol is placed on a map of the jurisdiction at the appropriate location. Color and/or symbol codes indicate the type and severity of the accident. Figure 8-4 shows a typical spot map.

Modern computer technology now allows such maps to be electronically generated from a well-designed accident data base. Computer record systems can also produce rankings of high-accident

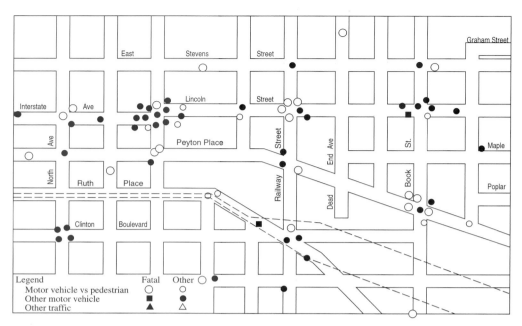

Figure 8-4 A typical accident spot map. [Used with permission of Prentice-Hall, Inc., from *Manual of Transportation Engineering Studies,* Institute of Transportation Engineers, p. 400. Copyright © 1994 Prentice-Hall, Inc.]

locations based on either total accidents occurring or accident rates. Often, the rankings produced by totals and rates are different. Some locations with high numbers of accidents reflect high volumes, and have relatively low accident rates. A small number of accidents at a remote location with low volumes may produce a high accident rate. Thus, while such rankings give the engineer a starting point, judgment must be applied in the identification and selection of sites most in need of improvement during any given budget year.

One way of determining which locations require immediate attention is to identify those with accident rates that are significantly higher than the average for the jurisdiction or area under study. To say that the accident rate at a specific location is significantly higher than the area average with 95% confidence, choose only those rates that fall in the highest 5% of area on the normal distribution (see Figure 8-5).

If the accident rate at one location is significantly higher than the average, then the accident rate, when converted to a *z*-value on the standard normal distribution, must be greater than 1.645—the *z*-value cor-

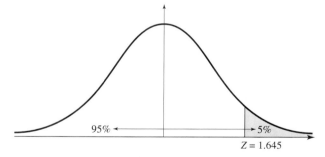

Figure 8-5 The standard normal distribution.

responding to a probability of 95% (the probability of a value being less than or equal to *z*). If the actual value of *z* is computed as:

$$z = \frac{x_1 - \bar{x}}{s} \qquad [8\text{-}2]$$

where: x_1 = accident rate at the location under consideration

$\bar{x}$ = average accident rate for locations within the jurisdiction or study area

s = standard deviation of accident rates for locations within the jurisdiction or study area

If the value of z must be 1.645 for 95% confidence, the minimum accident rate that would be considered to be significantly higher than the average may be taken to be:

$$x_1 \geq 1.645(s) + \bar{x} \qquad [8\text{-}3]$$

Locations with a higher accident rate than this value would normally be selected for specific study and remediation. It should be noted that in comparing average accident rates, similar locations should be grouped. Thus, accident rates for intersections are compared to other intersections, midblock rates are compared to other midblock rates, and so on.

E. Statistical analysis of before-after accident data

When an accident problem has been identified and an improvement implemented, the engineer must evaluate whether or not the improvement has been effective. For this purpose, a before-after accident analysis is conducted. The period of time considered before and after the improvement must be long enough to observe changes in accident occurrence. For most locations, periods ranging between three months and one year are selected. The lengths of the "before" and "after" periods must be the same.

The Normal Approximation test is often used to make this determination. This test is more fully discussed in Chapters 5 and 7. The statistic z is computed as:

$$z_1 = \frac{f_A - f_B}{\sqrt{f_A + f_B}} \qquad [8\text{-}4]$$

where: z_1 = test statistic, representing the reduction in accidents on the standard normal distribution

f_A = number of accidents in the "after" study period

f_B = number of accidents in the "before" study period

If $P\{z \leq z_1\} \geq 0.95$, the reduction in accidents may be taken to be statistically significant at the 95% confidence level. The probability level is found using the

Standard Normal Distribution table presented in Chapter 5.

Because of the small sample sizes involved in most before-and-after accident comparisons, it is generally more accurate to use the Poisson Distribution and a modified binomial test. Figure 8-6 shows criteria for rejecting the null hypothesis (that there has been no change in accident rate), according to the modified binomial test. The graph is entered with the "before" count. Using the "reduction" curve, a percentage is found on the vertical axis. This percentage is the minimum reduction that would be considered statistically significant.

Technically, there is a significant flaw in the way that most before-and-after accident comparisons are conducted. There is generally a base assumption that

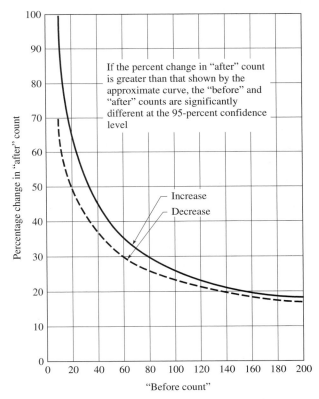

Figure 8-6 Rejection criteria for Poisson-distributed data based on binomial test. [Used with permission of Transportation Research Board, National Research Council, from R. Weed, "Revised Decision Criteria for Before-and-After Analyses," *Transportation Research Record 1068*, p. 11. Copyright © 1986 Transportation Research Board.]

any observed change in accident occurrence (or severity) is due to the corrective measures implemented at the location(s) in question. Because of the time span involved in most such studies, this may not be a correct assumption.

If possible, a control experiment or control experiments should be established. These control experiments involve locations with similar accident experience that are not treated with corrective measures. The controls establish the expected change in accident experience due to general environmental causes not influenced by corrective measures. For the subject location(s), the null hypothesis is that the change in accident experience is not significantly different from the change observed at control locations. Figure 8-7 illustrates this technique.

While desirable from a statistical point of view, the establishment of control experiments is often a practical problem, requiring that some high-accident locations be left untreated during the period of the study. For this reason, many before-and-after accident comparisons must be made without such controls.

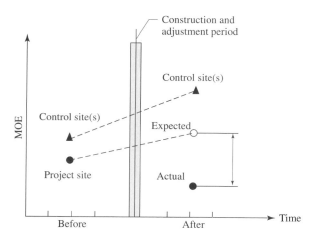

● Avg. project site MOE*
▲ Avg. control site MOE
○ Expected MOE

Figure 8-7 Before-and-after experiment with control sites. [Used with permission of Prentice-Hall, Inc., from *Manual of Transportation Engineering Studies,* Institute of Transportation Engineers, p. 368. Copyright © 1994 Prentice-Hall, Inc.]

Site analysis

Perhaps the most complex task in traffic safety is the analysis of site-specific accident data to identify contributing causes and to develop site improvements. Once a particular location has been identified as a "high accident" location, detailed information is required in two principal areas: (1) the occurrence of accidents at the location in question, and (2) the environmental and physical conditions existing at the location.

The former is obtained by reviewing the accident file for the location in question, perhaps supplemented by available summaries and/or computer records. The latter requires a detailed site investigation conducted by appropriate field personnel. These analyses result in two graphical documents: (1) the collision diagram, and (2) the condition diagram.

A. Collision diagrams

A *collision diagram* is a schematic representation of all accidents occurring at a given location over a specified period, generally from one to three years. Each collision is represented by a set of arrows, one for each vehicle involved, which schematically represents the type of accident and directions of all vehicles. Arrows are labeled with codes for vehicle types, date and time of accident, and weather conditions.

Arrows are placed on a schematic, not-to-scale drawing of the intersection, with no interior details shown. One set of arrows represents one accident. It should be noted that arrows are not necessarily placed at the exact location of the accident on the drawing. Several accidents may have taken place at the same spot. Arrows are placed to illustrate the occurrence of the accident, as close to the actual spot as possible while still clearly indicating each accident as a separate set of symbols.

Table 8-3 lists the standard symbols and codes used in the preparation of collision diagrams. Figure 8-8 illustrates a collision diagram for an intersection.

The diagram is virtually self-explanatory. The intersection has experienced primarily rear-end and right-angle types of collisions, with several injuries but no deaths occurring during the period shown. Many of the accidents appear to be clustered at night.

Table 8-3 Symbols Used in Accident Diagrams

Symbol used	Interpretation	Symbol used	Interpretation
Vehicle-type symbols		Accident-type symbols	
	Passenger car		Rear-end
(T)	Truck		Head-on
(B)	Bus		Right angle
(C)	Cycle		
(O)	Other		Other angle (opposing directions)
	Pedestrian		Other Angle (common directions)
Movement symbols			Sideswipe (common directions)
	Left turn		
	Right turn		Sideswipe (opposing direction)
	Straight		Out-of-control
Severity symbols			Collision with fixed object
	PDO		
	Injury		
	Fatal		

The diagram clearly points out these patterns, which now must be correlated to the physical and control characteristics of the site to determine contributing situations and corrective measures.

B. Condition diagrams

A *condition diagram* describes all physical and environmental conditions at the accident site under study. The diagram must show all geometric features of the site, the location and description of all controls (signs, signals, markings, lighting, etc.), and all relevant features of the roadside environments, such as the location of objects, driveways, land uses, and so on. The diagram must encompass a large enough area around the location to include all potentially involved features. This may range from several hundred feet on intersection approaches to $\frac{1}{4}$–$\frac{1}{2}$ mile on rural highway sections.

Figure 8-9 illustrates a condition diagram for an intersection in a suburban community. This is the same intersection illustrated in the collision diagram of Figure 8-8. The diagram includes several hundred feet of each intersection approach and clearly shows all driveway locations and the commercial land uses they serve. Control details include signal locations and timing, location of all stop lines, crosswalks, and even the location of roadside trees, which could block signal visibility lines.

C. Interpretation of results

This brief overview chapter cannot, of course, fully discuss and present all types of accident-site analyses. The objective is straightforward: Find contributing causes to the observed accidents shown in the collision diagram among the design, control, operational, and environmental features summarized on the condition diagram. This will involve virtually all of the traffic engineer's knowledge and experience, as well as his or her insight and professional judgment.

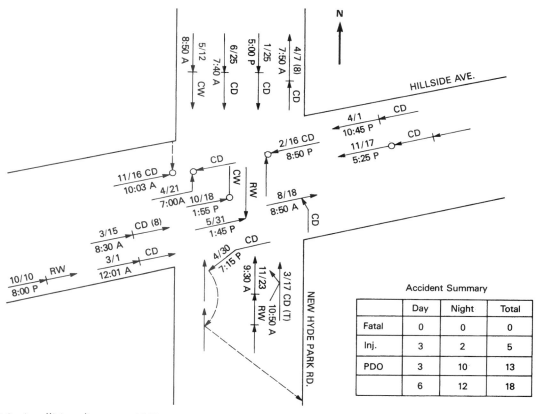

Figure 8-8 A collision diagram—1980.

Accidents are generally grouped by type. The predominant accidents illustrated in Figure 8-8 are rear-end and right-angle accidents. For each type of accident, three questions must be asked and answered:

1. What driver actions lead to the occurrence of such an accident?
2. What conditions existing at the location could contribute toward drivers taking such actions?
3. What changes can be made to reduce the chance of such actions occurring in the future?

Consider the rear-end collisions of Figure 8-8. Rear-end collisions occur when the lead vehicle stops suddenly or unexpectedly, and/or when the following driver follows too closely for the prevailing speed and environmental conditions. While tailgating by a following driver is not correctable by design or control, a number of factors may contribute to vehicles stop-

ping suddenly at the intersections depicted in Figures 8-8 and 8-9.

At signalized intersections, quick stops are often related to a mistimed yellow or clearance interval. If the interval is too short, vehicles attempting to continue through the intersection will have to stop suddenly to avoid being hit by crossing vehicles. Therefore, the timing of the clearance interval must be checked in cases such as these.

The condition diagram of Figure 8-9 shows an unusual number of driveways allowing access to and egress from the street right at or near the intersection area. Unexpected movements in and out of these driveways could cause mainline vehicles to stop suddenly. Another noticeable condition is that STOP lines are located well back from the sidewalk line, particularly in the northbound direction. Thus, vehicles are stopping at positions not normally expected, and

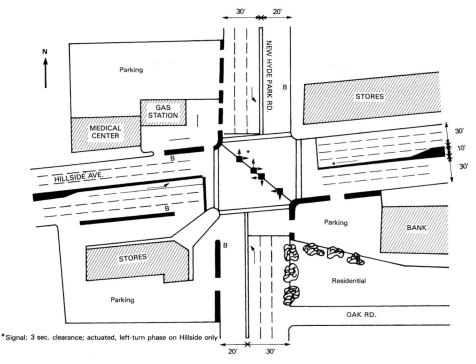

Figure 8-9 A condition diagram.

following drivers may be surprised and unable to respond in time to avoid a collision.

Potential corrective actions flow from this. Several driveways in the immediate intersection area should be closed, and STOP lines moved to more normal locations. The clearance intervals must be checked and retimed. Signal sight lines with respect to trees and so on should be checked. Further, since most of the accidents are occurring at night, lighting and visibility under these conditions should be studied.

Right-angle collisions clearly indicate a breakdown in the right-of-way assignment by the signal. Signal visibility should be checked, as well as the overall signal timing for reasonableness. A too-short clearance interval will result in vehicles being released into the intersection before vehicles from the competing direction have been cleared. An unreasonable signal timing will lead to vehicles jumping the green or otherwise disregarding it.

For the intersection of Figures 8-8 and 8-9, several factors compounded each other. Clearance intervals were indeed too short at this location, contributing to both rear-end and right-angle accidents. The placement of STOP lines back from the intersection, however, not only caused vehicles to stop at unexpected locations, but *increased* the required clearance time, owing to the increased distance to the other side of the intersection. By moving the STOP lines closer to the intersection, the required clearance interval can be reduced, and the needed increase in the actual clearance interval minimized. Signal visibility can be enhanced by installing 12-inch signal heads instead of the 8-inch signal heads now at the location.

Clearly, this analysis is illustrative. Each situation and location will have its own unique characteristics, requiring the application of the traffic engineer's skills in an insightful and innovative way. The tools of site analysis, the collision and condition diagrams, are not the end result of an analysis, but merely the most effective means of depicting complex information. As noted previously, accident-site analysis is quite complicated, using all of the traffic engineer's knowledge of design, operations, controls, and safety. The present treatment of the subject is included to make the reader aware of this important type of study, rather than to fully explain every detail of how it is done.

Traffic safety is not an isolated subject for the study of the traffic engineer. Rather, it pervades every aspect of everything the traffic engineer does. This chapter has provided an overview of the general subject and is not intended to be exhaustive. The importance of building safety into all traffic designs, controls, and operational plans is emphasized throughout this text.

D. Development of countermeasures

Of course, the ultimate goal of any analysis of accidents at a site is the development of countermeasures to mitigate the circumstances leading to those accidents. The previous section provided some examples illustrating the analysis and identification of underlying causes of accidents.

Each case, however, has its own unique characteristics that must be studied and analyzed in detail, using the tools discussed previously: collision and condition diagrams, related studies such as speed and sight distances, personal observation of operations at the site, and the background and experience of both the individual traffic engineer and his/her agency.

Table 8-4 gives a more comprehensive overview of probable causes and generally effective countermeasures compiled by the Federal Highway Adminis-

tration. While it does not cover all possible situations, it does cover all of the most commonly-occurring situations. The list of countermeasures is excellent, but could never be complete. Thus, the table serves as a good overview and guide to effective accident countermeasures that can be used in conjunction with detailed site investigations to assist in the design and implementation of improvements.

Like many other highway projects, accident countermeasures are often subject to economic comparisons of costs and benefits. This, of course, is a most difficult process, as it involves placing a monetary value on life (cost of a fatality) and limb (cost of injuries). Because of this, these analyses are never really straightforward.

Table 8-5 presents some general information on costs and benefits of various accident countermeasures, based on a nationwide sample of sites, while Table 8-6 contains estimates of accident costs compiled by two different agencies. These are presented here primarily for information purposes. Because this text does not cover economic analysis of alternatives, no examples are shown. When conducting such comparisons, however, local data and costs are often used instead of national averages, such as those presented here.

References 3–6 provide effective overviews of accident study techniques and analyses.

Table 8-4 A Summary of Accident Countermeasures

Accident Pattern	Probable Cause[a]	Possible Countermeasures[b]	Accident Pattern	Probable Cause[a]	Possible Countermeasures[b]
Left turn, head-on	A	1–11	Ran off roadway	E	15
	B	3, 6, 12–15		G	15, 19–22
	C	16, 17		H	23
	D	3		K	54
	E	15		U	55–58
				V	14, 53, 59
Rear-end at unsignalized intersection	A	4, 13, 18		W	60
	E	15		X	6
	F	14		Y	61
	G	15, 19–22			
	H	23	Fixed object	E	15
	I	10, 24		G	20, 22, 55, 62
	J	25		H	23
				T	53
Rear-end at signalized intersection	A	3, 4, 13, 18		U	14, 63
	G	15, 19–22		Z	58, 64–67
	H	23		AA	68
	J	25, 26			
	K	12, 14, 15, 27–32	Parked or parking vehicle	E	15
	L	16, 17, 33		T	69
	M	34		BB	35
				CC	70
Right angle at signalized intersection	B	6, 12, 14, 15 35, 36		DD	45, 50, 71
				EE	1, 43
	E	15, 16, 37			
	H	23	Sideswipe or head-on	E	15, 72, 73
	K	14, 27–32, 38		T	53
	L	11, 16, 17, 33, 39, 40		U	1, 55
				W	60
	N	14		X	6, 13, 74
	O	2, 11		Y	61
				FF	38, 75
Right angle at unsignalized intersection	B	6, 10, 12, 14, 15 24, 35, 36, 41, 42	Driveway-related	A	13, 18, 35, 55 72, 76
	E	15, 16, 37		B	12, 15, 23, 35
	H	23		E	15
	N	14		H	23
	O	10, 43		GG	77–81
	P	44, 45		HH	43, 79, 82
Pedestrian–vehicle	B	12, 25, 35, 46		II	6, 10, 74
	E	14, 15, 45, 47			
	H	23	Train–vehicle	B	12, 14, 24, 83–85
	I	10, 25, 26		E	15
	L	11		G	62
	P	26		K	23, 54
	Q	47, 48		T	36, 42, 53
	R	49		JJ	11
	S	14, 15, 47, 50		KK	86
	T	51–53		LL	87
				MM	88
Wet pavement	G	15, 19–22, 62	Night	K	14, 23, 59
	T	53		V	14, 59, 89
				X	14, 53, 59, 89
				FF	44, 90

Table 8-4 (continued)

aKey to probable causes:

A	Large turn volume	U	Inadequate roadway design for traffic conditions
B	Restricted sight distance	V	Inadequate delineation
C	Amber phase too short	W	Inadequate shoulder
D	Absence of left-turn phase	X	Inadequate channelization
E	Excessive speed	Y	Inadequate pavement maintenance
F	Driver unaware of intersection	Z	Fixed object in or too close to roadway
G	Slippery surface	AA	Inadequate TCDs and guardrail
H	Inadequate roadway lighting	BB	Inadequate parking clearance at driveway
I	Lack of adequate gaps	CC	Angle parking
J	Crossing pedestrians	DD	Illegal parking
K	Poor traffic control device (TCD) visibility	EE	Large parking turnover
L	Inadequate signal timing	FF	Inadequate signing
M	Unwarranted signal	GG	Improperly located driveway
N	Inadequate advance intersection warning signs	HH	Large through traffic volume
O	Large total intersection volume	II	Large driveway traffic volume
P	Inadequate TCDs	JJ	Improper traffic signal preemption timing
Q	Inadequate pedestrian protection	KK	Improper signal or gate warning time
R	School crossing area	LL	Rough crossing surface
S	Drivers have inadequate warning of frequent midblock crossings	MM	Sharp crossing angle
T	Inadequate or improper pavement markings		

bKey to possible countermeasures:

1	Create one-way street	46	Reroute pedestrian path
2	Add lane	47	Install pedestrian barrier
3	Provide left-turn signal phase	48	Install pedestrian refuge island
4	Prohibit turn	49	Use crossing guard at school crossing area
5	Reroute left-turn traffic	50	Prohibit parking
6	Provide adequate channelization	51	Install thermoplastic markings
7	Install stop sign	52	Provide signs to supplement markings
8	Revise signal phase sequence	53	Improve or install pavement markings
9	Provide turning guidelines for multiple left-turn lanes	54	Increase sign size
10	Provide traffic signal	55	Widen lane
11	Retime signal	56	Relocate island
12	Remove sight obstruction	57	Close curb lane
13	Provide turn lane	58	Install guardrail
14	Install or improve warning sign	59	Improve or install delineation
15	Reduce speed limit	60	Upgrade roadway shoulder
16	Adjust amber phase	61	Repair road surface
17	Provide all-red phase	62	Improve skid resistance
18	Increase curb radii	63	Provide proper superelevation
19	Overlay pavement	64	Remove fixed object
20	Provide adequate drainage	65	Install barrier curb
21	Groove pavement	66	Install breakaway posts
22	Provide "slippery when wet" sign	67	Install crash cushioning device
23	Improve roadway lighting	68	Paint or install reflectors on obstruction
24	Provide stop sign	69	Mark parking stall limits
25	Install or improve pedestrian crosswalk TCDs	70	Convert angle to parallel parking
26	Provide pedestrian signal	71	Create off-street parking
27	Install overhead signal	72	Install median barrier
28	Install 12-inch signal lenses	73	Remove constriction such as parked vehicle
29	Install signal visors	74	Install acceleration or deceleration lane
30	Install signal back plates	75	Install advance guide sign
31	Relocate signal	76	Increase driveway width
32	Add signal heads	77	Regulate minimum driveway spacing
33	Provide progression through a set of signalized intersections	78	Regulate minimum corner clearance
34	Remove signal	79	Move driveway to side street
35	Restrict parking near corner/crosswalk/driveway	80	Install curb to define driveway location
36	Provide markings to supplement signs	81	Consolidate adjacent driveways
37	Install rumble strips	82	Construct a local service road
38	Install illuminated street name sign	83	Reduce grade
39	Install multidial signal controller	84	Install train-actuated signal
40	Install signal actuation	85	Install automatic flashers or flashers with gates
41	Install yield sign	86	Retime automatic flashers or flashers with gates
42	Install limit lines	87	Improve crossing surface
43	Reroute through traffic	88	Rebuild crossing with proper angle
44	Upgrade TCDs	89	Provide raised markings
45	Increase enforcement	90	Provide illuminated sign

Source: FHWA 1981.

[Reprinted with permission of Prentice-Hall, Inc., from Robertson, Hummer, and Nelson (editors), *Manual of Transportation Engineering Studies*, Institute of Transportation Engineers, pp. 214 and 215. Copyright © 1994 Prentice-Hall, Inc.]

Table 8-5 Average Cost-Effectiveness of Various Safety Improvements

Type of Improvement to Construction Classification	Indexed Cost of Evaluated Improvements (millions)	Percent Reduction in Accident Rates after Improvements			Cost per Accident Reduced (thousands)		Benefit/Cost Ratio
		Fatal	Injury	Fatal + Injury	Fatal	Fatal + Injury	
Intersection and traffic control	562.3	37	15	15	344.5	18.7	4.0
Channelization turning lanes	297.7	48	23	24	510.9	19.7	2.8
Sight distance improvements	7.8	44*	31	32	371.4	22.8	3.6
Traffic signs	19.6	34	3	4	59.3	15.7	20.9
Pavement markings and/or delineators	33.7	15	(1)*	(1)*	751.8	—	1.6
Illumination	13.2	45	8	9	122.6	16.8	10.3
Traffic signals upgraded	63.1	40	22	22	412.1	8.6	4.0
Traffic signals, new	127.3	49	21	21	344.5	10.5	5.1
Structures	307.7	50	28	29	752.2	92.1	1.7
Bridge widened or modified	79.8	49	22	23	1,077.9	103.8	1.2
Bridge replacement	156.9	72	47	49	1,201.6	159.3	1.1
New bridge construction	26.2	77*	40	43	1,637.8	223.2	0.8
Minor structure replacement/improvement	39.0	36	20	21	277.1	39.8	4.5
Upgraded bridge rail	5.6	72*	41	45	189.5	39.4	6.5
Roadway and roadside	1,971.3	31	13	13	722.2	54.0	1.8
Widened travel way	511.0	9*	7	7	4,041.3	174.2	0.4
Lanes added	212.9	(2)	13	13	—	66.8	0.1
Median strip to separate roadway	56.8	73	17	19	382.4	72.8	3.2
Shoulder widening or improvement	88.3	28	11	12	497.9	37.9	2.6
Roadway realignment	329.9	61	32	34	1,193.2	111.1	1.1
Skid resistant overlay	468.4	26	18	19	837.0	30.3	1.8
Pavement grooving	12.6	34*	15	15	377.3	14.5	3.8
Upgraded guardrail	149.7	42	8	9	151.7	31.5	8.1
Upgraded median barrier	7.4	45*	28	29	192.8	10.8	7.0
New median barrier	58.9	62	0*	3*	224.7	213.6	5.4
Impact attenuators	10.7	31*	36	36	390.0	8.0	4.0
Flatten side slopes/regrading	36.5	(25)*	9	8*	—	102.2	—
Bridge approach guardrail transition	4.8	61*	44	45	200.9	25.8	6.3
Obstacle removal	15.0	49	22	23	202.5	16.0	6.4
Railroad-highway crossings	331.2	89	63	67	570.0	114.2	2.2
New flashing lights	55.0	91	74	77	551.4	103.5	2.2
New flashing lights and gates	138.1	92	84	86	591.8	115.3	2.1
New gates only	63.2	90	78	80	432.8	96.7	2.8

Note: Numbers in parentheses indicate increased accident rates.

*No significant change at the 95% confidence level.

[Reprinted with permission of Prentice-Hall, Inc., from Robertson, Hummer, and Nelson (editors), *Manual of Transportation Engineering Studies*, Institute of Transportation Engineers, p. 216. Copyright © 1994 Prentice-Hall, Inc.]

	Table 8-6 Estimates of Accident Costs	
Source	**Event**	**Cost per Person**
National Safety Council, 1991 (1990 dollars)	Fatality	$410,000
	A-Injury	38,200
	B-Injury	8,900
	C-Injury	2,900
	PDO	3,500 (per accident)
NHTSA, National Center for Statistics and Analysis (1986 dollars)	Fatality	360,000
	5-Injury	280,000
	(MAIS scale)	65,000
	4-Injury	15,000
	3-Injury	6,500
	2-Injury	3,100
	1-Injury	580 (per vehicle)
	PDO	

Sources: National Safety Council, "Estimated Costs of Traffic Accidents, 1990," Chicago, Ill., 1991; NHTSA, National Center for Statistics and Analysis.

[Reprinted with permission of Prentice-Hall, Inc., from Robertson, Hummer, and Nelson (editors), *Manual of Transportation Engineering Studies,* Institute of Transportation Engineers, p. 217. Copyright © 1994 Prentice-Hall, Inc.]

References

1. *Accident Facts,* 1995 Edition, National Safety Council, Itasca, IL, 1995.
2. Billingsley and Jorgenson, "Direct Costs and Frequencies of 1958 Illinois Vehicle Accidents, *Highway Research Record 12,* Transportation Research Board, National Research Council, Washington, DC, 1963.
3. *Manual of Transportation Engineering Studies,* 1st Edition, Institute of Transportation Engineers, Prentice-Hall, Englewood Cliffs, NJ, 1994, Chapter 11.
4. Pline James (editor), *Traffic Engineering Handbook,* 4th Edition, Institute of Transportation Engineers, Prentice-Hall, Englewood Cliffs, NJ, 1991.
5. "Accident Data Quality: A Synthesis of Highway Practice," *NCHRP Synthesis 192,* Transportation Research Board, National Research Council, Washington, DC, 1993.
6. "Safety Research: Accident Studies, Enforcement, EMS, Management, and Simulation 1990," *Transportation Research Record 1270,* Transportation Research Board, National Research Council, Washington, DC, 1990.

Problems

Problem 8–1

Consider the following data for the year 1997 in a small suburban community:

Number of accidents	360
Fatal	10
Injury	36
PDO	314
Number of fatalities	15
Area population	50,000
Registered vehicles	35,000
Annual VMT	12,000,000
Average speed	30 mph

Compute all relevant exposure and population-based accident rates for this data. Compare these to the national norms found in this chapter.

Problem 8–2

The data of Table 8-7 details information concerning pedestrian accidents in 1984. Using two (and no more) graphic displays, convey as much of this information as practicable, in as clear a manner as possible.

Problem 8–3

Consider the statistical display of Figure 8-10. What information does it convey, and how may it be interpreted?

Table 8-7 Distribution of Pedestrian Deaths and Injuries by Age and Action, 1984

Actions	All Ages	Age of Persons Killed or Injured							
		Under 5	5–9	10–14	15–19	20–24	25–44	45–64	65 and Over
All Actions	*100.0%*	*6.8%*	*12.3%*	*14.5%*	*8.3%*	*12.2%*	*24.8%*	*12.0%*	*9.1%*
Total Pedestrians	**100.0%**	**100.0%**	**100.0%**	**100.0%**	**100.0%**	**100.0%**	**100.0%**	**100.0%**	**100.0%**
Crossing or entering	52.5	47.7	65.5	50.2	48.3	43.9	47.4	56.8	66.1
at intersection	25.0	9.7	13.7	23.7	19.0	26.4	27.0	33.1	41.1
between intersection	27.5	38.0	51.8	26.5	29.3	17.5	20.4	23.7	25.0
Walking in roadway	23.1	31.3	9.9	34.4	17.4	30.8	23.0	19.5	17.0
with traffic	13.0	22.2	1.4	25.0	9.8	16.2	11.1	10.1	10.1
against traffic	10.1	9.1	8.5	9.4	7.6	14.6	11.9	9.4	6.9
Standing in roadway	1.0	0.4	0.2	0.3	1.9	1.3	1.6	1.0	0.5
Pushing or working on vehicle in roadway	1.1	0.5	0.2	0.3	1.6	1.9	1.8	1.3	0.4
Other working in roadway	1.0	0.2	0.2	0.2	1.1	1.2	1.5	1.5	0.6
Playing in roadway	2.1	6.6	6.6	3.4	1.8	0.8	0.4	0.2	0.1
Other in roadway	13.7	10.0	14.7	8.6	16.3	14.4	17.9	12.9	9.4
Not in roadway	5.5	3.3	2.7	2.6	11.6	5.7	6.4	6.8	5.9

[From *Accident Facts*, National Safety Council, p. 63, 1995.]

What additional information would be useful, but is not shown?

Problem 8–4

Consider the collision and condition diagrams of Figure 8-11. Discuss the probable causes of the accidents observed. Recommend improvements, and illustrate them on a revised conditions diagram. Would these recommendations

change if the land on the southeast corner of the intersection were vacant?

Problem 8–5

A before-after accident study results in 25 accidents during the year before a major improvement to an intersection, and 15 the year after. May this reduction in accidents be considered significant? Use the normal approximation test.

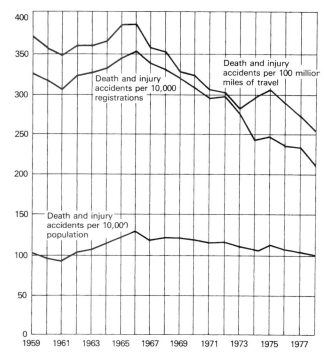

Figure 8-10   Death and injury accident rates, New York State—1977. [From *Motor Vehicle Statistics,* State of New York Department of Motor Vehicles, p. 3, 1978.]

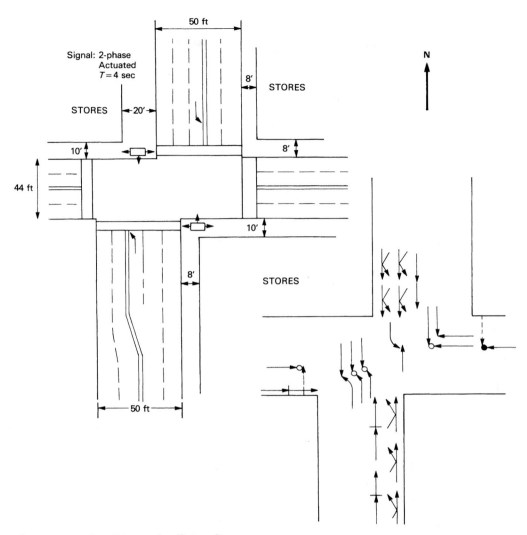

Figure 8-11   Condition and collision diagram.

9

Traffic Capacity
Analysis Concepts

One of the most critical needs in traffic engineering is a clear understanding of *how much* traffic a given facility can accommodate, and *under what operating conditions*. These are the issues addressed in traffic capacity analysis.

The basis for all capacity analysis is a set of analytic models that relate flow levels, geometric characteristics, and controls to measures of the resulting operating quality. These models may be based on extensive field data, theoretic algorithms, laws of physics, and/or simulation results. Their application allows traffic engineers to determine the ultimate traffic-carrying capacity of the facility, and to estimate operating characteristics at various flow levels.

In the United States, the standard reference for capacity analysis procedures is the *Highway Capacity Manual* (*HCM*). This document is published by the Transportation Research Board (TRB), and its contents are the responsibility of the TRB Committee on Highway Capacity and Quality of Service (HCQSC) and its subcommittees. Both the Federal Highway Administration (FHWA) and the National Cooperative Highway Research Program (NCHRP) support the development of capacity analysis models and procedures through funded research efforts.

There have been three full editions of the *HCM*. The first was published by the then Bureau of Public Roads in 1950 [1]. The document was primarily used as a design guide, and was intended to provide for minimal nationwide consistency in design practices for the rapidly-growing post-WWII highway system. It was based on scant data, and many of the basic relationships were developed through the theoretical application of professional judgment.

Following the publication of the 1950 *HCM,* the informal group of Bureau of Public Roads personnel that essentially wrote the manual became the initial members of the HCQSC. Subsequent publications of the *HCM* were handled by the TRB. The second edition of the *HCM* was published in 1965 [2]. The second edition reflected a significantly-improved data base, and more extensive knowledge concerning the operation of limited-access facilities. The concept of *level of service* was introduced, and procedures allowed for analysis of current or proposed operations, as well as for design use. Over time, the predominant use of the procedures of the 1965 *HCM* became analysis, as opposed to direct design usage. Many design applications were handled as trial-and-error analyses of various proposed configurations.

While the first two editions of the *HCM* were produced primarily through the direct efforts of volunteer committee members (with data provided by federal and state transportation agencies), the third edition was based almost entirely on formal research studies funded by FHWA and NCHRP. The HCQSC became a review body, and assisted in the preparation of final text for the third edition, which was published in 1985 [3]. The 1985 *HCM* was published in loose-leaf format, with the hopes that frequent updates of portions of the manual could be more easily accomplished. The manual also represented a significant move towards operational analysis as the primary use of procedures. Data bases were more comprehensive and better documented, and procedures were significantly more detailed and involved.

Because of the computational complexity of some methodologies of the 1985 *HCM,* led by the signalized intersection procedure, a set of software was developed shortly after completion of the third edition, under the sponsorship of the FHWA. The *Highway Capacity Software (HCS)* package [4] has become the "official" package for replicating the computational methodologies of the *HCM,* and it is regularly updated as changes to the manual occur. Recent surveys [5] show that the vast majority of applications of the *HCM* are done using software. In a sense, *HCS* has become the manual. This change has placed new burdens on the HCQSC to monitor not only the manual itself, but the principal software package that implements it. Other software packages have been privately developed to perform, and in some cases extend, models of the *HCM.*

Even though the 1985 *HCM* was published in loose-leaf form, it has not been possible to update it page by page due to the limitations of the publication process. One full chapter of the manual, "Multilane Rural and Suburban Highways," was replaced in 1992. In 1994, the TRB published an update of the third edition of the *HCM,* in which almost one-half of the material is revised [6]. While not a full fourth edition, this release continues the development of capacity and level of service models. In addition to introductory chapters, revised chapters are included for:

• Basic Freeway Sections
• Ramps and Ramp Terminals
• Signalized Intersections
• Unsignalized Intersections
• Urban and Suburban Arterials

Another significant revision of the HCM will occur in late 1997, about the same time that this text appears in print. It will include additional changes to procedures for basic freeway sections, signalized intersections, unsignalized intersections, and urban and suburban arterials. A new weaving chapter is included, as are addenda to several other affected chapters.

For the most part, this text is based on the material that will appear in the 1997 update of the *HCM.* Chapter 17, an analysis of signalized intersections, is based on the 1994 *HCM,* with a discussion of expected 1997 changes. Unfortunately, several important aspects of the 1997 signalized intersection technique were still under discussion as this text went to print.

Work on a full fourth edition of the *HCM* is now underway. It is expected to be published in the year 2000. The fourth edition will be quite different in form and substance than previous editions. In addition to a paper document, a CD-ROM presentation is being developed with moderate multimedia content. A new version of the *HCS* package will also be available on the same CD-ROM, allowing for full integration of the manual itself and the software that implements it. Coordinated by the HCQSC, the fourth edition is supported by an extensive research and production program funded by FHWA and NCHRP, and more recently by National Cooperative Transit Research Program (NCTRP). The fourth edition will deal more explicitly with the use and application of simulation models, and the use of capacity analysis output in related models (such as air quality and planning models).

Capacity

A. The concept of capacity defined

The *Highway Capacity Manual* defines the capacity of a facility as "*the maximum hourly rate at which persons or vehicles can be reasonably expected to traverse a point or uniform segment of a lane or roadway during a given time period under prevailing roadway, traffic, and roadway conditions."* This definition contains several important concepts:

1. The capacity of a facility depends on prevailing conditions. *Traffic conditions* refer to the mix of passenger cars, trucks, buses, and recreational vehicles in the traffic stream. Traffic conditions also include peaking characteristics, proportions of turning movements at intersections, and other factors describing the nature of traffic demand. *Roadway conditions* refer to geometric characteristics of the facility. These include type of facility, number and use of lanes, lane and shoulder widths, lane configuration, and horizontal and vertical alignment. The latter are often considered through surrogate measures that will be defined when used. *Control conditions* apply primarily to surface facilities, and most often refer to signals at individual intersections and on arterials. Controls affecting capacity also include STOP signs and lane use controls. If any of the underlying prevailing conditions change, the capacity of the facility also changes.

2. Capacity is defined for a "point or uniform section" of a facility. Capacity is estimated for segments having uniform traffic, roadway, and control conditions. Points at which any or all of these conditions change represent the boundaries of segments for which separate analyses will be necessary.

3. Capacity is the maximum *rate of flow* that can be accommodated by the facility segment. By definition, most capacity procedures deal with the rate of flow within the worst 15 minutes of the peak hour(s). Thus, the capacity of a facility most often *does not* represent the maximum number of vehicles that can be accommodated in a full hour. In the 1994 *HCM,* however, some facilities *may* be analyzed according to the full peak hour. The user must take care to implement the procedure properly when selecting this option.

4. Perhaps the most difficult concept concerning capacity is that of *reasonable expectancy.* Measuring capacity directly is difficult, at best. In truth, the measured capacity at a single location will show moderate to significant variation from day to day, week to week, and year to year. Further, local driving habits produce a variation in observed capacities for given types of facilities in different regions. Capacity is not, therefore, the highest flow rate ever observed on a given facility or facility type. Rather, it represents a value that can be "reasonably expected" to exist on a regular basis over time, and in different regions for similar facilities. It is not, therefore, impossible to observe actual flow rates that exceed the "capacity" indicated in the *HCM.* Higher values, however, cannot be counted on to exist at all times and in all locations. Thus, as a criteria for both analysis and design, values are based on what can be "reasonably expected" with consistency.

5. Capacity may be defined in terms of persons/hour or vehicles/hour, depending on the type of facility involved, and the purpose of the analysis. Most traffic facilities are analyzed in terms of vehicles/hour, although average occupancies can be used to convert to persons/hour with relative ease. Transit and pedestrian facilities are analyzed in terms of persons/hour, which is a more meaningful parameter for such facilities.

It should be noted that, while capacity is an important concept, operating characteristics at capacity are generally quite poor, and it is difficult (but not impossible) to maintain capacity operation without breakdown for long periods. Thus, a major aspect of capacity analysis is the determination of maximum flow rates that can be accommodated while maintaining prescribed operating characteristics. This leads to the level of service concept, described in the next major section.

B. Capacity values for ideal conditions

Capacity varies with all of the prevailing conditions noted previously. Most capacity analysis models, however, include the determination of capacity under *ideal roadway, traffic, and control conditions.* The value is generally a constant which is then modified to reflect prevailing conditions. For various types of facilities, basic capacity values under ideal conditions are described in the following sections.

1. Multilane uninterrupted flow. Multilane uninterrupted flow refers to freeways and to sections of rural and suburban multilane highways between signalized intersections, where signal spacing is sufficient to allow for uninterrupted flow.

Ideal conditions for such facilities include:

- 12-foot minimum lane width
- 6-foot minimum lateral clearances at the roadside
- all passenger cars in the traffic stream
- driver population consisting of familiar users of the facility
- for rural and suburban multilane highways, alignment sufficient to allow for free-flow speeds ≥60 mph

Under ideal conditions, multilane and freeway capacity values vary with the free-flow speed of the facility. Free-flow speed is technically defined as the theoretical speed of a traffic stream with "0" flow. In practical terms, speed is virtually constant for flow levels below 1000–1300 pcphpl. Thus, free-flow speed is a measurable quantity by which such facilities can be classified. Chapter 10 contains a more detailed discussion of free-flow speed.

Multilane highway capacity varies from 2200 pcphpl for a facility with a free-flow speed of 60 mph, to 1900 pcphpl for a facility with a 45-mph free-flow speed. Freeway capacity varies from 2400 pcphpl for a freeway with a 70-mph free-flow speed to 2250 for a freeway with a 55-mph free-flow speed.

These capacities are *average* per lane values. For example, a 70-mph free-flow speed freeway with three lanes in one direction has a capacity of 3 × 2400 = 7200 pcph. This flow, however, might not be uniformly distributed across the three lanes. Thus, one or more lanes may carry more than 2400 pcph, while others carry less. Also note that for multilane facilities, capacity is generally stated as maximum flow in *one direction*. Therefore, the capacity of a six-lane freeway is stated in terms of *three lanes in one direction*.

Note that these values reflect the 1997 update of the *HCM,* and that they may change in subsequent editions, reflecting the continuous changes in observed driver behavior.

2. Two-lane highways. Two-lane highways are unique among uninterrupted flow facilities. Since passing takes place in the opposing lane, traffic in one direction affects traffic in the other. Thus, for two-lane rural highways, capacity is expressed in terms of total two-directional flow.

Ideal conditions for two-lane rural highways are:

- design speed ≥60 mph
- 12-foot lane widths
- 6-foot minimum clear shoulders at the roadside
- level terrain
- no "NO PASSING" zones
- 50/50 directional split of traffic
- all passenger cars in the traffic stream

Under these conditions, a two-lane rural highway has a capacity of 2800 pcph in both directions. Note that there are more ideal conditions specified than for multilane highways. This is because there are more prevailing conditions that affect capacity of two-lane highways than affect multilane highways.

It should also be noted that virtually no actual two-lane highways have anything resembling ideal conditions. Thus, actual capacities, when adjusted for prevailing conditions, are often considerably lower than the ideal value cited here.

3. Interrupted flow. For interrupted flow, signalized intersections represent the most severe capacity restrictions, as it is only for these that full capacity values can be specified. At signalized intersections, however, signal timing significantly affects the capacity of a given lane or approach, as it controls the fraction of time that the intersection is available for flow from that lane or approach. Basic capacity for signalized intersections is defined in terms of the *saturation flow rate,* i.e., the capacity of the lane or approach assuming that the signal is green at all times.

The saturation flow rate at signalized intersections under ideal conditions is 1900 pcphgpl—passenger cars per hour of green per lane. The ideal conditions at a signalized intersection approach are:

- 12-foot lane widths
- level approach grade
- all passenger cars in the traffic stream
- no left- or right-turning vehicles in the traffic stream
- no parking adjacent to a travel lane within 250 ft of the stop line
- intersection located in a non-CBD area

Capacity values under ideal conditions from the 1997 *HCM* are summarized in Table 9-1.

Table 9-1 Basic Capacities under Ideal Conditions

Type of Facility	Basic Capacity
Freeways:	
70 mph free-flow speed	2400 pcphpl
65 mph free-flow speed	2350 pcphpl
60 mph free-flow speed	2300 pcphpl
55 mph free-flow speed	2250 pcphpl
Multilane Highways:	
60 mph free-flow speed	2200 pcphpl
55 mph free-flow speed	2100 pcphpl
50 mph free-flow speed	2000 pcphpl
45 mph free-flow speed	1900 pcphpl
Two-Lane Rural Highways	2800 pcph
Interrupted Flow	1900 pcphgpl

C. The *v/c* ratio and its use

A critical factor in any capacity analysis is the proportion of the facility's capacity being utilized by current or projected traffic. This value is the ratio of current or projected flow rate to the capacity of the facility, or:

$$v/c = \frac{rate\ of\ flow}{capacity} \qquad [9\text{-}1]$$

This ratio is often used as a measure of the sufficiency of existing or proposed capacity. In concept, a ratio greater than 1.00 can exist where a forecast demand flow rate is used to compare to an existing or estimated capacity. The actual rate of flow (departing a section of roadway) can never be greater than its actual capacity. In forecasting situations, a v/c ratio above 1.00 predicts that the facility will fail, i.e., be unable to discharge the demand arriving at the section for service. Such a situation will lead to queues and extensive delays.

Level of service

A. The level of service concept

A *level of service* is a letter designation that describes a range of operating conditions on a particular type of facility. Six levels of service are defined, using the letters A through F. Level of service A represents the best level of service, and generally describes opera-

tions of free flow (on uninterrupted flow facilities) and very low delay (on interrupted flow facilities). Level of service F represents the worst operating conditions. In many cases, it will signify that a breakdown has occurred, i.e., that arrival flow is greater than departure flow for a segment, resulting in the build-up of queues and delay. In other cases, it will signify that an operating parameter has exceeded a reasonable maximum based on user expectations. Other letters identify intermediate conditions. While LOS F signifies a breakdown, LOS E most often represents flow at or near capacity.

For each type of facility, levels of service are defined in terms of a single *measure of effectiveness* (MOE). An MOE is a parameter that describes traffic operations in terms discernible by motorists and their passengers. Three primary measures are used in the *HCM:*

1. *Speed and Travel Time:* One of the most discernible measures of service quality is the amount of time spent in travel. Therefore, speed and travel time measures are important MOEs used throughout the *HCM* to define levels of service.
2. *Density:* Density describes the proximity of other vehicles in the traffic stream. It is a surrogate measure for driver comfort and ease, and for the ability to maneuver within the traffic stream. This MOE is used to describe levels of service for multilane uninterrupted flow facilities in the *HCM.*
3. *Delay:* Delay is a generic term describing excess or unexpected time spent in travel. Many specific delay measures are defined and used as MOEs in the *HCM.* They are primarily used on interrupted flow facilities, where signals and other interruptions often cause delay. A unique delay measure, percent time delay, is used to define levels of service on two-lane rural highways.

Table 9-2 illustrates the specific measures of effectiveness used to define levels of service for various types of facilities in the 1997 *HCM.*

B. Service flow rates and service volumes

Figure 9-1 illustrates levels of service for an uninterrupted flow highway segment, defined in terms of density, the MOE for these types of facilities. Note

Table 9-2 Measures of Effectiveness in 1997 *HCM*

Type of Flow	Type of Facility	MOE
Uninterrupted	Freeway	
	Basic sections	Density (pc/mi/ln)
	Weaving areas	Density (pc/mi/ln)
	Ramp junctions	Density (pc/mi/ln)
	Multilane highways	Density (pc/mi/ln)
	Two-Lane highways	Percent time delay (%)
		Average upgrade speed (mph)
Interrupted	Signalized inter.	Control delay (sec/veh)
	Unsignalized inter.	Average total delay (sec/veh)
	Arterials	Average travel speed (mph)
	Transit	Load factor (pers/seat)
	Pedestrians	Space (sq ft/ped)

that each level of service represents a *range* of operating conditions, and that two points *within* a given level of service may represent operating characteristics that are more different than two points in *two different levels of service that are close to the boundary.* The letter designations for service quality are a convenient way of explaining often-complex concepts to various public groups and decision-makers. The engineer, however, has access to the MOE values, which are more precise, and which often are better descriptors of operations than a single letter-grade covering a sometimes broad range of conditions.

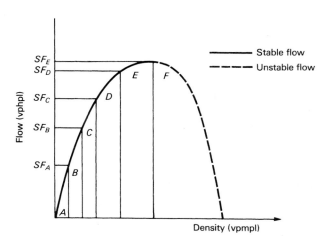

Figure 9-1 Levels of service for multilane uninterrupted flow illustrated.

Note also that for uninterrupted flow facilities, it is possible to define the maximum rate of flow that can be sustained for any given level of service (under ideal conditions). These values are shown in Figure 9-1, and are referred to as *service flow rates (SF)*. The service flow rate for a given LOS is the maximum rate of flow that can be sustained without violating the defined operating limits of that level. By convention, capacity is most often defined in terms of flow rates for a peak 15-minute period. Service flow rates, therefore, can be converted to equivalent full-hour volumes using the PHF:

$$SV_i = SF_i \times PHF \qquad [9\text{-}2]$$

where: SV_i = service volume for level of service i, vph
SF_i = service flow rate for level of service i, vph
PHF = peak hour factor

The service volume, SV, would then be the maximum full-hour volume that could be accommodated without violating the defined operating limits of that level *during the worst 15 minutes of the hour.*

While many capacity analysis methodologies allow the determination of service flow rates and service volumes, some procedures do not. In signalized intersections, for example, operations are so complex that the same MOE may occur under many different flow scenarios, making it impossible to determine a specific *SF* or *SV* for a given level of service. Chapters dealing with specific methodologies discuss this issue as appropriate.

C. Level of service criteria changes in the 1997 update of the *HCM* and beyond

The most significant change in the 1997 update is the conversion of the MOE for signalized intersections from *average individual stopped-time delay* to *control delay* (often referred to as approach delay). This would bring the signalized intersection methodology into conformance with the delay MOE used in evaluating unsignalized intersections (total delay and control delay are basically the same), and in the computation of average speed along an arterial. Criteria would be shifted to produce approximately the same levels of service as the current procedure.

Beyond the 1997 update, there has been much discussion and study on the LOS structure for the *HCM* 2000. The full fourth edition of the *HCM* is expected to focus much more heavily on system measures. Thus, levels of service may be needed to address long segments of facilities, corridors involving several facilities, or networks involving many facilities. A central theme being developed is that *travel time* is the measure most evident to users. Thus, an attempt will be made to have all procedures result in a speed- or time-based operational measure. The *HCM* 2000 will also include methodologies that yield more than one output parameter. There is already some consideration (for two-lane rural highways) of a level of service structure using more than one MOE. Such an approach would be a departure from the traditional, and would result in a matrix structure of criteria.

Adjusting capacity and service flow rate to reflect prevailing conditions

It might be reasonably stated that most capacity and level of service analysis methodologies do nothing more than address the effect of prevailing non-ideal conditions on the capacities illustrated in Table 9-1, and on service flow rates for the various levels of service.

Typically, the ideal capacity or service flow rate is drawn from a table or figure, and is modified by a series of multiplicative adjustment factors, each reflecting the impact of a given prevailing condition or set of conditions:

$$c = c_I \times f_1 \times f_2 \times \ldots \times f_i \qquad [9\text{-}2]$$

where: c = capacity of facility under prevailing conditions, vph (alternatively, this may be SF_i, the service flow rate for level of service i under prevailing conditions)

c_I = capacity of facility under ideal conditions, pcph (alternatively, this may be MSF_i, the maximum—or ideal—service flow rate under ideal conditions)

f_i = multiplicative adjustment factor for prevailing condition i

Different types of facilities have different categories of "prevailing conditions" that must be accounted for in the model. Generally, for each ideal condition specified, there is an adjustment factor to account for any non-ideal occurrence of the specified characteristic. Most of the models, however, are developed by calibrating each adjustment factor separately. There is little or no research on the accuracy of using several multiplicative adjustment factors together. Does a truck in a narrow lane have the same impact on traffic as the multiplication of the effect of a truck in a normal lane, and a narrow lane, each occurring separately? Such questions are left unanswered, and most often, unresearched.

Prevailing conditions, as noted, are grouped in categories of geometric, traffic, or control conditions. Each of these is discussed briefly in the sections that follow.

A. Geometric conditions affecting capacity and service flow rates

1. Horizontal and vertical alignment. The basic alignment of the facility generally has an impact on its capacity and service flow rates. As the alignment of a multilane facility becomes more restrictive, drivers must slow down and exercise more caution. This process most often results in reduced speeds for given flow levels, and a reduction in capacity under prevailing conditions. For two-lane rural highways, alignment directly controls passing opportunities, and may have a severe impact on capacity and service flow rates.

While methodologies of the 1965 *HCM* most often quantified alignment in terms of the *design speed,* this term has been dropped from the 1985 and 1994 versions. Design speed was primarily a measure applied to a specific roadway feature (i.e., a horizontal or vertical curve element). It was the maximum safe speed for a particular roadway element. It was difficult to apply this measure across a set of highway sections with varying vertical and horizontal alignment elements. In the 1985 *HCM,* and even more in the 1994 and 1997 updates, *free-flow speed* is used as a surrogate measure for alignment. Free-flow speed is defined as the average speed of traffic when there are no vehicles present, a value with only theoretical meaning. On the other hand, modern flow characteristics are such that speed remains virtually constant over a broad range of flows, and can therefore be measured in the field at low to moderate volumes (<1300 pcphpl). Such a speed reflects not only the horizontal and vertical alignment, but such parameters as density and activity levels at roadside sites, numbers of turning vehicles, and other difficult-to-quantify traffic elements.

As seen in Table 9-1, the capacity of multilane facilities tends to decline with decreases in free-flow speed. This is because for any given density, drivers are traveling at slower speeds on a facility with restricted geometry. Given that rate of flow is the product of speed and density, it is easy to see how this leads to a decline in capacity.

2. Lane width and lateral clearance. These two factors have very similar impacts on drivers. Narrow lanes force drivers to travel laterally closer to one another than is comfortable. Drivers compensate by driving slower at similar densities, or by leaving longer spacings between themselves and a lead vehicle. In either case, the capacity declines.

Restricted lateral clearance has a similar effect. Drivers will shy away from a barrier or objects at the roadside that are close enough to impose an obvious hazard to the driver. In so doing, the driver moves closer to the vehicles in the next lane, and once again, the normal compensation is to drive more slowly and/or leave longer longitudinal spacings between vehicles.

Figure 9-2 clearly shows this effect in a section of highway with extremely poor conditions. In the illustration, 10-ft lanes are complicated by dangerous median and roadside barriers immediately at the edge of the pavement. Note how virtually every vehicle is "hugging" the lane line to avoid getting too close to the roadside barriers. In this section, the situation is so bad that it is virtually impossible for two vehicles to travel side-by-side!

3. Grades. The impact of grades on traffic operations and capacity is complex. For most types of facilities, the 1997 *HCM* assumes that the combination of *heavy vehicles* and *grades* creates an impact. Heavy vehicles cannot maintain the same speed as passenger cars on grades of appropriate length and severity, and therefore create large gaps in the traffic stream that cannot be effectively filled by normal passing maneuvers. For facilities such as freeways and multilane rural highways, it is assumed that passenger car operation is unaffected by the presence of grades.

The exceptions to this approach are unsignalized and signalized intersections, and two-lane rural highways. In all of these cases, the methodology also considers the impact of grades on the operation of *passenger cars.* In each case, the models used are complex, and not consistent with each other.

Thus, while it is clear that grades can and do influence traffic behavior, the *HCM* has not yet developed a consistent way of treating this impact.

B. Prevailing traffic conditions affecting capacity

1. Directional distribution. The only type of facility affected by directional distribution is the two-lane rural highway. On this type of facility, where passing maneuvers in one direction must take place in the opposing lane of flow, flow in one direction has an important influence over flow in the other. The "ideal" capacity of 2800 pcph (in both directions) is based on a 50%-50% split of traffic in the two directions. For any other directional distribution, the capacity decreases, falling to a value of 2000 pcph when 100% of the traffic is in *one* direction. The latter value is related to the maximum average per lane capacity of a freeway that was in effect at the time the two-lane procedure was developed.

Figure 9-2 Impact of narrow lanes and lateral obstructions illustrated.

For other types of facilities, each direction of flow is considered separately. The directional distribution is important to results, however. A freeway with a 70%-30% directional distribution of traffic must be designed to accommodate 70% of the peak-hour traffic *in both directions.* What goes in direction 1 in the A.M. peak will return in direction 2 in the P.M. peak. This principle is extremely important at signalized intersections, where right turns in one peak period become left turns in the other.

2. Lane distribution. Most highway capacity analysis procedures ignore lane distribution as an explicit factor affecting flow. Sets of lanes operating in equilibrium are analyzed, and average per lane flows are used to characterize operations.

In Figure 9-3(a), each direction of a freeway is operating in equilibrium, and is analyzed separately. Within each direction, the lane distribution is ignored, although it is recognized that it is most likely *not* uniform. It is assumed that drivers select lanes to optimize their perceived operation in the traffic stream, and that over time, an equilibrium distribution is reached. For capacity and level of service analysis, the details of lane distribution are unimportant; only the results of the equilibrium are of interest.

Figure 9-3(b) illustrates an intersection approach with two exclusive left-turn lanes and three lanes for

through and right-turning vehicles. Vehicles in the left turn lanes will seek equilibrium, while those in the three through/RT lanes will also reach an equilibrium lane distribution. However, these two sets of lanes *must* be separately analyzed, because lane use regula-

(a) Equilibrium is established in each direction on a freeway.

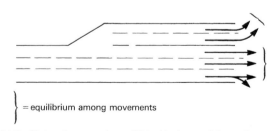

} = equilibrium among movements

(b) Equilibrium is separately established in the two left-turn lanes and remaining lanes of an intersection approach.

Figure 9-3 Lane distribution considerations in capacity and level of service analysis.

tions prevent left-turning vehicles from using the through/RT lanes, and vice-versa.

3. Heavy vehicles in the traffic stream. The single most important traffic characteristic affecting capacity and level of service is the presence of heavy vehicles in the traffic stream. The effect of such vehicles is twofold:

- Heavy vehicles are larger than passenger cars, and occupy more space.
- Heavy vehicles have operating characteristics generally inferior to those of passenger cars.

The second is the most important. As noted previously, heavy vehicles often are unable to maintain the same speed as passenger cars on grades of appropriate length and severity. Figure 9-4 illustrates the result: long gaps form in front of heavy vehicles on a grade that is not effectively filled by normal passing maneuvers.

Heavy vehicles are generally placed in one of four different categories:

a. *Trucks* are heavy vehicles engaged in the transport of goods, materials, or services requiring equipment. They come in a variety of shapes and sizes, from light vans and single-unit trucks to double-back tractor trailers. The average weight-to-horse-power ratio for trucks is in the 125–150 lbs/hp range, with the largest and heaviest trucks in the 300–400 lbs/hp range.

b. *Recreational Vehicles* involve motor homes and boats/race cars/etc. towed by passenger vehicles. Weight-to-horsepower ratios for this class of vehicle are generally in 30–60 lbs/hp range. Many recreational vehicles are awkward to handle, and are being driven by inexperienced drivers.

c. *Intercity or Through Buses* are heavy vehicles involved in the transportation of passengers. By definition, these buses *do not* stop to pick up or discharge passengers within the confines of the facility. Weight-to-horsepower ratios for this class of vehicle are in the 100–135 lbs/hp range. In many of the new procedures adopted in 1994 and 1997, intercity buses are no longer considered to be a separate type of heavy vehicle; rather, they are grouped with trucks in a single category.

d. *Local Buses* are transit vehicles that stop within the right-of-way to pick-up and/or discharge passengers. Weight-to-horsepower ratios are somewhat lower than for intercity buses, as transit buses generally have an automatic transmission and less powerful engines than their intercity brothers. Local buses pose an additional deleterious effect on capacity: when they stop to pick up or discharge

Figure 9-4 Impact of heavy vehicle operation on grades illustrated.

passengers, they are blocking a portion of the roadway.

In most cases, heavy vehicles are modeled by determining the passenger car equivalent of 1 truck, bus, or recreational vehicle (E_T, E_B, and E_R). This is the number of passenger cars displaced in the traffic stream by *one* truck, bus, or RV. These equivalents can then be manipulated into a form that yields a multiplicative adjustment factor. The details of how this is done are explained in Chapter 11.

C. Prevailing control factors affecting capacity

A number of control factors can affect capacity, although most are not explicitly accounted for in computational methodologies:

1. *Speed Limits:* Speed limits do not directly affect values of capacity, which tends to occur at relatively low speeds. Speed limits can, however, affect the *free-flow speed* of a facility, and therefore the characteristics of flow on the facility. This is particularly true where speed limits are unreasonably low and strictly enforced. In most cases, studies show that drivers are not terribly affected by speed limits unless they are strictly enforced.

2. *Lane Use Controls:* At signalized and other intersections, regulations creating separate left- and/or right-turning lanes have an impact on which vehicles can use certain lanes. This has a clear impact on flow in those lanes, and therefore, on the quality of operation.

3. *Traffic Signals:* Traffic signals dramatically affect the capacity and quality of flow on intersection approaches. The signal effectively regulates *how much time* vehicles on a given approach or set of lanes can legally move through the intersection. Any change in signal design and timing has, therefore, a dramatic impact on capacity and operations.

4. *STOP and YIELD Signs*: Again, these types of control influence the capacity and operation of intersection approaches subject to control. The 1985 *HCM* contained procedures for analysis of both types of control; the 1994 *HCM* restricts analysis to STOP-controlled intersection approaches.

There are no adjustment factors for any of these control conditions in the *HCM*. Rather, the impact of each is fundamental to analysis procedures used, and is explicitly considered in a more systematic way.

Summary

This chapter provides a basic overview of the principles of capacity and level of service analysis. Subsequent chapters deal with specific types of traffic facilities, and present specific methodologies for their analysis.

References

1. *Highway Capacity Manual,* 1st Edition, Bureau of Public Roads, Washington, DC, 1950.
2. *Highway Capacity Manual, Special Report 87,* Transportation Research Board, National Research Council, Washington, DC, 1965.
3. *Highway Capacity Manual, Special Report 209,* Transportation Research Board, National Research Council, Washington, DC, 1985.
4. "Highway Capacity Software," *User's Manual,* McTrans Center, University of Florida, Gainesville, FL, 1994.
5. Reilly, W., et al., "Highway Capacity Manual for the Year 2000," *Draft Final Report,* Catalina Engineering, Inc., Tucson, AZ, and Polytechnic University, Brooklyn, NY, July 1996.
6. *Highway Capacity Manual, Special Report 209,* 3rd Edition, Transportation Research Board, National Research Council, Washington, DC, (revised) 1994.

Problems

Problem 9–1 √

A freeway has three lanes in each direction. What is the capacity in one direction of the freeway if its free-flow speed is 65 mph, and if applicable adjustment factors are:

Lane width/lateral clearance = 0.90

Heavy vehicle presence = 0.85

All other conditions are ideal, and require no adjustment.

Problem 9–2 √

A two-lane highway in severe terrain has a number of prevailing conditions that reduce its capacity, as follows:

Terrain and inability to pass = 0.75

Heavy vehicle presence = 0.82

Lane width/narrow shoulders = 0.90

Direction distribution = 0.79

What is the capacity of the roadway in *both* directions if all other conditions may be considered to be ideal?

Problem 9–3 √

Sketch a density-flow curve for a freeway and illustrate the six levels of service on this plot.

10

Highway Capacity Analysis of Multilane, Uninterrupted Flow Facilities

The most straightforward application of the concepts of capacity and level of service, as discussed in Chapter 9, is to a class of highway facilities that provide for multilane, uninterrupted flow. For such facilities, the characteristics and operation of traffic depend on the interactions among drivers of vehicles in the traffic stream, and between these drivers and the geometric features of the roadway.

Uninterrupted flow defines a class of highway facilities on which there are no external interruptions to the traffic stream. "External causes" include such things as at-grade driveways and intersections, traffic signals, STOP or YIELD signs, and vehicles entering and leaving curbside parking places.

The *freeway* is the only type of facility that provides completely uninterrupted flow. There is no access to abutting lands, no at-grade intersections or driveways, no traffic signals. All access and egress are via ramps that are intended to allow merging and diverging to take place at reasonable speeds. When freeways break down, or experience congestion, it is due to causes within the traffic stream, i.e., the result of interactions among vehicles and the roadway environment.

Surface *multilane highways* do not provide purely uninterrupted flow. Since access to abutting lands is permitted, there are some driveways and intersections at grade. At busy intersections, traffic signals may be introduced. However, in many rural and suburban areas, there is considerable distance between interruptions on such facilities. In these cases, flow between interruptions is virtually "uninterrupted." Most studies show, for example, that at a maximum distance of two miles downstream of a traffic signal, the effects of platooned flow have been fully dissipated. In some cases, platoons fully disperse at distances as short as one mile from the nearest upstream signal. Sections that are at least this distance from the nearest signals (in both directions), can be considered to accommodate uninterrupted flow. Where signals are spaced more closely, the facility operates as an *arterial,* and the effects of platoon flow are always present.

Multilane highways can be subcategorized into three groups: divided, divided by a two-way left-turn lane, and undivided. Divided multilane highways have a median of at least 4 ft with a median barrier or curb, or a wider median without such a barrier. Medians are usually at least 20 ft wide before they are built without a barrier. The median effectively restricts left turns onto and off of the highway to those places where a median break allows such crossings to occur. In rural areas, long stretches of divided multilane highway may look exactly like a freeway. In some suburban areas, multilane highways are built with a center lane striped to allow left turns in both directions. This requires that the cross section accommodate an odd number of lanes, such as five or seven. Vehicles turning left off of the facility move into the turning lane and wait for a gap in opposing traffic. Those turning left onto the facility cross the near half of the facility, turning into the turning lane. They then seek a gap in traffic into which they can safely merge. These designs reduce the amount of disruption to the traffic stream caused by left-turning vehicles. An uncrossable median eliminates the problem entirely, while the provision of the two-way left-turn lane takes most of the friction out of the main traffic stream.

Undivided multilane highways are "divided" by a simple double yellow marking, which allows for continuous left-turn movements without restriction. Figure 10-1 illustrates the basic features of freeways and multilane highways in plan view.

Freeways generally have 4-, 6-, or 8-lane alignments, although occasional 10-lane segments (or segments with 5 lanes in one direction) exist. Wider freeway alignments generally provide for dual separated roadways in each direction, with no single segment having more than 3 lanes. Multilane highways generally have four or six lanes, although an occasional eight-lane alignment is found.

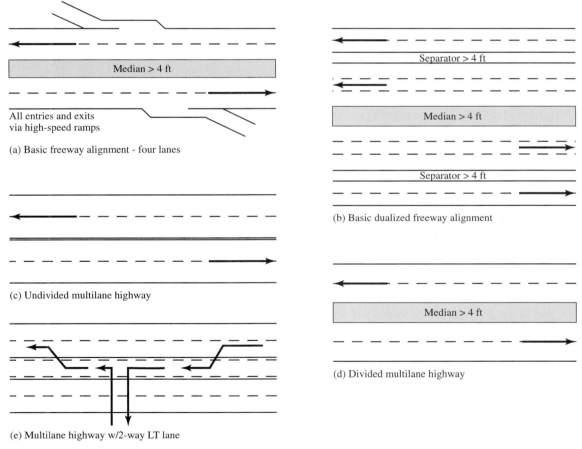

(a) Basic freeway alignment - four lanes

(b) Basic dualized freeway alignment

(c) Undivided multilane highway

(d) Divided multilane highway

(e) Multilane highway w/2-way LT lane

Figure 10-1 Freeway and multilane highway alignments.

Rural *two-lane, two-way highways* may also have sections operating at sufficient distances from fixed interruptions to provide for uninterrupted flow. Even under uninterrupted flow, however, such highways are unique, in that the flow in one direction interacts with flow in the other because passing maneuvers are made in the opposing lane. Thus, their characteristics are quite different from multilane facilities, where passing is accomplished using lanes fully dedicated to the driver's direction of flow. This type of highway facility is analyzed in Chapter 13.

This chapter discusses the capacity and level of service analysis of multilane uninterrupted flow sections, because the methodology for freeways and surface multilane highways are quite similar in structure, and because they share a number of common calibrations.

The methodologies discussed herein are from the 1997 revision of the *Highway Capacity Manual* [1]. Both freeway and multilane highway analysis methodologies have been significantly revised from the procedures of the 1985 *Highway Capacity Manual* [2]. Multilane analysis procedures in the 1985 *HCM* were basically reproduced from the 1965 *HCM* [3] with only minor editorial changes. A study sponsored by the National Cooperative Highway Research Program (NCHRP) [4] resulted in a significant revision, adopted in 1992. Freeway procedures were updated on an interim basis for the 1994 *HCM* based on results in the published literature, and on the multilane results which could be also reasonably applied to freeways. Another NCHRP study, completed in 1995 [5], resulted in further revisions, that are included in the 1997 update.

Freeways and multilane highways are referred to in terms of the total number of travel lanes on the facility. Thus, a 6-lane freeway refers to a freeway with 3 lanes in each direction. Analysis procedures, however, focus on determining the capacity and level of service of a single direction of flow. This is necessary, as there are many instances in which the conditions in one direction are quite different from those in the other. Each direction of a multilane flow facility operates independently of the other in uninterrupted flow situations. The capacity of a 6-lane freeway, for example, will be stated as the maximum rate of flow which can be accommodated in the *3* lanes in *one* direction.

Basic characteristics of multilane flow

Capacity and level of service analysis procedures for multilane uninterrupted flow begin with the calibration of a characteristic set of speed-flow-density relationships for highways operating under "ideal" conditions. Ideal conditions for uninterrupted flow generally implies no heavy vehicles in the traffic stream (all passenger cars), and drivers who are regular users of the facility.

Figure 10-2 shows the theoretical form of the speed vs. flow relationship for multilane uninterrupted flow. It has been modified from Reference [5] and reflects four distinct regions of flow, and illustrates several critical definitions.

- *Region 1* describes a range in which speed is insensitive to flow levels. The constant speed in this range is defined as the *free-flow speed*.
- *Region 2* describes a range in which speed begins to decline in response to increasing levels of flow. This region terminates at point 2, the point of maximum flow, which is defined as *capacity*.
- When arrival flow exceeds the capacity of a segment to discharge flow, a queue forms. The discharge from the queue is relatively stable, and is shown as *Region 3* in Figure 10-2. While the queue discharge flow is constant, the speed of traffic varies, depending on how far downstream of the discharge it is measured. Vehicles leaving a queue will

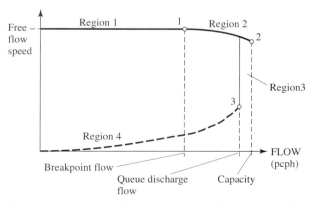

Figure 10-2 General form of multilane speed-flow relationships.

accelerate until their desired speed is reached, unless impeded from doing so by additional downstream breakdowns.

- *Region 4* depicts flow conditions *within the queue* that forms behind a segment or point at which arrival flow exceeds the capacity to discharge. Such a point is referred to as a "breakdown point."

It should be pointed out that the measurements made to calibrate a speed-flow relationship cannot be made at a single point. Regions 1 and 2 should be observed some distance downstream of a point that is expected to break down, such as a heavily-used on-ramp, but far enough downstream to avoid the effects of accelerating vehicles on speed measurements. When the breakdown occurs, queue discharge can be measured at any point downstream of the discharge (without other entry/exit points between the discharge and measurement locations). Speed should be measured at several downstream locations. Region 4 must be observed within the queue after breakdown, or upstream of the breakdown point.

The exact calibration of such a curve depends on the geometric and traffic conditions of the facility, as well as its general environment. The free-flow speed can vary considerably, as is discussed later in this chapter. Such characteristics as the number of roadside entrances or ramps per mile, lane widths and lateral clearances, and even the number of lanes on a facility can influence this value.

Point 2, where speed begins to decline with increasing flow, also varies. In general, the lower the free-flow speed, the higher the flow level to which it can be maintained. Over the past twenty years, drivers have become much more familiar with and skilled at driving on uninterrupted flow facilities. Hence, they are more aggressive, and average speeds have tended to increase, as have the flow levels to which these speeds can be maintained.

There is a great deal of discussion on the issue of whether or not "capacity" is higher than, or equal to the "queue discharge" flow. Depending on the location of study, either result can be achieved. When capacity is significantly higher than queue discharge flows, it tends to be a rather transitory condition that is not maintained for long periods. In such cases, the "queue discharge" flow may be of more interest, as it

is a more stable condition, although certainly not a desirable one.

Region 4 is shown as a dashed line because there is very little real knowledge of precise conditions here. Field studies show great variability, and attempts to calibrate generally result in a fuzzy wide band of points rather than a precise relationship that can be mathematically described.

For the analysis procedures of this chapter, curves have been adopted for a set of "ideal" conditions. These include no heavy vehicles in the traffic stream (all passenger cars) and all drivers are familiar with the facility (generally commuters).

Figure 10-3 shows the standard curves adopted for freeways. These curves were prepared by members of the Freeway Subcommittee of the HCQSC, based primarily on the work in Reference [5]. Other published work on freeway flow characteristics was also considered [6–15].

Figure 10-4 shows similar curves for uninterrupted flow sections of surface multilane highways. These curves resulted from a nationwide study sponsored by the National Cooperative Highway Research Program in the late 1980s [4].

A. General characteristics

The calibrated speed-flow curves for freeways and multilane highways share many common features, and a few that differ. In each case, a family of curves is presented, differentiated by the *free-flow speed* that each exhibits.

Free-flow speed has been defined as the speed that results when density and flow are "zero," i.e., the intercept on the speed scale. In practical terms, however, the free-flow speed is a constant value that prevails over a significant portion of these curves. Speed does not start to decline from the free-flow value until a flow rate of 1300 pcphpl is achieved on freeways. This is the value for a free-flow speed of 70 mph; breakpoints for lower free-flow speeds are even higher. Because of the higher amounts of general side and left-turning frictions on multilane highways, speeds begin to decline at flow rates in the 1200–1400 pcphpl range. This means that free-flow speed can be fairly easily measured on such facilities as the average speed of traffic streams with flow rates lower than 1000 pcphpl.

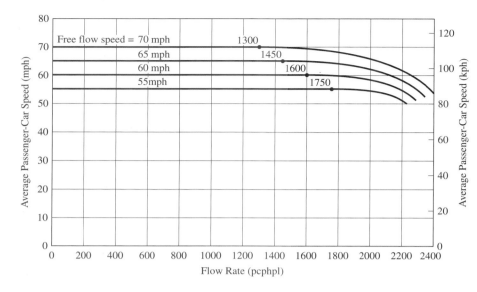

Figure 10-3 Speed-flow characteristics for freeways. [Used with permission of Transportation Research Board, National Research Council, from Draft Chapter 11 of the *Highway Capacity Manual, Special Report 209,* p. 11-3, 1996.]

Free-flow speed is a new concept in categorizing operational characteristics. All analysis procedures rely on the traffic engineer to identify the correct speed-flow curve for his/her facility. While this may be fairly easy for an existing facility (it can be measured in the field), it is impossible to do on future new or substantially altered facilities. For multilane highways, where a comprehensive funded research effort was conducted, an algorithm for estimating free-flow speed has been developed, and will be discussed in a later section. For freeways, no algorithm is provided

in the 1994 *HCM*, but one will exist in the 1997 update, and is included herein.

The multilane procedure hypothesizes that the free-flow speed is a function of such factors as **median type**, **lane widths and lateral clearances**, and the **number of roadside access points per mile**. For freeways, such features as lane widths, lateral clearances, number of interchanges per mile (interchange density) and the number of lanes appear to influence the free-flow speed.

The *general shape* of the families of curves presented in Figures 10-3 and 10-4 are similar. They all

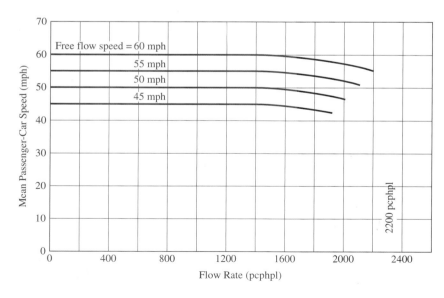

Figure 10-4 Speed-flow characteristics for uninterrupted flow sections of multilane highways. [Used with permission of Transportation Research Board, National Research Council, from *Highway Capacity Manual, Special Report 209,* 3rd Ed., p. 7-4. Copyright © 1994 Transportation Research Board.]

show substantial flow ranges over which speed is constant, and show that the speed drop at capacity is relatively slight, in the range of 5 to 15 mph from the free-flow speed. This reflects the relative comfort of drivers on modern congested highway systems, and explains why breakdowns often occur so quickly. Relatively small increments in demand can move a facility from a stable moving stream at high speeds to the unstable portion of the curve.

Note that none of the curves of Figures 10-3 and 10-4 include any depiction of the unstable parts of the curves. This recognizes the difficulty in properly calibrating the unstable flow regime, and the difficulty in determining how and where to make measurements of such flow (which occurs within queues). All capacity and level of service analysis procedures, however, deal with stable flow. While conditions that will lead to breakdown can be identified and assessed, analysis procedures usually end with the determination that such a breakdown exists. None of the methodologies adequately describes what happens during breakdowns, or during the process of recovery.

B. Capacity values

Both the freeway curves of Figure 10-3 and the multilane highway curves of Figure 10-4 show that capacity varies with the free-flow speed of the facility. The maximum freeway capacity is for 70-mph free-flow speeds, and is 2400 pcphpl. For each 5 mph reduction in free-flow speed, the capacity is reduced by 50 pcphpl, to 2250 pcphpl for 55-mph free-flow speeds. On multilane highways, for the "ideal" free-flow speed of 60 mph, a capacity of 2200 pcphpl is suggested. However,

this value decreases by 100 pcphpl for each 5-mph decrease in free-flow speed below 60 mph.

Table 10-1 summarizes the various values of capacity for freeways and multilane highways, and the approximate average speeds at which capacity occurs.

C. Levels of service

Levels of service for multilane uninterrupted flow facilities are defined on the basis of *density* in pc/mi/ln. As speed does not vary over a wide range of flows, it is not a good indicator of service quality. Density, which is a measure of proximity of other vehicles in the traffic stream, is directly perceived by drivers, and does vary with all flow levels. Density values are *defined* to mark the boundaries between levels of service. Each level of service then covers a range of density values.

For levels of service A through D, boundary conditions can be more or less arbitrarily defined; for level of service E, they cannot. By definition, the upper density bound of level of service E is the density at which capacity occurs. This is a characteristic of the adopted speed-flow curves of Figures 10-3 and 10-4. For freeways, the density at capacity is 45 pc/mi/ln. At higher densities, it is generally not possible to sustain stable flow. For multilane highways, the density at capacity varies somewhat with free-flow speed from 40 pc/mi/ln at 60 mph to 45 pc/mi/ln at 45 mph.

Other density limits were rationally determined to provide for reasonably uniform increments in service flow rate (complete uniformity is not rational, as the curves are non-linear), while maintaining reasonable definitions of different ranges of operation.

Table 10-1 Basic Values of Uninterrupted Flow Capacity

Type of Facility	Free-Flow Speed (mph)	Capacity (pcphpl)	Approx Speed at Capacity (mph)
Freeway	70	2,400	53
	65	2,350	52
	60	2,300	51
	55	2,250	50
Multilane	60	2,200	55
	55	2,100	51
	50	2,000	48
	45	1,900	42

Table 10-2 summarizes the maximum densities defined for the various levels of service on basic freeway sections and multilane highways.

Level of service A is intended to describe free-flow operation. At these low densities, the operation of each vehicle is not greatly influenced by others in the traffic stream. Speeds are not affected by flow in this range, and average speeds at the free-flow speed prevail. Lane changes within the traffic stream, as well as merging and diverging movements, are made relatively easily, as many large gaps in lane flows exist. Short duration, partial lane blockages may cause the LOS to deteriorate locally below level A, but do not cause significant disruptions to flow. The average spacing between vehicles is in the 23–26 car-lengths range.

At *level of service B*, drivers first begin to respond to the presence of other vehicles in the traffic stream, although average speeds remain at the free-flow speed level. Maneuvering within the traffic stream is still relatively easy, but drivers must be more vigilant in searching for gaps in lane flows. The traffic stream still has sufficient gaps to dampen the impacts of most minor partial lane disruptions, and the average spacing between vehicles is in the 18–20 car-lengths range.

At *level of service C*, the presence of other vehicles now begins to restrict maneuverability within the traffic stream. Average speeds remain at the free-flow speed level, but drivers now need to adjust their course to find gaps they can use to pass or merge. A significant increase in driver vigilance is required at this level. While there are still sufficient gaps in the traffic stream to dampen the impact of minor partial lane blockages, any significant blockage could lead to breakdown and the formation of queues. Vehicle spacings are in the 9–11 car-lengths range.

Level of service D is the range in which average speeds begin to decline with increasing flows. Density deteriorates more quickly with flow in this range. Thus, level D enters the range of flow conditions where breakdowns can occur quickly in response to smaller increases in flow. Maneuvering within the traffic stream is now quite difficult, and drivers often have to search for gaps for some time before successfully passing or merging. The ability of the traffic stream to dampen the effects of even minor lane blockages is severely restricted, and most such disruptions result in queue formation unless removed very quickly. The average vehicle spacing at this level is in the 7–9 car-lengths range.

The maximum density limit of *level of service E* defines capacity operation. For such an operation, there are no usable gaps in the traffic stream. Therefore, the impacts of even the slightest disruption to flow cannot be damped. Any such disruption will cause a breakdown, with queues forming rapidly behind the disruption. Maneuvering within the traffic stream is extremely difficult, as other vehicles must give way to accommodate either a lane-changing or merging vehicle. Vehicle spacings are in the 4–6 car-lengths range.

Table 10-2 Maximum Densities for Uninterrupted Flow Levels of Service

Level of Service	Maximum Density for Freeways (pc/mi/ln)	Maximum Density for Multilane Highways (pc/mi/ln)
A	10	12
B	16	20
C	24	28
D	32	34
E	45	40–45 based on free-flow speed
F	>45	>40–45 based on free-flow speed

Level of service F describes conditions in a queue that has formed behind a point of breakdown or disruption. Such disruptions can be accidents or incidents, or might involve regular points of congestion, such as merge areas, where the flow delivered to the merge point regularly exceeds the downstream or merge area capacity. Actual operating conditions vary considerably, and are subject to short term perturbations. As vehicles "shuffle" through the queue, there are periods when they are moving quite quickly, and others when they are stopped completely. Level of service F is used to describe the point of the breakdown as well, even though operations immediately downstream of such a breakdown may appear to be quite good. In forecasting situations, LOS F is predicted when the forecasted demand flow rate exceeds the estimated capacity of the facility.

Levels of service may be graphically illustrated on the basic speed-flow curves of Figures 10-3 and 10-4. Since density = flow/speed, a constant density can be shown on a speed-flow grid as a line of constant slope, beginning at the origin. Figures 10-5 and 10-6 show the level of service definitions in this way, for freeways and multilane highways, respectively. These graphs reinforce the concept of a level of service covering a range in operation conditions, and can be used directly in analysis. Figures 10-5 and 10-6 relate (for ideal conditions) flow and speed to levels of service defined by density. Knowing any two of these three variables, the curves can be entered to determine the third.

Tables 10-3 and 10-4 present the same information as Figures 10-5 and 10-6 in tabular form. In the tables, only boundary values are shown. For the defined maximum density of each level of service, these tables show the expected minimum average speed of traffic expected under ideal conditions (mph), the maximum ideal service flow rate (pcphpl), and the maximum v/c ratio. Tabular values have been rounded in many cases, and may differ slightly from curve values.

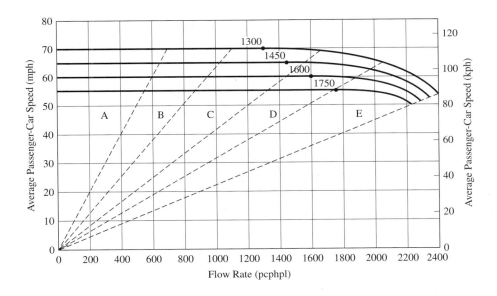

Note: Capacity varies by free-flow speed	
Free-flow speed (mph)	Capacity (pcphpl)
≥70	2400
65	2350
60	2300
55	2250

Figure 10-5 Levels of service on freeways. [Used with permission of Transportation Research Board, National Research Council, from Draft Chapter 11 of the *Highway Capacity Manual, Special Report 209*, p. 11-8, 1996.]

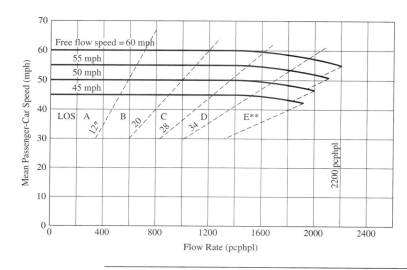

Figure 10-6 Levels of service on multilane highways. [Used with permission of Transportation Research Board, National Research Council, from *Highway Capacity Manual, Special Report 209,* 3rd Ed., p. 7-8. Copyright © 1994 Transportation Research Board.]

Table 10-3 Level of Service Criteria for Basic Freeway Sections

Level of Service	Maximum Density (pc/mi/ln)	Minimum Speed (mph)	Maximum Service Flow Rate (pcphpl)	Maximum v/c Ratio
Free-Flow Speed = 70 MPH				
A	10.0	70.0	700	0.29
B	16.0	70.0	1120	0.47
C	24.0	68.0	1632	0.68
D	32.0	64.0	2048	0.85
E	45.0	53.0	2400	1.00
F	var	var	var	var
Free-Flow Speed = 65 MPH				
A	10.0	65.0	650	0.28
B	16.0	65.0	1040	0.44
C	24.0	64.5	1548	0.66
D	32.0	62.0	1984	0.84
E	45.0	52.0	2350	1.00
F	var	var	var	var
Free-Flow Speed = 60 MPH				
A	10.0	60.0	600	0.26
B	16.0	60.0	960	0.42
C	24.0	60.0	1440	0.63
D	32.0	58.0	1856	0.81
E	45.0	51.0	2300	1.00
F	var	var	var	var
Free-Flow Speed = 55 MPH				
A	10.0	55.0	550	0.24
B	16.0	55.0	880	0.39
C	24.0	55.0	1320	0.59
D	32.0	54.5	1744	0.78
E	45.0	50.0	2250	1.00
F	var	var	var	var

[Used with permission of Transportation Research Board, National Research Council, from Draft Chapter 11 of the *Highway Capacity Manual, Special Report 209,* p. 11-9.]

Table 10-4   Level of Service Criteria for Multilane Highway Sections

LOS	Max Density pc/mi/ln	Min Speed mph	Max Service Flow Rate, pcphpl	Max v/c Ratio
A	12.0	60.0	720	0.33
B	20.0	60.0	1,200	0.55
C	28.0	59.0	1,650	0.75
D	34.0	57.0	1,940	0.89
E	40.0	53.0	2,200	1.00
F	VARIES	VARIES	VARIES	VARIES
Free-Flow Speed = 55 MPH				
A	12.0	55.0	660	0.31
B	20.0	55.0	1,100	0.52
C	28.0	54.0	1,510	0.72
D	34.0	53.0	1,800	0.86
E	41.0	51.0	2,100	1.00
F	VARIES	VARIES	VARIES	VARIES
Free-Flow Speed = 50 MPH				
A	12.0	50.0	600	0.30
B	20.0	50.0	1,000	0.50
C	28.0	50.0	1,400	0.70
D	34.0	49.0	1,670	0.84
E	43.0	47.0	2,000	1.00
F	VARIES	VARIES	VARIES	VARIES
Free-Flow Speed = 45 MPH				
A	12.0	45.0	540	0.28
B	20.0	45.0	900	0.47
C	28.0	45.0	1,260	0.66
D	34.0	44.0	1,500	0.79
E	45.0	42.0	1,900	1.00
F	VARIES	VARIES	VARIES	VARIES

Estimating free-flow Speed

Any analysis of freeways and/or multilane highways involves determining the appropriate free-flow speed of the facility, thereby identifying the correct speed-flow curve for use in the analysis.

While existing procedures for both types of facility stress that field measurement is the most accurate way of determining this, this is often not possible, especially when dealing with the analysis of future designs and situations that cannot be directly observed.

The 1994 *HCM* contains a recommended algorithm for predicting the free-flow speed on multilane highways; the 1997 update will contain a similar algorithm for freeways.

A. Estimating free-flow speed for multilane highways

The *HCM* recommends that free-flow speed be directly measured in the field whenever possible. On multilane highways, average speeds observed at flow levels less than 1400 pcphpl would be an appropriate indicator of free-flow speed, although measurements at flows under 1000 pcphpl are preferred. Such measurements reflect all of the prevailing conditions at the location under study, and require no further adjustment.

Where field measurement is not possible, the following equation may be used to estimate the prevailing free-flow speed:

$$S_F = S_{Fi} - f_m - f_{lw} - f_{lc} - f_a \quad [10\text{-}1]$$

where: S_F = prevailing free-flow speed, mph,
S_{Fi} = free-flow speed under ideal conditions, mph,
f_m = adjustment for median type,
f_{lw} = adjustment for lane width,
f_{lc} = adjustment for lateral clearance, and
f_a = adjustment for access points.

All adjustments are subtractive, and can be found in Table 10-5. The "ideal" free-flow speed, S_{Fi}, should be based on available highway speed data from the facility in question, or from similar facilities. The ideal free-flow speed may be taken to be 1 to 3 mph less than the 85th percentile speed. When the 85th percentile speed is 60 mph or more, 3 mph is deducted; when it is 50 mph, 2 mph is deducted; when it is 40 mph or less, 1 mph is deducted.

A second method for approximating the "ideal" free-flow speed is to relate it to existing or anticipated speed limits. Ideal free-flow speed may be taken to be 7 mph greater than the speed limit for speed limits of 40 and 45 mph, and 5 mph greater than the speed limit at higher speed limits. The relationship between ideal free-flow speeds and speed limits is approximate at best, and should be used with caution.

Once the "ideal" free-flow speed is established, the adjustments shown in Table 10-5 may be applied. Median types and lane widths are self-explanatory. Lateral clearance adjustments are based on the *total* lateral clearance on both sides of a one-way roadway. Left-side obstructions are in the median of the roadway, while right-side obstructions are located at the roadside. For undivided multilane highways, there is no median, and no median obstruction is assumed, as there is a separate adjustment for median

type. Since the "ideal" distance to an obstruction is 6 ft or more, 6 ft is the largest distance to an obstruction used, and a total of 12 ft is therefore the best case that can be used. For undivided highways, the distance to the left-side obstruction is always assumed to be 6 ft.

Some judgment must be used in assessing the impact of lateral obstructions. Drivers become accustomed to some types of obstructions, such as concrete median barriers, and may not react to their presence. When affected by lateral obstructions, drivers usually shift their lateral placement in the adjacent lane away from the obstruction, and/or slow down.

For multilane highways, the number of access points per mile is a major determinant of free-flow speed. An access point is defined as any driveway or unsignalized intersection with sufficient traffic to warrant the vigilance of highway drivers. In assessing the number of access points per mile, only right-side access points are included.

Two examples using equation 10-1 to determine free-flow speed for multilane highways are given below:

EXAMPLE 1

An existing undivided multilane highway is to be improved by widening from 4 to 6 lanes (all lanes = 12 ft), adding a median barrier, and reducing the number of access points per mile from 30 to 10. Lateral clearances will be improved from 3 ft to 6 ft at the roadside. There are no median lateral obstructions in the new design. General speed studies on highways with similar characteristics indicate an 85th percentile speed of 55 mph for the proposed design and 50 mph for the existing design. What is the expected free-flow speed of the facility both before and after the proposed improvements?

SOLUTION 1:   The free-flow speed is estimated from Equation [10-1]:

$$S_F = s_{Fi} - f_m - f_{lw} - f_{lc} - f_a$$

The ideal free-flow speed is estimated from the measured 85th percentile speed on similar highways. Using the general rule and straight-line interpolation:

Table 10-5 Adjustment Factors to Ideal Free-Flow Speed for Multilane Highways

(A) Adjustment for Median Type

Median Type	Adjustment to S_{Fi}
Undivided Highways	1.6 mph
Divided Highways (includes TWLTLs)	0.0 mph

(B) Adjustment for Lane Width

Lane Width	Adjustment to S_{Fi}
10 ft	6.6 mph
11 ft	1.9 mph
12 ft	0.0 mph

(C) Adjustment for Lateral Clearance

Total Lateral Clearance	4-Lane Roadways Adjustment to S_{Fi}	6-Lane Roadways Adjustment to S_{Fi}
12 ft	0.0 mph	0.0 mph
10 ft	0.4 mph	0.4 mph
8 ft	0.9 mph	0.9 mph
6 ft	1.3 mph	1.3 mph
4 ft	1.8 mph	1.7 mph
2 ft	3.6 mph	2.8 mph
0 ft	5.4 mph	3.9 mph

(D) Adjustment for Access-Point Density

Access Points per Mile	Adjustment to S_{Fi}
0	0.0 mph
10	2.5 mph
20	5.0 mph
30	7.5 mph
40 or more	10.0 mph

[Used with permission of Transportation Research Board, National Research Council, from *Highway Capacity Manual, Special Report 209*, 3rd Ed., p. 7-10. Copyright © 1994 Transportation Research Board.]

85th Percentile Speed	S_{Fi} is × mph Less than 85th %
60 mph	3.0 mph
55 mph	2.5 mph
50 mph	2.0 mph
40 mph	1.0 mph

S_{Fi} (new alignment) $= 55.0 - 2.5 = 52.5$ mph

S_{Fi} (existing alignment) $= 50.0 - 2.0 = 48.0$ mph

Adjustments to the ideal free-flow speed may be taken from Table 10-5, as follows. Adjustments are selected for both the improved and unimproved highway.

Adjustment	Existing Alignment	New Alignment
Median Type	−1.6 mph	0.0 mph
Lane Width	0.0 mph	0.0 mph
Lateral Clearance	−0.65 mph (interpolate)	0.0 mph
Access Points	−7.5 mph	−2.5 mph

For lateral clearance, the unimproved highway is a 4-lane facility with a 3-ft lateral clearance at the roadside and an assumed 6-ft clearance at the median, for a total clearance of 9 ft. The improved highway has 6 ft of clearance at both the roadside and median for a 12-ft total clearance, for a 6-lane facility. The estimated free-flow speeds may now be computed as:

S_F (existing) $= 48.0 - 1.6 - 0.0 - 0.65 - 7.5$

$= 40.25$ mph (40 mph)

S_F (improved) $= 52.5 - 0.0 - 0.0 - 0.0 - 2.5$

$= 50.0$ mph

Free-flow speeds are always rounded to the nearest mph.

EXAMPLE 2

A new multilane facility is to be built in a suburban area. It will have 4 lanes, ideal lane widths and lateral clearances, and will be undivided. Access points per mile are expected to stabilize at 20 per mile. A 55 mph speed limit is anticipated. Estimate the free-flow speed.

SOLUTION 2: The general equation for estimating free-flow speed is used. The ideal free-flow speed is estimated as 5 mph higher than the speed limit of 55 mph, or 60 mph. Adjustments are then selected from Table 10-5. Because lane widths and lateral clearances are ideal, there will be no adjustments for these factors, i.e., the adjustments for these are 0.0 mph. From Table 10-5a, the median type adjustment is -1.6 mph for an undivided highway, and from Table 10-5c, the adjustment for 20 access points per mile is -5.0 mph. Therefore:

$$S_F = 60.0 - 1.6 - 0.0 - 0.0 - 5.0$$

$$= 53.4 \text{ mph (53 mph)}$$

Again, we emphasize that direct field measurement of free-flow speed is the preferred method of determination. The analytic procedures presented herein allow for rough estimates to be made in cases where such measurement is not a realistic option. Given the general nature of the estimation procedures, results should always be rounded to the nearest whole mph.

B. Estimating free-flow speed for freeways

Free-flow speed for freeways is estimated as:

$$S_F = S_{Fi} - f_{lc} - f_{lw} - f_n - f_{id} \qquad [10\text{-}2]$$

where: S_F = prevailing free-flow speed, mph,
S_{Fi} = free-flow speed under ideal conditions, mph,
f_{lc} = adjustment for lateral clearance,
f_{lw} = adjustment for lane width,
f_n = adjustment for number of lanes, and
f_{id} = adjustment for interchange density.

For freeways, the "ideal" free-flow speed is usually taken to be 70 mph; in places where high speed limits (>70 mph) encourage higher speeds, 75 mph may be used. Adjustments are then given in Table 10-6.

Ideal clearances on freeways are 6 ft or more on the right, and 2 ft or more on the left (median). Most freeways have at least 2 ft of clearance to median barriers, so this is generally not an issue. No factors are available to treat median barriers that are closer than

Table 10-6   Adjustment Factors to Free-Flow Speed for Freeways

(A) Adjustment for Lane Width

Lane Width	Adjustment to S_{Fi}
≥12 ft	0.0 mph
11 ft	2.0 mph
10 ft	6.5 mph

(B) Adjustment for Right-Shoulder Lateral Clearance

Right-Side Lateral Clearance	Adjustment to S_{Fi} Lanes in One Direction		
	2	3	4
≥6 ft	0.0 mph	0.0 mph	0.0 mph
5 ft	0.6 mph	0.4 mph	0.2 mph
4 ft	1.2 mph	0.8 mph	0.4 mph
3 ft	1.8 mph	1.2 mph	0.6 mph
2 ft	2.4 mph	1.6 mph	0.8 mph
1 ft	3.0 mph	2.0 mph	1.0 mph
0 ft	3.6 mph	2.4 mph	1.2 mph

(C) Adjustment for Number of Lanes

Number of Lanes (One Direction)	Adjustment to S_{Fi}^{*}
≥5	0.0 mph
4	1.5 mph
3	3.0 mph
2	4.5 mph

(D) Adjustment for Interchange Density

Interchanges per Mile	Adjustment to S_{Fi}
≤0.50	0.0 mph
0.75	1.3 mph
1.00	2.5 mph
1.25	3.7 mph
1.50	5.0 mph
1.75	6.3 mph
2.00	7.5 mph

[Used with permission of Transportation Research Board, National Research Council, from Draft Chapter 11 of the *Highway Capacity Manual, Special Report 209*, Exhibits 11-19 through 11-22, pp. 11-21, 11-22.]

*Adjustment factors apply to urban and suburban freeways. For rural freeways, the adjustment is 0.0 mph for any number of lanes.

2 ft to the edge of the left lane; where such conditions exist, field measurements are recommended.

The NCHRP study [5] found a relationship between the number of freeway lanes and the free-flow speed, which is documented in the adjustment for number of lanes. This is a rather controversial adjustment, particularly in view of the fact that the ideal case is 5 lanes in one direction, an extremely rare occurrence. The adjustment suggests that there are no freeways with 2, 3, or 4 lanes in each direction operating at a free-flow speed of 70 mph. Again, field observations of speeds on local and regional freeway facilities may be useful in determining how to best apply this adjustment.

While access points per mile were a major determinant of multilane highway free-flow speed, the parallel parameter for freeways is the "interchange density," or the number of interchanges per mile. An "interchange" includes all ramps associated with a connection to a surface facility or another freeway. Each ramp is NOT separately counted. In computing the interchange density, a section of roadway 3 miles upstream to 3 miles downstream of the study section is included; the number of interchanges within this range is divided by 6 miles to obtain the "density."

Again, we emphasize that the estimation procedure for freeways presented in this section is based on drafts of material for the 1997 update. Some changes may be made before the 1997 *HCM* is published, and the reader is urged to check this document to review final adjustment factors.

An example using this procedure to estimate free-flow speed follows:

EXAMPLE 3

An older 6-lane urban freeway (3 lanes each direction) has 11-ft lanes, obstructions 2 ft from the roadside, reinforced concrete median barriers, and average interchange spacing of ½ mile. Provide a quick estimate of its free-flow speed, without taking field studies.

SOLUTION 3: This is a case in which the recommended methodology might be cautiously applied. The free-flow speed may be estimated using Equation 10-2:

$$S_F = S_{Fi} - f_{lc} - f_{lw} - f_n - f_{id}$$

The ideal free-flow speed is taken as 70 mph. Adjustments are selected from Table 10-6. The right-side lateral clearance is 2 ft to roadside obstructions. With an interchange spacing of ½ mile, the interchange density is 2.00 per mile.

Adjustment	Value
Lateral Clearance	−1.6 mph
Lane Width	−2.0 mph
Number of Lanes	−3.0 mph
Interchange Density	−7.5 mph

Then:

$$S_F = 70.0 - 1.6 - 2.0 - 3.0 - 7.5$$
$$= 55.9 \text{ mph (56 mph)}$$

C. Use of estimated free-flow speeds

The principal use of the measured or estimated value of free-flow speed is to determine the appropriate speed-flow curve for use in analysis procedures. Since both Figures 10-3 and 10-4 for freeways and multilane highways respectively provide for only four choices at 5 mph increments, the analyst can interpolate and insert a curve that better represents the facility under study.

Figure 10-7 illustrates this for the freeway sample problem above. A curve for a free-flow speed of 56 mph is interpolated between the 55 and 60 mph curves. This interpolated curve may then be used in additional analyses of the location under study.

Computational procedures

A. Basic relationships

Figures 10-3 and 10-4, and the resulting Tables 10-3 and 10-4, give maximum values of capacity and service flow rate for freeways and multilane highways operating under otherwise ideal conditions for the free-flow speeds shown. Thus, either the curves or the tables may be used to find the maximum allowable service flow rate for each level of service.

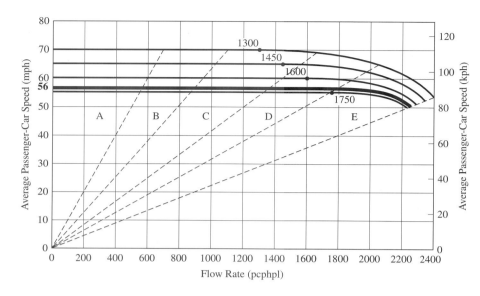

Figure 10-7 An interpolated speed-flow curve for freeway example computational procedures.

The principal "ideal" condition included in these figures and tables is the assumption that all vehicles are passenger cars. The presence of trucks and other heavy vehicles in the traffic stream can have a serious affect on these values. Heavy vehicles use more roadway time-space than passenger cars because they are a) larger than passenger cars, and b) have poorer operating characteristics that cause gaps to form in the traffic stream, gaps that cannot be efficiently filled by passing maneuvers. Thus, values of maximum service flow rate and capacity drawn from these figures and/or tables must be adjusted to reflect the prevailing mix of traffic at the location under study.

It is also assumed that most drivers are familiar with the facility, and are regular users. The basic ideal characteristics used reflect commuter or regular user flows. Predominantly recreational traffic and/or traffic streams dominated by occasional or unfamiliar users may also have a dramatic affect on operations.

The general equation for including these adjustments is as follows:

$$SF_i = MSF_i \, N \, f_{HV} \, f_p \qquad [10\text{-}3]$$

where: SF_i = service flow rate for level of service i under prevailing roadway and traffic conditions (in one direction), vph

MSF_i = maximum service flow rate for level of service i under ideal conditions (except for free-flow speed), taken from Figure 10-3 or Table 10-3 for freeways and Figure 10-4 or Table 10-4 for multilane highways, pcphpl

N = number of lanes in one direction

f_{HV} = adjustment factor for heavy vehicles in the traffic stream

f_p = adjustment factor for driver population

The maximum service flow rate, MSF_i, may be shown in the form:

$$MSF_i = c_j (v/c)_i \qquad [10\text{-}4]$$

where: c_j = capacity of facility with free-flow speed j, pcphpl

$(v/c)_i$ = maximum v/c ratio for level of service i, taken from Table 10-3 for freeways and Table 10-4 for multilane highways

The v/c ratio is often a useful measure, as it compares actual or forecasted demand traffic directly to the capacity as a ratio. Any prediction that the v/c ratio will be greater than 1.00 is an indication that insufficient capacity exists to handle the expected demand. In previous editions of the *HCM*, the v/c ratio was used extensively as a primary measure. Current methodologies use the MSF directly, and do not result in v/c computations, although they can easily be expressed in this format.

Both the actual service flow rate under prevailing conditions (*SF*) and the maximum service flow rate under ideal conditions (*MSF*) are based on rates of flow during the peak 15-minute period of the analysis hour, usually the peak hour. A service flow rate may be converted to an equivalent hourly service volume using the PHF:

$$SV_i = SF_i(PHF) \qquad [10\text{-}5]$$

where: SV_i = service volume over full hour for level of service *i*, vph

SF_i = service flow rate during peak 15 minutes for level of service *i*, vph

PHF = peak hour factor

Often, an analysis calls for converting an existing measured peak hour volume to an equivalent flow rate in pcph under ideal conditions. This can be done using the peak hour factor and the adjustment factors noted previously, and most often includes a conversion to "per lane" flows:

$$v = \frac{V}{PHF \, N \, f_{HV} \, f_p} \qquad [10\text{-}6]$$

where: v = equivalent flow rate during peak 15 minutes under ideal conditions, pcph

V = actual or projected hourly volume, vph

N = number of lanes in one direction other variables as previously defined

These basic relationships are the basis for operational analysis and design methodologies, using the characteristics depicted in the speed-flow relationships for multilane highway and freeway facilities. The sections that follow discuss each of the adjustment factors in greater detail, and present procedures for their determination.

B. Adjustment for heavy vehicles in the traffic stream

The heavy vehicle adjustment factor, f_{HV}, is applied to both freeway and multilane highway analyses. In fact, both use the same set of factors. Heavy vehicles affect traffic due to their size and operating characteristics.

Because of their size, they obviously occupy more space than passenger cars. The largest impact of heavy vehicles, however, is the result of their operating characteristics. Because heavy vehicles take longer to slow or stop, drivers of heavy vehicles generally leave more space between themselves and the vehicle in front of them than do passenger car drivers. On upgrades, heavy vehicles are not able to maintain their speed as well as passenger cars. This creates large gaps in the traffic stream as heavy vehicles follow passenger cars. When these gaps cannot be efficiently filled by passing maneuvers, the heavy vehicle effectively occupies as much roadway space as many passenger cars.

The heavy vehicle adjustment factor is based on the concept of passenger car equivalence. The impact of one heavy vehicle on the traffic stream is quantified as the number of passenger cars it displaces. This equivalence accounts for the displacement of passenger cars due to both the size of the heavy vehicle and the gaps it creates in the traffic stream as a result of their non-uniform operating characteristics.

Standard procedures provide models for estimating the passenger car equivalents of two classes of heavy vehicles:

1. Trucks and buses
2. Recreational vehicles

These equivalents represent a range of specific vehicles in the heavy vehicle population. Trucks and buses range from a weight-to-horsepower ratio of about 100 lbs/hp to as much as 350 lbs/hp. Recreational vehicles generally have weight-to-horsepower ratios of about 50–75 lbs/hp. Passenger cars are generally in the range of 20–25 lbs/hp.

The impact of heavy vehicles depends on the grade conditions of the highway location under study. Passenger car equivalents are specified for two conditions:

- *Extended General Highway Segments:* It is often possible to analyze the operation on an extended length of highway containing many individual upgrades and downgrades. This can be done where no single grade is steep enough or long enough to have a significant impact on heavy vehicle operation in the overall section. This type of analysis can be applied **where no single grade of 3 percent or greater is longer than ¼ mile, and where no single grade under 3 percent is longer than ½ mile.**

- *Specific Grades:* Any single grade that does not meet the criteria for "extended segment" analysis must be treated as an isolated segment. This is because such grades have a significant affect on heavy vehicle operations, and therefore, on the operation of the freeway as a whole. In such situations, the upgrade direction must be considered separately from the downgrade direction, as the impacts may be quite different.

1. Finding passenger car equivalents for heavy vehicles on extended general highway segments. Passenger car equivalents for trucks/buses and recreational vehicles are defined in terms of three general categories of terrain:

- *Level Terrain:* Level terrain is any combination of vertical and horizontal alignment that allows heavy vehicles to maintain approximately the same speed as passenger cars. This generally includes short grades of no more than 2%.
- *Rolling Terrain:* Rolling terrain is any combination of vertical and horizontal alignment that causes heavy vehicles to reduce their speeds substantially below those of passenger cars, but does NOT cause heavy vehicles to operate at crawl speeds for any significant length of time.
- *Mountainous Terrain:* Mountainous terrain is any combination of vertical and horizontal alignment that causes heavy vehicles to operate at crawl speeds for significant distances or at frequent intervals.

These definitions depend on operation of heavy vehicles at the "crawl speed." The crawl speed is the maximum speed that heavy vehicles can sustain on an extended upgrade of a given percent. Any truck will eventually decelerate to its crawl speed if an upgrade is long enough, after which it can maintain that speed virtually indefinitely on the grade.

Figure 10-8 illustrates the operation of heavy vehicles on grades. The figure depicts the operating characteristics of a typical truck with weight-to-horsepower ratio of 200 lbs/hp. It shows the speed of the truck vs. distance upgrade on grades of varying percent. All curves assume that the truck enters the grade at a speed of 55 mph.

For any given percent grade, the truck begins to slow as it advances up the grade. Eventually it reaches a minimum speed that it can maintain indefinitely on a grade of the given percent. As the grade gets steeper, trucks reach the crawl speed more quickly, and the crawl speed itself gets slower.

Once the appropriate category of terrain is determined for a given highway segment, the passenger car equivalents for trucks/buses and recreational vehicles may be selected from Table 10-7.

2. Finding passenger car equivalents of heavy vehicles on specific grade sections. Any single grade of 3% or more that is longer than ¼ mile, or any single grade of less than 3% that is longer than ½ mile, must be considered separately as a specific grade.

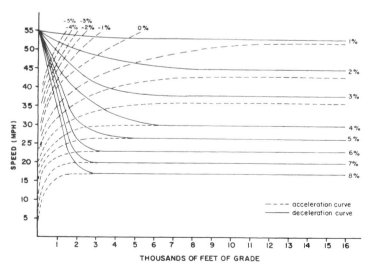

Figure 10-8   Grade performance of a typical truck (200 lbs/hp). [Used with permission of Transportation Research Board, National Research Council, from *Highway Capacity Manual, Special Report 209*, 3rd Ed., p. 3-32. Copyright © 1994 Transportation Research Board.]

Table 10-7 Passenger Car Equivalents on Extended General Highway Segments

Category	Level	Rolling	Mountainous
E_T for Trucks/Buses	1.5	3.0	6.0
E_R for Recreational Vehicles	1.2	2.0	4.0

The impact of heavy vehicles on such grades varies with the severity of the grade and the length of the grade. Tables 10-8 and 10-9 give the upgrade passenger car equivalents for trucks/buses and recreational vehicles. Table 10-10 gives the downgrade passenger car equivalents for trucks/buses. Downgrades may be treated as if they were *level terrain* for recreational vehicles.

3. Composite grades. Most highways are not designed so that each grade has a constant percentage. Rather, grades are composites, containing several subsections of different percentage connected by vertical curves. Thus, a single upgrade, for example, might consist of ½ mile at 3% followed by another mile at 4% and a final ½ mile at 2%.

This complicates the issue of assessing the impact of trucks on grades, as Tables 10-8, 10-9, and 10-10 refer only to constant grades of a given percentage. To use these tables, a constant grade equivalent must be found for a composite grade.

Finding an equivalent grade for a composite series of grades is best illustrated by specific example. Consider the simple case of 3000 ft of 3% upgrade followed by 5000 ft of 5% upgrade. One simple technique is to find the *average grade*. This can be found by taking the total rise (or fall) of the grade over the longitudinal distance over which the rise (or fall) was accomplished. For the example:

Rise on 3% grade = 3000 ft × 0.03 = 90 ft

Rise on 5% grade = 5000 ft × 0.05 = 250 ft

Total Rise on Grade   340 ft

As the 340 ft rise is accomplished over a length of 3000 ft + 5000 ft, or 8000 ft, the average grade is:

Average Grade = (340/8000) × 100 = **4.25%**

Tables 10-8 and/or 10-9 could then be entered to find the appropriate passenger car equivalents for a single grade of 8000 ft (1.52 miles) and 4.25%.

This simple procedure is relatively accurate for situations in which the total length of the grade is less than 4000 ft, or where no segment is steeper than 4%. Where a grade is *both* longer than 4000 ft total *and* contains segments steeper than 4%, a more precise procedure is needed. In the example above, the use of the average grade would *not* be appropriate, as the grade is 8000 ft long and contains a 5% segment.

Since the impact of heavy vehicles on grades is primarily due to their inability to maintain speed, a more precise procedure would be to find *a single grade of constant percent and length equal to the total length of the composite grade that results in the same final speed of heavy vehicles as the actual composite grade.* Thus, if after a series of composite upgrades, trucks have been forced to reduce their speed to 35 mph, then the equivalent constant grade would be the one resulting in a final speed of trucks of 35 mph after the same length as the composite grade.

A set of heavy vehicle acceleration/deceleration curves must be used for this purpose. Figure 10-8, shown previously, is the standard set of curves used in the *HCM* for this purpose. Figure 10-9 illustrates the solution for an equivalent grade on this basis for the example. The following points describe the graphic solution shown:

1. The initial grade segment is a 3% grade of 3000 ft. The curve is entered with a vertical line constructed at 3000 ft, finding the intercept with the 3% deceleration curve (Point 1). Constructing a horizontal line to the Y-axis, it is found that trucks are traveling at 41 mph after 3000 ft of 3% grade.

2. Since the 5% grade is entered at the end of the 3% grade, it can be assumed that trucks will *enter* the 5% segment at 41 mph, the final speed on the 3% segment. Point 2 is found as the intersection of the horizontal drawn at 41 mph and the 5% deceleration curve. Dropping a vertical to the *X*-axis, a speed of 41 mph is the same as would have been reached by trucks after 1200 ft of 5% grade. Thus,

Table 10-8   Passenger Car Equivalents for Trucks and Buses on Specific Upgrades

Grade (%)	Length (miles) Percent Trucks and Buses	Passenger-Car Equivalent, E_T								
		2	4	5	6	8	10	15	20	25
<2	All	1.5	1.5	1.5	1.5	1.5	1.5	1.5	1.5	1.5
2	0–¼	1.5	1.5	1.5	1.5	1.5	1.5	1.5	1.5	1.5
	¼–½	1.5	1.5	1.5	1.5	1.5	1.5	1.5	1.5	1.5
	½–¾	1.5	1.5	1.5	1.5	1.5	1.5	1.5	1.5	1.5
	¾–1	2.5	2.0	2.0	2.0	1.5	1.5	1.5	1.5	1.5
	1–1½	4.0	3.0	3.0	3.0	2.5	2.5	2.0	2.0	2.0
	>1½	4.5	3.5	3.0	3.0	2.5	2.5	2.0	2.0	2.0
3	0–¼	1.5	1.5	1.5	1.5	1.5	1.5	1.5	1.5	1.5
	¼–½	3.0	2.5	2.5	2.0	2.0	2.0	2.0	1.5	1.5
	½–¾	6.0	4.0	4.0	3.5	3.5	3.0	2.5	2.5	2.0
	¾–1	7.5	5.5	5.0	4.5	4.0	4.0	3.5	3.0	3.0
	1–1½	8.0	6.0	5.5	5.0	4.5	4.0	4.0	3.5	3.0
	>1½	8.5	6.0	5.5	5.0	4.5	4.5	4.0	3.5	3.0
4	0–¼	1.5	1.5	1.5	1.5	1.5	1.5	1.5	1.5	1.5
	¼–½	5.5	4.0	4.0	3.5	3.0	3.0	3.0	2.5	2.5
	½–¾	9.5	7.0	6.5	6.0	5.5	5.0	4.5	4.0	3.5
	¾–1	10.5	8.0	7.0	6.5	6.0	5.5	5.0	4.5	4.0
	>1	11.0	8.0	7.5	7.0	6.0	6.0	5.0	5.0	4.5
5	0–¼	2.0	2.0	1.5	1.5	1.5	1.5	1.5	1.5	1.5
	¼–⅓	6.0	4.5	4.0	4.0	3.5	3.0	3.0	2.5	2.0
	⅓–½	9.0	7.0	6.0	6.0	5.5	5.0	4.5	4.0	3.5
	½–¾	12.5	9.0	8.5	8.0	7.0	7.0	6.0	6.0	5.0
	¾–1	13.0	9.5	9.0	8.0	7.5	7.0	6.5	6.0	5.5
	>1	13.0	9.5	9.0	8.0	7.5	7.0	6.5	6.0	5.5
5	0–¼	4.5	3.5	3.0	3.0	3.0	2.5	2.5	2.0	2.0
	¼–⅓	9.0	6.5	6.0	6.0	5.0	5.0	4.0	3.5	3.0
	⅓–½	12.5	9.5	8.5	8.0	7.0	6.5	6.0	6.0	5.5
	½–¾	15.0	11.0	10.0	9.5	9.0	8.0	8.0	7.5	6.5
	¾–1	15.0	11.0	10.0	9.5	9.0	8.5	8.0	7.5	6.5
	>1	15.0	11.0	10.0	9.5	9.0	8.5	8.0	7.5	6.5

Note: If the length of grade falls on a boundary, apply the longer category; interpolation may be used to find equivalents for intermediate percent grades.

[Used with permission of Transportation Research Board, National Research Council, from *Highway Capacity Manual, Special Report 209*, 3rd Ed., p. 3-14. Copyright © 1994 Transportation Research Board.]

trucks enter the 5% grade segment *as if they had already been on a 5% for 1200 ft.*

3. Trucks will stay on the 5% grade for 5000 ft. This is added to the assumed 1200 ft equivalence point. At the end of the 5000 ft 5% segment, the speed of trucks will be the same *as if they had been on a constant 5% grade for 1200 + 5000 = 6200 ft. A vertical line is constructed at 6200 ft, and the intersection with the 5% deceleration curve is found (Point 3). Drawing a horizontal through this point to the Y-axis reveals that the final speed of trucks at the end of the composite grade will be 26 mph.

Table 10-9 Passenger Car Equivalents for Recreational Vehicles on Specific Upgrades

Grade (%)	Length (miles)	Passenger-Car Equivalent, E_R								
Percent RVs		2	4	5	6	8	10	15	20	25
<2	All	1.2	1.2	1.2	1.2	1.2	1.2	1.2	1.2	1.2
3	0–½	1.2	1.2	1.2	1.2	1.2	1.2	1.2	1.2	1.2
	>½	2.0	1.5	1.5	1.5	1.5	1.5	1.2	1.2	1.2
4	0–¼	1.2	1.2	1.2	1.2	1.2	1.2	1.2	1.2	1.2
	¼–½	2.5	2.5	2.0	2.0	2.0	2.0	1.5	1.5	1.5
	>½	3.0	2.5	2.5	2.0	2.0	2.0	2.0	1.5	1.5
5	0–¼	2.5	2.0	2.0	2.0	1.5	1.5	1.5	1.5	1.5
	¼–½	4.0	3.0	3.0	3.0	2.5	2.5	2.0	2.0	2.0
	>½	4.5	3.5	3.0	3.0	3.0	2.5	2.5	2.0	2.0
6	0–¼	4.0	3.0	2.5	2.5	2.5	2.0	2.0	2.0	1.5
	¼–½	6.0	4.0	4.0	3.5	3.0	3.0	2.5	2.5	2.0
	>½	6.0	4.5	4.0	4.0	3.5	3.0	3.0	2.5	2.0

Note: If the length of grade falls on a boundary, apply the longer category; interpolation may be used to find equivalents for intermediate percent grades.

[Used with permission of Transportation Research Board, National Research Council, from *Highway Capacity Manual, Special Report 209,* 3rd Ed., p. 3-14. Copyright © 1994 Transportation Research Board.]

Table 10-10 Passenger Car Equivalents for Trucks and Buses on Specific Downgrades

Percent Downgrade (%)	Length of Grade (miles)	Passenger-Car Equivalent, E_r			
		Percent Trucks/Buses			
		5	10	15	20
<4	All	1.5	1.5	1.5	1.5
4	≤4	1.5	1.5	1.5	1.5
4	>4	2.0	2.0	2.0	1.5
5	≤4	1.5	1.5	1.5	1.5
5	>4	5.5	4.0	4.0	3.0
≥6	≤4	1.5	1.5	1.5	1.5
>6	>4	7.5	6.0	5.5	4.5

[Used with permission of Transportation Research Board, National Research Council, from *Highway Capacity Manual, Special Report 209,* 3rd Ed., 3-16. Copyright © 1994 Transportation Research Board.]

4. The "equivalent constant grade" sought is one which, after 8000 ft, produces a final speed of trucks of 26 mph. This is found as the intersection of a horizontal at 26 mph and a vertical at 8000 ft (Point 4). The equivalent grade is 5%.

In this solution, the result lies on one of the deceleration curves, and the determination of equivalent grade is easy. If the solution point falls between curves, approximate interpolation is acceptable. The equivalent grade is: **5%, 8000 ft long.**

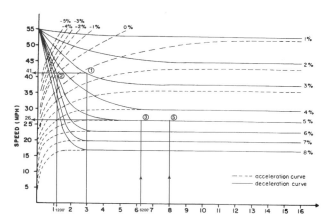

Figure 10-9 Solving for equivalent constant grade using truck deceleration curves.

This procedure can be followed for any number of consecutive grade sections, even extended grades involving both upgrade and downgrade sections. This is necessary, as no new grade section can be considered as a starting point unless trucks have returned to at least the 55 mph entry speed assumed in standard deceleration curves.

For any composite grade, the equivalent grade should be found to the point at which the impact of heavy vehicles is greatest. This is not always the final point on the grade. If, for example, 1 mile of 4% upgrade were followed by ½ mile of 2% upgrade, heavy vehicles would be at their slowest at the end of the 4% segment. Thus, passenger car equivalents for a 1 mile, 4% grade would be used, since conditions would improve as heavy vehicles accelerate to higher speeds along the 2% grade segment.

4. Finding the heavy vehicle adjustment factor from passenger car equivalents. Since the computational procedures for both freeways and multilane highways require the determination of a multiplicative adjustment factor, f_{HV}, to be applied to capacity and maximum service flow rates under ideal conditions, such a factor must be related to the passenger car equivalents defined in previous sections.

Consider the following problem: 1000 vph are observed on a freeway in generally rolling terrain. The traffic stream consists of 10% trucks, 2% buses, and 3% recreational vehicles. How many equivalent pcph are in the traffic stream?

From Table 10-7, it is determined that each truck or bus in rolling terrain displaces 3.0 passenger cars from the traffic stream, while each recreational vehicle displaces 2.0 passenger cars. To find the number of equivalent passenger cars in the traffic stream, each truck and bus is replaced by 3.0 passenger cars and each recreational vehicle by 2.0 passenger cars. Therefore:

Category	VPH	Equivalent Value	Equivalent PCPH
Pass Cars	1000 (0.85) = 850	× 1.0 =	850 pcph
Tr/Buses	1000 (0.12) = 120	× 3.0 =	360 pcph
RVs	1000 (0.03) = 30	× 2.0 =	60 pcph
TOTAL	**1000 vph**		**1270 pcph**

In essence, the number of vehicles in each category is found using the percentages of trucks, buses, and recreational vehicles in the traffic stream, and each is multiplied by the number of passenger cars one vehicle in that category displaces. Obviously, the "passenger car equivalent" for a passenger car is taken to be 1.0. If this process is reduced to an equation form, the following results:

$$V_{PCPH} = V_{VPH}(1 - P_T - P_R)$$
$$+ V_{VPH}P_T E_T + V_{VPH}P_R E_R \quad [10\text{-}7]$$

where: V_{PCPH} = volume or flow rate in pcph
V_{VPH} = volume or flow rate in vph
P_T = proportion of trucks and buses in the traffic stream
P_R = proportion of recreational vehicles in the traffic stream
E_T = passenger car equivalent for trucks and buses
E_R = passenger car equivalent for recreational vehicles

The first term of the equation represents the number of passenger cars in the traffic stream. This equation may be reduced to:

$$V_{PCPH} = V_{VPH}[1 + P_T(E_T - 1)$$
$$+ P_R(E_R - 1)] \quad [10\text{-}8]$$

For the sample problem solved above:

$$V_{PCPH} = 1000[1 + 0.12(3 - 1) + 0.03(2 - 1)]$$
$$= 1000(1.27) = 1270 \text{ pcph}$$

By definition, the adjustment factor, f_{HV}, converts a volume or flow rate in pcph to one in vph. The equation above may be manipulated into the form:

$$V_{VPH} = V_{PCPH}x\left[\frac{1}{1 + P_T(E_T - 1) + P_R(E_R - 1)}\right]$$

$$= V_{PCPH} f_{HV} \qquad [10\text{-}9]$$

and:

$$f_{HV} = \frac{1}{1 + P_T(E_T - 1) + P_R(E_R - 1)} \qquad [10\text{-}10]$$

For the example problem:

$$f_{HV} = \frac{1}{1 + 0.12(3 - 1) + 0.03(2 - 1)} = 0.7874$$

and:

$$1000 = 1270 \times 0.7874$$

C. Adjustment for driver population

The computational procedure for freeways also employs an adjustment factor representing the impact of driver population on capacity and maximum service flow rates. While the 1994 *HCM* had eliminated this adjustment from the multilane highway procedure, the adjustment is being re-introduced in the 1997 update. Several studies, primarily from the west coast, have shown that recreational or occasional users of a facility do not use the facility as efficiently as commuters, for whom the standard curves are calibrated. Thus, the same facility may not display the same capacity on weekends, when occasional recreational drivers dominate the traffic stream, as on weekdays, when commuters dominate. There is no definitive algorithm for this adjustment, although studies have shown that the decline in capacity on weekends could be as high as 10% to 15%. Thus, the 1997 *HCM* will continue to recommend the following:

$f_p = 1.00$ (for commuter or regular users)

$f_p = 1.00 - 0.85$ (for recreational or occasional users)

The selection of an exact value must be based on direct observation of characteristics at the subject site, or at a similar site.

Applications of the computational methodology

The elements of the computational methodology outlined in the previous section can be applied in three different ways:

- finding capacity and service flow rates for the various levels of service under prevailing conditions
- finding the prevailing level of service for an existing or projected highway segment
- finding the number of lanes needed to provide for a given level of service given existing or forecast traffic demand

The subsections that follow detail procedures for each of these, and illustrate them with examples.

A. Finding capacity and service flow rates

In this application, existing and/or forecast traffic and roadway conditions must be specified. The following information is needed:

- type of facility
- free-flow speed (measured or estimated)
- terrain conditions
- lane widths and lateral clearances
- number of lanes
- traffic composition (% trucks/buses, % RVs)

The computational analysis will result in the service flow rates that can be accommodated at any given level of service (capacity is the service flow rate at LOS E). Service flow rates can be converted to full-hour service volumes by applying the Peak Hour Factor. This information can then be compared to various existing or anticipated demand flows or hourly volumes to assess the level of service.

For this type of analysis, basic relationships of Equations [10-3] and [10-5] are used directly:

$$SF_i = MSF_i\, N\, f_{HV}\, f_p$$

$$SV_i = SF_i\, PHF$$

The following specific steps are followed:

1. Establish the facility type and free-flow speed. Free-flow speed is either measured in the field, or estimated using the algorithms presented herein (Table 10-5 for multilane highways; Table 10-6 for freeways).

2. Find the values of MSF for each level of service A through E (there is no value for LOS F, which is unstable). If the free-flow speed is an even value included in Table 10-3 (freeways) or Table 10-4 (multilane highways), values of MSF for each level of service may be taken directly from the tables. If the free-flow speed is an intermediate value, straight-line interpolation in the tables is appropriate.

3. Values of applicable adjustment factors are determined. Values of f_{HV} are based upon passenger car equivalents and terrain conditions, as described previously.

4. Compute service flow rates and service volumes for each level of service using the basic algorithms presented above.

EXAMPLE 1

An existing older freeway has the following characteristics: 4 lanes (2 in each direction), 11-ft lane widths, 2 ft of clearance to the nearest roadside obstructions, 2 ft of clearance to a median barrier curb, rolling terrain, 5% trucks/buses in the traffic stream, no RVs in the traffic stream, interchanges spaced at an average of 1 mile. The Peak Hour Factor is 0.91. Determine the service flow rates and service volumes for each level of service.

SOLUTION 1:   As the free-flow speed of this facility is not specified, it must be estimated using adjustments found in Table 10-6 and the algorithm of Equation [10-2]:

$$S_F = S_{Fi} - f_{lc} - f_{lw} - f_n - f_{id}$$

From Table 10-6:

f_{lc} = −2.4 mph (right clearance 2 ft, 2 lanes, one dir.)

f_{lw} = −2.0 mph (11 ft lanes)

f_n = −4.5 mph (2 lanes each direction)

f_{id} = −2.5 mph (1 interchange per mile)

For freeways, the ideal free-flow speed is usually taken to be 70 mph. Therefore, the estimated free-flow speed of this facility is:

$$S_F = 70.0 - 2.4 - 2.0 - 4.5 - 2.5$$
$$= 58.6 \text{ mph, SAY 59 mph}$$

As this is not one of the free-flow speeds found in Table 10-3, values of *MSF* are found by interpolation:

Level of Service	MSF (60 mph)	MSF (59 mph)	MSF (55 mph)
	Table 10-4	**Interpolated**	Table 10-4
A	600 pcphpl	**590 pcphpl**	550 pcphpl
B	960 pcphpl	**945 pcphpl**	880 pcphpl
C	1440 pcphpl	**1416 pcphpl**	1320 pcphpl
D	1856 pcphpl	**1834 pcphpl**	1744 pcphpl
E	2300 pcphpl	**2290 pcphpl**	2250 pcphpl

Now, adjustment factors f_{HV} and f_p must be determined. From Table 10-7, passenger car equivalents for trucks/buses and recreational vehicles in rolling terrain are:

$$E_T = 3.0$$
$$E_R = 2.0$$

Given that there are 5% trucks/buses, and no recreational vehicles in the traffic stream, the heavy vehicle adjustment factor is found using Equation 10-10 as:

$$f_{HV} = \frac{1}{1 + P_T(E_T - 1) + P_R(E_R - 1)}$$

and:

$$f_{HV} = \frac{1}{1 + 0.05(3 - 1) + 0.00(2 - 1)} = 0.909$$

Given that no driver population was specified, it will be assumed that it is a normal commuter population, i.e., that $f_p = 1.00$. Service flow rates and service volumes can now be computed as shown in Tables 10-11 and 10-12. This computation shows that the capacity of this facility under prevailing traffic and roadway conditions is 4163 vph, with correspondingly decreasing service flow rates for each better level of service.

Service flow rates, however, apply to the peak 15 minutes of flow within the hour of analysis, presumably the peak hour. Corresponding service volumes, applicable to full-hour demand volumes are found by multiplying the service flow rates of Table 10-12 by the peak hour factor. These tables may now be entered with any peak hour volume (Table 10-12) or

Table 10-11   Computing Service Flow Rates for Example 1

LOS	SF =	MSF x	N x	f_{HV} x	f_p
A	1073 vph	590	2	0.909	1.00
B	1718 vph	945	2	0.909	1.00
C	2574 vph	1416	2	0.909	1.00
D	3334 vph	1834	2	0.909	1.00
E	4163 vph	2290	2	0.909	1.00

Table 10-12   Computing Service Volumes for Example 1

LOS	SV = (VPH)	SF x (VPH)	PHF
A	976	1073	0.91
B	1563	1718	0.91
C	2342	2574	0.91
D	3034	3334	0.91
E	3788	4163	0.91

peak demand flow rate (Table 10-11) to find the expected level of service. For example, if a peak hour volume of 2000 vph were expected, the level of service (from Table 10-12) would be C, as the maximum allowable volume for LOS B is exceeded, and the maximum allowable value for LOS C is not.

B. Finding existing or forecast level of service

To determine the level of service on an existing facility, or to forecast the level of service on a future facility, all of the information required for service flow rate determinations will be needed, as well as the existing or forecast peak hour volume.

Level of service can be determined in two ways. The first is to compute service flow rates and service volumes for each level of service, and compare the existing or forecast flow to these values, as illustrated in the previous example.

This computational procedure is somewhat limited, however, in that more precise values of expected speed and density cannot be easily obtained from a table such as Table 10-12. A more common approach is to compute the effective maximum service flow rate

under equivalent ideal conditions for the existing or forecast peak hour volume.

As has been noted previously, an actual peak hour volume can be converted to an equivalent flow rate under ideal conditions using the same adjustment factors that are used to modify capacity and maximum service flow rates using Equation [10-6]:

$$v = \frac{V}{PHF \, N \, f_{HV} \, f_p}$$

where all values are as previously defined. Division by the peak hour factor converts the peak hour volume to the maximum rate of flow for a 15-minute period within the hour. Adjustment factors adjust a volume or flow rate for prevailing conditions to an equivalent value under theoretically ideal conditions. The effective maximum service flow rate under ideal conditions is converted to a "per lane" value through the inclusion of N in the equation.

The effective maximum service flow rate under ideal conditions is used to enter the appropriate speed-flow curve on Figure 10-5 (for freeways) or Figure 10-6 (for multilane highways) to determine (a) the prevailing or expected level of service, (b) the density, and (c) the average speed expected for the defined conditions. Densities and speeds are in terms of an equivalent ideal traffic stream, and may vary somewhat from field-measured values, which reflect prevailing conditions.

The following computational steps are followed:

1. Determine the facility type and the appropriate free-flow speed through field measurement or the estimation algorithms presented herein. If the free-flow speed is an intermediate value, inscribe an interpolated curve on a base of Figure 10-5 or 10-6.

2. Determine all appropriate adjustment factors.
3. Compute the effective maximum service flow rate under ideal conditions using the Equation [10-6].
4. Enter the appropriate speed-flow curve in Figure 10-5 or 10-6 to determine level of service, density, and speed.

EXAMPLE 2

A four-lane suburban multilane highway with a two-way left-turn lane carries a peak hour volume of 2600 vph in the heaviest direction. There are 12% trucks/buses and 2% recreational vehicles in the traffic stream. Studies indicate that the free-flow speed for this facility is 55 mph. The section under study is on a 3% grade, 1.0 mile long. The PHF is 0.87. What is the expected level of service for this facility?

SOLUTION 2:   Given that this facility is on an extended grade, the upgrade and downgrade directions must be separately considered. The peak traffic generally travels in one direction in the A.M. and the other in the P.M., so that *both* directions must handle the peak traffic load, even though the peak load travels only in one direction at a time.

Since the free-flow speed has been determined by field study, and the curve is a value already shown on Figure 10-6, no further consideration of this parameter is necessary. Because this is a multilane highway and drivers are presumed to be regular users, the only adjustment factor to be considered is the heavy vehicle factor, f_{HV}. Passenger car equivalents are determined from Table 10-8 and 10-9 for the upgrade, and from Table 10-10 for the downgrade:

Upgrade

E_T 4.0 (3% grade, 1 mile, 12% trucks/buses, Table 10-8)

E_R 2.0 (3% grade, 1 mile, 2% RVs, Table 10-9)

Downgrade

E_T 1.5 (< 4% grade, 12% trucks/buses, Table 10-10)

E_R 1.2 (assume level terrain, use Table 10-7)

The heavy vehicle adjustment may now be computed using Equation [10-10]:

$$f_{HV} = \frac{1}{1 + P_T(E_T - 1) + P_R(E_R - 1)}$$

$$f_{HV}(up) = \frac{1}{1 + 0.12(4 - 1) + 0.02(2 - 1)} = 0.725$$

$$f_{HV}(dn) = \frac{1}{1 + 0.12(1.5 - 1) + 0.02(1.2 - 1)} = 0.940$$

The effective maximum service flow rate under ideal conditions may now be computed for both upgrade and downgrade directions of the multilane highway, using Equation [10-6]:

$$v = \frac{V}{PHF\ N\ f_{HV}\ f_p}$$

Note that the driver population factor is taken to be 1.00, based upon the assumption of a driver population of familiar facility users.
Then:

$$v(up) = \frac{2600}{0.87 \times 2 \times 0.725 \times 1} = 2061\ pcphpl$$

$$v(dn) = \frac{2600}{0.87 \times 2 \times 0.940 \times 1} = 1590\ pcph$$

With these results, the 55 mph curve of Figure 10-4 may be entered to estimate the levels of service, speed, and density of the upgrade and downgrade peak hour traffic streams. Figure 10-10 illustrates this determination.

Figure 10-10 shows that the upgrade level of service is *E*, with an expected average speed of 51 mph. The downgrade level of service is *D*, with an expected average speed of 54 mph. Knowing the effective flow rate and the expected speed, the expected density may be computed as *v/S*, or:

$$D(up) = 2061/51 = 40.4\ pc/mi/ln$$

$$D(dn) = 1590/54 = 29.4\ pc/mi/ln$$

These densities can be checked vs. the LOS limits in Table 10-4, which confirms the graphic determination of LOS *E* for the upgrade and LOS *D* for the downgrade. Note also that the speeds and densities determined in this manner reflect equivalent ideal conditions. Actual speeds and densities under prevailing conditions may vary somewhat from these

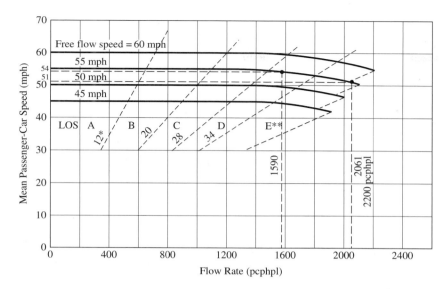

Figure 10-10 Solution for LOS and speed for example 2.

values because of the effect of trucks and other heavy vehicles. An important observation may be made from these results. The upgrade, operating at an effective maximum service flow rate of 2061 pcphpl, is very close to the capacity of a multilane highway with a 55 mph free-flow speed, which is 2100 pcphpl. On the other hand, the downgrade is operating well below capacity, at an effective maximum service flow rate of 1590 pcphpl.

An appropriate question is: How many more vph under prevailing conditions can the upgrade and downgrade handle before demand exceeds capacity, and a breakdown occurs?

For the upgrade, the two lanes have a capacity of 2×2100 or 4200 pcph. The effective flow rate (under ideal conditions) is 2×2061 or 4122 pcph. The difference is a flow rate of only 88 pcph, under equivalent ideal conditions. Converting this to a full-hour volume under prevailing conditions requires multiplication by the PHF and f_{HV}, or:

Available Capacity (upgrade) = $88 \times 0.87 \times 0.725$

$$= 56 \text{ vph}$$

Following similar logic for the downgrade, the two lanes have a capacity of 4200 pcph and an effective flow rate of 2×1590 or 3180 pcph. The difference is 1020 pcph, which is converted to a full-hour volume under ideal conditions:

Available Capacity (downgrade)

$$= 1020 \times 0.87 \times 0.940 = \textbf{834 vph}$$

Clearly, conditions on the upgrade are approaching a critical stage. An increase of more than 56 vph in demand will cause a breakdown. This is almost a negligible increase on a base volume of 2600 vph. This reflects the more serious impacts of heavy vehicles on the upgrade than the downgrade, where this problem does not exist. A potential solution to this problem would be consideration of a truck-climbing lane on the upgrade, subject to how this would affect roadside driveways and other conditions.

C. Design applications: Determining type of facility and number of lanes

The final application is design. Capacity and level of service analysis are used to help decide on the type of facility needed, and to determine the appropriate number of lanes for the facility. This requires projected geometric conditions for each type of facility under consideration, and a forecast DDHV, directional design hour volume—the forecast value of the peak hour volume.

Again, there are two ways of making this determination. Both involve trial-and-error computations, and establishment of a desired level of service during peak periods. In the first method, for each type of facility under consideration, the basic relationship:

$$SF_i = MSF_i \, N \, f_{HV} \, f_p$$

is utilized. The DDHV is converted to a flow rate, and is taken to be the effective service flow rate, *SF*. Then:

$$\frac{DDHV}{PHF} = SF_i = MSF_i \, N \, f_{HV} \, f_p$$

Solving this equation for *N* yields:

$$N = \frac{DDHV}{PHF \, MSF_i \, f_{HV} \, f_p} \qquad [10\text{-}13]$$

where all terms are as previously defined. This relationship often results in a fractional computation of *N*. Since a fractional lane cannot be built, and because the computed value represents the minimum number of lanes necessary to provide the desired level of service, a decision must be made to build to the next higher number of full lanes, or to accept a lower level of service. Often, integer values of *N* surrounding the result are assumed, and a level of service determination (as in the previous subsection) is made to assist in this decision. Note that the computation of *N* is for *one direction* of the facility. For general terrain sections, both directions will generally require the same number of lanes. On significant grades, the upgrade and downgrade should be considered separately, as the upgrade may require more lanes than the downgrade to provide an equivalent level of service.

A second approach is to assume various feasible values for *N* (2 or 3 for multilane highways, 2–5 for freeways), finding the resulting level of service for each. The results can then be considered and an appropriate facility type and number of lanes selected. This methodology requires multiple computations of the type illustrated in the previous subsection. If the first method is used, the following steps are followed:

1. Establish the *DDHV*, desired LOS, and the types of facility under consideration.
2. Establish basic design standards, such as lane widths, lateral clearances, design speeds, number of interchanges or driveways per mile, and anticipated speed limits.
3. Estimate the free-flow speed for each type of facility, using measurements on similar facilities, or the estimation algorithms provided herein.

4. Establish projected traffic and roadway conditions: composition of the traffic stream and terrain conditions. Find the appropriate adjustment factors for these conditions.
5. Find appropriate values of *MSF_i* from Table 10-3 (freeways) or 10-4 (multilane highways) for the desired LOS and the types of facilities under consideration.
6. Using the Equation [10-13], compute the number of lanes needed to provide the desired LOS for each facility type under consideration.
7. If desired, determine the level of service for integer values of *N* surrounding the results obtained in step 6.

EXAMPLE 3

A rural two-lane, two-way highway is expected to have a directional design hour volume (*DDHV*) of 3000 vph by the year 2000. It is to be reconstructed as a divided multilane highway or freeway to provide for no worse than level of service C during peak periods. The demand volume includes 15% trucks, and no buses or RVs. Terrain is generally rolling. Modern design standards are to be employed, with 12-ft lanes and adequate lateral clearances. If built as a multilane highway, there would be no more than 5 access points per mile. A freeway would have average interchange spacings of 2 miles or more. Both the freeway and multilane highway would have a design speed of 70 mph. This will produce an expected freeway free-flow speed of 65 mph. Similar multilane highways have an 85th percentile speed of 63 mph. The *PHF* is expected to be 0.82. What type of facility should be built, and how many lanes should it have?

SOLUTION 3: The free-flow speed of the possible freeway has been specified as 65 mph. The corresponding free-flow speed of the multilane highway must be estimated from the 85th percentile speed of 63 mph. The *ideal* free-flow speed is taken to be about 3 mph less than this, or 60 mph. The ideal free-flow speed is reduced by the adjustments found in Table 10-5. Given that lane widths and lateral clearances will be built to meet modern standards, there are no adjustments for these conditions. Since the highway is to be divided, there is no adjustment for this condition either. The only adjustment is for access points per mile, which may be interpolated between 0 for 0 access points/mile and -2.5 mph for 10 access points/mile. For 5 access points/mile, -1.25 mph is the appropriate adjustment. The free-flow speed for the multilane highway is, therefore, 60-1.25 or 58.75, say 59 mph. This is an almost negligible adjustment.

The general algorithm for determining N is Equation [10-13]:

$$N = \frac{DDHV}{PHF\ MSF_i\ f_{HV}\ f_p}$$

Appropriate values of MSF must be found for freeways (65 mph free-flow speed) and multilane highways (59 mph free-flow speed) for the desired level of service, which is C. From Table 10-3:

MSF_c (freeways, 65 mph) = 1548 pcphpl

From Table 10-4:

MSF_c (multilane, 59 mph, interpolated) = 1622 pcphpl

The driver population is assumed to be regular users, and lane widths and lateral clearances require no adjustment. Thus, the only adjustment factor to be used is the heavy vehicle adjustment, f_{HV}. From Table 10-7:

$$E_T(\text{rolling terrain}) = 3.0$$

$$E_R(\text{rolling terrain}) = 2.0$$

Then:

$$f_{HV} = \frac{1}{1 + 0.15(3 - 1) + 0.00(2 - 1)} = 0.769$$

The minimum value of N can now be computed for both the freeway option and the divided multilane highway option:

$$N\ (\text{freeway}) = \frac{3000}{0.82 \times 1548 \times 0.769 \times 1} = 3.07$$

$$N\ (\text{multilane}) = \frac{3000}{0.82 \times 1622 \times 0.769 \times 1} = 2.93$$

The result shows very little difference between the multilane divided highway and the freeway. To provide for LOS C, however, 3 lanes in each direction on the freeway would NOT be sufficient, while the same number of lanes on the multilane highway would be. This, however, could be very misleading, as the densities for the various levels of service are *higher* for multilane highways than for freeways, based on lower

driver expectations of such facilities. Operating conditions on the multilane highway will be worse than on the freeway.

To illustrate this, the level of service, speed, and density will be found for a divided multilane highway and a freeway of 3 lanes (in each direction) for the stated situation. Then:

$$v = \frac{DDHV}{PHF\ N\ f_{HV}\ f_p}$$

and:

$$v = \frac{3000}{0.82 \times 3 \times 0.769} = 1586\ \text{pcphpl}$$

This value is now used to enter Figure 10-5 for freeways, and Figure 10-6 for multilane highways. A 59 mph free-flow speed curve is interpolated on Figure 10-6 for this purpose. The solution is illustrated in Figure 10-11.

Although the freeway operates at level of service D, it is very close to the boundary for LOS C. The expected speed is 64 mph, and the density is 1586/64 or 24.8 pc/mi/ln. While the multilane highway does provide for level of service C, it is very close to the LOS D boundary. The expected average speed is 57 mph, and the density is 1586/57 = 27.8 pc/mi/ln. Thus, even though the multilane highway provides a better level of service than the freeway, the freeway provides a higher average speed and a lower density.

This analysis provides important information in deciding whether to build a 6-lane multilane divided highway or a 6-lane freeway. It alone, however, is not sufficient to make the decision. Any signalized intersections along the multilane route must be carefully examined for their impact on overall operations. Aspects of cost, both construction and maintenance, are also important. Development plans in the corridor might also have an impact on the final decision, as would comparative environmental impact statements.

The HCS package

Currently, the "official" software package that replicates all *Highway Capacity Manual* computations is the *Highway Capacity Software Package*. Originally developed at Polytechnic University and modified by

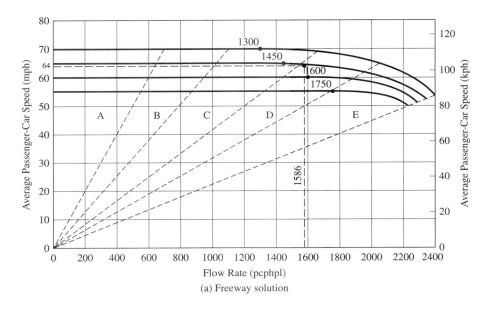

(a) Freeway solution

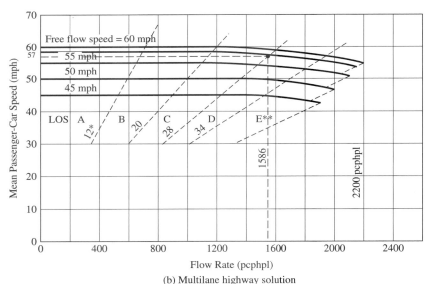

(b) Multilane highway solution

Figure 10-11 Solution for LOS and speed in example 3.

the Federal Highway Administration, this software is maintained and distributed through the McTrans Center at University of Florida at Gainesville. A version of the package including all of the updates included in the 1994 *HCM* is available; a version including all of the updates in the 1997 *HCM* is expected shortly after the manual itself.

Note, however, that the *HCS* package replicates only those procedures included in the current edition of the *HCM*. It also replicates only those computational sequences indicated in the *HCM* itself. This chapter has presented both computational applications found in the *HCM* and some that go beyond. The latter are not replicated in the *HCS* package.

References

The methodologies presented in this chapter are those in the current edition of the *Highway Capacity Manual* [1]. Its predecessors in 1985 [2], 1965 [3], and 1950 [16] are important historical references. Multilane methodologies are based on the results of NCHRP Project 3-35 [4]. Materials have been added from the draft final report of NCHRP Project 3-45 [5], scheduled to appear in the 1997 update of the *HCM*. References [17–19] contain useful presentation of the concept of freeway level of service. Various approaches to the development and calibration of passenger car equivalents are found in References [20–25]. Additional references [6–15] address studies of freeway speed-flow-density relationships, as previously noted.

1. *Highway Capacity Manual, Special Report 209,* 3rd Edition, Transportation Research Board, National Research Council, Washington, DC, (revised) 1997.
2. *Highway Capacity Manual, Special Report 209,* Transportation Research Board, National Research Council, Washington, DC, 1985.
3. *Highway Capacity Manual, Special Report 87,* Transportation Research Board, National Research Council, Washington, DC, 1965.
4. Reilly, W., Harwood, D., and Schoen, J., "Capacity and Quality of Flow of Multilane Highways," *Final Report,* JHK & Associates, Tucson, AZ, 1988.
5. Schoen, J., May, A., Reilly, W., and Urbanik, T., "Speed-Flow Relationships for Basic Freeway Segments," *Draft Final Report,* JHK & Associates and Texas Transportation Institute, Tucson, AZ, December 1994.
6. Hurdle, V., and Datta, P., "Speeds and Flows on an Urban Freeway: Some Measurements and a Hypothesis," *Transportation Research Record 905,* Transportation Research Board, National Research Council, Washington, DC, 1983.
7. Hall, F., Hurdle, V., and Banks, J., "Synthesis of Recent Work on the Nature of Speed-Flow and Speed-Occupancy (Density) Relationships on Freeways," *Transportation Research Record 1365,* Transportation Research Board, National Research Council, Washington, DC, 1992.
8. Hall, F., and Agyemang-Duah, K., "Freeway Capacity Drop and the Definition of Capacity," *Transportation Research Record 1320,* Transportation Research Board, National Research Council, Washington, DC, 1991.
9. Urbanik, T., Hinshaw, W., and Barnes, K., "Evaluation of High-Volume Urban Texas Freeways," *Transportation Research Record 1320,* Transportation Research Board, National Research Council, Washington, DC, 1991.
10. Persaud, B., and Hurdle, V., "Some New Data That Challenge Some Old Ideas About Speed-Flow Relationships," *Transportation Research Record 1194,* Transportation Research Board, National Research Council, Washington, DC, 1988.
11. Hall, F., and Hall, L., "Capacity and Speed-Flow Analysis of the Queen Elizabeth Way in Ontario," *Transportation Research Record 1287,* Transportation Research Board, National Research Council, Washington, DC, 1990.
12. Banks, J., "Flow Processes at a Bottleneck," *Transportation Research Record 1287,* Transportation Research Board, National Research Council, Washington, DC, 1990.
13. Chin, H., and May, A. "Speed-Flow Relationships of Uncongested Flow on Freeways," Institute for Transportation Studies, University of California, Berkeley, CA, 1990.
14. Hall, F., Pushkar, A., and Shi, Y., "Some Observation on Speed-Flow and Flow-Occupancy Relationships Under Congested Conditions," presented at the Annual Meeting of the Transportation Research Board, Washington, DC, January 1993. (To be published in Transportation Research Record).
15. Acha-Daza, J., and Hall, F., "Graphical Comparisons of Predictions for Speed Given by Catastrophic Theory and Other Classic Models," *Transportation Research Record 1398,* Transportation Research Board, National Research Council, Washington, DC, 1993.
16. *Highway Capacity Manual,* 1st Edition, Bureau of Public Roads, Washington, DC, 1950.
17. Roess, R., McShane, W., and Pignataro, L., "Freeway Level of Service: A Revised Approach," *Transportation Research Record 699,* Transportation Research Board, National Research Council, Washington, DC, 1980.
18. Roess, R., and McShane, W., "Capacity and Level of Service Concepts in the 1985 *Highway Capacity Manual,*" *ITE Journal,* April 1987.
19. Roess, R., and McShane, W., "Changing Concepts of Level of Service in the 1985 *Highway Capacity Manual:* Some Examples," *ITE Journal,* May 1987.
20. Linzer, E., McShane, W., and Roess, R., "Effects of Trucks, Buses, and Recreational Vehicles on Freeway Capacity and Service Volume," *Transportation Research Record 699,* Transportation Research Board, National Research Council, Washington, DC, 1980.

21. St. John, A., and Koppett, J., "Grade Effects on Traffic Flow, Stability, and Capacity," *NCHRP Report 185*, Transportation Research Board, National Research Council, Washington, DC, 1978.
22. Cunagin W. and Messer, C., "Passenger Car Equivalents for Rural Highways," *Final Report,* Herbert G. Whyte Associates and the Texas Transportation Institute, College Station, TX, May 1982.
23. Craus, J., Polus, A., and Grinberg, L., "A Revised Model for the Determination of Passenger Car Equivalents,"
Transportation Research, Vol. 14A, Pergamon Press, London, England, 1980.
24. "Review of Truck Weight/Horsepower Ratios as Related to Passing Lane Design," *Final Report,* NCHRP Project 20-7, Penn State University, State College, PA, 1978.
25. Krammes, R., and Crowley, K., "Passenger Car Equivalents for Trucks on Level Freeway Segments," *Transportation Research Record 1194,* Transportation Research Board, National Research Council, Washington, DC, 1988.

Problems

Problem 10–1

Estimate the free-flow speed of a 4-lane undivided multilane highway having the following characteristics: a) speed limit = 35 mph; previous study has 85th percentile speed of 45 mph; b) lane widths = 11 ft; c) obstructions are located 3 ft from the roadside edge in both directions; d) 20 access points per mile, each side of the roadway.

Problem 10–2

Estimate the free-flow speed of a 6-lane freeway with 12-ft lanes, roadside obstructions located 4 ft from the pavement edge, reinforced concrete median barriers located 2 ft from the left lane pavement edge, and interchanges spaced at an average of one mile.

Problem 10–3

Find the appropriate composite grade for the following grade sequences:

(a) 1000 ft of 3% grade, followed by 1500 ft of 2% grade, followed by 750 ft of 4% grade.
(b) 2000 ft of 4% grade, followed by 5000 ft of 3% grade, followed by 2000 ft of 5% grade.
(c) 4000 ft of 5% grade, followed by 3000 ft of 3% grade.

For each of the above cases, what is the appropriate value for E_T and E_R for use in analysis? There are 10% trucks in the traffic stream.

Problem 10–4

A freeway operating in generally rolling terrain has a traffic composition of 10% trucks and buses, and 5% recreational vehicles. If the observed peak hour volume is 3500 vph, what is the equivalent volume in pcph under ideal conditions?

Problem 10–5

Find the upgrade and downgrade service flow rates and service volumes for an 8-lane urban freeway with a free-flow speed of 65 mph. The facility has 11-foot lanes, with obstructions located 2 ft from the pavement edge in both directions. The median barrier is an old type, with a barrier curb located immediately at the left pavement edge in both directions. The traffic stream contains 5% trucks with no buses or RVs. The driver population consists primarily of daily commuters. The section in question is on a 4% upgrade, 1 mile in length. The PHF = 0.85.

Problem 10–6

An existing 6-lane divided multilane highway with a free-flow speed of 45 mph serves a peak hour volume 4000 vph, with 15% trucks, and no buses or RVs. The PHF is 0.90. The highway in question is in generally rolling terrain. What is the likely level of service for this scenario?

Problem 10–7

A long section of freeway is to be designed on level terrain. A level section of 5 miles, however, is followed by a 1-½ mile 5% grade. If the DDHV is 2500 vph with 10% trucks and 3% RVs, how many lanes will be needed on the a) upgrade, b) downgrade, and c) level terrain section to provide for a minimum of level of service C? Assume that acceptable lane widths and lateral clearances are to be provided, and that drivers are generally regular users of the facility. The PHF is 0.92.

11

Areas of Concentrated Turbulence on Uninterrupted Flow Facilities: Weaving, Merging, and Diverging

Chapter 10 addresses the analysis of basic multilane uninterrupted flow. Even on freeways, however, there are areas of concentrated turbulence caused by weaving, merging, and diverging movements. In these areas, even though there are no fixed interruptions to disrupt the traffic stream, the maneuvering of vehicles onto, off of, and across the freeway creates changes in the character of traffic flow that must be considered. In most cases, these movements, undertaken by a significant number of vehicles, cause lane changing well in excess of that occurring on a basic uninterrupted flow segment.

While "turbulence" is a good descriptor of operations in these areas, there are no generally accepted measures of "turbulence" that can be systematically applied. Attempts have been made to relate turbulence to lane-changing parameters, as well as to the variance of speeds through the section [1, 2]. The driver experiences this turbulence in a number of ways, including the need for additional vigilance. Speed changes tend to be more frequent, and speeds may decline somewhat from similar operations on basic sections.

Figure 11-1 illustrates the basic movements creating turbulence on uninterrupted flow facilities. *Weaving* occurs when one movement must cross the path of another along a length of facility without the aid of signals or other control devices (except guide signs). Such situations are created when a merge junction is followed closely by a diverge junction, as shown in Figure 11-1a. The flow entering on the left and leaving on the right must cross the path of vehicles entering on the right and leaving on the left.

Merging occurs when two separate traffic streams join to form a single stream. *Diverging* occurs when one traffic stream separates to form two separate traffic streams. Merging generally occurs at on-ramps to an uninterrupted flow highway segment, but also occurs when two significant facilities join to form one. Conversely, diverging most often occurs at off-ramps from uninterrupted flow segments, but also occurs where a major facility splits into two routes.

The difference between weaving and separate merging and/or diverging movements is unclear at best. Weaving occurs when a merge is "closely followed" by a diverge. When the two are close enough,

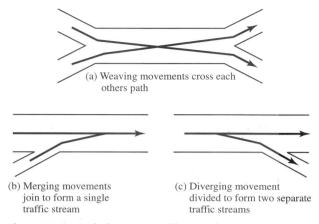

(a) Weaving movements cross each others path

(b) Merging movements join to form a single traffic stream

(c) Diverging movement divided to form two separate traffic streams

Figure 11-1   Turbulence areas illustrated.

vehicles tend to make their crossing maneuvers throughout the section. When far apart, most of the merging is completed well before diverging maneuvers start to occur. Little is definitively known about exact distances comprising "closely followed." In the 1965 *Highway Capacity Manual* [3], a curve defining "out of the realm of weaving" defined such limits. It was, however, based on only a few data points, and was mostly a rational extension of other relationships. Subsequent research has been unable to duplicate this curve, or find a definitive alternative. The 1997 *HCM* [4] indicates that weaving occurs when the merge area and subsequent diverge area are separated by less than 2000 ft or 2500 ft, depending on the specific geometry of the section. At greater distances, merging and diverging are treated as separate operations.

Even where merge and diverge areas are spaced within the noted limits, weaving does not always exist. When a single-lane on-ramp is closely followed by a one-lane off-ramp, weaving is said to exist if the two are connected by a continuous auxiliary lane. If no auxiliary lane exists, merging and diverging are again treated as separate operations. This distinction is not particularly logical, and is more a result of the history of weaving area research than any rational comparison of data from various sites.

The 1994 *HCM* had a number of inconsistencies between and among procedures for basic freeway sections, weaving areas, and ramp junctions. The weaving area methodology was the oldest in the 1994 manual, having been developed in the early 1970s.

The procedures for ramp analysis were relatively new, resulting from an NCHRP study completed in 1993 [5]. Complicating matters, the 1994 *HCM* included revisions to basic freeway section analysis that were inconsistent with a number of weaving area analysis components.

As the 1997 *HCM* was being developed, further revisions to the basic freeway section methodology were developed, resulting in minor additional revisions to ramp analysis procedures. Because of this, this book's authors developed revised weaving analysis procedures that would at least eliminate the major inconsistencies of the 1994 procedure. The revisions were subsequently adopted for inclusion in the 1997 *HCM*.

The procedures presented for weaving area and ramps herein, therefore, represent those of the 1997 *HCM*.

Analysis of weaving areas

A. Movements in a weaving area

In a typical weaving area, four component flows may exist. By definition, the two flows crossing each other's path within the section are called *weaving flows* while those that do not are called *non-weaving flows*. Figure 11-2 illustrates.

Vehicles entering on leg A and exiting on leg Y cross the path of vehicles entering on leg B and leaving on leg X. These are the weaving flows. Movements A–X and B–Y do not have to cross the path of any other movement, even though they may share lanes,

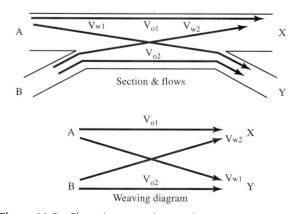

Figure 11-2   Flows in a weaving section.

and may make optional lane-changing movements in the weaving area.

By convention, non-weaving, or *outer* flows are given the subscript "o," while weaving flows are given the subscript "w." The larger of the two outer or weaving flows is given the subscript "1," while the smaller is given the subscript "2." A number of ratios are also commonly used in weaving analysis. The following weaving area volumes and ratios are, therefore, defined:

V_{w1} = larger weaving volume, vph

V_{w2} = smaller weaving volume, vph

V_{o1} = larger outer or non-weaving volume, vph

V_{o2} = smaller outer or non-weaving volume, vph

V_w = total weaving volume, $V_{w1} + V_{w2}$, vph

V_{nw} = total outer or non-weaving volume, $V_{o1} + V_{o2}$, vph

V = total volume in section, $V_w + V_{nw}$, vph

VR = volume ratio = V_w/V

R = weaving ratio = V_{w2}/V_w

The schematic line drawing beneath the section is called a "weaving diagram." In block form, it shows the weaving and non-weaving flows and their relative positions on the roadway. By convention, it is always drawn with flow moving from left to right. This is a convenient form to illustrate the component flows in a consistent way for analysis.

B. Critical geometric variables

Three geometric variables have a marked effect on the quality of weaving area operations:

- lane configuration
- length of the weaving area
- width (number of lanes) of the weaving area

Each of these has an impact on the amount of lane-changing that must occur, and its intensity.

1. Lane configuration. As has been noted, weaving vehicle streams cross each other's path as they move from one side of the roadway to the other. Vehicles must make lane changes to weave successfully. The

lane configuration, i.e., the alignment of entry lanes with exit lanes, can have a significant impact on the number of these lane changes. *Seven* different weaving configurations can be provided. Some of these are extremely rare, and some have similar, although not equal, characteristics. For this reason, the 1997 *HCM* groups configurations into *three* different categories, called Type A, B, and C configurations.

Type A configurations are illustrated in Figure 11-3. The feature common to Type A areas is that every weaving vehicle *must execute one lane change* to successfully complete the desired maneuver. Such a situation is created when the nose of the merge gore area is connected to the nose of the diverge area by a lane line. A lane line of this type is called a *crown line.* Every weaving vehicle must make one lane change across this line.

The most common Type A weaving configuration is the *ramp-weave section.* As shown in Figure 11-3a, the ramp-weave section is formed when a single-lane on-ramp is followed by a single-lane off-ramp with a continuous auxiliary lane connecting them. The crown line is the lane line separating the right-hand lane of the main roadway from the auxiliary lane. All weaving vehicles, both those entering the freeway and those leaving it, must cross between the auxiliary lane and the right lane of the main roadway. Additional lane changes can be made, but they are not *required* to achieve the desired destination.

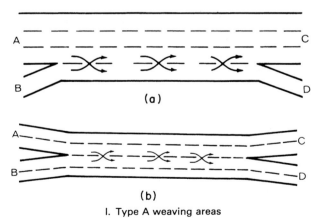

I. Type A weaving areas

Figure 11-3 Type A weaving configurations. [Used with permission of Transportation Research Board, National Research Council, Washington, DC, from *Highway Capacity Manual, Special Report 209,* 3rd Ed., p. 4-3. Copyright © 1994 Transportation Research Board.]

Figure 11-3b shows a similar configuration formed by a major merge junction followed by a major diverge junction. Where more than two input and output lanes have multiple lanes, the weaving area is termed a *major weaving section.* In the case shown, one lane line connects the merge and diverge nose, and a crown line is created. Again, every weaving vehicle must make one lane change across this line.

While the configurations of Figures 11-3a and b have similar lane-changing characteristics, they are different in one significant way. In a ramp-weave, on-ramp and off-ramp vehicles often enter or leave the section at reduced speeds due to the constrictive geometry of the ramps. Thus, the weaving area is one in which weaving vehicles are often accelerating or decelerating. In a major weave, merging and diverging roadways most often have high design speeds, and the need to accelerate or decelerate within the weaving area is not significant. It should be noted that the methodology of the 1997 *HCM* was calibrated specifically for ramp-weave configurations, and its application to similar major weave configurations is approximate.

Type B configurations are illustrated in Figure 11-4. Three sub-types are shown, although the variation illustrated in Figure 11-4a is by far the most prevalent. All have a unique characteristic: because of the lane configuration, at least one weaving movement can be accomplished *without making a lane change.* Further, the other weaving movement requires *no more than one lane change.* This requires a continuous lane in which a vehicle can enter on the right leg and leave on the left leg of the section, or vice-versa.

Such a lane, shown in Figure 11-4a, is provided by having *lane balance* at the exit gore. A "lane balanced" exit gore has one more lane departing than it has entering. Thus, vehicles in one lane can exit on either leg without making a lane change. Such designs can provide flexibility to handle varying demand splits on the exit legs. In the illustration, a vehicle traveling from leg B to leg C (a weaving movement) can do so without making a lane change. Vehicles in the other weaving movement, A to D, must make one lane change.

In Figure 11-4b, the same weaving lane-change situation is created by having a lane from each entry leg merge into a single lane at the entry gore area. In this case, the exit gore area is *not* lane balanced.

While the weaving situation in Figure 11-4b is similar to that in Figure 11-4a, the turbulence due to the

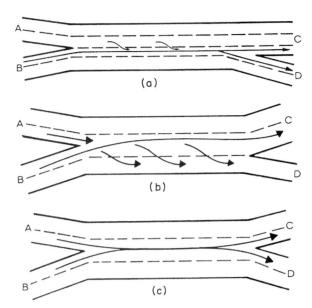

Figure 11-4 Type B weaving configurations. [Used with permission of Transportation Research Board, National Research Council, Washington, DC, from *Highway Capacity Manual, Special Report 209,* 3rd Ed., p. 4-3. Copyright © 1994 Transportation Research Board.]

merge required at the entry gore often makes this a less desirable alternative.

In Figure 11-4c, a design frequently used on collector-distributor roadways is shown. It accommodates a weaving movement in *both* directions without a lane change. This is accomplished by having both a merging lane at the entry gore area and lane balance at the exit gore area.

Again, note that the *HCM* model for Type B weaving areas was calibrated primarily for sites of the type shown in Figure 11-4a, with some data from sites similar to Figure 11-4b. There was no data for sites of the type shown in Figure 11-4c.

Type C configurations are illustrated in Figure 11-5. The common feature of a Type C configurations is that while one weaving movement can still be made without making a lane change, the second weaving movement requires *at least two lane changes.* A typical situation is shown in Figure 11-5a: one weaving movement requires no lane changes, while the other requires two. In Figure 11-5b, a unique type of weaving area—a two-sided—is illustrated. In such a section, a right-hand on-ramp is followed closely by a left-hand off-ramp, or a left-hand on-ramp is followed

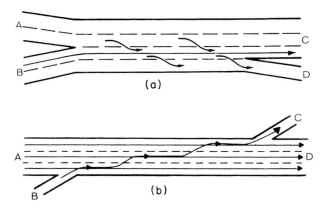

Figure 11-5 Type C weaving configurations. [Used with permission of Transportation Research Board, National Research Council, Washington, DC, from *Highway Capacity Manual, Special Report 209*, 3rd Ed., p. 4-4. Copyright © 1994 Transportation Research Board.]

closely by a right-hand off-ramp. Here, the ramp-to-ramp traffic must weave across the entire through flow of the uninterrupted flow facility. The through facility flow is, in effect, a weaving movement. In this case, the through flow (weaving) does not have to make any lane changes, while the ramp-to-ramp flow must execute lane changes across the width of the freeway.

The *HCM* model is calibrated completely to configurations of the type shown in Figure 11-5a. There is little recent data on two-sided weaves, which are included in this category only as the roughest of approximations.

Lane configuration depends on how entry and exit lanes "line up," creating continuous paths that do not require lane-changing. The operational difference can be immense. Consider a case in which 1000 vph weave from right to left with 500 vph from left to right. If a Type A configuration is present, each vehicle *must* make one lane change. Thus, a minimum of 1000 + 500 or 1500 lane-changes per hour must take place within the weaving area. If a Type B configuration is provided, allowing the primary movement to take place without a lane change, then only the 500 vph moving from left to right must change lanes *once*. Thus, 500 lane-changes per hour must take place. If a Type C configuration were provided, the minor weaving movement would have to make *two* lane changes. Thus, a total of $2 \times 500 = 1000$ lane-changes per

hour would have to take place. The configuration chosen can change the number of required lane changes by 1000 per hour, which has a tremendous impact on turbulence through the section.

It should be noted that other lane changes may take place in the weaving area. Configuration, however, determines how many lane changes weaving vehicles *must* make to successfully complete their desired movement. Drivers of both weaving and non-weaving vehicles may make additional discretionary lane changes, but they are not forced to do so by the geometry provided.

2. Length of the weaving area. While the configuration of lanes in a weaving area has a tremendous impact on the number of required lane changes, the length of the section is a critical determinant of the intensity of lane changing within the section. Since all of the *required* lane changes made by weaving vehicles must take place between the entry and exit gore areas, the length of the section determines the intensity of lane-changing. If 1000 vph must make a lane change in the weaving area, then the intensity of lane changing will be much higher in a section of 500 ft length than in one of 2000 ft. As the section gets shorter, then the number of lane changes per unit of length increases, creating greater turbulence.

The length of a weaving area is measured as illustrated in Figure 11-6. By convention, length is measured from a point at the entrance gore area where the distance between the right-most lane edge of the left leg and the left-most lane edge of the right leg are 2 ft apart to a point at the exit gore where the two are 12 ft apart. The original logic for this definition is not certain, due to relative antiquity. It was the method used for early weaving area studies conducted by the Bureau of Public Roads (now the Federal Highway Administration) during the late 1950s and early 1960s. For conformance, subsequent studies have followed the pattern. It is likely that the definition arose from the types of weaving areas prevalent at the time, many of them formed by interchanges with loop ramps. Because of the geometry of the typical loop ramp of that period, the angle of departure at the exit gore was larger than the merge angle at the entrance gore. The definition also reflects the behavior of drivers in response to paint markings in the gore area.

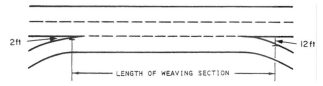

Figure 11-6 Length of a weaving area. [Used with permission of Transportation Research Board, National Research Council, Washington, DC, from *Highway Capacity Manual, Special Report 209*, 3rd Ed., p. 4-2. Copyright © 1994 Transportation Research Board.]

3. Width of the weaving area and its impact on operations. The total width of the intersection is measured in the number of lanes available for all flows, *N*. The width of the section has an impact on lane-changing, as it controls the maximum number of lane changes that may be made in any given direction as vehicles attempt to move across the facility.

Of greater interest, however, is the proportional use of lanes by weaving and non-weaving vehicles. Under normal circumstances, vehicles on a highway facility "compete" for space, and operations across the facility tend to reach an equilibrium in which all drivers are experiencing relatively similar conditions. In a weaving area, there is some degree of segregation of non-weaving from weaving flows. Non-weaving drivers tend to stay in outside lanes to avoid the turbulence caused by the intense lane-changing of weaving vehicles. Nevertheless, many lanes are shared by both weaving and non-weaving vehicles. Barring any external constraints, weaving vehicles will occupy N_w effective lanes of the weaving area, with non-weaving vehicles occupying the remaining lanes (and/or portions thereof).

In a very real sense, however, the lane configuration limits the total number of lanes that *can* be utilized by weaving vehicles, because of the lane changes that must be made. The following general statements can be made:

a. Weaving vehicles may occupy all of a lane in which weaving is accomplished without a lane change.
b. Weaving vehicles may occupy most of a lane from which a weaving maneuver can be accomplished with a single lane change.
c. Weaving vehicles may occupy a small portion of a lane from which a weaving maneuver can be completed by making two lane changes.

d. Weaving vehicles cannot occupy a measurable portion of any lane from which a weaving maneuver would require three or more lane changes.

This translates into limitations on the maximum number of lanes that weaving vehicles can occupy, based on the configuration of the section. These are illustrated in Figure 11-7.

In a typical Type A ramp-weave section, for example, almost all ramp vehicles are weaving, i.e., there is usually little ramp-to-ramp flow. Thus, the auxiliary lane is almost fully occupied by weaving vehicles. The shoulder lane of the freeway, however, must be shared with a substantial number of through vehicles. Studies have shown, therefore, that weaving vehicles rarely occupy more than 1.4 lanes of a ramp-weave section.

Type B weaving configurations are far more flexible. There is always one "through lane" for at least one of the weaving movements that can be fully occupied by weaving vehicles. In addition, the two lanes adjacent to the "through lane" allow weaving in both directions with only a single lane change; both of these lanes can be substantially used by weaving vehicles. There can be

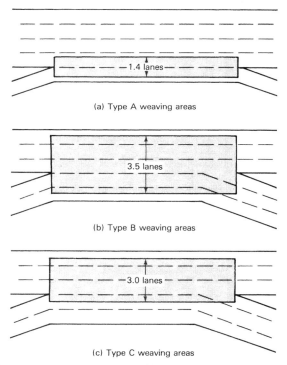

Figure 11-7 Maximum use of lanes by weaving vehicles.

some occupancy of the next adjacent lanes as well. Studies have shown that weaving vehicles can occupy up to 3.5 total lanes in a Type B configuration.

Type C weaving configurations are somewhat more restrictive than Type B sections. There is still a "through lane" for one weaving movement, in which a weave is completed without a lane change. Thus, weaving vehicles can fully occupy such a lane. *One of* the lanes adjacent to the through lane allows weaving with one lane change, and can be substantially occupied by weaving vehicles. The other, however, serves the minor weaving movement, and requires two lane changes. Thus, weaving vehicles can make some, but not significant use of this lane. The practical limit on lane use by weaving vehicles in a Type C configuration is 3.0 lanes, except for two-sided weaves, where the entire through roadway is occupied by weaving vehicles, regardless of the number of lanes present.

Given that configuration can effectively "constrain" the number of lanes occupied by weaving vehicles, two variables are defined:

N_w = number of lanes weaving vehicles must occupy to achieve balanced equilibrium operation with non-weaving vehicles, lanes

N_w (max) = maximum number of lanes that can be occupied by weaving vehicles, based on geometric configuration

When $N_w \leq N_w$ (max), weaving vehicles may reach their desired equilibrium with non-weaving vehicles, and a balanced, or *unconstrained operation* results. When $N_w > N_w$(max), weaving vehicles cannot achieve equilibrium operation. This case is called *constrained operation,* as weaving vehicles are constrained to using fewer lanes than they require for equilibrium. In such a case, weaving vehicles use fewer lanes and non-weaving vehicles use more lanes. Operations often result in weaving vehicles experiencing significantly worse conditions than non-weaving vehicles. A critical feature of the weaving model is the determination of which type of operation is likely to exist in any given circumstance.

C. The 1997 *HCM* computational methodology

The 1994 *HCM* methodology for analysis of weaving areas was (in 1996) the oldest procedure in the man-

ual. It was the first to be re-examined after publication of the 1965 *HCM*, and the process of developing the 1985 *HCM*, however illogically, began with a comprehensive study of weaving area operations, sponsored by NCHRP [6] in the early 1970s. In 1978, an FHWA study led to the modification of this procedure [7], and its publication in a TRB publication of "Interim Materials on Highway Capacity" in 1980 (8). A second weaving area analysis procedure, independently developed by J. Leisch, was also included in the interim materials. The inclusion of two vastly differing procedures in a single document led to a great deal of confusion. Subsequently, FHWA sponsored a study to fully document the Leisch procedure [9], and NCHRP sponsored an independent study to compare the two to a new data base [10]. The latter led to the development of a third analysis procedure. When the 1985 *HCM* was published, the final weaving chapter became a synthesis of these procedures developed as part of the NCHRP-sponsored effort to produce final materials for the manual [11]. Thus, despite a great deal of research effort, the methodology adopted, which was not updated in the 1994 *HCM*, represented a compromise of often incongruent concepts and ideas. This text presents an updated version of the weaving procedure. Though developed specifically for this text, it was subsequently presented to the Committee on Highway Capacity and Quality of Service and adopted for publication and use in the 1997 *HCM*.

1. Structure of the methodology. The 1997 *HCM* model is used only in operational analysis, i.e., given a full specification of traffic and geometric conditions, a level of service is predicted. The model was calibrated using volumes converted to peak flow rates under equivalent ideal conditions. The model follows the following steps, as illustrated in Figure 11-8.

a. Specify all traffic and geometric conditions for the site.

b. Convert all demand volumes to peak flow rates under equivalent ideal conditions.

c. Assume that operations are *unconstrained.* Estimate the resulting speed of weaving and non-weaving vehicles.

d. Using the results of c, check that operations are indeed unconstrained. If they are not, re-estimate speeds assuming *constrained* operations.

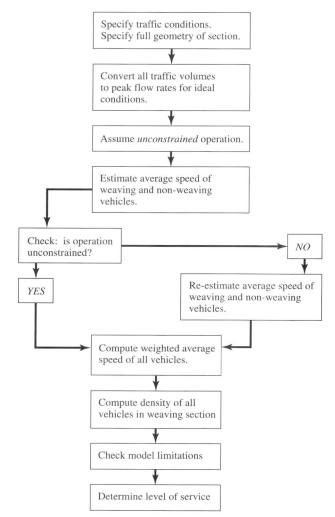

Figure 11-8 Flow chart of the weaving area model.

e. Determine the weighted average speed and density for the section.
f. Check input variables against limitations of the methodology.
g. Determine level of service from estimated densities.

Note that the model focuses on prediction of the speed of component weaving and non-weaving flows. The 97 model logically extends this to a prediction of density.

2. Converting demand volumes to peak flow rates under equivalent ideal conditions. The first computational step in a weaving analysis is the conversion of all demand volumes to peak flow rates under equivalent ideal conditions using the following algorithm:

$$v_i = \frac{V_i}{PHF\,f_{HV}\,f_p}$$ [11-1]

where: v_i = peak flow rate under equivalent ideal conditions for movement i, pcph
V_i = hourly volume under prevailing conditions for movement i, vph
PHF = peak hour factor
f_{HV} = heavy vehicle adjustment factor
f_p = driver population adjustment factor

The weaving model was developed for freeway weaving areas. Thus, the adjustment factors applied are drawn from current procedures for basic freeway sections, as discussed in Chapter 10. Later, this chapter will discuss the issue of how to apply these procedures to other types of facilities.

It is often useful to construct a weaving diagram, such as that illustrated in Figure 11-2, using converted flow rates, because these will be used throughout the model application.

3. Predicting the average speed of weaving and non-weaving vehicles. As has been discussed, under some circumstances, weaving and non-weaving vehicles may experience very different operating conditions, even though they share the same facility. For this reason, the 1997 *HCM* model predicts the speed of weaving and non-weaving vehicles separately.

The general form of the speed-prediction algorithm was developed by JHK & Associates as part of an NCHRP-sponsored study [10]:

$$S_i = S_{\min} + \frac{S_{\max} - S_{\min}}{1 + W}$$ [11-2]

where: S_i = average speed of vehicles ($i = w$ for weaving vehicles, nw for non-weaving vehicles), mph
$S_{\min}$ = minimum expected speed in weaving area, mph
$S_{\max}$ = maximum expected speed in weaving area, mph
W = weaving intensity factor

In the 1997 *HCM*, the maximum speed, $S_{\max}$, is set equal to the free-flow speed on the freeway plus 5 mph. The +5mph adjusts for the algorithm's tendency to under-predict higher speeds, even when the proper maximum is used. The assumed minimum speed is 15 mph, and the speed algorithm becomes:

$$S_i = 15 + \frac{S_{FF} - 10}{1 + W} \qquad [11\text{-}3]$$

where all terms have been previously defined. The use of a variable free-flow speed also allows for the application of the algorithm to weaving on other facility types. Non-freeways, such as multilane highways and collector-distributor roadways can be reflected in lower free-flow speeds, yielding lower speed predictions.

While there is a great deal of interest in arterial weaving, great care should be taken in applying what is essentially an *uninterrupted flow* methodology to an *interrupted flow* case. Nothing in this procedure addresses the effect of nearby signals on the operation of a weaving area in which platoon flow is a dominant feature.

The weaving intensity factor, W, takes the form:

$$W = \frac{a(1 + VR)^b(v/N)^c}{L^d} \qquad [11\text{-}4]$$

and:

VR = volume ratio
v = total adjusted rate of flow in the weaving section, pcph
N = total number of lanes in the weaving section
L = length of the weaving section, ft
a,b,c,d = constants of calibration

The constants of calibration in the weaving intensity factor (W) vary based on (1) whether the prediction is for the speed of weaving vehicles or non-weaving vehicles, (2) the configuration type, and (3) whether the operation is *constrained* or *unconstrained*.

The weaving intensity factor is based on a rationale constructed to produce logical sensitivities. As W increases, average speed decreases, as expected. Weaving intensity increases as the proportion of weaving traffic increases (VR), the average flow rate per lane increases (v/N), and as the length (L) decreases. All of these are expected trends. The term $(1 + VR)$ eliminates the numerical difficulties of raising a fractional number to a power.

Constants of calibration for Equation [11-4] are shown in Table 11-1.

Table 11-1 Constants of Calibration for the Weaving Intensity Factor

Type of Oper.	Calibration Constants for Prediction of Weaving Speed S_w				Calibration Constants for Prediction of Non-Weaving Speed S_{mw}			
	a	*b*	*c*	*d*	*a*	*b*	*c*	*d*
Type A Configurations								
U	0.226	2.2	1.00	0.90	0.020	4.0	1.30	1.00
C	0.280	2.2	1.00	0.90	0.020	4.0	0.88	0.60
Type B Configurations								
U	0.100	1.2	0.77	0.50	0.020	2.0	1.42	0.95
C	0.160	1.2	0.77	0.50	0.015	2.0	1.30	0.90
Type C Configurations								
U	0.100	1.8	0.80	0.50	0.015	1.8	1.10	0.50
C	0.100	2.0	0.85	0.50	0.013	1.6	1.00	0.50

U = Unconstrained operation; C = Constrained operation.

All speed predictions are initially done assuming that the type of operation is *unconstrained*. In the next procedural step, this assumption is checked. If it is shown to be correct, the speed predictions remain as computed. If the assumption is shown to be incorrect, speeds are re-estimated using calibration constants for *constrained* operation.

4. **Determining the type of operation.** As discussed previously, the type of operation depends on the ability of weaving vehicles to occupy enough of the available roadway space to achieve equilibrium with non-weaving vehicles. N_w has been defined as the number of lanes weaving vehicles must occupy to achieve equilibrium. N_w (max) has been defined as the maximum number of lanes that weaving vehicles can occupy based on the configuration provided. Given these definitions:

- If $N_w \leq N_w$ (max), the operation is *unconstrained*.
- If $N_w > N_w$ (max), the operation is *constrained*.

In unconstrained operation, the geometric configuration does not prevent weaving vehicles from occupying the number of lanes required for equilibrium operation. In constrained operation, equilibrium requires that weaving vehicles occupy more lanes than the configuration allows.

Equations [11-5], [11-6], and [11-7] are empirical algorithms for determining N_w for Type A, B, and C configurations respectively:

$$N_w = \frac{2.19 \, N \, VR^{0.571} \, L_H^{0.234}}{S_w^{0.438}} \qquad [11\text{-}5]$$

$$N_w = N\left[0.085 + 0.703VR + \frac{234.8}{L} - 0.018(S_{nw} - S_w)\right] \qquad [11\text{-}6]$$

$$N_w = N[0.761 + 0.047VR + 0.011L_H - 0.005(S_{nw} - S_w)] \qquad [11\text{-}7]$$

where: L_H = length of the weaving area, in hundreds of ft, and all other variables as previously defined

The results of these estimates must be compared with the maximum values for the appropriate configuration type to determine the type of operation.

Table 11-2 Criteria for Unconstrained vs. Constrained Operation

Configuration	N_w	N_w (max)
Type A	Equation [11-5]	1.4 lanes
Type B	Equation [11-6]	3.5 lanes
Type C	Equation [11-7]	3.0 lanes*

* Excludes 2-sided weaving areas, where N_w (max) = N.

[Used with permission of Transportation Research Board, National Research Council, Washington, DC, from *Highway Capacity Manual, Special Report 209,* 3rd Ed., p. 4-7. Copyright © 1994 Transportation Research Board.]

These have been discussed previously, and are summarized in Table 11-2.

5. **Limitations on weaving algorithms.** Table 11-3 shows limitations on the use of the weaving algorithms for speed and lane usage predictions. These reflect the limitations of the data base from which the algorithms were developed, and not all have the same meaning and interpretation.

"Weaving capacity" reflects the highest v_w values observed over a wide range of sites. While somewhat approximate, these limits are maximums. Thus, if higher weaving flows are predicted or anticipated, it is likely that the section *will break down,* i.e., that level of service F will result, regardless of what the speed and density predictions suggest. Thus, the interpretation of these limits is: *When weaving flows exceed the weaving capacity, algorithms are unreliable, and level of service F conditions are likely to arise.*

"Maximum v/N" reflects a similar consideration. Because of turbulence in the weaving area, maximum per lane flow rates are limited to a value somewhat below the capacity of a lane in a basic freeway section. Note that the capacity of a freeway lane is variable (c) based on the free-flow speed of the facility. The interpretation of the limit is similar to that for maximum weaving capacity: *When total flow per lane in the weaving area exceeds the maximum limit, algorithms are unreliable, and level of service F conditions are likely to arise.*

The "maximum volume ratio (*VR*)" limits are most interesting. They again reflect field data observations. The relationship to configuration is important, as it illustrates how different configurations can be adapted to various demand situations. In Type A configura-

Table 11-3 Limitations on Weaving Sections

Type of Config	Weav Cap v_w (max)[1]	Maximum v/N[2]	Max VR[3]		Max R[4]	Max Weav Length, L[5]
A	2000 pcph	(c − 100) pcphpl	N	VR	0.50	2000 ft
			2	1.00		
			3	0.45		
			4	0.35		
			5	0.22		
B	3500 pcph	(c − 100) pcphpl		0.80	0.50	2500 ft
C	3000 pcph	(c − 200) pcphpl		0.50	0.40	2500 ft

1. Section likely to fail at higher weaving flow rates.
2. Section likely to fail at higher total flows per lane.
3. Section likely to operate at lower than predicted speeds at higher VR ratios.
4. Section likely to operate at lower than predicted speeds at higher R ratios.
5. When length exceeds these limits, merge and diverge are treated as isolated ramps, and analyzed accordingly.

tions, for example, all weaving vehicles must change lanes once over the crown line. This effectively limits N_w (max) to 1.4 lanes, as previously discussed. As the freeway gets wider, the ability of weaving vehicles to use additional lanes is not enhanced. Thus, the proportion of total flow that can weave is related to the total number of lanes present, and gets smaller as lanes are added. With only two lanes (this would be collector-distributor roadway), all vehicles could weave. When four freeway lanes are present (plus an auxiliary lane), weaving vehicles are still substantially restricted to using parts of the two lanes adjacent to the crown line. Thus, the proportion of traffic in such a section that can weave is far lower than for the two-lane case.

Type B configurations comprise the only geometry that can handle more than 50% (0.50) weaving traffic with $N > 2$ lanes. The great flexibility of a "through lane" for one weaving movement, while the second weaving movement requires only one lane change, allows for the handling of large weaving flows that could conceivably dominate the section. Even Type C configurations are limited to a maximum VR of 0.50, as the secondary weaving flow must make two or more lane changes. Thus, even in a Type C section, at least one significant non-weaving flow will exist.

The maximum VR limit implies that for values higher than those shown, the computed speed esti-

mates are likely too high for the conditions that exist. This may imply that a breakdown will occur, or may simply imply a level of service worse than that predicted on the basis of speed estimates.

The limitation on weaving ratio, R, is not really an important feature. The maximum value of R is 0.50. Thus, for Type A and Type B sections, there is no limit on its value. For Type C configurations, values in excess of 0.40 suggest that the actual speeds will be worse than those predicted. Such a value of R, however, rarely occurs on a Type C section.

Maximum lengths, L, have an entirely different meaning from other limits. Where lengths exceed the limiting values, it is assumed that merge operations and diverge operations are independent. Thus, merging and diverging analysis procedures are applied to such cases, *not* the weaving procedure. These are, at best, rough estimates. The exact boundary between weaving operations and isolated merge and diverge operations is not known, and is difficult to calibrate.

6. Density-based LOS criteria. If for no other reason than consistency, the level of service criteria for uninterrupted weaving must be based on density. This allows the evaluation of weaving areas on a basis similar to that used on basic multilane uninterrupted flow segments and ramp junctions. The use of density on multilane uninterrupted flow facilities is motivated by the fact that speeds are often unaffected by flow through relatively high flow levels. Density tends to vary throughout the range of flows, and provides a more rational definition of level of service.

Knowing speed and flow in a section, a density can be computationally estimated. In weaving areas, however, a complication exists: speeds of weaving and non-weaving flows are separately predicted. Evidence shows that the speed of these components can vary substantially, particularly in constrained operation. It is more difficult to conceive of two separate density measures, because there is at least some, and perhaps substantial, sharing of lanes by weaving and non-weaving vehicles.

While not as clear as speed differentials, there is some segregation of weaving and non-weaving flows in every weaving area. For ramp-weaves, this segregation may be substantial. Thus, the concept of separate densities for weaving and non-weaving vehicles is not completely irrational.

Separate density measures can be estimated from the number of lanes occupied by weaving vehicles, N_w. For unconstrained operations, N_w is estimated using Equations [11-5], [11-6], or [11-7]. For constrained cases, $N_w = N_w$ (max). In either case, the number of lanes occupied by non-weaving vehicles, N_{nw}, is $N - N_w$. Once the use of lanes by weaving and non-weaving vehicles is known, densities can be computed as:

$$D_w = \frac{v_w/N_w}{S_w} = \frac{V_w}{N_w S_w} \qquad [11\text{-}8]$$

$$D_{nw} = \frac{v_{nw}/N_{nw}}{S_{nw}} = \frac{v_{nw}}{N_{nw} S_{nw}} \qquad [11\text{-}9]$$

where: D_w = average density for weaving vehicles, pc/mi/ln,

D_{nw} = average density for non-weaving vehicles, pc/mi/ln,

v_w = weaving flow rate, pcph,

v_{nw} = non-weaving flow rate, pcph,

N_w = number of lanes occupied by weaving vehicles,

N_{nw} = number of lanes occupied by non-weaving vehicles,

S_w = average speed of weaving vehicles, mph, and

S_{nw} = average speed of non-weaving vehicles, mph.

The 1997 update of the *HCM does not* allow computation of separate densities for weaving and non-weaving vehicles. Rather, a weighted average density for all vehicles is estimated. First a weighted average speed is found. The harmonic mean is used, as a space mean speed computation is desired:

$$S = \frac{v_{nw} + v_w}{\dfrac{v_{nw}}{S_{nw}} + \dfrac{v_w}{S_w}} \qquad [11\text{-}10]$$

where S is the weighted average speed for all vehicles in the section. The average density can then be estimated as:

$$D = \frac{v/N}{S} = \frac{v}{NS} \qquad [11\text{-}11]$$

where D is the weighted average density for all vehicles in the section.

Whether level of service is applied separately to weaving and non-weaving vehicles, or as a weighted average, it describes the operation of all vehicles in the section. Density boundaries are set slightly higher than for basic uninterrupted flow segments. This accounts for the increased turbulence of the weaving area, which will tend to result in lower speeds and higher densities for any given flow level.

While this is a good approach for density at levels of service describing operations at less than capacity, it is not a good approach for the LOS E/F boundary. The value of density at which breakdown occurs should logically be somewhat *less* than it is on basic uninterrupted flow sections. Due to turbulence, it is likely that breakdown will occur at somewhat lower densities than on open sections not subject to ramp or weaving turbulence.

Level of service criteria for weaving areas are shown in Table 11-4. According to the 1997 *HCM*, they are only applied to the average density of all vehicles in the section. If the user wished to expand this definition, the criteria could be separately applied to weaving and non-weaving densities in accordance with Equations [11-8] and [11-9].

7. Extension of the methodology to multiple weaving configurations. Multiple weaving areas are formed when one merge area is followed closely by two diverge areas, or where two closely-spaced merge areas are closely followed by a single diverge area. In such

Table 11-4   LOS Criteria for Weaving Areas

Level of Service	Maximum Density Freeways pc/mi/ln	Maximum Density Multilane Hways C–D Roadways pc/mi/ln
A	10	12
B	20	24
C	28	32
D	35	36
E	≤43	≤40
F	>43	>40

cases, several sets of weaving movements overlap, and the situation becomes more complex than for simple weaving areas.

The 1997 *HCM*, similar to its predecessors, provides analysis procedures for two-segment multiple weaving areas as described above. In practice, it is possible to have any number of closely-spaced merge and diverge points overlapping. Analysis of more than two overlapping sections, however, is not considered to be practical. Further, a general background level of weaving is considered in the proposed algo-

rithm for estimating free-flow speed on freeways, in the form of an adjustment for interchange density.

Figure 11-9 illustrates a single merge followed by two diverge points. As shown, movement 5 weaves with movements 3 and 4. Both of these weaving movements must take place within the first segment of the weaving section, as movement 5 exits at the first diverge point. In the first segment, movements 1 and 2 are outer flows on the left, and movement 6 is an outer flow on the right. Thus, a simple weaving diagram for the first segment of the weaving area is as shown.

Movement 2 weaves with movement 3. This weave can take place anywhere in the section. The few field studies that have been made, however, show that these vehicles tend to segregate from other weaving flows in segment 1, and wait to make their weaving maneuvers until they are in segment 2. Thus, all of these weaving movements are assumed to occur in the second segment of the multiple weaving area. In segment 2, movement 1 is an outer flow on the left, and movement 4 is an outer flow on the right.

Once separate simple weaving diagrams have been developed for each segment of the multiple weave, each segment is separately analyzed as if it were a

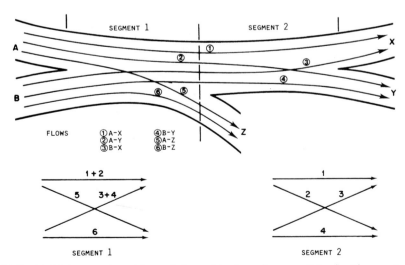

Figure 11-9 Multiple weaving: Merge followed by two diverges. [Used with permission of Transportation Research Board, National Research Council, Washington, DC, from *Highway Capacity Manual, Special Report 209*, 3rd Ed., p. 4-11. Copyright © 1994 Transportation Research Board.]

simple weaving section. The number of lane changes required of each weaving movement, however, has to be carefully considered to establish the correct configuration type for each segment in accordance with the principles discussed previously.

Figure 11-10 illustrates two merge areas followed by a single diverge area. In this case, movement 5 weaves with movements 3 and 4. These weaving movements must occur in the second segment of the weaving area, as movement 5 only enters at that point. Movement 1 is an outer flow on the left while movement 6 is an outer flow on the right.

Movement 2 also weaves with movement 3. While this weaving movement could take place anywhere in the section, sparse studies suggest that such vehicles weave early, in the first segment, so that they can avoid the turbulence of other weaving vehicles in the second segment. Thus, all of these weaving movements are assumed to occur in the first segment. Movement 1 is an outer flow to the left, and movement 4 is an outer flow to the right. Again, each segment is now analyzed as if it were a simple weaving section, with the number of

lane-changes required of weaving vehicles determining the type of configuration.

D. Sample problems in weaving area analysis

The following two problems illustrate weaving area analysis procedures.

SAMPLE PROBLEM 1: A FREEWAY RAMP-WEAVE SECTION

PROBLEM STATEMENT: Figure 11-11 illustrates a typical ramp-weave section on a freeway. It is formed by a single-lane on-ramp closely followed by a single-lane off-ramp on a 6-lane freeway (3 lanes in each direction). With the addition of an auxiliary lane, the weaving section has *four* lanes in one direction. Other relevant information concerning the section is shown in Figure 11-11. As in all weaving area analyses, existing or forecast conditions are specified, and the level of service is estimated. What level of service is expected under the conditions shown?

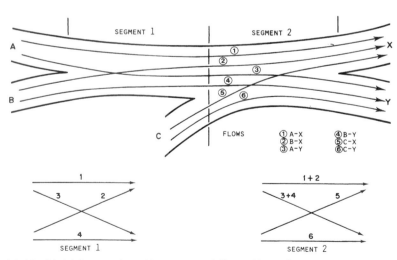

Figure 11-10 Multiple weaving: Two merges followed by a diverge. [Used with permission of Transportation Research Board, National Research Council, Washington, DC, from *Highway Capacity Manual, Special Report 209,* 3rd Ed., p. 4-12. Copyright © 1994 Transportation Research Board.]

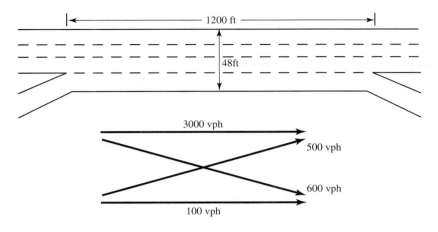

General Characteristics: Ideal lateral clearance
10% trucks, all mvts
level terrain
PHF=0.92
Free-Flow speed=70mph

Figure 11-11 Weaving section for sample problem 1.

SOLUTION: The first step in the solution is to convert all demand flows to equivalent pcph under ideal conditions. This requires the use of Equation 11-1:

$$v = \frac{V}{PHF\, f_{HV}\, f_p}$$

where: E_T (level terrain) = 1.5 (Table 10-7)

and: f_{HV} = $1/[1 + 0.10(1.5 - 1)]$
     = 0.952
   f_P = 1.0 (no indication of non-regular population)
   PHF = 0.92 (given)

Then:

v_{o1} = $3,000/(0.92 \times 0.952 \times 1)$ = 3426 pcph

v_{o2} = $100/(0.92 \times 0.952 \times 1)$ = 144 pcph

$v_{NW} = V_{o1} + V_{o2}$ = 3540 pcph

v_{w1} = $600/(0.92 \times 0.952 \times 1)$ = 685 pcph

v_{w2} = $500/(0.92 \times 0.952 \times 1)$ = 571 pcph

$v_w = v_{w1} + v_{w2}$ = 1256 pcph

$v = v_{NW} + v_W$ **= 4796 pcph**

and:

VR = 1256/4796 = 0.262

R = 571/1256 = 0.455

v/N = 4796/4   = **1199 pcphpl**

L = 1200 ft

Now, each of the weaving intensity factors must be computed using the volume conversions above. Constants a, b, c, and d are selected from Table 11-1, for Type A weaving sections.

Weaving Speed, Unconstrained

$$W = \frac{0.226(1 + 0.262)^{2.2}(1199)^{1.00}}{(1200)^{0.9}} = 0.766$$

Non-Weaving Speed, Unconstrained

$$W = \frac{0.020(1 + 0.262)^{4.0}(1199)^{1.30}}{(1200)^{1.0}} = 0.425$$

Weaving Speed, Constrained

$$W = \frac{0.280(1 + 0.262)^{2.2}(1199)^{1.00}}{(1200)^{0.9}} = 0.948$$

Non-Weaving Speed, Constrained

$$W = \frac{0.020(1 + 0.262)^{4.0}(1199)^{0.88}}{(1200)^{0.6}} = 0.369$$

Again, *unconstrained operation* is assumed. Speeds are now estimated for this condition using the revised speed algorithm presented in Equation [11-4]:

$$S_i = 15 + \frac{S_{FF} - 10}{1 + W}$$

The free-flow speed, S_{FF}, is given as 70 mph for this problem. Then:

$$S_w = 15 + \frac{60}{1 + 0.766} = 49.0 \text{ mph}$$

$$S_{nw} = 15 + \frac{60}{1 + 0.425} = 57.1 \text{ mph}$$

The assumption of unconstrained operation is now checked by computing N_w required to achieve such operation. Equation [11-5], for Type A sections, is used.

$$N_w = \frac{2.19(4)(0.262)^{0.571}(12)^{0.234}}{(49.0)^{0.438}} = 1.33 \text{ lanes}$$

Since N_w (max) is 1.4, the assumption that this section is *unconstrained* is confirmed.

Estimates of the weighted average speed for all vehicles in the section are now computed, to allow an estimation of average density in the section.

$$S = \frac{1256 + 3540}{\frac{1256}{49.0} + \frac{3540}{57.1}} = 54.7 \text{ mph}$$

$$D = \frac{1199}{54.7} = 21.9 \text{ pc/mi/ln}$$

For the level of service criteria presented in Table 11-4, level of service C prevails in the weaving section. If weaving and non-weaving vehicles are to be considered separately, then:

$$D_w = \frac{(1256/1.33)}{49.0} = 19.3 \text{ pc/mi/ln (LOS B)}$$

$$D_{nw} = \frac{(3540/2.67)}{57.1} = 23.2 \text{ pc/mi/ln (LOS C)}$$

CONCLUSION: The calculations indicate that the weaving area as described will operate at level of service C. Unconstrained operation prevails. Weaving vehicles have somewhat lower speeds *and* lower densities than non-weaving vehicles. This often occurs in Type A sections due to the reduced speeds at which ramp vehicles generally enter and leave the mainline.

SAMPLE PROBLEM 2: A WEAVING AREA ON A COLLECTOR-DISTRIBUTOR ROADWAY

PROBLEM: Figure 11-12 illustrates a collector-distributor roadway that is part of a complicated freeway interchange. The segment shown forms a weaving area that must be analyzed to insure that operations do not break down during peak periods.

Note that the volumes on the section are not particularly high, and thus breakdown would not be expected. Figure 11-12 shows a Type B configuration. The movement weaving from right to left may do so without making a lane change, while the movement weaving from left to right may do so with a single lane change.

SOLUTION: The first step in the solution is the conversion of the volumes to peak flow rates under equivalent ideal conditions using Equation [11-1]. As driver population is not unusual, f_p is 1.00. A heavy vehicle factor for 5% trucks and level terrain must be selected, and the *PHF* of 0.95 must be applied.

$$E_T \text{ (level terrain)} = 1.5 \text{ (Table 10-7)}$$

and:

$$f_{HV} = \frac{1}{1 + 0.05(1.5 - 1)} = 0.976$$

Then, component volumes can be adjusted to reflect the peak hour factor and the truck adjustment factor:

$$v_{o1} = 200/(0.95)(0.976) = 216 \text{ pcph}$$
$$v_{o2} = 400/(0.95)(0.976) = \underline{431 \text{ pcph}}$$
$$v_{nw} = v_{o1} + v_{o2} = 647 \text{ pcph}$$
$$v_{w1} = 300/(0.95)(0.976) = 324 \text{ pcph}$$
$$v_{w2} = 150/(0.95)(0.976) = \underline{162 \text{ pcph}}$$
$$v_w = v_{w1} + v_{w2} = 486 \text{ pcph}$$
$$v = v_{Nw} + v_w = 1133 \text{ pcph}$$

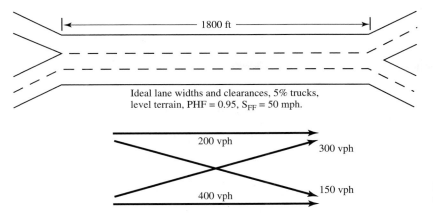

Ideal lane widths and clearances, 5% trucks, level terrain, PHF = 0.95, S_{FF} = 50 mph.

200 vph

300 vph

400 vph

150 vph

Figure 11-12 Sample problem 2—A C–D roadway weaving area.

Other key variables for use in subsequent computations include:

$$v/N = 1{,}133/3 \quad = 377.7 \text{ pcphpl}$$

$$VR = 486/1133 = 0.429$$

$$R = 162/486 = 0.333$$

$$L = \qquad\quad 1800 \text{ ft}$$

Unconstrained operation is once again the assumed condition. Weaving intensity factors for a Type B configuration, unconstrained operation are selected from Table 11-1. Appropriate values of VR, v/N, and L are inserted into the equations, resulting in:

For Weaving Speeds:

$$W = \frac{0.100(1 + 0.429)^{1.2}(377.7)^{0.77}}{(1800)^{0.5}} = 0.348$$

For Non-Weaving Speeds:

$$W = \frac{0.020(1 + 0.429)^{2}(377.7)^{1.42}}{(1800)^{0.95}} = 0.151$$

These values may now be used to estimate speeds in the weaving section using the speed algorithm of Equation [11-3]:

$$S_w = 15 + \frac{40}{1 + 0.348} = 44.7 \text{ mph}$$

$$S_{nw} = 15 + \frac{40}{1 + 0.151} = 49.8 \text{ mph}$$

The type of operation need not be checked, as N_w (max) for Type B configurations is 3.5 lanes, and there are only 3 lanes in the section. Therefore, the operation is unconstrained as was assumed.

A weighted-average speed can now be computed, and from that, an average density for the weaving area. It is compared to the LOS criteria of Table 11-4 to determine the prevailing level of service:

$$S = \frac{486 + 647}{\dfrac{486}{44.7} + \dfrac{649}{49.8}} = 47.5 \text{ mph}$$

$$D = \frac{377.7}{47.5} = 8.0 \text{ pc/mi/ln (LOS A)}$$

Separate densities for weaving and non-weaving vehicles could be computed, but would not be highly instructive in this case. A specific value of N_w would have to be computed using Equation 11-6 to do this. Even without doing so, however, it is seen that operations in the section are very good, as was anticipated from the low volumes specified. Note that by recognizing the reduced free-flow speed of the C-D roadway, the procedure is able to characterize operations as LOS A, and produces speed predictions that are not inconsistent with the free-flow speed of the section.

Analysis of ramps and ramp terminals

The *HCM* addresses three ramp components: (1) the ramp-freeway terminal, (2) the ramp roadway, and (3) the ramp-street terminal. The last is covered by methodologies applying to signalized and unsignalized intersections that are addressed in other chapters of this text. The first two are treated as part of procedures for freeway ramps and ramp terminals.

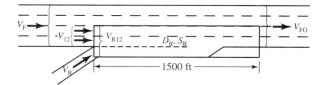

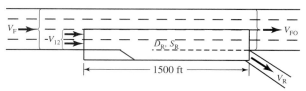

A. Structure of the ramp-freeway terminal methodology

The 1997 *HCM* defines *merge or diverge influence areas* as those parts of the freeway that are most significantly affected by the turbulence of merging of diverging movements in the traffic stream. This defined area includes the acceleration or deceleration lane, and lanes 1 and 2 of the freeway for a distance of 1,500 ft upstream of a merge and downstream of a diverge. Figure 11-13 illustrates the concept of the merge or diverge influence area.

The analysis methodology attempts to estimate the quality of operations in this influence area. Level of service criteria are based on the estimated density of traffic within the area. Figure 11-14 illustrates key input and output variables used in the 1997 *HCM* models.

Principal input variables include the total freeway volume approaching the merge or diverge (V_F), the volume on the ramp (V_R), the length of the acceleration or deceleration lane (L_A or L_D), and the free-flow speed of the ramp (which is heavily dependent on geometrics)(S_{FR}). If close enough to the subject ramp, adjacent upstream and downstream ramp parameters may also become important, and influence operations at the subject ramp. Volume on the adjacent ramp (V_U or V_D) and the distance to these ramps (D_U or D_D) become important parameters when this is the case.

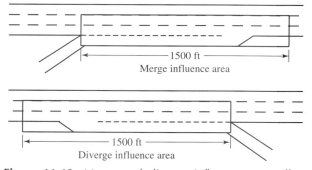

Figure 11-13 Merge and diverge influence areas illustrated. [Used with permission of Transportation Research Board, National Research Council, Washington, DC, from *Highway Capacity Manual, Special Report 209*, 3rd Ed., p. 5-3. Copyright © 1994 Transportation Research Board.]

Figure 11-14 Key variables for ramp junction analysis illustrated. [Used with permission of Transportation Research Board, National Research Council, Washington, DC, from *Highway Capacity Manual, Special Report 209*, 3rd Ed., p. 5-3. Copyright © 1994 Transportation Research Board.]

The first variable predicted in the methodology is v_{12}, the flow in freeway lanes 1 and 2 immediately upstream of the ramp junction. For off-ramps, "immediately upstream" is defined as immediately prior to the beginning of the deceleration lane. For on-ramps, this is the point immediately prior to the acceleration lane becoming parallel to the freeway lanes.

v_{12} is the freeway flow *entering* the merge or diverge influence area, and therefore has a major impact on operations within the influence area. For on-ramps, the ramp flow also enters the influence area, and v_{R12} is defined as $v_{12} + v_R$ for these cases. For off-ramps, the ramp flow is part of v_{12}.

Once the volume entering the influence area is determined, algorithms provide estimates for the density (D_R) and speed (S_R) within the influence area. Density is then used to define the level of service. Speed predictions are informational only, and do not influence level of service. Critical capacity checkpoints involve the total freeway flow leaving the ramp junction (on the freeway, v_{FO}) and the total flow entering the ramp influence area.

B. Converting volumes to equivalent flow rates under ideal conditions

As was the case in the weaving methodology, all hourly volumes must be converted to pcph under equivalent ideal conditions before applying any of the algorithms in the methodology. Equation [11-1] is applied to all freeway and ramp volumes:

$$v = \frac{V}{PHF\, f_{HV}\, f_p}$$

where all variables are as previously defined.

C. Estimating v_{12} immediately upstream of ramp influence areas

1. Merge areas. The general model for estimating v_{12} at merge areas is quite simple:

$$v_{12} = v_F P_{FM} \qquad [11\text{-}13]$$

where: v_{12} = flow rate entering the influence area (lanes 1 and 2) from freeway, pcph

v_F = total flow rate on freeway immediately upstream of the influence area, pcph

P_{FM} = proportion of freeway flow in lanes 1 and 2 immediately upstream of the influence area

A series of five algorithms is used to estimate the critical variable P_{FM}. The appropriate algorithm is based on the number of lanes on the freeway and the proximity of adjacent upstream or downstream ramps. All of the algorithms are regression models using a data base of over 70 ramp junctions collected throughout the United States [4]. Figure 11-15 shows the five algorithms, along with criteria for selection of the appropriate equation.

Note that for 4-lane freeways (2 lanes in each direction), the equation is trivial, in that the entire freeway flow is in lanes 1 and 2. Thus, P_{FM} is 1.00. Figure 11-15 also shows ranges of applicability for all equations. Where input parameters fall outside the applicable range, Equation [2] becomes the default equation for 6-lane freeways, and Equation [5] for 8-lane freeways.

2. Diverge areas. The general model for estimating v_{12} at diverge areas is somewhat different. It is assumed that *all* of the off-ramp traffic must be in lanes 1 or 2 immediately upstream of the ramp junction. Thus, the algorithm must estimate the proportion of *through freeway traffic* that remains in lanes 1 and 2. Thus:

$$v_{12} = v_R + (v_F - v_R)P_{FD} \qquad [11\text{-}14]$$

where: v_{12} = flow rate entering the influence area (lanes 1 and 2) from the freeway, pcph

v_F = total flow rate on freeway immediately upstream of the influence area, pcph

v_R = flow rate on the off-ramp, pcph

P_{FD} = proportion of through freeway traffic remaining in lanes 1 and 2 immediately upstream of the off-ramp

Figure 11-16 shows the five algorithms used to estimate P_{FD}. Once again, the selection is based upon the number of lanes on the freeway, and the proximity of adjacent upstream or downstream ramps. Again, all of the equations are regression-based, resulting from a nationwide study of over 70 ramp-freeway terminals. Again, for 4-lane freeways, the model is trivial. For 6-lane freeways, Equation [7] is the default where data falls outside the applicable ranges for Equations [8] and/or [9]. Equation [10] applies to all cases involving 8-lane freeways. While it is shown as a constant value, this is more a result of a small data base than a firm statistical conviction that the value is indeed constant.

D. Capacity of ramp-freeway junctions

The capacity of ramp-freeway junctions has several components that must be considered. Studies have shown that the turbulence of merge and diverge areas *does not* affect the capacity of the junction. Thus, the capacity of the junction is related to the capacity of incoming and outgoing roadways, and portions thereof.

For merge areas, there are two checkpoints of importance:

1. The total capacity of the merge area is controlled by the capacity of the downstream freeway section, assuming that it is free of other downstream constraints affecting the area under consideration.
2. The merge influence area may fail even if the total merge flow is below capacity. This occurs when too many vehicles attempt to enter the merge influence area. Thus, the total flow entering the influence area, $v_{R12} = v_{12} + v_R$, must be checked

$$v_{12} = v_F \times P_{FM}$$

Equations:

EQN 1	$P_{FM} = 1.00$
EQN 2	$P_{FM} = 0.5775 + 0.000028L_A$
EQN 3	$P_{FM} = 0.7289 - 0.0000135(V_F + V_R) - 0.003296S_{FR} + 0.000063D_U$
EQN 4	$P_{FM} = 0.5487 + 0.2628V_D/D_D$
EQN 5	$P_{FM} = 0.2178 - 0.000125V_R + 0.01115L_A/S_{FR}$

Relevant Statistics:

Statistic	EQN 1	EQN 2	EQN 3	EQN 4	EQN 5
R^2	N/A	0.93	0.96	0.89	0.97
SE	N/A	202	143	219	128
V_F Range	N/A	950-7792	950-7280	2038-5886	4012-9102
V_R Range	N/A	112-2310	160-1822	160-2310	244-672
L_A Range	N/A	325-2300	N/A	N/A	695-1335
S_{FR} Range	N/A	N/A	30-53	N/A	32-50
V_D Range	N/A	N/A	N/A	80-1122	N/A
D_D Range	N/A	N/A	N/A	1200-6000	N/A
D_U Range	N/A	N/A	450-2700	N/A	N/A

Selection Matrix:

Configuration	4-Lane Freeway	6-Lane Freeway	8-Lane Freeway
Isolated	EQN 1	EQN 2	EQN 5
w/Upstream On-Ramp	EQN 1	EQN 2	EQN 5
w/Upstream Off-Ramp	EQN 1	EQN 3 or EQN 2	EQN 5
w/Downstream On-Ramp	EQN 1	EQN 2	EQN 5
w/Downstream Off-Ramp	EQN 1	EQN 4 or EQN 2	EQN 5

Figure 11-15 Models for predicting v_{12} for on ramps. [Used with permission of Transportation Research Board, National Research Council, Washington, DC, from *Highway Capacity Manual, Special Report 209,* 3rd Ed., p. 5-5. Copyright © 1994 Transportation Research Board.]

against the capacity for this element, which has been observed to be limited to 4600 pcph.

For diverge areas, there are three checkpoints of importance:

1. The total capacity of the diverge is generally limited by the capacity of the approaching freeway section.
2. The section may fail even if total capacity is appropriate if too many vehicles attempt to enter the diverge influence area. For diverge areas, this is v_{12} (which includes v_R), which has been observed to be limited to 4400 pcph.
3. The section may also fail if the capacity of one of the departing legs of the diverge is insufficient to handle the demand. The departing freeway leg(s) is (are) controlled by the capacity of the downstream freeway section. The departing ramp leg is controlled by the capacity of the ramp, as indicated in Table 11-10 (discussed in a later section).

If any of these capacities is exceeded by demand, the section is assumed to fail, i.e., to be operating at level of service F. For such cases, no further analysis is conducted. Where operations are found to be stable (in the LOS A–E range), the analysis contin-

$$\boxed{v_{12} = v_R + (v_F - v_R)\,P_{FD}}$$

Equations:

EQN 6	$P_{FD} = 1.00$
EQN 7	$P_{FD} = 0.760 - 0.000025V_F - 0.000046V_R$
EQN 8	$P_{FD} = 0.717 - 0.000039V_F + 0.604V_U/D_U$
EQN 9	$P_{FD} = 0.616 - 0.000021V_F + 0.1248V_D/D_D$
EQN 10	$P_{FD} = 0.436$

Relevant Statistics:

Statistic	EQN 6	EQN 7	EQN 8	EQN 9	EQN 10
R^2	N/A	0.87	0.92	0.97	0.85
SE	N/A	156	119	77	138
V_F Range	N/A	3624-6190	3624-6190	3763-5973	5382-8278
V_R Range	N/A	502-1688	502-1688	502-696	468-1238
L_D Range	N/A	N/A	N/A	N/A	N/A
V_U Range	N/A	N/A	236-548	N/A	N/A
D_U Range	N/A	N/A	2000-4500	N/A	N/A
V_D Range	N/A	N/A	N/A	476-1219	N/A
D_D Range	N/A	N/A	N/A	950-1400	N/A

Selection Matrix:

Configuration	4-Lane Freeway	6-Lane Freeway	8-Lane Freeway
Isolated	EQN 6	EQN 7	EQN 10
w/Upstream On-Ramp	EQN 6	EQN 8 or EQN 7	EQN 10
w/Upstream Off-Ramp	EQN 6	EQN 7	EQN 10
w/Downstream On-Ramp	EQN 6	EQN 7	EQN 10
w/Downstream Off-Ramp	EQN 6	EQN 9 or EQN 7	EQN 10

Figure 11-16 Models for predicting v_{12} for off-ramps. [Used with permission of Transportation Research Board, National Research Council, Washington, DC, from *Highway Capacity Manual, Special Report 209*, 3rd Ed., p. 5-6. Copyright © 1994 Transportation Research Board.]

ues with the determination of density and level of service.

Table 11-5 summarizes the capacities related to freeway legs and ramp influence areas. Consult Table 11-10 for capacity of ramp roadways.

E. Levels of service at ramp-freeway junctions

Levels of service at ramp-freeway junctions are based on the density within the ramp influence area. Table 11-6 gives algorithms for estimating density in the in-fluence area, based on the ramp flow, flow in lanes 1 and 2, and the length of the acceleration or deceleration lane. It should be noted that these algorithms *apply only to cases of stable operation,* i.e., where no breakdown is present. Therefore, these predictive algorithms are employed only after capacity checks have been completed, and the existence of stable operations is confirmed.

Because the algorithms of Table 11-6 are only applied to cases in which no breakdown is occurring, the densities predicted are all, by definition, in the range of level of service A through E. Table 11-7

Table 11-5 Capacity Values for Merge and Diverge Areas

Freeway Free-Flow Speed (mph)	Maximum Upstream (v_{Fi}) or Downstream (v_{FO}) Freeway Flow (pcph)				Max Flow Entering Influence Area (v_{R12}) MERGE (pcph)	Max Flow Entering Influence Area (v_{12}) DIVERGE (pcph)
	No. of Lanes in One Direction					
	2	3	4	>4		
70	4800	7200	9600	2400/ln	4600	4400
65	4700	7050	9400	2350/ln	4600	4400
60	4600	6900	9200	2300/ln	4600	4400
55	4500	6750	9000	2250/ln	4600	4400

Note: For capacity of off-ramp roadways, see Table 11-10.

contains density criteria for levels of service in ramp influence areas.

The 1997 *HCM* also provides models for estimating the average speed within ramp influence areas (for cases in which no breakdown occurs). This is primarily to provide additional information, as speed is not a measure of effectiveness for level of service determinations. Table 11-8 shows these models. Note that the regression coefficients shown indicate that speed-prediction models are not nearly as reliable as those used for density predictions.

Table 11-6 Estimating Density in Ramp Influence Areas

Item	Equation or Value
Single-Lane On-Ramp Merge Area	
Model	$D_R = 5.475 + 0.00734V_R$ $+ 0.0078V_{12} - 0.00627L_A$
R^2	0.88
Std. error (pc/mi/ln)	2.68
Data periods (no.)	167
Single-Lane Off-Ramp Diverge Areas	
Model	$D_R = 4.252 + 0.0086V_{12}$ $- 0.009L_D$
R^2	0.93
Std. error (pc/mi/ln)	1.75
Data periods (no.)	86

F. Special applications

The analysis procedures discussed previously apply to single-lane on- or off-ramps on freeways. Merging and/or diverging movements take place in a number of other situations. The 1997 *HCM* provides a series of logical adaptations of the methodology to address these situations. In some cases, these applications were specifically researched as part of NCHRP 3-37 [5]; in others, material from other sources is adopted and used; in still others, rational extensions of the single-lane ramp methodology were devised.

1. Two-lane on-ramps. Figure 11-17 illustrates a typical two-lane on-ramp. Note that for this discussion,

Table 11-7 Level of Service Criteria for Ramp Influence Areas

Level of Service	Maximum Density (Primary Measure) (pc/mi/ln)	Minimum Speed (Secondary Measure) (mph)
A	10	58
B	20	56
C	28	52
D	35	46
E	>35	42
F	*	*

* Demand flows exceed the limits of Table 11-5.

Table 11-8 Models for Prediction of Speed in Ramp Influence Areas

Item	Equation or Value
Single-Lane On-Ramps, Stable Flow	
Model	$S_R = S_{FF} - (S_{FF} - 42) M_S$
	$M_S = 0.321 + 0.0039\ e^{(V_{R12}/1000)}$
	$\quad - 0.002\left(\dfrac{L_A\ S_{FR}}{1000}\right)$
R^2	0.60
SE (mph)	2.20
Data periods (no.)	132
Single-Lane Off-Ramps, Stable Flow	
Model	$S_R = S_{FF} - (S_{FF} - 42) D_S$
	$D_S = 0.883 + 0.00009\ V_R$
	$\quad - 0.013\ S_{FR}$
R^2	0.44
SE (mph)	2.46
Data periods (no.)	73

[Used with permission of Transportation Research Board, National Research Council, Washington, DC, from *Highway Capacity Manual, Special Report 209*, 3rd Ed., p. 5-8. Copyright © 1994 Transportation Research Board.]

a two-lane on-ramp implies that two lanes are merging onto the freeway. Many two-lane ramps taper to a single lane at the freeway junction. Such ramps are treated using standard procedures for single-lane ramps.

For this case, standard procedures are followed. Flow in lanes 1 and 2 of the freeway is computed as:

$$v_{12} = v_F P_{FM}$$

Instead of using the models presented in Figure 11-15 for P_{FM}, however, the following values are substituted:

- For 4-lane freeways: $P_{FM} = 1.0000$
- For 6-lane freeways: $P_{FM} = 0.5550$
- For 8-lane freeways: $P_{FM} = 0.2093$

In addition, when computing the estimated density in the merge influence area, L_{Aeff} is used instead of L_A:

$$L_{Aeff} = 2L_{A1} + L_{A2} \qquad [11\text{-}15]$$

Capacity values are unaffected when applied to two-lane on-ramps. The values of Table 11-8 are applied in the normal way.

2. Two-lane off-ramps. Figure 11-18 illustrates two common designs for two-lane off-ramp diverge areas. Again, in this context, a two-lane off-ramp is one that has two lanes at the point of diverge. Ramps that have a single lane at the diverge point and widen to two lanes on the ramp roadway are *not* included in this category.

As was the case for two-lane on-ramps, the general algorithm for determining the entering flow in lanes 1 and 2 of the freeway remains unchanged:

$$v_{12} = v_R + (v_F - v_R)P_{FD}$$

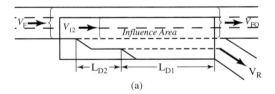

(a)

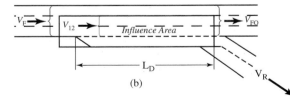

(b)

Figure 11-18 Typical two-lane off-ramps. [Used with permission of Transportation Research Board, National Research Council, Washington, DC, from *Highway Capacity Manual, Special Report 209*, 3rd Ed., p. 5-11. Copyright © 1994 Transportation Research Board.]

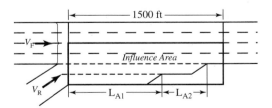

Figure 11-17 Typical two-lane on-ramp configuration. [Used with permission of Transportation Research Board, National Research Council, Washington, DC, from *Highway Capacity Manual, Special Report 209*, 3rd Ed., p. 5-10. Copyright © 1994 Transportation Research Board.]

Instead of using the models presented in Figure 11-16 for P_{FD}, however, the following values are substituted:

- For 4-lane freeways: $P_{FD} = 1.00$
- For 6-lane freeways: $P_{FD} = 0.45$
- For 8-lane freeways: $P_{FD} = 0.26$

If the geometry is similar to that shown in Figure 11-18(a), then L_{Deff} should be used in computing the density in the diverge influence area, where:

$$L_{Deff} = 2L_{D1} + L_{D2} \qquad [11\text{-}16]$$

Where the geometry is of the type shown in Figure 11-18(b), the length of the deceleration lane may be used directly without modification.

3. Ramps on 10-lane freeways (5 lanes in each direction). Though not common, some sections of urban freeway in the U.S. have five lanes in a single direction. These sections contain ramp junctions that must be analyzed and evaluated. The 1997 *HCM* suggests a rational technique: The volume in lane 5 of the freeway is estimated; it is then subtracted from the total freeway volume, yielding an estimate of the volume in the remaining four lanes of the freeway. The ramp analysis is then conducted as if the freeway were an 8-lane facility (4 lanes in each direction). Table 11-9

gives the recommended algorithms for estimating the volume in lane 5 of the freeway.

The effective volume for the remaining four lanes of the freeway is then given by the equation:

$$V_{4eff} = V_F - V_5 \qquad [11\text{-}17]$$

where: V_{4eff} = volume in lanes 1 through 4 of the freeway immediately upstream of the diverge, vph
V_F = total freeway volume immediately upstream of the diverge, vph
V_5 = volume in lane 5 of the freeway immediately upstream of the diverge, vph

Note that this exercise is done in mixed vph, *before* any of the volumes are converted to equivalent flow rates in pcph under ideal conditions. The ramp analysis may then proceed using V_{4eff} and treating the freeway as if it had 4 lanes in the subject direction.

4. Major merge and diverge sections. Figure 11-19 illustrates several typical configurations for major merge and diverge sections. A major merge consists of two multilane limited access roadways joining to form a single freeway segment; a major diverge fea-

Table 11-9   Determination of V_5 for Right-Hand Ramps on 10-Lane Freeway Segments (5 la. ea. dir.)

Total Freeway Flow, V_F (pcph)	Flow in Lane 5, V_5 (pcph)
Approaching Right-Hand On-Ramps	
> 8500	2500
7500–8499	$0.285V_F$
6500–7499	$0.270V_F$
5500–6499	$0.240V_F$
< 5500	$0.220V_F$
Approaching Right-Hand Off-Ramps	
> 7000	$0.200V_F$
5500–7000	$0.150V_F$
4000–5499	$0.100V_F$
< 4000	0

[Used with permission of Transportation Research Board, National Research Council, Washington, DC, from *Highway Capacity Manual, Special Report 209,* 3rd Ed., p. 5-12. Copyright © 1994 Transportation Research Board.]

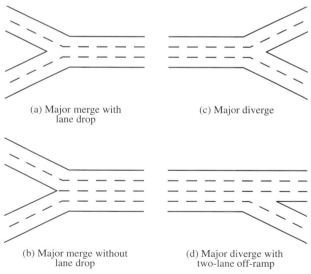

(a) Major merge with lane drop

(c) Major diverge

(b) Major merge without lane drop

(d) Major diverge with two-lane off-ramp

Figure 11-19   Major merge and diverge areas illustrated. [Used with permission of Transportation Research Board, National Research Council, Washington, DC, from *Highway Capacity Manual, Special Report 209,* 3rd Ed., p. 5-13. Copyright © 1994 Transportation Research Board.]

tures a freeway segment separating into two multi-lane limited access roadways. Such sections may be formed where multilane ramps are combined with lane drop or lane addition situations.

There is little definitive information on operations at such locations. Capacity checks are made for each entering and exiting roadway using the standard values of Table 11-5. Where projected demand will exceed these values, a breakdown is anticipated.

A model was calibrated for the density across all freeway lanes in a 1500 ft segment immediately upstream of a major diverge area:

$$D = 0.0175 \frac{v_F}{N} \qquad [11\text{-}18]$$

Density criteria from Table 11-10 can then be applied to determine level of service in the diverge influence area. The *HCM* does not provide an algorithm for estimating density in the vicinity of major merge sites.

5. Capacity of ramp roadways. Table 11-10 shows the capacity of ramp roadways. The table is based on data from recent studies [5], and from work done in the 1970s [12]. In the context of this table, the capacities cited are for the *ramp roadway* itself, NOT the ramp-freeway junction. At the ramp-freeway junction, there is no evidence that a two-lane on-ramp would be able to handle more flow than a single-lane on-ramp, unless a lane were added or deleted. In the latter case, the section would be treated as if it were a major merge site. At the ramp-freeway junction, a two-lane off-ramp is able to handle higher flows than a single-lane ramp, perhaps as high as 4000 pcph.

In a number of situations, a single-lane ramp terminal should be widened to accommodate two lanes on the ramp itself.

a. Where the length of the ramp is 1000 ft or greater, room for vehicles to pass slower-moving vehicles should be provided.

b. Where queuing at the ramp-street terminal may affect the flow of vehicles exiting the limited access facility, the addition of ramp lanes increases the amount of "storage" space provided.

c. When the ramp has a steep grade, a second lane provides the opportunity for other vehicles to pass.

When two-lane ramps are provided for any of these purposes, they are invariably tapered to a single lane at the merge or diverge point.

G. Worksheets for analysis

Figure 11-20 shows a worksheet provided by the 1997 *HCM* for summarizing the results of a ramp analysis. As the analysis procedure is not that complicated, the worksheet is not really necessary to guide computations. Worksheets are convenient, however, to summarize the data for each problem application.

H. Sample problems in ramp analysis

PROBLEM 1: AN ISOLATED ON-RAMP

PROBLEM: An isolated on-ramp on a 6-lane freeway with standard 12-ft lane widths and adequate clearances serves a demand of 800 vph (10% trucks). The freeway mainline approaching the ramp carries 3500 vph (10% trucks) during the P.M. peak period of commuter traffic. Terrain is level, the PHF is 0.90, and the ramp has an acceleration lane of total length 1000 ft. Free-flow speeds are 65 mph for the freeway and 40 mph for the ramp. At what level of service would this ramp be expected to operate?

SOLUTION: A sketch illustrating this section is included in Figure 11-21, which is the worksheet for this calculation. The first computation is the conversion of all demand volumes to flow rates in pcph under ideal conditions. For each demand flow, the

Table 11-10   Capacity of Ramp Roadways

Free-Flow Speed of Ramp S_{FR} (mph)	Capacity (pcph)	
	Single-Lane Ramps	Two-Lane Ramps
> 50	2200	4400
41–50	2100	4100
31–40	2000	3800
21–30	1900	3500
< 21	1800	3200

WORKSHEET FOR ANALYSIS OF RAMP-FREEWAY TERMINALS

UPSTREAM ADJACENT RAMP	LOCATION: _____ TIME PERIOD: _____ ANALYST: _____ TERRAIN: _____	DOWNSTREAM ADJACENT RAMP
Yes ☐ No ☐		Yes ☐ No ☐
Off ☐ On ☐		Off ☐ On ☐
D_U = _____ ft	S_{FF} = _____ mph S_{FR} = _____ mph	D_D = _____ ft
V_U = _____ vph	SKETCH (SHOW LANES, L_{AD}, V_R, V_F)	V_D = _____ vph

CONVERSION TO PCPH UNDER IDEAL CONDITIONS:

	vph	PHF	%HV	f_{HV}	f_P	$v = \dfrac{V}{PHF\ f_{HV}\ f_P}$
V_F						
V_R						
V_U						
V_D						

☐ MERGE AREAS	☐ DIVERGE AREAS

ESTIMATION OF V_{12}:

$V_{12} = V_F(P_{FM})$	$V_{12} = V_R + (V_F - V_R)P_{FD}$
P_{FM} = _____ Using Equation _____	P_{FD} = _____ Using Equation _____
V_{12} = _____ pcph	V_{12} = _____ pcph

CAPACITY CHECKS:

	ACTUAL	MAXIMUM	LOS F?		ACTUAL	MAXIMUM	LOS F?
V_{FO}		See table 11-5		$V_{FI} = V_F$		See table 11-5	
				V_{12}		4400: ALL	
V_{R12}		4600 ALL		$V_{FO} = V_F - V_R$		See table 11-5	
				V_R		See table 11-10	

LEVEL OF SERVICE DETERMINATION (IF NOT F):

$D_R = 5.475 + 0.00734V_R + 0.0078V_{12} - 0.00627L_A$	$D_R = 4.252 + 0.0086V_{12} - 0.009L_D$

D_R = _____ pc/mi/ln   LOS _____   Table 11-4 S_R = _____ mph

Figure 11-20 Worksheet for analysis of ramp-freeway terminals. [Used with permission of National Research Board, National Research Council, Washington, DC, from *Highway Capacity Manual, Special Report 209,* 3rd Ed., p. 5-5. Copyright © 1997 Transportation Research Board.]

PHF is given, and information is given which allows for the determination of f_{HV} and f_p. These factors are selected according to the procedures outlined in Chapter 10.

The driver population factor, f_p, is 1.00, as commuter traffic is present. For level terrain, the passenger car equivalent for trucks is 1.5 passenger cars/truck, yielding an f_{HV} of $1/[1 + 0.10(1.5 - 1)] = 0.952$ for both the freeway volume, and the ramp volume.

The PHF for both volumes is given as 0.90. The adjusted demand flow rates are then computed using Equation [11-1]:

$$V_F = \frac{3500}{0.90(1.00)(0.952)(1.00)} = 4085 \text{ pcph}$$

$$V_R = \frac{800}{0.90(1.00)(0.952)(1.00)} = 934 \text{ pcph}$$

UPSTREAM ADJACENT RAMP	LOCATION: _Sample 1_ TIME PERIOD: _PM peak_		DOWNSTREAM ADJACENT RAMP
	ANALYST: _R Roess_ TERRAIN: _Level_		

UPSTREAM ADJACENT RAMP
Yes ☐   No ☒

Off ☐   On ☐

3,500 vph (10% trucks)
36 ft
800 vph (10% trucks)
1,000 ft

D_U = _____ ft S_{FF} = **65** mph S_{FR} = **40** mph

V_U = _____ vph

SKETCH (SHOW LANES, L_{AD}, V_R, V_F)

DOWNSTREAM ADJACENT RAMP
Yes ☐   No ☒

Off ☐   On ☐

D_D = _____ ft

V_D = _____ vph

CONVERSION TO PCPH UNDER IDEAL CONDITIONS:

	vph	PHF	%HV	f_{HV}	f_P	$v = \dfrac{V}{PHF\, f_{HV}\, f_P}$
V_F	3,500	0.90	10	0.952	1.0	4,085
V_R	800	0.90	10	0.952	1.0	934
V_U						
V_D						

☒ MERGE AREAS	☐ DIVERGE AREAS

ESTIMATION OF V_{12}:

$V_{12} = V_F(P_{FM})$	$V_{12} = V_R + (V_F - V_R)P_{FD}$
P_{FM} = 0.6055 Using Equation 2	P_{FD} = _____ Using Equation _____
V_{12} = 2,473 pcph	V_{12} = _____ pcph

CAPACITY CHECKS:

	ACTUAL	MAXIMUM	LOS F?		ACTUAL	MAXIMUM	LOS F?
V_{FO}	5,019	See table 11-5	NO	$V_{FI} = V_F$		See table 11-5	
				V_{12}		4400: ALL	
V_{R12}	3,407	4600 ALL	NO	$V_{FO} = V_F - V_R$		See table 11-5	
				V_R		See table 11-10	

LEVEL OF SERVICE DETERMINATION (IF NOT F):

$D_R = 5.475 + 0.007834V_R + 0.0078V_{12} - 0.00627L_A$	$D_R = 4.252 + 0.0086V_{12} - 0.009L_D$

D_R = 25 pc/mi/ln   LOS C Table 11-4 S_R = 57 mph

Figure 11-21 Worksheet for sample problem 1.

The remainder of the solution uses these converted demand flow rates as inputs values. All flow rate results are in terms of pcph during the peak 15-minutes of the hour of interest.

Figure 11-15 indicates that v_{12} should be computed using Equation [11-2]. For the case of an isolated on-ramp on a 6-lane freeway, P_{FM} is computed as:

$$P_{FM} = 0.5775 + 0.000028L_A$$
$$P_{FM} = 0.5775 + 0.000028 \times 1000 = 0.6055$$

This value is then used to estimate v_{12} as:

$$v_{12} = v_F \times P_{FM} = 4085 \times 0.6055 = 2473 \text{ pcph}$$

Two capacity values must now be checked. The total downstream freeway flow rate departing the merge area $(v_{FO} = v_F + v_R)$ is $4085 + 934 = 5019$ pcph. This is less than the capacity for 6-lane freeways with a 65-mph free-flow speed of 7050 pcph, so no problem is anticipated. The total flow entering the ramp influence area $(v_{R12} = v_R + v_{12})$ is

934 + 2473 = 3407 pcph, which is also less than the capacity of 4600 pcph for such flows. Capacities are drawn from Table 11-5. The operation is expected to be stable, i.e., no queues will form under the conditions of this calculation.

The expected density in the merge influence area is now computed using the on-ramp equation of Table 11-6:

$$D_R = 5.475 + 0.00734V_R + 0.0078V_{12} - 0.00627L_A$$

$$D_R = 5.475 + 0.00734(934) + 0.0078(2473)$$
$$- 0.00627(1000)$$

$$D_R = 25 \text{ pc/mi/ln}$$

From Table 11-7, this is level of service C, as the density is less than the upper limit for LOS C. For supplemental information, the expected average speed of vehicles can be estimated using the on-ramp, stable flow equation of Table 11-8:

$$S_R = S_{FF} - (S_{FF} - 42)M_S$$
$$M_S = 0.321 + 0.0039e^{(3407/1000)}$$
$$- 0.002(1000 \times 40/1000) = 0.359$$
$$S_R = 65 - [(65 - 42) \times (0.359)] = 57 \text{ mph}$$

The results of this analysis indicated that the on-ramp displayed would be expected to operate at an acceptable level of service, C. No unusual turbulence nor any queuing would be expected to be present.

PROBLEM 2: CONSECUTIVE OFF-RAMPS

PROBLEM: Figure 11-22 illustrates the section under study in this calculation. Two consecutive off-ramps are spaced at 1500 ft on a section of freeway in generally rolling terrain carrying commuter traffic. All other pertinent information is shown in Figure 11-22. What is the expected level of service through this section?

SOLUTION: The solution of this problem involves separate analysis of the operation of each ramp-freeway terminal, and the drawing of reasonable conclusions concerning the operation of the entire section from this information.

The first computation involves converting the freeway volume and the ramp volumes to equivalent pcph under ideal conditions for the peak 15- minute period within the hour. Adjustment factors are drawn as appropriate from basic freeway criteria presented in Chapter 10. All adjustment factors (f_p and f_{HV}) are 1.00, since standard lane widths and clearances are provided, no trucks are present, and there is a commuter driver population. Therefore:

$$v_F = \frac{5300}{0.95(1.00)(1.00)} = 5579 \text{ pcph}$$

$$v_{R1} = \frac{400}{0.95(1.00)(1.00)} = 421 \text{ pcph}$$

$$v_{R2} = \frac{600}{0.95(1.00)(1.00)} = 632 \text{ pcph}$$

By implication, the freeway flow rate immediately upstream of the second ramp is 5579 − 421 = 5158 pcph. Figures 11-23 and 11-24 illustrate worksheets for each of the two ramps.

The first ramp is an off-ramp with an adjacent downstream off-ramp. Figure 11-16 suggests that

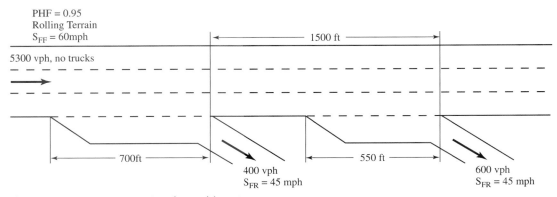

PHF = 0.95
Rolling Terrain
S_{FF} = 60mph

5300 vph, no trucks

1500 ft

700ft

550 ft

400 vph
S_{FR} = 45 mph

600 vph
S_{FR} = 45 mph

Figure 11-22 Freeway section for problem 2.

UPSTREAM ADJACENT RAMP	LOCATION: _Sample 2_ TIME PERIOD: _AM peak_	DOWNSTREAM ADJACENT RAMP
	ANALYST: _E Prassas_ TERRAIN: _Rolling_	

Yes ☐ No ☒	5,300 vph (No trucks) / → PHF = 0.95; Rolling Terrain / 700 ft / 400 vph	Yes ☒ No ☐
Off ☐ On ☐		Off ☒ On ☐
D_U = _____ ft	S_{FF} = **60** mph S_{FR} = **50** mph	D_D = _1,500_ ft
V_U = _____ vph	SKETCH (SHOW LANES, L_{AD}, V_R, V_F)	V_D = _600_ vph

CONVERSION TO PCPH UNDER IDEAL CONDITIONS:

	vph	PHF	%HV	f_{HV}	f_P	$v = \dfrac{V}{PHF\, f_{HV}\, f_P}$
V_F	5,300	0.95	0	1.0	1.0	5,579
V_R	400	0.95	0	1.0	1.0	421
V_U						
V_D	600	0.95	0	1.0	1.0	632

☐ MERGE AREAS	☒ DIVERGE AREAS

ESTIMATION OF V_{12}:

$V_{12} = V_F(P_{FM})$	$V_{12} = V_R + (V_F - V_R)P_{FD}$
P_{FM} = _____ Using Equation _____	P_{FD} = _0.601_ Using Equation _7_
V_{12} = _____ pcph	V_{12} = _3,522_ pcph

CAPACITY CHECKS:

	ACTUAL	MAXIMUM	LOS F?		ACTUAL	MAXIMUM	LOS F?
V_{FO}		See table 11-5		$V_{FI} = V_F$	5,579	See table 11-5	NO
				V_{12}	3,522	4400: ALL	NO
V_{R12}		4600 ALL		$V_{FO} = V_F - V_R$	5,158	See table 11-5	NO
				V_R	421	See table 11-10	NO

LEVEL OF SERVICE DETERMINATION (IF NOT F):

$D_R = 5.475 + 0.007834V_R + 0.0078V_{12} - 0.00627L_A$	$D_R = 4.252 + 0.0086V_{12} - 0.009L_D$

D_R = _28_ pc/mi/ln   LOS _C_   Table 11-4 S_R = _55_ mph

Figure 11-23 Worksheet for sample problem 2 (1st ramp).

Equation [7] or [9] be used for this case. The ramp flow in this case, 421 pcph, falls outside the range of calibration for Equation [9] (502–696). The methodology indicates that Equation [7] is therefore used:

$$v_{12} = v_R + (v_F - v_R)P_{FD}$$
$$P_{FD} = 0.760 - 0.000025(5579)$$
$$- 0.000046(421) = 0.601$$
$$v_{12} = 421 + (5579 - 421)(0.601) = 3522 \text{ pcph}$$

Capacity values for the first ramp are now checked. The total flow approaching the diverge area is 5579 pcph, which is lower than the capacity for a 6-lane freeway with a 60-mph free-flow speed: 6900 pcph. V_{12} is 3522 pcph, which is lower than the capacity for vehicles entering the diverge influence area of 4400 pcph. The ramp flow of 421 pcph is less than the capacity of an off-ramp with free-flow speed = 50 mph (2100, Table 5-10). Thus, the operation is expected to be stable.

UPSTREAM ADJACENT RAMP	LOCATION: _Sample 2_ TIME PERIOD: _AM peak_ ANALYST: _E Prassas_ TERRAIN: _Rolling_	DOWNSTREAM ADJACENT RAMP
Yes ☒ No ☐ Off ☒ On ☐	PHF = 0.95; Rolling Terrain 4,900 vph (No trucks) _ _ _ _ _ _ _ _ _ _ _ _ _ [36 ft] ←—— 550 ft ——→	Yes ☐ No ☒ Off ☐ On ☐
D_U = _1,500_ ft	S_{FF} = **60** mph S_{FR} = **45** mph	D_D = _____ ft
V_U = _400_ vph	SKETCH (SHOW LANES, L_{AD}, V_R, V_F)	V_D = _____ vph

CONVERSION TO PCPH UNDER IDEAL CONDITIONS:

	vph	PHF	%HV	f_{HV}	f_P	$v = \dfrac{V}{PHF\, f_{HV}\, f_P}$
V_F	4,900	0.95	0	1.0	1.0	5,158
V_R	600	0.95	0	1.0	1.0	632
V_U	400	0.95	0	1.0	1.0	421
V_D						

☐ MERGE AREAS	☒ DIVERGE AREAS

ESTIMATION OF V_{12}:

$V_{12} = V_F(P_{FM})$	$V_{12} = V_R + (V_F - V_R)P_{FD}$
P_{FM} = _____ Using Equation _____	P_{FD} = _0.602_ Using Equation _7_
V_{12} = _____ pcph	V_{12} = _3,357_ pcph

CAPACITY CHECKS:

	ACTUAL	MAXIMUM	LOS F?		ACTUAL	MAXIMUM	LOS F?
V_{FO}		See table 11-5		$V_{FI} = V_F$	5,158	See table 11-5	NO
				V_{12}	3,357	4400: ALL	NO
V_{R12}		4600 ALL		$V_{FO} = V_F - V_R$	4,526	See table 11-5	NO
				V_R	632	See table 11-10	NO

LEVEL OF SERVICE DETERMINATION (IF NOT F):

$D_R = 5.475 + 0.007834V_R + 0.0078V_{12} - 0.00627L_A$	$D_R = 4.252 + 0.0086V_{12} - 0.009L_D$

D_R = _28_ pc/mi/ln   LOS _C_   Table 11-4 S_R = _54_ mph

Figure 11-24: Worksheet for sample problem 2 (2nd ramp).

The expected density in the ramp influence area is computed using the single-lane off-ramp equation of Table 11-6:

$$D_R = 4.252 + 0.0086(3522) - 0.009(700)$$
$$= 28 \text{ pc/mi/ln}$$

From Table 11-7, this is level of service C, but barely. The off-ramp stable flow equation from Table 11-8 can be used to get a general estimate of the average speed in the ramp influence area. This compu-

tation is not shown here, but results in a speed of 55 mph, as shown on the worksheets.

The second ramp is an off-ramp with an adjacent upstream off-ramp. Figure 11-16 suggests that Equation [7] be used for this case:

$$v_{12} = v_R + (v_F - v_R)P_{FD}$$
$$P_{FD} = 0.760 - 0.000025(5158) - 0.000046(632)$$
$$= 0.602$$
$$v_{12} = 632 + (5158 - 632)(0.602) = 3356 \text{ pcph}$$

Capacity values may now be checked using Table 11-5. The total approach flow to the diverge is 4526 pcph, well within the capacity of 6900 pcph for 6-lane (60 mph) freeways; the v_{12} value of 3356 pcph is also lower than the capacity of 4400 pcph for this flow. The off-ramp capacity of 2100 pcph is sufficient to handle the demand. Again, no breakdowns are expected, and flow is expected to be stable.

Density is computed using the off-ramp equation of Table 11-6:

$$D_R = 4.252 + 0.0086(3356) - 0.009(550)$$

$$= 28 \text{ pc/mi/ln}$$

From Table 11-7, this is level of service C, being just at the upper limit for LOS C. An approximate indication of the average speed within the ramp influence area can be obtained from the single-lane off-ramp stable flow equation of Table 11-8. Not shown here, the result of this computation is 54 mph.

The section, considered as a total, is expected to operate at the upper edge of level of service C.

HCS software

The *HCS* package replicates current weaving and ramp analysis procedures. Some versions of *HCS* for the 1994 *HCM* continued to use passenger car equivalents from the 1985 *HCM*, which were revised in 1994. The user should take care to ascertain that their version does not include this serious error.

It is anticipated that the *HCS* package will be updated to include any and all revisions made in the 1997 update of the *HCM*.

Procedure Sources

Significant sources for the procedures presented in this text have been cited throughout the chapter. A number of interesting studies of weaving area operations have taken place since the formulation of current procedures in the 1985 *HCM*. Fazio [13] developed a methodology that quantified a lane-changing parameter based on configuration and volumes. A modified speed algorithm included this parameter. Extensive studies have been conducted at University of California at Berkeley on weaving analysis. The work has focused on predicting operating characteristics in individual lanes or cells of the weaving area [14–16]. Some of this work is based on a methodology included in the 1965 *HCM*, originially developed by Moskowitz [17]. Early work by Hess [18] is also of historic interest on the development of ramp analysis procedures.

References

1. Theophilopolous, N., "A Turbulence Approach at Ramp Junctions," Ph.D. Dissertation, Polytechnic University, Brooklyn, NY, June 1986.
2. Elefteriadou, A., "A Probabilistic Model of Breakdown at Freeway-Merge Junctions," Ph.D. Dissertation, Polytechnic University, Brooklyn, NY, June 1994.
3. *Highway Capacity Manual, Special Report 87,* Transportation Research Board, National Research Council, Washington, DC, 1965.
4. *Highway Capacity Manual, Special Report 209,* 3rd Edition, Transportation Research Board, National Research Council, Washington, DC, (revised) 1994.
5. Roess, R., and Ulerio, J., "Capacity of Ramp-Freeway Junctions," *Final Report,* NCHRP Project 3-37, Polytechnic University, Brooklyn, NY, 1993.
6. Pignataro, L., et al., "Weaving Areas-Design and Analysis," *NCHRP Report 159,* Transportation Research Board, National Research Council, Washington DC, 1975.
7. Roess, R., et al., "Freeway Capacity Analysis Procedures," *Final Report,* Project No. DOT- FH-11-9336, Polytechnic University, Brooklyn, NY, 1978.
8. "Interim Procedures on Highway Capacity," *Circular 212,* Transportation Research Board, National Research Council, Washington, DC, 1980.
9. Leisch, J., "Completion of Procedures for Analysis and Design of Traffic Weaving Areas," *Final Report, Vols. 1 and 2,* U.S. Department of Transportation, Federal Highway Administration, Washington, DC, 1983.
10. Reilly, W., et al., "Weaving Analysis Procedures for the New Highway Capacity Manual," *Technical Report,* JHK & Associates, Tucson, AZ, 1983.
11. Roess, R., et al., "The New Highway Capacity Manual," *Final Report,* NCHRP Project 3-28B, Polytechnic University, Brooklyn, NY, 1984.
12. Blumentritt, C., et al., "Guidelines for Selection of Ramp Control Systems," *NCHRP Report 232,* Transportation

Research Board, National Research Council, Washington DC, 1981.

13. Fazio, J., "Development and Testing of a Weaving Operational Design and Analysis Procedure," Master's Thesis, University of Illinois at Chicago, Chicago, IL, 1985.

14. Cassidy, M., and May, A., "Proposed Analytical Technique for Estimating Capacity and Level of Service of Major Freeway Weaving Sections," *Transportation Research Record 1320,* Transportation Research Board, National Research Council, Washington, DC, 1992.

15. Ostrom, B., et al., "Suggested Procedures for Analyzing Freeway Weaving Sections," *Transportation Research Record 1398,* Transportation Research Board, National Research Council, Washington, DC, 1993.

16. Windover, J., and May, A., "Revisions to Level D Methodology of Analyzing Freeway Ramp-Weaving Sections," *Transportation Research Record 1457,* Transportation Research Board, National Research Council, Washington, DC, 1995.

17. Moskowitz, K., and Newman, L., "Notes on Freeway Capacity," *Traffic Bulletin No. 4,* California Department of Public Works, Division of Highways, Sacramento, CA, July 1962.

18. Hess, J., "Ramp-Freeway Terminal Operation as Related to Freeway Lane Volume Distribution and Adjacent Ramp Junctions," *Highway Research Record 99,* Transportation Research Board, National Research Council, Washington, DC, 1965.

Problems

Problem 11–1

Consider the on-ramp shown in the figure at right. For the information given, at what LOS is the merge area expected to operate?

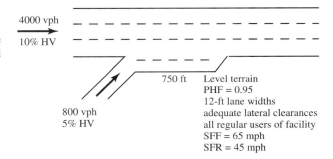

Problem 11–2

Consider the pair of ramps shown in the figure below.

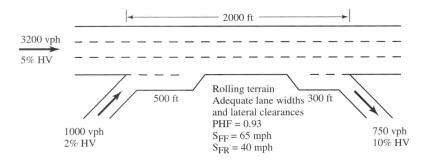

(a) Given the existing demand volumes, at what level of service is this section expected to operate? If problems exist, which elements appear to be causing the difficulty?

(b) It is proposed that the acceleration and deceleration lanes be joined to form a continuous auxiliary lane. This makes the section a weaving configuration. How will this affect the operation? Would you recommend the change?

Problem 11–3

At what LOS would the weaving area shown be expected to operate? All volumes are in pcph, and the PHF is 0.97. All lane widths and lateral clearances are adequate.

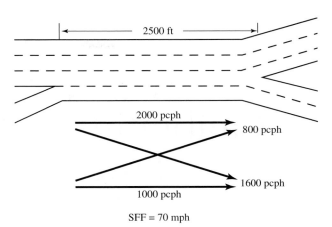

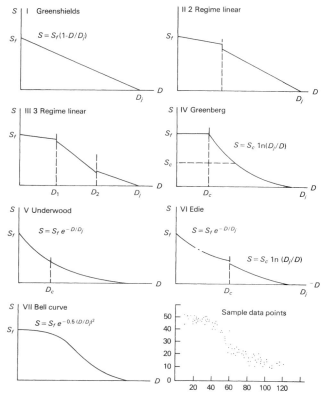

Figure 12-2 Illustration of speed-density hypotheses. [Used with permission of Transportation Research Board, National Research Council, J. S. Drake, J. L. Schofer, and A. D. May, Jr., *Traffic Flow Theory: A Monograph, Special Report 165,* p. 57. Copyright © 1975 Transportation Research Board.]

$$S = S_f - \frac{S_f}{D_j} D$$

which is of the simple linear format $S = a + bD$. A multiple linear regression analysis would yield values of a and b, where:

$$a = S_f, \qquad b = -\frac{S_f}{D_j}$$

The linear model is simple and straightforward. Both free-flow speed and jam density are easily determined, and (as will be seen) the model is easily manipulated to find flow-speed and flow-density relationships. Most recent studies, however, have indicated that speed-density data are not perfectly linear.

2. Piecewise linear models. Ellis [5] proposed that the linear model could be made to more closely reflect

observed data by fitting different regions of the data with different linear models. As shown in Figure 12-2(b) and (c), Ellis demonstrated both two-segment and three-segment curves. The three-segment curve identifies regions of free flow, impeded flow, and congested flow—a principle that has been adopted by others in more recent work. The great advantage of piecewise linear models is that nonlinear relationships can be approximately depicted using simple linear equations. These models have another distinctive characteristic: discontinuities at the boundaries between linear sections. These discontinuities can complicate the task of identifying capacity and can lead to multiple values for capacity.

3. Greenberg's logarithmic model. Greenberg hypothesized a logarithmic shape for the speed-density relationship of the form:

$$S = S_c \ln \frac{D_j}{D} \qquad [12\text{-}9]$$

which may be expressed in linear form as

$$S = S_c \ln (D_j) - S_c \ln (D)$$
$$= a + bD_1$$

where: $a = S_c \ln (D_j)$
$\qquad b = -S_c$
$\qquad D_1 = \ln (D)$

The major flaw in this model is that it collapses at low densities. This is best seen by inserting $D = 0$ into Equation [12-9]. For this reason, a maximum free-flow speed must be independently assumed or observed and superimposed on this model, as shown in Figure 12-2(d).

4. Underwood's exponential model. Underwood [7] proposed an exponential model of speed-density of the following form:

$$S = S_f \exp \left(\frac{-D}{D_c} \right) \qquad [12\text{-}10]$$

which may be expressed in simple linear form as

$$\ln (S) = \ln (S_f) - \frac{1}{D_c} D$$

$$S_1 = a + bD$$

where: $S_1 = \ln (S)$
$a = \ln (S_f)$
$b = -\dfrac{1}{D_c}$

This model is reasonable at low densities, as it collapses to $S = S_f$ when D is zero. It is unreliable, however, at high densities, as S asymptotically approaches zero without ever reaching it.

5. Edie's two-segment model. Edie [8] hypothesized that the most appropriate model would use Greenberg's equation for high densities and Underwood's equation for low densities. This creates the discontinuous model shown in Figure 12-2(f). Use of the Greenberg and Underwood equations for the regions of flow where they are most appropriate creates a model capable of accurately describing the entire range of speeds and densities, given that the data display a moderately concave shape. The discontinuity is near the point of critical density, which leads to discontinuities in flow-speed and flow-density at the point of capacity.

6. The bell curve. May [9] suggested that a bell-shaped curve might fit some speed-density data very well, according to empiric observations in several studies. The curve would be of the form:

$$S = S_f \exp\left[-0.5\left(\frac{D}{D_c}\right)^2\right] \qquad [12\text{-}11]$$

which may be expressed in simple linear form as

$$\ln (S) = \ln (S_f) - \frac{1}{2D_c^2} D^2$$

$$S_1 = a + bD_1$$

where: $S_1 = \ln (S)$
$a = \ln (S_f)$
$b = -\dfrac{1}{2D_c^2}$
$D_1 = D^2$

This curve shares one disadvantage with the Underwood model: it asymptotically approaches zero speed as D increases, without ever actually reaching it.

7. Comments. The models illustrated above are clearly not a complete set of those that can be and have been proposed over the years. It is important to

note that there is no one equation form that best fits all freeway flow data. In some cases, one model may be most appropriate, while elsewhere other models work better. The models presented are the most significant ones developed to date and present the student with a variety of forms for use. Linear forms of these models are shown to help in multiple linear regression analyses.

D. Derivation of flow-speed and flow-density relationships

Given a speed-density model, corresponding equations for flow-speed and flow-density may be algebraically defined. Consider the linear model proposed by Greenshields:

$$S = S_f\left(1 - \frac{D}{D_j}\right) = S_f - \frac{S_f}{D_j} D$$

To find the corresponding model for flow versus speed, the general relationship $v = S \times D$ is used. Manipulating this equation, $D = v/S$, which may be substituted in the speed-density equation:

$$S = S_f - \frac{S_f}{D_j} \frac{v}{S}$$

Solving this equation for v, the following results:

$$v = (D_j)S - \frac{D_j}{S_f} S^2$$

As is the case here, linear speed-density models results in parabolic flow-speed equations.

To find the flow-density equation, $S = v/D$ is substituted into the original speed-density model:

$$\frac{v}{D} = S_f - \frac{S_f}{D_j} D$$

Solving for v:

$$v = S_f D - \frac{S_f}{D_j} D^2$$

This is also parabolic.

Similar derivations may be demonstrated for any speed-density model form. Figures 12-3 through 12-9 illustrate the forms resulting from each of the models discussed in the previous section. The plots illustrate sample calibrations to each of the forms discussed using a common set of freeway flow data from the Eisenhower Expressway in Chicago [9].

It should be noted that for the data shown in Figures 12-3 through 12-9, the Edie hypothesis results in the best "fit" of the mathematical description to the data. The Edie hypothesis is a two-segment curve, with interesting implications on capacity, as will be seen. This is not to say, however, that the mathematical description proposed by Edie will the best fit to *all* freeway speed-flow-density data. Different sites in different areas of the country, changes in driver characteristics over time, differing driver populations, and other factors may yield different results.

Finding capacity and defining level of service from basic speed-flow-density curves

A. Finding capacity

Capacity is defined as the maximum rate of flow (for a 15-minute period) that can be achieved on a freeway section under prevailing roadway, traffic, and control conditions. Once speed-flow-density relationships are established, capacity may be defined as the peak of the speed density curve. Capacity can, therefore, be defined either graphically or mathematically from the calibrated relationships.

Consider, for example, Greenshields' hypothesis, which results in a parabolic flow-density model of the form:

$$v = S_f D - \frac{S_f}{D_j} D^2$$

The peak of this curve occurs at a point where the slope of flow versus density is zero; that is,

$$\frac{dv}{dD} = 0 = S_f - 2\frac{S_f}{D_j} D$$

Solving this equation for D yields $D = D_j/2$. Capacity, therefore, occurs when the density is one-half the jam density. This may now be substituted into the linear equation relating speed and density (Greenshields' hypothesis) to find the corresponding speed:

$$S = S_f - \frac{S_f}{D_j} D = S_f - \frac{S_f}{D_j} \frac{D_j}{2} = \frac{S_f}{2}$$

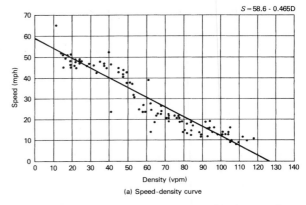

(a) Speed-density curve

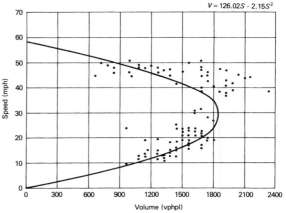

(b) Flow-speed curve

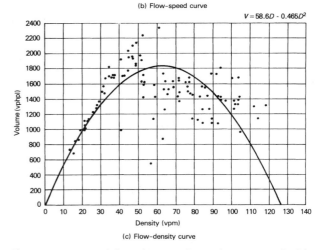

(c) Flow-density curve

Figure 12-3   Speed-flow-density relationships: Greenshield's hypothesis. [Used with permission of Transportation Research Board, National Research Council, Washington, DC, J. S. Drake, J. L. Schofer, and A. D. May, Jr., "A Statistical Analysis of Speed-Density Hypotheses," *Transportation Research Record 154*, pp. 77 and 78. Copyright © 1963 Transportation Research Board.]

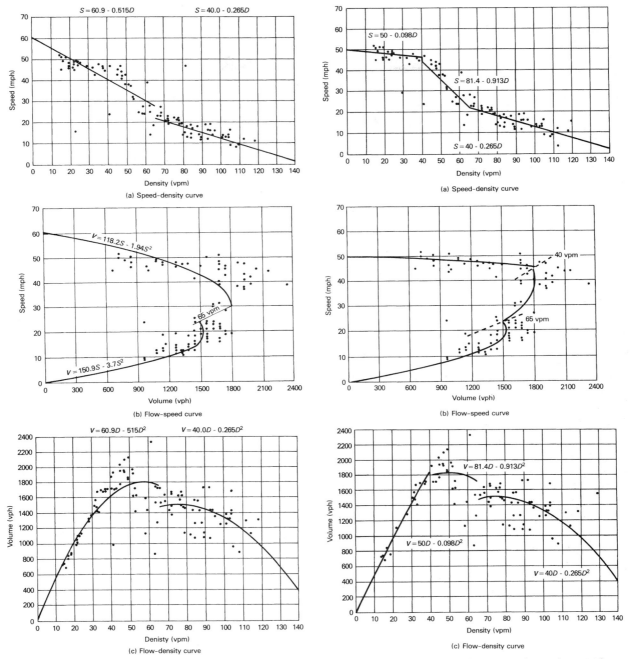

Figure 12-4 Speed-flow-density relationships: Two segment linear. [Used with permission of Transportation Research Board, National Research Council, Washington, DC, J. S. Drake, J. L. Schofer, and A. D. May, Jr., "A Statistical Analysis of Speed-Density Hypotheses," *Transportation Research Record 154*, pp. 78 and 79. Copyright © 1967 Transportation Research Board.]

Figure 12-5 Speed-flow-density relationships: Three-segment linear. [Used with permission of Transportation Research Board, National Research Council, Washington, DC, J. S. Drake, J. L. Schofer, and A. D. May, Jr., "A Statistical Analysis of Speed-Density Hypotheses," *Transportation Research Record 154*, pp. 80 and 81. Copyright © 1967 Transportation Research Board.]

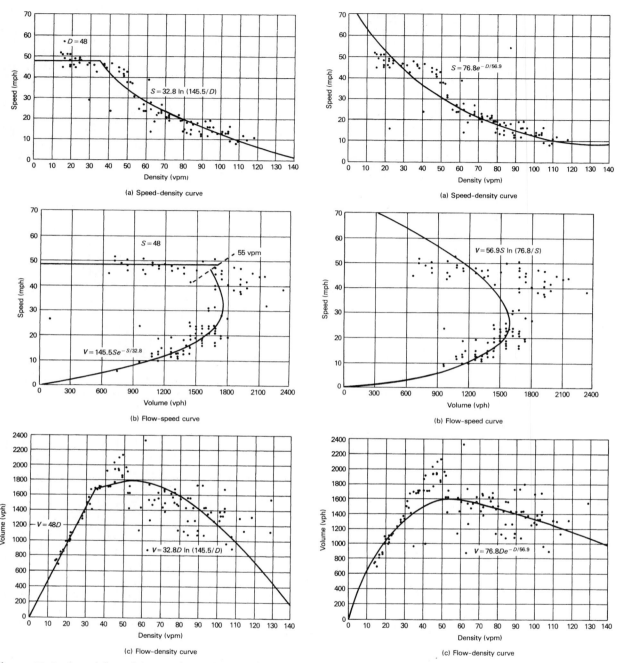

Figure 12-6 Speed-flow-density relationships: Greenberg hypothesis. [Used with permission of Transportation Research Board, National Research Council, Washington, DC, J. S. Drake, J. L. Schofer, and A. D. May, Jr., "A Statistical Analysis of Speed-Density Hypotheses," *Transportation Research Record 154*, pp. 81 and 82. Copyright © 1967 Transportation Research Board.]

Figure 12-7 Speed-flow-density relationships: Underwood hypothesis. [Used with permission of Transportation Research Board, National Research Council, Washington, DC, J. S. Drake, J. L. Schofer, and A. D. May, Jr., "A Statistical Analysis of Speed-Density Hypotheses," *Transportation Research Record 154*, pp. 83 and 84. Copyright © 1967 Transportation Research Board.]

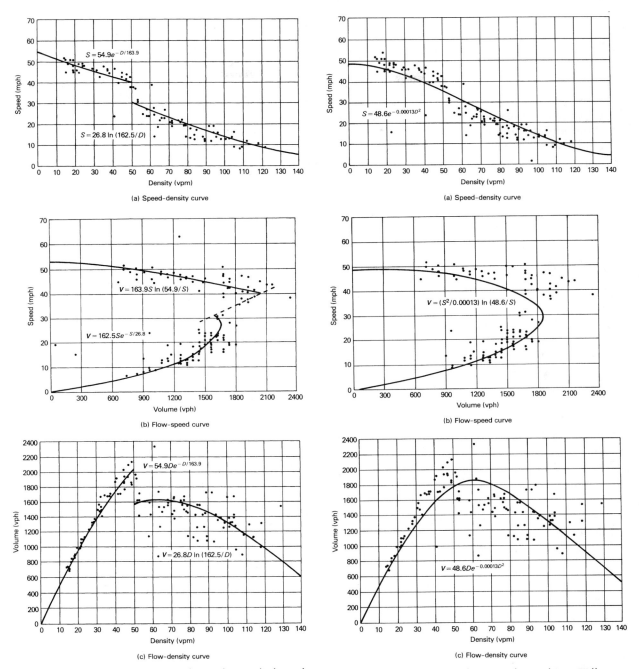

Figure 12-8 Speed-flow-density relationships: Edie hypothesis. [Used with permission of Transportation Research Board, National Research Council, Washington, DC, J. S. Drake, J. L. Schofer, and A. D. May, Jr., "A Statistical Analysis of Speed-Density Hypotheses," *Transportation Research Record 154*, pp. 84 and 85. Copyright © 1967 Transportation Research Board.]

Figure 12-9 Speed-flow-density relationships: Bell curve hypothesis. [Used with permission of Transportation Research Board, National Research Council, Washington, DC, J. S. Drake, J. L. Schofer, and A. D. May, Jr., "A Statistical Analysis of Speed-Density Hypotheses," *Transportation Research Record 154*, pp. 86 and 87. Copyright © 1967 Transportation Research Board.]

Thus, capacity also occurs when S is one-half the free-flow speed, $S_f/2$. As flow is the product of speed and density, the maximum rate of flow is

$$v_m = c = \frac{S_f}{2}\frac{D_j}{2} = \frac{S_f D_j}{4} \qquad [12\text{-}12]$$

Similar analyses can be done for other models as well. Solutions for Greenberg's and Underwood's hypotheses are shown below.

$$c\,(\text{Greenberg}) = S_c\frac{D_j}{e} \qquad [12\text{-}13]$$

$$c\,(\text{Underwood}) = D_c\frac{S_f}{e} \qquad [12\text{-}14]$$

Table 12-1 summarizes the comparative values of capacity, free-flow speed, and jam density for the various hypotheses illustrated in Figures 12-3 through 12-9. The range of values, particularly for free-flow speed, is broad, emphasizing the need to carefully analyze speed-flow-density data before adopting any particular form.

Capacity values also vary considerably, from 1612 vph to over 2000 vph—for stable flow values.

Multisegment curves involving discontinuities present a unique problem for the determination of capacity. If the maximum rate of flow is near the area of the discontinuity, two or more "capacity" values may arise. Consider the Greenshields hypothesis depicted in Figure 12-3. The curve is continuous and clearly displays a single peak value of 1846 vehicles per hour per lane. Now consider the Edie hypothesis depicted in Figure 12-8. The discontinuous curve clearly has two peaks, depending on which side of the discontinuity is selected. The low-density portion of the curve has a peak of 2060 vehicles per hour per lane, the high-density portion a peak of only about 1607 vehicles per hour per lane. The low-density side of the curve portrays stable flow, while the high-density side depicts congested or breakdown flow.

There is a great physical significance to these two descriptions of the flow-versus-density relationship. The Edie hypothesis suggests that there are two values of capacity: one when capacity is approached from stable flow, and another (lower) capacity when approached from forced flow. The physical significance of this is vitally important: Vehicles departing a freeway queue cannot do so at the same maximum rate of flow as vehicles in a stable moving stream. The Greenshields hypothesis does not recognize this characteristic. The practical impact of this is enormous on the ability to recover from a freeway breakdown. Consider the example illustrated in Figure 12-10.

Consider the impact of the situation illustrated in Figure 12-10 if the Edie hypothesis is correct. Assume for simplicity that the capacities under stable- and forced-flow conditions may be rounded to 2000 vphpl and 1600 vphpl, respectively.

Before the breakdown occurs, the freeway section shown operates at capacity, with 6000 vph arriving and a capacity of exactly $3 \times 2000 = 6000$ vph. When the breakdown occurs, one lane is blocked, and demand instantaneously becomes more than the available capacity, which at best is now 2×2000 vphpl =

Table 12-1 Comparative Values for Various Speed-Flow-Density Hypotheses

Model	Capacity (vphpl)	Free-Flow Speed (mph)	Jam Density (vpmpl)
Greenshields	1846	58.6	126.0
Two-segment linear	1801/1509	60.9	150.9
Three-segment linear	1814/1509	50.0	150.9
Greenberg	1761	48.0	145.5
Underwood	1612	76.8	—
Edie	2060/1607	54.9	162.5
Bell curve	1850	48.6	—

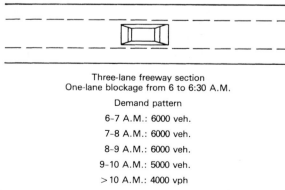

Three-lane freeway section
One-lane blockage from 6 to 6:30 A.M.

Demand pattern

6–7 A.M.: 6000 veh.

7–8 A.M.: 6000 veh.

8–9 A.M.: 6000 veh.

9–10 A.M.: 5000 veh.

>10 A.M.: 4000 vph

Figure 12-10 Illustration of a freeway breakdown.

Table 12-2 Queue Buildup and Dissipation for Figure 12-10, Assuming Discontinuous Speed-Flow-Density Characteristics

Time (A.M.)	Arrivals (veh)	Capacity (veh)	Queue Size (veh)
6:00–6:30	6000/2 = 3000	2 × 1600/2 = 1600	3000 − 1600 = 1400
6:30–7:00	6000/2 = 3000	3 × 1600/2 = 2400	1400 + 3000 − 2400 = 2000
7:00–8:00	6000	3 × 1600 = 4800	2000 + 6000 − 4800 = 3200
8:00–9:00	6000	4800	3200 + 6000 − 4800 = 4400
9:00–10:00	5000	4800	4400 + 5000 − 4800 = 4600
After 10:00	4000/hr	4800/hr	Queue decreases by 800/hr

Time to dissipate queue: 4600 veh/800 vph = 5.75 hr.
Time queue dissipates: 10:00 A.M. + 5.75 hr = 3:45 P.M.

Table 12-3 Queue Buildup and Dissipation for Figure 12-10, Assuming Continuous Speed-Flow-Density Relationships

Time (A.M.)	Arrivals (veh)	Capacity (veh)	Queue Size (veh)
6:00–6:30	6000/2 = 3000	2 × 2000/2 = 2000	3000 − 2000 = 1000
6:30–7:00	6000/2 = 3000	3 × 2000/2 = 3000	1000
7:00–8:00	6000	6000	1000
8:00–9:00	6000	6000	1000
9:00–10:00	5000	6000	1000 + 5000 − 6000 = 0

4000 vph. It is, however, worse than that. Once the breakdown occurs, and arrivals exceed the number of vehicles able to traverse the section, freeway queues and forced flow become the operating mode. Under the Edie hypothesis, this would provide a capacity of only 2 × 1600 vphpl = 3200 vph. Further, the stable-flow capacity of 2000 vphpl cannot be reachieved until the freeway queue is fully dissipated and stable flow resumes. Table 12-2 illustrates the buildup and dissipation of the freeway queue under these conditions.

Note that in the case illustrated by Table 12-2, a vehicle blockage lasting for only ½ hour creates a traffic jam that does not clear up until 9.75 hours after the time of the breakdown. Only when the full freeway queue is dissipated, some 9.75 hours later, does the facility regain its full stable-flow capacity of 6000 vph.

Consider the same problem, but now assume that there is only one value of capacity that does not change depending on whether it is approached from stable or forced flow. For simplicity, it is assumed that the single value of capacity is 2000 vphpl, and the analysis is redone in Table 12-3.

Table 12-4 Comparing the Two Solutions

	Discontinuous Assumption	Continuous Assumption
Maximum queue size (vehicles)	4600	1000
Maximum queue length (feet)	76,667	16,333
Time queue dissipated	3:45 P.M.	10:00 A.M.
Total time of disruption	9.75 hr	4.00 hr

Table 12-4 provides a startling comparison between the two analyses. Queue length (in feet) is estimated as the maximum queue size (in vehicles) × 50 ft/veh divided by three lanes. The use of 50 ft/veh is consistent with field observations of moving freeway queues. These studies generally indicate that, on the average, a vehicle in such a "shuffling queue" consumes between 40 and 50 ft of lane.

Clearly, the assumption of a discontinuous versus continuous speed-flow-density relationship can have a significant impact on capacity and on the analysis of freeway breakdown recovery. It must be noted, however, that there is no clear consensus among traffic engineers as to whether a discontinuous or continuous approach is more universally applicable. The 1994 *HCM* adopts standard speed-flow-density curves for ideal conditions and specifies a single value of freeway capacity. However, Chapter 6 of the *HCM* contains a detailed procedure for estimating the impacts of breakdowns that can be applied to discontinuous situations or assumptions. There is evidence in the literature to support both discontinuous and continuous theories. Which is the more accurate description of modern freeway operations may very well be a function of local driving customs and conditions. Despite the lack of clarity on this point, the engineer studying freeway operations must take this issue into account and should provide a mathematical description that best represents observed data.

B. Developing level of service criteria

The *HCM* specifies that density is the most appropriate measure by which to *define* levels of service for freeways. This is because speed is now seen to be constant through a large range of flows, and is therefore not a good measure of service quality. Of the two remaining macroscopic flow variables, flow is a point measure not discernible by drivers. This leaves density, which describes proximity to other vehicles, and which varies with flow throughout the full range of flow.

Note that level of service criteria are, for the most part, *defined*. Based on current speed-flow-density data, members of the TRB Committee on Highway Capacity and Quality of Flow make a collective judgment concerning the appropriate break points for the various levels of service.

Thus, density thresholds for levels of service A through D are established by collective professional judgment. The break point for LOS E, however, is not subject to judgment. By definition, it is the *critical density,* the density at which capacity occurs.

Figure 12-11 illustrates how level of service criteria may be established using a known speed-flow-density relationship. In this case, the Greenshields relationships, discussed earlier, are used as an example.

The maximum density for level of service E must be set at the critical density, which is 60 pc/mi/ln in Figure 12-11. Maximum densities for other levels of service may be set by judgment. For the illustration, the densities of the 1985 *HCM* are used, i.e.:

LOS A   12 pc/mi/ln
LOS B   20 pc/mi/ln
LOS C   30 pc/mi/ln
LOS D   42 pc/mi/ln

Figure 12-11 illustrates how corresponding maximum flows and minimum speeds may be determined. These can then be tabulated, as shown in Table 12-5. This type of table, and accompanying figures, then form the base of freeway analysis procedures.

Studies for the 1997 HCM update

Sponsored by NCHRP, a major data collection and analysis effort was conducted to determine appropriate speed-flow-density relationships for the 1997 update of the *HCM* [24].

As part of this effort, a data base consisting of 44 basic freeway sites was studied in different regions of the country.

One of the critical aspects studied was the potential of more than one value of capacity: Is there more than one? If so, which one should be used?

Unfortunately, as in previous studies, the results are inconclusive. The researchers developed four scenarios of what the typical speed-flow relationship might look like, and were unable to determine which was the most likely to occur.

Table 12-5   Level-of-Service Criteria Derived from Figure 12-11: An Illustration

Level of Service	Maximum Density (pc/mi/ln)	Minimum Speed (mph)	Maximum Flow (pcphpl)
A	12	54	800
B	20	50	1000
C	30	45	1350
D	42	39	1610
E	60	30	1800
F	>60	<30	<1800

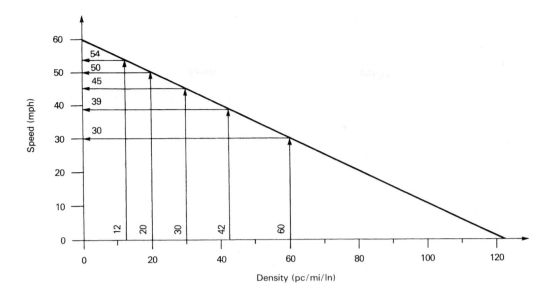

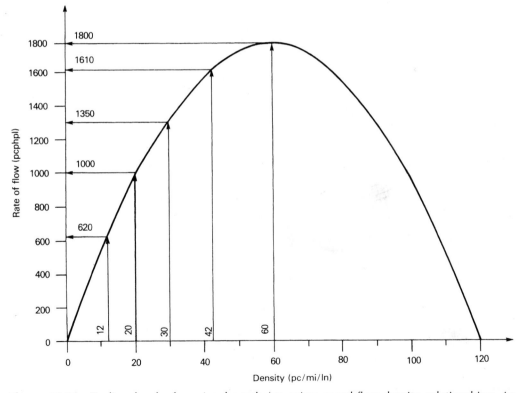

Figure 12-11 Finding level of service boundaries using speed-flow-density relationships: An Illustration.

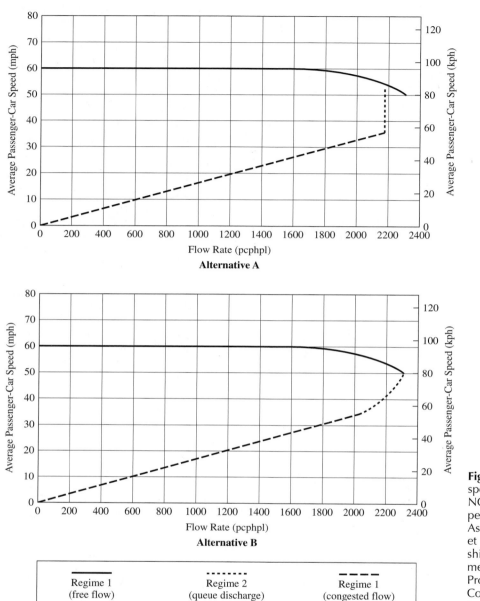

Figure 12-12 Alternative speed-flow-curves from NCHRP study. [Used with permission of JHK & Associates, from J. Schoen, et al., "Speed-Flow Relationships for Basic Freeway Segments," *Final Report,* NCHRP Project 3-45, pp. 4 and 5. Copyright © 1995 JHK & Associates.]

The four scenarios are illustrated in Figure 12-12. Note that all four scenarios are identical in the range of stable (free) flow. They differ in how forced flow and queue discharge flow occur. In Figure 12-12(a), the capacity under stable flow conditions is shown as higher than that under queue discharge or congested flow. Queue discharge is a constant, with varying speed depending on how far downstream of the queue discharge point the observation is taken.

In Figure 12-12(b), there is only one capacity, although the slope of the relationship changes radically at capacity. Queue discharge occurs with varying

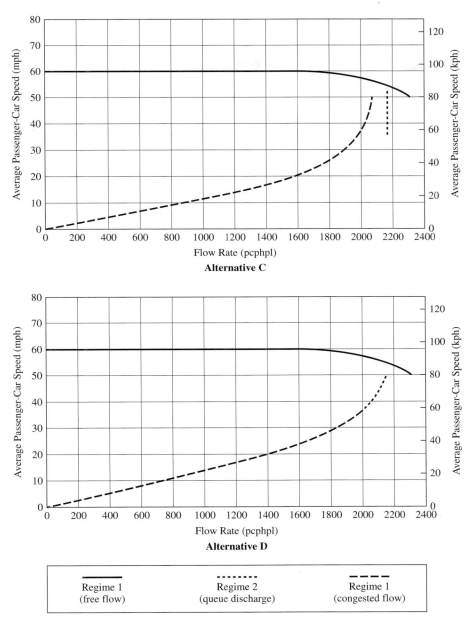

Figure 12-12 (Continued)

speeds and flows, and smoothly connects capacity operations with the beginning of congested flow.

Figure 12-12(c) shows *three* different values of capacity: one for stable or free flow, one for queue discharge, and yet another for congested flow.

Figure 12-12(d) depicts a discontinuous curve with two capacities (stable and unstable). The queue dis-

charge portion of the curve is, however, smoothly tied to the congested flow portion, and occurs with varying speed and a range of flow levels.

Figure 12-13 shows all of the data for 5-minute flow periods from all sites in the study. As can be seen, it would be equally easy to make an argument for any of the scenarios presented in Figure 12-12. For this

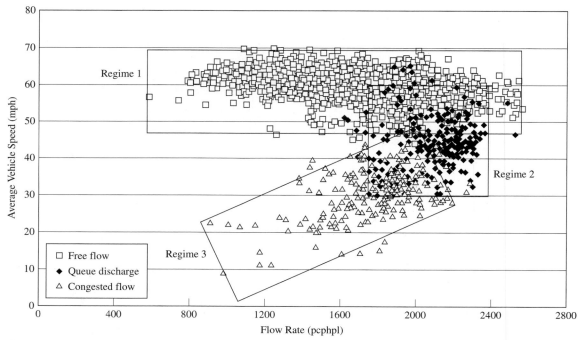

Figure 12-13 Data from NCHRP study. [Used with permission of JHK & Associates, from J. Schoen, et al., "Speed-Flow Relationships for Basic Freeway Segments," *Final Report,* NCHRP Project 3-45, pp. 3–6.]

reason, the 1997 update does not make a clear statement concerning the queue discharge and congested flow portions of the curve, and based its methodology entirely on the stable flow region.

The study also contains some interesting site by site analyses using time series data, i.e., plots of consecutive five-minute flow periods by time. When plotted with queue discharge periods identified, some interesting trends appear.

Figure 12-14 is a sample of three sites from the study. They are, however, fairly representative of most of the sites. In each of the three cases shown, flow levels stabilize, but do not drop, after the onset of queue discharge.

Since the onset of queue discharge is a clear indication that demand has exceeded capacity, thus forming a queue from which discharge can take place, these plots are a strong argument against two capacities. There are similar trends in the vast majority of the sites studied, but not all of them. Further, the levels of pre-queue flow and queue discharge flow do

vary in other sites. At some sites, queue discharge flow is initially significantly below pre-queue levels, but subsequently rises considerably, occasionally to levels almost as high as the pre-queue flow.

References [25–42] provide more detailed insight into these and other issues related to speed-flow-density relationships on modern freeways.

Calibration of adjustment factors for freeway capacity analysis

Previous sections of this chapter have addressed the measurement and calibration of basic speed-flow-density relationships for freeways operating under ideal conditions. These curves form the basis of the analysis methodology presented in Chapter 10 and for the definition of levels of service.

Capacity-analysis techniques, however, must also deal with conditions that are not ideal. Prevailing

Site 290T7; All Lanes; 5-min.

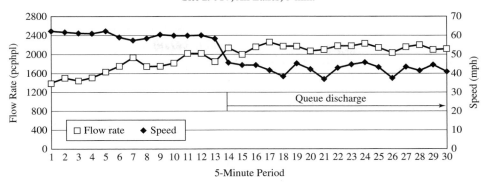

Site 290T8; All Lanes; 5-min.

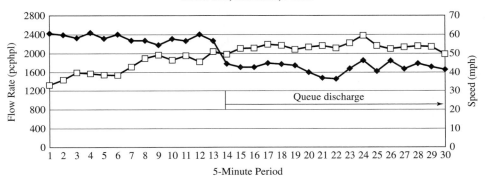

Site 290T9; All Lanes; 5-min.

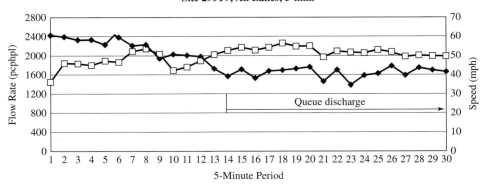

Figure 12-14 Time series data: 3 sites from NCHRP study. [Used with permission of JHK & Associates, from J. Schoen, et al., "Speed-Flow Relationships for Basic Freeway Segments," *Final Report,* NCHRP Project 3-45, Appendix 2. Copyright © 1995 JHK & Associates.]

conditions on a freeway rarely approach the definition of "ideal"—that is, primarily regular users of the facility in the driver population, and all passenger cars in the traffic stream. The last condition is, of course, the least likely to occur in practice, except on those parkways and similar facilities where trucks and other heavy vehicles are prohibited.

The basic relationship for freeways defined in Chapter 10 is as follows:

$$SF_i = MSF_i \times N \times f_{HV} \times f_p \quad [12\text{-}15]$$

where: SF_i = service flow rate for LOS i under prevailing conditions (vph)

MSF_i = maximum service flow rate per lane for LOS i under ideal conditions (pcphpl)

N = number of lanes in one direction on the freeway

f_{HV} = adjustment factor for the presence of trucks, buses, and recreational vehicles in the traffic stream

f_p = adjustment factor for driver populations dominated by unfamiliar or occasional users of the facility

Values of MSF_i are selected from tables in the *HCM*, which are similar to Table 12-5. These values are for ideal conditions and are determined from calibrated speed-flow-density curves as discussed herein. The issue to be addressed now is the determination or calibration of the adjustment factors that account for the differences between prevailing and ideal conditions.

In essence, each adjustment factor multiplies a calibrated flow value in pcph under ideal conditions to yield an equivalent flow value in vph under prevailing conditions. This may be generally expressed as

$$v(\text{prevailing conditions}) = v(\text{ideal conditions}) \times f \quad [12\text{-}16]$$

Therefore:

$$f = \frac{v(\text{prevailing conditions})}{v(\text{ideal conditions})} \quad [12\text{-}17]$$

This is simply a matter of definition. The calibration of any adjustment factor, therefore, is accomplished by finding equivalent flow values under ideal and specified prevailing conditions. This must be done in a controlled and scientific fashion and involves judgments concerning the definition of "equivalent." The subsections that follow discuss the three individual adjustment factors and their calibration, as well as a number of different theories concerning the concept of "equivalent" flows.

A. Calibrating the heavy-vehicle factor

The heavy-vehicle factor, f_{HV}, converts a rate of flow stated in terms of pcph to an equivalent flow in vph for a specified mix of vehicle types. Thus, by definition:

$$v(\text{vph}) = v(\text{pcph}) \times f_{HV}$$

and:

$$f_{HV} = \frac{v(\text{vph})}{v(\text{pcph})} \quad [12\text{-}18]$$

The *HCM* uses the passenger-car equivalent as an intermediate value to find the heavy-vehicle adjustment factor. The *passenger-car equivalent* is the number of passenger cars that would occupy the same amount of "space" as *one* truck, bus, or recreational vehicle in a specified traffic stream. With this definition, the passenger-car equivalent is easily converted to a heavy-vehicle factor:

$$f_{HV} = \frac{1}{1 + P_T(E_T - 1) + P_R(E_R - 1)} \quad [12\text{-}19]$$

where: P_T, P_R = proportion of trucks and buses, and RVs in the traffic stream

E_T, E_R = passenger-car equivalent for trucks and buses, and RVs in the traffic stream

Where trucks are the only form of heavy vehicle in the traffic stream, the relationship simplifies to:

$$f_{HV} = \frac{1}{1 + P_T(E_T - 1)} \quad [12\text{-}20]$$

This section will focus on this simpler relationship to better clarify the concepts involved in calibrating passenger-car equivalents.

The concepts of "equivalence" are not particularly clarified by the use of a "passenger-car equivalent" value. The same issues arise in calibrating values of E_T as arise in calibrating f_{HV}, which are, after all, only different algebraic presentations of the same thing. While some early researchers attempted to simplify the problem by calibrating E_T independently of its derivation, this approach often led to concepts of equivalence not well related to capacity. The 1965 *HCM*, for example, used a technique developed for two-lane highways to derive freeway E_T values. The "passenger-car equivalent" was defined in terms of relative numbers of passing maneuvers of cars by cars and trucks by cars [10]. Equation 12-18 was then used to obtain the heavy-vehicle adjustment factor, f_{HV}. However, relative numbers of passing maneuvers have little to do with space or time-space occupied by vehicles traversing a freeway section, and the resulting values of f_{HV} were of questionable relevance.

Equation [12-21] finds f_{HV} in terms of E_T. Since the functional definition of f_{HV} is clear (a ratio of equivalent flows), it is more instructive to solve Equation [12-20] for E_T in terms of f_{HV}:

$$E_T = \frac{\dfrac{1}{f_{HV}} - 1}{P_T} + 1 \qquad [12\text{-}21]$$

Remembering that f_{HV} is the ratio of equivalent flows in vph and pcph, this equation can be expressed as:

$$E_T = \frac{\dfrac{v(\text{pcph})}{v(\text{vph})} - 1}{P_T} + 1$$

For calibration purposes, it is now useful to recall that rates of flow can be related to average headways in a traffic stream. In a traffic stream consisting of trucks and passenger cars, four types of headways can exist, as previously enumerated: P-P, P-T, T-P, and T-T.

Flow in passenger cars per hour can be related to the headways of passenger cars following passenger cars—that is:

$$v(\text{pcph}) = \frac{3600}{H_{aPP}}$$

where H_{aPP} = average headway, P-P pairs (sec).

Similarly, the flow in vph is related to the average of all headways in the traffic stream:

$$v(\text{vph}) = \frac{3600}{H_a}$$

where: H_a = average of all headways (sec)

This can be expressed as

$$H_a = P_T^2 H_{aTT} + P_T(1 - P_T)H_{aTP}$$
$$+ (1 - P_T)P_T H_{aPT} + (1 - P_T)^2 H_{aPP}$$

where:
P_T = proportion of trucks in traffic stream

$1 - P_T$ = proportion of passenger cars in traffic stream

$H_{app}, H_{aPT}, H_{aTP}, H_{aTT}$ = average headways for the indicated paired vehicle types, (sec)

This relationship can now be substituted into Equation [12-21]. When simplified, the definition of the passenger-car equivalent simplifies to

$$E_T = \frac{(1 - P_T)(H_{aPT} + H_{aTP} - H_{aPP}) + P_T H_{aTT}}{H_{aPP}}$$
$$[12\text{-}22]$$

Some traffic analysts have suggested that the size of the headway depends primarily on the type of the *following vehicle* of a pair—that is, that

$$H_{aPP} = H_{aPT} = H_{aP}$$
$$H_{aTP} = H_{aTT} = H_{aT}$$

If this premise, which can be tested with field data, is accepted, then Equation [12-22] can be further simplified as

$$E_T = \frac{H_{aT}}{H_{aP}} \qquad [12\text{-}23]$$

Passenger-car equivalents, therefore, flow from the definition of the heavy-vehicle factor, and *must* be based on a ratio of headways. The selection of "equivalent" headways for use in such equations is not as straightforward. The following subsections deal with several different approaches to this problem.

1. Driver-determined equivalence. Krammes and Crowley [11] have suggested a straightforward means of determining equivalence of headways. A given traffic stream represents an equilibrium condition in which individual drivers have adjusted their vehicles' operation consistent with their subjective perception of optimality. Krammes and Crowley suggest that individual headways within a given traffic stream represent the drivers' view of "equivalent" operational quality, or level of service. This is an important concept. As the service flow rate is defined for a given level of service, it is rational to use the concept of level of service as a basis for equivalence.

Using this approach, during each 15-minute period of observation, headways would be classified by type, and equivalents would be computed using Equation [12-22] or [12-23]. Consider an example. The following data was obtained during a single 15-minute interval on a freeway. The traffic stream during this interval consisted of 10% trucks and 90% passenger cars.

Type of Headway	Number Observed	Average Value
P-P	400	3.0 sec
P-T	40	3.4 sec
T-P	40	4.2 sec
T-T	9	4.6 sec

Using Equation [12-22], the passenger car equivalent for trucks during this 15-minute interval may be calculated as

$$E_T = \frac{(1 - P_T)(H_{aPT} + H_{aTP} - H_{aPP}) + P_T H_{aTT}}{H_{aPP}}$$

$$= \frac{(1 - 0.10)(3.4 + 4.2 - 3.0) + 0.10(4.6)}{3.0}$$

$$= 1.53$$

Based on the Krammes and Crowley theory of equivalence, each truck consumes as much space or capacity as 1.53 passenger cars in the traffic stream described by the data.

It is also interesting to note how the result would change if the simpler approach of Equation [12-23] were applied to this data. First, average truck and passenger-car headways would have to be computed:

$$H_{aT} = \frac{N_{TP}H_{aTP} + N_{TT}H_{aTT}}{N_{TP} + N_{TT}}$$

$$H_{ap} = \frac{N_{PP}H_{aPP} + N_{PT}H_{aPT}}{N_{PP} + N_{PT}}$$

where: N_{TP} = number of T-P headways observed
N_{TT} = number of T-T headways observed
N_{PP} = number of P-P headways observed
N_{PT} = number of P-T headways observed

Then:

$$H_{aT} = \frac{(40 \times 4.2) + (9 \times 4.6)}{40 + 9} = 4.27 \text{ sec}$$

$$H_{aP} = \frac{(400 \times 3.0) + (40 \times 3.4)}{400 + 40} = 3.04 \text{ sec}$$

And from Equation [12-23]:

$$E_T = \frac{H_{aT}}{H_{aP}} = \frac{4.27}{3.04} = 1.40$$

Note that there is a difference of 0.23 between the two results. The difference exists because the assumption that headway depends only on the following vehicle is obviously not correct in this case. The result is, however, close, indicating that the simpler assumption may produce reasonable results. This is important for cases where there are more than two types of vehicles. Classification of headways by the type of trailing vehicle greatly simplifies the analysis of such cases.

Note that this example illustrates the calibration of *one* E_T value. From the *HCM*, E_T is shown as varying with P_T, the size of the freeway, and the terrain. Researchers may find that it varies with other variables as well, including flow. Thus, the calibration of *a set of values* or a relationship defining E_T would require the collection of headways at various sites for numerous 15-minute intervals. If E_T varies with three other variables, then a three-dimensional matrix of values must be created. This is often done by calibrating critical cells of the matrix and using regression or other statistical techniques to define the relationship over the full space. The relationship may then be presented for use as a table, a graph, or an equation.

2. Equivalent headways based on constant spacing. A second view of equivalence is to select headways of various vehicle types such that their *spacing* (in feet) is constant. This is done by plotting headways of trucks and passenger cars (at a given site) versus their spacing. Remember that spacing is related to density $(D = 5280/S_a)$ and that density is the defining parameter for level of service on freeways. Use of this theory results in passenger-car equivalents that define traffic streams of equal density and therefore, equal level of service.

Figure 12-15 illustrates how plots of headway versus spacing would be used to generate E_T calibrations.

The plot of headways versus spacings can be made from data covering any time period sufficient to define the relationships. The plots, however, would be valid only for the site in question and would relate to the size of freeway, terrain, grade, and length of grade present. E_T might be shown to vary with spacing (density) as the result of any given set of plots. This approach would not reveal variations in E_T based on P_T.

Note that the "equivalent" headways selected in this method would not have to occur during the same 15-minute time period. Equivalence is defined by equal spacings to tie the value of E_T directly to the defined performance measure, density. In the Krammes and Crowley approach, equivalence was based on headways within a given 15-minute period and therefore measured drivers' perception of equivalence as expressed through their observed driving behavior.

3. Equivalent headways based upon constant speed.

A plot of headways versus speeds of individual vehicles would take much the same form as the plot of headways versus spacings illustrated in Figure 12-15.

"Equivalent" headways could be similarly selected from such a plot by entering the curves with constant speed values. This would result in the definition of E_T values yielding an equivalent traffic flow operating at the same speed as the mixed traffic stream observed. This would be an attractive alternative if speed were the measure defining level of service, but it has little meaning in the context of current freeway procedures. A constant-speed method was used to calibrate heavy vehicle factors for the two-lane highway methodology of the 1985 *HCM*. Level of service is at least related to speed in a secondary way for such facilities [12].

4. Macroscopic calibration of the heavy-vehicle factor.

Since f_{HV} is defined as a ratio of equivalent flows in vph and pcph, it seems that a more straightforward approach would measure these directly. Figure 12-16 illustrates plots of flow versus density for similar geometric sites and time periods during which the percentage of trucks varies. Curves are illustrated for 10% trucks in the traffic stream and for 0% trucks in the traffic stream. Given that density is the level-of-service parameter, equivalent flow levels can be found by keeping density constant. The ratio of these flows yields a factor, f_{HV}, directly, rather than a passenger-car equivalent which is algebraically converted to a factor.

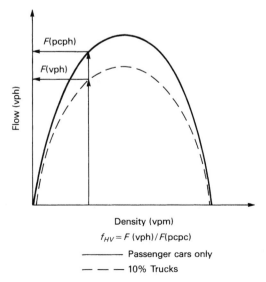

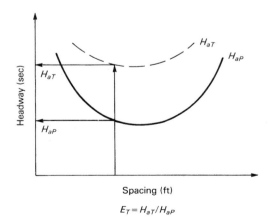

Figure 12-15 Calibration of passenger car equivalents using equal spacing.

Figure 12-16 Calibration of the heavy-vehicle factor from flow-density plots.

Clearly, the data-collection process is a difficult one for such a procedure. Curves would have to be established for various truck percentages in the traffic stream ranging from 0% to as high as 25% to 30%. Sites with varying terrain would have to be studied as well. Each point on a macroscopic flow-density curve is 15 minutes of data, whereas each point on a headway-spacing plot is a single vehicle. Therefore, while theoretically simple, macroscopic calibration of f_{HV} directly is difficult and often impractical.

A similar approach could be made using a plot of flow versus speed. As noted before, a constant-speed definition of the heavy-vehicle factor would be of questionable relevance to the methods of the *HCM*.

5. Comments. The literature contains numerous theoretical and practical treatments of passenger-car equivalents and the heavy vehicle factor [13–16]. No common concept of equivalence has emerged, nor do all researchers agree on specific calibration techniques. In practical terms, the amount of data needed to fully calibrate a set of passenger-car equivalents or heavy-vehicle factors is very large. The cost of obtaining and analyzing such data is often prohibitive. For this reason, most of the factors in the *HCM* and elsewhere are based on small data bases, with theoretical extensions of the data used to fill gaps and extend the range of the data.

B. Calibrating the driver population factor

All references to the driver population factor, f_p, in the *HCM* are to a poorly-defined range of potential values. The analyst is urged to make local measurements to pinpoint the appropriate value for use.

There are two reasons for this: (1) the lack of uniformity of driver populations, and our inability to completely specify it; and (2) observations show that there may be vast regional and local differences in this factor.

The factor basically allows for the consideration of non-commuter (or non-regular) users of a facility. Its principal use is in analyzing weekend traffic on heavily-used recreational routes. Often, when a facility is used by commuters during the week, and some mix including non-regular recreational users on the weekend, the facility will have vastly different oper-

ating characteristics. Such facilities are ideal for observing this effect.

The factor is most often calibrated by comparing observed capacity values during a normal weekday peak period with those observed on weekends. It is critical that known bottleneck locations be used in such studies to guarantee that what is observed is indeed capacity operation.

The factor is then calibrated as the ratio of the weekend capacity to the weekday capacity. The problem is that it is difficult to extend one measurement to other facilities and locations. The mix of regular and non-regular users is critical to overall behavior, and this may vary considerably from location to location.

Nevertheless, this is about the best that can be done at present, and it is a reasonable approach to getting a general estimate of a very volatile factor.

Adjustment factors to free-flow speed

With the 1994 *HCM* (for multilane highways) and the 1997 update (for basic freeway sections), free-flow speed has emerged as a significant parameter in capacity analysis methodology.

In the procedure for estimating free-flow speed, adjustments are applied. While the concept of the adjustment is similar to that used previously to "adjust" capacities or flow rates, the approach is very different. Adjustments are subtractive rather than multiplicative, and are indexed to an "ideal" free-flow speed, a concept that is itself somewhat complicated.

If data bases are sparse for adjustments to capacity and service flow rates, they are even sparser for free-flow speed adjustments. The lane width and lateral clearance adjustments were based upon very limited field data, as well as by the mathematical projection of capacity-based adjustment factors onto the speed scale of the speed-flow curve.

Other adjustment factors were based on small data bases showing somewhat systematic trends vs. underlying variables such as interchange density and others.

While free-flow adjustments have not been heavily researched, nor subjected to a great deal of analytic examination, their broadening use in the *HCM* is sure to spur new interest in the research community.

Calibration of procedures for weaving and ramp analysis

While it is indeed possible and often practical for engineers to modify *HCM* standards for basic freeway sections to reflect local behavior using some of the techniques discussed herein, it is virtually impossible to do this for weaving areas and ramps.

The amount of data required to calibrate the *HCM* procedures for these types of facilities is enormous and is beyond the means of most engineering projects. Both were calibrated with substantial government support by designated research teams.

The final calibration of the *HCM* procedure for weaving areas is detailed in a paper by Roess [17]. The 1985 *HCM* procedure was a combination of the concepts developed by several researchers who had recommended competing procedures during the early 1980s [18–20]. The ramp procedures of the 1985 *HCM* were calibrated in the early 1960s as the result of an in-house study by the FHWA [21] and a second study in California [22]. The 1985 *HCM* procedure modified these older studies to account for new information evolving from the weaving studies which impinged on ramp analysis. These modifications were documented in another paper by Roess [23].

The ramp analysis procedure appearing in the 1994 *HCM* was developed at Polytechnic University under NCHRP sponsorship, and is presented in a research report [43].

Summary

The material in this chapter discussed key issues and concepts involved in calibrating critical freeway-related algorithms for use in capacity analysis procedures.

The 1985 *HCM*, and its successor updates in 1994 and 1997, often base analysis methodologies on sparse data bases and relationships without the kinds of correlation coefficients that would be desired strictly on the basis of statistics.

Yet, these procedures are needed; and when necessary, collective professional judgment, exercised through the TRB Committee on Highway Capacity and Quality of Service (and its subcommittees) can fill gaps. Thus, analysis procedures are always under discussion and development. Differences of opinion give rise to enlightened discussion of the issues, and the thoughtful generation of new concepts and approaches to keep the state-of-the-art moving forward.

References

1. *Highway Capacity Manual, Special Report 209,* 3rd Edition, Transportation Research Board, National Research Council, Washington, DC, (revised) 1997.
2. Mood and Grabell, *Introduction to the Theory of Statistics,* 2nd Edition, McGraw-Hill, New York, NY, 1963.
3. Gerlough, D., and Huber, M., *Traffic Flow Theory: A Monograph, Special Report 165,* Transportation Research Board, National Research Council, Washington, DC, 1975.
4. Greenshields, B., "A Study of Traffic Capacity," *Proceedings of the Highway Research Board,* Vol. 14, Transportation Research Board, National Research Council, Washington, DC, 1934.
5. Ellis, R., "Analysis of Linear Relationships in Speed-Density and Speed-Occupancy Curves," Report, Northwestern University, Evanston, IL, December 1964.
6. Greenberg, H., "An Analysis of Traffic Flows," *Operations Research,* Vol. 7, ORSA, Washington, DC, 1959.
7. Underwood, R., "Speed, Volume, and Density Relationships," *Quality and Theory of Traffic Flow,* Yale Bureau of Highway Traffic, New Haven, CT, 1961.
8. Edie, L., "Car-Following and Steady-State Theory for Non-Congested Traffic," *Operations Research,* Vol. 9, ORSA, Washington, DC, 1961.
9. Duke, J., Schofer, J., and May, A., "A Statistical Analysis of Speed-Density Hypotheses," *Highway Research Record 154,* Transportation Research Board, National Research Council, Washington, DC, 1967.
10. *Highway Capacity Manual, Special Report 87,* Transportation Research Board, National Research Council, Washington, DC, 1965.

11. Krammes, R., and Crowley, K., "Passenger Car Equivalents for Trucks on Level Freeway Segments," *Transportation Research Record,* Transportation Research Board, National Research Council, Washington, DC, 1987.
12. Messer, C., "Two-Lane, Two-Way Rural Highway Level of Service and Capacity Procedures," *Final Report,* Texas Transportation Institute, College Station, TX, February 1983.
13. Linzer, E., Roess, R., and McShane, W., "Effect of Trucks, Buses, and Recreational Vehicles on Freeway Capacity and Service Volume," *Transportation Research Record 699,* Transportation Research Board, National Research Council, Washington, DC, 1979.
14. Craus, J., Polus, A., and Grinberg, "A Revised Method for the Determination of Passenger Car Equivalents," *Transportation Research,* Vol. 14A, No. 4, Pergamon Press, London, England, 1980.
15. Cunagin, W., and Messer, C., "Passenger Car Equivalents for Rural Highway," *Transportation Research Record 905,* Transportation Research Board, National Research Council, Washington, DC, 1983.
16. Roess, R., and Messer, C., "Passenger Car Equivalents for Uninterrupted Flow: Revision of the Circular 212 Values," *Transportation Research Record 971,* Transportation Research Board, National Research Council, Washington, DC, 1984.
17. Roess, R., "Development of Weaving Area Analysis Procedures for the 1985 *Highway Capacity Manual,*" *Transportation Research Record 1112,* Transportation Research Board, National Research Council, Washington, DC, 1988.
18. Leisch, J., "Completion of Procedures for Analysis and Design of Traffic Weaving Sections," *Final Report and User's Guide,* U.S. Department of Transportation, Federal Highway Administration, Washington, DC, 1983.
19. Reilly, W., Kell, J., and Johnson, J., "Weaving Analysis Procedures for the New Highway Capacity Manual," *Final Report,* JHK & Associates, Tucson, AZ, August 1984.
20. Pignataro, L., McShane, W., Roess, R., Crowley, K., and Lee, R., "Weaving Areas: Design and Analysis," *NCHRP Report 159,* Transportation Research Board, National Research Council, Washington, DC, 1975.
21. Hess, J., "Capacities and Characteristics of Ramp-Freeway Connections," *Highway Research Record 27.* Transportation Research Board, National Research Council, Washington, DC, 1963.
22. Moskowitz, K., "Waiting for a Gap in a Traffic Stream," *Proceedings of the Highway Research Board,* Vol. 33, Transportation Research Board, National Research Council, Washington, DC, 1954.
23. Roess, R., "Development of Modified Capacity Analysis Procedures for Ramps," *Transportation Research Record 772,* Transportation Research Board, National Research Council, Washington, DC, 1980.
24. Schoen, J., et al., "Speed-Flow Relationships for Basic Freeway Sections," *Final Report,* NCHRP Project 3-45, JHK & Associates, Tucson, AZ, May 1995.
25. Agyemang-Duah, and Hall, F., "Some Issues Regarding the Numerical Value of Freeway Capacity," *Proceedings of the International Symposium on Highway Capacity,* Karlsruhe, Germany, July 1991, Transportation Research Board, National Research Council, Washington, DC.
26. Banks, J., "Evaluation of the Two-Capacity Phenomenon as a Basis for Ramp Metering," *Final Report,* San Diego State University, San Diego, CA, 1991.
27. Banks, J., "Flow Processes at a Freeway Bottleneck," *Transportation Research Record 1287,* Transportation Research Board, National Research Council, Washington, DC, 1990.
28. Chin, H., and May, A., "An Examination of the Speed-Flow Relationship at the Caldecott Tunnel," *Transportation Research Record 1320,* Transportation Research Board, National Research Council, Washington, DC, 1991.
29. Chin, H., and May, A., "Speed-Flow Relationships of Uncongested Flow on Freeways," *Report No. UCB-ITS-WP-90-3,* Institute of Transportation Studies, University of California at Berkeley, Berkeley, CA, 1990.
30. Fong and Rooney, F., "Volumes and Capacities Along Urban California Freeways," Report, California Department of Transportation, Sacramento, CA, 1992.
31. Gunter and Hall, F., "Transitions in the Speed-Flow Relationship," *Transportation Research Record 1091,* Transportation Research Board, National Research Council, Washington, DC, 1986.
32. Hall, F., "An Interpretation of Speed-Flow Concentration Relationships Using Catastrophe Theory," *Transportation Research-A,* Vol. 21A, No. 3, 1987.
33. Hall, F., and Agyemang-Duah, "Freeway Capacity Drop and Definition of Capacity," *Transportation Research Record 1320,* Transportation Research Board, National Research Council, Washington, DC, 1991.
34. Hall, F., and Hall, L., "Capacity and Speed-Flow Analysis of the QEW in Ontario," *Transportation Research Record 1287,* Transportation Research Board, National Research Council, Washington, DC, 1990.

35. Hall, F., Hurdle, V., and Banks, J., "A Synthesis of Recent Work on the Nature of Speed-Flow and Flow-Occupancy Relationships on Freeways," *Transportation Research Record 1365,* Transportation Research Board, National Research Council, Washington, DC, 1992.

36. Hsu and Banks, J., "Effects of Location on Congested-Regime Flow-Concentration Relationships for Freeways," paper presented at the Transportation Research Board Annual Meeting, Washington, DC, 1993.

37. Persaud and Hurdle, V., "Some New Data that Challenge Some Old Ideas About Speed-Flow Relationships," *Transportation Research Record 1194,* Transportation Research Board, National Research Council, Washington, DC, 1988.

38. Ringert and Urbanik, T., "An Evaluation of Freeway Capacity in Texas," Report, Texas Transportation Institute, Texas A & M University, College Station, TX, September 1992.

39. Robertson, "A Study of Speed-Flow Relationship at Two Bottlenecks on Highway 401," Master's Thesis, University of Toronto, Toronto, Ontario, Canada, 1992.

40. Urbanik, T., et al., "Evaluation of High-Volume Urban Texas Freeways," *Transportation Research Record 1320,* Transportation Research Board, National Research Council, Washington, DC, 1991.

41. Wemple, Morris, and May, A., "Freeway Capacity and Flow Relationship," *Proceedings of the International Symposium on Highway Capacity,* Karlsruhe, Germany, July 1991, Transportation Research Board, National Research Council, Washington, DC.

42. Westland, "Potential Methods to Forecast the Actual Highway Capacity," *Proceedings of the International Symposium on Highway Capacity,* Karlsruhe, Germany, July 1991, Transportation Research Board, National Research Council, Washington, DC.

43. Roess, R., and Ulerio, J., "Capacity and Level of Service of Ramp-Freeway Terminals," *Final Report,* NCHRP Project 3-37, Polytechnic University, Brooklyn, NY, 1994.

Problems

Problem 12–1

A study of freeway flow at a particular site has resulted in a calibrated speed-density relationship, as follows:

$$S = 57.5(1 - 0.008D)$$

From this relationship:

(a) Find the free-flow speed and jam density.
(b) Derive equations describing flow versus speed and flow versus density.
(c) Determine the capacity of the site mathematically.
(d) Sketch the speed-density, flow-speed, and flow-density curves.

Problem 12–2

Answer all questions as in Problem 12-1 above for a calibrated speed-density curve as follows:

$$S = 61.2e^{-0.015D}$$

Problem 12–3

For each of the relationships described in Problems 12-1 and 12-2, find level-of-service thresholds for flow and speed, based upon the *HCM* definition of levels of service. Remember that critical density must correspond to the point of maximum flow.

Problem 12–4

A freeway with two lanes in one direction has a capacity of 2000 vphpl under normal stable-flow conditions. On a particular morning, one of these lanes is blocked for 15 minutes, beginning at 7 A.M. The arrival pattern of vehicles is as follows: 7–8 A.M.—4000 vph; 8–9 A.M.—3900 vph; 9–10 A.M.—3500 vph; after 10 A.M.—2800 vph.

(a) Assuming that the capacity of this section reduces to 1800 vphpl under unstable or forced-flow conditions, how long a queue will be established due to this blockage? When will the maximum queue occur? How long will it take to dissipate the queue from the time of the breakdown?
(b) Reconsider your analysis if the capacity of the section remains 2000 vphpl under forced-flow conditions.

Problem 12–5

The following headways were observed during a 15-minute period on an urban freeway:

Type of Headway	Number Observed	Average Value
P-P	128	3.1 sec
P-T	32	3.8 sec
T-P	32	4.3 sec
T-T	8	4.9 sec

Compute the effective passenger-car equivalent for this case (a) assuming that all headway types are different, and (b) assuming that headway values depend only on the type of trailing vehicles. Are your results different? Why? Which do you think is more correct?

13

Analysis of Two-Lane Rural Highways

Approximately 80% of the nation's almost four million miles of paved highway are considered to be "rural." Of these, 85% are two-lane highways, i.e., one lane for traffic in each direction, with passing maneuvers taking place in the opposing lane when visibility and opposing traffic conditions permit.

These roadways, which range from heavily-traveled intercity routes to sparsely-traveled links to isolated areas, provide a vast network connecting the fringes of urban areas, agricultural regions, resource development areas, and remote outposts. Because of the varied functions they serve, two-lane rural highways are built to widely-varying geometric standards.

Rural two-lane highways serve two primary functions in the nation's highway network:

- mobility
- access

As part of state and county primary highway systems, these highways serve a critical mobility function. Significant numbers of people rely on these highways for regular trip-making. Design standards for this type of two-lane highway generally reflect their use by higher volumes, and higher design speeds reflecting mobility needs are generally present.

Many two-lane rural highways, however, serve low volumes, sometimes lower than 100 vehicles per day. The primary function of such highways is to provide for basic all-weather access to remote or sparsely-developed areas. Because such highways are not used by large numbers of people or vehicles, their design speeds and related geometric features are often not a major concern.

Because of the varied functions that two-lane rural highways serve, such a highway in a remote mountainous area will look and operate very differently from the highway serving a busy intercity link.

Design standards

Since two-lane highways exist in varied situations, AASHTO [1] allows for considerable flexibility in basic design standards applied. Table 13-1 shows recommended design speeds vs. the ADT of the facility in question, and the general terrain through which it

Table 13-1 AASHTO Recommended Design Speeds on Rural Highways

Type of Terrain	Speeds for Various Design Volumes, kph (mph)					
			ADT Volume			
	<50 vpd	50–250 vpd	250–400 vpd	400–1500 vpd	1500–2000 vpd	>2000 vpd
LEVEL	50 (31.0)	50 (31.0)	60 (37.3)	80 (49.7)	80 (49.7)	80 (49.7)
ROLLING	30 (18.6)	50 (31.0)	50 (31.0)	60 (37.3)	60 (37.3)	60 (37.3)
MTNS	30 (18.6)	30 (18.6)	30 (18.6)	50 (31.0)	50 (31.0)	50 (31.0)

[From *A Policy on Geometric Design of Highways and Streets,* Washington, D.C.: The American Association of State Highway and Transportation Officials. Copyright 1994. Used by permission.]

Table 13-2 AASHTO Recommended Maximum Grades on Rural Highways

Type of Terrain	Design Speed, kph (mph)							
	30 (18.6)	40 (24.8)	50 (31.0)	60 (37.3)	70 (43.5)	80 (49.7)	90 (55.9)	100 (62.1)
LEVEL	8%	7%	7%	7%	7%	6%	6%	5%
ROLLING	11%	11%	10%	10%	9%	8%	7%	6%
MTNS	16%	15%	14%	13%	12%	10%	10%	NA

[From *A Policy on Geometric Design of Highways and Streets,* Washington, D.C.: The American Association of State Highway and Transportation Officials. Copyright 1994. Used by permission.]

travels. Note that current AASHTO geometric and other criteria are given in metric form. For ease of use, English conversion units are also shown. The major difference in using metric standards is that thresholds are rounded in metric form; when converted to English units, the breakpoints and thresholds fall at arbitrary intermediate levels. Table 13-2 shows maximum grades vs. design speed.

Passing on two-lane rural highways: A unique operational feature

On two-lane rural highways, passing is accomplished using the opposing lane when it is unoccupied. This is a unique operational feature, which causes a number of major effects.

Directional flows on two-lane highways interact as a result of passing maneuvers. As traffic in one direction increases, demand for passing maneuvers in that direction also increases. At the same time, traffic in the opposing direction generally also increases, thereby decreasing the number of opportunities to pass. Thus, a paradox exists on two-lane highways: As the need to pass increases, the ability to pass decreases.

Because of limitations on the ability to pass, the impact of heavy vehicles on traffic flow is considerably greater on two-lane than on multilane highways. Extensive queues may form behind any slow-moving vehicle, which cannot be efficiently dispersed without the ability to pass at will. The formation of platoons behind slow-moving vehicles is a major characteristic limiting the capacity of two-lane highways and is a major cause of deteriorating service quality on such facilities.

Because traffic in one direction interacts with traffic in the other, capacity cannot be defined for a single direction. Rather, the capacity of a two-lane highway is defined in terms of the total two-way traffic that can be accommodated.

To permit passing on a two-lane highway, drivers must be able to see a sufficient distance to appraise the approach of oncoming vehicles and execute a safe passing maneuver. This is called the *safe-passing sight distance*. In determining this value, AASHTO makes several assumptions concerning the maneuver [1]:

1. The overtaken vehicle travels at uniform speed.
2. The passing vehicle has reduced speed and trails the overtaken vehicle as it enters a passing section.
3. When the passing section is reached, the driver requires a short period of time to perceive the clear passing section and to react to start his/her maneuver.
4. Passing is accomplished under what may be termed a delayed start and hurried return in the face of opposing traffic. The passing vehicle accelerates during the maneuver, and its average speed during the occupancy of the left lane is 15 kph faster than that of the overtaken vehicle.
5. When the passing vehicle returns to its lane, there is a suitable clearance length between it and an oncoming vehicle in the other lane.

The minimum passing sight distance is then computed as the sum of four component distances:

d_1 = distance traveled during perception/reaction time and during the initial acceleration to the point of encroachment on the left lane

d_2 = distance traveled while the passing vehicle occupies the left lane

d_3 = distance between the passing vehicle at the end of its maneuver and the opposing vehicle

d_4 = distance traversed by an opposing vehicle for two-thirds the time the passing vehicle occupies the left lane

Figure 13-1 illustrates these component distances, and includes a graph that plots these distances versus average speed of the passing vehicle in mph. Table 13-3 shows values of passing sight distance recommended by AASHTO for various design speeds.

Capacity analysis procedures for two-lane highways

Two-lane highways are unique among facilities providing for uninterrupted flow in that the directional flows strongly interact. Passing is accomplished by use of the opposing travel lane, and thus, volume in

one direction influences capacity and operations in the other. For this reason, capacity analysis of two-lane highways addresses the total two-way capacity of the facility, and the level of service provided to the total two-way traffic volume.

Because two-lane highway analysis addresses both directions as a total, and because of the many factors affecting passing, the format of procedures is quite different than those of freeways and multilane highways.

A. Capacity and level of service

One unique feature of the *HCM* [2] two-lane highway analysis procedure is the definition of level of service. As on freeways, speed is relatively insensitive to flow on two-lane highways. Further, density, when applied to two-directional flow, is not as meaningful a descriptor as for uni-directional flow.

The 1985 *HCM* introduced the parameter "percent time delay" and subsequent editions continue to use this value to define levels of service. *Percent time delay* is the percentage of total travel time all vehicles spend in a platoon, behind a slow-moving vehicle, unable to pass. This is the most visible operational characteristic of two-lane highways. Drivers experience delay and substantial frustration when "stuck" behind a slow-moving vehicle in a platoon. Particularly for rural highways, on which trip lengths are often substantial, being delayed by a truck or other vehicle can add significant amounts of travel time to a trip. The only significant flaw in the use of percent time delay as a parameter is that it should be related to the length of the highway section in question. Being delayed 70% of the time means something quite different if it is for a 100-mile section than for a 1-mile section. Unfortunately, even the most recent research has not developed a reasonable means for incorporating section length into a level-of-service methodology.

Despite this, percent time delay is a powerful and descriptive parameter. It is, of course, quite difficult to measure directly in the field. For this reason, a surrogate measure is often applied. Percent time delay may be taken to be the same as the percentage of vehicles traveling at headways of less than 5 seconds. The latter is measurable. While researchers disagree over whether the headway value should be 3, 4, or 5 seconds, the *HCM* was calibrated using the 5-second surrogate. Therefore, when using the *HCM*, use the 5-second measure.

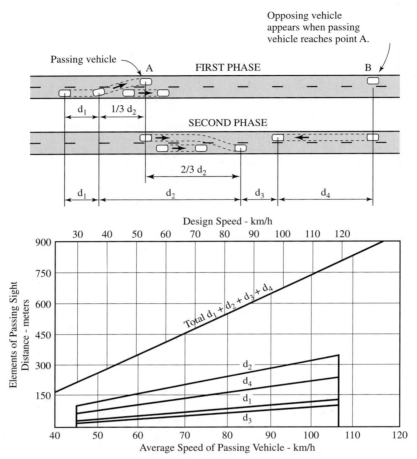

Figure 13-1 Elements of total passing sight distance for two-lane highways. [From *A Policy on Geometric Design of Highways and Streets,* Washington, D.C.: The American Association of State Highway and Transportation Officials, Copyright 1994. Used by permission.]

Figure 13-2 shows the relationship between percent time delay and total two-way flow on a two-lane highway under ideal conditions. Ideal conditions for a two-lane highway include:

- 12-foot lanes
- 6-foot shoulders
- level terrain
- 100% passing sight distance available
- all passenger cars in the traffic stream
- design speed of 60 mph or more
- 50/50 directional distribution of traffic

Capacity of a two-lane highway under ideal conditions is taken to be 2800 pcph total in both directions.

This value is rarely observed in the field, as few two-lane highways ever operate at capacity, for reasons which will be seen. It was established on the basis of a few field studies and comprehensive simulation analyses. This is considerably less than the 2200–2400 pcphpl that can be accommodated on a multi-lane highway, reflecting the restrictive effect of flow in one direction on flow in the other direction. It is, however, an increase over the 2000 pcph (total) stated in the 1965 *HCM* [3].

The relationship between percent time delay and flow is extremely interesting. At a flow level of 1200 pcph, less than one-half the capacity of an ideal two-lane highway, percent time delay is already over 60%.

Table 13-3 Elements of Passing Sight Distance

Speed Group (mph) Average Passing Speed (mph)	31–40 35	41–50 43	51–59 52	60–68 62
Initial Maneuver:				
a = avg acceleration (mph/sec)	1.40	1.43	1.47	1.50
t_1 = time (sec)	3.6	4.0	4.3	4.5
d_1 = distance travelled (ft)	148	213	295	361
Occupation of Left Lane:				
t_2 = time (secs)	9.3	10.0	10.7	11.3
d_2 = distance travelled (ft)	476	640	820	1,034
Clearance Length:				
d_3 = distance travelled (ft)	98	180	246	295
Opposing Vehicle:				
d_3 = distance travelled (ft)	312	427	541	689
Total Distance (ft)	1,034	1,460	1,902	2,379

[From *A Policy on Geometric Design of Highways and Streets,* Washington, D.C.: The American Association of State Highway and Transportation Officials, Copyright 1994. Used by permission.]

Percent time delay deteriorates rapidly with increased flow. This is because as flow increases, the demand to pass also increases, while ability to pass decreases. The impact of this situation on platoon formation and percent time delay is extremely detrimental. On freeways and multilane highways, level of service was less sensitive at low flow rates and more sensitive at high flow rates approaching capacity. For two-lane highways, the opposite is true. Level of service, as measured by percent time delay, is extremely sensitive at low flow levels, and less sensitive as capacity is approached.

In plain English, level of service on two-lane highways deteriorates rapidly at relatively low flow levels. As a matter of definition, levels of service were established by the TRB Committee on Highway Capacity and Quality of Flow as follows:

Level of Service	Percent Time Delay
A	≤30
B	≤45
C	≤60
D	≤75
E	>75
F	100

As a practical matter, from Figure 13-2 a 75% time delay, the limit for LOS D, occurs at a flow level of approximately 1600 pcph, or 57% of capacity. Thus, under ideal conditions, levels of service A through D

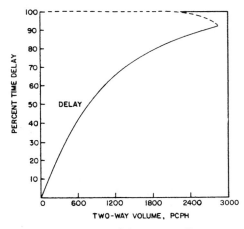

Figure 13-2 Percent time delay versus flow on two-lane highways: Ideal conditions. [Used with permission of Transportation Research Board, National Research Council, Washington, D.C., from *Highway Capacity Manual, Special Report 209,* 3rd Ed., p. 8-4. Copyright © 1994 Transportation Research Board.]

cover a range of 0 to 1600 pcph, while LOS E alone covers a range of 1600 to 2800 pcph—a range of 1200 pcph for a single level of service! Thus, service on a two-lane highway becomes poor at relatively low flow levels. Additional flow to the point of capacity simply cannot do too much additional damage to service quality!

This explains why few two-lane highways operate at or near capacity. Long before traffic reaches levels close to capacity, service has so seriously deteriorated that improvements have been formulated and implemented.

Figure 13-3 illustrates the relationship between speed and total flow on ideal two-lane highways. This is also an interesting relationship. Note that speed, even at capacity, remains fairly high—45 mph.

Speed on two-lane highways, however, is not a good measure of service. Many two-lane highways, particularly those serving primarily an access function, are located in terrain which does not permit operation at high speeds. Further, the relationship between flow and percent time delay does not appear to be seriously affected by design speed of the facility. Thus, speed is used only as a secondary measure for two-lane highways, and percent time delay is the parameter used to define levels of service.

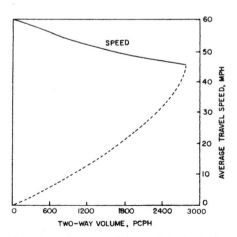

Figure 13-3 Speed versus flow on ideal two-lane highways. [Used with permission of Transportation Research Board, National Research Council, Washington, DC, from *Highway Capacity Manual, Special Report 209,* 3rd Ed., p. 8-4. Copyright © 1994 Transportation Research Board.]

There are two different computational methods for analysis of two-lane highways. The first applies to general terrain segments of level, rolling, or mountainous terrain. The second applies to specific isolated grades. Isolated grades are treated with a separate methodology, as the operating regime concerning passing is radically different on grades. The sections which follow detail these computational procedures.

B. Computational procedures for general terrain sections

The general terrain methodology is normally applied to sections of two-lane highway more than 2 miles long. Any grades that are both steeper than 3% *and* longer than ½ mile should be treated as isolated grades.

The relationship governing analysis of general terrain sections of two-lane highway is as follows:

$$SF_i = 2800\,(v/c)_i\,f_d\,f_w\,f_{HV} \qquad [13\text{-}1]$$

where: SF_i = service flow rate for LOS i, vph (total, both directions)
$(v/c)_i$ = maximum permissible v/c ratio for LOS i
f_d = adjustment factor for directional distribution
f_w = adjustment factor for narrow lanes and/or shoulders
f_{HV} = adjustment factor for heavy vehicles

The equation is always used in the form shown. In operational analysis, the service flow rate, SF, for each level of service is computed and compared to the actual or projected demand rate of flow. The demand rate of flow is usually converted from an hourly volume to a flow rate using the *PHF*:

$$v = \frac{V}{PHF} \qquad [13\text{-}2]$$

This procedure is used instead of a direct solution for the effective v/c ratio for freeways and multilane highways. This is because several of the adjustment factors for two-lane highways vary with level of service, and a direct solution for v/c would have to be iterated.

There is no "design analysis" for two-lane highways, as design analysis seeks to establish the number of lanes needed. This is not a variable for two-lane highways.

A simplified procedure for planning is presented in the 1985 and subsequent versions of the *HCM* and will be covered in a separate section of this chapter.

1. Values of *v/c*. Table 13-4 gives limiting values of *v/c* ratio for the various levels of service. The table also incorporates the variables of terrain and "percent no-passing zones." Note that among the ideal conditions for two-lane highways were level terrain and 100% available passing sight distance. Thus, Table 13-4 contains conditions that are not ideal. In actuality, Table 13-4 incorporates adjustments for terrain and passing sight distance that are not singled out for separate computation in the basic relationship of Equation [13-1]. For this reason, the *v/c* ratio at capacity (LOS E) is not always 1.00. For non-ideal conditions, the *v/c* ratios listed in Table 13-4 have already been reduced to reflect the non-ideal conditions.

Passing becomes increasingly difficult as the terrain becomes more severe. For this reason, capacity and service flow rates are lower in rolling and mountainous terrain than on level terrain.

Earlier, a methodology was presented for finding the minimum safe passing sight distance for two-lane highways. For most applications of capacity analysis, passing may be assumed to be permissible where sight distances are equal to or greater than 1500 ft. The "percent no-passing zones" is the percentage of the length of the section under study for which sight distance is less than 1500 ft. An average percentage for both directions is used. Thus, if 50% of the NB length and 40% of the SB length of a study section had sight distances of less than 1500 ft, the "percent no-passing zones" for the section would be taken to be 45%.

2. Adjustment for directional distribution. The adjustment factor for directional distribution is found in Table 13-5. The ideal condition is a traffic stream with 50% of the traffic in each direction. As the directional split becomes more unequal, the total capacity of a two-lane highway declines. At the point where the split is 100/0, that is, all traffic is in one direction, the capacity reduces to 2000 pcph, all in one lane.

On general terrain segments, it does not matter which direction the predominant flow is in, i.e., a

70/30 split has the same impact on capacity as a 30/70 split.

3. Adjustment factor for narrow lanes and shoulders. The adjustment factor for narrow lanes and shoulders, f_w, varies with level of service and is shown in Table 13-6. Note that for two-lane highways the factor addresses "usable shoulder width," rather than "lateral clearance." This is because the usable shoulder serves many functions on a two-lane highway, including an area for storage of stalled vehicles, and a place where slow-moving vehicles can pull over to allow others to pass. Some states now require that slow-moving vehicles periodically pull over to the shoulder to allow queued vehicles to pass. Restrictions on usable shoulder width have, therefore, a negative impact on overall operations on a two-lane highway.

4. Adjustment for heavy vehicles in the traffic stream. The presence of heavy vehicles in a two-lane traffic stream has an extremely negative impact on operations. As is the case on multilane highways, heavy vehicles are larger than passenger cars and therefore occupy more time-space on the facility. They cannot keep up with passenger cars, causing platoons to form behind them.

The latter impact is critical on a two-lane highway. Because passing opportunities are limited, the formation of platoons behind heavy vehicles severely restricts capacity. As more heavy vehicles enter a two-lane traffic stream, the demand for passing rises dramatically. At the same time, the presence of heavy vehicles in the opposing lane makes passing more difficult.

The heavy-vehicle factor on general terrain segments of two-lane highways is computed from passenger-car equivalents, just as for multilane highways:

$$f_{HV} = \frac{1}{1 + P_T(E_T - 1) + P_R(E_R - 1) + P_B(E_B - 1)}$$

where all terms are previously defined.

Passenger-car equivalents for trucks, RVs, and buses are given in Table 13-7. Note that PCEs for two-lane highways vary by level of service, reflecting the dynamics of passing of heavy vehicles, which becomes more difficult as traffic becomes more congested.

Table 13-4   Values of *v/c* Ratio for Various Levels of Service on General Terrain Segments of Two-Lane Highways

			v/c Ratio[a]					
			Level Terrain					
	Percent Time Delay	**Avg[b] Speed**	**Percent No-Passing Zones**					
LOS			**0**	**20**	**40**	**60**	**80**	**100**
A	≤30	≥58	0.15	0.12	0.09	0.07	0.05	0.04
B	≤45	≥55	0.27	0.24	0.21	0.19	0.17	0.16
C	≤60	≥52	0.43	0.39	0.36	0.34	0.33	0.32
D	≤75	≥50	0.64	0.62	0.60	0.59	0.58	0.57
E	>75	≥45	1.00	1.00	1.00	1.00	1.00	1.00
F	100	<45	—	—	—	—	—	—

			v/c Ratio[a]					
			Rolling Terrain					
	Percent Time Delay	**Avg[b] Speed**	**Percent No-Passing Zones**					
LOS			**0**	**20**	**40**	**60**	**80**	**100**
A	≤30	≥57	0.15	0.10	0.07	0.05	0.04	0.03
B	≤45	≥54	0.26	0.23	0.19	0.17	0.15	0.13
C	≤60	≥51	0.42	0.39	0.35	0.32	0.30	0.28
D	≤75	≥49	0.62	0.57	0.52	0.48	0.46	0.43
E	>75	≥40	0.97	0.94	0.92	0.91	0.90	0.90
F	100	<40	—	—	—	—	—	—

			v/c Ratio[a]					
			Mountainous Terrain					
	Percent Time Delay	**Avg[b] Speed**	**Percent No-Passing Zones**					
LOS			**0**	**20**	**40**	**60**	**80**	**100**
A	≤30	≥56	0.14	0.09	0.07	0.04	0.02	0.01
B	≤45	≥54	0.25	0.20	0.16	0.13	0.12	0.10
C	≤60	≥49	0.39	0.33	0.28	0.23	0.20	0.16
D	≤75	≥45	0.58	0.50	0.45	0.40	0.37	0.33
E	>75	≥35	0.91	0.87	0.84	0.82	0.80	0.78
F	100	<35	—	—	—	—	—	—

[a] Ratio of flow rate to an ideal capacity of 2800 pcph in both directions.

[b] Average travel speed of all vehicles (in mph) for highways with design speed ≥60 mph; for highways with lower design speeds, reduce speed by 4 mph for each 10-mph reduction in design speed below 60 mph; assumes that speed is not restricted to lower values by regulation.

[Used with permission of Transportation Research Board, National Research Council, Washington, DC, from *Highway Capacity Manual, Special Report 209*, 3rd Ed., p. 8-5. Copyright © 1994 Transportation Research Board.]

Table 13-5 Adjustment Factor for Directional Distribution

Directional Distribution	Factor, f_d
50/50	1.00
60/40	0.94
70/30	0.89
80/20	0.83
90/10	0.75
100/0	0.71

[Used with permission of Transportation Research Board, National Research Council, Washington, DC, from *Highway Capacity Manual, Special Report 209,* 3rd Ed., p. 8-9. Copyright © 1994 Transportation Research Board.]

5. Using the procedure. As noted previously, the procedure for general terrain segments is applied by computing the service flow rate, *SF,* for each level of service using Equation [13-1] and the tables discussed previously. These are compared to the actual rate of flow—either a present measured flow or a projected future flow—which is generally estimated from a known or projected hourly demand as $v = V/PHF$. The comparison allows for the determination of level of service and the approximate percent time delay to be expected on the facility.

Sample problems illustrating the procedure are presented later in this chapter.

Table 13-7 Passenger-Car Equivalents for Trucks, RVs, and Buses on General Terrain Segments of Two-Lane Highways

Vehicle Type	Level of Service	Type of Terrain		
		Level	Rolling	Mountainous
Trucks, E_T	A	2.0	4.0	7.0
	B and C	2.2	5.0	10.0
	D and E	2.0	5.0	12.0
RVs E_R	A	2.2	3.2	5.0
	B and C	2.5	3.9	5.2
	D and E	1.6	3.3	5.2
Buses, E_B	A	1.8	3.0	5.7
	B and C	2.0	3.4	6.0
	D and E	1.6	2.9	6.5

[Used with permission of Transportation Research Board, National Research Council, Washington, DC, from *Highway Capacity Manual, Special Report 209,* 3rd Ed., p. 8-9. Copyright © 1994 Transportation Research Board.]

C. Computational procedures for specific grades

Specific grades on two-lane highways are significantly different from grades on multilane highways. The existence of an extended upgrade aggravates the operation of heavy vehicles in the upgrade direction, causing more and longer platoons to form behind

Table 13-6 Adjustment Factor for Narrow Lanes and/or Shoulders

Usable[a] Shoulder Width (ft)	12-ft Lanes		11-ft Lanes		10-ft Lanes		9-ft Lanes	
	LOS A–D	LOS[b] E	LOS A–D	LOS[b] E	LOS A–D	LOS[b] E	LOS A–D	LOS[b] E
≥6	1.00	1.00	0.93	0.94	0.84	0.87	0.70	0.76
4	0.92	0.97	0.85	0.92	0.77	0.85	0.65	0.74
2	0.81	0.93	0.75	0.88	0.68	0.81	0.57	0.70
0	0.70	0.88	0.65	0.82	0.58	0.75	0.49	0.66

[a] Where shoulder width is different on each side of the roadway, use the average shoulder width.

[b] Factor applies for all speeds less than 45 mph.

[Used with permission of Transportation Research Board, National Research Council, Washington, DC, from *Highway Capacity Manual, Special Report 209,* 3rd Ed., p. 8-9. Copyright © 1994 Transportation Research Board.]

slow-moving vehicles than on general terrain segments. At the same time, the presence of the upgrade makes passing more difficult, causing drivers to be more conservative in attempting passing maneuvers.

Recent studies have also shown that passenger cars on two-lane upgrades do not maintain the same speeds as on general terrain segments. This makes the issue of passenger-car equivalents more difficult to deal with: One truck may be worth *x* cars on the grade—but what is one car on the grade equivalent to?

Directional distribution is also a more critical issue. On general terrain segments, a 70/30 directional distribution has the same impact as a 30/70 distribution. On sustained grades this is not the case. If 30% of the traffic is upgrade, the impact is very different from the case in which 30% of the traffic is in the downgrade direction.

Even basic level-of-service criteria are different for two-lane sustained grades. Level of service is related to the average upgrade speed, as indicated in Table 13-8.

The average upgrade speeds in Table 13-8 have been selected to produce approximately the same percent time-delay values for each LOS as for general terrain sections. As much of the data used to calibrate two-lane highway procedures was generated by simulation, it was not possible to exactly define percent time delay for specific grade sections.

Note also that it is not possible to define the upgrade speed at capacity. Capacity may occur at speeds anywhere between 25 and 40 mph, depending on the

severity and length of the grade. This complicates the computational procedure, as will be seen.

The general relationship governing the operation of specific grades on two-lane highways is

$$SF_i = 2800(v/c)_i\, f_d\, f_w\, f_g\, f_{HV} \qquad [13\text{-}3]$$

where: SF_i = service flow rate for LOS *i* (vph)
   $(v/c)_i$ = maximum *v/c* ratio that can be accommodated at LOS *i*
   f_d = adjustment factor for directional distribution
   f_w = adjustment factor for narrow lanes and/or shoulders
   f_g = adjustment factor for grade
   f_{HV} = adjustment factor for heavy vehicles

While this equation is quite similar to the one used for general terrain segments, its use and application differ significantly, as do the values of most of the adjustment factors.

For general terrain segments, the general equation was utilized to compute the service flow rates, *SF*, for each level of service. This will also be done for specific grades. The major difference is that capacity, or SF_E, cannot be easily defined, as the speed at which it occurs is variable. The subsections following detail the computational procedures used with Equation [13-3].

1. Finding basic values of *v/c* ratio. Table 13-9 gives basic values of *v/c* ratio for use in Equation [13-3]. Note that the table *does not* show *v/c* ratio versus level of service, but *v/c* ratios versus average upgrade speed. For levels of service A through D, LOS and average upgrade speed are related on a one-to-one basis. For LOS E, however, average upgrade speed varies, and it cannot be found at this point in the procedure. For this reason, Table 13-9 is organized with average upgrade speed as the independent variable. For convenience, the 1985 *HCM* recommends computing the service flow rate, *SF*, for average upgrade speeds of 55, 52.5, 50, 45, 40, 35, and 30 mph. As will be seen, this will allow the determination of capacity and service flow rates for all other levels of service.

Note further that some of the values of *v/c* in Table 13-9 are zero. For example, on a 7% grade with 20% "no-passing zones," the maximum allowable *v/c* ratio is 0.00 for an average upgrade speed of 55 mph. This simply means that even if there were only one vehicle

Table 13-8   Levels of Service for Specific Grades on Two-Lane Highways

Level of Service	Average Upgrade Speed, mph
A	≥55
B	≥50
C	≥45
D	≥40
E	≥25–40
F	<25–40

Table 13-9 Limiting Values of *v/c* Ratio for Two-Lane Highways, Specific Grade Sections

Percent Grade	Average Upgrade Speed (mph)	Percent No-Passing Zones					
		0	20	40	60	80	100
3	55	0.27	0.23	0.19	0.17	0.14	0.12
	52.5	0.42	0.38	0.33	0.31	0.29	0.27
	50	0.64	0.59	0.55	0.52	0.49	0.47
	45	1.00	0.95	0.91	0.88	0.86	0.84
	42.5	1.00	0.98	0.97	0.96	0.95	0.94
	40	1.00	1.00	1.00	1.00	1.00	1.00
4	55	0.25	0.21	0.18	0.16	0.13	0.11
	52.5	0.40	0.36	0.31	0.29	0.27	0.25
	50	0.61	0.56	0.52	0.49	0.47	0.45
	45	0.97	0.92	0.88	0.85	0.83	0.81
	42.5	0.99	0.96	0.95	0.94	0.93	0.92
	40	1.00	1.00	1.00	1.00	1.00	1.00
5	55	0.21	0.17	0.14	0.12	0.10	0.08
	52.5	0.36	0.31	0.27	0.24	0.22	0.20
	50	0.57	0.49	0.45	0.41	0.39	0.37
	45	0.93	0.84	0.79	0.75	0.72	0.70
	42.5	0.97	0.90	0.87	0.85	0.83	0.82
	40	0.98	0.96	0.95	0.94	0.93	0.92
	35	1.00	1.00	1.00	1.00	1.00	1.00
6	55	0.12	0.10	0.08	0.06	0.05	0.04
	52.5	0.27	0.22	0.18	0.16	0.14	0.13
	50	0.48	0.40	0.35	0.31	0.28	0.26
	45	0.79	0.76	0.68	0.63	0.59	0.55
	42.5	0.93	0.84	0.78	0.74	0.70	0.67
	40	0.97	0.91	0.87	0.83	0.81	0.78
	35	1.00	0.96	0.95	0.93	0.91	0.90
	30	1.00	0.99	0.99	0.98	0.98	0.98
7	55	0.00	0.00	0.00	0.00	0.00	0.00
	52.5	0.13	0.10	0.08	0.07	0.05	0.04
	50	0.34	0.27	0.22	0.18	0.15	0.12
	45	0.77	0.65	0.55	0.46	0.40	0.35
	42.5	0.86	0.75	0.67	0.60	0.54	0.48
	40	0.93	0.82	0.75	0.69	0.64	0.59
	35	1.00	0.91	0.87	0.82	0.79	0.76
	30	1.00	0.95	0.92	0.90	0.88	0.86

[a] Ratio of flow rate to ideal capacity of 2800 pcph, assuming passenger-car operation is unaffected by grade.

Note: Interpolate for intermediate values of "percent no-passing zone"; round "percent grade" to the next higher integer value.

[Used with permission of Transportation Research Board, National Research Council, Washington, DC, from *Highway Capacity Manual, Special Report 209,* 3rd Ed., p. 8-10. Copyright © 1994 Transportation Research Board.]

on a 7% two-lane highway upgrade, it would travel at a speed *under* 55 mph.

Table 13-9 also incorporates adjustments reflecting "percent no-passing zones" and severity of grade.

2. Adjustment factor for directional distribution.

The adjustment factor for directional distribution, f_d, is given in Table 13-10. It is based on the percent of traffic in the upgrade direction.

Note that for sustained grades, the directional distribution factor can be greater than 1.00. This means that a situation in which most of the traffic is traveling downgrade improves capacity and operations. This is not a surprising effect, as there are fewer vehicles that will travel at slow speeds on a downgrade, and the demand for passing in the downgrade direction would be expected to be minimal.

3. Adjustment factor for narrow lanes and/or shoulders.

The adjustment factor for narrow lanes and/or shoulders, f_w, is the same as that used for general terrain segments. It is found from Table 13-6, as previously discussed.

4. Adjustment factors for grade and heavy vehicles.

Both the grade factor, f_g, and the heavy-vehicle factor, f_{HV}, adjust ideal conditions (which include level terrain) to reflect operations on a sustained grade. As noted previously, this adjustment must account for the fact that trucks are different from passenger cars *and* that passenger cars on two-lane sustained grades operate differently from those on level sections.

Table 13-10 Adjustment Factor for Directional Distribution

Percent Traffic on Upgrade	Adjustment Factor
100	0.58
90	0.64
80	0.70
70	0.78
60	0.87
50	1.00
40	1.20
≤30	1.50

[Used with permission of Transportation Research Board, National Research Council, Washington, DC, from *Highway Capacity Manual, Special Report 209*, 3rd Ed., p. 8-11. Copyright © 1994 Transportation Research Board.]

Both adjustment factors are based on values of the passenger-car equivalent, E, which have been calibrated for a particular mix of heavy vehicles in the traffic stream: 14% trucks, 4% RVs, and no buses. This was the average mix of traffic on rural two-lane highways documented in a nationwide survey [4]. An analytic procedure allows for the modification of E to reflect the prevailing traffic mix.

Values of E, therefore, apply to all heavy vehicles in the traffic stream, regardless of type. This is a radically different approach than that taken for multilane highways and general terrain segments of two-lane highways. Values of E are given in Table 13-11.

Values of E vary with level of service, or average upgrade speed, as shown in the table. Note that the effect of heavy vehicles on a sustained upgrade can be enormous in extreme cases. For example, at 55 mph, one heavy vehicle on a 5% grade of 2 miles consumes as much capacity as *91* passenger cars. This reflects the impact of long gaps forming in front of slow-moving vehicles with the ability to pass restricted. For grades that are too long and/or steep to achieve the average upgrade speed stated, no passenger-car equivalent value is given.

The grade factor, f_g, adjusts for the difference between passenger-car operation on a sustained grade and on level terrain. It is found using Equations [13-4] and [13-5].

$$f_g = \frac{1}{1 + P_p I_p} \qquad [13\text{-}4]$$

$$I_p = 0.02(E - E_0) \qquad [13\text{-}5]$$

where: f_g = adjustment factor for grades
I_p = impedance factor for passenger cars on sustained upgrades
P_p = proportion of passenger cars in the traffic stream, expressed as a decimal
E = passenger-car equivalent for the standard mix of heavy vehicles on the percent and length of grade under consideration, obtained from Table 13-11 for values of average upgrade speed
E_0 = passenger-car equivalent for the standard mix of heavy vehicles on a 0% grade, obtained from Table 13-11 for values of average upgrade speed

Table 13-11 Passenger-Car Equivalents on Two-Lane Highways Sustained Grades

Grade (%)	Length of Grade (mi)	Average Upgrade Speed (mph)					
		55.0	52.5	50.0	45.0	40.0	30.0
0	All	2.0	1.8	1.6	1.4	1.3	1.3
3	¼	2.9	2.3	2.0	1.7	1.6	1.5
	½	3.7	2.9	2.4	2.0	1.8	1.7
	¾	4.8	3.6	2.9	2.3	2.0	1.9
	1	6.5	4.6	3.5	2.6	2.3	2.1
	1–½	11.2	6.6	5.1	3.4	2.9	2.5
	2	19.8	9.3	6.7	4.6	3.7	2.9
	3	71.0	21.0	10.8	7.3	5.6	3.8
	4	*a*	48.0	20.5	11.3	7.7	4.9
4	¼	3.2	2.5	2.2	1.8	1.7	1.6
	½	4.4	3.4	2.8	2.2	2.0	1.9
	¾	6.3	4.4	3.5	2.7	2.3	2.1
	1	9.6	6.3	4.5	3.2	2.7	2.4
	1–½	19.5	10.3	7.4	4.7	3.8	3.1
	2	43.0	16.1	10.8	6.9	5.3	3.8
	3	*a*	48.0	20.0	12.5	9.0	5.5
	4	*a*	*a*	51.0	22.8	13.8	7.4
5	¼	3.6	2.8	2.3	2.0	1.8	1.7
	½	5.4	3.9	3.2	2.5	2.2	2.0
	¾	8.3	5.7	4.3	3.1	2.7	2.4
	1	14.1	8.4	5.9	4.0	3.3	2.8
	1–½	34.0	16.0	10.8	6.3	4.9	3.8
	2	91.0	28.3	17.4	10.2	7.5	4.8
	3	*a*	*a*	37.0	22.0	14.6	7.8
	4	*a*	*a*	*a*	55.0	25.0	11.5
6	¼	4.0	3.1	2.5	2.1	1.9	1.8
	½	6.5	4.8	3.7	2.8	2.4	2.2
	¾	11.0	7.2	5.2	3.7	3.1	2.7
	1	20.4	11.7	7.8	4.9	4.0	3.3
	1–½	60.0	25.2	16.0	8.5	6.4	4.7
	2	*a*	50.0	28.2	15.3	10.7	6.3
	3	*a*	*a*	70.0	38.0	23.9	11.3
	4	*a*	*a*	*a*	90.0	45.0	18.1
7	¼	4.5	3.4	2.7	2.2	2.0	1.9
	½	7.9	5.7	4.2	3.2	2.7	2.4
	¾	14.5	9.1	6.3	4.3	3.6	3.0
	1	31.4	16.0	10.0	6.1	4.8	3.8
	1–½	*a*	39.5	23.5	11.5	8.4	5.8
	2	*a*	88.0	46.0	22.8	15.4	8.2
	3	*a*	*a*	*a*	66.0	38.5	16.1
	4	*a*	*a*	*a*	*a*	*a*	*28.0*

a Speed not attainable on grade specified.

Note: Round "percent grade" to next higher integer value.

[Used with permission of Transportation Research Board, National Research Council, Washington, DC, from *Highway Capacity Manual, Special Report 209,* 3rd Ed., p. 8-12. Copyright © 1994 Transporation Research Board.]

The adjustment factor for heavy vehicles, f_{HV}, adjusts for the presence of heavy vehicles in the traffic stream. It is found using Equations [13-6] and [13-7].

$$f_{HV} = \frac{1}{1 + P_{HV}(E_{HV} - 1)} \quad [13\text{-}6]$$

$$E_{HV} = 1 + (0.25 + P_{T/HV})(E - 1) \quad [13\text{-}7]$$

where: f_{HV} = heavy-vehicle factor
  E_{HV} = passenger-car equivalent for the prevailing mix of heavy vehicles in the traffic stream
  P_{HV} = proportion of all heavy vehicles in the traffic stream, expressed as a decimal
  $P_{T/HV}$ = proportion of trucks among heavy vehicles in the traffic stream (for example, 10% trucks, 5% RVs, 5% buses: $P_{T/HV} = 10/(10 + 5 + 5) = 0.50$)
  E = passenger-car equivalent for the standard mix of heavy vehicles for the percent and length of grade under consideration, found in Table 13-11 for values of average upgrade speed

5. Finding capacity. Once all adjustment factors have been determined, service flow rates, *SF*, may be determined for average upgrade speeds of 55, 52.5, 50, 45, 40, and 30 mph. This automatically determines the service flow rate for levels of service A through D, which correspond directly to speeds of 55, 50, 45, and 40 mph respectively. The speed at which capacity occurs, however, is variable, and cannot be directly computed using the service-flow-rate relationship. In effect, computations of service flow rate for various speeds provide a relationship between average upgrade speed and resulting service flow rate that can be plotted. It will be necessary to prepare such a plot to determine capacity and the speed at which it occurs.

As a result of the simulation studies undertaken to develop the two-lane highway analysis procedures [4], a relationship was established between the value of capacity of a two-lane sustained grade and the speed at which it occurs. The relationship is

$$S_c = 25 + 3.75\left(\frac{c}{1000}\right)^2 \quad [13\text{-}8]$$

where: S_c = critical speed at which capacity occurs (mph)
  c = capacity (in mixed vph)

This relationship may also be plotted. It is the intersection of Equation [13-8] with the relationship generated by computing service flow rates for various average upgrade operating speeds that defines capacity and the speed at which it occurs.

Because the determination of capacity is complex, the worksheet provided in the 1985 *HCM* is a useful tool in implementing the procedure for sustained grades on two-lane highways. It is a two-page form, as illustrated in Figure 13-4.

The first page of the form allows for summarizing computations of service flow rates at various average upgrade speeds. The second page allows for this to be plotted. Note that Equation [13-8], which is always the same, is already plotted on the worksheet. The intersection of this line with the plotted values of *SF* versus speed determines capacity. The lower part of the second page of the worksheet allows for service flow rates for LOS A through E to be summarized and compared to an actual or projected flow rate to determine level of service.

D. Sample problems for general terrain and sustained grade sections

The following sample calculations illustrate the computational procedures for sustained upgrades on two-lane highways.

SAMPLE PROBLEM 1: FINDING LEVEL OF SERVICE FOR A GENERAL TERRAIN SEGMENT

PROBLEM STATEMENT: A two-lane rural highway carries a peak-hour volume of 200 vph and has the following characteristics:

1. *Roadway Characteristics:* 70-mph design speed; 11-ft lanes; 2-ft shoulders; mountainous terrain; 80% no-passing zones; length = 10 miles.
2. *Traffic Characteristics:* 50/50 directional split; 5% trucks; 10% recreational vehicles; no buses; 85% passenger cars; *PHF* = 0.90.

At what level of service will the highway operate during peak periods?

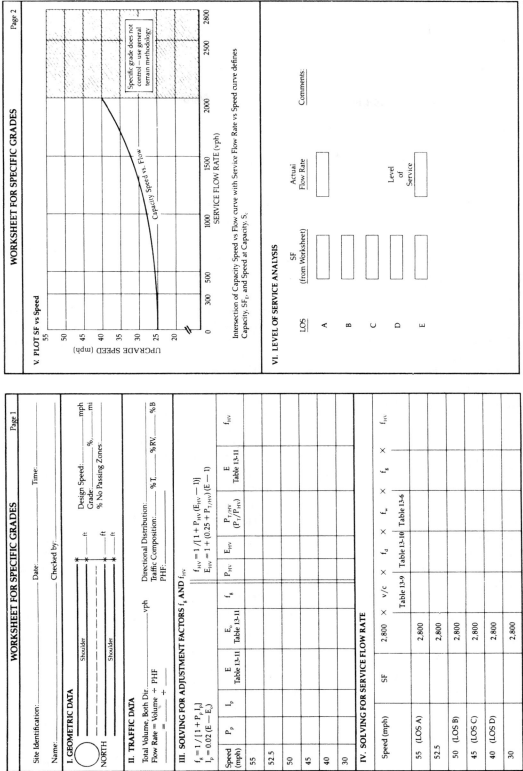

Figure 13-4 A worksheet for two-lane highway sustained grades. [Used with permission of Transportation Research Board, National Research Council, Washington, DC, from *Highway Capacity Manual, Special Report 209*, 3rd Ed., p. 8-16. Copyright © 1994 Transportation Research Board.]

SOLUTION: The solution is found by comparing the actual flow rate to service flow rates computed for each LOS. The actual flow rate is found as:

$$v = \frac{V}{PHF}$$

where:

$$V = 200 \text{ vph (given)}$$

$$PHF = 0.90 \text{ (given)}$$

and:

$$v = \frac{200}{0.90} = 222 \text{ vph}$$

Service flow rates are computed for general terrain segments as

$$SF_i = 2800 \, (v/c)_i \, f_d \, f_w \, f_{HV}$$

$$f_{HV} = \frac{1}{1 + P_T(E_T - 1) + P_R(E_R - 1) + P_B(E_B - 1)}$$

where: v/c = 0.02 (LOS A)   0.37 (LOS D)
           0.12 (LOS B)   0.80 (LOS E)
           0.20 (LOS C)
           (Table 13-4, mountainous, 80%
           no-passing zones)
       f_d = 1.00 (Table 13-5, 50/50 split)
       f_w = 0.75 (LOS A–D)
           0.88 (LOS E)
           (Table 13-6, 11-ft lanes, 2-ft shoulders)
       E_T = 7 (LOS A) E_R = 5.0 (LOS A)
           10 (LOS B, C)   5.2 (LOS B–E)
           12 (LOS D, E)
           (Table 13-7, mountainous)
       P_T = 0.05 (given) P_R = 0.10 (given)

Then:

$$f_{HV} \text{ (LOS A)} = \frac{1}{1 + 0.05(7 - 1) + 0.10(5.0 - 1)}$$

$$= 0.588$$

$$\text{(LOS B, C)} = \frac{1}{1 + 0.05(10 - 1) + 0.10(5.2 - 1)}$$

$$= 0.535$$

$$\text{(LOS D, E)} = \frac{1}{1 + 0.05(12 - 1) + 0.10(5.2 - 1)}$$

$$= 0.508$$

and:

$$SF_A = 2800 \times 0.02 \times 1.00 \times 0.75 \times 0.588$$

$$= 24 \text{ vph}$$

$$SF_B = 2800 \times 0.12 \times 1.00 \times 0.75 \times 0.535$$

$$= 135 \text{ vph}$$

$$SF_C = 2800 \times 0.20 \times 1.00 \times 0.75 \times 0.535$$

$$= 224 \text{ vph}$$

$$SF_D = 2800 \times 0.37 \times 1.00 \times 0.75 \times 0.508$$

$$= 395 \text{ vph}$$

$$SF_E = 2800 \times 0.80 \times 1.00 \times 0.88 \times 0.508$$

$$= 1001 \text{ vph}$$

If the actual flow rate of 222 vph (which represents the flow rate during the peak 15 minutes of flow) is compared to these values, it is seen that it is higher than the service flow rate for LOS B (135 vph) but is barely less than the service flow rate for LOS C (224 vph). Therefore, the level of service for the highway is C for the conditions described.

DISCUSSION: This problem illustrates several points. On severe terrain, such as the situation for this problem, "good" operating conditions can be sustained only at low flow rates. The capacity of the roadway is also severely limited, reaching only 1001 vph, which is approximately one-third of the ideal capacity of 2800 vph. Note that the v/c ratio used in the computation of capacity is only 0.80. This is because all v/c ratios in the two-lane methodology are referenced to the ideal capacity of 2800 vph, which cannot be achieved in severe terrain with passing-sight-distance restrictions.

SAMPLE PROBLEM 2: FINDING LEVEL OF SERVICE AND CAPACITY OF A SPECIFIC GRADE

PROBLEM STATEMENT: A rural two-lane highway in mountainous terrain has a grade of 7%, 2 miles long. It currently carries a peak-hour volume of 600 vph. Other relevant characteristics include:

1. *Roadway Characteristics:* 60-mph design speed; 11-ft lanes; 4-ft shoulders; 80% no-passing zones.
2. *Traffic Characteristics:* 80/20 directional split; 4% trucks; 10% recreational vehicles; 2% buses; 84% passenger cars; *PHF* = 0.91.

At what level of service does the grade operate? What upgrade speed can be expected during the peak 15 minutes of flow? What is the capacity of the grade? If the approach speed to the grade is 55 mph, what delay is incurred by vehicles climbing the grade?

SOLUTION: The finding of capacity for a specific grade requires plotting of the service-flow-rate-versus-speed curve. Service flow rates on a sustained two-lane highway grade are computed as

$$SF_i = 2800 \, (v/c)_i \, f_d \, f_w \, f_g \, f_{HV}$$

where: $f_g = \dfrac{1}{1 + P_p I_p}$

$I_p = 0.02(E - E_0)$

and:

$$f_{HV} = \dfrac{1}{1 + P_{HV}(E_{HV} - 1)}$$

$$E_{HV} = 1 + (0.25 + P_{T/HV})(E - 1)$$

Capacity is found at the point where this curve intersects the speed-at-capacity-versus-capacity curve on the worksheet. The upgrade speed is found by entering this curve with the actual flow rate.

To plot the curve, the procedure recommends computing service-flow-rate points for the following speeds: 55 mph (LOS A), 52.5 mph, 50 mph (LOS B), 45 mph (LOS C), 40 mph (LOS D), and 30 mph. These points would be plotted on the specific grade worksheet and a smooth curve constructed. Once capacity is determined, the service flow rates for every LOS will be known, and the actual LOS can be determined by comparing the actual flow rate to the computed values.

The following values are used in these computations:

$v/c = 0.00$ (55 mph)   0.05 (52.5 mph)
0.15 (50 mph)   0.40 (45 mph)
0.64 (40 mph)   0.88 (30 mph)
(Table 13-9, 7% grade, 80% no-passing zones)

$f_d = 0.70$ (Table 13-10, 80/20 split)

$f_w = 0.85$ (55–45 mph)
0.92 (40–30 mph)
(Table 13-6, 11-ft lanes, 4-ft shoulders)

$E = 88.0$ (52.5 mph)   46.0 (50 mph)
22.8 (45 mph)   15.4 (40 mph)
8.2 (30 mph)
(Table 13-11, 7% grade, 2 mi, no value given for 55 mph)

$E_0 = 1.8$ (52.5 mph)   1.6 (50 mph)
1.4 (45 mph)   1.3 (40–30 mph)
(Table 13-11, 0% grade)

$P_p = 0.84$ (given)

$P_{HV} = P_T + P_R + P_B = 0.04 + 0.10 + 0.02$
$= 0.16$

$$P_{T/HV} = \dfrac{P_T}{P_{HV}} = \dfrac{0.04}{0.16} = 0.25$$

Values of f_g may now be computed as follows:

$I_P(52.5) = 0.02(88.0 - 1.8) = 1.724$

$(50.0) = 0.02(46.0 - 1.6) = 0.888$

$(45.0) = 0.02(22.8 - 1.4) = 0.428$

$(40.0) = 0.02(15.4 - 1.3) = 0.282$

$(30.0) = 0.02(8.2 - 1.3) = 0.138$

$$f_g(52.5) = \dfrac{1}{1 + 0.84(1.724)} = 0.41$$

$$(50.0) = \dfrac{1}{1 + 0.84(0.888)} = 0.57$$

$$(45.0) = \dfrac{1}{1 + 0.84(0.428)} = 0.74$$

$$(40.0) = \dfrac{1}{1 + 0.84(0.282)} = 0.81$$

$$(30.0) = \dfrac{1}{1 + 0.84(0.138)} = 0.90$$

Values of f_{HV} are also computed:

$E_{HV}(52.5) = 1 + (0.25 + 0.25)(88.0 - 1) = 44.5$

$(50.0) = 1 + (0.25 + 0.25)(46.0 - 1) = 23.6$

$(45.0) = 1 + (0.25 + 0.25)(22.8 - 1) = 11.9$

$(40.0) = 1 + (0.25 + 0.25)(15.4 - 1) = 8.2$

$(30.0) = 1 + (0.25 + 0.25)(8.2 - 1) = 4.6$

$$f_{HV}(52.5) = \frac{1}{1 + 0.16(44.5 - 1)} = 0.13$$

$$(50.0) = \frac{1}{1 + 0.16(23.6 - 1)} = 0.22$$

$$(45.0) = \frac{1}{1 + 0.16(11.9 - 1)} = 0.36$$

$$(40.0) = \frac{1}{1 + 0.16(8.2 - 1)} = 0.46$$

$$(30.0) = \frac{1}{1 + 0.16(4.6 - 1)} = 0.63$$

Having computed all relevant factors, the total two-way service flow rates for the designated speeds may be computed:

Speed	$2800 \times$	$v/c \times$	$f_d \times$	$f_w \times$	$f_g \times$	$f_{HV} =$	SF
55.0	2800	0.00	0.70	0.85	****	****	0 vph
52.5	2800	0.05	0.70	0.85	0.41	0.13	4 vph
50.0	2800	0.15	0.70	0.85	0.57	0.22	31 vph
45.0	2800	0.40	0.70	0.85	0.74	0.36	178 vph
40.0	2800	0.64	0.70	0.92	0.81	0.46	430 vph
30.0	2800	0.88	0.70	0.92	0.90	0.63	900 vph

Note that the low or zero service flow rate for 55.0 mph indicates that this average upgrade speed is virtually impossible to maintain on the upgrade described in this problem.

These computations are summarized on the specific grade worksheet, shown in Figure 13-5. The curve defined by these points is also plotted on the worksheet. The intersection of the plotted curve with the speed-at-capacity-versus-flow-rate-at-capacity curve indicates that capacity is *1010 vph*, total in both directions, which occurs at an average upgrade speed of *28.0 mph*.

To find the existing level of service, the volume of 600 vph is converted to a flow rate for the peak 15-minute period:

$$v = \frac{V}{PHF} = \frac{600}{0.91} = 659 \text{ vph}$$

The plotted curve is entered on the worksheet with 659 vph, and the upgrade speed is found to be *35 mph*. As this speed is less than 40 mph, the minimum value for LOS D (Table 13-8), but greater than the speed at

capacity (28 mph), the level of service is E. This can also be determined by comparing the actual flow rate of 659 vph with the service flow rate for LOS D (40 mph) of 430 vph and capacity (1010 vph).

The last part of this problem asks us to find the delay incurred by vehicles traveling up the grade. "Delay" is defined as the difference in travel time experienced by vehicles traversing the upgrade at the existing speed and the travel time which would be experienced if they were able to maintain their approach speed on the grade. Thus:

Travel time at 55.0 mph

$$= (2 \text{ mi}/55 \text{ mph}) \times 3600 \text{ sec/hr}$$

$$= 130.9 \text{ sec/veh}$$

Travel time at 35.0 mph

$$= (2 \text{ mi}/35 \text{ mph}) \times 3600 \text{ sec/hr}$$

$$= 205.7 \text{ sec/veh}$$

$$\text{Delay} = 205.7 - 130.9$$

$$= 74.8 \text{ sec/veh}$$

SAMPLE PROBLEM 3: ANOTHER SPECIFIC GRADE

PROBLEM STATEMENT: A two-lane rural highway section consists of a 5% grade, 1 mile long. The peak hour demand is 400 vph, with a 70/30 directional split—70% upgrade in the P.M., 70% downgrade in the A.M., 5% trucks, 15% RVs, and a PHF of 0.88. The section has ideal lane widths and shoulders. Find the capacity of the section for the A.M. and P.M. peak hours, and the average upgrade speed during those periods.

SOLUTION: Use significant grade method. Plot curves for *SF* vs. Average Upgrade Speed for A.M. and P.M. peak hours.

a. The peak hour volume must be converted to a peak demand flow rate within the peak hour:

$$v = \frac{400}{0.88} = 455 \text{ vph}$$

b. Service flow rates for various upgrade speeds are computed as:

$$SF_i = 2800 \, (v/c)_i \, f_d \, f_w \, f_g \, f_{HV}$$

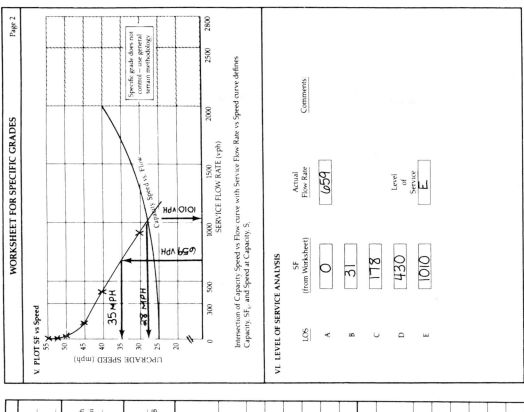

Figure 13-5 Worksheet for sample problem 2.

Page 2

WORKSHEET FOR SPECIFIC GRADES

V. PLOT SF vs Speed

Plot of SF vs Speed, with UPGRADE SPEED (mph) on the vertical axis (from 20 to 55) and SERVICE FLOW RATE (vph) on the horizontal axis (0 to 2800).

- 35 MPH
- 28 MPH
- 659 VPH
- 1010 VPH
- Capacity Speed vs. Flow

Specific grade does not control — use general terrain methodology.

Intersection of Capacity Speed vs Flow curve with Service Flow Rate vs Speed curve defines Capacity, SF_E, and Speed at Capacity, S.

VI. LEVEL OF SERVICE ANALYSIS

LOS	SF (from Worksheet)
A	0
B	31
C	178
D	430
E	1010

Actual Flow Rate: **659**

Level of Service: **E**

Comments:

Page 1

WORKSHEET FOR SPECIFIC GRADES

Site Identification: **SAMPLE PROBLEM 2**   Date: ____   Time: ____

Name: **R. ROESS**   Checked by: ____

I. GEOMETRIC DATA

Design Speed: **60** mph
Grade: **7** %   **2** mi
% No Passing Zones: **80**

Shoulder * **4** ft
* **22** ft
Shoulder * **4** ft

II. TRAFFIC DATA

Total Volume, Both Dir.: **600** vph
Flow Rate = Volume ÷ PHF
659 = **600** ÷ **0.91**

Directional Distribution: **4** % T. **10** % RV. **2** % B
Traffic Composition: **80/20**
PHF: **0.91**

III. SOLVING FOR ADJUSTMENT FACTORS f_g AND f_{HV}

$f_g = 1/[1 + P_p I_p]$
$I_p = 0.02 (E - E_o)$

$f_{HV} = 1/[1 + P_{HV}(E_{HV} - 1)]$
$E_{HV} = 1 + (0.25 + P_{T/HV})(E - 1)$

Speed (mph)	P_p	I_p	E Table 13-11	E_o Table 13-11	f_g	P_{HV}	E_{HV}	$P_{T,HV}$ (P_T/P_{HV})	E Table 13-11	f_{HV}
55										
52.5	.84	1.704	88	1.8	.41	.16	44.5	.25	88	.13
50	.84	.888	46	1.6	.57	.16	23.5	.25	46	.22
45	.84	.428	22.8	1.4	.74	.16	11.9	.25	22.8	.36
40	.84	.282	15.4	1.3	.81	.16	8.2	.25	15.4	.46
30	.84	.138	8.2	1.3	.90	.16	4.6	.25	8.2	.63

IV. SOLVING FOR SERVICE FLOW RATE

Speed (mph)	SF		v/c Table 13-9	f_d Table 13-10	f_w Table 13-6	f_g	f_{HV}
55 (LOS A)	0	2,800	.00	.70	.85	—	—
52.5	4	2,800	.05	.70	.85	.41	.13
50 (LOS B)	31	2,800	.15	.70	.85	.57	.22
45 (LOS C)	178	2,800	.40	.70	.85	.74	.36
40 (LOS D)	430	2,800	.64	.70	.92	.81	.46
30	900	2,800	.88	.70	.92	.90	.63

327

Computation For Problem 3

	Avg Upgrade Speed	E	E_o
	55 mph	14.1	2.1
	52.5 mph	8.4	1.8
	50 mph	5.9	1.6
	45 mph	4.0	1.4
	40 mph	3.3	1.3
	35 mph	3.05	1.3

Computing f_g:

Speed	$I_p = 0.02\,(E - E_o)$	$f_g = 1/[1 + P_p I_p]$
55 mph	0.02(14.1 − 2.1) = 0.24	1/[1 + (0.80)(0.24)] = 0.839
52.5 mph	0.02(8.4 − 1.8) = 0.132	1/[1 + (0.80)(0.132)] = 0.904
50 mph	0.02(5.9 − 1.6) = 0.086	1/[1 + (0.80)(0.086)] = 0.937
45 mph	0.02(4.0 − 1.4) = 0.052	1/[1 + (0.80)(0.052)] = 0.960
40 mph	0.02(3.3 − 1.3) = 0.040	1/[1 + (0.80)(0.040)] = 0.969
35 mph	0.01(3.05 − 1.3) = 0.035	1/[1 + (0.80)(0.035)] = 0.973

Computing f_{HV}:

Speed	$E_{HV} = 1 + (0.25 + P_{T/HV})(E - 1)$	$f_{HV} = 1/[1 + P_{HV}(E_{HV} - 1)]$
55 mph	1 + (0.25 + 0.25)(14.1 − 1) = 7.550	1/[1 + 0.20(6.550)] = 0.432
52.5 mph	1 + (0.500)(8.4 − 1) = 4.700	1/[1 + 0.20(3.700)] = 0.575
50 mph	1 + (0.500)(5.9 − 1) = 3.450	1/[1 + 0.20(2.450)] = 0.671
45 mph	1 + (0.500)(4.0 − 1) = 2.500	1/[1 + 0.20(1.500)] = 0.769
40 mph	1 + (0.500)(3.3 − 1) = 2.150	1/[1 + 0.20(1.150)] = 0.813
35 mph	1 + (0.500)(3.05 − 1) = 2.025	1/[1 + 0.20(1.025)] = 0.830

Computing A.M. Peak Service Flow Rates

Speed	$SF = 2800\ v/c\ f_d\ f_w\ f_g\ f_{HV}$	
55 mph	2800(0.08)(1.5)(1.0)(0.839)(0.432) =	122 vph
52.5 mph	2800(0.20)(1.5)(1.0)(0.904)(0.575) =	437 vph
50 mph	2800(0.37)(1.5)(1.0)(0.937)(0.671) =	977 vph
45 mph	2800(0.70)(1.5)(1.0)(0.960)(0.769) =	2,170 vph*
40 mph	2800(0.92)(1.5)(1.0)(0.969)(0.813) =	3,044 vph*
35 mph	2800(1.00)(1.5)(1.0)(0.973)(0.830) =	3,392 vph*

Computing P.M. Peak Service Flow Rates

In computing P.M. service flow rates, the only change is in the directional distribution factor, as 70% of the trucks are now going *upgrade* rather than *downgrade,* as in the A.M. All other factors remain unchanged.

Speed	$SF = 2800\ v/c\ f_d\ f_w\ f_g\ f_{HV}$	
55 mph	2800(0.08)(0.78)(1.0)(0.839)(0.432) =	63 vph
52.3 mph	2800(0.20)(0.78)(1.0)(0.904)(0.575) =	227 vph
50 mph	2800(0.37)(0.78)(1.0)(0.937)(0.671) =	508 vph
45 mph	2800(0.70)(0.78)(1.0)(0.960)(0.769) =	1129 vph
40 mph	2800(0.92)(0.78)(1.0)(0.969)(0.813) =	1583 vph
35 mph	2800(1.00)(0.78)(1.0)(0.973)(0.830) =	1764 vph

Where: v/c = 0.08 (55 mph); 0.20 (52.5 mph); 0.37 (50 mph); 0.70 (45 mph); 0.92 (40 mph); 1.00 (35 mph)-Table 13-9, for 100% NO PASSING zones
f_d = 1.5 (A.M.); 0.78 (P.M.)
f_w = 1.00 (ideal conditions)

Values of E and E_o are found in Table 13-11. Values of f_g and f_{HV} are computed from these as shown on page 328. Service flow rates for AM and PM peak periods are also computed as shown on page 328.

The asterisk requires that the details of the specific upgrade procedure be consulted. For values of $SF >$ 2,000 vph, the specific grade methodology is not valid. Thus, it cannot be used to find the capacity of the section. The capacity must be based on the general terrain methodology, as follows:

$$SF(\text{LOS E}) = 2800 \, v/c \, f_d \, f_w \, f_{HV}$$

where: v/c (LOS E) = 1.00 (Table 13-4) level terrain
f_d = 0.89 (Table 13-5)
f_w = 1.00 (Table 13-6)
E_T = 2.0 (Table 13-7) level terrain
E_R = 1.6 (Table 13-7) level terrain
f_{HV} = $1/[1 + 0.05(2 - 1) + 0.10(1.6 - 1)] = 0.901$,

and:

$SF(\text{LOS E}) =$
$2800(1.00)(0.89)(1.0)(0.901) = 2245$ vph

Note that for values of $SF \leq 2000$ vph, the specific upgrade technique is *valid,* and that these points may still be plotted on the worksheet.

c. The computed A.M. and P.M. service flow rates are plotted on the specific grade worksheet as shown. Note that the A.M. curve does not intercept the capacity vs. speed curve; thus capacity for the A.M. is determined by the general segment methodology as indicated (2245 vph). The capacity in the P.M. is governed by the intersection of the SF vs. speed and capacity vs. speed curves, and is seen to be 1775 vph. At the given demand flow rate of 455 vph, the average upgrade speed is expected to be 53.0 mph in the A.M. and 50.5 mph in the P.M.

E. General planning methodology

Because two-lane highways are often designed for rural situations with relatively low demands, it is convenient for analysts to evaluate capacity and level of service for such facilities on the basis of AADT

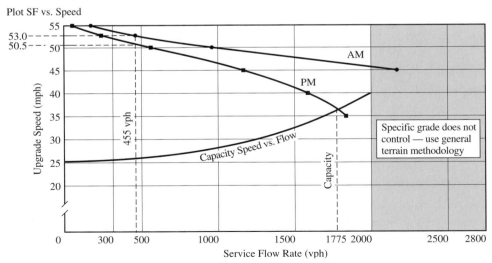

Figure 13-6 Service flow rate (vph)

volumes. Table 13-12 shows maximum AADT volumes for two-lane highways versus the worst level of service that would occur during any 15-minute analysis period of the day. The table also uses the *K*-factor, discussed previously. The *K*-factor is the percentage of daily traffic expected during the peak hour; it is a local or regional characteristic calibrated from regular state or local volume-counting programs.

To convert level-of-service criteria to AADT criteria, Table 13-12 incorporates many assumptions as to average conditions found on two-lane highways:

- 60/40 directional split
- 14% trucks, 4% RVs, no buses
- *PHF* based upon random arrivals
- 20% no-passing zones for level terrain
- 40% no-passing zones for rolling terrain
- 60% no-passing zones for mountainous terrain

Thus, Table 13-12 is a useful planning tool for general consideration of future two-lane highway conditions. It is not useful for detailed analysis purposes, owing to the nature of the assumptions made.

Consider the following problem: A two-lane highway carrying an AADT of 5000 vpd is located in level terrain in an area where the design-hour factor (*K*) is 0.14. The area has a traffic growth rate of 5% per year. The responsible highway agency's policy is to expand two-lane highways to four lanes before the level of service becomes E during peak periods. In how many years will expansion of the facility have to be completed under this policy? If it will take six years to construct a four-lane highway, how long will it be until the construction project should begin?

SOLUTION: The policy requires that expansion of the highway be completed before the AADT exceeds the maximum allowable value for LOS D. From Table 13-12, the maximum AADT for LOS D, for level terrain and a *K* factor of 0.14, is 9600 vpd.

The question now becomes: How many years will it take an AADT of 5000 vpd to grow to 9600 vpd at a rate of 5% per year? Therefore:

$$9600 = 5000(1 + 0.05)^n$$

$$n = 13.6 \text{ years}$$

Construction should begin in 13.6 − 6 years, or in 7.6 years.

Table 13-12   Maximum AADTs versus Level of Service during Peak Periods

K-Factor	Level of Service				
	A	B	C	D	E
0.10	2400	4800	7900	13,500	22,900
0.11	2200	4400	7200	12,200	20,800
0.12	2000	4000	6600	11,200	19,000
0.13	1900	3700	6100	10,400	17,600
0.14	1700	3400	5700	9600	16,300
0.15	1600	3200	5300	9000	15,200
Rolling Terrain					
0.10	1100	2800	5200	8000	14,800
0.11	1000	2500	4700	7200	13,500
0.12	900	2300	4400	6600	12,300
0.13	900	2100	4000	6100	11,400
0.14	800	2000	3700	5700	10,600
0.15	700	1800	3500	5300	9900
Mountainous Terrain					
0.10	500	1300	2400	3700	8100
0.11	400	1200	2200	3400	7300
0.12	400	1100	2000	3100	6700
0.13	400	1000	1800	2900	6200
0.14	300	900	1700	2700	5800
0.15	300	900	1600	2500	5400

Note: All values rounded to the nearest 100 vpd. Assumed conditions include 60/40 directional split, 14% trucks, 4% RVs, no buses, and *PHF* values from *HCM* Table 8-3. For level terrain, 20% no-passing zones were assumed; for rolling terrain, 40% no-passing zones; for mountainous terrain, 60% no-passing zones.

F. Operational and design improvements for two-lane highways

What happens where a capacity analysis of a two-lane highway indicates existing or future operations in an unacceptable range? Unlike other types of facilities where the *HCM* can be used to evaluate various design improvements (such as adding lanes), a two-lane highway either works acceptably or not. Yet, the decision to expand the highway to a four-lane facility has enormous economic consequences.

A number of improvements can be applied to two-lane highways short of expansion to a four-lane facility. Some of these involve various three-lane treatments, others involve periodic addition of passing and/or climbing lanes to the two-lane facility. The *HCM* presents these alternatives, but points out that at the present time, the precise capacity and level-of-service impacts of each of these improvements are not well understood, nor can they be quantified using available techniques.

The more prevalent of these improvements are briefly described in the following paragraphs.

1. Improvements to passing sight distance. Improvement of the alignment of a two-lane highway can decrease the number and length of "no-passing zones" and improve capacity and operations. This feature can be evaluated directly using the procedures in this chapter. This can, however, be an expensive undertaking, as vertical and horizontal alignment must be made less severe.

2. Addition of passing lanes. Where the alignment is such that the distance between passing opportunities is long and/or queuing is extensive, consideration should be given to the periodic provision of exclusive passing lanes for each direction. This can be done in several ways. A continuous three-lane alignment can be provided with the center lane alternatively assigned for exclusive use of one direction at a time. A third lane can be added periodically to provide for passing of vehicles in one direction. If conditions permit, the two-lane highway can be improved to four lanes periodically to provide for passing in both directions every so often.

A study of passing lanes in Canada [5] indicated that the maximum distance to a passing lane in a given direction should follow these guidelines:

Total Two-Way Volume (vph)	Maximum Distance to Next Passing Opportunity (mi)
400	5.0
300	6.5
200	9.0

In general, the minimum length of such passing lanes should be 1.00 to 1.25 miles. Provision of such lanes allows platoons to break up periodically, and while they do not improve the level of service on any given section, drivers are subjected to queues for shorter periods, and over a long trip, have significantly lower travel times.

3. Addition of climbing lanes. Addition of a heavy-vehicle climbing lane is often a useful treatment on sustained upgrades which can negate many of the negative impacts of heavy vehicles on such grades. The 1985 *HCM* gives three criteria for providing a climbing lane, all of which must be met to justify adding the lane:

- Upgrade flow rate exceeds 200 vph
- Upgrade truck flow rate exceeds 20 vph
- One of the following exists:
     LOS E or F exists on the grade;
     LOS on grade is two or more levels less than on approach;
     trucks must reduce speeds by more than 10 mph on the upgrade.

The last condition is most often met by a reduction in upgrade truck operating speeds. Figure 13-7 gives speed-reduction curves for a 200-lb/hp (typical) and a 300-lb/hp (heavy) truck which may be used to estimate the reduction in truck speeds on a two-lane highway upgrade.

4. Turnouts. Turnouts are short sections of pavement on the side of a two-lane highway provided to allow slow-moving platoon vehicles to periodically "turn out" of the traffic stream and allow following vehicles to pass. One study [6] indicated that turnouts are generally safe and are used by about 10% of platoon leaders. While they are not a substitute for periodic passing lanes, they can be useful in areas of severe terrain where other treatments are not possible.

Another study [7] indicated that the length of the turnout should correspond to the speed of approaching vehicles:

Approach Speed (mph)	Minimum Length of Turnout (ft)
25	200
30	200
40	250
50	375
55	450
60	535

Lengths over 500 ft are used only on downgrades exceeding 3% where high approach speeds are expected. Lengths over 600 ft are never used, as drivers may mistake these for passing lanes.

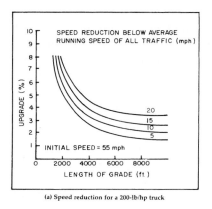

(a) Speed reduction for a 200-lb/hp truck

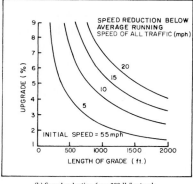

(b) Speed reduction for a 300-lb/hp truck

Figure 13-7   Speed reduction curves for trucks on two-lane upgrades. [Used with permission of Transportation Research Board, National Research Council, Washington, DC, from *Highway Capacity Manual, Special Report 209,* 3rd Ed., p. 8-30. Copyright © 1994 Transportation Research Board.]

Summary

This chapter has treated some of the special aspects of two-lane rural highways. The procedures presented herein are taken from the 1994 update of the *Highway Capacity Manual* [2], but they are unchanged from the 1985 *HCM* and will not change in the 1997 update. They are based on studies conducted at the Texas Transportation Institute at Texas A&M University [4,8] and several studies conducted in Canada [9,10,11]. Several innovative concepts were developed in these studies and applied in the *HCM* methodology. These include the variation of capacity with terrain, the use of passenger car equivalents for a *mix* of heavy vehicles, the impact of grades on passenger car operation, and the use of "percent time delay" as a measure of effectiveness.

No changes in these procedures will be incorporated into the 1997 update of the *HCM*, but significant NCHRP-funded research is underway that will produce new material for the full fourth edition of the *HCM*, expected in the year 2000. Likely changes may include the use of a multi-dimensional measure of effectiveness for level of service determinations and using similar criteria for general terrain sections and for grades of significant length. Changes in heavy vehicle equivalence are also expected. The work will be based on both new field data, and new simulation results.

Even on rural two-lane highways, periodic interruptions may occur. Any isolated signalized intersections or STOP-controlled intersections must be separately analyzed using the procedures for such cases.

References

1. *A Policy on Geometric Design of Highways and Streets,* American Association of State Highway and Transportation Officials, Washington, DC, 1994.
2. *Highway Capacity Manual, Special Report 209,* 3rd Edition, Transportation Research Board, National Research Council, Washington, DC, (revised) 1994.
3. *Highway Capacity Manual, Special Report 87,* Transportation Research Board, National Research Council, Washington, DC, 1965.
4. Messer, C., "Two-Lane, Two-Way Rural Highway Capacity," *Final Report,* NCHRP Project 3-28A, Texas Transportation Institute, College Station, TX, 1983.
5. "Development of Passing Lane Criteria," Ontario Ministry Transportation and Communications, Downsview, Ontario, Canada, 1975.
6. Rooney, F., *Turnouts: Traffic Operational Report 2,* Office of Traffic, California Department of Transportation, Sacramento, CA, 1976.

7. "Theoretical Analysis: Slow Moving Vehicle Turnouts," Oregon Department of Transportation, Salem, OR, 1978.
8. Messer, C., "Two-Lane, Two-Way Rural Highway Capacity Procedures," *Project Report,* NCHRP Project 3-28, Texas Transportation Institute, College Station, TX, 1983.
9. Krummins, A., "Capacity and Level of Service on Two-Lane Highways in Alberta," Master's Thesis, University of Calgary, Calgary, Alberta, Canada, 1981.
10. Yagar, S., "Capacity and Level of Service for Two-Lane Rural Highways," *Final Report,* Ontario Ministry of Transportation and Communications, Downsview, Ontario, Canada, 1983.
11. Werner, A. and Worrell, J., "Passenger Car Equivalents of Trucks, Buses, and Recreational Vehicles for Two-Lane Rural Highways," *Transportation Research Record 615,* Transportation Research Board, National Research Council, Washington, DC, 1976.

Problems

Problem 13–1

A rural two-lane highway segment in rolling terrain has a design speed of 60 mph, 12-ft lanes and 4-ft clear shoulders. The segment has 50% "no-passing zones." If current traffic on the facility is 350 vph (total, both ways), including 12% trucks and 6% RVs, what level of service is expected on the facility? The directional distribution of traffic is 60/40. How many years will it take for capacity to be reached if traffic grows at a rate of 8% per year? How many years will it take for LOS D to be exceeded at this rate?

Problem 13–2

A rural two-lane highway in level terrain has a design speed of 70-mph, 12-ft lanes, and 10-ft shoulders. There are no passing-sight-distance restrictions. New development will increase traffic on the facility to an AADT of 10,000 vpd with a *K*-factor of 0.10. The traffic will include 9% trucks. Directional distribution of traffic is 60/40. The total traffic department has a policy of improving two-lane facilities when LOS D is exceeded. Will the new development require improvements?

Problem 13–3

A sustained two-lane highway grade of 6%, 1.5 miles in length, carries peak-hour traffic of 400 vph with a direc-

tional distribution of 60/40 and a PHF of 0.90. No passing is permitted on the grade, and traffic includes 8% trucks and 8% RVs. Lane widths and shoulders are ideal. How do the capacity and level of service of the facility differ between A.M. peaks, when 60% of the traffic travels in the upgrade direction, and P.M. peaks, when 60% of the traffic travels in the downgrade direction? What average upgrade speeds are expected in A.M. and P.M. peaks?

Problem 13–4

Does the grade in Problem 13–3 justify an upgrade climbing lane for heavy vehicles according to the criteria of the *HCM*? Assume that the approach section to the grade is in level terrain.

Problem 13–5

Approximately what maximum AADT can be accommodated by a rural two-lane highway in level, rolling, and mountainous terrain without operating at worse than LOS D during peak periods? Without exceeding capacity during peak periods? The *K*-factor in the region is 0.12.

14

Traffic Control Devices

Chapters 1 and 2 discuss the issues concerning the rights of various governmental agencies to enact and implement traffic regulations. These rights are spelled out in the various state motor vehicle and traffic codes, along with a host of other related laws governing motor vehicle operation, vehicle inspection, and driver licensing procedures.

Traffic control devices are the media traffic engineers use to communicate with drivers. Virtually every traffic law, regulation, or operating restriction must be communicated through the use of devices that fall into three broad categories:

- traffic markings
- traffic signs
- traffic signals

It is important to recognize that traffic engineers have no direct control over any individual driver or group of drivers except through these media. Unlike rail transit controls, where a train passing a RED signal will trip a switch that automatically engages an emergency braking system, a motorist running past a RED signal does so unimpeded, except by conflicting vehicles or pedestrians. Thus, the traffic engineer has a critical responsibility to design control devices that communicate uncomplicated messages clearly, in a way that encourages proper observance.

This chapter introduces some of the basic principles involved in the design and placement of traffic control devices. Chapter 15 takes a detailed look at the control of surface intersections, and the options available. Chapters 16 and 17 treat the signalization of individual intersections in detail.

The manual of uniform traffic control devices

The principal standard governing the use, placement, and design of traffic control devices is the *Manual of Uniform Traffic Control Devices* (MUTCD) [1]. The Federal Highway Administration publishes a national MUTCD, which serves as a minimum standard and a model for individual state MUTCDs. As is the case with other federal highway mandates, the federal MUTCD is enforced by partial withholding of federal-aid highway funds from states that do not comply. Individual states have the option of adopting the federal MUTCD, or developing a state MUTCD. In the latter case, the state MUTCD must meet all of the minimum standards of the federal manual, but may impose additional or more stringent standards.

A. History and background

One of the principal objectives of the MUTCD is to establish *uniformity* in the use, placement, and design of traffic control devices. Communication is greatly enhanced when the same message is delivered in the same way and in similar circumstances at all times. Consider the confusion caused if all the states' STOP signs had different shapes, colors, and legends.

Early traffic control devices were developed in various locales with little or no coordination on their design, much less their use. Traffic control devices appeared on streets and highways in the U.S. as early as the 1910s. The first centerline appeared in Michigan in 1911. The first electric signal installation is thought to have occurred in Cleveland, Ohio in 1914. The first STOP sign was installed in Detroit in 1915, where the first three-color traffic signal was installed in 1920.

The first attempts to create national standards for traffic control devices occurred during the mid-1920s. Two separate organizations developed two manuals during this period. In 1927, the American Association of State Highway Officials (AASHO, the forerunner of AASHTO) published the *Manual and Specifications for the Manufacture, Display, and Erection of U.S. Standard Road Markers and Signs.* The manual addressed only rural signing applications. In 1930, the National Conference on Street and Highway Safety (NCSHS) published the *Manual on Street Traffic Signs, Signals, and Markings*, which addressed urban applications.

In 1932, the two groups formed a merged *Joint Committee on Uniform Traffic Control Devices,* and published the first complete MUTCD in 1935. This group continued to have responsibility for subsequent editions until 1972, when the Federal Highway Administration formally assumed responsibility for the manual. The original MUTCD was republished in 1937, with new editions appearing in 1939, 1942 (war emergency edition), 1948, 1954, 1961, 1971, 1978, and 1988. This chapter is based on the 1988 edition, as re-vised. Four revisions have been released since 1988 at this writing.

Work on a new MUTCD has been underway since the late 1980s. A new manual is expected in the 1998–2000 period, and will contain major changes in format and presentation of material.

For an excellent history of the MUTCD and its development, consult a series of articles by Hawkins [2–5].

B. General principles of the MUTCD

The MUTCD defines five requirements for a traffic control device. To be effective, a device must:

1. Fulfill a need
2. Command attention
3. Convey a clear, simple meaning
4. Command respect of road users
5. Give adequate time for proper response

In addition to the obvious meanings of these requirements, some subtleties should be carefully observed. The first implies that superfluous devices are NOT to be used. Each device must have a specific purpose, and must be needed for the safe and efficient flow of traffic. The fourth reinforces this. Respect is commanded only when drivers are conditioned to expect that all devices carry meaningful and important messages. Overuse or misuse of devices encourages drivers to ignore them. When this happens, drivers will then not pay full attention to those devices that *are* needed.

Items 2 and 3 affect the design of a device. Commanding attention requires proper visibility and a distinctive design that attracts the driver's attention. Clarity and simplicity of message is critical if the message is to be understood in the short time a driver has to consider an individual device. Use of color and shape as codes are important in this regard; legend, the hardest element of a device to understand, must be kept short and simple.

Item 5 affects the placement of devices. A STOP sign, for example, while always placed at the stop line of the intersection, must be visible for at least one safe stopping distance from the stop line. Guide signs requiring drivers to make lane changes, such as on a freeway, must be placed well in advance of the diverge gore area.

C. Contents of the MUTCD

The MUTCD contains:

1. Detailed standards for the physical design of the device, covering size, shape, colors, legend types, and specific legend.
2. Detailed standards and guidelines on where devices should be physically located or placed in relationship to the roadway.
3. Warrants, or conditions which justify, the use of a particular device.

The most detailed and definitive standards are for the design of the device. Here, little is left to judgment, and virtually every detail of the design is fully specified. Variance is generally not permitted. The standards sometimes allow for the use of several different sizes of device depending on the particular situation and need.

Placement standards and guidelines are also relatively definitive, but often allow for some variation within specified limits.

Warrants are given with various levels of specificity and clarity. Signal warrants, for example, are relatively detailed and precise. Warrants for STOP and YIELD signs, on the other hand, are relatively general. Because of the expense involved in signalization, much study has been devoted to defining conditions which require their use, resulting in more quantitative warrants than for other devices. Chapter 15 deals in detail with warrants related to various forms of intersection control. Proper implementation of warrants in the MUTCD requires appropriate engineering studies to be made to determine the need for a particular device or devices.

Three words within the MUTCD require special attention, as they describe the relative force with which each standard or criterion is given:

1. *SHALL:* The use of the word "shall" or "shall not" denotes a mandatory condition. Where imposed, such conditions *must* be met. Failure to observe conditions imposed with the "shall" or "shall not" qualification may create legal liability for the implementing agency.
2. *SHOULD:* The use of the word "should" or "should not" denotes an advisory, but not mandatory condition. The criteria so given are recommended. When not observed, some documentation explaining why there is no compliance should be maintained. The logic for non-compliance should be clear and convincing.
3. *MAY:* The use of the word "may" or "may not" denotes a permissive condition. No requirement on design or application is intended.

These words have enormous legal connotations. As indicated, failure to observe a mandatory condition exposes the presiding agency to lawsuits. Advisory conditions are usually followed unless there is an extraordinary reason not to; such reasons must always be carefully documented should legal questions arise.

Warrants are rarely given as a mandatory condition. Thus, there is considerable latitude in the use and application of particular devices. When used, however, design and placement criteria are most often mandatory. Ironically, a jurisdiction is more legally exposed when it places a device that does not follow design and placement conditions than it is when it fails to place a device which might be indicated, but with an advisory or permissive criteria.

This chapter presents some of the principles of the MUTCD, and shows a number of examples. Traffic engineers must consult the MUTCD directly whenever a device is placed, because it contains standards and criteria well beyond those illustrated herein. It is also important to consult the MUTCD directly as revisions and new editions (of the MUTCD) may well occur within the lifetime of this textbook. In addition, state MUTCDs should be consulted for minor, but locally important, deviations from the federal version.

Communicating with the driver

The driver is accustomed to being given a certain message in clear, standard ways, often with great redundancy. A number of mechanisms are used to convey messages. These mechanisms make use of and recognize human limitations, particularly with respect to eyesight. Messages are conveyed through the use of:

Color: Color is the most easily seen characteristic of a device. A color is recognizable long before even a general shape is recognizable, and well before legend can be read and understood. The principal colors used in traffic control devices are red, yellow, green, orange, black, blue, and brown. These are used to code certain devices, and to reinforce specific messages whenever possible.

Pattern: Pattern is used in the application of traffic markings. In general, double solid, solid, dashed, and broken lines are used. Each conveys a type of meaning with which drivers become familiar. The frequent and consistent use of similar patterns in similar applications contributes greatly to their effectiveness, and to the instant recognition of their meaning.

Shape: After color, the shape of a device is the next element to be discerned by the driver. Particularly in signing, shape is an important element of the message, either identifying a particular type of information that the sign is transmitting, or conveying a unique message on its own.

Legend: The last element of a device that the driver comprehends is the specific legend on the device. Signals and markings, for example, convey their entire message without the use of legend. Signs, however, often use specific legend to transmit the details of the message being conveyed. Legend must be kept simple and short, so that drivers do not divert their attention from the driving task, yet are able to see and understand the specific message being given.

Redundancy of message can be achieved in a number of ways. The STOP sign is a good example. This device has a unique shape (octagon), a unique color (red), and a unique one-word message (STOP). Any of the three elements alone is sufficient to convey the message. Each provides redundancy for the others.

In another example, a left-turn lane is reinforced with a left-turn signal, arrow and word markings on the pavement, and left-turn lane signing, as shown in Figure 14-1. Here, all three categories of control device are used together to reinforce a single message.

In the final analysis, the driver expects to see traffic control devices that are uniform and used in consistent ways. Redundancy of message is useful, and often necessary to properly convey a message. The MUTCD is the federal standard providing for this necessary uniformity in use, design, and placement of devices.

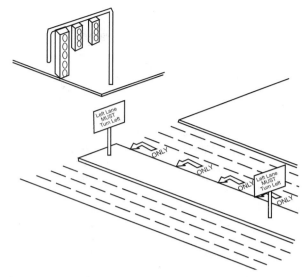

Figure 14-1 Left-turn lane: An example of redundancy in communicating with the driver.

The following sections of this chapter introduce some of the standards for critical traffic control devices. Again, the traffic engineer must consult current editions of the MUTCD, as well as applicable state MUTCDs, for a complete version of all standards for all devices.

Traffic markings

Traffic markings are the most frequently-used traffic control device. Markings serve a variety of purposes and functions, and fall into three broad categories:

- longitudinal markings
- transverse markings
- object markings and delineators

Longitudinal and transverse markings are applied to the roadway surface using a variety of materials, the most common of which are reflectorized paint and thermoplastic. Paint reflectorization is provided by mixing small glass beads in the paint, or by applying a thin layer of glass beads to the surface of a marking as it is placed. In the latter case, the reflectorized beads are on the surface, providing for maximum reflectorization. Traffic wear, however, can remove the beads before the paint itself is affected. In the former case, some reflectorization is preserved as the paint wears. Yet another means of providing reflectorization is through the use of supplemental pavement inserts. These are small reflectors either affixed to, or inserted in, the pavement. They are visible in wet and dry weather, and are wear-resistant. They are difficult to maintain in areas in which snow is prevalent, as snow plows can tear them from the pavement unless the reflectors are recessed.

Object markers and delineators are small object-mounted reflectors. Delineators are small reflectors mounted on lightweight posts.

A. Longitudinal markings

In this excerpt, the MUTCD gives nine key principals concerning longitudinal pavement markings which *shall* be observed at all times (mandatory conditions) [Reference 1, p. 3A-2]:

1. Yellow lines delineate the separation of traffic flows in opposing directions, or mark the left edge of the pavement of divided highways and one-way roads.
2. White lines delineate the separation of traffic flows in the same direction or mark the right edge of the pavement.
3. Red markings delineate roadways that shall not be entered or used by the viewer of those markings.
4. Broken lines are permissive in character.
5. Solid lines are restrictive in character.
6. Width of line indicates the degree of emphasis.
7. Double lines indicate maximum restrictions.

8. Markings which must be visible at night shall be reflectorized unless ambient illumination assures adequate visibility.
9. Raised pavement markers may serve as position guides for, may supplement, or in some cases may be substituted for other types of markings.

These principals result in the patterns and usages that drivers have become familiar with: center lines are yellow, and may be broken or solid; lane lines are white, and are generally broken. The figures that follow illustrate a number of standard applications of longitudinal traffic markings.

Figure 14-2 illustrates one of the most important uses of centerline markings. On two-lane highways, the centerline not only delineates the division of opposing flows (yellow is used), but it defines the safety of passing maneuvers, which are made in the opposing lane on such facilities.

The single-yellow-dashed centerline of Figure 14-2 (a) indicates that passing is safe in either direction. In Figure 14-2 (b), passing is *not* permitted from the direction having the solid yellow line, and *is* permitted from the direction having the broken yellow line. Where there is a double-yellow-solid line, passing is prohibited from both directions.

The placement of these lines is determined by an analysis of passing-sight-distance on each direction of the roadway. Passing-sight-distance, explained in greater detail in Chapter 13, is based on the requirements of the passing maneuver with an assumed vehicle approaching in the opposing lane at the limit of

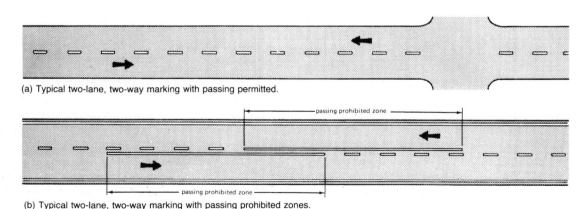

(a) Typical two-lane, two-way marking with passing permitted.

(b) Typical two-lane, two-way marking with passing prohibited zones.

Figure 14-2 Typical markings for a two-lane highway. [From *Manual of Uniform Traffic Control Devices*, Federal Highway Administration, 1988, p. 3B-4.]

the driver's sight distance. When the sight distance is sufficient to allow this complex maneuver to take place safely, a broken line is provided; when sight distance is insufficient, passing must be prohibited. On two-lane highways, passing restrictions shown with pavement markings should be supplemented by special signing as well.

Figure 14-3 shows four typical applications of longitudinal markings on multilane arterials. The first shows typical centerline, lane line, and edge mark-

ings on a four-lane arterial. The double-yellow-solid centerline prohibits crossings, except for left turns at designated driveways (unless specifically prohibited by signing).

Figure 14-3 (b) shows a similar arterial with left-turn channelization provided. The single-white-solid lines denoting the right edge of the left-turn lanes discourage, but do not absolutely prohibit crossings. Full prohibition would be shown using a double-white-solid line here.

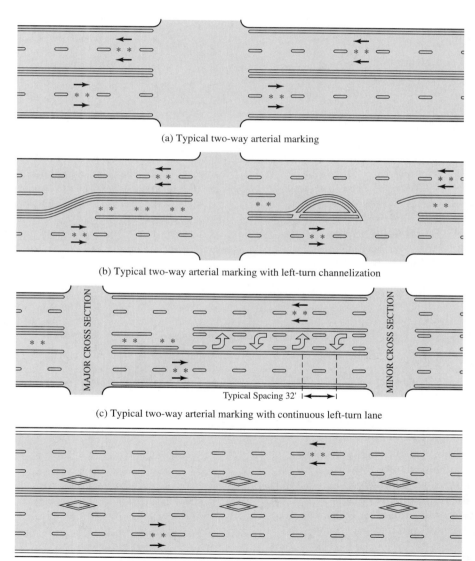

(a) Typical two-way arterial marking

(b) Typical two-way arterial marking with left-turn channelization

(c) Typical two-way arterial marking with continuous left-turn lane

Typical Spacing 32'

(d) Typical two-way arterial marking with special use lane

Figure 14-3 Typical markings for multilane two-way arterials. [From *Manual of Uniform Traffic Control Devices,* Federal Highway Administration, 1988, pp. 3B-5 and 3B-6.]

Figure 14-3 (c) shows a common, relatively recent treatment (in the last 15 years or so): an arterial with an odd number of lanes, where the center lane is used as a continuous left-turn lane for both directions. Vehicles making mid-block left turns off of the arterial first move into this lane, then seek a gap in the opposing traffic to turn through; when making a left-turn onto the arterial, a vehicle finds a gap in the closest direction of flow, and turns into the center lane, then merges with through traffic. The use of this device eliminates some of the disruptive effect of mid-block left turns caused by waiting vehicles. Markings on either side of the lane are yellow, using the pattern shown.

In Figure 14-3 (d), a typical centerline is used. A special diamond marking, however, designates the left lane in each direction as a "special use lane." Signing would have to state the specific restrictions on use of the lane, and hours of the day over which the restriction applies. A typical example would be a high-occupancy vehicle lane, or HOVL.

The MUTCD gives numerous other examples and illustrations of the use of various longitudinal markings for urban, suburban, and rural environments, including markings used in conjunction with raised medians, freeway merge and diverge junctions, and other applications. This text is not intended to replace the MUTCD itself; the reader is cautioned to refer directly to the federal or applicable state MUTCD for complete standards, guidelines, and illustrations.

B. Transverse markings

Transverse markings are those placed across travel lanes. There are three primary types of transverse markings: stop lines, crosswalks, and parking lines.

Stop lines are solid white lines between 12 and 24 inches in width extending across all approach lanes. The MUTCD indicates that stop lines *should* be used in both urban and rural areas where it is important to indicate the point behind which vehicles must stop in response to a STOP sign, traffic signal, police officer's command, or other legal requirement. When used in conjunction with a crosswalk, the stop line *should* be placed 4 feet in advance of, and parallel to, the crosswalk.

There are a number of different ways to mark *crosswalks*. The accepted designs are illustrated in Figure 14-4. The typical designs include marking the

(a) Standard crosswalk marking

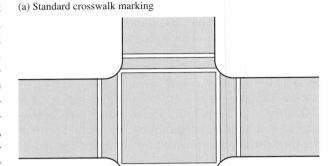

(b) Crosswalk marking with diagonal lines for added visibility

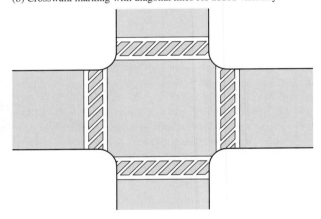

(c) Crosswalk marking with longitudinal lines for added visibility

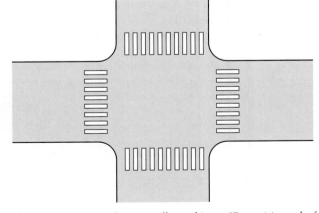

Figure 14-4 Typical crosswalk markings. [From *Manual of Uniform Traffic Control Devices,* Federal Highway Administration, 1988, p. 3B-24.]

crosswalk with two solid white lines at its boundary, adding diagonal solid white markings to the boundary lines, or vertical solid white lines with no boundary lines. The MUTCD also specifies special crosswalk markings (not shown here) for use in conjunction with exclusive pedestrian signal phases. While they *should not* be used indiscriminately, crosswalks *should* be marked at all intersections where there is substantial conflict between vehicle and pedestrian movements.

Typical *parking space markings* are shown in Figure 14-5. While never required, parking space markings improve efficiency in the use of parking spaces where turnover is high. They also assist in the management of curb space by clearly marking parking stalls, and making loading zones, bus stops, taxi stands, and other curb uses more obvious due to their lack of such markings. It is also common to mark stalls in conjunction with parking meters, to avoid the confusion of having drivers "straddling" meters.

As indicated in Figure 14-5, marked parking stalls are never placed within 20 ft of the far crosswalk line. The standard width of a parking stall is 20 ft.

C. Word and symbol markings

The MUTCD permits the placement of a small number of word and/or symbol markings on the pavement. Arrows, symbolizing lane use restrictions are frequently used, and are often accompanied by the word marking "ONLY."

Where word markings are used, they are elongated to appear in proportion to the driver of a moving vehicle. The most often used word markings include: STOP, SCHOOL, R × R, SCHOOL XING, and PED XING. Most word markings are supplemented by signs, as inclement weather (particularly snow) renders the markings difficult or impossible to read. Figure 14-6 illustrates arrow markings and the "ONLY" word marking.

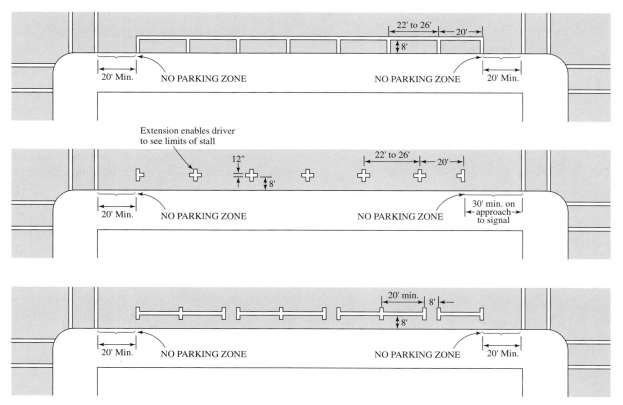

Figure 14-5 Typical parking lane markings. [From *Manual of Uniform Traffic Control Devices,* Federal Highway Administration, 1988.]

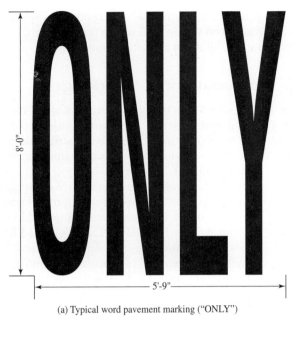

(a) Typical word pavement marking ("ONLY")

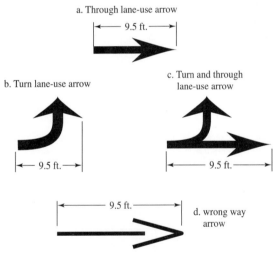

a. Through lane-use arrow

b. Turn lane-use arrow

c. Turn and through lane-use arrow

d. wrong way arrow

(b) Typical arrow pavement markings

Figure 14-6 Typical arrow and word pavement markings. [From *Manual of Uniform Traffic Control Devices,* Federal Highway Administration, 1988, pp. 3B-28 and 3B-29.]

D. Intersection markings

Intersections, both signalized and unsignalized, provide the opportunity for use of a wide variety of markings. Longitudinal, transverse, and word/symbol markings all find frequent application at intersections, and are employed to provide for safer and more orderly flow through the intersection.

Figure 14-7 illustrates three intersection applications of markings. In Figure 14-3(a), the critical feature is the offset of the N–S street. Dashed white markings are employed to guide vehicles on the N–S street through the intersection, lessening the opportunity for sideswipe accidents as vehicles traverse the offset. Crosswalks are also of particular importance in this case, as pedestrians may attempt to cross the E–W street on a vertical path, which would place them in conflict with a moving traffic lane. Stop lines on the E–W street emphasize where vehicles should stop, and the relationship between where vehicles stop and the designated pedestrian path.

Figure 14-7(b) illustrates an intersection of two one-way streets where heavy turning movements are expected. Solid white lines mark the desired turning path of vehicles making either of the two legal turns at the intersection. The lines guide turning vehicles into two departure lanes in each case, which makes the turning movements more efficient.

Figure 14-7(c) shows a complicated four-leg intersection using virtually every type of marking available. Two turning paths (on the north leg of the intersection) are channelized. Crosswalk markings across this and other approaches are most important, as they guide pedestrians in the desired crossing path, which involves two triangular refuge islands on the north approach. The existence of these islands, and their inclusion in the legal crossing path has an effect on signal timing parameters, as well as safety. Markings are also used to create left-turn lanes as well as a right-turn guide line for the northbound right turn.

The judicious use of transverse and longitudinal markings at intersections provides both drivers and pedestrians with movement paths that are intended to minimize conflict and maximize safety. At the same time, they encourage efficient traffic movement in an orderly fashion by delineating vehicle paths and placement on the pavement. Every motorist has had the experience of driving a section of roadway or intersection after repaving has been done, but before pavement markings have been replaced. The confusion and inefficiency is evident. Without the kind of guidance presented by transverse and longitudinal markings, drivers tend to behave more like pedestrians, moving

a Typical pavement marking with offset lane lines continued through the
   intersection and optional crosswalk lines and stop limit lines.

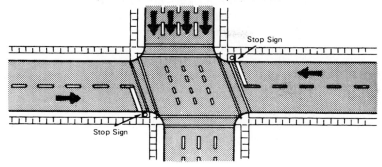

b Typical pavement marking with optional double turn lane lines, pavement
   messages, crosswalk lines, and stop limit lines.

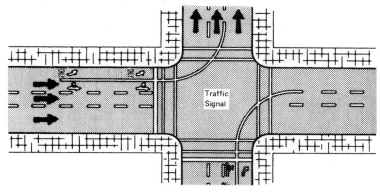

c Typical pavement marking with optional turn lane lines, crosswalk lines,
   and stop limit lines.

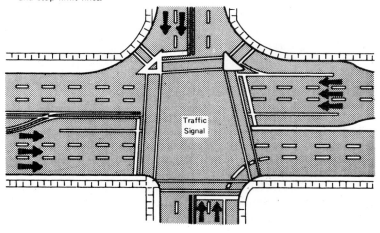

Figure 14-7 Intersection markings
illustrated. [From *Manual of Uniform Traffic
Control Devices,* Federal Highway
Administration, 1988, p. 3B-12.]

in staggered patterns and not systematically following any particular path.

E. Object markers and delineators

Object markers are reflectorized devices mounted on obstructions within or adjacent to the roadway. The MUTCD provides specifications for four different types of object markers, illustrated in Figure 14-8.

Type 1 markers are yellow with or without yellow reflectors, or yellow reflectors mounted on a black background. They are used primarily to mark obstructions within the travelled way, such as a bridge abutment in the middle of the road. Type 2 reflectors are yellow, or yellow reflectors mounted on a white background. These are used primarily to mark obstructions outside the travelled way, but close enough to the roadside to pose a potential hazard to motorists. Type 3 markers have alternating yellow and black stripes on a 45-degree angle. They may be used

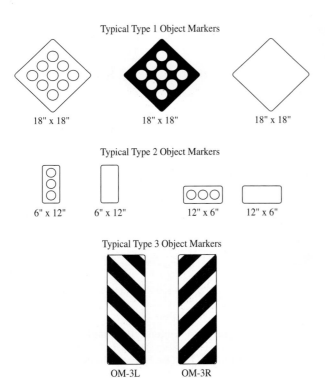

Typical Type 1 Object Markers

18" x 18"   18" x 18"   18" x 18"

Typical Type 2 Object Markers

6" x 12"   6" x 12"   12" x 6"   12" x 6"

Typical Type 3 Object Markers

OM-3L   OM-3R
12" x 36"   12" x 36"

Figure 14-8 Object markers illustrated. [From *Manual of Uniform Traffic Control Devices,* Federal Highway Administration, 1988, p. 3C-2.]

to mark objects either within or adjacent to the travelled way. End markers are red reflectors on a red background, or red reflectors on a black background. They are used to mark the end of a travelled way when there is no other vehicle path available, such as the end of a dead-end street.

In many cases, object markers will be used in conjunction with an appropriate warning sign alerting drivers to the upcoming hazard. The intent is to provide better visibility to drivers, particularly at night, of objects which could become a collision hazard. The MUTCD provides a range of sizes for these devices, and specific instructions for mounting heights.

Roadway delineators are reflectorized devices mounted at the roadside to demark roadway alignment. Generally mounted in series at a distance between 2 ft and 8 ft from the edge of the shoulder, delineators are aids to night driving and are considered to be guidance devices, not warning devices. They may be used continuously along the roadway, or may be used to delineate changes in the roadway alignment, such as changes in horizontal or vertical alignment, or changes in lane widths or number of lanes. The color of the delineator matches the edge line of the roadway being delineated—i.e., delineators for the left side of a one-way roadway are yellow; delineators for the right side of a one-way roadway are white. On straight section of roadway, delineators should be placed at regular intervals of between 200 and 528 ft. On horizontal curves, closer placement is desirable, with the MUTCD specifying the spacing based on the radius of the curve being delineated. For a 1000 ft radius, delineators are placed 90 ft apart; for a 500 ft radius, 65 ft apart; and for a 200 ft radius, 35 ft apart, for example.

Figure 14-9 illustrates a typical installation of roadside delineators around a horizontal curve.

Traffic signs

The MUTCD gives detailed specifications for and general guidance on the use of several hundred different traffic signs covering a wide variety of situations. While a general overview is given herein, the student and/or practitioner must consult the MUTCD directly for a complete coverage of the subject of traffic signs.

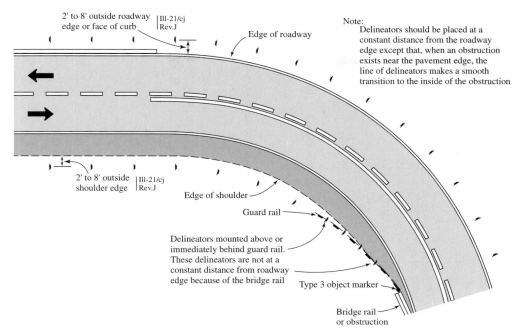

2' to 8' outside roadway
edge or face of curb | Ill-21/cj Rev.J

Edge of roadway

Note:
Delineators should be placed at a
constant distance from the roadway
edge except that, when an obstruction
exists near the pavement edge, the
line of delineators makes a smooth
transition to the inside of the obstruction

2' to 8' outside
shoulder edge | Ill-21/cj Rev.J

Edge of shoulder

Guard rail

Delineators mounted above or
immediately behind guard rail.
These delineators are not at a
constant distance from roadway
edge because of the bridge rail

Type 3 object marker

Bridge rail
or obstruction

Figure 14-9 Roadside delineation illustrated. [From *Manual of Uniform Traffic Control Devices*, Federal Highway Administration, 1988, p. 3C-4.]

Traffic signs fall into one of three general categories:

- regulatory signs
- warning signs
- guide signs

Color and shape are used to help identify these signs. *Regulatory signs* are generally black legend on a white background, and are either square or rectangular (long dimension vertical) in shape. They convey information concerning specific traffic regulations which the driver must obey. *Warning signs* are generally black legend on a yellow background, and are diamond-shaped. They are used to warn drivers of impending hazards that they are approaching. *Guide signs* give directional guidance to drivers. They are generally white legend on a green, blue, or brown background (color depends on type of guidance information being given), and are rectangular (long dimension horizontal) in shape.

A. Regulatory signs

Regulatory signs all convey information about a specific traffic regulation with which drivers must com-

ply. They are organized in six different categories according to the type of regulation conveyed.

1. Right-of-way series. The right-of-way series includes two unique signs that assign the right-of-way to selected legs of an at-grade intersection. These are the STOP and YIELD signs. Chapter 15 discusses the use and application of these signs in detail.

2. Speed series. A variety of speed signs may be used to post legal speed limits. These include the typical speed limit sign, truck, night, and minimum speed signs, as well as signs alerting drivers to changes in speed regulations. Figure 14-10 illustrates these signs.

Two kinds of speed limits may be applied: a linear speed limit and an area speed limit. Linear speed limits apply to a specific roadway, and carry the simple message "SPEED LIMIT" and a number indicating the limit in mph. Linear speed limit signs are placed whenever a change in limit takes place, and shortly after critical locations at which significant numbers of vehicles enter the roadway.

Area speed limits apply to all roadways within a given area. The sign usually indicates the type of area with the notation "___SPEED LIMIT." The blank

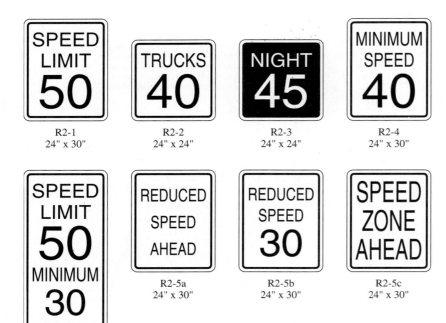

Figure 14-10 — R2-1 24" x 30", R2-2 24" x 24", R2-3 24" x 24", R2-4 24" x 30", R2-4A 24" x 48", R2-5a 24" x 30", R2-5b 24" x 30", R2-5c 24" x 30"

Figure 14-10 Signs of the speed series. [From *Manual of Uniform Traffic Control Devices,* Federal Highway Administration, 1988, pp. 2B-6–2B-9.]

denotes the type of area for which the limit applies. General terms include STATE, TOWN, VILLAGE, COUNTY, etc. Area speed limit signs should be placed at every crossing point where vehicles enter the area under control, and at critical interior points where reinforcement of the area limit is deemed important.

Separate truck speed limits are applied on high-speed roadways where heavy commercial vehicles must be limited to slower speeds than passenger cars for safety reasons. Safety is also the predominant factor in applying minimum speed limits. Very slow vehicles may present a safety hazard to themselves and others on a high-speed facility. Similarly, night speed limits are applied where night visibility conditions dictate slower speeds for safe operations. Where truck, night, and/or minimum speed limits exist, these are usually posted at the same location as the general limit, with the proviso that no more than three limits should be posted at any given location.

When the 55 mph national speed limit (and the short-lived 65 mph rural national speed limit) was in effect, the need for truck, night, and minimum speed limits was somewhat reduced. With the removal of all national controls on speed limits in November of 1995,

and the subsequent move to 70 mph and 75 mph state speed limits in many areas, these will take on new importance. In the most extreme case, Montana removed all daytime speed limits, relying instead on a general "safe and prudent" statute. When this was done, the application of a state truck speed limit and a state night speed limit were simultaneously enacted [6].

The removal of the national speed limit will refocus attention on the relationship between speed and safety. Some experts were predicting an increase in national fatalities in the range of 6000–7000 per year in 1995[7]. By the time this textbook is published, several years of experience without national speed limits will have occurred, and additional data will be available to closely examine this most critical issue.

3. Movement series. The movement series contains a wide variety of signs affecting specific vehicle maneuvers. These include turn prohibition signs, signs related to roadway alignment and required vehicle maneuvers, exclusion signs, and one-way street signs.

a. Turn Signs. Turn signs include turn prohibitions and lane use control signs. Several of these are illustrated in Figure 14-11. International symbology is

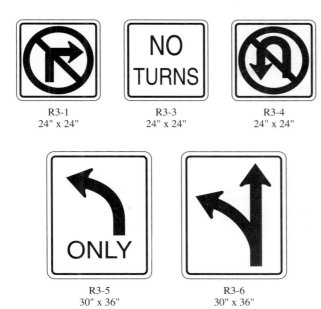

R3-1
24" x 24"

R3-3
24" x 24"

R3-4
24" x 24"

R3-5
30" x 36"

R3-6
30" x 36"

Figure 14-11 Illustrative turn signs. [From *Manual of Uniform Traffic Control Devices,* Federal Highway Administration, 1988, pp. 2B-10 and 2B-11.]

used to indicate prohibition of right turns, left turns, or U-turns. The now-familiar red circle with diagonal crossbar indicates prohibition of the illustrated action, and is used throughout the world to promote international standardization. This symbol, adopted at a 1973 United Nations conference on traffic safety, has become so familiar, it is widely used in non-traffic applications, such as to indicate "no smoking," and other generic prohibitions.

Turn prohibitions are generally used as a last resort. Where signalization cannot be used to safely accommodate turns, and where opposed or unsignalized turns may be unduly hazardous, serious consideration to prohibition must be given. Where the demand for the banned turning movement is moderate to significant, care must be taken to provide for alternative routes for the movement.

Lane use signs also make heavy use of arrow indications. In these signs, arrows, sometimes supplemented with the word message "ONLY," indicate movements which all vehicles in the lane must make.

Turn signs are also provided for indicating two-way left-turn lanes on urban and suburban arterials.

Some turn control signs may be used with time-specific applications. Turn prohibitions, for example, may be required during peak periods, but not during other times of the day. In such cases, signs are posted with a supplementary sign indicating the specific hours during which the prohibition applies. The MUTCD also allows for the placement of portable signs which are removed when not in effect, but this is a labor-intensive process, and mistakes in placement or removal of signs could lead to legal liability on the part of the agency with jurisdiction.

b. Alignment Signs. Alignment signs include those referring to required and/or prohibited movements required by the roadway alignment. This series includes signs designating diamond (special use) lanes, such as bus lanes, or general high-occupancy-vehicle lanes. Diamond lane signs are often accompanied by notations of specific hours of applicability, as many such lanes are operated only during peak periods.

Signs regulating passing on two- or three-lane highways are also included, as are signs related to truck climbing lanes and restrictions on truck use of lanes. The most common signs in the alignment series are those requiring vehicles to "keep left" or "keep right" around an obstruction, or when a divided highway is approached. Figure 14-12 shows a sample of the alignment series signs provided for in the MUTCD.

c. Exclusion Signs. Exclusion signs denote specific vehicles, pedestrians, and/or bicycles excluded from using a particular facility or portion of a facility. The most often used signs in this classification are the "DO NOT ENTER" and "WRONG WAY" signs posted to prevent vehicles from entering a one-way street or a ramp in the wrong direction. These have unique designs that make them quite distinctive and noticeable.

Other common exclusions include banning truck use, or prohibition of pedestrians and/or bicycles from certain facilities. A "NO MOTOR VEHICLES" sign is also provided for use on park roadways or other areas set aside for bicycles and/or pedestrians. Figure 14-13 shows a sample of exclusion signs provided for in the MUTCD.

d. One-Way Signs. One-way signs include the typical one-way arrows that must be posted at every junction where a designated one-way street can be entered. These are usually supplemented by "DO NOT ENTER" signs facing vehicles that might try to use the street in the wrong direction. Also included are

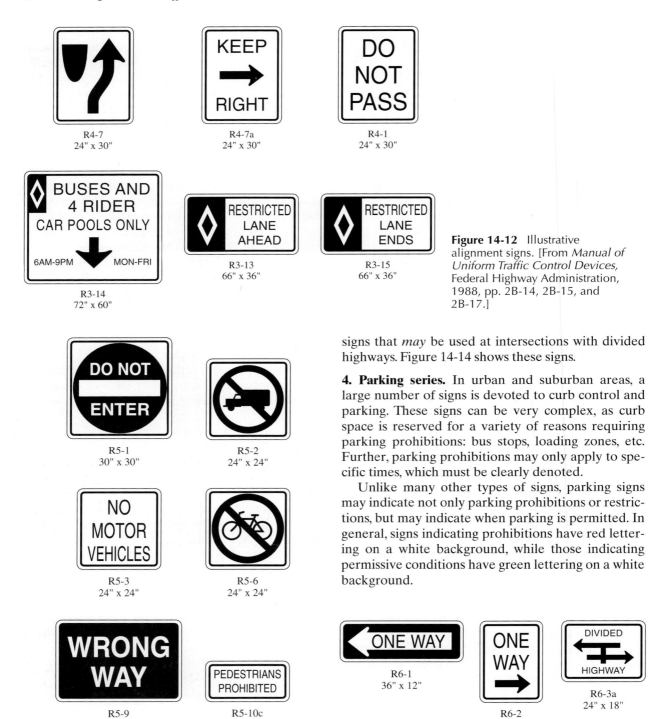

Figure 14-12 Illustrative alignment signs. [From *Manual of Uniform Traffic Control Devices,* Federal Highway Administration, 1988, pp. 2B-14, 2B-15, and 2B-17.]

signs that *may* be used at intersections with divided highways. Figure 14-14 shows these signs.

4. Parking series. In urban and suburban areas, a large number of signs is devoted to curb control and parking. These signs can be very complex, as curb space is reserved for a variety of reasons requiring parking prohibitions: bus stops, loading zones, etc. Further, parking prohibitions may only apply to specific times, which must be clearly denoted.

Unlike many other types of signs, parking signs may indicate not only parking prohibitions or restrictions, but may indicate when parking is permitted. In general, signs indicating prohibitions have red lettering on a white background, while those indicating permissive conditions have green lettering on a white background.

Figure 14-13 Illustrative exclusion signs. [From *Manual of Uniform Traffic Control Devices,* Federal Highway Administration, 1988, pp. 2B-19–2B-21.]

Figure 14-14 One-way signs. [From *Manual of Uniform Traffic Control devices,* Federal Highway Administration, 1988, pp. 2B-22 and 2B-23.]

In either case, the sign must clearly indicate the prohibition or permissive condition, in addition to specific hours of application. A sign must be placed at the beginning and end of the curb section affected, and at sufficient intermediate locations to insure that motorists will see the regulation. Arrows are placed on signs to indicate the direction (along the curb) in which the regulation applies.

Parking signs may also indicate prohibition of "standing" or "stopping." While each state defines these terms in their vehicle and traffic codes, the most common interpretations are:

- *Parking* is generally defined as a vehicle in a stopped position without the motor running.
- *Standing* is generally defined as a vehicle in a stopped position, attended by a driver, with the motor running.
- *Stopping* is generally defined as a motor vehicle in a stopped position.

Thus, a "NO STOPPING" regulation prohibits any stopping at the curb (except, perhaps, for buses at a designated bus stop). A "NO STANDING" regulation would allow a brief stop to pick up or discharge a passenger, but would not allow the driver to wait at the curb, or to park. A "NO PARKING" regulation allows both standing and stopping maneuvers.

The MUTCD also includes parking signs for rural applications. These are all red lettering on white backgrounds with specific legends indicating the prohibition. Typical messages include prohibitions on parking or stopping on the pavement.

Figure 14-15 shows a selection of commonly-used parking signs.

5. Pedestrian series. The pedestrian series includes both legend and symbol signs prohibiting hitch-hiking, a pedestrian prohibition sign, signs requiring pedestrians to use crosswalks, and a sign requiring pedestrians to walk on the left, facing traffic. These are illustrated in Figure 14-16.

6. Miscellaneous series. Every type of sign has a "miscellaneous" series for signs that do not fit into other defined categories. A wide variety of regulatory signs are included in this category, such as:

- signs used in conjunction with signals at signalized intersections
- a "KEEP OFF MEDIAN" sign
- signs indicating road closures

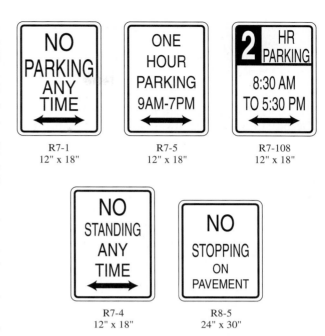

Figure 14-15 Illustrative signs from the parking series. [From *Manual of Uniform Traffic Control Devices,* Federal Highway Administration, 1988, pp. 2B-24 and 2B-27.]

Figure 14-16 Signs of the pedestrian series. [From *Manual of Uniform Traffic Control Devices,* Federal Highway Administration, 1988, pp. 2B-29 and 2B-30.]

- signs indicating vehicle weight limitations and restrictions
- signs restricting vehicles carrying hazardous cargo or substances

These are illustrative. With each revision of the MUTCD, new signs are added, often in this category. The practitioner must always consult the latest edition of the federal or applicable state MUTCD for the most up-to-date information on signs and other devices currently approved for use.

B. Warning signs

Warning signs provide drivers with information on impending conditions that are or may be hazardous. Warning signs call attention to conditions that generally require additional vigilance, a decline in speed, or a maneuver on the part of the driver. While warning signs are valuable aids to the safe and efficient movement of traffic, overuse should be avoided. Warning signs are not placed where conditions are apparent and easily discerned by the driver. Their use is most valuable where a condition is not likely to be observed without calling attention to it. Like any control device, overuse will breed disrespect for all devices.

Warning signs are usually diamond shaped, with black legend or symbols on a yellow background. Some signs have special shapes, such as the pennant-shaped "No Passing Zone" warning and the round "RR Xing" sign. These special shapes are used to warn of particularly hazardous conditions. While some warning signs still use legend messages, most use easily-understood symbols to depict the condition.

1. Types of warning signs. The MUTCD lists 11 types of conditions for which warning signs *may* generally be placed:

- changes in horizontal alignment
- intersections
- advance warning of control devices
- converging traffic lanes
- narrow roadways
- changes in highway design
- grades
- roadway surface conditions
- railroad crossings
- entrances and crossings
- miscellaneous

Figure 14-17 illustrates a selection of warning signs commonly in use. In most cases, warning signs are used where the condition(s) is(are) unexpected, or where visibility limits the ability of the driver to discern and react to the approaching hazard. Advance warning of control devices, for example, is always signed where visibility is not sufficient to give the driver full safe stopping distance when approaching a STOP or YIELD sign, or a traffic signal.

Grade warnings are posted primarily for drivers of commercial vehicles; warnings are needed for downgrades to advise drivers to shift into lower gears. Heavy vehicles can reach speeds on downgrades that exceed the normal braking capability of the vehicle. "Runaway trucks" in such situations are extremely dangerous to themselves and other vehicles on the roadway. Grade warning signs are often accompanied by supplementary signs showing the percent of grade or specifically indicating the need for low gear operation. Special signs indicating the presence of "runaway truck" ramps may also be posted where such lanes are present.

Railroad crossings are particularly hazardous locations. Such locations are always signed, and the MUTCD contains a separate section on the protection of at-grade railroad crossings which includes signing, pavement markings, crossing signals, crossing gates, and other treatments.

2. Posting distances. Warnings signs are primarily for the driver who is unfamiliar with the roadway. Thus, signs must be placed sufficiently in advance of the hazard/condition to allow the driver to see the sign, and to go through the full perception/reaction sequence before reaching it. The MUTCD provides suggested posting distances for warning signs under a variety of conditions.

Table 14-1 contains the recommended posting criteria. Three basic conditions are indicated in the table:

- *Condition A:* This condition is for situations in which difficult judgments are required of the driver. The assumed PIEV time for this condition is 10 seconds. Typical warnings requiring such judgments include merge, lane ending, and similar situations.
- *Condition B:* This condition is for situations that may require the driver to come to a full stop before the hazard is reached. Typical situations include

Figure 14-17 Selected warning signs from the MUTCD. [From *Manual of Uniform Traffic Control Devices,* Federal Highway Administration, 1988, pp. 2C-3–2C-17.]

crossroad, stop ahead, yield ahead, signal ahead, and similar warnings. The assumed PIEV time for this condition is 3 seconds.

- *Condition C:* This condition is for situations calling for drivers to decelerate to a specific advisory speed. Posting distances depend on approach speeds and the posted advisory speed to which drivers should decelerate. The assumed PIEV time is 3 seconds.

In addition to the PIEV times noted, the table assumes level terrain, 125 ft visibility distance for the

warning sign, braking distance for Condition B, and comfortable deceleration distance for Condition C.

Some warning signs advise of conditions that are not related to a specific location, such as animal or other crossings or soft shoulders. These should be posted at the most appropriate locations, and should be repeated as needed along the sections to which they apply.

3. The advisory speed panel. In general, whenever the safe speed through a hazard is at least 10 mph *less* than the posted speed limit, a warning sign should be

Table 14-1   Suggested Posting Distances for Warning Signs (feet)

Posted or 85th% Speed (mph)	COND A PIEV = 10 sec	COND B Stop	General Warning Signs PIEV = 3 sec					
			COND C—Deceleration to Advisory Speed of __					
			10 mph	20 mph	30 mph	40 mph	50 mph
20	175	(1)	(1)					
25	250	(1)	100					
30	325	100	150	100				
35	400	150	200	175				
40	475	225	275	250	175			
45	530	300	350	300	250			
50	625	375	425	400	325	225		
55	700	450	500	475	400	300		
60	775	550	575	550	500	400	300
65	850	650	650	625	575	500	375

(1) No posting distance provided. At these speeds, sign locations depend upon physical conditions at the site.
[From *Manual of Uniform Traffic Control Devices,* Federal Highway Administration, 1988, p. 2C–2a.]

accompanied by an advisory speed panel, as shown in Figure 14-18. Such a panel should only be used in conjunction with a warning sign; it is never used alone, or with any other type of sign. In most locations, the advisory speed sign is not enforceable. The advisory panel is mounted on the same post as the warning sign, normally immediately below the warning sign. The "safe speed" through the hazard should be established by an appropriate field study of the location.

As discussed previously, the MUTCD contains other warning signs in special sections of the manual covering work zones, school zones, and railroad crossings. The practitioner should consult these sections directly for more specific information concerning these special treatments.

W13-1
18" x 18"
24" x 24"

Figure 14-18   An advisory speed panel. [From *Manual of Uniform Traffic Control Devices,* Federal Highway Administration, 1988, p. 2C-19.]

C. Guide signs

Guide signs are of the utmost importance to users unfamiliar with a roadway system. They are critical to safety in many instances: nothing is more unsafe than a confused driver approaching an intersection or a diverge area.

Guide signs provide information to assist drivers in selecting appropriate routes to their desired destinations. Guide signs are, in general, rectangular with the long dimension horizontal, and are color-coded according to the type of destination information contained: white lettering on a green background for normal route and destination information; white on blue for information pertaining to motorists' services; white on brown for information on historic or landmark destinations. Route markers are also in this category, and come in a variety of shapes and colors depending on the system they mark.

The MUTCD provides guide signing information for three categories of facility: conventional roads, expressways, and freeways. Freeways have full control of access; expressways have partial control of access; conventional roads have little or no control of access.

Guide signing is somewhat different from other types, in that overuse is generally not a serious concern, unless it leads to confusion. Clarity and consistency of message is most important in guide signing. There are some general principles of importance:

- If a route services a number of destinations, the most important of these should be listed. Thus, a highway serving Philadelphia, for example, as well as several lesser suburbs, would consistently list Philadelphia as the primary destination.
- No guide sign should list more than three destinations on a single sign. This, in conjunction with the first principle, makes the selection of priority destinations a critical part of effective guide signing.
- Where roadways have both a name and a route number, both should be listed if possible. If only one can be listed, the route number should take precedence, as the unfamiliar driver is more likely to know the number than the name. Also, most maps list route numbers more prominently than names, which may change several times along the roadway's length.
- Wherever possible, advance signing of important junctions should be given. This is more difficult on conventional roadways, where junctions may be very closely spaced; it is critical on freeways and expressways where high approach speeds make advance knowledge of upcoming junctions a significant safety issue.
- Confusion or doubt on the part of the driver must be avoided at all cost. Sign sequencing should be logical and naturally lead the driver to the desired route selections. Overlapping sequences should be avoided wherever possible. Left-hand exit ramps and unusual junction features should be signed extremely carefully.

The size, placement, and lettering of guide signs varies considerably, and the manual gives information on numerous options. A number of site-specific conditions affect these design features, and there is more latitude and choice involved than for other types of highway signs. The MUTCD should be consulted directly for this information.

1. Route markers. One of the most important types of guide signs is the route marker. The MUTCD indicates that "route markers *shall* be used to identify and mark all numbered highways." Route markers have designs that are distinctive and unique to the system of which the route is a part. They are posted singly,

and in conjunction with other route markers and auxiliary markers to form "marker assemblies" for a variety of purposes.

All interstate routes are marked by the "interstate shield." The route number is in white letters on a blue background. At the top of the shield, the word "INTERSTATE" is in white on a red background strip. A special off-interstate business marker is used to note local business routes looping around sections of an interstate highway.

All U.S. routes are marked with a similar marker. A white shield is shown on a black, square background, with the route number shown in black letters in the white shield. Each state designs its own distinctive state route marker. Many have the outline of the state in solid white on a black background, with the route marker in black letters inside the state outline. All county route markers have the same shape, with yellow legend on a blue background. The name of the county is shown on each marker. Special markers are also provided for roadways within national parks and/or national forests. Figure 14-19 illustrates a selection of these route markers.

The MUTCD also prescribes a variety of rectangular auxiliary markers to be used in conjunction with route markers and route marker assemblies. These auxiliary markers are generally black lettering on a white background, and are rectangular (long dimension horizontal). They are used to indicate the type of route or marker assembly being signed, and include the following legends:

- JCT—junction
- cardinal direction (NORTH, SOUTH, EAST, WEST)
- ALT—alternate (or ALTERNATE)
- BY-PASS
- BUSINESS
- TRUCK
- TO
- END
- TEMPORARY
- various arrow indications

Route markers and auxiliary markers are combined to form several different types of route marker assemblies, each of which performs a unique function:

a. Junction Assemblies. Junction assemblies consist of one or more route markers and a junction

Figure 14-19 Route markers from the MUTCD. [From *Manual of Uniform Traffic Control Devices*, Federal Highway Administration, 1988, pp. 2D-5–2D-7.]

marker. Junction assemblies are used to indicate an upcoming junction with a numbered route.

b. Advance Route Turn Assemblies. An advance turn assembly consists of a route marker (or markers, if more than one route is involved), an advance arrow marker (or word message marker), and a cardinal direction marker, if necessary. Such an assembly gives

advance indication that the route(s) will make a turn at the next intersection or interchange.

c. Directional Assemblies. A directional assembly consists of a route marker or markers, a directional arrow, and a cardinal direction marker, if necessary. A directional assembly is used at an intersection, and indicates the path of a route through the intersection or interchange. A directional assembly with a straight through arrow is never used in the absence of other route markers indicating left and/or right turns.

d. Confirming or Reassurance Assemblies. These assemblies consist of a route marker or markers and a cardinal direction marker. They are placed shortly after a route has passed through an intersection or interchange, and are meant to confirm that the driver is on the intended numbered route.

e. Trailblazer Assemblies. A trailblazer assembly consists of a route marker or markers and the "TO" marker. These assemblies mark the route *to* a numbered route, and are used on major approach routes to the numbered route.

The MUTCD contains detailed instructions on the placement of these assemblies with respect to critical junctions, and to each other as a junction is approached. In general, the junction marker is first, followed by an (optional) advance turn assembly, followed by a turn assembly at the junction. On each numbered route departing the junction, a confirming assembly is placed. Directional guide signs must also be appropriately placed in this sequence.

Figure 14-20 illustrates a number of typical route marker installations. The figures also show the relative placement of directional guides and other appropriate signs in the junction sequence.

2. Destination signs: Conventional roadways. Destination signs are used on conventional roadways to indicate the distance to critical destinations along the route, and to mark key intersections or interchanges. On conventional roads, destination signs are in all capital white letters on a green background. Distance in miles to the indicated destination may be indicated to the right of the destination.

Destination signs are generally used at intersections of U.S. or State numbered routes, or junctions forming part of a route to such a numbered route. More than three destinations *shall not* be placed on a single destination sign. Distance signs are usually

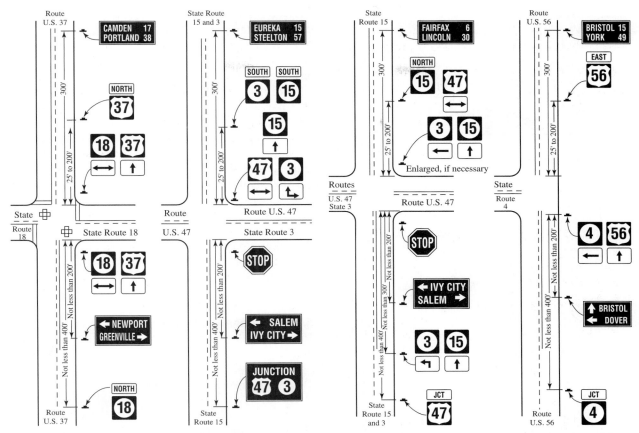

Figure 14-20 Typical route marker assembly installations. [From *Manual of Uniform Traffic Control Devices*, Federal Highway Administration, 1988, pp. 2D-16–2D-18.]

placed on important routes leaving a municipality or a major junction with a numbered route.

Local street name signs are also included as conventional roadway directional signs. Figure 14-21 shows a selection of these signs.

3. Destination signs: Expressways and freeways. Destination signs for expressways and freeways are similar, although there are different requirements for size and placement specified in the MUTCD. They differ from conventional road guide signs in a number of key ways:

• Destinations are indicated in initial capitals and small letters.

• Numbered routes are indicated by inclusion of the appropriate marker type on the guide sign.

• Exit numbers are included as auxiliary panels located at the upper right or left corner of the guide sign.

• At major junctions, diagrammatic elements may be used on guide signs.

As for conventional roads, distance signs are frequently used to indicate the mileage to critical destinations along the route. Every interchange and every significant at-grade intersection on an expressway is extensively signed with advance signing, and with signing at the junction itself.

The distance between interchanges is a major influence on guide signing. Where interchanges are

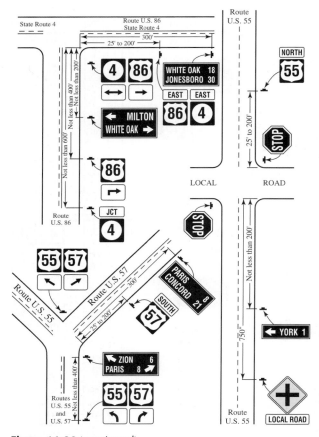

Figure 14-20 (continued)

freeway interchange signing for several different types of interchange.

4. Service guide signs. Another important type of information drivers require is directions to a variety of motorist services. Drivers, particularly those unfamiliar with the route, need to be able to identify where such services as fuel, food, lodging, medical assistance, campgrounds, and similar facilities can be found. The MUTCD provides for a series of white on blue service signs to provide this information. Most involve symbols indicating the type of service available. On freeways, large signs using word messages are used with exit number auxiliary panels to indicate the services available at a particular exit. Finally, on freeways, signing is used to indicate the specific services available (by brand name) at the upcoming interchange. Figure 14-23 illustrates a selection of these service guide signs.

5. Recreational and cultural interest area signing. Information on historic, recreational, and/or cultural

widely-spaced, advance guide signs can be placed as much as five miles from the interchange, and may be repeated several times as the interchange is approached. In general, however, advance signing only gives information on the *next* interchange, to avoid overlapping sequences. The only exception to this is a distance sign indicating the distance to the next several interchanges. Thus, in urban areas, where interchanges are closely spaced, sometimes at less than one-mile intervals, the advance sign for the next interchange is placed at the last off ramp of the previous interchange.

The MUTCD contains many detailed instructions for appropriate guide signing on expressways and freeways. Figure 14-22 illustrates several examples of

Figure 14-21 Selected directional guide signs for conventional roads. [From *Manual of Uniform Traffic Control Devices,* Federal Highway Administration, 1988, pp. 2D-21–2D-24.]

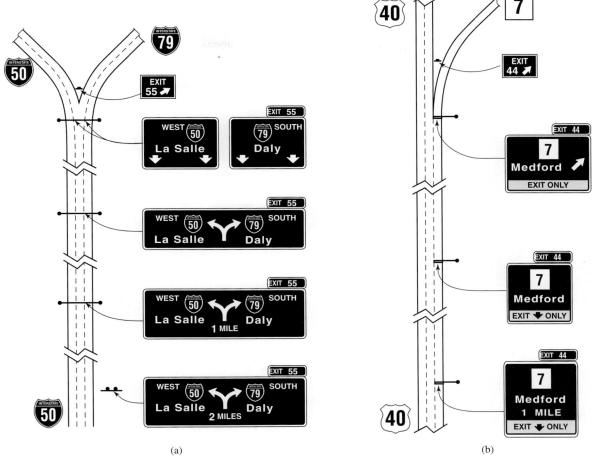

(a) (b)

Figure 14-22 Examples of freeway guide signing. [From *Manual of Uniform Traffic Control Devices,* Federal Highway Administration, 1988, pp. 2F-17–2F-33.]

interest areas is given on white on brown guide signs. Again, symbol signs are frequently used to indicate the specific type of area, but larger signs with word messages can be used as well. Figure 14-24 shows a selection of these signs.

6. Mileposts. Mileposts are small 6 × 9 inch vertical white on green panels indicating the mileage along the designated route. These are provided to allow the driver to estimate his/her progress along a route, and to provide a location system for accidents and other emergencies which may occur along the route.

Distance numbering is continuous within a state, with "zero" beginning at the south and west state lines, or at the junction at which a route begins. Where routes overlap, mileposts are continuous only for *one* of the routes. In such cases, the first mileposts beyond the overlap should indicate the total mileage travelled along the route which is *not* continuously numbered.

On some freeways, mileage markers are placed every 10th of a mile for a more precise location system. With the legislated change to metric measures under way, milepost markers will have to be replaced

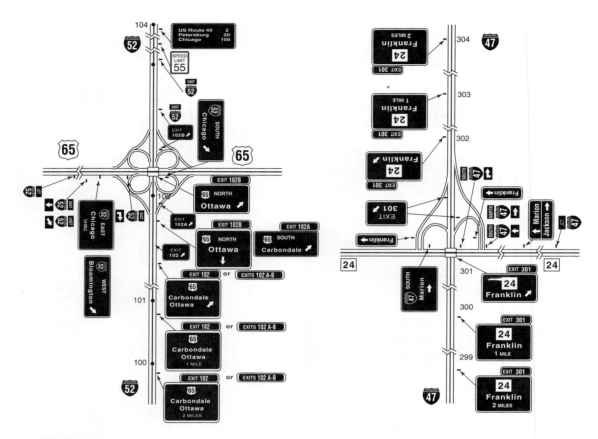

Figure 14-22 (Continued)

with kilometer and 10th-kilometer markers over the next several years.

Traffic signals

A "traffic signal" is defined by the MUTCD as "any power-operated traffic control device other than a barricade warning light or steady burning electric lamp, by which traffic is warned or directed to take some specific action." The most familiar type of signal is the traffic control signal, used primarily at intersections to direct traffic alternately to stop and to move. Other types of signals commonly used include pedestrian signals, lane use signals, and various types of beacon warning devices.

A. Traffic control signals

The MUTCD provides very specific warrants for the use of traffic control signals. These warrants are far more detailed than those specified for other devices. The cost of traffic signals is considerably higher than other types of devices, and the negative impact of their misapplication is also greater than for other

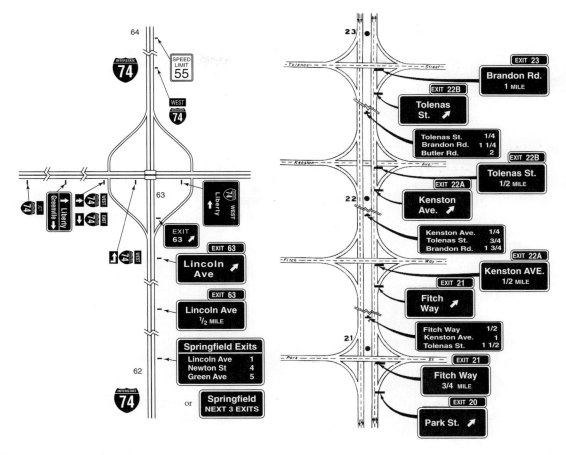

Figure 14-22 (Continued)

types of devices. Thus, the manual is clear that traffic control signals be installed *only* at locations that meet one or more of the eleven specified signal warrants. Further, it states that existing signals *shall be removed* if they are at a location that does not meet any of these warrants.

Warrants for traffic control signals, as well as for STOP and YIELD signs, are covered in detail in Chapter 15, Introduction to Intersection Control. The MUTCD also gives very detailed standards for the design, placement, and operation of traffic control signals.

When properly installed in accordance with warrants and standards, the MUTCD (page 4B-1) indicates that traffic control signals have one or more of the following benefits:

1. They can provide for the orderly movement of traffic.
2. Where proper physical layouts and control measures are used, they can increase the traffic-handling capacity of the intersections.
3. They can reduce the frequency of certain types of accidents, especially the right-angle type.
4. Under favorable conditions, they can be coordinated to provide for continuous or nearly continuous movement of traffic at a definite speed along a given route.

Figure 14-23   Selected service guide signs. [From *Manual of Uniform Traffic Control Devices,* Federal Highway Administration, 1988, pp. 2E-35 and 2G-5.]

5. They can be used to interrupt heavy traffic at intervals to permit other traffic, vehicular or pedestrian, to cross.

It is also noted that unwarranted, poorly-designed, or improperly-operated traffic control signals can cause excessive delay to drivers and pedestrians, encourage disobedience, induce the use of less adequate routes, and increase the frequency of certain types of accidents, particularly the rear-end type.

The MUTCD provides detailed meanings for the various signal indications which may be used:

Steady Circular Indications

GREEN: Vehicular traffic facing a "green ball" may enter the intersection to travel straight through or to turn left or right, except when prohibited by signs, lane markings, or design. Turning vehicles must yield to opposing through vehicles,

RA-030
Campfire

RA-110
Shelter (sleeping)

RA-130
Showers

RS-010
Skating (ice)

RS-060
Sledding

RS-070
Snowmobiling

RL-010
Amphitheater

RL-050
Playground

RL-100
Trail (hiking)

RW-020
Canoeing

RW-080
Ramp (launch)

RW-130
Swimming

YELLOWSTONE
NATIONAL PARK
2 MILES

CEDAR CREEK

WINTER SPORTS

GREAT SMOKY MTS
NATIONAL PARK

Figure 14-24 Selected recreational and cultural interest guide signs. [From *Manual of Uniform Traffic Control Devices,* Federal Highway Administration, 1988, pp. 2H-7, 2H-8, and 2H-14.]

and to pedestrians legally in a conflicting crosswalk. Unless a pedestrian signal is present, pedestrians may proceed across the roadway within any legal marked or unmarked crosswalk.

YELLOW: Vehicles are warned that the related green movement is being terminated or that a red indication will immediately follow. Entry on "yellow" is generally legal, but is prohibited on the "red" which may follow it. In the absence of pedes-

trian signals, pedestrians are prohibited from entering the street during a yellow indication.

RED: Vehicular traffic is prohibited from entering the intersection, and all vehicles must stop at a stop line or crosswalk line (or path, if unmarked). Right turning traffic may proceed cautiously after making a complete stop unless prohibited by signs. Left turns from a one-way street to another one-way street may also proceed cautiously after making a complete stop. In either case, vehicles must yield to pedestrians legally crossing the street. Not all states allow the one-way left turn to proceed on red; the applicable state MUTCD should be checked for this detail. Right-turn-on-red is prohibited by ordinance in some urban areas, such as New York City. Pedestrians facing a "red ball" are prohibited from entering the intersection.

Flashing Circular Indications

YELLOW: Drivers facing a flashing yellow may proceed through the intersection with caution.

RED: The flashing red carries the same requirement as a STOP sign: drivers may proceed only after coming to a full stop.

Steady Arrow Indications

GREEN: Traffic may execute the movement indicated by the arrow cautiously. Such traffic must yield to pedestrians legally crossing the street. A left green arrow is used only when the left-turn movement indicated is "protected," i.e., free of opposing through vehicular traffic. When a green arrow is the only green indication shown, pedestrians are prohibited from entering the intersection.

YELLOW: This indication has the same meaning as a circular yellow indication, except that it applies specifically to a movement controlled by a green arrow. Thus, a yellow arrow indicates that the related movement is about to be terminated, and/or that a red arrow (or ball) indication will immediately follow.

RED: This indication has the same meaning as a circular red indication, except that it applies specifically to a movement controlled by a green arrow.

Flashing Arrow Indications

Flashing yellow or red arrow indications carry the same meaning as flashing yellow or red circular indications, except that they apply specifically to the movement indicated by the arrow.

In general, a signal face should have three to five signal lenses, with some exceptions allowing for a sixth to be shown. Consult the MUTCD directly for these exceptions. Two lens sizes are provided for: 8 inches and 12 inches (diameter). While it is relatively

common to use 12-inch red lenses with 8-inch yellow and green lenses, the MUTCD prohibits use of 8-inch red lenses with 12-inch yellow and/or green lenses.

The larger 12-inch lens is *required* under the following conditions:

1. On signalized approaches where drivers view both traffic control and lane use signals simultaneously
2. Where the nearest signal face is between 120 and 150 ft beyond the stop line, unless a supplemental near-side signal indication is used
3. For signal faces located more than 150 ft from the stop line
4. For all signalized approaches for which the minimum visibility requirements for 8-inch lenses cannot be met

and *should* be used in the following situations:

5. Where 85th percentile approach speeds on a signalized approach exceed 40 mph
6. On approaches where signalization might be unexpected
7. For all arrow indications
8. All approaches with rural cross sections where only post-mounted signals are used

The larger lenses *may* be used in any situation where an engineering study indicates the need for extra visibility or target value.

Table 14-2 shows the visibility distance requirements for traffic signals. For through traffic, two signal faces must be provided. Where these visibility distances cannot be met, use of 12-inch lenses is man-

Table 14-2   Required Visibility Distances
for Signal Faces

85th Percentile Speed	Minimum Visibility Distance
20 mph	175 ft
25 mph	215 ft
30 mph	270 ft
35 mph	325 ft
40 mph	390 ft
45 mph	460 ft
50 mph	540 ft
55 mph	625 ft
60 mph	715 ft

[From *Manual of Uniform Traffic Control Devices,* Federal Highway Administration, 1988, p. 4B-11.]

dated, as is the placement of appropriate "signal ahead" warning signs, which may be supplemented by a "hazard identification beacon."

The arrangement of lenses on a signal face is also limited to approved sequences. The general sequence requires that the red signal be located on the top of a vertical display, and to the left on a horizontal display, followed by the yellow then the green. Where ball and arrow indications are located on the same face, arrow indications are on the bottom or right of the display. Figure 14-25 illustrates the most frequently used combinations of lenses. The MUTCD contains detailed discussion of the applicability of various signal face designs.

Figure 14-26 illustrates the preferred placement of signal faces. At least one of the two required signal faces (for through traffic) *shall* be located between 40 and 150 ft of the stop line, unless the physical design of the intersection prevents it. Horizontal placement should be within 20° of the centerline of the driver's eye, facing straight ahead.

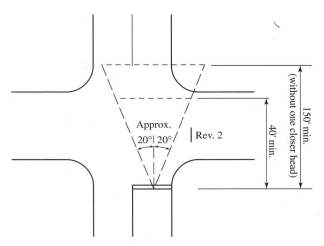

Figure 14-26 Desirable location of signal faces. [From *Manual of Uniform Traffic Control Devices,* Federal Highway Administration, 1988, p. 4B-13.]

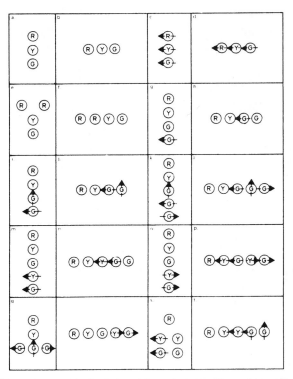

Figure 14-25 Typical signal face designs. [From *Manual of Uniform Traffic Control Devices,* Federal Highway Administration, 1988, p. 4B-9.]

Continuous operation of traffic control signals is critical to safe operation. No signal face should ever be "dark." At least one lens on each signal face must be illuminated at all times. In cases where signal operation is deemed unnecessary during overnight or other off-peak periods, signals must be operated in the flashing mode. Signal installations must be designed so that flashing operation can be maintained even when the controller is removed for repair or replacement.

During installation, inoperable signals should be bagged and turned to make it obvious to drivers that they are not in operation. In general, signals should be installed shortly before operation to minimize possible confusion to drivers.

Maintenance of traffic control signals is also of the utmost importance. A burned-out bulb or lamp can cause a "dark" signal face to appear. Other malfunctions can lead to other non-standard indications being shown. A regular bulb replacement schedule should be maintained, a schedule that anticipates reasonable service life. A maintenance group must be in place (either through contract with a private company or directly by the operating agency) with strict response time requirements in the event a malfunction is reported. Malfunctioning signals can lead to legal liability for accidents that occur as a result of the malfunction.

B. Pedestrian signals

Chapters 15 and 16 discuss the use and application of pedestrian signals in the overall context of intersection control and signalization. As for other devices, the MUTCD specifies design details for pedestrian signals. Figure 14-27 illustrates four alternative designs for pedestrian signals that are permitted by the MUTCD.

C. Other traffic signals

The MUTCD specifies design criteria for a variety of flashing yellow and/or red beacons. These are generally used to identify a hazard, or to call attention to a critical control device, such as a speed limit sign, a STOP sign, a YIELD sign, a DO NOT ENTER sign, or similar devices.

Lane use control signals are also described and specified. In general, overhead signals using red and yellow X's, and green downward arrows indicate whether a lane is available for use by vehicles traveling in the direction to which the signal face is visible. Such controls are used to control reversible lanes on bridges, in tunnels, and on streets and highways.

Traffic signal hardware and street display

While the MUTCD provides general standards for signal design elements, the hardware of a signal system is covered in a variety of other references. Because a variety of manufacturers make signal hardware, maintenance of standards, compatibility, and the ability to interchange components are critical issues. While not treated in detail herein, it is also critical to maintain signal equipment, which requires proper staffing, and an inventory and record-keeping system.

Traffic signal hardware covers a wide variety of equipment. From the traffic engineering point of view, functional components include:

- intersection controllers
- intersection display hardware
- arterial and system coordination hardware
- detectors (where needed)

Intersection controllers implement the signal timing by defining phases and sequencing, cycle lengths, and

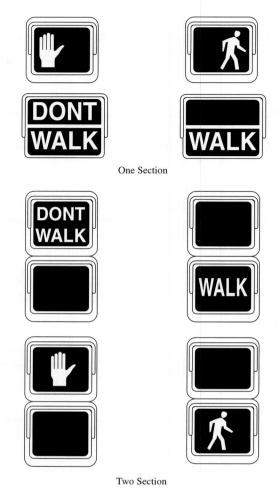

One Section

Two Section

Figure 14-27 Typical pedestrian signal indications. [From *Manual of Uniform Traffic Control Devices,* Federal Highway Administration, 1988, p. 4D-3.]

phase splits. They are connected to *display hardware* that informs drivers of the signal control plan. Such hardware includes signal heads and various types of supporting structures. Where signals are coordinated, master controllers and/or computers comprise *arterial and system coordination hardware.* Finally, where either intersection or system elements are demand-responsive, *detectors* must be used to provide information on vehicle presence that will interact with controllers to determine a signal timing pattern.

Of course, hardware also includes other important elements, including communications, wiring, power supply, conduit runs, underground or above-ground compartments for housing controllers, and lighting.

The *Manual of Traffic Signal Design* [8] and the *Traffic Detector Handbook* [9] are standard traffic engineering references that provide significant detail on all elements of traffic signal hardware.

A. Standards for traffic control equipment

The National Electrical Manufacturers Association (NEMA) is the principal trade group for the electronics industry in the U.S. Within the organization, there is a Traffic Control Systems Section charged with setting manufacturing guidelines and standards for traffic control hardware. Specifically, the group sets standards in accordance with the following philosophy [10]:

- Industry standards for traffic control equipment should be based on proven designs.
- Standards for interchangeable traffic control equipment should be downward compatible with existing equipment.
- The industry has an obligation to take the lead in developing hardware standards.
- Every precaution should be exercised to reduce the potential for malfunctions.
- Performance and reliability of traffic control equipment should be upgraded and should reflect the current state-of-the-art.

Having solicited committee members and comments from the International Municipal Signal Association (IMSA) and ITE, NEMA initially promulgated its Standards Publication TS1, "Traffic Control Systems," in 1976, and continues to update it periodically.

NEMA standards are not product designs, but rather descriptions and performance criteria for various product categories. The Standard covers such products as solid-state controllers, load switches, conflict monitors, loop detectors, flashers, and terminals and facilities. Reference [11] provides a good overview of what the NEMA standards mean and imply.

NEMA does not preclude any manufacturer from making and selling a nonconforming product. Many funding agencies, however, require the use of "NEMA controllers" and other "NEMA-type hard-

ware." While these requirements are vague, they have effectively limited the market for non-conforming hardware. Whether or not this retards hardware innovation is a complex issue that is not easily resolved.

B. Intersection signal controllers

In general, there are two types of intersection signal controllers: *pretimed* and *actuated*. These two forms of control are discussed in greater detail in Chapters 16, 17, and 18. *Pretimed* control provides for constant cycle lengths, phase sequences, and phase lengths. A single controller may provide for several different timing patterns for different times of the day. Its primary feature is that it functions without respect to demand patterns, and requires no detection. In *actuated* control, signal operation is affected on a cycle-by-cycle basis by current demand. Thus, actuated control requires detection to provide the controller with current information on arrivals.

Historically, pretimed controllers were electromechanical devices marked by simplicity, reliability, and reasonable cost. Early actuated controllers used hard-wired circuits and vacuum tubes, and were costly and not always reliable.

With the advent of transistors, integrated circuits, and microcomputers, a new generation of actuated controllers was created and the equipment became modular so that individual elements could be "pulled" and replaced in the field.

Modern solid-state controllers also exist for the pretimed function, and actuated equipment can be set to the pretimed mode through use of recall switches. Nevertheless, because of cost factors and high reliability, there is still substantial use of electromechanical pretimed controllers.

1. Electromechanical pretimed controllers. The primary functioning elements of the electromechanical pretimed controller are illustrated in Figure 14-28. In Figure 14-28a, a *synchronous motor* turns at a fixed rate (determined by the frequency of the power supply), and drives the *timing dial* through a *timing gear*. The timing gear can be changed easily, and it is the gear ratio that determines the rotation speed of the timing dial and thus the cycle length, which comprises one rotation of the timing dial.

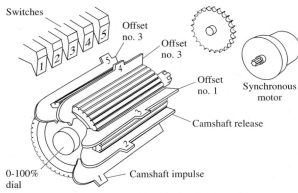

(a) Synchronous motor drives timing dial through gears

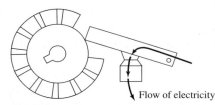

(b) Switches in "a" advance the camshaft

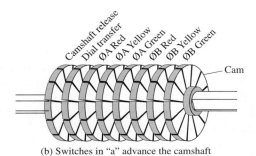

(c) Breaks in the cams allow electricity to flow to specific bulbs

Figure 14-28 Basic elements of an electromechanical controller. [From *Traffic Control Devices Handbook,* Federal Highway Administration, 1983, p. 439.]

A number of *keys* are inserted in the timing dial, each of which lifts a *switch.* Certain switch activations cause a *camshaft* to advance (Figure 14-28b), rotating a set of *cams,* most of which are directly related to signal indication.

The actual signal indication occurs because the teeth on a given cam are broken out (Figure 14-28c), allowing a contact to close a circuit so current can flow to designated bulbs in the signal heads. The cams

are broken out in a pattern that allows the logical sequence of green-yellow-red first on one phase and then another. Cams are wired to the appropriate bulbs so that they light at the appropriate time.

What can the engineer or technician easily change in the field? The timing gear can be replaced, causing the cycle length to change. The keys can be moved, changing the duration of individual signal phases and transitions. The phase *sequence* cannot be changed without changing the cams themselves, and this is *not* an easy procedure.

In early computer control systems, the central computer took over the cam advance function, superceding the timing dial. In this way, cycle length and phase durations could be controlled remotely.

Figure 14-29 shows a three-dial electromechanical controller as it would be installed inside the

Figure 14-29 Electromechanical controller inside a standard cabinet. [Courtesy of General Traffic Equipment.]

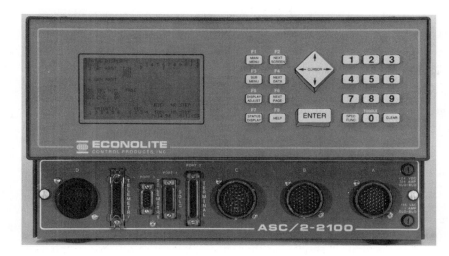

Figure 14-30 A modern actuated controller. [Courtesy of Econolite Control Products, Inc.]

equipment cabinet at the intersection. Some of the fixed wiring is hidden behind the panel near the dials in this illustration. By time-of-day or other control, a given dial would be selected for use. In this way, three different sets of cycle lengths and phase durations could be implemented.

2. Modern actuated controllers. Because the technology has advanced so rapidly in a competitive market, the details of most illustrations tend to be dated. With this caveat, refer to Figure 14-30, which shows a controller being marketed in 1996. Note several features:

- standardized plug interfaces
- touchpads, replacing knobs, thumb-wheels, and other input devices of earlier equipment
- function keys
- convenient information displays

Figure 14-31 shows the same unit with the cover opened, displaying the internal electronics.

The illustrated unit has a number of impressive features, including: allowance for up to 12 phases,

Figure 14-31 Controller with front panel open. [Courtesy of Econolite Control Products, Inc.]

eight concurrent groups, and two timing rings; all standard NEMA timing functions; 64 coordination patterns; three interconnection methods; preemption options; ability to use up to 64 vehicle detectors; telemetry, including a 1200 bps modem; diagnostics; and display and help screens.

C. Arterial and system hardware

To maintain a system of signals in coordination, either along a single arterial, or in a network, individual intersection controllers must be interconnected to achieve the necessary synchronization. For decades, the most common means of achieving interconnection have been (1) installation of dedicated wiring and (2) leasing service from the local telephone company. The former is a large capital expense and an agency responsibility to maintain the wiring, while the latter is a continuing operating expense.

Other ways of communicating between a master location and individual local controllers include:

- radio communications
- optical communications along line-of-sight
- leased service from cable TV operators on coaxial cable installed for their basic service
- fiber optics cable
- wireless communications using modern cellular technology

One other advance has been in the development of *time-based* coordination units that do not require synchronization, but rather depend on internal clocks, much as a quartz watch does.

Historically, most coordinated systems involve pre-timed controllers, as a prerequisite of coordinated control is a common cycle length for all interconnected intersections. A *master controller* is used to send coordination pulses to all intersection controllers. The master controller can have a tune clock that selects the plan to be implemented by time-of-day of the week. More sophisticated systems included signals actuated by using "coordination units" to assure that main-street green was not disrupted by side-street calls for service.

The next level of sophistication was hard-wired *traffic-adjusted* systems. The basic concept of such systems is the use of a limited number of detectors along an arterial to: (a) measure traffic flow levels, (b) compute the traffic in each direction as a percent of expected peak loading, and (c) use this information and user-set transition levels to determine the plan to be selected to best serve observed traffic. Later, hard-wired traffic-responsive systems used detector occupancy as well as volume in making the plan selection. Ultimately, for complex systems, the use of general-purpose digital computers greatly expanded the number of signals that could be coordinated. Chapter 24 is a survey of modern computer-controlled technology and its application.

Modern network control hardware tends to build upon the concepts of IC- and microprocessor NEMA controllers described in the previous section, with special units to serve as system masters and supporting software to allow user-friendly network control and report generation.

D. Detectors

Over the years, a variety of detectors have been used, both in providing on-line information to actuated controllers, and in data collection. These include:

- inductive loop detectors
- magnetic detectors
- magnetometer
- radar detectors
- sonic detectors
- photocell detectors
- pressure pads

Installations of all of these still exist in various locations throughout the nation. However, in recent years, the predominant type of detection is the *inductive loop*.

Loop detectors are typically formed by two or three turns of a 12-gauge or 14-gauge wire placed in slots cut into the pavement and brought back to an amplifier/oscillator in the control cabinet. The oscillator serves as a source of energy for the loop. A vehicle passing over or stopped within the loop causes a reduction in loop inductance, which causes an increase in the oscillator frequency. The increase activates a relay, sending an electrical output to the controller.

Figure 14-32 illustrates a standard installation of loops on a two-lane approach. Note that each lane has a separate detector. Corners are cut on an angle, as shown, so that sharp edges do not pose installation problems. Some agencies use wire placed inside plastic tubing prior to installation for the same reason. The pavement cut is sealed with epoxy or another substance after the wire's insertion.

Preformed loops are now available commercially for ease of installation. The loop is preformed in a concrete block; the concrete block is then installed as a unit into the pavement and connected to an oscillator/amplifier in the control box.

Ultrasonic detectors saw a great deal of use in the 1970s. They experienced some difficulties in the adjustment of the area of detection and with pavement surface problems. Recently, improved technology has

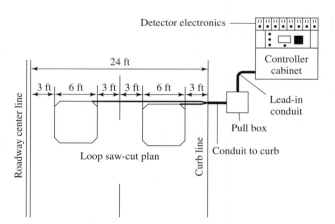

Figure 14-32 Typical installation of loop detector system. [Used with permission of Institute of Transportation Engineers, from *Traffic Detector Handbook*, 2nd Ed., JHK & Associates, p. 3. Copyright © Institute of Transportation Engineers.]

fostered a rebirth of interest in this type of detection. It is particularly useful in areas where poor pavement condition makes the use of loops (which are installed in the pavement) impractical from a maintenance standpoint. Figure 14-33 shows a typical installation.

The ultrasonic detector essentially sends an ultrasonic wave to the pavement, from which it is reflected back to the source. The time for the reflection to return is calibrated. When a vehicle is within the detection cone area, it is reflected back sooner, as the top of the vehicle is closer to the detector than the pavement.

Only one ultrasonic detector is generally placed on an intersection approach. Thus, the adjustment of the detection cone is critical to its proper operation, as it must detect vehicles in any moving lane on the approach.

A rapidly-developing type of detection that will have vast implications for current and future hardware systems is wide-area video imaging. Use of video has become more sophisticated in recent years with the development of supporting software. It is now possible to define detector locations anywhere within a video image (and in fact several locations can be defined within the range of a single image). Vehicles can be "detected" as the light intensity of the image on the pictals in the defined "detector" changes. This requires that the intensity of the background image be constantly recalibrated to adjust for different lighting conditions. In addition, care must be taken in terms of image angles to avoid "detecting" vehicle shadows as well as the vehicles themselves.

It is now possible to directly connect a wide-area video camera to a microprocessor in the controller cabinet to operate an actuated controller.

The great advantage of this emerging type of detection is the ability to cover a wide area of significant length and several lanes with a single device. It also allows the specific locations of individual detectors to be remotely altered by computer, as they are no longer physical devices located in the pavement. A typical installation is shown in Figure 14-34.

E. Display hardware

The MUTCD requires that at least one, and preferably two, signal faces be located within a cone of 20° to the left or 20° to the right of the "center of the approach lanes extended." While there is some controversy concerning the origin of the cone, it is generally taken to be the centerline of all moving approach lanes (including *uncontrolled* left- and right-turn lanes) at the stop line. Figure 14-35 illustrates two examples in which this is implemented.

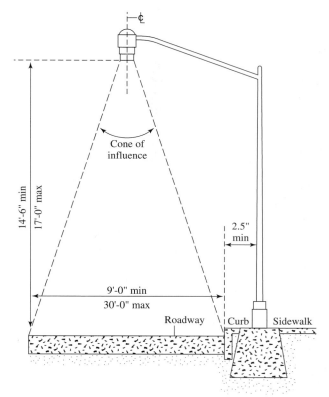

No. of lanes	¢
1	4' from curb (or edge of roadway)
2	Between lanes
3	Center line of middle lane

Figure 14-33 A typical ultrasonic detector installation. [Used with permission of Institute of Transportation Engineers, from *Traffic Detector Handbook,* 2nd Ed., JHK & Associates, p. 166. Copyright © Institute of Transportation Engineers.]

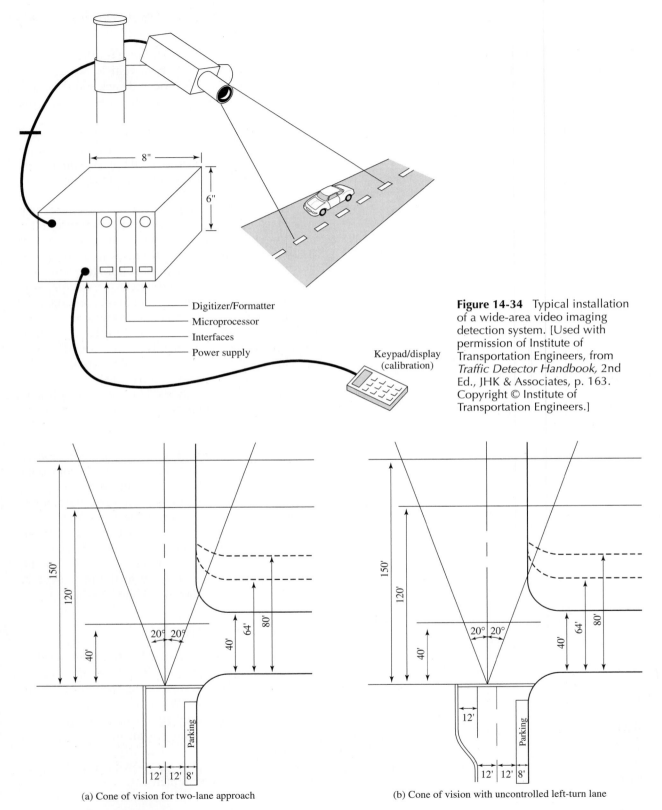

Figure 14-34 Typical installation of a wide-area video imaging detection system. [Used with permission of Institute of Transportation Engineers, from *Traffic Detector Handbook,* 2nd Ed., JHK & Associates, p. 163. Copyright © Institute of Transportation Engineers.]

Digitizer/Formatter
Microprocessor
Interfaces
Power supply

Keypad/display
(calibration)

(a) Cone of vision for two-lane approach

(b) Cone of vision with uncontrolled left-turn lane

Figure 14-35 Maximum visibility cones for signal head placement. [Used with permission of Prentice-Hall, Inc., from J. Kell and I. Fullerton, *Manual of Traffic Signal Design,* 2nd Ed., p. 44. Copyright © 1991 Prentice-Hall, Inc.]

There are three basic methods for mounting signal heads: (1) post-mounting, (2) mast-mounting, and (3) span-mounting. These three alternatives are illustrated in Figures 14-36, 14-37, and 14-38, respectively.

Post-mounted signal heads are generally the most inexpensive, and are used where the overall width of the intersection allows for placement of post-mounted heads within the required 20° vision cone required by MUTCD. Post mounting can be a problem in busy commercial areas, where signal heads would be in proximity to or in the line of sight of colorfully-lighted commercial displays.

Mast arms carry the signal heads out over the intersection, and allow them to be located closer to the centerline of the approach. They can also be used to hold more than one signal head for emphasis or added visibility.

Span mounting is most often used at wider intersections where neither post- nor mast-mounting provide sufficient visibility. Span mounting also allows for placement of several signal heads over specified lanes, which may be important where exclusive turning lanes are heavily used. Figure 14-38 shows four alternative patterns for span-mounting that are in general use, depending on the number of heads and their exact placement requirements.

Reference [8] gives a more detailed discussion of the advantages and disadvantages of each type of mounting with respect to other features of the intersection design and the demand flows.

F. Other hardware issues

As noted previously, there are many details of hardware that are not covered in this section, including wiring specifications and other details. Pedestrian signals, ramp controls and similar hardware are also not discussed, although the MUTCD and the *Manual of Traffic Signal Design* [8] provide useful information in these areas.

The reader is also reminded that issues of maintenance and operation are critical in traffic signal management. A signal that malfunctions, even if only for a very short while, represents a severe safety problem, and one for which the agency in charge is fully liable. While not treated in this text, the traffic engineer must be fully aware of his/her responsibilities in this area.

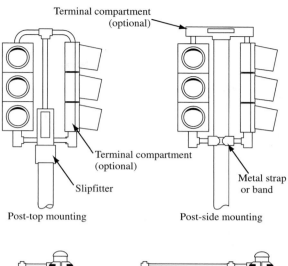

Post-top mounting   Post-side mounting

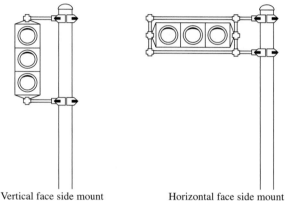

Vertical face side mount   Horizontal face side mount

(a) Post-mounting alternatives

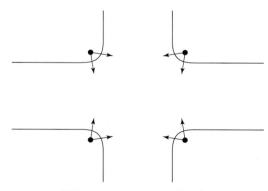

(b) Standard post-mounting locations

Figure 14-36 Post-mounted traffic signal heads. [Used with permission of Prentice-Hall, Inc., from J. Kell and I. Fullerton, *Manual of Traffic Signal Design,* 2nd Ed., p. 44. Copyright © 1991 Prentice-Hall, Inc.]

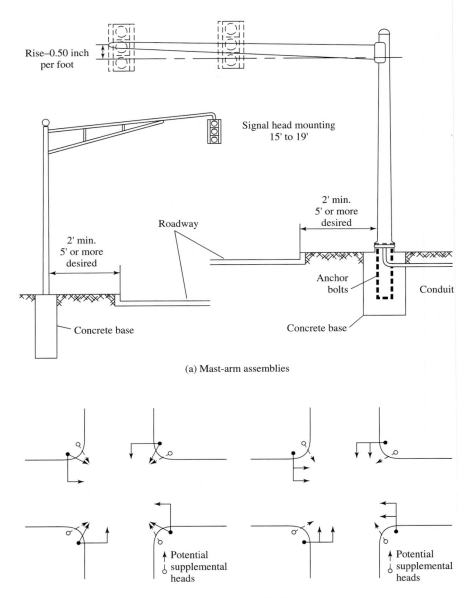

Rise–0.50 inch
per foot

Signal head mounting
15' to 19'

Roadway

2' min.
5' or more
desired

2' min.
5' or more
desired

Anchor
bolts

Conduit

Concrete base

Concrete base

(a) Mast-arm assemblies

Potential
supplemental
heads

Potential
supplemental
heads

(b) Typical mast-arm locations

Figure 14-37 Mast-mounted traffic signal heads. [Used with permission of Prentice-Hall, Inc., from J. Kell and I. Fullerton, *Manual of Traffic Signal Design,* 2nd Ed., p. 57. Copyright © 1991 Prentice-Hall, Inc.]

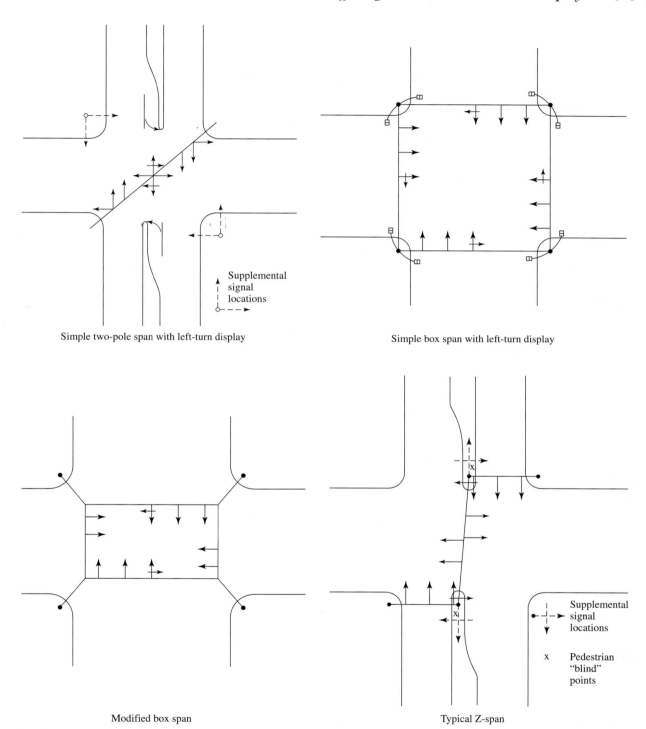

Simple two-pole span with left-turn display

Simple box span with left-turn display

Modified box span

Typical Z-span

Figure 14-38 Span-mounted traffic signal heads. [Used with permission of Prentice-Hall, Inc., from J. Kell and I. Fullerton, *Manual of Traffic Signal Design,* 2nd Ed., pp. 51–53. Copyright © 1991 Prentice-Hall, Inc.]

Summary and conclusion

This chapter has provided an overview of traffic control devices, the criteria of the MUTCD which govern their use, design, and placement, and other important references regarding traffic signal hardware. Again, the student and practitioner are reminded that the MUTCD and other references contain much detailed information not included herein, and that the

manual and other standard documents should be consulted directly whenever traf-fic control device installations are being considered and designed.

Chapter 15 will discuss the alternatives for intersection control in great detail. Subsequent chapters will address the timing and analysis of traffic control signals at intersections, and the complex issues of signal coordination.

References

1. *Manual of Uniform Traffic Control Devices,* U.S. Department of Transportation, Federal Highway Administration, Washington, DC, 1988 (amended through 1997).
2. Hawkins, H. G., "Evolution of the MUTCD: Early Standards for Traffic Control Devices," *ITE Journal,* July 1992.
3. Hawkins, H. G., "Evolution of the MUTCD: Early Editions of the MUTCD," *ITE Journal,* August 1992.
4. Hawkins, H. G., "Evolution of the MUTCD: The MUTCD Since WWII," *ITE Journal,* November 1992.
5. Hawkins, H. G., "Evolution of MUTCD Mirrors American Progress Since the 1920s," *Roads and Bridges,* Scranton Gillette Communications, Inc., Des Plaines, IL, July 1995.
6. Kowal, J., "Montana's Out Front—No Daytime Limit," *Newsday,* Sunday, December 10, 1995.
7. Schaer, S., "Pedal Power," *Newsday,* Sunday, December 10, 1995.
8. Kell, J., and Fullerton, I., *Manual of Traffic Signal Design,* 2nd Edition, Institute of Transportation Engineers, Prentice-Hall, Inc., Englewood Cliffs, NJ, 1991.
9. *Traffic Detector Handbook,* 2nd Edition, JHK & Associates, Institute of Transportation Engineers, Washington, DC, n.d.
10. Parris, C., "NEMA and Traffic Control," *ITE Journal,* August 1986.
11. Parris, C., "Just What Does a 'NEMA Standard' Mean?" *ITE Journal,* July 1987.

Problems

Problem 14–1

Define the terms "shall," "should," and "may" as they apply to standards and criteria given in the *Manual on Uniform Traffic Control Devices.*

Problem 14–2

Describe how color, shape, and legend are used to convey and reinforce messages given by traffic control devices.

Problem 14–3

Why is it important not to overuse regulatory and warning signs?

Problem 14–4   use MUTD

How far from the point of hazard should the following warning signs be placed?

(a) A "stop ahead" warning sign on a road with a posted speed limit of 50 mph.
(b) A "curve ahead" warning sign with an advisory speed of 30 mph on a road with a posted speed limit of 45 mph.
(c) A "merge ahead" warning sign on a ramp with an 85th percentile speed of 35 mph.

Problem 14–5

Why is the use of route markers an important guide to drivers? Describe the various types of route marker assemblies.

Problem 14–6

Many things are "standardized" in our society, by formal standards written into law or regulation, or by common practice. A clear, well-accepted standard use of "red" and "green" in traffic control is to indicate whether a driver is permitted to proceed or not. A less formal "standard" expectation is that fire trucks are painted red.

(a) In fact, studies have shown that lighter colors are more visible in such uses as fire trucks moving through traffic, and there have been moves to lime green and white fire trucks in some communities. However, the trend is very slow and may have faltered: the red fire truck is still the norm. Be prepared to discuss the expectation of the public as distinct from the technical fact of enhanced visibility, and the trade-offs (and education effort) involved in making the two coincide. Apply the discussion to the case of fire trucks and to the more general issue of standardization.

(b) For the purpose of discussion only, assume that a definitive study shows that the two new colors are much better than "red" and "green" for distinction and visibility to many more drivers under many more conditions (this is hypothetical; the authors know of no such work). Be prepared to discuss the issue of the ease with which the standard use of colors could be changed, how it might be done, and over what time frame (if at all).

(c) Now consider the same issue of standardization, but introduce the considerations of maintenance, interchangeability, and of "freezing" the technology by virtue of standardization. Apply the discussion to traffic controllers specifically, but do make comparisons to the signal colors and the fire trucks.

Problem 14–7

Refer to Reference [8] and tabulate the advantages and disadvantages of the various types of mounting specified in this chapter.

(a) From observations in your own area, find which type(s) of mounting are most common in the following situations:

CBD intersections

Arterials on the state road system

Urban arterials, not on the state road system

Comment. If possible, find what local practices are codified or otherwise formally stated regarding type of mounting.

(b) On an arterial with significant percentages of trucks, comment on the type(s) of mountings that may be most and/or least suitable, and the reasons for your judgment.

Problem 14–8

This example is an adaptation of a study conducted in Tampa, Florida by Tindale. It is a study of a relamping program in

place of a "respond to burnouts" approach. It is strongly recommended that this example be laid out on a spreadsheet.

Basics

Lamps in the field = 8500
Vehicle operating cost = $0.24/mile
Average hourly wage = $6.75/hour
Cost of lamp = $0.47/hour

Alternate 1: Respond to burnouts

Failure rate = 0.0187 per month
Typical call = 10 miles traveled at 35 mph
39 minutes consumed in repair
1-person crew

Alternate 2: Group Relamping

Plan is to replace all lamps once every 18 months

Average distance = 12 miles to first signal,
0.3 miles from signal to signal,
all traveled at 35 mph
Replacement-rate info = 0.3 miles from signal to signal,
21 lamps per intersection
6 intersections per day
8-hour work day (i.e., pay for 8 hr)
2-person crew
Failure rate = 0.00447 per month

The failure in Alternate 2 still requires the type of response described in Alternate 1.

(a) Compare the cost of the two alternatives on a yearly basis and decide which is more appropriate.

(b) Consider changes of ±25% in all unit costs, distances, and time. Rank them in terms of percent impact on total cost of the selected alternative. Do any of them individually cause the selected alternative to change?

(c) Create two additional alternatives, and use the given information to estimate relevant numbers as best you can. Alternate 3 is a variation on Alternate 1: when a burnout call is received, a two-person crew is dispatched and all lamps at that intersection are replaced. Alternate 4 is another variation on Alternate 1: the person responding to burnouts is in radio contact with the base, and moves from one burnout to the next, thus saving mileage and time.

Explain your estimates for the average distances and the failure rate for future burnouts. Is Alternate 4 real, considering the typical number of burnouts per day?

Decide on which alternative to select. Comment.

(d) Comment on the need to do some or all of this work during the off-peak.

(e) What would happen if the lamp life could be increased 100% for a 35% increase in lamp cost?

15

Introduction to Intersection Control

The most complex locations within any street and highway system are at-grade intersections. At intersections, vehicular flows from several different approaches making left-turn, through, and right-turn movements seek to occupy the same physical space. In addition to these vehicular flows, pedestrians also seek to use some of this space to cross the street.

At no other location within the street and highway system are so many potential and actual conflicts present. Figure 15-1 illustrates the potential for conflicts in a typical at-grade intersection of two two-way streets. When all of the possible movements are considered, there are 16 combinations of movements crossing each other's path within the intersection.

These conflicts include 4 between competing through movements, 8 between left turns and competing through movements, and 4 between competing left-turn movements. In addition, every left-turn or right-turn movement involves a merging conflict as the turning vehicle merges into a through traffic stream. Pedestrians crossing the street conflict with through vehicles on the street being crossed, as well as vehicles turning into the street being crossed.

The critical task of the traffic engineer is to control and manage these conflicts in such a way as to provide for safe and efficient movement through the intersection for both motorists and pedestrians.

Hierarchy of intersection control

Three fundamental levels of control can be provided at intersections: basic rules-of-the-road, STOP or YIELD control, and signal control, as illustrated in Figure 15-2. The analysis of which of these is most appropriate for any given situation is one of the most important conducted by traffic engineers, and often one of the most visible to local residents and interest groups.

Basic rules-of-the-road apply at any intersection where right-of-way is not assigned through the use of traffic signals, STOP, or YIELD signs. These rules are specified in each state's vehicle and traffic law, and motorists are required to know them. At intersections, all states follow a similar format. In the absence of

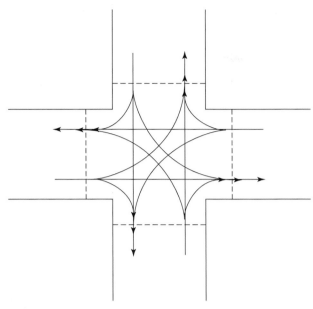

Figure 15-1 Conflicts at an at-grade intersection of two two-way streets.

INTERSECTION CONTROL OPTIONS

How much judgment can drivers safely exercise to avoid collisions? Three levels of control are available:

Level I: **Passive control-basic rules of the road apply**

- No control
- Guide signs only
- Warning sings with or without guide signs

Level II: **Assignment of right-of-way (ROW) to major street or rotational ROW**

- YIELD control
- Two-way STOP control
- All-way STOP control

Level III: **Positive alternate assignment of exclusive ROW**

- Traffic signals
  -Two phase
  -Multiphase
- Traffic control agent/officer

Figure 15-2 Levels of intersection control illustrated.

---

control devices, the driver on the left must yield the right-of-way to the driver on the right, when the vehicle on the right is approaching in a manner that may create an impending hazard to the vehicle on the left. In essence, the responsibility for avoiding conflicts falls to the driver on the left. Most state codes go on to specify that through vehicles have the right-of-way over turning vehicles in the absence of control devices.

Advance intersection warning signs and directional signs do not constitute "control devices" and do not change the application of the basic rules-of-the-road in any way, although they may contribute to the safety of the operation by focusing drivers' attention on both the existence and location of the intersection.

The most common application of *STOP or YIELD signs* is in a two-way format. In this case, drivers on the minor street in both directions must stop or yield, and right-of-way is clearly assigned to vehicles on the major street. When a STOP sign is in place, all vehicles on controlled approaches must come to a complete stop, and must wait for a safe gap in the major street traffic stream to proceed. A YIELD sign (in most states) requires drivers to slow to a maximum speed of 10 mph, and to yield the right-of-way to any vehicle approaching on the major street that would present a hazard to the minor street vehicle. Some states require drivers to slow to 8 mph in response to a YIELD sign. Where two-way STOP or YIELD control is in place, the responsibility for avoiding conflicts is clearly assigned to the minor street motorists.

All-way STOP signs are sometimes used at intersections where it would be difficult to determine a major and minor street, but where uncontrolled operation is deemed unsafe. Vehicles on all approaches are required to STOP, and drivers on the right have the initial right-of-way to proceed. Thus, right-of-way proceeds in a clockwise direction sequentially when there are vehicles waiting on all approaches.

All-way STOP control has historically been a subject of much debate among traffic engineers. Many do not like it because of the relative confusion it causes in drivers who rarely understand the right-of-way protocol. This sometimes results in increased numbers of minor accidents. Others believe that it can be useful in solving problems where signals are clearly not warranted, and where lesser methods have failed to provide relief. YIELD signs, of course, may never be used in the "all-way" mode.

Signalization is the ultimate form of intersection control. Its use is called for where vehicular and pedestrian flow are at levels that make it difficult or impossible for drivers to select gaps in conflicting traffic streams through which to safely execute their desired maneuvers. In its most basic form, a *two-phase signal* alternatively assigns full right-of-way to all movements on a given street. In this form, left-turning vehicles must still select gaps through the opposing through flow. *Multiphase signalization* almost always incorporates some form of "protection" for left-turning vehicles, that is, signal phases during which opposing through flows are stopped to allow designated left-turn movements to be made without conflict.

The following sections discuss how each of these levels of intersection control may be analyzed and assessed. In general, the Manual on Uniform Traffic Control Devices (MUTCD) [1] provides very detailed warrants for the imposition of traffic signals. These warrants have been developed over a period of years based on practical experience and federally-sponsored research efforts. The detail to which such warrants are presented underscores the significant expense of both street hardware and controllers, incurred when signals are installed. Warrants for STOP and YIELD signs are far less definitive, and require considerable interpretation to be applied. Finally, the MUTCD provides virtually no guidance on when operation under basic rules-of-the road can be safely applied. Other techniques must be employed to make this assessment.

Assessing the viability of basic rules-of-the-road

The primary prerequisite for safety under the basic rules-of-the-road is that all drivers must be able to see and assess the possibility of "impending hazards" posed by vehicles on conflicting approaches. Sight distances must be adequate for this purpose. The driver can only be given full responsibility for avoiding conflicts he/she can see in sufficient time to react.

At intersections, sight distances are generally limited by buildings or other view obstructions on the corners. Figure 15-3 illustrates the basic geometry of the "visibility triangle" at an intersection corner.

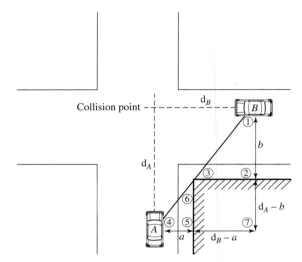

Figure 15-3   Visibility triangle at an intersection.

There are, of course, four such triangles at the typical intersection of two two-way streets.

The line of sight to a conflicting approach is limited by the edge of the building or other obstruction in the corner. At a point where both vehicles just see each other, Vehicle A is d_A ft from the point at which a collision could occur, and Vehicle B is d_B ft from this point. The sight triangle must be sufficiently large to insure that at no time could two vehicles be on these two conflicting paths at distances and speeds that might lead to an accident, without being able to see each other in time to take evasive or corrective actions.

Note that there are three similar triangles in Figure 15-3: △123, △147, and △645. From the similarity of △123 and △645, a relationship between the critical distances in Figure 15-3 can be established:

$$\frac{b}{d_B - a} = \frac{d_A - b}{a} \qquad [15\text{-}1]$$

and:

$$d_B = \frac{ad_A}{d_A - b} \qquad [15\text{-}2]$$

Thus, if the position of Vehicle A is known, the position of Vehicle B when first visible can be established. The equation could also be solved to yield the position of Vehicle A knowing the position of Vehicle B.

Two "rules" insure that sight distances are adequate for either vehicle to avoid an "impending hazard" posed by the other. Rule 1 requires that when the drivers of Vehicles A and B first see each other, *both have at least 1 safe stopping distance to the collision point.* If this is insured, then either vehicle will be able to stop before colliding, and less extreme avoidance measures can certainly be taken. The following computational steps are followed to test whether Rule 1 is satisfied:

1. Assume that Vehicle A is located one safe stopping distance from the collision point. Then:

$$d_A = 1.468 S_A t + \frac{S_A^2}{30(F \pm G)} \qquad [15\text{-}3]$$

where: S_A = speed of Vehicle A, mph
t = driver reaction time, sec
F = coefficient of forward rolling or skidding friction
G = grade (expressed as a decimal)

2. Based on the assumed position, determine the location of Vehicle B when it first becomes visible from Equation [15-2]. This determines the actual value of d_B, and is given the symbol d_B (act).

3. Since Rule 1 requires that Vehicle B also have one safe stopping distance to the collision point, compute the minimum required value of d_B:

$$d_B(\text{min}) = 1.468 S_B t + \frac{S_B^2}{30(F \pm G)} \qquad [15\text{-}4]$$

4. If d_B (act) $\geq d_B$ (min), then adequate sight distance for basic rules-of-the-road has been provided. If d_B (act) $< d_B$ (min), then adequate sight distance under Rule 1 does not exist, and operation under basic rules-of-the-road is not safe.

When Rule 1 fails, it is possible that Vehicle B is at a distance and speed that would produce a collision, yet cannot be seen by the driver of Vehicle A. This is inherently unsafe, and requires that some form of control be provided to assist drivers in avoiding potential conflicts.

A second rule is also used to assess safety. Rule 2 is illustrated in Figure 15-4. To avoid collision from the point at which drivers first see each other, *Vehicle A must travel 18 feet past the collision point in the same time that Vehicle B travels to a point 12 feet before the collision point.* Then:

$$\frac{d_A + 18}{1.468 S_A} = \frac{d_B - 12}{1.468 S_B} \qquad [15\text{-}5]$$

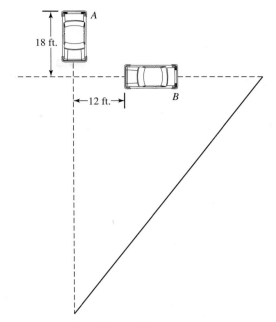

Figure 15-4 Rule 2 illustrated.

and:

$$d_B = (d_A + 18)\frac{S_B}{S_A} + 12 \qquad [15\text{-}6]$$

The steps in assessing the viability of basic rules-of-the-road under Rule 2 are the same as for Rule 1, with the exception of step 3. The minimum required distance for Vehicle B, d_B (min), is found using Equation [15-6] instead of Equation [15-4].

Neither rule is consistently less stringent than the other; the rule yielding the largest d_B (min) depends on the particular situation under study.

For safe operation under basic rules-of-the-road, sight distance for each of the four intersection corners (at a four-leg intersection) must be sufficient. It is also important to note that having adequate sight distance is a *necessary* but not *sufficient* condition for basic rules-of-the-road to be applied. High demand volumes, high approach speeds, or other traffic conditions may render operation under basic rules-of-the-road impractical or unsafe, even where adequate sight distance exists. Thus, a determination that adequate sight distance exists does not relieve the traffic engineer from the necessity of considering the warrants for signalization and/or STOP/YIELD control.

Figure [15-5] depicts a sample problem that will be used to illustrate these procedures. It shows the intersection of a one-way street with a two-way street. In such a situation, there are only two sight triangles to assess, as shown.

Step 1: Assume Vehicle A is one safe stopping distance from the collision point. Then, using Equation [15-3]:

$$d_A = 1.468(30)(1.0) + \frac{(30)^2}{30(0.35)} = 129.7 \text{ ft}$$

Step 2: Given that Vehicle A is 129.7 ft from the collision point, the actual position of Vehicle B when first seen can be determined from Equation [15-2]:

$$d_B(\text{act}) = \frac{(20)(129.7)}{129.7 - 42} = 29.6 \text{ ft}$$

Step 3: The minimum required distance for Vehicle B, d_B (min) can be computed using Rule 1 (Equation [15-4]) or Rule 2 (Equation [15-6]).

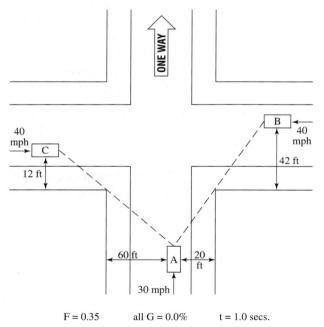

F = 0.35   all G = 0.0%   t = 1.0 secs.

Figure 15-5 Sample problem: Assessing the viability of operation under basic rules-of-the-road.

$$d_B(\text{min},R1) = 1.468(40)(1.0) + \frac{(40)^2}{30(0.35)}$$
$$= 211.1 \text{ ft}$$

$$d_B(\text{min},R2) = (129.7 + 18)\frac{40}{30} + 12 = 208.9 \text{ ft}$$

Step 4: In this case, the minimum distance requirements under Rules 1 and 2 are quite similar in either case. The minimum requirement of 211.1 ft or 208.9 ft is considerably more than the actual distance, 29.6 ft. Thus, this sight triangle *does not* provide the necessary sight distance for operation under basic rules-of-the-road.

Normally, the sight triangle formed between Vehicles A and C should also be checked. In this case, it is not necessary, since the failure of one sight triangle already requires imposition of at least some form of STOP/YIELD control. Nevertheless, to illustrate the computations for this corner:

Step 1: Vehicle A is assumed to be at one safe stopping distance from the collision point. This is the same as in the first computation, i.e., d_A = 129.7 ft.

Step 2: The actual distance for Vehicle C when it first becomes visible is computed using Equation [15-2]:

$$d_C(\text{act}) = \frac{(60)(129.7)}{129.7 - 12} = 66.1 \text{ ft}$$

Step 3: The required minimum distances under Rules 1 and 2 for Vehicle C are the same as for Vehicle B, as their approach speeds and other parameters are the same. Thus, d_B (min, R1) = 211.1 ft, and d_B (min, R2) = 208.9 ft.

Step 4: Once again, the minimum required distances under either rule are considerably larger than the actual distance of 66.1 ft. The second sight triangle does not provide the necessary sight distance for operation under basic rules-of-the-road either.

As both sight triangles in the sample problem fail to provide adequate visibility, operation under basic rules-of-the-road *cannot* be safely applied. Thus, regardless of volume levels, the minimum form of control considered should be two-way STOP or YIELD signs, although, as will be seen, imposition of YIELD and STOP control requires additional testing of visibility. If volumes or other conditions warrant, signal control may be applied.

Assessing the need for signalization: Warrants

The MUTCD [1] presents a detailed set of 11 warrants, each of which justifies the imposition of traffic signals at an intersection. Each warrant addresses a different set of conditions in which signal control has been found to be an effective and justifiable measure to insure safe and efficient operation of the intersection. Most of the warrants are based on long experience, and represent many years of practice and professional judgment. Some of the newer warrants have been recommended as a result of federally-funded research efforts. In either case, the warrants reflect empirical evidence, not abstract theory.

A. Data requirements

Because of the expense of traffic signal installations, and the delay caused to vehicles and their occupants, the MUTCD provides reasonably detailed warrants. The data required to assess need against these criteria is also detailed, and invokes thorough field studies. The MUTCD recommends that the following data be collected to study the need for a signal [Reference 1, pages 4C-1, 2]:

1. Traffic volumes entering the intersection from each approach in each of 16 consecutive hours of a typical day. The 16 hours selected should have the highest percentage of 24-hour traffic (of any other 16-hour period);
2. Traffic volumes by approach and movement, classified by vehicle type (passenger cars, light trucks, and heavy trucks), summarized for each 15-minute period during the two hours in the A.M. and the two hours in the P.M. during which traffic entering the intersection is greatest;
3. Pedestrian counts in each crosswalk during the same four hours covered by the vehicular counts of item 2, and during the hour of heaviest pedestrian traffic. In special situations, pedestrian traf-

fic may be classified by approximate age into three categories: under 13, 13–60, over 60. This is generally done when the make-up of the population suggests special attention to young or old pedestrians will be required;
4. 85th percentile speed of all vehicles on uncontrolled approaches to the intersection;
5. A *condition diagram* of the intersection showing all physical features, including lane widths and use restrictions, location of bus stops, location of all control devices, grades and other geometric details, pavement markings and channelization, parking signs and restrictions, location of utility poles and other objects at or near the intersection, distances to the nearest adjacent signals, etc.;
6. A *collision diagram,* showing all accidents occurring at the intersection by type, location, severity, time of day, and day of week for at least a one-year period, preferably three;
7. For the same time periods as identified in item 2, vehicle-seconds of delay determined separately for each approach;
8. For the same time periods as identified in item 2, the number and distribution of gaps in vehicular traffic on the major street when minor-street traffic has difficulty in safely crossing the intersection;
9. For the same time periods as identified in item 2, the 85th percentile speed of vehicles on controlled approaches measured at a point near to the intersection, but unaffected by the control;
10. For the same time periods as identified in item 2, pedestrian delay time for at least two 30-minute periods of an average weekday or like periods of a Saturday or Sunday should be determined.

Note that the collection of the data for a signal needs study covers virtually all of the areas and techniques of traffic data collection, analysis, and presentation covered in the first part of this text. It should also be noted that not all of the data recommended by the MUTCD is directly used in considering the criteria in signal warrants. The data will also be useful in considering the type of signal control that is most appropriate, and in such matters as the design of a phase plan.

In comparing field data to the criteria of signal warrants, the MUTCD states that "Traffic control signals *should not* be installed unless one or more of the signal warrants in this manual are met." Further, "If these requirements are not met, a traffic signal *should* neither be put into operation *nor continued* in operation (if already installed)" (*italics added*). The use of "should not" and "should" places these warrants in the strongly advisory category. They are not mandatory, but any variance should be carefully documented. Such documentation is important should the installation be a subject of litigation at a future time.

B. Existing warrants

In general, the warrants cover a wide enough range of conditions to justify the use of traffic signals in virtually all cases where the traffic engineer may wish to do so. Thus, cases in which signals are installed when none of the warrants are met are extremely rare. The warrants, however, give the traffic engineer a specific tool in dealing with public groups (who are often interested having signals installed) to explain why a signal is *not* installed at a particular location.

There are currently eleven warrants for signalization in the MUTCD, covering the following situations:

- minimum vehicular volume (8-hour)
- interruption of continuous traffic (8-hour)

- minimum pedestrian volume (8-hour)
- school crossing
- progressive movement
- accident experience
- systems warrant
- combination of warrants
- four-hour vehicular volume
- peak hour delay
- peak-hour vehicular volume

Figures 15-6 through 15-16 contain complete reproductions of all eleven warrants for traffic signal imposition. Note that warrants 9–11 are the most recent additions, and that they contain requirements for short periods of time. In some cases, where these are used as the primary justification for signal installation, the data needs discussed previously can be simplified and the length of time in the field shortened. This is important, as the collection of all of the data recommended is often a burden to small traffic agencies.

Warrant 1 (Figure 15-6) tests for the most common reason for imposing signal control: crossing volumes that are too high to permit drivers to safely pick gaps through which to pass. The minimum volumes are relatively low, but must exist for 8 hours of a typical day.

Warrant 1: Minimum Vehicular Volume

The Minimum Vehicular Volume warrant is intended for application where the volume of intersecting traffic is the principal reason for consideration of signal installation. The warrant is satisfied when, for each of any 8 hours of an average day, the volumes given in the table below exist on the major street and on the higher-volume minor street approach to the intersection. An "average" day is defined as a weekday representing traffic normally and repeatedly found at the location.

MINIMUM VEHICULAR VOLUMES FOR WARRANT 1

Number of lanes for moving traffic on each approach		Vehicles per hour on major street (total of both approaches)	Vehicles per hour on higher volume minor street approach (one direction only)
Major Street	Minor Street		
1	1	500	150
2 or more	1	600	150
1	2 or more	500	200
2 or more	2 or more	600	200

These major-street and minor-street volumes are for the same 8 hours. During those 8 hours, the direction of the higher volume may be on one minor approach during some hours and on the opposite approach during other hours.

When the 85th percentile speed of major-street traffic exceeds 40 mph in either an urban or a rural area, or when the intersection lies within the built-up area of an isolated community having a population of less than 10,000, the Minimum Vehicular Volume warrant is 70 percent of the requirement above.

Figure 15-6 Warrant 1: Minimum vehicular volume (8 hours). [From *Manual of Uniform Traffic Control Devices,* Federal Highway Administration, 1988, p. 4C-3.]

Thus, the peak hours would be expected to have volumes well in excess of the minimums.

While the "high-volume minor approach" may change over the 8-hour qualifying period, the choice of major and minor street must stay the same. In cases where it is not clear, the warrant can be tested treating each street as the "major" street for the 8-hour qualifying period.

The provision for reducing the minimum vehicular volume to 70% of stated values for high approach speeds or for low-population communities is applied to many of the warrants. High approach speeds make it more difficult for crossing drivers to safely select gaps. The increased danger is reflected by the reduction in warrant criteria. In small isolated communities, it is assumed that drivers are generally unfamiliar with congestion at any level, and that they may have greater difficulty in maneuvering through a crossing vehicle stream without the aid of control devices. The reduced warrant criteria compensate for this.

Warrant 2, Interruption of Continuous Traffic (Figure 15-7), is presented in the same format as the first, and also applies to an 8-hour qualifying period. In this case, the major street minimum volumes are higher than for Warrant 1, while the minor street volumes are correspondingly lower. The warrant addresses cases in which even low minor street flow has difficulty in crossing or merging with major street traffic that is basically continuous, i.e., without sufficient gaps to accommodate even a small minor street flow. When signals are installed under this warrant, it is often appropriate to use a semi-actuated signal. Such a signal keeps the green on the major street until a minor-street vehicle crosses a detector and "calls for" a minor-street green period. Types of signal control are discussed in greater detail in Chapter 16. The criteria of this warrant are also reduced for high major-street approach speeds and small isolated communities.

Warrant 3 (Figure 15-8) addresses the conflict between vehicular and pedestrian traffic at an intersection. Like Warrants 1 and 2, the minimum requirements must be met for 8 hours. When a signal is installed under this warrant, WALK/DON'T WALK indications are required. At isolated intersections, pedestrian push-buttons are recommended as well. Actuated signals are suggested when signals are installed at isolated intersections under this warrant.

Warrant 2: Interruption of Continuous Traffic

The Interruption of Continuous Traffic warrant applies to operating conditions where the traffic volume on a major street is so heavy that traffic on a minor intersection street suffers excessive delay or hazard in entering or crossing the major street. The warrant is satisfied when, for each of any 8 hours of an average day, the volumes given in the table below exist on the major street and on the higher-volume minor street approach to the intersection and the signal installation will not seriously disrupt progressive traffic flow.

MINIMUM VEHICULAR VOLUMES FOR WARRANT 1

Number of lanes for moving traffic on each approach		Vehicles per hour on major street (total of both approaches)	Vehicles per hour on higher volume minor street approach (one direction only)
Major Street	Minor Street		
1	1	750	75
2 or more	1	900	75
1	2 or more	750	100
2 or more	2 or more	900	100

These major-street and minor-street volumes are for the same 8 hours. During those 8 hours, the direction of the higher volume may be on one minor approach during some hours and on the opposite approach during other hours.

When the 85th percentile speed of major-street traffic exceeds 40 mph in either an urban or a rural area, or when the intersection lies within the built-up area of an isolated community having a population of less than 10,000, the Minimum Vehicular Volume warrant is 70 percent of the requirement above.

Figure 15-7 Warrant 2: Interruption of continuous traffic (8 hours). [From *Manual of Uniform Traffic Control Devices,* Federal Highway Administration, 1988, p. 4C-4.]

Warrant 3: Minimum Pedestrian Volume

A traffic signal may be warranted where the pedestrian volume crossing the major street at an intersection of mid-block location during an average day is:

> 100 or more for each of any four hours; or
> 190 or more in any one hour.

The pedestrian volume crossing the major street may be reduced as much as 50% of the values given above when the predominant pedestrian crossing speed is below 3.5 fps.

In addition to the minimum pedestrian volume stated above, there shall be less than 60 gaps per hour in the traffic stream of adequate length for pedestrians to cross during the same period when the pedestrian volume criterion is satisfied. Where there is a divided street having a median of sufficient width for the pedestrian(s) to wait, the requirement applies separately to each direction of vehicular flow.

Where coordinated traffic signals on each side of the study location provide for platooned traffic which will result in fewer than 60 gaps per hour of adequate length for the pedestrians to cross the street, a traffic signal may not be warranted.

This warrant applies only to those locations where the (distance to the) nearest traffic signal along the major street is greater than 300 ft and where a new traffic signal at the study location would not unduly restrict platooned flow of traffic. Curbside parking at non-intersection locations should be prohibited for 100 ft in advance of and 20 ft beyond the crosswalk.

A signal installed under this warrant should be of the traffic-actuated type with push-buttons for pedestrians crossing the main street. If such a signal is installed within a signal system, it should be coordinated if the signal system is coordinated.

Signals installed according to this warrant shall be equipped with pedestrian indications, conforming to requirements set forth in other sections of the (Manual on Uniform Traffic Control Devices).

Figure 15-8 Warrant 3: Minimum pedestrian volume (8 hours). [From *Manual of Uniform Traffic Control Devices,* Federal Highway Administration, 1988, pp. 4C-4 and 4C-5.]

Warrant 4 (Figure 15-9) addresses the special pedestrian case of school crossings. Specialized studies, not treated in this text, are required to establish the need for signal control at such locations. When a signal is placed under this warrant, WALK/DON'T WALK indications are required.

Signals installed under Warrant 5, Progressive Movement (Figure 15-10), are called "spacer signals." Their purpose is solely to help maintain progressive movement along a major street. Good progression requires that drivers stay in platoons moving through the system through a "green window" provided at

---

Warrant 4: School Crossing

A traffic control signal may be warranted at an established school crossing when a traffic engineering study of the frequency and adequacy of gaps in the vehicular traffic stream as related to the number and size of groups of school children at the school crossing shows that the number of adequate gaps in the traffic stream during the period when the children are using the crossing is less than the number of minutes in the same period. [Section 7A-3 (of the MUTCD)].

When traffic control signals are installed entirely under this warrant:

1. Pedestrian indications shall be provided at least for each crosswalk established as a school crossing.
2. At an intersection, the signal normally should be traffic-actuated. As a minimum, it should be semi-actuated, but full actuation with detectors on all approaches may be desirable. Intersection installations that can be fitted into progressive signal systems may have pretimed control.
3. At non-intersection crossings, the signal should be pedestrian-actuated, parking and other obstructions to view should be prohibited for at least 100 ft in advance of and 20 ft beyond the crosswalk, and the installation should include suitable standard signs and pavement markings. Special police supervision and/or enforcement should be provided for a new non-intersection installation.

Figure 15-9 Warrant 4: School crossings. [From *Manual of Uniform Traffic Control Devices,* Federal Highway Administration, 1988, pp. 4C-5 and 4C-6.]

Warrant 5: Progressive Movement

Progressive movement control sometimes requires traffic signal installations at intersections where they would not otherwise be warranted, in order to maintain proper grouping of vehicles and effectively regulate group speed. The Progressive Movement warrant is satisfied when:

1.   On a one-way street or a street which has predominantly unidirectional traffic, the adjacent signals are so far apart that they do not provide the necessary degree of vehicle platooning and speed control, or

2.   On a two-way street, adjacent signals do not provide the necessary degree of platooning and speed control and the proposed and adjacent signals could constitute a progressive signal system.

The installation of a signal according to this warrant should be based upon the 85th percentile speed unless an engineering study indicates that another speed is more desirable.

The installation of a signal according to this warrant should not be considered where the resultant signal spacing would be less than 1,000 ft.

Figure 15-10 Warrant 5: Progressive movement. [From *Manual of Uniform Traffic Control Devices,* Federal Highway Administration, 1988, p. 4C-6.]

successive signalized intersections. If signals are spaced too far apart, platoons begin to disperse due to differences in driver behavior, vehicles entering and leaving the traffic stream at unsignalized locations, and other side friction elements. Under this warrant, a signal may be placed between two widely-spaced intersections in a progressive system, even if the intersection itself does not warrant signalization. As stated in the warrant, the resulting signal spacing, after placing such a signal, should never be less than 1000 ft.

Warrant 6 (Figure 15-11) addresses the use of signals to correct accident problems at the intersection. The warrant refers to accidents " . . . of types susceptible to correction by traffic signal control." Traffic signals can be effective remedies to crossing accidents

and left-turning accidents, and for some types of pedestrian accidents. They are not particularly helpful in reducing side-swipe or head-on collisions, and may actually cause an increase in the number of rear-end collisions. Because the latter tend to occur at low speeds at signalized intersections, however, it is usually more important to reduce crossing and left-turn accidents, which are generally more severe. Where left-turn accidents are a severe problem, provision of a protected left-turn phase might also be considered.

Note also that the accident warrant cannot be used as the sole reason for placing a signal unless lesser control remedies (such as YIELD or STOP) control have been tried, and have failed to provide sufficient accident reductions. The four requirements of the

---

Warrant 6: Accident Experience

The accident warrant is satisfied when:

1.   Adequate trial of less restrictive remedies with satisfactory observance and enforcement has failed to reduce the accident frequency; and

2.   Five or more reported accidents, of types susceptible to correction by traffic signal control, have occurred within a 12-month period, each accident involving personal injury or property damage apparently exceeding the applicable requirements for a reportable accident; and

3.   There exists a volume of vehicular and pedestrian traffic not less than 80% of the requirements specified either in the Minimum Vehicular Volume warrant, the Interruption of Continuous Traffic warrant, or the Minimum Pedestrian Volume warrant; and

4.   The signal installation will not seriously disrupt progressive traffic flow.

Any traffic signal installed solely on the Accident Experience warrant should be semi-actuated (with control devices which provide proper coordination if installed at an intersection within a coordinated system), and normally should be fully traffic actuated if installed at an isolated intersection.

Figure 15-11 Warrant 6: Accident experience. [From *Manual of Uniform Traffic Control Devices,* Federal Highway Administration, 1988, p. 4C-6.]

warrant must *all* be satisfied to install a signal under this warrant.

Warrants 7 and 8 (Figures 15-12 and 15-13) address more general situations. Recent revisions, however, have made the warrants more specific, and limited the number of cases in which they could be applied as the sole justifications for installing a signal.

Warrant 7, the "Systems Warrant," addresses the use of signals to help establish "concentration and organization of traffic flow networks." The warrant addresses the case in which two "major routes" intersect, but where other warrants for signalization are not met. In such a case, installation of a signal essentially designates the intersection as a major or important one in the street network. Thus, in a case where future conditions are likely to meet other warrants, a signal might be installed under this warrant to help form and designate a major route system.

Warrant 8 addresses situations in which Warrants 1 and 2 are 80% satisfied, but neither warrant is met on its own. The most recent revisions to the warrants have limited the imposition of this warrant to "exceptional cases."

Warrants 9, 10, and 11 (Figures 15-14, 15-15, and 15-16) were added in 1985. Each addresses the critical need for signalization based on situations existing for less than the 8 hours required of the other most frequently used warrants. At many locations, the two A.M. and P.M. hours experiencing the most intense traffic determine both the design and control of the intersection. Where conditions during the peak periods are serious enough, signalization may be the only tractable solution, even if none of the 8-hour warrants can be met. Further, the existence of warrants addressing peak conditions simplifies the field studies required to assess the need for signalization by reducing the number of hours of interest. Since their introduction, these warrants have seen extensive use, and there is some interest in eliminating Warrants 1, 2, and 8.

Reference [2] reviewed the status of signal warrants at the time of the introduction of Warrants 9–11, noting that:

1. The volumes used in Warrants 1 and 2 have little quantitative basis, originating in the 1920s and 1930s as the consensus of experts serving on the AASHO (the predecessor of AASHTO) committee at the time.
2. The 8-hour requirement was likewise the expert consensus of these experts, being a period on which they could agree.

Warrant 7:   Systems Warrant

A traffic signal installation at some intersections may be warranted to encourage concentration and organization of traffic flow networks. The Systems Warrant is applicable when the common intersection of two or more major routes: (1) has a total existing, or immediately projected, entering volume of at least 1,000 vehicles during the peak hour of a typical weekday and has five year projected traffic volumes, based on an engineering study, which meet one or more of Warrants 1, 2, 8, 9, and 11 during an average weekday; or (2) has a total existing or immediately projected entering volume of at least 1,000 for each of any five hours of a Saturday and/or Sunday.

A major route as used in the above warrant has one or more of the following characteristics:

1.   It is part of the street or highway system that serves as the principal network for through traffic flow;
2.   It includes rural or suburban highways outside, entering, or traversing a city;
3.   It appears as a major route on an official plan such as a major street plan in an urban area traffic and transportation study.

Figure 15-12   Warrant 7: Progressive movement. [From *Manual of Uniform Traffic Control Devices,* Federal Highway Administration, 1988, p. 4C-7.]

Warrant 8: Systems Warrant

In exceptional cases, signals occasionally may be justified where no single warrant is satisfied, but where Warrants 1 and 2 are satisfied to the extent of 80% of more of the stated values.

Adequate trial of other remedial measures which cause less delay and inconvenience to traffic should precede installation of signals under this warrant.

Figure 15-13   Warrant 8: Combination of warrants. [From *Manual of Uniform Traffic Control Devices,* Federal Highway Administration, 1988, p. 4C-7.]

| Warrant 9: Four Hour Volumes |

The Four Hour Volume Warrant is satisfied when for each of any four hours of an average day, the plotted points representing the vehicles per hour on the major street (total of both approaches) and the corresponding vehicles per hour on the higher volume minor street approach (one direction only) all fall above the curve in Figure (A) for the existing combination of approach lanes.

When the 85th percentile speed of the major street traffic exceeds 40 mph or when the intersection lies within a built-up area of an isolated community having a population less than 10,000, the four hour volume requirement is satisfied when the plotted points referred to fall above the curve in Figure (B) for the existing combination of lanes.

FIGURE A: NORMAL CONDITIONS

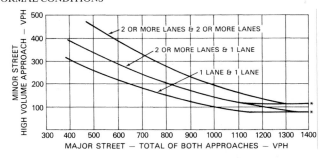

FIGURE B: MAJOR STREET APPROACH SPEED > 40 MPH OR POPULATION < 10,000 FOR A BUILT-UP AREA WITHIN AN ISOLATED COMMUNITY

*NOTE: 80 VPH APPLIES AS THE LOWER THRESHOLD VOLUME FOR A MINOR STREET APPROACH WITH TWO OR MORE LANES AND 60 VPH APPLIES AS THE LOWER THRESHOLD VOLUME FOR A MINOR STREET APPROACHING WITH ONE LANE.

Figure 15-14 Warrant 9: Four hour volumes. [From *Manual of Uniform Traffic Control Devices,* Federal Highway Administration, 1988, pp. 4C-7, 4C-11, and 4C-12.]

| Warrant 10: Peak Hour Delay |

The peak hour delay warrant is intended for application where traffic conditions are such that for one hour of the day, minor street traffic suffers undue delay in entering or crossing the major street. The peak hour delay warrant is satisfied when the conditions given below exist for one hour (any four consecutive 15-minute periods) of an average weekday.

The peak hour delay warrant is met when:

1.   The total delay experienced by traffic on one minor street approach (one direction only) controlled by a STOP sign equals or exceeds four vehicle-hours for a one-lane approach and five vehicle-hours for a two lane approach, and

2.   The volume on the same minor street approach (one direction only) equals or exceeds 100 vph for one moving lane of traffic or 150 vph for two moving lanes, and

3.   The total entering volume serviced during the hour equals or exceeds 800 vph for intersections with four (or more) or 650 vph for intersections with three approaches

Figure 15-15 Warrant 10: Peak hour delay. [From *Manual of Uniform Traffic Control Devices,* Federal Highway Administration, 1988, p. 4C-8.]

Warrant 11: Peak Hour Volume

The peak hour volume warrant is also intended for application when traffic conditions are such that for one hour of the day, minor street traffic suffers undue traffic delay in entering or crossing the major street.

The peak hour volume Warrant is satisfied when the plotted point representing the vehicles per hour on the major street (total of both approaches) and the corresponding vehicles per hour on the higher volume minor street approach (one direction only) falls above the curve in Figure (A) for the existing combination of approach lanes.

When the 85th percentile speed of the major street traffic exceeds 40 mph or when the intersection lies within a built-up area of an isolated community having a population less than 10,000, the peak hour volume requirement is satisfied when the plotted point referred to falls above the curve in Figure (B) for the existing combination of approach lines.

FIGURE A: NORMAL CONDITIONS

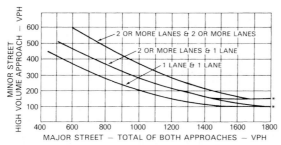

*NOTE: 150 VPH APPLIES AS THE LOWER THRESHOLD VOLUME FOR A MINOR STREET
APPROACH WITH TWO OR MORE LANES AND 100 VPH APPLIES AS THE LOWER
THRESHOLD VOLUME FOR A MINOR STREET APPROACHING WITH ONE LANE.

FIGURE B: MAJOR STREET APPROACH SPEED > 40 MPH OR POPULATION < 10,000 FOR A BUILT-UP AREA WITHIN AN ISOLATED COMMUNITY

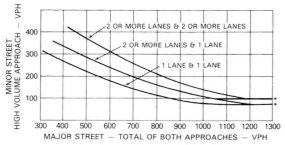

*NOTE: 100 VPH APPLIES AS THE LOWER THRESHOLD VOLUME FOR A MINOR STREET
APPROACH WITH TWO OR MORE LANES AND 75 VPH APPLIES AS THE LOWER
THRESHOLD VOLUME FOR A MINOR STREET APPROACHING WITH ONE LANE.

Figure 15-16   Warrant 11: Peak hour volume. [From *Manual of Uniform Traffic Control Devices,* Federal Highway Administration, 1988, pp. 4C-8–4C-10.]

3. Warrants 1 and 2 are based on minimum threshold volumes rather than a sliding scale or combined volume, so that intersections with a major street below the threshold and minor street very close to the same level might have more total conflicting volume (and not trigger the warrant) than an intersection that just meets each threshold.

Prior to 1985, most traffic signals were installed on the basis of Warrants 1 and 2. Given the lack of data supporting these warrants, and the fact that they represent the judgment of professionals over 60 years ago, this is somewhat disturbing. Warrants 9–11, on the other hand, have an extensive history of quantitative study and development. References [3, 4, and 5] detail some of the pioneering work, much of it sponsored by the National Cooperative Highway Research Program (NCHRP) and the Federal Highway Administration (FHWA).

Warrants 9 and 11 use continuous graphic displays as criteria rather than the tabular approach taken by the earlier Warrants 1 and 2. This ameliorates the difficulty cited previously, wherein the tabular criteria for one street barely "misses" the minimum value in a tabular array while the other is significantly higher than the threshold. The graphs, in effect, provide the "sliding scale" that is missing in Warrants 1 and 2.

C. Potential future warrants

There is ongoing discussion concerning further revisions to these warrants, including the deletion of Warrants 1 and 2, and the addition of warrants based specifically on gap acceptance field studies, and/or on individual delay per vehicle on a minor approach. Reference [6], for example, suggests a threshold of 25 seconds/vehicle of average side-street delay in *each* of the four peak hours in a day: If this threshold is exceeded in every one of these four peak hours, a signal would be installed. This warrant, however, had not yet been adopted in 1997.

One proposed warrant is based on a study of gaps in the major street traffic stream, and a determination of how many side street vehicles from one approach could pass through them. Gaps are categorized by their length (in seconds). Table 15-1 shows the number of side-street vehicles that can be expected to be able to use gaps of various sizes.

Once a field study identifies the number of gaps existing in each of the categories of Table 15-1, it is easy to estimate the total number of minor street vehicles that could be accommodated in one direction. The number of gaps in each category is multiplied by the number of vehicles each gap could accommodate.

Table 15-1 Availability of Gaps to Handle Side-Street Vehicles

Main Street Gap Size (sec)	No. of Vehicles Accommodated by One Gap of Indicated Duration
1–5	0
5–9	1
9–13	2
13–16	3
16–19	4
19–22	5
22–25	6
25–28	7
>28	8

[Used with permission of Institute of Transportation Engineers, from L. G. Neudorff, "Gap Acceptance Criteria for Signal Warrants," *ITE Journal.* Copyright © 1985 Institute of Transportation Engineers.]

The sum of these results is referred to as the "gap availability parameter," or GAP.

Figure 15-17 illustrates a model based on the GAP. It shows one of five calibrated figures, this one covering cases in which sight distance is adequate and right turns are 0–90%.

Figure 15-17 plots four points: the side-street volume per lane is plotted against the major street gap acceptance parameter (GAP) for each of the four peak hours of the day. If all four lie above the reference line for the appropriate maximum delay, the proposed warrant would be satisfied. If any one (or more) of the four points lies below the reference line the warrant would NOT be met.

The concept of a warrant based on gaps was analytically investigated in Reference [7].

Various local agencies may utilize additional warrants that have been developed for their specific area. The City of New York, for example, has experimented with additional warrants. One [8] provides a structured set of criteria for protected left-turn phasing at signalized intersections. It is based on left-turn related accidents and the comparison of left-turn demand with left-turn capacity. In another local usage, the NYC Bureau of Traffic uses the *Highway Capacity Manual (HCM)* [9] analysis procedure for unsignalized intersections as a trigger for doing field studies of delay. When a level of service at a STOP-controlled intersection is D or worse, field studies are done to see whether or not the peak-hour delay warrant is met. The 1994 and 1997 revisions to the *HCM* now give estimates of delay for unsignalized intersections. It remains to be seen whether predicted delays from this model will be used to evaluate the peak hour delay warrant directly.

SAMPLE PROBLEM

The intersection of Main Street (2 lanes each direction) and First Avenue (1 lane each direction) is currently controlled by STOP signs on First Street. Over the past three years, the intersection has experienced the following accident frequencies annually: 4 right-angle, personal injury accidents; 3 left-turning, personal injury accidents; 5 rear-end, property damage only accidents; 3 pedestrian accidents (with one fatality). During the peak hours, average delay per vehicle on the STOP-controlled approaches is 30 seconds/vehicle. Adjacent signals are located at 1000 feet in all directions, and the signal system is

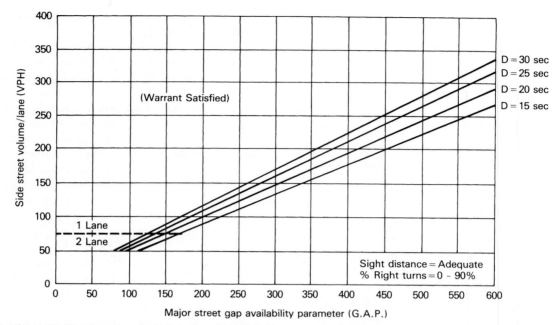

Figure 15-17 Sample criteria for a four-hour delay warrant based on threshold of individual side-street delay. [Used with permission of Institute of Transportation Engineers, from L. G. Neudorff, "Gap Acceptance Criteria for Signal Warrants," *ITE Journal.* Copyright © 1985 Institute of Transportation Engineers.]

coordinated. Installation of a signal at this location will not disrupt progressive movement, however. The data shown in Table 15-2 applies to the worst 12 hours of the day at the intersection, which is located near a large community shopping center. Approach speeds are 35 mph, and the intersection is located in a large metropolitan area.

On the basis of the information given, which signal warrants are met, which are not met, and which cannot be determined? What final recommendations for signalization would you make at this location?

SOLUTION: The first step in looking at signal warrants is to put the available information in a format

Table 15-2 Data for Sample Problem

Hour	Main St. EB (veh)	Main St. WB (veh)	First Ave. NB (veh)	First Ave. SB (veh)	Peds Xing Main St.
11–12A	400	425	75	80	115
12–01P	450	465	85	85	120
01–02P	485	500	90	100	125
02–03P	525	525	110	115	130
03–04P	515	525	100	95	135
04–05P	540	550	90	100	140
05–06P	550	580	110	125	120
06–07P	545	525	96	103	108
07–08P	505	506	90	95	100
08–09P	485	490	85	75	90
09–10P	475	475	75	60	50
10–11P	400	410	50	55	25

similar to that of the warrants themselves. For virtually all of the volume-driven warrants, the format is a comparison of *total major street volume* with the *highest one-direction volume on the minor street*. The volumes given in Table 15-2 should be reformatted to allow for direct comparisons on this basis. Such a reformatting is shown in Table 15-3.

The reformatted data can now be compared directly to various criteria in the eleven warrants for signalization. Each warrant is examined in turn.

Warrant #1: For 2-lane major street approaches and 1-lane minor street approaches, Warrant 1 requires a total major street traffic of at least 600 vph and a one-direction minor street traffic of at least 150 vph for eight hours of the day. If Table 15-3 is examined, it can be seen that *all* 12 hours meet the major street traffic criteria, but *none* meet the minor street traffic criteria. The approach speed and location of the intersection do not allow the criteria to be reduced. Therefore, this warrant *is not met*.

Warrant #2: For this warrant, total major street traffic must be at least 900 vph and the larger minor street volume must be at least 75 vph for 8 hours of the day. Table 15-3 shows that the *ten* hours between 12:00 Noon and 10:00 P.M. all meet both of these criteria. Therefore, Warrant 2 *is satisfied*.

Warrant #3: Warrant 3 requires a minimum of 100 peds/hr crossing the major street for four hours, or 190 peds/hr for one hour. Table 15-3 illustrates

Table 15-3 Reformatted Volumes for Warrant Analysis (Sample Problem)

Hour	Total Main Street Vol (veh)	Max. First Ave. Vol (veh)	Peds Xing Main St.
11–12A	825	80	115
12–01P	915	85	120
01–02P	985	100	125
02–03P	1050	115	130
03–04P	1040	100	135
04–05P	1090	100	140
05–06P	1130	125	120
06–07P	1070	103	108
07–08P	1011	95	100
08–09P	975	85	90
09–10P	950	75	50
10–11P	810	55	25

that while there are *no* hours with more than 190 peds/hr, there are *nine* hours (from 11:00 A.M. through 8:00 P.M.) with at least 100 peds/hr. This warrant, however, also requires that a gap study be made to determine whether or not the existing volume of pedestrians can safely cross through normally-occurring gaps in the major street traffic stream. Since this information is not available, the status of this intersection with respect to this warrant cannot be determined.

Warrant #4: As no school crossing information is given, the status of the intersection with respect to this warrant cannot be determined.

Warrant #5: No information on progression is provided. Thus, the status of the intersection with respect to this warrant cannot be determined.

Warrant #6: Installation of signalization under this warrant, the "accident warrant," requires that four criteria be met. The first requires that less restrictive controls have been tried: since First Ave. is already STOP-controlled, this criteria is met. Since both right-angle and left-turn collisions are susceptible to correction by signalization, and since 7 such accidents occur at this intersection each year, the criteria of at least 5 accidents (susceptible to correction by signalization) is also met. The third criteria requires that at least 80% of the requirements of Warrants 1, 2, or 3 be met. As Warrant 2 is fully met by this intersection, this criteria is also satisfied. The fourth criteria requires that progressive movement not be disrupted by installation of a signal. The problem statement indicates that this is so. Thus, all four criteria are met, and this warrant is *satisfied*.

Warrant # 7: Since no information is given concerning the region's highway system, it cannot be determined whether or not this warrant is satisfied.

Warrant #8: This is the "combination warrant" which requires that 80% of Warrants 1 and 2 be met, assuming that neither is individually satisfied. As Warrant 2 is fully satisfied, this warrant is not applicable.

Warrant #9: This is the "four-hour volume" warrant. Volumes in Table 15-3 must be plotted on Figure 15-14, graph A (for normal conditions). This is illustrated in Figure 15-18(a). Rather than plot all 12 hours, it is obvious from Table 15-13 that the hours between 3:00 P.M. and 7:00 P.M. are the worst in terms of total traffic. Figure 15-18(a) shows that only *one* of

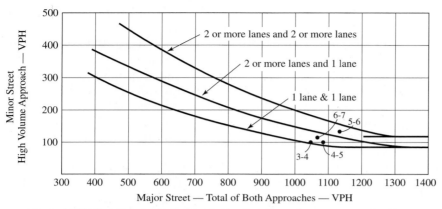

Note: 115 VPH applies as the lower threshold volume for a minor street apprach with two or more lanes and 80 VPH applies as the lower threshold volume for a minor street approaching with one lane.

(a) Testing the four-hour volume warrant

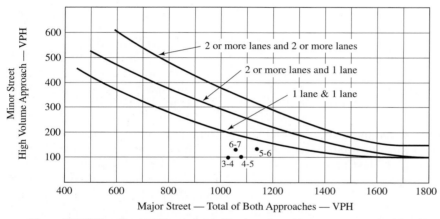

Note: 150 VPH applies as the lower threshold volume for a minor street approach with two or more lanes and 100 VPH applies as the lower threshold volume for a minor street approaching with one lane.

(b) Testing the peak-hour volume warrant

Figure 15-18 Warrants 9 and 11, sample problem 1.

these hours falls above the appropriate reference line (the middle one for 2-lane major street approaches vs. 1-lane minor street approaches). Thus, this warrant *is not met.*

Warrant #10: This warrant addresses delay to side-street vehicles on one minor street approach during the peak period. The single highest one-direction volume on First Avenue occurs between 5 and 6 P.M., when 125 vehicles use the SB approach. If each of these vehicles experiences 30 seconds of delay (given), then the total delay to these vehicles in the

peak hour is $30 \times 125 = 3750$ veh-sec, or 3750/3600 = 1.04 vehicle hours. This is less than the 4 hours of delay required by the warrant. This warrant is, therefore, *not met.*

Warrant #11: This is the "peak hour volume" warrant. The four worst hours of the day are plotted on Figure 15-16, graph A (for normal conditions). This is shown in Figure 15-18(b). None of the four worst hours is above the appropriate reference line (the middle one). Therefore, the peak hour volume warrant is *not met.*

CONCLUSION: A signal is called for under Warrants 2 (Interruption of Continuous Traffic) and 6 (Accident Experience). Consideration should be given to installing semi-actuated signals with detectors on the minor (First Ave.) approaches. Both warrants indicate that this is an appropriate remedy, and such signals would avoid undue delay and interruption of the major street (Main St.) traffic flow. Semi-actuated signals can also be placed within a coordinated system, so that progression patterns need not be disrupted.

Because pedestrian volumes are significant, and because pedestrian accidents appear to be a problem (3 per year, 1 fatality), use of pedestrian signals for those crossing the major street is advisable. Pedestrian push-buttons should also be provided, as this is a semi-actuated signal, and pedestrians may require crossing opportunities when there are no vehicles present.

Stop and yield control

If an analysis of intersection sight triangles indicates that operation under basic rules of the road is not feasible, and none of the warrants for signalization are met, then some form of STOP or YIELD control must be established. Even if sight distances under basic rules of the road are deemed sufficiently safe for such operation, other conditions may dictate that STOP or YIELD control is necessary or advisable. Three forms of control in this category may be considered:

1. YIELD control of minor approaches (one or two),
2. STOP control of minor approaches (one or two), and
3. Multiway STOP control of all approaches.

The use of STOP or YIELD control on minor approaches clearly assigns right-of-way to the major (uncontrolled) street, and places the burden for avoidance of hazards on minor street drivers. Multiway STOP control forces all vehicles to stop before entering the intersection, and is only used where neither intersecting street can be clearly identified as the "major" street.

A. Warrants

Figure 15-19 shows some of the warrants for installation of STOP signs (non-multiway). Note that the warrants are relatively general, and are only given under the "may" provision, which means that they are entirely advisory.

The MUTCD is far more certain about what uses are inappropriate. STOP signs *shall not* be installed at intersections having traffic signals, for example. This practice was relatively common in many jurisdictions where signals were turned off at night. The MUTCD now requires that the signals be operated in the flashing RED/flashing YELLOW mode, with the flashing RED on approaches expected to stop. The confusion to unfamiliar drivers faced with a green light and a STOP sign makes such a use of STOP signs impractical and hazardous.

Portable STOP signs *shall not* be used, except in emergencies. They *should not* be used for speed control, nor should they be placed on the through roadway of an expressway (with occasional at-grade intersections). The use of STOP signs for speed control within residential communities with a rectangular grid street system is relatively common, despite the non-binding caution not to do so. It is better to lay

Warrants for Non-Multiway STOP Signs
Because the STOP sign causes a substantial inconvenience to motorists, it should be used only where warranted. A STOP sign may be warranted where one or more of the following conditions exist: 1. Intersection of a less important road with a main road where application of the normal right-of-way rule is unduly hazardous. 2. Street entering a through highway or street. 3. Unsignalized intersection in a signalized area. 4. Other intersections where a combination of high speed, restricted view, and serious accident record indicates a need for control by the STOP sign.

Figure 15-19 Warrants for stop signs. [From *Manual of Uniform Traffic Control Devices,* Federal Highway Administration, 1988, p. 2B-2.]

out local streets with curved geometry such that high speeds are not feasible. There are also innovative design remedies for speed control on rectangular grids, but these tend to be expensive, and involve blocking through movements periodically. Because of this, many local areas resort to placing STOP signs at every other intersection (or at every intersection) to keep drivers from gaining too much speed.

The "unduly hazardous" provision of item 1 of Figure 15-19 refers not only to sight distance problems. Hazards may be caused by inadequate gap availability on the major street and/or high speeds on the major street. Accident experience involving right-angle and turning collisions also indicates such hazards, although the warrant sets no numerical standard on the number or severity of such accidents that would justify STOP control.

Provision 2 addresses the use of STOP signs to help designate through routes or streets by controlling all side streets entering the through facility. This provides for safety for side-street vehicles, and is part of the overall design strategy for creating major through facilities.

Provision 3 addresses situations (primarily in urban areas) where most intersections are signalized. Leaving any intersection uncontrolled in such an environment would transmit a false sense of safety to the driver, and is generally avoided. The fourth provision of the warrant is very broad, and allows for the placement of STOP signs in almost any situation in which the traffic engineer deems it necessary.

One of the more recent revisions in the MUTCD is a statement that prior to application of any of these warranting conditions, consideration should be given to lesser measures, in particular, the YIELD sign. The YIELD sign does not require a full stop unless there is a conflicting vehicle on the major street. It does, however, require the driver to slow down to 10 mph or less. Figure 15-20 gives the warrants for the placement of YIELD signs.

The first of these warrants is critical. It essentially indicates that YIELD signs can be used much the same way as STOP signs are, with the addition of one important characteristic: The "critical approach speed" must be greater than 10 mph.

The critical approach speed is the maximum safe speed at which a vehicle can approach an intersection and still have adequate sight distance to avoid the hazards of conflicting vehicles. Since most states require that drivers slow to 10 mph when YIELD signs are in place, placement of YIELD signs requires a critical approach speed in excess of this for safe operation.

One way to test for this condition is to use the procedures outlined for testing sight distances under basic-rules-of-the-road operation. The approach speed (for YIELD-controlled approaches) is set at 10 mph. If sight distances are sufficient for this condition, then a YIELD sign may be placed. If sight distances are NOT sufficient, a STOP sign must be used to assign right-of-way.

Figure 15-21 shows a nomograph from the *NYS Manual on Uniform Traffic Control Devices* [10]. For each of the four relevant visibility triangles at a standard 4-leg intersection, a point is plotted on the graph. Distance from the minor street vehicle to the nearest obstruction is plotted on the vertical axis; distance

---

Warrants for YIELD Signs
The YIELD sign may be warranted:
1. At the entrance to an intersection where it is necessary to assign right-of-way and where the safe approach speed on the entrance exceeds 10 mph.
2. On the entrance ramp to an expressway where an acceleration lane is not provided.
3. At intersections on a divided highway where the median between the roadways is more than 30 ft. wide. At such intersections, a STOP sign may be used at the entrance to the first roadway of the divided highway and YIELD sign may be placed at the entrance to the second roadway.
4. Where there is a separate or channelized right-turn lane, without an adequate acceleration lane.
5. At any intersection where a special problem exists and where an engineering study indicates the problem to be susceptible to correction by use of the YIELD sign.

Figure 15-20 Warrants for yield signs. [From *Manual of Uniform Traffic Control Devices*, Federal Highway Administration, 1988, pp. 2B-4 and 2B-5.]

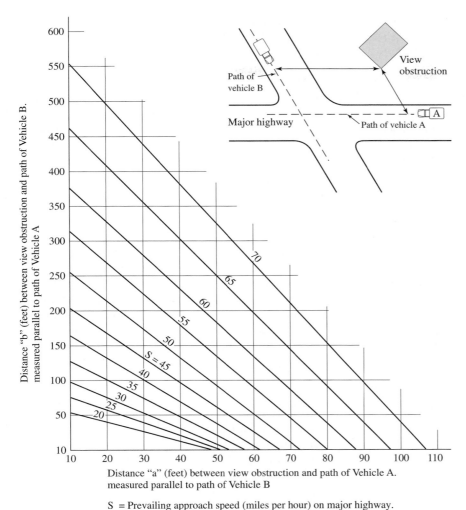

Figure 15-21 Nomograph for critical approach speed check. [From *Manual of Uniform Traffic Control Devices,* State of New York, Department of Transportation, Traffic and Safety Division, 1983, p. 37.]

from the major street vehicle to the nearest obstruction is plotted on the horizontal axis. Reference lines on the graph represent various approach speeds for major street vehicles. If all four points lie above the appropriate reference line, the critical approach speed is in excess of 10 mph, and use of a YIELD sign is safe. If any of the points lie below the reference line, then STOP signs are required. Even if one approach has adequate sight distance while the opposing approach does not, STOP signs would be used on both approaches. Common practice is not to have a YIELD sign on one approach and a STOP sign on the opposing approach. It should be noted that the nomograph of Figure 15-21 is constructed for a set of com-

mon parameters, such as reaction time, friction factors, deceleration rates, etc. If an unusual situation exists (significant grades, for example), the nomograph should not be used.

Items 2 and 3 of the warrants refer to relatively unique applications of YIELD signs. The first deals with STOP-controlled intersections where the major street is divided by a wide median (>30 ft). In such cases, the driver literally progresses as if there were two separate intersections with one-way roadways. A second sign is required at the entrance to the second major roadway being crossed as a reminder to the driver. Since there are rarely sight distance restrictions in the median, a YIELD sign is appropriate for this usage. If there are unusual obstructions in the median, the critical approach speed should be checked to insure that the use of a YIELD sign is safe.

The second unique usage is for the control of channelized or separated right-turn movements. At major signalized intersections, channelized right turns are often provided. This effectively removes them from the signalization scheme, as they are permitted to progress at all times. Such channelized right turns may also exist at unsignalized intersections. Where no adequate acceleration lane exists, these channelized right turns should be controlled by a YIELD sign.

The decision between use of a STOP or YIELD sign for assignment of right-of-way must be made carefully. Wherever sight distances are inadequate to support a safe approach speed of 10 mph or greater on the controlled approaches, STOP signs *must* be used. However, YIELD signs are never *required,* and STOP signs may be acceptably used in virtually all situations in which YIELD signs could be used. While the federal MUTCD does not encourage (or discourage) the use of YIELD signs, some state manuals do. The NYS manual, for example, contains the following language:

> In the absence of considerations which require otherwise, an intersection approach with a critical approach speed greater than 10 mph normally should be controlled with a YIELD sign [10, page 36.]

This statement includes the strongly advisory "should," and establishes a policy that the minimum necessary constraint should be implemented to provide for safe and effective control.

Even where STOP control is adopted, serious sight distance considerations must be checked. In essence, the driver of the stopped vehicle must be able to see conflicting vehicles approaching from the right and left for a distance sufficient to allow him/her to accelerate and make the desired maneuver (left turn, through, right turn). While not covered in detail here, AASHTO's *Policy on Geometric Design of Highways and Streets (1994)* contains detailed descriptions of these sight distance requirements.

Multiway STOP control is still relatively controversial. Some traffic engineers dislike this form of control, as it frequently confuses motorists, and generally causes more delay than a two-way STOP-controlled intersection would. Others believe it to be

quite useful in unusual situations where the more traditional two-way STOP control has not solved all accident and efficiency problems, but where signals are not warranted.

The MUTCD takes a cautious approach to this form of control, stating that "it should only be used where the volume of traffic on the intersecting roads is approximately equal" and that "a traffic control signal is more satisfactory for an intersection with a heavy volume of traffic." [Reference 1, page 2B-3.]

The MUTCD allows the use of multiway STOP control: 1) as an interim measure at an intersection where signals are urgently needed, 2) to solve an accident problem indicated by 5 or more accidents per year of the right-angle and left-turn type. In all cases, the total vehicular volume entering the intersection must be 500 vph or more for any 8 hours of the day, and the combined vehicular and pedestrian traffic on the minor street must be at least 200 units/hour for the same 8 hours. Where the 85th percentile approach speed on the major street is 40 mph or above, the volume requirements are 70% of these values.

SAMPLE PROBLEM

Consider the intersection shown in Figure 15-5. In this problem, it was previously determined that sight distances were not sufficient to allow the intersection to operate under basic rules-of-the-road. Thus, it is necessary that a STOP or YIELD sign be placed (at a minimum) on the minor approach, which is a one-way street. Which should be used?

SOLUTION: To determine whether or not a YIELD sign can be used, points representing the two sight triangles affecting minor street vehicles must be plotted on Figure 15-21, as shown in Figure 15-22.

Reference points are plotted on Figure 15-21, based on the distances to obstructions for the two sight triangles of interest. These points are plotted at (42, 20) and (12, 60). As shown in Figure 15-22, the two plotted points lie *below* the reference line (40 mph approach speed on the major approach), which means that the critical approach speed is *less* than 10 mph. Therefore, a YIELD sign should NOT be used in this situation. A STOP sign is required, assuming that the intersection does not meet any of the warrants for signalization.

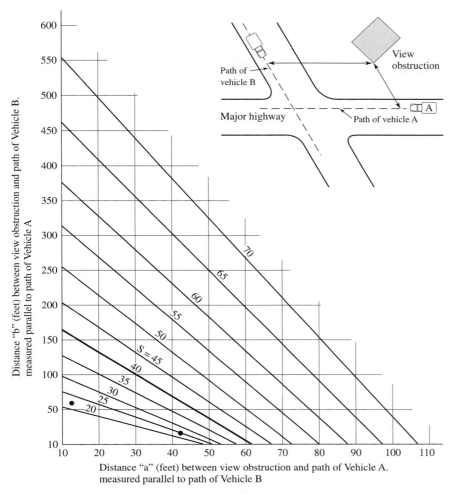

Distance "b" (feet) between view obstruction and path of Vehicle B, measured parallel to path of Vehicle A

Distance "a" (feet) between view obstruction and path of Vehicle A, measured parallel to path of Vehicle B

S = Prevailing approach speed (miles per hour) on major highway.

Figure 15-22 Sample problem on use of yield sign critical approach speed criteria.

Summary

This chapter has provided an overview of the three primary levels of intersection control available to the traffic engineer. The viability of operation under basic rules-of-the-road requires, but is not guaranteed by, adequate sight distance at all corners of the intersection. Warrants specify when signals can and should be used, and provide guidance for the imposition of STOP and YIELD control.

In the final analysis, traffic engineers must exercise judgment in applying the criteria and methodologies presented herein. Warrants often allow considerable latitude in interpretation and application. These guidelines, however, provide important and powerful information to traffic engineers which should be carefully considered in determining the most appropriate control option in any given situation. In all cases, the final determination must be consistent with both safety and relative efficiency of operation.

References

1. *Manual of Uniform Traffic Control Devices,* U.S. Department of Transportation, Federal Highway Administration, Washington, DC, 1988 (amended through 1997).
2. Wainwright, W. S., "Will Newly Improved Warrants Result in More Signals?," *ITE Journal,* December 1985.
3. "Warrants for Traffic Signals," *Final Report,* National Cooperative Highway Research Program Project 3-20/1, KLD & Associates, Huntington, NY, 1976.
4. *A Traffic Signal Warrant for Heavy Traffic Volumes Occurring During Short Periods of Time,* Wilbur Smith and Associates, Washington, DC, April 1975.
5. Henry, R. D., et al., "Peak Hour Traffic Signal Warrant," *National Cooperative Highway Research Program Report 249,* Transportation Research Board, National Research Council, Washington, DC, September 1982.
6. Neudorff, L. G., "Gap-Based Criteria for Signal Warrants," *ITE Journal,* February 1985.
7. Drew, D., *Traffic Flow Theory and Control,* McGraw-Hill, New York, NY, 1968.
8. Athanailos, E., "Guidelines for Left-Turn Signal Warrant Analysis," *Internal Memorandum,* New York City Department of Transportation, Bureau of Traffic, Long Island, NY, January 26, 1992.
9. *Highway Capacity Manual, Special Report 209,* 3rd Edition, Transportation Research Board, National Research Council, Washington, DC, (revised) 1997.
10. *NYS Manual of Uniform Traffic Control Devices,* New York State Department of Transportation, Albany, NY, 1983.

Problems

Problem 15–1

For the intersection of two rural roads shown below, determine: a) whether or not operation under basic rules-of-the-road may be safely applied, and b) whether STOP or YIELD signs are warranted or (in your judgment) desirable. Support your response with appropriate computations and rationale.

Problem 15–2

As in Problem 15-1, determine whether or not the intersection shown can be safely operated under basic rules-of-the-road, and whether or not STOP or YIELD control is warranted or desirable.

Problems 15–3 to 15–6

For each of the intersections shown in the accompanying figures, determine whether or not the data provided meets

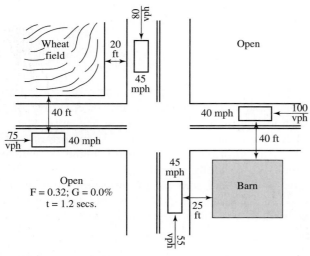

Figure for Problem 15–1

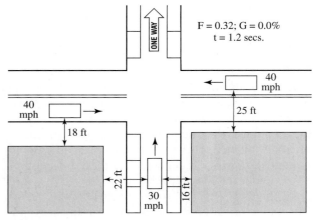

Figure for Problem 15–2

each of the 11 signal warrants. Indicate when not enough information is provided to assess a given warrant. Based on the results in each case: a) Is a signal warranted? b) What type of signal would you recommend, based on the avail- able information? c) Are pedestrian signals and/or push- buttons needed?

In all cases, assume that no hours for which data is not shown meet any of the 11 warrants.

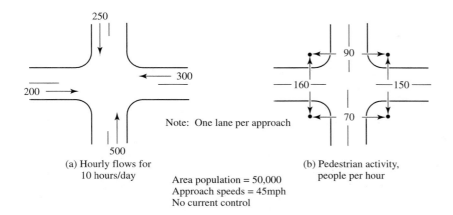

(a) Hourly flows for 10 hours/day

Note: One lane per approach

Area population = 50,000
Approach speeds = 45mph
No current control

(b) Pedestrian activity, people per hour

Figure for Problem 15–3

	Volumes (vph)			
Hour	NB	SB	EB	WB
1	30	30	25	25
2	30	30	50	50
3	50	50	75	100
4	50	50	150	150
5	75	100	250	200
6	100	250	400	300
7	125	400	500	350
8	150	450	500	350
9	200	375	450	300
10	250	300	200	200
11	200	250	150	150
12	150	150	150	150
13	100	100	150	150
14	100	100	150	200
15	100	75	150	200
16	250	100	200	250
17	325	125	350	250
18	375	150	400	300
19	400	150	350	450
20	425	150	350	450
21	325	100	200	200
22	150	75	100	100
23	100	50	50	50
24	50	25	50	50

Area Population = 75,000
Approach Speeds = 30 mph
Current Control = Multiway STOP

Figure for Problem 15–4

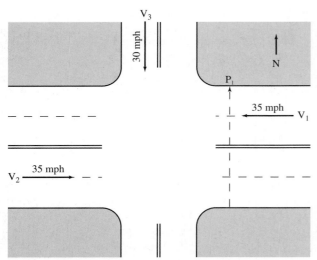

Volumes By the Hour

Time Period	$V_1 + V_2$ (Vehs/Hr)	V_3 (Vehs/Hr)	P_1 (Peds/Hr)
01:00–02:00 P.M.	850	100	200
02:00–03:00 P.M.	875	100	210
03:00–04:00 P.M.	925	110	205
04:00–05:00 P.M.	1050	140	193
05:00–06:00 P.M.	1250	108	180
06:00–07:00 P.M.	1100	125	170
07:00–08:00 P.M.	1000	100	180
08:00–09:00 P.M.	950	90	200
09:00–10:00 P.M.	900	80	150
10:00–11:00 P.M.	900	80	100

Area Population = 40,000
Approach Speeds As Shown
Accidents Per Year: 5 Rt. Angle; 6 Rear End; 2 Left-Turn
Current Control = Two-Way STOP

Note: V3 is the higher minor street volume.

Figure for Problem 15–5

Volumes By Hour (vph)

Time Period	Volume $V(1)$	Volume $V(2)$	Volume $V(3)$	Volume $V(4)$
10:00–11:00 A.M.	400	450	120	135
11:00–12:00 Nn	410	410	100	108
12:00–01:00 P.M.	395	400	95	103
01:00–02:00 P.M.	425	415	108	109
02:00–03:00 P.M.	450	425	120	125
03:00–04:00 P.M.	455	465	128	122
04:00–05:00 P.M.	500	505	150	155
05:00–06:00 P.M.	510	515	165	175
06:00–07:00 P.M.	480	450	135	125
07:00–08:00 P.M.	420	385	101	85
08:00–09:00 P.M.	380	350	90	80
09:00–10:00 P.M.	300	300	100	150

Area Population = 100,000
Approach Speeds = 30 mph
Current Control = Two-Way STOP
All approaches = 1 lane

Figure for Problem 15–6

16

Basic Principles of Intersection Signalization

In Chapter 15, the various forms of intersection control were presented and discussed. *Warrants,* presented in the *Manual of Uniform Traffic Control Devices* [1], provide general and specific guidelines for selection of an appropriate form of control. At many critical intersections, consideration of traffic volumes, potential conflicts, safety considerations, and driver convenience will lead to the decision to install traffic signals.

This chapter presents some of the key elements of traffic signals and their application to intersection control. Various analytic models are introduced to describe some of these principal elements. In Chapter 17, a signal timing methodology is introduced. In Chapter 18, a specific model, that of the 1994 *Highway Capacity Manual* [2] and its 1997 update, is introduced and applied to a variety of intersection signalization problems. The *HCM* Model of Chapter 18 contains virtually all of the elements described in this chapter, although some are not in exactly the same analytic form. The *HCM* Model is the most frequently-used tool for the analysis of signalized intersections, and it can be used to optimize signal

timing in a trial-and-error mode facilitated by the Highway Capacity Software package [3].

Terms and definitions

Traffic signals are complex devices that can operate in a variety of modes. A number of key terms and definitions should be understood before undertaking any substantive discussion:

1. *Cycle:* A signal cycle is one complete rotation through all of the indications provided. In general, every legal vehicular movement receives a "green" indication once within each cycle, although there are some exceptions to this rule.
2. *Cycle Length:* The cycle length is the time (in seconds) that it takes a signal to complete one full cycle of indications. It is given the symbol "C."
3. *Interval:* An interval is a period during which none of the lights at a signalized intersection changes. At any signalized intersection, there are many intervals included in the signal cycle, including:
   • *change interval:* the "yellow" indication for a given movement, called the "change interval";

each movement at the intersection receives such an interval between the GREEN and RED signal indications for that movement;

- *clearance interval:* the "all red" indication for a given movement, referred to as the "clearance interval"; after each "yellow" interval, a period during which *all* signal faces show RED is usually included, and is referred to as an "all red" indication; the sum of the change plus clearance intervals (yellow plus all red) for a given movement is given the symbol Y_i;
- *green interval:* the "green" indication for a particular movement or set of movements, given the symbol G_i;
- *red interval:* the "red" indication for a particular movement or set of movements, given the symbol R_i.

Of course, intervals for one movement may overlap intervals for other movements. The green, change, and clearance intervals for one set of movement is the red interval for all others.

4. *Phase:* A phase is the green interval plus the change and clearance intervals that follow it; it is a set of intervals that allows a designated movement or set of movements to flow and to be safely halted before release of another set of movements.

Traffic signals can operate in several different modes, as described below:

5. *Pretimed Operation:* In pretimed operation, the cycle length, phases, and all intervals are preset. Each cycle of the signal is exactly like another, and all interval and phase times are the same. "Three-dial" signal controllers allow for three different pretimed settings for different times of the day. An internal clock activates the appropriate timing at the appropriate times, which are also preset.

6. *Semi-Actuated Operation:* In semi-actuated operation, detectors are placed on the minor approaches to the intersection. The signal is green for the major street at all times, until and unless one of the minor street detectors is activated, indicating the presence of a vehicle waiting for service. Subject to constraints, such as minimum green times for the major street and others, the green is transferred to the minor street upon such a "call" for service. For semi-actuated signals, cycles have widely varying lengths, depending on the pattern of actuations by minor-street vehicles.

7. *Full-Actuated Operation:* In full-actuated operation, every intersection approach (including separate turning lanes) has a detector or detectors. Subject to limiting values preset in the controller, green time is allocated based upon detector actuations. In actuated control, each cycle is different from another, and both the sequence and length of intervals and phases can be altered in response to detected demand. Limitations include minimum and maximum green times, and minimum gaps between detector actuations required to retain the GREEN indication. Chapter 19 deals with the operation of actuated signals in detail.

8. *Computer Controlled:* Computer control is basically a system term. No isolated intersection is "computer controlled," unless the intersection controller is itself considered to be a computer. Rather, a computer links many signalized intersections (up to 100 and more) into a coordinated system. It selects or computes optimal progression patterns based on detectors placed at key locations, and implements a timing pattern in response to this. Within a computer-controlled system, however, most individual intersections will operate on a pre-timed basis, as constant and equal cycle lengths must be maintained at all intersections in the system. It is possible, however, to have the allocation of green time altered in response to detector actuations within a fixed cycle length.

Left turns at a signalized intersection can be handled in a number of ways:

9. *Permitted Left Turns:* A "permitted" left turn is made across an opposing through vehicle flow. In such cases, the driver is "permitted" to cross the opposing through flow, but must select an appropriate gap in the opposing stream through which to turn. This is the most common form of left-turn phasing at signalized intersections, used where left-turn volumes are reasonable, and where gaps in the opposing through flow are adequate to accommodate left turns safely.

10. *Protected Left Turns:* A "protected" left turn is made without an opposing through vehicular flow. The signal phasing "protects" left-turning

vehicles by prohibiting the opposing through movement. This requires separate signal phases for left turns and the opposing through vehicles, and leads to multiphase signalization, i.e., more than two phases at the intersection. Left turns are "protected" by intersection geometry on one-way streets, or on the stem of a T-intersection, or in any situation where an opposing vehicular flow is not present.

11. *Protected/Permitted or Permitted/Protected Left Turns:* More complicated signal phasing can be designed in which left turns (on a given approach or approaches) have a protected turn for part of the cycle and a permitted turn for another part of the cycle. This type of phasing is sometimes referred to as "compound phasing."

The terms "permitted" and "protected" are also used to describe right turns. In this case, however, the conflict is not with an opposing vehicular flow, but with pedestrians in the crosswalk through which right-turning vehicles must cross. When a right turn is "protected," the conflicting pedestrian flow is prohibited while right turns are being made. Protected right-turn phasing is fairly rare, and compound right-turn phasing is used only in the most complex situations involving heavy pedestrian flows.

Four basic mechanisms

Four basic mechanisms must be understood in building an analytic model or description of a signalized intersection:

- discharge headways at a signalized intersection
- the "critical lane" and "time budget" concepts
- the effects of left-turning vehicles
- delay and other measures of effectiveness

Each of these is discussed in the subsections which follow:

A. Discharge headways, saturation flow, lost times, and capacity

The basic characteristic to understand before modeling intersection operations is the manner in which vehicles depart, or discharge, from the intersection when a GREEN indication is received. Figure 16-1

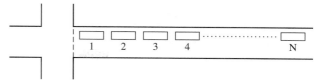

Figure 16-1 Vehicles in an intersection queue.

illustrates a group of *N* vehicles at a signalized intersection, waiting for the GREEN indication. When the GREEN is initiated, headways between departing vehicles will be observed as vehicles cross the curb line, as shown. The first headway will be the time between the initiation of the GREEN and the crossing of the first vehicle over the curb line. The second headway is the time between the first and second vehicles crossing the curb line, etc. Common practice is to measure the headways as the *rear* wheels of the reference vehicle cross the curb line.

Successive headways are now plotted as shown in Figure 16-2. Figure 16-2 is conceptual, and shows an ideal set of headways. Actual field measurements would vary around a trend similar to that depicted in Figure 16-2.

The first headway is relatively long, as it must include the first driver's reaction time, and the time necessary to accelerate. The second headway is shorter, because the second driver can overlap his/her reaction and acceleration time with the first driver's. Each successive headway gets a little smaller. Finally, headways tend to level out. This generally occurs when vehicles have fully accelerated by the time they reach

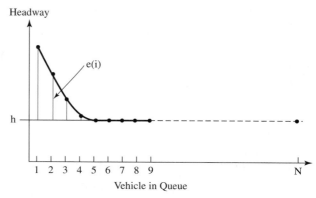

Figure 16-2 Headways departing signal.

the curb line. Most modern studies show that this "leveling off" begins with the fourth or fifth headway.

The level headway, which characterizes all headways beginning with the fourth or fifth vehicle, is defined as the *saturation headway,* and is shown in Figure 16-2 as h. This is the headway that can be achieved by a stable moving platoon of vehicles passing through a GREEN indication.

It is convenient to model behavior at a signalized intersection by assuming that every vehicle (in a given lane) consumes an average of h seconds of green time to enter the interaction. This gives rise to a related term, *saturation flow rate.* If every vehicle consumes h seconds of green time, and if the signal were *always* green, then s vehicles/hour could enter the intersection, where s is the saturation flow rate. Thus:

$$s = \frac{3600}{h} \qquad [16\text{-}1]$$

where: s = saturation flow rate, vphgpl
   h = saturation headway, sec
   3600 = seconds/hour

The units of saturation flow rate are "vehicles per hour of green time per lane." It can be multiplied by the number of lanes to yield units of "vehicles per hour of green time." If the signal were always green for the subject movement(s), the saturation flow rate would be the capacity of the lanes serving the movement(s).

The signal, of course, is not always green for any movement. Thus, some mechanism for dealing with the cyclic starting and stopping of a movement at a signal must be developed. In particular, the average headway is going to be *more than h* seconds, as the first 3 or 4 vehicles involve larger headways than h. Rather than deal with the complexities of an average headway that varies with the number of vehicles in the queue, it is easier to deal with a constant h seconds/vehicle, treating the additional headway consumed by the first several vehicles as a single value.

In Figure 16-2, each of the first 4 vehicles has a headway larger than h. The difference between the actual headway and h, for each of these vehicles, is denoted as "$e(i)$." These differences can be added for the first several vehicles:

$$l_1 = \sum e(i) \qquad [16\text{-}2]$$

where: l_1 = start-up lost time, sec
   $e(i)$ = (actual headway $- h$) for vehicle i
   i = 1 through n
   n = last vehicle with a headway $> h$

Treating start-up lost time as a single value simplifies the analysis of signalized intersections. For example, if the green time necessary to clear N vehicles per lane, per cycle through a signalized intersection were desired, it could be computed as:

$$T = l_1 + h(N) \qquad [16\text{-}3]$$

where: T = time to clear N vehicles through signal in a single lane, sec
   h = saturation headway, sec
   l_1 = start-up lost time, sec

Thus, if a signal were to be timed to accommodate an average queue size of 10 vehicles, and the start-up lost time was 3 seconds and the saturation headway was 2.2 seconds/vehicle, then:

$$T = 3 + 2.2(10) = 3 + 22 = 25 \text{ sec}$$

Therefore, each green phase should be at least 25 seconds long. This simplified approach, however, ignores the fact that cycle length and demand per phase are very much related.

A more sophisticated approach is to compute the amount of green time available to be used at a rate of one vehicle every h seconds. This concept is called *effective green time,* and is given the symbol g_i for movement i. For any given movement, the effective green time is the sum of the actual green time (G_i) plus the yellow and all red times (Y_i) minus applicable lost times. In addition to the start-up lost time, l_1, there is a lost time when a movement is stopped. This is defined as the clearance lost time, l_2. The clearance lost time is the time between the last vehicle entering the intersection (in a fully-utilized green phase) and the initiation of the green on the next phase. Thus:

$$g_i = G_i + Y_i - t_L \qquad [16\text{-}4]$$

where: g_i = effective green time for movement i, sec
   G_i = actual green time for movement i, sec
   Y_i = sum of yellow plus all red time from movement i, sec
   t_L = total lost time per phase, sec
   $t_L = l_1 + l_2$

The ratio of effective green time to the cycle length (g_i/C) is defined as the "green ratio" for movement i. This is the proportion of actual time available to movement i as effective green time. Since the saturation flow rate, s, is defined as the number of vehicles that can be moved in one lane in one hour assuming that the signal is always green, then the capacity of the lane can be computed as:

$$c_i = s_i \frac{g_i}{C} \qquad [16\text{-}5]$$

where: c_i = capacity of lanes serving movement i,
    vph or vphpl
   s_i = saturation flow rate for movement i,
    vphg or vphgpl
   g_i = effective green time for movement i,
    sec
   C = signal cycle length, sec

Consider the following sample problem:

SAMPLE PROBLEM

A given movement at a signalized intersection receives a 27-second green time, and 3 seconds of yellow plus all red out of a 60-second cycle. If the saturation headway is 2.4 seconds/vehicle, the start-up lost time is 2 seconds/phase and the clearance lost time is 1 second/phase, what is the capacity of the movement, per lane?

Two solutions will be illustrated.

SOLUTION 1: The first simply accounts for all of the 3,600 seconds of time available in the hour. All time during which vehicles *cannot* move at a rate of one vehicle every 2.4 seconds will be deducted. The remaining time *is* used at a rate of one vehicle every 2.4 seconds.

Since green and lost times are given on a per phase or per cycle basis, it is necessary to compute the *number of cycles* in an hour. For a 60-second cycle length, the number of cycles per hour is 3600/60 = 60 cycles per hour. Then:

Number of seconds in hour:		3600 sec
Deductions for:		
1. Red Time	$(60 - 27 - 2 - 1)60$	= 1800 sec
2. Start-Up	$(2)60$	= 120 sec
Lost Time		

3. Clearance	$(1)60$	=	60 sec
Lost Time			
Total Deductions:			-1980 sec
Time Available:			1620 sec

The red time is computed as the cycle length minus the green, yellow, and all red for the movement. Then the two lost times are deducted. This leaves 1620 seconds/hour available to be used at the rate of one vehicle every 2.4 seconds. Therefore, the capacity for the movement is:

$$c = \frac{1620}{2.4} = 675 \text{ vphpl}$$

SOLUTION 2: The result could also have been computed using equations [16-4] and [16-5]. From the information given, the effective green time for the subject movement is:

$$g = G + Y - t_L = 27 + 3 - 3 = 27 \text{ sec}$$

where: G = 27 seconds
   Y = 3 seconds
   t_L = 2 + 1 = 3 seconds

Note that in this case, with the yellow plus all red intervals equaling the sum of the start-up and clearance lost times, the effective green time, g, is equal to the actual green time, G. This is not an unusual case, as the equivalence often (but not always) holds for yellow plus all red intervals in the range of 3 to 5 total seconds. The two, however, do not occur at the same time, even when they are numerically equivalent. The capacity for the movement can then be computed as:

$$c = s\frac{g}{C} = \frac{3600}{h}\frac{g}{C} = \frac{3600}{2.4}\frac{27}{60} = 1500\,(0.45)$$
$$= 675 \text{ vphpl}$$

where the saturation flow rate is computed as per Equation [16-1] as 3600/h. The concepts of saturation headway, saturation flow rate, lost times, effective green time, and capacity are critical to the description of signalized intersection operations. The concepts are relatively straightforward, although their use and application in the *HCM* Model of Chapter 18 is more complicated.

For the remainder of this chapter, it is assumed that the value of h, and therefore, s, is known. In actuality, the saturation headway and flow rate vary widely depending on prevailing conditions for the movement in question. Such conditions as lane widths, approach grades, heavy vehicle presence, parking conditions, numbers of turning vehicles and conflicting vehicular and pedestrian flows, etc., all heavily influence the saturation headway and flow rate. Chapter 18 presents a detailed model for estimating the prevailing saturation flow rate, based on an *ideal* saturation flow rate that occurs under *ideal conditions*. Such conditions include 12-ft lanes, no grades, all passengers cars in the traffic stream, no parking on the approach, no local buses, no left or right turns, and a location outside the central business district.

The first work on measuring lost times and saturation headways was done by Bruce Greenshields in the mid-1940s. At that time, he proposed a model in the form of Equation [16-3] for the green time needed to process N vehicles at a signalized intersection [4]:

$$T = 3.7 + 2.1N$$

In this formulation, the start-up lost time is 3.7 seconds, and the saturation headway is 2.1 seconds. The saturation flow rate is 3600/2.1 = 1714 vphgpl. His studies included a number of intersections with varying conditions. Thus, his values represented averages over a range of conditions.

Reference [5] reported an update of Greenshields' equation in 1978, based on a study of 175 signalized intersections:

$$T = 1.1 + 2.1N$$

Surprisingly, despite the passage of 30 years, the saturation headway and flow rate results are the same as Greenshields'. The start-up lost time, however, was considerably lower, reflecting more aggressive driving habits and better acceleration performance of modern vehicles. Again, however, these results reflect a variety of underlying conditions existing at the 175 intersections studied. This study also attempted to distinguish characteristics between types of lanes (right, center, left), but the results tended to be somewhat inconsistent.

A comprehensive study of saturation flow rates at intersections in five cities was conducted in 1987–1988 to determine the effect of opposed left turns. It produced, however, an interesting view of saturation flow rates in general. Some of the data is summarized in Table 16-1 [6].

Table 16-1 Saturation Flow Rates and Headways from a Nationwide Study

Item	Single-Lane Approaches	Two-Lane Approaches
Number of approaches	14	26
Number of 15-min periods	101	156
Avg saturation flow rate	1280 vphgpl	1337 vphgpl
Avg saturation headway	2.81 sec/veh	2.69 sec/veh
Maximum saturation flow rate	1705 vphgpl	1969 vphgpl
Minimum saturation headway	2.11 sec/veh	1.83 sec/veh
Minimum saturation flow rate	636 vphgpl	748 vphgpl
Maximum saturation headway	5.66 sec/veh	4.81 sec/veh

These results show generally lower saturation flow rates (and correspondingly higher saturation headways) than previous studies. Since the study was intended to determine the effect of opposed left turns, however, all of the intersections studied contained such turns, which have a significant impeding effect.

The most remarkable result of this study, however, is the wide variation in saturation flow rates, even for a given intersection approach. The study measured saturation flow rates for each 15-minute study period. Even when underlying conditions remained relatively constant, measured saturation flow rates for a given intersection approach often varied by as much as 20% to 25%. In a doctoral dissertation using the same data base, Prassas [7] demonstrated that saturation headways and flow rates have a significant probabilistic component, making calibration of stable values difficult.

The variation in saturation flow rates persisted even when the effects of prevailing conditions were eliminated, either by ignoring "non-ideal" data, or through use of standard adjustment factors from the *Highway Capacity Manual*. Saturation flow rates under ideal conditions (12-ft lanes, no heavy vehicles, no turns, no local buses, etc.) varied from 1240 pcphgpl to 2092 pcphgpl for single-lane sites and from 1668 pcphgpl to 2361 pcphgpl for multilane approaches.

Another significant result of this data is that multi-lane approaches consistently show higher saturation flow rates than single-lane approaches. As will be seen in Chapter 18, single-lane approaches have a number of unique characteristics, one of which is that left- and right-turning vehicles use the same lane. Because of some of these unique characteristics, this result is not surprising.

In an interesting paper by Teply [8], field methodologies for measurement of saturation flow rates and lost times are analyzed. Teply points out that while most working definitions of saturation flow rates are consistent, there are a variety of field measurement techniques that do not produce consistent values. The literature contains a number of interesting references concerning saturation flow concepts and measurement techniques [9–15].

B. The "critical lane" and "time budget" concepts

The "time budget" and "critical lane" concepts are closely allied in signal analysis. The time budget is, in its simplest form, the allocation of time to various vehicular and pedestrian movements at an intersection through signal control. Time is a constant: there are 3600 seconds/hour to allocate, never more, never less.

The critical lane concept involves how (or to what) time is allocated. During any given signal phase, several lanes of traffic on one or more approaches are permitted to move. One of these will have the most intense traffic. This is the lane for which time must be allocated during the subject phase. It requires more time than any other lane moving at the same time; all other lanes require less time. Thus, if sufficient time is allocated for the critical lane, then all other lanes (for the subject signal phase) are accommodated as well.

There is *one* and *only one* critical lane in each signal phase. The time budget allocates 3600 seconds/hour to each of the signal phases based on the critical lane and its flow, and to lost times that are built into the cycle.

Consider the example illustrated in Figure 16-3. It shows two 4-lane arterials with a simple two-phase signal. Each street gets a single phase, with all movements accommodated. All left turns are, therefore, permitted. During each phase, 4 lanes of traffic are moving. One has the most intense traffic, and is the critical lane (labeled 1 and 2 in Figure 16-3). The two-phase signal allocates time for the two critical lane flows, and for

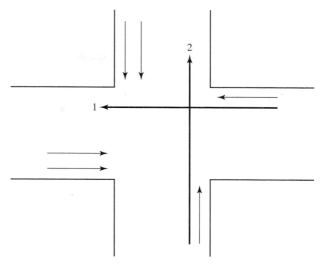

Figure 16-3 Critical lanes illustrated.

the lost times involved in starting and stopping each phase (start-up and clearance lost times).

1. The maximum sum of critical lane volumes: One view of capacity. The two critical lane volumes of Figure 16-3 are what the traffic signal must be timed to accommodate. One view of "capacity," not the traditional one of the *Highway Capacity Manual,* would be to consider the maximum sum of critical lane volumes that a signal can accommodate, given that the prevailing saturation headway and lost times are known.

By definition, each signal phase has one and only one critical lane. Thus, except for lost times in the cycle, *one* critical lane is always moving. Lost times (start-up and clearance) are incurred for each signal phase in each signal cycle. These are times during which NO lane is moving. The maximum sum of critical lane volumes may, therefore, be found by determining how much total lost time there is in the hour, and dividing the remaining time by the saturation headway.

If t_L is the total (start-up plus clearance) lost time per phase, and if the signal has N phases, then the total lost time *per cycle* (L) is:

$$L = Nt_L \qquad [16\text{-}6]$$

If C is the cycle length, then the number of cycles in the hour is $3600/C$. Thus the total lost time in the hour is found as:

$$L_H = L\,\frac{3600}{C} = Nt_L\,\frac{3600}{C} \qquad [16\text{-}7]$$

where L_H is the total lost time *per hour*. The time remaining in the hour to allocate to effective green time for the critical movements is, therefore:

$$T_G = 3600 - L_H = 3600 - Nt_L \frac{3600}{C} \quad [16\text{-}8]$$

where T_G is the time available for effective green allocation within the hour. The maximum sum of critical lane volumes that can be accommodated within the hour, therefore, is given by:

$$V_c = \frac{T_G}{h} = \frac{1}{h}\left[3600 - (N)(t_L)\left(\frac{3600}{C}\right)\right] \quad [16\text{-}9]$$

where V_C is the maximum sum of critical lane volumes, and h is the prevailing saturation headway.

If values of h and t_L are specified, Equation [16-9] may be plotted for various cycle lengths. Figure 16-4 plots values of V_C vs C for two-phase, three-phase, and four-phase signals. The saturation headway for Figure 16-9 is 2.15 sec/veh, and t_L is 3 sec/phase. The plot illustrates two important characteristics of the relationship among these critical variables:

1. As the cycle length increases, the capacity (in terms of the maximum sum of critical lane volumes) also increases. This is because lost times are constant *per phase*. As the cycle length is reduced, there are more cycles within the hour, and therefore more total lost time. This relationship starts to level out at high cycle lengths, and is limited to relatively modest capacity increases. For a two-phase signal, the maximum sum of critical lane volumes increases from 1473 vph to 1591 vph as cycle length goes from 50 seconds to 120 seconds.

2. Capacity also increases as the number of signal phases is reduced. Again, this is related to lost times. If there are three phases within each cycle, then three sets of lost times are included. If there are only two phases, then only two sets of lost times are included. This relationship is interesting, and explains why two-phase signalization is to be desired unless prevailing conditions make it impractical. On the other hand, it can also be misleading. The saturation headway (or saturation flow rate), assumed to be a constant herein, is affected by left-turning conditions. Any increase gained by holding the number of phases to a minimum may be lost by declines in the saturation flow rate due to left-turn conflicts (with opposing vehicles) that exist in a two-phase signal.

2. Applying the "time budget" and "critical lane" principles. Equation [16-9] may be used in many ways. It can be used directly to find the maximum sum of critical lane volumes for a given situation. It can also be used to help "size," i.e., plan the appropriate number of lanes for an intersection.

SAMPLE PROBLEM

Consider the intersection illustrated in Figure 16-5.

SOLUTION: As indicated in Figure 16-5, all volumes have been converted to through vehicle equivalents. This means that adjustments have already been made reflecting the impact of turning vehicles. The demand

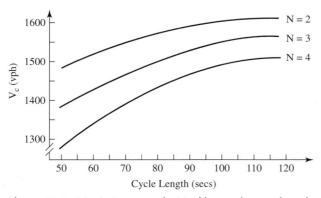

Figure 16-4 Maximum sum of critical lane volumes plotted.

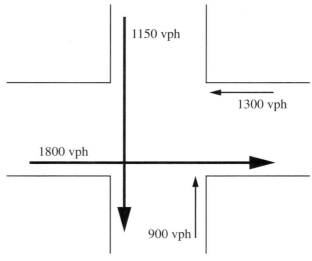

Figure 16-5 Intersection for sample problem.

volumes in vph are for the same characteristics as the saturation headway.

The maximum sum of critical lane volumes for this case is computed using Equation [16-9], as follows:

$$V_c = \frac{1}{2.3}\left[3600 - (2)(3)\left(\frac{3600}{40}\right)\right] = 1330 \text{ vph}$$

Thus, the sum of the critical lane volumes for two signal phases may never exceed 1330 vph. From Figure 16-5, the two critical movement flows are shown as 1800 vph (EB) and 1150 vph (SB). If each of these flows operated in a single lane, they would be the critical lane volumes, and their sum would be 1800 + 1150 = 2950 vph, well above the limiting value of 1330 vph.

The total of the critical lane volumes, however, can be reduced by breaking either the 1800 vph EB volume and/or the 1150 vph SB volume into several lanes. Figure 16-6 shows several scenarios for this, with the resulting sum of critical lane volumes.

The only option shown in Figure 16-6 that brings the sum of critical lane volumes below the limiting value of 1330 vph provides the EB flow with 3 lanes and the SB flow with 2 lanes. This reduces the critical lane volumes to 1800/3 = 600 vph (EB) and 1150/2 = 575 vph (SB) for a total of 1175 vph < 1330 vph. Additional lanes could be added, but are not required for the signal plan stated in the problem.

Even though the EB and SB volumes are critical, 3 lanes would also be provided in the WB direction, and 2 lanes in the SB direction. If the volumes shown represent the A.M. peak period, for example, they would doubtless reverse in the P.M. peak. Thus, at the intersec-tion, the east-west arterial will have 6 total lanes in both directions, and the north-south arterial 4 total lanes.

This problem could be explored from another point of view. If field conditions, for example, limited the size of both streets to 4 lanes each (2 in each direction), then the sum of the critical lane volumes would have been 1800/2 = 900 vph (EB) plus 1150/2 = 575 vph (SB), for a total of 1475 vph. This is greater than the 1330 vph maximum sum for the signal plan as stated. The following question could be posed: *what cycle length would be needed to accommodate a V_C of 1475 vph, given that other conditions are fixed, that is, h = 2.3 sec/veh, t_L = 3 sec/phase, and a two-phase signal is planned?*

Equation [16-9] could then be solved for an unknown cycle length, with all other values known:

$$1475 = \frac{1}{2.3}\left[3600 - (2)(3)\left(\frac{3600}{C}\right)\right]$$

$$C = \frac{(3600)(6)}{3600 - 1475(2.3)} = \frac{21,600}{207.5} = 104 \text{ sec}$$

This means that a cycle length of *at least* 104 seconds would be needed to accommodate a sum of critical lane volumes of 1475 vph, given the other constraints of the problem. In practical terms, this would imply a 110-second cycle, if this were a pretimed signal. Pretimed cycle lengths are available in 5-second increments from 30 to 90 seconds, and in 10-second increments from 90 to 120 seconds.

3. Adding consideration of the PHF and v/c ratio. In the sample problem of the previous section, a minimum

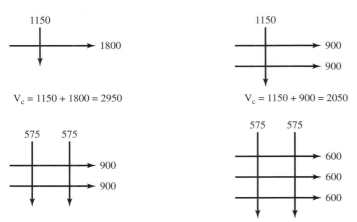

$V_c = 1150 + 1800 = 2950$

$V_c = 1150 + 900 = 2050$

$V_c = 575 + 900 = 1475$

$V_c = 575 + 600 = 1175$

Figure 16-6 Lane scenarios for sample problem.

cycle length was computed for a given value of V_c and other known parameters. This equation may be generalized as:

$$C_{min} = \frac{3600Nt_L}{3600 - V_c h}$$

which is often rewritten as:

$$C_{min} = \frac{Nt_L}{1 - \dfrac{V_c}{(3600/h)}} \qquad [16\text{-}10]$$

This computation, however, is based on full hour critical lane volumes, and does not take into account peaking within the hour. It also produces an *absolute minimum* cycle length, in which every second of effective green time would be utilized. In effect, it computes a cycle length that guarantees operation at a volume-to-capacity (*v/c*) ratio of 1.00. This is rarely desirable, and as will be seen later, results in high delay.

A *desirable* cycle length could be found by specifying a desired *v/c* ratio, i.e., the proportion of available capacity that would be utilized by the given sum of critical lane flows.

To account for peaking within the hour, the sum of critical lane volumes should be divided by the PHF. Similarly, the sum of critical lane volumes would be divided by the desired *v/c* ratio to insure that the appropriate proportion of capacity is utilized. When this is done, the desirable cycle length may be computed as:

$$C_{des} = \frac{Nt_L}{1 - \dfrac{V_c}{PHF(v/c)(3600/h)}} \qquad [16\text{-}11]$$

SAMPLE PROBLEM

In the sample problem of the previous section, consider the case providing three EB lanes and two SB lanes, with a V_C of 1,175 vph. It is now stipulated that a cycle length be chosen such that the *v/c* ratio during the peak 15 minutes of the hour is no more than 0.90, and that the *PHF* is 0.95 for this location.

SOLUTION: Then:

$$C_{des} = \frac{(2)(3)}{1 - \dfrac{1175}{(0.95)(0.90)(3600/2.3)}} = \frac{6}{1 - 0.878}$$

$$= 49.2 \text{ sec}$$

This indicates that a cycle length of 50 seconds would have to be provided to insure that the *v/c* ratio during the peak 15 minutes of the hour does not exceed 0.90. If the geometry were limited to 2 lanes for each critical movement (V_c = 1475 vph), then the desirable cycle length would be:

$$C_{des} = \frac{(2)(3)}{1 - \dfrac{1475}{(0.95)(0.90)(3600/2.3)}} = \frac{6}{1 - 1.102}$$

$$= -58.8 \text{ sec}$$

The negative result indicates that such a cycle length IS NOT POSSIBLE. A similar computation for a desired *v/c* ratio of 0.95 would also result in a negative answer, indicating that this is also not possible. A cycle length that would provide a *v/c* ratio of 1.00 *during the peak 15 minutes of the hour* is:

$$C_{des} = \frac{(2)(3)}{1 - \dfrac{1475}{(0.95)(1.00)(3600/2.3)}} = \frac{6}{1 - 0.99}$$

$$= 600 \text{ sec}$$

While this is physically possible, the cycle length required is well beyond the range of practical values used.

The results of all of these computations taken together are interesting. Given the original 40-second cycle length, the intersection with 3 lanes EB and 2 lanes SB operates at a *v/c* ratio of 1175/1330 = 0.883 (V_C actual/V_C capacity). This, however, is an average *v/c* ratio over the full hour. To provide for a maximum *v/c* ratio of 0.90 during the peak 15 minutes, a cycle length of 50 seconds is required for the 3 × 2 intersection.

If a 2 × 2 intersection is designed, a 104-second cycle would be needed to provide for an average *v/c* ratio of 1.00 during the full our. There is NO cycle length that would accommodate a maximum *v/c* of 0.90 during the peak 15 minutes, and even provision of a *v/c* ratio of 1.00 during the peak 15 minutes is impractical. This essentially indicates that the signal will fail during the peak 15 minutes. "Failure" implies that more vehicles will arrive during the peak 15 minutes than will be discharged. Queues will continuously grow during this period, and many vehicles will have to wait for more than one GREEN phase to be discharged. This is an undesirable condition, and suggests that the 2 × 2 intersection design is NOT practical.

This problem illustrates the great sensitivity of cycle length to critical lane volumes, and to the desired v/c ratio. Figure 16-7 further illustrates this point. It depicts Equation [16-11] for a 2-phase signal, with $h = 2.0$ sec/veh, $t_L = 3$ sec/phase, and $PHF = 1.00$.

While Figure 16-7 shows only a portion of the useful range of Equation [16-11], improvement in v/c ratio for any given sum of critical lane volumes clearly comes at the price of a steep increase in cycle length. This relates to the reduction in total lost time as cycle length increases, yielding higher capacities. Given the practical range of cycle lengths, 30–120 seconds for pretimed signals, and up to 180–240 seconds for actuated signals, the ability to increase capacity by increasing the cycle length is severely limited, and is effective primarily in cases where a small increase in capacity makes the difference between failure and stable operation.

C. The effect of left-turning vehicles and the concept of "through car equivalence"

The most difficult process to model at a signalized intersection is the left turn. Firstly, left turns are made in several different modes using two different inter-section design elements. Left turns may be made from a lane shared with through vehicles (shared lane operation), or from a lane dedicated to left-turning vehicles (exclusive lane operation). Traffic signals may allow for permitted or protected left turns, or some combination of the two.

Whatever the case, however, a left-turning vehicle will consume more effective green time traversing a signalized intersection than a through vehicle because of the nature of the movement, and where permitted operation is in effect, the impact of the opposing through flow. This latter case is illustrated in Figure 16-8.

A left-turning vehicle operating in a shared lane must wait for an acceptable gap in the opposing flow. While waiting, the vehicle blocks the shared lane, and other vehicles are delayed behind it. Some vehicles will change lanes to avoid the delay, while others are unable to, and must wait behind the left-turner until the turn is successfully completed. Virtually all models of the signalized intersection account for this in terms of "through car equivalents," i.e., how many through vehicles would consume the same amount of effective green time traversing the stop line as *one* left-turning vehicle?

If both the left lane and the right lane of Figure 16-8 were observed, an equivalence similar to the following could be determined.

In the same amount of time, the left lane discharges 10 through vehicles and 5 left-turning vehicles, while the right lane discharges 25 through vehicles.

Thus, in terms of effective green time consumed, 10 through vehicles plus 5 left-turning vehicles is

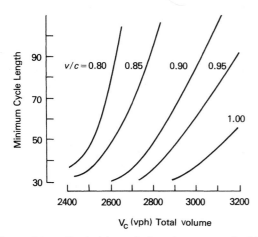

Figure 16-7 Desirable cycle length vs. sum of critical lane volumes (2-phase, $h = 2.0$ sec/veh, $t_L = 3$ sec/phase, $PHF = 1.00$).

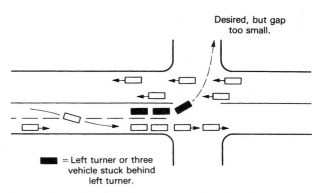

Figure 16-8 Permitted left turns at a signalized intersection.

equivalent to 25 through vehicles. If one left-turning vehicle were the equivalent of E_{LT} through vehicles, then the following relationship could be written:

$$10 + 5E_{LT} = 25$$

and:

$$E_{LT} = \frac{25 - 10}{5} = 3.0$$

where: E_{LT} = through vehicle equivalent of a left-turning vehicle, often referred to as the "left-turn equivalent."

It must be noted that this computation holds only for the characteristics of the intersection described. It is dependent on the opposing flow, and the number of lanes in which the opposing flow is distributed, as well as other factors.

Figure 16-9 illustrates the general form of the relationship between E_{LT} and opposing flow. In general, as the opposing flow increases, so does the left-turn equivalent. For any given level of opposing flow, the equivalent decreases as the number of lanes in which the opposing flow is distributed increases. This latter relationship, however, is not linear, as the task of selecting a gap in three lanes of traffic is more complex than that of selecting a gap in a smaller number of lanes. To illustrate how the left-turn equivalent can be used in modeling a signalized intersection, consider the following sample problem:

SAMPLE PROBLEM

An approach to a signalized intersection has 2 lanes, permitted left-turn phasing, 10% left-turns with an equivalent of 5, and a saturation headway *for through vehicles* of 2.00 sec/veh. Determine the equivalent saturation headway and saturation flow rates for all vehicles for this approach.

SOLUTION 1: One way to interpret the left-turn equivalent is that each left-turning vehicle consumes 5 times as much effective green time as through vehicles. Thus, each left-turning vehicle would have an equivalent headway of $5 \times 2.00 = 10.00$ sec/veh. If 10% of the vehicles on the approach are left turners, then the average saturation headway for all vehicles is:

$$h_{avg} = (0.10)(10.00) + (0.90)(2.00) = 2.80 \text{ sec/veh}$$

The saturation flow rate for the approach is therefore:

$$s = \frac{3600}{h_{avg}} = \frac{3600}{2.8} = 1286 \text{ vphgpl}$$

SOLUTION 2: Another approach is to calibrate a factor that would multiply the saturation flow rate for through vehicles to produce the actual saturation flow rate, including the impact of left-turning vehicles. The saturation flow rate for through vehicles, in this case, is $3600/2.0 = 1800$ vphgpl.

Such a multiplicative factor is calibrated as the ratio of the through saturation headway to the average saturation headway, incorporating the impact of left-turning vehicles. The computation for the average saturation headway may be generalized as:

$$h_{avg} = [(P_{LT}E_{LT}h)] + [(1 - P_{LT})h] \quad [16\text{-}12]$$

where: P_{LT} = proportion of left-turning vehicles,
E_{LT} = left-turn equivalent,
$1 - P_{LT}$ = proportion of non-left-turning vehicles, and
h = saturation headway for through vehicles.

Then:

$$f_{LT} = \frac{h}{[P_{LT}E_{LT}h] + [(1 - P_{LT})h]}$$

$$= \frac{1}{P_{LT}E_{LT} + (1 - P_{LT})}$$

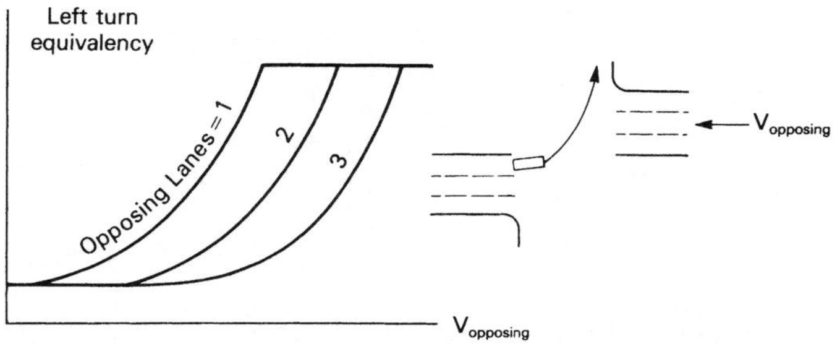

Figure 16-9 Relationship between left-turn equivalent and opposing vehicular flow.

which may be reorganized as:

$$f_{LT} = \frac{1}{1 + P_{LT}(E_{LT} - 1)} \quad [16\text{-}13]$$

where f_{LT} is the left-turn adjustment factor. For the sample problem:

$$f_{LT} = \frac{1}{1 + 0.10(5 - 1)} = 0.714$$

and:

$$s = 1800(0.714) = 1286 \text{ vphgpl}$$

which is the same result obtained previously by adjusting saturation headways directly.

It is important that the concept of through vehicle equivalence for left-turners be understood. Its use in left-turn adjustment factors is often obscured, but the concept remains the same—the amount of effective green time consumed by one left-turning vehicle is equal to E_{LT} times the effective green time consumed by the average through vehicle.

D. Delay and other measures of effectiveness at signalized intersections

1. Introduction. Because signalized intersections are basically points or nodes within a system of surface highways and streets, defining appropriate measures of effectiveness to describe the quality of operations is somewhat more difficult than defining uninterrupted flow facilities. A number of measures have been used in capacity analysis and simulation models, all of which quantify some aspect of the experience of traversing a signalized intersection in terms the driver comprehends. The most common of these include:

• delay
• queuing
• stops

Delay is a measure that most directly relates the driver's experience, in that it describes the amount of time consumed in traversing the intersection. Delay, however, can be quantified in many different ways. The most frequently used forms of delay are defined below:

a. *Stopped Time Delay:* Stopped time delay is defined as the time a vehicle is stopped while waiting to pass through the intersection.

b. *Approach Delay:* Approach delay includes stopped time, but also includes the time lost when a vehicle decelerates from its ambient speed to a stop, as well as while accelerating from the stop back to its ambient speed.

c. *Travel Time Delay:* Travel time delay is defined as the difference between the driver's desired total time to traverse the intersection and the actual time required to traverse it.

d. *Time-in-Queue Delay:* Time-in-queue delay is the total time from a vehicle joining an intersection queue to its discharge across the stop-line or curb-line.

These delay measures can be quite different, depending on conditions at the signalized intersection in question. Figure 16-10 illustrates the differences among stopped time, approach, and travel time delay for a single vehicle traversing a signalized intersection. Time-in-queue delay can only be illustrated by tracing a number of vehicles through the intersection.

Figure 16-10 shows a plot of distance vs. time for the progress of one vehicle. The desired path of the vehicle is shown, as well as the actual progress of the vehicle, which includes a stop at a "red" signal. In the figure:

• *Stopped time delay* includes only the time that the vehicle is actually stopped waiting at the "red" signal. It starts when the vehicle reaches a full stop, and ends when the vehicle begins to accelerate.
• *Approach delay* includes the stopped time, but adds the time lost due to deceleration and acceleration. It is measured as the time scale differential between the actual path of the vehicle, and its actual path extended as if the light had been "green" on arrival.

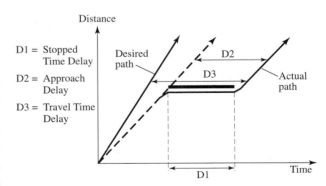

Figure 16-10 Delay measures illustrated.

• *Travel time delay* is measured as the time scale difference between the driver's desired time at any given distance from the origin, and the actual time. This value varies according to the distance at which it is measured. For a signalized intersection, it is measured at the stop-line, as the vehicle enters the intersection.

Delay measures can also be stated on an aggregate basis, or on an average per-vehicle basis. *Aggregate delay* would be stated in terms of the total vehicle-hours (or vehicle-seconds, or vehicle-minutes) of delay experienced by all vehicles traversing the intersection during some specified time period. *Average individual delay* is stated in terms of sec/veh (or hr/veh, or min/veh) of delay, also for some specified time period.

Delay is the most frequently-used measure of effectiveness for signalized intersections. Nevertheless, other measures are also useful. Length of queue at any given time (Q_T) is a useful measure, and is critical in determining when a given intersection will begin to impede the discharge from an adjacent upstream intersection. The number of stops made (N_S) is an important input parameter in air quality models.

Figure 16-11 shows a plot of total vehicles vs. time. Two curves are shown: (a) a plot of arriving vehicles, assumed here to be a uniform arrival rate, and (b) a plot of departing vehicles. For the purposes of this illustration, one "red" phase of a signal is depicted, and the rate of arrivals is assumed to be uniform.

Vehicles are assumed to arrive at a uniform rate of v vehicles per unit time, seconds in this case. This is shown by the constant slope of the arrival curve. Arriving vehicles depart instantaneously when the signal is green. When the red phase begins, vehicles begin to queue, as none are being discharged. When the signal turns green again, queued vehicles begin to depart *at the saturation flow rate, s* seconds per unit time. This departure rate continues until departure curve intersects the arrival curve, signifying the dissipation of the queue. The arrival and departure curves then coincide until the next red phase. This scenario, of course, assumes that all queued vehicles are handled within a single phase, with no overflow.

In this simple model:

• The total time (approach delay) for vehicle i to traverse the intersection ($W(i)$) is given by the time scale (horizontal) difference between the arrival and departure curves, as shown.
• The total number of vehicles queued at time t ($Q(t)$) is the vehicle scale (vertical) difference between the arrival and departure curves, as shown.
• The aggregate delay for all vehicles passing through the signal is the area between the arrival and departure curves.

Figure 16-12 extends this view of a single signal phase to a series of phases, and depicts three different types of operation. It also allows for a variable arrival function ($A(t)$), while retaining the departure function described in Figure 16-11 ($D(t)$).

Figure 16-12a shows a case in which no signal cycles fail, i.e., no vehicle is forced to wait for more than one green phase to be discharged. In such a case, the departure function "catches up" with the arrival function during each cycle of the signal. The total aggregate delay is the sum of all of the triangular areas between the arrival and departure functions. This type of delay is often referred to as "uniform delay," given the symbol "UD."

Figure 16-12b shows a case in which some of the signal cycles fail, i.e., some vehicles must wait for more than one cycle to be discharged. The departure function does not "catch up" to the arrival function during each cycle. Nevertheless, after a small number of cycles, the arrival and departure functions do meet. Such failures of individual signal cycles are due to the stochastic variability in arrivals. Thus, even where the discharge capacity over, for example, fifteen 60-

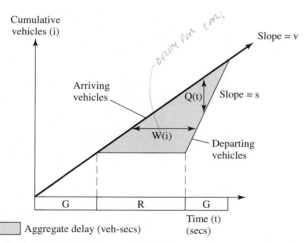

Figure 16-11 Delay, waiting time, and queue length illustrated.

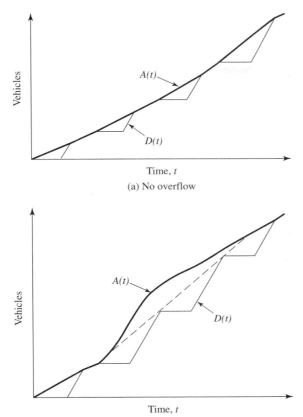

(a) No overflow

(b) Overflow due to stochastic variation in arrivals

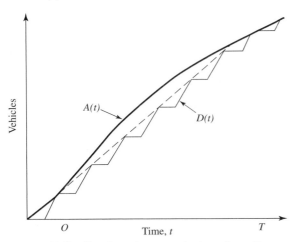

(c) Overflow due to long-term shortage of capacity

Figure 16-12 Three-delay scenarios illustrated. [Adapted with permission of Transportation Research Board, National Research Council, Washington, DC, from V. F. Hurdle, "Signalized Intersection Delay Model: A Primer for the Uninitiated," *Transportation Research Record 971*, pp. 97 and 98. Copyright © 1984 Transportation Research Board.]

second cycles is sufficient, *some* of those fifteen cycles may fail to discharge all arriving vehicles. In such a case, delay includes a uniform delay component, plus an overflow delay (OD) component. A line defining the maximum number of departures per cycle is shown. Its slope is a constant, and is the capacity of the intersection approach (c). The uniform delay component (UD) is the area between the capacity function and the departure function. The overflow delay component (OD) is the area between the arrival function and the capacity function.

Figure 16-12c shows a situation in which overflow exists in virtually every signal cycle for a significant length of time. In such cases, queuing becomes a serious problem, as overflow queues in one cycle *add* to the overflow queues from previous cycles. Uniform (UD) and overflow (OD) delay components also exist in this case, except that the overflow term may become extremely large due to the cumulative queues that form. Uniform and overflow delay are measured as in Figure 16-12b.

2. Webster's delay model. The modeling of signalized intersection delay can become quite complex. A 1984 paper by Hurdle [16] is an excellent review of many of the basic principles and problems inherent in the analytic modeling of this complex process, which always involves simplifying assumptions not well-tailored to the real world. While some of his explanations are repeated here, the reader is urged to consult the original work for a more complete review.

Virtually every model of delay at a signalized intersection starts with Webster's Delay Model. Initially published in 1958 [17], this model starts with a simple analytic approach to the computation of the uniform delay component. It makes the simplifying assumption that the arrival function is uniform, i.e., arrivals at a constant rate of v vehicles/second. This is essentially the situation illustrated in Figure 16-11. The derivation is based on the area of the triangle formed between the uniform arrival and departure functions. While the full derivation is not reproduced here, Figure 16-13 illustrates it, and some of the steps are discussed below.

The aggregate delay is the area within the shaded triangle of Figure 16-13. The area is simply ½ the base of the triangle (R) times the height (V). Because signal analysis is rarely done using red times, the

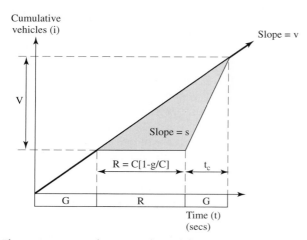

Figure 16-13 Webster's uniform delay formula illustrated.

duration of the red may be depicted as the proportion of the cycle length which is not green, or:

$$R = C\left[1 - \left(\frac{g}{C}\right)\right] \qquad [16\text{-}14]$$

The height of the triangle is found by setting the number of vehicles arriving during the time $R + t_c$ equal to the number of vehicles departing in time t_c, or:

$$V = v(R + t_c) = st_c$$

Substituting Equation [16-14] for R, and solving sequentially, first for t_c, then for V yields:

$$V = C\left[1 - \left(\frac{g}{C}\right)\right]\left[\frac{vs}{s - v}\right] \qquad [16\text{-}15]$$

The area of the triangle can then be determined. This gives the total vehicle-seconds of delay incurred by all vehicles arriving and discharging during the cycle:

$$UD_a = \frac{1}{2}C^2\left[1 - \frac{g}{C}\right]^2\left[\frac{vs}{s - v}\right] \qquad [16\text{-}16]$$

where UD_a is the aggregate uniform delay, in vehicle-seconds. To obtain the average delay per vehicle, this is divided by the number of vehicles processed during the cycle, which is the arrival rate, v, times the full cycle length, C. This includes the vehicles arriving on green that experience no delay in traversing the intersection. Dividing by vC and simplifying in a number of steps yields the classic form of the Webster Formula for uniform delay:

$$UD = \frac{C}{2}\frac{[1 - (g/C)]^2}{[1 - (v/s)]} \qquad [16\text{-}17]$$

where UD is the average uniform delay per vehicle, in sec/veh. Another familiar form of the equation makes use of Equation [16-5], substituting the product (v/c) (g/C) for v/s.

While the formula is derived for a single cycle, the assumed conditions of uniform arrivals make it valid for any period of time over which the arrival rate is constant.

The uniform delay formula, however, assumes a uniform arrival pattern. At isolated intersections, vehicle arrivals are more likely to be randomly distributed. A number of stochastic models have been developed, including those by Newall [18], Miller [19, 20], and Webster [17]. The models generally assume that arrivals are Poisson distributed, with an underlying average rate of v vehicles/unit time. They account for the "overflow delay" due to individual cycle failures, although the v/c ratio for the entire analysis period is always less than 1.00. The Webster formulation is the most frequently used:

$$D = \frac{C}{2}\frac{[1 - (g/C)]^2}{[1 - (v/s)]} + \frac{(v/c)^2}{2v[1 - (v/c)]}$$
$$- [0.65(c/v^2)^{1/3}(v/c)^{2+(g/C)}] \qquad [16\text{-}18]$$

The first term of the equation is the uniform delay component, UD. The second term accounts for the randomness of arrivals, and is theoretically developed. It is sometimes referred to as the "overflow delay" term, but this is somewhat of a misnomer, since it accounts only for individual cycle failures within an analysis period during which v/c is less than 1.00. For the purposes of this text, this is referred to as the "random delay" component, RD. The last is an adjustment based on a series of simulation runs. While in the first two terms, v/s and v/c are dimensionless (both must be in similar units), the third term must use flow rates in vehicles/second. The third-term "adjustment" results in a decrease of between 5% and 15% in the delay result. This is most often approximated by applying a multiplicative factor of 0.90 to uniform and random delay:

$$D = 0.90[UD + RD] \qquad [16\text{-}19]$$

Webster also derived an expression for the optimum cycle length to minimize delay, and then an approximation for the more complex precise form:

$$C_o = \frac{1.5L + 5}{1 - \sum (v/s)_c} \qquad [16\text{-}20]$$

where: C_o = optimal cycle for minimum delay, sec
 L = lost time per cycle, sec
 $\sum(v/s)_c$ = sum of v/s ratios for critical lanes or critical lane groups

Figure 16-14 illustrates the average delay for a set of demand levels, based on Webster's formulas. When the cycle length is too short for the demand, individual cycles begin to fail, and eventually a condition in which $v/c > 1.00$ is reached. Thus, delay increases rapidly for cycle lengths which are "too short." When the cycle length is too long, there is much unused green time. This forces vehicles to wait longer than necessary, and also increases delay. This trend, however, is more gradual than for short cycles, as no capacity constraint is involved. The optimal cycle length is minimum delay point for the appropriate curve. However, as Figure 16-14 illustrates, in a considerable range of cycle lengths, delay is relatively constant. As shown, cycle lengths in the range of 3/4 to 1–1/2 times the optimum value produce reasonable delay values. This flexibility in cycle length selection is important, as many external factors, including coordination constraints, limit the ability to select precisely optimal values.

3. Modeling overflow delay when $v/c > 1.00$. While Webster's formulas treat the delay due to individual cycle failures in the random delay term, they do not address the more significant issue of delay when demand exceeds capacity for a significant period of time. Consider the simplified situation illustrated in Figure 16-15. In this case, a constant demand, v, exceeds the capacity of the signalized approach to discharge vehicles. The capacity, c, is shown as a constant-slope line showing the maximum average discharge rate per unit time. It is defined by the end points of the discharge function in each signal cycle. The discharge function, as previously, shows no discharge during red, and a discharge rate equal to the saturation flow rate, s, during the green.

Where demand flow continuously exceeds capacity, the overflow delay component continues to grow with time. Thus in the case of oversaturation, the *duration* of the oversaturation affects the overflow delay. The uniform delay component in this situation is a special case of Equation [16-17], in which the v/c ratio is effectively 1.00. The uniform delay is the area between the capacity and discharge functions, and is equal to the delay that would occur if the arrival function and capacity functions coincided.

Taking Equation [16-17], substituting $(g/C)(v/c) = (v/s)$, and inserting a v/c ratio of 1.00 yields:

$$UD_o = \frac{C[1 - (g/C)]}{2} \qquad [16\text{-}21]$$

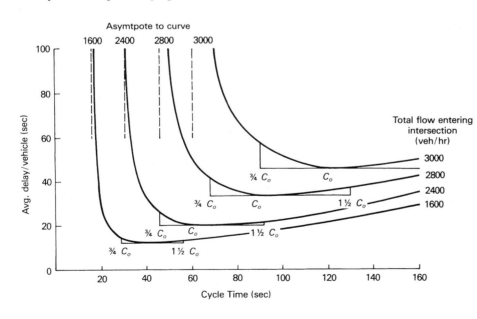

Figure 16-14 Average delay as a function of demand level and cycle length. [Used with permission of Her Majestys Stationery Office, London, U.K., from F. V. Webster, "Traffic Signal Settings," *Road Research Technical Paper No. 39*. Copyright © 1958 Her Majesty's Stationery Office.]

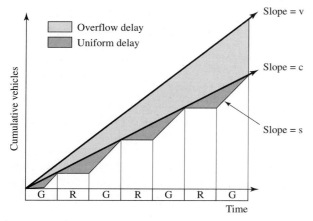

Figure 16-15 Overflow delay illustrated.

where UD_o is the uniform delay component when oversaturation exists on the approach under consideration.

The overflow relationship derives from the area between the arrival function and the capacity function, assuming that both have constant slopes. Figure 16-16 illustrates.

The total aggregate overflow delay experienced by vehicles *through time t = T* is equal to the area enclosed by the arrival function, the capacity function, and a vertical drawn at time = *T*. This is given by:

$$OD_a = \frac{1}{2} T(vT - cT) = \frac{T^2}{2}(v - c) \quad [16\text{-}22]$$

where OD_a is the aggregate delay. If this is averaged over the number of vehicles *discharged* during time *T*, cT, then:

$$OD = \frac{T}{2}[(v/c) - 1] \quad [16\text{-}23]$$

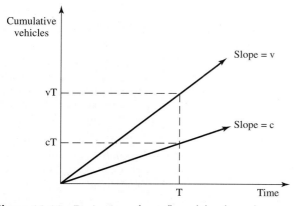

Figure 16-16 Derivation of overflow delay formula.

where *T* may be in seconds, minutes, or hours. The units of *OD* will correspond to the input: seconds/vehicle, minutes/vehicle, or hours/vehicle.

It is important that this formulation be understood:

- The relationship is time-dependent. As the period of oversaturation (i.e., $v/c > 1.00$) increases, the overflow delay increases. This is only logical, as queues continue to build throughout such a period.
- The relationship yields the *average delay per vehicle* from the onset of oversaturation to time *T*. It does *not* represent the delay to vehicles at the *end* of time *T*, which is much larger.
- The formulation does *not* include the delay experienced by vehicles arriving within *T* that occurs *after* time *T*. This is important, as some vehicles arrive *before T*, but are discharged *after T*. The component of their delay occurring after *T* is not included in Equation [16-22].

A formula may also be derived to describe the average overflow delay per vehicle occurring between times T_1 and T_2:

$$OD_i = \frac{(T_1 + T_2)}{2}[(v/c) - 1] \quad [16\text{-}24]$$

where OD_i is the average overflow delay per vehicle for time increment *i*. For the case where $T_1 = 0$, this collapses to Equation [16-23]. For all other increments (after the initiation of oversaturation), the average delay per vehicle is higher, and continues to increase as T_1 and T_2 increase.

This equation averages the delay based on the number of vehicles discharged during the period $T_2 - T_1$, and includes all delay incurred during that period. In this case, however, some of the vehicles discharged during the period arrived prior to T_1, and some vehicles arriving during the interval are not discharged until after T_2. Thus, the precise interpretation of the "average overflow delay" is not straightforward. The aggregate delay *does not* include *all* of the delay incurred by either vehicles discharged or arriving during the specified time interval. Further, the actual vehicles incurring the delay within the interval are not the same as those discharging during the interval, although there is overlap. The degree of overlap increases as the difference between the arrival rate, *v*, and the capacity, *c*, decreases.

4. Inconsistencies between stochastic and overflow delay models: A practical problem. Figure 16-17 illustrates a serious practical difficulty with the theoretical delay models introduced in previous sections. The figure is a plot of the random delay term of Webster's equation (from Equation [16-18]) and the overflow delay formula of Equation [16-23]. Average overflow delay is plotted vs. the v/c ratio for a case in which the cycle length is 60 seconds, the g/C ratio is 0.50, and the saturation flow rate is 3600 vphg. The latter represents two lanes.

The behavior of the two relationships in the vicinity of $v/c = 1.00$ is most interesting. The Webster equation depicts random delay for cases in which v/c is less than 1.00. It approaches a v/c of 1.00 from lower values. As the random delay term includes $[1 - (v/c)]$ in the denominator, the value goes to infinity as v/c approaches 1.00. The overflow delay formula, on the other hand, begins with a v/c ratio of 1.00, and has a value of "0" for that case. It increases linearly as v/c increases. Thus, the steady-state stochastic model of Webster "blows up" to extremely high values of delay as $v/c = 1.00$ is approached, while the overflow model goes to "0" delay as $v/c = 1.00$ is approached.

Much of the modern work in delay modeling represents attempts to bridge the gap between these two divergent theoretical approaches. Most studies conclude that at v/c ratios below 0.80–0.85, the sto-chastic model closely represents field conditions. At v/c ratios above 1.15–1.20 (approximately), the overflow delay model is a relatively good representation of delay, especially when T is limited to short periods. Unfortunately, most signalized intersections that are analyzed involve v/c ratios within the range of 0.80–1.20.

The dashed line in Figure 16-17 illustrates how a model "bridging the gap" should look. One model was developed as part of the TRANSYT signal optimization program, a standard package in regular use in the profession [21]. While the exact model is quite complex, an approximation is reported in Reference 22:

$$OD = \frac{15T}{v}(v - c)$$
$$+ \sqrt{(v - c)^2 + \frac{240v}{T}} \qquad [16\text{-}25]$$

where OD is the overflow delay which must be added to uniform delay to estimate total delay. OD is in sec/veh, T is in minutes, and v and c are in vph. This equation is reported as an approximation of the version used in TRANSYT-6. Other versions use somewhat different, but similar, relationships.

Another important model that has been used for a number of applications was developed by Akcelik [23, 24] for the Australian intersection analysis procedure:

$$OD = \frac{T}{4}\left[(v/c - 1) \right.$$
$$\left. + \sqrt{(v/c - 1)^2 + \frac{12(v/c - v_o/c)}{cT}}\right] \qquad [16\text{-}26]$$

where: $v_o/c = 0.67 + s(g/600)$

The equation is valid for cases in which $v/c > v_o/c$. Overflow delay is equal to zero when this is not the case. In this formula, c is in vph, s is in vphg, and T is in hours.

As shown in Figure 16-17, the "ideal" delay relationships should be asymptotic to the theoretical overflow delay curve at high v/c ratios, and to the stochastic delay curve at low v/c ratios. The exact shape of the curve between these is open to speculation. In preparing models for the 1985 *Highway Capacity Manual* [25], Reilly et al. [26] conducted extensive field studies to measure delay. They found that Equation [16-26] consistently overestimated field-measured values, and recommended that the theoretical results be reduced by 50% to better reflect field conditions.

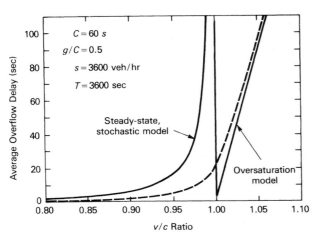

Figure 16-17 Random and overflow delay models compared. [Adapted with permission of Transportation Research Board, National Research Council, Washington, DC, from V. F. Hurdle, "Signalized Intersection Delay Model: A Primer for the Uninitiated," *Transportation Research Record 971*, p. 101. Copyright © 1984 Transportation Research Board.]

Since the 1985 *HCM* used stopped-time delay as a measure of effectiveness, not the approach delay predicted by Equation [16-26], a further adjustment was necessary. The study results suggested that approach delay was 1.3 times stopped delay. Time was also converted from hours to seconds. The first term of Equation [16-26] was, therefore, adjusted to:

$$\frac{T}{4} \times \frac{1}{1.3} \times \frac{1}{2} \times 3600 = 346.2T$$

Using this adjustment, T is in hours, while v and c are in vph, and the resulting stopped-time overflow delay (OD_s) is in seconds/vehicle. The resulting equation is:

$$OD_s = 346.2T\left[(v/c - 1) + \sqrt{(v/c - 1)^2 + \frac{12(v/c - v_o/c)}{cT}} \right]$$
$$[16\text{-}27]$$

Reilly's suggested formulation also included a somewhat different form of v_o/c which does not radically alter results.

Figure 16-18 illustrates how Equations [16-25], [16-26], and [16-27] compare to the stochastic delay model and the theoretical overflow delay model. Note that while Equation [16-27] was calibrated to a North American data base, it differs from the other two in that it is NOT asymptotic to the overflow delay model at high v/c ratios.

5. Delay models in the highway capacity manual. Reilly's equation was modified in Reference [27] and used in the 1985 and 1994 *Highway Capacity Manuals*. In those manuals, total average individual stopped delay (for random arrivals) is given by the formula:

$$d = 0.38C\,\frac{[1 - (g/C)]^2}{[1 - (g/C)(X)]}$$
$$+ 173X^2\left[(X - 1) + \sqrt{(X - 1)^2 + \frac{16X}{c}} \right] \quad [16\text{-}28]$$

where: d = total average individual stopped-time delay, sec/veh
  X = v/c ratio

The first term of this equation is Webster's uniform delay formula, divided by 1.3 to adjust for stopped-time rather than approach delay. The maximum value of v/c in the uniform delay term is explicitly limited to

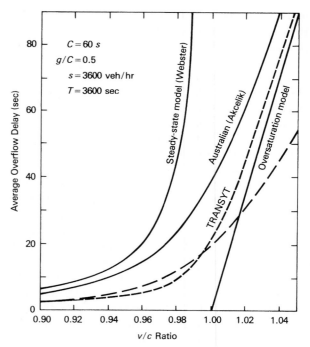

Figure 16-18 Delay formulas compared. [Adapted with permission of Transportation Research Board, National Research Council, Washington, DC, from V.F. Hurdle, "Signalized Intersection Delay Model: A Primer for the Uninitiated," *Transportation Research Record 971*, p. 102. Copyright © 1984 Transportation Research Board.]

1.00. The second term represents the 1985 *HCM* model for overflow delay. The 173 is from the term $T/4$, where the unit of time is a 15-minute analysis period, with results converted to seconds. Thus:

$$\frac{0.25}{4} \times 3600 \times \frac{1}{1.3} = 173$$

The X^2 term was inserted to make the overflow delay increase more quickly at high v/c ratios. The last term under the radical is a special case of the same term in Equation [16-26], where $T = 0.25$ hrs, and where modifications have been introduced to achieve a better fit to Reilly's measured delay values.

6. Theory vs. reality. Most of the models presented in this section are based on the assumption of a simple uniform arrival pattern. Webster and others have added terms that account for random arrivals with a constant underlying rate. In most practical applications, however, arrivals are neither uniform nor random. Figure 16-19 shows a comparison between uniform arrivals, random arrivals, and the platooned arrivals more likely to exist at most urban and suburban signalized intersections.

When arrivals are "bunched" or "platooned" as illustrated in Figure 16-19c, the exact timing of the arrivals of platoons has a significant effect on delay. When platoons arrive at the beginning of a green period, most vehicles can traverse the intersection without stopping. When platoons arrive at the beginning of a red period, then all of the vehicles in the platoon must stop and wait for the green.

Hurdle [16], in presenting his overview of delay equations, notes that "No claim is made that the formulas are *correct*, but rather that they yield answers which do not violate elementary logic in the region of *v/c* near unity where neither the steady-state nor the oversaturation models can be expected to yield reasonable results."

This view highlights the fact that most delay modeling has been done on a purely theoretical basis. Even Webster compared his theoretical results to simulation results rather than field data. Field studies, particularly extensive field studies, have been few and far between, with the Reilly study being one notable exception.

This is because delay is difficult to measure at best. Reference [28] contains an excellent overview of measurement techniques through the late 1970s, and compares results for 10 signalized intersections at which studies were conducted. Chapter 7 in this book presents a simplified point-sampling method for measuring stopped-time delay originally developed by

Berry [29, 30]. Reference [31] details a method for measuring time-in-queue delay by observing queue lengths at specified times in each signal cycle. Reference [32] presents a method for time-in-queue measurement using a delay meter. A volume-density method for travel time delay, wherein the number of vehicles occupying a section under study is observed at specified time intervals, is described in Reference [33]. Approach delay, the subject of most theoretical models, is the most difficult to measure in the field, and usually requires the use of time-lapse or video-tape photography. This allows detailed tracing of vehicles as they traverse the intersection. The Reilly study [28] of 10 intersections used such technology, and was able to compare various delay forms to each other. This study resulted in the 1.3 factor used to relate stopped-time and approach delay. As stopped-time delay is easier to measure, often field studies focus on this, using the factor to estimate approach delay. The correctness of the constant 1.3 conversion factor, however, is not universally accepted due to the relatively small data sample on which it was based.

7. Sample delay computations. The following sample computations illustrate the use of the delay models presented in this section.

SAMPLE COMPUTATION A: An intersection approach has an approach volume of 1000 vph, a saturation flow rate of 2800 vphg, a cycle length of 90 seconds, and a *g/C* ratio of 0.55. What average approach delay per vehicle is expected under these conditions?

In addition to the data given, it would be useful to compute the capacity of the approach, and the

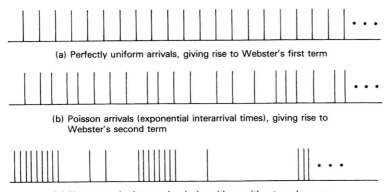

(a) Perfectly uniform arrivals, giving rise to Webster's first term

(b) Poisson arrivals (exponential interarrival times), giving rise to Webster's second term

(c) Not covered: platooned arrivals, with or without randomness

Figure 16-19 Arrival types illustrated.

effective *v/c* ratio. Capacity may be computed using Equation [16-5]:

$$c = s\frac{g}{C} = 2800(0.55) = 1540 \text{ vph}$$

and:

$$v/c = \frac{1000}{1540} = 0.65$$

Since this is relatively low value of *v/c*, the steady-state uniform delay model of Webster will be applied (Equation [16-17]):

$$UD = \frac{C}{2}\frac{[1-(g/C)]^2}{[1-(v/s)]} = \frac{90}{2}\frac{[1-0.55]^2}{[1-(1000/2800)]}$$

$$= 14.2 \text{ sec/veh}$$

Thus, each vehicle is expected to experience 14.2 seconds of approach delay traversing the intersection approach as described. Stopped-time delay is obtained by dividing the result by the 1.3 conversion factor: $UD_s = 14.2/1.3 = 10.9$ seconds/vehicle.

SAMPLE COMPUTATION B: A signalized intersection approach experiences chronic oversaturation during a typical two-hour P.M. peak period. For this time, vehicles arrive at a rate of 1100 vph. The saturation flow rate for the approach is 2000 vphg, with a 120-second cycle length, and a *g/C* ratio of 0.52. What is the total average approach delay expected during the two-hour period? during the last 15-minutes of the peak period?

Once again, the capacity of the approach, and the *v/c* ratio should be computed:

$$c = s\frac{g}{C} = 2000(0.52) = 1040 \text{ vph}$$

$$v/c = \frac{1100}{1040} = 1.058$$

The oversaturated condition is obvious from the *v/c* ratio, which exceeds 1.00. In such cases, there are two components of delay, uniform delay and overflow delay. Uniform delay for an oversaturated case is given by Equation [16-21]:

$$UD = \frac{C[1-(g/C)]}{2} = \frac{120(1-0.52)}{2}$$

$$= 28.8 \text{ sec/veh}$$

To this must be added the appropriate overflow delay. The average overflow delay for the two-hour peak period is given by Equation [16-23]:

$$OD(2 \text{ hrs}) = \frac{T}{2}[v/c - 1] = \frac{7200}{2}[1.058 - 1]$$

$$= 208.8 \text{ sec/veh}$$

Thus, over the full two-hour period during which oversaturation exists, the total average delay per vehicle is expected to be:

$$d(2 \text{ hrs}) = UD + OD = 28.8 + 208.8$$

$$= 237.6 \text{ sec/veh}$$

To obtain the average overflow delay per vehicle during the *last 15 minutes of the peak hour,* Equation [16-24] must be used:

$$OD_i(\text{last 15m}) = \frac{(T_1 + T_2)}{2}[v/c - 1]$$

$$= \frac{6300 + 7200}{2}[1.058 - 1]$$

$$= 391.5 \text{ sec/veh}$$

The uniform delay term for the last 15 minutes is the same as for other parts of the hour. Therefore, the total average approach delay per vehicle during the last 15 minutes of the 2-hour peak period is:

$$d(\text{last 15m}) = UD + OD_i = 28.8 + 391.5$$

$$= 420.3 \text{ sec/veh}$$

Obviously, the problems associated with the operation of an intersection approach at a *v/c* ratio over 1.00 for 2 hours are quite serious. In the last 15 minutes of the analysis period, it takes the average driver 420.3/60 = 7.0 minutes to traverse the intersection. Whether drivers would accept such a condition is difficult to say. In a situation such as that described, queues would doubtless build through any proximate upstream signalized intersection. Many drivers will begin to seek alternative routes, avoiding the location. Thus, the assumed constant demand throughout the two-hour peak period is probably not reasonable. The computation does, however, illustrate how fast delay builds when *v/c* is greater than 1.00.

It might be more reasonable to consider the average delay during the *first* 15 minutes of oversaturated operation. The uniform delay remains unchanged, and the overflow delay would be:

$$OD(\text{first 15m}) = \frac{900}{2}[1.058 - 1] = 26.1 \text{ sec/veh}$$

and the total approach delay would be:

$$d(\text{first 15m}) = 28.8 + 26.1 = 54.9 \text{ sec/veh}$$

This is not a particularly large average delay. The 1994 *HCM* would define this as level of service E, based on 54.9/1.3 = 42.2 sec/veh of stopped-time delay. Thus, it is not clear whether substantial diversion would occur during or immediately after the first 15 minutes of oversaturated operation. Driver characteristics and expectations, block lengths, and availability of alternative routes would all affect when and how drivers divert around the problem intersection.

SAMPLE COMPUTATION C: What average stopped-time delay per vehicle is predicted by the 1994 *HCM* for the problem described in Sample Computation B above? What is its meaning?

The 1994 *HCM* predicts the average stopped-time delay for vehicles during the first 15 minutes during which a given *v/c* ratio exists. Where *v/c* ratios are less than 1.00, delay is constant over time. Where *v/c* ratios are greater than 1.00, delay decreases for subsequent 15-minute periods, as illustrated in Sample Computation B above.

Equation [16-28] gives the 1994 *HCM* model for stopped-time delay, given random arrivals:

$$d = 0.38C\frac{[1 - (g/C)]^2}{[1 - (g/C)(X)]}$$
$$+ 173X^2\left[(X - 1) + \sqrt{(X - 1)^2 + \frac{16X}{c}}\right]$$

where: $C = 120$ seconds
$g/C = 0.52$
$X = v/c = 1.058$ (use 1.00 max. value for uniform delay term)
$c = 1{,}040$ vph

Then:

$$d = 0.38(120)\frac{[1 - 0.52]^2}{[1 - (0.52)(1.00)]}$$
$$+ 173(1.058)^2\left[(1.058 - 1)\right.$$
$$+ \left.\sqrt{(1.058 - 1)^2 + \frac{16(1.058)}{1040}}\right]$$

$$d = 21.9 + 43.6 = 65.5 \text{ sec/veh}$$

This results in considerably higher delay than the prediction using the theoretical overflow delay equation (for the first 15-minutes of oversaturation), as in Sample Computation b. The 65.5 seconds/vehicle of stopped-time delay compares to the 42.2 second/vehicle of stopped time delay of the first 15 minutes of oversaturated operation in Computation b. The uniform delay of 21.9 seconds matches the previous computation, adjusted to reflect stopped-time delay (28.8/1.3 = 22.2 sec/veh; the small discrepancy is due to the rounding of the 0.38 factor in the *HCM* equation from a more precise 0.384). The difference, then, is in the overflow delay equation. The *v/c* in this problem, 1.058, lies in the range of *v/c* ratios for which the steady-state stochastic model and the theoretical overflow delay model do not work well. In "bridging the gap," the *HCM* model yields higher overflow delay values than the theoretical equation.

8. Additional references. In addition to the many references cited within the material on signalized intersection delay, the literature is rich in published studies related to model development, analysis, and testing. Akcelik compares equations used in Australia, Canada, and the U.S. in Reference [34]. In Reference [35], Berry makes a number of interesting suggestions for improving the 1985 *HCM* model. Additional studies of interest are found in References [36–45], while applications of delay modeling to unsignalized intersections are found in References [46–50].

Summary

The four basic mechanisms involved in modeling signalized intersections—departure headways, the time budget and critical lane concepts, left-turn equiva-lency, and delay—are the fundamental building blocks of any approach to the analysis of intersections. In Chapter 17, some of these fundamentals are expanded and included in a technique for simple signal timing. In Chapter 18, the *HCM* model for signalized intersections is developed, discussed, and illustrated. It uses all of the fundamentals discussed here, occasionally in different formats, to build a complex model of traffic's most complex operation: signalized intersections.

References

1. *Manual of Uniform Traffic Control Devices,* U.S. Department of Transportation, Federal Highway Administration, Washington, DC, 1988 (amended through 1994).
2. *Highway Capacity Manual, Special Report 209,* 3rd Edition, Transportation Research Board, National Research Council, Washington, DC, (revised) 1994.
3. *Highway Capacity Software, User's Manual,* McTrans Center, University of Florida at Gainesville, Gainesville, FL, 1994.
4. Greenshields, B., "Traffic Performance at Intersections," *Yale Bureau Technical Report No. 1,* Yale University, New Haven, CT, 1947.
5. Kunzman, W., "Another Look at Signalized Intersection Capacity," *ITE Journal,* August 1978.
6. Roess, R., et al., "Level of Service in Shared-Permissive Left-Turn Lane Groups," *Final Report,* FHWA Contract No. DTFH-87-C-0012, Transportation Training and Research Center, Polytechnic University, Brooklyn, NY, September 29, 1989.
7. Prassas, E., "Modeling the Effects of Permissive Left Turns on Intersection Capacity," Ph.D. Dissertation, Polytechnic University, Brooklyn, NY, December 1994.
8. Teply, S., and Jones, A., "Saturation Flow: Do We Speak the Same Language," *Transportation Research Record 1320,* Transportation Research Board, National Research Council, Washington, DC, 1991.
9. Teply, S., "Saturation Flow Through a Magnifying Glass," *Proceedings: 10th International Symposium on Transportation and Traffic Flow,* Toronto University Press, Toronto, Canada, 1981.
10. Branston, D., and Van Zuylen, H., "The Estimation of Saturation Flow, Effective Green Time, and Passenger Car Equivalents at Traffic Signals by Linear Regression," *Transportation Research,* Vol. 12, Pergamon Press, London, U.K., 1978.
11. Kimber, R., and Semmens, "An Experiment to Investigate Saturation Flow at Signalized Intersections," *Traffic Engineering and Control,* March 1982.
12. Kimber, R., et al., "The Prediction of Saturation Flow for Road Junctions Controlled by Traffic Signals," *Digest of Research Report RR67,* Transportation Road Research Laboratory, Her Majesty's Stationery Office, Crowthorne, Berkshire, U.K., 1978.
13. *Traffic Capacity of Major Routes,* Road Transportation Research, Organization for Economic Cooperation and Development (OECD), Paris, France, July 1983.
14. "A Method for Measuring Saturation Flow at Signalized Intersections," *Road Note 34/196,* Transportation Road Research Laboratory, Crowthorne, Berkshire, U.K., 1963.
15. Akcelik, R., "Traffic Signals: Capacity and Timing Analysis," *Research Report 123,* Australian Road Research Board, Victoria, Australia, 1981.
16. Hurdle, V., "Signalized Intersection Delay Models: A Primer for the Uninitiated," *Transportation Research Record 971,* Transportation Research Board, National Research Council, Washington, DC, 1984.
17. Webster, F., "Traffic Signal Settings," *Road Research Technical Paper No. 39,* Road Research Laboratory, Her Majesty's Stationery Office, London, U.K., 1958.
18. Newell, G., "Approximation Methods for Queues with Application to the Fixed-Cycle Traffic Light," *SIAM Review,* Vol. 7, 1965.
19. Miller, A., "Settings for Fixed-Cycle Traffic Signals," *ARRB Bulletin 3,* Australian Road Research Board, Victoria, Australia, 1968.
20. Miller, A., "The Capacity of Signalized Intersections in Australia," *ARRB Bulletin 3,* Australian Road Research Board, Victoria, Australia, 1968.
21. Kimber, R., and Hollis, E., "Traffic Queues and Delays at Road Junctions," *TRRL Report 909,* Road Research Laboratory, Crowthorne, Berkshire, U.K., 1979.
22. Robertson, D., "Traffic Models and Optimum Strategies of Control—A Review," *Proceedings on Traffic Control Systems,* Vol. 1, Berkeley, CA, 1979.
23. Akcelik, R., "Time-Dependent Expressions for Delay, Stop Rate, and Queue Length at Traffic Signals," *Report No. AIR 367-1,* Australian Road Research Board, Victoria, Australia, 1980.
24. Akcelik, R., "Traffic Signals: Capacity and Timing Analysis," *ARRB Research Report 123,* Australian Road Research Board, Victoria, Australia, March 1981.
25. *Highway Capacity Manual, Special Report 209,* Transportation Research Board, National Research Council, Washington, DC, 1985 Edition.
26. Reilly, W., et al., "Capacity of Signalized Intersections," *Final Report,* NCHRP Project 3-28(2), JHK & Associates, Tucson, AZ, 1983.

27. Roess, R., and McShane, W., "Final Report on the New Highway Capacity Manual," *Final Report,* NCHRP Project 3-28(B), Transportation Training and Research Center, Polytechnic University, Brooklyn, NY, October 1986.

28. Reilly, W., and Gardner, C., "Technique for Measuring Delay at Intersections," *Transportation Research Record 644,* Transportation Research Board, National Research Council, Washington, DC, 1977.

29. Berry, D., "Field Measurement of Delay at Signalized Intersections," *Proceedings of the Highway Research Board,* Transportation Research Board, National Research Council, Washington, DC, 1956.

30. Berry, D., and Van Til, C., "A Comparison of Three Methods for Measuring Delay at Intersections," *Traffic Engineering,* Institute of Transportation Engineers, Washington, DC, December 1954.

31. Sagi, G., and Campbell, L., "Vehicle Delay at Signalized Intersections: Theory and Practice," *Traffic Engineering,* Institute of Transportation Engineers, Washington, DC, February 1969.

32. *SDS Delay Meter Manual,* SDS Technical Devices, Ltd., Winnipeg, Manitoba, Canada, n.d.

33. Solomon, D., "Accuracy of the Volume-Density Method of Measuring Travel Time," *Traffic Engineering,* Institute of Transportation Engineers, Washington, DC, March 1957.

34. Akcelik, R., "The Highway Capacity Manual Delay Formula for Signalized Intersections," *ITE Journal,* March 1988.

35. Berry, D., "Using Volume-to-Capacity Ratio to Supplement Delay as Criteria for Levels of Service at Traffic Signals," *Transportation Research Record 1112,* Transportation Research Board, National Research Council, Washington, DC, 1987.

36. Li, J., et al., "Overflow Delay Estimation for a Simple Intersection with Fully Actuated Signal Control," *Transportation Research Record 1457,* Transportation Research Board, National Research Council, Washington, DC, 1994.

37. Akcelik, R., and Rouphail, N., "Overflow Queues and Delays with Random and Platooned Arrivals at Signalized Intersections," *Journal of Advanced Transportation,* Vol. 28, Institute for Transportation, Durham, NC, 1994.

38. Akcelik, R., and Rouphail, N., "Estimation of Delays at Traffic Signals for Variable Demand Conditions," *Transportation Research,* Vol. 27A, No., 2, Pergamon Press, Oxford, U.K., 1993.

39. Rouphail, N., and Akcelik, R., "Oversaturation Delay Estimates with Consideration of Peaking," *Transportation Research Record 1365,* Transportation Research

Board, National Research Council, Washington, DC, 1992.

40. Ha, D., "A Dynamic Model for Intersection Delay with Time-Varying Demand," Dissertation, Polytechnic University, Brooklyn, NY, 1992.

41. Courage, K., and Maddula, S., "Evaluation of Signalized Intersection Delay Using Video Image Technology," *Compendium of Technical Papers,* 64th Annual Meeting of the Institute of Transportation Engineers, Institute of Transportation Engineers, Washington, DC, 1994.

42. Dowling, R., "Use of Default Parameters for Estimating Signalized Intersection Level of Service," *Transportation Research Record 1457,* Transportation Research Board, National Research Council, Washington, DC, 1994.

43. Heidemann, D., "Queue Length and Delay Distributions at Traffic Signals," *Transportation Research,* Vol. 28, No. 5, Elsevier Science, Ltd., Oxford, England, 1994.

44. Olszewski, P., "Modeling Probability Distribution of Delay at Signalized Intersections," *Journal of Advanced Transportation,* Vol. 28, No. 3, Institute for Transportation, Durham, NC, 1994.

45. Akcelik, R., and Chung, E., "Traffic Performance Models for Unsignalized Intersections and Fixed-Time Signals," *Proceedings of the Second International Symposium on Highway Capacity,* Transportation Research Board, National Research Council, Washington, DC, 1994.

46. Tonke, R., "Delays at Unsignalized Intersections Under Non-Stationary Traffic Flow Conditions," *HEFT 401,* Bundesmiinister Fur Verkehr, Bonn, Germany, 1983.

47. Chodur, J., et al., "Capacity and Traffic Conditions at Unsignalized Intersection Approaches Situated in Traffic Signal Networks," *Proceedings of the Second International Symposium on Highway Capacity,* Transportation Research Board, National Research Council, Washington, DC, 1994.

48. Abou-Henaidy, M., et al., "Gap Acceptance Investigations in Canada," *Proceedings of the Second International Symposium on Highway Capacity,* Transportation Research Board, National Research Council, Washington, DC, 1994.

49. Akcelik, R., "Gap-Acceptance Modeling by Traffic Signal Analogy," *Traffic Engineering and Control,* Vol. 35, No. 9, Printerhall, Ltd., London, U.K., 1994.

50. Tracz, M., et al., "Influence of Vehicular Delay on Safety Risks at Junctions," *Report No. VT 1A, Part 1,* Swedish Road and Transport Research Institute, Linkoping, Sweden, 1994.

Problems

Problem 16–1

Consider the headway data shown on next page. Data was taken from the center lane of a three-lane intersection approach for a total of 10 signal cycles. For the purposes of this analysis, the data may be considered to have been obtained under ideal conditions.

(a) Plot headways vs. position in platoon for the data shown. Sketch an approximate best-fit curve through the data.
(b) Using the approximate best-fit curve constructed in a), determine the saturation headway and the start-up lost time for the data.
(c) What is the saturation flow rate for this data?

Problem 16–2

A signalized intersection approach has 3 lanes, with no exclusive left- or right-turning lanes. The approach has a 35-second green out of a 75-second cycle. The yellow plus all red intervals for the phase are a total of 3 seconds. If the start-up lost time is 1.5 seconds/phase, the clearance lost time is 1.0 seconds/phase, and the saturation headway is 2.87 seconds/vehicle under prevailing conditions, what is the capacity of the intersection approach?

Problem 16–3

An equation has been calibrated for the amount of time required to clear *N* vehicles through a given signal phase:

$$T = 1.35 + 2.35N$$

(a) What start-up lost time does this equation suggest exists?
(b) What saturation headway and saturation flow rate is implied by this equation?
(c) A simple two-phase signal is to be placed at this location, and the two critical volumes are 550 vphpl and 485 vphpl. Using the equation above, estimate an appropriate signal timing for the two phases. Is iteration necessary? Why? How does the equation close to a solution?

Problem 16–4

What is the maximum sum of critical lane volumes that may be served by an intersection having a three-phase traffic signal with a cycle length of 75 seconds, a saturation headway of 2.75 seconds/vehicle, and a total lost time per phase of 3.1 seconds/phase?

Problems 16–5 and 16–6

For the two intersections shown, find the appropriate number of lanes for each lane group needed. Assume that all vph shown have been converted to compatible "through car equivalent" values for the conditions shown. Assume that critical volumes reverse in the other daily peak hour.

Problem 16–7

In the intersection of Problem 16–5, consider a case in which the E-W arterial has two lanes in each direction and

Q Pos	1	2	3	4	5	6	7	8	9	10

Data for Problem 1

Headways (sec) for Cycle No. —

Q Pos	1	2	3	4	5	6	7	8	9	10
1	3.5	3.4	3.0	3.6	3.5	3.1	3.2	3.5	3.0	3.5
2	2.9	2.6	2.9	2.7	2.5	2.6	2.9	3.1	2.6	3.0
3	2.3	2.5	2.3	2.0	2.7	2.7	2.4	2.5	2.8	2.3
4	2.1	2.4	2.3	2.4	2.6	2.1	2.0	2.6	2.2	2.2
5	2.2	1.9	2.0	2.3	2.1	2.0	2.1	1.8	1.9	1.8
6	1.9	2.0	2.1	2.2	1.8	2.3	2.2	1.8	2.1	1.7
7	1.9	2.1	2.1	2.3	1.9	2.3	2.1	2.0	2.2	2.0
8	x	2.2	2.1	1.9	2.0	2.1	2.3	2.1	x	2.1
9	x	1.9	x	2.2	x	2.2	1.9	x	x	1.8
10	x	1.9	x	2.1	x	x	2.1	x	x	2.0

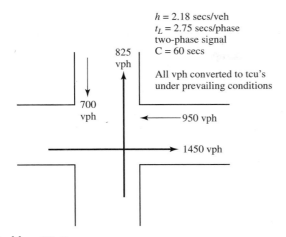

h = 2.18 secs/veh
t_L = 2.75 secs/phase
two-phase signal
C = 60 secs

All vph converted to tcu's
under prevailing conditions

825 vph
700 vph
950 vph
1450 vph

Problem 16–5

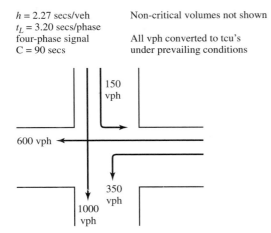

h = 2.27 secs/veh
t_L = 3.20 secs/phase
four-phase signal
C = 90 secs

Non-critical volumes not shown

All vph converted to tcu's
under prevailing conditions

150 vph
600 vph
350 vph
1000 vph

Problem 16–6

the N-S artery has only one lane in each direction. For this case:

(a) What is the absolute minimum cycle length that could be used?

(b) What cycle length would be required to provide for a v/c ratio of 0.90 during the worst 15 minutes of the hour if the PHF = 0.92?

(c) Compare these cycle lengths to the optimal delay cycle length suggested by Webster's equation.

Problem 16–8

At a signalized intersection, one lane is observed to discharge 18 through vehicles in the same time as the left lane discharges 9 through vehicles and 3 left-turning vehicles. For this case:

(a) What is the through vehicle equivalent, E_{LT}, for these left-turning vehicles?

(b) What is the left-turn adjustment factor, f_{LT}, for the case described?

(c) What variables can be expected to affect the observed value of E_{LT}?

Problem 16–9

An intersection approach volume is 1500 vph, and includes 7.5% left turns, with a through-vehicle equivalent of 3.0 tcu's/left turn. What is the total equivalent through volume on the approach?

Problem 16–10

An intersection approach has three lanes, permitted left turns, 8% left turns with a through vehicle equivalent of 4.50, and a saturation flow rate of 1750 vphgpl for *through vehicles* under prevailing conditions.

(a) What is the left-turn adjustment factor for the case described?

(b) Determine the saturation flow rate and saturation headway for the approach, including the impact of left-turning vehicles.

(c) If the approach in question has an effective green time of 45 seconds in a 75-second cycle length, what is the capacity of the approach in vph?

Problem 16–11

An intersection approach has a demand volume of 500 vph, a saturation flow rate of 1250 vphg, a cycle length of 60 seconds, and 35 seconds of effective green time. What average approach delay per vehicle is expected under these conditions? What average stopped time delay per vehicle is expected under these conditions?

Problem 16–12

A signalized intersection approach operates at an effective v/c ratio of 1.15 for a peak 30-minute period each evening. If the approach has a g/C ratio of 0.50 and the cycle length is 60 seconds:

(a) What is the average approach and stopped time delay per vehicle for the entire 30-minute peak period?

(b) What is the average approach and stopped time delay per vehicle during the last 5 minutes of the peak period?

(c) What is the average approach and stopped time delay per vehicle during the first 15 minutes of the peak period. Why is this period significant?

Problem 16–13

A signalized intersection approach experiences chronic oversaturation for a one-hour period each day. During this time, vehicles arrive at a rate of 2000 vph. The saturation flow rate for the approach is 3250 vphg, with a 100-second cycle length, and 55 seconds of effective green.

(a) What is the average approach and stopped time delay per vehicle for the full one-hour peak?

(b) What is the average approach and stopped time delay for the first 15 minutes of the peak period? Compare the delay predicted by theoretical equations vs. that predicted by the 1994 *HCM* equation.

(c) What is the average approach and stopped time delay per vehicle for the last 15 minutes of the peak hour?

17

Fundamentals of Signal Design and Timing

The development of signal timing plans and designs involves a number of important components:

1. Development of a phase plan and sequence
2. Timing of "yellow" and "all red" intervals for each phase
3. Determination of cycle length
4. Allocation of available effective green time to the various phases, often referred to as "splitting" the green
5. Checking pedestrian crossing requirements

Many aspects of these are tied to principles discussed in Chapter 16 and elsewhere in this text. The process is, however, not exact, nor is there often a single "right" way to plan, design, and time a signal.

This chapter discusses the key elements of signal design and timing, and provides a number of illustrations. Note that it is virtually impossible to develop a complete signal design and timing that will not be subject to fine-tuning when the proposed plan is analyzed using the *HCM* or some other complex model of signalized intersection operation. This is because

no straightforward design and timing process can hope to include all of the potential complexities that may exist in any given situation. Thus, initial design and timing is often a starting point for analysis using a more complex model.

Signal phasing and the development of phase plans

One of the most important aspects of signal design is the development of an appropriate phase plan for a given situation. While such aspects of signal design as the determination of cycle length and the splitting of available green time among critical movements may be formulated analytically, there are no such simple approaches to developing a phase plan. Further, any analytic approach to cycle length and green time determinations requires that the phase plan be specified. Thus, the development of a phase plan involves more professional judgment than the determination of timing parameters.

The key aspect of any phase plan involves a determination of which left-turn movements require protection, and how such protection should be provided. There are, of course, many other issues, including the provision of the most efficient signalization possible, but the issue of left-turn protection is paramount.

The most frequently used phase plan is one in which *no* left turns are protected. This is a typical two-phase signal plan in which all left turns are made against a conflicting opposing through movement. Left-turn protection may be provided through the use of (1) protected left-turn phases and lanes, (2) compound signal phasing involving protected + permitted or permitted + protected phasing, and/or (3) prohibition of left-turn movements. The latter requires reasonable alternative routes that allow drivers to access their desired origins/destinations without undue disruption.

Several important points should be remembered in establishing appropriate and effective signal phase plans:

- Phasing can be used to minimize hazard risks by separating competing movements (such as a left turn and its opposing through movement). However, decreased efficiency of operation, and increased delay, which often accompany an increase in the number of signal phases, are adverse impacts which must be considered and balanced.
- While increasing the number of phases increases the amount of lost time included in an hour, the off-setting increase in saturation flow rates due to the elimination of opposed left turns may more than offset this effect.
- A phase plan must be implemented in accordance with the standards and criteria of the MUTCD, and must be accompanied by the necessary signs, markings, and signal hardware needed to identify appropriate lane usage.
- The phase plan must be consistent with the intersection geometry, lane use assignments, volumes and speeds, and pedestrian crossing requirements.

For instance, it would not be practical to have an exclusive left-turn phase at a location where there is no exclusive lane for left-turners. In such a case, when the left-turn signal turns green, the first vehicle in line may NOT be a left-turner. Since everyone else must stop, the first vehicle will block the lane for *all* traffic. Thus, one of the simplest adages may be coined: When

an exclusive left-turn phase is provided, an exclusive left-turn lane for the movement must also be provided.

A number of typical and not-so-typical signal phase plans are presented and discussed in this section. Signal phase plans are generally illustrated using *phase diagrams* and *ring diagrams*. In both cases, movements allowed within a given phase are shown using arrows. In this text, only those movements allowed are shown; in some of the literature, movements not allowed are shown with a straight line at the head of the arrow, indicating that the movement is stopped in the subject phase.

Figure 17-1 illustrates some of the basic forms used in these diagrams. Some related definitions and interpretations follow:

- A solid arrow indicates a movement without opposition. All through movements are, by definition, unopposed. An unopposed left turn has no opposing through movement. An unopposed right turn

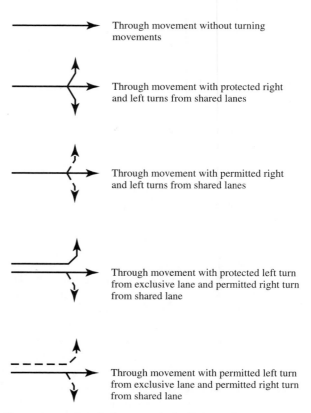

Figure 17-1 Signal phase symbols illustrated.

has no opposing pedestrian movement in the crosswalk through which the turn is made.

- Opposed left- and right-turn movements are shown as a dashed or dotted arrow.
- Turning movements made from a shared lane(s) are shown as arrows connected to the through movement arrow with which the lane(s) is (are) shared.
- Turning movements made from an exclusive lane(s) are shown as separate arrows, not connected to any through movement.

A *phase diagram* shows all movements being made in a given phase within a single block of the diagram. A *ring diagram* shows which movements are controlled by which "ring" on a signal controller. A "ring" of a controller generally controls one set of signal faces. Thus, while a phase involving two opposing through movements would be shown in one block of a phase diagram, each movement would be separately shown in a ring diagram. Chapter 14 described signal hardware and the operation of signal controllers in more detail.

A. Basic signalization: The two-phase signal

Figure 17-2 illustrates the simplest and most widely used form of signalization, the two-phase signal. Each street receives one phase during which all movements from that street are made. All left-turn and right-turn movements are made on a permitted basis, usually from shared lanes, although exclusive lanes may be provided for some or all left-turn movements, if de-

sired. This form of signalization is appropriate where the mix of left turns and opposing through flows is such that no unreasonable delays or unsafe conditions are created for and by left turners.

The phase diagram shows that all N-S movements occur in Phase A, while all E-W movements occur in Phase B. The ring diagram illustrates that the N and S signal faces, while following the same phasing, are controlled by separate rings of the signal controller. For the simple two-phase signal, the phase and ring diagrams are quite similar, and the ring diagram adds little to the understanding of the signal plan. For more complex phasings, as will be seen, the ring diagram is considerably more informative than the phase diagram. In this case, all phase changes occur at the same time on each ring of the controller, and the "phase boundaries" are easily identified. It should be noted that it makes little difference which rings the N and S movements are shown on; they could be reversed, as could the E and W movements.

B. Left-turn protection using exclusive left-turn phasing

The simplest way to provide left-turn protection is through the use of exclusive left-turn phasing. In this phase plan, both opposing left turns on a given street are provided with a simultaneous and exclusive phase, most often before the through phase for the same street, and occasionally after.

The issue of whether or not to provide left-turn protection on any or all intersection approaches is

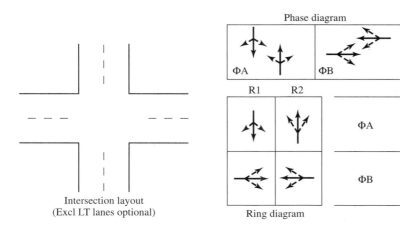

Figure 17-2 Illustration of a two-phase signal.

Intersection layout
(Excl LT lanes optional)

Ring diagram

complex, and involves many considerations. Three very general guidelines can be formulated:

1. Left-turn protection is rarely used for left-turn volumes of less than 100 vph.
2. Left-turn protection is almost always used for left-turn volumes of more than 250–300 vph.
3. For volumes between these values, the provision of left-turn protection must consider opposing volumes and number of lanes, accident experience, system signal constraints, and other related factors.

The first guideline recognizes that even when opposing flows are so heavy as to block all left turns, approximately two left turns per cycle can be expected during the yellow plus all red intervals. These are vehicles that enter the intersection looking for a gap in the opposing stream, but are unable to do so, completing their turn when the opposing flow stops at the end of the signal phase. Thus, with a 60-second cycle, approximately 120 left-turns per hour could be processed without providing an exclusive phase or phases.

The second guideline recognizes current practice. Even where opposing flows are light, a heavy volume of left-turning vehicles can present a difficulty from the points of view of capacity and safety.

In the middle range, provision of left-turn protection must consider the interaction of left turns and opposing flows, cycle lengths and green times, delay to left-turning vehicles, safety, and other factors. A left-turn flow of, for example, 150 vph, may be handled with no protection if opposing flows are light and have sufficient gaps. On the other hand, a heavy opposing through flow could easily lead the traffic engineer to provide such protection.

Even where volumes are under 100 vph, left-turn protection may be desirable where sight distances are limited, or where dog-leg or other unusual geometries place left-turning vehicles and opposing through vehicles in unexpected conflict situations.

Figure 17-3 illustrates a typical three-phase signal in which an exclusive left-turn phase is provided for one of the two intersecting streets. Note that any approaches having an exclusive left-turn phase *must* have an exclusive left-turn lane with sufficient length to accommodate expected queues during each signal cycle.

Several options can be created using the exclusive left-turn phase, in addition to the three-phase plan of Figure 17-3:

1. A *four-phase* signal may be created by providing an exclusive left-turn phase for both streets. Note that an exclusive left-turn lane would have to be provided for both the N and S approaches.
2. A *protected plus permitted* phase plan could be created by allowing a permitted left turn on the E and W approaches in ΦB. If a protected phase were provided for the N and S approaches, a *protected plus permitted* phase plan could likewise be created there.

In general, protected plus permitted (or permitted plus protected) phasing is used where the combina-

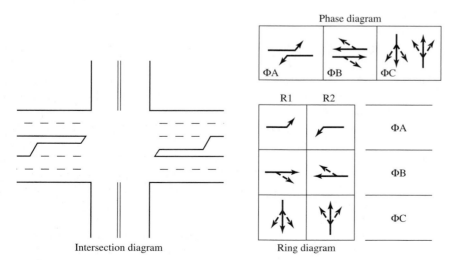

Intersection diagram   Ring diagram

Figure 17-3 Exclusive left-turn phase illustrated.

tion of left turns and opposing flow is so heavy that provision of fully protected left turns leads to undesirably long cycle lengths, or even unfeasible cycle lengths. Protected plus permitted phasing is more difficult for drivers to comprehend, and is more difficult to display. In some jurisdictions, such phasing is used only as a last resort, primarily for this reason. In other areas, the benefits of reduced delay to left-turning vehicles is considered significant enough to warrant frequent use of protected plus permitted phases. Practice on use of compound phasing, therefore, varies significantly on a regional and local basis.

C. Leading and lagging green phases: Splitting the exclusive left-turn phase

When exclusive left-turn phases are used, the two opposing left-turn movements are given the same amount of green time. This can be inefficient where the two left-turn volumes are significantly different. One of the earliest ways developed to address this, and other, unique situations is the leading and/or lagging green phase.

In a typical leading and lagging green signalization, one direction on the subject street is released while the other is held. Since the opposing flow is stopped,

left turns from this approach are protected. This is followed by a phase in which the second through movement is started and allowed to move simultaneously with the first. During this period, left turns are either prohibited, or made on a permitted (unprotected) basis. Finally, the initial movement is stopped while the opposing flow continues, giving the second left turn movement protection. Figure 17-4 illustrates this phasing.

This type of phasing is a form of "overlapping phases." In Figure 17-4, the E-W artery is shown using the leading and lagging green. Note that the full green time for the EB approach overlaps, but does not coincide with, the green for the WB approach.

One critical question arises: how many phases exist in this plan? In the phase diagram of Figure 17-4, it could be argued that there are four distinct phases. It could also be argued that phases A1, A2, and A3 form a single, overlapping phase, and that only two phases exist. Both analyses would be wrong. The correct answer is found by looking at the ring diagram. The boundary between phases A1 and A2 affects only one of the two signal rings. Similarly, the boundary between phases A2 and A3 affects only one of the two signal rings. The question is answered by counting the number of phase boundaries that each ring of the signal goes through in a single cycle. In this case, the

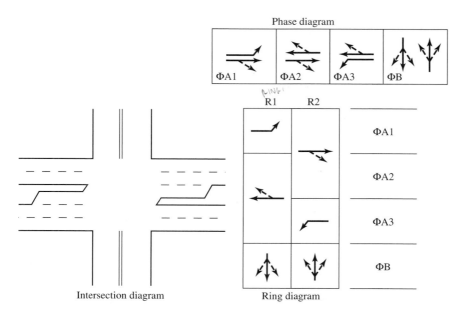

Figure 17-4 Leading and lagging green phases illustrated.

answer is *three* for both rings. Therefore, the leading and lagging phase plan, as shown, represents a *three-phase signal.*

The number of phases in a plan is critical, in that one set of lost times (t_L) is included in each phase. Increasing the number of phases increases total lost time per cycle, which can lead to decreased capacity and/or increased delay.

A number of interesting options can be based on the leading and lagging green:

1. A leading green may be used *without* a lagging green, or vice-versa. This is usually done where a one-way street or T-intersection creates a case in which there is only one left turn from the major street.
2. A *compound* phasing can be created by allowing permitted left turns to be made in Phase A2. In this case, the EB left turn would have a *protected plus permitted* phase, while the WB left turn would have a *permitted plus protected* phase. This can be especially useful where the geometry of the roadway does not permit an exclusive left-turn lane. The leading and/or lagging green with compound phasing is the only practical phase plan that can be used to provide for partial protection of left turns without having an exclusive left-turn lane.

3. Leading and/or lagging green phasing can be added to the N-S artery if the situation warrants it.

It should be noted that the National Electronics Manufacturing Association (NEMA) standards for signal controllers no longer include leading and lagging green phasing. Nevertheless, this type of phasing is still in use in many areas of the country, and controllers can be obtained to implement it.

D. Eight-phase actuated control

Modern actuated controllers give the traffic engineer a great deal of flexibility in dealing with variations in demand. Actuated controllers have the capability of not only varying the cycle length and green times in response to detector actuations, but of altering the order and sequence of phases. Such controllers can also skip phases in cycles where they are not needed.

Figure 17-5 illustrates the standard NEMA eight-phase controller, showing the required intersection layout (left-turn lanes are necessary), and a phase diagram. The phase diagram is different from those of Figures 17-2, 17-3, and 17-4, as it allows for alternative paths through the cycle. The illustration shows similar phasing for both intersecting arteries.

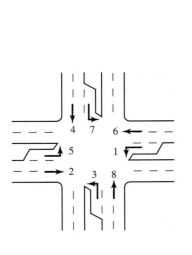

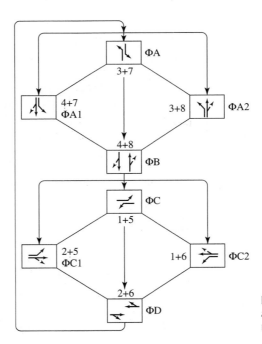

Figure 17-5 An eight-phase, actuated phase plan (with NEMA numbering) illustrated.

For both streets, the phase sequence is as follows:

1. The initial phase for a given street is an exclusive left-turn phase, during which both left turns move on a protected basis.
2. The initial phase is followed by a leading green phase in which one left-turn movement is stopped, while the other is allowed to continue with its through and right-turning movements. The choice of which left turn is terminated is based on detector actuations in the two left-turn lanes. If, for example, the EB left turn is fully served, but there are remaining vehicles in the WB left turn, the EB exclusive green would be terminated, and a leading phase for all WB movements initiated.
3. When the second left turn is fully satisfied, or when the maximum green time for the movement is reached, all left turns are stopped, and both through and right-turn movements proceed.
4. If, in any given cycle, no left-turn demand is indicated in either lane, the controller goes immediately to the simultaneous through and right-turn phase. Any left turners arriving during this phase will have to wait until the next cycle.
5. If, in any given cycle, left-turn demand is present in only one direction, the controller will immediately implement the appropriate leading green phase.

Actuated control is most often implemented at isolated locations, where coordination with other signals is not necessary. Coordinated systems place restrictions on individual intersection signal timing, such as a common, fixed cycle length, which greatly limit the flexibility that actuated control is intended to provide.

Given that the controller provides for the defining of eight separate signal phases, the question of the number of phases in operation is critical. Again, a ring diagram must be considered to obtain the correct response. This is shown in Figure 17-6. The situation shown assumes that the left-turn phases provided will be needed, i.e., that no phases are "skipped" due to lack of demand. This is a conservative approach, forcing the traffic engineer to account for the highest possible amount of lost time within each cycle.

Note that there are four possible paths for the signal to follow, depending on whether ΦA1 or ΦA2 is selected, and whether ΦC1 or ΦC2 is selected. Only one illustrative path is shown in Figure 17-6, as the re-

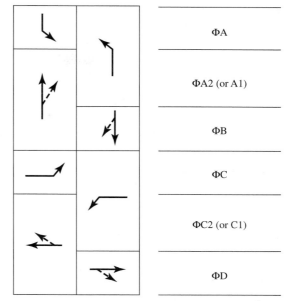

Figure 17-6 Ring diagram for eight-phase, actuated controller.

sulting conclusion on number and sequence of phases is the same for all possibilities.

If the sequence shown were to include Phase A1 instead of A2, the only change would be that the partial phase boundaries between Phases A and A1 and between Phases A1 and B would be reversed in the diagram. The same applies to a case in which Phase C1 were shown instead of Phase C2. The sequence on each of the rings, however, would remain unchanged.

If the number of phases is counted for either ring of the diagram, the conclusion is the same. There are *four* distinct phases in the signal operation, some of which overlap, as was the case with leading and lagging green phasing. The significance of this is that the total lost time per cycle in this case is $4 \times t_L$.

The type of phasing illustrated in Figures 17-5 and 17-6 is useful for relatively isolated locations where left turn volumes vary, but are generally heavy during the peak period. The actuated controller provides left-turn protection when needed, and has the ability to allocate different amounts of green time to each of the left-turn movements. When left-turn volumes are not a problem, the controller can skip phases, eliminating the need for other vehicles to wait, and reducing the amount of lost time in the cycle. This type of control is in common use in many sun belt cities, where arterial grids and signalized intersections are relatively widely-spaced (1.5–2.0 miles).

A pretimed signal phase plan can also be worked out in the pattern illustrated. In the pretimed case, however, the dominant direction given the "leading green" phase would be fixed for any given time period, and each cycle would follow the same pattern and timing.

E. Some special cases: Examples

Some of the basic signal phase plans have been introduced in previous sections. These can be combined in many innovative ways to most effectively meet the needs of any given intersection. Traditional exclusive left-turn phases on one street can be combined with leading and lagging greens on the other. Protected plus permitted phasing can be used on one street, while fully protected left-turn phasing can be used on the other.

The traffic engineer has a great deal of flexibility in designing an appropriate phase plan. The objectives should always include two considerations: efficiency of operation and safety to the motorist. Often, the efficiency benefits of complicated phasing must be weighed against the driver confusion they may cause. It is often unwise, for example, to introduce a particular phase plan that is not expected to be used anywhere else within a region. Designing the proper signal displays and street hardware is critical to implementing a signal plan with minimum confusion to drivers.

While the standard approaches discussed previously are sufficient to address most signalization problems, there are always unique situations that call for innovative approaches.

Figure 17-7, for example, illustrates the use of an exclusive pedestrian phase. Originally introduced in New York City by then Traffic Commissioner Henry Barnes, this type of phasing became known as the "Barnes Dance." It provides for a phase in which pedestrians are allowed to move freely across the intersection in any direction, including diagonal. It was intended to handle large volumes of pedestrians, difficult to accommodate within standard signal phase plans. All vehicular movement is stopped during the exclusive pedestrian phase.

Two major problems exist within this phasing: (1) the entire pedestrian phase must be included as additional lost time for vehicular movement, and (2) pedestrians (particularly in large numbers) do not easily clear the intersection at the end of the phase, making it very difficult for vehicular movement to begin. Eventually, this type of phasing was eliminated in NYC, but it has found uses in smaller urban areas where the number of pedestrians is moderate, and where pedestrians are well-disciplined in clearing the intersection for vehicles at the end of the phase.

Figure 17-8 shows three different phase plans for a T-intersection, each coordinated with a channelization design. In the first plan, no channelization is provided, and a three-phase plan separating all movements is specified. In the second design, median islands and a left-turn lane are provided on the major artery. This allows right turns from the stem to be made in Phase A. The protection of a median makes it easier to allow the WB through movements to continue in Phase B.

In the third option, the channelization design allows for the WB through movement to move contin-

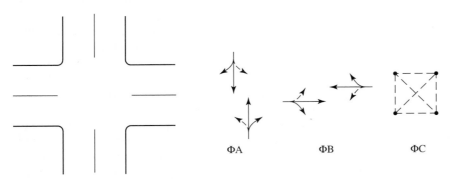

ΦA   ΦB   ΦC

Figure 17-7 An exclusive pedestrian phase illustrated.

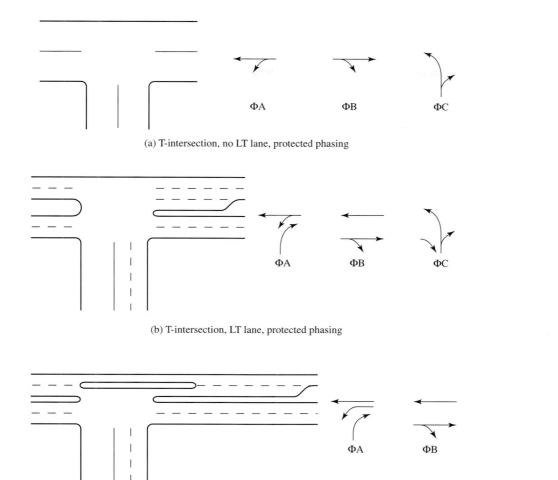

(a) T-intersection, no LT lane, protected phasing

(b) T-intersection, LT lane, protected phasing

(c) T-intersection, special geometry

Figure 17-8 Phasing options for a T-intersection.

uously (a permanent green), essentially removing it from the signalization plan. Also, EB right turns are permitted during Phase C.

Figure 17-9 shows a case which often becomes a traffic engineer's nightmare: a five-leg intersection. In this case, the fifth leg is a one-way artery (a ramp from an expressway), which "simplifies" the situation. A four-phase plan is shown, with only the EB left turn receiving a protected phase. Such cases become more complex when a number of left turns require partial or full protection. In most cases, the exact signal plan must be coordinated with the details of intersection geometry. Some movements may have to be prohib-

ited at such intersections to provide for efficient and safe signalization. Such locations virtually always involve long cycle lengths and high delay to motorists. When combined with high demand volumes, the situation often calls for major reconstruction and/or the banning of some movements.

In New York City, for example, Broadway created a major problem in traffic control. Manhattan was developed along a regular rectangular grid, with 800 ft between avenues (N-S) and 400 ft between streets (E-W, or crosstown). Such a regular grid, especially when coordinated with one-way streets and avenues, is relatively easy to control. Broadway, however, is a

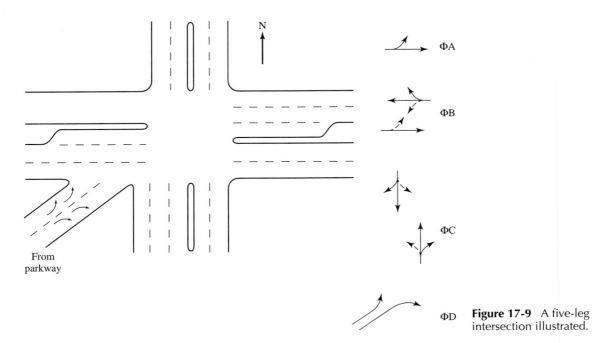

ΦA

ΦB

ΦC

From
parkway

ΦD

Figure 17-9 A five-leg intersection illustrated.

diagonal artery cutting across a major portion of the grid, creating many five-leg intersections with very heavy vehicular and pedestrian flows. The eventual solution, in addition to installing a one-way flow pattern in the late 1950s, was to disallow through flow on Broadway at many intersections. This effectively turned Broadway into a local collector with little or no through traffic. Through traffic was forced back onto the grid, and simplified the signalization of intersections involving Broadway.

F. Right-turn phasing and right-turn-on-red

While the use of protected left-turn phasing is common, and is the driving factor in designing a phase plan, the overwhelming majority of signalized intersections handle right turns on a permitted basis, most often from a shared lane.

Protected right-turn phasing is only used where the number of pedestrians is extremely high. Modern studies show that a pedestrian flow of 1700 peds/hr in a crosswalk can effectively block all right turns on green. This volume of pedestrians, however, exists very rarely, and only in major city centers. While provision of a protected right-turn phase helps motorists,

it may worsen pedestrian congestion on the street corner. In these extreme cases, it is often useful to examine the feasibility of pedestrian overpasses or underpasses. These are generally coordinated with barriers preventing pedestrians from entering the street at the corner.

Protected plus permitted right-turn phasing may be provided where there is an exclusive left-turn phase on the intersecting street. For example, if such a phase were to be provided for the NB and SB right turns, the permitted portion of the phase would occur during the N-S through green, while the protected portion of the phase would occur during the E-W left-turn phase.

Exclusive right-turn lanes are useful where heavy right-turn flows exist, particularly where right-turn-on-red is permitted. Such a lane allows right-turners to pass through vehicles stopped in the right lane on red. It can also be coordinated with channelized right turns. Where a channelized right-turn is provided, it can often be allowed to move at all times, generally controlled by a YIELD sign.

A study conducted by the City of Salem, Oregon [1] in 1994 provided some interesting insights and recommendations on right-turn treatments at signalized intersections. Figure 17-10 illustrates the recommended selection criteria for one-lane and two-lane approaches. The criteria were based on consideration of *v/c* ratios and delay. Safety was not considered. It must be noted that the criteria of Figure 17-10 are illustrative. They were developed for a particular city, and may not be readily transferable to other areas without extensive recalibration.

"Right-turn-on-red" (RTOR) was first authorized in California in 1937, and was permitted only in conjunction with a sign authorizing the movement [2]. In recent years, virtually all states permit RTOR unless it is specifically prohibited by a sign. The federal government encouraged this in the 1970s by linking the implementation of RTOR to receipt of federal-aid

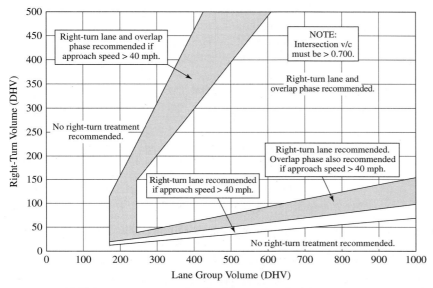

(a) Right-turn treatments at signalized intersections for 1-lane groups

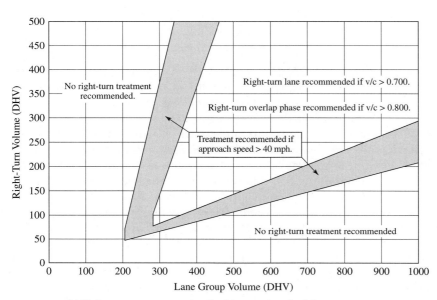

(b) Right-turn treatments at signalized intersections for 2-lane groups

Figure 17-10 Illustrative criteria for right-turn treatments. [Used with permission of Institute of Transportation Engineers, from R. A. Perez, "Guidelines for Right-Turn Treatments at Signalized Intersections," *ITE Journal*. Copyright © 1995 Institute of Transportation Engineers.]

highway funds. In some urban areas, like New York City, RTOR is still generally prohibited. In such cases, signs must be posted alerting drivers to this fact as they enter the area affected. All RTOR laws require that the vehicle stop before executing the right-turn movement on red.

The major issues regarding RTOR were and continue to be (1) the delay savings to right-turning vehicles, and (2) the increased accident risk caused. In one of the key works which led to the implementation of RTOR, McGee et al. [3] concluded that the delay savings to the average right-turning vehicle was 9% in CBDs, 31% in other urban areas, and 39% in rural areas. The delay savings to right turners is, of course, influenced by conditional probabilities that a through vehicle blocks the right-turner's access to the intersection. Thus, the effectiveness of RTOR is always greatly enhanced by provision of an exclusive right-turn lane of appropriate length. Delay reductions for right turners have related beneficial effects on energy consumption and air quality.

An early study of RTOR accidents [4] found that only about 0.61% of all intersection accidents involved RTOR vehicles, and these tended to be less severe than other intersection accidents, perhaps as a result of the low speed at which RTOR movements occur. The study also found no conclusive results from limited before–after accident studies involving RTOR implementation.

Another interesting study, conducted by an ITE council committee [5] synthesized a data base on driver behavior at RTOR locations.

G. Summary and conclusion

The subject of phasing, and the selection of an appropriate phase plan, is a critical part of effective intersection signalization. While there are general criteria available to help in the design and selection process, there are few firm and/or universally accepted standards. The traffic engineer must apply a knowledge and understanding of the various phasing options, and how they effect other critical aspects of signalization, such as capacity and delay.

Chapter 18 will present a detailed model for analyzing the likely operations resulting from any fully-specified signalization plan, together with defined geometry and demand volumes. This model is a use-ful tool for fine-tuning the phase plan and signal timing. Its trial-and-error approach, however, requires that a starting point be established. This will be further discussed in a later section of this chapter.

Some important details of intersection signalization

This section treats three important aspects of intersection signalization in more detail: (1) change and clearance intervals, (2) pedestrian requirements, and (3) additional details on left-turn treatments.

A. Change and clearance intervals

The terms "change" and "clearance" intervals are used in a variety of ways in the literature. They refer to the *yellow* and *all red* indications that mark the transition from GREEN to RED for every signal phase.

The MUTCD [page 4B-15] states the following with respect to change and clearance intervals:

A yellow change interval shall be used, where applicable, following each circular GREEN or GREEN arrow interval. . . .

The exclusive function of the steady yellow interval shall be to warn traffic of an impending change in the right-of-way assignment.

Yellow change intervals should have a normal range of approximately 3 to 6 seconds. Generally, the longer intervals are appropriate to higher approach speeds.

The MUTCD goes on to specifically prohibit the use of the yellow during the transition from RED to GREEN, a practice common in many European countries. More importantly, the MUTCD carries *no requirement* for an *all red* or *clearance* interval. Most state laws allow a vehicle to legally enter the intersection during a yellow indication. Upon receipt of the GREEN, a released vehicle has the responsibility to avoid conflict with any other vehicle legally within the intersection, including those entering the intersection on yellow from the conflicting street.

The Institute for Transportation Engineers (ITE) recommends that *both* a *yellow* change interval *and* an *all-red* clearance interval be provided [6]:

To a substantial extent, the need for (all) red clearance intervals is predicated on the local jurisdiction's policy regarding the necessity of an absolute provision of time for vehicles that entered on yellow to clear the area of conflict before the right-of-way is reassigned.

It is the policy of ITE that if clearance time is to be provided, it should be in the form of an (all) red clearance interval.

Not providing an all-red clearance interval allows that vehicles entering the intersection on yellow may still be in the intersection when a conflicting flow is given the GREEN. While drivers given the GREEN must still yield to conflicting vehicles and pedestrians legally within the intersection, an article by Parsonson et al. [7] points out that this is not a reasonable expectation. In a survey of 239 drivers, over 60% indicated that they were unaware of this legal responsibility. Also, 60% indicated that they did not bother to look for traffic from the conflicting street when given the GREEN indication. The article goes on to cite an accident case in which a traffic jurisdiction was held partially responsible for damages in part due to the failure to provide a clearance interval.

1. The ITE recommended practice on change intervals [6]. The recommended methodology for computing the appropriate length of a *yellow* or *change interval:*

$$y = t + \frac{S_{85}}{2a + 64.4g} \qquad [17\text{-}1]$$

where: Y = length of the yellow interval, sec
t = driver reaction time, sec
S_{85} = 85th percentile speed of approaching vehicles, or the speed limit as appropriate, fps
a = deceleration rate of vehicles, fps^2
g = grade of approach, expressed as a decimal
64.4 = 2 x the acceleration due to gravity, or 32.2 fps^2

This equation was derived from the time required for a vehicle to traverse one safe-stopping distance at its approach speed. Commonly used values for key parameters include a deceleration rate of 10 fps^2 and a reaction time of 1.0 sec.

The appropriate yellow time for a vehicle approaching a signal at a speed of 30 mph (44 fps) on a level approach would be:

$$y = 1.0 + \frac{44}{2(10) + 64.4(0)} = 3.2 \text{ sec}$$

Table 17-1 illustrates values for the *yellow* interval based on various approach speeds and grades.

Note that most of the values fall within the MUTCD-recommended range of 3 to 6 seconds for the yellow or change interval. In some jurisdictions, 5 seconds is used as a practical maximum for *y*; if larger values are needed, the excess is *added* to the all-red interval. One study [8] demonstrated that the percentage of vehicles encroaching on the RED indication increased as yellow times went from 3 to 5 seconds. Thus, violation rates and safety may be an issue with long yellow times.

2. ITE recommended practice on clearance intervals [6]. The *clearance* or *all-red* interval is timed to allow a vehicle that has just entered the intersection legally on a yellow interval to clear the intersection before giving the GREEN to a conflicting movement. The methodology considers several different situations, as indicated in the following equations:

Where there is no pedestrian traffic:

$$r = \frac{w + L}{S_{15}} \qquad [17\text{-}2a]$$

Where there is a likelihood of pedestrian crossings:

$$r = \max \left(\frac{w + L}{S_{15}}, \frac{P}{S_{15}} \right) \qquad [17\text{-}2b]$$

Table 17-1 Recommended Yellow Intervals—ITE (sec)

Speed (mph)	Speed (fps)	Grade				
		+4%	+2%	0%	−2%	−4%
20	29.4	2.3	2.4	2.5	2.6	2.7
25	36.7	2.6	2.7	2.8	3.0	3.1
30	44.0	3.0	3.1	3.2	3.4	3.5
35	51.4	3.3	3.4	3.6	3.7	3.9
40	58.7	3.6	3.8	3.9	4.1	4.4
45	66.1	3.9	4.1	4.3	4.5	4.8
50	73.4	4.3	4.4	4.7	4.9	5.2

Where significant pedestrian traffic exists, or where the crosswalk is protected by pedestrian signals:

$$r = \frac{P + L}{S_{15}} \qquad [17\text{-}2c]$$

where: r = length of the all-red clearance interval, sec
 w = distance from the departure stop line to the far side of the farthest conflicting traffic lane, ft
 P = distance from the departure stop line to the far side of the farthest conflicting pedestrian crosswalk, ft
 L = length of a standard vehicle, usually taken to be 20 ft
 S_{15} = 15th percentile speed of approaching vehicles, fps

Note that while the formula for the yellow change interval uses the 85th percentile speed, the computation of the all-red uses the 15th percentile speed. Both are conservative assumptions, which imply that resulting values for y and r will satisfy all but the most extreme 15% of the speed distribution. If a full speed distribution is not available for analysis, then the 85th percentile speed may be estimated as one standard deviation more than the average speed, while the 15th percentile speed can be estimated as one standard deviation less than the average speed. Where no measurement of the standard deviation is available, use 5 mph (7.34 fps).

Figure 17-11 illustrates distances w and P for use in Equation [17-2]. Distance w brings the front of the vehicle to the far edge of the most distant conflicting vehicular path. Distance P brings the front of the vehicle to the far edge of the most distant pedestrian crosswalk. In most situations, the distances are applied to the through vehicle path, as shown in Figure 17-11a. If the traffic engineer determines that the left-turning movement is the most critical, then the paths shown in Figure 17-30b are used.

Both equations 17-2a and 17-2c require that the vehicle clear the critical distance, w or P, but also the length of the vehicle, L. This insures that all conflicting vehicles have fully cleared the intersection before the conflicting flow(s) is (are) released. In equation 17-2b, full clearance is required for vehicular concerns, but the pedestrian clearance does NOT include the length of the vehicle. It is assumed that in a light to moderate pedestrian environment, pedestrians have the ability to avoid conflict with a vehicle, even if they are released just as a vehicle enters the crosswalk.

3. The dilemma zone. The functional purpose of the change plus clearance intervals is to guarantee that no driver is placed in a position where (a) (s)he is too close to the stop-line to safely stop when the conflicting flow is released, and (b) (s)he does not have enough time to safely cross the intersection before the conflicting flow is released. A driver in such a situation is in "the dilemma zone," illustrated in Figure 17-12.

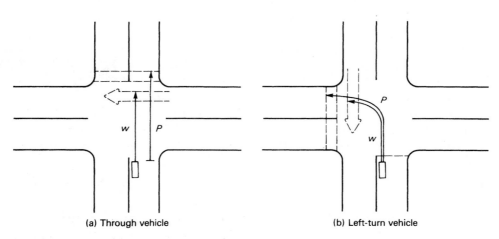

(a) Through vehicle   (b) Left-turn vehicle

Figure 17-11   Illustration of dimensions for all-red clearance interval.

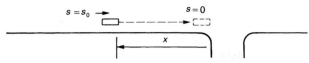

$v = 0 = (s_0 - at)$
$t = (s_0/a)$ secs to stop vehicle
$x = (s_0/2)(s_0/a)$ feet to stop vehicle

(a) Safe stopping during clearance interval

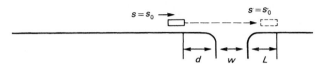

TIME $= (d + w + L)/s_0$

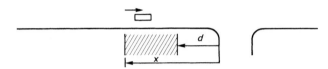

If $d < x$, there is a <u>dilemma zone</u>, an area from which a vehicle can neither stop safely nor cross completely in the time allowed.

(b) Decision not to stop during clearance interval

Figure 17-12 The dilemma zone illustrated.

The time required to safely brake the vehicle illustrated in Figure 17-12 (ignoring reaction time) is:

$$t_s = \frac{S_o}{a + 32.2g} \quad [17\text{-}3]$$

The distance traveled during this time is:

$$x = \frac{S_o}{2} \times \frac{S_o}{a + 32.2g} = \frac{S_o^2}{2a + 64.4g} \quad [17\text{-}4]$$

where: t_s = time to stop, sec
  x = braking distance while stopping, ft
  S_o = initial approach speed of vehicle, fps
  and other variables as previously defined

The time necessary for the vehicle to safely clear the intersection is:

$$t_c = \frac{d + w + L}{S_o} \quad [17\text{-}5]$$

where: t_c = time required to safely clear the intersection, sec
  d = distance from vehicle to stop line, ft, and other variables as previously defined

As shown in Figure 17-12b, when $d < x$, the driver may be caught in a virtual "no man's land" in which (s)he can neither stop nor safely clear the intersection. The solution is to insure that $x = d$ in determining the yellow plus all-red intervals. The appropriate sum of these intervals could then be determined by substituting Equation [17-4] (for x) into Equation [17-5] and adding an appropriate reaction time. Then:

$$Y = t + \frac{S_o}{2a + 64.4g} + \frac{w + L}{S_o} \quad [17\text{-}6]$$

where: Y = sum of yellow change plus all red clearance intervals, sec, and all other terms as previously defined

Note that, except for the use of 85th and 15th percentile speeeds, the first two terms of Equation [17-4] constitute the ITE recommended practice for yellow intervals, and that the last term constitutes the ITE recommended practice for all-red intervals (for vehicular requirements). Thus, following the ITE practice effectively eliminates the possibility of a "dilemma zone" occurring.

A recent ITE task force report [9,10] summarizes various practices in the U.S. regarding the timing of change and clearance intervals. The report is *not* a recommended practice, but does provide an interesting overview of different methodologies applied throughout the U.S.

SAMPLE PROBLEM

What change and clearance intervals should be used for an intersection approach with the following characteristics?

Average approach speed = 35 mph

Grade = −2.5%

Distance from stop line to far side of most distant lane = 48 ft

Distance from stop line to far side of most distant xwalk = 60 ft

Standard car length = 20 ft

Reaction time = 1.0 sec

Equation [17-1] is used to compute the appropriate length of the yellow interval. This equation uses the 85th percentile approach speed, which will be estimated as 5 mph *more* than the average speed, or $35 + 5 = 40$ mph, or $40 \times 1.468 = 58.72$ fps. Then:

$$y = t + \frac{S_{85}}{2a + 64.4g} = 1.0 + \frac{58.72}{2(10) + 64.4(-0.025)}$$

$$= 4.2 \text{ sec}$$

The solution for the appropriate all-red phase depends on the number of pedestrians present and/or the existence of pedestrian signals. Also, the speed is the 15th percentile speed, not the 85th percentile used in computing the yellow time. This speed is $35 - 5 = 30$ mph, or 44 fps. The possible results are found using Equations [17-2a–c]. Thus, if pedestrians are not a concern:

$$r = \frac{w + L}{S_{15}} = \frac{48 + 20}{44} = 1.5 \text{ sec}$$

If a pedestrian signal exists, or if there is a large number of pedestrians:

$$r = \frac{P + L}{S_{15}} = \frac{60 + 20}{44} = 1.8 \text{ sec}$$

If a moderate number of pedestrians exists, the all-red is the maximum of 1.5 seconds or:

$$r = \frac{P}{S_{15}} = \frac{66}{44} = 1.4 \text{ sec, USE 1.5 sec}$$

If an assumption of no significant pedestrian traffic is made, then $y = 4.2$ seconds and $r = 1.5$ seconds. This makes for a total change plus clearance interval of $Y = 4.2 + 1.5 = 5.7$ seconds. This computation guarantees that no dilemma zone occurs.

B. Pedestrian considerations at signalized intersections

The MUTCD gives a number of guidelines concerning pedestrians at signalized intersections. In general, pedestrians must be able to see signal indications. Thus, vehicular signal indications must be visible to pedestrians, or a pedestrian signal (WALK/DON'T WALK) should be used.

In particular [MUTCD, page 4D-1, 2]:

Pedestrian signal indications shall be installed in conjunction with vehicular traffic signals under any of the following conditions: (1) When a traffic signal is installed under the Pedestrian Volume or School Crossing warrant. (2) When an exclusive interval or phase is provided or made available for pedestrian movements in one or more directions, with all conflicting vehicular movements being stopped. (3) When vehicular indications are not visible to pedestrians, such as on one-way streets, at T-intersections; or when the vehicular indications are in a position which would not adequately serve pedestrians. (4) At established school crossings at intersections signalized under any warrant.

Pedestrian signal indications also may be installed under any of the following conditions: (1) When any volume of pedestrian activity requires use of a pedestrian clearance interval to minimize vehicle-pedestrian conflicts, or when it is necessary to assist pedestrians in making a safe crossing. (2) When multi-phase indications (as in split phase timing) would tend to confuse pedestrians guided only by vehicular indications. (3) When pedestrians cross part of the street, to or from an island, during a particular interval (where they should not be permitted to cross another part of that street during any part of the same interval).

In another stipulation, the minimum WALK phase should be 4 to 7 seconds in length.

1. Minimum crossing time and its relationship to vehicular green times. Conventional practice allows pedestrians to cross a street during the vehicular green, yellow, and all-red phases. The sum of these phases, therefore, must be sufficient to accommodate safe pedestrian crossings. If a minimum start-up time of 4 to 7 seconds is assumed, then the minimum time needed for pedestrians to safely cross a street is:

$$G_p = (4 \Leftrightarrow 7) + \frac{D_x}{S_p} \qquad [17\text{-}7]$$

where: G_p = minimum safe time for pedestrians to cross, often referred to as the "pedestrian green time," sec
D_x = crossing distance, ft
S_p = 15th percentile walking speed, fps

The general rule is that D_x should be taken as the distance from the departure curb to the *midpoint* of the farthest traffic lane to be crossed. Again, it is assumed that with a pedestrian in the middle of his/her lane, drivers will continue to yield the right-of-way, even if the GREEN is received. This is illustrated in Figure 17-13.

In determining the appropriate crossing distance, the specific geometrics of the intersection must be considered. Where crosswalks begin and/or end on the curve of the curbing, for example, the crossing distance is effectively longer due to the curvature. Where median or other channelizing islands are sufficient to provide pedestrian refuge, timing can accommodate a safe crossing in *two* cycles. Other special conditions may also need to be considered in establishing an appropriate value for D_x.

Common practice is to use a pedestrian start-up period of 4 seconds for low pedestrian flow rates of 10 peds/cycle or less. A start-up of 7 seconds is used when pedestrian flow rates are in the range of 10–20 peds/cycle. A walking speed of 4.0 fps is the most common value used today.

To provide pedestrians with a safe crossing, the signal timing must be such that:

$$G_p \leq G + Y \qquad\qquad [17\text{-}8]$$

where: G_p = minimum pedestrian crossing time needed, sec
　　　　G = vehicular green interval, sec
　　　　Y = vehicular change plus clearance intervals, sec

When this relationship is NOT SATISFIED, i.e., when the vehicular green, yellow, and all-red in-

tervals are LESS than the required pedestrian crossing time, the traffic engineer must either (a) change the signal timing to satisfy this requirement, or (b) install pedestrian detectors (pedestrian buttons) at the intersection.

When installed, a pedestrian push-button detector instructs the signal controller to provide a $G + Y$ period equal to G_p during the *next* available green phase. Thus, the pedestrian is guaranteed to have sufficient crossing time during the next cycle. This generally results in lengthening the vehicular green phase beyond its requirements. To help maintain progression patterns, the additional green time added to accommodate pedestrians is normally deducted from other phases within the same signal cycle. When a push-button detector is provided, pedestrian signals must also be installed.

The use of pedestrian push-buttons allows traffic engineers to time a signal for vehicular needs, taking care of pedestrians when they require service. Such an approach is not feasible where pedestrians regularly appear during every signal cycle. In such cases, the push-button is actuated during each cycle, and the overall signal timing for vehicles is not implemented; the vehicular signal timing should be adjusted to accommodate pedestrian requirements during every signal cycle.

Because of the way street systems are established, vehicular and pedestrian timing requirements are often inconsistent. Consider the case illustrated in Figure 17-14. This is a typical intersection of a major and a minor street. Due to the expected traffic distribution, the major street requires a long green time, while the minor street requires a much shorter one. Pedestrians, however, cross the major (and wider) street during the minor street vehicular phase, and the minor street during the major street vehicular phase. Thus, pedestrian requirements are for a longer green during the minor street phase, and a shorter green during the major street phase.

In Figure 17-14, the E-W artery would normally receive the larger green time, as traffic flow is more intense than on the minor N-S street. Pedestrians, however, must cross the wider E-W artery during the N-S green. They require more time to do this than to cross the narrow N-S street during the E-W green. Thus, if the green time were apportioned according to relative traffic flow, the allocation would be quite

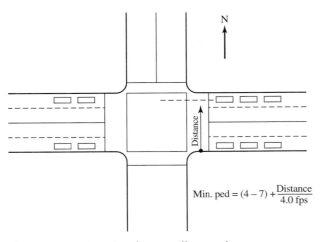

Figure 17-13 Crossing distance illustrated.

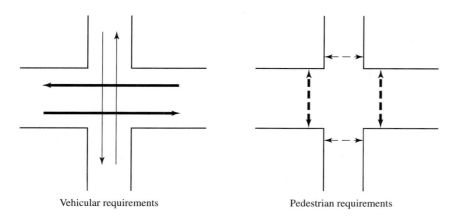

Vehicular requirements   Pedestrian requirements

Figure 17-14 Vehicular vs. pedestrian signal requirements.

different from an apportionment based on pedestrian crossing needs.

In practice, the objective is to base signal timing on vehicular requirements, with pedestrian requirements acting as an effective minimum requirement on green times, in the absence of a pedestrian push-button detector. It may be necessary in some cases, as will be illustrated later, to increase cycle lengths to accommodate pedestrians without seriously affecting vehicular green time allocations.

2. Relationship between vehicular signal indications and pedestrian signal indications. The relationship between vehicular signal indications and pedestrian signal indications should be clearly understood. Pedestrian indications have the following meanings:

• *WALK:* The constant WALK indication means that it is safe for a pedestrian to *start* crossing the street.
• *Flashing DON'T WALK:* The flashing DON'T WALK indication means that it is unsafe to start crossing the street. Those already in the crosswalk, however, have sufficient time to safely complete their crossing.
• *DON'T WALK:* The constant DON'T WALK indication means that it is unsafe for any pedestrian to be in the crosswalk.

Some jurisdictions use a flashing WALK instead of a constant WALK indication where right-turning vehicles will conflict with crossing pedestrians.

The flashing DON'T WALK indication is often referred to as the pedestrian clearance interval. This interval is far longer than a vehicle clearance interval,

because of the relatively low walking speeds of pedestrians compared to vehicular speeds.

Figure 17-15 illustrates three basic cases, and shows how pedestrian intervals would compare to vehicular intervals for the same approach for each. In Case 1, the pedestrian crossing time, G_p, is exactly equal to the $G + Y$ vehicular intervals. In such a case, the WALK is only displayed for the minimum 4–7 second pedestrian start-up period. The flashing DON'T WALK would have a length of $D_x/4.0$, where 4.0 fps is the assumed speed of pedestrians. The constant DON'T WALK would coincide with the vehicular red phase for the approach. In Case 2, the pedestrian crossing time, G_p, is less than the vehicular $G + Y$ intervals. In this case, the DON'T WALK still coincides with the vehicular red phase, and the flashing DON'T WALK is still $D_x/4.0$. The remaining time is available for the WALK interval. In Case 3, the vehicular $G + Y$ intervals are insufficient to provide for safe crossing. Thus, in most cycles, the DON'T WALK is permanently displayed. When the pedestrian push-button is actuated, the *next* green phase will be lengthened such that $G_p = G + Y$, as is illustrated in Case 1. In each case, remember that the Y interval includes the yellow plus all-red intervals, $y + r$.

SAMPLE PROBLEM

Consider the sample problem illustrated in Figure 17-16. It shows the intersection of a major artery and a minor street. Pedestrian flows are moderate, with at least a few pedestrians using every crosswalk during every signal cycle. Because there is little left-turning traffic, the simple two-phase signalization shown in

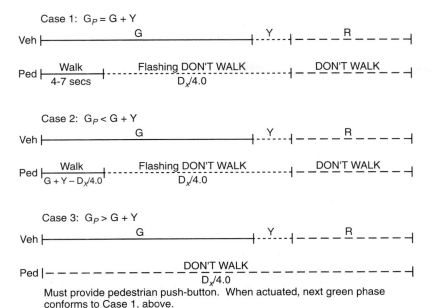

Case 1: $G_P = G + Y$

Veh | ————————— G ————————— | ⋯ Y ⋯ | – – – R – – – |

Ped | —— Walk —— | ⋯⋯⋯ Flashing DON'T WALK ⋯⋯⋯ | – – DON'T WALK – – |
        4-7 secs $D_x/4.0$

Case 2: $G_P < G + Y$

Veh | ————————— G ————————— | ⋯ Y ⋯ | – – – R – – – |

Ped | — Walk — | ⋯⋯⋯ Flashing DON'T WALK ⋯⋯⋯ | – – DON'T WALK – – |
     $G+Y-D_x/4.0$ $D_x/4.0$

Case 3: $G_P > G + Y$

Veh | ————————— G ————————— | ⋯ Y ⋯ | – – – R – – – |

Ped | – – – – – – – – – – DON'T WALK – – – – – – – – – – – |
                             $D_x/4.0$

Must provide pedestrian push-button. When actuated, next green phase conforms to Case 1, above.

Figure 17-15 Relationship between vehicular and pedestrian timing.

Figure 17-16 is in effect. Does the signal adequately accommodate pedestrians? If not, what should be done to provide for safe crossing?

The first step in addressing this problem is to determine the minimum crossing time needed for pedestrians. Because the pedestrian flows are in the 10 to 20 peds/cycle range, a start-up time of 7 seconds will be assumed. For pedestrians crossing the major street during Phase B, a crossing distance of 51 ft will be used, as this is the worst case for this phase. For pedestrians crossing the minor street during Phase A, a distance of 21 ft is used, as shown. Equation [17-8] is used:

$$G_p(\text{Phase A}) = 7 + \frac{21}{4.0} = 12.25 \text{ sec}$$

$$G_p(\text{Phase B}) = 7 + \frac{51}{4.0} = 19.75 \text{ sec}$$

To accommodate pedestrian safely, Phase A must be at least 12.25 seconds long, including $G + Y$. As

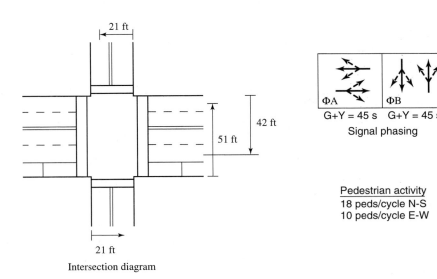

Intersection diagram

Pedestrian activity
18 peds/cycle N-S
10 peds/cycle E-W

G+Y = 45 s   G+Y = 45 s
Signal phasing

Figure 17-16 Sample problem in pedestrian requirements.

shown in Figure 17-16, Phase A is 45 seconds, and thus, pedestrians crossing the minor street are safe. Pedestrians crossing the major street in Phase B, however, require 19.75 seconds. The actual $G + Y$ is only 15 seconds, so these pedestrians are NOT accommodated safely.

To remedy the safety problem for pedestrians crossing the major street, two options might be considered. The most obvious would be to increase the length of Phase B to at least 19.75 seconds. Assuming, however, that the relative amounts of $G + Y$ provided to the two phases is appropriate, this balance should not be changed. If the length of Phase B is increased to a $G + Y$ of 20 seconds, and if the ratio of the green in Phases A and B is to be held constant, then:

$$\frac{(G + Y)_A}{20} = \frac{45}{15}$$

and:

$$(G + Y)_A = \frac{(20)(45)}{15} = 60 \text{ sec}$$

This retiming of the signal for pedestrian requirements suggests a cycle length of $C = 60 + 20 = 80$ seconds. To be viable, there would have to be no system or other constraints that would prevent an 80-second cycle from being implemented.

If the current 60-second cycle length must be preserved, then a design change would be needed. The parking lane shown in Figure 17-35 could be removed in favor of an 8-ft median island. Pedestrians would be forced to cross the major street in two successive signal cycles. Since their crossing distance would be reduced to approximately 24 ft (from curb line to island), the minimum crossing time for Phase B reduces to $7 + (24/4.0) = 13$ seconds, which is less than the 15 seconds available. Should this solution be adopted, pedestrian signals would have to be provided.

A third option, that of installing pedestrian pushbuttons, is not viable here, as pedestrians are expected to be present during virtually every signal cycle. Therefore, *every* cycle must provide safe crossing opportunities for pedestrians.

Other impacts of increasing the cycle length might include some increase in delay to vehicles and their occupants. If an island is constructed, then pedestrians will experience greater delay, as it will take two signal cycles to complete a safe crossing.

3. Pedestrian prohibitions. Prohibiting pedestrian crossings at an intersection is an extreme measure to be considered only when unusual hazards exist that cannot be ameliorated in any other reasonable way. This is generally not practical where any significant numbers of pedestrians exist, or where there is no alternative crossing location within reasonable proximity. The MUTCD prescribes signs both for posting a crossing prohibition, and for directing pedestrians to the nearest crosswalk. In cases where the combination of high pedestrian volumes, high vehicle speeds, and/or high conflicting vehicular volumes present unusual hazards, and where alternative crossing locations are not readily available, provision of pedestrian underpasses or overpasses should be considered.

Reference [11] reports on a nationwide survey of pedestrian signal usage in medium size cities, and contains some useful insights. Reference [12] summarizes the report of an ITE technical committee on interpretation and application of pedestrian requirements in the MUTCD.

C. Special considerations related to left turns at signalized intersections

In the section on signal phasing, alternative means of handling left turns were discussed and presented. Left-turning vehicles present one of the most serious challenges in intersection operations, and are often the principal factor in degraded performance at an intersection. The traffic engineer is faced with a critical dilemma:

- When left turns occur against an opposing flow, i.e., permitted phasing, they must wait for appropriate gaps in that flow, and generally impede the through flow on their own approach (unless a turn bay of sufficient length is provided).
- When left turns are moved separately from an opposing flow, i.e., protected phasing, the time dedicated to this movement is not available for through movements. Further, additional lost time is introduced into the signal cycle through the addition of phases.

There are several approaches to severe left-turning problems, in addition to the provision of protected signal phasing:

1. *Left-Turn Prohibitions:* Left-turn prohibitions may be introduced with caution where other solutions do not appear to be viable. Since such prohibitions generally involve what would be fairly high left-turn volumes (if the movement were allowed), the availability of alternative routes in critical. In a grid system, one left turn can be replaced by three right turns (around the block). This invariably increases the number of vehicle-miles travelled on the network, and may cause congestion at other intersections. Specific destinations should also be considered, as some left-turn prohibitions may make some specific destinations almost impossible to reach. In some cases, part-time left-turn prohibitions may be justified during peak periods, while the turns may be permitted during off-peak periods. The MUTCD contains signs which must be used in posting left-turn prohibitions.

2. *One-Way Streets:* A system of one-way streets essentially eliminates all opposed left turns. In such a system, left turns are very much like right turns, in that the primary conflicting movement is by pedestrians. Not all street systems, however, are amenable to one-way operation. One-way operation requires pairs of streets with similar capacities, close enough to each other and to major generators to effectively serve demand, that can be operated as a "one-way couplet," with one street in each direction. Trip-lengths are invariably increased on a one-way system, as many drivers will have to go around a block to reach their desired destination. Many businesses can be affected by a change from two-way to one-way operation, such as a gas station on a corner, around which no turns can be made with one-way operation. Implementation of these systems involves careful consultation and cooperation with local area businesses. One-way systems may also complicate bus transit routes and bus stop locations. Nevertheless, operation of a one-way system eliminates or greatly reduces serious left-turn problems.

One of the classic cases demonstrating the effectiveness of one-way street systems is Manhattan. A regular, rectangular grid system made it relatively easy (from an engineering point of view) to convert to one-way operation, with the exception of several major crosstown arteries. While turn problems (right and left) are still a problem due to massive numbers of pedestrians at many locations, opposed left turns have been eliminated, and signal coordination was greatly simplified. Business groups, however, were bitterly opposed to the plan, and delayed its implementation for many years.

3. *Design Solutions:* A number of design treatments can ameliorate left-turn problems. One common approach is the "jug-handle." In this approach, left-turning vehicles make a right turn into a connecting roadway, then a left-turn onto the cross-street. This approach, illustrated in Figure 17-17, is useful where (1) there is land available to build an appropriate jug-handle roadway, and (2) the cross street operation is not seriously disrupted by the addition of an intersection (signalized or unsignalized) for jug-handle traffic. This approach has been frequently used in New Jersey and other northeastern states.

A second approach is more recent. A novel design, called a "continuous flow intersection," has been proposed [13] as a solution for handling major left-turning volumes efficiently. It is illustrated in Figure 17-18, and essentially takes a complicated intersection with heavy left-turning volumes, and separates it into two signalized intersections, each of which can be signalized using a simple two-phase scheme. This approach, which has only been implemented a few times, requires space. Also, the distance between the two signalized intersections created must be carefully coordinated with signal timing to avoid spillback problems.

Other design solutions are also possible, and involve partial interchanges with fly-overs for critical movements. All design solutions to left-turn problems involve expensive construction and right-of-way

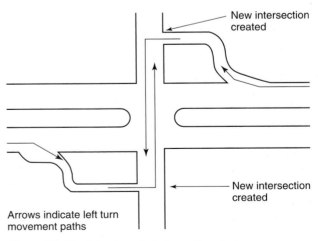

Figure 17-17 A jug-handle intersection design.

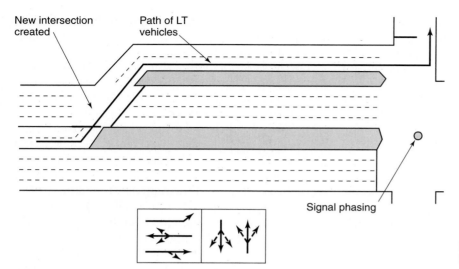

Figure 17-18 Continuous flow intersection illustrated.

costs. The benefits of implementation must be carefully weighed against the additional cost incurred.

The engineer facing decisions concerning left turn treatments must select carefully from among a wide range of options.

In some jurisdictions, the type of left-turn phasing used is dictated by local policy, based on a judgment concerning driver expectations, safety, and other factors. Reference [14] provides information concerning the use of *warrants* for left-turn phasing at signalized intersections, based on a survey of 1200 ITE members working for state or local transportation agencies. Approximately 77% of those responding indicated that their agency *had* adopted some form of warrant or analysis technique for installation of a protected left-turn phase. The most common techniques were based on:

- Accidents (85 of 335 responses)
- Volumes (143 of 355 responses)
  —cross-product of left-turn volume and opposing volume/lane (43 of 143)
  —minimum left-turn volumes (58 of 143)
- Delay and/or queues (29 of 355 responses)

The "cross product" rule states that if the product of the left-turning volume and the per-lane opposing flow exceeds a certain number (50,000 is a common example), then a protected left-turn phase should be provided.

There are a number of interesting and informative studies of left-turn treatments in the literature. In Texas, a simulation model was used to generate four different delay criteria for the installation of a left-turn phase [15]. A number of studies [eg. 16] have documented that protected left turns and other intersection management techniques for left-turning vehicles can substantially lessen accident experience. Agent [17] documents the use of left-turn phasing at intersections in Kentucky, where protected phasing is the norm. He concluded that protected plus permitted phasing is preferable to fully protected phasing due to the savings in delay that result from its use. He cautioned that such phasing, however, adds to the accident potential, and should not be used where speed limits exceed 45 mph, where left-turns must cross three or more lanes, and where double left-turn lanes exist. Warren [18] observed that for nine intersections, replacement of fully protected phasing with protected plus permitted phasing altered the *types* of accidents occurring. In these cases, left-turn accidents increased dramatically, while rear-end and total accidents decreased. Habib [19] reported that left-turning vehicles are about four times more hazardous than through traffic in terms of pedestrian accidents, and that pedestrians are hit twice as often by left-turning vehicles than by right-turning vehicles.

Table 17-2 summarizes some of the major points made in this section, and elsewhere in the chapter, concerning alternative left-turn treatments.

It should also be noted that wherever fully protected left-turn phasing is implemented, a left-

Table 17-2 Left-Turn Alternatives for Signalized Intersections

Option	Key Advantages	Key Disadvantages
Two-phase signalization	Minimized lost times Efficient where LT flow is low	Left turns are opposed Congestion can occur with many LTs
Two-phase signalization with exclusive LT lane	Removes waiting LTs from through lanes	Does not address the limits of opposing flow on LTs
Multiphase signalization with protected LTs	Provides unopposed LTs Reduces congestion caused by LTs	Requires exclusive LT lane Increases cycle length Increases lost time in cycle Many increase delay to some movements
Multiphase signalization with protected + permitted LTs	Minimized cycle length needed to provide for protected LTs Reduces delay to LTs	Complex phasing is difficult to convey; may confuse drivers
Prohibition of LTs	Avoids all LT problems	Diverts traffic to alternate locations, which may be negatively affected Causes driver inconvenience
One-way streets	Removes opposing flow for LTs	Requires compatible system geometry May increase average trip lengths and VMT

turn lane of appropriate length is also needed. A common rule-of-thumb for estimating the appropriate length of a left-turn lane is that the lane should accommodate between 1.5 and 2.0 times the average number of left-turning vehicles in a cycle. This is based on a Poisson distribution of arrivals that randomly show up in any cycle; 95% of all cycles will have *less* than 1.5 to 2.0 times the average number of left-turning vehicles. Messer [20] has refined the methodology for estimating left-turn lane lengths, accounting for variation with opposing flow, and presented specific guidelines.

Simple signal timing: Getting started

All of the aspects of intersection signalization treated in this chapter and in Chapter 16 are included in the *HCM* operational analysis model presented in the next chapter. The methodology, however, predicts operational parameters based on specified traffic, geometric, and signal timing conditions. While the existence of computational software that implements the modal makes trial-and-error analysis of alternatives relatively straightforward, the traffic engineer

should have a simple methodology for establishing an initial signal timing plan for such an analysis.

The 1997 *HCM* contains a "planning methodology" that can be used to develop an initial signal timing plan. The method is itself, however, quite complex. Also available is proprietary software [21] that optimizes signal timing by iterating through the 1994 *HCM* procedure.

The literature is also rich in various approaches to signal timing. The early work on departure headways and lost times by Bruce Greenshields is the basis for what is now called "critical lane" or "critical movement" analysis. Webster's work on signal optimization is still fundamental, and extensively used. Messer and Fambro's work on critical lane analysis [22] is a benchmark in the development of modern models. References [23–29] contain additional important works that contributed to the development of current methodologies, both at home and abroad.

An approximate signal timing, however, can be achieved somewhat more simply using some of the parameters specified in the *HCM,* and applying some of the concepts presented in this chapter and Chapter 16.

The methodology presented here uses a default value for the saturation headway, based on *HCM* adjustment factors, and specifically accounts for the effects of left-turning and right-turning vehicles to allow for rational decision-making concerning signalization options and the need for exclusive lanes. For simplicity, it is also suggested that initial signal timing deal only with fully protected or fully permitted phasing, with compound phasing remaining an option to be investigated using the *HCM* model presented in Chapter 18.

The 1997 *HCM* recommends the use of an *ideal* saturation flow rate of 1900 pcphgpl for signalized intersection analysis. The model includes nine different adjustment factors accounting for the following conditions: lane width, heavy vehicles, grades, parking, local buses, area type, lane utilization, right turns, and left turns. For the signal timing methodology developed herein, a saturation flow rate of $0.85 \times 1900 = 1615$ vphgpl is used. This corresponds to a saturation headway of $3600/1615 = 2.23$ sec/veh. This rate accommodates 12-ft lane widths, no parking or local buses, 5% heavy vehicles in the traffic stream, a +1% grade, and a CBD location. It does not account for left- or right-turning vehicles, which will be taken into account separately. Equation [17-11], which determines the desirable cycle length for a specified v/c ratio and PHF, will be used in this method. If a lost-time of 3 seconds/phase (t_L) is adopted, and the average headway of 2.23 seconds/vehicle is inserted, this equation becomes:

$$C_{des} = \frac{3N}{1 - \dfrac{V_c}{1615PHF(v/c)}} \quad [17\text{-}9]$$

where N is the number of signal phases, C is the cycle length, v/c is the volume to capacity ratio desired, and *PHF* is the peak hour factor.

Since equation [17-9] does not address the impact of right- and left-turning vehicles, this must be done separately, by computing the number of "through car equivalents" on each approach. While through car equivalent values for right and left turning vehicles are very complex issues, a relatively simple approach is taken here to determine an initial signal timing plan. Table 17-3 gives values of E_{LT}, the number of through car equivalents for a left turn, while Table 17-4 gives values of E_{RT}, the number of through car equivalents for a right turn. Values of E_{LT} are loosely based on values given in the 1994 *HCM*, modified to

Table 17-3   Through Car Equivalents for Left-Turning Vehicles, E_{LT}

Opposing Flow V_o (vph)	Number of Opposing Lanes, N_o		
	1	2	3
0	1.1	1.1	1.1
200	2.5	2.0	1.8
400	5.0	3.0	2.5
600	10.0*	5.0	4.0
800	13.0*	8.0	6.0
1000	15.0*	13.0*	10.0*
≥1200	15.0*	15.0*	15.0*

E_{LT} (protected left turns) = 1.05

*May indicate the LT capacity is only available through "sneakers" turning at the end of the cycle.

Table 17-4   Through Car Equivalents for Right-Turning Vehicles, E_{RT}

Number of Conflicting Pedestrians (peds/hr)	Equivalent
None (0)	1.18
Low (50)	1.21
Moderate (200)	1.32
High (400)	1.52
Extreme (800)	2.13

account for their different usage here, and vary with both the intensity of opposing flow and the number of lanes in which it is distributed. Values of E_{RT} are similarly based, and account for the number of pedestrians in conflicting crosswalks.

The recommended procedure assumes that basic intersection geometry is specified as part of the input information. If there are several alternatives available, these may be considered separately.

The methodology for establishing an initial signal timing is as follows:

1. Develop a reasonable signal phase plan in accordance with the principles discussed in this chapter. DO NOT include any compound phasing in the preliminary signal timing. Consider a protected left-turn phase for any left-turning movement that:

a. has a left-turning volume in excess of 200 vph,
b. has a cross-product of the left-turn volume (in vph) and the opposing through volume per lane (in vphpl) in excess of 50,000.
Other criteria based on local policies may be applied, and several phase plans may be tested.
2. Convert all left-turning and right-turning volumes to through car equivalents (tcu's) using Tables 17-3 and 17-4.
3. Establish a reasonable phase plan using the principles discussed in this chapter. Determine the actual sum of critical lane volumes, V_c, using this plan. Use volumes in tcu's for this purpose. Check the sum of critical lane volumes in tcu's for reasonableness. Make any adjustments necessary.
4. Using Equation 17-9, determine the desirable cycle length based on a desired v/c ratio, the PHF.
5. Allocate the available effective green time within the cycle in proportion to the critical lane volumes (in tcu's) for each signal phase.

Note that the procedure recommended does not yield a unique result, nor does it allow for development of an initial signal timing entirely by algorithm. The traffic engineer must apply some judgment in the process, and should be aware of applicable local or regional policies that may affect the process.

The resulting signal timing, illustrated in several sample problems that follow, is only an initial timing. The resulting design and timing should be analyzed using the *HCM* methodology discussed in Chapter 18, and should be fine-tuned to optimize the desired measure of effectiveness. Provision of compound phases should be considered as part of this fine-tuning process.

SAMPLE PROBLEM 1

Recommend an appropriate signal timing for the intersection shown in Figure 17-19. The PHF is 0.92, and moderate numbers of pedestrians are present. The intersection should operate at 0.90 of its capacity during the worst 15-minutes of the peak hour, for which volumes are shown in Figure 17-19.
1. The first consideration is whether or not protected left-turn phases are needed for any approach. This is done by checking the left-turn volumes and the cross-products of left-turn volumes and opposing

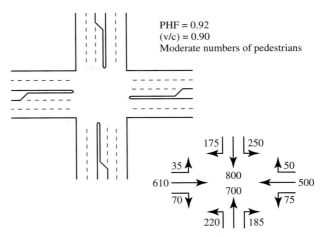

Figure 17-19 Intersection for Sample Problem 1.

through volumes against the criteria specified herein. For Sample Problem 1:

Eastbound Approach	$V_{LT} = 35 < 200$ vph x-prod = 35 × 500/2 = 8,750 < 50,000	**NO**
Westbound Approach	$V_{LT} = 75 < 200$ vph x-prod = 75 × 610/2 = 22,875 < 50,000	**NO**
Southbound Approach	$V_{LT} = 250 > 200$ vph	**YES**
Northbound Approach	$V_{LT} = 220 > 200$ vph	**YES**

Using the recommended guidelines, both the northbound and southbound approaches should receive a protected left-turn phase. The eastbound and westbound approaches, even though they have a left-turn lane, should not be initially assigned a protected phase.
2. All volumes should now be converted to equivalent "through car units" or tcu's. All through vehicles have an equivalent of 1.00. Equivalents for left-turning and right-turning vehicles are drawn from Tables 17-3 and 17-4 respectively. Straight-line interpolation is acceptable in either table, where appropriate.

These computations are illustrated in Table 17-5, below. Note that where two or more movements will share a set of lanes (a lane group), their total is added for convenience.
3. At this point, a suitable phase plan must be developed, and the critical lane volumes for each phase

Table 17-5 TCU Volumes for Sample Problem 1

Approach	Movement	Volume (vph)	Equivalent	Volume (tcu)	Shared Lane Grp (tcu)
EB	LEFT	35	4.00	140	<u>140</u>
	THROUGH	610	1.00	610	
	RIGHT	70	1.32	92	702
WB	LEFT	75	5.00	375	<u>375</u>
	THROUGH	500	1.00	500	
	RIGHT	50	1.32	66	566
SB	LEFT	250	1.05	263	<u>263</u>
	THROUGH	800	1.00	800	
	RIGHT	175	1.32	231	<u>1031</u>
NB	LEFT	220	1.05	231	<u>231</u>
	THROUGH	700	1.00	700	
	RIGHT	185	1.32	244	944

must be identified. In this case, protected left-turn phases are needed for the NB and SB approaches. As the two LT volumes are similar, it would be efficient to handle both in an exclusive LT phase. A ring diagram showing the proposed phase plan, together with lane volumes moving in each phase is shown in Figure 17-20.

In Phase A, the NB and SB left-turn movements are given protection. Since each of these movements operates out of a separate lane, the *per lane* volume is equal to the total volume for each movement, in tcu's, as computed in Table 17-5. Since the volumes are in the same units, the larger of two volumes, or 263 tcus/lane/hr, is the critical volume for this phase.

In Phase B, the through and right-turn movements from the NB and SB approaches have the green. Both of these combined movements have two lanes each. Thus, the *per lane* volumes shown in Figure 17-20 are the shared-lane volumes from Table 17-5 divided by 2. For the NB approach, 944/2 = 472; for the SB approach, 1,031/2 = 516. The SB volume is clearly higher, and the critical volume for this phase is 516 tcu's/lane/hr.

In Phase C, *four* sets of movements are given the green. The EB and WB left-turning movements have exclusive lanes; their *per lane* volume is equal to the movement volume. The EB and WB through and right-turning movements share two-lane approaches.

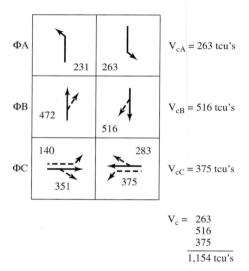

Figure 17-20 Ring diagram and critical volumes for Sample Problem 1.

Their *per lane* volume is, therefore, the shared-lane group volume from Table 17-5 divided by 2. For the EB approach, 702/2 = 351 tcu/lane/hr; for the WB approach, 566/2 = 283 tcu/lane/hr. The critical volume for this phase is the highest of the *four per lane volumes moving during the phase.* In this case, this is the WB left-turning movement, and the critical volume for the phase in 375 tcu/lane/hr.

The sum of critical lane volumes for this signal plan is, therefore, 263 + 516 + 375 = 1155 tcu/hr, as shown.

4. The desired cycle length can now be computed using Equation [17-8]:

$$C = \frac{(3)(3)}{1 - \frac{1154}{1615(0.92)(0.90)}} = \frac{9}{0.137} = 65.7 \text{ sec}$$

Assuming that a pre-timed signal is in use, use *70 seconds* as the cycle length, as timing dials are commonly available in 5-second increments.

5. The allocation of available effective green time will be in proportion to the critical lane volumes for each phase. The effective green time is the cycle length minus the lost time in the cycle, or 70 − (3)(3) = 61 seconds. Then:

$$g_A = 61(263/1154) = 13.9 \text{ sec}$$
$$g_B = 61(516/1154) = 27.3 \text{ sec}$$
$$g_C = 61(375/1154\,) = \underline{19.8 \text{ sec}}$$
$$61.0 \text{ sec}$$
$$L = \underline{9.0 \text{ sec}}$$
$$70.0 \text{ sec}$$

6.

Although not illustrated here, these effective green times would have to be converted to actual green times. This would involve determining appropriate values for the "yellow" and "all red" intervals in each phase, and the relationship:

$$g = G + Y - t_L$$

where $Y = y + r$, as discussed previously in this chapter. Pedestrian crossing times should also be checked to insure that these green times allow for safe crossings. If a deficiency for pedestrians is noted, the cycle length would normally be increased, and the green time reallocated in the same proportion as this solution. See previous sample problems for an illustration of this process.

In any event, this solution must be considered to be an initial signal timing. A full analysis using the methodology of Chapter 18 should be conducted to check all lane group *v/c* ratios and average delays. Improvements to the signal timing may be found by

trial-and-error using the Chapter 18 methodology, as implemented on commonly-available software.

SAMPLE PROBLEM 2

Find an appropriate signal timing for the intersection of two 2-lane downtown streets shown in Figure 17-21. The *PHF* is 0.85, and a *v/c* ratio of 0.85 is desired during the worst 15-minutes of the peak hour. Pedestrian activity is moderate.

1. The initial step in the analysis is consideration of any protected left-turn phases that may be necessary. In this case, if any protected left turns are needed, left-turn lanes on the affected approaches would have to be added. Another option would be to use compound phasing, probably in conjunction with leading and lagging greens.

Left-turn volumes and cross-products are compared to the recommended criteria for protected phasing:

Eastbound Approach:	$V_{LT} = 35 < 200$ vph X-prod = 35 × 250 = 8750 < 50,000	**NO**
Westbound Approach:	$V_{LT} = 40 < 200$ vph x-prod = 40 × 205 = 8200 < 50,000	**NO**
Southbound Approach:	$V_{LT} = 25 < 200$ vph x-prod = 25 × 175 = 4375 < 50,000	**NO**
Northbound Approach:	$V_{LT} = 40 < 200$ vph x-prod = 40 × 200 = 8000 < 50,000	**NO**

Therefore, no protected left turns are needed, and a simple two-phase signal may be implemented.

2. All volumes are now converted to tcu's, as shown in Table 17-6. Through-car equivalent values

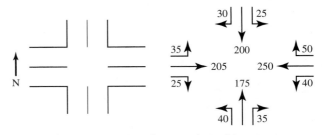

Figure 17-21 Intersection for Sample Problem 2.

Table 17-6   TCU Volumes for Sample Problem 2

Approach	Movement	Volume (vph)	Equivalent	Volume (tcu)	Shared Lane Grp (tcu)
EB	LEFT	35	3.13	110	
	THROUGH	205	1.00	205	348
	RIGHT	25	1.32	33	
WB	LEFT	40	2.50	100	
	THROUGH	250	1.00	250	416
	RIGHT	50	1.32	66	
SB	LEFT	25	2.33	58	
	THROUGH	200	1.00	200	298
	RIGHT	30	1.32	40	
NB	LEFT	40	2.50	100	
	THROUGH	175	1.00	175	321
	RIGHT	35	1.32	46	

are drawn from Tables 17-3 (left turns) and 17-4 (right turns). Straight-line interpolation in these tables is acceptable.

3. In this case, the development of a phase plan is quite straightforward. As no protected left turns are required, a simple two-phase signal will suffice, as shown in Figure 17-22.

In Phase A, northbound and southbound movements have the green. Comparing the two lane volumes, the northbound approach is seen to be critical, with a volume of 321 tcu/lane/hr.

In Phase B, eastbound and westbound flows move. Again, comparing the two lane volumes, the westbound approach is critical, with a volume of 416 tcu's/lane/hr. Thus, the sum of critical lane volumes for this intersection is 321 + 416 = 737 tcu.

4. The desired cycle length may now be estimated using Equation [17-8]:

$$C = \frac{(3)(2)}{1 - \frac{737}{1615(0.85)(0.85)}} = \frac{6}{0.37} = 16.2 \text{ sec}$$

This is less than the practical minimum cycle length of 30 seconds. Therefore, the signal will be timed using a cycle length of 30 seconds.

5. Effective green times are allocated in proportion to the critical lane volumes for each signal phase. The total amount of effective green time in the cycle is 30 − (2)(3) = 24 seconds. Then:

$$g_A = 24(321/737) = 10.5 \text{ sec}$$

$$g_B = 24(416/737) = \underline{13.5 \text{ sec}}$$

$$24.0 \text{ sec}$$

$$L = \qquad \underline{6.0 \text{ sec}}$$

$$30.0 \text{ sec}$$

6. As in Sample Problem 1, this preliminary signal timing should be checked against pedestrian requirements, and should be fully analyzed and fine-tuned using the *HCM* model presented in Chapter 18. "Yellow" and "all red" times should also be com-

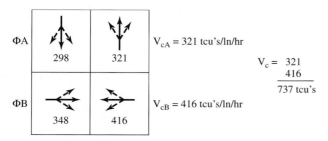

$V_{cA} = 321$ tcu's/ln/hr

$V_c = $ 321
       416
      ‾‾‾‾‾
      737 tcu's

$V_{cB} = 416$ tcu's/ln/hr

Figure 17-22   Ring diagram and V_c for Sample Problem 2.

puted, enabling the effective green allocation to be related to the actual green times that must be established in the controller.

SAMPLE PROBLEM 3

Figure 17-23 shows an intersection of a 6-lane arterial with left- and right-turn lanes and a 4-lane arterial with no turning lanes. The peak hour factor is 0.85, and the desired *v/c* ratio during the worst 15 minutes of the peak hour is also 0.85. There are no pedestrians at this location.

1. The need for protected left-turn phases is checked against the criteria recommended herein:

Eastbound Approach:	$V_{LT} = 300 > 200$ vph	**YES**
Westbound Approach:	$V_{LT} = 150 < 200$ vph	
	x-prod $= 150 \times 1200/3$	
	$= 60,000 > 50,000$	**YES**
Southbound Approach:	$V_{LT} = 30 < 200$ vph	
	x-prod $= 30 \times 500/2$	
	$= 7500 < 50,000$	**NO**
Northbound Approach:	$V_{LT} = 50 < 200$ vph	
	x-prod $= 50 \times 400/2$	
	$= 10,000 < 50,000$	**NO**

From this analysis, the eastbound and westbound left turns require protection. No protection is called for on the northbound and southbound approaches.

2. Conversions of all volumes to tcu's is illustrated in Table 17-7. As in previous examples, equivalent values are drawn from Tables 17-3 (left turns) and 17-4 (right turns). Straight-line interpolation is used to obtain intermediate values. As the E-W artery has exclusive RT lanes, right turns are kept in a separate lane group.

3. Figure 17-24 illustrates the recommended phase plan for this case. Given that the two movements requiring left-turn protection have vastly different volumes (300 EB and 150 WB) it will be more efficient to split the two protected phases rather than to run them simultaneously. A leading and lagging green phase for the E-W artery accomplishes this, and is chosen.

Determining the critical lane volumes is not a simple process, as the proposed phasing involves overlaps. First, the appropriate *per lane* volumes in each phase have to be determined.

- For the EB LT phase, the per lane volume is 315 tcu's/ln/hour, as there is only one lane. Similarly, for the WB LT phase, the per lane volume is 158 tcu's/ln/hr.
- For the EB TH & RT phase, 118 tcu's use the right-turn lane, while 1200 tcu's share three through lanes, with an average per lane volume of 400 tcu's/ln/hr.
- For the WB TH & RT phase, 295 tcu's use the right-turn lane, while 1000 tcu's share three through lanes, with an average per lane volume of 333 tcu's/hr/ln.

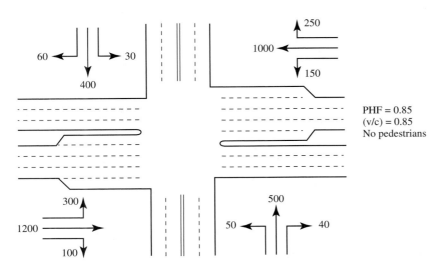

PHF = 0.85
(v/c) = 0.85
No pedestrians

Figure 17-23 Intersection for Sample Problem 3.

Table 17-7   TCU Volumes for Sample Problem 3

Approach	Movement	Volume (vph)	Equivalent	Volume (tcu)	Shared Lane Grp (tcu)
EB	LEFT	300	1.05	315	315
	THROUGH	1200	1.00	1200	1200
	RIGHT	100	1.18	118	118
WB	LEFT	150	1.05	158	158
	THROUGH	1000	1.00	1000	1000
	RIGHT	250	1.18	295	295
SB	LEFT	60	4.00	240	
	THROUGH	400	1.00	400	675
	RIGHT	30	1.18	35	
NB	LEFT	50	3.00	150	
	THROUGH	500	1.00	500	697
	RIGHT	40	1.18	47	

- On the southbound approach, a total of 675 tcu's share two lanes for an average flow of 338 tcu/ln/hr. Similarly, on the northbound approach, 697 tcu share two lanes for an average flow of 349 tcu's/hr/ln.

Once the appropriate lane volumes are determined for each phase of the signal, the critical path through the signal timing must be found. For phase B, with no overlaps, this process is the same as in previous problems, and is based on the largest per-lane volume in the SB and NB approaches. As shown in Figure 17-24, this total is 349 tcu/hr/ln, for the NB approach.

For phases A1, A2, and A3, the process is more complicated, as these phases overlap. As is shown in the ring diagram, there are two paths through phase A. The left ring starts with the EB LT and follows with the WB TH & RT. The right ring starts with the EB TH & RT and follows with the WB LT. The path with the highest total sum of lane volumes is the *critical path* for this phase, and determines the critical lane volume(s). As shown in Figure 17-24, the left ring is

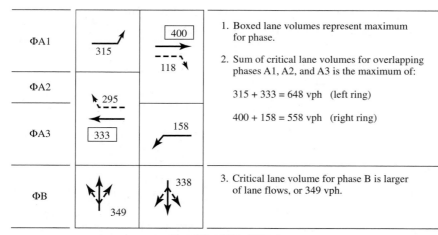

1. Boxed lane volumes represent maximum for phase.

2. Sum of critical lane volumes for overlapping phases A1, A2, and A3 is the maximum of:

   315 + 333 = 648 vph   (left ring)

   400 + 158 = 558 vph   (right ring)

3. Critical lane volume for phase B is larger of lane flows, or 349 vph.

$V_c = 648 + 349 = 997$ vph

Figure 17-24   Ring diagram and V_c for Sample Problem 3.

the critical path, with a total critical lane volume of 648 tcu's/ln/hr. Thus, the sum of critical volume for this signal is 648 + 349 = 997 tcu/hr. Note that both rings of the signal go through *three* phases. Thus, this is a 3-phase signal, involving three sets of lost times per cycle.

4. An appropriate cycle length may now be determined using Equation [17-8]:

$$C = \frac{(3)(3)}{1 - \frac{997}{1615(0.85)(0.85)}} = \frac{9}{0.15} = 60.0 \text{ sec}$$

As this is a standard value, it will be used.

5. Effective green time will be allocated in proportion to the critical lane volumes for each phase. Since there are overlapping phases, the initial timing focuses on the critical path through the signal, which includes the *left ring path* for phase A. The total amount of effective green time available in the cycle is 60 − (3)(3) = 51 seconds. Then:

$$g_{A1} = 51(315/997) = 16.1 \text{ sec}$$
$$g_{A2+A3} = 51(333/997) = 17.0 \text{ sec}$$
$$g_{B} = 51(349/997) = \underline{17.9 \text{ sec}}$$
$$51.0 \text{ sec}$$
$$L = 9.0 \text{ sec}$$
$$60.0 \text{ sec}$$

This, however, does not fully specify all of the green times for the signal. While the total length of phase A is 16.1 + 17.0 = 33.1 sec, the split between phases A2 and A3 is still not specified. This is generally done by splitting the 33.1 available seconds of effective green time in proportion to the *per lane* volumes for the noncritical path through phase A (in this case, the right ring). Then:

$$g_{A1+A2} = 33.1(400/558) = 23.7 \text{ sec}$$
$$g_{A3} = 33.1(158/558) = \underline{9.4 \text{ sec}}$$
$$33.1 \text{ sec}$$

The timing is now fully specified, with $g_{A2} = 17.0 - 9.4 = 7.6$ sec.

6. As in Sample Problems 1 and 2, pedestrian crossing times should be checked. Precise "yellow" and "all red" intervals should be computed for each phase. This initial signal timing should be analyzed and fine-tuned using the procedures described in Chapter 18.

SAMPLE PROBLEM 4

Figure 17-25 illustrates a T-intersection with general geometrics as shown. An appropriate signal timing is desired to provide for a *v/c* ratio of 0.85 during the worst 15 minutes of the peak hour. Pedestrian activity is low, and the *PHF* is 0.92.

1. Once again, the first step in the process is a determination of which left-turn movements require protection. There is, however, only one potentially opposed left turn in this intersection, the WB left turn. Checking this volume against the recommended criteria:

$$V_{LT} = 380 > 200 \text{ vph} \qquad \textbf{YES}$$

This movement will require a protected left turn.

2. All movement volumes are converted to tcu's using the equivalent values of Tables 17-3 (left turns) and 17-4 (right turns). Straight-line interpolation is used to find intermediate values. These computations are shown in Table 17-8.

3. Next, signal phasing and per-lane volumes need to found. As only the WB LT requires protection, a leading green will be provided for the WB approach. Since there is no opposing left turn, the WB TH movement will be permitted to go during this phase.

Lane volumes are quite straightforward, as both the WB and NB approaches assign each movement a dedicated lane. In the EB approach, a total of 821 tcu's/hr share two lanes for an average flow of 411 tcu's/ln/hr.

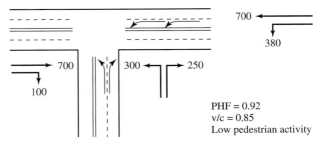

Figure 17-25 Intersection for Sample Problem 4.

Table 17-8   TCU Computations for Sample Problem 4

Approach	Movement	Volume (vph)	Equivalent	Volume (tcu)	Shared-Ln Grp Vol
EB	THROUGH	700	1.00	700	821
	RIGHT	100	1.21	121	
WB	LEFT	380	1.05	399	399
	THROUGH	500	1.00	500	500
NB	LEFT	300	1.05	315	315
	RIGHT	250	1.21	303	303

Figure 17-26 illustrates the signal phasing described, and shows the determination of critical lane volumes. Note that in phase A, the two rings have a *different number of phases.* The left ring, which is critical, goes through *two* phases, while the right ring goes through *a single* phase. Because the left ring was the critical path, the signal is treated as a *three-phase signal.* Had the right ring been the critical path, the signal would be treated as a *two-phase signal.* This, of course, affects the amount of lost time which must be accounted for in the cycle.

4. The desired cycle length is now estimated using Equation [17-8]:

$$C = \frac{(3)(3)}{1 - \frac{1125}{1615(0.92)(0.85)}} = \frac{9}{0.11} = 81.9 \text{ sec}$$

As this is not a standard cycle length, a cycle length of 90 seconds is chosen. (85 seconds would also be acceptable.)

5. Effective green time is now allocated in proportion to the critical lane volumes for each signal phase. There are $90 - (3)(3) = 81$ seconds of effective green time in the cycle, as defined. Then:

$$g_{A1} = 81(399/1125) = 28.7 \text{ sec}$$
$$g_{A2} = 81(411/1125) = 29.6 \text{ sec}$$
$$g_B = 81(315/1125) = \underline{22.7 \text{ sec}}$$
$$81.0 \text{ sec}$$
$$L = \underline{9.0 \text{ sec}}$$
$$90.0 \text{ sec}$$

These allocations completely define the signal timing.

6. As in all previous sample problems, pedestrian requirements should be checked, "yellow" and "all red" intervals for each phase should be computed, and the initial timing should be analyzed and fine-tuned using the procedures of Chapter 18.

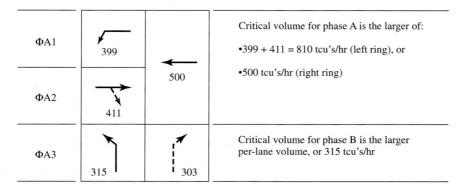

ΦA1 399
ΦA2 411
ΦA3 315   303

500

Critical volume for phase A is the larger of:

•399 + 411 = 810 tcu's/hr (left ring), or

•500 tcu's/hr (right ring)

Critical volume for phase B is the larger per-lane volume, or 315 tcu's/hr

$V_c = 810 + 315 = 1,125$ tcu's/hr

Figure 17-26 Ring diagram and V_c for Sample Problem.

Summary

This chapter has covered a wide range of issues and principles affecting traffic signals at individual intersections. These principles lead to a simplified approach to initial signal timing, which is presented and illustrated. In Chapter 18, the most frequently-used model of signalized intersection operation, the Highway Capacity Model, is introduced, explained, and its use illustrated. It adopts and utilizes all of the principles described in this chapter, albeit not always in the same analytic form presented here. It also treats several layers of complexity that are difficult to illustrate without use of computer programs or simulations.

References

1. Perez, R., "Guidelines for Right Turn Treatments at Signalized Intersections," *ITE Journal,* Institute of Transportation Engineers, Washington, DC, February 1995.
2. McGee H., and Warren, D., "Right Turn on Red," *Public Roads,* June 1976.
3. McGee, H., et al., "Right Turn on Red," *Volume 1—Final Report,* Contract No. FHWA-RD-76-89, U.S. Department of Transportation, Federal Highway Administration, Washington, DC, May 1976.
4. McGee, H., "Accident Experience with Right Turn on Red," *Transportation Research Record 644,* Transportation Research Board, National Research Council, Washington, DC, 1977.
5. ITE Technical Committee 4M-20, "Driver Behavior at RTOR Locations," *ITE Journal,* April 1992.
6. ITE Technical Committee 4A-16, "Recommended Practice: Determining Vehicle Change Intervals," *ITE Journal,* May 1985.
7. Parsonson, P., et al., "Yellow and Red Clearance Signal Timing—Drivers and Attorneys Speak Out," *ITE Journal,* June 1993.
8. Parsonson, P., "Management of Traffic Signal Maintenance," *NCHRP Synthesis of Highway Practice 114,* Transportation Research Board, National Research Council, Washington, DC, December 1984.
9. ITE Technical Council Task Force 4TF-1, "Technical Council Summary Report," *ITE Journal,* August 1994.
10. ITE Technical Council Task Force 4TF-1, "Determining Signal Change and Clearance Intervals," *Publication No. IR-073,* Institute of Transportation Engineers, Washington, DC, 1994.
11. Greenberg, F., "Pedestrian Signal Usage in the CBD of Medium Sized Cities," *ITE Journal,* April 1995.
12. Technical Committee 4A-35, "Pedestrian Treatments at Signalized Intersections," *ITE Journal,* Institute of Transportation Engineers, Washington, DC, June 1995.
13. Hutchinson, T., "The Continuous Flow Intersection: The Greatest New Development in Traffic Engineering Since the Traffic Signal?" *Traffic Engineering and Control,* Vol. 36, No. 3, Printerhall Ltd., London, U.K., 1995.
14. Lalani, N., et al., "A Summary of the Use of Warrants for the Installation of Left-Turn Phasing at Signalized Intersections," *ITE Journal,* April 1986.
15. Lin, H., and Machemel, R., "Developmental Study of Implementation Guidelines for Left-Turn Treatments," *Transportation Research Record 905,* Transportation Research Board, National Research Council, Washington, DC, 1983.
16. Griewe, R., "Intersection Management Techniques for the Left-Turning Vehicle," *ITE Journal,* Institute of Transportation Engineers, Washington, DC, June 1986.
17. Agent, K., "Guidelines for the Use of Protected/Permissive Left-Turn Phasing," *ITE Journal,* July 1987.
18. Warren, D., "Accident Analysis of Left-Turn Phasing," *Public Roads,* Vol. 48, No. 4, March 1985.
19. Habib, P., "Pedestrian Safety: The Hazards of Left-Turning Vehicles," *ITE Journal,* April 1980.
20. Messer, C., "Guidelines for Signalized Left-Turn Treatments," *Implementation Package,* Contract No. FHWA-IP-81-4, Texas Transportation Institute, Texas A & M University, College Station, TX, 1981.
21. *SIG/CINEMA, User's Manual,* KLD Associates and Polytechnic University, Huntington, NY, 1995.
22. Messer, C., and Fambro, D., "Critical Lane Analysis for Intersection Design," *Transportation Research Record 644,* Transportation Research Board, National Research Council, Washington, DC, 1977.
23. Peterson, B., and Imre, E., *Berakning av kapacitet, kolangd, fordrojning I vagrafikanaggningar,* (*Swedish capacity manual*), Statens Vagverk, Stockholm, Sweden, 1977.
24. Bang, K., "Capacity of Signalized Intersections," *Transportation Research Record 667,* Transportation Research Board, National Research Council, Washington, DC, 1978.

25. Berry, D., and Gandhi, P., "Headway Approach to Intersection Capacity," *Highway Research Record 453,* Transportation Research Board, National Research Council, Washington, DC, 1973.
26. Capelle, D., and Pinnell, C., "Capacity Study of Signalized Diamond Intersections," *Highway Research Bulletin 291,* Transportation Research Board, National Research Council, Washington, DC, 1961.
27. Bellis, W., "Capacity of Traffic Signals and Traffic Signal Timing," *Highway Research Bulletin 271,* Transporta-

tion Research Board, National Research Council, Washington, DC, 1960.
28. Reilly, E., and Steifert, R., "Capacity of Signalized Intersections," *Highway Research Bulletin 321,* Transportation Research Board, National Research Council, Washington, DC, 1970.
29. "Interim Methods on Highway Capacity," *Circular 212,* Transportation Research Board, National Research Council, Washington, DC, 1980.

Problems

Problem 17–1

What change (yellow) and clearance (all red) intervals are recommended for an intersection approach with an average approach speed of 42 mph, level grade, a distance of 40 ft from the STOP line to the far side of the most distant conflicting lane, and an additional 10 ft to the far side of the furthest conflicting crosswalk? Assume a standard vehicle length of 18 feet, and a driver reaction time of 1.5 seconds. Pedestrians are expected during virtually every signal cycle.

Problem 17–2

Consider the intersection illustrated below, and the signal timing as indicated. Are pedestrian crossings safely accommodated by this situation? If not, what signal timing would

be appropriate to accommodate safe pedestrian crossings? Assume a pedestrian crossing speed of 4 fps.

Problem 17–3

How would the answer to Problem 17–2 change if the E-W artery had no parking and a 20-foot median? Assume 12-ft travel lane widths.

Problems 17–4 through 17–8

For the intersections shown in the following illustrations, determine an appropriate initial signal timing. For each intersection, check to insure that pedestrians have adequate crossing time, and compute appropriate "yellow" and "all red" intervals for each phase.

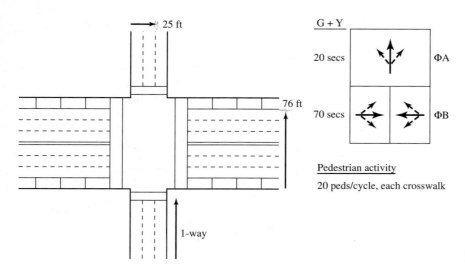

Intersection for Problem 17–2.

All volumes shown are in vph for prevailing conditions. Note that the simplified signal timing methodology of this chapter uses a default value for saturation flow rate that accounts for all prevailing conditions except turning vehicles, and that the standard value of t_L used is 3.0 seconds.

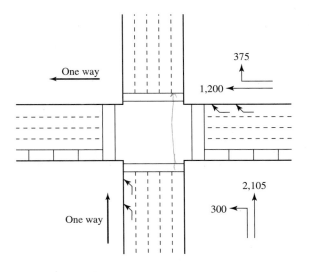

Lane widths = 12 ft
Parking widths = 8 ft
PHF = 0.87
Desired v/c ratio = 0.90
Low pedestrian activity
Walking speed = 4 fps
Average approach speed =
    40 mph, all approaches
Driver reaction time = 1.0 secs.

Intersection for Problem 17–4.

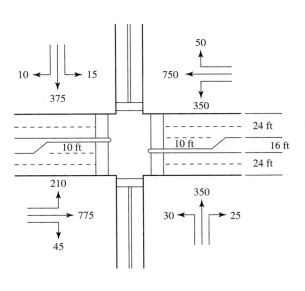

Lane widths as shown
PHF = 0.94
Desired v/c ratio = 0.95
Moderate pedestrian activity
Average approach speeds:
    30 mph N and S
    45 mph E and W
Walking speed = 4 fps
Driver reaction time = 1.2 secs.
X-walk width = 8 ft
Lost time = 3 secs per phase

Intersection for Problem 17–5.

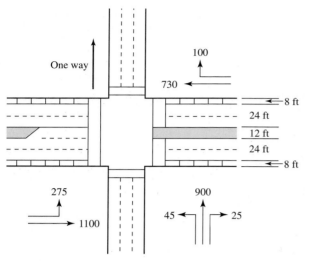

Lane widths as shown
PHF = 0.90
Desired v/c ratio = 0.92
Moderate pedestrian activity
Walking speed = 4.0 fps
Average approach
    speed = 40 mph
Driver reaction time
    = 1.0 secs.
Lost time = 3 secs per phase

Intersection for Problem 17–6.

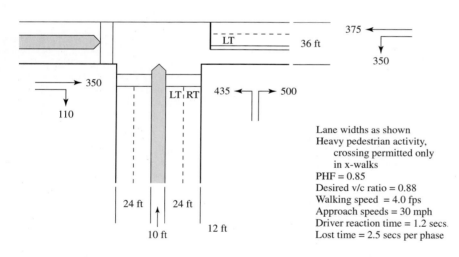

Lane widths as shown
Heavy pedestrian activity,
    crossing permitted only
    in x-walks
PHF = 0.85
Desired v/c ratio = 0.88
Walking speed = 4.0 fps
Approach speeds = 30 mph
Driver reaction time = 1.2 secs.
Lost time = 2.5 secs per phase

Intersection for Problem 17–7.

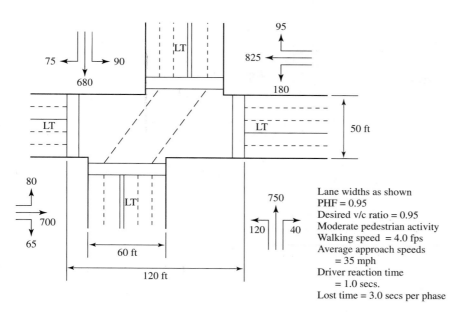

Lane widths as shown
PHF = 0.95
Desired v/c ratio = 0.95
Moderate pedestrian activity
Walking speed = 4.0 fps
Average approach speeds
     = 35 mph
Driver reaction time
     = 1.0 secs.
Lost time = 3.0 secs per phase   **Intersection for Problem 17–8.**

18

Analysis of Signalized Intersections

Signalized intersections are the most complex locations within a traffic system. In Chapter 16, significant principles of signalization were presented. In Chapter 17, a "simple" signal timing methodology was presented. A complete analysis of any signalized intersection, however, requires use of a more complex model in which the many variables affecting its operation can be assessed. In addition, compound signal phasing plans must have a means for assessment in such a model.

The most frequently-used model for signalized intersection analysis is contained in the *Highway Capacity Manual* [1]. The *HCM* is a standard document, and its use in analysis is required by most federal, state, and local agencies. For this reason, it is the model described in detail in this text. It is not, however, the only model in existence. The Australian Road Research Board has developed a model for use in Australia, and an associated computer package, called SIDRA [2,3]. A Canadian model has also been recently developed [4]. In addition, a number of simulation models have been developed that treat intersection and arterial operation in great detail.

These include NETSIM [5], TRANSYT-7F [6], and PASSER [7]. An overview of simulation models and their use is given in Chapter 25.

The models of the *HCM*, as well as those used in Australia and Canada, consist primarily of deterministic analytic algorithms developed from theoretical considerations and/or empirical data and regression analysis. With such models, a problem run many times always produces the same answer, and a user could (at least theoretically) reproduce all results by hand calculation, however difficult and time-consuming. Simulation models are based on simulated behavior of individual vehicles in the traffic stream. Traffic stream parameters are "measured" from the simulated stream flow that results from models of individual behavior. Because of the stochastic nature of such models, the same inputs do not produce exactly the same results after each run, and useful results are virtually always based on an average output of several runs. Further, it is virtually impossible to reproduce the output of simulation models by hand calculation.

The model in the 1994 edition of the *Highway Capacity Manual* (1994 *HCM*) has become sufficiently complex that virtually no practitioners implement the manual by hand calculation, even though detailed worksheets are provided for this purpose. The model includes a number of iterative features, and complex algorithms that would be difficult to implement by hand without error. The *Highway Capacity Software* package [8] is the "official" tool that replicates the procedures of the 1994 *HCM*. It is the most universally accepted tool to replicate the manual's results. In this text, a second package, *HCM-Cinema* [9] is used to illustrate problem solutions. While the HCS package produces only tabular output, *HCM-Cinema* produces graphic output that is quite useful for illustrative purposes. It also provides a link to a NETSIM simulation of the intersection, which provides additional information not obtained from a standard *HCM* signalized intersection analysis. *HCM-Cinema* is a proprietary package of KLD & Associates and the Polytechnic University, and its use herein is by permission.

The 1997 update of the *HCM* will include some detailed changes in the signalized intersection methodology. As this textbook went to print, several issues were still under debate. Anticipated 1997 revisions are briefly described in a section at the end of this chapter. All computations and illustrations are based on the 1994 *HCM*.

Conceptual framework for the 1994 HCM method

Chapter 16 focused on a number of critical principles of signalized intersection operation. All are incorporated into the 1994 *HCM* methodology. The treatment of these and other key concepts in the 1994 *HCM* model are discussed in this section.

A. Critical lane group concept

While Chapter 16 presented the signalization of intersections based on the *critical lane* moving in each phase, the 1994 *HCM* takes a slightly different approach to accomplish the same thing. The model focuses on lane groups operating in stable equilibrium. Where left- and right-turning vehicles share lanes with through vehicles, it is assumed that all lanes on the approach will operate in equilibrium as drivers optimize their own course through the intersection. Exclusive right- or left-turn lanes, however, must be

separately analyzed, as traffic regulations, implemented by signs and markings, prohibit turning vehicles from sharing through lanes and vice-versa. In such cases, exclusive turning lanes may operate very differently from through lanes.

Figure 18-1 illustrates the way the *HCM* treats the issue. Where several lanes operate in equilibrium, the *lane group* is treated as a total entity. Instead of dealing with a critical lane volume, and the saturation flow rate for that lane, the total volume in the lane group is compared to the total saturation flow rate for the lane group. This usage requires, however, that traffic volumes in lane groups of varying size be normalized for comparison.

B. The *v/s* ratio: Normalizing traffic volumes/flow rates

In Chapter 17, signal timing was accomplished by adjusting traffic volumes to account for turning movements. The desired cycle length was found using a default saturation flow rate that accounted for "typical" conditions at signalized intersections. The cycle length determination also accounted for peaking conditions within the hour, and a desired *v/c* ratio during peak operation.

The 1994 *HCM* accounts for eight specific conditions affecting intersection operations: lane width, heavy vehicle presence, grade, parking conditions, local bus blockage, location within the urban area, right turns, and left turns. All of these adjustments, however, are used to modify an *ideal* saturation flow rate to one that represents prevailing conditions for the lane group in question.

Thus, it is impossible to directly compare volumes from various lane groups directly. The prevailing

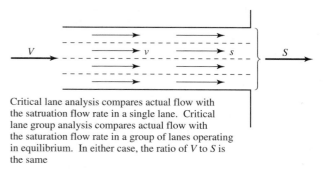

Critical lane analysis compares actual flow with the satruation flow rate in a single lane. Critical lane group analysis compares actual flow with the saturation flow rate in a group of lanes operating in equilibrium. In either case, the ratio of *V* to *S* is the same

Figure 18-1 Illustration of the critical lane group concept.

conditions on each are different, and each lane group may have a different number of lanes. Normalization is accomplished by dividing the actual flow rate, *v*, by the saturation flow rate, *s*, for the lane group. This ratio, *v/s*, is called the *flow ratio*. It is dimensionless, as the units and base conditions for *v* and *s* are the same. The *flow ratio* is used as the measure of intensity of flow in each lane group, and is used as the basis of comparison to identify critical lane groups.

C. Capacity

The 1994 *HCM* model does not yield a value for the capacity of the intersection. Rather, each lane group is separately considered, and a capacity for each is established. One might argue that the capacity of the intersection as a whole could be taken as the sum of the individual lane group capacities. This, however, ignores the fact that traffic demand would normally not reach its highest point on all approaches at the same time. Further, signal timings may change during various periods of the day, yielding significantly different capacities on individual lane groups, and indeed different sums. In effect, the "capacity" of the intersection as a whole is not a useful or relevant concept. The intent of signalization is to allocate sufficient time to various approaches and movements to accommodate demand. "Capacity" is provided to movements to satisfy movement demands.

This concept of capacity should not be confused with the maximum sum of critical lane volumes computed in Chapter 16. The latter considers only critical lanes of the intersection, and depends on a specified cycle length.

D. Level of service

The measure of effectiveness for signalized intersection level of service in the 1994 *HCM* is *average individual stopped-time delay*. A delay value is estimated for each lane group; results are then aggregated to obtain averages for each approach, and finally to obtain an average value for the intersection as a whole. Table 18-1 shows the criteria used.

The use of delay as a measure of effectiveness creates a number of problems in application and interpretation. Chapter 16 presented and reviewed delay models. In order of importance, the three variables affecting delay are cycle length, green time, and *v/c*

Table 18-1 Levels of Service at Signalized Intersections

Level of Service	Stopped Delay per Vehicle (sec)
A	≤5.0
B	5.1 to 15.0
C	15.1 to 25.0
D	25.1 to 40.0
E	40.1 to 60.0
F	≥60.0

[Used with permission of Transportation Research Board, Transportation Research Council, Washington, DC, from *Highway Capacity Manual, Special Report 209,* 3rd Ed., p. 9-6. Copyright © 1994 Transportation Research Board.]

ratio. All of the models, however, assume random arrivals. The variable having the largest impact on delay values is the quality of progression. This is accounted for using an adjustment factor applied to a delay estimate for random arrivals. The importance of this is that the *v/c* ratio has a relatively small effect on delay compared to other variables. This is radically different from level of service analysis of uninterrupted flow facilities, for which a *v/c* ratio of 1.00 has relatively well-defined operating conditions.

In signalized intersection analysis, a delay of over 60 seconds/vehicle (LOS F) may occur on a lane group with a *v/c* ratio under 1.00, even significantly so. Thus, situations arise in which the LOS is F because of high delay, but there is no evidence of a breakdown in flow. High delays occur frequently when cycle lengths are long and the green time for the subject movement is short. Exclusive left-turn phases, for example, often involve short green intervals in a long cycle length. Even if capacity is sufficient, the delays involved could exceed 60 seconds/vehicle. For signalized intersections, therefore, LOS F does not necessarily imply the "failure" of a lane group (i.e., insufficient capacity for existing or projected demand).

The reverse case is also possible, and is more troubling. Because the 1994 *HCM* delay model focuses on the *first* 15-minute interval during which the described flows exist, it is possible to have a lane group with a *v/c* ratio that *exceeds* 1.00, but has a delay under 60 seconds/vehicle (i.e., a LOS other than F). This permits cases in which there is a clear capacity deficiency to be labeled with a LOS that for other facilities implies operation without breakdown. The analyst *must*, therefore, be very careful in interpreting the meaning of a level of service designation for a signalized intersection. The *v/c* ratio must be considered in addition to the level of service to gain a complete view of the lane group's operation.

At its summer meeting in July 1995, the Transportation Research Board Committee on Highway Capacity and Quality of Service (the HCM oversight group), decided to change the definition of level of service F for signalized intersections in the fourth edition of the *HCM* (expected in 2000). LOS F is to be defined as *either* a delay >60.0 sec/veh and/or an implied *v/c* ratio greater than 1.00.

E. Critical analytic concepts

1. Saturation flow rate. In Chapter 16, it was assumed that the saturation headway or saturation flow rate reflecting prevailing conditions was known. One of the principal parts of the 1994 *HCM* model is a methodology for prediction prevailing saturation flow rate based on known traffic parameters. The algorithm takes the form:

$$s_i = s_o N \prod f_i \qquad [18\text{-}1]$$

where: s_i = saturation flow rate for lane group *i* under prevailing conditions, vphg
s_o = ideal saturation flow rate, pchgpl (usually taken to be 1900 pcphgpl)
N = number of lanes in the lane group
f_i = a series of multiplicative adjustment factors to account for a variety of non-ideal conditions

Specific adjustment factors are discussed in a later section. They are a major part of the 1994 *HCM* methodology, and many involve complex models themselves. Note that the algorithm includes *N* as a multiplier, and that *s* is a *total* saturation flow rate for all lanes of the lane group in question.

2. Capacity of a lane group. Saturation flow rate of a lane group is, in effect, the theoretical capacity of the lane group if 100% green time were available. As in Chapter 16, actual capacity of a lane group is related to the proportion of total time that is effectively green for the lane group:

$$c_i = s_i \frac{g_i}{C} \qquad [18\text{-}2]$$

where: c_i = capacity of lane group *i*, vph
s_i = saturation flow rate for lane group *i*, vphg
g_i = effective green time for lane group *i*, sec
C = cycle length, sec

3. *v/c* ratios. In signal analysis, the *v/c* ratio is often referred to as the "degree of saturation," and given the symbol *X*. This is convenient, as the term '*v/c*' appears in many equations that can be simplified using *X*. As in other *HCM* applications, the *v/c* ratio is the ratio of the actual or projected demand flow rate (during the peak period, usually defined as 15 minutes) in a lane group, and the capacity of the lane group.

Capacity is virtually always estimated from Equation [18-2], as it is difficult to measure in the field. Thus, when analyzing an existing facility under existing conditions, a measured flow rate is compared to an estimated capacity. To be meaningful, the existing flow rates should represent *arrival flows*. Often, however, it is easier to count *departure flows*, and this is what many intersection volume studies actually document. Where departure flows are used as the basis for a capacity analysis, a *resulting v/c ratio >1.00 cannot be accepted as accurate*. If the departure count is correct, then the capacity of the lane group must be equal to or greater than the observed flow. When analysis "predicts" a *v/c* ratio in excess of 1.00, only one interpretation is possible: capacity has been underestimated.

For future conditions, forecast flow rates are compared to estimated capacity values. In this case, an analysis resulting in a *v/c* ratio greater than 1.00 indicates that the forecast demand flow exceeds the estimated capacity of the lane group, and a problem will likely exist.

The difference in these two cases is important. The 1994 *HCM* gives a *prediction* of lane group capacity based on nationally observed averages and trends. In a given case, the actual capacity can be somewhat higher or lower. Thus, if a flow in excess of predicted capacity is accurately observed, the estimate of capacity needs to be "adjusted" to reflect the observation. An approach to doing this is discussed later in the chapter. For a future case, *both* the demand flows *and* the capacity are estimated values. Either or both could be high or low. As forecasted flows are, by definition, *arrival flows,* a predicted v/c ratio in excess of 1.00 is a clear indicator of breakdown. It is not, however, a 100% certainty.

The computation of a v/c ratio for a given lane group is done directly, by dividing a flow rate by the estimated capacity. Another expression can be derived by using Equation 18-2 for capacity:

$$X_i = \frac{v_i}{c_i} = \frac{(v/s)_i}{g_i/C} \qquad [18\text{-}3]$$

where: X_i = degree of saturation (v/c ratio) for lane group i, and other variables as previously defined

Since demands are eventually expressed as v/s ratios in the *HCM* model, this form of the equation is often convenient for use.

While the *HCM* does not define the capacity of an intersection as a whole, it does define a *critical v/c ratio* for the intersection. This ratio is defined as the sum of the critical lane group flows divided by the sum of the lane group capacities available to serve them:

$$X_c = \frac{\sum v_{ci}}{\sum \left(s_{ci}\dfrac{g_{ci}}{C} \right)} = \frac{\sum(v/s)_{ci}}{\sum \dfrac{g_{ci}}{C}}$$

where: X_c = critical v/c ratio for the intersection
  v_{ci} = flow rate in critical lane group i, vph
  s_{ci} = saturation flow rate for critical lane group i, vphg
  g_{ci} = effective green time for critical lane group i, sec
  $(v/s)_{ci}$ = flow ratio for critical lane group i
  C = cycle length, sec

The term $\sum g_{ci}/C$ is the total proportion of the cycle length that is effective green for all critical lane groups. Since the definition of a critical lane or lane group is that one and only one such lane or group must be moving during all phases, the only time a critical lane group *is not* moving is during the lost times. Thus, $\sum g_{ci}/C$ can be expressed as:

$$\frac{C - L}{C}$$

where: L = total lost time per cycle, sec

and:

$$X_c = \frac{\sum(v/s)_{ci}}{\dfrac{C - L}{C}} = \sum (v/s)_{ci} \frac{C}{C - L} \qquad [18\text{-}4]$$

This is the form used in the *HCM.*

As the value of X_c varies with cycle length, it is difficult to apply to future cases in which the exact signal timing may not be known. Thus, for future analyses, the *HCM* defines a value of X_c based upon the *maximum* feasible cycle length. This produces the *minimum* feasible value of X_c. For pretimed signals, 120 seconds is the usual maximum cycle length, but this is sometimes exceeded in special situations. For actuated signals, longer cycle lengths are not as rare. Equation [18-4] then becomes:

$$X_{cm} = \sum (v/s)_{ci} \frac{C_{max}}{C_{max} - L} \qquad [18\text{-}5]$$

where: X_{cm} = minimum feasible critical v/c ratio
  C_{max} = maximum feasible cycle length, sec

This latter value is more useful in comparing future scenarios, particularly physical design scenarios. The cycle length assumed is, in effect, held constant for all cases compared. Further, use of the maximum cycle length gives a view of the "best" critical v/c ratio achievable through signal timing, given the physical design and the phase plan specified.

The critical v/c ratio is an important indicator. If the value of X_c (or X_{cm} for future scenarios) is greater than 1.00, then the physical design, phase plan, and cycle length specified *do not provide sufficient capacity for the anticipated or existing critical lane group flows.* More capacity is needed. At a signalized intersection, additional capacity can be provided by any, or a combination of, the following:

• increasing the cycle length
• devising a more efficient phase plan
• adding a critical lane group or groups

As discussed in Chapter 16, increasing the cycle length can add some capacity to the intersection by reducing the total lost time in an hour. This is a limited effect, however, and the capacity gained through increasing cycle length alone is usually a small percentage of what was originally provided.

Devising a more efficient phase plan generally involves looking at protected left-turn phasing. If a permitted left turn has substantial opposing flow, adding a protected phase will often make the plan more efficient. On the other hand, if a protected phase has been provided for a marginal left-turn movement case, it may be more efficient to handle it as a permitted turn. Other issues may involve splitting the left-turn phases for opposing left turns where the volumes per lane are vastly different, as discussed in Chapter 17. Left-turn treatments can have a marked impact on the saturation flow rate, and can therefore have a significant impact on capacity.

In many cases, however, the cycle length and phase plan chosen may already be close to optimal. In these cases, the only way to increase capacity is to add lanes to one or more of the critical approaches. This will reduce the per lane flows on the critical approaches, and therefore the requirement for total green time. In the *HCM* model, this result is reflected somewhat differently. Increasing the number of lanes on a critical approach increases its total saturation flow rate. As the demand flow does not change, the effect is to *lower* the *v/s* ratio for the affected approach(es).

If the critical *v/c* ratio is *less* than 1.00, then the cycle length, phase plan, and physical design provided *are* sufficient to handle the demand flows specified. Having a critical *v/c* ratio under 1.00 *does not*, however, assure that every critical lane group (or even non-critical lane groups) has *v/c* ratios under 1.00. When the critical *v/c* ratio is less than 1.00, but one or more lane groups have *v/c* ratios greater than 1.00, the green time has been misallocated. The situation can be rectified by re-allocating green time among the critical lane groups in proportion to their *v/s* ratios.

F. Effective green times and the application of lost times

In Chapter 16, effective green time was defined as:

$$g_i = G_i + Y_i - t_L$$

where: g_i = effective green time for phase *i*, sec
 G_i = actual green time for phase *i*, sec
 Y_i = sum of the yellow plus all red intervals for phase *i*, sec
 t_L = sum of the start-up plus clearance lost times for phase *i*, sec

In terms of effective times, the signal cycle is divided into effective green time (g) and effective red time (r). To simplify the interpretation of t_L, the *HCM* model assumes that all of the lost time occurs *at the beginning of the phase*, i.e., that it is all start-up lost time. This is done to simplify the modeling process, and because field studies show that as much as 75% of actual lost times do occur as start-up losses.

Figure 18-2a illustrates the relationships among actual green times, effective green times, and lost times as assumed in the *HCM* model. For a given movement, the signal is effectively red during the actual red time and the lost times, which are applied at the beginning of the actual green phase.

Figure 18-2b illustrates the application of lost times to the beginning of a phase. While in many cases this is a simple exercise, it is more complex in cases of overlapping phases. In the figure, a lead-lag phasing is illustrated. Lost times are applied to the EB LT and EB TR movements in Phase 1a, because they begin in that phase. Lost times are applied to WB LT and WB TR movements in Phase 1b for the same reason. No lost times, however, are applied to any EB movement in Phase 1b, as these are continued from Phase 1a. In Phase 1b, the lost time applied to WB movements is additional effective green time for EB movements. In Phase 1c, no lost times are applied, since both of the WB movements were initiated in Phase 1b. Note that

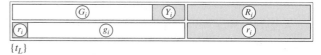

(a) Effective green and red times illustrated

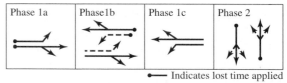

— Indicates lost time applied

(b) Lost time applied to beginning of a phase

Figure 18-2 Relationship among actual green times, effective green time and lost times in the *HCM* model. [Used with permission of Transportation Research Board, National Research Council, Washington, DC, from *Highway Capacity Manual, Special Report 209*, 3rd Ed., pp. 9-4–9-5. Copyright © 1994 Transportation Research Board.]

no lost time is applied when the left-turn movements go from permitted to protected or vice-versa. In Phase 2, all NB and SB begin, and lost times are applied here.

The proper application of lost times is an important concept in the *HCM* model. In Figure 18-2b, *three* sets of lost times are applied over four overlapping phases. The lost time for some movements in the illustrated phase plan, however, is effective green time for others. Accurate determination of capacity, *v/c* ratios, and delays for various lane groups requires accurate determination of effective green times. A systematic means of applying lost times, as illustrated, is an important part of doing so.

The 1994 HCM model

In many of its elements, the 1994 *HCM* model for signalized intersection analysis is relatively straightforward, building on many of the conceptual treatments described in Chapter 16. The model becomes complex when opposed left turns are involved. Permitted or partially permitted left-turn phasing requires that the complex interaction between left turns and opposing flows be carefully described and modeled. The models used for this must take into account many variables, and some aspects must be iterative.

Figure 18-3 illustrates the structure of the 1994 *HCM* model. The analysis methodology is modular, and works from a fully specified signalized intersection (volumes, geometrics, signal timing) to produce delay estimates and level of service determinations for each lane group, approach, and for the intersection as a whole. Alternative physical designs and signal timings can be analyzed on a trial-and-error basis, using appropriate software.

Recent surveys [9] indicate that very few users of the 1994 *HCM* signalized intersection methodology implement the model by hand computation. The vast majority use the HCS package or other appropriate software. The complexity of the opposed left-turn model component makes manual computation difficult and time-consuming. This text will illustrate one sample problem with all of its manual computations, utilizing worksheets provided in the 1994 *HCM*. For other sample problems, the HCM-Cinema program (described previously) will be used for illustrative purposes.

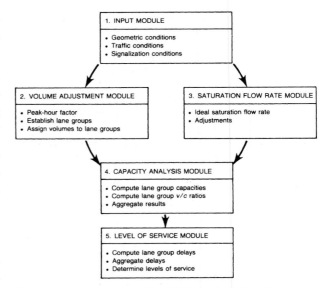

Figure 18-3 Structure of the *HCM* model. [Used with permission of Transportation Research Board, National Research Council, Washington, DC, from *Highway Capacity Manual, Special Report 209,* 3rd Ed., p. 9-9. Copyright © 1994 Transportation Research Board.]

A. Input module

The input module is simply a set of conditions that must be specified for analysis to proceed. It is the parametric description of the signalized intersection to be analyzed. Table 18-2 lists the parameters that must be specified to implement the 1994 *HCM* model, along with default values that may be used where specific data is not available. Note, however, that the use of default values will affect the accuracy of the results. Field or projected values should be used for all parameters whenever possible.

Most of the variables listed in Table 18-2 have been previously defined. Some are new, and some require additional discussion:

1. *Area Type:* The location of the intersection must be classified as being in the central business district (CBD) or not (Other). The calibration study conducted for the 1985 *HCM* [10] indicated that intersections in CBDs have saturation flow rates approximately 10% lower than similar intersections in other areas. This has been a controversial issue, as the definition of CBD is quite relative. Is the business district of a small satellite community

Table 18-2 Input Data Needs for Signalized Intersection Analysis

Type of Condition	Parameter	Symbol Used	Recommended Default Value(s)
Geometric	Area type	CBD, other	Other
	Number of lanes	N	(No default should be used)
	Lane width, ft	W	12 feet
	Grades, %	$\%G$	Level (0%)
	Existence of exclusive LT or RT lanes	(No symbol)	(No default should be used)
	Length of storage bay, LT/RT lanes, ft	L_s	(No default should be used)
	Parking conditions	Yes, no	No Parking
Traffic conditions	Volumes by movement, vph	V	(No default should be used)
	Ideal saturation flow rate, pcphgpl	s_o	1900 pcphgpl
	Peak hour factor	PHF	0.90
	Percent heavy vehicles, %	$\%HV$	2%
	Conflicting pedestrian flow, ped/hr	$PEDS$	NONE (0); LOW (50); MODERATE (200); HIGH (400)
	Local bus volume, buses/hr	N_B	0/hr
	Parking activity (if parking exists), mvts/hr	N_M	20/hr (if parking exists)
	Arrival type (1–6)	AT	Lane groups w/TH mvts—3 (uncoordinated) Late groups w/TH mvts—4 (coordinated) Lane groups w/o TH mvts—3
	Proportion of vehicles arriving on green	P	Use algorithm
Signalization conditions	Cycle length, sec	C	60–120 sec
	Green time, sec	G	Use Ch 19 procedure to allocate green times
	Yellow change interval, sec	y	$y + AR = 4$ sec
	All-red clearance interval, sec	AR	$y + AR = 4$ sec
	Actuated or pretimed operation	A or P	Pretimed
	Pedestrian push button?	YES or NO	(No default should be used)
	Minimum pedestrian green	G_p	Use algorithm
	Phase plan	(No symbol)	(No default should be used)
	Lost time per phase, sec	t_L	3 sec/phase

[Used with permission of Transportation Research Board, National Research Council, Washington, DC, from *Highway Capacity Manual, Special Report 209,* 3rd Ed., pp. 9-10–9-11. Copyright © 1994 Transportation Research Board.]

a CBD, or should it be treated as an "other" location with respect to the nearby major city? In general, if drivers are "used to" driving in a big city CBD, all locations in satellite communities would be classified as "other." In an isolated rural community, even a small business area would be classified as a CBD. The general theory is that the busier environment of the CBD causes drivers to be more cautious and less efficient than in other areas.

2. *Parking Conditions and Parking Activity:* If a lane group has curb parking within 250 ft of the stop line, the existence of a parking lane is assumed. Where such parking exists, the right-hand lane is disrupted for two reasons: (a) side-friction from parked vehicles, and (b) disruption due to vehicles entering and leaving curb parking spaces. Where parking exists, the number of parking movements per hour occurring within 250 ft of the stop line is an important variable. Any vehicle entering OR leaving a curb parking space constitutes a "movement." The number of movements can be counted in the field, estimated from parking duration and meter regulations, or from a default value.

A parking lane only affects the lane group in which it is included. Thus, a separate left-turn lane group on a street with parking is unaffected by parking, while the through + right-turn lane group is affected.

3. *Conflicting Pedestrian Flow:* Right-turning vehicles turn through the adjacent pedestrian crosswalk. The flow of pedestrians impedes right-turning vehicles and influences the saturation flow rate for the lane group in question. To accurately reflect this phenomenon, the pedestrian flow rate in each conflicting crosswalk is needed. Pedestrian flows between 1700 ped/hr and 2100 ped/hr in a crosswalk have been shown to fully block right-turners during the green phase.

4. *Local Bus Volume:* In signalized intersection analysis, a "local bus" is one that stops to pick up and/or discharge passengers within the intersection at either a near or a far side bus stop. Stopped buses disrupt the flow of other vehicles and influence the saturation flow rate of the affected lane group. A bus that passes through the intersection without stopping to pick up or discharge passengers is considered to be a "heavy vehicle."

5. *Arrival Type:* The single most important factor influencing delay predictions is the quality of progression. The 1994 *HCM* model uses "arrival type" to account for this impact. Six arrival types are defined as follows (1994 *HCM*, page 9-10):

Arrival Type 1: Dense platoon, containing over 80% of the lane group volume, arriving at the start of the red phase. This AT is representative of network links that may experience *very poor* progression quality as a result of conditions such as overall network signal optimization.

Arrival Type 2: Moderately dense platoon arriving in the middle of the red phase or dispersed platoon, containing 40% to 80% of the lane group volume, arriving throughout the red phase. This AT is representative of *unfavorable progression* on two-way arterials.

Arrival Type 3: Random arrivals in which the main platoon contains less than 40% of the lane group volume. This AT is representative of operations at *isolated and non-interconnected* signalized intersections characterized by highly dispersed platoons. It may also be used to represent coordinated operation in which the benefits of progression are minimal.

Arrival Type 4: Moderately dense platoon arriving in the middle of the green phase or dispersed platoon, containing 40% to 80% of the lane group volume, arriving throughout the green phase. This AT is representative of *favorable progression* quality on a two-way arterial.

Arrival Type 5: Dense to moderately dense platoon, containing over 80% of the lane group volume, arriving at the start of the green phase. This AT is representative of *highly favorable progression* quality, which may occur on routes with low to moderate side-street entries and which receive high-priority treatment in the signal timing plan design.

Arrival Type 6: This arrival type is reserved for *exceptional progression* quality on routes with near-ideal progression characteristics. It is representative of very dense platoons progressing over a number of closely spaced intersections with minimal or negligible side-street entries.

Arrival types were originally defined only in verbal terms. It was expected that traffic engineers would assign an appropriate type based on general observation of field conditions (for existing cases) and/or perusal of time-space diagrams (for future cases). To provide for a numerical guideline, the *platoon ratio* was created. The platoon ratio is defined as the proportion of vehicles arriving on green (P) divided by the g/C ratio for the lane group under study:

$$R_p = \frac{P}{g/C} = P\frac{C}{g} \qquad [18\text{-}5]$$

where: R_p = platoon ratio
P = proportion of total lane group vehicles arriving on green
C = cycle length, sec
g = effective green time, sec

Subsequent research [11] was able to establish a relationship between the platoon ratio and arrival type, as shown in Table 18-3.

Random arrivals should logically result in $R_p = 1.00$, as the proportion of vehicles arriving on green should be equal to the g/C ratio. Ratios higher than 1.00 reflect favorable progression situations, while ratios lower than 1.00 reflect unfavorable situations. The magnitude of the difference between R_p and 1.00 is a measure of the degree of favorability or unfavorability.

Table 18-3   Relationship Between Platoon Ratio and Arrival Type

Arrival Type	Range of Platoon Ratio, R_p	Default Value R_p	Progression Quality
1	≤0.50	0.333	Very poor
2	>0.50 and ≤0.85	0.667	Unfavorable
3	>0.85 and ≤1.15	1.000	Random arrivals
4	>1.15 and ≤1.50	1.333	Favorable
5	>1.50 and ≤2.00	1.667	Highly favorable
6	>2.00	2.000	Exceptional

The platoon ratio is an important variable, given that it determines the arrival type, which in turn has a significant impact on delay estimates and level of service. The proportion of vehicles arriving on the green may be generally estimated through field measurements or by considering an anticipated time-space diagram of the progression together with information of side street entries and exits.

When comparing different signalized intersection designs and timing plans, it is important that a common arrival type be used. High delays should not be simply dismissed or mitigated by presuming an improved progression quality. The many constraints on progression quality must be carefully studied to determine whether such an improvement is practical or cost-effective. For future scenarios, the 1994 *HCM* recommends that arrival type 3 be assumed for comparative purposes.

The 1994 *HCM* provides a worksheet on which all of the required input information can be summarized. It is shown in Figure 18-4.

B. Volume adjustment module

The volume adjustment module is, in some ways, a misnomer. In the 1994 *HCM*, virtually all "adjustments" are applied to saturation flow rate, not to volumes. Nevertheless, several important determinations and calculations are done in this module.

1. Conversion of hourly volumes to peak rates of flow. The 1994 *HCM* model, like most other procedures in the *HCM*, focuses on operational analysis of the peak 15-minute period within the hour of interest. Since demand volumes are entered as *full-hour vol-*

umes, each must be adjusted to reflect the peak 15-minute interval using the peak hour factor:

$$v_p = \frac{V}{PHF} \qquad [18\text{-}6]$$

where: v_p = flow rate during the peak 15-minutes of the hour, vph
V = hourly volume, vph
PHF = peak hour factor

Use of this conversion methodology assumes that all movements of the intersection *peak during the same 15-minute period.* This is a conservative assumption, but is rarely reflective of actual conditions.

An alternative to this analytic estimation of peak flow rates for existing cases is to record volume data in 5- to 15-minute intervals. The actual data can then be examined for the 15-minute period that represents the most intense traffic. Fifteen minute volumes in this period can then be multiplied by 4 to obtain rates of flow in vph. If peak 15-minute flow rates are used as inputs, instead of hourly volumes, the PHF used is set equal to 1.00—a value that produces no adjustment.

2. Establish lane groups for analysis. As noted earlier, the 1994 *HCM* model focuses on lane groups operating in equilibrium. Any set of lanes across which drivers may optimize their operation through unimpeded lane selection will operate in equilibrium conditions determined by those drivers. Any such set of lanes is analyzed as a single cohesive lane group.

In practical terms, an approach is considered to be a single lane group, except for cases of exclusive left- and or right-turn lanes. Where exclusive lanes are provided for turning vehicles, through vehicles may

INPUT MODULE WORKSHEET

Intersection: _____ Date: _____

Analyst: _____ Time Period Analyzed: _____ Area Type: ☐ CBD ☐ Other

Project No.: _____ City/State: _____

VOLUME AND GEOMETRICS

SB TOTAL

N/S STREET

WB TOTAL

LOST TIME PER PHASE (sec.): ☐

IDENTIFY IN DIAGRAM

1. Volumes
2. Lanes, lane widths
3. Movements by lane
4. Parking (PKG) locations
5. Bay storage lengths
6. Islands (physical or painted)
7. Bus stops

E/W STREET

EB TOTAL

NB TOTAL

TRAFFIC AND ROADWAY CONDITIONS

Approach	Grade (%)	% HV	Adj. Pkg. Lane		Buses N_b	PHF	Conf. Peds. (peds./hr)	Pedestrian Button		Arr. Type
			Y or N	N_m				Y or N	Min. Timing	
EB										
WB										
NB										
SB										

Grade: + up, – down
HV: veh. with more an 4 wheels
N_m: pkg. maneuvers/hr

N_b: buses stopping/hr
PHF: peak-hour factor
Conf. Peds.: Conflicting peds./hr

Min. Timing: min. green for pedestrian crossing
Arr. Type: Type 1-6, or P

PHASING

D I A G R A M

Timing	G = Y + AR =	G = Y + AR =	G = Y + AR =	G = Y + AR =	G = Y + AR =	G = Y + AR =	G = Y + AR =	G = Y + AR =

_____↗ Protected turns ___ ↗ Permitted turns - - - - - - Pedestrians Cycle Length _____ Sec.

Updated October 1994

Figure 18-4 Input module worksheet from the 1994 *HCM*. [Used with permission of Transportation Research Board, National Research Council, Washington, DC, from *Highway Capacity Manual, Special Report 209,* 3rd Ed., p. 9-36. Copyright © 1994 Transportation Research Board.]

not elect to use them, nor can turning vehicles elect to use through lanes. No equilibrium among turning vehicles and through vehicles can be reached. Where an exclusive turning lane exists, it must be analyzed as a separate lane group for analysis.

An intersection approach can, therefore, be analyzed as one, two, or three lane groups, as illustrated in Figure 18-5.

There is one complication to the establishment of lane groups: the *defacto left-turn lane.* Even where no exclusive left-turn lane is provided, it is possible that there are enough left-turning vehicles to completely occupy the left lane of the approach. This happens most often in cases where high opposing flows make permitted left turns very inefficient. With significant blockage to through vehicles in the left lane, the extreme is reached when *no* through vehicles use the left lane, even though there is no regulation to prevent them from doing so. In such cases, the left lane is a *defacto left-turn lane* and should be established as a separate lane group for analysis.

One lane group: All turns made from shared lanes with through vehicles.

Two lane groups: Exclusive LT lane, and shared TH/RT lanes.

Two lane groups: Shared LT/TH lanes and exclusive RT lane.

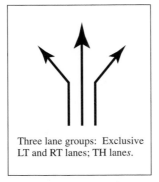

Three lane groups: Exclusive LT and RT lanes; TH lanes.

Figure 18-5   Lane group options for an intersection approach.

Unfortunately, there is no easy way to determine when this is going to occur, unless it is observed in the field. Thus, the 1994 *HCM* procedure is begun with the assumption that no such lane exists. Later in the methodology, the proportion of left-turning vehicles in the left lane (P_L) is estimated. If the estimated value of P_L is 1.00 (or higher—analytically possible, but physically impossible), the lane is established as an exclusive left-turn lane, and the problem reworked. This is one of the iterative features of the methodology that dissuades traffic engineers from doing manual solutions.

3. Lane utilization adjustment. The last adjustment made to volume is for unequal lane use. Where lane groups have more than one lane, equilibrium may not imply *equal* use of lanes. The 1994 *HCM* allows for an *optimal* adjustment to account for this.

$$v = v_p U \qquad [18\text{-}7]$$

where: v = flow rate adjusted for unequal lane use, vph

v_p = flow rate in peak 15-minute period unadjusted for lane use, vph

U = lane adjustment factor

The lane utilization factor adjusts the total lane group flow rate such that when divided by the number of lanes in the group, the result is the rate of flow expected in the most heavily-used lane.

The 1994 *HCM* makes use of this adjustment optional, as there is significant controversy over its meaning and accuracy. Many traffic engineers contend that as *v/c* ratios on a lane group approach 1.00, the distribution of flow over available lanes tends to equalize. Unfortunately, research results are mixed, and have not resolved this issue.

The meaning of the factor is also important. When a lane utilization adjustment is used, the resulting *v/c* ratios and delays reflect conditions in the most heavily-used lane of the group. This is particularly difficult where delay is concerned, as the delay/ vehicle *cannot* be multiplied by either the adjusted or unadjusted lane group flow rate to estimate aggregate delay.

If the factor is not used (i.e., set equal to 1.00), the resulting *v/c* ratios and delays reflect average conditions over the lane group. In this case, delay/vehicle *can* be multiplied by the lane group flow rate to obtain aggregate delay. The lane utilization factors recommended for use are shown in Table 18-4.

To illustrate the use and meaning of the lane utilization factor, consider a 3-lane through lane group serving a flow rate of 1000 vph. From Table 18-4, the appropriate lane utilization factor is 1.10. The adjusted flow rate would then be 1000 × 1.10 = 1100 vph. This means that the most heavily-used lane in the lane group is expected to serve 1100/3 = 367 vph, which is 36.7% of the actual demand of 1000 vph.

While use of the factor is optional, its use (or not) must be consistent when comparing designs and signal plans, or when various traffic growth scenarios are being analyzed.

4. Worksheet. Figure 18-6 shows the worksheet for the Volume Adjustment Module. The worksheet is useful in illustrating the order of computations. All intersection movements are entered in column 3 as hourly volumes or peak flow rates determined from field observations. The appropriate peak hour factor is entered in column 4, and may be different for different approaches and movements. If column 3 entries are peak flow rates, a value of 1.00 is used. Column 5 is used to enter peak flow rates computed using Equation [18-6]. In column 6, lane groups are established for analysis, using the rules discussed previously. Arrow indications are used. Where turning movements use shared lanes, they are combined into the "TH" row of the worksheet. In column 7, lane

group flow rates are computed by adding the movement flow rates included in each lane group. The number of lanes in the lane group is entered in column 8, and the lane utilization factor based on this is in column 9. In column 10, the lane group flow rate is multiplied by the lane utilization factor. In column 11, the proportion of left- and right-turns in each lane group is entered. These values are used in later computational steps.

C. Saturation flow rate module

The saturation flow rate module is the most important part of the 1994 *HCM* model. In this module, the prevailing total saturation flow rate for each lane group is estimated using the following algorithm:

$$s = s_o N f_w f_{HV} f_g f_p f_{bb} f_a f_{RT} f_{LT} \qquad [18\text{-}8]$$

where: s = total saturation flow rate for lane group, vphg
s_o = ideal saturation flow rate per lane, pcphgpl, usually taken to be 1900 pcphgpl
N = number of lanes in the lane group
f_w = adjustment factor for lane width
f_{HV} = adjustment factor for heavy vehicle presence
f_g = adjustment factor for grade
f_p = adjustment factor for parking conditions

Table 18-4   Lane Utilization Factors

Lane Group Movements	Number of Lanes in Lane Group	% of Traffic in Most Heavily Used Lane	Lane Utilization Factor, U
Through and shared turns	1	100.0	1.00
	2	52.5	1.05
	3	36.7	1.10
Exclusive left-turn lanes	1	100.0	1.00
	2	51.5	1.03
Exclusive right-turn lanes	1	100.0	1.00
	2	56.5	1.13

Note: Where greater numbers of lanes exist, field studies should be conducted to determine the appropriate value of *U*.

1 Appr.	2 Mvt.	3 Mvt. Volume (vph)	4 Peak Hour Factor PHF	5 Flow Rate v_p (vph) [3]/[4]	6 Lane Group	7 Flow Rate In Lane Group v_g (vph)	8 Number of Lanes N	9 Lane Utilization Factor U Table 18-4	10 Adj Flow v (vph) [7]*[9]	11 Prop. of LT or RT P_{LT} or P_{RT}
EB	LT									
	TH									
	RT									
WB	LT									
	TH									
	RT									
NB	LT									
	TH									
	RT									
SB	LT									
	TH									
	RT									

Figure 18-6 Volume adjustment worksheet. [Used with permission of Transportation Research Board, National Research Council, Washington, DC, from *Highway Capacity Manual, Special Report 209,* 3rd Ed., p. 9-38. Copyright © 1994 Transportation Research Board.]

f_{bb} = adjustment factor for local bus blockage
f_a = adjustment factor for area type
f_{RT} = adjustment factor for right-turning vehicles
f_{LT} = adjustment factor for left-turning vehicles

The *eight* adjustment factors each adjust the saturation flow rate to account for one prevailing condition that may differ from the defined ideal conditions. The models for six of these adjustment factors are relatively straightforward and easy to apply. The adjustment for right turns must deal with the complexity of the interaction between turning vehicles and pedestrians in the conflicting crosswalk. While somewhat complex, this adjustment is relatively easy to apply.

It is the last adjustment, for left-turning vehicles, that introduces several layers of great complexity. Left turns may be made from exclusive or shared lanes, and may have protected, permitted, or compound signalization. All of these cases are quite different, and require different analytic treatment. Where permitted or compound phasing is involved, the dynamic relationship among turning vehicles, opposing flow, and other vehicles in the lane group affected by left-turners cannot be simply described in analytic terms.

The sections that follow discuss the models used to determine each of these adjustment factors.

1. Lane width adjustment factor. The ideal lane width is defined as 12 feet, and it is for this value that the ideal saturation flow rate is defined. When narrower lanes exist, the increased side-friction between adjacent vehicles causes drivers to be more cautious, and increases headways (i.e., reduces saturation flow rate). It has also been found that wider lanes allow drivers to be more aggressive, reducing headways and increasing saturation flow rates. The model used in the 1994 *HCM* is:

$$f_w = 1.00 + \frac{W - 12}{30} \qquad [18\text{-}8]$$

where: f_w = adjustment factor for lane width
W = lane width, ft

Note that where $W < 12$ feet, a negative adjustment occurs; when $W > 12$ feet, the adjustment is positive. When $W = 12$ feet, the factor becomes 1.00. The model is empirical, i.e., it is based on field observation of saturation flow rates in lanes of varying width. The adjustment is modest, in that for each foot of lane width below or above the standard, 1/30th of the saturation flow rate is lost or gained. Values of the factor resulting from Equation [18-8] are shown in Table 18-5.

Where lane widths exceed 16 feet, it is assumed that two lanes exist with ½ of the width. In fact, when demand on such lane groups approaches capacity, drivers will make two lanes.

2. Heavy vehicle adjustment factor. The ideal saturation flow rate is stated in terms of pcphgpl, i.e., no heavy vehicles in the traffic stream. At a signalized intersection, any vehicle with more than four wheels on the ground during normal operation is considered to be a "heavy vehicle." Excluded from this category are local buses making stops within the confines of the intersection (either near or far side) to pick up or discharge passengers. An adjustment for the presence of these vehicles is implemented using a separate adjustment factor.

The basic algorithm for the heavy vehicle adjustment factor is the same as that used on other types of facilities:

$$f_{HV} = \frac{1}{1 + P_{HV}(E_{HV} - 1)} \qquad [18\text{-}9]$$

where: f_{HV} = heavy vehicle adjustment factor
P_{HV} = proportion of heavy vehicles in the lane group (decimal)
E_{HV} = passenger car equivalent for one heavy vehicle

For signalized intersections, the passenger car equivalent for one heavy vehicle, E_{HV}, is taken to be a constant value: 2.00. Note that E_{HV} does not vary with grade conditions, as is the case for uninterrupted flow facilities. There is a separate adjustment factor for grades at a signalized intersection. This factor assumes that *all* vehicles, not just heavy vehicles, are affected by grade.

Table 18-6 shows the adjustment factors that result from Equation [18-9].

3. Grade adjustment factor. In the analysis of uninterrupted flow, the effect of grades is always combined with heavy vehicle adjustments. Such procedures assume that the effect of grades is on the operation of heavy vehicles only, and that it is the heavy vehicles that affect other vehicles in the traffic stream.

At signalized intersections, the grade adjustment deals with the impact of an approach grade on the saturation headway (and therefore flow rate) at which vehicles cross the stop line. Studies have shown that the effect is not limited to heavy vehicles. A grade will affect the departure operation of passenger cars, whether or not there are heavy vehicles present. For this reason, a separate adjustment factor is necessary. The algorithm for the adjustment factor, shown in Table 18-7, is:

$$f_g = 1 - \frac{G}{2} \qquad [18\text{-}10]$$

Table 18-5 Lane Width Adjustment Factors, f_w

W (ft)	8	9	10	11	12	13	14	15	16
f_w	0.867	0.900	0.933	0.967	1.000	1.033	1.067	1.100	1.133

[Used with permission of Transportation Research Board, National Research Council, Washington, DC, from *Highway Capacity Manual, Special Report 209*, 3rd Ed., p. 9-14. Copyright © 1994 Transportation Research Board.]

Table 18-6   Adjustment Factor for Heavy Vehicles (f_{HV})

Percent Heavy Vehicles, %HV	Heavy Vehicle Factor, f_{HV}
0	1.000
2	0.980
4	0.962
6	0.943
8	0.926
10	0.909
15	0.870
20	0.833
25	0.800
30	0.769
35	0.741
40	0.714
45	0.690
50	0.667
75	0.571
100	0.500

4. Parking adjustment factor. The parking adjustment factor accounts for two deleterious effects on flow in a lane group containing a curb parking lane within 250 ft of the stop line: (a) the existence of the parking lane creates additional side friction for vehicles in the adjacent lane, thereby affecting the saturation flow rate, and (2) vehicles entering or leaving curb parking spaces within 250 ft of the stop line will disrupt flow in the adjacent lane, which will further affect the saturation flow rate. Because of the second effect, it is important to know the number of movements into and out of parking spaces within the 250 ft limit. As noted previously, each maneuver entering or leaving a parking space is counted as a separate *park-*

ing movement. The number of such movements per hour is given the symbol N_m.

It is generally assumed that the primary effect of a parking lane is on flow in the immediately adjacent lane. If the number of lanes in the lane group is more than one, it is assumed that the adjustment for other lanes is 1.00, as illustrated in Figure 18-8.

The algorithm for the parking factor is based on the following: a) the lane adjacent to the parking lane suffers a 10% loss in saturation flow rate due to the mere existence of the parking lane, b) the total adjustment due to parking, applied *only to the lane adjacent to the parking lane,* is P, and c) there is no adjustment to other lanes in a multilane group (i.e., factor = 1.00.) Then, where parking exists:

$$P = 0.90 - \frac{N_m}{200} \qquad [18\text{-}11]$$

and:

$$f_p = \frac{(N-1) + P}{N} = \frac{P + N - 1}{N} \qquad [18\text{-}12]$$

Equations [18-11] and [18-12] can be combined to obtain a single expression for the parking adjustment factor:

$$f_p = \frac{N - 0.1 - (N_m/200)}{N} \qquad [18\text{-}13]$$

where: f_p = parking adjustment factor
 N = number of lanes in the lane group
 N_m = number of parking movements in and out of adjacent parking spaces within 250 ft of the stop line, mvts/hr

This equation is subject to three conditions:

- $f_p = 1.00$ where no adjacent parking lane exists in the lane group.

Table 18-7   Grade Adjustment Factor, f_g

% Grade	≤−6	−4	−2	0	+2	+4	+6	+8	≥+10
G (decimal)	≤−0.06	−0.04	−0.02	0.00	+0.02	+0.04	+0.06	+0.08	≥+0.10
f_g	1.030	1.020	1.010	1.000	0.990	0.980	0.970	0.960	0.950

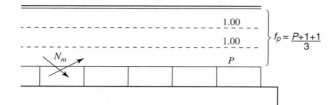

Figure 18-7 Parking adjustment factor illustrated.

- The maximum practical value of N_m is 180 mvts/hr; at this value, the factor becomes 0.05; no higher value may be entered into the equation.
- On a one-way street with parking on both sides of the street, the total number of parking movements on both sides is used.

Table 18-8 illustrates the values of f_p that result from Equation [18-13].

5. Local bus blockage adjustment factor. As noted previously, buses that stop within the confines of the intersection to pick up and/or discharge passengers must be separately considered. The 1994 *HCM* provides *two* different methodologies for considering local buses, one of which requires field studies for calibration to any given situation.

A general adjustment factor is prescribed for the majority of "ordinary" bus stop situations. "Ordinary" is not well-defined in the *HCM*, but might be interpreted as a relatively small number of local buses stopping ($0 \leq N_B \leq 40$), each picking up or dropping off no more than a handful of passengers. Unfortunately, the *HCM* methodology does not preclude using the general adjustment factor for more extreme cases, for which it invariably underestimates the deleterious effect of local buses.

The model, in a manner similar to the parking adjustment factor, assumes that the only lane affected by local buses is the right-most lane. For general cases, there is no differentiation between buses stopping *in* a travel lane and buses pulling into and out of a stop *not* in a travel lane (such as in a parking lane). It is assumed that there is no effect on other lanes, i.e., the factor for other lanes is 1.00. The algorithm for the general adjustment factor is:

$$B = 1.000 - \frac{N_B}{250} \qquad [18\text{-}14]$$

and:

$$f_{bb} = \frac{(N-1) + B}{N} = \frac{B + N - 1}{N} \qquad [18\text{-}15]$$

which may be combined as:

$$f_{bb} = \frac{N - (N_B/250)}{N} \qquad [18\text{-}16]$$

where: f_{bb} = local bus blockage adjustment factor
B = local bus blockage factor, as applied only to the right-most lane of the lane group
N = number of lanes in the affected lane group
N_B = number of buses stopping per hour

Table 18-9 shows the general adjustment factors that arise from the use of Equation [18-16].

		No. of Parking Mvts per Hour, N_m				
No. of Lanes in Group, N	**No. Parking in Group**	**0**	**10**	**20**	**30**	**40**
1	1.000	0.900	0.850	0.800	0.750	0.700
2	1.000	0.950	0.925	0.900	0.875	0.850
3	1.000	0.967	0.950	0.933	0.917	0.900
>3	1.000	Apply Eq. [18-13] directly				

Table 18-8 Parking Adjustment Factor, f_p

Table 18-9 Local Bus Blockage Adjustment Factor: General Case, f_{bb}

No. of Lanes in Group	No. of Local Buses Stopping per Hour, N_B				
	0	10	20	30	40*
1	1.000	0.960	0.920	0.880	0.840
2	1.000	0.980	0.960	0.940	0.920
3	1.000	0.987	0.973	0.960	0.947
<3	1.000	Apply Eq. [18-16] directly			

The general adjustment factors of Table 18-9 should not be applied where there exists an unusually high number of buses stopping (>40 buses/hr), or where large numbers of passengers are boarding and/or alighting, such as at terminal stops, or at transfer points with rail and/or other bus lines. In such cases, each bus occupies a greater amount of time in the stop than anticipated by the general factors.

In such cases, limited field studies should be conducted to measure *bus dwell times,* that is, the average amount of time that a bus spends in the stop discharging or picking up passengers. If the bus is stopping in a moving traffic lane, then it blocks the lane for this time, and for the time needed to decelerate and accelerate. If the bus stops out of a moving lane, the dwell time is of little interest, and the blockage involves the bus pulling into and out of the off-line stop from and into the adjacent moving lane.

The amount of time that the right-most lane of traffic is blocked due to local buses is given by:

$$T_{LB} = 3 - 4 \text{ sec/bus} \qquad [18-17]$$

where the bus stops out of a moving lane, and:

$$T_{LB} = \left(\frac{g}{C}\right)(D + L) \qquad [18-18]$$

where the bus stops in a moving lane of traffic.

where: T_{LB} = time lost per bus, sec/bus
D = dwell time per bus, sec
L = accel/decel time per bus, usually 2–3 sec/bus

g = effective green time for the lane group, sec
C = cycle length, sec

The inclusion of the g/C factor accounts for buses that stop to discharge and/or pick up passengers during the "red" phase, when they would have to stop anyway. If the ideal saturation headway is 3600/1900 = 1.89 sec, then each local bus may be said to have a passenger car equivalent of:

$$E_{LB} = \frac{T_{LB}}{1.89} \qquad [18-19]$$

Using the standard formula for converting an equivalent to an adjustment factor:

$$f_{bb} = \frac{1}{1 + P_{LB}(E_{LB} - 1)} \qquad [18-20]$$

where: f_{bb} = local bus blockage adjustment factor
E_{LB} = passenger car equivalent of one local bus
P_{LB} = proportion of total lane group flow consisting of local buses, in decimal form (N_B/v)

While this second approach does a better job of modeling the impact of extraordinary local bus operations, it still ignores the difference between near side and far side bus stops, a consideration included in the 1965 *HCM*. In major cities with significant local bus operations, the additional effort of field studies is a worthwhile investment in a more accurate treatment of the signalized intersection. Where bus stop location is a significant issue, a separate study of near-side vs. far-side bus stop operations may also be useful.

6. Area type adjustment factor. This adjustment is one of the more controversial features of the 1994 *HCM* signalized intersection model. Data collected as the 1985 *HCM* was prepared suggest that saturation flow rates in CBDs tended to be 10% less than similar intersections in other parts of the urban or suburban area. The data were, however, not statistically conclusive, and there is some question as to whether this factor is a surrogate for impacts not accounted for in the *HCM* model, or whether it double-counts impacts taken into account elsewhere in the model.

Its use is *not,* however, optional. There is no algorithm for this adjustment, as it depends only on the location of the signalized intersection: either CBD, or other.

Table 18-10 shows the factors used.

7. Right-turn adjustment factor. Right-turning vehicles, in general, conflict with pedestrians using the adjacent crosswalk, as illustrated in Figure 18-8.

While it might appear that modeling this interaction should be relatively straightforward, the problem is complicated by the fact that right turns may be handled under seven different scenarios, which are enumerated in the *HCM*:

1. Exclusive RT lane with protected RT phase (no pedestrians)
2. Exclusive RT lane with permitted RT phase
3. Exclusive RT lane with protected + permitted RT phase
4. Shared RT lane with protected RT phase
5. Shared RT lane with permitted RT phase
6. Shared RT lane with protected + permitted RT phase
7. Single lane approach (permitted phasing assumed)

While all seven cases occur, the majority of signalized intersections fall into Case 5, with a shared RT lane and permitted RT phasing. Fully-protected right-turn phasing is rare, and usually involves provision of a pedestrian underpass or overpass with surface crossings prohibited. Compound (protected + permitted or vice-versa) right-turn signal phasing is rarely used.

Right turns affect the saturation flow rate for two reasons: the difficulty of the movement increases saturation headways regardless of pedestrian interference, and any pedestrian interference further increases headways.

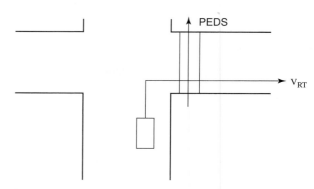

Figure 18-8 Interaction between right-turning vehicles and pedestrians.

Despite this complexity, the *HCM* offers two algorithms, both based on empirical studies conducted during the early 1980s:

For Cases 1–6: Exclusive or shared lanes/protected, permitted, or protected + permitted phasing:

$$f_{RT} = 1.0 - P_{RT}[0.15 + (PEDS/2100)][1 - P_{RTA}]$$
[18-20]

For Case 7: Single-Lane Approaches:

$$f_{RT} = 0.90 - P_{RT}[0.135 + (PEDS/2100)]$$
[18-21]

where: f_{RT} = right-turn adjustment factor
P_{RT} = proportion of right turns in the lane group, expressed as a decimal; $P_{RT} = 1.00$ for exclusive RT lane(s)
$PEDS$ = pedestrian flow rate, in pedestrians/ hour, using the conflicting crosswalk; if $PEDS > 1700$ ped/hr, 1700 is used
P_{RTA} = proportion of right turns using a protected RT phase; $P_{RTA} = 1.00$ for a fully-protected RT phase; $P_{RTA} = 0.00$ for a fully-permitted RT phase

Note that Equation [18-21] is a special case of Equation [18-20]. It is Equation [18-20] multiplied by 0.90, with $P_{RTA} = 0.00$. Observations indicate that single-lane approaches are approximately 10% less efficient than multilane approaches.

Table 18-10 Area Type Adjustment Factor, f_a

Type of Area	Area Type Factor, f_a
CBD	0.90
All other areas	1.00

These equations indicate that a f_{RT} of 0.00 is reached when the conflicting pedestrian flow reaches 1700 ped/hr. In such a case, some right-turning vehicles "sneak" through after the signal changes. To reflect this, *the minimum value of f_{RT} is 0.05 under all circumstances.*

There is also a discontinuity in Equation [18-21] for single-lane approaches. By definition, $f_{RT} = 1.00$ when there are no right-turning vehicles. The moment a single right-turning vehicle is introduced, the factor reduces to 0.90 or less.

Table 18-11 shows the factors that result from application of Equations [18-20] and [18-21] for the seven right-turn cases. In general, intermediate values may be found by straight-line interpolation, *except* for the interval $P_{RT} = 0.00$ to 0.20 for single-lane approaches, due to the discontinuity noted in the previous paragraph. For this range, Equation [18-21] should be directly applied.

8. Left-turn adjustment factor. Were it not for the left-turn adjustment factor, the 1994 *HCM* signalized intersection methodology would be relatively straightforward, and manual computations, while still difficult, would still be a reasonable task.

There are six ways in which left turns may be handled at a signalized intersection:

1. Exclusive LT lane with protected LT phasing
2. Exclusive LT lane with permitted LT phasing
3. Exclusive LT lane with compound LT phasing
4. Shared LT lane with protected phasing
5. Shared LT lane with permitted phasing
6. Shared LT lane with compound phasing

Except for Case 4 (shared lane, protected phasing), which is quite rare, all of the other cases are in regular use throughout the U.S. Those cases involving permitted or compound phasing are extremely complex, and the models used to describe these types of operation are, therefore, similarly complex.

Case 1 (exclusive lane, protected phasing) is the most straightforward. For this case, a constant factor is used:

$$f_{LT} = 0.95$$

The constant value reflects the additional headway usually consumed by vehicles due to the nature of the left-turning movement. It *does not* consider pedestrian interference. This is because the left-turning vehicle experiences pedestrian interference at the far side of the intersection. Saturation flow is measured across the stop line, and is not likely to be greatly influenced by far-side pedestrian interference except in extreme cases. This is, however, a weakness in all of the left-turn models.

Table 18-12 summarizes left-turn adjustment factor approaches in the 1994 *HCM*. The modeling of permitted left-turn phases and of compound phases is treated in major sections D and E, which follow.

9. Worksheet. Figure 18-9 shows the worksheet provided in the 1994 *HCM* for the saturation flow rate module. Filling column 12, the left-turn adjustment factor, will often require a lengthy analysis.

D. Modeling permitted left turns

Table 18-12 indicates that for permitted left turns, a "special procedure" must be used to find the appropriate left-turn adjustment factor. For protected/permitted phasing, this procedure is also applied to the permitted portion of the phase.

1. Subdividing the green phase. Figure 18-10 illustrates the general case of left turns from a shared lane with permitted phasing. It also illustrates three critical portions of the green phase, each of which must be taken into account in considering the effect of left turns.

The figure shows a subject approach with its opposing flow. When the GREEN phase is initiated, vehicles on both approaches begin to move. Vehicles from the standing queue on the opposing approach move through the intersection *with no gaps.* Thus, *no left turn from the subject approach may proceed during the time it takes this opposing queue to clear.* If a left-turning vehicle arrives in the subject approach during this time, it must wait, *blocking the left-most lane,* until the opposing queue has cleared. After the opposing queue has cleared the intersection, left turns from the subject approach may be made through gaps in the unsaturated opposing flow. The rate at which they can be made, and their impact on the operation of the subject approach, is based on the number of such turns that must be made and the magnitude and distribution of the opposing flow. Another basic concept is that left-turning vehicles have no impact on the

Table 18-11   Right-Turn Adjustment Factor, f_{RT}

| | | | Proportion of RTs in Lane Group, P_{RT} | | | | | |
| | | | CASES 4, 5, 6 | | | | | CASES 1, 2, 3 |
Case	P_{RTA}	PEDS	0	.2	.4	.6	.8	1.0
2 and 5	0	0	1.00	.970	.940	.910	.880	.850
		50 (Low)	1.00	.965	.930	.896	.861	.826
		100	1.00	.960	.921	.881	.842	.802
		200 (Mod.)	1.00	.951	.902	.853	.804	.755
		400 (High)	1.00	.932	.864	.796	.728	.660
		800	1.00	.894	.788	.681	.575	.469
		1200	1.00	.856	.711	.567	.423	.279
		≥1700	1.00	.808	.616	.424	.232	.050
3 and 6	.20	0	1.00	.970	.940	.910	.880	.850
		50 (Low)	1.00	.966	.932	.899	.865	.831
		100	1.00	.962	.925	.887	.850	.812
		200 (Mod.)	1.00	.955	.910	.864	.819	.774
		400 (High)	1.00	.940	.879	.819	.758	.698
		800	1.00	.909	.818	.727	.636	.545
		1200	1.00	.879	.757	.636	.514	.393
		≥1700	1.00	.840	.681	.521	.362	.202
	.40	0	1.00	.970	.940	.910	.880	.850
		50 (Low)	1.00	.967	.934	.901	.869	.836
		100	1.00	.964	.929	.893	.857	.821
		200 (Mod.)	1.00	.959	.917	.876	.834	.793
		400 (High)	1.00	.947	.894	.841	.789	.736
		800	1.00	.924	.849	.773	.697	.621
		1200	1.00	.901	.803	.704	.606	.507
		≥1700	1.00	.873	.746	.619	.491	.364
	.60	0	1.00	.970	.940	.910	.880	.850
		50 (Low)	1.00	.968	.936	.904	.872	.840
		100	1.00	.966	.932	.899	.865	.831
		200 (Mod.)	1.00	.962	.925	.887;	.850	.812
		400 (High)	1.00	.955	.910	.864	.819	.774
		800	1.00	.940	.879	.819	.758	.698
		1200	1.00	.924	.849	.773	.697	.621
		≥1700	1.00	.905	.810	.716	.621	.526
	.80	0	1.00	.970	.940	.910	.880	.850
		50 (Low)	1.00	.969	.938	.907	.876	.845
		100	1.00	.968	.936	.904	.872	.840
		200 (Mod.)	1.00	.966	.932	.899	.865	.831
		400 (High)	1.00	.962	.925	.887	.850	.812
		800	1.00	.955	.910	.864	.819	.774
		1200	1.00	.947	.894	.841	.789	.736
		≥1700	1.00	.938	.875	.813	.750	.688

Table 18-11 (continued)

Case	P_{RTA}	PEDS	Proportion of RTs in Lane Group, P_{RT}					CASES 1, 2, 3
			CASES 4, 5, 6					
			0	.2	.4	.6	.8	1.0
1 and 4	1.00	0	1.00	.970	.940	.910	.880	.850
7	—	0	1.00	.873	.846	.819	.792	.765
		50 (Low)	1.00	.868	.836	.805	.773	.741
		100	1.00	.863	.827	.790	.754	.717
		200 (Mod.)	1.00	.854	.808	.762	.716	.670
		400 (high)	1.00	.835	.770	.705	.640	.575
		800	1.00	.797	.694	.590	.487	.384
		1200	1.00	.759	.617	.476	.335	.194
		≥1700	1.00	.711	.522	.333	.144	.050

[Used with permission of Transportation Research Board, National Research Council, Washington, DC, from *Highway Capacity Manual, Special Report 209,* 3rd Ed., p. 9-16. Copyright © 1994 Transportation Research Board.]

subject approach *until the first left-turning vehicle arrives.*

The following portions of the green phase are, therefore, critical variables in modeling permitted left turns:

g_q = average amount of green time required for the opposing standing queue to clear the intersection, sec

g_f = average amount of green time before the arrival of the first left-turning vehicle on the subject approach, sec (note that for an exclusive LT lane, g_f is 0.0 sec)

g_u = average amount of green time *after* the arrival of the first left-turning vehicle that is *not blocked* by the clearance of the opposing standing queue, sec

Figure 18-10 illustrates the relationship among these three important variables. Note that the value of g_u depends on whether g_q or g_f is larger:

$$g_u = g - g_q \qquad g_q \geq g_f \qquad [18\text{-}22a]$$
$$g_u = g - g_f \qquad g_f > g_q \qquad [18\text{-}22b]$$

Determining g_u in this way includes only the time that left-turning vehicles may filter through an unsaturated opposing flow; the time before clearance of the op-

posing queue and/or before the arrival of the first left-turning vehicle is NOT included.

2. Basic structure of the permitted left-turn model. The model for determining the left-turn adjustment factor for permitted left turns must consider how left-turning vehicles are impacted during various portions of the green phase, and how those left-turning vehicles affect the general operation of the lane group. The modeling process starts by determining a left-turn adjustment factor that applies *only* to the left-most lane from which left turns are made. This factor, f_m, is later averaged to find the total impact on the lane group. Where there is only *one* lane in the lane group, $f_m = f_{LT}$.

In deriving an appropriate algorithm for f_m, there are three critical time periods to consider:

g_f — Before the first left-turning vehicle arrives in the subject approach, left turns have *no* impact on the left lane. Thus, during this period, an effective left-turn factor of 1.00 should be applied.

$g_q - g_f$ — If the first left-turning vehicle arrives *before* the opposing standing queue has cleared, it must wait for a minimum $g_q - g_f$. While the vehicle waits, the left lane is blocked for all

P_{LTo} = proportion of left-turning vehicles in the opposing single-lane approach, expressed as a decimal

n = number of opposing vehicles in the period $g_q - g_f$, roughly estimated as $(g_q - g_f)/2$. Note that "n" is subject to a minimum value of 0

While this section has discussed the general structure of the left-turn adjustment factor models of the 1994 *HCM*, a significant number of details must be added. Models are needed to estimate the three critical portions of the green phase, g_q, g_f, and g_u. Several parts of the model depend on the variable P_L, the proportion of vehicles in the left lane. While P_{LT} is known—the proportion of left-turning vehicles in the lane group—P_L must be estimated. Where there is an exclusive left-turn lane or lanes, both P_{LT} and P_L are 1.00 by definition. Where the subject lane group has only one lane, P_{LT} and P_L equal. For all other cases, an estimation procedure is needed. The following sections detail the algorithms used for these estimates.

3. Estimating g_f. The algorithms used to estimate g_f and g_q primarily resulted from an FHWA-sponsored national research effort, and were developed from a substantial data base [12]. Some of the equations were somewhat modified by members of the Signalized Intersection Subcommittee of the TRB Committee on Highway Capacity and Quality of Service based on theoretical considerations. For the most part, these algorithms replace those of the 1985 *HCM*, which were entirely based on theory.

There are two algorithms for estimating g_f, depending on whether the subject approach is a multilane or single-lane approach. There is a logical basis for differing models for multilane and single-lane approaches. The single-lane approach is the only situation in which both left and right turns share the same lane. Both the arrival and departure of vehicles are, therefore, somewhat different from the multilane case, due primarily to the additional care and vigilance drivers must exercise in the single-lane case. The general model for f_m already includes special consideration of single-lane opposing approaches.

When the subject approach has more than one lane:

$$g_f = Ge^{-(0.882\, LTC^{0.717})} - t_L \qquad [18\text{-}30\text{a}]$$

When the subject approach has one lane:

$$g_f = Ge^{-(0.860\, LTC^{0.629})} - t_L \qquad [18\text{-}30\text{b}]$$

where: g_f = average time to arrival of first left-turning vehicle in subject lane group, sec $(0.0 \le g_f \le g)$

G = actual green time for lane group, sec

LTC = left-turns per cycle, computed as $[V_{LT}\, C/3600]$, vpc

v_{LT} = left-turn flow rate in subject lane group, vph

t_L = total lost time per phase, sec

Field measurements of g_f used in calibration were indexed to the start of actual green time. As the 1994 *HCM* assumes that all lost time is applied at the beginning of the phase, a value of g_f indexed to the start of the effective green time must have t_L deducted. When this is done, g_f reflects the portion of effective green, g, to the arrival of the first left-turning vehicle. This adjustment is made to many algorithms in the 1994 *HCM*; each time it is made, it reflects the same consideration.

For exclusive left-turn lane groups, g_f is 0.00 by definition. The form of the equation guarantees that the value of g_f is in the range of 0.00 to g. If no left-turning vehicle arrives during the effective green (which would occur only if v_{LT} were 0 vph), then g_f is equal to the full effective green time, g.

4. Estimating g_q. The average time it takes the opposing standing queue to clear the intersection depends on whether the *opposing approach* has more than one lane:

For opposing approaches with more than one lane:

$$g_q = \frac{v_{olc}\, qr_o}{0.5 - [v_{olc}(1 - qr_o)/g_o]} - t_L \qquad [18\text{-}31\text{a}]$$

For single-lane opposing approaches:

$$g_{q(s)} = 4.943\, v_{olc}^{0.762}\, qr_o^{1.061} - t_L \qquad [18\text{-}31\text{b}]$$

where: g_q = average time for opposing standing queue clear the intersection from a multilane approach, sec, $(0.0 \le g_q \le g)$

$g_{q(s)}$ = average time for opposing standing queue to clear the intersection from a single lane approach, sec, $(0.0 \le g_q \le g)$

v_{olc} = opposing flow rate in vehs/lane/cycle, computed as $[v_o C/3600 N_o]$

v_o = opposing flow rate, in vphg (do *not* include flow from exclusive LT or RT lanes on the opposing approach)

N_o = number of opposing lanes (do *not* include exclusive LT or RT lanes on opposing approach)

qr_o = queue ratio for opposing flow; proportion of opposing flow originating in opposing standing queues, estimated as $[1 - R_{po}(g_o/C)]$

R_{po} = platoon ratio for opposing flow, taken from Table 18-3 for the appropriate arrival type, or from direct field observations

C = cycle length, sec

g_o = effective green for the opposing flow, sec

t_L = total time lost per phase, sec

Note that the term $[v_{olc}(1 - qr_o)/g_o]$ in Equation [18-31a] may not exceed 0.49.

The basis of Equation [18-31a] is theoretic, while Equation [18-31b] was empirically developed. This incongruence of approach reflects the overall development of the 1994 *HCM* model, which draws from many sources and several different funded research efforts.

Equation [18-31a] is based on the assumption that the number of vehicles per lane departing the intersection during g_q must be the same as those arriving during the red interval, plus those that join the end of the queue during g_q. This equivalence may be stated as:

$$0.5 g_q = v_{olc} qr_o + g_q \left[v_{olc} \frac{1 - qr_o}{g} \right]$$

where:

$0.5\,g_q$ = number of vehicles departing during g_q, assuming 2 sec/veh, or 0.5 veh/sec

$v_{olc}qr_o$ = number of vehicles arriving during the red interval

$g_q[v_{olc}(1 - qr_o/g]$ = number of vehicles arriving during g_q

Solving this equation for g_q yields Equation [18-31a], except for the deduction of t_L, which is again done to index the start of g_q at the start of effective green, rather than actual green. Equation [18-31b] was developed via regression analysis on an empirical data base.

5. Estimating P_L. The remaining variable to be estimated is P_L, the proportion of left-turning vehicles in the left lane. The proportion of left-turning vehicles in the total lane group, P_{LT}, is known from input data. P_L is then estimated as:

$$P_L = P_{LT}\left[1 + \frac{(N - 1)g}{(f_s g_u + 4.5)}\right] \qquad [18\text{-}32a]$$

$$f_s = \frac{875 - 0.625 v_o}{1000} \qquad [18\text{-}32b]$$

where: P_L = proportion of left turns in left lane, expressed as a decimal

P_{LT} = proportion of left turns in lane group, expressed as a decimal

v_o = opposing flow rate, vph

f_s = left-turn saturation factor

g_u = unsaturated portion of the green phase for the subject lane group, sec

g = green phase for the subject lane group, sec

N = number of lanes in the lane group

The derivation of this equation is somewhat tortuous. It may even be argued that it is incomplete. By definition, P_L and P_{LT} may be expressed as:

$$P_L = \frac{V_{LT}}{V_1} \qquad P_{LT} = \frac{V_{LT}}{V_1 + V_2}$$

where: V_{LT} = left-turn flow rate, vph

V_1 = total flow rate in left lane, vph

V_2 = total flow rate in all other lanes (except left lane), vph

Then:

$$\frac{P_L}{P_{LT}} = \frac{V_1 + V_2}{V_1}$$

and:

$$P_L = P_{LT}\left[1 + \frac{V_2}{V_1}\right]$$

This defines the basic structure of Equation [18-32a]. An appropriate value, however, must be inserted for the ratio, V_2/V_1. The ratio is taken to be equal to the relative effective green times that each flow has available.

For V_2, the total flow in lanes other than the left lane, it is assumed that the entire green time is available. Because there may be more than one lane for V_2, the green time available is $(N - 1)g$, where N is the total number of lanes in the lane group. In effect, $N - 1$ lanes each have g seconds of effective green available to service V_2.

For V_1, the logic is more complex, and is at best incomplete. It is assumed that left-turning vehicles may progress only during the unsaturated portion of the green time, g_u. However, each left-turning vehicle uses more green time than a through vehicle. The magnitude of this is reflected in the through-car equivalent for left turns, E_L. At this point, however, rather than using the value E_{L1}, consistent with the general model, a default value of E_L is employed:

$$E_L \text{ (default)} = \frac{1600}{1400 - v_o}$$

where 1600 vphgpl is an assumed default value for saturation flow rate, and $1400 - v_o$ represents a rough estimate of the saturation flow rate of left-turning vehicles through an opposing flow. To find the equivalent green time available in the left lane (to left-turners), g_u is divided by E_L (default). To simplify this, f_s is defined as $1/E_L$ (default), producing the term $f_s g_u$. To account for two sneakers per cycle, 4.5 seconds of green are added to this, assuming a saturation headway of 2.25 sec/veh (3600/1600). From this logic, the ratio of V_2/V_1 is set equal to $[(N - 1)g]/[f_s g_u + 4.5]$, and Equation [18-32a] results.

This algorithm has two major problems: (1) its use of a default value for E_L is unnecessary and inconsistent with other parts of the model, and (2) the expression for equivalent green time for V_1 assumes that *only* left-turning vehicles are present in the left lane. The former is easily corrected by using E_{L1}, defined previously. The latter is more fundamental.

Rouphail, in an unpublished memorandum to the Signalized Intersection Subcommittee of the TRB Committee on Highway Capacity and Quality of Service, suggests a correction documented in a doctoral dissertation by Prassas [12]. He recommends that a) g_f be added to the effective green time for V_1, b) E_{L1} be substituted for the default value, and c) that

the "sneaker" term be reduced to reflect a default saturation flow rate of 1700 vphgpl. This produces:

$$P_L = P_{LT}\left[1 + \frac{(N - 1)g}{g_f + (g_u/E_{L1}) + 4.24}\right] \quad [18\text{-}33]$$

Even in this form the algorithm has remaining difficulties. In this form, it is assumed that there are only left-turning vehicles in the left lane *during the period g_u*. Since this is assumed to be a shared lane group, some through vehicles use the left lane during g_u as well. The use of E_{L1} as an equivalent during this period ignores the fact that through vehicles during g_u will have an equivalent of 1.00. Further, the assumption of 2 sneakers during each phase is inconsistent with the Equation [18-24], which assumes that the number of sneakers is $1 + P_L$. Including these additional complexities, however, would lead to an iterative set of algorithms that would be difficult to comprehend and to implement.

It should be noted that, for consistency, all problem solutions herein use the 1994 *HCM* algorithms of Equations [18-32a] and [18-32b]. All current software implementing the 1994 *HCM*, including the HCS package and HCM-Cinema (used herein) incorporate these equations. The 1997 revisions of the manual, however, are expected to include further modification of the estimation procedure for P_L.

The determination of P_L has another function in the overall model. If for a shared multilane group, P_L is 1.0 (the maximum feasible value, although the algorithm may yield higher values), then the left lane must be treated as a *defacto left turn lane*. It is then established as a separate lane group, and the analysis is redone.

6. Summary. The algorithms presented in this section permit the estimation of g_f, g_q, g_u, and P_L for various combinations of multilane and single-lane subject and opposing approaches. These values may now be inserted into Equation [18-23] (multilane opposing approach) or Equation [18-27] (single-lane opposing approach) to find f_m and Equation [18-25] to find f_{LT}. To help in sorting through the various combinations and sequences of algorithms that may be applied in estimating f_{LT} for permitted phasing, Table 18-14 is provided as an index. Figures 18-11 and 18-12 show worksheets to use in making these computations.

When the worksheets are used, care must be taken to make the indicated substitutions for multilane approaches opposed by single-lane approaches and vice-versa.

Table 18-14 An Index to Algorithms for Estimating f_{LT} for Permitted Left Turns

Opposing Approach	Algorithm for Estimating:					
	g_f	g_q	g_u*	P_L	f_m	f_{LT}
Subject Approach: Multilane						
Multilane	Eq. [18-30a]	Eq. [18-31a]	[Eq. 18-22a] or	Eq. [18-32]	Eq. [18-23]	Eq. [18-25]
Single	Eq. [18-30a]	Eq. [18-31b]	Eq. [18-22b]]	Eq. [18-32]	Eq. [18-27]	Eq. [18-25]
Subject Approach: Single Lane						
Multilane	Eq. [18-30b]	Eq. [18-31a]	[Eq. [18-22a] or	$P_L = P_{LT}$	Eq. [18-23]	$f_{LT} = f_m$
Single	Eq. [18-30b]	Eq. [18-31b]	Eq. [18-22b]]	$P_L = P_{LT}$	Eq. [18-27]	$f_{LT} = f_m$
Subject Lane Group: Exclusive LT						
Multilane	$g_f = 0.00$	Eq. [18-31a]	[Eq. 18-22a or	$P_L = 1.0$	Eq. [18-23]	$f_{LT} = f_m$
Single	$g_f = 0.0$	Eq. [18-31b]	Eq. [18-22b]]	$P_L = 1.0$	Eq. [18-27]	$f_{LT} = f_m$

*Eq. [18-22a] is used when $g_q \geq g_f$; Eq. [18-22b] is used when $g_f > g_q$.

E. Modeling the left-turn adjustment factor for compound (protected/ permitted) phasing

The most complicated left-turn case to be modeled is the combination of protected and permitted phasing. The 1985 *HCM* does not address this case in any detail, and contains several fundamental errors in its presentation. The 1994 *HCM* makes considerable progress, and presents more realistic ways to address this complex situation.

1. Compound phasing in shared lane groups. Protected plus permitted phasing from *shared lane groups* is still handled in a very general way, using left-turn adjustment factors that assume a generalized split of demand between the protected and permitted portions of the phase. This case is, however, quite rare, making it difficult to conduct field observations of this type of operation. This type of phasing occurs when leading and lagging green phases are implemented without exclusive left-turn lanes. Such phasing is the only way to provide for partially protected left turns when exclusive lanes cannot be provided.

For this case, the left-turn factor is given by:

$$f_{LT} = \frac{1400 - v_o}{(1400 - v_o) + (235 + 0.435v_o)P_{LT}}$$

[18-34a]

for values of $v_o \leq 1220$ vph, and:

$$f_{LT} = \frac{1}{1 + 4.525P_{LT}}$$ [18-34b]

for values of $v_o > 1220$ vph,

where: f_{LT} = left-turn adjustment factor applied to the total protected plus permitted phase
v_o = opposing flow rate, in vph
P_{LT} = proportion of left-turning vehicles in the shared lane group

When a protected plus permitted phasing exists on a shared lane group, the combination of the protected and permitted portions of the phase are treated as a unit, as a single lane group. In so doing, the effective green time for the phase is the total of the effective green times for both the protected and permitted portions of the phase.

In computing delay for this case, the standard delay model is used, even though this represents only a gross estimation for protected plus permitted turns.

The derivation of these algorithms is not well-documented, and involves many gross simplifications and assumptions. Research sponsored by both NCHRP and FHWA is now underway to provide a more detailed understanding of this complicated case.

2. Compound phasing in exclusive left-turn lane groups. In most cases, protected plus permitted phasing is implemented in conjunction with exclusive

SUPPLEMENTAL WORKSHEET FOR PERMITTED LEFT TURNS ***For Use Where the Subject Approach is Opposed by a Multilane Approach***				
APPROACH	EB	WB	NB	SB
Enter cycle length, C				
Enter actual green time for lane group, G				
Enter effective green time for lane group, g				
Enter opposing effective green time, g_o				
Enter number of lanes in group N				
Enter number of opposing lanes, N_o				
Enter adjusted left-turn flow rate, v_{LT}				
Enter proportion of left turns in lane group, P_{LT}				
Enter adjusted opposing flow rate, v_o				
Enter lost time per phase, t_L				
Compute left turns per cycle: $LTC = v_{LT} \, C/3600$				
Compute opposing flow per lane, per cycle: $v_{olc} = v_o \, C/(3600 \, N_o)$				
Determine opposing platoon ratio, R_{po} (Table 18-3 or Eq. [18-5])				
Compute $g_f{}^* = G \exp(-0.882 \, LTC^{0.717}) - t_L$, $g_f \le g$				
Compute opposing queue ratio: $qr_o = 1 - R_{po} \, (g_o/C)$				
Compute g_q, using Equation [18-31a] $g_q \le g$				
Compute g_u: $g_u = g - g_q$ if $g_q \ge g_f$ $g_u = g - g_f$ if $g_q < g_f$				
Compute $f_g = (875 - 0.625 \, v_o)/1000$, $f_g \ge 0$				
Compute $P_L\dagger = P_{LT}[1 + \{(N-1)g/f_g g_u + 4.5)\}]$				
Determine E_{L1} (Table 18-13)				
Compute $f_{\min} = 2(1 + P_L)/g$				
Compute f_m: $f_m = [g_f/g] + (g_u/g)[1/\{1 + P_L(E_{L1} - 1)\}]$ min $= f_{\min}$; max $= 1.00$				
Compute $f_{LT} = [f_m + 0.91 \, (N-1)]/N\ddagger$				

* For special case of single-lane approach opposed by multilane approach, see text.

† If $P_L \ge 1$ for shared left-turn lanes with $N > 1$, then assume de facto left-turn lane and redo calculations.

‡ For permitted left turns with multiple exclusive left-turn lanes $f_{LT} = f_m$.

Figure 18-11 Worksheet for permitted LT's—Multilane opposing approaches. [Used with permission of Transportation Research Board, National Research Council, Washington, DC, from *Highway Capacity Manual, Special Report 209,* 3rd Ed., p. 9-41. Copyright © 1994 Transportation Research Board.]

SUPPLEMENTAL WORKSHEET FOR PERMITTED LEFT TURNS
For Use Where the Subject Approach is Opposed by a Single-Lane Approach

APPROACH	EB	WB	NB	SB
Enter cycle length, C				
Enter actual green time for lane group, G				
Enter effective green time for lane group, g				
Enter opposing effective green time, g_o				
Enter number of lanes in group N				
Enter adjusted left-turn flow rate, v_{LT}				
Enter proportion of left turns in lane group, P_{LT}				
Enter proportion of left turns in opposing flow, P_{LTo}				
Enter adjusted opposing flow rate, v_o				
Enter lost time per phase, t_L				
Compute left turns per cycle: $LTC = v_{LT}\, C/3600$				
Compute opposing flow per lane, per cycle: $v_{olc} = v_o\, C/3600$				
Determine opposing platoon ratio, R_{po} (Table 18-3 or Eq. [18-5])				
Compute $g_f^* = G \exp(-0.860\, LTC^{0.629}) - t_L,\ g_f \le g$				
Compute opposing queue ratio: $qr_o = 1 - R_{po}\,(g_o/C)$				
Compute $g_q = 4.943\, v_{olc}^{0.762}\, qr_o^{1.061} - t_L\ \ g_q \le g$				
Compute g_u: $g_u = g - g_q$ if $g_q \ge g_f$; $g_u = g - g_f$ if $g_q < g_f$				
Compute $n = (g_q - g_f)/2,\ n \ge 0$				
Compute $P_{THo} = 1 - P_{LTo}$				
Determine E_{L1} (Table 18-13)				
Compute $E_{L2} = e(1 + P_{THo}^{\ n})P_{LTo}$				
Determing $f_{min} = 2(1+P_{LT})/g$				
Compute $f_{LT}^* = f_m = [g_f/g] + [(g_q - g_f)g][1/\{1 + P_{LT}(E_{L2}-1)\}] + [g_u/g][1/(1+P_{LT}(E_{LT}-1)]$ min $= F_{min}$; max $= 1.00$				

* For special case of multilane approach opposed by single-lane approach or when $g_f > g_q$, see text.

Figure 18-12 Worksheet for permitted LT's—single lane opposing approaches. [Used with permission of Transportation Research Board, National Research Council, Washington, DC, from *Highway Capacity Manual, Special Report 209*, 3rd Ed., p. 9-42. Copyright © 1994 Transportation Research Board.]

left-turn lanes. For this case, the 1994 *HCM* provides a more detailed model for use. Critical changes to the standard model include:

a. Protected and permitted portions of the phase are treated as separate "lane groups" for purposes of the saturation flow rate and subsequent capacity analysis computations.

b. It is assumed that the capacity of the *first* portion of the phases is fully utilized. This means that if the protected phase comes first in the sequence, demand flow is assumed to use all of the available capacity in this portion of the phase. The only exception to this is when demand is not sufficient to fully utilize available capacity. All remaining demand flow is assigned to the *second* portion of the phase. This is a reasonable assumption, and it allows distinguishing between protected plus permitted and permitted plus protected phasing. It is still, however, a simplification, and actual operations may differ.

c. Items a and b, taken together, mean that such critical values as saturation flow rate, capacity, and *v/c* ratios are separately computed for protected and permitted portions of the phase.

d. In applying the special procedure for determining the left-turn adjustment factor for the permitted portion of the phase, several adjustments to standard computational models must be made. These are discussed in detail in the following sections.

3. The left-turn adjustment factor for protected portion of compound left-turn phases.

If the saturation flow rate is to be separately estimated for the protected and permitted portions of a combined phase, this will require separate computation of the left-turn adjustment factor for each portion of the phase. Other adjustment factors will be unaffected, and are equal for both parts of the phase.

For the protected portion of the phase, this is straightforward, as the left-turn adjustment factor for all protected left-turns in exclusive left-turn lane groups is 0.95.

Determination of the effective green, g, for the protected portion of the phase depends on whether it comes first or second in the sequence. Remember that, for convenience, the total lost time per phase, t_L, is allocated to the beginning of the phase. Thus, if the protected portion of the phase was first in the sequence, effective green would be:

$$g_{PT} = G_{PT} + Y_{PT} - t_L \qquad [18\text{-}35a]$$

If the protected phase is second in the sequence, the lost time is not deducted, as it would have occurred during the permitted portion of the phase. Then:

$$g_{PT} = G_{PT} + Y_{PT} \qquad [18\text{-}35b]$$

where: g_{PT} = effective green time, protected portion of protected plus permitted phase, sec

G_{PT} = actual green time, protected portion of protected plus permitted phase, sec

Y_{PT} = actual "yellow arrow" or "yellow plus all red" clearance for the protected

left-turn; when first in the sequence, the yellow LT arrow is followed by a green ball allowing permitted turns; when second in the sequence, the yellow LT arrow is followed by an "all red" clearance interval, sec

t_L = total lost time per phase, sec, assigned at the beginning of the movement

4. Left-turn adjustment factor for the permitted portion of a compound left-turn phase.

For the permitted portion of the phase, finding the left-turn adjustment factor requires the use of the special procedure for permitted left turns. This special model requires the determination of g_f, g_q, and g_u. The standard equations generally used for these determinations must be modified when protected plus permitted phasing is present. They must also be notified when a fully permitted left-turn is opposed by an approach with a leading green phase. The consideration of g_f is basically a moot point, however, because for exclusive LT lanes, g_f is always "zero."

These modifications are necessary because the standard equations are indexed to specific times relative to the beginning of the movement in question. When used to estimate the impact on left turns, only the portion affecting the permitted portion of the phase should be taken into account.

To better explain this, consider the standard case of a fully permitted left-turn phase, as illustrated in Figure 18-13.

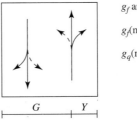

g_f and g_q indexed to start of effective green

$g_f(\min) = 0$ $g_f(\max) = g$

$g_q(\min) = 0$ $g_q(\max) = g$

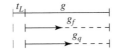

Figure 18-13 Standard case: Fully permitted left-turn phasing. [Used with permission of Transportation Research Board, National Research Council, Washington, DC, from *Highway Capacity Manual, Special Report 209*, 3rd Ed., p. 9-22. Copyright © 1994 Transportation Research Board.]

In this case, the standard equations for estimating g_f and g_q use the actual green time for the phase, G, as input. The resulting estimates of g_f and g_q are indexed to begin t_L seconds after the initiation of G. This is because the total lost time per phase is counted at the beginning of a movement, both as a matter of convenience, and because the start-up lost time is usually significantly larger than the clearance lost time, which actually occurs at the end of a movement. The value of g_u is found as $g - g_q$ or $g - g_f$, depending on whether g_q or g_f is the larger value.

Figure 18-14 shows a leading green phase. In this configuration, the NB LT is a protected plus permitted phase, and the SB LT is a fully permitted phase opposed by a leading green. Both cases require adjustments to the results obtained from standard models used to estimate g_f and g_q. For convenience, results from standard models use the usual notation for all variables. Adjusted values to be applied to these special cases are marked with an asterisk (*). The NB and SB permitted left turns are discussed in the following sections.

For the NB Permitted Left Turn

a. The effective green time for the NB permitted left turn is:

$$g^* = G_2 + Y_2$$

Note that no lost time is deducted as the permitted portion of the phase is the *second* in the sequence. Lost time, t_L, would be deducted during the protected portion of the phase.

b. While the diagram shows the comparison of g_f and g_f^*, this is irrelevant for an exclusive LT lane, as both values would be "0" by definition. In an exclusive LT lane, it is assumed that a left-turning vehicle is already present when the signal turns green.

c. In computing g_q for the NB permitted left turn, G_2, for the opposing SB through movement, would be used as an input. The result is a value of g_q that automatically deducts t_L from the beginning of the subject phase. Since this deduction is not appropriate for the NB permitted left turn:

$$g_q^* = g_q + t_L$$

d. Given the above adjustments:

$$g_u^* = g^* - g_q^*$$

again, recognizing that $g_f^* = g_f = 0$ for an exclusive LT lane.

For the SB Permitted Left Turn

a. Because the SB left turn begins in the permitted phase (there is no protected phase for this movement), the effective green computation includes

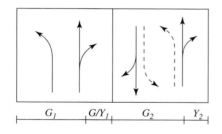

Figure 18-14 Leading green phase (PT + PM). [Used with permission of Transportation Research Board, National Research Council, Washington, DC, from *Highway Capacity Manual, Special Report 209,* 3rd Ed., p. 9-22. Copyright © 1994 Transportation Research Board.]

the deduction of lost time at the beginning of the movement:

$$g^* = G_2 + Y_2 - t_L$$

b. Because the SB permitted left turn can be made from either an exclusive lane group or a shared lane group, the computation of g_f must be considered.

- If an exclusive LT lane is present, both g_f and g_f^* are "0" by definition.
- If a shared lane group is present, g_f is computed using G_2 as an input, as this is the period during which the SB through and left-turn movement begins. The computation results in a value of g_f that already accounts for the deduction of t_L at the beginning of the phase. As the SB movements begin in the permitted portion of the phase, this deduction is appropriate, and:

$$g_f^* = g_f$$

Thus, no adjustment to the standard computation is necessary in this case.

c. In computing g_q for the permitted SB LT, several difficulties arise. The model for this determination predicts the time for the opposing queue to clear *from the time the opposing movement begins.* The opposing NB through movement begins to move in the protected portion of the phase. Thus, to compute g_q, the input value of actual green is $G_1 + G/Y_1 + G_2$. Note that during the period G/Y_1, the NB LT sees a "yellow arrow" while the through movement continues to receive a "green ball." When this is done, the resulting value of g_q begins in the protected portion of the phase after adjusting for the lost time, t_L. For the purposes of the SB permitted left turn, however, only the portion of g_q interfering with the permitted left turn is of interest. This portion should also include a deduction for lost time, as the SB movement begins in the permitted phase. Thus:

$$g_q^* = g_q - G_1 - G/Y_1$$

Note that the minimum value of g_q^* is "0" and the maximum value is g^*.

d. Given the above adjustments:

$$g_u^* = g^* - g_q^* \qquad \text{if } g_q^* \geq g_f^*$$
$$g_u^* = g^* - g_f^* \qquad \text{if } g_f^* > g_q^*$$

Figure 18-15 illustrates the case of a lagging green. This case is much simpler than that of a leading green, as all movements start in the permitted portion of the phase, and the deduction of lost time at the beginning of the phase occurs as usual, without adjustment.

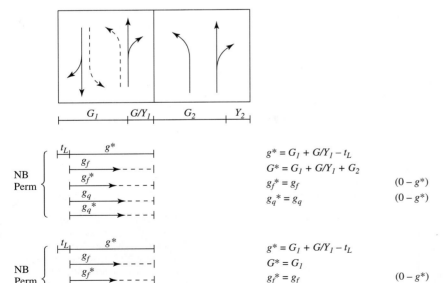

$$g^* = G_1 + G/Y_1 - t_L$$
$$G^* = G_1 + G/Y_1 + G_2$$
$$g_f^* = g_f \qquad (0 - g^*)$$
$$g_q^* = g_q \qquad (0 - g^*)$$

$$g^* = G_1 + G/Y_1 - t_L$$
$$G^* = G_1$$
$$g_f^* = g_f \qquad (0 - g^*)$$
$$g_q^* = g_q \qquad (0 - g^*)$$

Figure 18-15 Lagging green phasing (PT + PM). [Used with permission of Transportation Research Board, National Research Council, Washington, DC, from *Highway Capacity Manual, Special Report 209,* 3rd Ed., p. 9-23. Copyright © 1994 Transportation Research Board.]

Two key adjustments must be addressed in this case. When estimating g_f for the NB left turn or g_q for the SB left turn, the input value of actual green time is $G_1 + G/Y_1 + G_2$. Note again that $g_f = 0$ by definition for an exclusive LT lane.

These computed values, therefore, could exceed the effective green for the permitted portion of the phase:

$$g^* = G_1 + G/Y_1 - t_L$$

Thus, the effective maximum for both g_f^* and g_q^* is g^*. Because there must be an exclusive LT lane in the NB direction, both g_f and g_f^* are "0" by definition. As shown in Figure 18-15, $g_q^* = g_q$, requiring no adjustment other than observance of the maximum practical value.

Figure 18-16 combines the cases illustrated in Figures 18-14 and 18-15 to produce the traditional leading and lagging green phasing. This phasing provides an unopposed LT phase for both directions on the street in question. The combined adjustments required to handle this case are described below.

NB Permitted Left-Turn Phase

a. The effective green time for the NB permitted left-turn phase may be taken as:

$$g^* = G_2 + G/Y_2$$

Note that there is no deduction for lost time, as the NB left-turn movement begins in the protected phase, and would be deducted there.

b. The value of actual green time used to compute g_q is the green time for the opposing SB through movement: $G_2 + G/Y_2 + G_3$. The standard computation for g_q includes a deduction for lost time. As there is no lost time assigned to the NB left turn, the result must be adjusted:

$$g_q^* = g_q + t_L$$

The maximum value of g_q^* is "g^*."

c. Once again, as left-turns are made from an exclusive lane, g_f and g_f^* are by definition, "0."

d. As $g_f = 0$, then $g_u^* = g^* - g_q^*$.

SB Permitted Left Turn Phase

a. The effective green time for the SB permitted left turn must account for the lost time, as the SB left turn begins in the permitted phase. Thus:

$$g^* = G_2 + G/Y_2 - t_L$$

b. The actual green time used to compute g_q is that associated with the NB through movement: $G_1 + G/Y_1 + G_2$. The value computed must be adjusted to

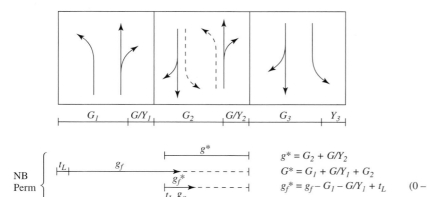

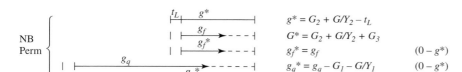

Figure 18-16 Leading and lagging green phasing ((PT + PM). [Used with permission of Transportation Research Board, National Research Council, Washington, DC, from *Highway Capacity Manual, Special Report 209*, 3rd Ed., p. 9-23. Copyright © 1994 Transportation Research Board.]

take into account only the portion of g_q that blocks the permitted SB left turn. Thus:

$$g_q^* = g_q - G_1 - G/Y_1$$

The practical range of g_q^* is from "0" to "g^*."

c. Once again, as left-turns are made from an exclusive lane, g_f and g_f^* are by definition, "0."

d. As $g_f = 0$, then $g_u^* = g^* - g_q^*$.

Figure 18-17 illustrates another case in which compound phasing might arise. This involves actuated signalization operating in the standard "quad eight" mode, in which a fully protected left-turn phase is followed by a leading green with a protected left turn in one direction, followed by a shared through phase in which left turns are permitted.

The element in this signalization is that during each phase, one of the left-turn movements has an interruption between its protected and permitted portions of the phase. For that left turn, *two* lost times are involved, as the movement literally starts and stops *twice* during each cycle.

For the case shown in Figure 18-17.

NB Permitted Left-Turn Movement

a. The effective green for the NB left-turn movement does not involve a lost time, as it moves continuously from the protected to the permitted portion of the phase. Thus:

$$g^* = G_3 + Y_3$$

b. The computation of g_q for the NB permitted left turns begins with the actual green time for the SB through movement: G_3. The resulting computation already accounts for the deduction of a lost time, which is NOT appropriate in this case. Thus the adjustment:

$$g_q^* = g_q + t_L$$

The practical range of g_q^* is from "0" to "g^*."

c. Once again, as left-turns are made from an exclusive lane, g_f and g_f^* are by definition, "0."

d. As $g_f = 0$, then $g_u^* = g^* - g_q^*$.

SB Permitted Left-Turn Movement

a. The SB left-turn movement starts anew in the permitted phase, and must therefore incorporate one lost time:

$$g^* = G_3 + Y_3 - t_L$$

b. In computing g_q, the actual green time entered corresponds to the actual green time for the NB through movement: $G_2 + G/Y_2 + G_3$. The value

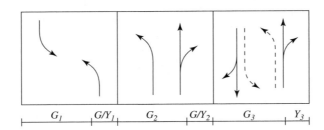

$$g^* = G_3 + Y_3$$
$$G^* = G_1 + G/Y_1 + G_2 + G/Y_2 + G_3$$
$$g_f^* = g_f - G_2 - G/Y_2 + t_L \qquad (0 - g^*)$$
$$g_q^* = g_q + t_L \qquad (0 - g^*)$$

NB
Perm

$$g^* = G_3 + Y_3 - t_L$$
$$G^* = G_1 + G_3$$
$$g_f^* = g_f \qquad (0 - g^*)$$
$$g_q^* = g_q - G_2 - G/Y_2 \qquad (0 - g^*)$$

NB
Perm

Figure 18-17 Quad-eight phasing (PT + PM). [Used with permission of Transportation Research Board, National Research Council, Washington, DC, from *Highway Capacity Manual, Special Report 209*, 3rd Ed., p. 9-24. Copyright © 1994 Transportation Research Board.]

thus computed must be adjusted to take into account only the portion that "blocks" opposing left turns during the permitted part of the phase, or:

$$g_q^* = g_q - G_2 - G/Y_2$$

The practical range of values for g_q^* is "0" to "g^*."

c. Once again, as left-turns are made from an exclusive lane, g_f and g_f^* are by definition, "0."
d. As $g_f = 0$, then $g_u^* = g^* - g_q^*$.
e. It should be noted that dealing with this case is entirely approximate. As the protected and permitted portions of the phase are separated, it is impossible to tell which is "first" or which is "second." Thus, the initial assumption that the capacity of the first portion of the phase is fully utilized and all remaining flow assigned to the second portion of the phase cannot be effectively implemented. Demand must be arbitrarily split between the two portions of the phase, perhaps assuming equal v/c ratios. Making the problem more difficult is the fact that this signalization is actuated, and the direction in which the divided phase occurs may vary from cycle to cycle.

These examples provide a variety of base cases that can be referred to when dealing with the analysis of protected + permitted or permitted + protected signal phasing. In applying these special procedures, manual computation becomes extremely difficult. Not only are the cases and sub-cases difficult to keep track of, but the sheer numerical volume of the manipulations involved makes it virtually impossible to do by hand without errors. These complexities, which should be understood, make the use of software the overwhelmingly-preferred way to implement these procedures.

F. Capacity analysis module

Sections D and E have dealt with the difficulties of describing left-turn impacts on saturation flow. The models of these sections result in a determination of f_{LT} for permitted left-turn cases and compound left-turn cases respectively. With the final adjustment factor determined, the saturation flow rate module can now be completed.

It is in the capacity analysis module that the first substantive results of signalized intersection analysis are realized.

1. **Determining v/s ratios.** The volume adjustment module produces lane groups with total flow rates adjusted for the PHF and lane distribution. The saturation flow rate module produces total saturation flow rates for each lane group, adjusted for eight types of prevailing conditions. The capacity analysis module begins by computing the ratio of these results (v/s) for each lane group.

2. **Determining critical lane groups and the sum of critical lane v/s ratios.** In Chapter 17, critical lane groups were determined by comparing adjusted per lane flows in each lane group using a ring diagram. As volumes are not uniformly adjusted in the 1994 *HCM* model, per lane flows cannot be directly compared. Thus, critical lane groups are identified by comparing v/s ratios. The approach and methodology is the same as presented in Chapter 17. Ring diagrams are still used to identify overlapping portions of the signal phase. Figure 18-18 illustrates the use of v/s ratios to find critical lane groups.

The total length of phases A and B is controlled either by the left ring (the WB through movement), or by the right ring (the combination of the WB left turn and the EB through/right-turn movement). The v/s ratio for the WB through movement, 0.45, is compared to the *sum* of the v/s ratios for the WB left turn and the EB through/right-turn movements, 0.20 + 0.35 = 0.55. The right ring involves the highest *sum* of v/s ratios, and is the critical path.

Phase C is discrete. The larger v/s ratio for the two lane groups in the phase determines which is critical. In this case, the NB right-turn lane group is critical, with a v/s ratio of 0.35.

Thus, the critical lane groups are the WB LT, the EB TH/RT, and the NB RT. As there are *three* critical movements (there could have been only two in this case), this signalization involves *three* sets of lost times in each cycle.

Having identified the critical lane groups, the sum of the critical lane group v/s ratios, $\Sigma(v/s)_{ci}$, may also be determined. In the sample case, the sum is 0.20 + 0.35 + 0.35 = 0.90. The sum of critical lane group v/s ratios is an interesting variable. It essentially identifies the proportion of real time that must be devoted to effective green. In the sample case, the signal timing must allocate 0.90 of real time as effective green. Conversely, only $1 - 0.90 = 0.10$ of real time is

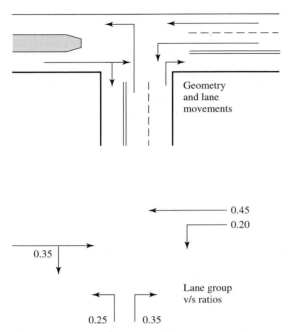

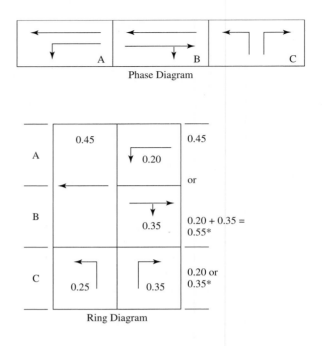

Figure 18-18   Finding critical lane groups using v/s ratios.

available to allocate to lost times. If $\Sigma(v/s)_{ci}$ is greater than 1.00, it is clear that the specified geometric design and signalization are inadequate to handle the specified demand flows.

If t_L is 3 sec/phase for the intersection of Figure 18-18, then the lost time per cycle for the 3-phase signal is $3 \times 3 = 9$ seconds per phase. The 9 sec/cycle of lost time must consume no more than 0.10 of the cycle. This suggests a minimum practical cycle length:

$$C_{\min} = \frac{9}{0.10} = 90 \text{ sec}$$

which may be generalized as:

$$C_{\min} = \frac{n t_L}{1 - \Sigma (v/s)_{ci}} \qquad [18\text{-}36]$$

Note that the signal timing has already been specified as an input to the model, and is needed to find the left-turn adjustment factor (for permitted or compound left-turn phasing). Thus, there is an iterative process at work in which signal timing affects v/s ratios, while resulting v/s ratios can be used to affect signal timing. In a later section, use of v/s ratios to revise signal timing is discussed in greater detail.

3. Determining lane group capacities and *v/c* ratios. Individual lane group capacities can be determined from saturation flow rates using Equation [18-2]:

$$c_i = s_i \frac{g_i}{C}$$

and v/c ratios can then be directly computed by dividing the lane group demand flow rate by the capacity:

$$X_i = \frac{v_i}{c_i} \qquad [18\text{-}37]$$

The critical v/c ratio for the intersection may also be found from the sum of critical lane group v/s ratios using Equation [18-4]:

$$X_c = \Sigma (v/s)_{ci} \frac{C}{C - L}$$

With the computation of v/c ratios for the intersection as a whole and for individual lane groups, the results of the capacity analysis module are complete. As discussed previously, a value of $X_c > 1.00$ indicates that the cycle length, phase plan, and geometry specified are inadequate to handle critical flows in the intersection. An increase in the cycle length, a more efficient phase plan, and/or addition of lanes to critical lane groups would be necessary to remedy the situation. If $X_c \leq 1.00$, the specified cycle length, phase plan, and geometry are adequate. If $X_c \leq 1.00$, and X_i for one or more lane groups is greater than 1.00, the situation can be remedied by reallocation of green time within the specified cycle length and phase plan.

Figure 18-19 shows a worksheet which can be used to summarize and guide computations in the capacity analysis module.

4. Modifying signal timing based on *v/s* ratios. The results of the capacity analysis module may indicate a need to adjust the cycle length and/or reallocate green time. While this can be done on a trial-an-error basis, v/s ratios can be used for a more straightforward approach.

Equation [18-4] for X_c can be solved for the cycle length, resulting in:

$$C = \frac{LX_c}{X_c - \Sigma\,(v/s)_{ci}} \qquad [18\text{-}38]$$

Note that Equation [18-36] is no more than a special case of this equation, where X_c is 1.00, and $L = n\,t_L$. In a similar fashion, the *v/c* ratio for a lane group may be expressed as shown in Equation [18-3]:

$$X_i = \frac{(v/s)_i}{g_i/C}$$

This equation may be solved for g_i, resulting in:

$$g_i = (v/s)_i \frac{C}{X_i} \qquad [18\text{-}39]$$

In general, green is allocated to provide for equal X_i in all critical lane groups. To accomplish this, each X_i for a critical lane group must be set equal to X_c. It is also possible to set X_i to 1.00 (or close to 1.00) for minor movements, such as a protected left turn, assigning all excess green time to through movements. This policy almost always results in very high delays to the minor movements, however.

Consider the sample problem of Figure 18-18, presented earlier. These principles could be used to estimate a signal timing. If, for example, it were desired to have a signal timing that resulted in $X_c = 0.95$, Equation [18-38] would be used, and:

$$C = \frac{9(0.95)}{0.95 - 0.90} = 171 \text{ sec}$$

This compares to the minimum cycle length of 90 seconds which was determined previously. It is also un-

reasonably high for most applications. Thus, a conclusion that a critical v/c ratio of 0.95 cannot be achieved may be reached. Note that the denominator of the equation, $X_c - \Sigma(v/s)_{ci}$, indicates that $X_c < \Sigma(v/s)_{ci}$ can never be achieved. In this case, the minimum cycle length is 90 seconds, and the desired X_c of 0.95 cannot be achieved. The maximum normal cycle length is 120 seconds. If this were adopted, the resulting X_c will be:

$$X_c = 0.90\,\frac{120}{120 - 9} = 0.973$$

This is the best achievable result, assuming that the signalization is restricted to the normal range of cycle lengths.

A cycle length of 120 seconds is selected, and green times are allocated using Equation [18-39], with all critical lane groups X_i set at 0.973. Then:

$$g_A = 0.20\,\frac{120}{0.973} = 24.6 \text{ sec}$$

$$g_B = 0.35\,\frac{120}{0.973} = 43.2 \text{ sec}$$

$$g_C = 0.35\,\frac{120}{0.973} = 43.2 \text{ sec}$$

where $g_A + g_B + g_C + L = 24.6 + 43.2 + 43.2 + 9.0 = 120$ seconds.

The sample problem of Figure 18-18 *does not* contain any permitted or compound left-turn phasing. Thus, if these signal timings were introduced, the resulting v/c ratios would be exactly as intended. In cases including permitted or compound phasing, the left-turn factor, and therefore saturation flow rates and v/s ratios, depend on signal timing. Thus, the process is iterative, and resulting v/c ratios approach those specified. If a reasonable signal timing methodology is used initially, specified signal timings should not produce terribly unreasonable results. Even where a totally inadequate signal timing is initially proposed, however, the timing can be refined using the procedure outlined herein, and the solution reworked. Once a reasonable timing is established, small trial-and-error changes using software should result in optimal timing without extraordinary effort.

G. Level of service module

The last step in the analysis process is the estimation of average individual stopped delays for each lane

1 Lane Group Movements	2 Phase type (P, S, T)	3 Adj. Flow Rate (v)	3 Adj. Sat. Flow Rate (s)	5 Flow Ratio (v/s) [3]/[4]	6 Green Ratio (g/C)	7* Lane Group Capacity (c) [4]x[6]	8 Lane Group v/c Ratio (X) [3]/[7]	9 Critical Lane Grp. [√]

* Permitted left turns subject to minimum capacity of $(1 + P_L)(3600/C)$ in column 7.

Cycle length, C _____ sec.

Lost time per cycle, L _____ sec.

$Y = \text{Sum } (v/s)_{ci} =$ _____

$$X_C = Y \times \frac{C}{(C - L)} = \underline{\qquad}$$

Figure 18-19 Worksheet for capacity analysis module. [Used with permission of Transportation Research Board, National Research Council, Washington, DC, from *Highway Capacity Manual, Special Report 209,* 3rd Ed., p. 9-44. Copyright © 1994 Transportation Research Board.]

group. These values may be aggregated to find weighted average delays for each approach, and finally for the intersection as a whole. Once delays are determined, Table 18-1 is used to establish a level of service to each lane group, approach, and the intersection as a whole.

1. Delay models for standard cases. Delay prediction models were extensively discussed in Chapter 16. The 1994 *HCM* uses the following algorithms:

$$d_i = d_{1i}DF + d_{2i} \qquad [18\text{-}40]$$

$$d_{1i} = 0.38C\frac{[1 - (g_i/C)]^2}{1 - (g_i/C)X_i} \qquad [18\text{-}41]$$

$$d_{2i} = 173X_i^2[(X_i - 1) + \sqrt{(X_i - 1)^2 + (mX_i/c_i)}] \qquad [18\text{-}42]$$

where: d_i = average stopped delay per vehicle for lane group *i*, sec/veh

d_{1i} = average stopped uniform delay component per vehicle for lane group *i*, sec/veh

d_{2i} = average stopped overtime delay component per vehicle for lane group *i*, sec/veh

DF = delay adjustment factor for progression quality and/or actuation

C = cycle length, sec

g_i = effective green time for lane group *i*, sec

X_i = v/c ratio for lane group *i*, (maximum value for d_{1i} is 1.00)

m = delay calibration term depending on arrival type

c_i = capacity of lane group *i*, vph

The delay adjustment factor, *DF*, and the delay calibration term, *m*, are obtained from Table 18-15. Both factors are based on *arrival type,* which was specified as part of the input data, and discussed in the section on Input Module. The table applies a delay adjustment *either* for actuated signalization, or for the quality of progression (as reflected in arrival type), but not both. The benefits of actuation are minimal when movements are coordinated. Because *DF* is applied only to d_1, the model also recognizes that the benefits of coordination diminish as v/c approaches and exceeds

1.00. Note that the factor becomes "0" for excellent progression (arrival types 4 or 5) and high g/C ratios.

Left turns from exclusive lane groups or phases are generally considered to be uncoordinated. Arrival type 3 is assumed for such cases, unless specific information is available to suggest otherwise.

Average stopped delays for each lane group are aggregated to obtain values for each approach, and for the intersection as a whole:

$$d_{Aj} = \frac{\sum d_i v_i}{\sum v_i} \qquad [18\text{-}43]$$

$$d_i = \frac{\sum d_{Aj} v_j}{\sum v_j} \qquad [18\text{-}44]$$

where: d_i = average stopped delay per vehicle for lane group *i*, sec/veh

d_{Aj} = average stopped delay per vehicle for approach *j*, sec/veh

d_I = average stopped delay per vehicle for the intersection as a whole, sec/veh

v_i = rate of flow, lane group *i*, vph

v_j = rate of flow, approach *j*, vph

Figure 18-20 shows a worksheet that may be used to summarize and/or guide computations in the level of service module.

2. Delay models for protected plus permitted phasing from exclusive left-turn lane groups. The general model discussed above applies to all cases of fully permitted or fully protected phasing, and to the case of compound phasing from a shared lane group. The latter case is understood only in the most approximate of terms, and the model's application to this case is similarly approximate.

Where compound left-turn phases are provided with an exclusive left-turn lane or lanes (it should be noted that compound phasing is not generally used when more than one exclusive lane is present), the model for the uniform delay component must be altered to reflect varying arrival and departure patterns. *Five* different cases may arise in such a situation:

a. A *leading left-turn phase* is provided, but no queued left-turning vehicles remain at the end of either the protected or permitted portions of the phase.

b. A *leading left-turn phase* is provided, and a queue of left-turning vehicles remains at the end of the

Table 18-15 Uniform Delay Adjustment Factor, *DF*

Controller-Type Adjustment Factor (*CF*)

Controller Type	Noncoordinated Intersections	Coordinated Intersections
Pretimed (no traffic-actuated lane groups)	1.0	*PF* as computed below
Semiactuated:		
Traffic-actuated lane groups	0.85	1.0
Nonactuated lane groups	0.85	*PF* as computed below
Fully actuated (all lane groups traffic-actuated)	0.85	Treat as semiactuated

Progression Adjustment Factor (*PF*)
$$PF = (1 - P)f_p(1 - g/C) \text{ (see Note)}$$

Green Ratio (*g/C*)	Arrival Type (AT)					
	AT-1	AT-2	AT-3	AT-4	AT-5	AT-6
0.20	1.167	1.007	1.000	1.000[3]	0.833	0.750
0.30	1.286	1.063	1.000	0.986	0.714	0.571
0.40	1.445	1.136	1.000	0.895	0.555	0.333
0.50	1.667	1.240	1.000	0.767	0.333	0.000
0.60	2.001	1.395	1.000	0.576	0.000	0.000
0.70	2.556	1.653	1.000	0.256	0.000	0.000
Default, f_p	1.00	0.93	1.00	1.15	1.00	1.00
Default, R_p	0.333	0.667	1.000	1.333	1.667	2.000
Incremental delay calibration term, *m*	8	12	16	12	8	4

Note: 1. Tabulation is based on default values of f_p and R_p. 2. $P = R_p\, g/C$ (may not exceed 1.0). 3. *PF* may not exceed 1.0 for AT-3 through AT-6.

[Used with permission of Transportation Research Board, National Research Council, Washington, DC, from *Highway Capacity Manual, Special Report 209*, 3rd Ed., p. 9-28. Copyright © 1994 Transportation Research Board.]

protected period, but not at the end of the permitted period.

c. A *leading left-turn phase* is provided, and a queue of left-turning vehicles remains at the end of the permitted period, but not at the end of the protected period. Note that it is not possible to have a queue at the end of *both* the permitted and protected portions of the phase, as the *v/c* ratio is not allowed to exceed 1.00 for the purposes of the uniform delay estimation.

d. A *lagging left-turn phase* is provided, and there is no queue of left-turning vehicles after the permitted portion of the phase. If this is the case, there will be no queue after the protected portion of the phase either, since it follows the permitted portion.

e. A *lagging left-turn phase* is provided, and a queue of left-turning vehicles remains after the permitted portion of the phase. If the *v/c* ratio is kept below 1.00 for the purposes of estimating uniform delay, then this queue will be fully serviced during the protected portion of the phase.

Figure 18-21 illustrates the accumulation and discharge of vehicles that occurs in each of these basic cases. As can be seen, obtaining the area under these shapes to determine aggregate delay, and then average individual delay, is far more complex than for the simple case of a fully-permitted or fully-protected phase. In those cases, the resulting shape is a simple triangle, and Webster's delay equation is derived, as discussed in Chapter 16.

Cycle, sec	First Term Delay				Second Term Delay			Lane Group		Approach	
1 Lane Group Movements	2 *v/c* Ratio, *X*	3 Green Ratio, *g/C*	4 Unknown Delay, d_1 (sec/veh)	5 Delay Adj. Factor, *DF*	6 Lane Grp. Capacity, *c* (vph)	7 d_2 Cal. Term, *m*	8 Incremental Delay, d_2 (sec/veh)	9 Delay [4]/[5] +[8] (sec/veh)	10 L O S	11 Delay (sec/veh)	12 L O S
EB											
WB											
NB											
SB											

Intersection delay _____ sec/veh   Intersection LOS _____

Figure 18-20 Worksheet for the level of service module. [Used with permission of Transportation Research Board, National Research Council, Washington, DC, from *Highway Capacity Manual, Special Report 209,* 3rd Ed., p. 9-46. Copyright © 1994 Transportation Research Board.]

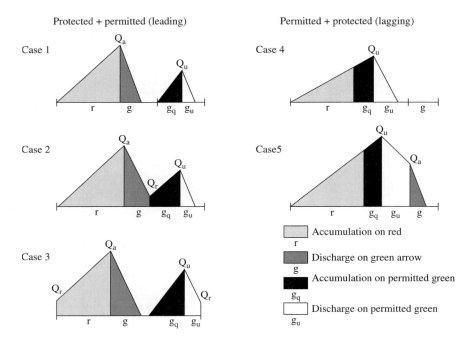

Protected + permitted (leading)

Case 1

Permitted + protected (lagging)

Case 4

Case 2

Case5

Case 3

Accumulation on red
r

Discharge on green arrow
g

Accumulation on permitted green
g_q

Discharge on permitted green
g_u

Figure 18-21 Model for uniform delay for compound phasing illustrated. [Used with permission of Transportation Research Board, National Research Council, Washington, DC, from *Highway Capacity Manual, Special Report 209*, 3rd Ed., p. 9-30. Copyright © 1994 Transportation Research Board.]

Figure 18-22 shows a special worksheet provided in the 1994 *HCM* to obtain uniform delay for these cases. It is complex and difficult. Software is the only practical means to implement this portion of the 1994 *HCM* model.

The model for protected/permitted delay is a significant improvement over previous approaches to this difficult situation. It is not, however, without problems, particularly when taken together with the assumed operation, i.e., that the *first* portion of the phase is 100% utilized, with only remaining demand using the *second* portion of the phase. An incongruence occurs when demand volume is barely sufficient to fully utilize the first portion of the phase, which may occur when the protected portion of the phase comes first. In such a situation, few, or even no, vehicles utilize the permitted portion of the phase. Under these circumstances, the delay model will still show a significant decrease in delay compared to a fully protected phase because of the different models used. Care should be taken, therefore, not to overemphasize the importance of reduced delays gained through compound phasing when the protected portion of the phase (leading only) is sufficient to handle all or most of the left-turn demand.

H. Analysis of actuated signals

The 1994 *HCM* model presented in this section requires that signal timing be specified as part of the input information. This includes semi-actuated and actuated signals. This presents practical difficulties, in that actuated signals have varying cycle lengths and green splits, albeit limited by maximums and minimums established in the controller.

In general, the *average* signal timing should be used in analysis. This will produce the most accurate results on capacity of various lane groups. The delay model incorporates an adjustment that reflects the delay benefits of actuated control. The difficulty is how to establish what the average signal timing is, or in the case of a future case, what it will be.

For existing cases, the signal timing can be observed in the field. Average values for cycle length and the various green phases can then be determined. Where future scenarios are under consideration, this is not possible. Even where future demand scenarios on an existing signal are studied, the average timing should change in response to the new demand configuration if the actuated signal is operating properly.

SUPPLEMENTAL UNIFORM DELAY WORKSHEET FOR LEFT TURNS WITH PRIMARY AND SECONDARY PHASES

———— INPUT DATA ————		EBLT	WBLT	NBLT	SBLT
Adj. LT vol from Vol. Adjustment Worksheet,	v	_____	_____	_____	_____
Adj. LT vol from Vol. Adjustment Worksheet,	X	_____	_____	_____	_____

Signal timing intervals:

Primary phase effective green	g	_____	_____	_____	_____
Secondary phase green intervals	g_q	_____	_____	_____	_____
(From Supplemental Permitted LT Worksheet)	g_u	_____	_____	_____	_____
Cycle length, C _____ Red (C-g-g_q-g_w)	r	_____	_____	_____	_____

Arrival and Departure rates (veh/sec)

Arrivals: v/(3600(max(X, 1.0)))	q_a	_____	_____	_____	_____
Primary ph. departures: s/3600	s_p	_____	_____	_____	_____
Secondary ph. departures: $s(g_q + g_u)/(g_u$x3600)	s_s	_____	_____	_____	_____

———— **COMPUTATIONS** ————

	Protected + Permitted (Leading Lefts)	Protected + Permitted (Lagging Lefts)				
X_{perm}	$q_a(g_q + g_u)/s_s g_u$	$q_a(r + g_q + g_u)/s_s g_u$	_____	_____	_____	_____
X_{prot}	$q_a(r + g)/s_p g$	N/A	_____	_____	_____	_____

CASE

1. $X_{perm} <= 1.0$ & $X_{prot} <= 1.0$ 4. $X_{perm} <= 1.0$
2. $X_{perm} <= 1.0$ & $X_{prot} >= 1.0$ 5. $X_{perm} > 1.0$
3. $X_{perm} > 1.0$ & $X_{prot} <= 1.0$

_____   _____   _____   _____

Uniform queue sizes at transition points

Queue at beginning of green arrow	Q_a	_____	_____	_____	_____
Queue at beginning of unsaturated green	Q_w	_____	_____	_____	_____
Residential queue	Q_1	_____	_____	_____	_____
Uniform delay from formulas below	d_t	_____	_____	_____	_____

CASE	Q_a	Q_w	Q_s	DELAY FORMULAS
1.	$q_a r$	$q_a g_q$	0	$D_1 = [.38/(q_a C)] [rQ_a + Q_a^2/(s_p-q_a) + g_q Q_g + Q_a^2/(s_s-q_a)]$
2.	$q_a r$	$Q_w + g_a g_q$	$Q_s- g(s_p-q_a)$	$D_1 = [.38/(q_a C)] [rQ_a + g(q_a+q_g) + g_q(Q_s + Q_w) + Q_a^2/(s_s-q_a)]$
3.	$q_s + q_a r$	$g_a g_q$	$Q_g- g_u(s_s-q_a)$	$D_1 = [.38/(q_a C)] [g_q Q_g + g_u(Q_w + Q_s) + r(Q_s + Q_a) + Q_a^2/(s_p-q_a)]$
4.	0	$q_a(r + g_q)$	0	$D_1 = [.38/(q_a C)] [(r + g_n)Q_u + Q_a^2/(s_p-q_a)]$
5.	$Q_w - g_u(s_s - q_a)$	$q_a(r + g_q)$	0	$D_1 = [.38/(q_a C)] [(r + g_n)Q_u + g_u(Q_u + Q_a) + Q_a^2/(s_p-q_a)]$

Figure 18-22 Worksheet for uniform delay for exclusive LT lanes with compound phasing. [Used with permission of Transportation Research Board, National Research Council, Washington, DC, from *Highway Capacity Manual, Special Report 209,* 3rd Ed., p. 9-46. Copyright © 1994 Transportation Research Board.]

Average signal timing can be estimated using the simplified timing methodology of Chapter 17, or using Equations [18-38] and [18-39] with *v/s* ratios. When this is done, a high target *v/c* ratio is generally assumed—in the range of 0.90 to 0.95. The purpose of actuated signals is to limit unused green time during peak periods. If timed properly, a high *v/c* ratio will result.

For semi-actuated signals, this process is somewhat less useful. Given that the green remains on the major street unless a side-street "call" is sensed, periods of unused green time on the major street are to be expected. Further, with a lightly used side street, the cycle length can reach very high values, as the green stays on the major street for extended periods of time between side-street calls. For semi-actuated signals, a lower *v/c* ratio—in the range of 0.80–0.85—may be a better assumption. In allocating green times within an estimated average cycle length, the side street phase would be allocated minimal green time, i.e., a value of *v/c* close to 1.00. All remaining green time would be allocated to the major street.

At best, this approach "predicts" a highly approximate average signal timing for an actuated signal. Further, the prediction does not respond to timing features of an actuated controller, such as minimum and maximum green times, and the minimum gap required to retain the green on a given phase. The approach also assumes that these critical controller features are properly set, and that detectors are appropriately placed. Poorly-timed actuated signals can be extremely inefficient, and may produce significantly lower *v/c* ratios, and higher delay.

For future cases, it is often more convenient to use an analysis based on the maximum cycle length. The green time would still be allocated in proportion to adjusted volumes or *v/s* ratios. This is a reasonable approach when comparing many different scenarios. It would not, however, effectively illustrate the full benefits of actuated control for any given demand scenario.

Sample Problem 1: With full details

As has been noted repeatedly, few actual analyses using the 1994 *HCM* model are conducted manually. Most rely on software for implementation.

In this section, a sample problem is worked using the HCM-Cinema software package. This product replicates the 1994 *HCM* and produces all of the worksheets discussed herein. In this regard, it is the same as the HCS package. In addition, however, HCM-Cinema runs a NETSIM simulation of the intersection, producing additional outputs not available from the HCS package. The primary reason HCM-Cinema is used herein is that it also produces a graphic of the intersection with input volumes and signal timing. Thus, for illustrative purposes, it is more useful than the HCS package, which produces only tabular output.

For this problem, most of the computations will be repeated manually to enable the student to relate the output to the specific algorithms discussed herein. The problem will also be used to demonstrate the NETSIM portion of the output of this program, and to discuss how it relates to highway capacity and level of service analysis.

The sample used is Sample Problem 1 from Chapter 17, illustrated in Figure 17-19. In that problem, the intersection of two divided four-lane arterials was shown. Each approach had an exclusive left-turn lane. As a result of the signal timing exercise, a three-phase signalization was devised: E-W (all)—19.8 sec; N-S (left turn only)—13.9 sec; N-S (through + right turn only)—27.3 sec. E-W left turns are, therefore, permitted, while N-S left turns are protected. The sample problem statement indicated that the PHF was 0.92, and that moderate numbers of pedestrians were present in all crosswalks. The latter translates to a default value of 200 ped/hr in each crosswalk. Because the simple signal timing method of Chapter 17 did not require it, several other pieces of data are added here: 5% heavy vehicles in all lane groups, 11-ft left-turn lanes, 12-ft through and right-turn lanes, no parking, no local buses, and a location outside the CBD. Arrival type 3 is assumed (random arrivals).

Figure 18-23 shows the principal output of the HCM-Cinema analysis. It shows summary output from the 1994 *HCM* analysis, as well as a diagram showing the intersection and its volumes and signal timing. The summary output illustrates the various lane groups established for analysis. In this case, the four left-turn lanes must be considered to be separate lane groups. Thus, each approach has two lane groups: the exclusive LT lane, and the TH + RT lanes. For

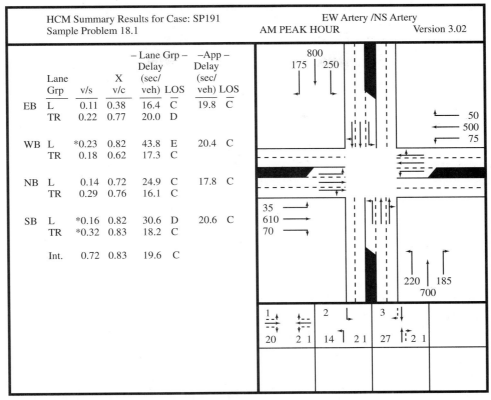

Figure 18-23 HCM-Cinema summary output for Sample Problem 1.

each of these lane groups, the resulting *v/s* ratio, *v/c* ratio, delay, and level of service are shown. Aggregated delays and levels of service for each approach are summarized, as are values for the intersection as a whole.

Note that the signal timings entered are rounded to the nearest full second. The HCM-Cinema program does not allow entry of signal timings to tenths of seconds. Also, yellow intervals of 2 seconds and all red intervals of 1 second are assumed for each phase; t_L is assumed to be 3 seconds/phase. The sections that follow describe the manipulations of each module in detail.

A. Volume adjustment module

The volume adjustment worksheet for this problem is shown in Figure 18-24. The first three columns show the given demand volumes by movement. The computer output has a column *not* included in the *HCM* worksheet. This is the fourth column, headed "Growth

Factor." This is provided to allow analysts to increase demand volumes by a factor to reflect future growth trends, or new development traffic. As this is not an issue in this problem, these factors have all been entered as 1.00. The fifth column is simply the original volumes multiplied by the growth factor. This column is also *not* included in the *HCM* worksheet. Again, as all growth factors were entered as 1.00, the resulting volumes are the same as those originally entered.

The peak hour factor is shown in the sixth column. Using Equation [18-6], all input volumes are divided by the PHF to obtain values of v_p, the flow rate during the peak 15 minutes of the hour. Computations for the EB approach are illustrated below:

$$v_{pEBL} = \frac{35}{0.92} = 38 \text{ vph}$$

$$v_{pEBT} = \frac{610}{0.92} = 663 \text{ vph}$$

VOLUME ADJUSTMENT WORKSHEET
==

App	Mvt	Cur-rent Vol (vph)	Growth Factor	Mvt Vol (vph)	PHF	V_p Peak Mvt Flow (vph)	Lane Grp.	V_g Lane Group Flow (vph)	N Lns	U Lane Util Fact	V Adj. Flow (vph)	Proportion LT	RT
EB	L	35	1.00	35	0.92	38	L	38	1	1.00	38	1.00	0.00
	T	610	1.00	610	0.92	663	TR	739	2	1.05	776	0.00	0.10
	R	70	1.00	70	0.92	76							
WB	L	75	1.00	75	0.92	82	L	82	1	1.00	82	1.00	0.00
	T	500	1.00	500	0.92	543	TR	597	2	1.05	627	0.00	0.09
	R	50	1.00	50	0.92	54							
NB	L	220	1.00	220	0.92	239	L	239	1	1.00	239	1.00	0.00
	T	700	1.00	700	0.92	761	TR	962	2	1.05	1010	0.00	0.21
	R	185	1.00	185	0.92	201							
SB	L	250	1.00	250	0.92	272	L	272	1	1.00	272	1.00	0.00
	T	800	1.00	800	0.92	870	TR	1060	2	1.05	1113	0.00	0.18
	R	175	1.00	175	0.92	190							

Figure 18-24   Volume adjustment results for Sample Problem 1.

$$v_{pEBR} = \frac{70}{0.92} = 76 \text{ vph}$$

In the eighth column of Figure 18-24, analysis lane groups are established. In this case, this is relatively straightforward. Exclusive LT lanes must be treated as separate lane groups, as there can be no equalizing of traffic between these lanes and others on the approach. Given this, all other lanes of each approach form additional lane groups. The analysis proceeds with *eight* lane groups: one LT lane group and one TH + RT lane group on each approach. The ninth column is used to combine appropriate movement flow rates into lane group flow rates. As LT lane groups do not combine movements, these flow rates do not change. The TH and RT flow rates on each approach, however, must be added, as these flows combine in a single lane group. Thus:

$$v_{gEB}(\text{TH + RT}) = 663 + 76 = 739 \text{ vph}$$
$$v_{gWB}(\text{TH + RT}) = 543 + 54 = 597 \text{ vph}$$
$$v_{gNB}(\text{TH + RT}) = 761 + 201 = 962 \text{ vph}$$
$$v_{gSB}(\text{TH + RT}) = 870 + 190 = 1060 \text{ vph}$$

The tenth column indicates the number of lanes in each lane group: 1 for the LT lane groups, and 2 for the TH + RT lane groups. The eleventh column lists the lane utilization factor, U, taken from Table 18-4. This value is 1.00 for one-lane groups, and 1.05 for two-lane groups. There is no change in the LT lane group flow rates. For the TH + RT lane groups:

$$v_{EB}(\text{TH + RT}) = 739 \times 1.05 = 776 \text{ vph}$$
$$v_{WB}(\text{TH + RT}) = 597 \times 1.05 = 627 \text{ vph}$$
$$v_{NB}(\text{TH + RT}) = 962 \times 1.05 = 1010 \text{ vph}$$
$$v_{SB}(\text{TH + RT}) = 1060 \times 1.05 = 1113 \text{ vph}$$

The eleventh and twelfth columns merely list the proportion of left and right turns in each lane group. For all LT lane groups, the proportion of left turns is 1.00, and 0.00 for right turns. For the TH + RT lane groups, the proportion of left turns is 0.00. The proportion of right turns is:

$$P_{RT}(\text{EB TH + RT}) = 76/739 = 0.103, \text{ rounded to } 0.10$$
$$P_{RT}(\text{WB TH + RT}) = 54/597 = 0.090$$
$$P_{RT}(\text{NB TH + RT}) = 201/962 = 0.209, \text{ rounded to } 0.21$$
$$P_{RT}(\text{SB TH + RT}) = 190/1060 = 0.179, \text{ rounded to } 0.18$$

B. Saturation flow rate module

The results of the saturation flow rate module are shown in Figure 18-25. Each lane group begins with an ideal saturation flow rate of 1900 pcphgpl, which is entered into the third column. The first adjustment is to multiply by the number of lanes in each group: 1 for the LT lane groups, and 2 for the TH + RT lane groups.

Columns five through twelve indicate the adjustment factors for eight critical prevailing conditions. The first six are relatively trivial:

- *Lane Width Adjustment Factor*, f_w: Obtained from Table 18.5. For LT lane groups, with 11-ft lane widths, the factor is 0.967. For TH + RT lane groups, with 12-ft lane widths, the factor is 1.000.
- *Heavy Vehicle Adjustment Factor*, f_{HV}: Obtained from Table 18-6. All movements have 5% heavy vehicles. The factor for this is 0.952.
- *Grade Adjustment Factor*, f_g: Obtained from Table 18-7. All grades are level, which is the standard condition. Thus, the factor is 1.000.
- *Parking Adjustment Factor*, f_p: Obtained from Table 18-8. There is no parking on any lane group. The factor for this, which is the standard condition, is 1.000.
- *Local Bus Blockage Adjustment Factor*, f_{bb}: Obtained from Table 18-9. As there are no local buses, this factor is 1.000.
- *Location Adjustment Factor*, f_a: Obtained from Table 18-10. For a location outside the CBD, this factor is 1.000.

The *right turn adjustment factor*, f_{RT} is obtained from Table 18-11, and is somewhat more complicated. For all LT lane groups, where there are no right turns, this factor is 1.000. For the TH + RT lane groups, a factor based on the proportion of right-turning vehicles in the lane group and the volume of conflicting pedestrians must be selected. Since all right turns are made from shared right-turn lanes with permitted phasing, *Case 5* is appropriate for finding factors. There are *200* conflicting pedestrians in each crosswalk. Thus:

EB TH + RT: for Case 5200 ped/hr, and 0.10 right turns, the factor must be interpolated between values of 1.00 (for 0.00 RTs) and 0.951 (for 0.20 RTs); the result is a factor of 0.975.

WB TH + RT: for Case 5200 ped/hr, and 0.09 right turns, the factor must be similarly interpolated; the result is 0.978.

NB TH + RT: for Case 5200 ped/hr, and 0.21 right turns, the factor must be interpolated between values of 0.951 (for 0.20 RTs) and 0.902 (for 0.40 RTs); the result is 0.949.

SB TH + RT: for Case 5200 ped/hr, and 0.18 right turns, the factor must be interpolated between values of 1.00 (for 0.00 RTs) and 0.951 (for 0.20 RTs); the result is 0.956.

The *left-turn adjustment factor*, f_{LT} is taken from Table 18-12. For all of the RT + TH lane groups,

SATURATION FLOW ADJUSTMENT WORKSHEET

App	Lane Group	Ideal Sat. Flow	N Lanes	Lane Width f_w	Heavy Veh f_{HV}	Grade Grade f_g	Pkg. Pkg. f_p	Bus Block f_{bb}	Area Type f_a	Right Turn f_{RT}	Left Turn f_{LT}	s Adj. Sat. Flow vphg
EB	L	1900	1	0.967	.952	1.000	1.00	1.00	1.00	1.00	.200	350
	TR	1900	2	1.000	.952	1.000	1.00	1.00	1.00	.975	1.00	3527
WB	L	1900	1	0.967	.952	1.000	1.00	1.00	1.00	1.00	.200	350
	TR	1900	2	1.000	.952	1.000	1.00	1.00	1.00	.978	1.00	3538
NB	L	1900	1	0.967	.952	1.000	1.00	1.00	1.00	1.00	.950	1662
	TR	1900	2	1.000	.952	1.000	1.00	1.00	1.00	.949	1.00	3433
SB	L	1900	1	0.967	.952	1.000	1.00	1.00	1.00	1.00	.950	1662
	TR	1900	2	1.000	.952	1.000	1.00	1.00	1.00	.956	1.00	3458

Figure 18-25   Saturation flow rate module for Sample Problem 1.

where there are no left turns, this factor is 1.00. For the NB LT and SB LT lane groups, where protected phasing exists, the factor from Table 18-12 is 0.950. The EB LT and WB LT lane groups, however, involve permitted phasing, and must use the special procedure for this case. Figure 18-22 shows the worksheet for computation of these factors. Key computations are illustrated below.

g_f: As both EB LT and WB LT lane groups contain only left turns, g_f is 0.00 for both lane groups, by definition.

g_q: Equation [18-31a] is used to compute this factor. Note that each LT lane group is opposed by a 2-lane TH + RT lane group:

$$g_q = \frac{v_{olc}qr_o}{0.5 - [v_{olc}(1 - qr_o)/g_o]} - t_L$$

where: v_{olc} (EB) = 627 (70)/(3600 × 2)
                      = 6.10 vpcpl

v_{olc} (WB) = 776 (70)/(3600 × 2)
               = 7.54 vpcpl
$qr_o = 1 - R_{po}(g_o/C)$
$R_{po} = 1.000$ for arrival type 3 (Table 18-3)
qr_o (EB/WB) = 1 − 1(20/70) = 0.714

$$g_{qEB} = \frac{6.10 \times 0.714}{0.5 - [6.10(1 - 0.714)/20]} - 3$$

= 7.54 sec

$$g_{qWB} = \frac{7.54 \times 0.714}{0.5 - [7.54(1 - 0.714)/20]} - 3$$

= 10.74 sec

g_u: As $g_q > g_f$, $g_u = g - g_q$. Then:
g_u(EB) = 20.00 − 7.54 = 12.46 sec
g_u(WB) = 20.00 − 10.74 = 9.26 sec

P_L: As the problem involves exclusive left-turn lane groups, P_L is 1.00 for both the EB and WB LT lane groups, by definition.

```
WORKSHEET FOR PERMITTED LEFT TURNS OPPOSED BY A MULTILANE APPROACH
==================================================================================
                                            EB        WB       NB      SB
Cycle Length C, (sec)                       70        70
Actual Green, G                             20.0      20.0
Effective Green, g (sec)                    20.0      20.0
Opposing Effective Green, go                20.0      20.0
Number of Lanes, N                          1         1
Opposing Lanes, No                          2         2
Adjusted Left-Turn Flow Rate, vLT           38        82
Proportion of LT, PLT                       1.00      1.00
Opposing Flow Rate, vo (vph)                627       776
Lost Time Per Phase, tL                     3.0       3.0
Left Turns per Cycle, LTC=vLT*C/3600        0.74      1.59
Opp Flow (/Ln/Cycle), volc=vo*C/(3600*No)   6.10      7.54
Opposing Platoon Ratio, Rpo                 1.00      1.00
gf=G**(-0.860*LTC**.629)-tL, gf<=g          0.00      0.00
Opp. Queue Ratio, gro=1-Rpo*(go/C)          0.71      0.71
gq                                          7.54      10.74
gu=g-gq (if gq<=gf then gu=g-gf)            12.46     9.26
fs=(875-.625*vo)/1000, fs>=0                0.48      0.39
PL=PLT[1+{(N-1)*g/(fs*gu+4.5)}]             1.00      1.00
EL1                                         3.91      5.62
fmin=2*(1+PL)/g                             0.20      0.20
fm=[gf/g]+[gu/g][1/{1+PL(EL1-1)}]           0.20      0.20
fLT = [fm + .91 * (N-1)] / N                0.20      0.20
```

Figure 18-26 Special worksheet for permitted left-turn factor, Sample Problem 1.

The left-turn adjustment factors can now be computed using Equation [18-23]. To use this equation, a value of the left-turn equivalent, E_{L1}, must be selected from Table 18-13. For an exclusive LT lane group with more than two signal phases (this is a 3-phase signal) and two opposing lanes, equivalents are selected based on opposing flow. For the EB LT lane group, the opposing flow is 627 vph. The equivalent must be interpolated between values of 3.6 (for 600 vph opposing flow) and 5.9 (for 800 vph opposing flow). The result is an equivalent of 3.91. The WB LT lane group has an opposing flow of 776 vph. The equivalent must be interpolated between the same two values. The result is an equivalent of 5.62. Then:

$$f_m = \frac{g_f}{g} + \frac{g_u}{g} \frac{1}{1 + P_L(E_{L1} - 1)}$$

$$f_{mEB} = \frac{0}{20} + \frac{12.46}{20} \frac{1}{1 + 1.00(3.91 - 1)} = 0.159$$

$$f_{mWB} = \frac{0}{20} + \frac{9.26}{20} \frac{1}{1 + 1.00(5.62 - 1)} = 0.082$$

Both of these values, however, are subject to the minimum value based on "sneakers" as defined by Equation [18-24]:

$$f_m(\text{min}) = \frac{2(1 + P_L)}{g} = \frac{2(1 + 1)}{20} = 0.20$$

Since the minimum value of f_m exceeds either of the computed values, the minimum must be used. Thus, f_m for both the EB LT and WB LT lane groups is 0.20. As these are exclusive LT lane groups of one lane, $f_{LT} = f_m = 0.20$. This factor, however, indicates that virtually *all* left turns are being made as sneakers, and that no effective filtration is possible through the heavy opposing flow. This information may be useful in considering whether or not to install an exclusive LT phase for the E-W street.

All of the adjustment factors for the saturation flow rate module are now complete. The total saturation flow rate for each lane group is the multiplication of 1900 pcphgpl by N and all of the adjustment factors:

$s(\text{EB LT})$ = 1900(1)(0.967)(0.952)(1)(1)(1) $\times$ (1)(1.000)(0.20) = 350 vphg

$s(\text{EB TH+RT})$ = 1900(2)(1.000)(0.952)(1)(1)(1) $\times$ (1)(0.975)(1.00) = 3527 vphg

$s(\text{WB LT})$ = 1900(1)(0.967)(0.952)(1)(1)(1) $\times$ (1)(1.000)(0.20) = 350 vphg

$s(\text{WB TH+RT})$ = 1900(2)(1.000)(0.952)(1)(1)(1) $\times$ (1)(0.978)(1.00) = 3538 vphg

$s(\text{NB LT})$ = 1900(1)(0.967)(0.952)(1)(1)(1) $\times$ (1)(1.000)(0.95) = 1662 vphg

$s(\text{NB TH+RT})$ = 1900(2)(1.000)(0.952)(1)(1)(1) $\times$ (1)(0.949)(1.00) = 3433 vphg

$s(\text{SB LT})$ = 1900(1)(0.967)(0.952)(1)(1)(1) $\times$ (1)(1.000)(0.95) = 1662 vphg

$s(\text{SB TH+RT})$ = 1900(2)(1.000)(0.952)(1)(1)(1) $\times$ (1)(0.956)(1.00) = 3458 vphg

C. Capacity analysis module

The output worksheet from the capacity analysis module is shown in Figure 18-27. This worksheet combines the outputs of the volume adjustment and saturation flow rate modules to find v/s ratios, capacities, and v/c ratios.

In many ways, the capacity analysis module is quite straightforward. Column 5 in Figure 18-27 takes lane group flow rates from the volume adjustment module, v, and divides them by lane group saturation flow rates from the saturation flow rate module, s. For example, the v/s ratio for the EB LT lane group is 38/350 = 0.11. Others follow similarly.

Once all of the v/s ratios are determined, critical lane groups can be identified. In this case, there are three discrete signal phases without overlaps, and the process is relatively easy.

- In Phase 1, all EB and WB flows move simultaneously. Thus, the four v/s ratios for the two LT lane groups and the TH + RT lane groups are examined to find the highest value. The WB LT lane group, with a v/s ratio of 0.23 is the highest, and identifies this as the critical lane group for Phase 1. Note that this is another indication that the permitted left turn may be a problem. It would be preferable if one of the TH + RT turn groups were critical, as they carry the larger volumes. The g/C ratio for this phase is 20/70 = 0.29.
- In Phase 2, the NB LT and SB LT moves. The larger v/s ratio is 0.16, and identifies the SB LT lane group as critical for this phase. The g/C ratio for this phase is 14/70 = 0.20.

```
                    CAPACITY ANALYSIS WORKSHEET
================================================================================
              v          s         v/s       g/C          c           X
       Lane   Adj Flow   Adj Sat   Flow      Green     Capacity      v/c
App.   Group  (vph)      (vphg)    Ratio     Ratio     (vph)        Ratio
-----  ------ ---------- --------- ------    ------    ----------   ------
EB     L          38        350    0.11      0.29        100         0.38
       TR        776       3527    0.22      0.29       1008         0.77

WB   * L          82        350    0.23      0.29        100         0.82
       TR        627       3538    0.18      0.29       1011         0.62

NB     L         239       1662    0.14      0.20        332         0.72
       TR       1010       3433    0.29      0.39       1324         0.76

SB   * L         272       1662    0.16      0.20        332         0.82
     * TR       1113       3458    0.32      0.39       1334         0.83
```

*Critical Lane Group

Sum (v/s) crit = 0.72   Xc = 0.83
Cycle Length, c = 70 Sec   Lost Time Per Cycle, L = 9.0 Sec

Figure 18-27   Capacity analysis worksheet for Sample Problem 1.

• In Phase 3, the NB and SB TH + RT lane groups move. The SB TH + RT is critical, as it has the higher *v/s* ratio of 0.32. The *g/C* ratio for this lane group is 27/70 = 0.39.

Capacity for each lane group is the saturation flow rate multiplied by the *g/C* ratio. Therefore:

$$c(\text{EB LT}) \qquad\quad = 350 \times 0.29 = 100 \text{ vph}$$

$$c(\text{EB TH + RT}) = 3527 \times 0.29 = 1008 \text{ vph}$$

$$c(\text{WB LT}) \qquad\quad = 350 \times 0.29 = 100 \text{ vph}$$

$$c(\text{WB TH + RT}) = 3538 \times 0.29 = 1011 \text{ vph}$$

$$c(\text{NB LT}) \qquad\quad = 1662 \times 0.20 = 332 \text{ vph}$$

$$c(\text{NB TH + RT}) = 3433 \times 0.39 = 1324 \text{ vph}$$

$$c(\text{SB LT}) \qquad\quad = 1662 \times 0.20 = 332 \text{ vph}$$

$$c(\text{SB TH + RT}) = 3458 \times 0.39 = 1334 \text{ vph}$$

With capacities now computed, the determination of *v/c* ratios is simply accomplished by dividing the lane group flow rate, *v*, by the computed capacities, *c*:

$$X_{EB\,LT} = 38/100 = 0.38$$

$$X_{EB\,T/R} = 776/1008 = 0.77$$

$$X_{WB\,LT} = 82/100 = 0.82$$

$$X_{WB\,T/R} = 627/1011 = 0.62$$

$$X_{NB\,LT} = 239/332 = 0.72$$

$$X_{NB\,T/R} = 1010/1324 = 0.76$$

$$X_{SB\,LT} = 272/332 = 0.82$$

$$X_{SB\,T/R} = 1113/1334 = 0.83$$

The critical *v/c* ratio is computed from the sum of the critical lane group *v/s* ratios, which is 0.23 + 0.16 + 0.32 = 0.71. Note that the computer output indicates a total of 0.72. This is because the *v/s* ratios have been rounded herein to the nearest hundredth. The computer does all mathematics exactly. If the *v/s* ratios were shown to three or four decimal places, the total would be greater than 0.715, which would round to 0.72. The correct value, 0.72, is used in subsequent computations. Then, using Equation [18-4], the critical *v/c* ratio is computed as:

$$X_c = 0.72 \frac{70}{70 - 9} = 0.83$$

The *v/c* ratios for the three critical approaches are all similar: $X_{WB\,LT} = 0.82$; $X_{SB\,LT} = 0.82$; $X_{SB\,T/R} = 0.83$. Thus, the timing developed using the Chapter 17 methodology produced a scheme in which the critical lane group *v/c* ratios were approximately equal. However, the timing scheme developed in Chapter 17 was intended to produce a critical *v/c* ratio of 0.90. There are several reasons for this discrepancy. First, the minimum cycle length computation (Chapter 17) was 66 seconds; a 70-second cycle was used, which marginally increases capacity and lowers *v/c* ratios. The most important reason, however, is that the Chapter 17 methodology assumes a default value for saturation flow rate that is apparently somewhat too low for the intersection as described. Nevertheless, on the basis of *v/c* ratios, the estimated signal timing is quite reasonable, and appears to work well.

D. Level of service module

In the final analysis module, delays for each lane group, approach, and for the intersection as a whole are computed using Equations [18-40], [18-41], and [18-42]. It is noted that *arrival type 3* was assumed for this problem, so that the delay adjustment factor, *DF*, is 1.00 for all lane groups, and $m = 16$ for all lane groups. Thus, for each lane group:

$$d_i = d_{1i}(1.00) + d_{2i} = d_{1i} + d_{2i}$$

The level of service worksheet is shown in Figure 18-28.

Uniform Delay, d_1

$$d_{1i} = 0.38C \frac{[1 - (g/C)]^2}{[1 - (g_i/C)X_i]}$$

$$d_{1\,EB\,LT} = 0.38(70)\frac{[1 - 0.29]^2}{[1 - 0.29(0.38)]} = 15.2 \text{ sec/veh}$$

$$d_{1\,EB\,T/R} = 0.38(70)\frac{[1 - 0.29]^2}{[1 - 0.29(0.77)]} = 17.4 \text{ sec/veh}$$

$$d_{1\,WB\,LT} = 0.38(70)\frac{[1 - 0.29]^2}{[1 - 0.29(0.82)]} = 17.7 \text{ sec/veh}$$

$$d_{1\,WB\,T/R} = 0.38(70)\frac{[1 - 0.29]^2}{[1 - 0.29(0.62)]} = 16.5 \text{ sec/veh}$$

$$d_{1\,NB\,LT} = 0.38(70)\frac{[1 - 0.20]^2}{[1 - 0.20(0.72)]} = 19.9 \text{ sec/veh}$$

$$d_{1\,NB\,T/R} = 0.38(70)\frac{[1 - 0.39]^2}{[1 - 0.39(0.76)]} = 14.2 \text{ sec/veh}$$

$$d_{1\,SB\,LT} = 0.38(70)\frac{[1 - 0.20]^2}{[1 - 0.20(0.82)]} = 20.4 \text{ sec/veh}$$

$$d_{1\,SB\,T/R} = 0.38(70)\frac{[1 - 0.39]^2}{[1 - 0.39(0.83)]} = 14.8 \text{ sec/veh}$$

Overflow Delay, d_2

$$d_{2i} = 173X_i^2\left[(X_i - 1) + \sqrt{(X_i - 1)^2 + \frac{mX_i}{c_i}}\right]$$

$$d_{2\,EB\,LT} = 173(0.38)^2\left[(0.38 - 1)\right.$$

$$\left. + \sqrt{(0.38 - 1)^2 + \frac{16(0.38)}{100}}\right]$$

$$= 1.2 \text{ sec/veh}$$

$$d_{2\,EB\,T/R} = 173(0.77)^2\left[(0.77 - 1)\right.$$

$$\left. + \sqrt{(0.77 - 1)^2 + \frac{16(0.77)}{1008}}\right]$$

$$= 2.6 \text{ sec/veh}$$

$$d_{2\,WB\,LT} = 173(0.82)^2\left[(0.82 - 1)\right.$$

$$\left. + \sqrt{(0.82 - 1)^2 + \frac{16(0.82)}{100}}\right]$$

$$= 26.1 \text{ sec/veh}$$

$$d_{2\,WB\,T/R} = 173(0.62)^2\left[(0.62 - 1)\right.$$

$$\left. + \sqrt{(0.62 - 1)^2 + \frac{16(0.62)}{1011}}\right]$$

$$= 0.8 \text{ sec/veh}$$

```
                      LEVEL OF SERVICE WORKSHEET
=================================================================================
          ---------Delay 1---------    ------Delay 2------   --Ln Grp--   ---App---
          X       g/C      d1     DF     c      m      d2     Delay        Delay
    Lane  v/c     Green    (sec  Adj.   Cap    Calib  (sec    (sec          (sec
App Grp.  Ratio   Ratio    /veh) Fact   (vph)  Param  /veh)   /veh)  LOS    /veh)  LOS
--- ----- ------ ------   ------ -----  ------ ------ ------  ------  ----  ------  ----
EB   L    0.38    0.29    15.2   1.00    100   16.0    1.2    16.4    C     19.8    C
     TR   0.77    0.29    17.4   1.00   1008   16.0    2.6    20.0    C

WB   L    0.82    0.29    17.7   1.00    100   16.0   26.1    43.8    E     20.4    C
     TR   0.62    0.29    16.5   1.00   1011   16.0    0.8    17.3    C

NB   L    0.72    0.20    19.9   1.00    332   16.0    5.0    24.9    C     17.8    C
     TR   0.76    0.39    14.2   1.00   1324   16.0    1.9    16.1    C

SB   L    0.82    0.20    20.4   1.00    332   16.0   10.2    30.6    D     20.6    C
     TR   0.83    0.39    14.8   1.00   1334   16.0    3.4    18.2    C
```

Cycle = 70 Sec

Intersection
19.6 C

Figure 18-28   Level of service worksheet for Sample Problem 1.

$$d_{2\,NB\,LT} = 173(0.72)^2 \left[(0.72 - 1) \right.$$
$$\left. + \sqrt{(0.72 - 1)^2 + \frac{16(0.72)}{332}} \right]$$
$$= 5.0 \text{ sec/veh}$$

$$d_{2\,NB\,T/R} = 173(0.76)^2 \left[(0.76 - 1) \right.$$
$$\left. + \sqrt{(0.76 - 1)^2 + \frac{16(0.76)}{1324}} \right]$$
$$= 1.9 \text{ sec/veh}$$

$$d_{2\,SB\,LT} = 173(0.82)^2 \left[(0.82 - 1) \right.$$
$$\left. + \sqrt{(0.82 - 1)^2 + \frac{16(0.82)}{332}} \right]$$
$$= 10.2 \text{ sec/veh}$$

$$d_{2\,SB\,T/R} = 173(0.83)^2 \left[(0.83 - 1) \right.$$
$$\left. + \sqrt{(0.83 - 1)^2 + \frac{16(0.83)}{1334}} \right]$$
$$= 3.4 \text{ sec/veh}$$

Total Delay, d

$$d_{EB\,LT} = 15.2 + 1.2 = 16.4 \text{ sec/veh (LOS C,}$$
Table 18-1)

$$d_{EB\,T/R} = 17.4 + 2.6 = 20.0 \text{ sec/veh (LOS C,}$$
Table 18-1)

$$d_{WB\,LT} = 17.7 + 26.1 = 43.8 \text{ sec/veh (LOS E,}$$
Table 18-1)

$$d_{WB\,T/R} = 16.5 + 0.8 = 17.3 \text{ sec/veh (LOS C,}$$
Table 18-1)

$$d_{NB\,LT} = 19.9 + 5.0 = 24.9 \text{ sec/veh (LOS C,}$$
Table 18-1)

$$d_{NB\,T/R} = 14.2 + 1.9 = 16.1 \text{ sec/veh (LOS C,}$$
Table 18-1)

$$d_{SB\,LT} = 20.4 + 10.2 = 30.6 \text{ sec/veh (LOS D,}$$
Table 18-1)

$$d_{SB\,T/R} = 14.8 + 3.4 = 18.2 \text{ sec/veh (LOS C}$$
Table 18-1)

Aggregate Delay for Approaches

$$d_{EB} = \frac{16.4(38) + 20.0(776)}{38 + 776} = 19.8 \text{ sec/veh}$$
(LOS C)

$$d_{WB} = \frac{43.8(82) + 17.3(627)}{82 + 627} = 20.4 \text{ sec/veh}$$
$$\text{(LOS C)}$$

$$d_{NB} = \frac{24.9(239) + 16.1(1010)}{239 + 1010} = 17.8 \text{ sec/veh}$$
$$\text{(LOS C)}$$

$$d_{SB} = \frac{30.6(272) + 18.2(1113)}{272 + 1113} = 20.6 \text{ sec/veh}$$
$$\text{(LOS C)}$$

Aggregate Delay for the Intersections

$$d_I = \frac{[19.8(814) + 20.4(709) + 17.8(1249) + 20.6(1385)]}{814 + 709 + 1249 + 1385}$$

$$= 19.6 \text{ sec/veh (LOS C)}$$

The delay results are not startling, nor do they indicate any particular problem. The aggregate intersection delay of 19.6 sec/veh (level of service C) is acceptable for almost any location. By approach, all of the delays are in a narrow range around the intersection value, and no gross inequity is indicated. Where lane group delays are involved, the WB LT and SB LT lane groups (both are critical lane groups) stand out because of the relatively high value of overflow delay in both cases. The overflow delay in these cases arises from the likelihood of some individual cycle failures within the analysis period, given the relatively high *v/c* ratios, and the fact that both, but particularly the WB LT, have low capacities. As noted previously, however, minor left-turn movements frequently experience higher delays than through vehicles, and this situation is not necessarily inequitable.

In general, this analysis demonstrates that the simple signal timing approach of Chapter 17 can lead to very reasonable and workable signal timings.

E. NETSIM results from HCM-Cinema

Traffic simulation, including NETSIM and other simulators, is discussed in Chapter 25. As noted, however, the HCM-Cinema program used to generate worksheets and problem solutions herein also produces simulation results for the intersection using NETSIM. While the principles of NETSIM will not be discussed in this chapter, it is useful to review the kind of results available through HCM-Cinema for intersection analysis. Figure 18-29 shows the summary of NETSIM outputs for the sample problem intersection.

NETSIM Summary for Case: SP191 Sample Problem 18.1				
App	Lane Group	Queues Per Lane Avg/Max (veh)	Avg Speed (mph)	Spillback in Worst Lane (% of Peak Period)
EB	L	1/ 2	6.4	0.0
	TR	6/ 6	10.9	0.0
	All		10.7	0.0
WB	L	2/ 4	2.2	0.0
	TR	5/ 7	11.1	0.0
	All		9.7	0.0
NB	L	5/ 9	4.5	0.0
	TR	6/ 8	11.9	0.0
	All		10.3	0.0
SB	L	6/ 8	4.4	0.0
	TR	7/ 10	11.9	0.0
	All		10.3	0.0
Intersection			10.2	

Figure 18-29 Summary NETSIM output for Sample Problem 1.

For each lane group, the summary output includes average and maximum queues, average speed through the intersection area, and spillback in the worst lane (in terms of percent of the peak hour).

Queue information is of significant value. The average size of the queue per lane in each lane group indicates the number of vehicles queuing during the average signal cycle. The maximum queue lengths, however, are of greater interest. For example, the output indicates a maximum queue size of 9 vehicles for the NB LT lane group. This translates to a queue length of 9 × 20 = 180 ft, where 20 ft is taken as the average spacing of queued vehicles. The problem specified the length of the left-turn bay as 200 ft. This is just sufficient to hold the maximum queue expected. For through/right-turn lanes, the maximum queue size should be compared to the block length to determine whether spillback into the next intersection is likely.

Average speed is based on the travel time it takes a vehicle to traverse the intersection, where the default distance defined in HCM-Cinema includes 600 ft on the approach and departure side of the intersection. The speed of each vehicle is the distance divided by the total time (including stops, deceleration, and acceleration) to traverse this distance. As can be seen, the left-turning vehicles experience the slowest speeds, reflecting generally larger stopped delays and slower operating speeds.

Spillback data shows the *percent of the analysis period* during which the worst lane of the lane group overflows the distances set in HCM-Cinema. For the sample problem, this was 200 ft for the LT lane groups, and the default value of 600 ft for all others. It should be noted that the item analysis assumes adequate turn bay length. If the NETSIM analysis showed spillback from the left-turn bay, this would put into question the results of the HCM analysis. No spillbacks are indicated in the data.

More detailed NETSIM output is available through HCM-Cinema, including percentage of cycles with turn bay overflow, and for shared lanes, percentage of cycles where a turning vehicle is prevented from entering the intersection by a queue of non-turners. HCM-Cinema also produces an animation of the intersection, as well as fuel consumption and air pollution data.

It should be noted that NETSIM also produces estimates of delay. These, however, are not consistent with the concept and measurement of stopped delay as described herein. HCM-Cinema, therefore, suppresses this particular output.

F. Alternative considerations

The original signal timing process did not indicate the need for protected left turn phasing on the E-W arterial. The full analysis, however, yielded some results that lead to an opposite conclusion: Virtually all left turns from the EB and WB approaches are handled as "sneakers," and the delay, particularly to WB left-turners, is quite high compared to other lane groups.

This hypothesis is easily checked using software. The only part of the input information that changes is the phase plan and timing. Various trials using different timings can be easily tested; alternatively, the signal timing can be re-worked assuming a 4-phase plan with E-W protected left turns.

Figure 18-30 shows the summary results for a 4-phase plan. It was developed within the 70-second cycle length, since the original analysis results in X_c of 0.83, indicating that there is some "room" within the existing cycle. A short exclusive LT phase for the E-W street is introduced by deducting green time from the E-W through phase, the N-S LT phase, and the N-S through phase in approximate inverse relation to the v/s ratios for those lane groups in the original analysis. Note that the creation of a fourth phase introduces another set of lost times into the cycle, increasing t_L from 9 sec/cycle to 12 sec/cycle.

From the summary results, it is obvious that the addition of a fourth phase does not improve the operation of the intersection. The value of X_c rises to 0.91, which is not disturbing. Delay, however, also increases to 26.0 sec/veh for the intersection as a whole. Further, the WB LT (the reason for concern about a permitted phase), also has more delay than in the original plan. Note that additional trials with somewhat longer cycle lengths did not result in delay values comparable to or less than the original results. Thus, it is logical to conclude that the introduction of an LT phase for the E-W street is *not* a productive option.

Another option might be to take the signal timing of Figure 18-30, which includes the E-W LT phase, and to add permitted left turns during the E-W and N-S through/right-turn phases. This produces compound phasing for all left turns. Figure 18-31 shows the summary results of this case. While delays are reduced from the 4-phase case, they remain higher than for the original 3-phase case, in which EB and WB left turns are permitted. The delays to left-turning vehicles are, however, substantially reduced with this option. Unfortunately, providing the fourth phase increased the lost time per cycle, and reduced the green time available for through movements. The decline in delays to left-turning vehicles is more than offset by increases to vehicles in through/right-turn lane groups.

The results for the compound phasing option, however, also highlight an anomaly in the 1994 *HCM* model. Figure 18-32 shows the results of the capacity analysis worksheet for the compound phasing option of Figure 18-31. Note that it indicates that *no* vehicles are using the permitted portions of the compound left-turn phases. This follows the general rule that the 1994 *HCM* follows: Demand must fully utilize the first portion of the phase before vehicles are assigned

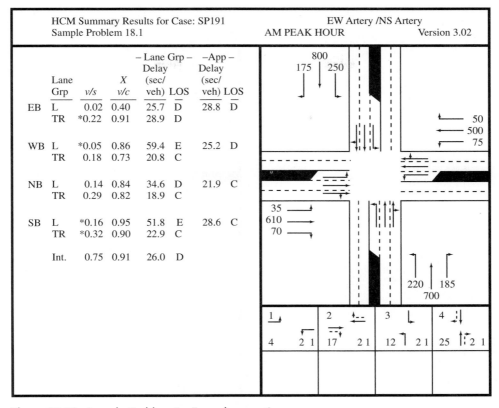

Figure 18-30   Sample Problem 1: Four-phase option.

to the second. As the protected portions of the phase were adequate to handle the demand, the addition of permitted phasing does not cause any vehicles to be assigned to it. If, then, no vehicles are using the permitted portion of the phase, how can a significant delay reduction be experienced? The delay model for compound phasing is, unfortunately, not coordinated with the assumed use of compound phases in other parts of the model. The results are, therefore, inconsistent.

Reality is undoubtedly somewhere in between. As some left-turning vehicles will obviously arrive during the permitted portion of the compound phase, some will doubtless progress during this period—they are not going to wait for the next protected phase, even if they move as "sneakers" at the end of the permitted portion of the phase. Thus, some delay benefits from adding permitted turns is reasonable. Whether the delay model of the 1994 *HCM* is the best depiction of this delay is open to question.

Other options could be applied to this problem, including splitting EB and WB LT phases, or even providing one for the WB LT movement and not for the much smaller EB LT. None, however, would greatly enhance the operational results of the original proposal.

Sample Problem 2: Looking at alternatives

Figure 18-33 illustrates a signalized intersection that will be evaluated using the 1994 *HCM* model. Various scenarios and alternatives for improvement will also be considered and discussed. Detailed computations for each alternative, however, are not shown, in the interests of space. HCM-Cinema was once again used to generate results, and summary outputs will be presented.

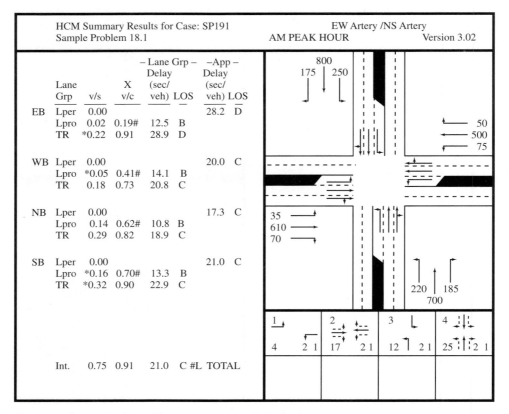

Figure 18-31   Sample Problem 1: Compound LT phasing option.

A. Base case

A 1994 *HCM* analysis of the intersection in Figure 18-33 yields the results illustrated in Figure 18-34. The SB and WB lane groups are critical, operating at *v/c* levels close to 1.00. Delays on the two critical lane groups are comparable, and are reasonably high. Delay for the intersection as a whole is 30.0 sec/veh, with $X_c = 0.98$. The overall LOS is D, and no lane group operates at anything worse than LOS D.

The permitted left turns appear to work acceptably on both facilities. To consider the impact of the permitted left turns, the left-turn adjustment factors from the saturation flow worksheet should be consulted. They are: $f_{LTEB} = 0.562$; $f_{LTWB} = 0.698$; $f_{LTNB} = 0.560$; and $f_{LTSB} = 0.517$.

The saturation flow rates are reduced from the ideal by these proportions to reflect the impact of opposed left-turning vehicles. While the effect is a serious one, the intersection as a whole operates acceptably under existing conditions.

Note that the graphic included in the HCM-Cinema summary output *does not* show the detail of parking lanes on the NB and SB approaches. The results, however, do account for its presence, and for the 30 mvts/hr which are estimated to exist.

B. Adding NB volume

In the first scenario, a small shopping center is opening just south of the intersection. During the P.M. peak hour (which is under analysis here), this shopping center is expected to generate an additional 300 vph in the northbound direction. The additional vehicles generated are expected to travel straight through the intersection. Thus, the NB through volume, originally 600 vph, becomes 900 vph. Figure 18-35 shows the summary output for this case.

The addition of 300 vph NB has caused several things to occur:

1. The sum of critical *v/s* ratios rises to 1.51, and $X_c = 1.62$. This is a clear indication that the original

		v	*s*	*v/s*	*g/C*	*c*		*X*	
App	Lane Group	Adj Flow (vph)	Adj Sat (vphg)	Flow Ratio	Green Ratio	Capacity (vph)		*v/c* Ratio	
EB	Lper	0	350	0.00	0.29	103		0.00	
	Lpro	38	1662	0.02	0.06	95	198#	0.40	0.19#
	*TR	776	3527	0.22	0.24	857		0.91	
WB	Lper	0	350	0.00	0.29	103		0.00	
	*Lpro	82	1662	0.05	0.06	95	198#	0.86	0.41#
	TR	627	3538	0.18	0.24	859		0.73	
NB	Lper	0	250	0.00	0.40	103		0.00	
	Lpro	239	1662	0.14	0.17	285	388#	0.84	0.62#
	TR	1010	3433	0.29	0.36	1226		0.82	
SB	Lper	0	250	0.00	0.40	103		0.00	
	*Lpro	272	1662	0.16	0.17	285	388#	0.95	0.70#
	*TR	1113	3458	0.32	0.36	1235		0.90	

HCM Analysis: SP191

Capacity Analysis Worksheet

Sum(*v/s*)crit = 0.75   *Xc* = 0.91   Cycle = 70   Lost Time = 12

* Critical Lane Group   # Left Movement Total

Figure 18-32 Sample Problem 1: Capacity worksheet for compound phasing option.

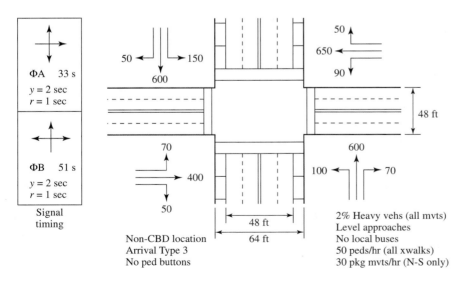

Figure 18-33 Intersection for Sample Problem 2.

Signal timing

ΦA   33 s
y = 2 sec
r = 1 sec

ΦB   51 s
y = 2 sec
r = 1 sec

Non-CBD location
Arrival Type 3
No ped buttons

2% Heavy vehs (all mvts)
Level approaches
No local buses
50 peds/hr (all xwalks)
30 pkg mvts/hr (N-S only)

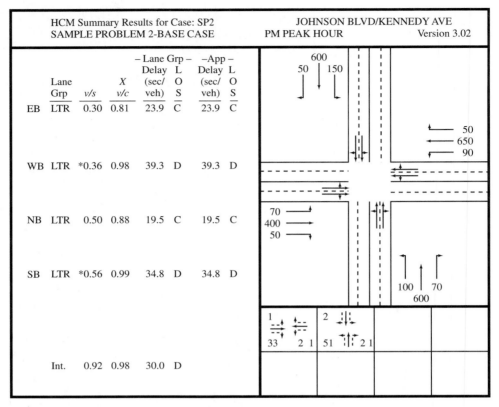

	Lane Grp			− Lane Grp −		−App −	
	Lane Grp	v/s	X v/c	Delay (sec/ veh)	L O S	Delay (sec/ veh)	L O S
EB	LTR	0.30	0.81	23.9	C	23.9	C
WB	LTR	*0.36	0.98	39.3	D	39.3	D
NB	LTR	0.50	0.88	19.5	C	19.5	C
SB	LTR	*0.56	0.99	34.8	D	34.8	D
	Int.	0.92	0.98	30.0	D		

Figure 18-34 Sample Problem 2: Base case output.

geometrics, phase plan, and cycle length are insufficient to handle the new demand volumes. Reallocation of the green time will not remedy the situation under these circumstances. Lanes will have to be added, the signal phasing changed, and/or the cycle length increased to effect an acceptable solution.

2. The analysis has indicated the existence of a *defacto left-turn lane* on the SB approach, and analyzed it as an exclusive LT lane. If left-turn adjustment factors are considered, it is seen that f_{LTSB} = 0.078: Over 92% of the saturation flow rate is lost due to the permitted left turn from this approach. This impact has occurred because the opposing flow—NB—has been increased to 900 through vehicles. As a result, SB left-turning vehicles are moving primarily as sneakers. Because of this, they are blocking the left lane most of the time, to the point where *all* through and right-turning vehicles are using the right lane of the SB approach.

3. NB and SB approaches clearly fail, both from the point of view of unacceptable *v/c* ratios (>1.00), and delays. No delay values for these approaches are shown, as the *v/c* ratios exceed 1.2. For such cases, the 1994 *HCM* delay algorithm is unreliable. As queues on the NB and SB approaches continue to grow throughout the period that these flows exist, delays also grow continuously. Level of service F is indicated, because the delays will be considerably higher than 60 sec/veh.

The addition of 300 vph to the NB approach has caused the intersection to break down. Because this would lead to building queues and eventual spillback into adjacent intersections to the north and south, such a situation cannot be tolerated. The next several

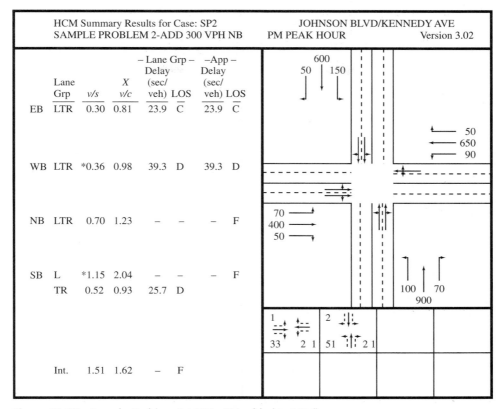

Figure 18-35 Sample Problem 2: 300 vPH added to NB flow.

sections explore various approaches to mitigating this situation.

C. A potential remedy: Addition of LT bays and protected phasing for NB and SB approaches

The previous analysis indicates that the addition of 300 NB vehicles creates substantial problems for the SB permitted left turn. One straightforward way to correct the situation would involve the addition of exclusive left-turn bays and signal phases for the NB and SB approaches. Since there is parking on both of these approaches, an additional lane can be provided by eliminating curb parking for a minimum of 250 ft from the stop lines.

Figure 18-36 shows the summary results for this case. Note that the original 90-second signal cycle has been retained, and that the allocation of green time was "optimized" on the basis of both *v/c* ratios and delays by trial-and-error using HCM-Cinema. In practical terms, finding the "best" signal timing by trial-and-error took about 7 trials, and about 15 minutes using the software.

The addition of the exclusive LT lanes and phasing brings the intersection to an acceptable operating condition. The average delay for the intersection is reduced to 29.4 sec/veh, which is lower than the base case, before the addition of the 300 vph NB. X_c is 0.95, and the resulting LOS is D. The delay to SB left-turning vehicles is high compared to other vehicles: 49.5 sec/veh, which is LOS E for this lane group.

D. Varying the cycle length

The previous analysis has confirmed that provision of exclusive LT lanes and phases in the NB and SB directions will mitigate the impacts of the additional

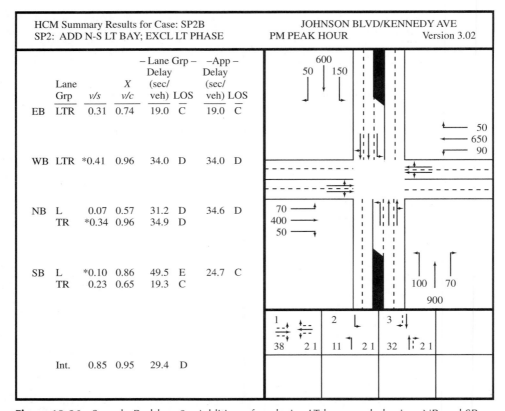

Figure 18-36   Sample Problem 2: Addition of exclusive LT lanes and phasing, NB and SB.

300 vph on the NB approach. As the 90-second cycle length was originally optimized based on the base condition, the issue of an optimum cycle length for the new situation should be investigated.

The minimum cycle length can be determined from Equation [18-36]. The sum of critical *v/s* ratios is taken from Figure 18-36 as 0.85. While this value depends somewhat on the cycle length and green splits, this computation gives a good indication of the range of cycle lengths that can be considered:

$$C_{min} = \frac{L}{1 - \Sigma (v/s)_{ci}} = \frac{9}{1 - 0.85} = 60 \text{ sec}$$

The three-phase signal plan is now tried for cycle lengths between 60 seconds and 120 seconds, the practical maximum for a pretimed signal. Green splits are arranged to keep *g/C* ratios for each phase approximately equal to the case illustrated in Figure 18-36. It should be noted, however, that HCM-Cinema only allows green times to be entered to the nearest full second. Thus, the *g/C* ratios could not be held exactly con-

stant for each cycle length. Table 18-16 lists the overall intersection delays and critical *v/c* ratios that result from various cycle lengths (in increments of 10 seconds).

From Table 18-16, the optimal cycle length is in the range of 70 seconds. Note that the delay range is relatively small until cycle lengths of 110 seconds or higher are reached. Any cycle length in the 70–100 second range would lead to acceptable results, and the final determination would most likely depend on system constraints. Had cycle lengths smaller than 60 seconds been tried, X_c values would have exceeded 1.00, and delays would have been extremely high—or out of the range in which the model yields a numerical estimate.

E. Another signal timing option: Leading SB LT phase

When 300 vph was added to the NB approach, serious difficulties were encountered with the SB left turn. It would be interesting to see if a better solution than reached so far could be found by providing *only* the

Table 18-16 Sample Problem 2: 3-Phase Timings—Various Cycle Lengths

Cycle Lengths (sec)	X_c	Delay, d (sec/veh)	Level of Service	Comments
60	0.98	27.3	D	X_{WB} = 1.01; SBLT LOS = E
70	0.96	26.7	D	all X < 1.00; SBLT LOS = E
80	0.95	27.8	D	all X < 1.00; SBLT LOS = F
90	0.95	29.4	D	all X < 1.00; SBLT LOS = E
100	0.94	30.7	D	all X < 1.00; SBLT LOS = E
110	0.94	33.1	D	all X < 1.00; SBLT LOS = E
120	0.94	35.6	D	all X < 1.00; SBLT LOS = E

SB left turn with protection. In the scenario posed here, a leading SB phase is provided, followed by a single combined NB/SB phase. NB left turns would be made on a permitted basis during this phase. SB left turns *would not* be permitted in this phase, thereby providing for a fully protected SB left turn.

This analysis was done using the 70-second optimal cycle length determined in section D, although the issue of cycle length can be legitimately re-examined for a different phase plan. Figure 18-37 shows the summary results for this case, which represents the optimum from among various green split trials.

There are several problems with the plan. Average delay for the intersection increases to 27.1 seconds, and the NB left turn, which is not protected, fails, with X = 1.01, and a delay of 86.2 seconds/vehicle. An attempt was made to provide more time for the combined NB/SB phase, thus giving more time for the permitted NB left turn. This was done by adding a permitted SB left turn during this phase, thus providing a protected + permitted SB left turn. This enabled the leading SB phase to be shortened to accommodate a longer through phase. The results of this are shown in Figure 18-38. The NB left turns achieve improved service, and X is now below 1.00 for this movement (0.97). The delay to NB left-turning vehicles is still very high—72.9 seconds—resulting in level of service F.

F. A final phasing option: Leading and lagging N-S compound phasing

From the previous analyses, it is clear that the NB left turn also requires protection to avoid unreasonable delays. A possible refinement is to split the left turn protection for NB and SB flows by providing a lead-ing *and* lagging phase. In this analysis, left turns are permitted during the combined N-S through phase. Thus, the SB left turn has a protected + permitted phase, while the NB left turn has a permitted + protected phase. Figure 18-39 shows the summary results of this analysis.

Overall delay is reduced to 22.6 seconds/vehicle (LOS C), and delays to NB and SB left-turning vehicles are significantly reduced. Again, the substantial decrease in left-turn delays is inconsistent with the assumed use of protected and permitted phases in other parts of the 1994 *HCM* model. Nevertheless, it is reasonable to assume that some turns will be made during the permitted portion of the phase, and that delays would be significantly reduced as a result.

Note that the phasing diagram of Figure 18-39 shows *four* sets of yellow and all red times, even though an examination of a ring diagram would show that this is a *three-phase* signal, and only three sets of lost times are included in the cycle. This simply involves understanding the way HCM-Cinema interprets entered timings. The yellow plus all red in Phase 3 (Figure 18-39) is interpreted as effective green time for SB movements. Remember that lost times are deducted at the *beginning* of a movement, and that SB flows are initiated in Phase 2. The yellow and all-red times in Phase 4 are interpreted as effective green time for NB movements, as these were initiated in Phase 3. The program automatically deducts only three sets of lost times from the cycle.

G. Summary

This sample problem is intended to demonstrate the ability of the 1994 *HCM* model to analyze a wide

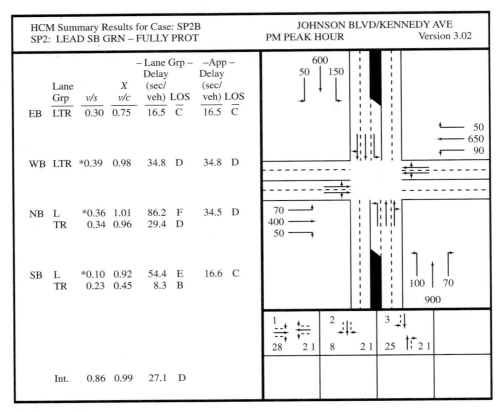

	Lane Grp	v/s	X v/c	– Lane Grp – Delay (sec/ veh)	LOS	–App – Delay (sec/ veh)	LOS
EB	LTR	0.30	0.75	16.5	C	16.5	C
WB	LTR	*0.39	0.98	34.8	D	34.8	D
NB	L	*0.36	1.01	86.2	F	34.5	D
	TR	0.34	0.96	29.4	D		
SB	L	*0.10	0.92	54.4	E	16.6	C
	TR	0.23	0.45	8.3	B		
Int.		0.86	0.99	27.1	D		

HCM Summary Results for Case: SP2B
SP2: LEAD SB GRN – FULLY PROT

JOHNSON BLVD/KENNEDY AVE
PM PEAK HOUR   Version 3.02

Figure 18-37 Sample Problem 2: A leading SB phase—fully protected.

range of signalized intersection options, and to provide the analyst with information on both *v/c* ratios and delays that permit a comprehensive evaluation of these options. In the sample problem illustrated, the final signal timing option resulted in the best combination of *v/c* ratios and delays. Before implementing this plan, system constraints and local policies would be considered as well. Some jurisdictions avoid compound phasing, while others use it frequently. Leading and lagging signalization is not used in some areas. The information provided by a comprehensive analysis, however, is sufficient to allow the traffic engineer to make reasonable and informed choices.

All of the options, including many signal timing trials not shown, were completed in less than one hour using HCM-Cinema. The HCS package would have produced the same numerical results in the same amount of time, but would not have provided graphic output. By hand, these computations would doubtless have taken many days.

While the use of software to implement the 1994 *HCM* model is a practical necessity, traffic engineers must be aware of what every value means, and where it originates. As new versions of software are released, there are always "bugs" to be found. The software user must be knowledgeable enough to recognize an irrational and/or incorrect result when it arises.

The 1997 HCM: Revisions and updates

At its January 1997 meeting, the Highway Capacity and Quality of Service Committee of the Transportation Research Board approved a number of revisions and refinements to the signalized intersection

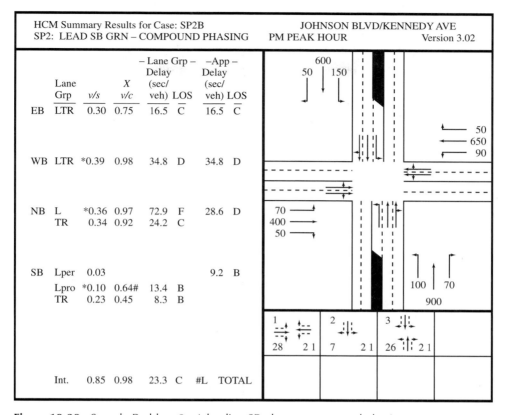

Figure 18-38 Sample Problem 2: A leading SB phase—compound phasing.

A. Level of service criteria

methodology that will appear in the 1997 update of the *HCM*. This section attempts to summarize these changes, which will be incorporated into new versions of the HCS and HCM-Cinema software.

Level of service criteria will be revised to reflect *total delay,* which will be called control delay, rather than the current *stopped delay.* This change will make the delay parameter consistent with that used in the unsignalized intersection and arterial methodologies. Because of this change, new thresholds have been adopted, as shown in Table 18-17.

B. Treatment of yellow and all-red times

The treatment of yellow and all-red times will be separated. Currently, the total of the two is treated as a single entity. This will allow for more realistic computations, and allows default values for lost time to be related to the all-red time.

C. Lane utilization adjustment

The lane utilization factor, U, is being removed from the Volume Adjustment Module, and is to be replaced by an adjustment factor, f_{LU}, to be applied in the Saturation Flow Rate Module. This adds a ninth adjustment factor to be applied to the ideal saturation flow rate, and makes the adjustment for lane utilization similar in format to all other adjustments, which are applied to saturation flow rate. The factors are shown in Table 18-18.

D. Left-turn equivalents

The values of left-turn equivalents (E_{L1}) have been revised and greatly simplified, as shown in Table 18-19.

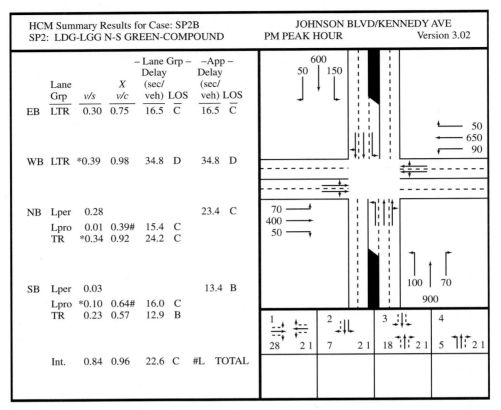

	Lane Grp	v/s	X v/c	– Lane Grp – Delay (sec/veh)	LOS	–App – Delay (sec/veh)	LOS
EB	LTR	0.30	0.75	16.5	C	16.5	C
WB	LTR	*0.39	0.98	34.8	D	34.8	D
NB	Lper	0.28				23.4	C
	Lpro	0.01	0.39#	15.4	C		
	TR	*0.34	0.92	24.2	C		
SB	Lper	0.03				13.4	B
	Lpro	*0.10	0.64#	16.0	C		
	TR	0.23	0.57	12.9	B		
	Int.	0.84	0.96	22.6	C	#L	TOTAL

Figure 18-39 Sample Problem: Leading and lagging greens (N-S) with compound phasing.

Table 18-17 Level of Service Criteria for Signalized Intersections, 1997 *HCM*

Level of Service	Total Delay/Vehicle
A	≤10 sec
B	>10 sec and ≤20 sec
C	>20 sec and ≤35 sec
D	>35 sec and ≤55 sec
E	>55 sec and ≤80 sec
F	>80 sec

[From Draft Chapter 9, *Highway Capacity Manual,* 3rd Ed. (1997 revision), Signalized Subcommittee of the Highway Capacity and Quality of Service Committee, 1996.]

Table 18-18 Lane Utilization Factor, f_{LU}, 1997 *HCM*

Lane Group Movements	No. of Lanes In Group	Lane Utilization Adjustment, f_{LU}
Through or shared	1	1.00
	2	0.95
	3*	0.91
Exclusive LT	1	1.00
	2*	0.97
Exclusive RT	1	1.00
	2*	0.88

*If more than this number of lanes exists, field studies are recommended to determine the appropriate value of f_{LU}.

[From Draft Chapter 9, *Highway Capacity Manual,* 3rd Ed. (1997 revision), Signalized Intersection Subcommittee of the Highway Capacity and Quality of Service Committee, 1996.]

Table 18-19 Left-Turn Equivalents (E_{L1}), 1997 *HCM*

Type of LT Lane	Effective Opposing Flow [v_o/f_{LUo}]						
	1	200	400	600	800	1000	1200
Shared	1.4	1.7	2.1	2.5	3.1	3.7	4.5
Exclusive	1.3	1.6	1.9	2.3	2.8	3.3	4.0

[From Draft Chapter 9, *Highway Capacity Manual*, 3rd Ed. (1997 revision), Signalized Intersection Subcommittee of the Highway Capacity and Quality of Service Committee, 1996.]

The values of E_{L2}, used only when opposing approaches are single-lane, do not change, but a minimum value of 1.00 has been established.

For opposing flows in excess of 1200 vph, a complex formula is used to determine the appropriate equivalent for use.

E. Estimating the proportion of left turns in the left lane (P_L)

The formula for estimating the proportion of left turners in the left lane has been revised to:

$$P_L = P_{LT}\left[1 + \frac{(N-1)g}{g_f + \frac{g_u}{E_{L1}} + 4.24}\right]$$

F. Changes in the delay formula

The 1997 *HCM* revises LOS criteria to reflect control delay. The delay equations, therefore, must be adjusted to reflect this change. Several other changes have been incorporated as a result of an NCHRP study.

The control delay is now estimated as:

$$d = d_1 PF + d_2 + d_3$$

where:

$$d_1 = \frac{0.50C[1 - (g/C)]^2}{1 - (g/C)X}$$

and:

$$d_2 = 900T\left[(X-1) + \sqrt{(X-1)^2 + \frac{8kX}{cT}}\right]$$

The maximum value of X in computing d_1 is 1.00, as is the case at the present time. The d_3 term is added to estimate delay occurring due to residual queues that may be in place at the start of the peak period T. A new appendix will be added to the chapter to illustrate its computation. The appendix will serve as an effective reference, but no one will seriously compute this value by hand.

The inclusion of a variable T in the 1997 *HCM* formulation allows the analyst to select a peak period of varying length. This is an important addition, because overflow delay is quite sensitive to the period of time over which overflow is experienced.

Table 18-20 gives values of k for use in computations.

G. Other revisions

The 1997 *HCM* will contain several other notable revisions. The appendix on measurement of stopped delay in the field has been revised to reflect the measurement of control delay. An appendix has been added to provide a more detailed procedure for estimation of average signal timings for actuated signals. The latter results from a recently completed NCHRP contract.

Table 18-20   Recommended k Values for Pretimed and Actuated Controllers

Unit Extension (Actuated)	Degree of Saturation, X					
	≤ 0.50	0.60	0.70	0.80	0.90	≥ 1.00
2.0 sec	0.04	0.13	0.23	0.32	0.41	0.50
2.5 sec	0.08	0.17	0.25	0.33	0.42	0.50
3.5 sec	0.13	0.20	0.28	0.35	0.43	0.50
4.0 sec	0.15	0.22	0.29	0.36	0.43	0.50
5.0 sec	0.23	0.28	0.34	0.39	0.45	0.50
Pretimed	0.50	0.50	0.50	0.50	0.50	0.50

[From Draft Chapter 9, *Highway Capacity Manual*, 3rd Ed., Signalized Intersection Subcommittee of the Highway Capacity and Quality of Service Committee, 1996.]

References

1. *Highway Capacity Manual, Special Report 209,* 3rd Edition, Transportation Research Board, National Research Council, Washington, DC, (revised) 1994.
2. Akcelik, R., "SIDRA for the *Highway Capacity Manual,*" *Compendium of Papers,* 60th Annual Meeting of the Institute of Transportation Engineers, Orlando, FL, 1990.
3. *SIDRA 4.1 User's Guide,* Australian Road Research Board Ltd., Australia, August 1995.
4. Teply, S., et al., *Canadian Capacity Guide for Signalized Intersections,* 2nd Edition, Institute of Transportation Engineers, District 7—Canada, June 1995.
5. *TRAF User Reference Guide, Version 4.2,* Office of Safety and Traffic Operations R&D, U.S. Department of Transportation, Federal Highway Administration, Washington, DC, February 1994.
6. *TRANSYT-7F, User's Guide, MOST Volume 4,* U.S. Department of Transportation, Federal Highway Administration, Washington, DC, December 1991.
7. *PASSER II-90 User's Guide, MOST Volume 3,* U.S. Department of Transportation, Federal Highway Administration, Washington, DC, December 1991.
8. *HCS User's Guide, Release 2,* McTrans Center, University of Florida, Gainesville, FL, 1995.
9. *HCM-Cinema User's Guide, Version 3.0,* KLD Associates and Polytechnic University, Brooklyn, NY, 1990.
10. Reilly, et al., "Signalized Intersection Capacity Study," *Final Report,* NCHRP Project 3-28(2), JHK & Associates, Tucson, AZ, December 1982.
11. Roess, R., et al., "Levels of Service in Shared-Permissive Left-Turn Lane Groups at Signalized Intersections," *Final Report,* Transportation Training and Research Center, Polytechnic University, Brooklyn, NY, September 1989.
12. Prassas, E., "Modeling the Effect of Permissive Left Turns on Intersection Capacity," Ph.D. Dissertation, Polytechnic University, Brooklyn, NY, January 1995.

Problems

Problem 18-1

Consider the intersection shown in Figure 18-40. A preliminary capacity analysis has resulted in the *v/s* ratios shown. For the phase plan shown:

(a) What is the minimum feasible cycle length?

(b) Find the cycle length required to provide for various reasonable X_c values. From these results, recommend a cycle length for implementation.

(c) Allocate effective green time to the various phases such that all critical lane groups have approximately equal X values.

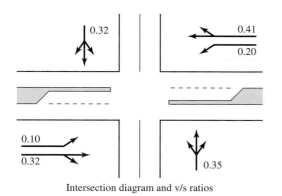

Intersection diagram and v/s ratios

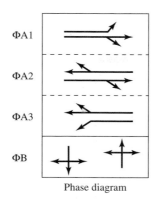

Phase diagram

Figure 18-40 Intersection for Problem 1.

Problem 18–2

Consider Sample Problem 3 in Chapter 17; it is shown in Figure 17-23. The problem specifies that there are no pedestrians, and that the peak hour factor is 0.85. The following information may be added:

> There are 7% heavy vehicles in all movements.
> The SB approach is on a 3% downgrade.
> The NB approach is on a 3% upgrade.
> Lane widths are 11 feet.
> The intersection is located in an outlying area.
> There are no local buses.
> Curb parking is prohibited.

Using the signal timing developed in the sample problem, conduct an analysis of intersection operations using the 1994 *HCM* model. How do the results compare with those anticipated by the signal timing methodology of Chapter 17? Can you recommend and defend any improvements based on your analysis?

Problems 18–3 through 18–7

These problems relate to Problems 17-17 through 17-21, respectively. Analyze each of these intersections using the 1994 *HCM* model. Assume that signal timings were determined as in Chapter 17. In each case, assume that heavy vehicles make up 5% of total traffic, no local buses, pedestrian activity as indicated, and level grades. These are all CBD-located intersections. In each case, compare the results with those anticipated by the signal timing methodology of Chapter 17, and make and defend recommendations for improvements, where appropriate.

Problem 18–8

The intersection of Washington Ave. and Jefferson St. is illustrated with all pertinent information on the input worksheet shown in Figure 18-41.

(a) For the signal timing, design, and volumes shown, determine the *v/c* ratio, delay, and level of service for each lane group, approach, and for the intersection as a whole.

(b) Recommend any improvement to the design, phase plan, or signal timing that would result in improved operations. Demonstrate these improvements using the 1994 *HCM* model for signalized intersections.

Problem 18–9

The input worksheet for Grand Blvd. and Crescent Ave. is shown in Figure 18-42. It is a simple intersection of two one-way arterials in a busy CBD.

(a) Determine the delays, levels of service, and *v/c* ratios for each lane group, approach, and for the intersection as a whole, using the design and signal timing shown.

(b) Vary the cycle length in increments of 10 seconds from 30 to 120 seconds. Allocate green times according to two rules: (1) to keep critical lane group *v/c* ratios equal, and (2) to maintain the same allocation ratio currently in place.

(c) Plot the resulting average delay for the intersection as a whole vs. cycle length for the two allocation policies.

(d) Comment on the results.

Problem 18–10

The intersection of Sunset Ave. and Mountain Rd. is located in an outlying area. The controller is fully actuated, and the signal timing shown in Figure 18-43 represents observed average timings during the analysis period. Determine the *v/c* ratio, delay, and level of service for each lane group, approach, and for the intersection as a whole.

Problem 18–11

The intersection of Main St. and First Ave. is located in a CBD area, and is shown in Figure 18-44.

(a) Find the *v/c* ratio, delay, and level of service for each lane group, approach, and for the intersection as a whole for the conditions shown.

(b) Make and defend recommendations for improving intersection operations where appropriate.

(c) How does the situation change if a movie theater is erected nearby, and causes an additional 175 vph SB TH, an additional 50 vph EB LT, and an additional 60 vph WB RT?

Problem 18–12

A detailed diagram of the intersection of Flatbush Ave. and Tillary St., located in downtown Brooklyn, New York, is shown in Figure 18-45. Perform a complete analysis of the intersection, and recommend needed changes in design and signalization. Test the effectiveness of recommended changes vs. existing conditions.

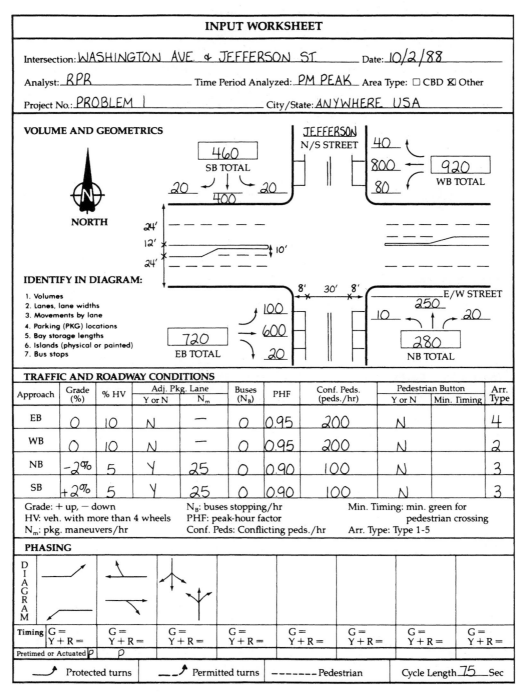

Figure 18-41 Input worksheet for Problem 18–8.

INPUT WORKSHEET

Intersection: GRAND BLVD. & CRESCENT AVE.   Date: 12/09/88

Analyst: RPR   Time Period Analyzed: PM PEAK   Area Type: ☒ CBD ☐ Other

Project No.: PROBLEM 2   City/State: SOMEPLACE USA

VOLUME AND GEOMETRICS

CRESCENT N/S STREET

SB TOTAL

WB TOTAL

NORTH

6 @ 11′

IDENTIFY IN DIAGRAM:

1. Volumes
2. Lanes, lane widths
3. Movements by lane
4. Parking (PKG) locations
5. Bay storage lengths
6. Islands (physical or painted)
7. Bus stops

BUS STOP   4 @ 13′   GRAND   E/W STREET

200   1600

3000   100

3,200   1,700

EB TOTAL   NB TOTAL

TRAFFIC AND ROADWAY CONDITIONS

Approach	Grade (%)	% HV	Adj. Pkg. Lane Y or N	Adj. Pkg. Lane N_m	Buses (N_B)	PHF	Conf. Peds. (peds./hr)	Pedestrian Button Y or N	Pedestrian Button Min. Timing	Arr. Type
EB	O	15	N	—	40⁺	0.90	400	Y		5
WB										
NB	O	5	N	—	0	0.90	400	Y		3
SB										

Grade: + up, − down N_B: buses stopping/hr   Min. Timing: min. green for
HV: veh. with more than 4 wheels   PHF: peak-hour factor   pedestrian crossing
N_m: pkg. maneuvers/hr   Conf. Peds: Conflicting peds./hr   Arr. Type: Type 1-5

PHASING

D I A G R A M								
Timing	G = Y + R =	G = Y + R =	G = Y + R =	G = Y + R =	G = Y + R =	G = Y + R =	G = Y + R =	G = Y + R =
Pretimed or Actuated	P	P	P					

⟋ Protected turns   ⟋ Permitted turns   - - - - - Pedestrian   Cycle Length 60 Sec

Figure 18-42 Input worksheet for Problem 18–9.

INPUT WORKSHEET

Intersection: SUNSET AVE. + MOUNTAIN RD. _____ Date: _____

Analyst: RPR _____ Time Period Analyzed: AM _____ Area Type: ☒ CBD ☐ Other

Project No.: PROBLEM 3 _____ City/State: JEFFERSON, NM _____

VOLUME AND GEOMETRICS

NORTH

MOUNTAIN RD.
N/S STREET

SB TOTAL

300
1400 ← | 1700 |
WB TOTAL

36'

12'

36'

IDENTIFY IN DIAGRAM:

1. Volumes
2. Lanes, lane widths
3. Movements by lane
4. Parking (PKG) locations
5. Bay storage lengths
6. Islands (physical or painted)
7. Bus stops

200
1800
| 2000 |
EB TOTAL

48'

SUNSET AVE. E/W STREET
1300
200 ← ↑ → 100
| 1600 |
NB TOTAL

TRAFFIC AND ROADWAY CONDITIONS

Approach	Grade (%)	% HV	Adj. Pkg. Lane Y or N	Adj. Pkg. Lane N_m	Buses (N_B)	PHF	Conf. Peds. (peds./hr)	Pedestrian Button Y or N	Pedestrian Button Min. Timing	Arr. Type
EB	0	10	N	—	0	0.95	LOW	Y	—	3
WB	0	10	N	—	0	0.95	LOW	Y	—	3
NB	0	10	N	—	0	0.95	LOW	Y	—	3
SB	—	—	—	—	—	—	—	—	—	—

Grade: + up, − down
HV: veh. with more than 4 wheels
N_m: pkg. maneuvers/hr

N_B: buses stopping/hr
PHF: peak-hour factor
Conf. Peds: Conflicting peds./hr

Min. Timing: min. green for pedestrian crossing
Arr. Type: Type 1-5

PHASING

D I A G R A M								
Timing	G = Y + R =	G = Y + R =	G = Y + R =	G = Y + R =	G = Y + R =	G = Y + R =	G = Y + R =	G = Y + R =
Pretimed or Actuated	A	A	A					

⟋ Protected turns ___⟋ Permitted turns ------- Pedestrian Cycle Length_____Sec

Figure 18-43 Input worksheet for Problem 18–10.

INPUT WORKSHEET

Intersection: MAIN STREET & FIRST AVENUE _____ Date: _____

Analyst: RPR _____ Time Period Analyzed: PM _____ Area Type: ☒ CBD ☐ Other

Project No.: PROBLEM 4 _____ City/State: SOMEWHERE, U.S.A. _____

VOLUME AND GEOMETRICS

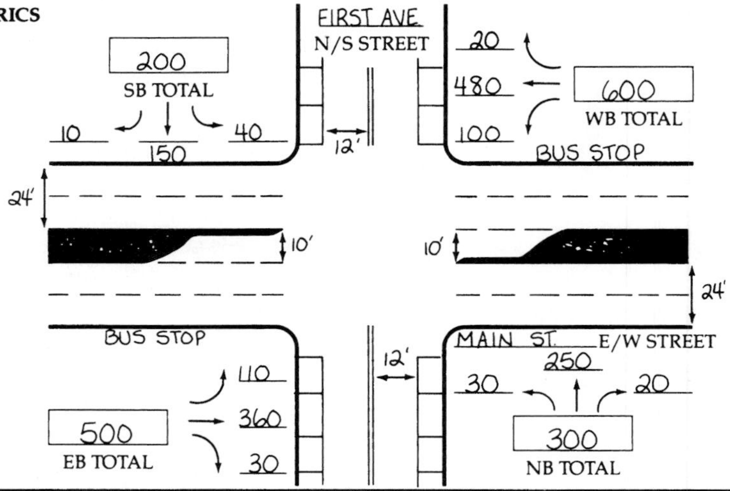

FIRST AVE
N/S STREET

200
SB TOTAL

20
480
100
600
WB TOTAL
BUS STOP

10   40
150

12'

NORTH

24'

10'

10'

24'

IDENTIFY IN DIAGRAM:

1. Volumes
2. Lanes, lane widths
3. Movements by lane
4. Parking (PKG) locations
5. Bay storage lengths
6. Islands (physical or painted)
7. Bus stops

BUS STOP

110
360
30

500
EB TOTAL

12'

MAIN ST.   E/W STREET
250
30   20

300
NB TOTAL

TRAFFIC AND ROADWAY CONDITIONS

Approach	Grade (%)	% HV	Adj. Pkg. Lane Y or N	Adj. Pkg. Lane N_m	Buses (N_B)	PHF	Conf. Peds. (peds./hr)	Pedestrian Button Y or N	Pedestrian Button Min. Timing	Arr. Type
EB	0	10	N	—	20	0.95	100	Y	—	4
WB	0	10	N	—	20	0.95	100	Y	—	4
NB	0	5	Y	10	0	0.95	200	Y	—	2
SB	0	5	Y	10	0	0.95	200	Y	—	2

Grade: + up, − down N_B: buses stopping/hr   Min. Timing: min. green for
HV: veh. with more than 4 wheels   PHF: peak-hour factor   pedestrian crossing
N_m: pkg. maneuvers/hr   Conf. Peds: Conflicting peds./hr   Arr. Type: Type 1-5

PHASING

DIAGRAM								
Timing G = Y + R =	G = Y + R =	G = Y + R =	G = Y + R =	G = Y + R =	G = Y + R =	G = Y + R =	G = Y + R =	
Pretimed or Actuated P	P	P						

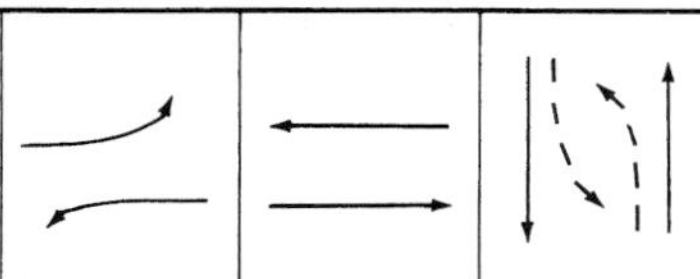

⟶ Protected turns   ⟶ Permitted turns   ------- Pedestrian   Cycle Length 75 Sec

Figure 18-44 Input worksheet for Problem 18–11.

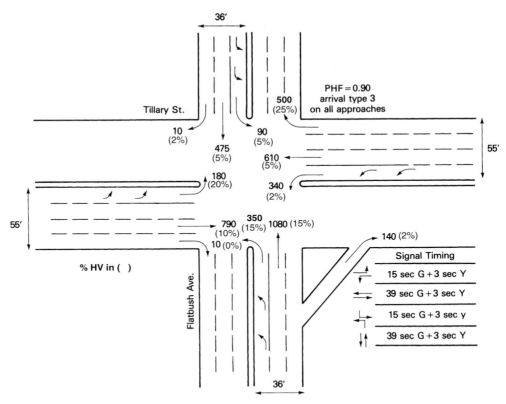

Figure 18-45 Diagram of Flatbush Ave. and Tillary St.

19

Actuated Signals and Detection

Pretimed signals operate with constant cycle lengths, phase sequences, and interval timings. Traffic demand, however, varies with time, and often displays short-term perturbations that can cause an isolated signal cycle, or a short series of cycles to fail. Consider the case shown in Figure 19-1, which illustrates five consecutive cycles of a selected signal phase. The phase has a fixed capacity of 10 vehicles/phase, or a total of 50 vehicles for the five phases shown. The illustration also shows a demand that is exactly equal to this capacity: 50 vehicles. They do not, however, arrive at a uniform rate of 10 per cycle, and this causes problems.

The problem is that while demand may vary from cycle to cycle, capacity (with a pretimed controller) is constant. In the situation depicted in Figure 19-1, capacity was sufficient for the total demand occurring over the five green phases illustrated. In reality, however, a queue of six vehicles remains unserved at the end of the five green phases, because more than 10 vehicles arrived for service during the *last two green periods*.

It is just this type of problem that actuated control attempts to address. Through the use of detectors, an actuated controller is provided with information concerning current demand, and is able to reallocate green times on a cycle-by-cycle basis in response to that information. In Figure 19-1, if the controller had varied the amount of green time allocated to the movement in question in response to the observed demand pattern, less green time would have been allocated during green Phases 1 and 2, and more would have been allocated in green Phases 4 and 5. The result would have been no queue, or a smaller one, depending on the timing, which would in turn result in considerably less delay to vehicles.

Actuated control and controllers

There are three basic types of actuated control, each with controllers that are somewhat different in their design:

1. *Semi-Actuated Control:* Semi-actuated control includes detection only on minor side-street approaches to the intersection. The green remains on

542

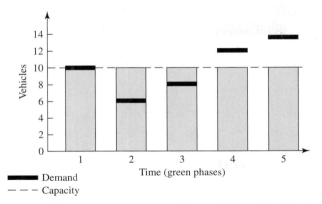

Figure 19-1 Variation in arrival demand at a signalized intersection.

the main street until a "call" for service on the side-street is registered. This type of control is frequently used when side-street traffic is relatively light, but signalization is required to periodically interrupt the main street flow to allow side-street vehicles to safely cross. This type of control is often adopted when signal warrant 2 is the principal reason for placement of the signal.

2. *Full-Actuated Control:* In full-actuated control, all approaches have detectors, and phases are sequenced according to "calls" for service on all approaches. This type of control is common at busy, but relatively isolated intersections, where demand fluctuations during the day would cause any fixed timing to be inefficient and/or ineffective.

3. *Volume-Density Control:* Volume-density control is basically the same as full-actuated control with additional demand responsive features, as discussed later in this chapter.

The basic characteristic of all forms of actuated control is that the cycle length and phase splits, and even the phase sequence, may vary from cycle to cycle in response to detector actuations. This makes such controllers inappropriate for use in most coordinated signal systems, where all signals must operate on a single fixed cycle length to maintain offsets and progression patterns. At critical locations within a coordinated system, actuated controllers may be used to alter the allocation of green time within a fixed cycle length, but this deprives the controller of most of its ability to vary cycle length to meet demand.

Detection for actuated signalization

The vast majority of actuated signal installations use *inductive loops* for detection purposes. In some areas, pressure plate and sonic detectors are used, but these are becoming relatively rare occurrences. Refer to Chapter 14 for a more detailed discussion of detectors.

The most common form of detection is *point detection.* In such a scheme, a single detector is placed for each approach lane to be actuated. The detector relays information as to whether a vehicle has passed over the detector. *Area detection* is provided by using a *long induction loop,* or a series of point detectors. These are generally used in conjunction with volume-density controllers, which can vary some settings based on the presence of a vehicle anywhere in the detection area, or to "count" the number of vehicles stored in the detection area.

Modern video technology is also rapidly developing. Wide-area video detection systems are now receiving intensive study, and may be available for practical applications within a reasonable horizon of 5 to 10 years. The great advantage of such systems, described in Chapter 14, is that the pavement need not be disturbed, and a single "detector" (a video camera in this case) can be used to monitor a number of lanes and approaches.

Actuated control features and operation

Each actuated phase (for semi-actuated operation) and all phases (for full-actuated operation) have the following features that must be set on the controller:

- *Minimum Green Time:* Each phase has a minimum green time; older controllers divided this time into two portions—an *initial green interval,* and a *unit extension.* The initial green interval was intended to provide sufficient time for all vehicles potentially stored between the detector and the stop line to enter the intersection; the unit extension allowed another vehicle to travel from the detector to the stop line.
- *Passage Time Interval:* The passage time interval allows a vehicle to travel from the detector to the stop

line, and is analogous to the "unit extension" of older controllers. The passage time setting, however, also defines the maximum gap between vehicles arriving at the detector to retain a given green phase. Where the actual passage time is too short for the latter purpose, the "passage time" setting may be increased. On some older controllers, passage time and unit extension settings may be separately established.

- *Maximum Green Time:* Each phase has a maximum green time. If demand is sufficient to retain a given green phase to this limit, the green will arbitrarily terminate, assuming that there is a "call" on another phase.

- *Recall Switch:* Each phase has a recall switch; when "on," the green is recalled from a terminating phase, whether or not there is demand; when "off," the green is retained on the previous phase until a "call" for service is received.

- *Yellow* Change Interval and *All Red* Clearance Interval: These are established as fixed times in the same manner as described for pretimed controllers in Chapter 17.

Figure 19-2 illustrates the operation of an actuated phase based on these three settings. When a green indication is initiated, it will be retained for *at least* the specified minimum green period. Additional detector actuations may occur during this minimum green period. If they occur, and there is at least one passage time left before the minimum green terminates, no green time is added. If a vehicle arrives during the minimum green, and there *is less than one passage time* left before its termination, an amount of green time equal to the passage time is added *from the time of the actuation;* this is what is happening for the first actuation shown in Figure 19-1.

The controller now enters the extension portion of the phase. If a subsequent actuation occurs *within* one passage time interval, another passage time interval is added to the green (again, from the time of the actuation, NOT the end of the passage time interval). This process continues.

The green is terminated by one of two mechanisms: a) a passage time elapses without an additional actuation, or b) the maximum green time is reached, and there is a call on another phase. Thus, the length of a phase is constrained to a range of the minimum

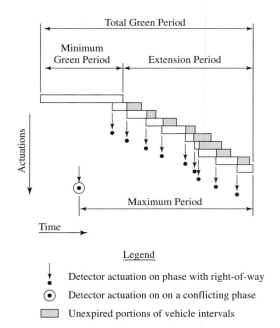

Figure 19-2 Operation of an actuated phase. [Used with permission of Institute of Transportation Engineers, from *Traffic Detector Handbook,* 2nd Ed., JHK & Associates, p. 66. Copyright © Institute of Transportation Engineers.]

green to the maximum green. The maximum green may be violated only if the recall switch on the next phase is "off" and no demand exists on any other phase.

The gap time of a single stream of vehicles observed by a detector as vehicles pass over it is somewhat less than the actual gap. This is because a vehicle activates a loop as it passes over, but does not deactivate it until the rear of the vehicle clears the loop. The error between apparent and actual gap is the time it takes the length of the vehicle to traverse the detector.

Another practical consideration involves multiple lanes. Detectors for a given phase, even when multiple lanes are involved, are most often connected to the controller using a single lead-in cable. In this case, the gap time may involve a vehicle clearing one detector, with a subsequent vehicle encroaching on another. Thus, the probability of short gaps being observed to extend the green is higher where multiple lanes are involved. This can be avoided if each detector is separately wired to the controller, but this is an expensive and infrequent practice.

Volume-density controllers are generally used with area detectors, or with point detectors set back considerable distances from the stop line. This type of control is recommended when approach speeds are high (always when ≥45 mph; often when ≥35 mph). These controllers have two additional features (beyond the minimum green, passage time, and maximum green):

- *Variable Initial Timing:* The "minimum green" is essentially made variable, affected by the number of vehicles "counted" as crossing the detector during the previous "yellow" and "red" phases on the approach. For area detection, the number of vehicles stored in the detection area at the initiation of the green is used. The variable initial timing is made of a *minimum green* (different from that used for other controller types), a *seconds per actuation* setting, and a maximum initial interval. The *minimum green* in this case is set at an arbitrary low value, usually between 5 and 8 seconds. The setting for "seconds per actuation" defines how much initial green time is added for each stored actuation (beyond those that are accommodated by the minimum green). The maximum initial interval defines the cut-off for total minimum green, and should be approximately the same as the minimum green used for other types of controllers. Figure 19-3 illustrates this process.
- *Gap Reduction:* Because volume-density controllers are often used in conjunction with long detector set-backs, the passage time may be fairly high, making for an inefficient minimum gap to retain the green. In such cases, the passage time and the minimum desirable gap are separately established, and the controller establishes a mechanism for gradually reducing the minimum gap from the passage time to the desirable minimum gap setting. This is done by setting the "time before reduction" and "time to reduce" in addition to the passage time and the minimum desirable gap. The minimum gap starts at the passage time. When a call on a conflicting approach is received, the "time to reduction" is initiated. At the end of this period, the gap is linearly reduced to the minimum desirable level over the "time to reduce." Figure 19-4 illustrates this process.

The volume-density controller has two big advantages over full-actuated controllers that are particularly important when dealing with long detector

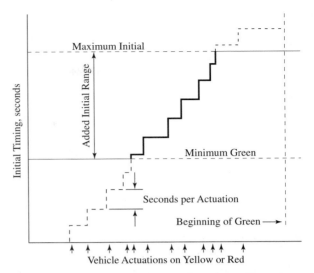

Figure 19-3 Variable initial timing for volume-density controllers. [Used with permission of Institute of Transportation Engineers, from *Traffic Detector Handbook*, 2nd Ed., JHK & Associates, p. 68. Copyright © Institute of Transportation Engineers.]

set-backs: The initial green allocated can vary to reflect the number of stored vehicles, eliminating the need to assume that the entire area between the detector and the stop line is filled; and the long passage time required by long detector set-backs can be reduced to reflect a more reasonable minimum gap.

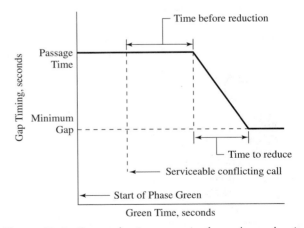

Figure 19-4 Gap reduction process for volume-density controllers. [Used with permission of Institute of Transportation Engineers, from *Traffic Detector Handbook*, 2nd Ed., JHK & Associates, p. 68. Copyright © Institute of Transportation Engineers.]

Both of these allow more efficient operation in situations where high speed of approaching vehicles would otherwise lead to inefficient timings.

Signal timing parameters and detector placement

One of the principal parameters affecting some of the timing parameters noted is the placement of the detector; specifically, how far it is from the stop line. The following sections discuss timing parameters, and how each can be addressed with respect to detector placement.

A. Minimum green time

For all actuated phases, the minimum green time must be established. This is generally taken to be equal to an initial interval that allows all vehicles potentially stored between the detector and the stop line to enter the intersection. For actuated (*not* volume-density controllers), it must be assumed that the entire distance between the detector and the stop line is occupied by stored vehicles. This is because actuated controllers do not "count" the number of such vehicles (volume-density controllers do), but merely register whether any such vehicles are present. Thus, safety demands that a full queue be assumed.

An initial interval must allow all potentially stored vehicles between the detector and the stop line to enter the intersection. A "start-up" time of 4 seconds is incorporated, in addition to 2 seconds for each vehicle (the latter based on a saturation flow rate of 1800 pcphgpl). Thus:

$$G_{\min} = 4 + \left[2 \times \text{Integer} \left(\frac{d}{20} \right) \right] \qquad [19\text{-}1]$$

where: $G_{\min}$ = initial interval (sec),
   d = distance between detector and stop line, ft
   20 = assumed distance between stored vehicles, ft
   4 = assumed start-up time, sec
   2 = assumed saturation headway, sec

Consider a location where the detector is located 50 ft from the stop line, and approach speeds are 30 mph. Then:

$$G_{\min} = 4 + \left[2 \times \text{Integer} \left(\frac{50}{20} \right) \right] = 4 + 2(3)$$

$$= 10 \text{ sec}$$

If a volume-density controller were in place, a minimum green between 5 and 8 seconds would be arbitrarily established. For each vehicle counted as being stored, 2 to 3 seconds of additional minimum green would be added. A minimum green of 10 seconds would be established, based on the computation illustrated above. In this case, the range of potential minimum green values would be relatively small, but that is related to the relatively close placement of the detector to the stop line. Most volume-density situations involve much larger distances.

B. Passage time and the allowable gap

Passage time is the time it takes a vehicle to travel from the detector to the stop line at its approach speed:

$$P = \frac{d}{1.468S} \qquad [19\text{-}2]$$

where: P = passage time, sec
    d = distance from detector to stop line, ft
    S = approach speed of vehicles, mph

Equation [19-2] may be used to compute the passage time for any given detector location. The passage time, however, is also used as the maximum allowable gap between vehicles at the detector that will retain the green. Consider the case of the 30 mph approach with a detector placed 50 ft from the stop line:

$$P = \frac{50}{1.468(30)} = 1.14 \text{ sec}$$

The passage time of 1.14 seconds would be inappropriate as an allowable gap. Effectly, headways at the detector must be less than this value in order to retain the green. As saturation headways are generally in the 2.0–3.0 second range, depending on prevailing conditions, it would be almost impossible to retain the green beyond the minimum with such an allowable gap.

Thus, the passage time becomes a minimum value for the allowable gap. In cases where the passage time results in an inappropriately low allowable gap, it is arbitrarily increased to an acceptable level. In general, allowable gaps range between 3 and 4 seconds for most conditions.

C. Maximum green times

Maximum green times are generally set by working out an optimal cycle length and phase splits as if the controller were pretimed. This can be done using the procedures of Chapter 17, or by trial-and-error using the *HCM* model of Chapter 18. The usual strategy would then be to increase the green times so computed by a factor of 1.25 or 1.50 to set the maximum greens.

D. Some detector location strategies

It is possible to estimate an optimal detector placement, given the approach speed of traffic and a desired minimum green time. Short minimum greens are desirable, as they do not build in significant amounts of unused green time should demand on any given phase not be sufficient to fully utilize the minimum green.

Consider a location with an approach speed of 40 mph. If a detector placement is desired to yield a minimum green time of 10 seconds, and a reasonable allowable gap is 3 seconds, where should the detector be placed?

Using Equation [19-1], and solving for distance d (ignoring the integer function for this purpose):

$$d = 10G_{min} - 40 \qquad [19\text{-}3]$$

For the problem posed:

$$d = 10(10) - 40 = 60 \text{ ft}$$

To obtain a minimum green time of 10 seconds with a 40 mph approach speed, the detector should be 60 feet away from the stop line. This is, of course, approximate, as the integer function is ignored in Equation [19-3]. In this case, the result is an even multiple of 20 ft, and the answer is exact.

Another approach is to set the detector back a distance equal to what can be traveled in 3 to 4 seconds, which is the normal range of allowable gaps. Then:

$$d = 1.468S(3) = 4.404S \qquad [19\text{-}4a]$$

or:

$$d = 1.468S(4) = 5.872S \qquad [19\text{-}4b]$$

For the problem originally posed, and using Equation [19-4a], this results in:

$$d = 4.404(40) = 176 \text{ ft}$$

This approach, however, does not yield a desired minimum green time, designated in Equation [19-3]. The minimum green for this condition is:

$$G_{min} = 4 + 2 \text{ integer} \left(\frac{176}{20}\right) = 20 \text{ sec}$$

Because of this, many agencies limit the maximum set-back of the detector to between 120 and 170 feet.

Table 19-1 shows recommended values of detector set-back based on the 3-to-4-second rule of Equations [19-4a] and [b], minimum green time, and passage time as a function of approach speed. Note that as approach speeds increase, longer set-backs are recommended for the detector, resulting in longer minimum green times.

However, many practical considerations could interfere with the use of recommended values. For one thing, a detector can never be placed further back from the nearest point at which vehicles can enter the approach. If there were a driveway located 50 feet from the stop line, the detector could not be placed any further back from this location, lest a vehicle enter the approach *without* tripping the detector. This becomes a larger problem where curb parking is permitted, as vehicles can enter the approach virtually to the stop line itself. In such cases, detectors must be located in close proximity to the stop line, and parking is generally prohibited for a distance of 20 ft from the stop line. The recommended placements and timings of Table 19-1 are easier to implement in suburban settings and at major isolated intersections of roadways with no curb parking and no driveways located near the intersection itself.

Pedestrian requirements

Pedestrian requirements at an actuated signal are no different than for pretimed control. The primary difference is that minimum green times rarely, if ever, safely accommodate pedestrian crossings. Thus, most actuated phases must include a pedestrian pushbutton and an actuated pedestrian phase, as described in Chapter 17. Because of the long crossing

Table 19-1 Recommended Detector Locations and Timing Parameters

Approach Speed		Detector Set-Back (To front of loop)		Minimum Green	Passage Time
mph	kph	ft	m	sec	sec
15	24	40	12	8.0	3.0
20	32	60	18	10.0	3.0
25	40	80	24	12.0	3.0
30	48	100	30	14.0	3.5
35	56	135	41	18.0	3.5
40	64	170	52	22.0	3.5
45+	72+	Volume-density or multiple detectors recommended.			

Note: Volume-density could be considered at speeds of 35 mph (56 kph) or above.

[Used with permission of Institute of Transportation Engineers, from *Traffic Detector Handbook,* 2nd Ed., JHK & Associates, p. 67 and 69 Copyright © Institute of Transportation Engineers.]

times required for pedestrians, actuated control is often inappropriate where significant numbers of pedestrians are present.

An example: Semi-actuated control

In many circumstances, semi-actuated control can be of benefit, including:

- The main street is an arterial and the off-peak side-street demand is low and quite random, such that the main street should indeed have the green whenever possible. An example is a residential street with low and random demand during off-peak hours.
- The main street is an arterial and the side-street demand peaks for short terms due to a local traffic generator, such that the side-street will require significant green time only at isolated intervals. Examples of such situations are fast-food establishments, schools, churches, factories, and other businesses that discharge traffic in discrete batches.
- A signal is needed, but it would disrupt progressive movement in every cycle if installed as a pretimed signal. It must be installed as a semi-actuated signal with an "inhibit" feature (which allows initiation of side-street green only at prescribed times to minimize disruption to progression) to keep it from randomly interrupting main street flow. This way,

disruption to progression is minimized, and occurs only when demand is present to require it.
- A signal is installed in response to a warrant unrelated to vehicular volume, such as the pedestrian warrant, the accident warrant, or part of school crossing protection programs.

The common characteristic of all semi-actuated installations is, however, that there is a clearly identifiable major street, and a truly minor street. Consider the example of such a location shown in Figure 19-5. To simplify computations, all volumes have been adjusted to equivalent "through car units (tcu's)" using the procedures of Chapter 17. Approach speeds are 25 mph on the side street and 40 mph on the main street. Due to driveway placements, the detector cannot be placed more than 30 feet from the stop line. The problem requires determination of all appropriate timing parameters, and the location of the detectors.

Solutions

1. Detector location and minimum green. The problem statement indicates that the detector placement can be no more than 30 feet from the stop line due to driveway placements. This is less than the recommended 80-foot placement given in Table 19-1. The recommended placement also results in a 12-second minimum green, which may be a bit high for a semi-actuated signal where the side-street green is expected

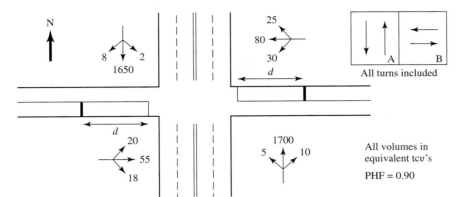

All turns included

All volumes in
equivalent tcu's

PHF = 0.90

Figure 19-5 A semi-actuated
signal example.

to be minimal. Using Equation [19-3], the optimal detector placement will be estimated, assuming a desired minimum green time of 8 seconds, the smallest value used for non-volume-density controllers.

$$d = 10(8) - 40 = 40 \text{ ft}$$

Even this placement is further back than the 30 feet allowed by driveway entrances. It is, therefore, reasonable to assume that the detector will be placed at 30 feet. The minimum green is then found using Equation [19-1]:

$$G_{\min} = 4 + \left[2 \times \text{Integer} \left(\frac{30}{20} \right) \right]$$

$$= 8 \text{ sec}$$

The detector will be placed 30 feet from the stop line on both minor approaches, and the minimum green for the actuated phase (side street) will be 8 seconds. Note that the minimum green time is the same as the original 8 seconds, even though the detector is closer to the stop line. This is due to the effect of the integer function.

2. Passage time and allowable gap. The passage time for a detector placed 30 feet from the stop line is given by Equation [19-2]:

$$P = \frac{30}{1.468 \times 25} = 0.82 \text{ sec}$$

This is far too short for an allowable gap, as no two vehicles ever travel that close to one another. Thus, a larger value will be set on the controller. For 25 mph, Table 19-1 recommends 3.0 seconds, which will be used.

3. Maximum green time. Maximum green times are found by doing a trial signal timing as if the signal were pretimed. From Chapter 17, the optimal cycle length is estimated as:

$$C = \frac{3N}{1 - \dfrac{V_c}{1615 PHF(v/c)}}$$

where: C = cycle length, sec
N = number of phases
3 = total time lost per phase, sec
V_c = sum of the critical lane volumes, in tcu's
PHF = peak hour factor
v/c = desired v/c ratio for the cycle length

For the problem as stated, there are 2 phases. The time lost per phase is assumed to be 3 seconds. The peak hour factor is given as 0.90. The desired v/c ratio should be relatively high, as there should be little unused green time in an actuated signal. Thus, a value of 0.95 will be used.

It is now necessary to determine the value of V_c, the sum of the critical lane volumes. The volumes shown in Figure 19-5 have already been converted to tcu's, which simplifies this consideration.

- For Phase A: The total NB volume is 5 + 1700 + 10 = 1715 tcu/hr, distributed over 2 lanes, resulting in a per-lane volume of 1715/2 = 858 tcu/hr (rounded up). The total SB volume results in a per lane volume of (8 + 1650 + 2)/2 = 830 tcu/hr. The larger is clearly the critical lane volume: NB − 858 tcu/hr.

- For Phase B: The total EB volume is $20 + 55 + 18 = 93$ tcu/hr, in one lane. The total WB volume is $25 + 80 + 30 = 135$ tcu/hr, also in one lane. The latter is clearly the critical lane volume for this phase.
- The sum of critical lane volumes, V_c, is therefore, $858 + 135 = 993$ tcu/hr.

Then:

$$C = \frac{2(3)}{1 - \dfrac{993}{1615(0.90)(0.95)}} = 21.43 \text{ sec}$$

This would be an unreasonably short cycle length for a pretimed signal. In this usage, however, it is being used only to estimate the maximum green for the actuated side-street phase. Rounding to 22 seconds, the effective green time allocated to the side-street (Phase B) green would be:

$$g_B = (22 - 6)\frac{135}{993} = 2.18 \text{ sec}$$

This is, of course, smaller than the minimum green time of 8 seconds, and is therefore not a reasonable basis for establishing the maximum green.

This is a familiar scenario for semi-actuated signals, where side-street volumes are often very low, yielding very small proportional green times in a pretimed computation. There is no computational basis for establishing the maximum green other than judgment. It is possible to make the maximum green the same as the minimum green, i.e., 8 seconds. In this event, every side-street green phase would be exactly 8 seconds long, and could not be extended. In 8 seconds, 3–4 vehicles could be accommodated, if that many vehicles were present. Another option would be to allow some extension of the green to a value of 12–15 seconds, thereby accommodating an additional 1–3 vehicles in a phase if necessary. The judgment should be based on knowledge of demand patterns at the intersection. If short-term peaks yielding as many as 6–7 vehicles in a given cycle are present, the latter course is most appropriate. If demand is more smoothly distributed throughout the peak hour, the constant 8-second option makes sense.

4. Minimum main street green. Even though the main street phase (Phase A) is NOT actuated, a mini-

mum green time must be established. This feature prevents the side-street from recapturing the green at frequent intervals, even if only for short periods. The side-street may not recapture the green until the main street has experienced some minimum continuous green time. This is generally established to be synchronized with other nearby signals on the arterial.

A strategy for setting this limit may be based on the relative critical lane volumes estimated in part 3 of the solution, and the minimum side-street green. The minimum side-street green is 8 seconds. The minimum main street green would be set in proportion to the critical lane volumes for the side street and the main street:

$$\frac{g_{A\min}}{V_{cA}} = \frac{g_{B\min}}{V_{cB}}$$

and:

$$g_{B\min} = g_{A\min}\frac{V_{cB}}{V_{cA}}$$

Then:

$$g_{B\min} = 8\frac{858}{135} = 50.9 \text{ sec}$$

Rounding, the minimum main street green would be established as 51 seconds.

5. Yellow and all-red intervals. The methodology for setting yellow and all-red intervals is discussed in Chapter 17. Yellow "change" intervals are based on the 85th percentile approach speed of approach vehicles, which may be estimated as 5 mph more than the average speed, i.e., $25 + 5 = 30$ mph for the side street, and $40 + 5 = 45$ mph for the main street. Level grades are assumed, and the standard motorist reaction time of 1.0 second is applied. The standard deceleration rate of 10 fps² is also used. Then:

$$y = t + \frac{S_{85}}{2a + 64.4g}$$

$$y_{\text{side}} = 1.0 + \frac{30 \times 1.468}{(2)(10)} = 3.2 \text{ sec}$$

$$y_{\text{main}} = 1.0 + \frac{45 \times 1.468}{(2)(10)} = 4.3 \text{ sec}$$

All-red "clearance" intervals are based on 15th percentile approach speeds, which may be estimated as 5 mph less than average speeds. For this case, $25 - 5 = 20$ mph on the side-street and $40 - 5 = 35$ mph on the main street. Using a standard 20-ft length of vehicles, and assuming 12-ft lane widths, and only a few pedestrians present:

$$r = \frac{w + L}{S_{15}}$$

and:

$$r_{side} = \frac{40 + 20}{20 \times 1.468} = 2.3 \text{ sec}$$

$$r_{main} = \frac{24 + 20}{40 \times 1.468} = 0.75 \text{ sec}$$

These values are now set as fixed interval times on the controller.

6. Pedestrian requirements. Pedestrian needs must be checked for safety. The *minimum* green times for both phases must be sufficient to allow pedestrians to cross the street. Where this is NOT provided, a pedestrian push-button must be installed to trigger a longer minimum green when needed by pedestrians.

When the main street has the green, the minimum green time is 51 seconds. Pedestrians must cross the side street, which is 24 ft wide. As noted in Chapter 17, standard practice allows that the pedestrian must be able to reach the center of the furthest travel lane crossed during the green plus yellow plus all-red intervals.

$$G_p = (4 \Rightarrow 7) + \frac{D_x}{v_p}$$

During the main street green, a 4 second start-up time and a 4 fps walking speed will be assumed. Then:

$$G_{p,main} = (4) + \frac{18}{4} = 8.5 \text{ sec}$$

This is considerably less than the minimum green of 58 sec, plus the yellow of 4.3 sec and the all-red of 0.75 sec. No pedestrian push-button is needed for pedestrians crossing the side street on the main street green, and no WALK-DON'T WALK signals are needed.

Pedestrians cross the main street during the side-street green, which has a minimum green time of 8

seconds, a 3.2 second yellow, and a 2.3 second all-red (13.5 seconds, total). Pedestrians, however, must have at least:

$$G_{p,side} = (4) + \frac{42}{4} = 14.50 \text{ sec}$$

This does not meet the minimum pedestrian requirement, and a pedestrian push-button must be provided. WALK-DON'T WALK signals are also required. A 4-second WALK interval would be followed by a flashing DON'T WALK, displayed until the end of the vehicular yellow. The solid DON'T WALK would be displayed during the remainder of the cycle.

An example: Full-actuated control

Consider the problem illustrated in Figure 19-6. The intersection shown is at an isolated location, and has approach speeds of 35 mph on all approaches. A full-actuated signal is to be provided, and all relevant timing parameters and the detector location must be established. The geometry and volumes are the same as those of Sample Problem 1, in Chapter 17. The volumes converted to tcu's are taken from that problem and are shown in Figure 19-6, as is an appropriate phase plan determined in Chapter 17.

Solutions

1. Minimum green time and detector placement. For 35 mph approach speeds, Table 19-1 recommends that detectors be placed 135 ft from the stop line, and that minimum green times be set at 18 seconds. This detector placement will be assumed if there are no physical constraints.

The recommended minimum green time from Table 19-1 may be checked against a computed value using Equation [19-1]:

$$G_{min} = 4 + \left[2 \times \text{Integer}\left(\frac{135}{20}\right) \right] = 4 + 2(7)$$

$$= 18 \text{ sec}$$

which is how the tabular value was determined.

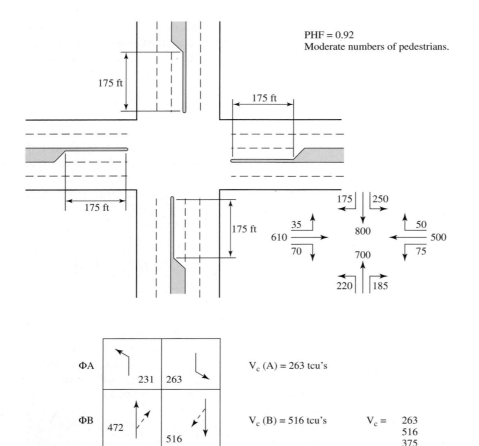

PHF = 0.92
Moderate numbers of pedestrians.

V_c (A) = 263 tcu's

V_c (B) = 516 tcu's

V_c (C) = 375 tcu's

$$V_c = \begin{array}{c} 263 \\ 516 \\ 375 \\ \hline 1,154 \text{ tcu's} \end{array}$$

Figure 19-6   An example: Full-actuated signal.

2. Passage time and the allowable gap. The passage time may be computed from Equation [19-2] for a detector set-back of 135 feet:

$$P = \frac{135}{1.468 \times 35} = 2.63 \text{ sec}$$

This is, in effect, the minimum value that can be prescribed. Table 19-1 recommends the use of 3.5 seconds for the allowable gap for 35 mph. This is only slightly larger than the passage time, and will be adopted for this case.

3. Maximum green times. The signal will be timed as if it were a pretimed signal, using the critical lane vol-

umes and the ring diagram shown in Figure 19-6. Note that a high v/c ratio is presumed, as that is the objective of having an actuated signal. Thus, v/c is set equal to 0.95 for this computation. The *PHF* is given as 0.92.

$$C = \frac{3N}{1 - \dfrac{V_c}{1615PHF(v/c)}}$$

Then:

$$C = \frac{(3)(3)}{1 - \dfrac{1155}{1615(0.92)(0.95)}} = 49.5 \text{ sec; SAY 50 sec}$$

Green times are allocated in proportion to the critical lane volumes in each of the phases shown in the ring diagram of Figure 19-6:

$$g_A = (50 - 9)(263/1155) = \quad 9.4 \text{ sec}$$

$$g_B = (50 - 9)(516/1155) = 18.3 \text{ sec}$$

$$g_C = (50 - 9)(375/1155) = \underline{13.3 \text{ sec}}$$

$$41.0 \text{ sec}$$

$$L = \qquad\qquad\qquad \underline{9.0 \text{ sec}}$$

$$50.0 \text{ sec}$$

Maximum green times would be set at 1.5 times these values or:

$$g_A(\text{max}) = \quad 9.4 \times 1.5 = 14.1 \text{ sec}$$

$$g_B(\text{max}) = 18.3 \times 1.5 = 27.5 \text{ sec}$$

$$g_C(\text{max}) = 13.3 \times 1.5 = 20.0 \text{ sec}$$

These values, however, are basically inconsistent with a minimum green time of 18 seconds, as established previously. Two approaches can be taken:

- The minimum green time must be reduced, and the detector therefore moved closer to the stop line.
- The maximum green times must be extended to higher values.

Given the volume levels, and the resulting maximum green time recommendations, the former seems to be a more rational course. If the detector is moved to 40 feet from the stop line, the minimum green value becomes:

$$G_{\text{min}} = 4 + 2 \text{ integer } (40/20) = 8 \text{ sec}$$

This revised location of detectors, and the revised minimum green will be adopted for this location.

The maximum cycle length permitted by this timing would be 14.1 + 27.5 + 20.0 + 9.0 = 70.6 seconds.

The long setbacks and resulting high minimum green values of Table 19-1 reflect more heavily-loaded intersections, where the longer minimum green times do not result in excessive amounts of unused green time. In the problem given, the peak flows simply do not justify this approach.

4. Yellow and all-red times. The yellow time is the same for all approaches, as a common average approach speed of 35 mph exists. The yellow time is based on the 85th percentile approach speed, which can be estimated as 35 + 5 = 40 mph. Then, assuming level terrain and standard values for t and a:

$$y = t + \frac{S_{85}}{2a + 64.4g}$$

$$y = 1.0 + \frac{40 \times 1.468}{(2)(10)} = 2.9 \text{ sec}$$

All-red "clearance" intervals are based on 15th percentile approach speeds, which may be estimated as 5 mph less than average speeds. For this case, 35 − 5 = 30 mph on all approaches. Using a standard 20-ft length of vehicles, and assuming 12-ft lane widths, and only some pedestrians present:

$$r = \frac{w + L}{S_{15}}$$

$$r = \frac{60 + 20}{30 \times 1.468} = 1.8 \text{ sec}$$

5. Pedestrian requirements. Pedestrians must be able to cross to the center of the furthest travel lane (a distance of 54 feet for all approaches) within a period equal to the minimum green (8.0 seconds) plus the yellow (2.9 seconds) and the all-red (1.8 seconds). This time is also the same for all approaches, totalling 12.7 seconds.

At an assumed 4 fps, and with a 4-second start-up time, the minimum pedestrian crossing time is:

$$G_p = 4 + \frac{54}{4} = 17.5 \text{ sec}$$

Therefore, a pedestrian push-button must be provided for all approaches. When actuated, it will initiate a minimum green of 17.5 − 2.9 − 1.8 = 12.8 seconds. Pedestrian WALK-DON'T WALK signals are also required for all approaches. They will display a solid DON'T WALK unless the pedestrian actuator is pushed. In the *next* green phase, a minimum green sufficient for safe crossing will be initiated. The WALK indication will be shown for 4 seconds, followed by a flashing DON'T WALK for the remainder of the green plus yellow period.

Summary

This chapter has merely scratched the surface of the highly complex subject of actuated signalization. Timing such signals is almost as much an art as a science, and more than one solution is possible. Further, because the actual operation of the signal is based on individual vehicle inter-arrival headways, field conditions may not always be as expected. The techniques illustrated in this chapter provide general guides to the setting of the various parameters involved.

References

The most comprehensive information on actuated signalization is found in References [1] and [2]. Reference [3] is a study of regularity of arrivals at signalized intersections, and makes a strong case for the use of actuated signals. Reference [4] is a recommended procedure for choosing the most appropriate form of signalization for an intersection. Reference [5] reports on NEMA standards for traffic signal controllers.

1. Kell, J., and Fullerton, I., *Manual of Traffic Signal Design,* 2nd Edition, Institute of Transportation Engineers, Prentice-Hall, Inc., Englewood Cliffs, NJ, 1991.

2. *Traffic Detector Handbook,* 2nd Edition, JHK & Associates, Institute of Transportation Engineers, Washington, DC, n.d.
3. McShane, W., and Crowley, K., "Regularity of Signal Detectors—Observed Arterial Traffic Characteristics," *Transportation Research Record 596,* Transportation Research Board, National Research Council, Washington, DC, 1976.
4. Tarnoff and Parsonson, "Selecting Traffic Signal Control at Individual Intersections," *NCHRP Report 233,* Transportation Research Board, National Research Council, Washington, DC, June 1986.
5. Parris, C.A., "NEMA and Traffic Control," *ITE Journal,* August 1986.

Problems

Problem 19–1

The side-street detector at a semi-actuated location is located 80 ft from the stop line. The recommended allowable gap is 3.0 seconds. The approach speed on the side street is 25 mph; on the main street, 35 mph. There are two phases. The minimum main street green is to be 50 seconds. The side street has a critical lane volume of 175 tcu/hr and the main street has a critical lane volume of 1200 tcu/hr.

(a) Find the desired minimum green for the side street. Comment on any assumptions made.
(b) Recommend a side-street maximum green and justify your recommendation.
(c) Estimate a worst-case cycle length. Comment.

Problem 19–2

A side-street location at a semi-actuated signal installation has approach speeds of 30 mph. It is desired that the minimum green time be no more than 8 seconds. How far from the stop line should the detector be placed?

Problem 19–3

There is a semi-actuated intersection with negligible side-street traffic. The signal has been installed for safety reasons. Whenever a nearby freeway breaks down, diverted traffic results in the situation shown in Figure 19-7. Because of system constraints, the maximum cycle length should not exceed 90 seconds when this condition occurs.

(a) Recommend settings for the minimum side-street green, and a detector location.
(b) Recommend settings for the maximum side-street green and the minimum main street green.
(c) Suppose a different type of incident occurs, resulting in volumes (with a PHF of 1.00) of 1100 vph WB and 800 vph SB. What will occur, given your recommended timing?

Problem 19–4

Refer to the intersection illustrated in Figure 19-8. A full-actuated controller is to be designed for this situation.

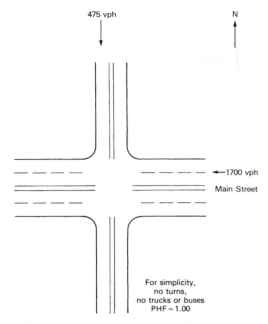

Figure 19-7 Intersection for Problem 19–3.

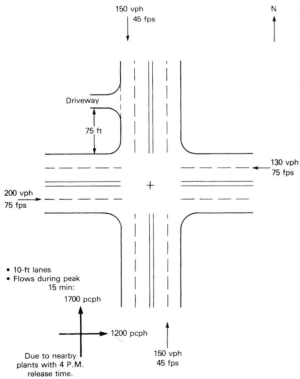

Figure 19-8 Intersection for Problem 19-4.

Determine all necessary timing parameters, and the appropriate location for detectors. Indicate any assumptions made.

Problem 19–5

A full-actuated controller has the following settings on each of two phases, denoted as Phase A and Phase B. The settings are the same for both phases:

Minimum green	8.0 sec
Passage time	3.5 sec
Maximum green	20.0 sec
Yellow	3.0 sec
All red	2.0 sec

(a) Comment on the likely location of detectors.
(b) Assume that a Phase A green begins at time $t = 0.0$ sec. The following arrivals occur at the detectors on the two approaches (all times are shown in cumulative seconds):

Phase A	Phase B
2.10	
7.80	
9.10	
11.70	
14.70	
	16.10
16.90	
19.10	
	19.50
22.10	
24.30	
26.20	
	27.30
29.20	29.30
32.10	
34.80	
38.00	
40.70	
44.00	
	45.10
	46.90
	48.50

(1) Describe the operation of this signal through the period shown in detail. Draw a diagram indicating the extension periods and times when the green is transferred to the next phase.

(2) Is there any logical explanation for the fact that there were no Phase B detector actuations between $t = 29.30$ and $t = 45.10$ sec? Does the clustering of actuations after $t = 45.10$ sec offer any insight?

(3) Redo parts (1) and (2) assuming that the vehicle arriving at $t = 22.10$ sec does not exist. Is it likely that the Phase B detector indications might change? Which? Why?

20

Calibration of Parameters for Critical Movement Analysis

The critical movement analysis technique of the 1997 *HCM* for evaluation of signalized intersections consists of two primary algorithms. The first gives an estimate of the prevailing saturation flow rate for the signalized intersection approach under study [1]:

$$s = s_o N f_w f_{HV} f_g f_p f_{bb} f_a f_u f_{RT} f_{LT} \qquad [20\text{-}1]$$

where: s = prevailing saturation flow rate for the intersection approach, vphg

s_o = saturation flow rate per lane for ideal geometric and traffic conditions, pcphgpl

N = number of lanes on the approach

f_w = adjustment factor for lane width

f_{HV} = adjustment factor for heavy vehicles

f_g = adjustment factor for grade

f_p = adjustment factor for parking

f_{bb} = adjustment factor for bus blockage

f_a = adjustment factor for area type

f_u = adjustment factor for lane utilization

f_{RT} = adjustment factor for right turns

f_{LT} = adjustment factor for left turns

The ideal saturation flow rate, s_o, applies when the following "ideal" conditions exist:

1. Lane width = 12 ft
2. No heavy vehicles in the traffic stream
3. Level grade
4. No parking adjacent to the approach
5. No local buses in the traffic stream
6. Intersection in an outlaying area
7. No right or left turns from the approach

Adjustment factors are applied multiplicatively to account for the impact of nonideal conditions on the prevailing saturation flow rate.

The second primary algorithm involved in signalized-intersection analysis is used to predict the average individual stopped delay per vehicle:

$$d_1 = 0.38C \frac{[1 - (g/C)]^2}{[1 - (g/C)X]}$$

$$d_2 = 173X^2 \left[(X - 1) + \sqrt{(X - 1)^2 + \frac{mX}{c}} \right]$$

$$d = d_1(DF) + d_2 \qquad [20\text{-}2]$$

where: d_1 = uniform delay, sec/veh
d_2 = incremental delay, sec/veh
d = total stopped delay, sec/veh
g = effective green phase for lane group, sec
C = cycle length, sec
c = capacity of lane group, vph
X = v/c ratio for lane group
m = adjustment for early or late platoon arrivals
DF = delay adjustment factor (for progression)

The first term of the delay estimate describes the delay that would occur if vehicle arrivals at the intersection were absolutely uniform. This is the first term of Webster's delay formulation [2]. The second term describes incremental or additional delay that occurs because arrivals are not uniform and because individual signal cycles begin to fail as X approaches, then exceeds 1.00.

The *Highway Capacity Manual* encourages users to calibrate many basic values to reflect local driving characteristics. This chapter explores methodologies that can be used to calibrate many of the values involved in signalized-intersection analysis. These methods can be applied to modify key values for local conditions and to conduct basic calibration studies for the methodology itself.

Because the estimation of saturation flow rates is based primarily on field observations and calibration of algorithms to those observations, many aspects of this estimation can be recalibrated for local conditions. The delay algorithm is based primarily on theory, with some modifications based on delay observations. Thus, it is a much more difficult task to "recalibrate" this equation.

Saturation flow rates

A. Measuring prevailing saturation flow rates

The *HCM* prescribes a methodology for field measurement of the prevailing saturation flow rate on an approach. It involves the observation of vehicle headways as they cross into the intersection. Headways are generally measured at STOP line of the approach in question. The reference point is generally the crossing of the rear axle of a vehicle over the STOP line. The

first headway is taken as the time between the initiation of the green indication and the crossing of the rear axle of the first vehicle over the STOP line. Subsequent headways are taken as the time between the rear axles of successive vehicles crossing the STOP line.

Figure 20-1 shows a field sheet for recording these headways. Note that each lane is separately observed, and that the saturation flow rate for each lane is separately computed. The total saturation flow rate for an intersection approach is the sum of the individual lane saturation flow rates.

Correct computation of the prevailing saturation flow rate, *s*, requires strict observation of when conditions are saturated. Since it is generally assumed that the first four vehicles in a queue experience start-up lost time, the first four headways of any queue are *not* considered to reflect saturated conditions. Saturated conditions strictly end when the last vehicle present in the standing queue as the green is initiated clears the STOP line. Practically speaking, vehicles that join the end of the queue after the green is initiated but before the last vehicle in queue clears the STOP line may be included if, in the judgment of observers, they are maintaining similar headways to vehicles in the standing queue.

Thus, observation of the prevailing saturation flow rate requires standing queues that are at least five vehicles in length (preferably much longer), and a careful noting of which vehicle is the last in queue for each cycle observed.

The example shown in Table 20-1 illustrates the computation of prevailing saturation flow rate for a given lane of an intersection approach. The lane in question is a central lane with no turning movements. Heavy vehicles are indicated with the notation, "H." A line marks the last vehicle in queue.

Note that the first four headways of each observed cycle are discarded, as these reflect the total of saturation headway plus start-up lost time. Further, headways beyond the last queued vehicle are also discarded. Thus, for the first cycle, headways 5 through 8 are included as reflecting saturated conditions. For Cycle 2, headways 5 through 12 are used; for Cycle 3, headways 5 through 10; for Cycle 4, headways 5 through 12; for Cycle 5, headways 5 through 11; for Cycle 6, headways 5 through 12.

Thus, the sum of all observed saturation headways over the six-cycle observation period is 96.0 seconds, as shown. There were 41 saturation headways ob-

FIELD SHEET – SATURATION FLOW STUDY

Location:_____

Date:____/____/____ Time:_____ City:_____

_____Bound Traffic; Approaching From the_____

Observers:_____ Weather:_____

Movements Allowed
☐ Thru
☐ Right Turn   Identify all Lane Movements
☐ Left Turn   & The Lane Studied

N

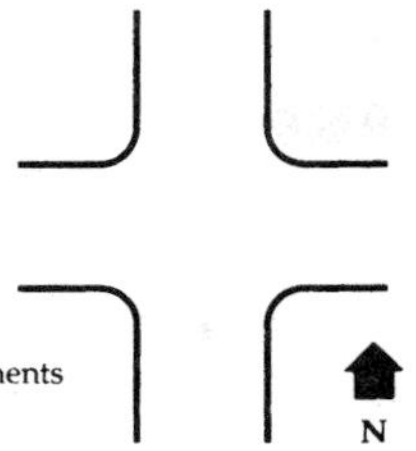

Veh. in Queue	Cycle 1			Cycle 2			Cycle 3			Cycle 4			Cycle 5			Cycle 6		
	Time	HV	T	Time	HV	T	Time	HV	T	Time	HV	T	Time	HV	T	Time	HV	T
1																		
2																		
3																		
4																		
5																		
6																		
7																		
8																		
9																		
10																		
11																		
12																		
13																		
14																		
15																		
16																		
17																		
18																		
19																		
20																		
End of Saturation																		
End of Green																		
No. Veh. > 20																		
No. Veh. on Yellow																		

HV = Heavy Vehicles (Vehicles with more than 4 tires)
T = Turning Vehicles (L = Left, R = Right)
Pedestrians and buses which block vehicles should be noted with the time that they block traffic, i.e.,
P12 = pedestrians blocked traffic for 12 sec
B15 = bus blocked traffic for 15 sec

Figure 20-1 Field sheet for observation of prevailing saturation flow rate. [Used with permission of Transportation Research board, National Research Council, Washington, DC, from *Highway Capacity Manual, Special Report 209*, 3rd Ed., p. 9-73. Copyright © 1994 Transportation Research Board.]

served in this total. The average saturation headway is therefore:

$$h = \frac{96.0}{41} = 2.34 \text{ sec}$$

The observed saturation flow rate is

$$s = \frac{3600}{h} = \frac{3600}{2.34} = 1538 \text{ vphgpl}$$

This is the observed prevailing saturation flow rate for the lane in Table 20-1. Other lanes of the approach would have been similarly observed and analyzed. The saturation flow rate for the entire approach would be the sum of the individual lane saturation flow rates. For example, if the approach had three lanes, with the saturation flow rates shown below, the approach saturation flow rate would be computed as:

Lane 1: $s = 1450$ vphgpl

Lane 2: $s = 1538$ vphgpl

Lane 3: $s = 1475$ vphgpl

Approach: $s = 4463$ vphg

The approach saturation flow rate *is not* based on the average of all of the saturation headways observed in all lanes. Such a procedure would weight the

Table 20-1 Example of Field Observation of Prevailing Saturation Flow Rate

Vehicles in Queue	Observed Headways (sec) Cycle Number						Sum of Sat. Headways	No. of Sat. Headways
	1	2	3	4	5	6		
1	3.5	2.9	3.9	4.2H	2.9	3.2	0.0	0
2	3.2	3.0	3.3	3.6	3.5H	3.0	0.0	0
3	2.6	2.3	2.4	3.2H	2.7	2.5	0.0	0
4	2.8H	2.2	2.4	2.5	2.1	2.9H	0.0	0
5	2.5	2.3	2.1	2.1	2.2	2.5	13.7	6
6	2.3	2.1	2.4	2.2	2.0	2.3	13.3	6
7	3.2H	2.0	2.4	2.4	2.2	2.3	14.5	6
8	2.5	1.9	2.2	2.3	2.4	2.0	13.3	6
9	4.5	2.9H	2.7H	1.9	2.2	2.4	12.1	5
10	6.0	2.5	2.4	2.3	2.7H	2.1	12.0	5
11		2.8H	4.0	2.2	2.4	2.0	9.4	4
12		2.5	7.0	2.9H	5.0	2.3	7.7	3
13		5.0		4.1		6.0	0.0	0
14		7.5					0.0	0
15							0.0	0
							96.0	41

total saturation flow rate by the number of observed saturation headways in each lane. Saturation flow is based on headways in a given lane, and total saturation flow rate for an approach is additive over the lanes comprising the approach.

B. Measuring ideal saturation flow rate

The field observation of a prevailing saturation flow rate replaces the need to estimate it using Equation [20-1] and the procedures of the *HCM*. This approach, however, has limited value, as it can apply only to an existing intersection under existing traffic loads.

The *HCM* suggests that the ideal saturation flow rate of 1900 pcphgpl may be modified according to local observations. This has far broader applicability, in that a locally calibrated value may now be used in conjunction with Equation [20-1] and the *HCM*.

Field observation of ideal saturation flow rates is a more difficult procedure, in that ideal conditions are rarely found in the field. In general, sites will be sought that have ideal geometric conditions: 12-ft lanes, no parking, level grades, and so on. Where possible, three-lane approaches will be sought, so that observations may focus on the center lane, from which

no turns are made. Heavy vehicles, however, are another matter, as few sites will have no heavy vehicles.

Assuming that geometric conditions at a site are ideal, which headways can be assumed to be reflective of "ideal" conditions? Any headway affected by a heavy vehicle or a turning vehicle is *not* ideal. It must be assumed that such vehicles affect not only their own headways, but those of vehicles that follow them. Thus, only headways that occur *before* the arrival of a heavy vehicle or turning vehicle may be treated as "ideal." As with the measurement of prevailing saturation flow rates, the first four headways in any queue are also discarded, as they contain start-up lost time.

If, in the problem of Table 20-1, geometric conditions are ideal, only Cycles 2 and 3 contain "ideal" headways. In every other cycle, a heavy vehicle appears prior to or in the fourth queue position. In both Cycles 2 and 3, the first heavy vehicle is the ninth vehicle. Thus, headways 5 through 8 in each of these cycles could be considered to reflect ideal conditions. Table 20-2 illustrates the computation of ideal saturation flow rate using these headways.

This result can now be used as a basic parameter in Equation [20-1] and the *HCM*. When this is done, the analytic procedure will more accurately reflect local

Table 20-2   Computation of Ideal Saturation Flow Rate for Data of Table 20-1

Vehicles in Queue	Observed Headway (sec)	
	Cycle Number	
	2	3
5	2.3	2.1
6	2.1	2.4
7	2.0	2.4
8	1.9	2.2
SUM	8.3	9.1
	17.4	

$$h_o = \frac{17.4}{8} = 2.18$$

$$s_o = \frac{3600}{2.18} = 1651 \text{ pcphgpl}$$

conditions and driving characteristics. Of course, the calibration of an ideal saturation flow rate for use in analysis would not be based on six cycles in one lane of one intersection. A number of sites would be observed over a longer period of time. It may be necessary to classify approaches by facility type (arterial, collector, local street) or subcategory, with different values of s_o applying to each.

As will be seen, s_o is the easiest parameter involved in intersection analysis to calibrate locally. Since it is a value that has been observed to vary, it is generally a good idea to have local calibrations of this variable available when doing signalized intersection analysis.

Lost times

A. Measurement of start-up lost time

Observation of start-up lost time is based on the headways of the first three vehicles in the queue and requires observation of the ideal saturation headway as an input. Start-up lost time is a critical input into signalized-intersection capacity computations, as it represents time not used by any vehicle flow at the saturation flow rate. Capacity of a signalized intersection approach is given by

$$c = s(g/C)$$

$$g = G + Y - l_1 - l_2 \qquad [20\text{-}3]$$

where: c = capacity of approach, vph
s = prevailing saturation flow rate, vphg
g = effective green time, sec
C = cycle length, sec
G = actual green time, sec
Y = yellow plus all-red interval, sec
l_1 = start-up lost time, sec
l_2 = clearance lost time, sec

Lost time is calibrated for ideal conditions relative to the ideal saturation headway. While standard procedures call for start-up lost time to apply to the first four headways in each queue, various studies have indicated that start-up lost time may involve as many as the first six vehicles in queue. This is most effectively determined by plotting vehicle headways versus position in queue for many cycles and finding the point at which headways tend to level out, as shown in Figure 20-2. The following point is critical, however: Once the point at which start-up lost time disappears is found, then only headways from this point on are included in the calibration of saturation flow rate, and only headways previous to this point are included in the calibration of start-up lost time.

In the studies made during the development of the *HCM*, it was found that start-up lost time generally involved only the first four vehicles in queue. Thus, if a detailed determination of this factor is not undertaken, this would be the most reasonable assumption to make.

Table 20-3 illustrates the computation of start-up lost time for a single observed queue in a lane with a calibrated "ideal" saturation headway of 2.0 seconds. Note that since the determination of start-up lost time involves "ideal" conditions, any queues with

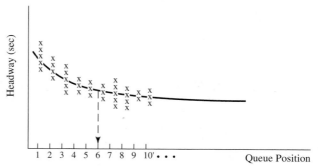

Figure 20-2   Finding the point at which start-up lost time dissipates.

Table 20-3   Illustration of Computation of Start-Up Lost Time

Vehicles in Queue	Headway (sec)	Headway >2.0 sec
1	3.5	1.5
2	3.0	0.5
3	2.4	0.4
4	2.2	0.2
Start-up Lost Time = Σ =		2.6 sec

heavy vehicles or turning vehicles within the first four queue positions would not be used. Start-up lost time is defined as the total additional headway consumed by the first n vehicles in the queue above and beyond the saturation headway. In the example of Table 20-3, the ideal saturation headway is 2.0 sec. Thus, the start-up lost time is the difference between the observed headway and 2.0 sec for the first four vehicles.

Again, calibration of a start-up lost time for a local area would involve observations at a number of sites over numerous signal cycles.

B. Measurement of clearance lost time

Clearance lost time occurs at the end of each green phase. It can be observed only when approaches in all signal phases are fully saturated, such that all green time in the cycle is used.

Clearance lost time is defined as the time between the crossing of the last vehicle in Phase A over the STOP-line and the initiation of the green for Phase B. This time will generally be shorter than the yellow plus all-red intervals provided for clearance, and represents the actual time that the intersection is not used by vehicles each time the signal phase changes.

Clearance lost time must be observed directly at a number of locations over a number of signal cycles.

Adjustment factors

The *HCM* allows for the modification of the ideal saturation flow rate by up to nine adjustment factors, one for each of the following potential non-ideal prevailing conditions:

1. Lane width (12 ft)
2. Heavy vehicles (0%)
3. Grade (0%)
4. Parking (none)
5. Bus blockage (none)
6. Area type (non-CBD)
7. Right turns (0%)
8. Left turns (0%)
9. Lane distribution (1997 update only)

These factors are, by definition, 1.00 when the ideal conditions shown in parentheses exists. When conditions are worse than the defined ideal, the factor is less than 1.00, accounting for the reduction in saturation flow rate due to the condition. In some cases, factors greater than 1.00 are also possible. Where a downgrade exists, saturation flow rates are higher than for level grades. Lane widths greater than 12 ft also produce higher saturation flow rates than for the standard "ideal" condition.

Calibration of all of these factors involves the controlled observation of saturation headways under conditions in which one variable is not ideal. By definition a factor adjusts an ideal saturation flow rate to a prevailing rate representing existing conditions. Thus:

$$s_p = s_o \times f_i$$

$$f_i = \frac{s_p}{s_o} \qquad [20\text{-}4]$$

where: s_p = prevailing saturation flow rate per lane, vphgpl
s_o = ideal saturation flow rate per lane, pcphgpl
f_i = adjustment factor for nonideal condition i

Since saturation flow rates are directly related to saturation headways, the following may be derived:

$$s_o = 3600/h_o$$

$$s_p = 3600/h$$

$$f_i = \frac{s_p}{s_o} = \frac{3600/h}{3600/h_o}$$

$$f_i = \frac{h_o}{h} \qquad [20\text{-}5]$$

where: h_o = ideal saturation headway, sec/veh
h = prevailing saturation headway, sec/veh

The subsections that follow discuss issues related to the calibration of specific factors.

A. Simple factors: Area type, lane width, and grade

These three are referred to as *simple factors* as they relate to only one variable, and field studies need merely to observe saturation headways under a variety of conditions for each.

The *area-type factors*, f_a, has only two values; one associated with non-CBD environments, the other with CBD environments. Observations have indicated that the general level of complexity in the CBD environment makes signalized intersections less efficient than similar intersections in non-CBD areas. In theory, any number of "environments" could be defined on the basis of development type or density. In the 1965 *HCM*, such a factor was based on the "metropolitan area population" and the *PHF*. This was found to be difficult to interpret and apply. It was replaced in the 1985 *HCM* by two categories.

Calibration would involve observation of saturation headways at sites which were otherwise geometrically ideal in both CBD and non-CBD environments. Only headways unaffected by turning or heavy vehicles would be included in the calibrations, as in previous examples. Given that "non-CBD" is the defined "ideal" condition, consider the following data:

$$h(\text{non-CBD}) = 2.15 \text{ sec/veh}$$

$$h(\text{CBD}) = 2.26 \text{ sec/veh}$$

Applying Equation [20-5]:

$$f_a(\text{CBD}) = \frac{2.15}{2.26} = 0.95$$

The *lane-width factor*, f_w, represents the impact of lanes narrower or wider than the defined "ideal" 12-ft lane on saturation flow rate. Observations of saturation headways would be taken at sites with a variety of lane widths, where other geometric conditions are ideal. Again, only headways not influenced by heavy or turning vehicles would be included in calibrations. Consider the following data:

$$h(\text{10-ft lanes}) = 2.6 \text{ sec/veh}$$

$$h(\text{11-ft lanes}) = 2.4 \text{ sec/veh}$$

$$h(\text{12-ft lanes}) = 2.1 \text{ sec/veh}$$

$$h(\text{13-ft lanes}) = 2.0 \text{ sec/veh}$$

$$h(\text{14-ft lanes}) = 1.9 \text{ sec/veh}$$

Equation [20-5] is again employed, with the 12-ft lane used as the base condition, as follows:

$$f_w(\text{10-ft lanes}) = \frac{2.1}{2.6} = 0.81$$

$$f_w(\text{11-ft lanes}) = \frac{2.1}{2.4} = 0.88$$

$$f_w(\text{12-ft lanes}) = \frac{2.1}{2.1} = 1.00$$

$$f_w(\text{13-ft lanes}) = \frac{2.1}{2.0} = 1.05$$

$$f_w(\text{14-ft lanes}) = \frac{2.1}{1.9} = 1.11$$

Factors for lanes wider than 12 ft are greater than 1.00, indicating that saturation flow rates increase as lane widths go beyond 12 ft. Single lanes wider than 15 ft are somewhat impractical, as they will often be used as two narrow lanes under heavy loading conditions.

The calibration of the *adjustment factor for grades*, f_g, follows a pattern similar to that for lane widths. A number of sites with various approach grades, both positive (up) and negative (down), are observed. They should have otherwise ideal geometries, and headways affected by turning and heavy vehicles are not included. Level grade is the base condition and is therefore used as the reference point for calibration factors. Consider the following example:

$$h(+4\%) = 2.9 \text{ sec/veh}$$

$$h(+2\%) = 2.5 \text{ sec/veh}$$

$$h(0\%) = 2.0 \text{ sec/veh}$$

$$h(-2\%) = 1.8 \text{ sec/veh}$$

$$h(-4\%) = 1.7 \text{ sec/veh}$$

Then:

$$f_g(+4\%) = \frac{2.0}{2.9} = 0.69$$

$$f_g(+2\%) = \frac{2.0}{2.5} = 0.80$$

$$f_g(0\%) = \frac{2.0}{2.0} = 1.00$$

$$f_g(-2\%) = \frac{2.0}{1.8} = 1.11$$

$$f_g(-4\%) = \frac{2.0}{1.7} = 1.18$$

Again, for downgrades, factors are greater than 1.00, indicating an increase in saturation flow rate over that observed on level grades.

B. Parking factor

The parking factor accounts for the frictional impact of a parking lane on saturation flow rate in the adjacent traffic lane and the blockage of the adjacent traffic lane by vehicles moving in and out of parking spaces. Both of these operational impacts are limited to the traffic lane immediately adjacent to the parking lane. Since adjustment factors apply to a lane group of *n* lanes, the number of lanes becomes another parameter to account for in calibrations.

Headway observations are made only on lanes adjacent to curb parking. Site selection is more difficult, as otherwise ideal conditions—12-ft lanes and no grade—should be sought. Headways affected by turning or heavy vehicles would not be included. Thus, sites with low right-turning percentages should also be sought. In addition to these limitations, parking activity is defined as the number of movements (in or out) within 250 ft of the intersection. Headways must be observed at sites covering a reasonable range of this variable.

The base condition is a site with no parking lane adjacent to traffic lanes. Sites must be separately selected and observed to provide information for this base condition. All other sites would have parking lanes adjacent to a traffic lane.

Consider the following observations made at sites with otherwise ideal geometric conditions:

h(no parking) = 2.0 sec/veh

h(parking, 0 mvts/hr) = 2.1 sec/veh

h(parking, 10 mvts/hr) = 2.3 sec/veh

h(parking, 20 mvts/hr) = 2.4 sec/veh

h(parking, 30 mvts/hr) = 2.6 sec/veh

h(parking, 50 mvts/hr) = 2.9 sec/veh

Note that all of these headways are for the right traffic lane, which would normally be the one adjacent to curb parking. The first step in the calibration factor is to compute, using Equation [20-5], adjustment factors for the right lane only. These factors will be denoted f_{pr}. Using the "no parking" condition as a base:

$$f_{pr}(0 \text{ mvts/hr}) = \frac{2.0}{2.1} = 0.95$$

$$f_{pr}(10 \text{ mvts/hr}) = \frac{2.0}{2.3} = 0.87$$

$$f_{pr}(20 \text{ mvts/hr}) = \frac{2.0}{2.4} = 0.83$$

$$f_{pr}(30 \text{ mvts/hr}) = \frac{2.0}{2.6} = 0.77$$

$$f_{pr}(50 \text{ mvts/hr}) = \frac{2.0}{2.9} = 0.69$$

At this point, depending on the number of observations available, two options are possible. Average values of the factor for various numbers of parking movements per hour can be taken directly and displayed in tabular form. A second option would be to find a mathematical relationship between the factor and the number of movements per hour, either by regression analysis or by simple plotting. The latter would normally require more data points but would avoid the need to interpolate in what could be a non-linear table for intermediate values of parking movement.

Once values of f_{pr} are established, values of f_p for various numbers of lanes in a lane group are easily computed. The parking factor for lanes not adjacent to a parking lane is assumed to be 1.00. The average factor for a group of lanes may then be computed as

$$f_p = \frac{f_{pr} + 1.0(N-1)}{N} \quad [20\text{-}6]$$

where N = number of lanes in the lane group.

Consider the following example. The parking factor for a lane adjacent to a curb parking lane has been found to be 0.85. What is the parking factor for this case if there are three lanes in the lane group? Applying Equation [20-6]:

$$f_p = \frac{0.85 + 1.0(3 - 1)}{3} = \frac{2.85}{3} = 0.95$$

Using this procedure, values of f_{pr} can be calibrated from field data, and a table of f_p values can be constructed for different values of N, as shown in the *HCM*.

C. Heavy-vehicle factor

As the signalized intersection procedure of the *HCM* contains a separate factor for the influence of grade on saturation flow rates, the heavy-vehicle factor relates only to the percentage of such vehicles in the traffic stream. Heavy vehicles are defined as any vehicle with more than four wheels touching the ground during normal operation.

As in previous calibrations, the heavy-vehicle factor is based on a comparison of a prevailing headway influenced by heavy vehicles to the ideal saturation headway. Calibration observations are made at sites with ideal geometric conditions, and generally in lanes from which no turns are made. Since the impact of heavy vehicles is sought, observations and calibrations will use all headways in such a lane, not just those unaffected by heavy vehicles.

Refer back to the sample problem illustrated in Table 20-1. In this example, six vehicle queues at an intersection with ideal geometric conditions (in a lane with no turning vehicles) were observed. The prevailing saturation headway was 2.34 sec/veh. Table 20-2 illustrated the computation of the ideal saturation headway from the same data, resulting in 2.18 sec/veh. The only difference between these two computations is the impact of heavy vehicles on the result.

In Table 20-1 are 6 heavy vehicles out of 41 observed saturation headways, where headways from the fifth vehicle in queue to the end of saturation are considered. This represents $(6/41) \times 100 = 14.6\%$ heavy vehicles in the traffic stream.

The truck factor for this case can be calibrated simply using Equation [20-5]:

$$f_{HV} = \frac{2.18}{2.34} = 0.932$$

Observations would have to be similarly taken at locations with a range of heavy-vehicle presence to construct the full table of adjustment factors.

There is another way to look at this calibration. If the 41 observed saturation headways in Table 20-1 had been "ideal," they would have consumed $41 \times 2.18 = 89.4$ sec. In fact, those 41 headways consumed $41 \times 2.34 = 95.9$ sec. Therefore, the 6 heavy vehicles in those headways caused an additional $95.9 - 89.4 = 6.5$ sec to be consumed, or $6.5/6 = 1.083$ additional seconds per heavy vehicle. Note that this additional time is consumed not only by the heavy vehicles themselves, but by vehicles following in the queue which may have been delayed. This computation, however, *assigns* all of the additional time to heavy vehicles.

Thus, the ideal saturation headway is 2.18 sec/veh, while the effective saturation headway per heavy vehicle could be taken as $2.18 + 1.083 = 3.263$ sec/heavy vehicle. These values could be used to calibrate a heavy-vehicle equivalent, as for uninterrupted flow. It could be said that 1 heavy vehicle consumes as much time as $3.263/2.18 = 1.497$ passenger cars. Using this as a value of E_{HV}, and applying the equation for translation of equivalents to factors:

$$f_{HV} = \frac{1}{1 + P_{HV}(E_{HV} - 1)}$$

$$f_{HV} = \frac{1}{1 + 0.146(1.497 - 1)} = 0.932 \quad [20\text{-}7]$$

This is the same result as achieved with the first computation, and it demonstrates the consistency of equivalency theory with the definition of factors.

D. Bus blockage factor

Chapter 12 of the 1997 *Highway Capacity Manual* gives a procedure for calibration of *bus blockage factors*, f_{bb}. The table of factors in the *HCM* is applicable to average cases in which buses are not very frequent, and where dwell times are relatively short.

Based on numerous observations of buses stopping to load and unload passengers, the *HCM* presents a procedure for estimating the average time loss, T_L, for one bus. This is equivalent to the headway per bus, where all delay to subsequent vehicles is assigned to the bus.

For buses stopping out of a travel lane, $T_L = 3$–4 sec/bus. For buses stopping in a travel lane:

$$T_L = \frac{g}{C}(D + 6) \qquad [20\text{-}8]$$

where: T_L = time loss, sec/bus
$\ g$ = effective green time, sec
$\ C$ = cycle length, sec
$\ D$ = average dwell time per bus, sec

Given that T_L is the effective headway per bus, where all excess time beyond the ideal saturation headway is assigned to the bus, the following relationships may be used to find the bus blockage factor:

$$E_B = \frac{T_L}{h_o} \qquad [20\text{-}9]$$

$$f_{bb} = \frac{1}{1 + P_B(E_B - 1)} \qquad [20\text{-}10]$$

where: E_B = bus equivalent, and
$\ P_B$ = proportion of buses in the traffic stream.

Consider a case in which local buses stop in a travel lane with average dwell times of 10 sec. The g/C ratio is 0.60 for the approach on which buses stop, and buses make up 10% of the traffic on the approach. Find the bus blockage factor, given that the ideal saturation headway at this location is 2.0 sec/veh.

First, T_L is computed as

$$T_L = \frac{g}{C}(D + 6) = (0.6)(10 + 6) = 9.6 \text{ sec/bus}$$

Then,

$$E_B = \frac{T_L}{h_o} = \frac{9.6}{2.0} = 4.8$$

and

$$f_{bb} = \frac{1}{1 + 0.10(4.8 - 1)} = 0.72$$

Calibration of bus blockage factors is recommended by the *HCM* for all cases in which the number of buses is unusually high, or where dwell times are longer than normal—that is, situations in which more than 5 or 6 passengers are boarding and/or alighting. Observations of g/C ratios and dwell times are the primary inputs into calibrations of this factor, as illustrated.

E. Right-turn factors

Factors for right and left turns are the most complex in the signalized-intersection analysis procedure, and are therefore the most difficult to calibrate.

Headways of right-turning vehicles are longer than for through vehicles, and headways of vehicles behind right turners in a queue can also be affected. The most significant variable influencing the extent of this effect is the magnitude of the pedestrian conflict with right-turning vehicles. Since the extent and timing of pedestrian–right-turning conflicts is based on both the design and signalization of the intersection, seven separate cases are defined by the *HCM*:

1. Exclusive RT lane and protected RT phase
2. Exclusive RT lane and permitted RT phase
3. Exclusive RT lane and protected + permitted phase
4. Shared RT lane and protected RT phase
5. Shared RT lane and permitted RT phase
6. Shared RT lane and protected + permitted RT phase
7. Single-lane approach

A *protected RT phase* is one in which no conflicting pedestrians are permitted to use the crosswalk while right turns are permitted. A *permitted RT phase,* by far the most prevalent type of signalization, is one in which vehicles are permitted to turn right with care through a conflicting pedestrian flow in the crosswalk.

A *shared RT lane* is one in which through vehicles share the lane with right-turning vehicles. An *exclusive RT lane* is one that only right-turning vehicles are permitted to use.

Other parameters affecting right-turning vehicles include the percentage of right turners in the traffic stream, the number of pedestrians using the conflicting crosswalk, and the proportion of right turns made during protected portions of protected + permitted phasing.

The computation of any one value of f_{RT} is not difficult. Again, other factors should be ideal—i.e., ideal geometrics and no use of headways affected by heavy vehicles. The average prevailing saturation headway in a right-turn lane is then compared to the ideal saturation headway. This yields an adjustment factor for the right-turn lane, which may be averaged over all lanes of a lane group, as was the case for parking factors:

$$f_{RTr} = \frac{h_o}{h} \qquad [20\text{-}11]$$

$$f_{RT} = \frac{f_{RTr} + (N - 1)}{N} \qquad [20\text{-}12]$$

where: f_{RTr} = right-turn factor for right lane only
 f_{RT} = right-turn factor for lane group
 N = number of lanes in the lane group
 h_o = ideal saturation headway, sec/veh
 h = prevailing saturation headway in right lane, sec/veh

The tables in the *HCM* relate the right-turn factor to conflicting pedestrian volumes, proportion of right-turning vehicles in the lane group, portion of right-turning vehicles using the protected portion of protected + permitted phasing, and the geometric/control case which exists. With this number of variables, it is virtually impossible to calibrate localized RT factors without a major research effort beyond the means of most practicing traffic engineering departments.

F. Left-turn factors

The left-turn adjustment factor is even more complicated than the right-turn factor. Left turns may occur under the same eight basic conditions of signalization and geometry as cited for right turns. In the case of left turns, protected turns are those made with the opposing through movement prohibited, while permitted turns are made through an opposing vehicular flow.

Headways for exclusive left-turn lanes with protected phasing can be easily observed and related to ideal saturation headways to determine an adjustment factor. Such headways are only marginally higher than the ideal, owing to the turning movement being made. As there is no opposing flow and no sharing of lanes, left-turning vehicles face no vehicular interference and do not influence other vehicles. This, however, is the only simple case.

The *HCM* presents a complex derived model for the impact of permitted left turns on prevailing saturation flow rates. The model is based on the division of the effective green phase into three portions:

g_q = blocked portion of the green phase, sec; left turns blocked by clearance of opposing vehicle queue
g_f = initial portion of g_q; time until first left-turning vehicle arrives for service; during this time, through vehicles in shared LT/TH lane may proceed, sec
g_u = unsaturated portion of the green phase, sec left-turning vehicles filter through an unsaturated opposing vehicular flow

The model used in the estimation of these times is derived from basic characteristics analytically. It has not been calibrated with field data or studies.

A project conducted at Polytechnic University in 1989, sponsored by the Federal Highway Administration, collected a significant data base to calibrate a model for determining an appropriate left-turn factor for permitted left turns [3]. Prevailing saturation flow rates are being observed at five sites in each of four cities for 12 hours apiece. The study assumes that all factors in the 1985 *HCM* were correct. Therefore:

$$s = s_o N f_w f_{HV} f_g f_p f_{bb} f_a f_{RT} f_{LT}$$

If the product of all applicable adjustment factors except the left-turn factor is defined as F, then

$$s = s_o N F f_{LT}$$

and

$$f_{LT} = \frac{s}{s_o N F} \qquad [20\text{-}12]$$

This approach had some risks in that it assumes that all 1985 *HCM* values are correct, except the left-turn factor. Its advantage is that sites without otherwise ideal conditions may be observed for calibration data.

Once field values of f_{LT} were imputed from the data as above, regression analysis was used to develop predictive algorithms, a number of which were adopted in the 1994 and 1997 *HCMs*, as presented in Chapter 18.

If the *HCM* is less than precise in its treatment of permitted left turns, it is even more approximate in its handling protected plus permitted phasing, as was discussed in Chapter 18. In the 1985 *HCM*, it was assumed that *all* left turns occurred during the protected portion of the phase, with iterations occurring should the capacity of that phase be insufficient. In the 1994 *HCM*, the approach was modified. It was assumed that the vehicles used 100% of the *first* portion of the phase (i.e., the protected portion of a protected plus permitted phase, and the permitted portion of a permitted plus protected phase), with all other vehicles using the second portion of the compound phase. Early versions of the HCS package [4] assumed that the two portions of the phase balanced to equal *v/c* ratios, but this was abandoned, as it did not exactly replicate the *HCM*.

None of these assumed behaviors exactly match field conditions at all intersections. They merely provide a basis for approximate modeling of *v/c* ratios and delay under conditions of compound phasing.

Again, calibration of left-turn adjustment factors involves complex models. They can be effectively calibrated only with significant research efforts that are well beyond the financial means of most highway agencies. Thus, this factor is rarely calibrated on a local basis.

Normalizing signalized-intersection analysis

In many cases, it will be difficult or expensive to calibrate individual factors involved in signalized-intersection analysis on a localized basis. As noted, in addition to the ideal saturation flow rate, eight adjustment factors can be calibrated. Nevertheless, in many cases it will be clear that the values given in the *HCM* are not correct for local conditions, as the results of analysis will be at variance with field observations.

It is possible to "normalize" the *HCM* procedure by observing departure volumes on fully saturated signalized-intersection approaches—conditions that denote capacity operation.

Consider the case of a three-lane intersection approach with a 30-second effective green in a 60-second cycle. Assume further that the product of all of the adjustment factors from the *HCM* for the prevailing conditions at the site is 0.80. Then:

$$s = s_o NF = 1900(3)(0.80) = 4560 \text{ vphg}$$

$$c = s(g/C) = 4560\left(\frac{30}{60}\right) = 2280 \text{ vph}$$

Despite this result, departure volume counts on this approach under fully saturated conditions have

measured a peak 15-minute rate of flow of *2400vph* leaving the approach. Assuming that this observation is correct, the capacity estimated by the 1985 *HCM* is too low. This could be due to s_o or any one of the adjustment factors being too low, or some combinations of these.

It may be too difficult to calibrate every one of these factors to determine which among them are inappropriate for the intersection under study. What can be done is to reverse the logic of the equations to determine the "effective" ideal saturation flow rate that would make the computed capacity agree with the observed value:

$$s = \frac{c}{g/C} = \frac{2400}{0.50} = 4800 \text{ vphg}$$

$$s_o = \frac{s}{NF} = \frac{4800}{3 \times 0.80} = 2000 \text{ pchgpl}$$

This computation *does not* indicate that the actual ideal saturation flow rate for this location is 2000 pcphgpl. What this computation has done is normalize the ideal saturation flow rate to account for inaccuracies in the ideal saturation flow rate and *all adjustment factors* that caused the predicted capacity to be lower than the observed value.

This "normalized" ideal saturation flow rate may now be used in other analyses concerning the subject approach. If such "normalizing" studies at several locations reveal a common areawide value, it may be applied to other intersections in the area as well.

This approach is quite productive where *HCM* procedures need modification but where resources are insufficient to calibrate individual factors in the analysis.

The delay equation

As noted previously, the delay equation of the *HCM* is based on extensive theoretical development and limited field calibrations. Using the Webster delay equation as a basis, various researchers have fit the transition between stable delay at reasonable *v/c* ratios to unstable delay at *v/c* ratios > 1.00, where delay increases rapidly and compounds as queues continue to increase. The *HCM* formulation was recommended by the Highway Capacity and Quality of Service Committee, based on the work of Akcelik [5], JHK & Associates [6], and Roess and Messer [7]. For an excellent treatment of the origin of these equations, consult Reference [8]. Subsequent work by Fambro Rouphail and others has led to additional modifications in the 1997 update of the *HCM*.

Appendix III of Chapter 9 of the 1994 *HCM* recommends a simple methodology for measuring delay at a signalized-intersection approach, which was presented in Chapter 7.

The 1997 update of the *HCM* will present a modified version of this procedure for field measurement of control (or approach) delay, the parameter of which will be used to define level of service.

Using this technique, which requires manual observation or photographic techniques, field values of delay may be obtained. Using the theoretical models described in the literature as a starting point, such data may be used to calibrate models to more accurately predict delay in a local area. This again is a costly procedure involving a significant research effort.

References

1. *Highway Capacity Manual, Special Report 109,* 3rd Edition, Transportation Research Board, National Research Council, Washington, DC, 1985.
2. Webster, R., "Traffic Signal Settings," *Road Research Technical Paper No. 39,* Road Research Laboratory, Her Majesty's Stationery Office, London, U.K., 1958.
3. Roess, R., Ulerio, J., and Papayanoulis, V., "Left-Turn Adjustment Factors for Shared-Permitted Left-Turn Lanes at Signalized Intersections," *Interim Report,* Polytechnic University, Brooklyn, NY, March 1988.
4. Shenk, E., McShane, W., Ulerio, J., and Roess, R., *Highway Capacity Software, User's Manual,* Polytechnic University, Brooklyn, NY, 1986.
5. Akcelik, R., "Traffic Signals: Capacity and Timing Analysis," *Australian Road Research Report 123,* Australian Road Research Board, Kew, Victoria, Australia, 1981.
6. "Signalized Intersection Capacity Study," *Final Report,* NCHRP Project 3–28(2), JHK & Associates, Tucson, AZ, December 1982.
7. Roess, R. and Messer, C., "The New Highway Capacity Manual," *Final Report,* NCHRP Project 3–28B, Polytechnic University, Brooklyn, NY, 1986.
8. Hurdle, V., "Signalized Intersection Delay Models: A Primer for the Uninitiated," *Transportation Research Record 971,* Transportation Research Board, National Research Council, Washington, DC, 1984.

Problems

Problems 20–1 through 20–4 deal with the data shown in Table 20-4. This figure shows headway data collected in three lanes of a three-lane signalized-intersection approach with ideal geometric conditions. Turning movements are denoted by L or R, and heavy vehicles are denoted by H. The line indicates the end of the saturated queue.

Problem 20–1

Determine the prevailing saturation flow rate for the intersection approach represented by the headway data in Table 20-4.

Problem 20–2

Determine the ideal saturation flow rate for the intersection approach represented by the headway data in Table 20-4.

Problem 20–3

Determine the start-up lost time for the intersection approach represented by the headway in Table 20-4.

Table 20-4 Data for Problems 1 Through 4

Data for Lane 1, Left Lane

Veh. in Queue	Observed Headways (sec)				
	Cycle 1	Cycle 2	Cycle 3	Cycle 4	Cycle 5
1	2.8	2.9	3.0	3.1	2.7
2	2.6	2.6	2.5	3.5H	2.6
3	3.9L	2.3	2.2	2.9	2.5
4	10.2H	2.1	2.0	2.5	2.0
5	8.7	4.0L	1.9	2.2	1.9
6	3.0	9.9L	2.2	2.0	1.9
7	<u>2.9</u>	9.8	2.9H	1.9	3.6HL
8	5.0	3.3	2.6	<u>1.8</u>	9.0
9	7.1	2.8	<u>2.1</u>	7.0	<u>4.0</u>
10	9.0	2.2	4.0	8.0	4.9
11		<u>1.9</u>	5.0		9.0
12		5.5			
13		4.0			
14					
15					

Data for Lane 2, Center Lane

Veh. in Queue	Observed Headways (sec)				
	Cycle 1	Cycle 2	Cycle 3	Cycle 4	Cycle 5
1	2.8	2.9	2.9	2.7	2.9
2	2.7	2.5	2.5	2.6	2.3
3	2.3	2.2	2.1	2.3	2.1
4	2.1	2.0	2.0	1.9	2.1
5	2.8H	1.9	1.8	1.9	1.9
6	2.3	1.9	2.0	1.9	2.0
7	2.6H	2.0	2.1	1.8	2.4H
8	2.1	<u>2.1</u>	1.9	2.0	<u>2.5H</u>
9	<u>1.9</u>	4.5	1.8	1.9	6.0
10	5.0	4.4	<u>2.1</u>	<u>2.0</u>	9.0
11			5.6	7.1	
12			3.3		
13					
14					
15					

Table 20-4 (continued)

Data for Lane 3, Right Lane

Veh. in Queue	Observed Headways (sec)				
	Cycle 1	Cycle 2	Cycle 3	Cycle 4	Cycle 5
1	3.0	2.8	3.1	3.9R	2.8
2	2.5	2.5	2.7	2.8	2.6
3	2.1	2.1	2.8R	2.1	2.1
4	1.9	1.9	2.3	1.9	1.8
5	2.5H	2.0	3.2RH	1.9	1.9
6	2.3	2.1	2.5	1.8	1.9
7	2.4R	2.5R	2.3	1.7	2.1
8	2.2	2.1	2.0	3.7	1.8
9	4.4	1.9	1.8	5.0	1.9
10	6.0	3.5	2.6R		4.7
11		4.0	7.0		
12		5.0			
13		2.9			
14					
15					

Problem 20–4

Determine the heavy-vehicle factor that applies to the headway data given in Table 20-4. To what period of time does this factor apply? Calibrate the factor directly, as well as through a determination of the passenger-car equivalent for heavy vehicles.

Problem 20–5

The following saturation headways for passenger cars were measured at sites that were geometrically ideal, except for varying lane widths. Determine the appropriate lane-width adjustment factors for this case.

Site No.	Lane Width (ft)	Sat. Headway (sec)
1	9	2.70
2	10	2.50
3	11	2.35
4	12	2.30
5	13	2.20
6	14	2.15
7	15	2.10

Problem 20–6

A busy bus stop at a downtown location is at an intersection with a 40-sec effective green time out of a 90-sec cycle. If buses stop in a travel lane with average dwell times of 18 sec, what is the appropriate bus blockage factor? Buses make up 5% of the traffic stream at this location.

Problem 20–7

The capacity of an intersection approach is estimated using the *HCM* method, with standard values as follows:

$$s_o = 1900 \text{ pcphg}$$
$$N = 2 \text{ lanes}$$
$$F = 0.75$$
$$\frac{g}{C} = 0.60$$

If a capacity of 1900 vph were actually observed at this location, what normalized value of s_o would adjust the *HCM* procedure to yield the correct estimate?

21

Techniques for Addressing Freeway System Congestion

This chapter presents an overview of analysis techniques used to address *freeway system congestion:*

- freeway entrance-ramp control
- incidents and capacity reductions
- congestion due to a bottleneck
- cumulative demand and capacity analysis

The chapter contains a more precise treatment of demand/capacity analysis than found in most of the literature, and notes the differences in approach (and results).

Freeway entrance-ramp control

Since the early 1960s, freeway ramp controls have been installed throughout the United States and elsewhere, as stand-alone projects or as part of an overall freeway surveillance and control system. Figure 21-1 shows a ramp control installation. The systems in Los Angeles, Chicago, New Jersey (Turnpike), and New York (INFORM) are some of the larger systems. Reference [2] is an interesting historic state-of-the-art report.

In addition to the *freeway* management systems, some of the early control work on limited-access facilities was on river tunnels, notably the Holland and Lincoln Tunnels connecting New York and New Jersey. Because of high demand and reduced capacity on the upgrade, metering of the tunnel inputs was imposed to avoid congested operation.

A. Strategies

There have been a number of basic strategies for inserting vehicles into the mainline traffic, each with different demands on sophistication of control and detectorization.

1. Simple metering. The simplest implementation is the use of a fixed metering rate, with an optional detector for sensing the presence of a vehicle. The detector allows the signal to rest in red, avoiding po-

Figure 21-1 A ramp metering installation. [Courtesy of INFORM, New York Department of Transportation.]

Mainline Occupancy*	Metering Rate (veh/min)
≤10%	12
11–16%	10
17–225%	8
23–28%	6
29–34%	4
>34%	3

*"Occupancy" is the percent time a detector is covered or activated by vehicles. It relates directly to density.

tential confusion to a driver approaching the signal, due to the short greens. The ramp-control signal, mounted close to driver level, generally provides two indications, green and red only. Figure 21-2 illustrates the installation.

The metering rate is determined by the expected mainline volume and by a decision on how much volume can be allowed in on the particular ramp. The green indication is generally 2 to 3 sec long, sufficient to pass one vehicle.

As an illustration, suppose that a metering rate of 300 vph were assigned to the ramp. This is one vehicle every 12 sec, so that a setting of a 2 sec of green followed by 10 sec of red could be used.

2. Demand-responsive metering. The concept of "simple metering" can be extended by use of information from upstream and/or downstream detectors in the mainline, so that the ramp metering rate is computed in real time to respond to current (perhaps averaged) demand levels and mainline conditions.

To determine the condition of the mainline, various installations have used volume and/or occupancy and have keyed to either upstream observations, downstream observations, or differences between the two. Reference [3] shows the following example of the metering rate at a "local-actuated" ramp control:

3. Gap-acceptance metering. One of the early advanced strategies was *gap-acceptance metering*, whereby a series of detectors in the shoulder lane of the upstream would identify "acceptable gaps" and match a ramp vehicle to the gap by timing the release of the ramp vehicle to maximize the likelihood of a match.

Gap acceptance was said to have special advantage for ramps with poor sight distance. Due to its sophistication and detectorization requirements, combined with small incremental benefits (if any), it is not a serious option in current operational projects. For a more complete discussion and related analysis, see [4].

4. Pacer and Greenband systems. The *Pacer* and *Greenband* systems are logical extensions of the gap-acceptance concept, for one of the concerns with the gap-acceptance option was whether the ramp vehicle would actually be in the right place at the right time. References [5] and [6] present the basic concepts of the systems, both of which were tried experimentally. Like the gap-acceptance concept, they are not routinely used as current operational options.

The *Pacer* system used a series of lights along the ramp to lead the vehicle along, with the pace of the lights matched to the gap sensed on the mainline.

The *Greenband* system followed the same principle, but used a band of acrylic panels backed by floodlights every 2 feet to provide an image of a moving band. Reference [5] reports that the Greenband system was preferred by drivers who had used both.

B. Warrants

The MUTCD [7] contains guidance on the installation of ramp controls and also provides guidance on the types of studies needed, including attention to

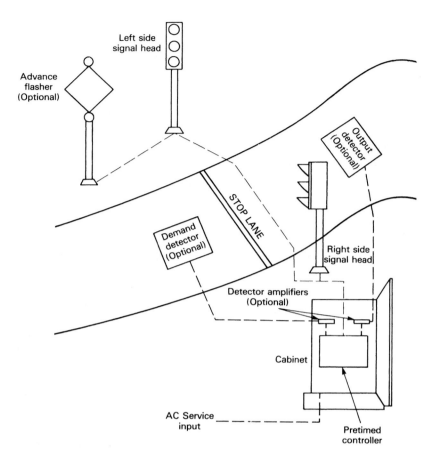

Figure 21-2 Principle hardware components of a pretimed ramp control. [Used with permission of Transportation Research Board, Transportation Research Council, Washington, DC, from C. W. Blumentritt, C. Pinnell, and W. R. McCasland, "Guidelines for Selection of Ramp Control Systems," *NCHRP Report 232*, p. 59. Copyright © 1981 Transportation Research Board.]

impacts on the local street system and the existence of alternate routes.

C. Advantages

Entrance-ramp control has a number of potential advantages, including the following:

- The freeway mainline operation can be greatly improved by restricting access and perhaps encouraging drivers to use alternate paths, such as existing frontage roads.
- Arrivals from a nearby surface street signal are "smoothed out" by the metering and do not load onto the freeway as a periodic pulse of vehicles.
- Certain types of accidents can be alleviated, such as ramp/merging accidents and rear-end accidents on a congested mainline.
- Emissions, fuel consumption, and vehicle operating costs can be decreased.

- Network routings can be beneficially influenced.

At the same time, it must be recognized that:

- There is no evidence that ramps with such active control have better *capacities.* Indeed, the purpose of the ramp control is generally to assure that the ramp operates below its capacity level.
- Ramps from which alternate paths do not exist are poor candidates for entrance control, due to the formation of large queues awaiting service.
- Likewise, ramps which are "dead ends" due to termination of the frontage road or other such reason are poor candidates.
- The potential effects of alternate paths—adverse and beneficial—must be taken into account in the advance planning.

Figure 21-3 shows an interesting example of traffic diversion that influenced the effectiveness of the

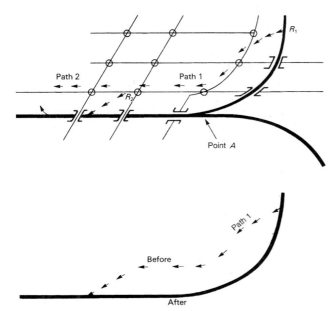

Figure 21-3   Effect of ramp control at one location.

ramp control at R_2. Due to congestion at Point A resulting from the merging of two limited-access facilities, vehicles were *already* diverting from R_1 to the surface streets to use R_2 as a short cut, which is causing congestion at the merge point that is backing up into Point A. With R_2 metered sufficiently, not only did it make R_2 less attractive, but it relieved the congestion at Point A, making the direct connection more attractive. Thus, rather than choosing Path 2, a significant number of vehicles simply abandoned Path 1 and stayed on the limited-access road, beyond control. Rather than achieving the diversion at R_2, the net effect was an *increase* in effective demand at Point A.

Incidents and capacity reductions

The cumulative demand—capacity analysis is a powerful tool for analyzing the effect of situations that result in capacity reductions, short term or longer term.

The principal adverse impacts include:

Weather

Incidents

Accidents

Work zones

A. Insight into effect of capacity reductions

There is little hard, quantitative information on the general effect of certain conditions. However, it is instructive to appreciate how sensitive the traffic network often is to disruption. Consider a peak period during which the drivers have distributed themselves so as to make their "best use" of the network, and as a result it is very common that

$$\frac{v}{c} = 0.93$$

in much of the network.[1]

Now consider a 15% loss in capacity, perhaps due to rain. The new v/c ratio in much of the network would be

$$\frac{v}{0.85c} = \frac{v/c}{0.85} = \frac{0.93}{0.85} = 1.09$$

That is, much of the network went from a functioning system to 9% above capacity, simply because of some rain.

A relevant digression: many people, looking at the chaos in a traffic network on a rainy day, start speculating that "A lot of people must have taken their cars because of the bad weather." That is, they assume that the demand *must* have jumped up, because the network is so atypically bad. However, the implication of the above computation is that even modest decreases in capacity (due to rain, mild snow, a short incident, and the like) can have truly dramatic impact on the v/c ratio, driving much of the system over 1.00.

Consider the following situations:

Capacity Reduction	Original v/c Ratio		
	0.85	**0.90**	**0.95**
10%	0.94	1.00	1.06
15%	1.00	1.06	1.12
20%	1.06	1.12	1.19
25%	1.13	1.20	1.27

where the entries are the new v/c ratios.

[1]If this were not the case, drivers would try to use the lower v/c links if at all possible, causing it to be the case.

Historically, facilities have been designed to their "good weather" and "incident-free" capacities. An interesting policy issue is the acceptability of designing—or the need to design—a facility to compensate for poor weather due to local climate and/or incidents. (The probability that some part of an even midsized system is adversely impacted in a given peak period is very high.)

B. Shifts in traffic patterns due to capacity reductions

There is no question that drivers will use knowledge of the network to optimize their own trips.[2] Indeed, the existing traffic assignment is the product of such a process. If a capacity reduction will exist for some extended period, many drivers can and will reroute if feasible paths exist. A number of "microassignment" models exist to help the transportation professional anticipate the effect of such reroutings.

If the capacity reduction is unexpected (e.g., an accident or other random incident), the inclination and ability for drivers to reroute will depend on a number of factors, not the least of which are the existence of alternate routes and the duration of the delay.

Regarding how much delay is acceptable, Reference [8] simply notes that in one jurisdiction "demands that would cause individual delay at one location of more than a half hour on a routine basis, are ignored on the premise they do not occur. It is assumed that this demand would use another route, would spread out and lengthen the peak period, would use another travel mode or the trip would not be made at all."

C. Effect of weather

Quantitative information is sparse, but some does exist. One study found that rain reduced capacity by 14% to 19% [9,10]. Another found a typical figure of 8% for rain [11], with some variation observed. It appears that 10% to 20% reductions in capacity are typical, and higher percentages are quite possible.

---

[2]Absent such knowledge, the need for advance notice, guidance, and communication is very real.

There are at least three practical problems with collection of "poor-weather" data: (1) the random nature of the event makes it difficult to schedule crews, (2) the adverse condition makes the data effort arduous and can affect accuracy, (3) it is difficult to quantify the weather parameter over a wide data base—how much rain is "heavy"? Is inches per hour sufficient, or do short downpours count disproportionately? How about snow, and its "wetness," which varies with region? How does early sanding affect the data?

Even if automated data collection lessens the import of the first two practical problems, the quantification of the "environmental" parameter is a real challenge. For this reason, making sensitivity studies over some plausible range (corresponding to the numbers cited, for instance) seems to have special value.

D. Effect of incidents and accidents

The term *incident* includes vehicle breakdowns, roadside distractions, and spilled loads. In most usages it includes accidents.

A number of factors must be considered regarding an incident or other event:

- frequency
- effect on capacity
- duration
- actions needed for public health and safety
- other responses needed

For instance, some incidents and accidents require ambulances, fire equipment, wreckers to clear large vehicles, and appearances by environmental agencies.

With regard to *effect on capacity,* Reference [12] estimated that for a three-lane facility (each direction):

An Incident	Percent Capacity Reduction
Removed to shoulder	33%
Blocking one lane	50%
Blocking two lanes	75%

Reference [13] reported the following, based on a survey of 28 ramp-control systems in the United States and Canada:

An Incident	Percent Capacity Reduction for *N* Lanes			
	N = 2	*N* = 3	*N* = 4	*N* = 5
Removed to shoulder	25%	16%	11%	—
Blocking one lane	68%	47%	44%	25%
Blocking two lanes	100%	78%	66%	50%

Numbers shown are rounded; Reference [13] also showed confidence bounds, which were of the order of ±5% for most numbers and ±10% for some of the larger numbers. The data was insufficient to estimate the "removed to shoulder" case for *N* = 5.

With regard to *frequency* of incidents, Reference [13] notes that in its survey, the ramp-control systems reported an average of 5.28 incidents per year per peak hour per lane-mile. This is notably lower than reported in [14], based on generalized statistics.

To appreciate the regularity with which disturbances occur, consider a 10-mile section of a six-lane limited-access facility, as shown in Figure 21-4. Reference [14] reported that

- The *incident* rate was estimated at 200 per million vehicle miles per year.
- The 10-mile section is expected to have 10,000 incidents during the peak periods per year.

That is, each *day* some 3.85 incidents are expected in *each mile* (both directions) during the four-hour peak period. Almost one incident is expected in each mile, every hour.[3]

Further, not counting drivers who stop in a lane but get to the vehicle to a shoulder, the statistics show that a one-lane blockage incident occurs somewhere in the 10 miles on average *every working day,* and one which blocks two or more lanes occurs about twice per month.

Other information is also available for accident histories. Annual statistics can be used to relate different reportable accident categories to at least millions of vehicle miles (MVM) of travel. More limited and site-specific information is available on other types of incidents.

[3]In this context, recall that facilities are designed for the good weather, incident-free condition.

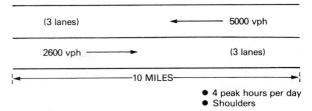

Figure 21-4 Summary of road cited in Reference [14] illustration.

Reference [15] reports that for one facility of interest, it was estimated that peak-period incidents were responsible for more delay than recurrent peak-period congestion at the location in question.

E. Components of incident response

The last issue raised with regard to incidents was *duration*. This in turn is closely linked with incident response.

Incident response consists of three elements, followed by a period in which the effect persists:

T_1 = time from the occurrence of an incident to the placement of a "call" for service

T_2 = time from receipt of a "call" for service and the arrival of help at the incident site

T_3 = time to clear the incident

T_4 = time to clear the effect of residual queues

Further, while many incidents are remedied by drivers without assistance, they too have effects: although we can say $T_1 = T_2 = 0$ in these cases, T_3 is not zero, nor is T_4.

Reference [13] reported the following, based on its survey of ramp-control systems:

Incident Type	Percent of Incidents	Time to Clear Incident	Of Which, Some Was to Clear to Shoulder
Vehicle or person on shoulder or median	48%	21.9 min	—
One-lane blockage	45%	18.2 min	First 5–10 minutes
Two-lane blockage	5%	23.6 min	First 10–15 minutes

Based on the description in [13] (i.e., "(time) to complete clearing"), these values are estimates of T_3.

All the numbers shown above had wide ranges in the survey responses (the confidence bounds almost equaled the numbers shown).

There has been much research emphasis on means by which T_1 can be reduced by means of better observations with closed-circuit TV (CCTV) or by means of detector algorithms (e.g., [16]). However, it is the *total* response time $T = (T_1 + T_2 + T_3)$ that is relevant from the view of traffic operations and relief of congestion.

Consider that the time T_1 depends on the technology available (CCTV, detectors, and so on) *and* the communications received from the field (CB reports, volunteer spotters, and the like). The time T_2 depends on a number of factors, primarily related to the proximity of necessary response vehicles and the ease with which they can get to the scene. That in turn depends on the level of the traffic relative to the reduced capacity, the existence of shoulders or other routes for emergency use, and the terrain. (In one meeting, a person from Texas simply reported that the tow trucks drove down the frontage road and then crossed to the incident over the level terrain.)

It is plausible to think in terms of the relative magnitudes of the times being:

	As Percent of *T*
$T_1 \simeq$ 5 minutes	12.5%
$T_2 \simeq$ 15 minutes	37.5%
$T_3 \simeq$ 20 minutes	50.0%

If so, then an interesting question is how one gets the best reduction in the overall time T, which is the quantity of importance in mitigating the congestion.

Note that a 2-minute reduction in T_1 represents 40% of the stated value, and requires considerable work in detection algorithms and/or hardware, based on past experience. The same reduction in T_2 represents 13% of the stated value, and probably requires system-management actions—location of repair vehicles, readiness for response, and other preplanning. For T_3 it is 10% of the stated value and might involve some "low-tech" approaches to a quick cleanup and removal (which in turn may have some institutional obstacles).

F. Work zones

For the safety of the work crew and the orderly conduct of the effort, it has always been necessary to delineate "work zones" on highways by proper use of markings, signing, and other measures. The *MUTCD* [7] contains a special section on the proper delineation of work zones, which is also printed as a separate document.

Work zones, however, have obvious impacts on the capacity available to the drivers, if only because one or more lanes are frequently taken out of service. In addition, both the existence of the work and the nature of it have an effect on the per-lane capacities in many cases.

For many years, the conventional wisdom was that the default number for per-lane capacity under mainline disruptions was 1500 vphpl. Thus, an engineer might well have assumed 1500 vphpl for each available lane at a work zone.

Based on work reported in the 1980s, the numbers in the *HCM* [16] seem much more appropriate as *default* values. Refer to Table 21-1 for an illustration. However, the underlying data has enough variation from site to site as to justify that practicing engineers have local data based on their own sites and/or checks on the specific site to make sure that the default values are reasonable.

The cumulative demand/capacity analysis technique can be used to good effect in (1) determining the impact of a construction or maintenance activity, and (2) scheduling the time of short-term activities.

Table 21-1   Average Measured Work-Zone Capacities

Number of Lanes		Average Capacity (vphpl)
Normal	Open	
3	1	1,170
2	1	1,340
5	2	1,370
4	2	1,480
3	2	1,490
4	3	1,520

[Adapted with permission of Texas Transportation Institute, from C. Dudek, *Notes on Work Zone Capacity and Level of Service.* Copyright © 1984 Texas Transportation Institute.]

Clearly, long-term capacity reductions due to construction require advance planning, including alternate route advisories whenever possible. These present special—and very common—challenges to the engineer.

Congestion due to a bottleneck

A section of roadway to which more demand is delivered than can be processed is referred to as a "bottleneck."

A. Different flow-density curves

A section of roadway may be thought of as defined by its "flow–density" curve, if one appreciates that (1) this curve is related to the speed–density curve, which is more basic, and (2) the analysis to follow is based on the "steady-state" or equilibrium conditions, and transition effects make the depiction more complex. (However, the principal effects are well represented by the analysis to be given.)

Consider the two flow–density relations of Figure 21-5 for sections of a three-lane road (each direction), with Curve I defining Sections 1 and 3, and Curve II defining Section 2. Section 2 clearly has a lower capacity; this might be due to a grade, a surfacing condition, or other factors.

Further, consider that the demand flow rate is Q_1 and is less than the lower capacity value.

- Section 1 has a space mean speed S_1 and a density D_1, defined by Curve I. The demand is served and flows on into Section 2.
- At the given demand, Section 2 has a space mean speed and density defined by Curve II, and the density D_2 is *higher* than the prior density D_1. Because the speed is given by the chord of the curve (see the indicated slopes), it follows that the speed S_2 is *lower* than in Section 1. Thus, the driver experiences lower speed and a greater proximity to other drivers.

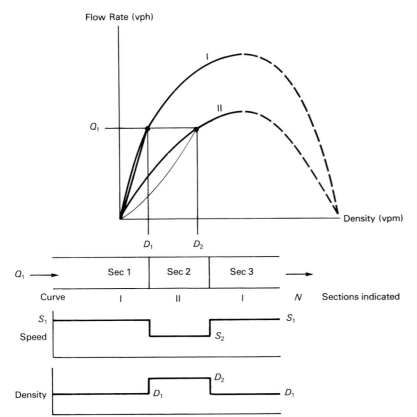

Figure 21-5 Two sections of road with different flow-density curves and demand lower than both capacities.

Nonetheless, the demand is served and flows on into Section 3.

- Section 3 has the same demand and curve as Section 1. There is no reason for the curve to rest on a flow–density pair to the right of the curves (i.e., the dashed parts). Compared to Section 2, the driver experiences better speed and lower density. Indeed, the driver returns to the conditions of Section 1.

The speed and density profiles by section are shown in Figure 21-5 for the given flow. The driver passes through the sections, experiencing this profile.

However, what would have happened if the demand flow rate had been greater than the capacity of the second section? Consider Figure 21-6, which depicts this situation. Note that:

- The demand flow rate Q_1 can be served at some point in Section I, illustrated by the Point 1 in the roadway. In this part of the section, the speed and density are as shown for the corresponding Point 1 and Curve I.

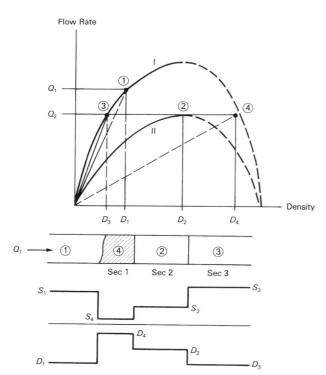

Figure 21-6 Two sections of road with different flow-density curves and demand lower than only one capacity.

- This demand cannot be passed to Section 2, simply because it exceeds the capacity of Section 2. The most that can be passed is Q_2, corresponding to the capacity of the section.
- Thus, in Section 2, it is the flow Q_2 which exists. This operates at Point 2 on Curve II and is at a lower speed and higher density than the traffic at Point 1.
- Only a flow level Q_2 can be passed to Section 3. Without a mechanism to force operation on the right (dashed) side of the curves, Section 3 operates at Point 3: it has a *higher* speed and *lower* density than even Point 1.

While this may seem strange, realize that Section 2 serves as the bottleneck, holding back the demand. Section 3 is the same quality road as Section 1 but has less flow—the true demand simply cannot reach it.

This situation is complicated by the fact that there is an accumulation of vehicles somewhere: the difference $(Q_1 - Q_2)$ passes Point 1 but cannot get into Section 2. Thus, they are stored upstream of Section 2, actually within Section 1. Thus, part of Section 1 stores vehicles *and* experiences an outflow of only Q_2. Clearly, it is not in the same mode of operation as Section 3, and is therefore not operating at Point 3. Rather, it is operating at the same flow rate, but on the *right* side of the curve, at Point 4.

The speed and density profiles by section are also shown in Figure 21-6. Note that the *best* speed and lowest density is downstream of the bottleneck; the *worst* speed and highest density is just upstream of the bottleneck. Thus, *an assumption that the section with the poorest speed is actually the bottleneck is wrong and would lead to an erroneous identification:* the real bottleneck is the section just *downstream* of the worst section, where the traffic is recovering some performance.

B. Rate of growth

An interesting problem is the proper identification of the rate of growth of the storage area.

Figure 21-7 shows the situation at an arbitrary time and at one hour later. The expansion of the storage area now (1) adds the hour's accumulation of $(Q_1 - Q_2)$ vehicles, *and* (2) encompasses an area in which there already were vehicles at density D_1. Thus, the growth is defined by a total addition of

$$[(Q_1 - Q_2) + (S)(D_1)] \text{ vehicles} \qquad [21\text{-}1]$$

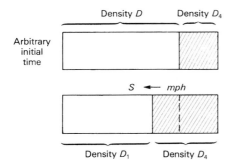

Figure 21-7 Rate of growth of stored vehicles.

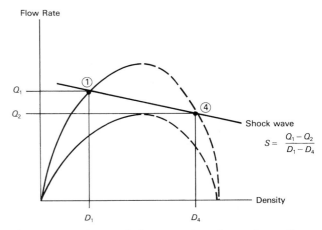

Figure 21-8 Geometric interpretation of rate of growth.

in the hour, with the speed of growth S not known.

However, it is also logical that the added growth is also defined by its *new* density, D_4. Thus the added growth includes $(S)(D_4)$ vehicles, so that

$$[(Q_1 - Q_2) + (S)(D_1)] = (S)(D_4)$$

or

$$S = \frac{Q_1 - Q_2}{D_4 - D_1} \qquad [21\text{-}2]$$

which is the speed of the growth of the queued vehicles. This is the "shock wave" traveling *up* the traffic stream from the bottleneck interface, due to the discontinuity.

Reference [18] is the landmark work on the kinematics of such "shock waves" or disturbances in traffic flow in a continuous flow. The authors, Lighthill and Whitham, used the analogy of traffic to a compressible fluid flow. In addition to the situation depicted above, they also covered more detailed cases in which the shock wave forms at a bottleneck and later dissipates as the demand decreases.

Equation [21-2] has a fascinating and logical geometric interpretation. As shown in Figure 21-8, it is the chord between Points 1 and 4 and has a negative slope, indicating that it travels *against* the direction of the vehicles.

To appreciate the scale, assume that

$$D_1 = 55 \text{ vpm}, \qquad D_4 = 100 \text{ vpm}$$
$$Q_1 = 1900 \text{ vph}, \qquad Q_2 = 1700 \text{ vph}$$

on a per-lane basis, and note that $S = (1900 - 1700)/(100 - 55) = 4.4$ mph. That is, the queue of stored vehicles grows at 4.4 mph for these numbers.

C. Types of bottlenecks

Bottlenecks may occur because of some permanent geometric feature, because of some construction activity, or because of some incident. The most common permanent bottleneck situations are (1) downstream of a freeway on-ramp, and (2) at an upgrade section, preceded and followed by zero grades. The first is a case in which demand is fed in beyond the existing capacity; the second is a case of reduced capacity due to the grade in one section.

Another common bottleneck permanent situation is a lane drop, such as two two-lane roads merging into a three-lane road, or a simple-lane drop along a mainline. A variation on this is the convergence of many lanes into fewer, or the discontinuity of a frontage road.

D. Identification of bottlenecks

Some bottleneck situations are easy to identify, such as a frontage-road discontinuity. However, in many cases, it is necessary to identify both the bottleneck situation *and* the true demand.

1. Single bottlenecks. Figure 21-9 shows a simple situation in which the demand flow rate Q feeds the six indicated sections.

What happens if $Q = 4600$ vph in this illustration? Certainly, the driver experiences some variation in speed and density as the trip is made. However, the demand is served in all sections and can be measured anywhere.

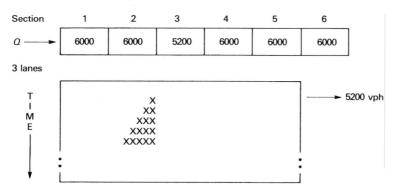

Figure 21-9 Simple case of a single bottleneck.

What happens if Q = 5600 vph? The demand cannot get through Section 3, and a queue develops *in Section 2*. This is illustrated in Figure 21-9. Further, the output flow to Sections 4 and beyond is only 5200 vph.

Note that the demand cannot be measured except upstream of the queue that develops (*not* just "upstream of the bottleneck"). Given the speed with which the queue can propagate upstream, this can be difficult, particularly if there are ramps in the area.

2. Hidden bottlenecks downstream. As shown in Figure 21-10, there are two sections with reduced capacity. Of course, in the field, this is not truly known and must be discovered by analysis.

Note that if Q = 4600 vph, there is no problem with serving the demand, although there is some variation in speed and density as one drives along the road.

However, if Q = 5600 vph, there is a severe problem with Section 3, resulting in a significant queue development in Section 2 (once again). This queue is *at*

least (5600 − 4800) = 800 vph[4] over the assumed three lanes.

Now even with three lanes, a queue of 1067 vph is 1067/3 = 356 vehicles per lane. At an average spacing of 50 ft per vehicle[5] this is a growth of (50)(356) = 17,800 ft or 3.4 miles in an hour.

Clearly, the bottleneck of Section 3 will be dramatic in its effect on Sections 1 and 2 and the overall performance. Downstream of Section 3 there is no obvious problem to be detected by travel-time runs, for the flow rate in these sections is 4800 vph.

---

[4]If D_1 = 60 vpmpl and D_2 = 120 vpmpl, then S = 4.4 mph by Equation [21-2], and the growth is 800 + 4.4(60) = 1067 vph by Equation [21-1].

[5]Most people initially assume 20 to 25 ft per vehicle in such a queue. These numbers are quite reasonable for a queue stopped at a traffic signal. However, the "queued" vehicles on a freeway are generally shuffling forward at level of service F, with significant gaps and an overall "accordion" effect, resulting in an average of 40 to 50 ft.

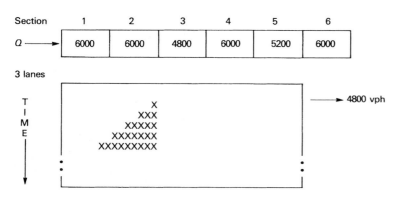

Figure 21-10 Two bottlenecks, one "hidden" downstream.

However, the bottleneck of 5200 vph in Section 5 does exist. If Section 3 is improved in a rehabilitation/ reconstruction project to 6000 vph (or any number much higher than 5200 vph), then once the demand finally passes Section 3 and hits Section 5, the new bottleneck is blatantly obvious.

Rather than face the cruel truth that the "new" bottleneck is an old one which was overlooked, some will state (and believe) that (1) it is new demand that developed during the years of the Section 3 work, or (2) it is diverted demand, attracted by the new capacity of the road, and overwhelming it. Sometimes these reasons are even true. However, sometimes it is also true that the proper analysis was never done to identify and fix both bottlenecks.

Given that the "demand" of 4800 vph released from Section 3 may not be sufficient to see the characteristic speed "dip" through the second bottleneck, due to the variability of real data, how then might the bottleneck be detected? One answer is the use of the capacity-analysis procedures applied to each section in order to estimate its capacity.

3. Hidden bottlenecks, upstream. Figure 21-11 shows the case of a "hidden" bottleneck upstream, using the same capacities as in the preceding example (albeit in different sections).

For a time, two distinct queues are seen. However, the downstream queue soon overwhelms the upstream one, effectively hiding the bottleneck. Indeed, given the wisdom that the section with the queue is *not* the bottleneck but rather upstream of it, Section 4 is overlooked.

Now *if* the travel time runs are made while there were two distinct queues and *if* they are detected in the data, then some insight into the existence of two bottlenecks is gained. However, the two queues can blend into one rather quickly, and perhaps only one travel-time run occurs during the time when they are distinct; one of the authors drives through such a situation in which the queues form and blend in some 20 minutes.

4. Should all bottlenecks be fixed? Engineers are trained to a frame of mind that states, "If it doesn't work, fix it." However, this is soon conditioned by some sense of engineering economics.

Consider the situation of Figure 21-12, with the vertical profile as shown. The low capacity in Section 5 is due to the road following the terrain into and out of a valley. Significant capacity gains might involve a viaduct (shown dashed) or extra lanes. If the number of lanes in place is such as to preclude another lane, and the viaduct is not cost effective, it may be that the capacity of Section 5 will remain as it is.

If that were to be the case, then a follow-up question is: Should any money be spent on Section 2, given that Section 5 will always have the indicated capacity? Aside from adverse impact on sections upstream of Sections 1 and 2 (which are not shown), the answer may actually be, "No, leave Section 2 as it is."

Cumulative demand and capacity

One of the most powerful tools for estimating the impact of freeway congestion is a relatively straightforward plot of cumulative demand and cumulative

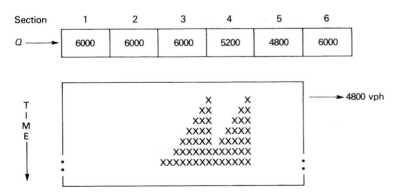

Figure 21-11 Two bottlenecks, one "hidden" upstream.

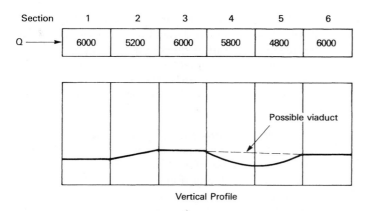

Figure 21-12   Considering whether improvement can be made.

capacity, on the same axis. Such a technique is presented in the *HCM* [16] and was also used in a key reference on work-zone planning [19]. Reference [20] reported on other related work and described a PC-based program to generate estimates.

The fact that such a technique was included in the *HCM* is of great significance. Since the first edition of the *HCM* in 1950, the emphasis was: "Use this manual to design facilities consistently, and according to the agreed state of the art." The emphasis on operations was limited. Level of service F was looked upon as a failure, not to be discussed in polite company. Indeed, the second edition of the *HCM* technically defined *five* operating levels of service, A through E. The usage of level of service F as the sixth level emerged, but it was not defined as an *operating* level.

By the third edition (the 1985 *HCM*, updated in 1994), transportation professionals recognized that level of service F is sometimes an unpleasant reality, and that some estimate of *how bad* things were was needed. The cumulative demand–capacity plots are focused on this end.

A. Conventional technique

To begin, there must be a plot of the demand flow rate and the capacity as a function of time, or the equivalent information in tabular form.

To illustrate, consider demand and capacity numbers as follows for a three-lane facility (per direction):

Time	Demand	Capacity
5:00– 6:00 A.M.	2500 vph	4000 vph
6:00– 7:00 A.M.	5000 vph	4000 vph
7:00– 8:00 P.M.	5000 vph	4000 vph
8:00– 9:00 A.M.	3000 vph	4000 vph
9:00–10:00 A.M.	3000 vph	4000 vph
10:00–11:00 A.M.	3000 vph	4000 vph

The "rules" are simple:

1. The problem starts only when demand exceeds capacity.[6] Thus, in the table of information above, the problem begins at 6:00 A.M. because demand is less than capacity in the earlier period(s).
2. From the problem initiation time to the end, tabulate and then plot the cumulative demand and capacity curves.
3. From the plot and/or table, determine the end time (the point at which cumulative demand falls below cumulative capacity).
4. Tabulate the queue as a function of time, in anticipation of the descriptive statistics.[7]
5. Compute the descriptive statistics as specified in the next section of this chapter.

---

[6]The most common mistake on examinations in the authors' classes was overlooking this requirement.

[7]The analysis in the next subsections will demonstrate that there is more to this than appears in most of the literature.

Figure 21-13(a) shows the plot of demand and capacity as a function of time. This is *not* a cumulative plot. However, it is useful to decide the point at which to start the analysis (i.e., at 6:00 A.M.).

The tabulation is as follows:

Time	Cumulative Demand	Cumulative Capacity	
	0	0	←Note
6:00– 7:00 A.M.	5000 vph	4000 vph	espec-
7:00– 8:00 A.M.	10,000 vph	8000 vph	ially, at
8:00– 9:00 A.M.	13,000 vph	12,000 vph	6:00 A.M.
9:00–10:00 A.M.	16,000 vph	16,000 vph	←Note end, with equality

This is also shown in plotted form as Figure 21-13(b).

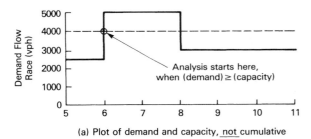

(a) Plot of demand and capacity, not cumulative

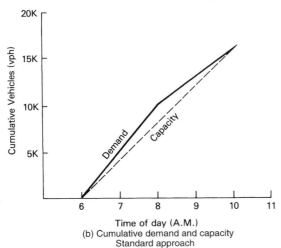

Time of day (A.M.)
(b) Cumulative demand and capacity
Standard approach

Figure 21-13 Basic plots for cumulative demand-capacity analysis. *Caution:* Do not use this approach without reading the next section, and considering the better "Approach 2."

Note that the cumulative capacity catches up with the cumulative demand at 10:00 A.M., which is when the analysis is therefore at an end.

B. Descriptive statistics

A number of very useful descriptive statistics can be obtained with relatively little difficulty. These include:

• number of vehicles affected
• total duration of congestion
• maximum number of vehicles queued
• maximum queue length
• maximum duration of individual delay
• total vehicle-hours of delay
• average delay per affected vehicle

According to the standard usage, the necessary basic quantities are illustrated in Figure 21-14. For instance,

$$\text{VEH}_{max} = \text{the total number of vehicles affected by the event, veh}$$

$$T_{max} = \text{the corresponding duration, hr}$$

It is possible to arbitrarily pick one vehicle (at least conceptually), enter the vertical axis of Figure 21-14 at the proper number, trace across to that vehicle's arrival time and departure time, thus obtaining the delay for that vehicle.

Likewise, in this approach, it is possible to arbitrarily pick a *time* on the horizontal axis and estimate the queue present at that time—or, to be precise, the principal part of the queue.

C. Need for an enhanced technique

Further consideration of the descriptive statistics led the authors to discover an inconsistency between the basic theory as developed in such references as [18] and the widely reported approach to cumulative demand–capacity analysis. The difference can be significant, and can be estimated.

APPROACH 1: is the commonly accepted and—on the surface—very logical computation of the queue. As shown in Figure 21-14, the difference between the cumulative demand and the cumulative capacity is "obviously" the queue. Indeed, this quantity is used in such key references as [16] and [19] and [20] and the works that have used these as references. The authors have happily used this approach.

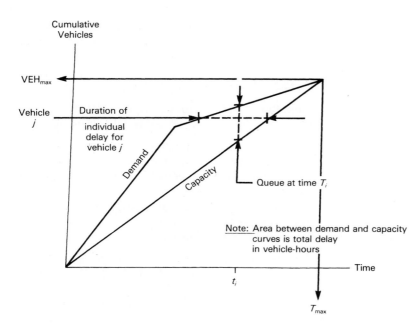

Figure 21-14 Standard interpretation of descriptive statistics from cumulative demand-capacity curve. *Caution:* Do not use this approach without considering the more precise "Approach 2."

Thus, drawing from the tabulation underlying Figure 21-13, the queue is estimated as:

Time	Cumul. Demand (veh)	Cumul. Capac. (veh)	Estimated Queue	
			Total	Lane
	0	0	0 veh	0 veh
6:00– 7:00 A.M.	5000	4000	1000 veh	333 veh
7:00– 8:00 A.M.	10,000	8000	2000 veh	667 veh
8:00– 9:00 A.M.	13,000	12,000	1000 veh	333 veh
9:00–10:00 A.M.	16,000	16,000	0 veh	0 veh

with the last column being averaged over the three lanes initially assumed. Indeed, Figure 21-13 is based on these numbers.

APPROACH 2: is more precise and includes the "extra" vehicles caught up in the growing queue. As illustrated in Figure 21-7, the section of road occupied by the queue $(Q_2 - Q_1)$ vehicles *also* was occupied by an additional number of vehicles at density D_1, giving rise to Equations [21-1] and [21-2].

To continue the illustration, assume the upstream flow–density curve is defined by

$$Q = 0.4734(D)(130 - D)$$

on a *per-lane* basis, corresponding to a 6000-vph capacity over three lanes:

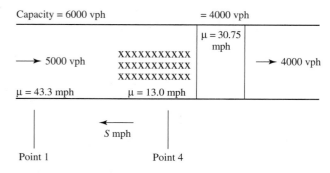

Thus $D_1 = 38.5$ vpmpl and $D_4 = 102.5$ vpmpl (using the 4000-vph capacity of the bottleneck), so that from Equation [21-2], $S = [(5000/3) - (4000/3)]/(38.5 - 102.5) = -5.2$ mph.[8]

---

[8]Note that the 102.5 vpmpl corresponds to an average vehicle spacing of $5280/102.5 = 51.5$ ft per vehicle (including the vehicle itself).

From Equation [21-1], the number of vehicles included is

$$\left[\left(\frac{5000}{3}\right) - \left(\frac{4000}{3}\right)\right] + (5.2)(38.5)$$

$$= \underline{533 \text{ vehicles per lane}}$$

which is 60% higher than Approach 1 at the end of one hour (i.e., at 7:00 A.M.).

By 8:00 A.M. the queued vehicles are 1066 vehicles per lane, 60% higher than the Approach 1 estimate. The queue is 10.4 miles long, at a density of 102.5 vpmpl, rather than $667/102.5 = 6.5$ miles long by Approach 1.

After 8:00 A.M. the queue shrinks, owing to the decreased demand (3000 vph). As shown in Figure 21-15, the "shock wave" now moves forward. Based on $D_1 = 19.0$ vpmpl (using $Q_1 = 3000/3$ vphpl), it follows that $S = [(3000/3) - (4000/3)]/(19.0 - 102.5) = +4.0$ mph, which characterizes the collapse rate.

The density within the area being released from the level of service F operation is D_4; it becomes density D_1. The number of *vehicles* released from the queued status is

$$\text{QUEUE DECREASE} = (S)(D4) \text{ vehicles/lane} \quad [21\text{-}3]$$

By 9:00 A.M. the queue has shrunk to $(10.4 - 4.0) = 6.4$ miles, and $(4.0)(102.5) = 410$ vehicles per lane have been released from queued status.

Given constant demand thereafter, the queue continues to shrink at the same rate, reducing to zero at 10:36 A.M.. (At 10:00 A.M. the queue is still $(6.4 - 4.0) = 2.4$ miles long, and it takes $2.4/4.0 = 0.60$ of an hour more to disappear).

Thus, the queue is not only longer, but takes 36 minutes longer to disappear, than indicated by Approach 1.

The conventional wisdom is that the simple difference between the cumulative-demand and cumulative-capacity curves yields the queued vehicles, and that the area between the curves yields the vehicle-hours of delay experienced by these vehicles. The authors are suggesting that this is not so, based on the principles shown in Figure 21-7 and cast into Equations [21-1] and [21-2].

Given the importance of this difference, it is critical that the point be reinforced. Consider Figure 21-16, which shows a distribution of vehicles on the road during queue formation. The density in the upstream part is D_1. Think of this in the following way:

- There are $(D_4 - D_1)$ "holes" to be filled in each mile of upstream space, in order to go from a free-moving situation to the shuffling high-density queue characterized by D_4.
- If the net number of vehicles joining the queue in that hour is $(Q_1 - Q_2)$, then the number of miles filled is $(Q_1 - Q_2)/(D_4 - D_1)$.
- That is, the queue grows at a rate of $(Q_1 - Q_2)/(D_4 - D_1)$ mph.
- That is also what Equation [21-2] states. The minus sign there simply shows that the direction of growth is toward the upstream.

The essential difference between the "standard" approach used in References [16], [19], and [20] and this

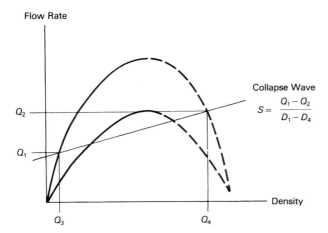

Figure 21-15 The speed with which the queue dissipates.

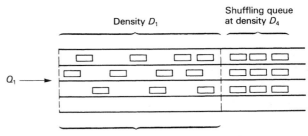

Think of this as having $(D_4 - D_1)$ "holes" to fill in an hour. How many vehicles does it take to do it?'

Figure 21-16 The explanation for the difference in the two approaches.

enhanced approach is that only $(D_4 - D_1)$ "holes" per mile exist to be filled, not D_4 "holes" per mile.

D. Enhanced technique for bottlenecks

This subsection presents an enhanced technique *for bottlenecks and other "permanent" obstructions,* including incidents whose duration extends past the congestion period. For incidents of shorter duration, there is an additional consideration (the queue starts clearing from the front, perhaps in addition to clearing at the rear).

The enhanced technique cannot make use of the cumulative demand–capacity *plot,* for both the "demand" and "capacity" cumulative plots have physical meaning, but the distance between them on the plot does *not* indicate all impacted vehicles.

The recommended steps in the enhanced technique are:

1. The problem starts only when demand exceeds capacity.
2. From the problem initiation time to the end, tabulate the cumulative demand and capacity. Do *not* plot this.
3. For each hour (or shorter period, if you wish), recall the flows Q_1 and Q_2 and also estimate the densities D_1 and D_4. Have all these numbers on a per-lane basis. To estimate D_1 and D_4 use the flow–density curve for the "normal" upstream roadway. Obtain this from *HCM* or appropriate local source. As a default, use

$$Q = 0.4734(D)(130 - D) \quad [21\text{-}4]$$

which is already per lane and has a jam density of 130 vpmpl and capacity of 2000 vphpl.[9]

4. Use the numbers from Step 3 to estimate the queue growth rate (i.e., the shock-wave speed S) from Equation [21-2]:

$$S = \frac{Q_1 - Q_2}{D_1 - D_4} \quad [21\text{-}2]$$

making sure that *per-lane* numbers are used.

[9]The 1994 and 1997 *HCM* updates use a higher number.

5. Use the speed S to estimate the total queue from Equation [21-1]:

$$\text{QUEUE GROWTH} = (Q_1 - Q_2) + (|S|)(D_1) \text{ veh/lane}$$
$$\text{when } S < 0 \quad [21\text{-}1]$$

$$\text{QUEUE DECREASE} = (Q_1 - Q_2) - (S)(D_4) \text{ veh/lane}$$
$$\text{when } S > 0 \quad [21\text{-}5]$$

Continue until the queue dissipates, taking care to *decrease* the queue when S is positive.

6. Plot the queue as a function of time (optional, but useful).
7. Estimate the following descriptive statistics:
   - total duration of time
   - number of vehicles affected
   - maximum number of vehicles queued
   - maximum queue length
   - maximum duration of individual delay
   - total vehicle-hours of delay
   - average delay per affected vehicle
8. For your own information, compare the answers by the two approaches. Estimate Part 1 of the queue, which is simply the difference between cumulative demand and cumulative capacity, expressing it on a per-lane basis, and compare to Step 5.

Table 21-2 summarizes the differences in the cited measures, as computed by the two approaches for the illustrative problem used in this section.

E. Comment

The "enhanced technique" referred to as Approach 2 is in fact consistent with the original work by Lighthill and Whitham [18], whereas Approach 1 is not.

Given the differences shown in Table 21-2, it is logical to wonder why an "Approach 1" analysis did not result in sufficient discrepancies from the field observations as to excite comment from concerned users.

As a practical matter, the cumulative demand–capacity analysis is not yet sufficiently widely used as a tool to cause such observations. Further, the results *are* highly sensitive to demand and particularly to capacity estimates. Thus, observed discrepancies might lead one to the conclusion that (for example) work-zone capacity estimates have to be improved.

Table 21-2 Comparison of the Two Techniques for Cumulative Demand–Capacity Analysis; Illustrative Case

Measure	Approach 2: Enhanced Technique	Approach 1: Original Technique	Actual* is Larger by
Total duration of time	4.6 hr	4.0 hr	15%
Number of vehicles affected	18,400	16,000	15%
Maximum number of vehicles stored	3200	2000	60%
Maximum queue length (mi)	10.4	6.5	60%
Maximum individual delay	48 min	30 min	60%
Total veh-hr delay	7355	4000	83.9%
Average delay per vehicle	24 min	15 min	60%

*"Actual" is taken as the answers by the enhanced technique (Approach 2).

References

1. Sumner, R., et al., *Freeway Management Handbook, Volume I, Overview,* Contract No. DOT-FH-11-9706, U.S. Department of Transportation, Washington, DC May 1983.
2. Everall, P. F., "Urban Freeway Surveillance and Control: The State of the Art," *Final Report,* U.S. Department of Transportation, Federal Highway Administration, (revised) Washington, DC, June 1973.
3. Blumentritt, C. W., Pinnell, C., and McCasland, W. R., *Guidelines for Selection of Ramp Control Systems,* NCHRP Report No. 232. Transportation Research Board, National Research Council, May 1981.
4. Drew, D., *Traffic Flow Theory and Control,* McGraw-Hill, New York, NY, 1968.
5. *Merging Control Systems,* U.S. Department of Transportation, Federal Highway Administration, Offices of Research and Development, Washington, DC, May 1971.
6. True, J., and Rosen, D., "Moving Merge—A New Concept in Ramp Control," *Public Roads,* Vol. 37, No. 7.
7. *Manual of Uniform Traffic Control Devices,* U.S. Department of Transportation, Federal Highway Administration, Washington, DC, (amended) 1994.
8. Newman, L., "Freeway Operations Analysis: Course Notes," University of California, Institute of Transportation Studies, University Extension, Berkeley, CA 1986.
9. Jones, E. R., and Goolsby, M. E., "The Environmental Influence of Rain on Freeway Capacity," *Highway Research Record 321,* Transportation Research Board, National Research Council, Washington, DC, 1970.
10. Jones, E. R., and Goolsby, M. E., "Effect of Rain on Freeway Capacity," *Research Report 14-23,* Texas Transportation Institute, Texas A&M University, College Station, TX, August 1969.
11. Kleitsch and Cleveland, "The Effect of Rainfall on Freeway Capacity," *Report TRS-6,* Highway Safety Research Institute, University of Michigan, Ann Arbor, MI, 1971.
12. Goolsby, M. E., "Influence of Incidents on Freeway Quality of Service," presented at 50th Annual TRB Meeting, January 1971.
13. Blumentritt, C. W., Pinnel, C., and McCasland, W. R., "Guidelines for Selection of Ramp Control Systems," *NCHRP Report 232,* Transportation Research Board, National Research Council, Washington, DC, May 1981.
14. Urbanek, G. L., and Rogers, R. W., "Alternative Surveillance Concepts and Methods for Freeway Incident Management, Vol. 1: Executive Summary," *Final Report.* FHWA-RD-77-58, U.S. Department of Transportation, Federal Highway Administration, Washington, DC, March 1978.
15. McDermott, J. M., "Automatic Evaluation of Urban Freeway Operations," *Traffic Engineering,* January 1968.
16. *Highway Capacity Manual, Special Report 209,* Transportation Research Board, National Research Council, Washington, DC, 1985.
17. Dudek, C., "Notes on Work Zone Capacity and Level of Service," Texas Transportation Institute, Texas A&M University, College Station, TX, 1984.
18. Lighthill, M. J., and Whitham, G. B., "On Kinematic Waves: Part II, A Theory of Traffic Flow on Long

Crowded Roads," *Proceedings of the Royal Society,* Vol. A229, No. 1178, 1955.

19. Abrahms, C. M., and Wang, J. J., *Planning and Scheduling Work Zone Traffic Control,* Implementation Package FHWA-IP-81-6, U.S. Department of Trans-

portation, Federal Highway Administration, Washington, DC, October 1981.

20. Morales, J. M., "Analytic Procedures for Estimating Freeway Traffic Congestion," *Public Roads,* Vol. 50, No. 2, September 1986.

Problems

Problem 21–1

For the relation $Q = 0.4734(D)(130 - D)$, plot the following, and comment:

(a) Flow versus density.
(b) Speed versus flow.
(c) Flow versus occupancy.

Problem 21–2

For the relation $Q = 0.4734(D)(130 - D)$ and several capacity levels, namely

1600 vphpl

1700 vphpl

1800 vphpl

1900 vphpl

prepare a table of shock-wave speeds for demand levels that exceed the capacity level by 50, 100, . . . vphpl, up to a total of 2000 vphpl demand level. Comment.

Problem 21–3

Use the cumulative demand–capacity analysis technique (Approaches 1 *and* 2) on the illustrative case of the text, recreating Table 21-2.

Problem 21–4

Construct a spreadsheet implementation of two approaches for the cumulative demand–capacity analysis, and test it by re-creating the work of Problem 21–3. Set the spreadsheet up so that the consecutive time periods need not be one hour each. In this way, the sheet can be used for analysis of the impact of accidents and incidents. In particular, it can be used for Problem 21–5 and 21–6 (which could, of course, be done by hand). Include the default relation for flow–density, given by Equation [21-4] on a per-lane basis.

Include the comparison table to the "original" technique for reference purposes. (What we have called the "original" or "standard" technique is properly so called only by repe-

tition in certain key documents in the 1970s and 1980s. The true original work dates to the mid-1950s [18], is correct, and is the basis for the "enhanced technique." However, there will be many who will ask, "OK, I understand this 'enhanced technique' may be more accurate, but are the answers really substantially different?")

Problem 21–5

Re-solve the illustrative cumulative demand–capacity problem of the text for the following cases:

Incident Duration	Discharge Headway during Incident	Discharge Headway after Incident
10 min	2.7 sec/veh	2.0 sec/veh
	2.4 sec/veh	2.0 sec/veh
20 min	2.7 sec/veh	2.0 sec/veh
	2.4 sec/veh	2.0 sec/veh
30 min	2.7 sec/veh	2.0 sec/veh
	2.4 sec/veh	2.0 sec/veh

(a) Prepare summary tables and/or graphs that give insight into the effect of incident duration and discharge headway (show the discharge headway in terms of saturation flow rate as well). Comment.
(b) What would have happened if the demand had been 4600 pcph, and not 5300 pcph?

Problem 21–6

(a) Re-solve Problem 21–5 with after-incident discharge headways of 2.3, 2.4, 2.5, and 2.6 sec/veh.
(b) Comment on the sensitivity of the answers with respect to the discharge saturation flow rate that prevails after the incident is cleared.

Problem 21–7

Using the results of Problems 21–5 and 21–6, comment on how the difficulty in measuring the discharge saturation flow rate (or the inclination to not do so) would logically make it difficult to determine whether the "standard" or "enhanced" technique (Approach 1 or 2, respectively) is the correct procedure. Comment on other factors that might make it difficult to determine which technique is the correct procedure.

Problem 21–8

Consider the case of a maintenance operation requiring the closure of the median lane of a three-lane freeway segment. The work will require four hours to complete, including placing and removing traffic-control devices. Data obtained from a nearby counter during the previous two weeks were used to estimate the following demand pattern:

Time Period	Demand Volume (vph)
9–10 A.M.	2920
10–11 A.M.	3120
11–noon	3200
12–1 P.M.	3500
1–2 P.M.	3830
2–3 P.M.	3940
3–4 P.M.	4620
4–5 P.M.	5520

(a) Assume work is to begin at 9:00 A.M. Use the enhanced and conventional techniques to estimate the impact of this activity, with the following capacities:
   (1) 1500 vphpl
   (2) 1450 vphpl
   (3) 1420 vphpl

(b) Solve part (a) again, assuming the work is to begin at 10:00 A.M.

(c) Solve part (a) again, assuming the work can be completed in three hours.

Problem 21–9

Consider the case of a maintenance operation requiring the closure of two lanes of a four-lane freeway segment. The work will be done from 9:00 A.M. to 4:00 P.M., including placing and removing traffic-control devices. The following demand pattern is estimated.

Time Period	Demand Volume (vph)
9–10 A.M.	4000
10–11 A.M.	3500
11–noon	2500
12–1 P.M.	2000
1–2 P.M.	2000
2–3 P.M.	2000
3–4 P.M.	2000

(a) Using the capacity from Table 21-1, use the enhanced and conventional techniques to estimate the impact of this activity.

(b) Solve part (a) again, assuming the work is to begin at 9:30 A.M. (The lost time will be made up by additional day(s) on the site, if needed.)

(c) If the work will be in 12 days rather than 11 days, is the total delay over the full period a net savings, or just a lower daily average? Support your answer.

22

Signal Coordination for Progressive and Congested Conditions

In situations where signals are relatively closely spaced, it is necessary to coordinate their green times so that vehicles may move efficiently through the *set* of signals. It serves no purpose to have drivers held at one signal watching wasted green at a downstream signal, only to arrive there just as the signal turns red.

In some cases, two signals are so closely spaced that they should be considered to be one signal. In other cases, the signals are so far apart that they may be considered independently. However, vehicles released from a signal often maintain their grouping for well over 1000 feet [1]. Common practice is to coordinate signals less than one-half mile apart on major streets and highways.

Factors affecting coordination

There are four major areas of consideration for the engineer considering signal coordination:

1. Benefits
2. Purpose of signal system
3. Factors lessening benefits
4. Exceptions to the coordinated scheme

These are discussed below. It should be noted first that all but the most complex coordination plans require that *all signals have the same cycle length*. While some signals might hold stopped vehicles for longer than they have to for strictly local purposes, the overall effect will be beneficial. If the overall effect is not beneficial, then the coordination serves no purpose.

In order to better understand some of the discussion, refer to Figure 22-1. This figure illustrates the path (trajectory) that a vehicle takes as time passes. At $t = t_1$, the first signal turns green. After some lag, the vehicle starts and moves down the street. It reaches the second signal at some time $t = t_2$. Depending on the indication of that signal, it either continues or stops.

The difference between the two green initiation times is referred to as the *signal offset,* or simply as the *offset*. In general, the offset is defined as the difference between green initiation times, measured in terms of the downstream green initiation relative to the upstream green initiation. In Figure 22-1 it is t_2

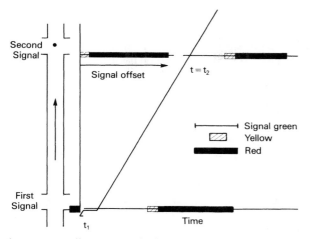

Figure 22-1 Illustrative vehicle trajectory.

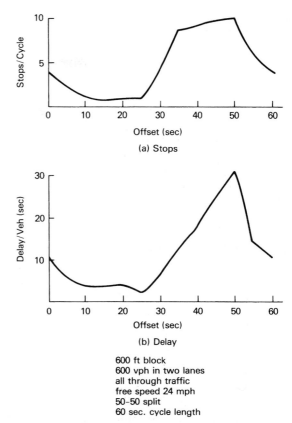

600 ft block
600 vph in two lanes
all through traffic
free speed 24 mph
50-50 split
60 sec. cycle length

Figure 22-2 Illustration of the effect of offset on stops and delay.

minus t_1. This is how the term will be used in this chapter and the rest of the text, unless otherwise specified.

There are other definitions of offset. For instance, some of the literature defines the offset of signals relative to one reference upstream signal. Some signal hardware uses the "offset" of *red* initiation, rather than green; other hardware uses the center of green as the reference point. Some hardware uses offset in seconds; other hardware uses offset as a percentage of the cycle length. Caution is therefore advised in using a set of computed offsets to set values on specific hardware.

A. Benefits

The prime benefit of coordination is improvement of service provided, usually measured in terms of stops and delay. Figure 22-2 illustrates the effect of offset on stops and delay for a platoon of vehicles leaving one intersection and passing through another (as in Figure 22-1). We see here the effect of allowing a poor offset to exist; the delay can climb to 30 sec per vehicle, and the stops to 10 per cycle.

It is common to consider the benefit of a coordination plan in terms of a "cost" or "penalty" function: a weighted combination of stops and delay, plus perhaps other terms:

$$\text{cost} = A \times (\text{total stops}) + B \times (\text{total delay})$$
$$+ \text{ other terms} \qquad [22\text{-}1]$$

The object is to make this disbenefit as small as possible. The weights A and B are coefficients to be specified by the engineer or analyst.

The coefficients may be selected according to a judgment of how important the two are to the public. For example, perhaps one stop is as bothersome as 5 seconds of delay, so that $A = 5B$.

The values of A and B may also be selected so as to reflect the estimated economic cost of each stop and delay. The amounts by which various timing plans reduce the cost shown in Equation [22-1] can then be used in a cost–benefit analysis to evaluate alternative plans.

In practice, numeric values of the improvement in stops and delay are usually obtained only with timing plans done with signal-optimization computer packages, such as the *TRANSYT* program [2, 3]. For those done manually, the engineer usually tries to make the number of vehicles stopped as small as possible, or tries to minimize delay. This is usually acceptable.

The conservation of *energy* and the preservation of the *environment* have grown in importance over the years. Given that vehicles must (or will) travel, fuel conservation and minimum air pollution are achieved by keeping vehicles moving as smoothly as possible at efficient speeds. This can be achieved by a good signal-coordination timing plan. Reference [4] reports on the results of one national demonstration of how signal optimization aids energy conservation.

Another benefit of signal coordination is the maintenance of a *preferred speed.* The signals can be set so as to encourage certain speeds: vehicles going much faster than this design speed will only have to stop frequently.

The fact that vehicles can be sent through successive intersections in moving *platoons* is also a benefit. In a well-formed platoon, the time headway between vehicles is generally somewhat shorter than can be achieved when they start from a stop. This is true despite their greater spacing due to their greater speed, leading to a more efficient use of the intersection.

It is also possible with good coordination to stop fewer vehicles. On short blocks with heavy flows, this is particularly important, for if all vehicles are stopped, the queue that results may overflow the available *storage* (the space available to store vehicles).

B. Purpose of the signal system

Usually the physical layout of the street system and the major traffic flows determine the purpose of the signal system.

First, one must consider the *type of system:* one-way arterial, two-way arterial, one-way, two-way, or mixed network. Although the existing system is a good starting point, it may sometimes happen that—for any number of reasons—the best solution is still not satisfactory. The engineer will then have to consider changing some streets. This must be done with sensitivity to capacities in both directions and many other issues.

Next, one must consider the *movements to be progressed.* On a two-way arterial, one or both directions may be progressed (that is, given the advantage of the coordination). If both are to be progressed, there will generally have to be some compromise between the

two. In a grid of signals, preferential paths must be determined and progressed.

It is then necessary to set an objective: For what purpose are the signals to be coordinated? The common objectives include maximum bandwidth ("windows" of green for traveling platoons), minimum delay, minimum stops, and minimum combination of stops and delay.

Last, it is necessary to recognize that there are limitations on what can be done. These are described below in Exceptions to the Coordinated Scheme.

C. Factors lessening benefits

Among the factors limiting the benefits of signal coordination are the following:

- inadequate roadway capacity
- existence of substantial side frictions, including parking, loading, double parking, and multiple driveways
- complicated intersections, involving multiphase control
- wide variability in traffic speeds
- very short signal spacing
- heavy turn volumes, either into or out of the street

Heavy turn-out volumes may impede platoons or destroy their structure by the loss of vehicles from the middle of the platoon. Left-turn volumes may interfere with platoons heading in the other direction.

Heavy turn-in volumes cause the stop and delay curves of Figure 22-2 to become less sharp, so that there is less benefit to setting the offset to a particular value. This is so because the turn-in volumes enter the street a half-cycle or so after the main platoon. Someone *must* be stopped, and the larger the turn-in volume, the less the benefit of determining who.

Figure 22-3 shows the effect of turn-in volume on the delay and stops, as a function of offset. These curves were generated with the TRAF-NETSIM traffic simulation model using a constant total volume on a simple network.

$V_1 + V_2 = 1500$ vph

2 lanes

$C = 60$ sec

The TRAF/NETSIM model is a well-validated microscopic simulation model developed for FHWA [5,6], available with animation on the PC [7,8].

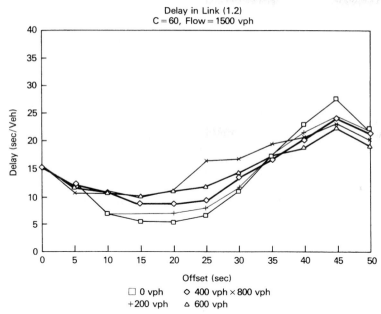

(a) Delay as a function of offset for various turn-in volumes V_2

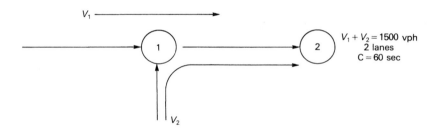

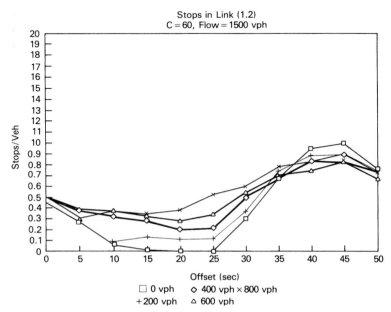

(b) Stops as a function of offset for the same turn-in volumes V_2

Figure 22-3 Delay and stops as affected by turn-in volume, for various offsets.

D. Exceptions to the coordinated scheme

It is misleading to think that all signals may easily be coordinated. Very often an intersection is sitting right in the middle of what the engineer chooses to call "his" system, requiring four phases and a 120-sec cycle length. Rather than requiring the entire system to be 120 sec, he/she elects to think of two separate systems, one on each side of this troublesome intersection. Perhaps the engineer can set the progression at 60 or 90 sec, so that the problem intersection may be at some multiple of the system.

Another situation that arises is that one intersection cannot handle the volumes delivered to it at any cycle length. This is referred to as a *critical intersection*. Some engineers choose to detach this intersection from their system. Others build the progression around it, delivering vehicles to it in a way that does not cause storage problems in upstream blocks. This last approach requires changing the purpose for which the progression is being designed. This is addressed later in the chapter.

The time–space diagram and ideal offsets

The *time–space diagram* is is simply the plot of signal indications as a function of time for two or more signals. The diagram is scaled with respect to distance, so that one may easily plot vehicle positions as a function of time. Figure 22-1 is a time–space diagram for two intersections.

The standard conventions are used in Figure 22-1: a green signal indication is shown by a blank or simple line (———), amber by a shaded line (▨▨▨▨) and red by a solid line (█████). The thin line rather than the blank is frequently used for green in this chapter so that the green may be located easily at the proper distance.

Figure 22-4 shows a time–space diagram for the intersections. For the purpose of illustrating trajectory (path), a northbound vehicle going at a constant speed of 40 fps is shown.

Offset has already been defined as the difference between the green initiation times at two adjacent intersections. More precisely, it is the green initiation time (of the phase of interest) at the downstream intersection minus the green initiation (of the phase of interest) at the upstream intersection. It is usually expressed as a positive number between zero and the cycle length. It is sometimes convenient to think of it as a negative number, usually no more than one-half a cycle length.

The "ideal offset" is defined as the offset that will cause the specified objective to be best satisfied. For the objective of minimum delay, it is the offset that will cause minimum delay. In Figure 22-2, the ideal offset is 25 sec for that case and that objective.

More often, the ideal offset is exactly the offset such that, as the first vehicle of a platoon just arrives

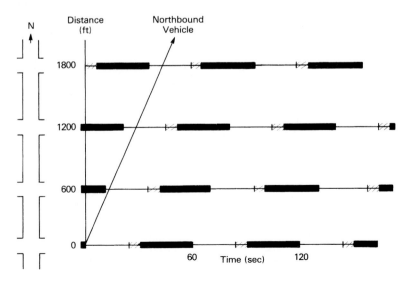

Figure 22-4 A time–space diagram for four intersections.

at the downstream signal, the downstream signal turns green. It is usually assumed that the platoon was moving as it went through the upstream intersection. If so, the ideal offset is given by

$$t(\text{ideal}) = \frac{L}{S} \qquad [22\text{-}2]$$

where $t(\text{ideal})$ = ideal offset, sec
L = block length, ft
S = vehicle speed, fps

If the vehicle were stopped, and had to accelerate after some initial start-up delay, the ideal offset could be represented by Equation [22-2] plus some term representing the start-up time at the first intersection.

Equation [22-2] will generally be used without an added term for start-up (which might add 2 to 4 sec). Usually, this will reflect the ideal offset desired for maximum bandwidth, minimum delay, and minimum stops. Even if the vehicle is stopped at the first intersection, it will be moving in most of the system.

Note that the penalty for deviating from the ideal offset is usually *not* equal in positive and negative deviations. In Figure 22-2, an offset of $(25 + 10) = 35$ sec causes much more harm than an offset of $(25 - 10) = 15$ sec, although both are 10 sec from the ideal offset.

Signal progression on one-way streets

Signal progression on a one-way street is relatively simple. For the purpose of this section, it will be assumed that a cycle length has been chosen and that the green allocations at each signal have been determined.

A. Determining ideal offsets

Consider a one-way arterial as shown in Figure 22-5, with the link lengths indicated. Assuming no vehicles are queued at the signals, the ideal offsets can be determined if the platoon speed is known. For the purpose of illustration, let us assume a desired platoon speed of 60 fps. Using Equation [22-2], the offsets are determined to be:

Signal	Relative to Signal	Ideal Offset
6	5	1800/60 = 30 sec
5	4	600/60 = 10 sec
4	3	1200/60 = 20 sec
3	2	1200/60 = 20 sec
2	1	1200/60 = 20 sec

Note that neither the cycle length nor the splits have entered into the computation.

In order to see the pattern which results, the time–space diagram should be constructed according to the following rules:

1. The vertical should be scaled so as to accommodate the dimensions of the arterial, and the horizontal so as to accommodate at least three to four cycle lengths.
2. The beginning intersection (Number 1, in this case) should be scaled first, usually with main-street green (MSG) initiation at $t = 0$, followed by periods of green and red (yellow may be shown for precision). See Point 1 in Figure 22-6.
3. The main-street green (or other offset position, if MSG is not used) of the next downstream signal should be located next, relative to $t = 0$ and at the proper distance from the first intersection. With this point located (Point 2 in Figure 22-6), fill in the periods of green, yellow, and red for this signal.
4. Repeat the procedure for all other intersections, working one at a time. Do be careful to note that the offset of one signal is relative to the immediately

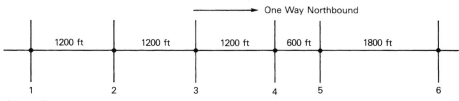

Figure 22-5 Case study: Progression on a one-way street.

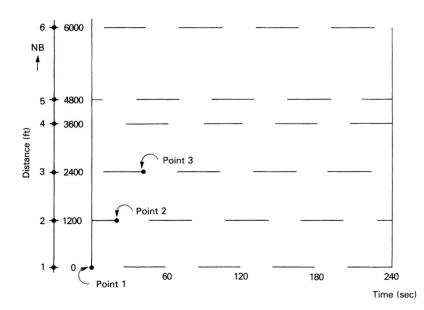

Figure 22-6 Time–space diagram for case of Figure 22-5.

preceding one. Thus, for Signal 3, the offset is located at Point 3, *20* sec later than Point 2. It is, of course, also 20 + 20 = 40 sec later than Point 1.

Figure 22-6 shows the time–space diagram for the illustrative problem being used. The yellow intervals are not shown due to the scale. Note that if the offsets had been expressed as relative to Signal 1, then (1) the simple addition of individual link offsets would have resulted in the correct numbers (e.g., for Signal 3, 20 + 20 = 40 sec), or the total length could have been used (e.g., for Signal 3, (1200 + 1200)/60 = 40 sec); and (2) the offsets sometimes exceed the cycle length but can be expressed as a number between zero and the cycle length, due to their repetitive pattern.

In general, any such offset can be expressed in modular arithmetic as

$$\text{Offset} = \underset{C}{\text{mod}} \{\text{OFFSET}\} \qquad [22\text{-}3]$$

where C is the cycle length. This can be done by subtracting the cycle length repeatedly until the offset is expressed as a number between zero and the cycle length.

Figure 22-6 has some interesting features, which can be explored with the aid of Figure 22-7.

First, if a vehicle (or platoon) were to travel at 60 fps, it would arrive at each of the signals just as they turn green; this is indicated by the heavy dashed line

in Figure 22-7, and is to be expected. After all, the offsets were chosen to achieve this.[1]

Second, this heavy dashed line also represents the speed of the "green wave" visible to a stationary observer at Signal 1, looking downstream. The signals turn green in order, corresponding to the planned speed of the platoon, and give the visual effect of a wave of green opening before the driver.

Note that if the speed of the vehicle (or platoon) were slower—say 40 fps—then the visible "green wave" would still be at 60 fps, but the platoon of vehicles would lag behind it, diverging from it.

EXERCISE: Plot the time–space diagram of Figure 22-7, and show the green wave at 60 fps, with the lead vehicle in a platoon going at 50 fps. Comment on the visual effect and on the effect on the path of the vehicle. Repeat for a vehicle speed of 70 fps.

Third, note that there is a "window" of green in Figure 22-7, with its end indicated by the second dotted line which is also the trajectory of the *last* vehicle that could travel through the progression, without stopping at 60 fps. This window is called the *bandwidth*

---

[1]Should the reader have trouble visualizing how the line represents the vehicle, note that the position is given by

$$x = vt = 60t$$

and the line is simply a plot of x versus t.

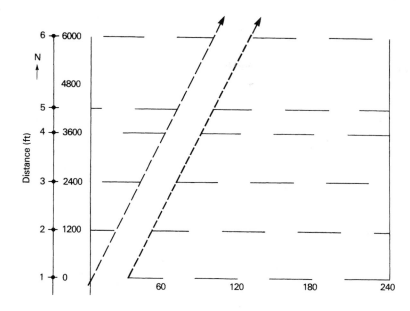

Figure 22-7 Vehicle trajectory and "green wave" in a progressed movement.

and is addressed in Section D of this chapter. It is a measure of how large a platoon of vehicles can be passed without stopping.

B. Effect of vehicles queued at signals

It sometimes happens that there are vehicles stored in the block waiting for a green light. These may be stragglers from the last platoon, vehicles that turned into the block, or vehicles that came out of parking lots or parking spots. The ideal offset must be adjusted to allow for these vehicles, so as to avoid unnecessary stops. The situation without this allowance is depicted in Figure 22-8.

The ideal offset is therefore given by

$$t_{\text{ideal}} = \frac{L}{S} - (Qh + \text{Loss}_1) \qquad [22\text{-}4]$$

where: Q = number of vehicles queued per lane, veh
h = discharge headway of queued vehicle, sec/veh
Loss_1 = loss time associated with vehicles starting from rest at the first downstream signal

The lost time is counted *only* at the first downstream intersection, at most: If the vehicle(s) from the pre-ceding intersection were themselves stationary, their start-up causes a shift that automatically takes care of the start-up at later intersections.

For a typical value of h, 1.9 sec/veh can be used. Likewise, 2.0 sec can be used as a default for the (first) start-up lost time. If different values are justified based on local data or on the fact that the arriving platoon was itself starting up at the upstream signal (so that everything is shifted by the same time), the equation values can be adapted.

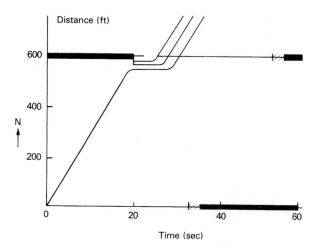

Figure 22-8 Effect of vehicles queued at a signal.

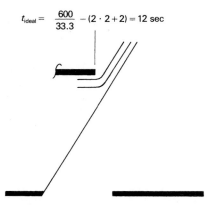

$$t_{\text{ideal}} = \frac{600}{33.3} - (2 \cdot 2 + 2) = 12 \text{ sec}$$

Figure 22-9 Adjustment in green initiation to assure smooth flow of arriving platoon.

Figure 22-9 shows the situation for use of the modified ideal offset equation [i.e., Equation [22-4]].

Figure 22-10 shows the time–space diagram for the case study of Figure 22-7, given queues of 2 vehicles per lane in all links. Note that the arriving vehicle platoon has smooth flow, and the lead vehicle has 60 fps travel speed. The visual image of the "green wave," however, is much faster, due to the need to clear the queues in advance of the arriving platoon.

The "green wave" or *progression speed*, as it is more properly called, is traveling at varying speeds as it moves down the arterial. The speed can be computed as follows:

Link	Link Offset (sec)	Speed of Progression (fps)
Signal 1 → 2	(1200/60) − (4 + 2) = 14	1200/14 = 85.7
2 → 3	(1200/60) − (4) = 16	1200/16 = 75
3 → 4	(1200/60) − (4) = 16	1200/16 = 75
4 → 5	(600/60) − (4) = 6	600/6 = 100
5 → 6	(1800/60) − (4) = 26	1800/26 = 69.2
Total offset = 78 sec		

Figure 22-10 shows some of the raggedness associated with the progression-speed changes, but they do not appear dramatic on the scale being used. The stationary observer at Signal 1 will see some raggedness but probably perceive an average speed of progression of 6000 ft per 78 sec, or about 77 fps. Thus, the "green wave" will appear to move ahead of the platoon, clearing queued vehicles in advance of it.

This positive depiction does, however, overlook the fact that the "window" available for moving a pla-

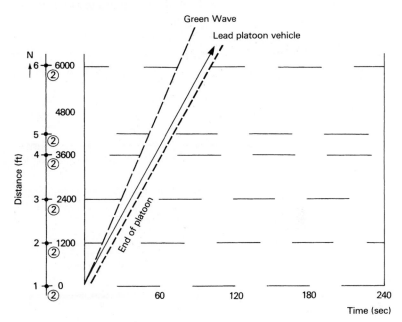

Figure 22-10 Effect of queue clearance on progression speed.

toon nonstop is now much smaller. Refer to the dotted line in Figure 22-10. Thus, while clearing out the queue in advance of the platoon, the green time at the signals is used for the queued vehicles.

C. A note on queue estimation

The development of the preceding subsection was done with a very neat implicit assumption that the queue is known at each signal. In fact, this task is not an easy one. However, if we know that there *is* a queue and know its approximate size (small, medium, large), the link offset can be set better than by pretending that no queue exists.[2]

Consider that the sources of the queued vehicles include, as illustrated in Figure 22-11:

1. Vehicles turning in from upstream side streets during *their* green (which is main-street red)
2. Vehicles leaving parking garages or spaces
3. Stragglers from previous platoons, or even part of a previous platoon truncated by insufficient green

There can be great cycle-to-cycle variation in the actual queue size, although its average size may be estimated. Even at that, queue estimation is a difficult and expensive task.

Even the act of adjusting the offsets can influence the queue size. For instance, the arrival pattern of vehicles from the side streets may be altered. Queue estimation is therefore a significant task in the real world, and simple statements such as "Given that the queue is known to be . . ." must be viewed with caution.

The special problem of progressions on two-way streets and in networks

The task of progressing traffic on a one-way street has been relatively straightforward. To highlight the essence of the problem on a two-way street, consider

---

[2]When the queue and the arriving platoon exceed the ability of the signal to process them, the procedures described later in this chapter for oversaturated operation may be in order. In such cases, the value of "progressive movement" is superseded by the need to avoid the spread of congestion.

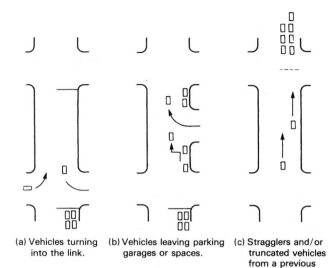

(a) Vehicles turning into the link. (b) Vehicles leaving parking garages or spaces. (c) Stragglers and/or truncated vehicles from a previous platoon.

Figure 22-11 Sources of queued vehicles.

that the arterial shown in Figure 22-7 is not a one-way but rather a two-way street. Figure 22-12 shows the trajectory of a *south*bound vehicle on this arterial: The vehicle is just fortunate enough not to be stopped until Signal 2, but is then stopped again for Signal 1, for a total of 2 stops and 40 seconds of delay. It is *not* possible to have a vehicle platoon pass along the arterial nonstop.

Of course, had the offsets or the travel times been different, it might have been possible to have nonstop southbound platoons.

A. Offset determination on a two-way street

Note that if any offset were changed in Figure 22-12 to accommodate the southbound vehicle(s), then the northbound vehicle or platoon would suffer. For instance, if the offset at Signal 2 were decreased by 20 sec, then the pattern at that signal would shift to the left by 20 sec, resulting in a "window" of green of only 10 sec on the northbound, rather than the 30 sec in the original display (see Figure 22-7).

The fact that the offsets are interrelated presents one of the most fundamental problems of signal optimization. Note that inspection of a typical cycle [see Figure 22-13(a)] yields the obvious conclusion that the offsets in the two directions add to one cycle

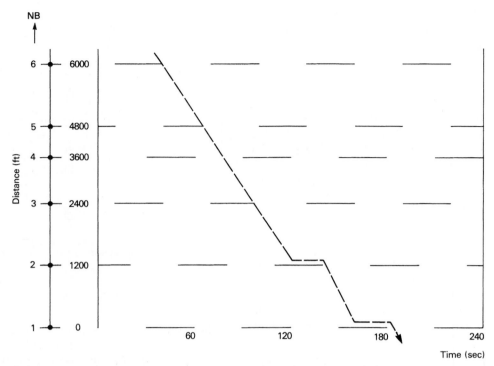

Figure 22-12   Moving southbound on a two-way arterial set for northbound progression: An illustration.

length. However, for longer block lengths [see Figure 22-13(b)] the offsets might add to two (or more) cycle lengths. Indeed, when queue clearances are taken into account, the offsets might add to zero cycle lengths.

Note that Figure 22-13 illustrates both actual offsets *and* travel times, which are distinct. While the engineer might desire the *ideal* offset to be the same as the travel time, Figures 22-12 and 22-13 neatly illustrate that once the offset is specified in one direction, it is automatically set in the other.

The general expression for the two offsets in a link on a two-way street can be written as

$$t_{NB,i} + t_{SB,i} = nC \qquad [22\text{-}5]$$

where the offsets are *actual* offsets, n is an integer (positive, zero, or negative) and C is the cycle length.

Any actual offset can be expressed as the desired "ideal" offset, plus an "error" or "discrepancy" term:

$$t_{\text{actual}(j,i)} = t_{\text{ideal}(j,i)} + e_{(j,i)} \qquad [22\text{-}6]$$

where j represents the direction and i represents the link. (If the links are numbered independently in each direction, the j can be dropped.)

In a number of signal optimization programs that can be used for two-way arterials, the objective is to minimize some function of the discrepancies between the actual and ideal offsets. The simplest form is perhaps the sum of the squares or of the discrepancies, weighted by the link volumes:

$$Z = \sum_{j,i} \{[v_{(j,i)}][t_{\text{actual}(j,i)} - t_{\text{ideal}(j,i)}]^2\} \qquad [22\text{-}7]$$

which can be written as

$$Z = \sum_{j,i} \{[v_{(j,i)}][e_{(j,i)}]^2\} \qquad [22\text{-}8]$$

where Equation [22-4] is used for the ideal offsets and Equation [22-5[for constraints on the offsets. The fact that the n must be found for each link adds to the complexity of the resultant mathematical programming problem.[3]

---

[3]The same optimization programs are generally capable of being applied to networks, or grids. Rather than a mathematical programming solution, some use "gradient search" (hill-climbing) techniques to seek a solution.

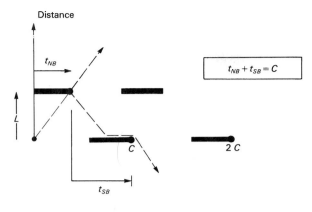

(a) Offsets add to one cycle length

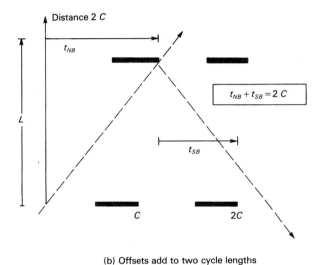

(b) Offsets add to two cycle lengths

Figure 22-13 Offsets on a two-way arterial are not independent.

B. Offset determination in a grid

The relative difficulty of finding progressions on a two-way street, compared to on a one-way street, might lead one to conclude that the best approach is to establish a system of one-way streets, to avoid the problem.

A one-way street system has a number of advantages, not the least of which is elimination of left turns against opposing traffic. However, the total elimination of the constraints imposed by the "closure" of loops within the network or grid is not possible. Refer to Figure 22-14(a), which highlights the fact that if the cycle length, splits, and three offsets are specified, the offset in the fourth link—denoted Link D in this illustration—is determined and cannot be independently specified.

Figure 22-14(b) extends this to a grid of one-way streets, in which all of the north–south streets are independently specified. The specification of *one* east–west street then "locks in" all other east–west offsets. Note that the key feature is that an *open tree* of one-way links can be completely independently set, and that it is the closing or "closure" of the open tree which presents constraints on some of the links.

To develop the constraint equation, refer to Figure 22-15 and walk through the following steps, keying to the green in all steps:

Step	Description
1	Begin at Intersection 1 and consider the green initiation to be time $t = 0$.
2	Move to Intersection 2, noting that the link offset in Link A specifies the time of green initiation at this intersection, relative to its upstream neighbor.
3	Recognizing we must ask, "When do the westbound vehicles get released at Intersection 2?", note that this occurs after the NS green is finished. Thus we are now at $$t = 0 + t_A + g_{NS,2}$$ and facing west at Intersection 2.
4	Move to Intersection 3, noting similarly to Step 2 that the link offset in Link B specifies the time of green initiation at this intersection, relative to its upstream neighbor.
5	Asking "When do the southbound vehicles get released at Intersection 3?" note that this occurs after the EW green is finished. Thus we are now at $$t = 0 + t_A + g_{NS,2} + t_B + g_{EW,3}$$ and facing west at Intersection 2.
6	Moving to Intersection 4, it is t_c which is added.
7	Turning at Intersection 4, it is the NS green which is relevant.
8	Moving to Intersection 1, it is t_D which is relevant.
9	Turning at Intersection 1, it is the EW green which is relevant.

However, we are now back where we started. Thus, this is either $t = 0$ or a multiple of the cycle length.

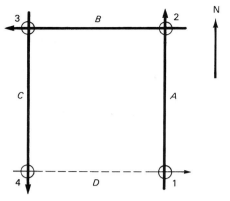

(a) Specification of cycle length, splits, and three offsets determines the offset in Link D

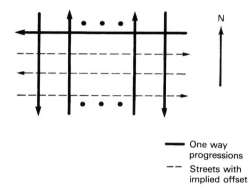

——— One way progressions

– – – Streets with implied offset

(b) Similar specification in a grid determines most of the system

Figure 22-14 Illustration of the "closure" effect in a grid.

Thus we can write that

$$nC = t_A + g_{NS,2} + t_B + g_{EW,3}$$
$$+ t_C + g_{NS,4} + t_D + g_{EW,1} \quad \text{[22-9]}$$

where the only caution is that the g values should really include the change and clearance intervals.

Note that Equation [22-9] is a more general form of Equation [22-5], for the two-way arterial is a special case of a network.

The interrelations stated in Equations [22-9]—for there are a *set* of them for any network—are constraints on freely setting all offsets. Note that these equations do allow more latitude, in that one can trade off between green allocations and offsets; to get a better offset in Link D, one can adjust the splits as well as the other offsets.

This section has shown the underlying reason for the "closure" constraints on two-way arterial and in networks of signalized intersections, motivating the presentation by use of Figure 22-13. It has also developed Equations [22-5] and [22-9], to express these constraints mathematically.

The fundamental result, however, may be stated simply: "If you set the offsets in one direction on a two-way street, then you also set them in the other direction. In a network, you can set any 'open tree' of links, but links that close the tree already have their offsets specified."

It is also clear that compromises must be reached in determining the offsets on such facilities, unless accident and good fortune intervene.

The remainder of this chapter focuses on related concepts, and on manual solutions and insights that can be gained from them.

The reader is advised to check the literature for the optimization programs in current use. TRANSYT [2] is used extensively for arterials and networks, PASSER II [9] for certain arterials, and NETSIM [7,8] for network simulation, as of this writing.

While it is sometimes necessary to consider networks in their entirety, it is common traffic engineering practice to decompose networks into non-interlocking arterials whenever possible. Refer to Figure 22-16 for an illustration.

The bandwidth concept and maximum bandwidth

The concept of bandwidth has already been introduced, by reference to "windows" of green through which platoons of vehicles can move.

The bandwidth concept is very popular in traffic engineering practice, because (1) the windows of green are easy visual images for both working professionals and public presentations, and (2) good solutions can often be obtained manually, by trial and error.

The most significant shortcoming of designing offset plans to maximize bandwidths is that internal queues are overlooked in the bandwidth approach.[4]

---

[4]References [7] and [8] address a computer-based maximum bandwidth solution which is said to go beyond the historical formulations.

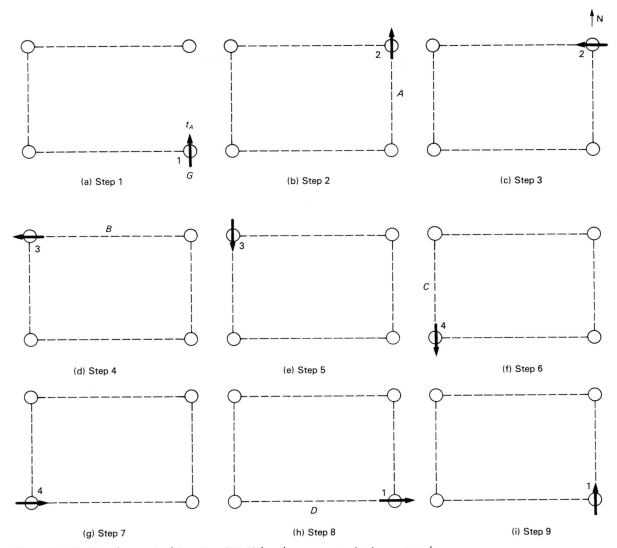

Figure 22-15 Development of Equation [22-9] for closure constraint in a network.

When internal queues exist, historic bandwidth-based solutions can be misleading and erroneous.

A. Bandwidth and efficiency of a progression

The efficiency of a bandwidth (measured in seconds) is defined as the ratio of the bandwidth to the cycle length, expressed as a percentage:

$$\text{efficiency} = \frac{\text{bandwidth}}{\text{cycle length}} \times 100\% \quad [22\text{-}10]$$

An efficiency of 40% to 55% is considered good. The bandwidth is limited by the minimum green in the direction of interest.

Figure 22-17 illustrates the bandwidths for one signal-timing plan. The northbound efficiency can be estimated as $(17/60)100\% = 28.4\%$. The southbound is obviously terrible—there is *no* bandwidth through the defined system. The northbound efficiency is only 28.4%. This system is badly in need of retiming, at least on the basis of the bandwidth objective.

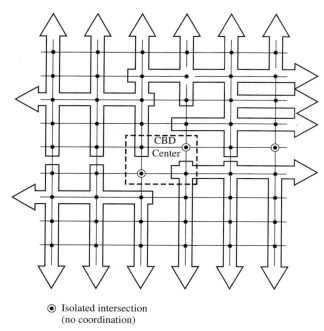

● Isolated intersection
(no coordination)

Figure 22-16 Decomposing a network into a non-interlocking system. [Courtesy of U.S. Department of Transportation, Federal Highway Administration, from *Traffic Control Systems Handbook.*]

In terms of *vehicles* that can be put through this system without stopping, note that the northbound bandwidth can carry 17/2.0 = 8.5 vehicles per lane per cycle in a nonstop path through the defined system. Thus, the northbound direction can handle

$$\frac{8.5 \text{ veh}}{\text{cycle}} \times \frac{\text{cycle}}{60 \text{ sec}} \times \frac{3600 \text{ sec}}{\text{hr}} = 510 \text{ vph } per\ lane$$

very efficiently *if* they are organized into 8-vehicle platoons when they arrive at this system.

If the per-lane demand volume is less than 510 vphpl and if the flows are so organized (and if there is no internal queue development), the system will operate well in the northbound direction, even though better timing plans might be obtained.

The computation just executed can be formalized into an equation as follows:

$$\text{nonstop volume} = \frac{3600(BW)(L)}{(h)(C)} \text{ vph}$$

[22-11]

where: BW = measured or computed bandwidth, sec

  L = number of through lanes in indicated direction

  h = headway in moving platoon, sec/veh

  C = cycle length

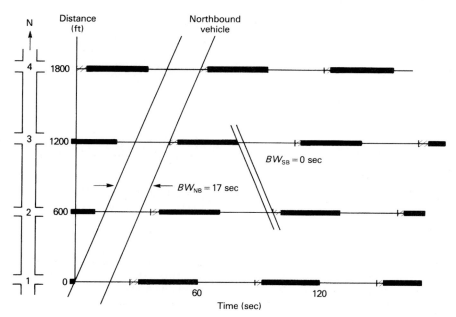

Figure 22-17 Bandwidths on a time–space diagram.

Note that we were not concerned in the sample computation with the fact that the answer was 8.5 vehicles, even though half-vehicles cannot be processed too easily. First, we anticipated multiple lanes. Second, we were willing to assume that eight or nine vehicles are possible in any cycle even if there were only one lane.

Nonetheless, Equation [22-11] does not contain any factors such as lane-utilization factors from Chapter 18 and is intended only to indicate some limit beyond which the offset plan will degrade, certainly resulting in stopping and internal queueing.

B. Finding bandwidths: A trial-and-error approach and a case study

The engineer usually wishes to design for *maximum bandwidth* in one direction, subject to some relation between the bandwidths in the two directions. Sometimes, one direction is completely ignored. Much more commonly, the bandwidths in the two directions are designed to be in the same ratio as the flows in the two directions.

There are both direct trial-and-error and somewhat elaborate manual techniques for establishing maximum bandwidths. There are also computer programs that do the computations for maximum bandwidth. Considering that these programs are available, and that other techniques are also available, it is not worthwhile to present an elaborate manual technique herein. Rather, attention will focus on the basic technique and trade-offs.

Refer to Figure 22-18, which shows four signals and decent progressions in both directions. For purposes of illustration, assume it is given that a signal with 50:50 split must be located midway between Intersections 2 and 3. Refer to the possible effect, illustrated in Figure 22-19; it would appear that there is no way to include this signal without destroying one or the other through band, or cutting both in half.

It may, of course, be the unfortunate truth that there is no way in some cases. This particular example, however, is constructed to illustrate an approach to such problems.

The engineer must move the offsets around until a more satisfactory timing plan develops. A change in cycle length may even be required. The changes in offsets may be explored by:

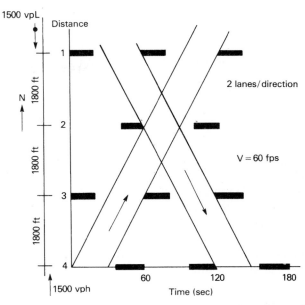

Figure 22-18 Case study: Four intersections with good progressions.

- copying the time–space diagram of Figure 22-19
- cutting the copy horizontally into strips, one strip per intersection
- placing a guideline over (or next to) the strips, so as to indicate the speed of the platoon(s) by the slope

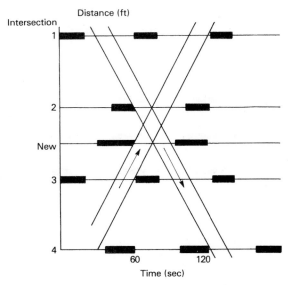

Figure 22-19 Effect of inserting a new signal into system.

of the guideline (the guideline may be a ruler, triangle, or a string fastened by thumbtacks into a board).

- Sliding the strips relative to each other, until some improved offset pattern is identified

With a little practice, the engineer learns how to achieve good progressions through reasonably sized systems. *There is no need to produce new strips for each cycle length considered: all times can be made relative to an arbitrary cycle length "C."* The only change necessary is to change the slope(s) of the guideline(s) representing vehicle speeds.

Note that the northbound vehicle takes $3600/60 = 60$ sec to travel from Intersection 4 to Intersection 2, or—given $C = 60$ sec—one cycle length. Had the cycle length been $C = 120$ sec, the vehicle would have arrived at Intersection 2 at $C/2$, or one-half the cycle length.

Figure 22-20 uses this approach to specify one solution to the problem introduced by the additional intersection. The solution shown is for $C = 120$ sec and has a 40-sec bandwidth in both directions for an efficiency of 33%. The 40-sec bandwidth can handle $(40/2.0) = 20$ vehicles per lane per cycle. From Equation [22-12], if the demand volume is greater than $3600(40)(2)/(2.0)(120) = 1200$ vph, then it will not

be possible to process the vehicles nonstop through the system.

As indicated in the original information (see Figure 22-18), the northbound demand is 1500 vph. Thus there will be some difficulty, in the form of excess vehicles in the platoon: they can enter the system, but cannot pass Signal 2 nonstop. They are "chopped off" the end of the platoon, to exist as queued vehicles in the next cycle. They are released in the early part of the cycle and arrive at Signal 1 at the beginning of its red. Figure 22-20 illustrates this, showing that these vehicles then disturb the *next* northbound through platoon.

Note that Figure 22-21 illustrates the limitation of the bandwidth approach when internal queuing arises, disrupting the platoon in the bandwidth. Had the demand been less than 1200 vph, no problems might have occurred, and the bandwidth solution would have been just fine.

For completeness, Figure 22-21 also shows the southbound platoon pattern, suggesting that the demand of exactly 1200 vph might give rise to minor problems of the same sort at Signals 3 and 4.

If the reader wishes to continue the trial-and-error attempt at a "good" solution, note that:

- If the green initiation at Intersection 1 comes earlier (it would help the main northbound platoon

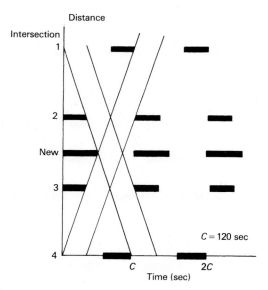

Figure 22-20 A solution to the case study with $C = 120$ seconds by increasing the slope of the vehicle guideline.

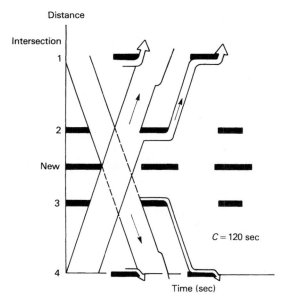

Figure 22-21 Effect on platoons at original demand volumes.

avoid the queued vehicle interference), the southbound platoon is released sooner and gets stopped or disrupted at Intersection 2.

• Likewise, Intersection 2 cannot help the northbound without harming the southbound.

• Nor can Intersection 3 help the southbound without harming the northbound.

Of course, some green can be taken from the side street and given to the main street.

It is also possible that the engineer may decide to give the northbound a better bandwidth because of its larger demand volume.

C. A historical perspective on the use of bandwidth

The preceding illustration showed insights that can be gained by simple inspection of a time–space diagram such as in Figure 22-17, using the concepts of bandwidth, efficiency, and an upper bound on demand volume that can be handled nonstop. Challenged to find a better solution, the reader might well inspect Figure 22-17 and imagine sliding the pattern at Signal 4 to the right and the pattern at Signal 1 to the left, allowing the northbound to be improved and allowing some hope for the southbound.

The authors have found interesting and basic questions arising in their classes: Why bother with this, when good computer solutions are available? Indeed, why did people waste time with a formulation that overlooks something as basic as the internal queues?

The questions are so interesting because they reveal (1) a bias toward computer solutions on the part of even the students who have work experience, an attitude that says, "The computer is obviously the best way, so let's learn it that way," and (2) a lack of true awareness of the radical advances in computational power which have occurred in the last 20 years, as well as (3) a lack of awareness that engineering solutions—even today—are developed within the context of the tools available to implement the solutions.

It is that last point that has motivated the remarks contained in this subsection, for the engineer in training must appreciate that the power of the solution cannot exceed the tools that can be brought to bear. An elegant mathematical formulation requiring two hours of computation on a supercomputer is somewhat irrelevant in most engineering offices.

The determination of good progressions on an arterial must be viewed in this context: Only 25 years ago, hand-held calculators did not exist; 20 years ago, calculators had only the most basic functions; some 15 years ago, personal computers were at best a new concept. Previously, engineers used slide rules for their multiplication and division, and did addition or subtraction by hand.

Even in the 1960s, when most larger firms had mainframe computers (or powerful and expensive minicomputers), access was by batch input of punched-card decks and involved turn-arounds measured in hours. Engineers still used slide rules for most day-to-day work.

"Optimization" of progressions could not depend on mathematical formulations such as expressed in Equations [22-7] and [22-8], subject to constraints of the form in Equations [22-5] and [22-9], simply because even one set of computations could take days with the tools available. The use of Equation [22-4] to include queue clearances would make the task even more infeasible.

Accordingly, graphical methods were developed. In some of the very early literature (1930s and 1940s), detailed procedures were laid out (e.g., [11]). Iterative, trial-and-error approaches were good for most solutions, but the more comprehensive techniques were used (and taught) for the more difficult cases. "Time–space boards" existed so that the signal patterns at the various intersections could be slid back and forth, in a more formal (and frequently used) implementation of the strips of paper discussed in the preceding subsection; cords over the boards represented vehicle speeds; and the time axis was normalized to numbers of cycle lengths.

By the mid- to late-1960s, the more difficult solutions were being sent to batch processing on mainframe computers, using programs that simply transported the "maximum-bandwidth" solution to the computer (e.g., [12,13]).

The first optimization programs that took queues and other details into account began to appear (e.g., [14,15]), leading to later developments that produced the signal-optimization programs in common use in the late 1980s (primarily [2]).

As computers became more accessible and less expensive, the move to computer solutions accelerated in the 1970s. New work on the maximum-bandwidth

operations in the community for decades to come. Indeed, the pattern could be set even until the technology of personal vehicles traveling on streets with at-grade crossings is superseded, much as the automobile superseded the horse.

It is also no overstatement to say that many professionals with other specialties and interests are oblivious to the issue but would appreciate its relevance to their interests when it is properly and clearly stated. The architect is concerned with form, but also with proper operation. The developer is concerned with return on investment, but also in operations that make the developments function properly. The town planner is concerned with form and function, but often has little formal training to appreciate the issue.

With this as background, the actual progressions can be considered.

A. Alternate progression

For certain block lengths with 50:50 splits and uniform block lengths, it is possible to select a feasible cycle length such that

$$\frac{C}{2} = \frac{L}{S} \qquad [22\text{-}12]$$

where: C = cycle length, sec
L = block length, ft
S = platoon speed, fps

is satisfied.

In this situation, the progression of Figure 22-23 can be obtained. There is no limit to the number of signals which can be involved.

The name for this pattern derived from the "alternate" appearance of the signal displays: as the observer at (or upstream of) Signal 1 looks downstream, the signals alternate—green, red, green, red, and so forth. When they switch, they again alternate—red, green, red, green, and so forth.

The key to Equation [22-12] is that the ideal offset in either direction (with zero internal queues) is L/S, so that the sum of the two desired offsets just happens to be

$$\frac{L}{S} + \frac{L}{S} = \frac{2L}{S} = C$$

by virtue of the fact that Equation [22-12] is satisfied. That is, the travel time to each platoon is exactly one-

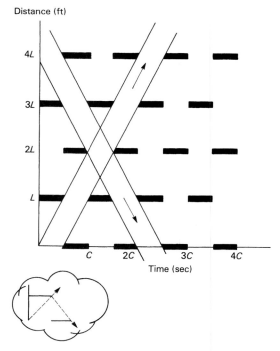

Figure 22-23 Alternate system illustrated.

half the cycle length, so that the two travel times add up to the cycle length. This is illustrated in the lower left corner of Figure 22-23.

The *efficiency* of the signal system is 50% in *each* direction, because all of the green is used in each direction. The upper limit on the platooned volume that can be carried in each direction without stops is typically [from Equation 22-11]:

$$\frac{3600(BW)(\text{lanes})}{(h)(C)} = (900)(\text{lanes}) \text{ vph}$$

As indicated initially, this is an approximation, and an upper bound; the capacity of the through lane group according to the procedure of Chapter 18 would be a more precise indicator.

If the splits are not 50:50 at some signals, note that (1) if they favor the main street, they simply represent excess green, suited for accommodating miscellaneous vehicles, and (2) if they favor the side street, they reduce the bandwidths.

As a practical matter, note the range of the block lengths for which alternate patterns might occur: platoon speeds might range from 30 to 50 mph (say 45 to

75 fps), and cycle lengths from 60 to 90 sec. Thus, using Equation [22-12], note

Cycle Length	Platoon Speed	→	Matching Block Length
60 sec	45 fps		1350 ft
60 sec	75 fps		2250 ft
90 sec	45 fps		2025 ft
90 sec	75 fps		3375 ft

All of these signal spacings imply a high-type arterial, often in a suburban setting.

B. Double alternate system

For certain block lengths with 50:50 splits and uniform block lengths, it is not possible to satisfy Equation [22-12], but it is possible to select a feasible cycle length such that

$$\frac{C}{4} = \frac{L}{S} \qquad [22\text{-}13]$$

is satisfied. In this situation, the progression of Figure 22-24 can be obtained.

The key is that the ideal offset in either direction (with zero internal queues) over *two* blocks is $2L/S$, so that the sum of the two desired offsets just happens to be

$$\frac{2L}{S} + \frac{2L}{S} = \frac{4L}{S} = C$$

by virtue of the fact that Equation [22-13] is satisfied. That is, the travel time of each platoon along *two* consecutive blocks is exactly one-half of a cycle length, so that two such travel times (one in each direction) add up to the cycle length. This is illustrated in the lower left corner of Figure 22-24. There is no limit to the number of signals that can be involved in this system, just as there was no limit with the alternate system.

The name for this pattern is derived from the "double alternate" appearance of the signal displays: as the observer at (or upstream of) Signal 1 looks downstream, the signals alternate in pairs—green, green, red, red, green, green, and so forth. When they switch, they again alternate in pairs—red, red, green, green, red, red, and so forth.

The *efficiency* of the double alternate signal system is 25% in *each* direction, because only half of the

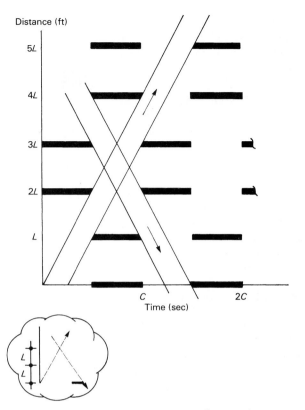

Figure 22-24 Double alternate system illustrated.

green is used in each direction. The upper limit on the platooned volume that can be carried in each direction without stops is typically 450 (lanes) vph, as an approximation.

As with the alternate system, if the splits are not 50:50 at some signals, note that (1) if they favor the main street, they simply represent excess green, suited for accommodating miscellaneous vehicles, and (2) if they favor the side street, they reduce the bandwidths.

Considering the range of block lengths for which double alternate patterns might occur, using Equation [22-13], note

Cycle Length	Platoon Speed	→	Matching Block Length
60 sec	45 fps		675 ft
60 sec	75 fps		1125 ft
90 sec	45 fps		1012 ft
90 sec	75 fps		1688 ft

Some of these signal spacings imply a high-type arterial, often in a suburban setting. However, with the shorter cycle lengths, some urban facilities could also have the necessary block lengths.

C. Simultaneous system

For very closely spaced signals, or for rather high vehicle speeds, it may be best to have all the signals turn green at the same time. This is a simultaneous system. Refer to Figure 22-25 for an illustration.

The *efficiency* of a simultaneous system depends on the number of signals involved. For *N* signals, it is

$$\left[\frac{1}{2} - \frac{(N-1)L}{(S)(C)}\right]100\% \qquad [22\text{-}14]$$

For four signals with $L = 400$ ft, $C = 80$ sec, and $S = 45$ fps, the efficiency is 16.7%. For the same number of signals with $L = 200$ ft, it is 33.3%.

It is clear that simultaneous systems are advantageous only under a limited number of special circumstances. The foremost of these special circumstances is very short block lengths.

The simultaneous system has an additional advantage, however, that is not at all clear from a bandwidth analysis: under very heavy flow conditions, it forestalls breakdown and spillback. This is so because (1) it allows for vehicle clearance time at the downstream intersection where queues inevitably exist during heavy flow, and (2) it cuts platoons off in a way that generally prevents blockage of intersections. This works to the advantage of cross traffic. (This congestion-inhibiting advantage arises because—for typical numbers—the simultaneous system comes quite close to the timing plans that would result if the explicit objective were to "inhibit spillback during heavy flow." Such plans are described later in this chapter.

Insights from the importance of signal spacing and cycle length

This section synthesizes much of the information presented on signal coordination, so that the reader is better equipped to use the information in engineering practice.

At this point, it should be clear that:

- While there are a number of "named" progressions—forward, backward, flexible, and so on—they all have their roots in the desire for ideal offsets, as reflected in Equation [22-4].
- For certain "appropriate combinations" of cycle length, block spacing, and platoon speed, some very satisfactory two-way progressions can be implemented.
- Other progressions can be designed to suit individual cases, using the concept of ideal offset and queue clearance, trial-and-error bandwidth-based approaches, or computer-based algorithms such as described in References [2], [3], and [9].

Thus, there are only a few "basic concepts" involved.

The traffic engineer may well be faced with a situation that looks intimidating, but for which the community (or its representatives) seek to have smooth flow of traffic along an arterial, or in a system. What is an orderly way to use the knowledge at hand in order to approach a solution?

First and foremost, it would be useful to appreciate the magnitude of the problem. While it sounds silly to the beginner, it is often true that the existing system has not been touched in a number of years. Thus, the splits, offsets, and cycle length might be totally out of date for the existing traffic demand. Even

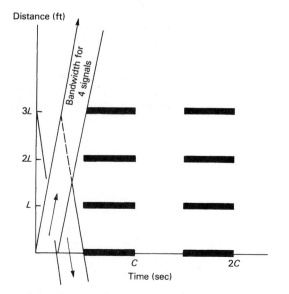

Figure 22-25   Simultaneous system illustrated.

if the *plan* is not out of date, the settings in the field might be totally different than those originally intended and/or set.

Thus, a logical first step is simply to ride the system and inspect it. As you sit at one signal, do you see the downstream signal green, but with no vehicles being processed? Do you arrive at signals that have standing queues, but were not timed to get them moving before your platoon arrived? Do you arrive on the red at some signals? Is the flow in the other direction significant, or is the *traffic* really a one-way pattern, even if the *streets* are two-way?

Second, it would be very useful to sketch out how much of the system can be thought of as an "open tree" of one-way links. This can be done with a local map and an appreciation of the traffic flow patterns. Refer to Figure 22-16. A distinction should be made among

- streets that *are* one-way
- streets that can be *treated* as one-way, due to the actual or desired flow patterns
- streets that must be treated as *two-way*
- larger grids in which streets (one-way and two-way) interact because they form unavoidable "closed trees" and are each important in that they cannot be ignored for the sake of establishing a "master grid," which is an open tree
- smaller grids in which the issue is not coordination but rather local land access and circulation, so that they can be treated differently

Downtown grids might well fall into the last category, at least in some cases.

For the purpose of the present discussion, the next most important issue is the cycle length dictated by the signal spacing and platoon speeds.

Third, therefore, attention should focus on the combination of

cycle length

block length

platoon speed

and their interaction. This, of course, is most relevant for two-way streets that must be treated as such and for one-way grids. In particular, is there a cycle length such that $L/S = C/2$ is possible? If so, an alternate system can be used, with an efficiency of 50% (unless other splits are needed). If not, is there a cycle length such that $L/S = C/4$ is possible? If so, a double alternate system can be used, with an efficiency of 25% (unless other splits are needed).

The presentations of Figures 22-24 and 22-25 are deficient in one regard; because they are plotted with the same distance between intersections, it is not obvious that each is suited over a certain range of block lengths. Figure 22-26 shows the three progressions of the preceding section—alternate, double alternate, and simultaneous—on the same scale. The basic "message" is that as the average signal spacing decreases, the type of progression best suited to the task changes.

Figure 22-27 illustrates a hypothetical arterial that comes from a low-density suburban environment

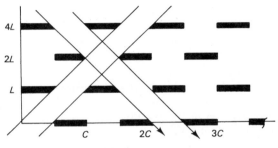

(a) Alternate pattern

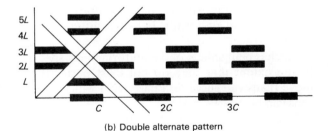

(b) Double alternate pattern

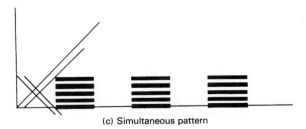

(c) Simultaneous pattern

Figure 22-26 Comparison of scales on which some standard patterns are used.

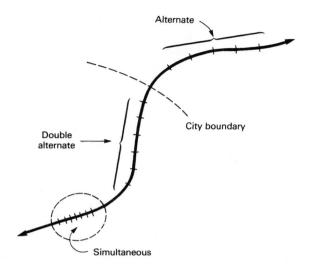

Figure 22-27 A hypothetical use of several patterns along the same arterial.

with larger signal spacings, into the outlying area of a city, and finally passes through one of the city's CBDs. As the arterial changes, the progression used may also be changed, to suit the dimensions.[6]

Note that the basic lesson here is that a *system* (e.g., the arterial of Figure 22-27) can sometimes be best handled by breaking it up into several smaller systems. This can be done with good effect on even smaller systems, such as ten consecutive signals, of which a contiguous six are spaced uniformly and the other four also uniformly, but at a different block length.

Much is being made of the uniform block spacings. To the extent that they do not exist perfectly, the above plans can serve as a base from which adaptations can be made.

To the extent that existing or proposed signals disrupt what would generally be a suitable pattern, serious consideration might be given to their elimination or to allowing a disruption in only one direction at that (those) signal(s).

Note that the alternate and double alternate plans will work beautifully, *if* there is no excessive internal

[6]Of course, if the flow is highly directional—as it well may be from the suburbs in the morning—then the suggestions of Figure 22-27 are superseded by the simple expedient of treating the street as a one-way street and imposing a forward progression, with queue clearance if needed.

queue generation and if the demand volumes do not exceed 900 vphpl and 450 vphpl, respectively. When the demand volumes are higher, life becomes more complicated.

One way of simplifying things is to meter access to such arterials, holding the demand below these levels by the green allocation at the termini signals. (For alternate progressions this is not difficult, for the full green is used for input demand. Four double alternate signals, however, it may not be feasible in most cases.)

Note that the focus in this item on the suitability of the cycle length has been significant. It is simply amazing how often the cycle length is poorly set *for system purposes*. There was an example in this chapter (see Figures 22-18 to 22-20) in which the cycle length was set at one value to good effect, but had to be reset dramatically in order for the system to function after a new signal was inserted into the system.

A good part of the problem may be due to the historic focus on the *intersection* as the basic building block of the system. In Chapter 18 an emphasis was placed on the fact that the intersection performance *and* capacity are both relatively insensitive to the cycle length, over a significant range. Thus, there is often little advantage to setting the cycle length based primarily on intersection-based concerns. However, this is how people have historically addressed the problem: do the intersection analyses, and piece together a system.

This approach is faulty. Given the relative insensitivity of intersections to cycle length (over a wide, practical range), it is most critical that *the cycle length be set primarily based on system considerations, using the rationale of this chapter heavily in such a determination*. Indeed, the authors feel so strongly about this point that they almost reorganized the order of chapters, so that this chapter appeared *before* Chapter 18, so as to instill this bias toward the system considerations determining the cycle length.

Figure 22-28 summarizes the interaction between the three key system parameters—cycle length, signal spacing, and platoon speed.

Having stressed taking the benefit of geometry whenever possible, it is perhaps necessary to conclude the section on a less optimistic note.

Fourth, therefore, is the necessity to recognize that if the geometry is not suitable, one can adapt and "fix up" the situation to a certain extent. The more sophisti-

First, can the two-way street be treated as a
one-way street based on highly directional flow?
If "yes" then do so. If not, then proceed:

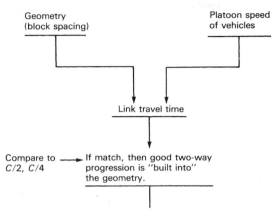

Figure 22-28 The importance of basic inter-relations.

cated signal-coordination/optimization programs may
be needed for the task. Even with these, future problems can be expected, for the underlying base is not
sound: As the volumes shift over the years, the fundamental shortcoming will be revealed again and again.
Indeed, the traffic work needed may be a family business, to be handed down from generation to generation,
until some fundamental changes are made (conversion
to one-way pairs, new technology, pruning of some signals, and the like).

Another issue to address, of course, is whether the
objective of progressed movement of traffic should
be maintained. The next sections address the need to
have a different objective in face of oversaturated
traffic networks.

Oversaturated traffic

The problem of oversaturation is not just one of degree but of kind—extreme congestion (i.e., oversaturation) is marked by a new phenomenon: intersection
blockage. This blockage ("spillback") causes the
spread of congestion along routes that might otherwise not be affected, for the productivity of upstream
intersections is ruined by it.

Because this intersection blockage can so degrade
the network, its removal must be the prime objective
of the traffic engineer. Although stops and delay will

doubtlessly increase when such blockages occur, they
are but secondary exhibitions of the basic problem.
Further, because most signal-optimization algorithms
do not explicitly take blockage into account, delay
and stops are poor proxies in attempting to solve the
blockage problem by such means. Thus, it is strongly
advocated that removal or avoidance of "spillback"
be the prime and explicit objective in the regime of
extreme congestion.

The overall approach can be stated in a logical set
of steps:

- Address the root causes of congestion—first, foremost, and continually.
- Update the signalization, for poor signalization is
frequently the cause of what looks like an incurable
problem.
- If the problem persists, use novel signalization to
minimize the impact and spatial extent of the extreme congestion.
- Provide more space, by use of turn bays and parking restrictions.
- Consider both prohibitions and enforcement realis-
tically—is it a futile effort? Will it only transfer the
problem?
- Take other available steps, such as right-turn-on-
red, recognizing that the benefits will generally
not be as significant as either signalization or more
space.
- Develop site-specific evaluations where there are
conflicting goals, such as providing local parking versus moving traffic, when the decision is ambiguous.

This list was constructed in Reference [18] with
some allowance for ease of implementation: it is generally easier to change signalization than to remove
urban parking; it is generally easier to treat spot locations than entire arterials; and so forth. At the same
time, relative benefits were also considered.

This chapter addresses some of the key technical
concepts underlying congestion relief on surface
streets. The focus is on signal-based remedies, namely:

- metering plans
- shorter cycle lengths
- equity offsets
- imbalanced split

Some note is made of nonsignal remedies, but the
essence of these remedies is "provide more space."

For further detail, the reader is referred to [18] and [19] and to the results of [20].

Signal remedies

It is difficult to overstate how often the basic problem is poor signalization. Once the signalization is improved through:

- reasonably short cycle lengths
- proper offsets (including queue clearance)
- proper splits

many problems disappear. Sometimes, of course, there is just too much traffic. At such times *equity offsets,* to aid cross flows, and *different splits,* to manage the spread of congestion, may be appropriate if other options cannot be called upon. These options may be used as distinct treatments or as part of a *metering* plan.

A. Metering plans

Three forms of metering can be applied within a congested traffic environment, characterized by demand exceeding supply (i.e., *v/c* deficiencies):

- internal
- external
- release

Internal metering refers to the use of control strategies within a congested network so as to influence the distribution of vehicles arriving at or departing from a critical location. The vehicles involved are stored on links defined to be part of the congested system under control, so as to eliminate or significantly limit the occurrence of either upstream or downstream intersection blockages.

Note that the metering concept does not explicitly minimize delay and stops, but rather manages the queue formation in a manner that maximizes the productivity of the congested system.

Figures 22-29 and 22-30 show situations in which internal metering might be used: (1) controlling the volume being discharged at intersections upstream of a critical intersection (CI), thus creating a "moving storage" situation on the upstream links, (2) limiting the turn-in flow from cross streets, thus preserving the arterial for its through flow, and (3) metering in the face of a backup from "outside."

External metering refers to the control of the major access points to the defined system, so that inflow rates into the system are limited if the system is already too congested (or in danger of becoming so).

External metering is convenient conceptually, because the storage problem belongs to "somebody else," outside the system. However, there may be limits to how much metering can be done without creat-

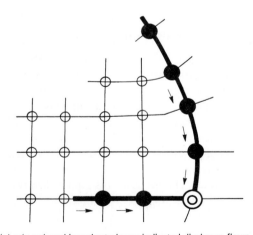

(a) *g/c* reduced in order to lower indicated discharge flows.

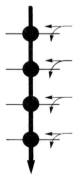

(b) Cross street (*g/C*) lowered to preserve actorial for through flow.

● Internally metered intersection   ◎ Critical intersection   ○ Undersaturated intersection

Figure 22-29 Internal metering used to limit volume arriving at critical location.

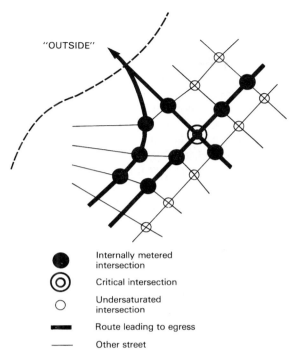

"OUTSIDE"

- ● Internally metered intersection
- ◎ Critical intersection
- ○ Undersaturated intersection
- ▬ Route leading to egress
- ── Other street

Figure 22-30 Application of internal metering in the face of a backup from "outside."

ing major problems in the "other" areas. Figure 22-31 shows a network with metering at the access points.

As a practical matter, there must be a limited number of major access points (such as river crossings, a downtown surrounded by water on three sides, a system that receives traffic from a limited number of radial arterials, and so forth). Without effective control of access, the control points can potentially be bypassed by driver reroutings.

Release metering refers to the cases in which vehicles are stored in such locations as parking garages and lots, from which their release can in principle be controlled. The fact that they are stored "off street" also frees the traffic engineer of the need to worry about their storage and their spillback potential.

Release metering can be used at shopping centers, megacenters, and other concentrations. While there are very practical problems with public (and property-owner) acceptance, this could even be—indeed, has been—a developer strategy to lower discharge rates so that adverse impacts are avoided. Such strategies are of particular interest when the associated roadway

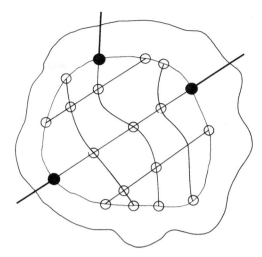

Figure 22-31 External metering: An illustration.

system is distributing traffic to egress routes or along heavily congested arterials.

B. Shorter cycle lengths

Chapters 17 and 18 demonstrated that increasing the cycle length does *not* substantially increase the capacity of the intersection. Indeed, as the cycle length increases, so do the stored queue lengths and the discharged platoon lengths formed. The likelihood of intersection blockage increases, with substantial adverse impacts on system capacity. This is particularly acute when short link lengths are involved.

Note that a critical lane flow of v_i nominally discharges $v_i C/3600$ vehicles in a cycle. If each vehicle requires D ft of storage space, the downstream link would be

$$\left(\frac{v_i C}{3600}\right)D \le L \qquad [22\text{-}15]$$

where L is the available downstream space in feet. This may be set by the link length or by some lower value, perhaps 150 ft less than the true length (to keep the queue away from the discharging intersection, or to allow for turn-ins).

Equation [22-15] may be rearranged as

$$C \le \left(\frac{L}{D}\right)\left(\frac{3600}{v_i}\right) \qquad [22\text{-}16]$$

Note that v_i in this case is the *discharge* volume per downstream lane, which may differ from the demand volume, particularly at the fringes of the "system" being considered. Refer to Figure 22-32 for an illustration of this relation. Note that only rather high flows (maximum $f \geq 800$ vphpl) and short blocks will create very severe limits on the cycle length. However, these are just the situations of most interest for extreme congestion situations.

C. Equity offsets

Offsets on an arterial are usually set to move vehicles smoothly along the arterial, as is logical. If no queues exist on the arterial, the ideal offset is L/S, where L is the signal spacing in feet and v is the vehicle speed in feet per second. If a queue of Q vehicles exist, the ideal offset t_{ideal} is

$$t_{ideal} = \frac{L}{S} - Q \times h \qquad [22\text{-}17]$$

where h is the discharge headway of the queue, in seconds. Clearly, as Q increases, t_{ideal} decreases, going from a "forward" progression to a "simultaneous" progression to a "reverse" progression.

Unfortunately, as the queue length approaches the block length, such progressions lose meaning, for it is quite unlikely that both the queue *and* the arriving vehicles will be passed at the downstream intersection. Thus the arrivals will be stopped *in any case.*

At the same time, the cross-street traffic at the upstream intersection is probably poorly served because of intersection blockages. Figure 22-33 illustrates the time at which t_{ideal} would normally cause the upstream intersection to switch to green (relative to the downstream intersection).

Consider the following, illustrated in Figure 22-34: Allow the congested arterial to have its green at the upstream intersection until its vehicles just *begin* to move; *then* switch the signal, so that these vehicles flush out the intersection, but no new vehicles continue to enter.

At the same time, this gives the cross-street traffic an opportunity to pass through a clear intersection. This concept, defined as *equity offset,* can be translated into the equation:

$$t_{equity} = g_1 C - \frac{L}{S_{acc}} \qquad [22\text{-}18]$$

where g_1 is the *upstream* main street (i.e., the congested-intersection) green fraction and V_{acc} is the speed of the "acceleration wave" shown in Figure 22-35.

A typical value is 16 fps. Comparing Figures 22-33 and 22-35, it is clear that equity offset causes the upstream signal to go red just when "normal" offsets would have caused it to switch to green in this particular case. This is not surprising, for the purpose is *different*—equity offsets are intended to be fair (i.e., equitable) to cross-street traffic.

Simulation test using a microscopic simulation model (NETSIM) have shown the value of using equity offsets: Congestion does not spread as fast as otherwise and may not infect the cross streets at all.

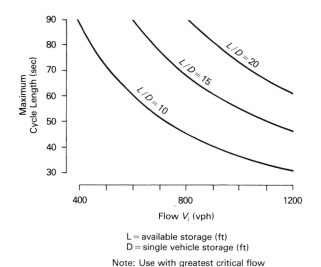

L = available storage (ft)
D = single vehicle storage (ft)

Note: Use with greatest critical flow

Figure 22-32 Maximum cycle length as a function of spacing.

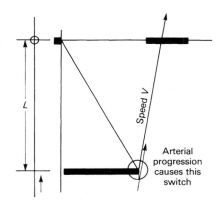

Figure 22-33   Ideal offset with queue filling block.

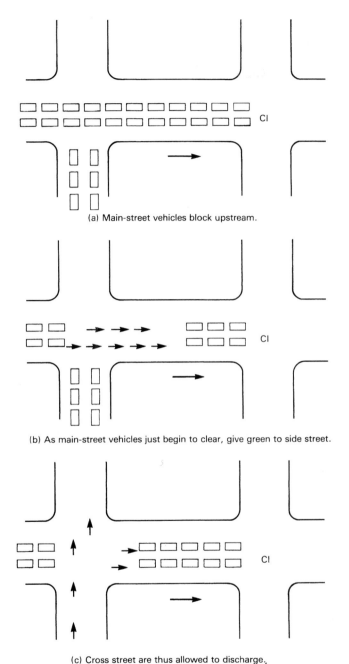

(a) Main-street vehicles block upstream.

(b) As main-street vehicles just begin to clear, give green to side street.

(c) Cross street are thus allowed to discharge.

Figure 22-34 Concept of equity offsets to clear side streets.

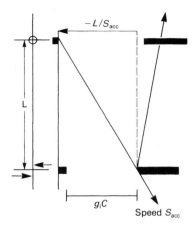

Figure 22-35 Equity offset to benefit cross street.

Figure 22-36 (a) shows a test network used to test the equity-offset concept. Link 2 is upstream of the critical intersection (CI). For the demands and signal splits shown it is likely to accumulate vehicles, with spillback into its upstream intersection likely. If this occurs, the discharge from Link 1 will be blocked and its queue will grow. In the extreme, congestion will spread.

The equity offset is computed as

$$t_{\text{equity}} = (0.60)(60) - \frac{600}{16} = -1.5 \text{ sec}$$

using Equation [22-18]. (At 25 ft per vehicle and a platoon speed of 50 fps., Equation [22-36] would have yielded $t_{\text{ideal}} = (600/50) - (24)(2) = -36$ sec for progressed movement. Of course, progressed movement is a silly objective when 24 vehicles are queued for 30 sec of green.)

Figure 22-36(b) shows the side-street queue (i.e., the Link 1 queue) as a function of the main-street offset. Note that an offset of -36 sec is the same as an offset of $+24$ sec when $C = 60$ sec, due to the periodic pattern of the offsets. Figure 22-37(b) shows the *best* results for allowing the side street to clear when the equity offset (offset $= -1.5$ sec) is in effect, and—in this case—the *worst* results when the queue-adjusted "ideal offset" (offset $= 24$ sec) would have been in effect.

The above discussion assumes that the cross-street traffic does not turn into space opened on the congested arterial. If a significant number of cross-street

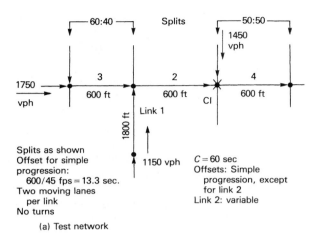

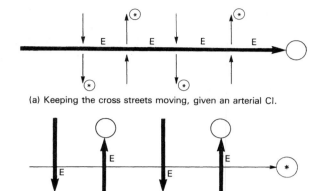

(a) Keeping the cross streets moving, given an arterial CI.

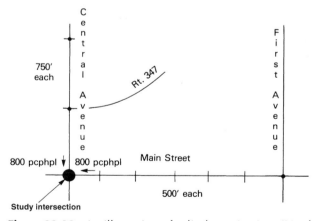

(b) Keeping an arterial moving, given cross-town CIs affecting the cross flows.

○ = CI   (*) = Flows released by use of equity offsets   E = Links on which equity offset were used

Figure 22-37 Use of equity offsets for different purposes.

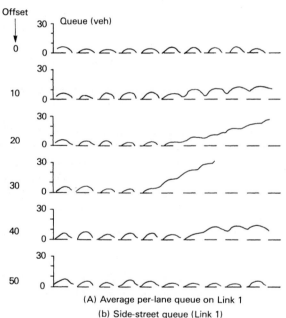

(A) Average per-lane queue on Link 1
(b) Side-street queue (Link 1)

Figure 22-36 Equity offsets avoid side street congestion, despite spillback.

vehicles do turn into the arterial, a modification in the offset is appropriate to assure that the upstream traffic on the congested arterial also has its fair share. Such a treatment is addressed in [1].

The equity-offset concept has been used to keep side-street cross flows moving when an arterial backs up from a critical intersection (CI). It may also be used to keep an arterial functioning when the cross streets back up across the arterial from *their* critical

intersections. Refer to Figure 22-37 for a comparison of these cases.

D. Imbalanced split

For congested flow, the standard rule of allocating the available green in proportion to the relative demands could be used, but it does not address an important problem. Consider the illustration of Figure 22-38. If

Figure 22-38 An illustration of split determination. [Used with permission of Transportation Research Board, National Research Council, Washington, DC, from "Traffic Determination in Oversaturated Street Networks," *NCHRP Report 194*, p. 123, Copyright 1978. Transportation Research Board.]

the prime concern is to avoid impacting Route 347 and First Ave. (but with little concern for the minor streets in between, if any), it is not reasonable to use a 50:50 split.

Considering that the relative storage available is 750 ft in one direction and 3000 ft in the other, and we wish *neither* to be adversely affected, the impact could be delayed for the longest time by causing the excess-vehicle queues to grow in proportion to their available storage. The two critical-lane discharge flows f_i would have to be set such that

$$\frac{d_1 - f_1}{d_2 - f_2} = \frac{L_1}{L_2}$$

and

$$f_1 + f_2 = \text{CAP} \qquad [24\text{-}19]$$

where d_i are the demands (vphpl), L_i is the storage, and CAP is the sum of the critical-lane flows (i.e., the capacity figure).

For the illustrative problem, using CAP = 1550 vphpl, the above equations result in $f_1 = 954$ vphpl and $f_2 = 759$ vphpl, where direction 1 is the shorter distance. This is a 56:44 split.

Note that in the extreme, if only one direction has a cross route that should not be impacted, much of the green could be given to that direction (other than some minimum for other phases) in order to achieve that end.

Nonsignal remedies: Some considerations

If a problem cannot be remedied by signalization, the next major set of actions are summarized in two words: *more space*. Left-turn bays and, where appropriate, right-turn bays can aid individual movements as well as remove impediments to the through flows.

Without question, additional lanes are beneficial. However, this tends to be an arterial-long solution and one which the engineer must be "backed into."

Two-way left turn lanes offer special advantages, particularly along strip development sites. This remedy (and a number of others) are addressed in a more general context in Chapter 24.

One-way systems, arterials with unbalanced lanes, and reversible lanes offer advantages but also represent either major implementation problems or very site-specific treatments.

One-way systems require studies quite beyond congestion, although congestion may be the prime motivator for such a study.

Unbalanced lanes require certain volume patterns to be of use.

Before instituting an *enforcement* program, the engineer must decide:

- Can it be enforced strictly enough to realize most or all of the projected benefit? Curb-parking prohibition to provide a moving lane is an example.
- Will it simply transfer or even accentuate the overall problem? Circulation of vehicles that would otherwise be double-parking is a prime example.

Only then can the engineer consider that there is a potential benefit.

The question of turning and other *prohibitions* arises: these can only be used if alternatives exist for the traffic involved. Often, this is not the case.

Summary

This chapter has introduced the basic considerations and concepts of signal coordination for undersaturated flows on one-way and two-way arterials, and in networks.

Chapter 24 contains a section that focuses on some related issues, such as the use of multiple and sub-multiple cycle lengths, coordination of multiphase signals, and diamond interchanges.

This chapter also addresses oversaturated conditions on surface streets. The problem of congestion and saturation is widespread and is not often approached in any consistent manner. Definite measures can be taken, but preventive action addressing the root causes must be given a high priority. Among the possible measures, those relating to signalization generally can have the greatest impact. There are different signal plans for avoiding spillback and for "living with" spillback. The nonsignal remedies are in no way to be minimized, particularly those that provide space either for direct productivity increases or for removing impediments to the principal flow.

References

1. *Highway Capacity Manual, Special Report 209,* Transportation Research Board, National Research Council, Washington, DC, 1985.
2. Courage, K., and Wallace, C., *TRANSYT/7F User's Guide,* Federal Highway Administration, Washington, DC, 1991.
3. Wallace, C. E., "At Last—A TRANSYT Model Designed for American Traffic Engineers," *ITE Journal,* August 1983.
4. *National Signal Timing Optimization Project: Summary Evaluation Report,* U.S. Department of Transportation, Federal Highway Administration, Washington, DC, May 1982.
5. *A User Guide: Traffic Network Analysis with NETSIM,* Implementation Package FHWA-IP-80-3, U.S. Department of Transportation, Federal Highway Administration, Washington, DC, January, 1980.
6. Kubel, et al., "What Network Simulation (NETSIM) Can Do for the Traffic Engineer," *Public Roads,* March 1978.
7. *NETSIM Traffic Simulation on the Microcomputer,* Federal Highway Administration, Office of Traffic Operations. Distributed through the McTrans Center, University of Florida, Gainesville, FL, 1994.
8. Andrews, B., Lieberman, E., Santiago, A. J., "The NETSIM Graphics System," *Transportation Research Record 1112,* Transportation Research Board, National Research Council, Washington, DC, 1988.
9. *PASSER II-90 Microcomputer User's Guide,* Texas Transportation Institute, Texas A&M University, College Park, TX, 1991.
10. *Signal Operations Analysis Package,* Implementation Package FHWA-IP-79-9, U.S. Department of Transportation, Federal Highway Administration, Washington, DC, July 1979.
11. Petterman, J. L., "Timing Progressive Signal Systems," *Traffic Engineering,* Vol. 17, Part I, February 1947, pp. 194–99; Part II, March 1947, pp. 242–49.
12. Morgan, J. T., and Little, J. D., "Synchronizing Traffic Signals for Maximal Bandwidth," *Operations Research,* Vol. 12, 1964, pp. 896–912.
13. Yardini, L. A., "Algorithms for Traffic-Signal Control," *IBM Systems Journal,* Vol. 4, 1965, pp. 148–61.
14. Chang, A., "Synchronization of Traffic Signals in Grid Networks," *IBM Journal of Research and Development,* July 1967.
15. *SIGOP: Traffic Signal Optimization Program Users Manual,* Peat, Marwick, Livingston & Co., New York, NY, December 1968.
16. Little, J. D. C., Kelson, M. D., and Gartner, N. H., "MAXBAND: A Program for Setting Signals on Arteries and Triangular Networks," *Transportation Research Record 795,* Transportation Research Board, National Research Council, Washington, DC, 1981.
17. Cohen, S. L., "Concurrent Use of the MAXBAND and TRANSYT Signal Timing Programs for Arterial Signal Optimizations," *Transportation Research Record 906,* Transportation Research Board, National Research Council, Washington, DC, 1983.
18. "Traffic Control in Oversaturated Street Networks," National Cooperative Highway Research Program, *(NCHRP) Report 194,* Transportation Research Board, National Research Council, Washington, DC, 1985.
19. *Traffic Control in Saturated Conditions,* Organization for Economic Co-operation and Development (OECD), Paris, France, 1981.
20. "Traffic Signal Control for Saturated Conditions," NCHRP Project 3-38(4), in progress, KLD Associates, Inc., scheduled completion date March 31, 1989.

Problems

Problem 22–1

Refer to Figure 22-39. Trace the lead NB vehicle through the system. Do the same for the lead SB vehicle. Use a platoon speed of 50 fps. Estimate the number of stops and the seconds of delay for each of these vehicles.

Problem 22–2

Refer to Figure 22-40. Find the NB and the SB bandwidths (in seconds). Determine the efficiency of the system in each direction and the maximum number of platooned vehicles that can be handled nonstop. There are three lanes in each direction. The progression speed is 50 fps.

Problem 22–3

(a) If vehicles are traveling at 60 fps on a suburban road, and the signals are 2400 feet apart, what cycle length would you recommend? What offset would you recommend?

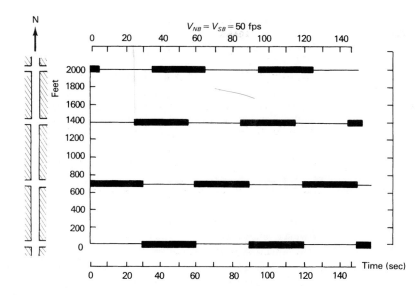

Figure 22-39 Time–space diagram for Problem 1.

(c) If an unsignalized intersection is to be inserted at 600 ft from one of the signalized intersections, what would you recommend?

Problem 22–4

You have two intersections 3000 ft apart and have achieved some success with a 50:50 split, 60-sec cycle length, and simultaneous system.

(a) Draw a time–space diagram and analyze the reason for your success.

(b) A developer who owns the property fronting on the first 2000 ft of the subject distance plans a major employment center. She plans a major driveway and asks your advice on its location. What is your recommendation?

Problem 22–5

(a) Consider four intersections, spaced by 500 ft. The platoon speed is 40 fps. Recommend a set of offsets for the eastbound direction, considering only the eastbound traffic.

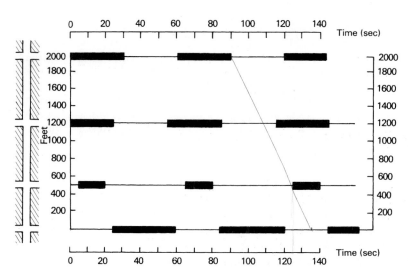

Figure 22-40 Time–space diagram for Problem 2.

(b) If there are queues of three vehicles at each of the intersections, recommend a different set of offsets (if appropriate).

Problem 22–6

Construct a time–space diagram for the following information and estimate the northbound bandwidth and efficiency for platoons going at 50 fps:

Signal No.	Offset	Cycle Length	Split (MSG first)
6	16 sec	60 sec	50/50
5	16 sec	60 sec	60/40
4	28 sec	60 sec	60/40
3	28 sec	60 sec	60/40
2	24 sec	60 sec	50/50
1		60 sec	60/40

All offsets are relative to the preceding signal. All signals are two-phase. There are two lanes in each direction.

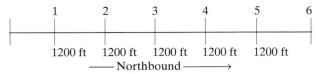

Also, estimate the number of platooned vehicles that can be handled nonstop on the northbound. Repeat for the southbound.

Problem 22–7

For the situation of Problem 22–6, design a better timing plan (if possible), under two different assumptions:

(a) Only the northbound flow is important.
(b) The two directions are equally important.

Problem 22–8

Find the offset desired for a link of 1500 ft, no standing queue at the downstream signal, and a platoon traveling at 40 fps. Re-solve if there is a standing queue of eight vehicles per lane.

Problem 22–9

Develop an arterial progression for the situation shown in Figure 22-41. Use a desired platoon speed of 40 fps. For simplicity, the volumes shown are already corrected for turns and PHF. What intersection level(s) of service do you have?

Problem 22–10

Throughout the chapter, the emphasis was on platoons of vehicles moving through the system, with no desire to stop. However, buses travel slower than most passenger cars and must stop. This problem addresses the timing of signals solely for the bus traffic.

(a) For the situation shown in Figure 22-42, time the signals for the eastbound bus. Draw a time–space diagram of the solution.
(b) Now consider the *westbound bus*. Locate the westbound bus stops approximately every two blocks and adjust the offsets to make the best possible path for the westbound bus, without adversely affecting the eastbound bus. Draw the revised time–space diagram.
(c) Show the trajectories of the EB and WB lead passenger cars going at 60 fps.
(d) Estimate what happens to EB and WB platoons of vehicles going at 60 fps, in terms of parts of the platoon being cut off, forming queues in future cycles, and so forth.

Problem 22–11

A major development is proposed abutting a suburban arterial as shown in Figure 22-43. The arterial is 60 ft wide, with an additional 5 ft for shoulders on each side, and no parking. There is moderate development along the arterial now. Platoons of vehicles travel at 60 fps in each direction. The center lane shown in Figure 22-5 is for turns only. The proposed development is on the north side, with a major driveway to be added at 900 ft along the arterial, requiring a

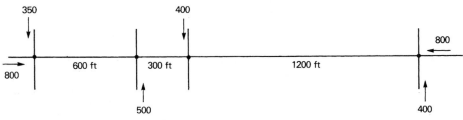

Volumes shown are critical movement volumes, with all corrections already done.

Figure 22-41 Arterial sketch for Problem 9.

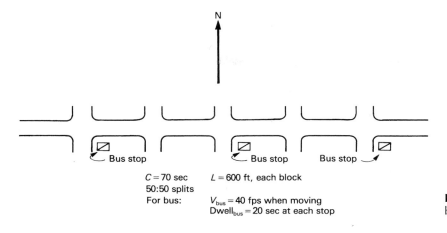

C = 70 sec   L = 600 ft, each block
50:50 splits
For bus: $V_{bus} = 40$ fps when moving
Dwell$_{bus} = 20$ sec at each stop

Figure 22-42 Arterial sketch with bus stop locations for Problem 10.

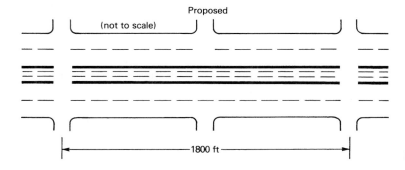

Figure 22-43 Arterial sketch for Problem 11.

signal. Evaluate the impact of this development in detail. Be specific, and illustrate your points and recommendations.

Problem 22–12

Refer to Figure 22-44. Second Street is southbound with offsets of +15 sec between successive signals. Third Street is northbound with offsets of +10 sec between successive signals. Avenue A is eastbound, with a +20-sec offset of the signal at Second Street and Avenue A relative to the signal at Third Street and Avenue A. Given this information, find the offsets along Avenues B through J. The directions alternate, and all splits are 60:40, with the 60 on the main streets (2nd and 3rd Streets).

Problem 22–13

Refer to Figure 22-45. Find the unknown offset X. The cycle length is 80 sec. The splits are 50:50.

Problem 22–14

Given three intersections spaced 600 ft apart, each with $C = 60$ sec and 50:50 split, find an offset pattern that equal-

izes the bandwidth in the two directions. [*Hint:* Set the first and the third relative to each other, and then do the best you can with the second intersection. This is a good way to start.]

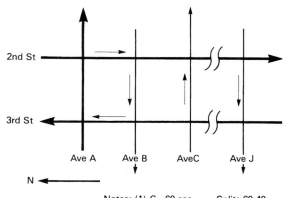

Notes: (1) $C = 60$ sec   Splits 60:40
(2) Block lengths 600 ft in all cases
(3) All streets are one-way.

Figure 22-44 Network sketch for Problem 12.

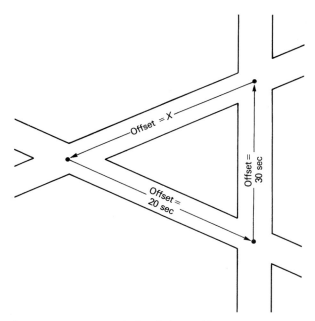

Figure 22-45   Network sketch for Problem 13.

Problem 22–15

Refer to Figure 22-46. Copy the figure, and cut horizontal strips (one per intersection) so as to allow them to move easily, in order to solve this problem. Find a set of offsets that will best maximize the bandwidths equally in the two directions. Submit the plot of the solution *and* a table of offsets. For the plot, tape together the strips provided.

Problem 22–16

Given an arterial with 20 consecutive signals, spaced at 1500 ft with vehicles moving at 50 fps, which coordination scheme is the best—simultaneous, alternate, or double alternate? What cycle length should be used?

Problem 22–17

Given the following information for the indicated arterial:

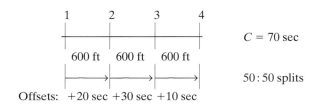

$C = 70$ sec

50 : 50 splits

Offsets: +20 sec +30 sec +10 sec

(a) Plot the time–space diagram.
(b) Find the two bandwidths. Show them graphically and find the numeric values. If they do not exist, say so.
(c) An intersection is to be placed midway between Intersections 3 and 4, with $C = 70$ sec and 50:50 split. Recommend an appropriate offset.

Problem 22–18

(a) For the one-way grid of Figure 22-47 N streets by M streets, show the following:
(1) There are $(N - 1)(M - 1)$ independent equations of the form of Equation 22-7 each of which places a

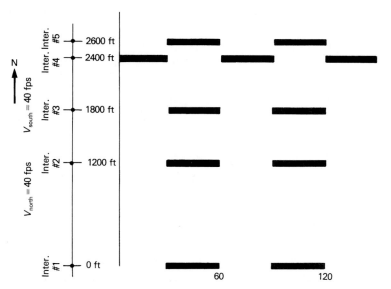

Figure 22-46   Time–space diagram for Problem 15.

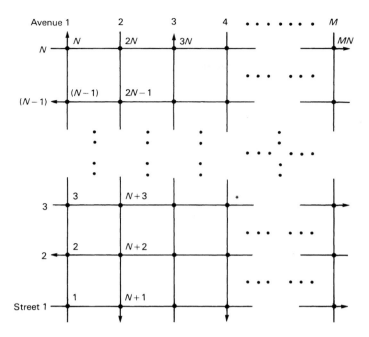

Avenue 1   2   3   4 • • • • • • • M

*Street "i" and Avenue "j" intersect at Intersection [N(j − 1) + i]

Figure 22-47   Sketch of network for Problem 18.

constraint among the signal-timing variables. Write the general form of such an equation, for notation keyed to the intersection numbers. [Note that there are really two parts to establishing the number of equations: Demonstrate that there are no more than the cited number (they can be written, but are not independent), and demonstrate that there are the cited number.]

(2) There are $[M(N − 1) + N(M − 1)]$ offsets to be determined, and thus the same number of variables in the objective function, if it is of the form of Equation [22-7] or [22-8].

(b) Given that the problem is to minimize the objective function subject to constraints, suggest a method for doing so. Note that there are unspecified integers $n(j,i)$ in each of the constraint equations. You must also consider how to set these, or how to enumerate all (or enough) reasonable combinations. If your background allows, comment on the dimensionality of the stated problem and the formal means by which such problems can be addressed.

▶ **NOTE:** Unless otherwise stated, all problems to follow are to be done on a per-lane basis, and all quantities are given that way (e.g., queue, volume).

Problem 22–19

Create a table of maximum cycle lengths based on Equations [22-15] and [22-16] for a range of discharge volumes (vphpl) on the horizontal and link lengths (ft) on the vertical. Include a sketch of the critical intersection, the link in question, and the discharge volume in question. [*Hint:* Is the sketch below correct?]

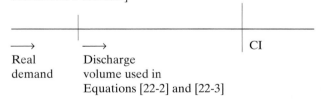

Real demand

Discharge volume used in Equations [22-2] and [22-3]

Use the following discharge volumes:

400, 600, 800, 1000, 1200 vphpl

and link lengths of 200, 400, 600, 800 ft.

Is an assumption of 50:50 split at the critical intersection (CI) necessary? Why or why not?

Problem 22–20

For an intersection with a 600-ft link upstream of it, plot the required ideal offset as a function of queue size. Assume

60-fps platoon speed, 60-sec cycle length, and splits as indicated (MSG first):

(a) At what value of discharge volume from Intersection 1 (the CI) does the idea of progressive movement become totally meaningless? Why is it the CI discharge volume determines this?

(b) What is the queue length generated by the volume level which makes progressed movement totally meaningless (if it were an arrival volume)?

(c) What is the equity offset which would allow the cross traffic to function at Intersection 2? Plot this on the same plot as for the ideal offsets. Comment.

Problem 22–21

Solve Problem 22–20 if the cycle length had been 90 sec. Comment.

Problem 22–22

Refer to Figure 22-48. Identify the candidate critical intersection(s) in the illustrated network, and justify your selection(s). For simplicity, assume that there are no turning volumes (except as indicated), and that no corrections to volume or saturation flow rate are needed. Assume 70-sec cycle, lost time of 3 sec per phase, two-phase signals. All volumes shown are demand volumes. *All streets are two moving lanes in the indicated directions, except as indicated on one northbound street.*

Problem 22–23

(a) What would have happened in the network used in Problem 22–22 if all of the splits had been 50:50, based on a traffic study done 15 years ago?

(b) What would have happened in the network used in Problem 22–22 if all of the splits had been 50:50, the offsets simultaneous, and the cycle length 90 sec? Assume 60 fps desired platoon speeds.

Problem 22–24

What will happen in the network used in Problem 22–22 if the traffic demand grows by 15%? Be specific and detailed. Include some comments on each intersection.

Problem 22–25

Given the demand volumes and geometrics shown in Figure 22-49 and the need to avoid interference with the indicated major streets for as long as possible,

(a) Determine a cycle length, split, and offsets which will (1) avoid the interference with the upstream major streets for as long as possible, and (2) allow cross-street traffic at intervening minor streets to cross the arterial.

(b) Estimate the time it takes for the queues to develop from $Q = 0$ at $t = 0$ to the point at which they interfere with the upstream major streets.

▶ **NOTE:** The last three problems may require more time and/or effort than the preceding problems but are in-

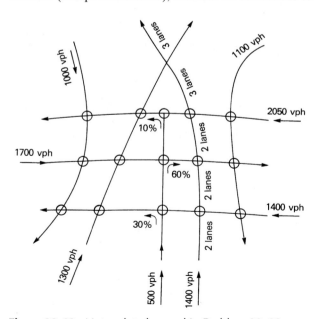

Figure 22-48 Network to be used in Problem 22–22.

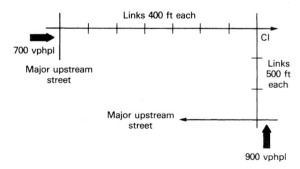

Figure 22-49 Network to be used in problem 22–24.

teresting and even rewarding. They may serve as special as-signments or a challenge to the student.

Problem 22–26

(a) Plot the queue length as a function of time for a demand volume of d vehicles per hour per lane, a cycle length of 80 sec, a 50:50 split, a lost time of 3 sec per phase, and a 2.0-sec/veh discharge headway. Assume zero initial queue. All vehicles arrive in a platoon from an upstream signal with enough green to assure that the platoon does indeed arrive, and the same cycle length. The pla-toon speed is 50 fps. All signals are two-phase. Assume an 800-ft link, and plot for the following conditions:
  (1) Offset = 14 sec.
  (2) Offset = 29 sec.
  (3) Offset = 44 sec.
  (4) Offset = 59 sec.
  (b) Repeat the problem for the following values of d:

Case	Demand Volume d (vphpl)
1	350
2	700
3	832
4	900
5	1000

Tabulate the maximum queue as a function of offset and de-mand volume. Comment, and explain the results. If any "maximum" continues to grow, explain why and tabulate values after 15 minutes.

Problem 22–27

Given the result of Problem 22–25, propose a procedure by which to measure the queue in the field, using conventional detectors.

First, you must decide the queue value you wish to mea-sure. For the Q used in the ideal offset equation, at what point do you wish to measure queue? For the needs of de-ciding when to invoke equity offset or imbalanced splits, which value or threshold of queue do you wish to measure?

Second, you must decide what variables must be ob-tained at the same time as the queue observation. Do they include demand volume, discharge volume, green alloca-tion, and/or offsets?

Problem 22–28

Equation [22-19] gives a relation for imbalanced splits, which is intended to equalize the time at which the queues on the competing approaches reach some identified points upstream (see Figure 22-38). Show that the resulting green allocation is given by a relation *of the form*

$$g_A = \frac{\dfrac{d_A}{s_A} + \left(\dfrac{W_A}{W_B}\right)\left[\left(1 - \dfrac{L}{C}\right) - \dfrac{d_B}{s_B}\right]}{1 + \dfrac{W_A}{W_B}}$$

where: L = lost time per cycle, sec
  d_i = demand volume on Approach i, vphpl
  s_i = adjusted saturation flow rate on Approach i = (vphpl)
  W_i = Storage$_i$ − $d_i C$
  C = cycle length, sec
  Storage$_i$ = space available to selected upstream point on Approach i, ft

and, as in Figure 22-38, the space selected for storage may cover more than one link. Note that the g_i is a decimal frac-tion, and has no units itself. Also,

$$(g_A + g_B)C + L = C$$

Note the emphasis on the words "of the form": The *units* of the proposed relation must be checked, and adjustment constants used where appropriate. Thus, the proposed rela-tion may not be correct.

23

Computer Traffic Signal Control Systems for Arterials and Networks

---

Digital computers are now used to control traffic signals along arterials and in networks in many cities throughout the world. This chapter acquaints the reader with the basic issues and concepts involved in computer control of surface street traffic and presents some of the experiences with such control.

With the current emphasis on ITS, computer control of systems is now classified as Advanced Transportation Management Systems (ATMS) and the control centers themselves as Transportation Management Centers (TMCs). However, the real existence of such systems predates the term "ITS" by a few decades.[1]

Basic principles and flow of information

The original concept[2] was that the power of the digital computer could be used to control many traffic

---

[1]In ATMS and TMC, the letter "T" initially meant "Traffic" but the application is broader.

[2]The first installations occurred in the early 1960s, following the introduction of computers that had circuits based on transistors.

---

signals from one central location, allowing the development of control plans which would usher in a new era of efficient vehicular movement in very busy, heavily loaded street systems.

A. The most basic system

Figure 23-1 shows the most basic concept: the computer sends out commands that control the signals along one or more arterials. There is no "feedback" of information from detectors in the field, and the traffic-signal plans are *not* "responsive" to actual traffic conditions.

How are the plans for such a system developed? They were typically based on engineers using data from field studies to generate plans either (1) by hand, using techniques such as discussed in Chapter 23, or (2) by computer, using packages available at the time. The computer solutions were run on another machine, or in "off" hours on the control computer when it was not being used for control of the traffic signals.

The key fact to recognize is that the actual control plans were generated "off-line" based on earlier traf-

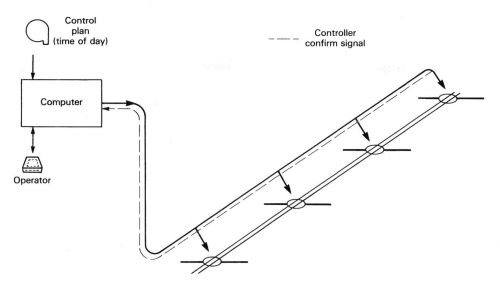

Control
plan
(time of day)

Controller
confirm signal

Computer

Operator

Figure 23-1 Characterization of the most basic computer control system.

fic data. They were *not* developed in "real time" by a high-speed computer based on the latest traffic data.

Compared to the popular conception of "computer control" in the early days, this depiction of: (1) no feedback of traffic information; (2) no responsiveness to changing conditions; (3) control plans often generated in the "back room" by conventional means does conjure an image of a very limited, perhaps deficient system. Indeed, one is tempted to observe that it is "only" a multidial controller of the most basic sort.

In actual fact, it is the image that is deficient, for this "limited" system has *major advantages* that can completely justify its existence. These include:

1. *Ability to Update Signals from a Central Location.* As a practical matter, signals are not updated in many areas simply because sufficient staff does not exist to do the task. Sending one or two people along an entire arterial to retime the signals individually at each intersection is a time-consuming task. The ability to do this from a central location opened the potential for getting a necessary task done conveniently.

2. *Ability to Have Multiple Plans and Special Plans.* In many localities a three-dial controller is quite sufficient: if traffic is generally regular, three basic plans (A.M. peak, P.M. peak, off-peak) can meet the need nicely.

The computer opens the possibility to have an *N*-dial controller, with special plans stored for Saturday, Sunday, severe rain, games at the local stadium, and so forth. With appropriate plans stored for each such event, the plans can be "called up" by time of day, or by operator intervention. The plans can be said to be stored in a "library" and called up as needed, most often by time of day.

3. *Information on Equipment Failures.* The early systems simply took control of electromechanical controllers, driving the cam-shaft from the central computer[3] and receiving a confirmation signal (typically, A-phase green confirm). Failure to receive this signal indicated trouble, perhaps the controller "hanging up" temporarily. The information provided by the control computer allowed such failures to be detected and repair crews dispatched.

4. *Performance Data on Contractor or Service Personnel.* With a failure detected and notification made, the system can log the arrival of the crew and/or the time at which the intersection is returned to active service.

These advantages alone can justify the existence of a computer control system, and greatly enhance the service provided to the public.

---

[3]By implication, the cycle length, phase durations, and offsets can be controlled. The number of phases cannot be varied, nor can the order of phases be changed.

B. Collection of traffic data

Figure 23-2 shows the preceding system, but with the refinement that detectors in the field are feeding information back to the central location. This refinement makes use of the special "talent" of the computer to receive great amounts of such information and to process it. However, as carefully structured in Figure 23-2, the information is *not* being used in an "on-line" setting: it still does not influence the current plan selection.

Nonetheless, this enhancement is valuable, for it provides the basic data for doing the off-line development of up-to-date plans, for identifying seasonal and other adjustments, and for observing general growth in the traffic level and/or changes in the pattern. Typically, the computer is being used as the tool for the collection of permanent or long-term count data.

C. Traffic data used for plan selection

Figure 23-3 shows a computer control system that actually uses the traffic data to aid in plan selection. This may be done in one of three principle ways:

1. *Use Library; Monitor Deviations from Expected Pattern.* This concept uses a time-of-day approach, looking up in a library both the expected traffic pattern and the preselected plan matched to the pattern. The actual traffic pattern (as estimated from the field data) can be compared to the expected, and—if a deviation occurs—the computer can then look through its library for a closer "match" and use the appropriate plan.

   The check can be done before putting the plan into effect, or there can be periodic checking to evaluate whether the current plan should be superseded.
2. *Use Library; Match Plan to Pattern.* This is a variation on the first concept, with the observed pattern being matched to the most appropriate prestored pattern, and the corresponding plan being used. The feature missing is the history of what is *expected* to be happening, based on time of day.
3. *Develop Plan On-Line.* This concept depends on the ability to do the necessary computations within a deadline either as a "background" task or on a companion computer dedicated to such computa-

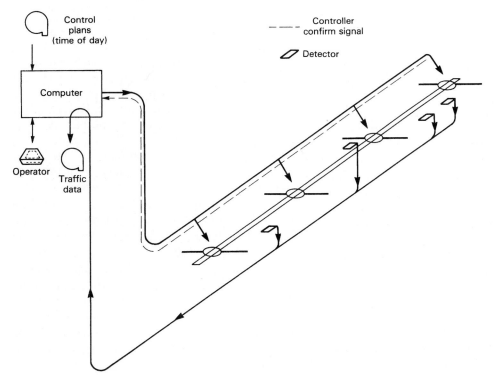

Figure 23-2 Information from the field added to basic system.

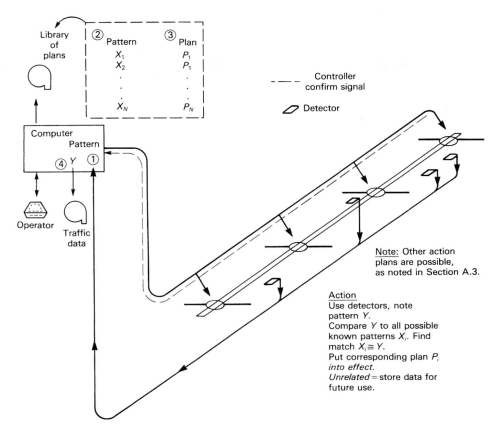

Controller
confirm signal

Detector

Note: Other action
plans are possible,
as noted in Section A.3.

Action
Use detectors, note
pattern Y.
Compare Y to all possible
known patterns X_i. Find
match $X_i \cong Y$.
Put corresponding plan P_i
into effect.
Unrelated = store data for
future use.

Figure 23-3 Computer control system with detector information used.

tions. This approach presumes an advantage to tailoring the control plan to the specific traffic data.

Note that the time between plan updates is constrained by the speed with which the on-line plan computations can be done. Further, the desire to have more frequent updates implicitly assumes that the real traffic situation can be known precisely enough to differentiate between consecutive update periods.

Some major demonstration/research computer control projects focused on the issues of time of day versus responsive control, and the frequency of plan modification in the responsive control mode, ranging from once per 15 minutes to once per 1 or 2 minutes. This is discussed later in the chapter.

Some systems introduced variations on the above, such as having a limited local responsiveness at intersections, designed to better serve individual vehicles that would be "averaged out" in any over-all prediction.

The illustration of Figure 23-3 shows one computer. As a practical matter, computers are often specialized to the task at hand; this was particularly so in the 1960s. Specifically, one computer design might be best for input-output and another design best for fast computation. Figure 23-4 highlights this by showing the extreme: distinct machines for overall control, detector monitoring, display-map service, plan computation, and data logging.

The display map has typically been a large stylized map of the system (often to scale), with colored indications showing the main-street signal indication, and other indications or display numbers showing traffic levels at detectors. The display map became a standard feature of computer control systems, for both technical purposes and for communication with the visiting public and elected officials. Computer graphic displays and large-screen displays are replacing large wall display maps as the preferred mode of communication.

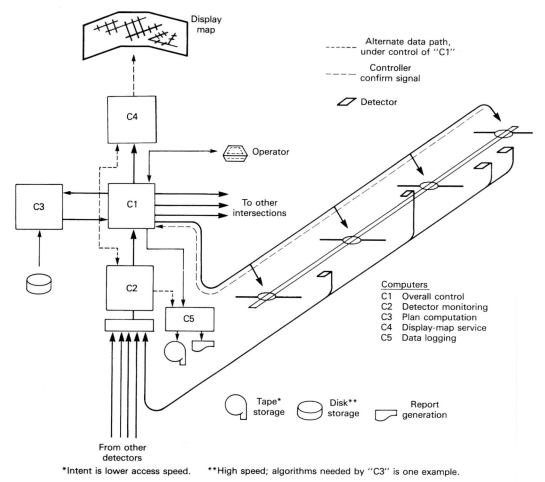

Figure 23-4   The control system of Figure 23-3, with several specialized computers for various tasks.

Issues influencing the evolution of computer control systems

To understand the current state of the art in computer control of traffic signals, as well as the evolution of systems since the 1960s, it is necessary to set a perspective:

- The computer of the early 1960s was a very expensive mainframe, based on discrete transistor technology as the major innovation. Minicomputers existed, but smaller, faster mainframes were the primary em-

phasis. Neither microprocessors nor integrated circuits (ICs) existed, nor did microcomputers.
- The cost of computers (and the expected power) oriented people to single, centralized machines.
- Future computers would be faster and even more reliable—more of the same, but better.
- The time-based controller—which might have influenced the direction of some localities—did not exist.
- The 1960s saw focus on (1) making sure the hardware worked and (2) making sure that the potential for future, more sophisticated control policies was not lost by hardware-system decisions that precluded future options.

The second part of the last item had tremendous implications for data-handling needs. With regard to a detector in the field, what had to be sent back to central for potential use, now or in the future?

Refer to Figure 23-5 for an illustration of the ways in which detector information could be "packaged" in order to save communications burden. However, any decision other than "send it all back" did run the risk of precluding a later, more advanced control policy by not being able to meet its data needs at the central location. For instance, it was not certain which variables would be needed, nor what control intervals would be used:

Variables	Control Period
Count	15 minutes
Speed	5 minutes
Occupancy	1 minute
Queue	shorter?

Further, some variables might be needed for *control*, and others for *evaluation* of performance, by computation of such *measures of effectiveness (MOEs)* as average queue size and/or overall system delay.

While these issues are still not completely resolved, *operational* systems are regularly installed that limit the information flow back to central and/or are significantly decentralized.

As the early systems were developed, there was also an underlying assumption that the quality of data observed could be refined and made more precise by the simple expedient of using a sufficient number of detectors. Several experiences have made traffic engineers more cautious in this regard:

- Even the most research-oriented facilities lack all the detectors for truly detailed observation of even traffic counts: one detectorized lane (not one detector per lane) is common.
- Quantities such as "queue at green initiation" and "queue for queue-management control" require detectors in different places (and numbers) than simple counts would dictate.
- Point detectors have severe limits in estimating vehicles in a space or over an area.
- It is extremely rare that all loop detectors will be working at any given time. Limited performance based upon the existence of failed detectors must be expected.
- New policies based on "fuzzy logic" are evolving.

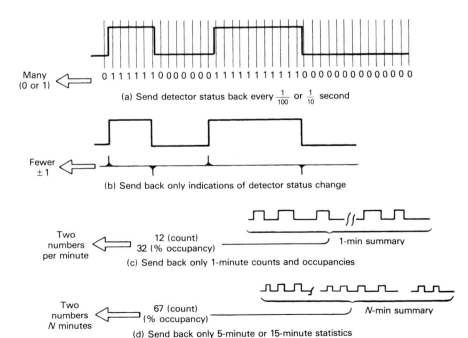

(a) Send detector status back every $\frac{1}{100}$ or $\frac{1}{10}$ second

(b) Send back only indications of detector status change

(c) Send back only 1-minute counts and occupancies

(d) Send back only 5-minute or 15-minute statistics

Figure 23-5 Different ways in which detector information can be sent to central.

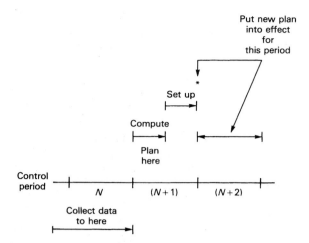

Figure 23-6 Need to compute control plan requires use of estimated (projected) traffic, not actual.

Further, there is the problem that the detector observations are not used directly, but are *projected* to a future time period (see Figure 23-6), so that the control policy computations may be done based on the estimated future traffic situation.

This reality raises questions of *observability* (how well can we "see" what is really going on in the real world?) and *controllability* (can we use the information in such a way as to exercise effective control of the network?). To date, there is no definitive work on this subject of the "limits of control."

General description of the control system

It is important to make a distinction between the *actual* traffic conditions and the *estimated* or predicted conditions. It is also important to recognize the relative roles of detection, prediction, and control.

Further, it is important to recognize that two types of controls can be used to influence the driver. These can be classified as:

- *"hard" controls,* which the driver must obey under penalty of law. These are primarily signalization (cycle length, phasing, splits, offsets), but could include turn prohibitions;
- *"soft controls,* which provide the driver with information for independent decisions, primarily related to route selection. These controls include variable

message signs, radio news, personal route guidance, and CB communications with other drivers.

These are indicated by the words *signalization* and *advisories* in Figure 23-7.

Figure 23-7 shows a generalized block diagram of the traffic control system. Each block represents a major function. The overall operation may be described as follows:

- *Traffic Network Block.* The drivers know their origin/destinations (O/Ds) and—taking into account the signalization and the condition (state) of the network—select their associated routings, resulting in the *actual flows and performance,* shown as the output or product of the Traffic Network block. The process can be influenced by special conditions, such as accidents and incidents that limit the available capacity in the network.
- *Detection System.* The input to the detection system is the actual flows and performance. However, the detectors do not *see* the true flows and other variables, but rather have some limited view, due to the nature of the detectors used.

Current technology is such that counts, speeds, occupancy, and area presence (using long loops) can be observed to varying degrees of precision and accuracy, depending on the number and placement of the point detectors in common use. Queues can also be measured with greater detection, or generated by an analytic relation dependent upon counts and/or occupancies.

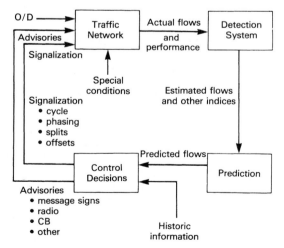

Figure 23-7 One view of the traffic process.

The output of the *Detection System* block is the *estimated flows and other indices.*

Note that the O/Ds cannot be observed directly. This is a sufficiently strong limitation of current technology that O/Ds are not even shown as an input to the detection system. Automatic vehicle identification (AVI) systems do hold the potential for deducing routings from information obtained at various points in the system.

- *Prediction.* As shown in Figure 23-6, the information used at a later stage (in the Control Decisions block) is not the estimated current flows, but rather the *predicted flows* (and other variables/indices) one or two time periods in the future. This is the function undertaken in the Prediction block.
- *Control Decisions.* The final block indicates that the input information is some combination of historic information and the predicted flows (plus other variables and indices). In this box one of the major functions is performed, the one most associated with the use of computer control—the decisions on control settings, *signalization* and *advisories,* by means of a "control policy." The control policy is an algorithm or decision process on how to use the available information in order to decide upon the control settings. The first section in this chapter discussed several basic approaches to the control policy.

As comprehensive as this block diagram might appear, it is deficient in some aspects. In particular, the block marked Traffic Network is more complex, because drivers will modify their routings based on their own perceptions of the network's performance and the controls imposed.

Figure 23-8 shows a more complete block diagram, in which the larger, more heavily outlined box provides greater detail on the driver decisions:

- *Traffic Network.* The Traffic Network produces a set of *actual travel times.*
- *User Perception.* The drivers combine their (limited) ability to observe these directly with information from the advisories (radio, personal route guidance, cell phones, CBs, and message signs) and their own experience to generate a set of *perceived travel times* as shown in the output of the User Perception block. Note that the perceived travel times need not conform to any reality. In the extreme, the driver may ignore all reports on the ac-

tual condition of other links and routes and have direct knowledge of only one link. Thus, routing decisions will be based on this somewhat distorted view of the world.

A significant issue is always the credibility of the various information sources. Are they accurate and up to date? Can they be believed? Drivers carry with them a set of perceptions that determine how seriously they take information.

- *Micro Assignment.* Based not on actual travel times, but on the distribution of perceptions, the drivers select new routings. Further, they do this continually as they take their trips through the network, with decisions being more significant at some points than others. This is the function indicated in the Micro Assignment block. While many behavioral models may be postulated, most formulations are simply based on travel times. The output of this block is a set of assigned volumes which have been located onto the network. Because this in turn influences the travel times, the actual set of computations is an *iterative* process, as indicated by the heavy arrow circling within the three boxes.

The only result seen by the real world is the *actual flows and performance,* shown as the output of the overall box. This is the input to the Detection System, as before.

While this is an interesting conceptual formulation, there is little hard information on how user perceptions are influenced by advisories provided and on how these feed a micro assignment model. At present, Figure 23-8 provides a framework, but not an operating model.

One point is very relevant for both surface street and corridor models: The drivers do not respond to "what is good for the system" but rather to what is good for their own personal trips. In general, this is somewhat different from what is good for the system.

Communications

A primary concern with traffic control by computer is the communications burden. Actually, there are two burdens—the amount of information to be transmitted, and the cost of the communications system (including leased or dedicated lines).

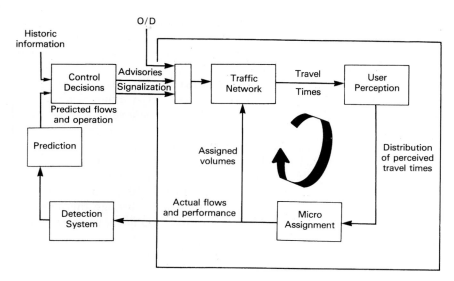

Figure 23-8 A more detailed model of the traffic process.

The issue of the amount of information to be transmitted to the central control was addressed earlier in conjunction with Figure 23-5. Even with a decision to return all information to the central location, there are several ways in which this can be done. Signals may be transmitted over a line for each signal (Figure 23-9(a)). Several signals may share a line by time-slicing the signals (time-division multiplexing, or TDM; Figure 23-9(b)). Several signals may share a line by having each signal ride on a different "carrier" frequency (frequency-division multiplexing, or FDM; Figure 23-9(c)).

The more information put onto a line, the greater is the line capacity needed. Voice-grade is perhaps the lowest-quality line; data-grade lines have higher capacity and can carry a number of "channels" of data (and are more expensive). Coaxial cable has much greater capacity and is becoming omnipresent due to cable TV (CATV) installations; leased channels on CATV have been used in several locations [1]. Fiber optics is one of the latest technologies available for use [2]. Wireless communication is also used for some applications.

Figure 23-10 shows the trend in traffic-control systems equipment cost during the 1970s [3]. Note that communications is some 20% of the total cost. In annual operating costs (as distinct from annualized capital cost), it can represent up to 40% of the bill. The communications burden in terms of cost is very significant.

Reference [1] cites a typical 1982 cost of laying telephone lines at $10 per foot, and notes that with a representative arterial length of 50,000 ft, the installation cost just for the line (excluding the communication gear) is one-half million dollars. Further, it notes that the reliability and availability problems are significant.

The issue is not just cost per foot, but number of signals that can be carried; clearly, most of the cost is installation (trenching, laying conduit, resurfacing, and so on). Fiber optics and coaxial cable have much greater channel capacity than conventional wire or data cables.

A current issue: Decentralization

The experience gained to date with computer control has moved such systems from "experimental" to "routine operational." As one looks at the use of computer control today, the following lessons emerge:

• In operational systems, it is now clear that almost all benefits can be obtained by features and policies known at the time of system installation.

• Communications costs are a very significant part of capital expenses, and often an even more significant part of operating costs.

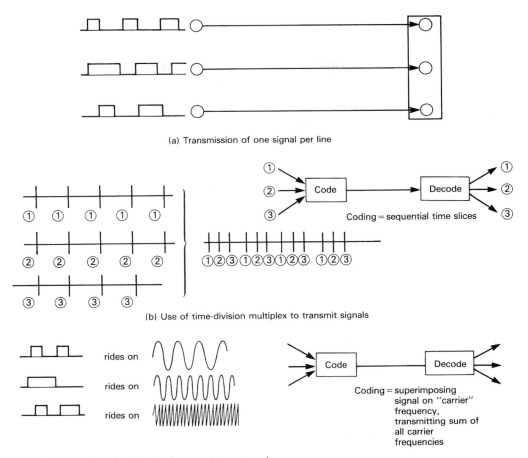

(a) Transmission of one signal per line

Coding = sequential time slices

(b) Use of time-division multiplex to transmit signals

rides on

rides on

rides on

Coding = superimposing signal on "carrier" frequency, transmitting sum of all carrier frequencies

Figure 23-9 Three methods of transmitting signals.

- The limits of detection, and the very reliability of detectors, are better understood. At least parts of the system will be degraded on any given day by the simple failure of detectors.
- The issues of system reliability and of availability of the system are of considerable importance.

At the same time, advances in technology have provided (1) less expensive, more reliable computers, (2) the ability to assign complex functions to local controllers, and (3) the ability for time-base coordination.

All these factors lead to a present trend toward *decentralized* control of computer-controlled signal systems and to a mix of subsystems. More computing is done in the field, less information is sent back to "Central," and far less communications are needed. Some "subsystems" could even consist of time-based controllers that receive their overall settings by radio from the central controller, with no wire interconnections at all. Figure 23-11 illustrates a possible configuration of a decentralized system.

While some future flexibility is lost in principle, distributed systems have the major advantage that the total system is rather immune from total failure. Further, the computing burden is simply not concentrated on one machine, which would escalate the machine requirements.

Toronto and other early projects

The earliest major project in computer control of traffic on surface streets was the Toronto, Ontario,

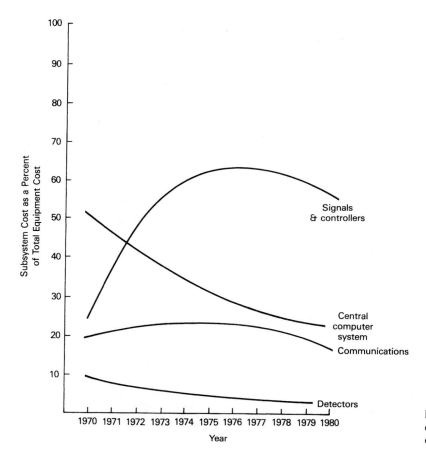

Figure 23-10 Relative costs of major equipment subsystems for a traffic control system.

system, which became operational in 1963 [4]. This system involved 864 intersections and represented one of the most comprehensive systems in the world.

Because the Toronto system was oriented to exploring various control policies, much of this section is devoted to this pioneering effort, now in operation for some 35 years. First, however, other early systems are noted.

A. Early systems, other than Toronto

In 1963, some 100 signals in West London were brought under computer control, with an 8% improvement in system operation as a result [4]. A similar system was initiated in Glasgow in 1967, with a 10% to 12% improvement in travel time over a baseline of locally actuated signals. The system began with 80 intersections and grew to some 500 intersections by 1985 [5]. Figure 23-12 shows the network initially controlled in Glasgow.

The city of Munich, Germany, reported its system operational in 1967, with 540 signals under control [6].

The improvements cited for Glasgow are for a time-of-day computer control, first with a simplified optimization for offsets and splits (12%), and then for a more complex optimization scheme (10%).

In 1965, the first system was installed in the United States, in San Jose, California. The system began with 59 intersections, and another 20 were later added. The results can be summarized as follows [4]:

Type of Control	Basis for Comparison	
	Baseline	Optimized 3-Dial
3-Dial volume actuated	11.1%	1.1%
Pattern settings by optimization scheme	14.3%	4.5%

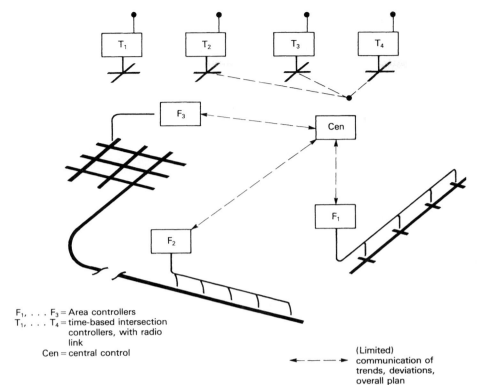

$F_1, \ldots F_3 =$ Area controllers
$T_1, \ldots T_4 =$ time-based intersection
controllers, with radio
link
Cen = central control

(Limited)
⟵ ╌ ╌ ╌ ➤ communication of
trends, deviations,
overall plan

Figure 23-11 An illustration
of a decentralized system
configuration.

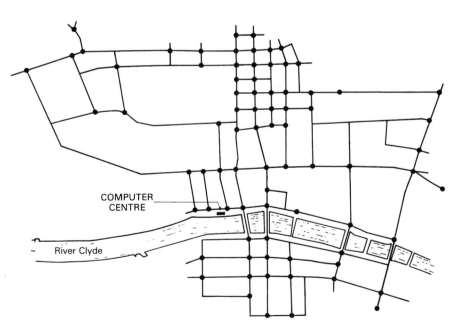

COMPUTER
CENTRE

River Clyde

Figure 23-12 The initial
network in the Glasgow area
traffic control. [Used with
permission of Printerhall Limited,
U.K., from J. Halroyland, J. A.
Hillier, "Area Traffic Control in
Glasgow," *Traffic Engineering +
Control.* Copyright © 1969
Printerhall Limited.]

The baseline was a single-dial system, timed by conventional means (no optimization program).

The City of Wichita Falls, Texas, had 77 signals under computer control in 1966. The basic policy was a library selection of plans, based on field data used to select the best match to a set of patterns for which control plans had been predetermined. Cycle-by-cycle split changes were allowed at critical intersections, based on detector observations.

The results reported for Wichita Falls include a 16.3% reduction in vehicle stops, a 31.1% decrease in average vehicle delays, and an 8.5% reduction in accidents. Further, in the peak directions, an increase of vehicle speed from about 20 mph to more than 30 mph was reported [8]. The baseline for comparison was a single-dial system in the CBD.

In even the early systems, very high benefit–cost ratios were computed based on observed improvements. Reference [4] reported that Toronto and Wichita Falls recovered their capital outlay in less than six *months,* and San Jose was estimated at six *years.*

B. Widespread use of computer control

In 1972, Reference [4] reported that nine communities in the United States had installed computer control systems, and that some 23 others were installing or studying computer control.

In 1979, Reference [9] reported on a FHWA survey that identified 201 computer control systems in the United States, either operational, under construction, or in preliminary engineering (some had no status reported). Reference [4] observed that there are additional systems not reported in that survey.

C. The Toronto system

The Toronto computer control system stands alone in its scale, pioneering effort, and success.[4] Consider the following:

- It was the first computer control system, installed in 1963, and subject to all the risks of a pioneering effort.

[4]While other projects have certainly had similar successes in terms of travel-time improvements and such, Toronto achieved its success in a large-scale pioneering effort.

- There were 864 intersections involved.
- The capital outlay was recovered within six months, in terms of user benefits.
- By 1974, the number of intersections was 1022.
- The Metropolitan Department of Roads and Traffic invested energy and professional staff in a continual upgrading and evaluation of improved control policies.
- In cooperation with other agencies within Canada, the Metropolitan Department of Roads and Traffic undertook a major effort in 1974–1976 to "study, develop, test, and evaluate existing and new traffic signal control strategies, including both off-line signal optimization techniques and real-time computer traffic responsive control concepts."

The last effort cited resulted in a series of three very substantial reports, on the state of the art [10], the evaluation of off-line strategies [11], and the development and evaluation of a real-time computerized traffic-control strategy [12].

The evaluation of off-line optimization programs in the 1974–1976 work used three computer programs judged to be the best available at the time:

1. SIGOP
2. TRANSYT
3. Combination method

These are described in References [13], [14], and [15] respectively. As of this writing, TRANSYT is now dominant, with PASSER II [42] and others also used.

The SIGOP program used an offset optimization algorithm to minimize the discrepancy between the actual offsets and a set of ideal offsets (calculated by the program or specified by the user). The TRANSYT program optimizes splits and offsets by minimizing a "network performance index" which is the sum of weighted link delays and stops, employing a traffic-flow model to generate flow patterns which include the effects of platoon dispersion. The GLC combination method determined a set of signal offsets to optimize a combination of total delay and stops, given a set of splits.

After an extensive evaluation project, the report [11] concluded that:

[I]t is doubtful whether the floating car speed and delay survey is an appropriate technique for accurately measuring on-street levels of performance . . . the field sampling rate was necessarily limited. . . .

The use of system service rates and travel times led to somewhat inconclusive results primarily due to the fact that aggregated system data tends to conceal fluctuations of volume and travel time on individual links. . . .

[T]he link performance evaluation technique seemed to have produced the most conclusive results.

These quotes are extracted because of the powerful lessons contained in them, drawn from one of the most successful computer control projects in existence: (1) it was not feasible to get enough travel-time runs to identify differences, if they existed, and (2) the system-level aggregated statistics hid some variations, simply by averaging them out.

In a related paper [16] it is stressed that:

Whichever optimization program is chosen to design urban network signal settings, it is imperative that the user have a thorough understanding of the selected program and also a comprehensive knowledge of the signal system. In addition, a commitment must be made to carefully review the program output to ascertain its validity. While these off-line signal optimization programs can be utilized as engineering aids in network signal setting design, they should not be used as replacements for engineering judgment and expertise.

The paper also cites a number of weaknesses with the SIGOP program (which is no longer in use), related to the "high number of arbitrary factors," but observes that "Despite its weaknesses, SIGOP performed surprisingly well . . . ," noting the high level of experience of the personnel making the judgments, given the history of the Toronto project.

Indeed, the three programs all performed comparably to the base condition, the existing signalization, which had been refined over years using a predecessor to SIGOP known as SIGRID. However, it was noted that TRANSYT had had greater successes elsewhere, and that:

[T]he superiority of TRANSYT was not evident from the results of the Toronto study. This is perhaps due to the fact that the program was used without prior calibration of some of the program parameters for local conditions (such as the smoothing factor used in the platoon dispersion model) . . . [T]here is sufficient reason to expect that it will perform much better if the program is calibrated.

This quote is singled out because of the stress on checking the validity of the "default values" or para-

meters in such models. Given the common use of such tools as the (later version of) TRANSYT, it is almost certain that most users do not do this systematically.

Note that although the Toronto test program did not calibrate TRANSYT to the specific locale, the results were comparable to the well-refined existing signal plan. Thus, while other users may not get the full benefit without local calibration, they will still get rather good results—if their experience is as fortunate as that in Toronto.

The Toronto work also involved the development and evaluation of an on-line optimization program known as RTOP (real-time optimization program), which is of the "second-generation" type.[5] RTOP used a 15-minute control period. The prediction algorithm uses information from three sources: historic trends, current trends, and a directional relationship (the last one is based on volume trend on a "representative" link). Further detail is contained in [12].

In the two areas in which RTOP was tested (one central, one suburban), it surpassed the existing signal plans in the central area but was much less effective in the suburban area. The factors judged to be contributory were: (1) the traffic fluctuations were sharper in the suburban area, making it harder to follow a trend, given the 15-minute period used, (2) the detector density was less in the suburban area, providing less accurate volume estimates, and (3) the larger number of signals in the suburban area led to greater computation times, sometimes exceeding the available time and thus causing the last policy to be "held over" for one more period.

UTCS, the urban traffic control system

The Urban Traffic Control System (UTCS) was an FHWA demonstration and research project in traffic-control systems, and another landmark project. The national "testbed" was Washington, DC. Reference [17] provides a good overview of the project and its impact.

---

[5]This term is defined in the next section. See Table 23-1 for the characteristic of each "generation" of control.

The stated objectives of the UTCS project were to [17]:

- develop and test, in the real world, new computer-based control strategies that would improve traffic flow
- document system planning, design, installation, operation, and maintenance to assist traffic engineers with installing their own systems
- stimulate modernization of traffic control equipment

In 1972 the system was initiated with 114 intersections under control. This was extended by 1974 to 200 intersections.

The plan was to demonstrate and evaluate three "generations" of control, each more sophisticated than its predecessor. The three generations are:

- *First generation* uses a library of prestored timing plans, each developed with off-line optimization programs. The plan selected can be based on time of day (TOD), measured traffic pattern (traffic responsive, or TRSP), or operator specification. The update period is 15 minutes.

  First generation allows critical intersection control (CIC) and has a bus priority system (BPS). For further information on the BPS, see References [18,19].

As is necessary, first generation has a signal transition algorithm. (Signal-plan transitions were addressed in Chapter 22.)

- *Second generation* uses timing plans computed in real time, based on forecasts of traffic conditions, using detector observations input into a prediction algorithm.
- *Third generation* was conceived as a highly responsive control, with a much shorter control period than second generation and without the restriction of a cycle-based system. Third generation included a queue management control at critical intersections (CIC/QMC).

Table 23-1 summarizes the principal features of the three generations of control. This terminology—"first generation" and so forth—has become pervasive in the discussion of traffic control systems.

Only the first two generations were implemented in Washington, DC, due in good part to the third-generation detectorization requirements, which exceeded the level present in the testbed.

One of the very interesting products of the overall UTCS project is the microscopic traffic simulator known as TRAF-NETSIM (named "UTCS-1" in its original form). This simulation program has been used in a variety of research and operations environments.

Table 23-1 Comparison of Key Features: Three Generations of Control

Feature	First Generation	Second Generation	Third Generation
Optimization	Off-line	On-line	On-line
Frequency of update	15 Minutes	5 Minutes	3-6 Minutes
No. of timing patterns	Up to 40 (7 used)	Unlimited	Unlimited
Traffic prediction	No	Yes	Yes
Critical intersection control	Adjusts split	Adjusts split and offset	Adjusts split, offset, and cycle
Hierarchies of control	Pattern selection	Pattern computation	Congested and medium flow
Fixed cycle length	Within each section	Within variable groups of intersections	No fixed cycle length

[From "The Urban Traffic Control System in Washington, D.C.," U.S. Department of Transportation, Federal Highway Administration, 1974.]

First-generation software was applied in New Orleans, controlling 60 intersections in an arterial environment. A time-of-day policy tested resulted in an 8.8% reduction in vehicle-minutes of travel; the traffic-responsive policy tested resulted in an 8.5% reduction [21].

The UTCS first-generation software was first coded in assembly language, but FHWA later had it coded in FORTRAN to make it more portable to other hardware systems. Some improvements were made to the basic first-generation software and tested in Charlotte, North Carolina. This led to the "extended" version of first generation, which became operational in Charlotte in 1978. The software became the official FHWA-supported version of UTCS for a number of years and was known as the "UTCS First Generation FORTRAN IV Overlay Software (Extended Version)" [22].

In 1977, FHWA initiated the first-generation "enhanced" project. Reference [24] provides a functional description of the enhanced UTCS software, circa 1979. The enhanced software was tested in Broward County, Florida (1982), and Birmingham, Alabama (1984). In May of 1985, FHWA distributed a policy statement on the support for the UTCS-Enhanced software [see 23].

The policy statement indicated, among other things, that FHWA will *not* further enhance the software or documentation and that the private sector will likely develop and maintain versions of their own. This is consistent with a trend in the 1980s that the federal government disengage from areas in which it might compete with the private sector.

The second generation of UTCS has not been developed by FHWA, akin to the first generation. However, documentation does exist for second-generation extended software, which has been installed in Overland Park, Kansas [25].

As of 1984, some 40 cities had, or were planning on having, UTCS-based systems [17].

Projects throughout the world[6]

The preceding sections have emphasized the work in North America (Canada and the United States) and

[6]Much of this section is due to E. Lieberman of KLD Associates, Huntington Station, NY, and is used with his permission.

some of the pioneering projects in the early 1960s. There have also been other significant projects undertaken in

- Great Britain
- Australia
- Spain
- Japan
- Germany
- France

These are addressed in this section.

A. Great Britain

The initial projects in West London and Glasgow have already been cited.

More recent developments, implemented in Glasgow and Coventry, have concentrated on adaptive control. The method known as SCOOT (split, cycle and offset optimization technique) is designed to minimize congestion [26]. The basic philosophy of this method is adjustment of signal timing in small, frequent intervals. SCOOT uses the signal-optimization logic previously developed for the TRANSYT signal-timing program [27]. Detector data is stored in the computer in terms of "cyclic flow profiles" [28]—that is, histograms of traffic-flow variation over a signal cycle. These "profiles" are used to develop a timing pattern that achieves the optimum degree of coordination. Detectors are located at the upstream end of key links; the measured occupancy of these detectors indicates queue lengths that may become critical. This information is then used to adjust signal timing so as to reduce the likelihood of the queue's blocking the upstream junctions. The TRRL report on the SCOOT program concludes:

> At its present stage of development, the traffic responsive SCOOT method of signal coordination is likely to achieve savings in delay which average about 12 percent compared to control by a high standard of up-to-date fixed time plans. . . . SCOOT is likely to be most effective where traffic demands are heavy and approach the maximum capacity of the junctions where the demands are variable and unpredictable and where the distances between junctions are short. SCOOT is likely to give further benefits compared to fixed time plans which, as is often the case, are out of date. Although the evidence is limited, it would appear that the delay reductions achieved by SCOOT are likely to double from 12 to over

20 percent when the fixed time plans are from 3 to 5 years old.

B. Australia

Australia shares, with the United States and England, the lead in theoretical and conceptual development for network computer traffic control under congested conditions. For instance, A. J. Miller [29] has developed some of the basic approaches for both intersection and network control. Although originally developed for undersaturated conditions, the method of approach has been found useful in the development of control strategies for the congested regime. The most significant development in the implementation of computer control signal systems in Australia has been in Sydney.

The Sydney Co-ordinated Adaptive Traffic (SCAT) System is a distributed-intelligence, three-level, hierarchical system using microprocessors and minicomputers [30]. The system is capable of real-time adjustment of cycle, split, and offset in response to detected variations in demand and capacity. It is designed to calibrate itself.

For control purposes, the total system is divided into a large number of comparatively small subsystems varying from one to ten intersections. This system configuration is in software. As far as possible, the subsystems are chosen to be traffic entities, and for many traffic conditions they will run without relation to each other. As traffic conditions demand, the subsystems "marry" with adjacent subsystems to form a number of larger systems or one large system. This "marriage" of subsystems is calculated in much the same way as are the interrelationships between intersections within a subsystem. Thus, there is a hierarchy of control as distinct from a hardware hierarchy.

Recent improvements in the control algorithms are designed to lead to improved real-time evaluation of both changes in offset patterns and the marriage of adjacent subsystems. The effects of possible changes in both intra- and intersubsystems' offset patterns are evaluated using actual volumes, and bandwidth parameters based on progression at free speeds [31].

If the degree of saturation exceeds a preset level (i.e., congested flow), cycle length is increased, with the additional time assigned to the phase showing saturation. At the same time, coordination will be forced into operation if congestion due to critical queues is imminent. There is no direct critical-queue detection; the system philosophy depends on detectors near the stop line. Critical queues are inferred from the detection of excessive decreases in flow at upstream intersections.

C. Spain

Two-level, hierarchical, fully adaptive computer traffic-control systems have been implemented in Barcelona [32] and Madrid [33]. At the higher level, cycles are selected, subareas defined, and coordination sequences established. At the lower level, within each subarea, offsets and splits are computed. Maximal bandwidth techniques [34] are used for undersaturated conditions. For saturated (congested) traffic flow, delays and stops are optimized by an algorithm, which assumes equal distribution of traffic over the entire green part of the signal cycle for every intersection. The algorithm selects optimum offsets for every pair of intersections and the associated split.

A check is made on resulting queue length and on the speed of backward propagation of the queue to determine possible conflicts (blockage). If such is the case, the optimal offset is modified iteratively, until an offset is found that results in the longest permissible queue. Signal splits are optimized through a minimum-delay criterion and adjusted to reflect route and network effects. Green time may thus be reduced to diminish the probability of excessive queues at downstream intersections or when excessive queues are noted by occupancy detectors.

D. Japan

The world's largest computer-controlled signal system—ultimate size, 8000 intersections—is being installed in Tokyo [35]. Large-scale systems are being installed in other Japanese cities; the Osaka and Nagoya systems will also, ultimately, control well in excess of 1000 intersections [36]. These systems use a number of different control criteria ranging from minimizing stops under light traffic conditions to maximizing capacity when traffic demand is heavy. The control mode is assigned on the basis of the degree of congestion computed from detector volume and occupancy data. Splits are selected on the basis of volume ratios and modified so as to balance queue lengths on all approaches. Offsets are adjusted in response to the derivative of delay with respect to offset. The computer-controlled signal system is a part of an integrated TSM system that also includes advisory routing information using radio, telephone, and changeable message signs.

E. Germany

The major effort at computerized network signal control in Germany is the PBIL system installed, for a full-scale field test, in Aachen [37]. The PBIL system operates by minimizing delay, which is defined as the difference between actual travel time and expected travel time under free-flow conditions. When critical queue lengths on the approaches to critical intersec-

tions are exceeded, the delay for the critical approach input into the optimizing algorithm is artificially increased and the critical intersection and the immediately adjacent related one (star network) are taken out of the system. The control algorithm then determines splits and offsets so as to minimize delay for this network.

F. France

Although a great deal of theoretical development work on congestion control has been done in France [e.g., 38], only one network computer-controlled signal system has been installed. This system, in Bordeaux, uses 1-GC control but is noteworthy for the extensive amount of traffic metering included [39].

Summary

This chapter has provided an overview of the principles and issues related to the use of computers to control traffic-signal systems; many of these remarks are also relevant to the control of traffic in freeway corridors.

This chapter has also provided information on the range of projects that have been implemented since the early 1960s, when Toronto made its pioneering effort.

Table 23-2 presents a list of benefits that can accrue to the drivers and to the overall community by the implementation of computer control.

Even though "effect on vehicle" and "fuel consumption" could have been listed under the more encompassing—and more common—heading of "vehicle operating costs," this was not done, because reduction in fuel consumption is *more* than a simple cost savings to the driver. Therefore, a summary might

Table 23-2 List of Benefits That Can be Attributed to Traffic Computer Control

	Quantitative	Qualitative

Motorist	+ Effect on vehicle:
	  number of stops
	  idle time
	+ Fuel consumption
	+ Travel-time savings
	+ Safety
		+ Smoother trip

Community	+ Energy-consumption reduction + Reduced total travel time for given VMT	+ Emissions + Noise + Public image

contain an estimate of total gallons saved, as well as the economic benefit to the driver.[7]

[7]As an aside, it is interesting to consider "minimize fuel consumption" as an explicit objective in a control system. While such an objective can be related to stops and delay, the relative weighting is not the same as is sometimes used for economic analysis or for driver preference. Indeed, Reference [40] addresses such an objective for a single intersection. One might be tempted to apply this object at all intersections. *This would be an error.* Reference [41] demonstrates that fuel consumption on a trip or through a network is directly correlated to the trip travel time. Thus, the minimization of fuel consumption is equivalent to the minimization of total travel time in the network.

Table 23-3 shows some of the advantages of computer control systems, *given four alternative centralized-control scenarios.* The emphasis is placed on "centralized control" because distributed control may have additional advantages not shown, such as reliability and availability.

The percentage X_i shown in Table 23-3 is intentionally left unspecified. On a scale of 100%, what should be the value of X_i%, given the list of advantages cited? Problems 23–1 to 23–3 at the end of the chapter address some of the issues underlying this table.

Table 23-3   Benefits of Computer Control, Related to System Sophistication

Benefit	Most Basic	First	Second	Third
+ Signal coordination				
+ Change timing easily				
+ Equipment status				
+ Monitor performance of repair crews	↓ X_1%			
+ Data collection for future policies		↓ X_2%		
+ Responsiveness to major variations			↓ X_3%	
+ Responsive to all variations (highly responsive)				↓ X_4%
Detector needs	None	Low	Moderate	High

*Terms are defined based on usage in UTCS.

References

1. Basnett, M. S., "CATV for Traffic Control System Interconnect: A Big Difference on the Budgetary Bottom Line," *ITE Journal,* June 1982.
2. Russo, R., "Fiber Optics Technology in Communications," *ITE Journal,* March 1985.
3. Cimento, A. A., "Traffic Control Systems Hardware," *Proceedings of the International Symposium on Traffic Control Systems,* Report UCB-ITS-P-79-2, U.S. Department of Transportation, Washington, DC, August 1979.
4. Stockfish, C. R., *Selecting Digital Computer Signal Systems,* Report No. FHWA-RD-72-20, U.S. Department of Transportation, Federal Highway Administration, Washington, DC, 1972.
5. Mowatt, A. M., and Young, A. D., "CITRAC—The First Five Years," *ITE Journal,* May 1985.
6. Bolke, W., "Munich's Traffic Control Centre," *Traffic Engineering and Control,* September 1967.
7. Holroyd, J., and Hillier, J. A., "Area Traffic Control in Glasgow," *Traffic Engineering and Control,* September 1969.

8. Wilshire, R. L., "The Benefits of Computer Traffic Control," *Traffic Engineering,* April 1969.

9. *CCSAG Newsletter,* Vol. 2, No. 4, Institute of Transportation Engineers, Washington, DC, December 1979.

10. *Improved Operation of Urban Transportation Systems: Volume 1, Traffic Signal Control Strategies, A State-of-the-Art,* Metropolitan Toronto Department of Roads and Traffic, Toronto, Canada, March 1974.

11. *Improved Operation of Urban Transportation Systems: Volume 2, The Evaluation of Off-Line Area Traffic Control Strategies,* Metropolitan Toronto Department of Roads and Traffic, Toronto, Canada, November 1975.

12. *Improved Operation of Urban Transportation Systems: Volume 3, The Development and Evaluation of a Real-Time Computerized Traffic Control Strategy,* Metropolitan Toronto Department of Roads and Traffic, Toronto, Canada, November 1976.

13. *SIGOP: Traffic Signal Optimization Program, User's Manual,* NTIS PB-182-835, U.S. Bureau of Public Roads, 1968.

14. Robertson, D.I., "TRANSYT: A Traffic Network Study Tool," *Report LR 253,* Road Research Laboratory, Crowthorne, Berkshire, U.K., 1969.

15. Huddart, K., and Turner, E., "Traffic Signal Progressions—GLC Combination Method," *Traffic Engineering and Control,* Vol. 11, No. 7, November 1969.

16. Rach, L., et al., "An Evaluation of Off-Line Traffic Signal Optimization Techniques," prepared for 54th Annual TRB Meeting, Washington, DC, 1975.

17. Stockfish, C. R., "The UTCS Experience," *Public Roads,* Vol. 48, No. 1, June 1984.

18. Raus, J., "Urban Traffic Control/Bus Priority System (UTCS/BPS): A Status Report," *Public Roads,* Vol. 38, No. 4, March 1975.

19. MacGowan, J., and Fullerton, I. J., "Development and Testing of Advanced Control Strategies in the Urban Traffic Control System," *Public Roads,* Vol. 43, No. 3, December 1979.

20. *The Urban Traffic Control System in Washington, D.C.,* U.S. Department of Transportation, Federal Highway Administration, Washington, DC, September 1974.

21. "Application of UTCS First Generation Control Software in New Orleans," *Final Report,* FHWA-RD-78-3, U.S. Department of Transportation, Federal Highway Administration, Washington, DC, January 1978.

22. "Urban Traffic Control System First Generation FORTRAN IV Overlay Software (Extended Version)," *Executive Summary, Report No. FHWA-TS-79-222,* U.S. Department of Transportation, Federal Highway Administration, Washington, DC, May 1979.

23. "Functional Description: Enhanced First Generation Software," *Technology Sharing Report FHWA-TS-79-228,* U.S. Department of Transportation, Federal Highway Administration, Washington, DC, August 1979.

24. "FHWA Announces Policy on Support of the UTCS-Enhanced Software," CCSAG Newsletter, *ITE Journal,* July 1985.

25. Kessman, R. W., *Overland Park Traffic Control System Software Documentation,* Contract No. DTFH61-82-00004, Federal Highway Administration, Washington, DC, July 1983.

26. Hunt, P. B., et al., "SCOOT—A Traffic Responsive Method of Coordinating Signals," *TRRL Report 1014,* Road Research Laboratory, Crowthorne, Berkshire, England, 1981.

27. Robertson, D. I., "TRANSYT: A Traffic Network Study Tool," *Report LR 253,* Road Research Laboratory, Crowthorne, Berkshire, U.K., 1969.

28. Robertson, D. I., "Cyclic Flow Profiles," *Traffic Engineering and Control,* Vol. 15, No. 4, June 1974.

29. Miller, A. J., "A Computer Control System for Traffic Networks," *Proceedings of the Second International Symposium on the Theory of Traffic Flow,* London, U.K., 1963, OECD, Paris, France, 1965.

30. Sims, A. G., and Dobinson, K. W., "S.C.A.T.—The Sydney Coordinated Adaptive Traffic System—Philosophy and Benefits," in *Proceedings of the International Symposium on Traffic Control Systems,* Vol. 2B, University of California, Berkeley, CA, 1979.

31. Luk, J. Y. K., and Sims, A. G., "Selection of Offsets for Sub-Area Linkage in SCATS," *Australian Road Research,* Vol. 12, No. 2, June 1982.

32. Garcia Roman, J., Lopez Montejano, A., and Sanchez Hernandez, D., "New Area Traffic Control System in the City of Barcelona," in *Traffic Control and Transportation Systems,* American Elsevier Publishing, New York, NY, 1974.

33. Guehrer, H. H., "Area Traffic Control—Madrid," *Proceedings of the First International Symposium on Traffic Control,* IFAC/IFIP, Versailles, France, 1970.

34. Little, J. D., Martin, B. V., and Morgan, J. T., *Synchronizing Traffic Signals for Maximal Bandwidth,* Department of Civil Engineering, Massachusetts Institute of Technology, Cambridge, MA, 1969.

35. Inose, H., Okamoto, H., and Yumoto, N., "A Multi-Computer Urban Traffic Control and Surveillance System in Tokyo," in *Traffic Control and Transportation Systems,* American Elsevier Publishing, New York, NY, 1974.

36. Hasegawa, T., "Traffic Control Systems in Japan," in *Research Directions in Computer Control of Urban Traffic Systems,* ASCE, New York, NY, 1979.

37. Albrecht, H., and Phillips, P., "Ein Programmsystem zur verkehrsabhaengingen Signalsteuerung nach dem

Verfahren der Signalprogrammbildung (PBIL)," *Strassenbau und Strassenverkehrstechnic, Heft 240,* Bundesminister fuer Verkehr, Bonn, W. Germany, 1977.

38. Ministere des Transports, *Traitement de la Saturation: Approche theorique et applications pr.atiques,"* Center d'Etudes des Transports Urbains, Bagneux, France, 1982.

39. Morrish, D. W., "Area Traffic Control in Bordeaux: A Contrast with British Practice," *Traffic Engineering and Control,* Vol. 21, No. 8/9, August 1980.

40. Courage, Parapar, "Delay and Fuel Consumption at Traffic Signals," *ITE Journal,* November 1975.

41. Evans, L., Herman, R., and Lam, T., *Gasoline Consumption in Urban Traffic,* Society of Automative Engineers, Detroit, MI, February 23-27, 1976.

42. *PASSER II-90 Microcomputer User's Guide,* distributed by the McTrans Center, Gainesville, FL, 1991.

Problems

Problem 23–1

Refer to Table 23-3. Consider the following, simply as a starting position:

$$X_1 = 85\%, \qquad X_2 = 90\%, \qquad X_3 = 95\%, \qquad X_4 = 97\%$$

(a) Present logical arguments as to the circumstances under which X_1 could be as high as 85%.

(b) Is it meaningful to suggest that even the third generation of control cannot achieve 100% of the advantages that could accrue, as is implicit in the statement that $X_4 = 97\%$?

Problem 23–2

Refer to Table 23-3.

(a) Is it plausible that all advantages listed could be expressed in quantitative, real-dollar impacts? That is, can you trace the cost implications of each of the listed advantages?

(b) Do they appear as "benefits" or "costs" in the typical economic analysis?

Problem 23–3

Refer to Table 23-3, with full appreciation that each of the systems listed is oriented to *centralized computer control.*

(a) What advantages must be added to the list in order to add one or more decentralized systems to the alternatives and obtain a fair comparison?

(b) Is a simple addiction of other advantages sufficient, or must you restructure the analysis in order to obtain a meaningful comparison?

(c) Are the advantages or other items you listed in **(a)** and **(b)** quantifiable? If quantifiable, can they be translated to dollar cost items in an economic analysis?

Problem 23–4

The last footnote in the chapter suggests that a network with each intersection optimized in accord with [40] is not the optimal solution for the total system. Further, it suggests that the proper system function to minimize is total travel time, based upon the findings in [41]. Analyze these suggestions and either confirm them or refute them, using sound reasoning and any necessary analytic support.

24

Arterial Design and Management

This chapter looks at the arterial as an overall facility, and concentrates on its functional design, the proper performance measure, and its management. Some operational aspects are introduced in the context of the overall management of the facility. As part of the attention to facility management, such topics as one-way street systems, HOV and other special use lanes, and bus priority are introduced.

The initial emphasis, however, is on *functional* design, and not the physical design of the facility according to AASHTO policies, which are addressed in the AASHTO Green Book. The chapter begins with some design guidelines articulated by Kramer.

Kramer's concept of an ideal suburban arterial

In a paper that could serve as a classic position paper on the proper design and operation of a suburban arterial, Kramer [1] enumerates two design principles that he maintains are *essential* to be adopted and followed at *all* intersections of a suburban arterial with public streets and private driveways, in addi-

tion to standard AASHTO, FHWA, and other applicable criteria:

Principle 1

. . . establish an absolute minimum percentage of green time that will be displayed to arterial through traffic. At every location where all crossing or entering (design year) traffic volumes cannot be accommodated within the remaining percent of green time allocated to those movements, *a full or partial grade separation is mandated.*

Principle 2

All locations having traffic movements that will be permitted to fully cross both directions of the arterial at grade, or otherwise cause both directions of the arterial to stop simultaneously, *must be predetermined before reconstruction* and a series of signal cycle lengths preestablished that will provide for full-cycle and/or half-cycle offsets for these critical at-grade intersections over the design life of the facility.

The same principles could apply to higher class urban arterials.

Kramer observed that at-grade crossings of the arterial should involve indirect turning movements, and that this should be assured by raised median barriers.

The second principle stated by Kramer is the one advocated throughout this text: The signal spacing dominates all other considerations, and the cycle length must be picked to be in harmony with the signal spacing (i.e., the geometry).

Kramer also identifies ten characteristics of an ideal suburban arterial:

1. Its three or four lanes in each direction of travel would receive a minimum of two-thirds to three-fourths of the signal cycle as green time at all intersections encountered along its entire length.
2. Each direction of travel would be signalized for progressive movement so that traffic would simultaneously flow as smoothly in each direction as if it were two parallel one-way streets.
3. Through traffic would be protected (by signalization) from conflicting left turns from the opposing direction.
4. Direct left turns would be provided from the arterial at frequent intervals, and would be protected by signalization from conflicting through traffic movements from the opposing direction.
5. The facility would accommodate all maneuvers of increased truck sizes and combinations.
6. Pedestrians crossing this arterial would be provided protected signal phasing and be free from (lawful) conflict with any vehicular traffic crossing their path; and the spacing of pedestrian crossings would be so convenient as to discourage pedestrian crossing at unprotected locations.
7. The facility would also provide for transit operations that would not impede through traffic movement at any bus stop.
8. Transit bus operations would be enhanced by providing stops at all convenient locations in close proximity to protected pedestrian crossings.
9. The geometric design of the facility would accommodate the infusion of additional major traffic generators with minimal adverse effect to the road user; i.e., through traffic could continue to receive a minimum of two-thirds to three-fourths of the signal cycle as arterial green time.
10. Signalization timing and offset programs for this arterial would be independently variable for each direction to take into account changes in traffic volumes, provide for special event (stadium) traffic, and accommodate an uninterrupted flow for

emergency vehicles having on-board preemption equipment.

Moreover, Kramer holds that all of these characteristics can be provided at reasonable construction costs within the existing right of way for typical divided suburban arterials, allowing that some spot acquisitions (taking of land) might be needed.

The great significance of Kramer's concept, and the reason that the authors have highlighted it, is that it provides a design philosophy for an entire class of facilities. Moreover, this class of facilities is of great importance in coming years, due to these factors:

- the decentralization (relative to the historic urban CBD focus) of employment and other activities into "megacenters" throughout suburbs and outlying areas, in effect giving rise to sets of interrelated small cities linked by the facilities addressed by Kramer
- the related importance of bidirectional levels of service, as discussed later in this chapter

Arterial performance

Arterial level of service in the *HCM* is based on the *average travel speed* of the *through* vehicles for the segment, section, or entire arterial under consideration. This is the basic measure of performance. There is no numeric computation of "arterial capacity"; capacity is defined at intersections and other critical points.

The average running time may be computed from

$$\text{ART SPD} = \frac{3600(\text{length})}{(\text{running time per mile})(\text{length}) + (\text{total of intersection approach delay})} \quad [24\text{-}1]$$

where: ART SPD = arterial or segment average travel speed, mph
length = arterial or segment length, miles
running time per mile = total of the running time per mile on all segments in the arterial or section, sec

total intersection = total of the approach
approach delay   delay at all intersections
              within the defined
              arterial or section, sec
              (This is easily related to
              stopped delay)

The 3600 is the conversion factor to compute ART SPD in miles per hour.

In special cases, there may be unusual midblock delays due to pedestrian crosswalks at which vehicles must regularly stop. There may be other such factors. Such delays may be added as a third term in the denominator of Equation [24-1].

The average travel speed is strongly influenced by the number of signals per mile and the average intersection delay. On a given facility, such factors as inappropriate signal timing, poor progression, and increasing traffic flow can substantially degrade the arterial LOS. Arterials with high signal densities are even more susceptible to these factors. Arterial LOS D will probably be observed even before substantial intersection problems, but both such problems and even poorer Arterial LOS values are not far behind arterial LOS D.

The arterial levels of service are defined in Table 24-1.

Table 24-1 Arterial Levels of Service

	Arterial Class		
	I	**II**	**III**
Range of free-flow speeds (mph)	45 to 35	35 to 30	35 to 25
Typical free-flow speed (mph)	40 mph	33 mph	27 mph

Level of Service	**Average Travel Speed (mph)**		
A	≥35	≥30	≥25
B	≥28	≥24	≥19
C	≥22	≥18	≥13
D	≥17	≥14	≥ 9
E	≥13	≥10	≥ 7
F	<13	<10	< 7

[Used with permission of Transportation Research Board, National Research Council, Washington, DC, from *Highway Capacity Manual, Special Report 209,* 3rd Ed., p. 11-4. Copyright © 1994 Transportation Research Board.]

The through vehicle is the measure

The *HCM* defines arterial performance in terms of *through* vehicles. This is appropriate, given the primary function of an arterial, namely moving through vehicles.[1,2]

As part of [3], one of the authors had a number of TRAF-NETSIM simulations done, with the average speed of all vehicles and of through vehicles *only* being reported. Figure 24-1 shows some of these results. In this figure, arterial vehicles that just joined the arterial (by upstream turn-in) or are leaving (by left or right turn) are *not* included as through vehicles even if they are part of the same lane group.

Vehicles that have just entered an arterial can expect a different (and poorer) treatment in the first arterial link, just as they can expect a different (and poorer) treatment in their last arterial link, as they seek to turn off the arterial. Therefore, the measure should reflect only the *true* "through" portion of their trip:

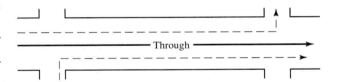

The differences are most interesting. As shown in Figure 24-1, the average travel speed of the through vehicles even in a very simple case is some 4–5 mph higher than the average travel speed of all vehicles.

The implication for the *HCM* is strong, because the intent of the arterial quality of flow measure is to focus on the through traffic, the defined users of arterials. If the arterial users have an average travel speed some 4–5 mph higher than that predicted by the *HCM*, then they are in reality getting a better level of service than the *HCM* predicts.

[1]Nonetheless, the *HCM* uses a delay formula for all lane group possibilities. Even when applied to a lane group with *only* through lanes, some of the included vehicles could have just joined the group, and be out of sync.
[2]Further, TRAF-NETSIM's standard speed measure includes all arterial vehicles.

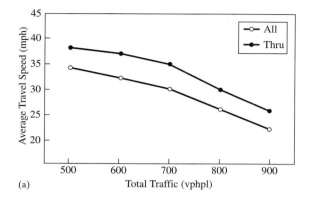

(a)

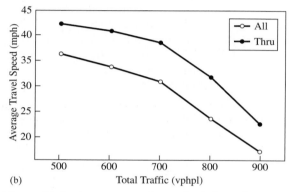

(b)

Figure 24-1 Average travel speed of through versus all vehicles, an illustration. [From W. McShane, et al., "Insights into Access Management Details Using TRAF-NETSIM," presented at the Second National Conference on Access Management, 1996.]

Looked at another way, if the intent is that the arterial users achieve a certain average travel speed (say 40 mph), then they can do this at higher flow rates than previously thought, because they are traveling faster than the average as computed in the *HCM* or by such tools as NETSIM.

Another immediate implication is that certain disruptions—driveways on the mainline—can cause the level of service to degrade even faster than previously thought, because the average travel speed of the real through (non-driveway, non-turning) traffic is very sensitive to these disruptions. *After the work in [3] is digested, it may well be that more traffic is allowed on an arterial for a given level of service, but that disruptions in the form of poorly placed or too numerous driveways are even more strongly discouraged.*

Signal spacing in a planning context

The emphasis on the importance of *signal spacing* and *signal coordination* in the treatment of this chapter introduces factors not explicitly considered in many planning analyses, but now incorporated into the *HCM* [2]. Two of the authors participated in Florida's consideration of these issues in its planning guidelines. Actually, the concept of arterial quality of flow helps to bring into focus several arterial planning issues:

1. The arterial function must be preserved. To preserve this function in the face of development over a period of many years, it may be necessary to have the through traffic segregated from the local traffic and from the land-use access. This might mean reserving sufficient right-of-way width. This also implies that the arterial class must be preserved.

2. The signal spacing must not be compromised. An equation later in the chapter makes it clear that increases in the number of signals per mile can degrade the arterial performance, or—at the very least—put very stringent demands on intersection performance.

There is another aspect of numbers of signals per mile, which has to do with the interaction of link spacing, platoon speeds, and cycle length. This was discussed in Chapter 22: Arbitrary placement of new signalized intersections can destroy the ability to progress vehicle platoons in both directions on an arterial.

Given the growth of "megacenters" imbedded within suburban or urban areas, the argument can be made that future arterials are less likely to have highly directional flows (A.M. inbound, P.M. outbound) than today's arterials, thus making the need for bidirectional coordination even more important.

3. Signal coordination is at least as important as some physical improvements. Cases in this chapter will show that intersection level of service can vary by two levels in some cases, due solely to the quality of progression. This is not atypical, and can be extended to arterial level of service easily.

Thus, in evaluating the state of arterials in a road system as regards traffic performance, it is not sufficient to look only at *v/c* ratios: These are important but do not tell the whole story. It is also important to know that the arterial has coordination equipment, and to know the level of coordination in effect. The addition and use of coordination hardware can become as important in delivering arterial quality of flow as lane additions in some cases. Unfortunately, as long as information on coordination and its use is absent from the arterial system data base, remedies must be skewed toward solely physical improvements.

A spreadsheet can be used as an efficient basis for investigating some of these issues, simply by making a number of test runs. Recall that

$$DHV = (K)(D)(AADT) \qquad [24\text{-}2]$$

where *DHV* is the design-hour volume, *K* is the design-hour factor (the fraction of daily traffic in the design hour), *D* is the directionality factor, and the *AADT* is the average annual daily traffic.

It is also possible to create a sheet that will compute the average travel speeds for a range of conditions. The volumes may be related to *AADT* by Equation [24-2].

With additional work, it is also possible to use a spreadsheet format to find the volumes (and thus the *AADT*s) for which the average travel speed "breakpoints" from one level of service to another occur. This too was done, with the following conditions specified, based on representative values for a Class I arterial in Florida (they can be changed in the spreadsheet format):

	Default Used
Arrival type	4
Cycle length	120 sec
g/C	0.50
K	0.09
D	0.58
PHF	0.92
Left turns	7%
Saturation flow rate (per lane)	1700

Pretimed signals and left turn bays were assumed.

The results shown in Table 24-2 are illustrative, powerful indicators of the import of the role of signal spacing in affecting the arterial quality of flow: As the number of signals per mile decreases from five to two, the permitted *AADT* increases by 16% to 23% (depending on number of lanes per direction); level of service C simply cannot be attained with five signals per mile. The effect of quality of progression can be studied in a similar way. Note that because this sketch planning explicitly considers both *signal spacing and quality of progression,* specific assumptions or statements must be made about them. Even more important, the planner must face decisions on the representative values of such factors as the "quality of progression"; this may involve a policy statement on the level of signal coordination expected on the state's arterials, by arterial class and function.

Although not obvious from the information presented, there are at least two major implications of adopting a table such as shown in Table 24-2: (1) The information with which to properly use the table should exist in the arterial data base, and (2) the perception of how much of the state's road system is rated in need of attention can be significantly altered by the *AADT* levels found.

With regard to the first point, note that the proper use of a table such as Table 24-2 requires knowledge of

Geometrics:
  number of lanes
  link lengths
Traffic:
  AADT
  K and *D* factors
Signalization:
  C and *g/C*
  quality of progression

The last category is generally most absent from such data bases.

With regard to the second point, it is important to realize the distinction between *perception and reality:* If as a result of applying the best state-of-the-art method, the percent of the system rated "in need of attention" increases from 20% to 30%, does this mean that the percent so rated has grown overnight? Or does it mean that we now properly perceive reality, that it was indeed 30% but we simply did not know it?

The authors are inclined to the latter view. At the same time, they recognize that this does place a burden of explanation on those who must write annual "state of the system" reports issued to local and state officials and to the public. It also may require some special explanation to other agencies that share in the

Table 24-2 Illustrative Table of Maximum AADT Levels for Indicated Arterial Levels of Service

Key Assumptions: $K = 0.09$ $D = 0.58$

Lanes per Direction	Signalized Intersections per Mile	Arrival Type	Maximum AADT for Indicated Arterial Level of Direction (Primary Direction)		
			C	D	E
1	5	4	*	11,100	14,200
1	4	4	8400	12,900	15,300
1	3	4	11,700	14,700	16,300
1	2	4	14,800	16,400	17,500
1	1	4	17,200	18,500	19,800
2	5	4	*	23,600	29,900
2	4	4	17,300	27,300	31,700
2	3	4	24,700	30,800	33,300
2	2	4	30,800	33,500	35,500
2	1	4	34,900	37,400	39,900
3	5	4	*	36,300	45,900
3	4	4	26,300	42,100	48,200
3	3	4	38,100	47,000	50,300
3	2	4	47,100	50,600	53,600
3	1	4	52,700	56,200	60,000

Other assumptions: $C = 120$ sec; $g/C = 0.50$; $PHF = 0.92$; left turns = 7%; saturation flow rate (per lane) = 1700.
*Cannot be achieved.

funding of improvements on facilities rated "in need of attention."

Fortunately, the best explanation rests with the fact that the underlying procedures represent the best state-of-the-art knowledge, and—as a very practical matter—also represent the fact that the state of the art is catching up with the best knowledge and practice. In the case of signalized intersections, this means recognizing that drivers use delay at signals as their primary measure of performance, not v/c ratios. In the case of arterials, this means incorporating the reality that numbers of signals per mile and signal coordination influence the quality of the trip.

An overall approach to arterial management

Five basic elements will be discussed in this section, building on Kramer's principles and guidelines:

- Advance planning
- Design and design elements
- Redesign as part of rehabilitation work
- Reallocation of arterial space as needed
- Other aspects of operation

These elements are used for the purpose of assuring the arterial function, namely the efficient movement of *through* traffic.

A. Advance planning

Two aspects of advance planning must be addressed:

1. Preserving the arterial function
2. Future need for two-way operation

1. Preserving the arterial function. It is essential to learn from prior experience. Perhaps the most important lesson is that a state or regional arterial system can be put in place, only to be degraded over time by localized growth in communities along its route. To preserve the arterial function in the face of such growth, it is necessary to think in terms of:

- *separating local frictions* from arterial traffic, where "local frictions" include parking, double parking, land access, deliveries, and perhaps local bus service
- *providing alternate means* in the initial plan to meet all of these future needs, lest the pressure to "accommodate" them in the future become unbearable
- *allowing for efficient platooned movement* by proper signal spacing on two-way arterials and by use of one-way pairs
- *removing built-in frictions* such as left turns across competing flows, by use of one-way facilities and by design features such as turn lanes in the median (to allow EB lefts to become WB rights, for instance)

This advance planning may influence not only the basic layout of various routes, but also the right of way needed for full development of some facilities (particularly two-way arterials). Refer to Figure 24-2, which shows an innovative and a standard treatment of a shopping center driveway.

2. Future need for two-way operation. Historically, arterials have served "tidal flow": The A.M. peak period is inbound, and the P.M. is outbound. Generally, traffic engineers and others think of arterials in these terms, and impacts are assessed (sometimes implicitly) in these terms.

In fact, the directional split has been changing over the years. The development of distributed centers in a region ("megacenters," concentrations of 0.5 million square feet or more) can accentuate this, leading to true bidirectional peaks. For two-way arterials, a bidirectional peak means that two-way progressions are essential. This in turn means that signal spacing becomes critical and must be taken into account: The standard approach of treating a two-way arterial as a de facto one-way arterial (with tidal flow) will no longer suffice. Requirements in impact assessments have not generally caught up with this trend. However, it is an essential element of future planning.

B. Design and design elements

In order to accomplish the planning objective, good functional (and detailed) design is essential.

Chapter 22 addressed the *signal-spacing requirements,* emphasizing that poor spacing will assure that

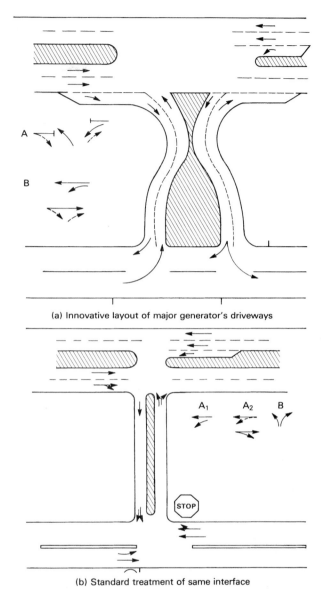

(a) Innovative layout of major generator's driveways

(b) Standard treatment of same interface

Figure 24-2 Driveways at a major generator along an arterial.

future generations of traffic engineers will be kept busy coping with an inherent problem. Nothing more will be said here, other than that the importance of signal (and intersection) spacing cannot be overemphasized on a two-way arterial or in a network.

To assure that *local activity* such as land access, parking, and short trips does not disrupt the arterial function, some arterials now have an "inner" and "outer" roadway, just as some freeways do; refer to Figure 24-3. This construction also ensures that the arterial function is "built into concrete" and defined for the future as well.

Discussions have appeared in the literature (e.g., [4]) for many years concerning "future arterial design," in which *limited-access* arterials are built as intermediate facilities between freeways and the surface street system. These facilities would include design features to minimize left turns (see below), pedestrian conflicts, and even number of signals. Such arterials would have the advantage of providing a "transition" from the freeway to the local streets and vice versa, in terms of free-flow speed and quality of flow.

Discussions on future arterial design also focus on *one-way pairs* in both urban and suburban settings; this is discussed later in the chapter.

To avoid *left turns* across opposing flow, turning opportunities can be built into medians sufficiently wide to allow left turns to be converted into right turns; re-

fer to Figure 24-4. Some attention must be paid to the distance *D* to avoid a concentrated weaving activity as the turn vehicles move to the right following the turn. Other factors to consider are the radii needed for the turning vehicles, the turning volume (storage, weaving), the increased trip lengths, and—of course—the existence of the necessary median width. The benefits can include reduced number of phases at the signal, and thus greater flexibility in setting the cycle length, reduced lost time per cycle, and/or less equivalent (pce) demand for service at the intersection.

As pointed out in Reference [1], the turning opportunities can be built into the cross street as well as into the arterial itself; refer to Figure 24-5. A hybrid approach, combining one direction's left turns on the arterial and the other direction's lefts on the cross street, is also possible.

A number of other design concepts can be used to alleviate *vehicle–vehicle conflicts* and to enhance *pedestrian safety*. Figure 24-6 shows a simple configuration in which the two directions are "decoupled"

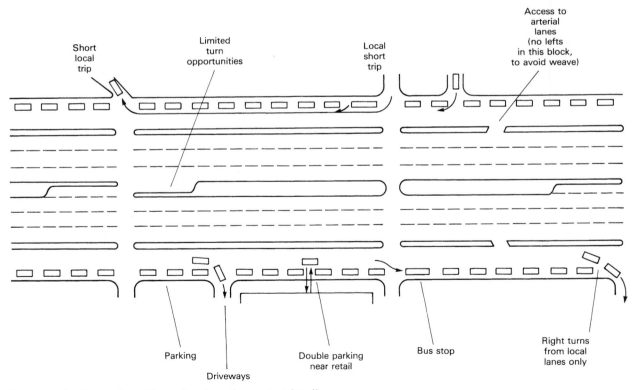

Figure 24-3 Separation of local functions from arterial traffic.

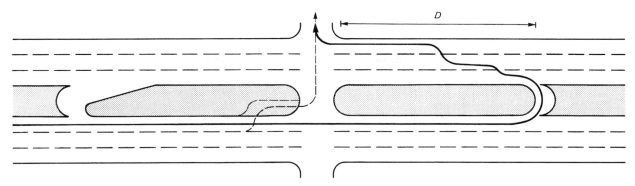

Figure 24-4 Median turn opportunities allowing elimination of left turns.

from each other by virtue of the fact that no north–south traffic crosses the centerline. As a result, the intersection can be treated as two *independent* T-intersections for signalization.

This design also has the advantage that pedestrians crossing the arterial do not encounter a vehicular flow crossing their path, because the left turns out of the cross street do not exist.

Of course, this design does require the NB vehicles who wish to go south or west (and the SB who wish to go north or east) to find other paths. The turn-arounds of Figure 24-4 can serve this function. For higher

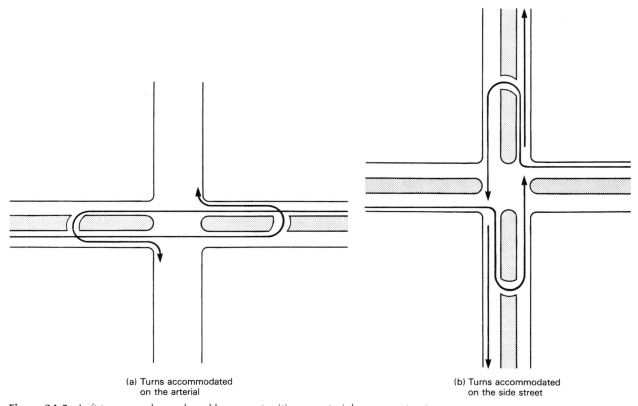

(a) Turns accommodated	(b) Turns accommodated
on the arterial	on the side street

Figure 24-5 Left turns can be replaced by opportunities on arterial or cross street.

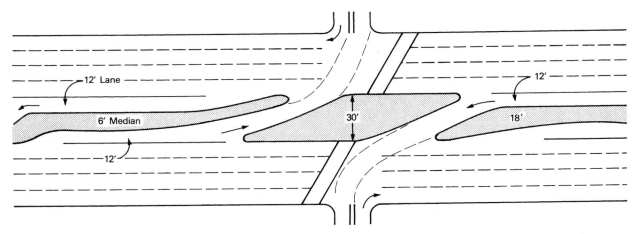

Figure 24-6 Design features that allow the two directions to be timed independently. [Used with permission of Institute of Transportation Engineers, from R. P. Kramer, "New Combinations of Old Techniques to Rejuvenate Jammed Suburban Arterials," *Strategies to Alleviate Traffic Congestion.* Copyright © 1988 Institute of Transportation Engineers.]

volumes, through lane overpasses (or underpasses) can serve the function.

Figure 24-7 shows a configuration that might be used when the cross "streets" are the driveways of major generators, such as shopping centers or office complexes. For standard trip-generation rates at shopping centers, Reference [1] indicates that this particular design can accommodate up to 2000 vph from *each* center while still maintaining 67% of the green for the arterial (this corresponds to 800,000 sq ft of development at each center).

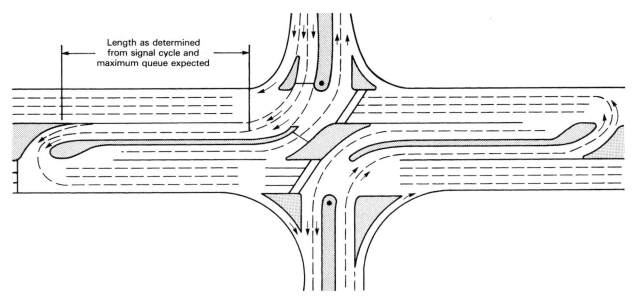

Figure 24-7 At-grade intersection fed by two major generators. [Used with permission of Institute of Transportation Engineers, from R. P. Kramer, "New Combinations of Old Techniques to Rejuvenate Jammed Suburban Arterials," *Strategies to Alleviate Traffic Congestion.* Copyright © 1988 Institute of Transportation Engineers.]

C. Redesign as part of rehabilitation work

Even when some desirable features are not included in the initial design, rehabilitation offers another opportunity to "do it correctly" in order to greatly enhance the facility for future decades.

This point deserves to be stressed and deserves great attention for the simple reason that much of the road system will routinely be rehabilitated during the careers of those reading this text.

In addition, other opportunities for enhancing the design arise as new developments are planned and related mitigation measures are put in place. When the overall design is enhanced at such opportunities (beyond the needs of the subject project, for instance), the question of equitable sharing of costs—and of "impact fees"—becomes very relevant.

D. Reallocation of arterial space as needed

In rehabilitation work, much can be done, particularly within rights of way typical of suburban arterials. However, urban arterials and even suburban arterials dominated by strip development often lack the right of way with which to introduce radical changes. Further, there are improvements that can—and sometimes must—be introduced prior to major rehabilitation.

In addition to the obvious remedy of updating the signalization,[3] the next most viable remedy is often the reallocation of the street space. This may take a number of forms:

- changing parking regulations, to allow curb use by trucks or other vehicles that might otherwise double-park
- removing parking, to provide a moving lane, or to provide right-turn bays
- reducing lane widths, to provide additional lane(s), left-turn bays, or two-way turn lanes

---

[3]In 1973, one of the authors observed in [5] that poor and/or out-of-date signalization seemed to be at the root of many congestion problems. In 1987, engineers were still able to make the same observation, unfortunately with the same clear justification (see "Traffic Signal Retiming: It Works!" [6]).

In addition, lane usage may be varied by time of day (i.e., reverse some lane directions) in order to increase capacity in the peak direction.

E. Other aspects of operation

Because arterial management is an overall process and perspective, it is also necessary to look at the individual components, decisions, and elements, in the context of the impact on the overall operation.

On the *intersection* level, the operations aspects that generally deserve the most attention for this purpose are:

- turn bays (left and right):
  - –existence
  - –length
- RTOR
- turn prohibitions
- arrival patterns of platoons
- signalization

For instance, right turn on red (RTOR) allows some localized delay reductions. However, it might also contribute to an imbalance between the numbers of upstream arterial and turn-in vehicles entering a link, or might inhibit discharge from a generator (e.g., a parking lot) within a link.

On the *arterial* level, the operations aspects that generally deserve the most attention for this purpose are:

- signal spacing
- parking
- transit
- delivery activity
- land-access function
- special-use lanes

Special-use lanes include HOV lanes (high-occupancy vehicles), reversible lanes, and two-way turn lanes.

Table 24-3 shows the several classes of *transportation system management* (*TSM*) actions that might be taken in an overall approach to facility management. In this context, TSM is defined as follows [7]:

> TSM is a planning and operating process designed to conserve resources and energy and to improve the quality of urban life. All existing transportation facilities are viewed as elements of a single system; the objective is to

Table 24-3   Classes of TSM Actions

Class	Strategy Group	Actions
Traffic Management Aimed at improving vehicle movements by increasing the capacity and safety of the existing facilities and systems	Traffic Operations	Intersection and roadway widening One-way streets Turn-lane installation Turning-movement and land-use restrictions New freeway lane using shoulders
	Traffic Control	Local intersection signal improvement Arterial signal system Area signal system Freeway diversion and advisory signing Freeway surveillance and control

	Roadway Assignment	Exclusive bus lane—arterial
		    Take-a-lane
		    Add-a-lane
		Bus-only street
		Contraflow bus lane
		Reversible lane systems
		Freeway HOV bypass
		Exclusive HOV lane—freeway
		    Take-a-lane
		    Add-a-lane

	Pedestrian and Bicycle	Widen sidewalks Pedestrian grade separation Bikeways Bike storage Pedestrian control barriers
Transit Management Designed to increase ridership by providing expanded and more efficient public transportation	Transit Operations	Bus route and schedule modifications Express bus service Bus traffic signal preemption Bus terminals
	Simplified Fare Collection Transit Management	Marketing program Maintenance improvements Vehicle fleet improvements Operations monitoring program
	Inter-Modal Coordination	Park and ride facilities Transfer improvements
Demand Management Oriented toward reducing trips or number of vehicles by encouraging other types of transportation services	Paratransit	Carpool matching programs Vanpool programs Taxi/group riding programs Dial-a-ride Jitney service Elderly and handicapped service
	Work Schedule	Staggered work hours and flex-time Four-day week
Restraint Measures Aimed at discouraging vehicle use mostly through restrictive controls	Parking Management	Curb parking restrictions Residential parking control Off-street parking restrictions HOV preferential parking Parking-rate changes
	Restricted Areas	Area licensing Auto-restricted zones Pedestrian malls Residential traffic control
	Commercial Vehicle	On-street loading zones Off-street loading zones Peak-hour on-street loading prohibition Truck route system
	Pricing	Peak-hour tolls Low-occupancy vehicle tolls Gasoline tax Peak/off-peak transit fares Elderly and handicapped fares Reduced transit fares

organize these individual elements into one efficient, productive, and integrated transportation system.

The same reference further states that:

> TSM . . . is an important component of a comprehensive transportation plan. It should be considered *before* embarking on a capital-intensive set of options. . . . It should respond to current and future needs.

There is a distinct and important emphasis on (relatively) low-cost improvements and management techniques prior to new construction.

Access management

Chapter 2 identified access management as one of the emerging themes in traffic engineering, and noted that several states—led by Colorado, Florida, and now New Jersey—are creating the explicit legislative and administrative infrastructure needed. A number of the points addressed in the previous section (and in the first section, on Kramer's guidelines) touch on access management issues. This section summarizes some of the operational aspects related to access management.

The primary operational measures that may be taken in access management are:

- achieving proper signal spacing
- minimizing conflicts by proper median treatments
  –two-way left-turn lanes (TWLTL)
  –restricted/raised medians
- minimizing frictions by controlling driveway number, placement and design
- separating and/or directing flows by use of back streets, side street access, lanes divided from the through lanes for local service (frontage roads, in effect)

Much has been said in this text about the first item, and it will not be addressed further in this section, other than to note that it is perhaps *the* primary measure.

The several operational measures just listed do have overlaps. For instance, installing a raised median does determine what driveway movements are feasible. Likewise, separating or directing flows to other access points is in effect influencing the number—or

existence—of driveways. The same is true of concentrating flows into fewer driveways.

Some comments are in order. Two-way left-turn lanes (TWLTLs) are very popular in some jurisdictions, because they (1) remove turning traffic from through lanes, (2) do not require radical changes in access to existing land uses, and (3) allow some movements such as lefts from a driveway to be made in two stages—one move to the TWLTL, followed by another merging into the traffic, so that two independent and smaller gaps are needed, not one combined and larger gap. Refer to Figures 24-8 and 24-9 for an illustration of a TWLTL and of the "two phase" operation.

At the same time, some of the literature has focused on the reality that raised medians have lower midblock accident experiences than TWLTLs. This is somewhat obvious, if only because the number of conflicts are reduced when the median is raised; refer to Figure 24-10. However, it does not tell the complete story, for in some cases the raised median is not a viable option. Reference [8] reports that at midblock locations, the accident rate per million vehicle miles of traffic is:

2.43 accidents/MVM for undivided

1.66 accidents/MVM for TWLTL

1.09 accidents/MVM for restrictive medians

Reference [9] also addresses such differences, including the statistical significance of its findings.

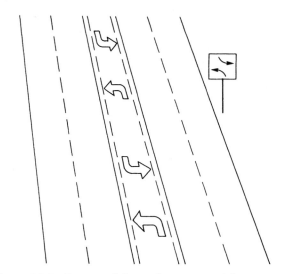

Figure 24-8 Two-way left-turn lane on arterial.

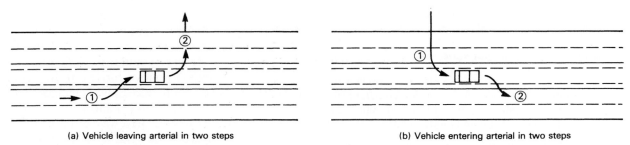

(a) Vehicle leaving arterial in two steps   (b) Vehicle entering arterial in two steps

Figure 24-9   Typical maneuvers benefiting from two-way left-turn lane.

Reference [10] is a 1996 TRB Circular on driveway and street intersection spacing, and is especially relevant. It includes a discussion of practices in various states and other jurisdictions. It also includes a discussion of minimum driveway spacings to avoid facing the driver with too many overlapping decisions.[4] Refer to Figure 24-11 for one illustration of the problem.

Reference [3] uses TRAF-NETSIM to gain insight into the effects of driveways, including eliminating left turns at the driveway and having decel/accel lanes as-

---

[4] The same issue of minimizing the decision tasks facing the driver is central to the AASHTO Green Book, and was discussed in Chapter 3 of this text in that regard.

sociated with the driveway. Figure 24-12 shows the left-turns-eliminated results on the westbound through traffic for the case indicated, with the initial case being 30% lefts and 70% rights and the second case being the same volume but 100% right turns (as assured by a raised median or signing, for instance). There was no median storage area in this case, and the results are quite plausible due to frictions. There was no significant effect on the eastbound through traffic, and it is not shown.

The same reference found that the presence of decel lanes into the driveway had a significant (2 mph) benefit to the eastbound through traffic, but that an accel lane had little benefit to eastbound through traffic (although it may have benefited the departing

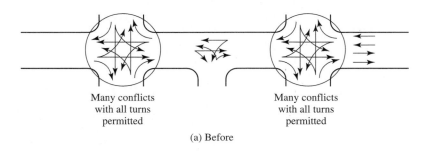

(a) Before

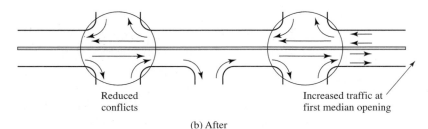

(b) After

Figure 24-10   Conflicts are reduced by raised median limiting driveway movements. [Courtesy of Urbitran Associates.]

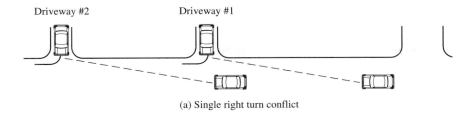

Driveway #2   Driveway #1

(a) Single right turn conflict

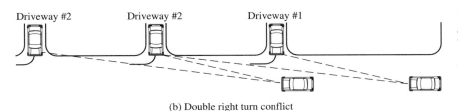

Driveway #2   Driveway #2   Driveway #1

(b) Double right turn conflict

Figure 24-11 Right turn conflict overlap. [Used with permission of Transportation Research Board, National Research Council, Washington, DC, from "Driveway and Street Intersection Spacing," *Circular 456*. Copyright © 1996 Transportation Research Board.]

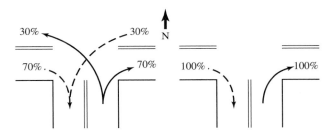

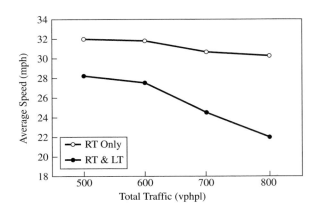

Figure 24-12 The effect of eliminating left turns at the driveway. [From W. McShane, et al., "Insights into Access Management Details Using TRAF-NETSIM," presented at the Second National Conference on Access Management, 1996.]

driveway traffic itself). Even when there was a +2 mph benefit to the through traffic, it must be noted that this recovered only one-third of a −6 mph disbenefit due to the *existence* of the driveway.

The question of redirecting flows to back streets, side streets, and/or restricting local access to frontage roads seems straightforward: If it can be done, the number and intensity of driveways on principal arterials can be minimized. Two of the related issues are: (1) Do the alternative path and access exist? (2) Are the intersections properly designed to accept the additional load from the "minor" streets, which now include this redirected traffic?

One-way streets and networks

One-way streets are especially attractive because:

- signal progression is a trivial task along the street, with no special geometric constraints such as the "closure" condition on a two-way street
- there are no opposing flows to create operational problems for left-turning vehicles
- there are generally related benefits for safety and capacity

For the most part, the capacity benefits arise because there are no left turns across opposing flow, with the associated high pce values, and the safety benefits arise because of the reduced number of conflicts.

The *Transportation Handbook* [11] reported a conversion of two-way to one-way operation that resulted in

37% reduction in average trip time

60% reduction in number of stops

38% reduction in accidents

at the same time that a 19% increase in ADT occurred.

Figure 24-13 shows a sketch of the conversion of a set of two-way streets to a one-way system, highlighting the potential for increased trip lengths.

The greatest issues related to one-way operation are generally: (1) identifying pairs or "couplets" of streets so that a "return path" exists for the traffic, (2) addressing the concern of business over the potential loss of customers due to the changed nature of the street, and (3) potential increases in trip distances for transit vehicles and pedestrians, as well as

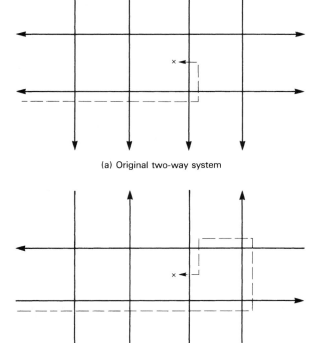

(a) Original two-way system

(b) Replacement one-way system

Figure 24-13   Conversion of a two-way system to one-way. *Note:* Dashed line indicates vehicle with increased trip length.

for other vehicles. For instance, some pedestrians would have to walk an extra block to get to a rerouted bus line, in one of the two directions. The buses themselves might have additional mileage due to the use of two streets.

The effect on trip distances (pedestrian, transit routes, all other vehicles) may represent the most significant disadvantage of introducing one-way streets. However, on balance, the advantages often outweigh the disadvantages, particularly as traffic volumes grow.

Table 24-4 summarizes some of the related advantages and disadvantages, most of which derive from those cited above.

Special-use lanes and streets

The term *special-use* is intended to cover any designated or restricted use of a lane or entire street, other than the standard designation of "left, through, right" or shared use. Special use includes:

- high-occupancy vehicle lanes
- bicycle lanes
- two-way turn lanes
- reversible lanes

For completeness, we will also include "unbalanced flow" in this section.

In addition to special *lane* uses, some streets have been restricted as to the types of vehicles allowed. For instance, some urban shopping malls are restricted to transit vehicles, to encourage pedestrian activity and to provide service for the shoppers. Facilities might also be restricted to trucks or to transit (for other reasons), creating "truckways" as well as "transitways" (in addition to creating a special jargon).

The criteria for implementation of a *high-occupancy vehicle (HOV)* lane on a surface street vary, as does the definition of "high occupancy vehicle." In general, HOV lanes are used by buses, with some allowance for taxis, vans, and other special carriers (on freeways, HOVs are now often defined so that passenger cars carrying 2 or more, or 3 or more, persons may also use the lane). Right-turning vehicles are allowed to enter surface street HOV lanes only to complete their maneuver (unless the HOV lane is channelized, at which time they may be totally restricted). Markings for a typical HOV are illustrated in Figure 24-14.

Some HOV lanes operate in a "contraflow" mode. That is, the HOV traffic—buses—travels in a specially

Table 24-4　Advantages and Disadvantages of One-Way Streets

Advantages

Improved ability to coordinate signals

Removal of left turns across competing flow

Related safety and capacity benefits:

Capacity	*Safety*
Low left-turn pce	Intersection conflicts removed
Fewer phases possible	Midblock conflicts removed
Less delay	Improved driver field of vision

Related quality of flow benefits in increased average speed/decreased travel time

Better quality of flow benefits transit and even transit operating costs

Better utilization of "extra" widths, and allowance for odd number of lanes on given facility (e.g., 3 or 5 lanes possible on one-way operation, but uncommon on two-way street)

Two-way turn lanes not needed

More opportunities to maneuver around double-parked or slow vehicles

Ability to preserve parking longer than otherwise possible, due to capacity benefits

Disadvantages

Increased trip lengths for some/most/all vehicles, pedestrians, transit routes

Some businesses affected (corner locations could be "wrong" corner; peak volumes could be at wrong time of day; e.g., gas station)

Signal coordination in grid still a problem in principle; in fact, mitigated by likelihood that "open tree" will be identified (see Chapter 22)

Transit route now (at least) a block apart for two directions

For transit routes, 50% reduction in number of right-side lanes in a given direction; potential problem when multiple routes concentrated into fewer right-side lanes, particularly if bus stops with longest dwell times occur at same locations for multiple routes

Concern by business that "character" of street will change due to better quality of flow

Fewer turning opportunities (lefts, rights) in total grid at the same time that number of turns increases due to greater trip lengths, more circuitous path to destination (in many cases)

Additional signing needed to designate "one way," turn prohibitions, and restricted entry as required by MUTCD; revisions in signal head locations and displays also needed

"Transit route" = "Bus route," in general.

designated lane *against* the flow of traffic on the street, with the designation accomplished by cones or channelization.

Bicycle lanes are mentioned for completeness. In some cities, special bike lanes are designated, marked, and sometimes channelized as a matter of policy for recreational purposes. In some towns in the United States (e.g., university towns in good climates), bicycles are a significant mode of transportation and bike lanes are designated because of the traffic volume. Bicycle–vehicle conflicts at intersections require attention.

Perhaps the greatest "special-use" innovation in recent decades has been the growth in the use of *two-way turn lanes*. On suburban and urban arterials with multiple relatively low-volume driveways (typical of strip development, for instance), dedication of a center lane for turns in either direction allows for storage

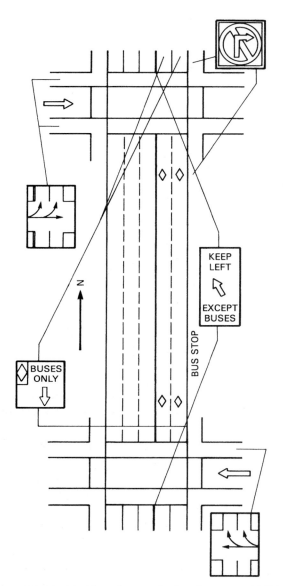

Figure 24-14   Markings for a typical surface street HOV.

the United States, Reference [11] cites one facility operated on a 6:2 split of eight lanes, reversed by time of day to match the demand. The concerns with reversible lanes relate to the misuse of lanes by the driver (particularly the unfamiliar driver), despite the signalization over the lanes.

Reference [12] notes that some jurisdictions have combined two-way left-turn lanes and reversible lanes on the same arterial "because of a combination of peak-period congestion and increased roadside development" and addresses the control-devices needs for such installations.

Unbalanced flow is a term indicating that the number of lanes in the two directions is not symmetric. This application is only suitable where the network configuration assures that the P.M. peak flow on the particular street is different than the A.M. peak flow.

Goods activity on arterials

Trucks and other goods-related vehicles have a significant impact on arterial operation, both because of their pce effect and because of their pickup and delivery (PUD) activity.

A number of cities have well-designed backstreet or "alley" systems for goods delivery, zoning requirements on a number of off-street loading bays, and/or curb-use regulations that accommodate truck needs to a large degree. However, in many areas, the basic mode of operation is that truck double-parking is endemic, with trucks parking within some 100 feet of the land use they are serving (e.g., see [13]). If the location of the land use is such that the truck tends to block a moving lane at either the entry or discharge end of a link, the impact on the arterial traffic can be very significant. Indeed, it is equivalent to the short-term loss of one lane, with associated turbulence as vehicles move around the obstacle. For *v/c* ratios already close to 1.00, this can be a severe impact.

A number of observations are in order:

• There is a growing body of knowledge on *trip-generation rates* of various land uses (retail, office, residential) for truck activity, with the rate often expressed in terms of trips per 100 sq ft of space for a given land use. Within retail, the rate varies significantly by business (e.g., fast food, shoe store, department store).

and for vehicles to make their maneuvers in two distinct steps.

Reversible lanes have been in use for many years, and the MUTCD specifies standard marking and signal/sign designations.

Clearly, reversible lanes have the great advantage of matching lane availability to the peak demand. In

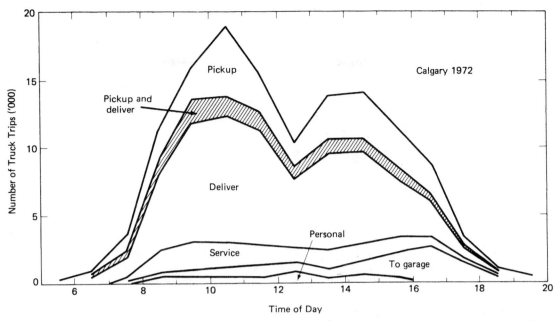

Figure 24-15 Truck trips by time of day in 1972 Calgary study. [Used with permission of Prentice-Hall, from W. S. Homburger, *Transportation and Traffic Engineering Handbook,* 2nd Ed.. Copyright © 1982 Prentice-Hall, Inc.]

- There are associated characteristic time-of-day distributions and duration-of-stay distributions for each land use.
- Combining the rates and temporal distributions with the spatial distribution of land uses and the proclivity of truckers to be in very close proximity to the land use being visited (for security of cargo, even more than for convenience), a detailed estimate of truck activity can be obtained.
- Given this estimate of truck activity, a positive program of mitigation (off-street bays, curb space allocation, and so on) can be planned *or* the adverse impact can be estimated according to double-parking and lane blockages.

To illustrate just some of these considerations, refer to Figures 24-15 and 24-16, which show (respectively) the temporal distribution of truck trips by time of day and purpose in a 1972 study and the temporal distribution of trucks as a percentage of the traffic stream in a 1985 study. The profile is (fortunately) rather characteristic: Truck activity peaks outside of the general commuting peak hours.

Remedies based on "making the truck traffic go away" are often counterproductive for many reasons. Consider some examples:

- Chasing double-parked trucks away simply puts them in motion, circulating throughout the network, driving up the total VMT as they circle the block.
- Levying fines is an added cost of doing business, but is often inexpensive compared to downtown storage space (in some downtown areas, package delivery trucks can be stationary for much of the day, with the truck being used as a base of operations).
- Restricting numbers of trucks may not be viable. Some industries simply do not have sufficient on-premises storage to accommodate even one day's inventory of raw materials, for historic reasons in the development of the industry in the particular city.
- Restricting delivery hours to "off hours" may not be viable for the same reason, plus the reality that the business must then be staffed for off-hours acceptance of delivery.

Truck policies that are too restrictive affect the economic viability of the industry within the city or region, thus attaining the ultimate in counterproductivity

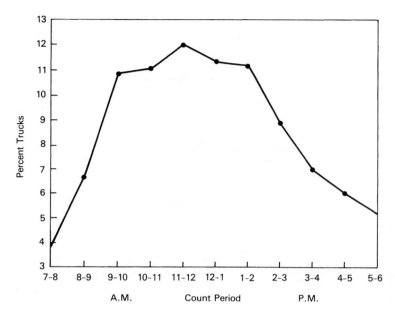

Figure 24-16   Percent of trucks in traffic stream in 1985 study, Austin, Texas. [Used with permission of Institute of Transportation Engineers, from D. G. Gerard, "Truck Operations on Arterial Streets," *Strategies to Alleviate Traffic Congestion.* Copyright © 1988 Institute of Transportation Engineers.]

for a locality—loss of jobs, tax base, and economic activity.

Against this must be balanced traffic operations and efficiency, leading one to a clear conclusion regarding the need for effective advance planning of well-estimated truck needs.

Transit vehicles on urban streets

There are many considerations related to transit vehicles on arterials, ranging from the justification for an HOV lane to the adverse impact of transit vehicles on the other traffic.

This section focuses on bus transit, but it is clear that light rail transit (LRT) on arterials has its own special set of problems and considerations. Even in a separated right of way, the need for vehicular traffic to cross that right of way introduces signal-coordination needs between the LRT signal system and the traffic control signals.

Within bus transit, there are a number of points to consider in even a survey section on the subject:

Bus-stop location

Bus priority systems

Characteristics of bus routes:
   loading patterns

   route capacity
   dwell times

Length of bus stop

Passenger-car equivalent (pce)
   if bus stops in moving lane

Passenger-car equivalent (pce)
   if bus uses bus stop

These points are addressed in brief in subsections below to provide an insight into the issues involved. For a greater operational knowledge, a complete reading of [2] plus other cited literature is recommended.

Note that some of the estimates provided in this section can be used to modify bus impacts (pce) as described in Chapter 18, based on more detailed knowledge of the bus operation.

A. Bus-stop location

There are a number of references on the subject of bus-stop location, including a 1967 recommended practice [14]. Basically, there are three distinct choices, each with its own merits:

• far side (of intersection)
• near side (just prior to intersection)
• midblock

Traffic engineers often favor the "far-side" bus stop because it allows the bus to pull in directly, does not trap the bus prior to the signal when the green is displayed, and minimizes problems for vehicles wishing to turn right. However, multiple considerations make it impossible to always put the bus stop in one location. These include: location of transfer points (e.g., rail line, other bus route); location of major attractors of bus riders (e.g., office building, department stores); traffic pattern relative to pedestrian paths to/from bus stop; existence of multiple bus routes, with potential of overloading a given bus stop.

B. Bus priority techniques

The early work in the United States dates from the FHWA testbed Urban Traffic Control System (UTCS) in Washington, DC [15,16]. Some of the early efforts led to an assessment that bus priority on the main street just means incurring delay on the side street, and this has entered the folklore of traffic engineering. Reference [17] is an older survey of the literature.

The European experience is nicely summarized in [18], as part of an effort by the Chicago Transit Authority to assess the technology and the potential as part of their own planning and implementation strategies. Bus priority is used extensively, and the technology is well described and routinely employed. However, the environment is generally radically different than that in the United States, because there is a distinct policy emphasis on transit as *the* priority mode, with auto traffic restricted or de-emphasized. Table 24-5 shows some key features of several European traffic signal priority projects.

Work in North America includes a study in the 1980s on several bus priority studies by the Toronto Transit Commission [19]. Several important issues are discussed, including:

1. Considering bus travel time savings as a way of reducing fleet requirements and operating costs, in addition to more obvious objectives such as reducing person delay
2. The identification of four "normal" signal methods related to priority (phase extension, truncation, skipping, and special phase), plus two methods to reduce delays to other road users (compensation by additional green, inhibition of later requests for a certain period)

3. The limits to providing bus priority when intersections are oversaturated, or have high v/c ratios
4. The differences that can occur due to near-side versus far-side bus stop location

The report also provides some then-current information on case studies conducted elsewhere (England, Australia, several U.S. cities), each yielding significant reductions in bus delay or travel time. Lastly, it assesses several policies for Toronto, recommending a central computer/limited coordination system due to relatively low hardware, software, and staffing costs, with expected good effect.

Other literature has paid special attention to light rail transit, notably in dedicated rights of way. TRAF-NETSIM was used in conjunction with other tools (TRANSYT-7F and HCS software) to assess the impacts of LRT priority treatment within its exclusive right of way in the North Central Corridor, wherein signals are shared with other traffic [20]. For a planned LRT in Chicago, also with dedicated right of way but shared signals, another project used TRAF-NETSIM, in conjunction with the TransSIM II[5] LRT/bus transit simulation model [21].

Some field comparisons with the paired TRAF-NETSIM/TransSIM II™ models were reported in [22], with generally favorable results. Other work is also being done related to bus transit priority signalization [23–29]. This body of work highlights a focus on modeling, rather than on developing new control algorithms. There is no exploration of the operational effects of ITS technologies, and they are not included in the modeling explicitly.

The literature reminds us that: (1) schedule adherence is an important issue; (2) better bus route travel times may have considerable operating cost savings; (3) queueing and the disruptions it implies may be at least as important as delay; (4) cross streets can be adversely impacted without some compensating time; (5) buses are not usually present on every cycle in many areas, so the opportunity for compensation exists; (6) person delay is a standard and important measure, and one which common tools—the *HCM*, for instance—do not treat explicitly; (7) in some venues, the real issue may be transit ridership delay, primary over passenger car delay.

[5] TransSIM II is a registered trademark for the specific transit simulator.

Table 24-5 Features of Selected European Traffic Signal Priority Projects

Elements/Cities	London	Stuttgart	Zurich	Nancy	Angouleme
Traffic Control System					
Central control	✓		✓		
Isolated		✓		✓	✓
UTC system	✓			✓	Future
Associated Priority Facilities					
With bus lanes	✓		✓	✓	
Without bus lanes	✓	✓	✓	✓	✓
Relation to AVL System					
Combined with AVL		Future		✓	✓
Not combined with AVL	✓	✓	✓		
Strategies Employed					
Green extension	✓	✓	✓	✓	✓
Red truncation	✓	✓	✓	✓	✓
Red interruption		✓	✓		
24-hour priority	✓	✓	✓	✓	✓
Priority cut-off		✓	✓	✓	✓
Compensation Following Priority					
Green extension		✓	✓		
Red extension	✓				
Conditions of Priority					
Reduced delay	✓				
Full priority		✓	✓		✓
Late buses only				✓	Future
Technology Employed					
Loops	✓	✓	✓		
Beacons		✓			
Radio		✓		✓	✓
Selection Procedure					
Individual intersection analysis			✓	✓	✓
Full line implementation		✓	✓		
System implementation					
Area implementation	✓		✓		

[From: *Traffic Systems Control Handbook,* U.S. Department of Transportation, Federal Highway Administration, 1996.]

Indeed, Items 4 and 5 of this enumeration remind us that signals may have two timing needs, one for the "bus present and going through" mode and the other for "no bus in need" mode. Further, it is to everyone's advantage to have a control system that can adapt to the bus's *absence* as well as its presence. We ourselves are inclined to think of this on the strategic level as well as the tactical—how do we adjust *all* system signals, given the locations and needs of all buses on the system?

In this context, let us enumerate candidate objectives and related measures of effectiveness (if there is any ambiguity or problem):

Objective	MOE(S)/Notes
1. Schedule adherence	Measurable; good for riders; important to influence/control "herding" on busy routes
2. Bus route travel time	Measurable; influences equipment needs and operating costs
3. Total person delay	Need to guess/estimate occupancies; need equipment sensitive to vehicle type; need to address whether all people (main and cross street; main street only); need to address local or arterial or system
4. Transit person delay	Same technical problems as preceding; may not be feasible to convince public; real problem that autos interfere with bus movement if not adequately served themselves by signal plan
5. Control queue lengths	Maybe not an objective, as much as a constraint, for interference argument; however, literature emphasizes queue issue

There are other, higher level and more strategic objectives we have not listed. More efficient, reliable transit can influence ridership and thus mode split. We lack real information on such elasticities, and also

believe that the Project Statement focuses on the more operational issues of control strategies and how to do them effectively, not these broader issues.

The definition of the *scenarios* and the matching *objective(s)* virtually defines what must be done. The open question is whether the technology can support the solution, or—more suitably—what level of technology is justified, given the probable cost and the benefits.

Consider the following cases in which the scenario and the objective virtually define the transit priority strategy:

Scenario	Objective	Transit Priority Strategy
Suburban route, low frequency, light to moderate ridership, modest arterial volumes, two-lane road	Schedule adherence	Bus has on-board ability to request/set priority
Suburban routes, converging at a shopping mall	Minimize person delay at access driveway/intersections	Area detection, capable of identifying buses; sets local controller
Urban route, frequent service, 10 signals per mile or more, long route length, AVLS, central control from TMC	Schedule adherence primary; low total person delay secondary	Identify actual locations of buses, estimate intersection arrival times, modify overall signal plan accordingly

Each of the illustrations chosen has a different control approach, matched to the need: One uses local control, activated by an individual bus; another uses an area/zone detection system, anticipating that too many competing needs may be triggered otherwise; the third takes a strategic view of the route, fully utilizing the AVLS and TMC features.

C. Characteristics of bus routes

Levinson observes [4] that in many cities, more than half of all peak-hour person-trips on downtown streets are carried in buses, citing several cases in which the number exceeds 80% in some key arterials in certain cities. He further observes an empiric distribution of *loading pattern* that startled the authors when they first encountered it:

> A reasonable design assumption is that 50% of the maximum load point volume is served at the heaviest CBD busway stop.

This does assume that there are at least three downtown stops (otherwise, it would be larger).

This is startling because it simply states that virtually *all* bus routes are "many-to-one" collectors (or "one-to-many" in the reverse direction), with the effective person-capacity of an entire route determined by the activity at one bus stop. This goes beyond the more reasonable statement that "In most cases station capacity rather than way capacity is the critical constraint"—that is, the stops (and dwell times) determine route capacity, not lane capacity.

No matter how startling the statement or its implications are, we offer the reader the same challenge we gave ourselves: Think of a bus route on which this is *not* the case. We failed, and so did everyone else to whom we have offered the challenge so far; the statement may be startling, but it is well founded.

At a given bus stop (for instance, the critical bus stop), the *dwell time* of the bus can be estimated according to [2] by

For boarding only (one-way flow):

$$D = (b)(B) \qquad [24\text{-}3a]$$

For alighting only (one-way flow):

$$D = (a)(A) \qquad [24\text{-}3b]$$

Two-way flow through door:

$$D = 1.2\,[(a)(A) + (b)(B)] \qquad [24\text{-}3c]$$

where the clearance time is added to obtain the bus headway:

$$h' = D + t_c \qquad [24\text{-}4]$$

where 15 sec clearance time is common (10 sec is the absolute minimum). The other terms are defined as follows:

A = number of alighting passengers *per bus* in peak 15 minutes

B = number of boarding passengers *per bus* in peak 15 minutes

a = alighting service time (sec/passenger): 1.7 to 2.0 sec/passenger is typical (use 2.0 in this text)

b = boarding service time (sec/passenger): 2.6 sec/passenger for single coin 3.0 sec/passenger for exact fare 3.5 sec/passenger for exact fare, standees on bus

The above numbers are typical; Table 12-10 of Reference [2] has additional refinements. The "1.2" was added to Equation [24-3c] as allowed in [2] to account for heavy flow through the door used for entrances *and* exits.

Table 24-6 computes some typical dwell times for combinations of A and B, assuming that a 15-sec clearance time is used.

The capacity of the bus stop (assuming a single position) is given in [2] as

$$f' = (g/C)\,\frac{3000}{t_c + D(g/C)} \quad \text{buses per hour} \qquad [24\text{-}5]$$

where g/C is the green-time-to-cycle-length ratio and f' is the capacity of a single-position bus stop (bus "berth").

Table 24-7 gives some illustrative bus capacities based on the same assumptions as the preceding table, for $g/C = 0.60$.

Note that the bus capacities of the "berth" or stop are rather low. For 8 passengers boarding per bus and only 2 passengers alighting per bus (albeit all through the single door), the capacity is 51 buses per hour. This means that only

$$(8)(51) = 408 \text{ passengers}$$

Table 24-6   Some Illustrative Dwell Times

Boarding Passengers	Alighting Passengers			
	2	4	6	8
2	12.0	16.8	21.6	26.4 sec
4	19.2	24.0	28.8	33.6
6	26.4	31.2	36.0	40.8
8	33.6	38.4	43.2	48.0
10	40.8	45.6	50.4	55.2
12	48.0	52.8	57.6	62.4

Equation [24-3c] used, assuming two-way flow through front door, exact fare, no standees, 2.0-sec/pass value for a.

Table 24-7   Some Illustrative Single-Position Bus-Stop Capacities

Boarding Passengers	Alighting Passengers			
	2	4	6	8
2	81	72	64	58 buses
4	68	61	56	51
6	58	53	49	46
8	51	47	44	41
10	46	42	40	37
12	41	39	36	34

Dwell times from Table 24-6; clearance times of 15 sec; $g/C = 0.60$.

can be taken away from this stop in an hour (*if the PHF* for the buses is 1.00). If this is the busiest station and we use the 50% concentrated-load rule of thumb, then the capacity of this route is limited to 816 passengers per hour. But what would happen if there were (say) 600 passengers waiting to board?

Focus on the common-sense explanation: If the 600 passengers tried to board 51 buses, it would be 600/51 = 11.76 boarders per bus. Assuming a proportionate increase in those alighting, this is (11.76/8) 100% = 147% of the planned amount—and of the computed dwell time. Thus, the dwell time goes up 47%, and the buses-per-hour figure goes *down*, because it is related to dwell time by Equation [24-5]:

$$f' = (g/C)\frac{3000}{t_c + D(g/C)} \quad \text{buses per hour}$$

This represents the most that can utilize the (single-position) bus stop in the hour.

Now this can be expressed in two equations as follows: First, the number of buses times *B* boarding passengers per bus should equal the stated demand (e.g., the 600 who wish to board):

$$\text{boarding demand} = (B)(f') \quad [24\text{-}6]$$

Equation [24-5] can be substituted into this, so that the relation is now between *D* and *B*, with all else fixed.

Second, there is *another* relation between *D* and *B*, namely Equation [24-3c]:

$$D = 1.2[(a)(A) + (b)(B)]$$

It is reasonable to assume that the ratio of *A* to *B* stays the same, so that only two variables—*B* and *D*—are unknown in these two equations (i.e., Equations [24-3c] and [24-6]).

We can plot *D* as a function of *B* in each relation, on the same axes, and look for the intersection of the two relations. We can also tabulate:

Assume B	Solve for D in Eq. [24-3c]	Substitute D into Eq. [24-5]	Solve for "Demand" in Eq. [24-6]	If Match, Success; If None at All, Impossible
8	33.6	$f' = 51.2$	408	
12	50.4	39.8	477	
16	67.2	32.5	521	
24	100.8	23.8	572	
30	126.0	19.9	596	
32	134.4	18.8	602	⟵ Match

Note: Equation [24-3c] used with *A:B* ratio constant at 2:8.

Note that *if* a bus showed up once per minute, there would be 600 boarders/60 buses = 10 boarders per bus, and it would take 50.4 sec of dwell time *plus* 15 sec of clearance time, for a total of 65.4 sec: 5.4 sec more than we have. Buses would back up. By cutting down on buses per hour, we attain the objective.

For further insight, the reader is encouraged to solve Problem 24–15 at the end of this chapter.

D. Length of bus stop

Actually, another effective means of handling an increased demand is simply to lengthen the bus stop so as to handle more than one bus at a time. This is addressed in [2]. However, the additional "berths" are not as effective as the first, and there is in effect a law of diminishing returns. Table 24-8 shows this effect. Thus, by the simple expedient of sufficiently lengthening the bus stop, the original number of 408 passengers per single berth could be increased up toward 1020 passengers; diminishing returns would dictate that the limit not be approached.

E. Passenger-car equivalents of a bus

Reference [2] offers guidance on the pce values of buses as follows:

- For moving buses on surface streets, a pce of 1.5 is appropriate.
- For buses that stop in a lane *not* used by moving traffic, the time loss to other vehicles is approximately 3 to 4 sec per bus.

Table 24-8 Efficiency of Multiple On-Lane Bus
Berths (Longer Bus Stops)

Number of Berths	Cumulative Number of Effective Berths
1	1.00
2	1.75
3	2.25
4	2.45
5	2.50

[Adapted with permission of Transportation Research Board, National Research Council, Washington, DC, from *Highway Capacity Manual, Special Report 209,* Table 12-9, p. 12-21. Copyright © 1994 Transportation Research Board.]

- For buses that stop in a lane used by moving traffic, the time loss for the lane in which the buses operate is given by

$$T_L = (g/C)(N)(D + L) \text{ seconds per hour} \qquad [24\text{-}7]$$

where the left side of the equation is time loss to other vehicles (actually, time used by the buses), N is the number of buses per hour, and L is time loss due to bus maneuvering, beyond the dwell time D. Typically, L is 6 to 8 sec. ($L = 6$ will be used in this text as the default condition.)

Equation [24-7] can be divided by the headway h and number of buses per hour N to obtain a pce value for a typical bus that stops in a moving lane:

$$\text{pce} = (g/C)(D + L)/h \qquad [24\text{-}8]$$

Values for such pce's can be used in a modification to the procedure of Chapter 18 if necessary. However, initial results from other work (circa 1989) indicate that Equation [24-8] *overestimates* the pce factor for buses in reserved-use lanes. This is probably due to the fact that two or more buses frequently stop simultaneously and thus the "follower(s)" are not adversely impacted by the "lead" stopped bus, so that the net flow of buses is higher than the pce implied by Equation [24-7].

Special signalization issues

Let us now address four arterial management issues related to signalization:

- transitions from one plan to another
- coordinating multiphase signals
- multiple and submultiple cycle lengths
- diamond interchanges

These are discussed in subsections below.

A. Transitions from one plan to another

Very little appears in the literature on finding a "best" or optimum way of moving from one plan to another in an orderly and efficient way. Nonetheless, it is an important problem; some engineers feel that the transition from one plan to another during peak loads is more disruptive than having the wrong plan in operation.

The fundamental problem is to get from "Plan A" to "Plan B" without allowing:

- red displays so short as to leave pedestrians stranded in front of moving traffic
- such short green displays that drivers get confused and have rear-end accidents as one stops but the other does not
- excessive queues to build up during excessively long greens
- some approaches to be "starved" for vehicles due to long red displays upstream, thus wasting their own green

Further, based on lessons learned in one demonstration system, Reference [30] reports that:

> [N]o more than two signal cycles should be used to change an offset, and the offset should be changed by lengthening the cycle during transition if the new offset falls within 0 and 70 percent of the cycle length. The cycle should be shortened to reach the new offset if the offset falls within the last 30 percent (70–100 percent) of the cycle.

The most basic transition algorithm is the "extended main-street green" used in conventional hardware: At each signal, the old plan is kept in force until main-street green (MSG) is about to end, at which time MSG is extended until the time at which the *new* plan calls for its termination. Clearly, some phase durations will be rather long. However, the policy is simple, safe, and easily implemented.

Reference [31] reported on the test of six transition algorithms (some of which were boundary cases and not field-implementable algorithms), because of the logical importance of effective transitions in computer-controlled systems, which update their plans frequently. Over the range of situations simulated (volume increasing, decreasing, constant), the "extended main-street green" algorithm was no worse than any of the special designs.

B. Coordinating multiphase signals

Multiphase signals (more than two phases) are sometimes required by local policy, dictated by safety considerations (for instance, when lefts must cross a very wide opposing direction), or needed to reduce the pce of the left turners in the face of an opposing flow.

When multiphase signals exist along a two-way arterial, they actually introduce another "degree of freedom" in attempts to get good progressions in two directions. Consider the time–space diagram of Figure 24-17, with the northbound progression set first, as shown. The usual challenge is to find a "best" southbound progression that does not disrupt this northbound success; the usual constraint is that the southbound and northbound greens must occur at the same time, so that perhaps only part of the "window" can be used for southbound platooned movement. This is illustrated in Figure 24-17.

However, there *is* some new flexibility. Refer to Figure 24-18, which shows that the SB through green can be "moved around" by the simple expedient of

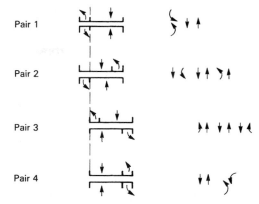

Figure 24-18 Candidate phase plans at each intersection of a multiphase arterial.

locating the protected left turns in various places. In this particular example, it gives the SB through a flexibility of ±10 sec relative to the (fixed) NB through-green initiation.

Observe that the SB window can be made wide by "pushing" the SB through at any intersection to an extreme in most cases. Further, the direction of the "push" generally alternates SB down the arterial (first one extreme and then the other) except for fortuitous spacings. Thus, the actual selected settings will frequently alternate between "Pair 2" and "Pair 3" in Figure 24-18.

Crowley [32] and Messer et al. [33] have both addressed the optimization of signal progressions along two-way multiphase arterials. Messer used his work as the basis for the PASSER program, which implemented this policy.

C. Multiple and submultiple cycle lengths

Coordinated systems operate on the principle of moving platoons of vehicles efficiently through a number of signals. In order to do this, a common cycle length is almost always assumed.

Chapter 22 emphasized that the selection of cycle length is a *system* consideration, and Chapter 16 also pointed out that (1) delay is rather insensitive to cycle-length variation over a range of cycle lengths, (2) capacity does not increase significantly with increased cycle length, and (3) real net capacity is likely to decrease if large platoons are encouraged, because of storage and spillback problems.

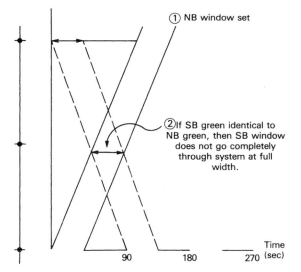

Figure 24-17 Illustrative problem for multiphase signal coordination.

Nonetheless, there are situations in which multiple or submultiple cycle lengths can work to advantage, or when other combinations are necessitated. As a matter of definition: If the system is at $C = 60$ sec and one intersection is put at $C = 120$ sec, it is a "multiple" of the system cycle length. If, on the other hand, the system is at $C = 120$ sec and one intersection is put at $C = 60$ sec, it is a "submultiple" of the system cycle length.

Other combinations are, of course, possible, but the pattern they induce will only repeat after the lowest common period (a "supercycle length," so to speak) has passed. For a 60-sec and a 90-sec pair of cycle lengths, the common period is 180 sec. For a 60-sec and a 75-sec cycle length, the common period is 300 sec.

Figure 24-19 shows one of the effects of having a multiple cycle length in the system: The platoon discharged from the greater cycle length (greater phase duration) moves into the downstream link, to be processed in two parts; with very good offset, this could be no problem, for much of the platoon is kept moving. However, for poor offsets, the entire platoon could become a queue, if only for a short time.

A number of situations might give rise to use of multiple or submultiple cycle lengths:

• If there is a very closely spaced diamond interchange somewhere along an urban arterial which has $C = 120$ sec (or even $C = 90$ sec), then $C = 60$ sec might well benefit the diamond operation by keeping platoons small and avoiding internal storage problems and even spillback.
• At a very wide intersection of two major arterials, at least one of which has $C = 60$ sec, the added lost time per phase (due to longer clearance intervals associated with the wide intersection) may present a problem, and it may be best to reduce the number of cycles per hour at this one intersection by increasing the cycle length to $C = 120$ sec—if storage permits.
• If the turns dictate that multiphasing is required and if the geometry of the overall arterial indicates that the *system* cycle length should not be changed, then it may be best to allow this one intersection to have a different (greater) cycle length.
• At the intersection of two major arterials, each with its own system cycle length dictated by its own geometry, it may be necessary to accept a different cycle length at the common intersection.

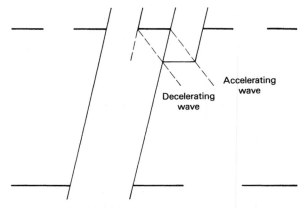

(a) $C = 120$ sec; feeding downstream with excellent progression

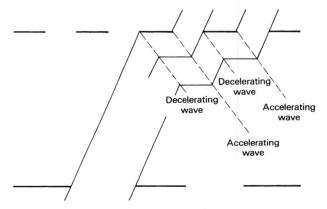

(b) $C = 60$ sec; feeding downstream with terrible progression

Figure 24-19   One of the effects of a multiple cycle length in the system.

Other examples could be constructed, but these serve for illustration and are representative.

In considering the use of multiple or submultiple cycle lengths, attention must be paid to upstream *and* downstream storage, relative g/C ratios, and the length of the common period (the "least common denominator"). Some savings can be achieved in particular cases (e.g., [34]), but usually at the expense of a markedly more complicated analysis.

D. The diamond interchange

Figure 24-20(a) shows a sketch of a typical or "conventional" diamond interchange at the juncture of an arterial and a freeway. Such diamond interchanges are relatively inexpensive, do not need signalization

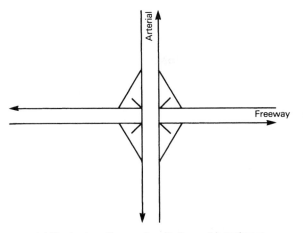

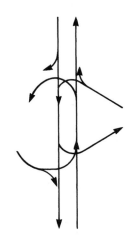

(a) The basic or "conventional" diamond interchange

(b) Movements in a conventional diamond

Figure 24-20 The conventional diamond interchange.

for typical initial volumes, and do not consume much space. They are well suited to locations where an interchange is needed for service, but the volumes are modest.

Unfortunately, volumes do grow at such locations, due to local development and/or the simple expansion of the urban area. By the time this growth is a problem, the contiguous land has often been developed and its cost is prohibitive (not to mention the practical and political problem of acquiring such land). Thus, the option of a total redesign is often not open.

Historically, much of the literature has been concerned with signal optimization at diamond interchanges (see, for instance, References [35] and [36]). The reason is simple: With the space unavailable, signalization is one of the few hopes for coping with the problem.

The inherent problems of a conventional diamond interchange under heavy volumes are considerable: As illustrated in Figure 24-20(b), there are numerous conflicting movements. Further, the bridge over the highway is relatively short (typically, 300 ft) and must be used for storage of left turners during certain phases. Last, volumes from the freeway tend to back up onto the freeway, substantially degrading its performance. All of this is exacerbated by periodic intersection blockages as queues develop due to the left turns from the arterial onto the freeway.

The true problem is that the initial design did not anticipate the traffic growth, and the initial economic analysis—if any—did not include "life-cycle" costs reflecting traffic growth, delay costs, travel-time costs, accident costs, *and* land and construction capital costs [37].

One design alternative that can be considered is the *split diamond* illustrated in Figure 24-21(a)

- The storage leading off the freeway is greater, for it includes the EW space between the NB and SB sections of the "split" arterial.
- There are no left-turn flows crossing or competing for green with opposing flows. Refer to Figure 24-22(b).
- All signals can therefore be two-phase, simplifying the operation. Refer to Figure 24-22(c).
- The EW storage space and the two-phase operation allow for narrower bridge widths.
- Indeed, if the split of the arterial is sufficiently wide, drivers may not realize that they are driving through a "diamond" configuration, for the two arterial directions could be considerable distances from each other, and the enclosed land could be fully developed.

Some signal optimization is in order, for the "closure" equations for optimum progressions must be tailored to the geometry and the traffic patterns.

There are other diamond configurations, and variations on each. However, the conventional and split serve to introduce the principal issues in this rather familiar—and troublesome—configuration.

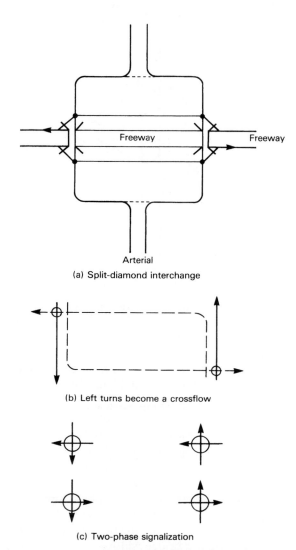

(a) Split-diamond interchange

(b) Left turns become a crossflow

(c) Two-phase signalization

Figure 24-21   Aspects of a split-diamond interchange.

One of the inescapable lessons of any consideration of the diamond interchange is that the true solution is much more than an optimum signalization. The literature is filled with better signalization schemes because the *given* condition in so many localities has always been, "We have a problem, but cannot provide more space: What can we do?" The answer is then, "Patch and cope, using signalization."

For the reader, however, the true solution—and lesson—is to avoid such dead ends by initial design, if at all possible. Cost-effective alternatives based on

life-cycle costs are one method of enhancing the chance of "building in" a better solution.

As an exercise, the reader should draw the analogy to the lesson of Chapter 24, reinforced in a different context by Kramer regarding suburban arterials: *Do not build future problems into the design, but rather avoid such future problems by good design principles and by awareness of the inherent issues.*

HCM procedure for arterials

The *HCM* procedure involves seven steps, shown in Figure 24-22. The essence of the procedure is computation of the arterial's average travel speed and comparison with the level-of-service definitions in Table 24-1. In order to appreciate the procedure fully, some understanding of *arterial classes* and of *arterial running speed* is required. These terms are addressed in subsections to follow.

It must be understood, however, that the value of the procedure is in the methodological approach and the level-of-service definitions. Specific values for average travel speed can be obtained from a number of sources, including local data, validated simulations, or default estimates from the *HCM* itself.

If field data is available, the framework can be used to determine the level of service of a given arterial without reference to running-time and intersection-delay estimates of the *HCM*. Rather than considering field evaluation as a lesser method, the transportation specialist should consider this as a better and more accurate alternative.

It will be seen that field data on free-flow speed will help in determining the arterial class and also in estimating the running time per mile. In cases where the specific arterial does not yet exist, data on free-flow speed at comparable facilities in the same city or area would be most useful.

The basic element on the arterial is the *segment,* or unidirectional link, from one signal to the next. Figure 24-23 illustrates the segment concept for one-way and two-way arterials. Note that there can be unsignalized intersections within a segment: The definition is from signal to signal.

The methodology is applied to the set of segments in a given direction and to the overall arterial. In addition to level-of-service determination, a plot of speed profile (average travel speed) is very useful. On

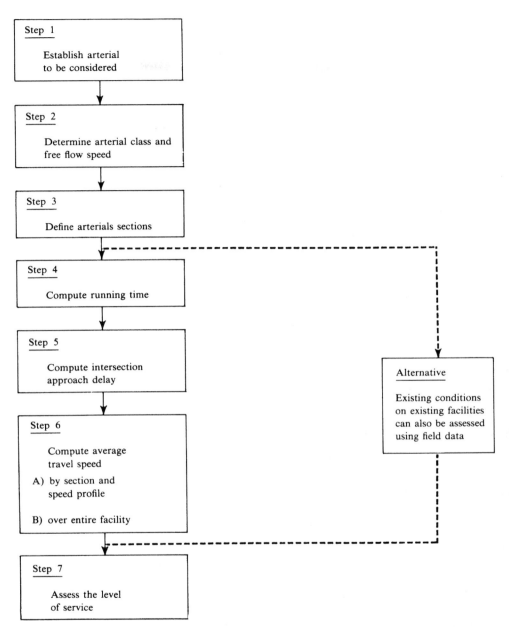

Figure 24-22   Arterial level-of-service methodology. [Used with permission of Transportation Research Board, National Research Council, Washington, DC, from *Highway Capacity Manual, Special Report 209,* 3rd Ed., p. 11-5. Copyright © 1994 Transportation Research Board.]

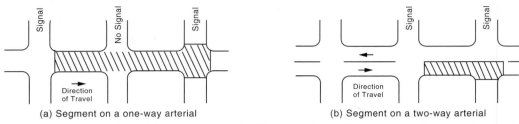

Figure 24-23   Illustration of arterial segments. [Used with permission of Transportation Research Board, National Research Council, Washington, DC, from *Highway Capacity Manual, Special Report 209,* 3rd Ed., p. 11-7. Copyright © 1994 Transportation Research Board.]

two-way arterials, the methodology must be applied *twice* (once in each direction.)

A. Arterial class

In Table 24-1 the definitions of level of service on arterials recognize major differences among arterial "classes" and among the expectations that drivers have on those different arterials. In effect, it is as if the methodology is an "umbrella" for several different, related facilities.

Consider the arterials depicted in Figure 24-24. The first part of the figure shows a divided arterial with left-turn bays, longer block lengths, and separation from the local-access traffic. The second shows an arterial with one lane in each direction, much shorter blocks, and a narrower right of way. In the second case, some would question whether the street *is* an arterial. However, there are such streets that do carry sufficient through traffic to be so classified.

In the two illustrations shown, drivers logically have different expectations of the service they will be provided on such streets. The "expectation" is influenced by a set of factors (parking, right-of-way width, intersection spacing, pedestrians, and so on) in a way that would be difficult to articulate, but that is most obviously reflected in the speeds with which a driver is satisfied for the given street.

The expectation for an arterial can be expressed in terms of the *free-flow speed* drivers expect on an arterial. The *HCM* describes the arterial class in terms of the street's function and its design, and closely links the result to the free-flow speed. Indeed, an ambiguity is resolved by reliance on the free-flow speed.

B. Arterial speeds

There are three relevant speeds on an arterial:

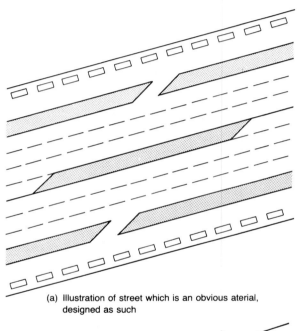

(a) Illustration of street which is an obvious aterial, designed as such

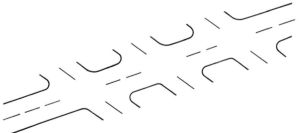

(b) Illustration of a street which is an aterial only by virtue of amount of through traffic

Figure 24-24   Illustration of two arterials clearly with different driver expectations.

1. Free-flow speed
2. Running speed
3. Average travel speed

Free-flow speeds. The *free-flow* speed is the speed most drivers would choose on the arterial if they had green indications and were alone in their direction of movement (i.e., they were not part of a platoon) but had all other prevailing conditions. That is, they would have to be conscious of block spacing, contiguous land use, right-of-way characteristics (profile, medians, and so on), pedestrian activity, parking, and all other such factors.

It would be nice if there were some quantified relations between the factors cited and free-flow speed. However, the most extensive research on the subject in the early 1980s [38] was not able to establish such relations; additional work in the future may do so, but there is no wide data base supporting such relations at this time (circa 1996). Actually, it is probably easier to get consensus on free-flow speed on a particular facility than it is to establish the data base for the preferred relations.

EXERCISE: As an exercise with a group (three or more students, or a class), identify two local streets representative of those shown in Figure 24-24 and known to most members of the group. Let each person form an opinion of the free-flow speed on each street, and then discuss the speeds as a group. Emphasize or review the factors cited that describe the driver's "environment" on the street. Do not give undue weight to the speedster of the group, who will claim to go at 60 mph whenever possible.

Experience with such groups has shown the authors that a consensus will be reached relatively quickly, and a better understanding of how the factors influence the desired speed will also be obtained.

Three major items characterize the arterial—environment, traffic, and signals. The free-flow speed is determined by the total "environment."

As such, the free-flow speed may vary by time of day. An urban arterial can have different free-flow speeds at 6:00 P.M. and 3:00 A.M. However, as we will see, in most cases this will not influence the identification of arterial class.

It does influence how *observable* free-flow speed is: Free-flow speed should be measured at just the time when all the factors are present, except for the prevailing traffic levels (which are also present, of necessity) and red indications. Thus, common advice would

be to measure the speed of individual vehicles away from platoons at midblock, away from these influences, as an approximation of free-flow speed.

Running speed. The *running speed* or *average running speed* is the driver's desired speed with both the environment and the traffic considered. That is, it is the driver's desired speed when he or she is in platoon and must consider the other vehicles going in the same direction. It might be 5 to 10 mph lower than the free-flow speed.

Average travel speed. The *average travel speed* is the actual speed with the additional effect of signals and all other stops added. It is the measure by which level of service is defined.

To summarize, note that:

Speed	Factors Considered	Comment	Best Arrived At by
Free-flow speed	Environment	Driver's expectation, traveling alone	Consensus, with midblock measurement an approximation
Running speed	Environment, traffic	Driver's expectation, in platoon	Measurement, with *HCM* default table if needed
Average travel speed	Environment, traffic, *and* signals	Actual speed	Measurement or computation

C. Arterial running time

There are a number of ways in which both running time *and* intersection-approach delay may be obtained, including (1) travel-time studies, which include both components; (2) output of well-established and calibrated models or signal-optimization programs, such as TRANSYT or NETSIM; (3) information on running times from local data, and computation of intersection delay based on Chapter 7 or other procedures; and (4) default values of running times and computation of intersection delay based on the methods just cited.

The remainder of this chapter will generally focus on the last two approaches and will present some background on the arterial-running-time default values. When other methods are used to obtain the average travel speed or its component parts, the only cautions are that (1) the analyst must be comfortable (and correct) in understanding which type of delay is being computed and how it relates to the "intersection approach delay" called for in the arterial methodology, and (2) when models such as NETSIM and TRANSYT are used, they must be properly calibrated or the analyst must recognize that default values—sometimes buried in the model—are being accepted, just as surely as the default values in other approaches are being superseded.

There is a table of default values in the *HCM* for average running speed, expressed in terms of running time per mile (*HCM* Table 11-4). This table shows the effect of segment length (i.e., signal spacing) directly. It also allows for arterial-class and free-flow-speed differences. Factors such as the presence of parking, side frictions, local development, and number of driveways are not considered explicitly. They do influence the free-flow speed, so that observation of free-flow speed is considered a proxy for such factors (of necessity).

The FHWA data base [38] underlying the default relations was not able to quantify such factors individually, due to the experimental design as well as the limits of regression analysis to discern small effects given available sample sizes. For instance, it is logical that there is a dependence of segment running time on traffic flow rate. It logically exists, but it is not strong. Certainly, it is not as strong as the effect of segment length on segment running time. Nor is it as strong as the substantial variation of intersection approach delay with traffic flow rate.

Fortunately, as a practical matter, computations of *arterial travel speed* for different traffic flow rates would be dominated by the changes in intersection approach delay, whether or not the segment-running-time dependence were clearly identified. Thus the absence of such an explicit factor does not affect the practical result, namely the computation of arterial travel speed.

The final version of the default table was created by an FHWA effort, in conjunction with the Arterials Subcommittee of the relevant TRB Committee [39] and the NCHRP contractor [40] responsible for the text of the 1985 *HCM*; the authors were involved in this effort. FHWA cleaned the data and finalized the regression analyses.

The default table must be viewed as a mosaic constructed by the inspection of many arterial segments and observation of travel times on those segments. It is blended together by regression analysis and some adaptation, but if one were constructing a new facility, the data base did not *vary* the segment length or any underlying variable on any single facility in the same sense a design engineer might vary a parameter in selecting a segment length.

The correct delay to use in the arterial evaluation is the total *approach* delay, which can be estimated as:

$$D = 1.3d \qquad [24\text{-}9]$$

where: D = intersection approach delay (sec/veh)
d = intersection stopped delay (sec/veh)

and where the intersection stopped delay is computed in accordance with Chapter 18.

If for any reason the capacity is not readily available or if the *adjusted demand flow rate* (denoted v, with units of vph) is desired, recall that the v/c ratio X_i is defined by $X_i = v_i/c_i$. The adjusted demand flow rate is computed by correcting for the peak-hour factor and the lane-utilization factor, as in Chapter 18.

In certain applications in which approximations are needed or desired (such as a *planning application* of the methodology), it may also be useful to recall a default relation for the capacity of the lane group:

$$c_i \simeq 1700 \times N \times (g_i/C) \qquad [24\text{-}10]$$

where N is the number of lanes in the lane group and both C and g/C have been defined above.

When Equation [24-10] is used to compute a capacity value (rather than using the multiple correction factors of Chapter 18, the evaluation becomes highly approximate. This may be used in "planning" applications of the arterial methodology. Note that some detailed information on signal timing and quality of progression is needed in *all* applications of the arterial methodology.

D. Potential for intersection and arterial LOS balance

The arterial level of service reflects solely *how good the trip is for through vehicles, over the defined segment or trip length.*

Intersections and arterials serve two distinct functions and have quality-of-flow measures suited to their function. The intersection's function is to move vehicles in competing flows past a *point*. The arterial's function is to move vehicles along a longitudinal *distance*.

To gain insight, Equation [24-1] can be rewritten in terms of intersections per mile in the following way:

$$\text{ART SPD} = \frac{3600}{(\text{running time per mile}) + 1.3\,(N)(\text{stopped delay per intersection})} \qquad [24\text{-}11]$$

where N is the number of intersections per mile.

An intersection with a stopped delay of 4.9 sec per vehicle is certainly level of service A in terms of its function. However, for a Class II arterial with a free-flow speed of 35 mph and 10 intersections per mile, the arterial average travel speed is $3600/[145 + 1.3(10)(4.9)] = 17.2$ mph. This could not be rated A under any circumstances.

It *would have* been convenient to have the intersection and arterials level of service "match" or balance, had this been logical. The engineer or planner must now present an analysis that shows ten consecutive intersections at LOS A, resulting in an overall trip (in this example) with LOS D:

Arterial

LOS D

Intersections

LOS A   . . .   LOS A   . . .   LOS A

This can be explained only in terms of the *function* of the two traffic facilities, as presented above: How well is each doing its job?

Of course, the extra complexity (and to the engineer appearing at a public hearing, inconvenience) is testimony to the importance of the signal-spacing factor: It can and does affect the quality of the arterial trip.

E. Design implications of arterial level of service

The discussion above leads to an interesting implication: Even great intersection performance may not be good enough to obtain good arterial performance, if there are too many signals per mile.

Stated another way, for even reasonable numbers of signals per mile, it is true that good arterial performance requires great intersection performance in many cases.

Consider an existing arterial with observed running speed of 40 mph and five signals per mile, determined to be a Class I arterial. Local officials desire the arterial to let drivers average between 30 and 35 mph. Using Equation [24-11] and noting that a running speed of 40 mph implies a running time of $3600/40 = 90$ sec per mile,

$$35\text{ mph} = \frac{3600}{90 + 1.3(5)(\text{delay})}$$

so that each intersection must have (on average) 1.98 sec of stopped delay per vehicle for the lane group containing the through traffic. For an average travel speed of 30 mph, the answer would have been 4.62 sec per vehicle; for 32.5 mph, 3.19 sec per vehicle.

There are only two ways to assure such performance in most circumstances: (1) Take green time from the side street to give to the main street, with consequent delay and inconvenience to the side-street vehicles, and (2) design the arterial to achieve the target intersection delay (for the arterial through vehicles) by some combination of signal coordination, number of lanes, and/or other factors.

Focusing on the latter item, the simple fact is that what would have been looked upon as *over-design* based only on the operation of an intersection has become *necessary* to achieve proper arterial operation.

The engineer or planner faced with this problem must be able to make it well understood that *excellent* intersection operation is often needed for *proper* arterial operation. Indeed, this need becomes more acute as the number of signals per mile increases.

The engineer or planner must also be able to focus on the desires and specification of the user (the driver), as reflected by the local officials. A request for certain arterial performance (e.g., 30 to 35 mph in the illustration) will frequently result in intersection design requirements that would in fact be overdesign if the intersection were isolated, or were not part of an arterial system.

Summary

This chapter placed a certain emphasis on the role of underlying design principles in setting the framework for a good facility-management approach. It also introduced some additional information, to encourage the reader to think in terms of the components of the traffic stream—transit, goods vehicles, passenger cars—and pedestrian activity. Moreover, these must be viewed in the context of providing support for the economic activity of the community.

At the same time, this chapter did *not* emphasize some management tools which are ITS-based, in part because they were addressed in Chapter 2:

- Satelite-based *vehicle location systems* are now a reality, and finding a market.
- *Dynamic route guidance* will be able to provide the driver with up-to-date information, and at the same time gain insight for traffic engineers into *network O-D patterns* needed for planning and modeling (although the societal acceptability of acquiring such data for even benign purposes has not yet been fully explored).
- The on-board electronics and *computing power* of newer vehicles virtually dictates that substantial innovations are assured in coming years. Indeed, they are underway.

- Communications capabilities and existing banking/billing systems have made *automated toll collection* an operational reality, and can lead to the politically sensitive issues of *automated congestion road pricing*.
- The increases in computing power and communications can lead to *automated vehicle control,* with associated essential increases in roadway capacity, well beyond our limits to construct new conventional facilities.
- The communications technology for route guidance can lead to situations in which the sign inventory is replaced by *sign images* projected before the driver in a "heads-up" display.

The authors recognize the sheer enjoyment of looking to this future, but also recognize that few prognosticators of the past have had meaningful insights into their future, the pace and timing of technological change, or its implications.

We will therefore close this chapter with an invitation to the reader to speculate on the timing and impact of major shifts in our transportation technology *and* the related travel demand needs (which are rooted in all other shifts, changes, and opportunities in our society), particularly as they relate to the facility-management concerns of this chapter.

References

1. Kramer, R. P., "New Combinations of Old Techniques to Rejuvenate Jammed Suburban Arterials," *Strategies to Alleviate Traffic Congestion, Proceedings of the 1987 National Conference,* Institute of Transportation Engineers, Washington, DC, 1988.
2. *Highway Capacity Manual, Special Report 209,* 3rd Edition, Transportation Research Board, National Research Council, Washington, DC, (revised) 1994.
3. McShane, W., et al., *Insights into Access Management Details Using TRAF-NETSIM,* presented at The Second National Conference on Access Management, August 1996.
4. Levinson, H. S., "Operational Measures—Future," report presented at the 32nd Annual Meeting, Institute of Transportation Engineers, Denver, CO, August 1962, published in the *ITE Proceedings,* 1962.
5. "Traffic Control in Oversaturated Street Networks," *NCHRP Report 194,* Transportation Research Board, National Research Council, Washington, DC, 1988.

6. Poteat, V. P., "Traffic Signal Retiming: It Works!" *Strategies to Alleviate Traffic Congestion, Proceedings of the 1987 National Conference,* Institute of Transportation Engineers, Washington, DC, 1988.
7. "Planning Urban Arterial and Freeway Systems: Proposed Recommended Practice," Institute of Transportation Engineers Technical Committee 6Y-19, *ITE Journal,* April 1985.
8. Long, G. D., et al., "Safety Impacts of Selected Median and Access Design Features," report to Florida Department of Transportation, Transportation Research Center, University of Florida, Gainesville, FL, May 1995.
9. Bowman, B. L., and Vecellio, R. L., "The Effect of Urban/Suburban Median Types on Both Vehicular and Pedestrian Safety," paper presented at the 73rd Annual Meeting of the Transportation Research Board, January 1994.

10. "Driveway and Street Intersection Spacing," *Circular 456,* Transportation Research Board, National Research Council, Washington, DC, March 1996.

11. Homburger, W. S., et al. (editors), *Transportation and Traffic Engineering Handbook,* 2nd Edition, Prentice-Hall, Englewood Cliffs, NJ, 1982.

12. Rosenbaum, M., "Traffic Control for Reversible Flow Two-Way Left-Turn Lanes," *Public Roads,* June 1986.

13. Crowley, K. W., and Habib, P. A., *Mobility of People and Goods in the Urban Environment—Facilitation of Urban Goods Movement,* December 1975.

14. *A Recommended Practice for Proper Location of Bus Stops,* Institute of Transportation Engineers, Washington, DC, 1967.

15. *Evaluation of UTCS/BPS Control Strategies,* U.S. Department of Transportation, Federal Highway Administration, Washington, DC, March 1975.

16. Tarnoff, P. J., "The Result of Urban Public Traffic Control Research: An Interim Report," *Traffic Engineering,* Vol. 45, No. 4, April 1975.

17. Yedlin, M., et al., *Bus Signal Priority Strategies: A Literature Review and State of the Art Assessment,* Contract No. DOT-FH-11-9609, Federal Highway Administration, Washington, DC, December 1979.

18. "Automatic Vehicle Location/Control and Traffic Signal Preemption: Lessons from Europe," NTIS PB95-1309512, Chicago Transit Authority, September 1992.

19. "Main Line Traffic Signal Priority Study, Phase 4, Final Report," NTIS PB92-153279, Municipality of Metropolitan Toronto, Toronto, Canada, April 1989.

20. Luedtke, P., Smith, S., Lieu, H., and Kanaan, A., "Simulating DART's North Central Light Rail Line Using TRAF-NETSIM," *ITE Compendium of Technical Papers,* Institute of Transportation Engineers, Washington, DC, 1993.

21. Bauer, T., Medema, M., and Jayanthi, S. V., "Testing of Light Rail Signal Control Strategies by Combining Transit and Traffic Simulation Models," *Transportation Research Record 1494,* Transportation Research Board, National Research Council, Washington, DC, 1995.

22. Venglar, S. P., Fambro, D. B., Bauer, T., "Validation of Simulation Software for Modeling Light Rail Transit," *Transportation Research Record 1494,* Transportation Research Board, National Research Council, Washington, DC, 1995.

23. Yager, S., "Efficient Transit Priority at Intersections," *Transportation Research Record 1390,* Transportation Research Board, National Research Council, Washington, DC.

24. Yager, S., and Han, B., "A Procedure for Real-Time Signal Control That Considers Transit Interference and Priority," *Transportation Research—Part B,* Vol. 28, No. 4, 1994.

25. Sunkari, S. R., Beasley, P. S., Urbanik, T., and Fambro, D. B., "Model to Evaluate the Impacts of Bus Priority on Signalized Intersections," *Transportation Research Record 1494,* Transportation Research Board, National Research Council, Washington, DC, 1995.

26. Cisco, B. A., and Khasnabis, S., "Techniques to Assess Delay and Queue Length Consequences of Bus Preemption," *Transportation Research Record 1494,* Transportation Research Board, National Research Council, Washington, DC, 1995.

27. Chang, G.-L., Vasudevan, M., and Su, C.-C., "Bus-Preemption Under Adaptive Signal Control Environments," *Transportation Research Record 1494,* Transportation Research Board, National Research Council, Washington, DC, 1995.

28. Khasnabis, S., Karnati, R. R., and Rudraraju, R. K., "A NETSIM-based Approach to Evaluate Bus Preemption Strategies," presented at Annual Meeting, Transportation Research Board, Washington, DC, January 1996.

29. Khasnabis, S., Reddy, G. V., and Hoda, S. K., "Evaluation of the Operating Cost Consequences of Signal Preemption as an IVHS Strategy," *Transportation Research Record 1390,* Transportation Research Board, National Research Council, Washington, DC, 1992.

30. Bissell, H. H., and Cima, B. T., "Dallas Freeway Corridor Study," *Public Roads,* Vol. 45, No. 3, 1982.

31. Ross, Pal, "An Evaluation of Network Signal Timing Transition Algorithms," *Transportation Engineering,* September 1977.

32. Crowley, K. W., "Arterial Signal Control," Ph.D. Dissertation, Polytechnic Institute, Brooklyn, NY, 1972.

33. Messer, C. J., et al., *A Variable-Sequence Multiphase Progression Optimization Program, Highway Research Record 445,* Transportation Research Board, National Research Council, Washington, DC, 1973.

34. Kreer, J. B., "When Mixed Cycle Length Signal Timing Reduces Delay," *Traffic Engineering,* March 1977.

35. Messer, C. J., et al., "Optimization of Pretimed Signalized Diamond Interchanges Using Passer III," *Transportation Research Report 644,* Transportation Research Board, National Research Council, Washington, DC, 1977.

36. Messer, C. J., et al., "A Real-Time Frontage Road Progression Analysis and Control Strategy," *Transportation Research Report 503,* Transportation Research Board, National Research Council, Washington, DC, 1974.

37. Oh, Y. T., "The Effectiveness for the Selections of Various Diamond Interchange Designs," Ph.D.

Dissertation, Polytechnic University, Brooklyn, NY, January 1988.

38. Shapiro, S., et al., "Quality of Flow on Urban Arterials: Phase II," *Final Report,* Contract No. DTFH61-80-C-00136, U.S. Department of Transportation, Federal Highway Administration, Washington, DC, 1985.

39. Transportation Research Board Committee on Highway Capacity and Quality of Service (TRB Committee A3A10).

40. *New Highway Capacity Manual,* NCHRP Project 3-28B, Polytechnic University with Texas Transportation Institute (subcontractor), Brooklyn, NY, March 1985.

Problems

Problem 24–1

An arterial has a free-flow speed of 45 mph, and an observed running time of 75 sec per mile. Each of its intersections has 4.5 sec of stopped delay per vehicle for the through-lane group. For 8 signals per mile, compute the arterial average travel speed and the arterial level of service. Do the same for 12 signals per mile.

Problem 24–2

An arterial has the same traffic demand, phasing, and splits on its northbound and southbound directions. Yet field studies show markedly different average travel speeds (and thus levels of service) in the two directions. Specify the most obvious reason(s) for this.

Problem 24–3

A field study has shown the following information along a northbound one-way arterial:

Block	Running Time (sec)	Intersection Approach Delay (sec/veh)	Midblock Special Delays (sec/veh)
1	18.0	5.4	—
2	21.5	7.9	—
3	19.3	10.1	—
4	23.0	10.1	15.0
5	22.0	10.1	—
6	19.7	8.3	—
7	17.4	6.0	—

The special midblock delay is a pedestrian crossing. The arterial has been found to be Class I. Evaluate the arterial level of service, by segment and overall, and the intersection levels of service at each intersection. Plot the speed profile along the arterial, and show the overall travel speed on the same plot. Comment. The length of each link is 0.2 miles.

Problem 24–4

An existing arterial is to be totally rehabilitated and upgraded to be the principal access to a town's industrial and commercial development corridor. The arterial is to be a divided facility with left-turn bays and protected left turns, plus two through lanes in each direction. The free-flow speed is estimated to be 53 mph based on other facilities in the area. Signal spacing is to be 0.25 mile, with excellent control of access, no parking, and no significant pedestrian activity.

The evaluation is desired for the eastbound A.M. period, which is characterized by the following estimated demand volumes:

Segment	Demand Volume (vph)	Percent Left Turns
1	1800	5%
2	1750	10%
3	1650	5%
4	1775	5%
5	1600	5%
6	1700	5%
7	1550	10%
8	1675	10%

The segments are numbered from east to west. The peak-hour factor used in the area for this type of facility is 0.86. Because of the flexibility of the development phase, it is not feasible to provide estimates of signal progression quality, g/C, or cycle length. However, a cycle length of 80 sec may be assumed. Evaluate the arterial level of service and the arterial capacity.

Problem 24–5

A number of test car runs in each direction on a two-way arterial yields the following information:

Segment	Northbound	
	Cumulative Avg. Travel Time (sec)	Average Stopped Delay (sec/veh)
NB Start $\longrightarrow$	0.0	
1	23.0	4.1
2	47.2	6.2
3	82.4	13.2
4	122.9	17.3
5	161.8	16.1
6	196.3	12.7
7	226.4	9.3
8	255.1	8.2
9	281.8	6.7
10	307.5	5.9

Segment	Southbound	
	Cumulative Avg. Travel Time (sec)	Average Stopped Delay (sec/veh)
1	414.0	24.2
2	366.3	22.8
3	320.9	21.7
4	276.9	19.7
5	235.3	17.8
6	194.2	20.2
7	149.9	16.3
8	111.5	17.1
9	72.1	13.7
10	37.0	14.6
SB Start $\longrightarrow$	0.0	

The travel times are cumulative, and include all stopped time. All segments are 0.20 mile long. The observed free-flow speed is 48 mph. The segments are numbered from south to north.

Determine the level of service in each segment and overall, for each direction. Plot the arterial speed profile in each direction.

Problem 24–6

Consider the eastbound direction of a Class II arterial, with 28 mph running speed and the following information at each signal for the lane group containing the through traffic;

$$C = 70 \text{ sec}$$
$$g/C = 0.60$$
$$X_i = 0.80$$
$$c = 1950 \text{ vph}$$

The arterial segments are 0.15 mile each. The signals are pretimed.

Investigate the effect of the quality of progression by considering all possibilities, and tabulating the arterial segment average travel speed and LOS that results, as well as the intersection stopped delay and LOS. [Recall that the quality of progression affects the stopped delay directly; use Equation [24-1] or [24-11] for the analysis.

Problem 24–7

Refer to Table 24-2. Assume that all conditions specified are in effect. For an arterial with four signals to the mile and two through lanes in each direction, specify the AADT which can be accommodated at LOS C. If a third lane is added in each direction, how much more AADT can be added while maintaining the same level of service? If the third lane is not added, but the AADT grows to the value found, what happens to the level of service?

Problem 24–8

If the arrival type is 5 rather than 4, solve all parts of Problem 24–7 again.

Problem 24–9

Consider the intersection and volumes shown in Figure 24-25. Use the intersection procedure of Chapter 19 to determine the v/c ratio, stopped delay, and level of service by lane group for

(a) Two-phase operation, cycle length of your choice.
(b) Three-phase operation, cycle length of your choice. Identify the lost time per phase and the sum of critical volumes in each case. [*Related Thoughts:* Should a two-phase operation be allowed when three lanes have to be crossed? Should a two-phase operation be allowed with the turn volumes shown for the EB and WB? Why or why not? (Look at the required timing in detail.) Note that (a) basic principles from other chapters must be kept in mind, (b) safety aspects must be kept in mind, and (c) "rules of thumb" from other chapters are sometimes illustrated in later problems.]
(c) Consider that the left turns can be converted into right turns as shown in Figure 24-7. How will the intersection then operate? Do a detailed analysis, and explain any improvement (or degradation). Sketch the revised intersection layout.
(d) If the left turns are converted as shown in Figure 24-6(b), how will the intersection operate? Which do you recommend, based on (1) overall total delay, and (2) primary concern with the arterial?

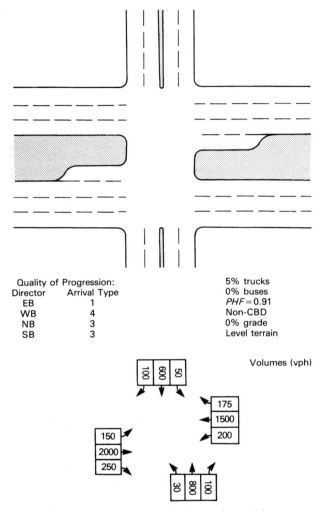

Quality of Progression:

Director	Arrival Type
EB	1
WB	4
NB	3
SB	3

5% trucks
0% buses
PHF = 0.91
Non-CBD
0% grade
Level terrain

Volumes (vph)

Figure 24-25 Intersection and volumes for Problem 24–9.

Problem 24–10

If the EB lefts had been 200 vph and the WB lefts 150 vph (rather than the other way around), how would this have affected the answers to each part of Problem 24–1?

Problem 24–11

You are to prepare a set of "design guidelines" for the two configurations of Figure 24-4 expressed in terms of traffic parameters and available geometrics, considering such aspects as:

Left-turn volumes

v/s ratios on the arterial and cross streets

Median turn setback distance *D*, for three possibilities:
    $D \simeq 350$ ft
    $D \simeq 500$ ft
    $D > 800$ ft

Also, specify some minimum median widths to allow (a) passenger cars only to turn, (b) all standard-design vehicles to turn. Further, estimate the increased travel distance and/or travel time for the left-turn vehicles as a function of the distance *D* and other parameters (if possible).

Note: The purpose of this problem is to introduce you to—or remind you of—the issues that go into a design selection, and the need to express such issues in terms of parameters available from the preliminary data.

Note: A good analysis of this problem may involve many test runs of the intersection performance over a range of conditions, and may constitute a good term project rather than a simple homework. Listing the factors and sketching ideas about the answer may constitute a challenging homework problem.

Problem 24–12

The text provides an estimate of 2000 vph from each major generator in Figure 24-7 (the generators are on the north and south sides of the arterial).

(a) Using Kramer's design characteristics so that the arterial (*g/C*) must be 0.67 or better, and using typical discharge headways and lost times, derive this estimate, justifying or revising it. Also specify or analyze:

(b) The location of all signals needed in Figure 24-7, and the coordination needed among them (if any), plus an overall phasing plan;

(c) The amount of through traffic (in addition to the traffic from the generators) that can be handled by the arterial. If necessary, assume that the directional split from each generator is 50:50 east–west;

(d) The effect on the analysis in part (c) if the directional split were such that 75% of all generator traffic (total of *both* generators) went (1) to the west, or (2) to the east. Note that this might occur because of the location of roads leading into/out of the area;

(e) The minimum length of the storage area indicated in Figure 24-7, for the three directional splits (50:50, 75:25, 25:75);

(f) Any modification to this minimum length based on interaction between various flows ("weaving"), such as the eastbound traffic heading north and the traffic from the northern generator which is to be eastbound.

Problem 24–13

Refer to Figure 24-26 and Table 24-9 for a description of a simple two-by-two grid of two-way streets, and their related demand volumes.

(a) Assess the *v/c* ratios, estimated delay, and level of service by approach using the procedure of Chapter 18 and summarize the results on an overlay of the sketch given. Comment.

(b) Assign the volumes to the proposed one-way grid shown in the insert on Figure 24-26 such that the same turns occur and the totals coming from/going to the various points of the compass (i.e., north, south, east, west) are the same as originally. Prepare a new version of Table 24-9.

(c) Assess the same information as in part (a), but for the proposed one-way system. Compare the results. Find reasons for any improvements or degradations. [*Note:* Keep the same cycle length, and continue to favor the

Table 24-9 Demand Volumes [a,b] for Problem 24–13

		Intersection			
		#1	#2	#3	#4
EB	L	150	150	100	100
	T	1200	900	*	*
	R	50	50	50	50
WB	L	50	50	50	50
	T	*	*	600	450
	R	100	100	50	50
NB	L	50	50	50	50
	T	*	1300	*	1100
	R	50	50	50	50
SB	L	50	50	50	50
	T	600	*	600	*
	R	50	50	50	50

[a]All volumes in vph.

[b]Volumes marked with an asterisk (*) can be derived from the given volumes by balancing. Indeed, they *must* be, in order to do Problem 24–13.

EB and NB in the setting of the progressions. Revise the split if appropriate.]

(d) Repeat part (c) for cycle lengths of 60 and 80 sec. Comment. Is there any cycle length you would prefer (in addition to these)? Why or why not?

Problem 24–14

(a) Equation [24-5] is

$$f' = (g/C) \frac{3000}{t_c + D(g/C)} \quad \text{buses per hour}$$

Show that it goes asymptotically to $f' = 3000/D$, so that the upper limit on boarding demand (single position) is

$$\text{boarding demand} = (B)(f') \longrightarrow 3000(B/D)$$

and that in the related illustrative problem of this chapter, this number is approximately 714 passengers per hour (single position).

(b) Explain why it is impossible to attain a higher number, given the assumptions. Why can't 1200 passengers be handled by a set of charter buses loading 50 people per bus at this bus stop? (That is, why can't we just load up 1200/50 = 24 buses and be done with it?) What assumptions—or realities—prevent it?

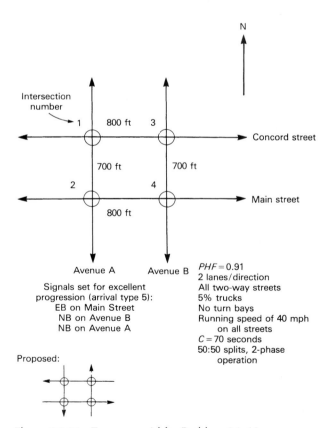

Intersection number

1   800 ft   3

Concord street

700 ft   700 ft

2   4

Main street

800 ft

Avenue A   Avenue B

Signals set for excellent progression (arrival type 5):
EB on Main Street
NB on Avenue B
NB on Avenue A

PHF = 0.91
2 lanes/direction
All two-way streets
5% trucks
No turn bays
Running speed of 40 mph on all streets
C = 70 seconds
50:50 splits, 2-phase operation

Proposed:

Figure 24-26 Two-way grid for Problem 24–13.

Problem 24–15

(a) Use Equation [24-8] to estimate typical bus pce for buses that stop in a moving traffic lane. Use Table 24-6 for information related to dwell times. Tabulate the pce values for $g/C = 0.40, 0.50$, and 0.60.

(b) Explain *specifically* how this information can be used in the intersection evaluation procedure of Chapter 19. If necessary, show an illustrative computation using the "default" conditions of Chapter 18 and the value(s) obtained from Equation [24-8].

Problem 24–16

Justify why (or why not) the loss time of Equation [24-7] *includes* the base-level time for the bus itself, despite the explanatory words that it is just the "loss time."

Note: The practical implication is really whether a computed pce of 4.0 (Equation [24-8] is derived directly from Equation [24-7]) is additional, so that the total pce for the bus is $(4.0 + 1.0) = 5.0$ or may be even $(4.0 + 1.5) = 5.5$, with the latter based on a moving bus pce of 1.5.

Problem 24–17

(a) Develop a set of rules for signal transition from Plan A to Plan B, such that the transition is complete within three cycle lengths.

(b) Apply the rules to the transition from Plan A to Plan B for a set of 6 signals with spacing between signals of 1800 ft, running speed of 60 fps in each direction, with

Plan A	Alternate settings
	50:50 splits
	$C = 60$ sec

Plan B	Simultaneous settings
	60:40 splits
	$C = 75$ sec

(c) Revise the rules so as to achieve the transition after two cycles.

(d) Test again, using the case of part (b).

Problem 24–18

Refer to Figure 24-19. Draw a similar diagram for a three-intersection sequence:

```
         Intersection
    #1        #2        #3
 ───→ * ───→ * ───→ * ───────
      C_b       C_a       C_b
```

for each of two cases:

| *Case 1:* | $C_a = 60$ sec, | $C_b = 120$ sec |
| *Case 2:* | $C_a = 120$ sec, | $C_b = 60$ sec |

with $g/C = 0.60$ in each case, 2.0-sec discharge headway, and all passenger cars. Use a link length of 1000 ft. Comment.

Problem 24–19

Repeat Problem 24–18 for a link length of 500 ft. Comment.

Problem 24–20

Create a spreadsheet capable of producing the information shown in Table 24-2. Use the spreadsheet to investigate the effect of arrival type 2 versus arrival type 4 for the condition specified in the assumptions of Table 24-2.

25

Traffic Simulation: Principles and Tools

Mathematical models are often constructed to describe physical processes. In some cases, the process and the model are *deterministic,* such as those describing an apple falling from a tree, a spacecraft on its flight to the moon, or the deflection of a beam. In other cases, the process and the model are *stochastic,* such as the description of queues in a bank, or at a toll plaza, or on a freeway.

It is not always clear which approach to use, and there are in fact "deterministic queuing" models of traffic congestion based on averaged demand and capacity patterns, as well as stochastic models of spacecraft trajectory based on random forces.

Whichever approach is taken, computers are frequently used as practical tools in the solution of the models. In computer applications, we wish to distinguish between simple uses as a *computational* tool and *simulation* of the process.

In computational applications, we generally have the equations or relations, but write computer code (C++, Fortran) or use a spreadsheet (Quattro, Excel, Lotus) to avoid the hand computations involved, for reasons of speed and accuracy. For instance, the equa-

tions for determining the left-turn factor for a permitted left turn can be programmed, so that a person can avoid these tedious, time-consuming, and error-prone computations.

In this spirit, both the HCS and HCM/Cinema software are primarily computational tools, because they simply execute the relations defined in the *Highway Capacity Manual* [1] in an efficient way. HCM/Cinema, however, does incorporate a simulation element for the purposes of illustration and visualization.

In simulation the most essential element is that the process has significant random components, and that these are explicitly treated. These may be the inter-arrival times of people at a bank or vehicles on a highway. A component may be the decision of an individual vehicle to make a left turn, or to select a particular desired free-flow speed, or to follow a certain acceleration pattern. The computer simulation attempts to incorporate this randomness as an explicit part of the exercise, so that the results reflect the randomness of the real world.

Some people make a distinction between what is really "random" and what only appears to be "random" because of our limited knowledge of the situation. For instance, if we are standing at the side of the road, the decision of the next vehicle to make a left turn (or not) may appear random. However, if we knew the origin and destination of each vehicle, and the trip times by various paths, the decision may not appear to be random at all.

Historically, traffic simulation models match the data realities of their era, and attempt to anticipate the uses to which the model will be put. Practical decisions also are made according to how much data is available to calibrate and validate the model, and in what form (and completeness) that data can be expected to exist.

Some traffic simulation models have treated each left turn as an independent and random decision, with no vehicle identity maintained through the network. If the purpose of the model is to analyze network statistics or even aggregate corridor statistics, this might be fine. However, if a traffic control policy or local incident would cause traffic re-routing in the real world, and if the simulation model is "blind" to vehicle routing, then the simulation model cannot be expected to mimic the response of the real world.

As we approach the year 2000 and take into account the advances in sensing, communications, and computing, it will be a great challenge to make sure that our computer models reflect the real information available to drivers for traffic decisions. In fact, the authors fully expect that some of the current traffic simulation models will prove totally inadequate for this challenge, but will be the logical basis from which the next generation of models will be created.

Basics of simulation

Simulation is used extensively in manufacturing, traffic engineering, and other areas. The simulation models themselves can be classified into generic tools and application-specific models. Modern manufacturing simulations allow the user to define a production line or process by dragging icons of process steps into a logical order in a Windows environment, and to define the characteristics of each process step as well as the workload (demand) characteristics. Likewise, the report statistics may be defined by the user. The actual mechanisms of the simulation are rather invisible to the user.

Traffic simulation models tend to be more application-specific, so that TRAF-NETSIM is tailored to only vehicular traffic on surface street networks. The network definition has become more user-friendly over the years, but is not the same drag-and-click approach of the generic manufacturing models. CORSIM [3] includes both TRAF-NETSIM and FRESIM—tailored to freeway traffic—and has rather user-friendly input.

A. Random number generation

The most basic feature of simulation is randomness, and yet computers are deterministic by their very nature. How then does one generate random numbers on a computer?

The answer is that one creates a computer code that generates a sequence of numbers that *appears* to be random. In fact, there is a pattern, but it repeats only after millions of numbers. Sequential numbers in the chain do not appear to be correlated to each other when standard autocorrelations are done on the chain, and other mechanisms for looking for patterns also tend to miss the deterministic nature of the algorithm generating the numbers. These "pseudo-random" number generating codes are now used extensively and are rather sophisticated in masking the underlying relation. Indeed, they are so routine that spreadsheets now incorporate random-number-generating capabilities.

In many applications, the user can specify a starting or "seed" number for the chain. By specifying a different number, the user picks up the chain in a different place each time, and in a well designed code, no discernable correlation between the two chains exists.

The user can also specify the same number, and be assured that exactly the same numbers are generated in exactly the same pattern. This is extremely useful when one wishes to see how two different control policies affect *exactly* the same traffic, something that is impossible in the real world. (From a statistical point of view, it also allows paired t-tests to be run on the performance data from a set of N replications under two different control policies, if the same set of N different seed numbers is used in the N runs for each policy.)

Lastly, the most common pseudo-random-number generators produce a sequence of numbers that appears to be uniformly distributed on the range (0,1).

B. Time-based versus event-based simulations

It is rather natural to think of moving ahead in discrete steps of time, say one second in the future. With knowledge of vehicle speeds and positions, a car-following relation, a lane-changing rule, and certain other rules, we can then estimate the next positions (and speeds) of individual vehicles. We can also estimate whether a new vehicle entered the system in each entry lane on each link. Further, we can gather information needed for the performance indices and vehicle trajectories. This approach is *discrete time-based* simulation. Most traffic models use this approach.

PROBLEM

Construct a means of determining whether the next vehicle turns left, given that 20% of the vehicles turn left.

SOLUTION: Generate a random number X from the uniform distribution with range (0,1). If $x \leq 0.20$, then the next vehicle turns left. Otherwise, it does not.

PROBLEM

Determine whether a vehicle enters a given lane in discrete time-based simulation with a one second time step, assuming exponential interarrivals with a mean of 3.0 seconds.

SOLUTION: The probability Y that a vehicle will arrive in the next one second is $Y = 1 - e^{-1/3}$, where the "3" is the mean interarrival time. Thus $Y = 0.283$. Generate a random number X from the uniform distribution with range (0,1). If $X \leq Y$, then a vehicle did arrive.

Such decisions are the building blocks of a discrete time-based simulation.

Another approach is *event-based* simulation. Consider a single waiting line on which there are two important events: a customer service is completed, and a new customer arrives. Rather than estimating the probability of each event in the next second, we can generate the time t_1 to the next completion-of-service and the time t_2 to the next arrival, each generated from an appropriate distribution. We can then jump ahead in time by $t_3 = \min(t_1, t_2)$ seconds, and continue to jump ahead from one event to another.

Event-based simulation of neatly contained systems (such as the bank teller line mentioned earlier) generally involves fewer steps over the simulation period than a time-based simulation of the same process, and can therefore be much faster running and even require less computer memory. However, the events must be very well defined, and the actual simulation code tends to be built around the events. If the process mechanisms are redefined—one customer line, multiple servers or various types of customers and toll booth types—the number and definition of events can change, causing a total revision.

Time-based simulations are not only "natural" to our thought process, but they can be modular: The rules for car-following and for lane changing are separable, even if they interact; desired free-flow speeds can be tagged to vehicles easily, and follow vehicles through the system. The modular construct is important, for we have certainly learned that traffic simulation models evolve as experience is gained, and as new needs are defined. Also, the power of modern desktop computers makes the older concerns for computational burden and memory efficiency less important than they once were.

C. Modeling the mechanisms

The first issue is actually *enumerating* the mechanisms of the proposed simulation model, and defining their interactions. This done, it is then necessary to model the individual mechanisms, link them, use them, and refine them in some iterative process that introduces reality. Consider the simple case of traffic traveling on an arterial. The primary mechanisms might be:

- vehicle arrives
- vehicle travels in lane at desired speed
- vehicle interacts with others (car following)
- vehicle changes lane, or not (overtaking? turning? when? why?)
- signal indication influences vehicle
- vehicle decelerates
- vehicle accelerates

This does not include the ways in which the vehicle may interact with pedestrians, geometrics (grade of road, for instance), weather, or sun glare. Nor does it include the ways in which cross traffic is considered, or many other factors.

Nonetheless, having defined these basic mechanisms, the immediate challenge is to establish the details of the mechanisms, the links to other mechanisms (because they are generally interdependent), and the calibration/validation data needs.

Moreover, there must be a guiding principle that anticipates the uses to which the model will be put. This is often elusive, because users find new applications and because the state of the art changes. Nonetheless, the need exists.

Consider the simple decision to affix an identity tag to each vehicle as it enters the network, which it retains as it moves through the network. This allows: (1) future applications to assign a route to that particular vehicle, and to update that route periodically; (2) desired speed and accel/decel patterns to be linked to that vehicle; (3) location data to be stored at each increment of time, allowing trajectories to be reconstructed. Without such an identity tag, the same vehicle might bounce through the network by Brownian motion, subject to a series of random turn decisions (with the turn percentage being a characteristic of the intersection), with no meaningful path information recoverable.

D. Calibrating the mechanisms and/or the model

If the mechanisms are constructed as linked modular entities, it should be possible to calibrate each mechanism individually. Consider the left turn mechanism under permissive signalization, which is basically a gap acceptance rule that considers the size of the available gap, the speed of the approaching opposing vehicle, and perhaps the type of opposing vehicle. It might also consider the type of left turning vehicle, the "pressure" from queued vehicles behind the turner, the number of lanes to be crossed, and other factors.

The challenge is to define the mechanism in a way that is both realistic and capable of calibration with an affordable amount of data. The starting point is often the traffic theory literature. Once the data plan is constructed, it must be executed at sufficient sites to assure credibility.

At this level of detail, it may be that the model as an entity is not calibrated as such, but that it is run for "reality checks" on whether the overall performance is credible.

E. Validating the mechanisms and/or the model

Validation is a distinct operation from calibration, and requires data reserved or collected for the purpose. Calibration data cannot be used to validate a model, simply because it is then a self-fulfilling prophesy.

Validation can be done on two levels, the microscopic checking of individual mechanisms and the macroscopic checking of aggregate performance measures. The latter category may verify that arterial travel times, average speeds, and delay conform to real world observations when observed traffic data (volumes, composition, etc.) are fed into the model. Because this is a statistical test, usually operating with a null hypothesis that the model and real world results are the same, a validation may require a significant amount of data.

Microscopic validation of individual mechanisms is done less frequently, simply because of the data needs. However, it is logical that it be part of every research project in which particular mechanism(s) are pivotal in determining the aggregate results, or the specific performance being investigated as part of the research.

A close look at the details of the simulation model may reveal items in which a new and detailed mechanism *calibration* is needed before the anticipated research investigation can be done. For instance, TRAF-NETSIM has a mechanism by which vehicles can turn into or out of driveways. However, this mechanism does not include any details on the geometrics of the driveways, and therefore TRAF-NETSIM in its present form (as of this writing) cannot be used to investigate such features.

Issues in traffic simulation

A number of issues in planning a traffic simulation study deserve special attention.

A. Number of replications

Assuming that the traffic model is as random as the real world, at least in its internal mechanisms, the resulting performance measures will be *samples* or *observations* from a set of possible outcomes.

That is, each performance measure is a random variable, with a mean and variance (among other properties).

Because of this, several runs (or "replications") of the situation are needed, each with its own set of seed random numbers. If one desires a certain confidence bound, a considerable number of replications might be required. If one can only afford a limited number of replications, then the resultant confidence bound might be disappointing.

A rule of thumb has emerged in traffic simulations that three replications are the minimum, and many users have translated this to mean that three replications will suffice. *This is without foundation, and confidence bounds must be considered in each case.*

Consider the following nine replications in which the average speed is read from the results:

Run	Average speed (mph)
1	45.2
2	52.5
3	43.7
4	48.4
5	47.3
6	53.2
7	46.7
8	42.9
9	50.1

From these results, one can estimate a mean of 47.8 mph and a standard deviation of 3.6 mph. Further, the 95% confidence bounds on the mean are ±2.4 mph. If ±1.0 mph were necessary, then 51 replications would have been required, rather than nine. Now if one could only afford nine replications (or had time for only nine), then the 95% confidence bound on the mean is unavoidably ±2.4 mph.

Some situations are not as bleak as this particular example. There is also some advantage to be gained when two control policies are to be compared, in terms of their effect on the performance measure. Consider the case in which nine replications are done with each of two control policies, using the same nine sets of seed numbers for each policy. This "pairs" specific sets of runs and allows us to construct the following:

Run	Control Policy One, Average Speed (mph)	Control Policy Two, Average Speed (mph)	Paired Difference (mph), CP2-CP1
1	45.2	48.1	2.9
2	52.5	54.3	1.8
3	43.7	44.3	0.6
4	48.4	51.4	3.0
5	47.3	50.2	2.9
6	53.2	55.8	2.6
7	46.7	48.3	1.6
8	42.9	45.2	2.3
9	50.1	53.5	3.4

If a test were done on the data without pairing, under the hypothesis of "the two means are the same," the variability in the data would probably yield a decision to *not* reject this hypothesis. However, by pairing the runs according to the seed numbers, the differences by pairs can be computed, as shown in the last column above. In this particular case (which we arranged to be so dramatic), *all* of the differences are positive, with a mean of 2.3 mph and a standard deviation of 0.9 mph. Indeed, the 95% confidence bounds on mean difference are ±0.6 mph, and a hypothesis of "zero difference" is easily rejected. While not all cases are so dramatic, the reader must understand the advantages of a well-planned set of runs.

B. Length of run

There is also a rule of thumb that traffic simulation runs (specifically, with TRAF-NETSIM) should be 15 minutes long. This can be very misleading. Rather than follow such a rule of thumb, the user must focus on the defining events, determine how often they occur, and select the run duration so that a reasonable number of these cases occur in the observation period.

Consider the case in which the productivity of an approach is being considered, and there are two defining events—the vehicle at the head of the queue is a left turner who traps everyone else, or it isn't. If the first situation occurs only 10% of the time, and by definition can occur only once every cycle length, then a 15-minute period with a 90-second cycle length will have *no* such blockages 35% of the runs, and only one such blockage another 39% of the runs.

Lengthening the run duration will dramatically lower these probabilities, if that is desired.

The authors have found that runs of 1–2 hours of simulated time are frequently desired when a number of such "rare" events should be included in the typical period. Another situation which may lead to longer runs is taking the effect of buses into account, because the interarrival times in some cases is 3–5 minutes based on local transit schedules.

C. Detail of specific detailed mechanisms

We have already noted that driveway geometrics are not included in TRAF-NETSIM, limiting the analysis that can be done on the effect of driveway location/number/design on access management measures. Consider another case, that of bus traffic in an urban area. If the simulation model specifies a dwell time distribution but does not link it to the interarrival time between buses, an important mechanism contributing to platooning of buses can be overlooked (because delayed buses *in the model* do not have more people waiting for them, and early-arriving buses do not have fewer). If a user is looking at overall performance, this may not be a problem. But if the user is trying to study bus platooning specifically, this can be a major problem, and the mechanism might have to be calibrated and the model revised.

D. Avoiding using the model beyond its limits

This is simply another aspect of the point just made, but is a particular challenge when a user is trying a new application. A working knowledge of the model is needed, on a level that only the developers and a few others might have.

E. Selecting performance measures for the model

The traffic engineering profession has a number of well-established measures (volume, flow rate, speed, delay) and a number of evolving ones, particularly as relate to multimodal considerations. Even so, the measures defined in some simulation models may not conform to the standard definitions and usage. For in-

stance, there are many forms of "speed" used in both practice and traffic models.

F. User-friendly input and output

Whereas the preceding subsections focus on some of the important application issues, the most important user issues tend to be in how user-friendly the input/output is, and how efficiently it can link to existing data bases, if at all.

There have been considerable advances in user-friendly input for traffic simulation models. In addition, the use of animation has helped the visualization of the output. Lessons learned from virtual reality can be expected to influence future model refinements.

A set of traffic models

There are a number of traffic simulation models, but none as widely validated and used as TRAF-NETSIM. We will focus on the pair of street network and freeway microscopic models (TRAF-NETSIM and FRESIM, respectively), now available in an integrated simulation tool known as CORSIM [3]—a corridor simulation model.

CORSIM is available as a user-friendly PC-based tool, and its component models have very effective graphical displays and animations.

TRAF-NETSIM

TRAF-NETSIM is a microscopic simulation model that represents the movements of vehicles on an urban network. Each vehicle in the traffic stream is treated as a unique entity. Each vehicle's trajectory and characteristics are updated every interval based on the vehicle's reaction to external stimuli, such as traffic signals, stop or yield signs, other vehicles' movements (which include analysis of behavioral characteristics), and pedestrian activity (although pedestrian activity is not specifically simulated).

Detailed measures of effectiveness (MOEs) are updated every second and are reported as totals to the user at the end of the analysis period (or the user can specify that statistics be reported for some intermediate interval).

Because the model is microscopic, it requires detailed data inputs to accurately represent the real world situation being simulated. The input types that are needed for TRAF-NETSIM can be classified into three groups [3]: geometric inputs, traffic inputs, and control inputs.

The *geometric input data* describes the physical network over which the vehicles travel. The network is defined in terms of nodes (intersections) and links connecting the nodes. The user must input the number of lanes on each link and in each turn bay, the length of the total link and of any turn bays, grade, how the lanes are channelized, and any special alignment of the lanes. Figure 25-1 shows a sample network and the link representation of the network. As part of the input process, each link must be defined in terms of lanes, turn bays, link length, and such.

The *traffic input data* describes the number and type of vehicles moving on the network. Volumes that enter the network at the entry points are input in vehicles per hour. Internally, the turning movements that leave each node are entered as percents or vehicles per hour. If vehicles per hour are entered, these will automatically be converted to percentages by the program. The composition of the traffic is entered, i.e., buses, trucks, carpools, and passenger cars; defaults are provided for the operating characteristics of each type of vehicle—for example, acceleration rate, speed, vehicle length—but the user can change the defaults if desired.

The initial version of NETSIM was created for the FHWA's testbed in Washington, DC, the Urban Traffic Control System (UTCS), and was designated UTCS-1. For more than twenty years, it has been refined, applied, and validated. It was used in congested network studies (e.g., [4]), tests of alternate geometric and control strategies [5–7], and real estate development [8].

The NETSIM outputs include link and network measures of performance, such as average travel speed, queues, overflows, throughput, and occupancy.[1] Emissions estimates are also available. Table 25-1 shows part of an illustrative NETSIM output.

[1] For links: It is measured as percent link occupancy, based on spatial occupancy, not percent time a detector is covered.

After the NETSIM model moved to the PC environment, graphics and animation were added to the output options [9]. The animation outputs are created by storing vehicle locations into a file during a NETSIM run, and processing that file after the run is completed.

Visualization packages

The entire process of visualizing traffic outputs is receiving great attention as this text goes to press, and the reader can expect substantial advances in the state of the art. Figure 25-2 shows a three-dimensional rendering of an intersection, with vehicles in motion based on a TRAF-NETSIM simulation. The perspective can be changed, and both the traffic professional and the general public can see the problems develop—and be remedied—in a controlled environment in which different control policies can be tested on exactly the same traffic.

FRESIM

FRESIM is a companion model, following the same conceptual development as TRAF-NETSIM, but for freeways [10]. It is a microscopic simulation, in which individual vehicles obey car-following rules, entry and exit rules, lane changing, and so forth, with stochastic elements in their characteristics and behavior.

FRESIM's inputs consist of geometric data and traffic data. The output reports show statistics for each link showing delay time, moving time, density, speed, and others. Figure 25-3 shows a sample output [10].

Specifying tomorrow's traffic simulation model

Clearly, traffic models are evolving. The power of modern computers, the low cost of computer memory, and the advances in commercial software products (spreadsheets, visualization, GIS data bases) have cleared the way for even greater advances. The demands of intelligent transportation, particularly with regard to a data-rich environment (area sensors, cell phones and other locators) and instant communication

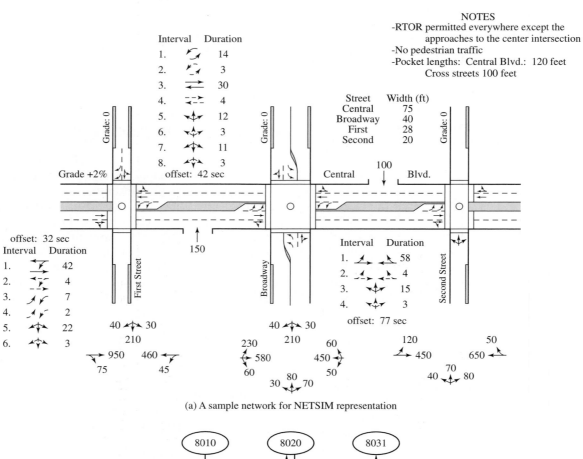

(a) A sample network for NETSIM representation

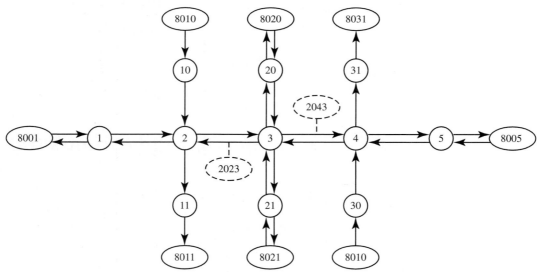

(b) The link representation of the same network

Figure 25-1 A network for NETSIM coding. [Courtesy of *TRAF-NETSIM Instructor's Guide*, U.S. Department of Transportation, Federal Highway Administration.]

Table 25-1 Part of an Illustrative TRAF-NETSIM Report

Cumulative NETSIM Statistics at Time 7:13:25

Elapsed Time is 0:13:25 (805 seconds), Time Period 1 Elapsed Time is 805 Seconds

Link	Vehicle		Vehicle Minutes			Ratio Move/Total	Minutes/Mile		Seconds/Vehicle					Average Values	
	Miles	Trips	Move Time	Delay Time	Total Time		Total Time	Delay Time	Total Time	Delay Time	Queue Time	Stop Time	Stops (%)	Volume (vph)	Speed (mph)
(8010, 10)		314												1404	
(10, 1)	29.73	314	51.3	168.4	219.7	0.23	7.39	5.66	42.0	32.2	23.9	22.8	64	1404	8.1
(1, 2)	66.97	268	115.6	86.1	201.6	0.57	3.01	1.29	45.1	19.3	12.2	11.8	33	1198	19.9
(2, 3)	83.75	268	144.5	93.2	237.7	0.61	2.84	1.11	53.2	20.9	10.7	10.2	47	1198	21.1
(3, 4)	41.24	242	71.2	39.0	110.2	0.65	2.67	0.95	27.3	9.7	4.9	4.8	18	1082	22.5
(4, 5)	34.65	229	59.8	28.6	88.4	0.68	2.55	0.83	23.2	7.5	3.4	3.3	10	1024	23.5
(5, 6)	15.91	224	27.5	46.5	74.0	0.37	4.65	2.93	19.8	12.5	9.8	9.7	18	1001	12.9
(6, 20)	19.02	201	32.8	4.8	37.7	0.87	1.98	0.25	11.2	1.4	0.0	0.0	0	898	30.3
(8030, 30)		161												720	
(30, 1)	9.43	166	18.9	106.3	125.2	0.15	13.27	11.27	45.2	38.4	30.3	29.3	80	742	4.5
(1, 35)	10.68	190	21.4	4.4	25.8	0.83	2.41	0.41	8.1	1.4	0.0	0.0	0	849	24.9
(8035, 35)		161												720	

[Data acquired using TRAF-NETSIM, U.S. Department of Transportation, Federal Highway Administration.]

Figure 25-2   Visualization of a simulated intersection in three dimensions. [Courtesy of KLD Associates, Inc.]

with the vehicle operators, are a driving force in defining the next generation of models.

The following help describe the environment we see for future traffic models:

1. Vehicles may receive route information before entering the network, and define their paths based on it. Further, they may update the path decisions dynamically, based on new information. Historic traffic assignment models will not suffice, and traffic simulation models can no longer assume static characteristics (for instance, turn rates implied by historic routings). Indeed, the two families of models may blend together.
2. Visualization of the output, even including a driver's eye view of the trip, will be very important.
3. Commercial software products in other fields will greatly enhance the value and user-friendliness of traffic simulation models. Packages are now available for visualization, icon-based network definition, report generation, and computation well beyond what is now in use in traffic simulation.
4. Links to existing GIS and other data bases will grow in importance.
5. The data-rich environment is here, and will become even more widespread. Some toll pass systems allow network conditions and even routings to be determined easily. Cellular phones can provide tremendous information on network condition and path selection, and telecommunications companies can provide incentives for people to volunteer the use of such information. Area sensors with sophisticated software processing are rather well advanced.
6. The emphasis on multimodal transportation will lead to newer performance indices, and to the explicit treatment of several modes on a level of detail previously associated only with microscopic vehicular traffic simulation.

CUMULATIVE FRESIM STATISTICS AT TIME 7 15 0

LINK STATISTICS

LINK	VEHICLES IN	OUT	LANE CHNG	CURR CONT	AVG CONT	VEH MILES	SECONDS/VEHICLE VEH MIN	TOTAL TIME	MOVE TIME	DELAY TIME	M/T	VEH·MIN/VEH·MILE TOTAL	DELAY	VOLUME VEH/LN/HR	DENSITY VEH/LN·MILE	SPEED MILE/HR	LINK TYPE
(1, 2)	749	750	104	3	3.5	43.7	52.4	4.1	3.7	0.3	0.92	1.20	0.10	1026.	20.5	50.01	FRWY
(2, 3)	800	803	209	17	17.1	227.7	256.4	19.2	18.6	0.6	0.97	1.13	0.04	1070.	20.1	53.28	FRWY
(3, 4)	803	798	86	13	11.4	151.3	170.7	12.8	12.3	0.5	0.96	1.13	0.04	1066.	20.0	53.19	FRWY
(21, 2)	50	50	0	0	1.0	9.5	14.7	17.6	17.3	0.2	0.99	1.54	0.02	202.	5.2	38.84	RAMP

NETWORK STATISTICS

VEHICLE·MILES = 432.2, VEHICLE·MINUTES = 494.2, MOVING/TOTAL TRIP TIME = 0.961,

AVERAGE CONTENT = 33.0, CURRENT CONTENT = 33.0, SPEED (MPH) = 52.47,

TOTAL DELAY (VEH·MIN) = 19.22, TRAVEL TIME (MIN)/VEH·MILE = 1.14, DEALY TIME (MIN)/ VEH·MILE = 0.04

POINT PROCESSING OUTPUT

Evaluation period beginning time • 1 (seconds)
Evaluation period ending time • 900 (seconds)

Link	Lane ID No.	Distance from HPST. Node (ft)	Loop Length (ft)	Station No.	Detector type	Volume (VPH)	Mean speed (mph)	Mean headway (sec)	Mean occupancy rate
(21, 2)	1	750.00	6.0	1	single short loop	200	33.884	17,899	1,687
(21, 2)	1	975.00	6.0	2	single short loop	200	11.865	17,974	1,688
(1, 2)	1	50.00	6.0	4	single short loop	428	40.454	1,860	6,911
(1, 2)	2	50.00	6.0	4	single short loop	1088	40.050	1,104	8,151
(1, 2)	1	50.00	6.0	4	single short loop	984	40.944	1,651	7,109
(1, 2)	1	100.00	6.0	4	single short loop	876	44.592	4,101	5,865
(1, 2)	2	100.00	6.0	4	single short loop	1148	45.100	3,136	7,467
(1, 2)	1	100.00	6.0	4	single short loop	974	48.012	1,672	6,141
(1, 2)	1	450.00	6.0	6	single short loop				

Figure 25-3 A sample FRESIM output report. [From *FRESIM User Guide, Version 4.5,* Turner Fairbank Highway Research Center, U.S. Department of Transportation, Federal Highway Administration, 1994.]

7. Faster-than-real-time models will be used in selecting control policies, and in providing drivers with data for their own path selection algorithms, so that a fully interactive and fully informed network will exist.

A new generation of traffic simulation models will grow out of the modeling knowledge and experience gained to date, but capable of handling the dynamic traffic environment caused by ITS technology and information flow.

Summary

This chapter presented the basic concepts of simulation in a vehicular traffic application, addressed some of the underlying issues, and introduced the most commonly used models.

References

1. *Highway Capacity Manual, Special Report 209,* 3rd Edition, Transportation Research Board, National Research Council, Washington, DC, (revised) 1994.
2. *TRAF User Reference Guide, Version 4.2,* U.S. Department of Transportation, Federal Highway Administration, February 1994.
3. *TSIS User's Guide, Version 4.0 beta, CORSIM User's Guide Version 1.0 beta,* Kaman Sciences Corporation, January 1996.
4. Rathi, A. K., and Lieberman, E. B., "Effectiveness of Traffic Restraint for a Congested Network," *Transportation Research Record 1232,* Transportation Research Board, National Research Council, Washington, DC, 1989.
5. Maki, R. E., and Brauch, D. R., *Signal Timing Optimization and Evaluation, Route M53, Macomb County, Special Report 194,* Transportation Research Board, National Research Council, Washington, DC, 1981.
6. Schafer, B. F., *Comparison of Alternative Traffic Control Strategies at T-Intersections, Special Report 194,* Trans-
portation Research Board, National Research Council, Washington, DC, 1981.
7. Bruce, E. L., and Hummer, J. E., "Delay Alleviated by Left Turn Bypass Lanes," *Transportation Research Record 1299,* Transportation Research Board, National Research Council, Washington, DC, 1991.
8. Papacostas, C. S., and Wiley, M., "Use of TRAF-NETSIM to Estimate the Traffic Impacts of an Urban Resort Area Development," *Microcomputers in Transportation* (J. Chow, editor) ASCE, 1992.
9. Andrews, B., et al., "The NETSIM Graphics System," *Transportation Research Record 1112,* Transportation Research Board, National Research Council, Washington, DC, 1989.
10. *FRESIM User Guide, Version 4.5,* Turner Fairbank Highway Research Center, U.S. Department of Transportation, Federal Highway Administration, Washington, DC, April 1994.

Problems

Problem 25–1

Describe the fundamental differences between

deterministic and stochastic
computation and simulation
time-based and event-based

providing examples in each case.

Problem 25–2

Use the uniform random number generator in a spreadsheet to generate 700 random numbers. Compute the mean and standard deviation of these numbers, and compare them to the theoretic values. Prepare a histogram of the 700 values. Does it appear to be uniform? Compute the confidence bounds on the estimate of the mean, if possible.

Problem 25–3

Use the same 700 numbers in Problem 2 in order to generate the interarrival times for vehicles in one lane of an ar-

terial, where the interarrival times are known to be exponentially distributed with a mean of 2.5 minutes. Compute the mean and standard deviation of these interarrival times, and prepare a histogram of these values. Compare to the theoretic expectation.

Problem 25–4

For the results of Problem 3, plot the flow rates for consecutive five minute periods at the observation point, and estimate the average flow rate, the hourly demand, and its standard deviation. Comment on how these are related to the interarrival time parameters, if they are.

Problem 25–5

Decide whether the average travel speed as used in *HCM* Chapter 11, is space mean speed or time mean speed, and compare it to the standard output(s) of TRAF-NETSIM. Are they the same? Can they be made to link to each other?

Index

AADT (average annual daily traffic), 62,
    121–22, 125–30, 141
    two-lane highways, 329–30
AAWT (average annual weekday traffic),
    62, 125
Acceleration performance, 46–50
Access management, 1, 17, 32–36
    good traffic engineering, 33
    mobility as goal, 32
    performance measures, 34–35
    transportation planning tools, 32–33
Accident
    computer record systems, 187–88
    costs, 202
    data collection, 184
    and freeway systems, 576
    investigations using skid distances,
      54–55
    manual filing systems,185–87
    and project-specific actions, 32
    record systems, 184
    reducing occurrence of, 182
    reducing severity of, 182–83
    reporting, 184
    site analysis, 194–205

    statistics, 188–94
    studies, 181–205
Accident, site analysis, 194–205
    collision diagrams, 194–95
    condition diagrams, 195
    countermeasures, 198–200
    interpretation of results, 195–98
Accident statistics, 188–94
    before-after accident data,
      193–94
    high-accident locations, 191–93
    rates, 189–90
    statistical displays, 190–91
    types of, 188–89
Activity centers, 5
Actuated signal and detection, 542–56
    controllers, 542–43
    detection, 543
    detector locations, 547
    full-actuated control, 551–53
    operation, 543–46
    pedestrian requirements, 547–48
    self-actuated control, 548–51
    signal timing, 546–47
Actuated signals, analysis of, 510–12

Adjustment factor
    area type, 483–84
    bus blockage, 482–83
    coverage counts, 144–45
    critical movement analysis, calibration,
      562–68
    driver population, 239
    free-flow speed, 304
    freeway capacity analysis, 298–304
    grade, 480
    heavy vehicles, 480
    lane utilization, 531
    lane width, 480
    left turn, 485
    and movement analysis, 565–66
    parking, 481–82
    right turn, 484–86
Adjustment volume module, and *HCM*
    model, 475, 513–14
ADT (average daily traffic), 62, 125
AHS (automtic highway system), 19, 26
Analysis
    bus blockage, 565–66
    capacity module, and *HCM* model, 517–19
    critical lane, 451